S0-DYT-168

The Connoisseur Complete Encyclopedia of Antiques

THE CONNOISSEUR COMPLETE ENCYCLOPEDIA OF ANTIQUES

SPRING
BOOKS

First published in Great Britain in 1962 by
The Connoisseur, London

First published in this redesigned form in Great Britain in 1975 by
The Connoisseur, London

This book was designed and produced by
Rainbird Reference Books Ltd
40 Park Street
London W1
for The Connoisseur, London

This edition published in 1988 by Spring Books
An imprint of Octopus Publishing Group PLC
59 Grosvenor Street
London W1

Distributed by The Hamlyn Publishing Group
Bridge House, London Road,
Twickenham, Middlesex, England

Copyright © The Connoisseur 1962
Copyright © The Connoisseur and Rainbird Reference Books Ltd 1975

All rights reserved. No part of this publication may be reproduced or transmitted in any form or by any means, electronic or mechanical, including photocopy, recording, or any information or storage or retrieval system now known or to be invented, without permission in writing from the publisher except by a reviewer who wishes to quote brief passages in connection with a review written for inclusion in a magazine, newspaper or broadcast.

ISBN 0 600 55725 1

Printed in Hong Kong

Contents

Acknowledgments

The publishers and producers wish to acknowledge that material appearing in this work is adapted from *The Concise Encyclopedia of Antiques* Volumes 1–5 and *The Concise Encyclopedia of American Antiques* Volumes 1–2.

The contributors include:

Josephine L. Allen
Edward H. H. Archibald
Amos G. Avery
John Ayres
F. W. Barker
John I. H. Baur
David Bland
John Boardman, M.A.
Alf Bøe, B.Litt.
Handasyde Buchanan
Kathryn C. Buhler
Adrian Bury, Hon. R.W.S.
Ralph E. Carpenter, Jr
R. A. G. Carson, M.A.
John Carter
R. A. Cecil
R. J. Charlestone
Erwin O. Christensen
Helen Comstock
Ruth Bradbury Davidson
Frank Davis
Bernard Denvir
Shirley Spaulding DeVoe
G. Wingfield Digby
M. L. D'Otrange-Mastai
Martha Gandy Fales
Ian Finlay
John Fleming
Peter Floud, C.B.E.
Geoffrey Godden
F. M. Godfrey, Ph.D.
Arthur Grimwade, F.S.A.
Rupert Gunnis
Yvonne Hackenbroch
Reginald G. Haggar
The Hon. Richard Hare
J. F. Hayward
Luke Herrmann, M.A.
G. Heywood Hill
John Hillier
M. T. Hindson, A.I.B.
Hugh Honour
G. Bernard Hughes
Mrs Therle Hughes
Eric de Jonge
E. T. Joy
Henry J. Kauffman
H. H. Knowland
P. Lasko
Frances Lichten
Raymond Lister
Nina Fletcher Little
H. Alan Lloyd, F.S.A., F.B.H.I.
Agnes Lothian
Jeremy Maas, M.A.
Harold McCracken
Lord Mackintosh
Joseph V. McMullan
Francis Maddison
Paul Magriel
Sydney J. Maiden
Jonathan Mayne
Barbara Morris
Howard M. Nixon
Sydney P. Noe
Gregor Norman-Wilcox
Oliver van Oss
Arnold Palmer
Virginia D. Parslow
Josephine H. Peirce
Harold L. Peterson
E. H. Pinto
C. F. Pitman, M.A., F.M.A.
Ada Polak
Tamara Talbot Rice
B. W. Robinson, M.A., F.R.A.S.
F. Gordon Roe, F.S.A.
Elizabeth E. Roth
Marvin D. Schwartz
Carolyn Scoon
Robert Sherlock
Horace Shipp
Harold S. Sniffen
Kenneth Snowman
Frank O. Spinney
Capt. A. V. Sutherland-Graeme, F.S.A. (R.)
Denys Sutton
Patrick Synge-Hutchinson
M. W. Thomas, Jr
James Tudor-Craig, F.S.A.
Malcolm Vaughan
C. Malcolm Watkins
Frank Weitenkampf
Geoffrey Wills
Alice Winchester
Franz Windisch-Graetz
Gordon Winter
Rudolf Wunderlich
John Cook Wyllie

New material for 1975 edition:

Cottie Burland–*Antiquities*
J. B. Donne–*Ethnographica*
Malcolm Easton–*The Aesthetic Movement; The Arts and Crafts Movement; Art Nouveau; Art Deco*, etc.
George Savage–*Oriental Antiques*

Introduction

When I began collecting antiques over twenty years ago, there was no *Connoisseur Encyclopedia* to help me. So I invented my own method of self-education, which was to cut up old copies of *The Connoisseur* and paste cuttings into a scrapbook under headings: Clocks, Wax Portraits, Papier Mâché and so on. My grandmother called this 'cutting up one book and sticking it in another'; but I suppose what I was really doing was creating for myself a rudimentary *Connoisseur Encyclopedia.* A few years later, *The Connoisseur* did it for me, far more professionally. As my father was a contributor to the original edition, we received an early set; and I have continually returned to the *Encyclopedia* for help and instruction. When, as often happens, a reader writes in with a query, I usually find that the easiest and best way to help him is to refer him to the relevant section of the work.

Antiques encyclopedias – and since the pioneer *Connoisseur* production there has been a huge number of them, good, bad and indifferent – can and should serve three main purposes. First, they act as a guide to the beginner, showing him the vast range of collecting subjects, allowing him to sample them, and giving him initial instruction in the subject he finally chooses. I have more than once heard someone come into a bookshop and ask 'Have you anything on antiques?'. In a way, the question is repellent: it immediately suggests that the inquirer has been watching a television programme, goggled at high prices mentioned, and decided to 'collect for investment'. Even if the intention is less mercenary, the question can still seem absurd: for no one person can hope to know about 'antiques' – he will be hard put to it to become even moderately expert on a subject as circumscribed as tortoiseshell boxes. The opportunities for promiscuity of the beginner are limitless: 'The world was all before them, where to choose.' The antiques encyclopedia, far from being the temptation towards dabbling it might initially seem, is usually the first step towards specialization. A man at a ball may dance with many girls, but he only takes one home.

The second function of the antiques encyclopedia is as a reference work. What is Gemellion? Paktong? Pilgrim's sign? Slipware? Pirlie pig? Posset pot? Binder's ticket? *Piqué? Monté à cage?* The answers to all these will be found in *The Connoisseur Encyclopedia.* 'Galloon', one discovers, is not just tennis colours round a straw hat, or 'balloon' spoken by a novice ventriloquist, but 'the plain, ribbon-like outer border of a tapestry. The factory and weaver's mark, when used, are woven into the galloon.' A *repoussé* nose is different from a *retroussé* one. The *Encyclopedia* can also save one from embarrassing mistakes in the order of Chinese dynasties or silver marks.

The third purpose of the encyclopedia is to give one an all-round general knowledge of antiques, a sea deep enough to float the barque of one's specialism. The different antiques subjects impinge upon each other at so many points that it is impossible to study a subject in isolation. Take English ceramics, for example. To understand Wedgwood wares, one needs to know something of the general history of Neoclassicism; also of the Industrial Revolution, in which Wedgwood was a leading spirit; also of Matthew Boulton, for whose metalwork (*q.v.*) Josiah Wedgwood provided jasper medallions. Porcelain is continually based on silver models, being a cheap substitute for silver; and one of the most sought-after factories, Chelsea, had a silversmith, Nicholas Sprimont, as its founder. A knowledge of Chinese and Continental porcelain also becomes necessary, partly so that the English products can be distinguished from them, and partly so that the influence of both on English wares can be detected. Enamels and glass are materials so closely allied to porcelain that no student or collector of ceramics can afford to live in ignorance of them. The cross-pollination of the arts is continual. An encyclopedia of antiques is the best way to begin building up a background of reference to one's own subject.

Since I was not the originator of *The Connoisseur Encyclopedia,* I can speak of that original conception and its working-out without the suspicion of *amour-propre.* An ideal balance was maintained, it seems to me, between on the one hand the profound and complex subjects, such as French furniture, where the encyclopedia could give only a broad introduction and a reading list, and on the other hand minority subjects of great collecting appeal, such as barometers, looking glasses and silhouettes, on which more or less all there was to say could be said within the compass of an encyclopedia section. A nice balance was also kept between academic scrupulousness and popularizing attractiveness of presentation. Writers such as Mr Hugh Honour and Mr John Fleming combined both qualities to an unusual degree. Other contributors ranged from Miss Agnes Lothian, the devoted archivist of the Society of Apothecaries (who wrote on pharmacy jars) to Mr Geoffrey Godden, a greatly respected dealer, who is a leading expert on English ceramics. The mixture was stimulating and readable, and we feel the revised encyclopedia is no less so.

But perhaps the biggest change which has taken place since *The Connoisseur Encyclopedia* first appeared in the 1950s is the way in which the frontiers of the antique have been pushed ever nearer our own times. In volume four of *The Concise Encyclopedia*, which was published in 1959, my predecessor as Editor, Mr L. G. G. Ramsey, referred to the gradually developing interest in Victoriana in these terms:

> *It often seems that beautiful and interesting objects are vanishing so swiftly from the market that it will soon be well nigh impossible to find anything worth collecting. Museums are buying on a larger scale than ever before and proving formidable rivals to the private collector. Yet it is always possible for a discerning individual to be in advance of official taste and to acquire for comparatively small sums the objects which will be the museum pieces of tomorrow. Hence the popularity of Victoriana, especially among younger collectors.*

This new edition of the *Encyclopedia* incorporates articles on Art Nouveau and Art Deco – the two collecting subjects which succeeded Victoriana as the avant-garde in collecting during the 1960s. The Art Nouveau revival was begun by the Beardsley and Mucha exhibitions at the Victoria and Albert Museum in the early 1960s, and given further impetus by excellent books on the subject by Robert Schmutzler, Mario Amaya and Maurice Rheims. There is now a book on Italian 'Liberty' style (as they call Art Nouveau) too; and visiting Sicily this year I was surprised and delighted to find a book by Gianni Pirrone on *Palermo Liberty* – surely the most esoteric art study ever committed to print. Shops such as John Jesse's in London and Lillian Nassau's in New York began to specialize in Art Nouveau; and the foundation of Sotheby's, Belgravia, in the late 1960s, for the sale of both Victoriana and Art Nouveau, gave new encouragement to collectors of these subjects.

The revival in Art Deco – the decorative arts of the 1940s and 1950s – began with a Paris exhibition of 'Les Années 25' in 1966, and was carried further in books by myself and Martin Battersby, by Art Deco exhibitions at Brighton, New York, Minneapolis, and the Geffrye Museum, London, and by permanent museum displays at the Victoria and Albert, the Brighton and Geffrye Museums and elsewhere. Sotheby's, Belgravia, added Art Deco to its stock-in-trade; in 1971 a French Deco sofa fetched some £13,000 in Paris; and in 1973 the antiques establishment of Britain, personified by the Grosvenor House Fair committee, gave official sanction to the 'new antiques' by extending their deadline for exhibits from 1830 to 1930 – growing young gracefully. In April 1974 I had the mixed pleasure of seeing a frosted glass hairdresser's door which I had bought from a demolition squad for £5 in 1964, sold for £300 at Sotheby's, Belgravia. (Mixed, because I had sold it for £30 some years before.) It has become accepted that Art Nouveau and Art Deco are not just silly collecting fads or interior decorators' dreams, but subjects comprising the work of really great designers, from Mucha and Rennie Mackintosh in Art Nouveau to Puiforcat and Ruhlmann in Art Deco.

Inevitably the tendency for new, later, periods to be co-opted into the realm of the 'antique' will continue; and I am sure that editions of *The Connoisseur Encyclopedia* subsequent to this will need to take account of 'Austerity/Binge', the label attached for convenience to the period of the decorative arts from 1940 to 1960, including the wartime arts of austerity, 'Festival of Britain style' and the Rock culture. 'Psychedelic' posters of the 1960s and the wonderfully imaginative record sleeves of the present day are bound to become collectors' pieces of the future, as will the toy spacemen, 'action men', 'Easy Rider' motorcycles and miniature weather-forecasting stations now in the toyshops; besides the works of exquisite hand-craftsmanship which continue to be made, such as the engraved glass goblets of Laurence Whistler, the wood engravings of Joan Hassall or the silver of Gerald Benney, all of which have been discussed and illustrated in *The Connoisseur* magazine in recent years. It is an odd kind of connoisseur whose connoisseurship stops short at fifty or a hundred years before his birth.

Bevis Hillier

THE AESTHETIC MOVEMENT; THE ARTS AND CRAFTS MOVEMENT; ART NOUVEAU; ART DECO, ETC.

A reappraisal of these eighty years in the history of the decorative arts comes most appropriately at the present time. For, after a long succession of cults and taboos, the wheel is seen to have turned full circle. Presented (at the Geffrye Museum, London) with the contrasting tableaux of a 'High Victorian' and a 'Voysey' Room, we are a good deal less sure of the superiority of the latter. Fussiness expresses a human need; austerity may strike a dictatorial note. Thanks largely to Mr Bevis Hillier, there exists a new understanding of the qualities, intrinsic or associational, of what has been only recently – and not without some ambiguity – christened 'Art Deco': the hand-made and machine-made products of the 1920s and 1930s. Ugly yesterday, they are acquiring fresh fascination with every moment that passes. The fine arts had already extended their boundaries to include photography, the strip-cartoon and commercial packaging: it was inevitable that this would lead to a general change of attitude towards the so-called sins against good taste, function and truth to material. Indeed, there are signs – and they come with the authority of the saleroom – that the change has taken place. And long before the rest of us learned to look with an unprejudiced eye at Schmied's bindings or Edgar Wood's glass, a pair of inspired collectors, the late Charles and Lavinia Handley-Read, had been quietly reversing critical judgments stretching back to the Great Exhibition of 1851. We may as well, then, begin our brief survey at this peak of British 'philistinism' which drew such bitter protests from the serious-minded of the day.

(For detailed coverage of certain types of antiques of the Victorian period see also American Victorian Furniture and Victorian Furniture in Furniture section and Victorian Embroidery in Needlework and Embroidery section.)

Right Gothic sideboard designed by Philip Webb, *c.* 1862. Ebonized wood with panels of gilt leather and painting. Victoria & Albert Museum

Left Porcelain dish designed by A. W. N. Pugin, Minton, exhibited in 1851. Victoria & Albert Museum

Morris & Co.

Though the decorative art on display in 1851 may now seem liberally enough supplied with cusps and finials, it leaned in fact somewhat coquettishly towards the *style Pompadour* and combined a mixture of sacred and profane particularly offensive to the followers of Augustus Pugin (who had died within a year of the Exhibition's opening). The missionary spirit of the Aesthetic Movement, like that of the Arts and Crafts Movement – and we shall be discussing both very shortly – can be traced direct to the architects of the Gothic Revival. Devotion to the medieval style of architecture drew its imitators back into the imagined world, into something like the piety, of the old builders. This had been the inspiration of Pugin, received into the Catholic Church in 1835, and of John Ruskin in a vision which came to him in 1854 while climbing in Switzerland. Above all,

Far left Wash-hand stand by William Burges, given by Sir John Betjeman to Evelyn Waugh, known as 'The Betjeman Benefaction'

Ruskin condemned the self-sufficiency of the artist working in isolation: the watchword of reform must be Partnership. In this, Ruskin both influenced, and was himself influenced by, the little band of painters who in 1848 founded the Pre-Raphaelite Brotherhood. The early works of D. G. Rossetti, William Holman Hunt and J. E. Millais demonstrated the need to return to older, purer techniques and, though Hunt alone of the three was a practising Christian, their vigorous handling of religious topics (owing something to the German Nazarenes who had similarly abjured Raphael) injected fresh life into the anaemic painted sermons of the period. A few years later, inspired in turn by Pugin and Ruskin, a young architect's apprentice, William Morris, joined Rossetti and the enthusiasts engaged upon designing frescoes for the Oxford Union Society. It was in 1859–60 when the Red House, built for him by Webb, required furnishing and decorating, that Morris turned his attention to the applied arts. In the following year, dissatisfied with what seemed to him the vulgar frippery supplied by the trade, he established a business of his own.

Assisted, in fact, by as loyal a group of friends as the Gothic ideal prescribed, Morris scored an early success at the International Exhibition of 1862 in London. Among the firm's showpieces were the St George's Cabinet, designed by Webb and painted by Morris himself; Rossetti's stained-glass 'Parable of the Vineyard'; patterned fabrics; iron and copper work; jewelry; and tiles. Soon, however, Morris's wallpapers achieved an even more remarkable success, and the stamp of Edward Burne-Jones's personality began to be felt. The two young men worked harmoniously together, and between them they may be said to usher in the movement sometimes known as 'Art' and sometimes as 'Aesthetic', of which the second label is the more meaningful. Morris's hard-won business acumen and the common sense, rare in a poet, that always seem to have distinguished him have nothing to do with the affectations ridiculed by W. S. Gilbert in *Patience.* It is true that he began as a pigheaded medievalist; but he ended by accepting that – for Socialism's sake – one must come to some sort of terms with the machine. The chairs, beds, settles, tables produced under his aegis stand four-square, exploit the traditional woods, eschew fuss. We see in Edward Burne-Jones's contributions, richly

Left Morris & Co. period room, the walls covered with Pomegranate wallpaper (1864), the floor with Lily Wilton carpet of the 1870s. The furniture includes a cabinet painted by Edward Burne-Jones with scenes from 'The Prioress' Tale', a settle from Red House and the St George's cabinet on the right which was painted by William Morris in 1862. The framed series of tiles above the cabinet depicts the story of the Sleeping Beauty and was designed by Burne-Jones in 1862. On the central table designed by Philip Webb is a pair of copper candlesticks he designed for Red House in 1860. Victoria & Albert Museum

Right Original design for Avon chintz by William Morris, *c.* 1886. Watercolour on paper. William Morris Gallery

imagined but languorous, the feminine side of the coin. His 'Briar Rose' pictures, however, identified a lost world and imposed it upon contemporaries only a little less influentially. Both men had thought of entering holy orders, and the Aesthetic Movement derived from them a didactic manner, a missionary zeal, it never quite lost.

(*See also* Needlework and Embroidery for 'Morris' embroideries.)

'Japonesque'

Oddly enough, neither Morris nor Burne-Jones cared for the art of Japan, opened to the Western world in 1853 after centuries of isolation. A certain William Burges, keen medievalist too, was the first to collect Japanese prints in Britain, a strange contradiction, it might seem, when one looks at his heavy, gilt and glass-encrusted furniture; but improvising on themes of the *long ago* and *faraway* was very much the same Romantic exercise. Burges himself did not actually reach the point of adapting the patterns of these 'hitherto unknown barbarians' to his own use. That initiative was taken by E. W. Godwin, whose skilful variations on Japanese fret enchant the eye in the unexpected context of a chair or a commode. Godwin expressed himself gracefully in a second style, the 'Queen Anne', being responsible for the first batch of redbrick houses in Bedford

Left Cabinet of oak inlaid with various woods, designed by J. P. Seddon and painted with subjects based on the honeymoon of King René of Anjou by Ford Madox Brown, Edward Burne-Jones, William Morris and Dante Gabriel Rossetti, 1862. Victoria & Albert Museum

Right The Peacock Room, originally the dining-room at 49 Prince's Gate, London, designed by Thomas Jeckyll, 1876–7, and painted by James McNeill Whistler for F. R. Leyland. The painting is Whistler's *La Princesse du Pays de la Porcelaine*. Courtesy of the Smithsonian Institution, Freer Gallery of Art, Washington D.C.

Writing cabinet by William Burges of painted and gilt wood, exhibited in 1862. The style and decoration is inspired by his study of 12th-century French Gothic. Victoria & Albert Museum

Park, West London, the original garden-suburb deliberately planned for the aesthetically-minded. He worked much with James McNeil Whistler: whose White House was to Godwin's design. Light, primrosy schemes of interior decoration, as visualized by the Master, were undertaken by him.

Whistler, indeed, gave a considerable personal impetus to the vogue for Japan, through his passionate collecting of blue-and-white china and, more subtly, through his paintings. His most celebrated association with an architect was not, however, with Godwin, but with Thomas Jeckyll. The result, the 'Peacock Room', is preserved in the Freer Gallery, Washington. Mr Peter Ferriday's researches show that it was the fine-spun shelving, half-Gothic, half-Japanese, that gave Whistler the idea of covering his patron's Spanish leather with golden peacocks and thus providing the artistic sensation of 1877. The shelves in F. R. Leyland's house had been designed by Jeckyll for a display of priceless Japanese porcelain. But people of more modest means were already being offered a wide variety of fascinating pastiches from English studio and commercial potteries. These spread the taste for the Oriental more effectively, perhaps, than any other form of craftsmanship or manufacture. Nor was it just a question of applying designs featuring bamboo-shoots and prunus-blossom to traditional native shapes: the silhouette of vases, jugs and bowls underwent a radical transformation. A blue-and-white vase appears in Whistler's painting 'Caprice', of 1864. He could have bought it from the shop of Farmer and Rogers of London which, in 1875, became Liberty. A. L. Liberty played an important role in the popularizing of Japanese, or pseudo-Japanese, manufactures right through into the 1880s, when another less exotic mode began to compete with it.

Arts and Crafts

'I do not want art for a few,' declared Morris; but the austere products of Morris & Co. were still luxury goods and found their way chiefly into the houses of

Left Ebonized side chair designed by E. W. Godwin, with ladder back and circular cane seat raised on turned tapering legs. The chairs show strong Japanese influence. Sotheby's Belgravia

Below Sideboard of ebonized wood with silver-plated fittings and inset panels of Japanese leather paper designed by E. W. Godwin, 1867, and made by William Watt. Victoria & Albert Museum

Oak writing-desk designed by A. H. Mackmurdo for the Century Guild, *c.* 1886. William Morris Gallery

This amalgamation of forces between William Lethaby and Lewis Day drew in Henry Holiday, T. M. Rooke and the versatile Walter Crane. Their aim was to raise the status of decorative art to that enjoyed by the fine arts, an aim perhaps partially achieved by the arrival of yet another body, still in 1884, less shy of blowing its own trumpet, the Arts and Crafts Exhibition Society. As Miss Gillian Naylor has pointed out, the term 'Arts and Crafts', which now entered into general use, was invented by T. J. Cobden-Sanderson, a member of the Society who had been a disciple of Morris and would go on (in 1900) to found The Doves Press. In spite of an occasional determination to go it alone and an inherited dread of the machine, which characterized some of the finest men in the Arts and Crafts Movement like William de Morgan the potter and C. R. Ashbee, chiefly known for his silversmithing, there was witnessed during the 1880s an increasing tendency on the part of industry to make use of the consultant designer. Liberty's of London has already been mentioned (though its insistence upon anonymity deprived the originating craftsman of some part of his reward), and a number of other firms stocked and sold this simpler, more discreetly decorated Guild

Far right Dish by William de Morgan, late 19th century. Earthenware painted with a peacock in 'Persian' colours. Victoria & Albert Museum

the socially-privileged. In spite of the many composite tasks carried out in the workshops belonging to the firm, involving as they did several pairs of hands, Morris remained the team's undisputed leader. And being a Socialist didn't prevent his having his feet firmly on the ground. When an idealistic younger generation looked to him for encouragement, he somewhat damped their ardour, dismissing the idea of corporate workshops as impracticable. Such had been the experience of A. H. Mackmurdo who, in 1882, founded the Century Guild. Nevertheless, the spate of similar organizations which followed during the same decade – the Art-Workers' Guild (1884), the Guild and School of Handicraft and the Arts and Crafts Exhibition Society (both of 1888) – was inspired by Morris's example, as well as by the still influential writings of Ruskin.

Like Morris, Mackmurdo became a self-taught craftsman in many fields. From Ruskin (whom he got to know well) derived the notion of the guild-system itself: 'to render all branches of art the sphere no longer of the tradesman, but of the artist'. Though Mackmurdo shared many of Morris's ideas, the style of the Century Guild reflects the outlook of a younger generation, one that could not escape altogether the impact of the Japanese upon furniture and ceramics, and one that in a few remarkable instances anticipates Art Nouveau. The most striking of these are Mackmurdo's own title-page for his *Wren's City Churches* and the back of a chair designed by him, now in the William Morris Gallery, Walthamstow, London: both probably belonging to the year 1883. His close associate, Selwyn Image (later, Slade Professor at Oxford), produced a cover for Mackmurdo's journal, *Hobby Horse*, which seems, on the contrary, to go back to the Pre-Raphaelites. This magazine heralds an awakening interest in typography and an appreciation of the artist's contribution to the printed page not met with again till Ricketts and Shannon brought out *The Dial* towards the end of the decade.

The same year in which *Hobby Horse* appeared, 1884, saw the foundation of the Art-Workers' Guild.

work. Ashbee's furniture and silverware designs, however, were dealt with in the workshop of his own School of Handicrafts; while William de Morgan produced his fine tiles and lustrework in private partnership.

If the 'trade' were on the whole sympathetic to new developments in glass and textiles, they found Arts and Crafts furniture too austere for their taste. The simple (but not unsophisticated) 'cottage' design seemed in its *stylelessness* positively ugly. By way of reply, a group of architects set up the firm of Kenton & Co. Among its partners were Lethaby, Ernest Gimson and Sidney Barnsley. Gimson laid particular stress on fitness for purpose and suitability to the wood used. The Morris tradition held good: simplicity (though unaccompanied now by Morrisian grandeur) remained the fundamental objective. Ever since Webb designed his massive candlesticks to match the stout oak of Morris & Co., developments in metalwork had gone hand-in-hand with other decorative design. Some of Christopher Dresser's electro-plated tableware continued to demonstrate the Anglo-Japanese style at its most imaginative during the 1880s. Among those not afraid to avail themselves of mass-production methods in this field was W. A. S. Benson, designer for his own manufacturing company in Hammersmith, London. His products in copper and brass were greatly valued by Samuel Bing, proprietor of the celebrated Art Nouveau shop in Paris (to which we shall be returning later), and a number of fine pieces of Benson's design are in the metalwork collection of the Nordenfjeldske Kunstindustrimuseum at Trondheim.

The career of C. R. Ashbee as silversmith is of special interest. Following it, we cross the threshold of the twentieth century, and see how the Morrisian-Socialist ideals stand up to the vastly accelerating mechanization of the modern age. For the Guild and School of Handicrafts, already mentioned, symbolize Ashbee's dedication to social reform as sharply as his concern for higher standards in design. Though critical of some of its aims, he lived in Toynbee Hall, where Oxbridge graduates (he was one himself) shared the life of the Whitechapel poor. His Guild depended for membership upon the classes he taught here, and inherent in its attitude throughout can be glimpsed a certain pride in learning skills the hard way. This, he felt, and with some justice, would stop his apprentices picking up the characterless finish which degraded commercial silver. The Catholic Revival, which had greatly benefited art-metalworkers with commissions for altar-plate, from Morris and Burges onwards, continued to keep the Guild workshops busy; but Ashbee's best-known pieces are for domestic use: bowls and dishes most often to be distinguished by their hammer-dinted surfaces, attenuated wire handles and single semi-precious stones. But we are not quite ready to pursue the fortunes of the Guild after Ashbee transported it, lock, stock and barrel, to the country in 1902.

Left, below Bowl designed by C. R. Ashbee and made by the Guild of Handicraft Ltd, 1895–6. Silver, embossed and chased with a leaf design, with cast legs. Victoria & Albert Museum

Below Hand-raised silver candlestick designed by R. C. Silver and made by W. H. Haseler, Birmingham, for Liberty & Co., 1906–7. The design was first published in *The Studio*, vol. XIX, 1900. Victoria & Albert Museum

'Fin-de-Siècle'

Emphasis has been placed on the quasi-religious atmosphere in which higher standards of taste were pursued by Morris and the Arts and Crafts designers. In England, in the 1880s, art was still equated with edification, and Ruskin's spiritual call-to-arms in *The Stones of Venice* was read and re-read by every industrious apprentice. Yet Victorian idealism was already in process of erosion. English artists learned the fundamentals of their profession in France, and in France, by the end of the 1870s, the Japanese vogue together with the new philosophy of Naturalism had changed the whole course of painting. And from France, too, came James McNeil Whistler, not just to paint golden peacocks in the houses of the rich, but to preach the doctrine of Art for Art's Sake and topple Ruskin off his throne.

What Whistler successfully challenged was the sanctity of artistic labour as such, the necessity of exact representation and the 'confounding' (as he called it) of Beauty with Virtue: a pretty formidable programme in its entirety. The chief events of his career thus embarked upon may be reckoned the Ruskin slander action of 1877, the Ten O'Clock Lecture of 1885 and the publication of *The Gentle Art of Making Enemies* in 1890. Yet hostile to a didactic art as he made himself out to be, Whistler was as busy a publicist and proselytizer as Ruskin himself. By skilful, persistent self-advertisement he got some way towards banishing the excessive patterning of walls, proving instead the efficacy of simple (sometimes graduated) washes of light colour; and he revolutionized the framing and hanging of pictures upon these walls, so altering the whole appearance of the typical English dining- and drawing-room. His association with Godwin has been earlier alluded to: the result of one joint enterprise can be seen in a contemporary photograph of their stand at the Paris Exhibition of 1878, entitled 'Harmony in Yellow and Gold'. Whistler cherished a purpose as solemn as Morris's or Ashbee's, but he chose to adopt a deliber-

Left Affiliating an Aesthete by George du Maurier in *Punch*, 19 June 1880

ately flippant manner of expressing it. Hitherto, in England, artistic reformers had gone to great trouble to *court* acceptance for their innovations. Whistler took pleasure in antagonizing the general public – critics included – who responded by making fun of the late-blossoming Aestheticism we hear about from W. S. Gilbert and see caricatured in the *Punch* drawings of George du Maurier.

It is obvious from the languorous poses of the women, their style of dressing and hairdressing, that Rossetti and Burne-Jones were leading idols of the cult; as also, from the Empire bonnets and high-waisted frocks worn by that unconsciously comic family of girls, the Cimabue-Browns, that Kate Greenaway was another. This was late in the 1870s or early in the 1880s. The fact that the Cimabue-Brown children are nursing sunflowers instead of dolls points to a further contributory influence, that of Oscar Wilde. With his successful career at Oxford just behind him, Wilde upheld the special charm of the lily and the sunflower, thus demonstrating his own dependence on Pre-Raphaelitism, Japanese art and the English decorative art, as we have seen, so profoundly influenced by it. Along with these catalysts of the *Fin-de-Siècle* must be numbered the exotic periods of Walter Pater (in such an essay as that on Leonardo in his *Studies of the History of the Renaissance*, of 1873) and the life-style of Whistler, who was soon to accuse Wilde of pilfering his witticisms. Wilde's imagination had been fired by the Greek ideal – he did not care for Gothic cathedrals – and in a period of hectic conversions to the Catholic faith, he adopted a frankly pagan attitude to life. With Théophile Gautier's *Mademoiselle de Maupin* as his model, he proclaimed in the preface to *The Portrait of Dorian Gray* (1891): 'All art is quite useless.' At first a somewhat naïve propagandist for the simple life and social equality on the lines laid down by Morris, Wilde began to sound the note of mockery, interspersed with a diabolism that takes us back to Gustave Moreau.

The family tree bearing Wilde and Aubrey Beardsley as its latest fruits is indeed a complicated growth. To the almost soporific eroticism of Burne-Jones is added the hiss of evil from *A Rebours*, J.-K. Huysmans' novel of sensation which mentions actual works by the painters Moreau and Odilon Redon. Though several of the drawings are inferior to his best, the Beardsley-illustrated English edition of Wilde's *Salome* uniquely harnessed the Satanic talents of the author to those of the artist who best expresses, for the next four years, the morbid introspection of the Decadence. Beardsley did not walk down Piccadilly with a poppy or a lily in his hand: he cared little for nature at the florist's or in the raw. Though his work suffered terribly from the insensitivity of line-block reproduction, it demonstrated that hand-engraving, still employed by Morris at the Kelmscott Press, was now outmoded. In Leonard Smithers Beardsley had a publisher, disreputable in character, but with a real feeling for typography, as witness the assembled parts of *The Savoy* magazine. All in all, the perverse touch, the preciosity and the cynicism of this brief era provided a stimulating alternative to the highly artificial 'Olde England' of Morris and the younger generation of artist-craftsmen. And then, in 1898, came Beardsley's death at twenty-six, followed a bare two years later by Wilde's. What part Beardsley had played in introducing the broader character of the 1890s in the various branches of decorative art is difficult to estimate, but there are women's evening-gowns by Worth, a year or two after his death, which seem to confirm the ubiquity of *Yellow Book* influence. And the cover designed by him for Vincent O'Sullivan's *The Houses of Sin* (1897), trailing a typically horrific arabesque, is in complete accord with the New Art.

Art Nouveau [1]

For years after its first appearance in 1898, edition after edition of Walter Crane's *The Basis of Design* rolled off the presses and by 1925 the conscientious reader (a student, most likely) must have wondered what the author meant when, on the last page, he read of the 'sinister powers and false ideals that now oppress [art]'. Crane's own picture-books for children are much more to be prized than his collected lectures as an art-school principal. *Pan-Pipes* (a book of old songs), for instance, is a remarkable piece of collaboration with Edmund Evans, the colour-engraver, as well as between the Japanese aesthetic and Morris's. To other tasks the artist's natural innocence adapted itself less effectively, and no doubt *The Yellow Book* filled him with dismay. But he had now to face something beyond Beardsley's flirtations with the forces of evil – and in a field where he, primarily a decorative artist, felt the intrusion most keenly.

For Art Nouveau, in which there has been so extraordinary a revival of interest in recent times, swept away the masculine solidity of design as taught by Morris and understood by Crane, substituting for it an asymmetry positively frivolous. Not surprisingly, the headquarters of the new mode were established in Paris. Before Samuel Bing opened his shop of that name in the rue de Provence, just off the fashionable boulevard Haussmann, in 1895, and Julius Meier Graefe his rather similar Maison Moderne (giving a fresh twist to the adjective 'moderne') three years later, Gauguin and the Pont Aven painters had anticipated this development in non-commercial terms. Having absorbed the Japanese influence, they were discarding the accepted rectangular boundaries of a picture, as, for example, in such a work as Gauguin's 'La Belle Angèle', of 1889. And if exotic vegetation becomes the hallmark of Art Nouveau, this, too, had been liberally provided by the Symbolists throughout the 1880s, their swirling plants as different as possible from, say, the 'Peonies' of Manet. In the year of 'La Belle Angèle', Paris celebrated the hundredth anniversary of the French Revolution with a Universal Exhibition. And from 1889 the decoration of metal and ceramics achieved a hectic virtuosity, matched soon in the more delicate crafts, too, notably in jewelry.

On the whole, Art Nouveau steers clear of precious materials, the craftsman seeking admiration rather for his ingenious working of the semi-precious. Gilding and bronzing were much in evidence. We note a strong popular demand for mechanically-reduced sculpture by the Baroque and eighteenth-century French masters. The same eclectic taste led to a proliferation of mass-produced casts after J.-B. Carpeaux and originated by a charming *pasticheur*, A.-J. Dalou (at the peak of his career, when a political exile

Far right Loïe Fuller at the Folies Bergère, poster by Jules Chéret, 1897

in England in the 1870s). On a considerably smaller scale still, table-ornaments took the form of ecstatic, half-swooning girls, nude or in windswept drapery, like the group that makes up Léonard's 'jeu d'écharpe' (1900); girls that, again, if a dish be required, may be half-transformed into the ever-recurring motif of the water-lily. Art Nouveau pottery used to be dismissed as vulgar: but this will hardly do for the *émail velouté* of Edmond Lachenal or the restrained, sensitive workmanship of Emile Decoeur. The prince of Art Nouveau jewellers was of French extraction, though the scene of Carl Fabergé's activities happened to be St Petersburg. So exclusively bound up with Romanov family custom are his most impressive commissions, the Imperial Easter Eggs, that it is a surprise to find among the products of the St Petersburg House a green-gold *minaudière* bearing an elegant pattern of lily-of-the-valley with leaves rippled in the vogue manner.

In the nearly related field of carved and jewelled glass, the leading craftsmen were Emile Gallé and René Lalique. In Gallé's work there are delicate hints taken from both the Chinese and Japanese, and flowers and insects are created from applied enamel and tinted encrustations within the glass. He applied the gifts of a great artist to the most trivial accessories of female attire, including combs, fans, buckles. And with a variety of activity characteristic of Art Nouveau, Gallé turned effortlessly from jewelry and glass to furniture. At the Universal Exhibition held in Paris in 1900 he showed an exquisite worktable, retaining in its carved or inlaid decoration the serpentine flower-forms with which the style had been initiated. The eighteenth-century Rococo element persisted, too, as is apparent in the floral sprays carved in other woods and applied to an ash screen. Art Nouveau, indeed, carries a rich profusion of echoes from the past: included among them, the irrepressible curving Empire line that distinguishes Samuel Bing's chair, also of about 1900. What remains constant is the formalized, at times even abstract, plant-motif.

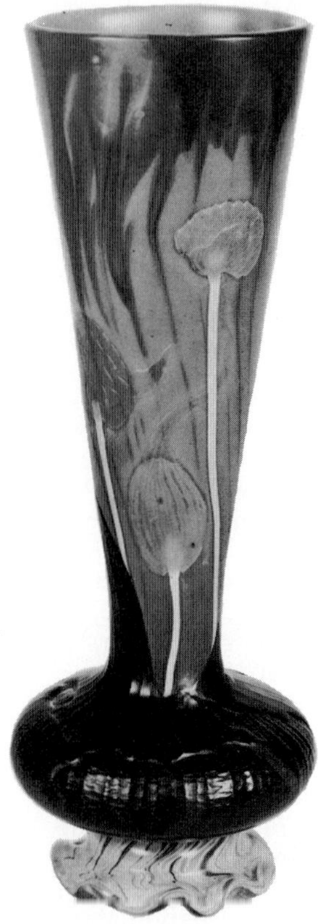

Above Marqueterie de verre vase by Emile Gallé, *c.* 1900. This technique was launched by Gallé in 1897 and involved pressing semi-molten glass into the surface of the piece before it was cooled

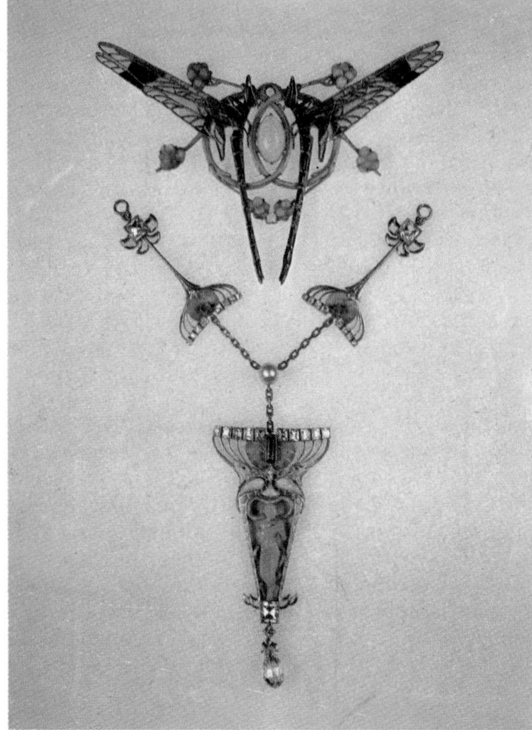

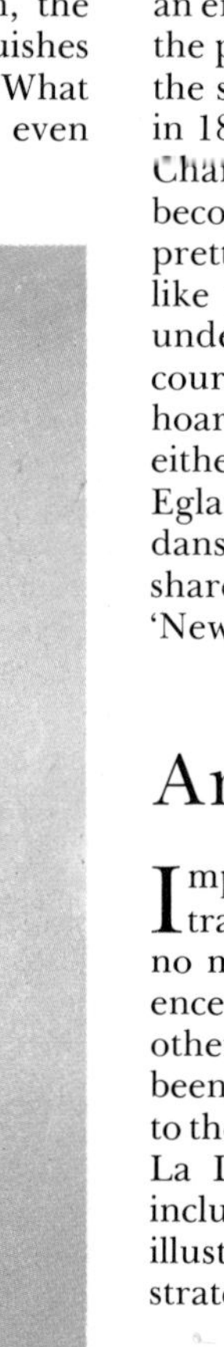

Right, top Hair piece by René Lalique. *Bottom* Pendant by Philippe Wolfers, Belgian, late 19th century

Art Nouveau furniture continued to press its claims right up to the 1914 watershed; but with this Universal Exhibition at the exact turn of the century, the climax of French craftsmanship in this style had already been reached. The year 1900 also brings to an end the splendid French contribution to the art of the poster, an art France had virtually created. Here the swirling rhythms seem to have been introduced in 1889 by Bonnard's admirable design for 'France-Champagne'. Vulgarized by Jules Chéret, they become the gay gyrations of an endless succession of pretty girls; then are congealed into the spaghetti-like patterns of Alphonse Mucha, for some years under Sarah Bernhardt's special patronage. But of course the undisputed master of the *grand-boulevard* hoardings during the 1890s was Toulouse-Lautrec, either for featherweight levity ('Troupe de Mlle Eglantine') or for massive strength ('Aristide Bruant dans son Cabaret'). These wonderful lithographs share in, and transcend, the extravagances of the 'New Art'.

Art Nouveau [2]

Important as was the part played by Paris in centralizing and promoting Art Nouveau, it exercised no monopoly. Indeed, to keep strictly to the sequence of events, we must go back to Brussels. Among other claims to distinction, the Belgian capital had been the scene of the first concert devoted exclusively to the works of Debussy. It took place in the gallery of La Libre Esthétique in 1894, in a setting which included posters by Toulouse-Lautrec and Beardsley illustrations from *Salome.* Nothing better demonstrates the wide-ranging application of a change in taste: not only did Debussy himself produce pastel-drawings in the Art Nouveau manner, in his music, too, he sedulously cultivated the arabesque, melodic equivalent of the arabesque, or flowing line, in art.

It was also in Brussels that a vulgar, moneyed but audacious patronage allowed Victor Horta his head over the designing of the celebrated Hôtel Tassel in 1892–3. Here the richly curvilinear ironwork in the entrance-hall has long been accepted as the flourish with which Art Nouveau was fairly launched. Henry van de Velde, another Belgian, developed the same sinuous, incisive rhythms. His house in Uccle (Brussels) deeply impressed Bing and led to a number of commissions in Paris; and, following on this, it was Van de Velde, Symbolist painter turned architect, rather than Horta, who commanded attention, above all – with disciples like Obrist and Endell – in Germany.

The headquarters of what came to be called the *Jugendstil* (when the art journal *Jugend* made its appearance in 1896) were located in Munich. In painting, any feather in the Germans' cap was borrowed from James Ensor or plucked outright from the eagle's-wing of Edvard Munch, who had already enjoyed a *succès de scandale* in Germany in 1892 and would be responsible for importing from Norway the seeds of Expressionism. The anti-Establishment groups (*Sezession*) in Munich and Berlin – another was led by Gustav Klimt in Vienna in 1897 – excelled in graphic work. Here again Munch's influence proved a doubly liberating force, since he himself was engaged in producing prints of some of his most striking compositions in paint. The stories about artists by Thomas Mann, particularly *Tonio Kröger* and *Der Tod in Venedig* (first published in 1903 and 1912), admirably convey the strains of feverish intellectualism and morbid sensuality which characterize this Teutonic Art Nouveau.

Project design for the dining room of the House of an Art Lover by Charles Rennie Mackintosh, 1901–2. Colour lithograph. University of Glasgow

Left Banister of the main staircase in the Hôtel Solvay, Brussels, gilt bronze and mahogany, designed by Victor Horta, 1895–1900

In Britain, meanwhile, appeared the extraordinary phenomenon of the new Glasgow School of Art, a building already under construction (1896–7) at the time of Van de Velde's earliest successes. The School, therefore, seems to have been of entirely independent origin. In fact, the influence of the architect, Rennie Mackintosh, was to be exercised rather in a move towards austerity than in helping to prolong the reign of Art Nouveau in all its extravagance. Mackintosh's building rises above Scott, Dalhousie and Renfrew Streets like a fortress, the ironwork alone weaving some twisting patterns round it. Mackintosh's interiors even in non-institutional buildings tended towards the ascetic: bare white walls, the minimum of ornament. Yet an irrepressible element of Celtic romanticism would break through; particularly, and not always pleasantly, in the series of tea-rooms (also in Glasgow) for Miss Cranston, to whom he was introduced in 1896: he was, indeed, carried away at times by the enthusiasm of a group which included such artists as the Macdonald sisters, one of whom he married. To this extent parochial, it might be supposed that Mackintosh's work would have been chiefly welcomed by expatriate Scots in London and that his

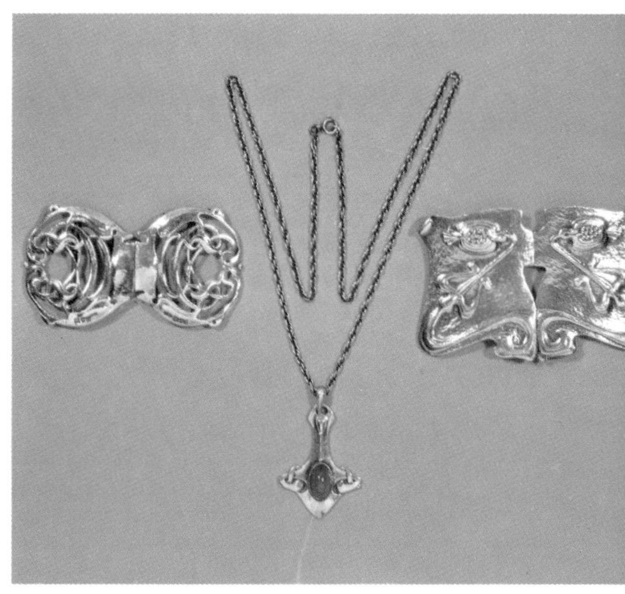

Right Jewelry designed by Archibald Knox. Waist clasp (*left*), silver with interlaced Celtic design, 1904. Waist clasp (*right*), silver with repoussé design on hammered ground, 1900. Pendant and chain (*centre*), set with cabochon-cut chrysoprase

eccentric, 'Spook School', spindle-back chairs, for instance, would have found little favour on the Continent. Precisely the opposite happened: Mackintosh was ignored south of the Border and hailed with great éclat in Germany. This is explained by the admiration felt by German designers for William Morris, which focused their attention upon Morris's native successors, among them the remarkable C. F. A. Voysey, a pioneer in total-planning (the client having, not only his house, but his spoons and forks, designed for him!). Though Morris's battle against the machine had really been lost long before his death in 1896, the example of his robust, wide-ranging activities can be seen all over Europe in the continuing determination of architects to produce their own furniture, tiles, fabrics, china and glass: 'Our whole new movement', wrote the influential Hermann Muthesius, in *Das Englische Haus* (1904–5), 'is built on the results which England has achieved from 1860 up to the mid-Nineties.' The Vienna Secessionists first came into their own at an exhibition at the Gartenbaugesellschaft in 1898. One saw the avant-garde divided here as elsewhere now into the gay, extravagant *Jugendstil* of J. M. Olbrich and the immaculately purposeful forms and colour restraint of Josef Hoffmann.

But if a retreat from extravagance was pretty generally in evidence in Britain, Germany and Austria, Art Nouveau of an astonishing exoticism continued to satisfy the Spanish architect, Antoni Gaudí. Barcelona, where he practised, was the centre of the Catalan 'Modernismo' from which sprang the youthful Picasso; and it is difficult to imagine where else such a radical attitude towards structure and ornament would have been tolerated. The echoes from England are rarer here, though the Pre-Raphaelites were much admired and a Jeckyll-like sunflower-motif can be found repeated in the iron garden-fence of the Vincens house, dating back to 1878. Yet while the snaking floral patterns in and on the Güell house, of about ten years later, are remarkable enough examples of an Art Nouveau barely dreamed of elsewhere, perhaps the greatest interest Gaudí's work holds for us is its pointing, whole generations ahead, to the importance of 'texture', whether extemporized out of uneven brick and stone, or from an apparently fortuitous jetsam of fractured glass and pottery; the message being brought home even more in the window grilles of the Güell Colony chapel – for there we find Gaudí experimenting with discarded machine parts rather in the manner of the Surrealists or the modern Scottish sculptor, Eduardo Paolozzi. Gaudí's genius awakened no immediate response, however. Barcelona's most gifted sons spread their wings and flew off to Paris, and the revolutionary Cathedral of the Sagrada Familia, with its incredible snail's-horn finials, remains unfinished to this day.

Art and Industry

W. B. Yeats, in one of his autobiographical volumes, remarks upon the return to normality that the twentieth century brought with it. The *Fin-de-Siècle* gracefully fizzled out, and Art Nouveau itself (except, perhaps, for Louis Comfort Tiffany's interesting development, in the United States, of what he called 'favrile' glass) never again reached the standard of originality displayed at the Paris Exposition of 1900.

Impatient of the stagy Social-Realism of the Newlyn School, and reacting strongly against the condescension of Whistler and Wilde towards all things non-urban, the younger generation of British artists and writers began to celebrate once more the beauties of nature. The romance of the 'open road' proved irresistible. Yeats and Lady Gregory studied the language of the Irish tinkers; Sampson (Liverpool University Librarian) and Augustus John, the deep Romani of North Wales. The move was towards simplicity, to the simple ballad of W. H. Davies and the *alla prima* panel that John and Innes slipped into their portable colour-boxes.

The decorative arts already bore the stamp of Morris's personality. Visions of a 'pack-horse on the down' and a London 'small and white and clean' might be too self-indulgently nostalgic for the first decade of the twentieth century, but – even forty years on from the foundation of Morris & Co. – traditional standards of fine craftsmanship set one dreaming of oak carved amid the bracken where the tree had been felled. C. R. Ashbee came as near as he could to this when, in 1902, he shifted his Guild and School of Handicrafts, lock, stock and barrel, from London's East End to the beautiful little Cotswold town of Chipping Campden. About sixty specialists, from printers to blacksmiths, were involved. It was a noble enterprise, but, unlike the *Werkbund* in Germany, without the necessary stability a link with industry would have given it. This is not to deny the influence for good that could still be exercised by

Cabinet on stand, designed and hand made by Sidney Barnsley, *c.* 1910. Quarter-cut English oak with black and white inlay, simple gouged decoration and hand-made iron handles

Box and cover of ebony and figured walnut, painted by Alfred and Louise Powell, by Ernest Gimson, *c.* 1905

the Arts and Crafts Movement upon machine-production, even in its latter years. Typography and book-design notably benefited. And by the sheerest chance a young but interested observer of the Cotswold invasion was Gordon Russell, who would later incorporate the same ideals of honesty and simplicity in the quite different context of mass-production. The Chipping Campden commune did not, in fact, promote the demand for hand-workmanship. Ashbee had reckoned without the economic depression which marked the closing years of the Edwardian age. In 1908 the Guild was finally disbanded. Its founder, however, had been coming to terms with the inevitable; and, not uninfluenced by his friend Frank Lloyd Wright, saw that there was less to fear than supposed from the intensification of factory techniques, providing Britain could follow America and Germany in determining that man, not the machine, ended up as master.

Kenton & Co., that other somewhat utopian project, had failed in 1892, when, like Ashbee but a little earlier, three of its most distinguished designers, Ernest Gimson and the Barnsley brothers, Ernest and Sidney, moved to the Cotswolds, reaching Sapperton in 1902. With the same respect for directness in design, these makers of furniture (all of them trained as architects) delighted in elaborate enrichment: as may be understood from Sidney Barnsley's particularly fine oak coffer, painted by Alfred and Louise Powell, of about 1910. And though C. F. A. Voysey's peak performances in architecture were not to be repeated in the twentieth century, he continued to turn out the chairs, rush-seated and bearing the symbol of the cut-out heart, which so well demonstrate the Arts and Crafts Movement's essentially rural, olde-worlde, character.

With the advent of war, nevertheless, Voysey too had to renounce some of the independence of private practice for employment from 1915 till 1919 as chief designer to the Liquor Control Board. Nor would it have benefited these survivors of the Morris tradition had they been following avant-garde fashions instead. For Roger Fry's artists' co-operative, the Omega Workshops in Fitzroy Square, London, founded in 1913 and pioneering hand-printed tex-

The Voysey Room at the Geffrye Museum, London

tiles and painted furniture in the Post-Impressionist and near-abstract modes, was also dealt its death-blow by the war. In the influential circle of Fry and Clive Bell, author of the important *Art* (1914) which propounded the theory of Significant Form, a Gallic gaiety prevailed. One had to go outside London, to Birmingham, to rediscover the earnest, socio-religious attitude towards art. There in the crafts of tempera-painting, jewelry and book-illustration, devout spirits like Maxwell Armfield, Arthur and Georgina Gaskin, Charles and Margaret Gere, F. L. Griggs and F. Cayley Robinson were rightly attracting attention, but the line they pursued could often be discouragingly archaizing and parochial.

Ashbee had learned to look to Germany for a solution to the fifty-year-old conflict between craftsmanship and mechanization. W. R. Lethaby, too, had a high regard for the Germans. In 1896, this leading member of the Art-Workers' Guild became co-principal of the new Central School, gathering round him some of the most distinguished contemporary designers to act as full- and part-time staff. Though he set his sights high, Lethaby stressed the merits of common sense and efficiency; the type designed by Edward Johnston, a teacher at the Central, for the London Underground providing perhaps the perfect example of what he meant. Lethaby believed in the 'scientific method' and was prepared to see as much beauty in a fine piece of engineering as in the handmade article. Like many others, he was greatly impressed by the work of the German designers shown at the Cologne Exhibition of 1914.

The *Werkstätte* display of that year included items made up of mass-produced parts, yet in which the machine's role had been highly discreet. All the budding geniuses of design throughout Europe were in sympathy with the geometric style which had its origin on the assembly-line. The office of Peter Behrens, where the Swiss Le Corbusier found himself working alongside Walter Gropius and Mies van der Rohe, was a far cry from Edgbaston, with its sentimental Goose Girls and romantic amethyst-drop necklaces. The new *Zeitstil* seemed to spring out of nowhere in a dozen different forms, though all obedient to the same central theme. One thinks of Futurist art in Italy, already playing at something akin to cybernetics; of the svelte, machine-tooled monsters masquerading as men and women in Wyndham Lewis's drawings of the same period; of Marcel Duchamp shocking America at the Armory Show (1913); of Le Corbusier's own gradually-forming determination to discard the Garden City concept for a planning-system as rigidly reduced to the straight line and the right-angle as Piet Mondrian was beginning to work out for his paintings. Thrust and counter-thrust in this process were to be expected. Hermann Muthesius, the man behind the *Werkstätten* in Germany, was often hard at work defending the union of designers and architects with manufacturing interests. Finally, England proved not too crudely patriotic to learn from the enemy when, in 1915, she formed her own version of the *Werkbund*, the Design and Industries Association.

By that time, the poet's 'rural pen' had been temporarily cast aside: his songs were of the battlefield. The paint peeled off Augustus John's caravans in the garden at Alderney Manor; and both he and Lucien Pissarro (naturalized, 1916) just escaped arrest while sketching out of doors. Apart from Bloomsbury's pacifists hoeing the bean-row in Sussex, culture had deserted the countryside. For those on leave, it was the city that offered, at its glittering centre, the prophylactic dreamed of in the trenches. Colonel Herbert Read, in London to receive his D.S.O. at the Palace, did not return to Yorkshire, but relaxed in the plush and gilt of the Café Royal – and accompanied the Sitwells to the Ballet.

Iridescent glass vases attributed to Professor Rudolf Bakalowits of Graz, Austria, *c.* 1902

Balletomania

What the avant-garde enthused in about 1918 was a somewhat draggle-tailed Diaghilev Company, rescued from Spain by Sir Oswald Stoll. *Schéhérazade* still provided the highlight of the repertory, but inevitably lacked the excitements of the first Paris production of 1910, with Nijinsky (now insane in Switzerland) missing from the cast. The Russian influence, and particularly that of the Ballets Russes, upon Western European design has been a little neglected. Alongside the thin-line style, sparing of colour, which developed out of Primitive Cubism and consciously, or unconsciously, conveyed the growing subordination of the handworker to the machine, occurred a renaissance of Eastern exoticism. Its provenance – while we must not forget the liberation of colour hastened by Henri Matisse and André Derain in Paris itself – was Russia.

The process may be traced back to 1906, to the Russian Exhibition at the Grand Palais in the French capital. The impresario was Sergei Diaghilev and the designer-in-chief Léon Bakst. There followed a series of concerts of Russian music at the Paris Opéra in 1907. But Russia's overtures were not all of the musical kind: in 1909, for instance, an Anglo-

Russian Trust, of a pattern repeated in other countries, came into existence. Relentless publicity built up Russia as the investor's paradise. Long-held doubts of the reliability of that far-distant and mysterious Empire were smoothed away and Imperial railway-stocks, rubber-stamped by the Duma, prospered accordingly – till war broke out and with effect from December 1917 all foreign debts were finally repudiated by the Bolsheviks. During the honeymoon-period between 1910 and 1914, however, the zest of Diaghilev's productions swept artists and designers off their feet. Nineteen-ten was the year in which, as has been said, *Schéhérazade* was first performed in Paris. The luscious music had been culled from Rimsky-Korsakov; Michel Fokine directed; but the most remarkable feature of the entertainment consisted in the costumes and settings by Bakst. As an easel-painter, Bakst could be, and often was, third-rate. Where stage-spectacles were concerned, his barbaric over-emphasis wonderfully oiled the wheels of production. The shuddering reds and greens of Shahryar's harem derived, perhaps, from Fauvism; but the textural enrichment – the blaze of stencilled pattern, silks, silk-twills, satins, gold thread, encrustations of pearls that sent the price of individual costumes soaring up to forty pounds – together with the arbitrary mixture of Persian delicacy and Russian bombast was all Bakst's own.

It is significant that Middleton Murry decided on the title of his revolutionary magazine *Rhythm* in Paris, during the winter of 1910–11, after consultation with the Paris-domiciled painter J. D. Fergusson. When *Rhythm* published in its first number (summer, 1911) a drawing by an American artist also living in Paris, Anne Estelle Rice, 'to express as plainly as possible the rhythm for which she strives', it turned out to be an impression of *Schéhérazade*. During the autumn and winter of 1911 and throughout 1912, *Rhythm* carried drawings relating to *L'Après-Midi d'un Faune*, *Le Spectre de la Rose* and *Le Dieu Bleu*. A full-page caricature of Ida Rubinstein in *Salomé* also appeared. And an even closer link with the Ballets Russes becomes evident when the magazine published drawings by Natalia Gontcharova and Michel Larionov, Bakst's most able colleagues. Murry himself, however, was unable to define 'rhythm', to describe exactly what part it played in a modern work of art and why it was so important. Rollo Myers spoke of 'large vibrations distilled from Nature'; Laurence Binyon used the metaphor, 'waves of wind in the corn'. Later, in a joint statement, Murry and Katherine Mansfield declared that the *quest* for Rhythm was nothing less than the unending movement of life itself, compounded of freedom, reality and individuality fused into the genius of the artist. Looking back now, we recognize easily enough an equivalent for the tremendous visual experience that Paris went through in 1910. To the 'movement' created by Bakst's settings, a movement of colour (an emerald green 'flecked with red', a 'shimmering' blue, a 'burning' crimson: the epithets are from Cyril Beaumont's first-hand recollections), was added, of course, the movement of the dance itself. The inimitable Pavlova and Karsavina headed a superb troupe. Nijinsky in particular astounded the public by a flowing movement so light and magically prolonged that it approached levitation.

Though the magazine *Rhythm* displayed the works of Marquet, Derain, Herbin and Friesz, as well as Picasso, to its readers, its world was necessarily a restricted one. In the wider sphere of French painting, and – astonishingly enough – something like two years later, much the same sublimation of ideas taken from the Dance made itself manifest at the Salon des Indépendants of 1913. Here it was given the name Orphism. The chief protagonists included Robert and Sonia Delaunay and Frank Kupka. Their aim was to give to Cubism the colour and movement – physical life – it so desperately lacked. For Robert Delaunay, the result was a group of compositions made up of brilliant-hued, bubble-like shapes, entitled 'Les Disques' and 'Formes circulaires cosmiques'. Later, he, too, adopted the word 'rythme' to suggest what he was seeking from abstract colour. What is of greater interest is that out of these discs and circular forms developed the typical fabric patterns of the Twenties, which continued throughout the decade. Even here, through the numerous mutations brought about by different minds and media involved, it would be foolish to underestimate the personal influence of Bakst himself. By way of the exclusive Houses of Poiret, Fortuny and Cartier, then of the big stores on both sides of the Atlantic, the hot colour, the rich texture, the 'Greek' or folksy Russian pattern units, inspired by the opulent ripple of the dance – its 'rhythm' – and having the stamp of his genius, changed the character of every department of the decorative arts.

Art Deco [1]

When the mists of war cleared away, and in the rest of Europe the florid, exotic and alien became the new *chic*, the case of Germany was different. Outlawed by the victorious Allies, but fully backed by the government of Saxe-Weimar, Walter Gropius and his associates took the bit between their teeth. Here was a return to the stark and the streamlined to cut time and costs, a need, never more pressing, for an alliance between art and the machine. Chronologically, the Bauhaus, founded in 1919, pioneered design in the Twenties and Thirties. In practice, however, because of Germany's isolation, this School, or 'House' of Building, did not make itself felt abroad till the end of the first decade.

During the intervening period, Paris effortlessly regained her ascendancy. The society she catered for was very different from the official patronage extended to the *Formlehre* group in Weimar. It consisted of the 'rich rich' (as Cole Porter distinguished them from the merely 'rich'): those who flocked to the centre of gaiety with money – much of it newly made – to burn. For them Jacques Ruhlmann provided something quite outside time or fashion; not what they wanted, which would doubtless have been a jazzy variation on Bakst, but what he wanted: rooms of exquisite austerity, the fluted, tapering legs of his furniture sinking into rugs of barbaric splendour, these latter, like the wall-decorations, offering the only real concessions to modernity, for the all-pervasive spirit was Empire. So, in introducing 'Art Deco', we meet with immediate contradictions. The term, now in everybody's mouth, while suggesting a style, is really a combination of styles, though very broadly capable of division into two recognizable

Above Enamelled-glass hanging shade, the octagonal domed glass bowl etched and enamelled on the inside with abstract geometric motifs in yellows, blues, mauves, etc. Signed in cameo, Loys Lucha, *c.* 1925. Sotheby's Belgravia

Above Wall light by Edgar Brandt, 1925. Victoria & Albert Museum

Below Pot by Bernard Leach, the St Ives Pottery, Cornwall

characters, 'rounded' for the Twenties, 'angular' for the Thirties. Further, there is a gaiety about the decorative arts of the period 1920–29, just as there is a perceptible *Angst* about those which follow through from the Depression to the outbreak of World War II. And, as has always been so, the decorative arts reflect a mood earlier and more vividly expressed in the fine arts, in music or in literature.

In the Twenties, one's search was for amusement. Whether it is T. S. Eliot's *The Waste Land* or Erik Satie's *Relâche* or one of Marie Laurencin's Sapphic maidens sniffing at a rose: all have their serious side, yet invoke, and were created to invoke, a smile. So much is still true of Ruhlmann's Spartan expensiveness. The juxtaposing of Percier-and-Fontaine-style chandeliers, and couches reminiscent of Mme Récamier, with Sonia Delaunay's Cubist rugs and fashion-plate painted-panels by Jean Dupas sustains the desired whimsicality. Though in general sparing of anything too 'modern', Ruhlmann and his peers, designers like André Groult and Charles Martin, provided the new nabobs and their wives with some striking developments where chairs were concerned. There is the 'Early Christian' tub in dusty tones of velvet; the three-sided silken box, cavernously relaxing; then, after various experiments in *glass*, the bent-metal 'barbarity' of Le Corbusier, the prototype of which had been Bauhaus-Viennese (Marcel Breuer) and German (Ludwig Mies van der Rohe). Ornament was stripped to the minimum in these luxurious apartments. One might, however, let oneself go on a piece of richly-convoluted ironwork commissioned from Subes. And then there was always a deliberately-placed piece of sculpture on which the eye could focus with a different kind of satisfaction.

After Auguste Rodin's death in 1917, Aristide Maillol was clearly the master in this field. For decorative purposes, however, carvings were in greater demand than bronzes, and for the heavy forms associated with Maillol and his imitators began to be substituted an emaciation equally mannered, the chief contributory causes for the volte-face being the vogue for African wood-carvings and for the carvings of the Yugoslav Ivan Mestrović. But sculptors, getting wind of this market, sprang up everywhere, each with his own brand of sophisticated naïveté which, as we look back on it, carries an unmistakable family-likeness. America is well represented by Paul Manship; White Russia by Chana Orloff; while, in Britain, the spoils were shared by Frank Dobson, Maurice Lambert and Sir Charles Wheeler. Rather stiffly formalized, these invariably female or animal figures provide another perfect souvenir of the entire interwar period. They first appear in splendid apartments hung with damask and carpeted in zebra-skin; but later something very like them crops up on the 'lounge' mantelpieces of the petty bourgeoisie: the end of the road, very likely, being a girl-footballer in gold-sprayed plastic and a commercial-pottery fawn. Dobson flourished mainly in the narrow world of Bloomsbury; Lambert found himself the darling of the Maharajas; but, since he worked right through the Twenties and into the Thirties on Sir Herbert Baker's Bank of England and India and South Africa Houses, Wheeler's sculpture is all around us in London and repays examination, as a kind of Jean Dupas in stone.

Nevertheless, Paris remained the centre of novelty, and sometimes of genius. As its Métro entrances had been monuments to Art Nouveau, so its shop-fronts provided excellent examples of the newer mode. The term 'Art Deco' itself was of French coinage, deriving from the impressive display of early-Twenties products shown at the International Exhibition of Decorative Art held in Paris in 1925 and first becoming current about ten years later as a shortened form of *Art Décoratif*, 'Art Déco'. In 1927 France's luxury liner, the *Ile-de-France*, set out on her maiden voyage. This had been planned as a red-letter day for the leading designers, who combined to produce an hypnotic shop-window, attracting all eyes to French taste and ingenuity. Included were a chapel (a great novelty), where hung a luminous Christ in *verre moulé*; a vast dining-room, glittering with Lalique glass, by Pierre Patou; a tea-room in which Ruhlmann's exquisite austerity scored a signal triumph; and the grand salon of Louis Suë and André Mare, its river nymphs rising in gilded splendour between the abstract-patterned Aubusson carpet and electric-lights hidden under elaborate mouldings and roses.

Some of the wealthiest of the *Ile-de-France*'s passengers, however, were renewing a cult of simplicity in the decoration of their own homes; with a preference for the severe, blanched style of Mrs Syrie Maugham, wife of the novelist. Indeed, as the post-war decade began to approach what would be a harrowing close, Syrie Maugham and the American Elsie de Wolfe (Lady Mendl) were turning interior-design into a métier for the woman of fashion. The simplicity, even severity, could have something to do with economics. The needs of the new-rich had been satisfied by now: the elegant less rich, or (in the modest terminology which made it preferable to refer to a house as a 'cottage') new-poor, were perhaps making a virtue of necessity, so that designers had to fall in with the wishes of a second wave of clients. In fact, the *à la mode* bleakness of Knightsbridge and Chelsea was curiously echoed in St Ives, Cornwall, in the work of the studio-potter, Bernard Leach, who, won over to subtle Oriental glazes of brown and grey, succeeded in outlawing colourful ceramics for generations to come.

It cannot be said that the restraint of an élite in Paris, Mayfair or the Cornish peninsula determined the character of popular decorative art during the Twenties. Impresarios of cheap entertainment moved from the fairground into the motion-picture business. 'Flea-pits' had sufficed for the war years; now something more than a screen and projector was required. All but the destitute attended cinema performances regularly, often with every change of bill. This vast public revelled in auditoriums throbbing to the Wurlitzer and bathed in magically-kaleidoscopic light, where painted cypresses, set behind three-dimensional balustrades, transported you to the Pincio or Generalife Gardens. The ticket-booth might be protected by a Moorish grille, the 'ladies' parlour' entered by way of an Old English lychgate. In certain instances – especially in America – the whole edifice reproduced an historic style, that of a Gothic cathedral or Florentine palace, or, inspired in 1922 by the discovery of the fabulous tomb of Tutankhamun, an Egyptian temple. Grauman's Theatre in that idiom (to be distinguished from another in the Chinese) was one of the sights of Hollywood. Even Britain had its

'Luxors', complete with entrance-pylons and hypostyle foyers.

The cinema supplied too popular a form of escape for the Wall Street crash of 1929 to interfere disastrously with its building-programme. But many producers of so-called luxury art goods went out of business. Among the hardest hit were studio-craftsmen who had been enjoying a boom in etchings and woodcuts, and those making use of their skills to publish fine-paper, lavishly illustrated books. The French proved the most adept in this field, as in so many others, and some of the finest bargains to be picked up in Charing Cross Road during the years between the wars included works decorated by such engravers as Daragnès, Hermann Paul and Alfred Latour. And in France there flourished a happy agreement, on other occasions, which permitted a draughtsman pure and simple to hand over his designs to a professional wood cutter, the result retaining the vigour of the sketch and at the same time marrying perfectly with the type.

It will be fitting to leave the Twenties on a note of gaiety, however, and the hand that most characteristically, because most extravagantly, evokes this is Erté's. A lesser figure than Bakst, Erté (born Romain de Tirtoff) began to achieve his success as a designer for the theatre a year or two before Bakst's death. He graduated from the fashion house of Paul Poiret, and a costume like 'Fedora' (for Ganna Walska: 1920) sticks close enough to contemporary dress, in contradistinction to his more celebrated fantasies commissioned by the Folies Bergère and Metro Goldwyn Mayer. Erté's importance as a grand interpreter of the *post-bellum* was recognized in 1966 at the exhibition 'Les Années 25' at the Musée des Arts Décoratifs, Paris.

Art Deco [2]

The 1930s, lacking the hectic abandon of the Twenties, are only now beginning to acquire a recognizable character of their own. It would be tempting, but still dangerous, to ascribe an increasing formalism to any one influence. The Depression, which lingered on till 1934, may have encouraged the client, and then the consultant, to adopt a plainer style for straightforward budgetary reasons. It is also true that the Bauhaus, opposed to ornament on principle, commanded greater attention abroad at a time when, from 1928 onwards, it was having to put up with increased hostility from the Nazis at home. The events of 1933 forced its distinguished teachers, present and past, to leave Germany and, receiving no support from the Soviet Union, spread their ideas throughout Western Europe and the New World: for some while, however, they remained architects speaking only to architects. Then again, as Mr Bevis Hillier argues, we ought to take into account the very great and accelerating interest aroused by Mexican art. Louis Henri Sullivan, the genius of high building, had contented himself with the axiom, 'form follows functions'. Now those who welcomed the cultural revolution which produced the celebrated mural-painter Diego Rivera made meaningful comparisons between a thirty-five-storey skyscraper and the Pyramid of Cuicuilco.

All the same, the cube teapot and multifaceted pendant light-fitting could have sprung from exemplars nearer home than that. 'Modernism', understood as the offspring of Braque and Picasso, was at last coming to roost in the High Street. Helped along by McKnight Kauffer posters, advertisements featuring scent-bottles designed by René Lalique and Etienne Drian's lean but sprightly fashion-drawings available in old waiting-room 'glossies', everyone was becoming acclimatized to hard-edge elegance. To 1930 belongs one of the most remarkable examples of 'modernism for the people', Oliver Bernard's illuminated-glass foyer and staircase for the Strand Palace Hotel – the dismembered units of which are today stored in the vaults of the Victoria and Albert Museum, London. In the same year, Oswald Milne redecorated Claridges Hotel, one of the patrician establishments, in a manner noticeably less imaginative and awesomely bleak. How much further, designers must have been asking themselves, could they *afford* to pursue simplicity? An Arctic waste of a room, even if its few furnishings were the most expensive of their kind, represented a Quixotic gesture on the part of the entrepreneur.

The French, certainly, were not prepared to allow the Depression to interfere with their commerce in luxurious accessories. Extremes of functionalism met with disapproval in Paris. Furniture's bare bones disappeared under the softest velvets and silk-shantungs, and there was a discreet return to reminders of the past – most often, of the eighteenth century. And when it came to another floating showroom, the *Normandie*, though launched in an inauspicious year, 1932, was every bit as dazzling as the *Ile-de-France*. Many of those who, like Ruhlmann, Dupas and Lalique, had worked on the earlier ship contributed to the splendour of the new one. As the decade got into its stride, the London decorator, still looking to Paris for inspiration, felt a need similar to his French counterpart's to enliven the repetitious harmonies in beige-and-white leather and Nigerian

Modernist cocktail service in clear glass with jazzy streaks enamelled in black with wedge-shape double bases, possibly from the Baccarat workshops, *c.* 1930. Sotheby's Belgravia

Vanity case by Lacloche Frères, Paris. Face of irregular silhouette and enamelled in flesh colour, white and black, with a sophisticated caricature of Enrico Caruso. The inside is gilt with two hinged covers concealing powder compartments, and with a hinged mirror opening to reveal ivory writing pad. Engraved inside with a facsimile signature of Enrico Caruso and with maker's mark and French poinçons, *c.* 1930. Sotheby's Belgravia

Below Peacock lamp of clear glass with acid-etched vertical ribs, the 'stopper' decorated with a pair of moulded and acid-etched peacocks, by René Lalique, *c.* 1925. Victoria & Albert Museum, Handley-Read Collection

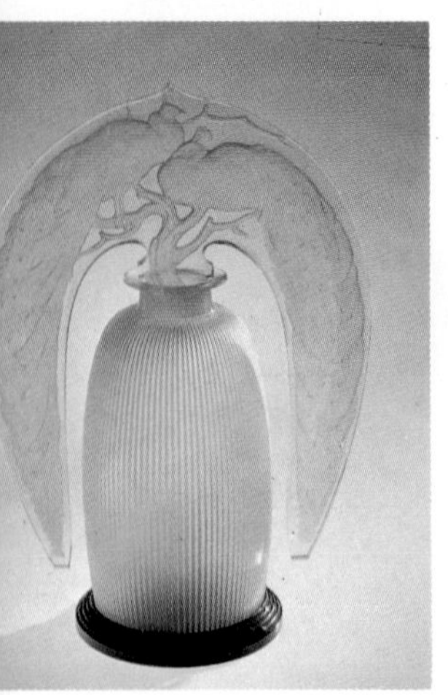

cherrywood with some element out of a totally different world.

In *Eminent Victorians* (1918) Lytton Strachey had vented the disapproval of his circle on the heroes and heroines they had been brought up to respect. For the next ten years, Victorian art seemed as contemptible as Victorian morality. Landseer and the Prince Consort, in particular, were derided. The turn of the tide was marked by the enormous success of Noel Coward's *Bitter Sweet* in 1929. From having been repulsive, the Victorians became quaint. For its smaller but influential public, Sir John Betjeman's first slim book of verse, *Mount Sion* (1932), proved another eye-opener. One perceived just how charming bustles really were and what affectionate humour nineteenth-century church-restoration could provoke. And when Charles Ginner, in 1935, chose for the subject of a painting a straightforward view of the Albert Memorial, it must be taken as the final and profound retraction of the anti-Victorian article of faith. The fact is that growing fears of the Police State, with its impressive but evilly-motivated functionalism, had begun to give super-efficiency, even that of Le Corbusier's house as a 'machine for living' (*Vers une Architecture*, 1923) a bad name. Well might the architect protest: 'Think of the inconveniences it saves you!' To this, like Aldous Huxley's Savage, any contemporary poet would have replied: 'But I like the inconveniences.' (*Brave New World*, 1932.)

But the unemployment-haunted, bromide-seeking general public was neither so well-informed nor so logical. It shopped around, acquiring now mass-produced *bric-à-Braque*, now won back to shoddy historicism. English suburban villas in the new ribbon development would be supplied with a sun-ray pattern gate (thought to derive from pre-Columbian models), though continuing to pay tribute to Sir Walter Scott with the name 'Kenilworth' painted on it. Inside, the honours were shared between the 'stepped' mirror over the mantelpiece and the Jacobethan, 'Drageway' dining-suite. When the war everyone dreaded showed signs of becoming a reality less than ten years after the Wall Street crash, an understandable impatience with the results of so much muddled thinking and desperate keeping up with the Joneses led to Betjeman's hope that 'friendly bombs' might fall on Slough, in his view the Sodom and Gomorrah of proletarian hideousness. The author, of course, had been joking: in 1937, when *Continual Dew* was published, bombs could still be the subject of jokes. A bare four years later, in the midst of hostilities, Sir Herbert Read (who is reported to have remarked once, in conversation: 'Beauty? I thought we were talking about art') wrote a pamphlet entitled *To Hell with Culture*; *Democratic Values are New Values.* For Culture is an ever-changing concept. Betjeman's version would not have done for Read, who collected Avinash Chandras and Ernst van Leydens; and neither would have felt at home with Sir William Llewellyn, President of the Royal Academy from 1928 to 1938, when he equated aesthetic perfection (on a Pathé news-reel) with Watteau and eighteenth-century cabinet-making. Now none of these interpretations will stand up to the cold, hard light as we enter the last quarter of the twentieth century. The vogue for Art Deco is a sign of it. In our present mood, the way for which has been paved by Pop Art and 'New Tendency', we set the highest value on that which seems best to express the spirit of the age which brought it into existence, however vulgar in Sir William Llewellyn's eyes it may have appeared. This is what fascinates us about the jazz-patterned, rectangular hairbrush, the shield-faced crystal clock and the cigarette-lighter spurting flame out of an onyx galleon. Originating from some of the most exclusive designers of the Twenties and Thirties, from a Jean Puiforcat or a Gabriel Argy-Rousseau, they would be multiplied in every kind of plastic and make-believe metal before the second decade was over. One day, it is safe to forecast, collectors will be vying not only for the archetype, but for the 'trash'. If anyone doubts this, let him examine the *Archive of Source Material for Twentieth Century Art* presented to the University of St Andrews by Eduardo Paolozzi, and recently catalogued. It includes Fold-Away Farms and Frankenstein Kits, Comic Playing-Cards and Just-Married Kissing Couples. The hour of the folk-artifact has arrived!

Collecting in the New Fields

The salerooms began to take serious note of Art Nouveau and Art Deco in the early 1960s. It was not clear at first who was buying, or why. Now the principal collectors are known to come from the United States, Germany and France. Americans like to concentrate on style, Germans on technical processes, the French on collecting as a means of re-creating a complete environment. The most spectacular collection so far has been that of a Frenchman, M. Doucet. Half of this was bequeathed to the Musée des Arts Décoratifs, and the other half came under the hammer in 1972, establishing among other things today's high valuation of the best craftsmanship in the new area. Meanwhile, we have seen a parallel awakening of interest in objects of an ephemeral character. Openly accepted as 'kitsch', they are given semi-ironical, 'glass-dome' treatment, mainly by young people with a curiosity in the life-style of the day-before-yesterday. These young people vary from wealthy pop-singers to penniless students, the objects they collect from Lalique motor-mascots to hard junk. Here, the junky end of the scale is ignored and a summary supplied of items, worthwhile but not necessarily for the wealthiest only, which may be expected to crop up from day to day in the auction-rooms during the mid-1970s.

Art Nouveau

GLASS

Gallé, Tiffany and Lalique are the most highly respected names here. A fine example by Gallé, appearing on the market a short while ago, was a vase flattened in form with a flared neck, its amber ground overlaid in pink on white and carved with a floral motif. (Overlay glass vases by d'Argental, Müller Frères and Legras have run Gallé close, too.) Tiffany favrile-ware may be seen at its best in iridescent golden vases of slender, flared shape; and, in the same colouring, Tiffany dishes and liqueur-glasses have been in evidence. The Daum brothers were

Left Silver-mounted green-glass decanter with maker's mark for the Guild of Handicraft and London assay marks 1901

Left, below A collection of painted underglaze earthenware tiles by William de Morgan

Right, below Cymric silver covered box made for Liberty & Co., *c.* 1900. Bethnal Green Museum

also fine workers in glass and fellow-members, with Gruber, of Gallé's 'Nancy School', and have still, perhaps, to enjoy the recognition they deserve. Lalique was a jeweller in the first place, his designs for glass dating from after the 1900 Exhibition: collectors will have reason to become familiar with the engraved signature 'R. Lalique' on bowls and vases of the earlier phase of his activities in this medium.

POTTERY

The collector can choose between vases, bowls, dishes, but will certainly direct part of his attention to plaques and pottery figures. Vase motifs include Leda and the Swan, stylized scrolls and floral sprays and endless nymphs in flowing draperies. A typical pottery plaque covered in an iridescent blue glaze, bears an angel playing a guitar. The various commercial pottery-manufacturers – Carlton, Pilkington, Doulton, etc. – are worth careful examination; and a lookout should be kept for examples of Martinware (freakish birds, acting as tobacco-jars, are among its favourite productions). Apart from the French, Austrian and Dutch pieces are common, the latter from factories in Gouda and Arnhem; and pottery groups from all over Europe reiterate the theme of dancers in flowing robes with flowers in their hair.

METALWORK

Repoussé-and-chased silver objects are common. The distinguishing mark is the stylized plant decoration, frequently sprays of roses, irises or peonies, whatever be the article, from a sweetmeat-dish to a hand-mirror. Pairs of candelabra in silvered metal are also characteristic of the period and easily acquired, leading us almost into the realm of sculpture, since each individual candelabrum is likely to represent a female figure whose drapery may fall to a circular base, the candle nozzles spreading out on either side on scrolled branches. Pewter was another favoured metal for candlesticks, again turning up in pairs: to be matched with pewter trays and pot-pourri bowls. One may look out, too, for the Liberty pewter, bearing the 'Tudric' mark, in which complete tea-services are still available. Bronze was another metal dear to the designers of Art Nouveau, so the collector can expect to meet with bronze inkwells in a number of fantasy shapes and bronze dishes formed into the ever-popular water-lily leaves.

Above Clock by Liberty & Co., pewter with enamelled face, *c.* 1900

CLOCKS AND LAMPS

Collectors have recently shown themselves keenly interested in acquisitions of this kind. It may be a German clock with arabesqued figures on the dial and an inset of mottled yellow glass, or with a pewter face carrying sunflower and poppy-spray motifs, or, more ambitious, a Tiffany grey-and-green jade clock with gold mounts. Equally sought after are stained-glass and bronze-metal lamps in the Tiffany style, characterized by moulded and chased stems and shades divided into flower-panels, and high prices are paid for Legras lamps and shades carved with Japanese-type landscapes.

FURNITURE

For those who want to see their Art Nouveau objects effectively displayed, there is the *étagère* of the period, often with the inlaid signature of Louis Marjorelle, one more able designer of the Nancy School. A master of the marquetry plant-motif in a variety of woods but usually on a satinwood ground, he can be seen represented by nests of tables with delightful arched feet and by bronze-handled trays curiously decorated in inlay. It is equally possible to pick up table-nests by Gallé, again with elaborate marquetry designs cut from fruitwoods. In this essentially French sphere of elegance, are pieces by C. Viardot, rather earlier in date but still manifestly of Art Nouveau inspiration. Offering a complete contrast, with their almost intimidating severity, a pair of armchairs by Rennie Mackintosh recently came up for auction. They were of oak, box-shaped and still with the original striped seat-covering, and fetched a considerably higher price than a set of four by the less celebrated Glasgow designer George Walton. On the other hand, very fair specimens of the spindle-back chair can be acquired for a song outside the auction-room and the exhibition-for-sale gallery. One sees them everywhere in England, even in cellars and out-houses, their rush-seats in ruins, but by no means irredeemable.

SCULPTURE

If figures adapted to electric-lamps and inkstands be excepted, the metal statuette (usually of bronze with a gilt or greenish finish) remains the chief containing vessel of the Art Nouveau style. Though greatly outnumbered in the salerooms now by the more flippant figures of the 1920s and 1930s, these earlier works were mass-produced in their own day, the best of them French (as the foundry mark will confirm). Well-known names to look out for in the signatures applied to subjects representing dancers – the favourites, Loïe Fuller and Cléo de Mérode – and water-nymphs are Müller, Angles, Raoul Larche and J. Caussé. Some of these figures were originally modelled in biscuit, as was the bronze Loïe Fuller by Théodore Rivière, just over 10 inches (25 cm) high, which recently appeared for auction, a typical example of swirling drapery. A number of bronze busts and statues on the same small scale, of origin other than French, became popular during the 1890s, many of them difficult to place with complete assurance under the Art Nouveau heading, though Sir Alfred Gilbert, author of the Piccadilly Eros, probably qualifies. Collectors will do well to prowl round premises due for demolition. Flanking the entrance to one of London's oldest stores and almost hidden behind booths and flower-stalls is a magnificent over-life-size double-group symbolic of the seasons by P. Gasq, a very rare example of large Art Nouveau sculpture and clearly of no particular value to its present owners.

Above Gilt-bronze lamp in the form of the American dancer, Loïe Fuller, by Raoul Larche

Right Stool by Liberty & Co., in imitation of the Egyptian style, *c.* 1880. Victoria & Albert Museum

POSTERS

While Toulouse-Lautrec posters are only for the very wealthy collector and the other classic lithographs produced during the 1890s by such great artists as Steinlen and Anquetin are also out of ordinary folk's reach, the tremendous upsurge of demand for these is popularly satisfied by modern reproductions. The move has since been towards lesser French designers with the unique gaiety of Jules Chéret and the solid virtues of Eugène Grasset. Georges de Feure and R.-G. Hermann-Paul are others to look out for; but without doubt the greatest come-back by a minor figure has occurred in the case of Alphonse Mucha, whose posters for Sarah Bernhardt would provide the collector with his greatest prize in this field. Sheets by Mucha which reach the salerooms vary from lettered posters like a recent 1898 *Job* to decorative panels in the same vein but without titling, both having been drawn on the stone. One has even seen a biscuit-box, decorated with a design after Mucha of about 1900, fetch the price of a respectable watercolour-drawing.

Art Deco

GLASS

This is a fruitful area of activity for the modest collector. It is also one of the most characteristic media of the craftsman during the 1920s and 1930s. While it would not be true to say that glass then became universally clear and colourless – there are too many examples of enamel, interior splashing, mottling and tinting, etc., for that – it produces an overall impression readily distinguishable from the glowing exuberance of Art Nouveau. Of special interest are geometrical pieces. A particularly attractive example which could have been acquired a short while ago took the form of a liqueur service, the individual glasses of flattened-hexagonal shape responding delightfully to the pressure of fingers and thumb.

These services were produced both in the 1920s and in the 1930s, like another category, the vase engraved with a stylized female figure, Simon Gate's versions of which have been much in demand. Extending from the earlier period right through the years between the wars, Lalique glass always has a place of its own in the saleroom. Nor is it exceptionally dear. Variety of treatment marks the Lalique output: in the one item, part of the surface will be polished, part acid-frosted; designs alternate between the abstract and the highly naturalistic; grey is a favourite tint, but with competition from a number of pale stains: purple, blue, sepia. Every kind of object, decòrative and/or utilitarian is available, scent and automobile manufacture well to the fore – you can acquire with a glass bird-of-prey the original chromed-metal mount that secured it to the radiator.

POTTERY

Moorcroft earthenware, all tropical blues and oleaginous reds, bridges the periods of Art Nouveau and Art Deco, though it will not be everyone's taste in studio ceramics. Early post-war Pilkington's Royal Lancastrian bowls and vases painted by W. S. Mycock and Richard Joyce may then lead one on to the Charles and Nell Vyse polychrome groups, a kind of Art Deco High Baroque at peak production during the later 1920s and beginning of the 1930s. Then, by way of Morleyware, Carltonware and Royal Staffordshire, one moves on to the 'Bizarre' inven-

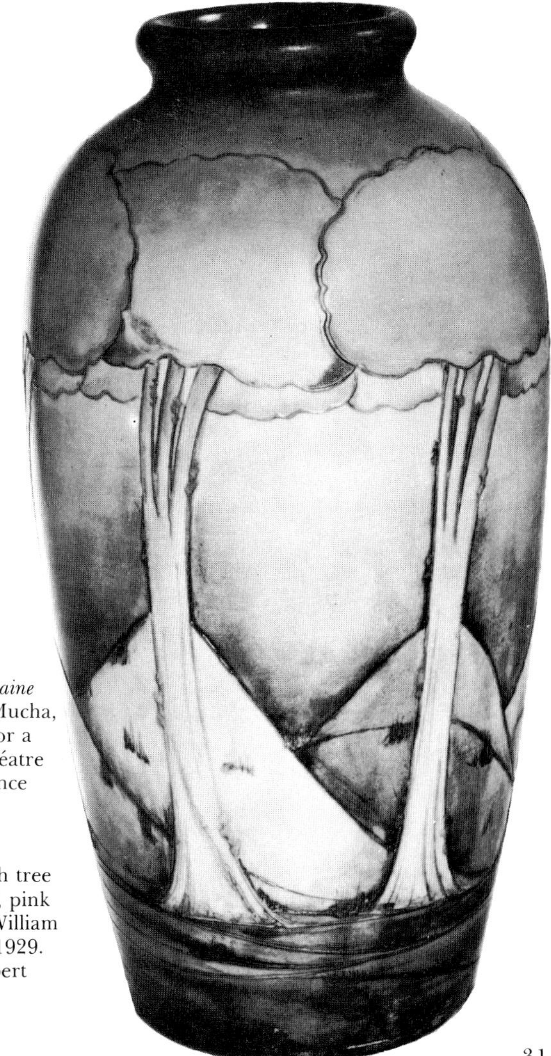

Left La Samaritaine by Alphonse Mucha, 1897, poster for a play at the Théatre de la Renaissance with Sarah Bernhardt

Right Vase with tree design in buff, pink and blue, by William Moorcroft, *c.* 1929. Victoria & Albert Museum tions of Clarice Cliff: tea-services, with such extras as biscuit barrels and jampots, which really did break new ground. Cubist teacup-handles contrast with Orphist teapots, the belly and handle forming a perfect circle. (One curiosity of Art Deco, now to be seen in the saleroom, is the further transformation of the teapot into a racing-car. One grips this by means of a hollowed-out boot, the spout projects from the bonnet and the lid-finial is formed out of the driver's head.) Clarice Cliff designed for several pottery companies, but mainly for Newport and Wilkinson, and the pieces carry the appropriate marks together with a facsimile signature. Pottery masks, busts and figures abound, but do not normally possess the charm of the period's small sculpture.

METALWORK

We can, in fact, pick up metalwork teapots of the 1920s and 1930s quite as remarkable as anything in pottery. An example was provided recently with the Paris mark of Gerard Sandoz, designed during the late 1920s. This was in silvered metal, with Cubist-style body and spout and ebony handle. Mirror-frames are among the most interesting products of the same period, and Edgar Brandt one of their leading designers. A useful 'environment' piece, of this kind – if not by Brandt, then in his manner – appeared a short while ago in wrought iron, triangular in form, with scrolled border and spiralled rosettes. Among smaller articles for day-to-day use are the nostalgic metal cigarette- and vanity-cases, lacquered, enamelled or gilt, which still survive in large numbers. One type of collector's item, somewhat off the beaten track, is the Art Deco dressing-case. Often unimpressive externally, the hide case showing signs of wear, this will prove a revelation when opened. Bottles, brushes, mirror, etc., in a recent instance, were all mounted in silver with geometric enamel decoration in black, red, green and pseudo-lapis lazuli, the date about 1930. For the metalwork enthusiast with a taste for large-scale work still *in situ*, a study of the lift-doors in some of the more ambitious shops of the period is recommended. Inspired by the zigzag horizontal bands and bronze reliefs featuring deer, fountains and exotic birds which enlivened the ground-floor lift-entrances, one take-over company in London has designed its entire new premises in accord with the original Art Deco shell it now occupies. Others less imaginative will no doubt send such historic relics to the scrap-metal yard – which the collector will do well to haunt.

Silvered metal teapot in Cubist style by Gérard Sandoz, the truncated cylindrical body with geometric spout, Paris, late 1920s. Sotheby's Belgravia

FURNITURE

Though no one has yet quite fixed the precise advent of Art Deco, it could and should embrace the extraordinarily precocious modernism of the Omega Workshops, dating mainly from 1913 to 1916. It must be admitted, however, that any furniture directly attributable to Roger Fry, Fred Etchells or Gaudier-Brzeska must now be hard to find. One can only wait patiently for lost pieces still in private hands to materialize on the open market, pieces like the table, with an inlaid Jazz design, of which there was a photograph in the London Hayward Gallery's 1974 Vorticist exhibition. The home of Mr Duncan Grant, who worked on a number of decorative projects with Fry and Vanessa Bell, contains a wealth of painted screens, tables and overmantels, etc., giving one an idea of what may be hidden away in less appropriate surroundings. The strictly professional furniture of the 1920s has charms of a less pictorial kind, and designers like Sir Ambrose Heal and the Russells fought gallantly against the notion, by no means universally abandoned, that if you can't buy antiques you must buy reproductions. Sir Gordon Russell and his brothers stressed the newness of their productions by following the example of Gimson and other designers in showing the natural wood; and this becomes the feature that will draw or repel you, according to taste, where the furniture of the 1930s is concerned: its almost unvarying light-to-blond colour and growing subordination to the 'unit'. If an unstained-oak dressing-table, articulated with peg-handles and surmounted by a circular mirror and locked to a matching chest-of-drawers (style of 1934), is too astringent for the collector, he can always watch out for one of Betty Joel's contemporary bedroom-pieces which – perhaps because of her connection with the film-studios – have an alluring yet by no means vulgar panache about them.

SCULPTURE

One of the most unexpected features of the past few years has been the sustained demand for female statuettes of the 1920s and 1930s. These fetch high prices at auction and find immediate buyers in the shops. While many of the market-stall versions in spelter (a rather unpleasant alloy, mainly zinc) can be vulgar in the extreme, the finest specimens – made of bronze and ivory – reach a high standard of craftsmanship and in no way offend the susceptibilities. Subjects are restricted in range, departing little from the dancing or bathing girl; though some figures do portray male dancers or musicians, and there is the recurring theme of Pierrot and Columbine. The aase, veined marble or onyx and geometric in most cases, is very much part of the piece. Names to look for are C.-P.-J.-R. Colinet, M. Bouraine, Lorenzl and Hanin, though the most prolific artist in the genre was undoubtedly F. Preiss. Such a piece as

Preiss's 'Invocation', lately up for auction, provided a good example of his shortcomings, however, and readers of catalogues are warned against black-and-white photographs, when colour is the sculptor's weak point and he goes in for cold-painting bronze in metallic blue. By contrast, however, at least two first-class specimens of the Art Deco statuette have appeared on the market recently. One was a bronze *No-No-Nanette*-style dancer in cloche hat and short swirling skirt (much formalized), the head and hands in ivory; the other, a masterpiece-in-little, took the form of a girl dancer in a pink-and-grey cat-suit sparkle-finished with great effect. The sculptures' spontaneous gaiety and charming marble and onyx plinths entirely justified the very high prices now given for works by this able designer, D. H. Chiparus.

PAINTINGS, DRAWINGS AND PRINTS, 1890–1940

If such a subject seems unpromisingly vast for the brief mention that can be made of it here, the opportunities for the collector are too significant to be passed over in silence. After the rise to fame of the American abstract-painters following World War II, it became fashionable to decry all non-Continental late nineteenth- and twentieth-century art of a figurative character. Undisturbed by this, a few dealers and collectors demonstrated their faith in artists who had not the appeal of novelty which 'abstract' still possesses, but whose qualities might otherwise be regarded as durable. There are pictures produced during these fifty years which enter rather obviously into the category of Art Nouveau or Art Deco, and others subtle enough to evade the mere label. These latter indicate the area in which the most interesting discoveries await the patient searcher. A good example is provided by the English painter Malcolm Drummond (1880–1945). He had been entirely forgotten when, in 1963, the first one-man show of his paintings and drawings, together with a single token of his etchings, was mounted in London. It was soon realized that not only did Drummond paint extremely well, but that the pre- and post-World War I periods lived again with a unique vividness in his neglected works. Galleries, national and otherwise, hastened to acquire Drummonds, and he is now one of the most highly admired artists of the Camden Town Group. Among others who have sprung to vigorous life again in recent times are all the Bloomsbury painters (Roger Fry and Vanessa Bell, in particular); the Glasgow School, represented by J. D. Fergusson, Samuel Peploe and F. C. B. Cadell; and – perhaps the most extraordinary phenomenon of all – A. J. Munnings, the horse-painter, the prices of whose pictures at auction have broken record after record in these last years.

The collector of Art Nouveau and Art Deco should not, therefore, narrow his field to expensive sketches by Mucha and Erté, but keep an eye open for artists at present little known or quite unknown. For genuine quality will always ultimately be crowned by recognition, as has happened very recently in the belated appreciation given to the paintings of Brake Baldwin (1885–1915) and the watercolours of Edith Lawrence (1890–1973). There is a tremendous amount of such material awaiting rediscovery, to be enjoyed for its own sake and to contribute towards the period atmosphere in which other acquisitions will show to best advantage.

ANTIQUITIES

In the present context one must limit 'antiquities' to objects of greater age than those generally described as antiques. It would be reasonable to say that they are human works made before about 1500 A.D. The many cultures, the varied materials and their different uses make the study of antiquities fascinating, but also require that most collections should be selective, based either on the materials used or the civilization illustrated.

The following chapter has been divided geographically, each area having its own time sequence. We have confined ourselves to works of the higher civilizations, omitting the strange beauties of stone implements made by the prehistoric hunters, and beginning with the first farmers who were able to live a settled life some seven thousand years ago. The earliest of these people lived in what is now called the Middle East.

Middle Eastern

The Sumerians, the first truly civilized people, came from the north east into the plains of southern Iraq, bringing agriculture and animal husbandry with them at least as early as the fifth millennium B.C. They worked in gold, making personal jewelry, cups and gold beads which were combined with crystal, lapis lazuli and chalcedony. From hard stones they made free-standing figures of gods and important persons, and they modelled animal figures, particularly bulls and eagles, with a great understanding of form.

Their pottery is very simple, usually wheel-thrown, of cream colour, very thin and never glazed. In the earliest periods pottery was coiled and painted with black oxides with figures of birds, mammals and people in simplified form. Their skills in pottery allowed the development of clay tablets as writing materials. The tablets are inscribed with linear abstractions of pictorial signs in the early Jemdet Nasr period, and later the syllabic signs are still further abstracted and impressed by a triangular stylus, which made cuneiform (wedge-shaped) marks. Often their building bricks were stamped with inscriptions giving details of the name of the building and the city ruler who made it.

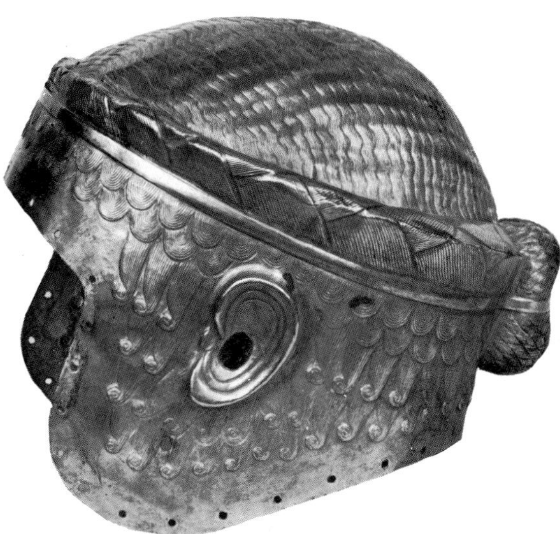

Right Sumerian golden helmet

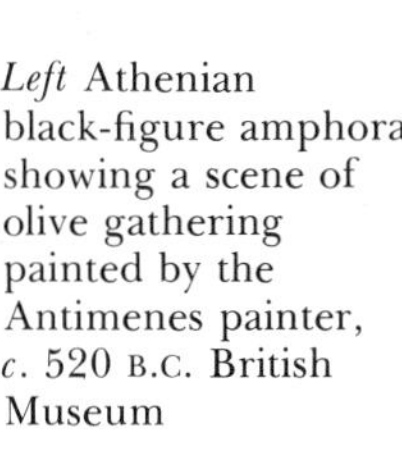

Left Athenian black-figure amphora showing a scene of olive gathering painted by the Antimenes painter, *c.* 520 B.C. British Museum

The vigorous art style of Sumerian carving reflects their quality of energetic advancement in the arts and sciences. They were great poets and competent astrologers, altogether a people who began many things which were the true roots of civilized living.

The Akkadians, a Semitic people who were to found Babylon and many another great city state, succeeded the Sumerians in Iraq in about 2350 B.C. They were also living in a bronze age, and their metal statuettes, less commonly in *repoussé* work than the earlier Sumerian works, have great dignity. The Akkadians also made fine jewelry in gold, usually with symbolic animal ornaments, and elegant and efficient pottery, all wheel-thrown but not of great variety. In their great days they carved relief figures of gods on basalt boundary stones which often include long cuneiform inscriptions in the Akkadian language, which is akin to Hebrew. A special class of small objects is formed by the cylinder seals carved in intaglio and perforated so that they could be rolled over clay to leave a relief design and often a short inscription. The seals are carved in a variety of hard stones and are testimony to the great skill of the engravers. Weapons, such as swords, arrow-heads and mace-heads, are usually made of cast bronze.

These arts of the Akkadians were greatly revived in the eighth and seventh centuries B.C., particularly in the reign of Nebuchadnezzar, and were then more decorative and more numerous because of the riches of the wider world of those times. However, the earlier epoch at Mari on the Euphrates produced fine painted and encaustic tiles which compare well with the blue and yellow glazed tiles of Nebuchadnezzar's city.

To the west of the rivers of Iraq were deserts crossed by the trade routes of the fertile crescent. The peoples of this region, the Syrians and Canaanites, spoke Semitic dialects, founded great trading cities and were among the wealthiest people of the world in the second millennium B.C. However, the earliest of all cities was made in their region by the people of Jericho, who, even before the invention of pottery, were using a kind of gypsum plaster to model realistic faces on human skulls in the fifth millennium B.C. The earliest people making pottery in Syria were adept at carving and painting designs on pottery and on walls. Frescoes of bulls and birds decorated temples as well as pots. Seals were made of

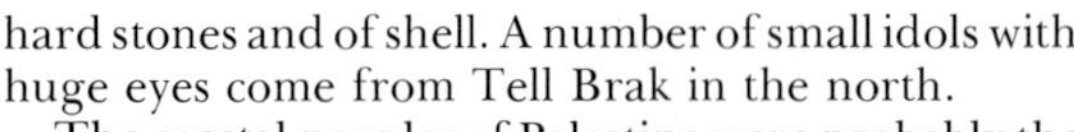

Above Mesopotamian bowl decorated in the centre with calligraphy 9th–10th century A.D.

hard stones and of shell. A number of small idols with huge eyes come from Tell Brak in the north.

The coastal peoples of Palestine were probably the first makers of glass, about 2000 B.C. They acquired great skill and sold the beautiful bottles and phials to Egypt and Babylon. The glass is a soda-sand mixture and very light in weight. It is mostly highly coloured, even sometimes displaying millefiori techniques. However, clear glass developed later and was always unusually good in form. Also from coastal Palestine come fine carvings in ivory, notably those produced by the Phoenicians, and many bronze weapons and figurines. Perhaps the greatest Semitic achievement was the development of an alphabet in about 1400 B.C., cuneiform in the north, but linear (derived from Egyptian hieroglyphics) in the south. It is to be seen painted on potsherds, and sometimes inscribed on rock slabs, and even on some Phoenician sarcophagi.

A very different world of culture arose to the north east of Mesopotamia during the third millennium B.C. This included hill peoples who made coiled buff pottery and vases of stone; they extended in various small groups as far as Baluchistan. These hill peoples seem to have had a considerable influence on the development of the Indus Valley culture centred around two great brick-built cities at Mohenjo Daro and Harappa. Pottery from the Indus Valley was mostly wheel-thrown, and washed over with a reddish-brown slip on which geometric patterns were painted in black. Bronze was known, and very rare small figurines were produced. There was also some stone carving. But the main artistic impulse in the Indus Valley seems to have centred on making small square seals, depicting rhinoceros, buffalo, elephant and occasionally a seated god. Many have a few symbols from the still undeciphered script used in this ancient culture of between 2500 and 1800 B.C.

There can be little doubt that the Indus Valley cultures developed under the influences coming from the wide region from northern Turkey and Iran through to Baluchistan. The region was inhabited by tribes who may have been seasonally nomadic. They produced pottery, often of great beauty though nearly always monochrome. The ceramics of Amlash in Eastern Turkey have become famous, but there were many other regions which produced good work, and the small bronzes from the northern part of the region, especially from Ordos, inner Mongolia, are works of art of great beauty.

The area that extended from Turkey to Iran was one of the earliest homes of art. There were many areas in which coiled and painted pottery was produced, and the painted walls of Çatal Hüyük (sixth and seventh millennia B.C.) discovered in recent years, have shown that the mesolithic population had great artistic skills. Into a culturally divided land the Hittites moved from the east in about 1500 B.C. They settled in central Turkey, producing rather crude pottery but fine stone carvings, jewelry and cuneiform tablets. Later they were overthrown (*c.* 700 B.C.), and the range of cultures there and in Syria show considerable Assyrian influence.

In Iran, the great Achaemenid kings of the middle of the first millennium B.C. who built Persepolis brought a fine tradition of metalwork in arms and personal adornment. Silver and gold were much used for drinking vessels, and the art was spread by the Scythians to the shores of the Black Sea. The Persians used fine stone seals, some of them of roller type and all engraved with gods and animals. Indirectly this intaglio art influenced the origin of matrices for striking the earliest coins, made in Lydia before it fell under Persian dominion. In fact the whole of the Middle East was greatly influenced by Persian art, so we find ceramics, ivory, glass and jewels all showing Persian artistic influence. It even spreads to archaic Greece and founded a tradition which developed its own styles later. The later Persian art of the Sassanian period (*c.* 200 B.C.–A.D. 700) includes highly developed work in silver, glass and gold. It is near-realistic and very elegant and was a decisive influence on the development of Islamic arts.

Arabia, the cradle of Islam, had trading relations to east and west from time immemorial. The arts developed richly and fine pottery, ivory and stone carvings were made and exported throughout the first millennium B.C. Influences from both Egypt and Mesopotamia are noticeable. Later, in about the third century B.C., Hellenistic art had a greater influence through the Ptolemaic and Seleucid empires. In the incense-trading country on the shores of the Red Sea there was a developing king-

Left Persian pottery, Rayy, with blue glazes, late 12th–early 13th century

Far left, above Glass bottle of 'alabaster' shape, dark blue with yellow and white wavy lines, Phoenician, probably 5th century B.C. Victoria & Albert Museum

Right South Arabian alabaster plaque carved with figure of woman, 1st century B.C.–1st century A.D., from Haid bin 'Agil, the necropolis of Timna'. Christie, Manson & Woods

Kasman wall tiles from a prayer niche at a mosque at Meshhed, printed in lustre and blue with Arabic symbols, Persian, early 13th century. Victoria & Albert Museum

dom of Saba (*c.* 1000 B.C.) which spread its influence northwards through the great Nabatean trading centre of Petra. As befits a trading nation, the arts were not original but followed the patterns liked by most other peoples around the Levant. However, a group of towns in the south developed at about the same time an independent style in sculpture, partly because they used a fine hard stone, rather like alabaster, which could be made into portrait heads and carved tomb slabs. The style ranges in its expression from realism to severe formality and simplicity. Many of these slabs have inscriptions in linear and decorative characters which can be translated. Various later cultures have flourished in Arabia, and beautiful Islamic ceramics dating from the first quarter of the seventh century A.D. can be found, reflecting a local tendency to directness of statement but rather less rich in decoration than those from the surrounding areas.

Egyptian and North African

Egypt spans a fairly limited area of the Nile Valley which in time became more and more concentrated and culturally exclusive. In predynastic times there seems to have been wider links with the Sahara. Some of the rock pictures of the central Sahara show a pastoral life into which occasional Egyptian types of design appear and the flaked-stone cultures show some traces of Egyptian contacts. But the main cultural influences which changed the Nilotic culture of upper Egypt came from the east in about 4000 B.C. The invaders differed in costume from the earlier peoples and were bearded.

However, the predynastic period was marked from the earliest times by fine pottery, some of redware with reduced fired black upper sections, others of red with brown linear paintings depicting boats and animals. The pottery is often accompanied by large stone bowls and elegant beakers. The hard stone, sometimes granite or vari-coloured conglomerates, was abraded into most beautiful shapes. Schist and green slate were much used for ceremonial 'palettes' and as small pendants in the form of animals. Fine beads were made from quartz, turquoise and chalcedony. Ivory was much used for ornament and for handles of weapons, carved in low relief with the help of stone tools. Weapons include stone-headed maces, often carved. In the later phases of the period we find the first appearance of hieroglyphic writing.

After Upper and Lower Egypt had been politically united in the late fourth millennium B.C., there was a fairly continuous progress in all the arts. Pottery was wheel-turned and not very adventurous, though some of the larger wine jars were beautifully painted with designs of flowers. Jewelry was at first simple, and small sculpture was strongly realist though somewhat stiff in posture. The work improved through the Fourth Dynasty (*c.* 2300 B.C.), and then a decline came. In the later period, after the Eleventh Dynasty (*c.* 2150 B.C.), there was a great revival in which relief sculptures became important, and jewelry became more complex. Faïence replaced pottery for important ceremonial use, and was used for decorative beads. Metalwork increased both in quantity and elegance. More small stone figures were made, with a greater degree of realism. Relief carvings also became more realistic and yet kept to the conventions of profile presentation.

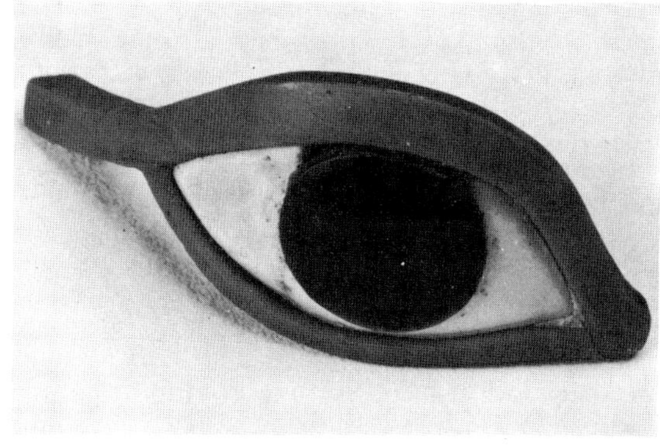

Right Eye inlay, the lining in opaque blue glass, the white of eye in opaque white glass, the pupil dark brown glass. Egyptian, probably second half of the 1st millennium B.C. Pilkington Glass Museum

Below Egyptian pre-dynastic bowl, built up by hand from coils and fired upside down in a wood fire, *c.* 4000 B.C.

There was an interregnum during the Hyksos invasions of Egypt (*c.* 1700 B.C.), though many beautiful small objects are known in all materials. However, after the expulsion of the Hyksos a great revival of luxury arts took place in an increasingly rich Egypt. Many fine wooden objects, spoons, pillows, and furnishings were made and wooden shrines with delicate carvings reached a very high standard. During the short reign of Akhenaten (*c.* 1379–1362 B.C.) a new style was introduced both in fresco painting and realistic carving. There are some parallels with Cretan work here. After the worship of the traditional god of Egypt, Amun, returned in

Scarab of blue glass paste from neck bead net of a mummy, *c.* 600 B.C., Egypt. Pilkington Glass Museum

1351 B.C., the arts continued with a great luxuriousness. Small bronzes of the gods became common, and figurines in gold and silver were made in quantity. There were many more ornaments, including polychrome ceramic jewelry; faïence was more common, and iron was in full use for tools. Frescoes from tombs became more brilliant. Mummies and mummy-cases were even more elaborately decorated and papyri have survived in greater numbers.

Gradually a decline in the arts occurred, and demotic script almost replaced the hieroglyphic except for religious sculptures. Eventually Egypt was overthrown by the Persian invasion (*c.* 525 B.C.). A short Egyptian revival followed with a more realistic style in sculpture, but the campaigns of Alexander the Great led to the country's being controlled by the Greek family of the Ptolemies (332–30 B.C.). The weight of tradition, however, kept Egyptian native religion and art throughout the Ptolemaic period. Greco-Egyptian sculpture was a charming hybrid style, and is most marked in the regions around the great city of Alexandria. The last of the Ptolemies, the brilliant and unfortunate Cleopatra IX, was unable to stave off a period of Roman administration in which the arts of the Egyptians declined and the generalized classic Mediterranean styles took over.

By this time the whole of the North African coast had become Roman in culture. The history of the area began with native North African cultures producing pottery and jewelry in the second millennium B.C. The early civilization had formed around trading posts of Greek and Phoenician merchants. These grew into city states, of which Cyrene (*c.* 630 B.C.–A.D. 660) and Carthage (*c.* 800–201 B.C.) were excellent and successful establishments.

Carthage is mostly represented by inscribed stelae and small funerary cists. This Punic work, simple and sometimes grotesque, is inscribed in the Phoenician alphabetic script, and there is some fine jewelry. The later Roman Carthage was also a flourishing city with a brilliant trading organization. Its art, together with that of most cities of the Maghreb (Africa north of the Sahara – *Africa* to the Romans), includes statuary and inscribed tablets. The styles are Roman, becoming increasingly realistic as the imperial period progresses. Pottery was not highly developed, metalwork was in the Roman styles and often very beautiful, and glass was important and among the best in the Roman Empire.

The Greek trading posts, the cities of what is now Libya, produced fine pottery, and by trading with the homeland acquired first-class works of art for private and public display. The Roman conquest did little to change the arts: language remained Greek and the cultural pattern became international.

The centre of international culture for some centuries became the Ptolemaic Egyptian city of Alexandria from 331 B.C. onwards. This great polyglot market was a trading emporium in which objects from the whole civilized world could be found. It was a centre of fine glass-making and in its workshops the metallurgists perfected techniques of gilding and gave rise to many alchemical traditions. In painting, a school of Greco-Egyptian art flourished, represented by many excellent encaustic portraits from mummy cases of the period. Of equally high standard was the work of Alexandrian jewellers.

The high point of Alexandrian culture was the

Miniature jug in the form of the head of a negress, Alexandrian style of 300–100 B.C. Bronze. British Museum

Museion and Library. From the ruins, after the tragedy of the Arab destruction in A.D. 642, many small artistic works were retrieved, and many Egyptian papyri on a variety of subjects were found in cemeteries, so that all of the old learning was not lost. Among the manuscripts preserved have been many illustrated works of the Gnostic churches of Africa. Alexandria was a great centre of heresies, and many strange manuscripts and inscribed amulets and seals remain from the time just before the Arab invasions. The burning of the Library was an isolated incident. On the whole the rule of the Arab Caliphs was beneficent, and Egypt and the Maghreb as a whole became centres of Islamic art. Throughout North Africa, metalwork and ceramics flourished, glass achieved new standards of excellence and tiles were of exquisite formal beauty. The arts of Arab North Africa were among the most beautiful in the Islamic world.

A special group of cultures developed to the south

Far right Bowl, decorated with the semi-stylized patterns of the early Iron Age, Cypriot, *c.* 1000–750 B.C. Victoria & Albert Museum

Above Marble figure of a woman, made in one of the Cycladic islands, 2500–2000 B.C. British Museum

of Egypt – the Meroitic kingdom, which lasted for a thousand years. It is of earlier origins but probably developed in the main when Egyptians moved south at the time of the Persian invasions of the sixth century B.C. and its great days were in the early centuries of the Christian era. The kingdom survived into Roman times, and it was probably the source of Egyptian ideas which reached West Africa. At all times its arts, which included sculpture, jewelry and pottery, were strongly African in style rather than Egyptian.

Another kingdom which owed much to Egyptian influence was Ethiopia. The early Coptic Christian Church Christianized the kingdom, but its traditional history and its arts show a close contact with Arabia. In later times (*c.* A.D. 600) the city of Aksum became important, and small sculptures, jewelry and some sculpture of Aksumite style survive. The later works of early Abyssinian art include religious crosses, wall paintings and a number of very beautiful formal books executed in the fifteenth and sixteenth centuries A.D.

Classical

The oldest remains of the classical cultures are found in the Mediterranean. There are the remarkable stone temples of Malta with their series of stone figures, the elegant semi-abstract figures and fine pottery of the Cyclades and the earliest Cretan cultures, dating back to the third millennium B.C. The peoples of the Cyclades and Crete were seagoing folk, and their first trading voyages to the islands of the Aegean seem to have been for obsidian, which was invaluable for making cutting tools. The traders also visited southern Greece and the coasts of Asia Minor.

A new influence, possibly from northern Syria, initiated the growth of the Minoan culture in Crete, the cultural centre of which was at Knossos. Pottery developed, notably cups and large rhytons, carving in steatite reached a high degree of excellence in naturalistic work, and frescoes, painted pottery and goldsmiths' work soon equalled them. As time went on, the Cretans established trade relationships with Egypt, which were fully developed about 1400 B.C. After a period of cataclysmic earthquakes the Cretan culture seems to have given way to influence from Greece, whence the system of 'linear B' writing had been introduced, eventually replacing the older 'linear A'.

The centre of the mainland Greek culture in the second millennium B.C. was Mykenae, one of several cities where the rulers lived in palaces which may have had their origins in the Danubian cultures. Mykenean gold work is of the finest, and cut jewels were used for seals both in Crete and on the mainland. Mykenean jewelry is also exceptionally fine. Precious stones were drilled and carved, gold was used both for gem settings and for drinking vessels, but the level of artistic achievement was lower than in the earlier Minoan culture in Crete. This is best shown in vase painting, which degenerated into a sketchy style, though it later solidified into the strong designs of the geometric phase of Greek ceramics.

The 'classical' Greeks were grouped in city states ruling small territories. In the arts they developed steadily, from an Archaic phase (*c.* 800–500 B.C.), largely reflecting Persian and Egyptian influences, to a formal but realist tradition. In addition to monumental sculpture, small stone figures were made, and bronzes became expressions of a realist art. The production of ceramics was notable; not only painted vases but also small ceramic figures of people and animals were made. At first vases were painted with scenes in which the human figures were black; later a

Hellenistic bronze figure of Herakles, *c.* 300 B.C. Christie, Manson & Woods

red-figure ware took over, with an increased skill in drawing realistic figures. There is a strong local variation in ceramics. Corinthian wares with different forms and floral decorations, as well as processions of mythical animals, contrast strongly with Athenian wares. The traditions of ceramic art continued under the Roman domination of Greece which started in the late second century B.C.; in this later phase the country became more luxurious and ornaments of gold more elaborate. Small ceramic figures reach a high point in the beautiful coloured figurines from Tanagra. Coinage in silver, gold and electrum was among the most beautiful ever made; it is said to have originated in Lydia and spread from the Greek cities in Asia Minor. Painters flourished, but little is known of their work except from vase paintings and mosaic copies usually from the Roman period.

Italian art begins with the pottery of many tribal groups of the third millennium B.C., sometimes of high quality but not approaching the wares made in the various Greek colonies around the coasts. In the late eighth century B.C. the Etruscans invaded north-eastern Italy and set up a group of city states, only loosely united. They excelled as craftsmen in bronze, and made fine jewelry, often of gold, and using a technique of almost microscopic incrustation. Much of their own pottery is complex in form but lacking inspiration. However, they imported the finest pottery from Greece. Their small sculptures in bronze, stone and terracotta reach heights of realism not met with before, and they made temples adorned with large and remarkable terracotta sculptures, some of them up to 8 feet (2.5 m) high. In their tombs they painted frescoes of subjects taken from daily life and mythology. Their dead were cremated, but the ashes laid in miniature sarcophagi, often with a painted figure of the deceased sculptured on the lid, also in a strictly realistic style. Scenes from the Greek classics are often found engraved on the backs of Etruscan bronze mirrors, and large and beautiful bronze vessels with human figures in the round are not uncommon.

Rome was a small city state, ruled for many years by Etruscan kings. It revolted (*c.* 330 B.C.), and the Roman republic slowly absorbed all of Italy into a unified civilization. The Roman arts aimed at realism, in a truly Etruscan manner. The early Roman bronzes and sculptures are sound but not brilliant works, apart from their copper coinage, which displays a Roman strength of character. The great days of Roman art came with the growth of the imperial power, starting about 27 B.C., and the emperors adorned the capital with buildings and sculpture. Gold, jewelry, mosaics, encaustic painting, metalwork and glass reached high standards and were produced in great quantities. The centre of a great empire, Rome attracted visitors from other lands and traditions became more cosmopolitan. Standards, however, remained high until the period of wars of survival against the barbarians in the fourth and fifth centuries A.D. led to a simplification of art. Constantine had already moved the capital to Byzantium (Constantinople) in A.D. 313.

Roman art flourished throughout the Empire. Some variations in local styles can be discerned, but from Britain to the borders of Persia, and from the Rhine and the Danube to the Sahara there was a unity of culture. In the whole area Roman-style cities grew up with Roman sculpture, architecture and painting. In the west there were some special features such as the production of the red terra sigillata ceramics from the Rhineland and southern France. Everywhere mosaics adorned the floors of villas. Wine was drunk from silver cups, and objects of everyday life included carvings in bone and ivory, fine glassware, and a multiplicity of brooches and jewels. Silver dishes were cast in moulds, and potters worked in domed kilns to produce an interesting variety of local wares. Inscribed memorials show the mixture of population in every part of the Empire including Londinium (London) which was second only to Rome in population. The North African cities, though smaller than the capital, were equally splendid.

The dissensions between rival claimants to the Empire, and later the incursions of barbarians, brought the mighty social construction to ruin. Attila the Hun spared Rome at the request of a Christian pope (A.D. 452), while a Christian Roman emperor ruled from Byzantium.

Christian art in the Roman Empire was a phenomenon which grew steadily even in times when the religion was officially unrecognized. The arts were represented by catacomb paintings and sculptures on the marble sarcophagi, and because persecutions, although cruel, were intermittent, a surprising amount of early Christian art has survived. There is a real decline in quality but there is an appealing simplicity and directness. Figures in frescoes are less free, and even the mosaics become simplified. The marble sarcophagi no longer depict naked gods and heroes, but show discreetly dressed people in scenes from the Gospels. Naturally the raising of Lazarus is a favourite theme. Early Christian glass includes a number of vessels in which medallions in gold leaf have been enclosed in two layers of glass.

When Constantine gave the Church freedom and protection, building of basilica churches with splendid mosaics and frescoes flourished and in Italy they developed through the style of the churches in Ravenna towards the beginnings of medieval Christian art.

The Roman tradition can be seen in the art of Byzantium until its fall in the middle of the fifteenth century, and even after that in the art of the orthodox churches of eastern Europe. Byzantine art is rich, and includes sculpture in a variety of stones, massive jewelry, renowned mosaic work, and attractively engraved glassware. Painting survives in a few magnificent books of the Gospels, and there was a wealth of ceremonial jewelry, rings and chains of office, as well as silver caskets and chalices. The ending of Roman art was never debased; it was active and alive until the fall of Constantinople.

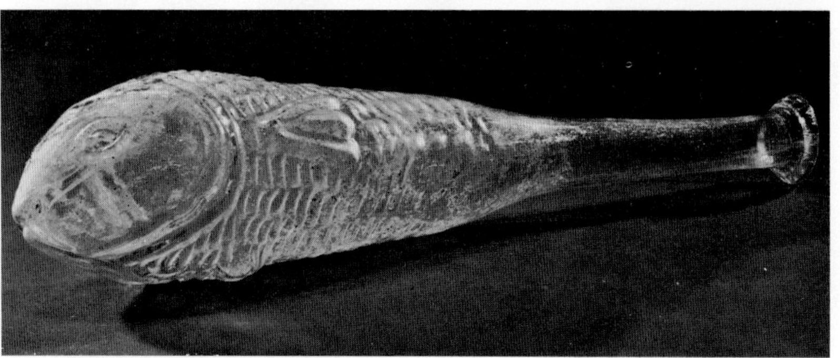

Mould-blown vase in the shape of a fish, transparent pale blue glass, from Western Roman Empire, 1st century A.D. Pilkington Glass Museum

Western and Northern European

Because of intensive recent archaeological research, the earliest arts of Europe are fairly well known. The palaeolithic paintings in the French caves and the beautiful ivory carvings from eastern as well as western Europe, dating from about 20,000 to 10,000 years ago, are among the treasures of mankind. Some of the smaller pieces of *art mobilier* are available outside museums, but on the whole palaeolithic art is rare.

Later, in the neolithic period, the peoples of southern and western Europe produced coiled pottery and made personal ornaments of incised clay, amber beads and pendants, and of jet, which they discovered. From Spain come many pendant slabs of stone and bone with incised designs, some of them accentuating eyes as a kind of magical symbol.

Towards the end of the neolithic phase, about 2000 B.C., people in the west were erecting great stone monuments which are often associated with the first appearance of bronze tools, and exquisitely delicate gold work, mostly used for pendants and box covers. The surface of the latter was decorated with incised linear geometric designs, whose meaning is no longer known.

The use of gold continued into the Bronze Age (*c.* 1700–700 B.C.), and work became more widely spread. The golden lunulae of Ireland, for example, were very beautiful and their designs are also found incised on ornaments made of Whitby jet. There seems to have been an international trade on a small scale in gold from Ireland, amber from the Baltic, tin from Spain and Czechoslovakia, and salt from Austria. Amber in particular was traded to the Mediterranean. Bronze Age pottery appears to be heavy and often coarse, but the decorated beakers of Western Europe and many larger burial urns are technical masterpieces with well chosen decoration, though always of a geometric rather than naturalistic style of design.

In the Bronze Age metal was not common and its use for weapons and ornaments seems to have centred around the courts of chiefs. It came into more general use later with the introduction of iron. The European Iron Age developed very gradually, starting about 750 B.C., but the distribution of ore was wide and eventually iron weapons became common over the whole area. In general pottery is less well made in the early Iron Age, but bronze work reaches new heights and there are some very beautiful and complex ornaments cast from wax models.

The apogee of the arts in the Iron Age was achieved by the Celtic-speaking peoples. Their origins are not clear, but it has been suggested that they at first moved through the urn-field cultures of the Rhineland and thence to the Alpine area. Their first clear identification is as the people of the Hallstatt culture in Austria (*c.* 750 B.C.). They made attractive bronze figurines, iron swords and spears, and ceramics, including pots with the characteristic spiral designs of Celtic art. Later the centre of Celtic arts was at La Tène in Switzerland. However, by about 500 B.C. Celtic peoples extended from northern Spain to the Rhine delta, and from Ireland to Galatia (central Asia Minor). Their small carvings and bronze, some of which was set with enamel, were widespread, as were their pottery, iron weapons, glass beads and pendants. The accoutrements of their warriors, swords and helmets, were magnificent. Horns and cymbals abound, and a number of stone heads are known to represent their head-hunting traditions. Horse-trappings show some of their best design work, and from Britain come remarkable bronze mirrors with engraved backs.

To the north, the Germanic-speaking peoples bordering the Celts had some customs in common with them, but, unlike the Celts, they never came under Roman domination. Their arts descended from the Scandinavian Bronze Age and later included the bracteates and helmets whose form ultimately derived from late Roman originals. They were very fond of large decorated brooches which held cloaks in position on the shoulder. These brooches become an index of the dispersal of the European tribes caused by the raids of the Huns. The Franks entered France, the Angli and Saxons went with their allies, the Jutes, to Britain, and the Goths to Greece, Italy and Spain. One group, the Visigoths, made a kingdom in North Africa. Everywhere their splendid jewelry and metalwork has been found, as well as carvings in ivory and bone. The African and Spanish kingdoms were overthrown by the Islamic advance and, in Spain, after the invasion in 711 A.D., Islamic arts reached high levels of beauty, especially in ceramics, including the world famous reduced-copper wares.

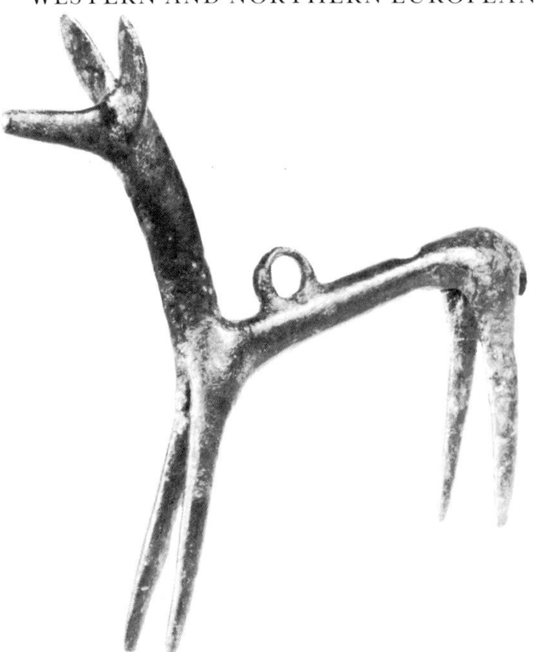

Celtic bronze figure of a deer, 1st century B.C. or earlier. Christie, Manson & Woods

Wessex/Middle Rhine type beaker decorated with horizontal and vertical hatchings, *c.* 1600 B.C. City Museum and Art Gallery, Hanley, Stoke-on-Trent

The Battersea Shield, dating from the 1st century A.D., discovered in the River Thames at Battersea. Bronze, inlaid with red glass. One of the finest existing examples of Celtic art

The later history of the Germanic tribes is one of the development of Christian arts in western Europe. Most of them evolved a style derived from Roman antecedents but with a lively sculptural tradition of its own both in stone and ivory. A high point was the work centred upon the palace style of Charlemagne (742–814) at Aachen. The strongest echoes of the older traditions came from Ireland, where Celtic traditions mixed with Viking art to produce a special style of great charm, exemplified in ecclesiastical ornaments and manuscripts such as *The Book of Kells*.

The Vikings, who came from all parts of Scandinavia during the eighth to tenth centuries A.D., carried Nordic art traditions as far as Iceland and raided throughout the Atlantic and Mediterranean coasts. The influence of their wood carving styles is apparent in Romanesque sculpture in Normandy and Britain.

A common inspiration showed in the minor arts and the Romanesque architecture of Europe. It was expressed in enamel and bronze reliquaries, pectoral crosses, rings and a remarkable series of illuminated manuscripts which made their mark in the so-called Dark Ages as an inspiration to artists and princes. Metalwork was highly finished, and gold and silver was used for church vessels and ornaments.

Knight jug decorated with a dark green lead glaze, Nottingham or Lincoln, 1250–70

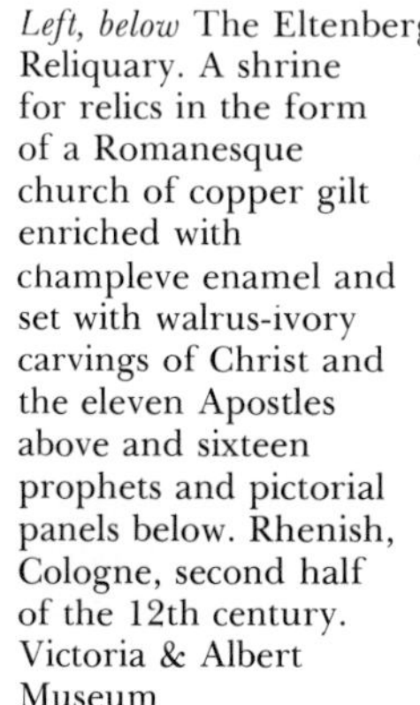

Left, below The Eltenberg Reliquary. A shrine for relics in the form of a Romanesque church of copper gilt enriched with champleve enamel and set with walrus-ivory carvings of Christ and the eleven Apostles above and sixteen prophets and pictorial panels below. Rhenish, Cologne, second half of the 12th century. Victoria & Albert Museum

Left, bottom Panel of stained and painted glass 'The Temptation in the Wilderness' (Command that these stones be made bread), French, Troyes, 13th century. Victoria & Albert Museum

Below Ram-shaped aquamanile in buff-ware with green glaze and decorated with green-glazed pellets, found on a pottery kiln site on North Cliff, Scarborough, late 13th–early 14th century

The unity of western Christendom combined with the basic Germanic traditions of western Europe to produce the 'Gothic' art in the twelfth century. These included almost every known skill, among them pottery, especially the elongated jugs with green glazes, enamels and precious metals, wood carvings, paintings in encaustic, frescoes, and illuminated manuscripts. There was great unity, though in Italy the classical tradition was still very strong. During the whole of this period of unity there was a steady development towards realism. The influence of the Renaissance in Italy spread through Europe quite slowly, but the spirit of realistic presentation in art was already widespread. The main innovation was the use of perspective in painting. Arms and armour developed into definite styles and in textiles, including tapestries and embroidery, splendid examples remain, mainly of ecclesiastical vestments, some embroidered in brilliant colours and gold.

In eastern Europe a similar development of the arts took place, but this was in the Byzantine tradition deriving originally from the eastern Roman Empire. The symbolic image of the religious icon was the dominant note, but the sacred paintings were embel-

lished with ornaments of gold and precious stones. Carvings and painted panels from the iconostases of orthodox churches express the same brilliant but austere traditions. Continuity with the classical past is to be found in the long series of manuscripts in which the illustrations show the gradual transition from the early freedom of Byzantine painting through to the vertical formalism of the derived traditions, which still flourish in eastern Europe. The older works of art, dating from the tenth and eleventh centuries, include fine enamel work and reliquaries made in the form of churches. Vestments differ from those of the west, usually having less brilliance of colour, but are equally rich and are splendidly adorned.

The Scandinavian traditions, although politically important in the formation of Russia, are not clearly defined in early Russian art. The basic Slavonic culture became linked with Byzantine tradition. There were contacts with the Far East through trade and various Mongol and Tartar invasions, but it is the general tendency to perpetuate Byzantine traditional arts that is apparent everywhere.

Gandhara grey schist head of Buddha, 3rd or 4th century B.C. Gandhara in north west India was the meeting point of Indian and Graeco-Roman culture and was the centre of a flourishing school of sculpture and architecture

South East Asian

NOTE. Antiquities from China and Japan are covered elsewhere in the encyclopedia in the relevant sections, e.g. Metalwork and Pottery and Porcelain.

The earliest contacts between the Western World and the high civilizations of the Far East came via trade routes of Roman times passing through Armenia, northern Persia and Turkestan. All regions had cultures of their own centred on the river valleys. From the second millennium B.C. there were many types of pottery and the Bronze Age cultures of the first millennium B.C. also produced some beautiful small figures and ornaments. There were periods of cultural unity, enforced at first by Persian and Chinese expansions, in the early centuries A.D., both of which at one time reached the Caspian Sea. Greek influence under the Seleucids (*c.* 312–64 B.C.) was strong and coins of this period have rare beauty. In the eastern regions of Turkestan, Chinese influence was greatest, trading posts were frequent and many fine locally made works in wood and stucco are known. There are also, from the third to the ninth centuries A.D., examples of Manichaean fresco painting and inscriptions. The mountainous terrain kept many peoples separate from one another, so local styles in pottery and wood carving vary. To the north were nomadic peoples, including the Huns, who have left little behind them apart from some metalwork. To the western end of their range, within the Russian sphere, some of the Siberian tribes left remarkable bronze horse-trappings, woodwork and even carpets dating back to the sixth century B.C.

Much later, from the fourth to tenth centuries A.D., the area acquired a more unified culture, and there are ancient books in local scripts which, from the Armenian area, are Christian. Samarkand and Bokhara produced Islamic books and fine tiles. In Turkestan were ruined towns which have yielded frescoes, wood carvings and books both of Buddhist Mahayana belief and also of Manichaean learning.

Through the ancient trade routes the armies of Alexander the Great penetrated into India. After his death, the dominions he controlled split up into separate kingdoms. In particular Gandhara (north west India and east Afghanistan) has remains of Buddhist cities and monasteries which contain many miles of carved friezes illustrating the life of the Buddha and the stories of his previous incarnations. They are mainly carved from grey schist and are of late classical styles under artistic influences from the Roman Levant. Some of the monasteries were decorated with stucco sculpture painted in naturalistic colour. Bronze vessels and coins and some beautiful jewelry, particularly necklaces and seal rings of semi-precious stones set in gold, have also been found at Gandhara. A certain austerity, perhaps due to the colder climate, marks the difference between Gandharan and early Indian art. The existence of the Gandharan civilization stresses the importance of early trade routes from the Levant towards the Far East. These contacts were greatly restricted when the development of Islam deterred traders from the Christian West in the seventh century A.D.

India and Pakistan have long been regions of great artistic activity. The early cultures of the Indus Valley (third millennium B.C.) were succeeded by Aryan kingdoms (second millennium B.C.), which produced new artistic styles. These, apart from some pottery and early Iron Age works, which were already developed, suddenly became fully developed under the influence of Buddhist art. This flowered from the second century B.C. to the second century A.D. in the realistic sculpture of a group of large monasteries, some of the finest examples of which are the stupas at Bharut and Sanchi, north central India. The graceful figures carved on the limestone palisades and gateways set the style which has ever since inspired Indian arts. Metalwork was developed in the earliest phases of Buddhist art, the iron pillar of Asoka being a magnificent example, and became an important part of later Indian art.

In southern India, the Hindu states produced sculpture, woodwork and bronze figures of great ele-

gance and rhythmic beauty over many centuries from about the fourth century A.D. Each area had its own style, and there is also a development through time, usually in the direction of greater complexity. The spread of the Jain system of belief which had begun about the sixth century B.C. produced a simplification and a rather grand austerity of presentation. Although jewelry was made at this time, most existing Indian jewelry is of the medieval and later periods. Jade carvings of the Mughal period are particularly beautiful.

In what is now Pakistan the introduction of Islam forbade the representation of the human figure and brought about the full development of geometric and floral ornament in sculpture. This was nevertheless accompanied by a rich achievement in miniature painting, which derived eventually from Persian art, was very popular and influenced painting throughout the subcontinent. Tiles and glass were also made in the Islamic tradition.

With the expansion of Indian trade into the Malayan Peninsula from the fifth to ninth centuries A.D., traders came into contact with the Chinese and there was an increasing mixture of the two cultures, stretching from the arts of Sri Lanka to those of Vietnam. In Sri Lanka there are beautiful Hindu and Buddhist figures. The kings of Kandy in the fifteenth century A.D. ruled a city which produced fine jewelry and peculiarly beautiful decorated knives. Sri Lanka is also the land of precious stones, particularly rubies and pearls and many of its jewels are beautifully adorned with them.

The influences of southern Buddhism, the Hinayana tradition, spread throughout South East Asia. A most important centre in Indonesia was the great temple of Boro Budur in Java. But there are also many magnificent Hindu temples in Indonesia. Ivory and metalwork, such as the beautiful wavy-bladed Indonesian krises, date back to the Majapahit empire of the twelfth to fourteenth centuries.

The area once known as Indochina has never been united and its different kingdoms show strongly marked individual styles of art. Burma, Cambodia, Thailand, Laos and Vietnam formed into varying political patterns. Their art has been first Hindu and then Buddhist throughout their history. Many beautiful bronze vessels and figures of Buddha and his disciples were made for temple services. Gold and fine jewels were always part of the regalia of kings and courtiers. Sculpture in hard stones was of a very high standard of design and technical finish. Pottery everywhere shows Chinese influence, but individual workshops provided a great variety of wares, often with rather thick white glazes. The cultures of importance belong to the period from about A.D. 300 to 1500. Fine domestic objects include *repoussé* bowls, betel-cutters and weapons, all of complex designs that probably originated in India but were varied locally. In the eastern kingdoms there has long been influence from China, which was accentuated when Kubla Khan invaded the country in the late twelfth century.

Further south the Malay Peninsula, the seat of several sultanates, received most of its influence from India, but the native genius simplified much of the complexity of medieval design and they produced remarkable metalwork in iron, silver and especially in gold.

The Indonesian islands were also ruled by independent sultans. Their antiquities are mostly Buddhist and Hindu, and they include excellent stone sculptures and a wide variety of bronzes, mostly used in religious and court ceremonials. Many objects are inscribed with a script derived from India.

Far to the north is Tibet, once a group of warlike mountain states, then part of the Chinese Empire, and recently independent. Its antiquities are almost entirely concerned with Mahayana Buddhism and inscribed rocks with the formula *Om mani padme hum*, the famous Buddhist prayer, abound. The bronzes are of exquisite workmanship, but few are ancient; that is, from before about A.D. 1500. The Tibetan area is midway between India and China, and both countries influenced its art very considerably.

North, Central and South American

No great works of art were produced in the Americas before agricultural village life had developed. In what is now the United States cultures known as Adena and Hopewell developed around the Ohio River from about 200 B.C. to A.D. 600. They made stone figures of people and a great number of pipe bowls carved in steatite representing the local fauna, and several showing human heads. Decorative objects in shell and mica suggest that

Far left Illustration from Wariat-i-Babari by Ram Das, depicting the Emperor Basar receiving Uzbeg and Rauput, envoys, in the garden at Agra on 18 December 1528. The Emperor sits on a throne with a canopy and in the background is the Fort at Agra. Moghul, *c.* 1590. Victoria & Albert Museum

Head of Bhairava of embossed copper, painted and gilt and set with imitation gems. Probably from Nepal, *c.* 17th century. This deity is not as popular in Tibet as in Nepal where it is used in a ritual during which devotees take liquid piped from behind the mask through the hole in the mouth

Nepalese gilt-bronze seated figure of Buddha, 15th century

there might have been contacts with Mexico. The artistic remains of these people are of the highest quality and widely collected.

About A.D. 1200–1400, around the Ohio River and the Mississippi, works of art engraved on shell and embossed in copper sheets (the copper was derived from the region of the Great Lakes) mark the Middle Mississippi culture. These works of art present human figures, gods, and magical birds and a favourite theme is an eagle-man. The figures seem to be alive and active, and they reflect a typically American Indian way of life. Their quality is high.

Over the whole of the eastern United States carved and shaped stones used as whistles, flute-stops etc. are to be found dating from about A.D. 700–1400. The workmanship is superb, and the abstract forms have great beauty. They are not, however, representative of any high culture, but are collectors' pieces because of their intrinsic quality.

In the south-western states a civilization began in the early centuries A.D. At first the remains are mainly basketry, but by the sixth century beautiful pottery was being produced. This pottery of the Anasazi cultures and the nearby Hohokam is a grey ware painted mainly with black abstract linear designs. The Hohokam is normally represented by bowls with interior painting. The Anasazi culture, passing through corrugated wares, gradually developed until it became represented by the Pueblo culture (*see* Ethnographica). These matt-surfaced, grey and black pots were all coiled and decorated freehand. They are widely collected, and modern reproductions are made, though these are usually more formal than the originals.

High cultures reached the Mexican area by about 1000 B.C. The earliest, the Olmec culture, have left fine pottery vessels, hand-coiled and painted with grotesque figures. More important are the Olmec jades, bluish and usually highly polished, with formal incised patterns and often modelled features with incised details. Masks, axe-blades etc. are characteristically decorated with ritual faces that have everted upper lips, suggesting jaguar masks.

In southern Mexico and Guatemala the Olmec, who had ceased their activity by the fifth century B.C., were succeeded by the Maya peoples in about the second century A.D. They made magnificent hand-moulded pottery, painted mostly in orange and red on a buff background. Their low-fired earthenware comprises beakers, bowls and dishes. They have artistic quality and were obviously intended for temple service. The Maya also worked in jade, preferring the green varieties, and produced ear-ornaments, beads of many forms, and pendants with relief sculpture. Some of the jades are inscribed in the Maya syllabary as are carved limestone stelae. Also in limestone are carved heads, and relief plaques of the second to eighth centuries.

In western Mexico the arts of two cultures have become popular. The Tarascos from the fourth to seventh centuries A.D. made amazingly live ceramic figures, mostly in a burnished red ware. They include human figures about 20 inches (50 cm) high, and charming animals, mostly dogs. South of the Tarascos the Zapotec kingdom lasted from the second century B.C. to the fifteenth century A.D. Elaborate pottery incensarios, with figures and masks of the gods in relief are characteristic. They vary from 6 inches (15 cm) to 30 inches (76 cm) in height, and the style changes with the period. Always in grey clay, a few of them are coated with stucco, mostly grey, but a few are tinted.

In south-eastern Mexico the Huaxtecs and Totonacs both made pottery figurines, sometimes painted with natural bitumen. They date from the early centuries A.D. and changed style as history proceeded until the Spanish Conquest in 1521. Shell ornaments with incised designs are important from this area. Many larger pottery figurines (up to 2 feet; 61 cm) of considerable beauty were made.

In the Central Mexican highlands many cultures flourished. Teotihuacán (second century B.C. to seventh century A.D.) produced pottery, sometimes painted with designs over a thin coating of lime plaster. There are great numbers of attractive pottery figurines, and decorated spindle whorls from this site. Tula was a centre of the Toltec empire from A.D. 650 to 980. Its pottery is poor and the figurines lack inspiration, but in the latter part of this period a 'plumbate' ware was produced in southern Mexico and traded through Central America, presumably because its greenish semi-gloss looked rather like jade. Tenochtitlán (Mexico City) was the centre of the Aztec culture (*c.* 1325–1520). Attractive but plain domestic pottery is plentiful, and mosaic work, gold ornaments and jade, worked for the Aztecs by their Mixtec neighbours, are to be found. There are also many small stone figures of gods and serpents. They are made of grey lava and a few of creamy limestone.

Beyond the southern limits of the Mexican and Maya cultures we find several styles in the art of Costa Rica, Nicaragua and Panama. Fine painted pottery was made, and significantly great quantities of gold and tumbaga (an alloy of gold and other metals, usually copper) were produced. Styles vary locally, but alligators, ocelots and monkeys mix with humans in the plethora of golden pendants, mostly between 2 inches (5 cm) and 4 inches (10 cm) in height. Modern reproductions are made because of the high artistic

Above Maya pottery effigy vessel in the shape of a man, Guatemala, pre-classic period (2000 B.C.–A.D. 200). Museum of Mankind, London

Maya jade plaque carved in relief. Museum of Mankind, London

qualities of the originals which date mostly from between the seventh and eleventh centuries A.D.

South of Panama, three cultures in Colombia have produced good pottery and much gold. The Chibcha from around Bogotá made rather grim pottery figures of chiefs (the originals of the El Dorado legend), and cast plaques with relief decoration in gold wire which vary from gold to differing forms of tumbaga. From the Cauca River valley come most beautifully finished golden figurines and vessels, all highly burnished and of elegant form. They belong to the Quimbaya, a group of Indian tribes living in villages and producing pottery vessels and figures often decorated by reserve dyeing of the burnished surfaces.

Further south golden pendants, nose-clips, ear-ornaments etc. come from the Sinú and cognate tribes. The varieties of design are immense and the workmanship is impeccable. The dating of the Colombian cultures is somewhat uncertain, but between the eighth and twelfth centuries most of the best work was done, though the Chibcha apogee was about 1400.

From the coast of Ecuador comes a great variety of ceramic figurines and vases. Some gold and bronze was also worked. Small pottery figurines dating from about 3000 B.C. from the Valdivia region are the oldest ceramics so far known from the Americas. As time went on, many other tribal cultures developed and their ceramics, which are all hand-moulded, show much greater complexity. The most realistic and well finished were those from the La Tolita region in the north, which date from between 500 B.C. and A.D. 500.

The most complex and the richest of all ancient American cultures was centred in Peru. There was a long succession of civilizations, all rich in works of art in gold, silver, tapestry and ceramics. Earliest was the Chavín culture (*c.* 1000 B.C.) in the high Andes, but only small stone carvings are available in the market. From the southern part of the Peruvian coast the Cupisnique culture, greatly influenced by Chavín, left a strong pottery in grey clay, some of which was carved with figures of gods, some painted with resin colours. The Cupisnique textiles are rather plain, but in the succeeding Paraccas culture, from about 900 B.C., we have great sheets of textile with all-over embroideries of gods and animals in brilliant colour. The Paraccas culture also produced decorated golden ornaments and rather plain ceramics. This culture is succeeded by the Nasca culture of the last centuries B.C. and early centuries A.D. Pottery vessels have charming designs of birds and flowers, and designs in polychrome slip showing human figures and gods. Globular vessels, beakers and small bowls in a fine red ware were made by hand-modelling. Brilliantly coloured textiles abound, first embroidery and later tapestry weaving. Gold was much used for pendants, and semi-precious stones are used as inlays in gold and strung together as necklets.

The Nasca culture was the last important one in southern Peru. It is overwhelmed by the culture from Tiahuanaco, beside Lake Titicaca in Bolivia. Tiahuanaco art is marked by strongly reticulated patterns both on pottery and in the textiles which included some square caps in a velvet technique. Sometimes textile designs become so formalized as to seem abstract. Small stone carvings reproducing patterns from the large sculptures at Tiahuanaco

appear on the market, but many of these are of modern manufacture. Of similar style is the art of Huari culture, far to the north of Tiahuanaco, which spreads from the mountains of Peru over the coastal regions. It is marked by some rather large pottery vessels with polychrome quadrated decoration. These two cultures cover the period from about 500 to 800 A.D. On the northern coast the Huari culture overthrew the earlier Mochica civilization, but did not totally destroy its traditions.

The Mochica, from the second century B.C. to the sixth century A.D., was characterized by well-made pottery, globular vases with stirrup spouts, and some textiles and woodwork. The ceramics were covered with a cream slip and painted with linear designs showing warriors and gods in reddish-brown iron pigments. There are also modelled pots, which include a number of representations of human heads and which achieve the rare status of true portraiture. The Mochica were succeeded by the Chimu (*c.* 1100), who formed a great and powerful coastal empire. They were great metal workers, using gold, silver and bronze for vessels and for ornament. Woodwork is in the form of carved paddles and centre-boards for balsa rafts. There are also a number of false heads for mummy-packs, sometimes covered with silver or gold masks. The textiles embrace a great range of techniques, including tie-dyeing and kilim weaves.

The brilliant Chimu kingdom was overthrown by the Incas (*c.* 1450) who have left a simpler and stronger design series. They preferred geometric pattern on textiles, and produced five standard forms of ceramic vessels (also painted with geometric designs) and a number of wooden beakers, called kero, which in later times were decorated with paintings in coloured mastic. The circumstances of the Spanish conquest ensured that most Inca gold and silver was melted down. Textiles are few but splendid and a great number of knotted string quipús (record-tallies) have been found in Inca graves.

After about 1540 the arts in Peru were entirely in the Spanish tradition, and American Indian arts have only a minimal existence. In northern Argentina the Diaguita-Calchaquí continued to make some of their large pottery burial urns in effect, the arts of the pre-Columbian area in all the American regions came to an end about 1600.

Glossary

Terracotta vessel decorated with a design of birds and fish, Nasca, A.D. 600. Museum of Mankind, London

Terracotta vessel with a design of running men, possibly messengers, Mochica, Chicama Valley, A.D. 600. Museum of Mankind, London

Art mobilier. Term used in many contexts for small and portable works of art. In the context of archaeology it particularly refers to small ivory and bone carvings of palaeolithic age.

Betel cutter. Hinged object not unlike nut crackers, but the upper part has a steel blade used for slicing the betel nut before it is dipped in lime and wrapped in sirih leaf for chewing.

Bracteates. Plaques, usually circular, worn as pendants beneath the collar.

Cast silver ware. Many Roman silver bowls and dishes were made by casting in a mould. First the form was made with its low relief sculpture in wax. From this the fireclay moulds were cast and baked. These in turn were placed in the furnace and molten silver was poured in. Finishing was by chasing and burnishing.

Chalcedony. Silicious stone similar to flint, usually in colours from honey to red and translucent. It takes a very high surface polish.

Clay tablets. Used in the Middle East for writing. The clay was very fine in texture, made into pillow-shaped blocks to fit in the palm of the hand while symbols were impressed by the stylus.

Coining. At first, in the seventh century B.C., coins were struck on a flat anvil by an intaglio-cut (*q.v.*) die. Later the anvil was also cut so that the two sides of the coin were struck by one blow.

Electrum. A natural alloy of gold and silver originally mined in Lydia. It contains 15–35 per cent of silver and is an attractive pale yellow colour.

Encaustic. 1. A system of painting in which the pigments are mixed with wax and applied to the surface of wooden panels. The pigment is melted with a hot iron or is laid on the wood and heated by ironing *in situ.* 2. Tile in which the design is inset in another colour of clay before burning and glazing.

Faïence. Term derived from the ceramics of Faenza in Italy. It is applied in Egyptian archaeology to a mixture of crushed quartz and a little clay fused in the fire and then covered with a blue copper carbonate glaze which gives it the characteristic blue to green colours.

Iconostasis. A screen across the nave of an Orthodox church, obscuring the priest and the altar from the people during the most sacred parts of the Mass. It obtains its name because it is usually painted over with religious pictures (icons).

Incrustation. Patterns in almost microscopic granules of gold are characteristic of much Etruscan jewelry. Such patterns were drawn on gold surfaces in resin, which acted as a flux. Fine gold filings were then dusted on; they adhered only to the resin. When heated, the gold powder formed into tiny globules, which then adhered to the main surface before it began to melt. The term is also used to describe the decoration of surfaces with an overall covering of jewels, glass fragments, shells etc.

Intaglio. Carving inward from the surface. In seals, all the forms are carved in reverse, so that they should appear in relief and in the right sequence on the final seal.

Kilim weaves. *See* Tie-dyeing.

Lapis lazuli. Dark blue semi-precious stone, in antiquity usually left with a semi-matt finish.

Lunula. Golden moon-shaped plate with twisted ends for suspension. Worn as gorgets.

Mastic. A resin tapped from the bark of suitable bushes. It fries by oxydization. Often mixed with mineral powder colours it was used for the decoration of wooden objects as an inlay. When dry it has an attractive glossy surface.

Millefiori. 'A thousand flowers'. Flower-like patterns drawn out from rods of different-coloured glass. Sections are cut and set into the surface of a glass vase.

Obsidian. Natural volcanic glass, usually found as volcanic 'bombs' lying on mountain slopes. The material flakes easily and produces very sharp blades.

Plumbate. In Mexican archaeology a term used for a low fired pottery on which a slip coating has fused to form a smooth greenish surface reminiscent of dull jade. It was named plumbate ware because of a superficial resemblance to lead glazed pottery.

Reduced copper. A system of ceramic decoration in which designs were painted on a vessel in copper oxides. It was then fired in a box in a reducing atmosphere in which closely packed charcoal produced carbon dioxide. The copper was purified and no oxygen remained to dull its lustre. These vessels are often called lustre wares.

Reduced firing. Excluding oxygen from a pottery vessel while it is being fired. The blackened tops of predynastic pottery were probably produced by smothering the ends of the pots with grass in the last phase of burning.

Reserve dyeing. The surface of pottery was painted with designs in wax. Then the pot was painted over with a black dye. On firing, the wax burnt away and the dyed surface remained black on a buff vessel.

Rhyton. Drinking vessel, derived originally from horns. In later times the curved narrower end was often modelled as a human or, more commonly, an animal head.

Schist. Metamorphic rock composed of fine layers which easily flake apart from each other. A typical example is slate.

Steatite. A massive, fine-grained form of talc. The soft smooth-surfaced rock is easily carved and is found in many parts of the world. It is usually grey or greenish in colour.

Stucco. A fine plaster, often compounded with glue to form relief ornament in interior decoration. For exterior work it was usually painted.

Terra sigillata. A red ware, made of reddish clay formed in a mould. A fine slip added to the surface acquired a high gloss in firing to give the normal finish to what was a very popular ware of the first to fourth centuries A.D.

Tie-dyeing and **Kilim weaves.** In tie-dyeing, areas of the textile were tied tightly so that when it was dipped in dye the colour did not take in the tied sections. In Kilim weaving areas of one colour were separated from the next colour by a gap in the cloth due to the inward turning of weft threads.

Tumbaga. A Malay word used to describe low-grade gold alloys. The admixture of copper and sometimes other metals, including platinum and silver, varies immensely. In the Chibcha culture of Colombia such alloys may have been used with a social connotation, the purest gold being used for the great chiefs.

Velvet technique. A weaving technique in which short lengths of dyed fibre were tied to the main threads of the textile. They projected outwards and, when trimmed to an even height, made an all-over pile in any desired pattern.

ARMS AND ARMOUR

There still exists among the uninformed a certain prejudice against the collection of arms and armour on the grounds that they represent the least sympathetic aspect of man's evolution. Whatever one's moral judgment of the preoccupation of the nobility in the past with the profession of arms may be, it should not be forgotten that until nearly the end of the eighteenth century a finely ornamented sword performed a decorative function in male costume analogous to that of jewelry in the female costume of the time. The best armours of the fifteenth and sixteenth centuries too have a sculptural quality that gives them a not unimportant place in the history of the plastic arts.

Armour

From the fall of the Roman Empire in the West until the early fourteenth century most armour was made of mail worn over a padded undergarment and accompanied by a plate helmet and a shield. But from as early as the beginning of the thirteenth century there is evidence to show that subsidiary defences of plate were coming into use. The first of these was probably a breastplate concealed under the fabric surcoat that was regularly worn over the armour from the end of the twelfth century onwards. By the late thirteenth century this plate had developed into a complete defence for the trunk formed of large overlapping plates riveted to a fabric lining or cover, now usually called the coat of plates. During the second half of the century also plates of metal or hardened leather (*cuirbouilli*) were attached to the mail at the elbows, knees, and shoulders, while gauntlets constructed in the same manner as the coat of plates were introduced. During the first quarter of the fourteenth century complete plate defences for the limbs were generally adopted, and from *c.* 1330 mail was relegated to a subsidiary role.

The armour for the trunk remained concealed by fabric throughout the fourteenth century, but in the period round about 1420 the coverings were generally discarded. By this date armour had achieved what was virtually its full development, and the majority of subsequent changes were ones of form rather than of basic construction. The complete harness now consisted of breast- and backplate, each formed of a single plate of steel, fauld – from *c.* 1430 equipped with tassets – cuisses, poleyns, greaves, sabatons, pauldrons, vambraces, gauntlets, and helmet.

Armour reached the highest point of its development during the second half of the fifteenth century. Much fine work was produced after this, but from early in the sixteenth century there were indications of the beginning of a decline. For example, a fashion started for elaborately embossed decoration which, though often of superb quality, made the armour quite useless for anything other than parade purposes. From the middle of the sixteenth century the weight of armour began to be increased as a result of improvements in the quality and power of firearms, and in consequence soldiers began to discard the less essential pieces, beginning with the legs. By the early seventeenth century the defensive equipment of the pikemen, who were now the only infantry to wear armour, had been reduced to a cuirass with large tassets and an open helmet. The heavy cavalry wore three-quarter armours until *c.* 1650, but from the 1620s there was an increasing tendency for the lighter units to use only a cuirass, an open helmet, and an elbow gauntlet in conjunction with a buff coat. This equipment became general for all cavalry in the second half of the century. It remained in use until *c.* 1700, after which date armour was gradually discarded.

From the second quarter of the fourteenth century until the seventeenth century special armour was used for the joust and tournament. For the most part this resembled the normal war armour of the period, except that it was fitted with various reinforcing plates.

Arms

SWORDS

The commonest form of sword throughout the Middle Ages had a straight two-edged blade and a guard formed by a single crossbar (quillon). As early as the fourteenth century, however, an additional guard was occasionally provided in the form of a single loop alongside the base of the blade; this enabled the user to hook his finger over one quillon, so obtaining a better grip on the sword. During the sixteenth century the introduction of the practice of duelling, as opposed to armoured combat in the lists, and the corresponding development of the science

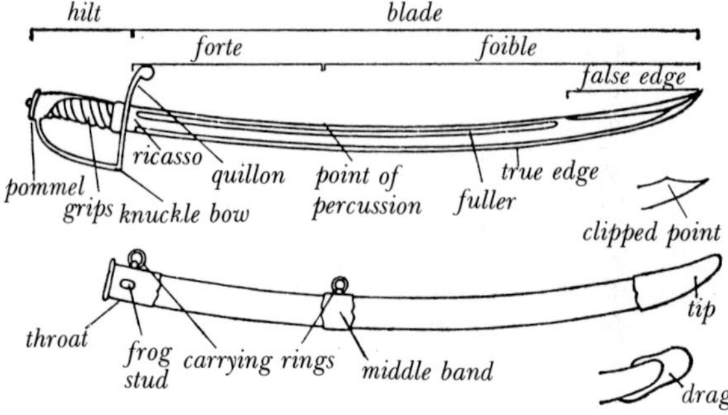

Suit of foot-jousting armour made for the Elector Christian I of Saxony, one of twelve made by Anton Pfeffenhauser, all to have been presented to the Elector on Christmas day 1591. Augsburg mark, *c.* 1590. Christie, Manson & Woods

Above Congressional naval presentation sword and scabbard of the War of 1812. U.S. Naval Academy Museum

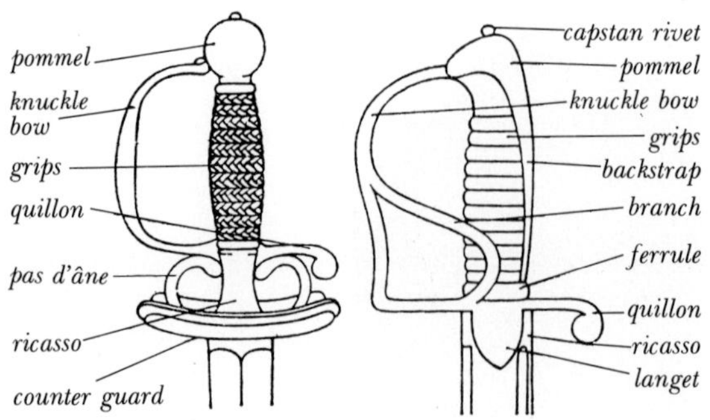

of fencing, led to the adding of more supplementary guards, finally producing the swept-hilt rapier of the second half of the sixteenth century. This remained in vogue until the second quarter of the seventeenth century, when a lighter form of rapier was introduced with a simple shellguard and a single curved bar over the knuckles, ultimately developing into the smallsword. In southern Italy, and more particularly in Spain, at this period, the swept hilt was superseded by the cup hilt, with a guard formed by a circular bowl supplemented by straight quillons and a knucklebar, which remained in use until the eighteenth century.

The two-hand sword, which had been used occasionally from the fourteenth century onwards, enjoyed a brief period of popularity in the sixteenth century, picked men being specially trained to its use. The basket-hilted sword, usually with a broad blade, was introduced in the middle of the sixteenth century; it has survived in a modified form until the present time.

(*See also* Backsword, Broadsword, Cinquedea, Claymore, Cutlass, Falchion, Hand-and-a-half sword, Hanger, Heading sword, 'Pappenheimer', Rapier, Sabre, Schiavona, Smallsword, Swept hilt.)

DAGGERS

The dagger, the diminutive of the sword designed chiefly for thrusting, was common in a variety of forms from the earliest times. It appeared as an adjunct to the sword in the late thirteenth century, usually being worn on the right hip. During the sixteenth and seventeenth centuries it played an important role in fencing.

(*See* Ballock knife, Bayonet, Cinquedea, Ear dagger, Lefthand dagger, Quillon dagger, Rondel dagger, Stiletto.)

Below, left Cup-hilted rapier of chiselled steel, Italian, 17th century. *Right* left-handed dagger signed 'Antonio Cilenta de Neapoli fecit'. Victoria & Albert Museum

STAFF WEAPONS

This category includes any weapon mounted on a haft. Apart from the club and the spear – the earliest of all weapons – and their derivatives, nearly all forms were derived from agricultural implements. A wide variety of different types exists, only a few of which can be included in the Glossary.

(*See* Bill, Glaive, Guisarme, Halberd, Hammer, Lance, Mace, Partizan, Pike, Vouge.)

FIREARMS

It now seems quite certain that gunpowder was discovered in the East, but it was apparently used there only for pyrotechnic devices and weapons. Guns, which were almost certainly a Western invention, are first recorded in Europe at the beginning of the second quarter of the fourteenth century. They did not start to become common until after *c.* 1350, but by *c.* 1400 were in general use. The earliest handguns, which first appeared in the middle of the fourteenth century, consisted simply of a barrel attached to a wooden or metal pole and were ignited with a piece of smouldering tinder held in the free hand. Early in the fifteenth century the earliest form of match lock appeared and made possible the development of a gun that could be aimed and fired in much the same way as a modern one. The butts of many of these guns were designed to be held against the cheek, not the shoulder, and an improved version of this form remained common in Germany until the eighteenth century.

Hand firearms did not start to play a major role in warfare until the end of the fifteenth century, but by the second half of the sixteenth century they had become the most important of all military arms. This was partly a result of improvements in their design, but was chiefly because of improvements in the quality of gunpowder. A development of particular importance was the introduction of the wheel lock in the second decade of the sixteenth century. This, by obviating the inconvenient and telltale match, made possible the production of both a practical cavalry firearm, the pistol, and a satisfactory sporting gun. The result was that firearms began for the first time to be used generally by the upper classes, who demanded finely made and finely decorated guns. Henceforth the gunmaker was assured of the kind of patronage that made it possible for him to improve his products. The sixteenth century, therefore, was a period of experiment, but after the general adoption of the flint lock in the second quarter of the seventeenth century no major development took place for nearly two hundred years. The invention of the percussion lock in 1807, however, led to another period of experiment, lasting for the greater part of the nineteenth century, during which most of the different types of firearms in use at the present day were evolved.

Though the majority of firearms in use prior to *c.* 1850 were single-shot muzzle loaders, experiments with breech-loading and repeating mechanisms were made at regular intervals from the early sixteenth century onwards. Apart from some revolvers, all were more or less failures, partly because of the fouling produced by gunpowder, which prevented most breech mechanisms from functioning after a few shots, and partly because of the problem of obturation, that is the prevention of the backward leak of

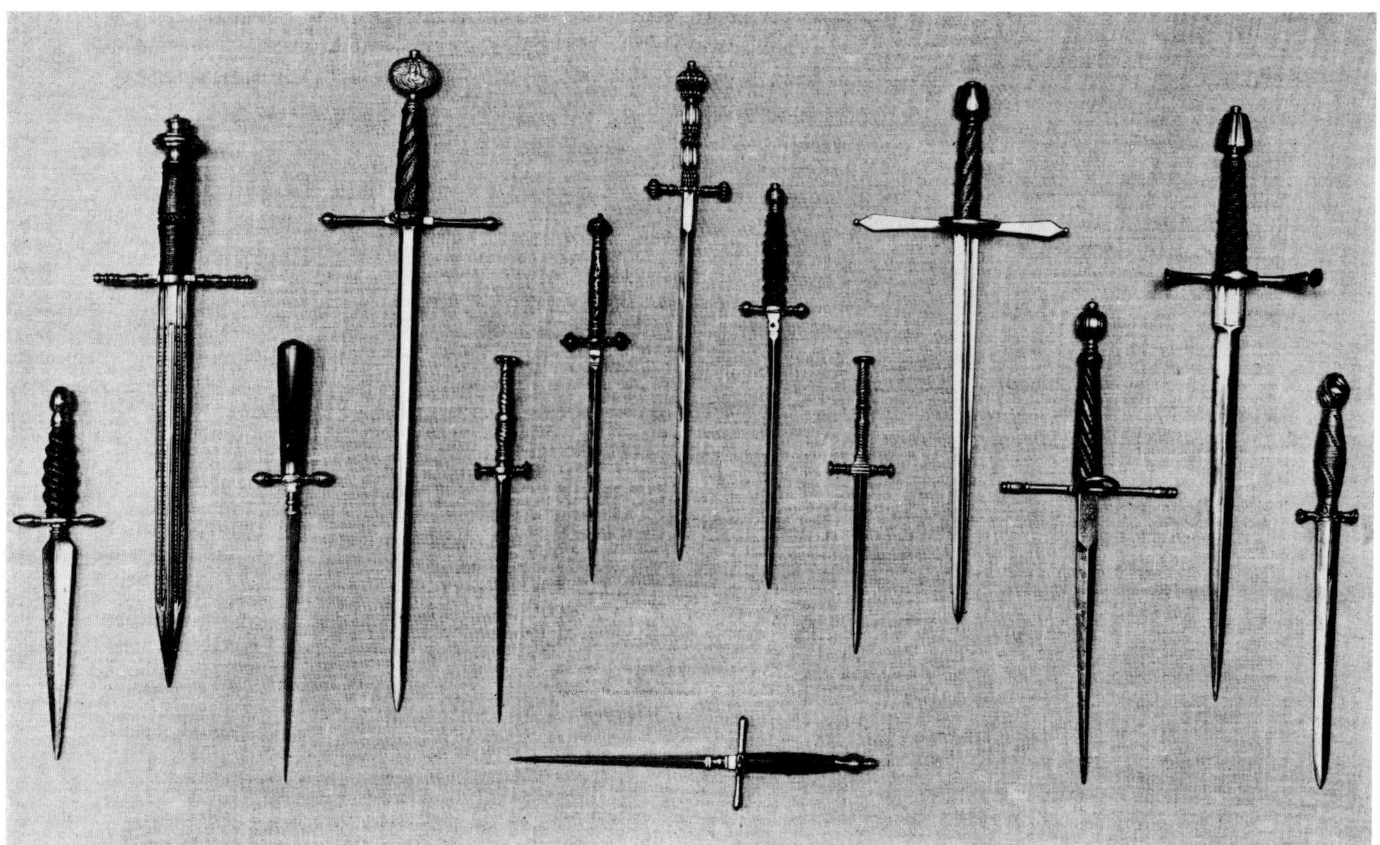

Collection of Italian daggers, early 17th century. Victoria & Albert Museum

gases through the breech mechanism. Only with the adoption of the self-obturating brass cartridge in the third quarter of the nineteenth century did really satisfactory breech-loading and repeating arms, other than revolvers, become possible.

Centres of Production

Most of the major European countries had their own armourers and weaponsmiths, but certain centres became especially famous for the making of arms and armour. Little is recorded about such centres in the early Middle Ages, but we know that by the fourteenth century northern Italy, in particular Milan, and southern Germany were supplying large quantities of armour and weapons to the rest of Europe. Of the German centres Augsburg, Nuremberg, Landshut, and Innsbruck were especially noted for armour, and Passau and Solingen for swords. The smiths of Solingen, in fact, supplied a very high proportion of all the blades used in Europe from the late sixteenth to the late eighteenth century, many of which they unashamedly signed with the names of eminent foreign makers. In the sixteenth and seventeenth centuries blades made in Toledo were greatly esteemed, though this city seems never to have become as great a centre of production as Solingen.

During the sixteenth century Milan, Nuremberg, and Augsburg developed an important trade in firearms. Other noted centres were Suhl in Germany and Brescia in northern Italy, the latter being especially noted for arms with elaborately chiselled steel mounts. But from the middle of the seventeenth century until the great Birmingham arms industry started to develop in the late eighteenth century, by far the most important centre of firearms production in Europe was the city of Liège in Belgium.

Glossary

The glossary which follows includes all major technical terms which the beginner collector will encounter in a study of European and American arms and armour. Oriental armour has not been included. Most of these terms have their individual translations in French, Italian, German, and Spanish. These will be learned by the serious student in the course of acquiring knowledge.

Armet. A term used in fifteenth- and early sixteenth-century texts, apparently to denote a close helmet (*q.v.*). Modern writers generally confine it to the early form of this helmet with hinged cheek pieces overlapping and fastening at the chin, and usually having at the back a steel disc (rondel) on a short stem.

Arquebus. A term derived from the German *Hackenbüchse* (hooked gun) applied originally to a handgun with a flat lug on the underside of the barrel that could be hooked over a parapet to serve as a recoil stop. In the second half of the sixteenth century it denoted a light musket and in the seventeenth century a heavy carbine. The term is now often applied loosely to any wheel- or match-lock gun.

Backstrap. A metal strap along the outside or back of the grip of a pistol or revolver.

Backsword. A sword having a blade with a back on one side and a single cutting edge on the other.

Above Arquebus, the stock inlaid with mother of pearl and staghorn partly tinted, German, *c.* 1620. Victoria & Albert Museum

Ballock knife. A form of dagger used from the fourteenth to the seventeenth centuries with a guard formed by two lobate protuberances. It is often called a kidney dagger by modern writers.

Bands. Loops of metal encircling the barrel and stock of a firearm as a means of fastening these two structures together.

Barbute. A fifteenth-century open helmet of Italian origin. It was tall, at first with a pointed apex, later becoming rounded, and extended over the cheeks, leaving only the eyes, nose, and mouth exposed. Some examples closely resemble the classical Greek Corinthian helmet, on which they may perhaps have been directly based.

Barrel tang. A metal strap attached to the breech of the barrel of a firearm and projecting towards the butt. It was used to anchor the barrel more firmly in place.

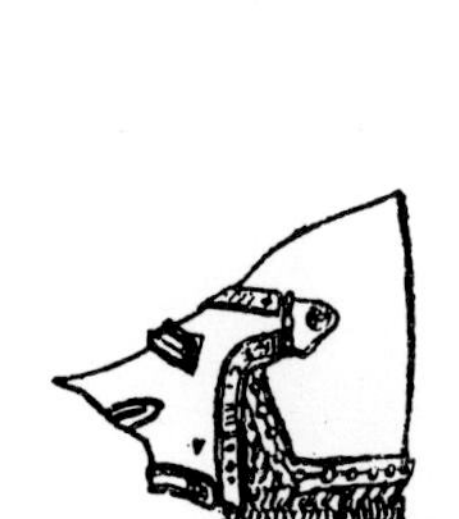

Bascinet

Bascinet. The characteristic light helmet of the fourteenth and early fifteenth centuries. At first rounded, it later became conical in shape and usually had a mail curtain (aventail) laced to its lower edge, protecting the throat and neck. In the second half of the fourteenth century it was often worn with an acutely pointed 'pig-faced' visor, a form for which the rare medieval term 'hounskull' is now generally used. In the fifteenth century the helmet again became rounded, and the aventail was replaced by a plate gorget; in this form it remained in use for fighting on foot in the lists until the beginning of the sixteenth century.

Bastard sword. *See* Hand-and-a-half sword.

Battery. *See* Steel.

Bayonet. A dagger, or short sword, fitted to a musket to convert it into a pike. Known early in the seventeenth century, it was not generally adopted for military purposes until the second half of that century. At first simply a dagger with round grip, tapered to fit into the musket muzzle, a form which remained in use until well into the eighteenth century, but this was gradually superseded by the socket bayonet introduced in the late seventeenth century. This had a tubular hilt fitting over the muzzle, the blade being set to one side so that the musket could be fired with the bayonet fixed. It was superseded in the nineteenth century by the sword bayonet, attached to a lug on the barrel by a spring catch and with a hilt like that of a sword.

Besagew. A small plate, usually circular, suspended over the front of each armpit on armours of the fourteenth to the sixteenth century.

Bevor. A chin defence, at first separate but from the early sixteenth century forming part of the close helmet (*q.v.*).

Bill. A staff weapon derived from the hedging bill, which it resembles.

Blade sight. An upright elongated front sight of a firearm.

Bluing. A heat or chemically induced oxidation used to colour iron or steel in shades of blue and black.

Blunderbuss. A short firearm with a large bore flaring at the muzzle, designed to scatter shot in a wide pattern and do considerable execution in a confined area. For this reason it was particularly popular as ships' arms for repelling boarders, and for defending streets and staircases. Apparently introduced into England from the Continent in the middle of the seventeenth century where it was used until well into the nineteenth century. The period of the blunderbuss's greatest popularity in America was the eighteenth century. Although popular myth insists that the Pilgrims were armed with them, very few of these guns were used in this country prior to 1700, and certainly none was used at Plymouth. Many eighteenth- and early nineteenth-century blunderbusses are equipped with a hinged spring bayonet, which is thrown forward into the fixed position when a catch is released.

Bootleg pistol. Peculiar form of percussion-cap pistol made largely in Massachusetts, with the hammer underneath the barrel and the grips at a rightangle.

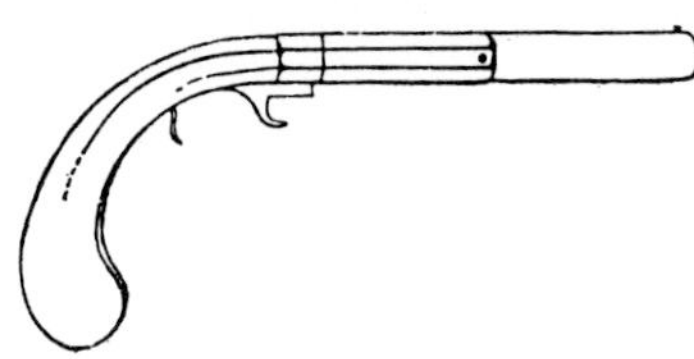

Bore. The interior of the barrel of a firearm. Also used as a designation of the diameter of the interior of the barrel in terms of the number of spherical lead balls of corresponding diameter in a pound weight. In this connotation it is synonymous with gauge.

Breech. The rear of the barrel of a firearm.

Breech loader. A firearm receiving its charge at the breech.

Breech plug. A cylindrical plug screwed in at the breech of muzzle-loading firearms to close the bore.

Brigandine. A light, flexible body defence consisting of small, overlapping metal plates riveted to the interior of a canvas or leather jacket. It was usually covered with coloured silk or velvet, the rivet heads on the exterior being gilt to produce a decorative effect. The term first occurs at the end of the fourteenth century, but the majority of surviving examples date from the sixteenth and early seventeenth centuries.

Broadsword. A sword with a straight double-edged blade. The term is applied chiefly to the basket-hilted cavalry sword of the seventeenth and eighteenth centuries. It survived in the Scottish basket-hilted sword, often erroneously called a claymore.

Browning. A process to colour the iron or steel parts of a firearm in shades of brown. Sometimes this was done through artificial oxidation, and sometimes a lacquer was used.

Buff coat. A coat of thick buff leather, usually with full skirts and often sleeved. It was thick enough to withstand a sword cut and became very popular, particularly for cavalry, when armour was falling into disuse in the seventeenth century.

Buffe. The sixteenth- and seventeenth-century term for a chin defence, more especially the type worn with the burgonet (*q.v.*).

Burgonet. An open helmet, used chiefly by light horsemen in the sixteenth and early seventeenth centuries. It usually had a peak (fall) over the eyes and hinged cheek pieces fastening under the chin. It was sometimes worn with a deep chin piece (buffe).
Butt. The portion of a long arm which fits against the shoulder, or the terminus of the grip of a pistol.
Butt cap. A metal covering for the butt of a pistol.
Butt plate. A metal plate used to cover and protect the extreme end of the butt of a shoulder arm.
Cabasset. *See* Morion.
Caliber or **calibre.** The diameter of the bore of a firearm expressed in hundredths of an inch.
Caliver. A light musket used in the sixteenth century.
Cap. A small charge of a percussion-igniting compound, usually fulminate of mercury, sealed within a paper or metal container and used to ignite the main charge of a firearm.
Carbine. A short shoulder arm intended for the use of mounted troops.
Cartridge. A combination of the ball and powder charge for a gun fastened together in a single container. The earliest cartridges were wrapped in paper or cloth. Later metal cartridges were developed which contained their own detonating charges as well.

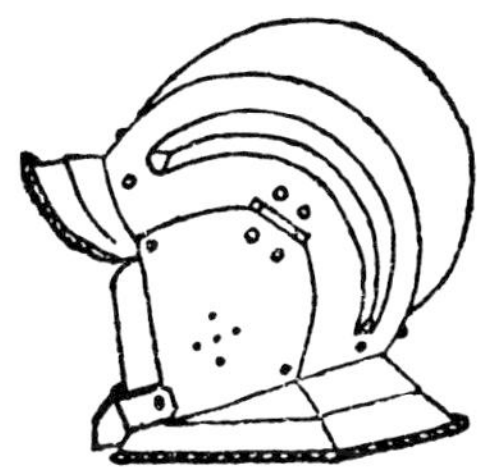
Burgonet

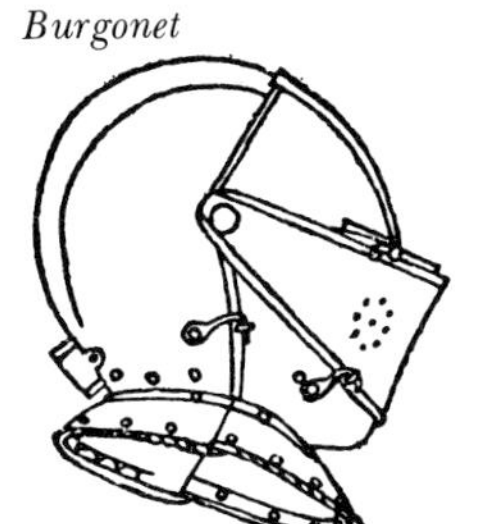
Close helmet

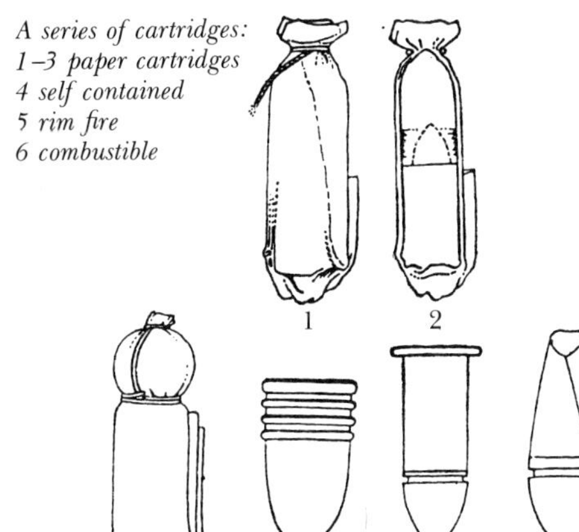

A series of cartridges:
1–3 paper cartridges
4 self contained
5 rim fire
6 combustible

Chamber. That portion of the bore of a firearm which receives the charge.
Chanfron. The plate defence for a horse's head, introduced early in the fourteenth century and remaining in use until well into the seventeenth.
Cinquedea. An Italian term for a dagger of uncertain form. It is now applied to a type of large dagger or short sword with a flat, triangular blade some five fingers wide near the hilt (the term being thought to derive from the Italian *cinque dei*), and often elaborately etched and gilt. It was essentially a civilian weapon, used chiefly in Italy, in the late fifteenth and early sixteenth centuries.
Claymore. From the Gaelic *claidheamh-mòr* (great sword). The Scottish two-hand sword introduced in the sixteenth century. Of very large proportions, it usually had straight quillons inclining at a sharp angle towards the broad, straight blade. In the seventeenth century the quillons became curved and were supplemented by two (sometimes only one) large solid shells bent towards the hilt. Since the eighteenth century the term has been applied erroneously to the basket-hilted Scottish broadsword.

Claymores

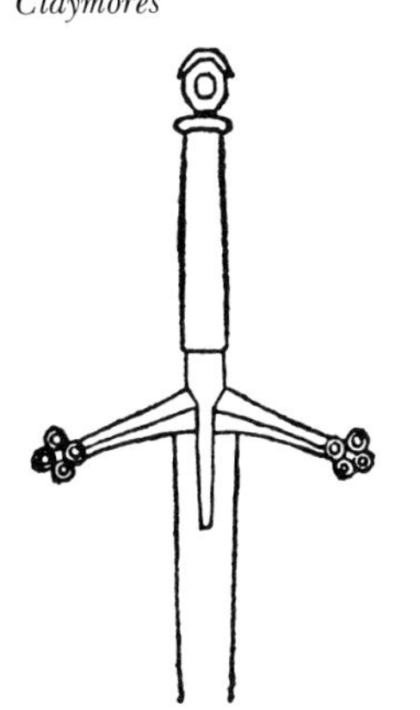

Close helmet. A close-fitting, visored helmet completely enclosing the head. The term is now usually confined to the type of headpiece introduced early in the sixteenth century, with the visor and chin piece pivoting at the sides, as opposed to the armet (*q.v.*), which has hinged cheek pieces fastening at the chin.
Cock. The pivoted arm of a flint-lock or snaphance mechanism which holds the flint and snaps forward to bring it in contact with the steel in order to produce the spark necessary to ignite the charge.
Colichemarde. *See* Smallsword.
Counterguard. Comprises those structures in addition to the quillons which are interposed between the hilt and the blade of a sword. It may take the form of a solid plate or a network of bars.
Couter. An elbow defence.

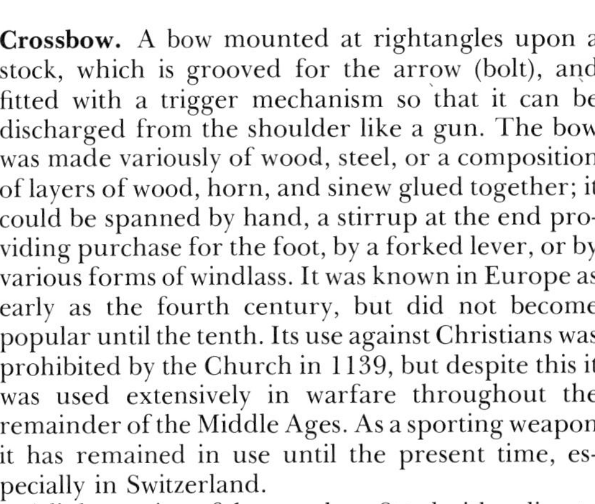
Right Sporting crossbow and cranequin, German, early 17th century. Christie, Manson & Woods

Crossbow. A bow mounted at rightangles upon a stock, which is grooved for the arrow (bolt), and fitted with a trigger mechanism so that it can be discharged from the shoulder like a gun. The bow was made variously of wood, steel, or a composition of layers of wood, horn, and sinew glued together; it could be spanned by hand, a stirrup at the end providing purchase for the foot, by a forked lever, or by various forms of windlass. It was known in Europe as early as the fourth century, but did not become popular until the tenth. Its use against Christians was prohibited by the Church in 1139, but despite this it was used extensively in warfare throughout the remainder of the Middle Ages. As a sporting weapon it has remained in use until the present time, especially in Switzerland.

A light version of the crossbow fitted with a sling to fire bullets or stones, and known as a stonebow, was much used from medieval times onwards for shooting small game. It remained popular, particularly in Lancashire and East Anglia, until well into the nineteenth century. The sixteenth-century term *brodd* is often applied to this sort of bow, though its original meaning is uncertain.

Above Cuirassier armour, German, *c.* 1620–30. Christie, Manson & Woods

Far right Flint-lock fowling piece, signed on the lock and barrel by Wilson, London. Silver mounts by Jeremiah Ashley, London, 1749–50. Victoria & Albert Museum

Cuirass. The breast- and backplate of an armour together.
Cuirassier armour. Armour for the heavy cavalry of the first half of the seventeenth century, consisting of a close helmet and defences covering the whole of the body down to the knees.
Cuisse. A thigh defence.
Culet. The seventeenth-century term for the hooped buttock defence attached to the backplate.
Cup hilt. A modern term for the type of rapier hilt, introduced in the second quarter of the seventeenth century, in which the main guard is formed like a bowl. It was used chiefly in Spain and Italy.
Cutlass. A term first appearing in the sixteenth century, denoting a short, single-edged sword, usually curved, the successor of the medieval falchion (*q.v.*). In the eighteenth and early nineteenth centuries it was a standard naval weapon.
Cutlass pistol. A type of single-shot percussion-cap pistol with a heavy cutting blade mounted underneath the barrel, patented by George Elgin in 1837 in the United States.

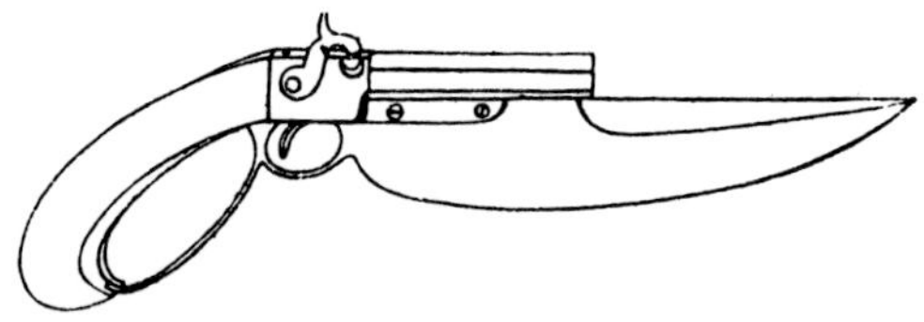

Cylinder. The portion of a revolver which holds the chambers for the charges. It revolves around an axis and presents its loads successively to the breech of the barrel.
Dagger. The diminutive of the sword, designed to be used chiefly for thrusting, and common in a variety of forms from the earliest times.
Deringer. One of the foremost U.S. gunsmiths was Henry Deringer of Philadelphia. A fine craftsman, noted for the excellent workmanship on his products, Deringer at first made both rifles and duelling pistols, but shortly after 1825 he began to concentrate on short pocket pistols with large calibres. These little weapons, ranging from 3¾ inches (9.5 cm) to 9 inches (22.9 cm) in over-all length, had calibres varying from 0.33 to 0.51 inches (approx. 1 cm to 1.3 cm). Thus considerable power was packed into arms that could be carried easily and inconspicuously almost anywhere. They were always fired with percussion caps and were almost always rifled. Deringer's pistols quickly became immensely popular, especially in the south and west, and his name became synonymous with the type of pistol he had developed. In fact, often spelled derringer, it was soon applied to any short pocket pistol, even cartridge arms with two or more barrels, and in that connotation it is still in use today. Because of the pistol's popularity, there were many imitators, some of whom put Deringer's name or slight variants such as Beringer on their own products, hoping to fool the unsuspecting. Deringer himself died in 1868, three years after one of his pistols had achieved national notoriety in the hands of John Wilkes Booth when he assassinated President Abraham Lincoln.
Dirk. Term applied to: (i) the characteristic long sheath knife of the Scottish Highlander, which seems to have developed from the early seventeenth-century form of ballock knife (*q.v.*); (ii) the light dagger carried by some naval officers, especially midshipmen, in the late eighteenth and nineteenth centuries.

Ear dagger. A form of fifteenth- and sixteenth-century dagger with the pommel formed by two flattened discs, like ears, set at an angle. It was of Eastern origin but was much used in Spain and occasionally elsewhere in Europe.
Elbow gauntlet. A form of gauntlet, introduced in the late fifteenth century, with a cuff extending to the elbow. In the seventeenth century the armour for the arms was often confined to a gauntlet of this type worn on the bridle hand, whence it is often called a bridle gauntlet.
Escutcheon plate. A metal plate set in the wrist of either a pistol or shoulder arm as a place to engrave the name or monogram of the owner or other similar data.
Falchion. A short, curved, single-edged sword, known as early as the twelfth century. The medieval form had a broad, cleaver-like blade.
False edge. *See* Sabre.

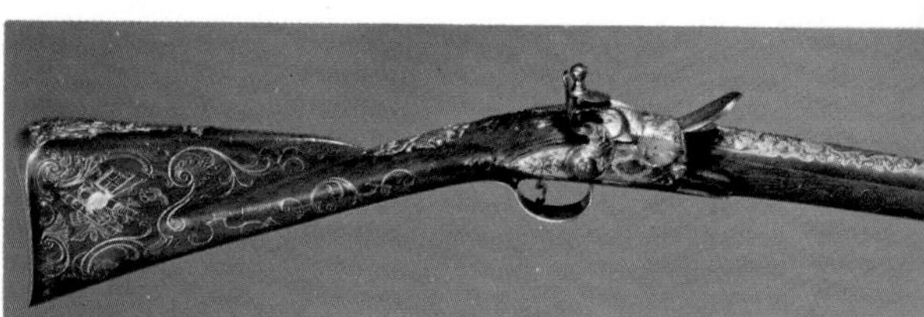

Flint lock. A term used from the late seventeenth century onwards to denote the snaphance (*q.v.*). Most modern writers confine it to the form of lock with the pan cover and steel made in one. This first appeared in the late sixteenth century and completely supplanted the earlier form during the second quarter of the seventeenth century everywhere except in Italy. The earliest version of this lock had a horizontal sear working through the lockplate, as on the early snaphance. The fact that the pan cover and steel were made in one, however, meant that once the gun had been primed the cock had to be kept pulled back. This led to the introduction of a safety device in the form of a small pivoted hook (so-called dog catch) which engaged in a notch at the rear of the cock and held it in the half-cocked position. In *c.* 1600 a separate half-cock sear appeared, a feature that remained in use in Spain on the miquelet lock (*q.v.*) until the nineteenth century. Elsewhere what has been termed the true flint lock came into general use during the second quarter of the seventeenth century. This, which had a vertical sear engaging in one of two notches in an internal tumbler (for half- and full-cock), was probably invented between 1610 and 1615 by Marin le Bourgeoys (d. 1634) of Lisieux, France. It remained in wide use until the second quarter of the nineteenth century.
Foible. The portion of the blade of a sword near the point which is weak from the standpoint of leverage. Usually it comprises from half to two-thirds of the length of the blade.
Forestock. The portion of a gunstock in front of the trigger guard.
Forte. The strong portion of the blade of a sword, usually about one-third, nearest the hilt.
Frizzen. *See* Steel.
Frog. A sleeve-like device, normally of leather, used to attach the sword to the belt. Usually the scabbard was thrust through the sleeve and a stud on its throat engaged in a hole in the frog.

Glaive with device of Wilhelm V of Bavaria, German, dated 1580. Bayerisches Armee-museum, Munich

Hanger

Gauge. *See* Bore.

Glaive. A staff-weapon with a large cleaver-like blade. Early writers also applied the term to the lance, and later poets to the sword.

'Gothic' armour. A modern term for the style of plate armour, characterized by slender elegant lines, and decorated with cusped borders and shell-like rippling, developed particularly in Germany in the fifteenth century. The term is extended to cover the fifteenth-century Italian style, which was rounder in form than the German, and usually had smooth, plain surfaces.

Grandguard. A reinforcing piece worn with sixteenth- and early seventeenth-century tilt armours. It covered the left side of the breastplate and the lower left side of the helmet.

Greave. The plate armour for the lower part of the leg, excluding the foot.

Greenwich armour. Armour made in the only English royal workshop, founded at Greenwich by Henry VIII in 1515. It was staffed largely by foreign workmen, of whom one of the most important was Jacob Halder, master workman, 1576–1607. He was almost certainly responsible for an album of drawings of armours made at Greenwich, now in the Victoria and Albert Museum, which has made possible the identification of a number of surviving suits, several of which are in the Tower of London. The workshop was closed down in about 1637.

Guisarme. A term applied in the later Middle Ages to a long-handled axe. Modern writers use it to denote a form of bill (*q.v.*).

Halberd. A staff weapon with a flat axe blade balanced by a fluke and with a long, sharp spike above. Introduced in the fifteenth century, it survived as a parade weapon, and as the arm of certain non-commissioned officers, until the nineteenth century.

Half-armour. A light armour covering the whole body excepting the legs, and often also excluding the arms.

Hammer. In a percussion-cap or cartridge gun the movable arm which strikes the primer and sets it off either directly or through the use of a firing pin. Modern collectors often use the term incorrectly to refer to the cock of a flint arm. In the eighteenth and early nineteenth centuries it was synonymous with steel (*q.v.*).

Hand-and-a-half sword. A large sword with a long grip that could be used with either one or two hands. It appears to have been known as a bastard sword in the fifteenth and sixteenth centuries.

Handgun. The earliest form of hand firearm, introduced early in the fourteenth century. It consisted simply of a tubular barrel attached to a long wooden stock designed to be held under the arm, and ignited at the touchhole by hand.

Hanger. (i) A light, single-edged civilian sword used by horsemen, huntsmen, and sailors in the seventeenth and eighteenth centuries; (ii) the triangular buckled sling attached to the belt, in which a rapier was carried in the late sixteenth and early seventeenth centuries.

Haute piece. One of the upstanding neckguards found on the pauldrons (*q.v.*) of some armours of the first half of the sixteenth century.

Heading sword. An executioner's sword, usually with a plain cruciform hilt long enough to be used with two hands, and a broad, straight, two-edged blade with a rounded or squared point. It was employed on the Continent, and especially in Germany, from the sixteenth to the early nineteenth century.

Helm. A large headpiece, covering the entire head and face and reaching nearly to the shoulders, introduced at the end of the twelfth century. The top was at first flat, but by the middle of the thirteenth century had become conical, giving an improved glancing surface. During the first half of the fourteenth century the helm was often worn over the bascinet (*q.v.*) in warfare, but was subsequently relegated to the tiltyard, where it remained in use until well into the sixteenth century. In its later form it was usually bolted down to the breast and back.

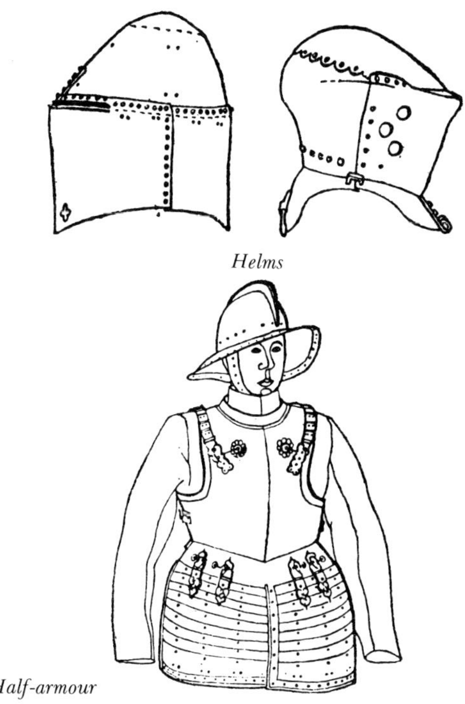

Helms

Half-armour

Hunting sword. A short, light hanger (*q.v.*) with a straight or very slightly curved blade and usually no knuckle-bow. Originally designed to be worn while hunting, as its name implies, it was often affected by high-ranking officers during the eighteenth century.

Jack. This was a cheaper form of the brigandine (*q.v.*), its plates, which were often of horn, being held in place by stitching.

Japanese swordguards. Engelbrecht Kaempfer (1651–1716), whose *History and Description of Japan* was widely consulted at the beginning of the eighteenth century, particularly praised the Japanese for their skill in metalwork, and nowhere is this exhibited to better effect than in the multifarious decorations of the *tsuba.* This, and the *kashira* (the pommel cap) and the *fuchi* (an oval ring which encircles the base of the hilt) are often decorated with great skill and artistry. It is certain that the Japanese swordsman was expected to be skilful enough not to need a swordguard for its proper purpose of protecting the hand if an opponent's blade slid upwards towards the hilt, since in many cases this would have damaged a considerable work of art. It is, perhaps, noteworthy that swordguards become increasingly ornamental with the more settled and peaceful conditions of the Edo period (1615–1867), and in 1870 the *samurai* were forbidden to carry swords as they had done throughout the preceding centuries.

The decorated swordguard seems to have started in the fifteenth century. Before this time most of them were of plain iron or leather with iron reinforcement, although piercing and other restrained forms of ornament were sometimes used. Those mainly sought are more elaborately pierced and often minutely chiselled. They are frequently inlaid with silver, gold, or one of the bronze alloys (like *shakudo* or *sentoku* – *see* Chinese and Japanese Bronzes in Metalwork section) and damascening is occasionally seen, using the term in its proper sense of inlaying designs with wire hammered into a triangular engraved groove opening on the surface at the apex. Engraving with a burin (the normal engraver's tool) is to be found on some examples, and even file cuts are occasionally employed decoratively, as well as punch marks. Some later *tsuba* are decorated with great ingenuity, which was much admired.

Subjects of decoration are, making due allowance for the difference in media, very similar to those employed to decorate other small works of art, and the styles of the swordguard makers are also to be seen on other small objects of metalwork.

The *tsuba* is at present being studied in detail, and the literature on the subject is increasing. The names of many of the srtiats, and the schools they founded, are being established, and much more is now known about them. They represent a type of Japanese art not uncommon in the West, since *tsuba* have been imported since the last quarter of the nineteenth century, and some notable collections, since dispersed, were formed before 1900.

'Kentucky' or **Pennsylvanian rifle.** Developed by the Dutch, German, and Swiss colonists in Pennsylvania. These people had long used rifles in their native lands, and they set out to adapt them to meet the needs of their new environment. They lengthened the barrel, decreased the calibre, and evolved a style of ornamentation that soon set these U.S. rifles completely apart from their European predecessors. The evolution of the U.S. rifle began quite early in the eighteenth century, and its final distinctive form was reached possibly by 1740–5. It was a fine, accurate gun in the hands of a man who knew how to use it, but it was slow to load and had no bayonet, so that it was not well adapted for the formal warfare of the period. The early rifles were simple, with straight lines and thick butts. The lavish inlays and sharply dropping butt did not develop until after 1790.

Kettle hat. An open helmet, usually with a brim, used from the thirteenth to the early sixteenth centuries, when it was replaced by the morion (*q.v.*). Sometimes referred to as the *chapel-de-fer* or war hat.

Key. A wedge-shaped device used to fasten the barrel of a firearm to the stock through corresponding slots in the forestock and lugs on the underside of the barrel. The term is also now applied sometimes to the spanner for winding a wheel lock.

Kidney dagger. *See* Ballock knife.

Lance. The horseman's spear. From the fourteenth to the early seventeenth centuries it was often equipped with a large metal guard for the hand (vamplate).

Lands. The uncut portions of the original surface left between the grooves in the bore of a rifled gun.

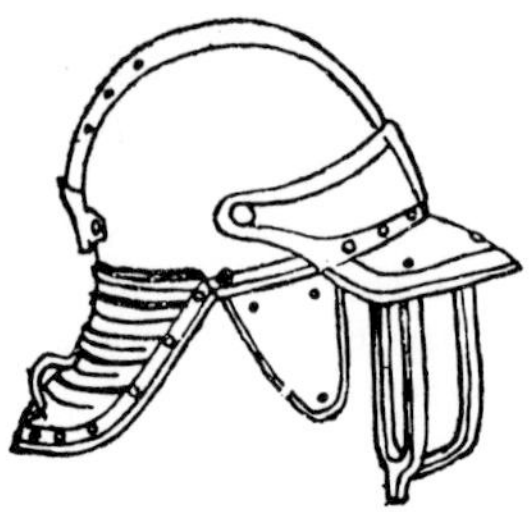

'Lobster-tail' helmet

Lefthand dagger. The dagger used in conjunction with the rapier in sixteenth- and early seventeenth-century fencing. It usually had quillons (often strongly arched to entangle an opponent's sword blade) and a side ring, but a special form, with a triangular knuckleguard, was used in Italy and Spain in conjunction with the cup-hilt rapier (*q.v.*). It remained in use in the latter country until well into the eighteenth century.

'Lobster-tail' helmet. A modern term for a form of burgonet (*q.v.*) worn by cavalry in the seventeenth century. It had a laminated tail, hinged cheek pieces, and a peak (often pivoted), with one or more bars extending from it over the face. The English form with three bars was the characteristic helmet of the Civil War.

Lock. The mechanism of a firearm used for igniting the explosive.

Lockplate. The basic iron or steel plate on which the movable parts of a gun lock are mounted.

Long arm. Those small arms designed to be fired from the shoulder. Synonymous with shoulder arm.

Lucerne hammer. A staff weapon with a hammerhead balanced by a fluke and with a long spike above. On late sixteenth- and seventeenth-century examples the hammer is often formed by three claws.

Mace. A horseman's club. From the fourteenth century onwards the head was normally flanged. On examples of the fifteenth century and later the haft was usually of metal like the head.

Magazine. A device for holding a number of cartridges together to facilitate loading for successive discharges. Also the part of a repeating firearm containing cartridges for successive discharges.

Mail. Armour made of interlinked rings which, on most European examples, are riveted. It was known in Europe at least as early as the second century B.C., and was the normal defence during the early Middle Ages. It was relegated to a subordinate role with the general adoption of plate armour in the fourteenth century, but nevertheless remained in common use until well into the seventeenth. The extension of the term to cover all forms of defensive armour and the word chainmail are both of comparatively recent date.

Maingauche dagger. *See* Lefthand dagger.

Manifer. A large, often rigid, gauntlet for the bridle hand worn with jousting armours from the fourteenth century onwards.

Match lock. The earliest form of mechanical ignition for a gun, introduced in the first quarter of the fifteenth century, in which an arm holding a lighted match (cord made of tow soaked in a solution of saltpetre) is brought into contact with priming powder at the touchhole by pressure on a trigger. Despite the invention of the wheel and flint locks, it remained in use for military purposes, on account of its cheapness, until the end of the seventeenth century.

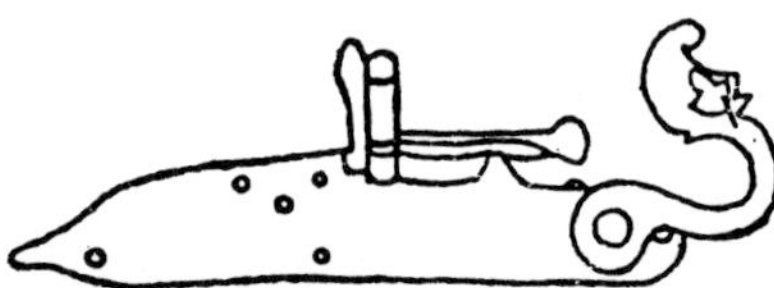

'Maximilian' armour. A modern term for the style of fluted armour which came into use in Italy and, more particularly, in Germany during the reign of the Emperor Maximilian I (1494–1519). It is rarely

Far right
Seven-barrelled flint-lock box-lock pepperbox revolver signed Twiggy, London, late 18th century. Christie, Manson & Woods

found after *c.* 1540, but examples dating from as late as *c.* 1560–70 are occasionally encountered. Modern writers sometimes use the rare sixteenth-century English term for fluted, 'crested', to describe this style.

Minié bullet or **Minié ball.** A cylindro-conoidal projectile with a cavity in its base which expanded when the powder charge was fired and caused the bullet to fit the bore tightly and thus take the spin imparted by the rifling. It was named after Captain C. E. Minié of the French Army, who originally developed the principle on which it functioned. Because this type of bullet allowed a muzzle-loading rifle to be loaded as rapidly as a musket, it ended the supremacy of the musket as a military arm.

Miquelet lock. A modern term for a form of flint lock (*q.v.*) used in southern Italy and Spain from the early seventeenth century onwards. It was a development from the early form of flint lock with two sears (giving half- and full-cock respectively) operating through the lockplate. It went out of use in Italy in the first half of the eighteenth century, but survived in Spain until well into the nineteenth century.

Morion

Morion. An open helmet much used by foot soldiers in the second half of the sixteenth century. Contemporary texts mention two forms: (i) the Spanish morion, called a cabasset by many modern writers, with a pear-shaped, pointed skull and a narrow, flat brim; (ii) the comb morion, with a high comb and a curved brim peaked before and behind. The modern term peaked morion refers to an intermediate type with a curved brim, and a pointed apex terminating in a small stalk.

Musket. A military match- or wheel-lock firearm introduced in the third quarter of the sixteenth century. It was heavier than any other hand firearm of the period and had to be fired from a forked rest. The rest was discarded in the second quarter of the seventeenth century, and henceforth the term was applied to any heavy military long gun.

Musketoon. A short musket.

Muzzle. The distal or front end of the barrel of a firearm.

Nipple. The small tube at the breech of a percussion-cap firearm on which the cap is placed.

Pan. The receptacle on the outside of the barrel or lockplate of a firearm used to hold the priming powder. Sometimes called the flash pan or priming pan.

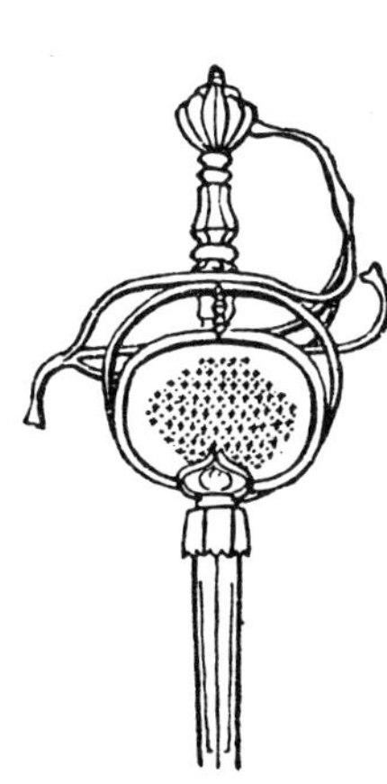
Pappenheimer

'Pappenheimer'. A heavy rapier with a form of swept hilt (*q.v.*) incorporating two large perforated shells. It was used during the first half of the seventeenth century and was named after the celebrated imperialist general of the Thirty Years' War, Gottfried Heinrich, Count von Pappenheim (d. 1632). Sometimes referred to incorrectly as a Walloon sword.

Partizan. A staff weapon with a long head formed like an equilateral triangle, usually with two small pointed lugs at the base. Introduced in the fifteenth century, it survived as a parade weapon until the nineteenth century.

Pasguard. A reinforcing plate worn over the left couter (*q.v.*) on sixteenth- and early seventeenth-century jousting armours.

Patch box
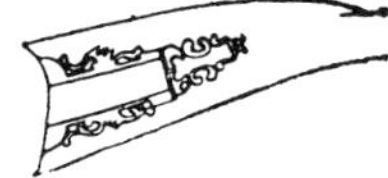

Patch box. A receptacle in the side of a rifle butt designed to hold greased patches or small pieces of equipment.

Pauldron. Plate defence for the shoulder.

Pepperbox. Percussion-cap muzzle-loading pistol which achieved great popularity in the United States during the 1830s and 1840s. This was by no means a U.S. invention. It had developed gradually for well over a century and a half, but it found a definite market at this period, and Americans were quick to make improvements and alterations in the basic design. Fundamentally, the pepperbox was a series of barrels grouped around a central axis that could be fired one after another by a single hammer. Some were single-action, some double-action. On some the barrels revolved automatically and on others it was necessary to turn them by hand. Normally these pistols had from three to six barrels, but occasionally there were more – eight, ten, twelve, and even eighteen. When first developed, they were the fastest-firing guns of their time, and they were widely carried as personal arms both by civilians and soldiers. The most prolific maker of U.S. pepperboxes was Ethan Allen of Grafton and Worcester, Massachusetts, in partnership with Charles Thurber and later with T. P. Wheelock. Second was the firm of Blunt & Syms of New York City, but there were many others. Even in the cartridge era there were pistols that still qualified as pepperboxes, notably those four-barrelled pocket pistols made by Christian Sharps of Philadelphia.

Percussion lock. The latest form of ignition for a firearm, involving the use of a detonating compound. The first patent for a lock of this type was taken out in 1807 by the Rev. Alexander Forsyth (d. 1843). As put on the market, this had a small, flask-shaped magazine which could be rotated on a central spindle, and which contained detonating powder in the lower end and a spring-loaded striker in the upper. By turning the magazine through 180 degrees a small amount of powder was deposited in a recess in the central spindle, connecting through a channel to the touchhole; when the magazine was returned to the normal position this powder was detonated by the striker, which was itself struck by a hammer-like cock (1).

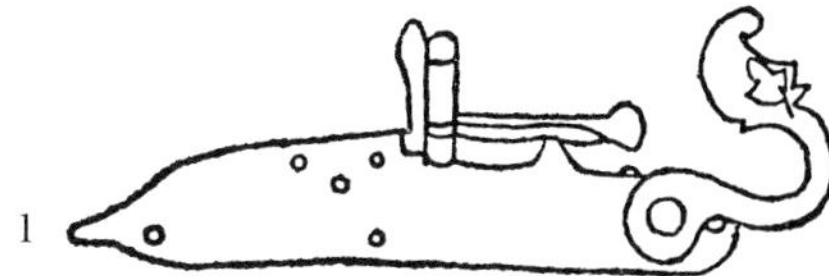

Improvements made on the Forsyth lock included the pellet or pill lock, in which the detonating powder was replaced by a pellet, sometimes enclosed in a paper cap, and the tube lock, which used a tubular metal primer held by a spring clip. All types were superseded by the percussion-cap system, apparently invented between 1818 and 1820, in which a thimble-shaped copper cap containing detonating powder was placed on a hollow nipple communicating with the chamber, and fired by the action of the cock. Many flint-lock guns were converted to this

system, which remained in use until the second half of the nineteenth century (2).

Petronel. A large pistol, or short arquebus, fitted with match or wheel lock and used in the late sixteenth and early seventeenth centuries. It had a curved stock, which was rested against the chest when fired.

Pike. A long infantry spear, usually with a small, leaf-shaped head. During the sixteenth and seventeenth centuries, when the pikeman played a major part in military tactics, it often attained a length of as much as 22 feet (6.8 m).

Pill lock. *See* Percussion lock.

'Pisan' armour. A misleading modern term for a type of late sixteenth-century armour, apparently produced chiefly in Milan. Its chief characteristic consists of bands of coarsely etched decoration of confused design.

Pistol. The smallest type of firearm, designed to be fired with one hand, introduced *c.* 1530. It was fitted at first with a wheel lock and subsequently snaphance, flint and percussion lock, but in Europe with a match lock. The earliest pistols were used chiefly by the cavalry, being carried in large holsters attached to the saddle, but in the late sixteenth century smaller forms were devised to be carried in the belt, and later in the pocket. Numerous attempts were made to produce a revolving pistol, but none was really successful until the invention of the Colt percussion revolver (*see* Revolver), patented in 1836.

Right Pair of flint-lock pistols made for Philip V by Nicolas Bis, Madrid, 1720. Steel mounts enriched with gold, the ramrod handles of ivory. H.M. Tower of London Armouries

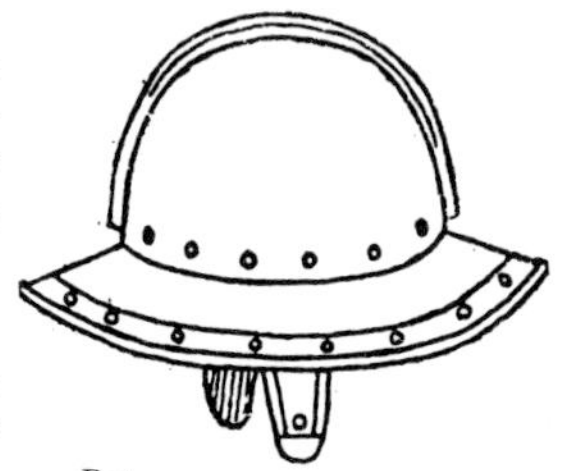

Pot

Below Case pair of flint-lock presentation pistols with silver mounts, bearing marks used up to 1809, traditionally given by Napoleon I to his brother Joseph Bonaparte on his being given the crown of Spain, probably in 1808. Made by Nicolas Noel Boutlet, Versailles. Christie, Manson & Woods

Left Scroll-butt flint-lock pistols of steel, Doune, Scottish, *c.* 1730–40. Glasgow Museum and Art Gallery

Plackart. A reinforcing breastplate.

Point of percussion. The point which divides the forte (*q.v.*) from the foible (*q.v.*), the theoretical spot at which a blow should be struck to achieve its greatest force.

Pole axe. A term applied from the fifteenth to the seventeenth centuries to a long-handled axe or hammer for use in fighting on foot. It is now confined to axes of this type only.

Poleyn. A plate defence for the knee.

Pommel. The shaped terminal of the hilt of a sword or dagger, designed to counterbalance the weight of the blade. The term is also applied to the rounded end of a pistol butt.

Pot. A term used in the seventeenth century apparently to designate any type of open helmet. Modern writers usually confine it to the large, wide-brimmed variety used by seventeenth-century pikemen.

Powder flask. Flask for carrying the black powder used for charging muzzle-loading guns. It was made in a variety of different shapes and materials, and was usually fitted with some kind of measuring device. A smaller flask was often carried for the finer powder used in priming.

Quillon. One of the branches of the crossguard of a sword.

Quillon dagger. A modern term applied to any dagger with quillons (*q.v.*).

Ramrod. A rod of wood or metal used to force home the charge in a muzzle-loading firearm.

Ramrod pipes or **thimbles.** The metal tubes on the underside of a muzzle-loading firearm which hold the ramrod.

Rapier. A sword with a long, straight blade, introduced in the sixteenth century. It was at first designed for thrusting and cutting, but as the science of fencing developed emphasis was laid increasingly on the former. It was primarily a civilian weapon, and in the sixteenth and seventeenth centuries was usually used in conjunction with a dagger or a cloak held in the left hand.

Rerebrace. Plate armour for the shoulder and upper arm. The term was generally replaced by pauldron (*q.v.*) during the first half of the fifteenth century.

Revolver. A firearm with a rotatable cylinder containing chambers for the charge that can be brought in turn into the firing position behind a single barrel, or one with a group of rotatable barrels. The term is applied especially to a pistol working on the former system.

Experiments were made with revolving firearms at regular intervals from the second quarter of the sixteenth century onwards. But the first really satisfac-

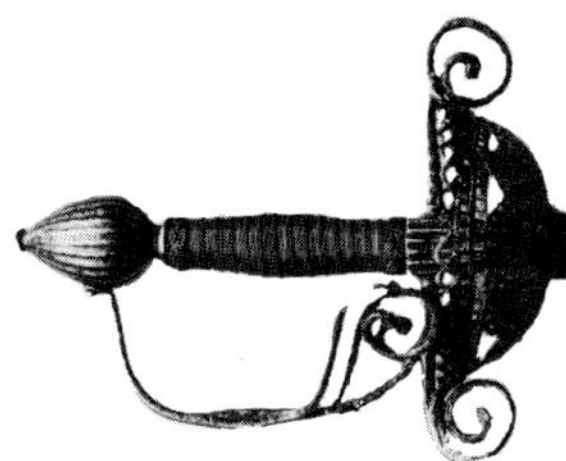

Above Rapier with pierced cup hilt, English *c.* 1630. Victoria & Albert Museum

Below Colt percussion revolver, five-shot, single action, .265 calibre, introduced in 1857. H.M. Tower of London Armouries

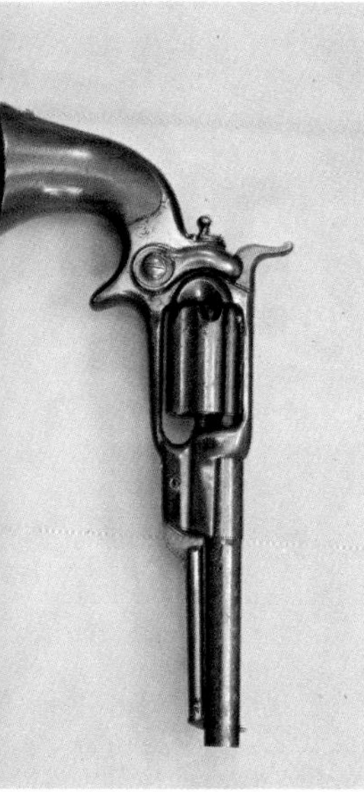

Below Peace-maker Colt Model 1873 revolver. Also known as the 'Frontier Six-Shooter' or the 'Single-Action Army' H.M. Tower of London Armouries

tory system was that patented in England in 1818 by the American Elisha H. Collier. This was a flint lock with an automatic priming device and an ingenious mechanism for locking the barrel and the appropriate chamber in the cylinder together at the moment of discharge. Only a small number of Collier's revolvers, both pistols and long arms, was made, and his invention was not a commercial success. In 1835, however, another American, Samuel Colt, was granted patents in England and France, and in 1836 in the United States, for the percussion revolver that was to be the prototype for all subsequent successful revolvers.

Despite the importance of Colt's invention, he had considerable difficulty in selling it. His first manufacturing plant was established at Paterson, New Jersey, in 1836, and it produced pistols, rifles, carbines, and shotguns, all with revolving cylinders. Orders were slow in coming, however. The venture failed, and the factory was sold. Today the revolvers made at this factory are known as 'Colt Patersons' and they are much sought after by collectors.

In 1847 Colt finally succeeded in obtaining a government contract for 1,000 of his pistols based on an improved design suggested by Capt. Samuel Walker of the Texas Rangers. With this order Colt was able to resume manufacturing his pistols, and soon his fortunes prospered. The Walker Colts were extremely large guns, 15½ inches (39.4 cm) long, but poorly made. They saw considerable service in the Army, and those specimens that have survived are considered by modern collectors the most valuable of all standard Colt models.

Following the Walker, the trend was to decrease the size of the revolver and improve its construction. There were three subsequent models for dragoons and two pocket pistols before the advent of the so-called 1851 Navy revolver. This well-balanced .36 calibre arm was the most popular of all Colt percussion-cap military revolvers, and it was widely used by both the Army and Navy as well as by civilians from its first production through the Civil War and as long as percussion-cap revolvers were used. In 1860 Colt developed a .44 calibre revolver for the Army which also was widely used during and after the Civil War. In addition to these principal models, Colt produced numerous others, both pistols and long guns, to meet almost every possible need. Examples of all models were frequently engraved and they had carved grips of bone, ivory, special woods, or even silver, for presentation purposes. Colt himself died in 1862, well before the company that he founded had reached its greatest peaks of production.

From the late 1840s onwards many revolvers, all more or less based on Colt's invention, were made both in Europe and the United States. Notable among these were the English Deane-Adams and Webley and the American Remington. *See also* Pepperbox.

Ricasso. A modern term for the oblong, blunt section at the base of some sword and dagger blades.

Rifle. A firearm with a series of spiral grooves down the inside of the barrel designed to make the projectile fly more truly by causing it to rotate on its own axis.

According to an unconfirmed tradition, rifling was invented at the end of the fifteenth century, but it was used rarely, if at all, before the late sixteenth century. From this time onwards many sporting guns were made with rifled barrels, especially in Germany. During the seventeenth and eighteenth centuries a number of experiments were made with rifled military arms, but the rifle was not widely adopted for service use until well into the nineteenth century. *See also* 'Kentucky' rifle.

Rifle musket. A term used during the nineteenth century to designate a firearm of musket size with a rifled bore.

Rifling. The grooves cut into the sides of the bore of a firearm which impart the spin to the projectile. Also the act of cutting these grooves.

Rondel dagger. A form of dagger used from the fourteenth to the early sixteenth century with a disc-shaped guard. Most examples have a pommel of similar form to the guard.

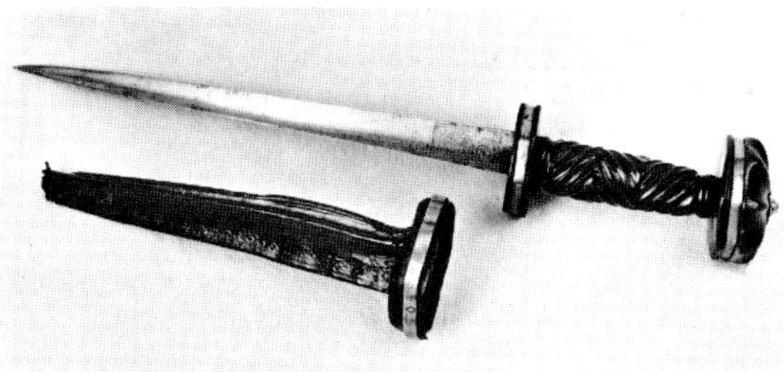

Rondel dagger, German, second half of 15th century. Kunsthistorisches Museum, Vienna

Sabaton. A laminated plate defence for the foot.

Sabre. A sword with a single edge designed primarily for cutting. Usually there is also a short edge along the back near the point which is termed the false edge. Some sabre blades are sharply curved and some are only slightly curved or absolutely straight. These straight or only slightly curved blades are frequently called cut-and-thrust blades.

Sallet. The characteristic helmet of the fifteenth century, usually worn with a deep chin piece (bevor). Its form generally followed that of the modern sou'wester, although it comes well down over the face, either having a movable visor, or a vision slit in its forward edge. The German type usually has a long, graceful, pointed tail, often laminated. The barbute (*q.v.*) is regarded as one of the forms of this helmet.

Schiavona

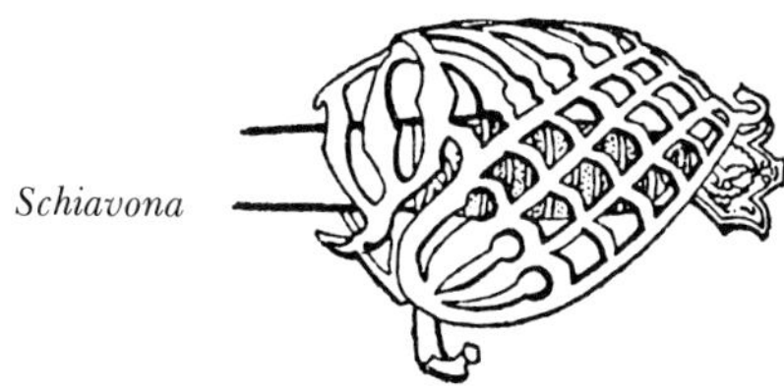

Schiavona. A basket-hilted sword with a straight, two-edged blade, used during the seventeenth and eighteenth centuries by the Dalmatian troops (stradiots) in the employ of Venice. It is often erroneously described as the prototype of the Scottish basket-hilted broadsword.

Screw plate. An elongated plate opposite the lock of a firearm which acts as a washer for the screws holding the lock in position. Sometimes also called the side plate, key plate, or nail plate.
Shield. Probably the earliest form of defensive arm. Shields have been used from prehistoric times, and made of a variety of materials, including wood, leather, wickerwork, metal, etc. They were usually attached to the left arm by straps (*enarmes*) or, when not in use, hung round the neck on a sling (*guige*). The earliest shields seem to have been mainly circular, oval, or rectangular, but in the eleventh century the tall kite shape appears, remaining in use until the thirteenth century, when the 'flat-iron' (heater) form was introduced. This survived until well into the fifteenth century, when a large variety of shapes appeared, many of which had a notch (*bouche*) cut in the upper edge for the lance. In the sixteenth century the majority of shields were circular, one of the most popular types being the buckler (introduced as early as the thirteenth century), which was held in the left hand by means of a crossbar on the inside. Shields have at all times been the subject of adornment, particularly with the owner's coat-of-arms or personal device after the introduction of heraldry in the twelfth century. Many of those made for parade purposes in the sixteenth century were of metal elaborately embossed or etched and gilt.

Shield, steel with intricate gold decoration, Persian, late 16th century. Victoria & Albert Museum

Short arms. A classification name often applied to pistols of all kinds.
Side plate. *See* Screw plate.
Skean Dhu. The small knife worn in the stocking with Highland Scottish dress. It appears to have been first introduced in the early nineteenth century.
Small arms. A military term applying to all arms carried on the person and designed to be fired without a support.
Smallsword. A light civilian sword with a simple hilt, often richly decorated, which succeeded the rapier (*q.v.*) in the third quarter of the seventeenth century, with the beginnings of fencing as it is known today. The slender blade, although designed principally for thrusting, was at first double-edged, but from *c.* 1700 one of hollow triangular section became almost universal. The eighteenth-century French term

Smallswords

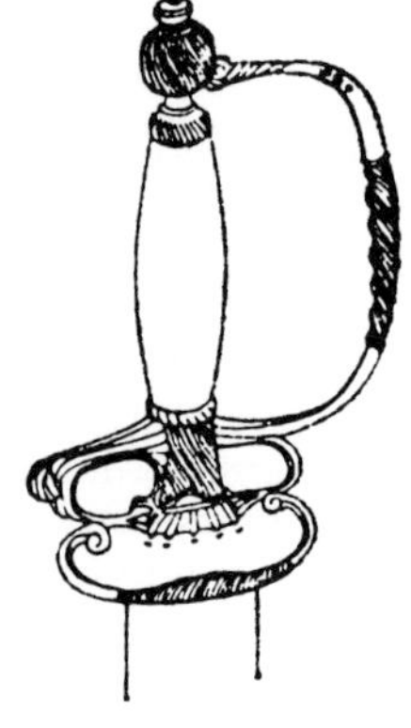

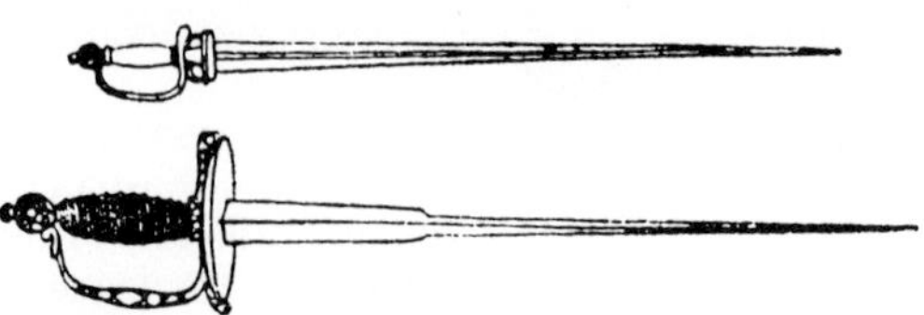

colichemarde often used by collectors, designates a blade which is wide near the hilt and narrows suddenly half-way along (see above). The smallsword remained in active use until the end of the eighteenth century, and still survives in the sword worn with modern court dress.
Smoothbore. Any firearm without rifling.
Snaphance. A type of gun lock first recorded in the middle of the sixteenth century. It is fitted with a pan (*q.v.*) with a flat steel (*q.v.*) pivoted above it. When the gun is discharged a specially shaped flint, held in the jaws of a spring-operated cock, strikes the steel, throwing it back and at the same time sending a shower of sparks into the priming. On the earliest form of the lock the pan was fitted with a separate cover that had to be opened manually immediately before firing, but this was soon replaced by a cover that opened automatically as the cock fell. The early lock also had a horizontal sear, the tip of which projected through the lockplate and engaged with a projection on the heel of the cock, holding the latter back until released by the trigger.

Modern writers usually confine the term snaphance to the form of lock with a separate steel and pan cover, and flint lock (*q.v.*) to the form on which these features are combined. In fact, the first term was applied indiscriminately to both constructions until the second half of the seventeenth century when it went out of use. Other than in certain parts of Italy, where it survived until the early nineteenth century, the snaphance was generally superseded by the flint lock in the second quarter of the seventeenth century.

Spontoon. A miniature partizan (*q.v.*) carried by infantry officers from the seventeenth to the late eighteenth century.
Spurs. Early spurs were of the prick type, with a single spike, usually pyramidal or cone-shaped and often mounted on a ball to prevent deep penetration. There is some evidence for the introduction of the rowel spur, with a wheel equipped with points instead of the single spike, in the middle of the thirteenth century, but it did not become common until the second quarter of the fourteenth. In the second half of the fifteenth century spurs had straight necks of great length, while those of the seventeenth had their necks bent down almost at rightangles.
Steel. That portion of a flint lock or snaphance (*qq.v.*) that serves as a steel for the flint to strike against and so produce sparks. It is sometimes called the battery or frizzen, the latter term being a modern corruption of the dialect word frizzle. During the eighteenth and nineteenth centuries it was also known as the hammer.

Stiletto. A form of quillon dagger (*q.v.*), introduced in the sixteenth century, with a stiff, narrow blade designed for stabbing only. The gunner's stiletto has a scale on the blade for converting weight of gun shot into diameter of bore.
Stirrup guard. A form of knucklebow which resembles half of a stirrup.
Stock. The wood or metal structure of a firearm used to hold the barrel and lock together in proper position and to provide a suitable means of holding the arm.

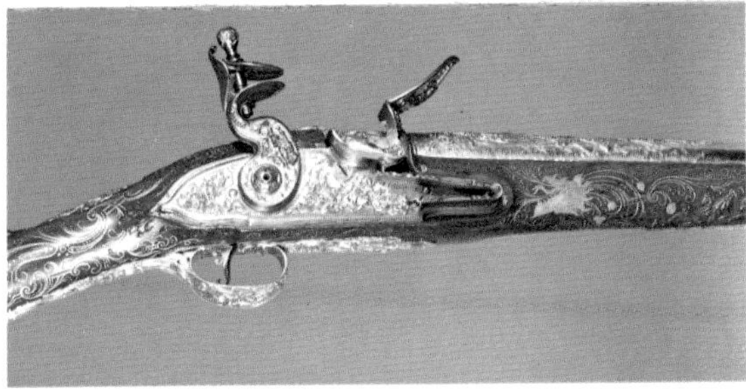

Detail of the stock of an air gun, walnut inlaid with silver, by Kolbe, London, *c.* 1750. Victoria & Albert Museum

Swept hilt. A modern term for the type of rapier hilt, introduced in the sixteenth century, in which the guard consists of a complicated series of curved bars.

Left Swept-hilt rapier, the blade probably by Sandrino Scacchi, Flemish, *c.* 1630. Christie, Manson & Woods

Right Saxon wheel-lock holster pistol, struck with the mark of Abraham or Anton Dressler of Dresden, dated 1577. Christie Manson & Woods

Swivel gun. A heavy military firearm shaped like a normal rifle or musket but designed to be fired from a swivel mount. Such guns were popular from the seventeenth to the early nineteenth century.

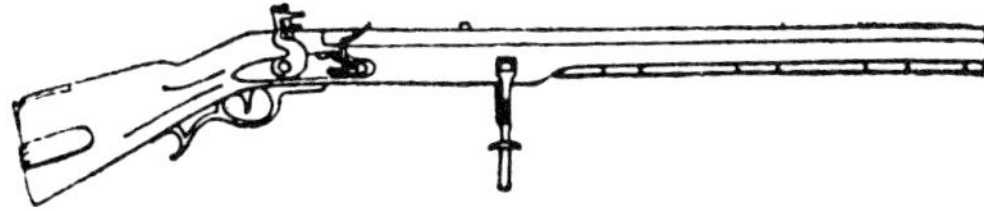

Tace. A form of tasset (*q.v.*). Incorrectly used by nineteenth-century writers as a synonym for fauld.
Tang. (i) The narrow portion of the blade which passes into the hilt; (ii) *see* Barrel tang.
Tapul. A rare sixteenth-century term of uncertain meaning connected with armour. Incorrectly used by nineteenth-century writers to denote a projecting central ridge to a breastplate.
Tasset. One of a pair of defences for the upper thighs which hung from the fauld. Tassets appeared in the second quarter of the fifteenth century, when they were usually pointed and made of a single plate. From the beginning of the sixteenth century they were normally rounded or straight at the bottom and made of a number of horizontal lames. From the second quarter of the sixteenth century light horsemen's armours were sometimes fitted with knee-length tassets in place of cuisses. This form became usual after *c.* 1600.

Below Breastplate and tassets, painted black with gilt ornament of vertical panels of trophies, English, first half of 17th century. Victoria & Albert Museum

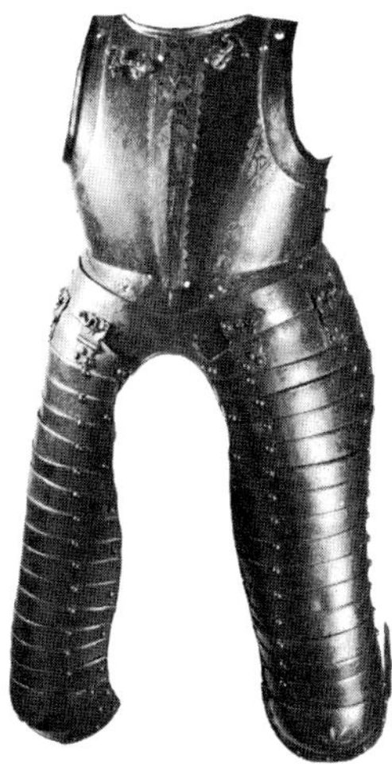

Three-quarter armour. An armour extending to the knees only.
Touchhole. A small hole or channel used to convey the sparks from the priming charge outside the barrel of a firearm to the propelling charge inside the barrel.
Trigger. The lever which activates the lock mechanism of a firearm and sets off the discharge.
Tschinke. A light wheel-lock gun, generally rifled, used for bird shooting in the area of Germanic culture during the seventeenth century. The butt usually takes a sharp downward curve while the lock has an external mainspring.
Tsuba. *See* Japanese swordguards.
Tube lock. *See* Percussion lock.
Tuile. A nineteenth-century term, no longer used by the enlightened, for the early one-piece pointed tasset (*q.v.*).
Vambrace. Plate armour for the arm from below the shoulder to the wrist, and including the couter (*q.v.*). Modern writers divide it for convenience into the upper cannon and the lower cannon, above and below the couter respectively.
Vamplate. *See* Lance.
Vouge. Probably originally the French equivalent of the English bill (*q.v.*). Used by modern writers to denote a staff weapon with a cleaver-like pointed blade attached by two rings to the haft.
Walker Colts. *See* Revolver.
War hammer. A short staff weapon, used by horsemen, with a hammerhead balanced by a pointed fluke.

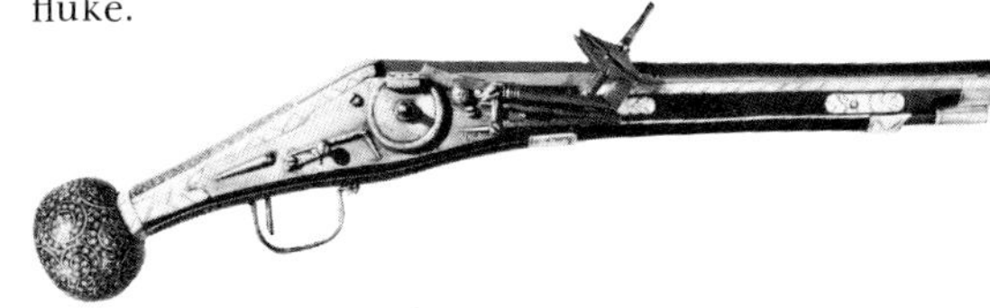

Wheel lock. Mechanism for igniting a firearm, in which a piece of pyrites, held in the jaws of a cock, is pressed against the grooved edge of a wheel projecting through the bottom of the pan (*q.v.*). The wheel is made to rotate by a spring, released by the trigger, so striking a shower of sparks from the pyrites and igniting the priming powder. The lock is usually wound by means of a spanner, but on rare examples this is effected automatically when the cock is drawn back.

The earliest known illustration of a wheel lock occurs in the *Codex Atlanticus* of Leonardo da Vinci (d. 1519), who has a very strong claim to being regarded as the inventor of the system. It was probably being made in Italy as early as 1510, but the earliest definite record of its existence comes from a German source of 1515. In 1517 and 1518 the Emperor Maximilian banned the use and manufacture of the lock in his territories, which probably accounts for the fact that the vast majority of surviving examples date from after the second decade of the sixteenth century. Wheel locks are rarely found on military weapons, probably because they were expensive to make, but were much used on sporting and target guns, especially in Germany, until well into the eighteenth century.
Wrist. The slender portion of the butt stock of a firearm immediately behind the lock.

60
Moore
JPSWICH

BAROMETERS, CLOCKS, AND WATCHES

There would seem to be little connection between barometers, which are dependent for their functioning on a natural phenomenon, and clocks and watches, which are actuated by man-designed mechanical means, but in England the earliest barometers were made by clockmakers.

Italy and France in the mid-seventeenth century saw the inception and proof of the idea that the weight of air varies. When this principle was brought to England, London became the first centre of production for barometers. The names of Tompion, Quare, Graham, Ellicott may be mentioned as well as those of John Patrick and Francis Hawksbee (the inventor of the vacuum pump), who were instrument makers. Later provincial production appeared, mainly anonymous and following current furniture design. Charles Orme of Ashby-de-la-Zouch and John Whitehust of Derby were among the most outstanding in this field. In the United States barometers were mainly imported.

The field of clocks is a much older and wider one, and we have records of weight-driven turret clocks in England at the end of the thirteenth century, as well as on the Continent. We do not know whether the clocks in England were made by an Englishman or by a Continental visitor.

From this period there was steady progress on the Continent, with the invention of the spring drive in the middle of the fifteenth century and the personal clock, or watch, in the last quarter of that century. Production in England reappeared only towards the end of the sixteenth century, and from then onwards it was centred in London. The craft gradually extended over the whole country during the eighteenth century, but relatively few makers achieved renown, and they were not grouped in any locality.

In the United States the chief centres of production were in the Eastern Atlantic states – Connecticut, Massachusetts, New Hampshire, and Rhode Island – but some earlier clocks had come from Philadelphia.

Barometers

The word barometer derives from the Greek root *baros*, meaning weight. Thus, we have an instrument for measuring the weight of the atmosphere.

Scientists in the first half of the nineteenth century had noticed that water could not be raised above about 33 feet (10 m) with a single-stage suction pump. The French philosopher René Descartes (1596–1650) had rejected the idea of the existence of a vacuum, and so had undermined the idea that Nature's abhorrence of a vacuum was the explanation of the action of water pumps, thus leading the way to the correct explanation – that is, pressure resulting from the weight of the atmosphere. He claimed to have anticipated Torricelli, an Italian, who conceived the idea of experimenting with mercury, because of its much greater density, and in 1643 found that the atmosphere would support a column of about 30 inches (76 cm) of mercury; but he did not appreciate that the height of the column varied with the state of the atmosphere. That the atmosphere has weight was shown by Galileo, who, in his book *Two New Sciences* (1638), estimated that the weight of the air was about one four-hundredth of that of the same volume of water. Torricelli was acquainted with Galileo and succeeded him as Grand Ducal mathematician on Galileo's death in 1642.

Descartes also claimed that in 1647 he had suggested to Blaise Pascal (1623–62) the idea of experimenting with a mercury column at the bottom and top of a tower. This experiment Pascal carried out on the tower of the church of St Jacques in Paris, and established the fact that the height of the mercury column was greater at the bottom of the tower than at the top, thus demonstrating that the weight of the atmosphere varied with height.

On 19 September 1646, under Pascal's direction, his brother-in-law, Florin Perier, carried out the historic full-scale experiment on Puy-de-Dôme in Auvergne.

At a meeting of the Royal Society on 6 December 1677, Dr Robert Hooke (1635–1703), that great seventeenth-century genius, affirmed that he had 'for these 15 or 16 years constantly observed the Barascope and that he had always found that in the said instrument the ☿ [☿ is the symbol for mercury] was always very exceeding low and fell to that stacion very suddenly whensoever any considerable Storme of Wind and Raine had happened in that time. . . .' And on 12 December 1695 Dr Hooke read 'an account of the several Barometers he had invented. That he was the first that had observed the changes of the height of the Mercury to answer the changes of the Weather.' From this we gather that Hooke was actively noting the connection between the barometer level and the weather since about 1661.

At this date there was no recognized scale, and Hooke probably used a scale of his own contrivance. Fahrenheit was the first to devise a scale with fixed points. His first scale was divided between 90 and −90. A siphon barometer by Robleau in the Science Museum, London, uses this scale. The zero point occurs in the middle of the scale and is designated 'Temperate'. The earliest date for this scale, as we know it today, is given as 1717.

Also in the Science Museum there is a reproduction of the 'Torricellian Experiment'. The tubes are inverted and filled with mercury. A finger is then

Act of Parliament clock by Thomas Moore of Ipswich (1720–89)

placed over the open end and removed when this is below the level of the mercury in the cistern. The mercury in the tube then runs out until the column remaining represents the height of mercury that the atmosphere can support at that moment. Torricelli thought that if there were any force due to the vacuum it would be greater in the larger vacuum. But as the two columns are of equal height, it shows the force to be wholly external and equal.

This simple device, by which changes of atmospheric pressure on the surface of the cistern are reflected in the height of the column in the tube, is that adopted by the earliest barometer makers. Later the siphon barometer was invented. In this type the tube for the mercury column turns up at the bottom to form a J, the short end being left open to the atmosphere. Both systems were employed side by side for a hundred years or more, the cistern being more common in England and the siphon on the Continent.

On 30 December 1663, the Journal of the Royal Society records that Dr Hooke produced 'a little engine to make the ascent and descent of Quicksilver in glasse-canes more discernible. It was ordered to prepare against the next Meeting a tube with Mercury and fit the Instrument to it.'

Hooke's original sketch, from the records of the Royal Society, shows a small compensated weight floating on the surface of the mercury in the shorter arm, which is open to the air. To the weight is attached a silken thread carrying at the other end the compensating weight, the silken thread being wound round the arbor, or shaft, of the indicating hand. Thus, any movement of the surface of the mercury is transmitted to the arbor of the indicator and magnified to any desired extent by regulating the length of the indicating hand.

This remained one of the principal types of barometer until the coming of the aneroid barometer towards the middle of the nineteenth century. Early wheel barometers with finely designed cases were made in the latter years of the seventeenth century by Tompion, Quare, and other leading clockmakers of that time. But since these are very rare, and nearly all are already held in royal or museum collections, none is illustrated here.

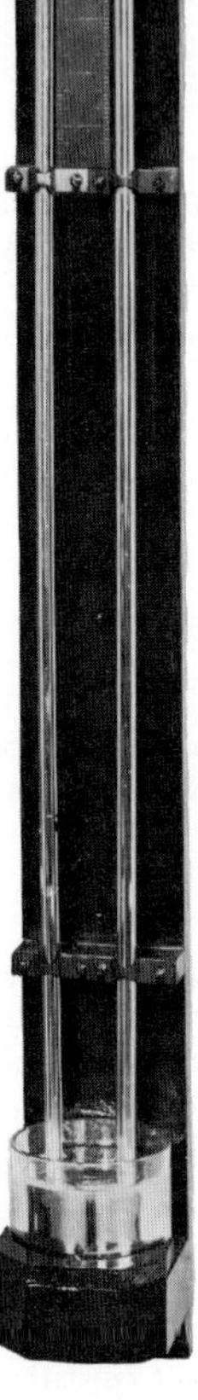

Above The first Torricelli barometer with stand, 1643. Science Museum

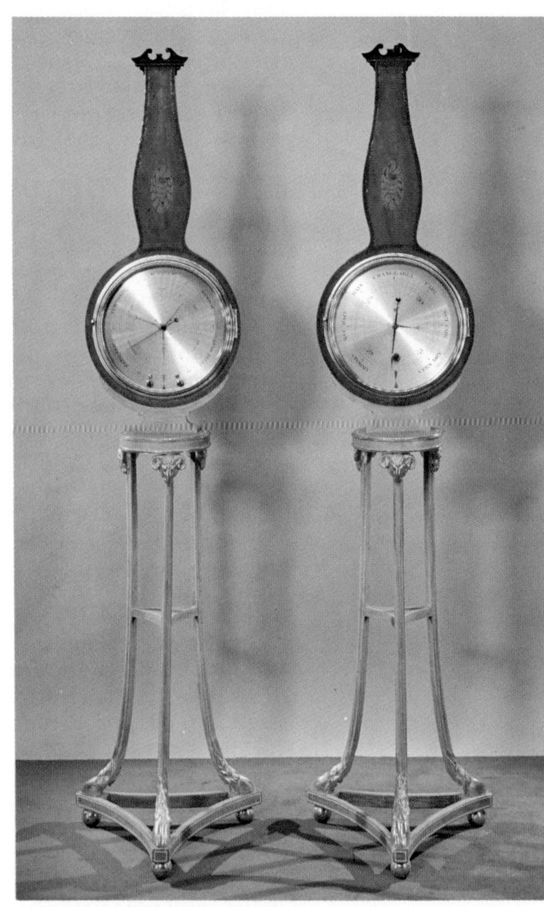

Right Pair of wheel barometers and stands by Bettaly. Mallet & Son, London

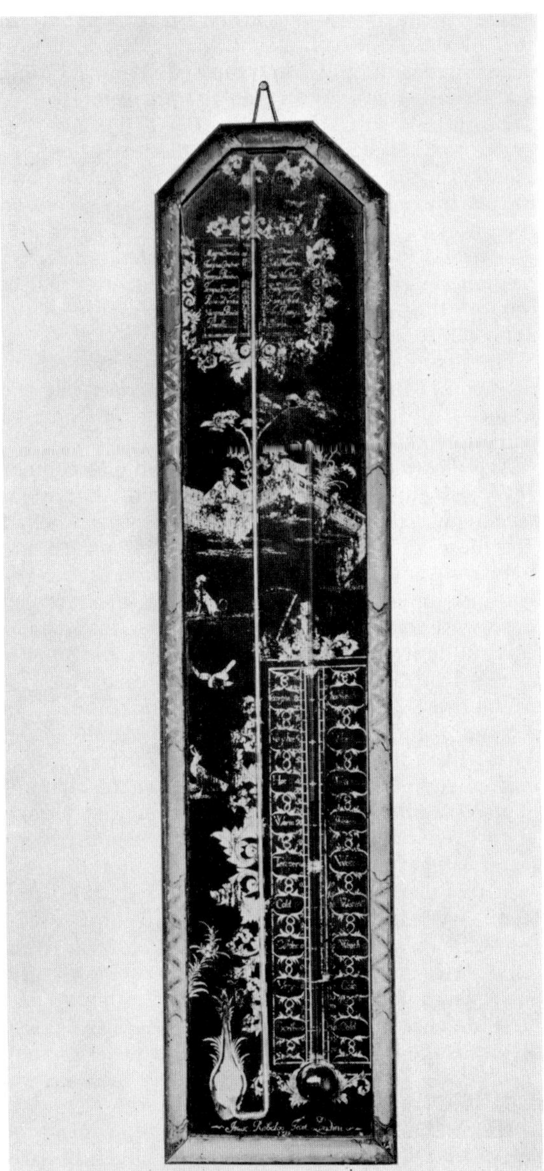

Left Syphon barometer, by Robleau, with Fahrenheit's early thermometer scale, 1719. Science Museum

James Gatley made a pleasing burr-walnut wheel barometer *c.* 1770 with a gut hygrometer. The small ivory setting knob for the barometer can be withdrawn and used to set the hygrometer, for which gut is used instead of the beard of a wild oat or the cod of a vetch, as recommended by Hooke in 1666. At the bottom of the barometer is a spirit level to check that the barometer hangs truly vertical, and, as is the case with most barometers, a thermometer is provided. For really accurate observations, allowance has to be made for the effect of temperature on the height of the mercury column.

One of the various ways of extending the reading scale of the barometer suggested by Hooke may have been the diagonal barometer, sometimes known as the signpost or yardarm type. The maximum variation of the mercury at ground level is about 3 inches (7.6 cm), and all the variations in the ordinary vertical tube have to be registered within these limits.

A very interesting and early example of the diagonal barometer was made by John Boll in 1666. The construction was quite simple: three siphon barometers were used, each having a vertical tube about 1 inch (2.5 cm) longer than that preceding and having a rise of about 1 inch in about 20 inches (2.5 cm in 51 cm) of inclined arm. Thus, these three tubes of 28 (71.1), 29 (73.7), and 30 inches (76.2 cm) in length start recording only when the mercury reaches the height at which their respective bends are situated. The maximum anticipated variation of about 3 inches (7.6 cm) in this country is spread over 60 inches (152.5 cm) of tube, thus giving a spread of 1 inch (2.5 cm) for each twentieth part of an inch (0.5 cm) variation in the height of the mercury column.

The early barometers were not portable, and an early attempt to remedy this is recorded in the Royal Society's Journal, 28 May 1668, when 'Mr Boyle brought in his Travelling or Portable Barascope, devised by himself to compare, by the help thereof the weight of the Atmosphere at the same time, not only in differing parts of the same country, but in differing Regions of the World: which is thus contrived, that the vessel containing both the sustained and stagnant Mercury is all of one piece of glasse of like bigness . . .'

Just what this means is not clear, but it seems to be a siphon in which the return part is of the same diameter as the main tube.

Hooke's wheel barometer was not altogether successful. It is reported that it was liable to be jerky in movement and not easy to adjust. On 3 February 1685, he produced a tube in which a column of lighter spirits of wine was supported by a column of mercury. The tube was so long as to be unwieldy, but the idea developed into the double barometer where the top of the lefthand tube is evacuated as the pressure falls, and the mercury in this tube falls and the spirit in the righthand tube rises over the extended scale for the oil. Low readings are therefore at the top.

Hooke made a careful study of the relationship between atmospheric pressure and storms and in Vol. II of the Royal Society's Journal of 6 December 1677 he reported that 'whenever the said ☿ was observed to fall suddenly very low, it had alwaies been a forerunner of a very great Storme to follow, sometimes within 12 houres and therefore he hoped that his Instrument might be of very good use at sea in order to the foreshowing of an ensuing Storme'. On 2 January 1677, he pursues the idea, and, after dealing with the difficulties of using a wheel barometer at sea, he suggests 'as a better alternative, a Weather Glasse made with pure Air and Quicksilver, which latter is left open to the Pressure of the Air and so becomes agitated by a double principle of Motion, i.e. by Heat and Air Pressure . . .'. To ascertain the changes due to heat, he provides a sealed thermometer with spirits of wine and graduates the two together in an oven. A table of differences is established, so that the resultant differences should be that due to air pressure.

This idea of Hooke, thrown out in 1677–8, seems, like so many of his ideas, to have lain dormant for many years. He returns to the question of a marine barometer in December 1694. At a meeting on the 5th of that month he was authorized to spend forty shillings on an example of his marine barometer. At a meeting on 13 November 1695, this instrument was presented and was ordered to be hung in the Meeting Room. What is possibly this instrument is seen in the Museum for the History of Science, Oxford. The thermometer with spirits of wine is on the right and that with mercury on the left.

In principle this idea is the air thermoscope or weatherglass, invented at the end of the sixteenth or the beginning of the seventeenth century, later forming the basis of the Sympiesometer, patented by Adie in 1818. A more simple type of marine barometer was developed (*see* Glossary).

In the meantime, in spite of Robert Boyle's idea in 1668, barometers were not portable. The Minute Book of the Royal Society for 16 January 1694/5, however, records: 'Mr Daniel Quare, Watchmaker, produced his Barometer so contrived as to be Portable, and even Inverted without spilling of the Quicksilver, or letting in any Air or excluding the pressure of the Atmosphere, which the Society were pleased to Declare, That it was the first of that sort they had seen. Mr Quare desired to be excused from Discovering the Secret thereof.'

Quare's secret was the use of a plug at the end of a screwed thread, which could be used to seal off the bottom of the tube under the mercury.

The first self-recording barograph was made in 1765 for King George III by Alexander Cumming and is now in Buckingham Palace. A second, made by Cumming for his own use in 1766, is now in the possession of Mr Geoffrey Howard. A pointer is carried by a ring floating on the surface of the mercury and, rising and falling with this, traces a continuous line on the outer dial, which is fitted with a graduated vellum disc and revolves once a year.

By the end of the seventeenth century practically all the problems had been solved.

Once established, the barometer was of easy con-

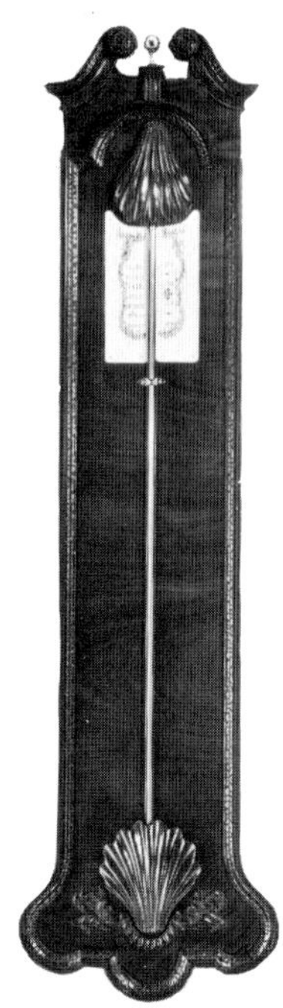

Above Mahogany barometer made in the Chippendale period, *c.* 1760. Glaisher and Nash Ltd., London

Above Wheel barometer, in a mahogany and tulipwood veneer case, by Thomas Chippendale and Justin Vulliamy, 1768–9. Nostell Priory, Yorkshire

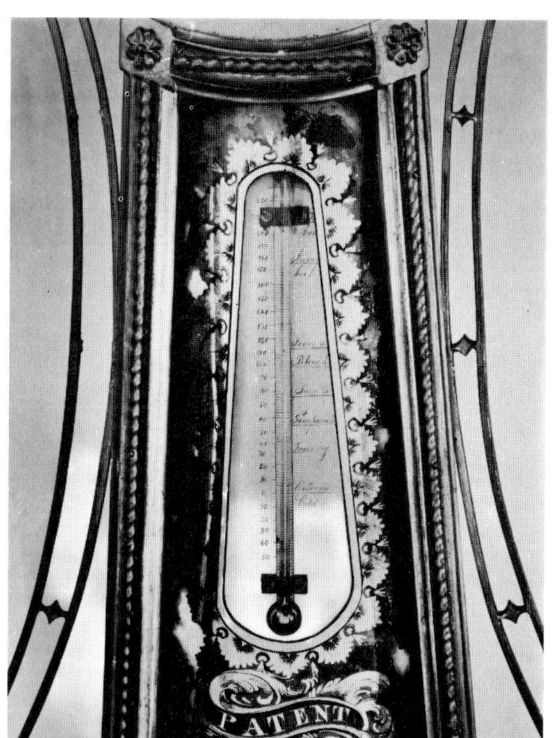

Left Detail of barometer set into American girandole clock by Lemuel Curtis (1790–1851)

struction. After the early years of the eighteenth century, with the possible exception of Patrick, there are no great names of barometer makers. One finds good and bad examples in both London and provincial productions.

American Clocks and Watches

The production of American timepieces in any quantity extends back little more than two hundred years, as compared to more than three times that in Europe.

CLOCKS

It is now impossible to say positively who was the first clockmaker in America. In 1638 Thomas Nash was one of the early settlers of New Haven, Connecticut. That Nash was a clockmaker is indicated by the inventory of his estate in 1658. Among his tools is listed: 'one round plate for making clocks'.

It is well established from inventories of their estates that many of the wealthier early colonists had clocks. It may be assumed that most of these had been brought over as original household equipment or had been imported later. In addition, some of the larger towns had one or more public clocks quite early; Boston had a tower clock in 1657. Undoubtedly the oldest American-made tower clock now in existence is one in Guilford, Connecticut, which was installed in the meeting house there in 1726 by Ebenezer Parmele.

There are other men of whom some scant records exist of clockmaking activities before 1700. But for two or three exceptions, no clocks by these early makers are known to be in existence today.

From about 1715 there were a number of clockmakers to whom existing clocks can certainly be attributed. Benjamin Chandlee, who was the first of a large family of clockmakers, came from Ireland to Philadelphia in 1702 and was apprenticed to Abel Cottey, the first established clockmaker of Philadelphia. Peter Stretch, who was born in England and there learned his trade under English masters, came to Philadelphia in 1702 and became a community leader as well as a prosperous clockmaker. Benjamin Bagnall from England appeared in Boston as a clockmaker about 1710. William Claggett, born in Wales about 1715, went later to Newport, Rhode Island. Slightly later than these were Gawen Brown, who came to Boston some time before 1750; and David Blaisdell, one of a family of clockmakers, who was in Amesbury, Massachusetts, by 1740.

By 1750 a number of skilled clockmakers were at work in Philadelphia and surrounding areas. The most famous of the Philadelphia group was David Rittenhouse (at work *c.* 1750–90), scientist, mathematician, astronomer, and a President (1791) of the American Philosophical Society. A large grandfather clock by Rittenhouse, now in the Drexel Institute of Technology, Philadelphia, is a superb example of the finest in American clocks.

The clocks made by the eighteenth-century clockmakers were mostly of the grandfather type. Each clock was individually made by hand and fitted to the case, which had also been made in the same shop or by a local cabinet maker. It was not until towards the end of the century that clockmakers were making unordered clocks in quantity. These early tall clocks usually had brass eight-day movements, although a few thirty-hour movements are found. The dials were usually of brass with cast brass spandrels. A few small and simple hang-up, or wag-on-the-wall, clocks were made for the less wealthy customers or by less skilled craftsmen. Members of the Blaisdell family of Massachusetts made a number of such quaint little clocks, examples of which may be rarely found.

From 1750 to 1800 clocks, principally tall or grandfather, were made in increasing numbers. About the middle of the eighteenth century a few clockmakers in Connecticut were making innovations. The most revolutionary of these new ideas was the use of wood in movements to replace brass, which was both expensive and difficult to obtain.

Benjamin Cheney, together with his younger brother Timothy, of East Hartford, Connecticut, is usually credited with making, about 1745, the earliest of the existing Connecticut wooden movements.

These early Connecticut wooden clocks were clumsy, thirty-hour grandfather clocks which were wound by pulling down on cords. They usually had brass dials, or brass-covered wood dials and were often in attractive cases. Although crudely made, they were satisfactory timekeepers and were inexpensive. These earliest wooden clocks by the Cheneys, Gideon Roberts, John Rich, and others of Connecticut are now rare and keenly sought by collectors.

The influence of these craftsmen of central Connecticut spread to Massachusetts. Benjamin Willard was born in 1743 in Grafton, Massachusetts. About 1760 he went to East Hartford as an apprentice of Benjamin Cheney. After completing his apprenticeship he returned to Grafton and opened (*c.* 1765) a clock shop at the old family home. His three younger brothers, Simon, Ephraim, and Aaron, also became noted clockmakers. From Grafton the four brothers moved to Roxbury, Lexington, and Boston and independently established profitable clockmaking businesses. From these Willard brothers there developed an extensive clockmaking industry in eastern Massachusetts, southern New Hampshire, and Rhode Island. Clockmakers of this 'Willard' or 'Boston' school made clocks of many types of the highest quality. Little attempt was made to produce an inexpensive clock, as was the trend in Connecticut. No wooden movements were produced by any of these men.

Simon Willard is the most famous of the four brothers on account of his patented (1802) timepiece, which is now known as the banjo clock. He worked first at Grafton (1774–80), and from 1780 to 1839 in Roxbury. Among his many apprentices who became prominent clockmakers were Abel and Levi Hutchins, Elnathan Taber and Daniel Munroe, besides his sons, Simon, Jr, and Benjamin.

Aaron Willard produced large quantities of clocks and is particularly noted for developing the Massachusetts shelf clock. He opened a shop near Simon's in Roxbury about 1780 and later moved to Boston, where he established a small factory. He was succeeded by his sons, Aaron, Jr, and Henry. Aaron, Jr, is often credited with originating the lyre clock.

Two other clockmakers at work in Connecticut during the last part of the eighteenth century deserve special notice, particularly because of their

Right Girandole wall clock by Lemuel Curtis, *c.* 1816, the case decorated in gold leaf with an architectural view in the banjo end. Old Sturbridge Village, Sturbridge, Mass.

Long-case clock by Benjamin Whitman (1774–1857), early 19th century. Yale University Art Gallery

influence on the beginnings of clockmaking as a great industry. Thomas Harland, a skilled clockmaker from England, settled in Norwich in 1773. Daniel Burnap, the most noted of Harland's apprentices, opened his own shop in East Windsor about 1780, and ultimately surpassed his master as a craftsman. Clocks by either of these makers are rare and choice. Soon after Burnap opened his shop at East Windsor he took as an apprentice Eli Terry, born in 1772. After completing his apprenticeship, Eli Terry opened his own shop in 1793, in Plymouth, Connecticut. The first clocks that Terry made were brass movements for tall clocks. However, he soon turned his attention to producing wooden clocks. About 1803 Terry began to use water power to turn his machines. In 1806 he accepted an order for 4,000 clocks. To meet the demands for such numbers he devised standardized or interchangeable parts. He now made large numbers of identical parts which went to an assembly line where the complete clocks were put together, the first application of the modern manufacturing methods to clock production.

These early wooden clocks of Eli Terry were thirty-hour movements intended for grandfather cases. In most instances they were sold without cases and the buyer had a case made to his own specification, or the movement could be used as a wag-on-the-wall. Many others began to copy Terry's methods and by 1815 the making of wooden clocks was an important industry. Clocks of this period with no indication of the maker are not especially valuable.

Eli Terry invented a shelf clock about 1814. He produced some seven or more known models, culminating about 1818 with a design which was made in large numbers by Terry and his sons and was extensively copied until about 1840, when the introduction of an inexpensive brass movement brought all production of wood movements to an end. Probably in 1817 the first pillar and scroll was produced. Some of these first models are recognized by having the escape wheel and pendulum in front of the dial. All of these early models are very rare.

Being cheaper and more portable than a tall clock, the new wood-movement shelf clock soon became popular, and the production of tall-clock movements ceased about 1825. By 1830 wooden shelf-clock cases had been simplified by Chauncey Jerome and others to a much plainer form. To compete with the eight-day brass clocks being made by the Massachusetts clockmakers certain Connecticut makers were producing a few shelf clocks with eight-day brass movements.

In 1838 Noble Jerome, at the suggestion of his brother, Chauncey, devised a simple thirty-hour weight movement of rolled brass. This type of clock almost immediately forced all wooden clocks out of production, for it was cheaper and better in every way. No wood-movement clocks were in commercial production after about 1842. The simple ogee case, which had occasionally been used with wooden movements before 1838, became the predominant style. It was now found profitable to export large numbers of these cheap clocks to England and other countries.

Factory-produced inexpensive steel springs first became available in America soon after 1840. The use of coiled springs for power made it possible to design smaller cases. Small clocks of many types began to appear before 1850 and were produced in increasing numbers. This period of mass production of inexpensive clocks yielded very few items which may now be considered desirable from the collector's standpoint.

Few antique clocks can now be found which do not need some restoration. The restoration of such damage to fine clocks should be entrusted only to qualified craftsmen.

A signed clock usually commands a higher price than a similar one not signed, and one signed by a famous maker even higher. There are many fine unsigned clocks available which in beauty and mechanical quality are equal to any by famous makers, and which may be acquired at much lower prices.

Far right Ogee shelf or wall clock by Jerome and Company, *c.* 1830, the case of figured walnut veneer

Above Acorn shelf clock by the Forrestville Manufacturing Co., Bristol, Connecticut, mahogany, *c.* 1850. Collections of Greenfield Village and the Henry Ford Museum, Dearborn, Michigan

WATCHES

The watch collector must be a true specialist; he must be informed on the complex history of American watchmaking; he must also be familiar with the fine mechanical characteristics of the many types of watches. Within the field of watch collecting an even narrower specialization will probably be made by the serious collector. He may try to collect watches by early makers, watches by extinct companies, or mechanically unusual ones. He will need to examine carefully every old watch to make sure that no important example is overlooked. American-made watches dating before 1800 are practically non-existent, and those before 1850 are rare. All of these old watches are key winders and are usually of large size.

Many of the early American clockmakers also advertised as watchmakers. The few watches which they produced were entirely handmade. Most examples of watches made before 1815 and signed with American names are so similar to contem-

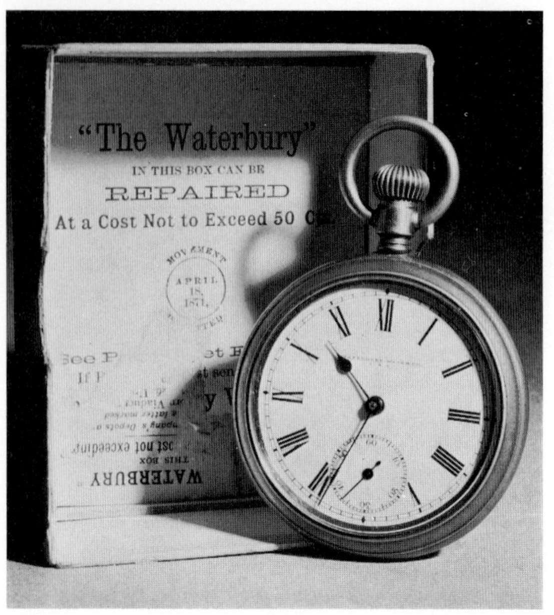

Left Waterbury watch with the box in which it was sold. The dial is modelled on the American fullplate watch

Right Fullplate watch, by the American Waltham Watch Company, 1885, the dial and movement in its case

porary English pieces that it is generally assumed that they were English imports or assembled from imported parts. They are all very rare.

It is impossible to say who made the first complete American watch. In 1809 Luther Goddard opened a small shop in Shrewsbury, Massachusetts, for the production of watches. It is not certain what proportion of the watch was imported and what was locally made. However, Goddard is usually credited with the first manufacture of watches in quantity in America. By 1817, when production ceased, about 500 watches had been made.

Probably the first manufacture of an all-American watch was begun in Hartford, Connecticut, in 1837 by the brothers, Henry and James Pitkin. The Pitkins had also designed and made the crude machinery with which the watches were manufactured. Owing partly to competition from the lower-priced Swiss watches, the company ceased operations about 1845, when fewer than 1,000 watches had been produced.

In 1843 Jacob Custer of Norristown, Pennsylvania, was granted a patent for watches. Custer and other craftsmen, about the middle of the nineteenth century, constructed a few watches of their own design. These watches often have unusual features and are extremely rare.

The modern American methods of watch manufacturing had their origin in the shop of Edward Howard (a clockmaker) and Aaron Dennison of Boston about 1850. From this small beginning grew the great Waltham Watch Company. The first model, an eight-day watch, was produced in 1850. For making watch parts, Howard and Dennison invented machines which, with only minor changes, are used in modern watch factories. In 1885 the company became the American Waltham Watch Co., which produced some of the finest watches ever made.

In 1864 Don J. Mozart was making, in Providence, Rhode Island, a very unusual watch with what he called a 'Chronometer lever escapement'. In 1867 with others he formed the New York Watch Co., which in 1877 became the Hampden Watch Co., later moving to Canton, Ohio, as the Dueber-Hampden Watch Co. The early watches by Mozart are very rare.

The inexpensive ('Dollar') watch of 1890–1920 had its beginning with the invention in 1877 by D. A. A. Buck in Worcester, Massachusetts, of a watch which could sell for four dollars. These were first manufactured in Connecticut by Benedict & Burnham, which later became the Waterbury Watch Co. Inexpensive watches were also later made by the Ingersoll Co., New Haven Watch Co., and others.

A great many mechanical innovations in watch movements have been designed by American makers. In the design of escapements used there is great variation.

It has been the usual custom for watchmakers and watch companies to sign and number watch movements. From these numbers the age of the watch can be ascertained. *The Book of American Clocks* lists by years the serial numbers used by some of the American watchmakers.

British Clocks and Watches

When clocks as we know them today, i.e. a series of wheels and pinions geared together with a weight as a motive force, first came into use is a matter of conjecture. The only early records are monastic manuscripts, and these use the term 'horologium' indiscriminately, whether referring to a sundial, a water clock, or a mechanical clock.

A water clock is usually a device whereby the recording of time was effected by the constant inflow or outflow of a regulated stream of water. There has recently come to light an eleventh-century Chinese manuscript describing a clock, which, although actuated by a constant stream of water, caused a step-by-step indication of the time in which may be discerned the germ of the escapement as we know it today.

In Europe there are certain rough guides. Dante describes the motion of a clock in his *Paradiso* of 1321, and we have definite written evidence of a very elaborate astronomical clock being in existence in Strasbourg about 1350. In 1344 Jacopo Dondi of

Padua, Italy, constructed a clock of which details are not known, but which was sufficiently outstanding for its time to earn for him the title of Dell' Orologio (of the clock), a title still carried by his descendants today. In 1364 his son, Giovanni, completed his astronomical clock, which showed the movements of the sun, moon, and five planets as well as the nodes. His drawing of this clock is the oldest known depiction of a mechanical clock.[1] If by the middle of the fourteenth century there were men capable of making very complicated astronomical clocks, we can assume that the earliest and simplest mechanical clock, with weight and foliot, was evolved a good deal earlier. A date of 1280–1300 is assumed. At all events, the unknown inventor or inventors of the verge escapement with foliot and the locking-plate striking arrangement, with its fan, or air brake, were geniuses; they had nothing earlier to guide them.

In England there has been discovered lately documentary evidence of three turret clocks being made for King Edward III in the years 1365–70. Unfortunately only the names of the clock keepers are given and not those of the makers. The oldest surviving mechanical clock in the world is that made for Salisbury Cathedral, and it is now there in its restored state; the second oldest is that which was made in 1392 for Wells Cathedral in Somerset; it is now in the Science Museum, London. From the maker's marks it is thought that both were made by the same hand.

The weight-driven clock is not portable, but the use of a coiled spring as a driving force made this practical. There is a spring-driven clock in the background of the portrait of a Burgundian nobleman of date about 1450, and King Charles VII of France bought a clock *sans contrepois*, that is without weights, in 1459. Spring-driven clocks so small that they could be carried on the person are first heard of in Italy about 1485; there were both timepieces and striking movements.

The unequal force of an uncoiling spring was corrected by the introduction of the fusee, possibly in Italy or Flanders. This invention has now been ante-dated to about 1445–50; a manuscript has been found, now in the Royal Library in Brussels, which shows several clocks, one of which is a table clock fitted with a fusee. Previously Jacob the Zech was credited with the invention of the fusee on the basis of his clock dated 1525, now with the Society of Antiquaries in London.

The attribution of the invention of the portable timepiece or watch to Peter Henlein of Nuremberg is now seen to be wrong, although there is no doubt he did much to popularize it by producing a great many of them.

The South German method of equalization of power was the stackfreed, and since this is much less efficient and was later universally replaced by the fusee, it seems likely that the two systems were developed independently and more or less concurrently; both localities were the cradles of early clockmaking.

It has heretofore been assumed that the foliot preceded the balance wheel, but Dondi's drawing of his clock, already referred to, shows a balance wheel, so that it is probable that the two progressed simultaneously. Neither has much advantage over the other as regards efficient timekeeping; both are very poor.

For the years between the fourteenth century and the late sixteenth century there are no records of clockmaking in England. Such examples as survive are mainly the work of foreign refugees in London, such as Nicholas Vallin, a Fleming, and Nicholas Urseau or Orseau, who, possibly, made the Windsor Castle clock. Towards the end of the seventeenth century English and Scottish names, such as David Ramsay, Randolf Bull, Michael Nowen, and Richard Grinkin, appear, and in 1632 the Clockmakers of London were granted their Charter. From this period onwards English clocks and watches took their place in the world's production, and for 150 years remained supreme.

One of the original Members of the Court of Assistants, under the Mastership of David Ramsay, was Edward East, who died in 1695 aged ninety-three. His work is distinguished by a great simplicity combined with good proportions. He was Clockmaker to both King Charles I and King Charles II.

In 1657 came the momentous discovery of the pendulum by Christiaan Huygens. Galileo had earlier perceived the principle of the pendulum, but there is no evidence to show that he developed it other than as an accurate recorder of oscillations to be counted by an observer. Huygens's work can be described as independent, and certainly he was the first to apply the pendulum to clocks.

The vastly improved timekeeping of pendulum clocks, even with the verge escapement, over foliot and balance, was due to the fact that the pendulum was the controller of the driving force, whereas formerly the driving force controlled the clock. Most clocks were converted to this new method of timekeeping, and it is very rare today to find a clock with its original foliot or balance.

Only thirteen years later came the revolutionary invention of the anchor escapement by William Clement. This largely abolished circular error and made timekeeping sufficiently accurate for use in astronomical observations.

Eight day table clock by Samuel Knibb, last half of 17th century. Clockmakers' Company Collection, London

[1] This clock has been reconstructed and can be seen in the Smithsonian Institution in Washington D.C.

The brothers Joseph and John Knibb of London and Oxford are noted for their fine productions of both long-case and bracket clocks. Joseph Knibb introduced what is known as 'Roman Striking', the blows up to four being struck on one bell and the five, either alone or in conjunction with a one, being indicated by a single stroke on a different-toned bell. Joseph also introduced the skeleton dial, in which the whole of the chapter ring is cut away except where actually engraved. This was doubly expensive, as it also involved a matted dial of about twice the normal area.

In 1675 Christiaan Huygens introduced the spiral balance spring for watches. This did for the watch what the pendulum had done for clocks in the matter of improved timekeeping. Robert Hooke claimed priority, and there are grounds for his support, but he did not make any public claim until after Huygens had published his invention, when he charged him with plagiarism. The truth is that both men probably worked independently.

We are now entering the age of the 'Great Ones' of English Horology. Thomas Tompion is justly famed as the chief contributor to England's supremacy in clockmaking at this time. Tompion's main contribution to clockmaking was his genius in designing complicated movements and the meticulous finish to all his work. Later George Graham and John Harrison made further improvements to timekeeping, as opposed to clockmaking, which kept England in the lead for the whole of the eighteenth century.

George Graham's deadbeat escapement, about 1715, held the field for astronomical observations for over 200 years. Graham's mercury pendulum is still in use today, as is John Harrison's gridiron pendulum, although recent researches tend to show that this invention should rather be credited to his younger brother, James. Graham's cylinder escapement for watches, about 1725, put his work in the lead for eighty years or so, until the lever escapement, invented about 1759 by Thomas Mudge, became more generally adopted in the early part of the nineteenth century.

John Harrison's name is always associated with the winning of the prize of £20,000 for the solution of the problem of 'the Longitude', i.e. making a timepiece sufficiently accurate to enable mariners to ascertain their longitude when at sea. Harrison's efforts, starting with long-case clocks made entirely of wood (he was a carpenter by trade), progressing through the three trial machines that took the form of clocks of unique design, and ending with his finally successful piece, in the form of a large watch, can properly be included in this brief survey. But Harrison's work was too complicated and expensive for general use, and it remained for John Arnold and Thomas Earnshaw to introduce the simplified types of chronometers that are the basis of those made today.

Above Precision or regulator clock by George Graham, London, no. 728, with dead beat escapement in case of wainscot oak

Left, above Veneered ebony bracket clock by Thomas Tompion

Right Circular ship's clock by George Graham, *c.* 1735. British Museum

Left Bracket clock probably by John Martin, signed Martin. Marquetry case with handle and gilt finials, square brass face, *c.* 1700. Victoria & Albert Museum

In 1760 James Cox invented his atmospheric Pressure Clock, which was wound up either on the rise or fall of the air pressure. This is the forerunner of the Atmos Clock of the 1920s which today operates on the change of temperature.

Above Two-tune musical watch by Timothy Williamson, London, *c.* 1780–85. White enamel dial with hour, minute and lunar dials and tune indicator. Contemporary watch-stand of ivory, ebony and tortoiseshell

Far left 'Fabulous Clock' by James Cox, London. The key is signed and dated, 1766. Chased gilt-metal case with agate background; the small clock movement is connected with a mechanism below showing the phases of the moon

In 1765 Alexander Cumming made for King George III the first self-recording barograph. A carrier floating on the surface of a mercury column held in its upper end a pencil which rose or fell with the change in atmospheric pressure and recorded its positions by tracing a line on a graphed-paper disc that was rotated by the clock once every six months. A second clock by Cumming inspired Luke Howard to make the recordings he later collated and published as his *Climate of London* (1820). On this book is based the whole of modern meteorology, so that a clockmaker can be considered instrumental in the founding of this science.

Up to the beginning of the eighteenth century astrology played an important part in day-to-day life, and clocks embodying the relative aspects of the planets are not infrequent. Clocks indicating the day of the month and those showing the phases of the moon are common. From time to time, but more rarely, we find dials to tell the time of high tide, at first for London, where the Thames was the main highway, and later for marine ports.

In the latter part of the seventeenth century and in the early eighteenth, when clocks were only to be found in the spacious rooms of large mansions, we find various systems of complicated striking, which indicate the time at more frequent intervals than one hour. Until clocks became sufficiently cheap, handles were attached so that they could be carried from room to room. In those made towards the end of the eighteenth century the handles were ornamental, in keeping with the decoration of furniture at the time. Movement of bracket clocks from room to room accounts for the retention of the verge escapement in this type for a hundred years or so after the invention of the much superior anchor escapement – the verge does not require the accurate levelling called for by the anchor.

Again, we find repeating clocks in use until about the time of the invention of matches; the repeating watch, being carried on the person, indoors and outdoors, was favoured until a later period.

BRITISH CLOCKMAKERS OF IMPORTANCE (1600–1830)

All clocks and watches before 1700 are interesting, as are many in the period 1700–35; there are fewer exceptional makers, until in the last thirty or forty years of the eighteenth century and thereafter, the clock or watch that is to be prized for its horological, as opposed to its furnishing or utilitarian value, is the exception rather than the rule.

The dates given are the approximate years between which signed pieces may be expected. For this purpose the first date is when the man is twenty-five or enters the Clockmakers' Company. The last date is the known or estimated date of death.

Antram, George	1707–1723
Arnold, John	1757–1799
Barker (*Wigan*)	2nd half 18th c.
Bradley, Langley	1697–1738
Clement, William	2nd half 17th c.
Cole, Ferguson	1818–1880
Colston, Richard	1682–1709
Cox, James	1740–1788
Delander, Daniel	1702–1733
Duchesne, Claude	1693–1730
Earnshaw, Thomas	1774–1829
East, Edward	1627–1697
Ebsworth, John	1667–1710
Ellicott, John	1731–1772
Emery, Josiah	1750–1797
Finney (*Liverpool*) Various members,	1730–1830
Fromanteel (*London*) Various members,	1625–1725
Garon, Peter	1695–1730
Goode, Charles	1686–1730
Gould, Christopher	1682–1718
Graham, George	1713–1751
Gray, Benjamin	1681–1764
Harrison, John	1715–1776
Hilderson, John	2nd half 17th c.
Hindley, Henry (*York*)	1726–1771
Holmes, John	1787–1815
Jones, Henry	1664–1695
Knibb, John (*Oxford & London*)	*c.* 1650–1710
Knibb, Joseph	*c.* 1650–1711
Knifton, Thomas	1640–1662
Lister, Thomas (*Halifax*)	1770–1814
McCabe, James	1781–1811
Margetts, George	1779–1810
Markwick, A family	1666–1805
Moore, William	1704–1720
Mudge, Thomas	1740–1794
Norton, Eardley	1750–1795
Pinchbeck, Christopher	1695–1732
Pinchbeck, Christopher, Jr	1735–1783
Prior, George	1765–1810
Prior, George (Son)	1815–1830
Quare, Daniel	1674–1724
Ramsay, David (*Edinburgh & London*)	1590–1655
Recordon, Louis	1778–1824
Reid, Thomas (*Edinburgh*)	1771–1831
Robinson, Francis	1696–1750
Roskell, Robert	1798–1830
Selwood, William	1633–1652
Staunton, Edward	1666–1710
Tomlinson, William	1699–1745
Tompion, Thomas	1671–1713
Vallin, Nicholas	1580–1630
Vulliamy, Benjamin	1775–1820

Vulliamy, Benjamin Lewis	1809–1854
Vulliamy, Justin	1730–1790
Watson, Samuel (*Coventry & London*)	1675–1715
Webster, William	1697–1725
Whitehurst, John (*Derby & London*)	1738–1788
Williamson, Joseph	1697–1725
Windmills, Joseph	1671–1725

Above Table clock by Eardley Norton, London, tortoiseshell case with metal mounts, late 18th century

All makers are in London, except where specified.

Glossary

BAROMETERS

Banjo. The type in which the case resembles this instrument.
Barograph. A self-recording barometer actuated by clockwork.
Capacity error. That introduced by the alteration in the level of the cistern or siphon reservoir by the inflow or outflow of mercury from the vertical tube.
Cistern. The type in which the lower open end of the vertical tube is placed below the level of the mercury in open reservoir. The earliest type.
Diagonal (also called Signpost and Yardarm). A type in which the recording part of the tube is at an obtuse angle with the lower upright part, so that the possible variation of the mercury height of about 3 inches (7.6 cm) may be spread over the inclined length of the tube.
Double. A type in which the mercury column is divided into two approximately equal halves fixed vertically side by side and connected by a tube filled with a lighter fluid substance, such as oil or air.
Fortin. A type in which the level of the cistern is adjusted to a fixed pointer before a reading by difference is taken, thus eliminating capacity error (*q.v.*).
Marine. A type in which part of the bore in the vertical tube is constricted in order to minimize a movement of level in the vertical tube by reason of the ship's motion. This type must also be capable of plugging when not in use.
Meniscus. The surface of a liquid in a tube. It is usually curved, owing to surface-tension effects.
Portable. A type in which the cistern or siphon can be entirely enclosed, and in which the mercury can be plugged in the vertical tube.
Siphon. A type in which the reservoir is situated in the return portion of a J-shaped tube.
Wheel. A siphon-type in which the variation of the mercury level is magnified and registered on a circular dial.

CLOCKS AND WATCHES

Acorn clock. A type of Connecticut shelf clock, in shape suggesting an acorn. *c.* 1850. Rare.
Act of Parliament Clock. A misnomer applied to a timepiece, usually weight-driven, with seconds pendulum having a large unglazed dial and a small trunk. According to legend, these clocks were first

From left to right Banjo, or wheel barometer, rosewood. Admiral Fitzroy's Barometer, named after the hydrographer and meteorologist, made of ash in the gothic style, 1880s. Pillar or stick barometer

put into inns and post taverns for use of the general public, many of whom had sold their clocks and watches when Pitt introduced his Act in 1797 levying 5*s* per annum on all clocks and watches. Such distress was caused in the trade that the Act was repealed in the following year.

Alarm. A mechanical attachment which, at a predetermined time, rings a bell or activates some other alarm. Found on many types of portable clocks, but rarely on tall clocks. The time for the release of the alarm is usually determined, or 'set', by a brass disc numbered 1–12, or by a third hand.

Arbor. The shaft or axle to which pinions and wheels (*qq.v.*) are attached.

Architectural clock. A clock in which the hood, in long-case, and the top in mantel clocks, is in the style of a classical pediment, with or without supporting columns. Usually a sign of work in the third quarter of the seventeenth century, although these pediment tops were revived for a short period early in the nineteenth century.

Arch top, plain. A case, usually in bracket clocks, where the arch rises directly from the sides of the case.

Astrological dials. These are embodied in many early clocks and watches and show the relation or aspect of the planets to one another at any time. They are usually shown as related to the moon, whose phases are to be seen through an aperture in the dial for this purpose. The distances in degrees are shown by the Trines △ (120°), Quartiles □ (90°), Sextiles ⚹ (60°), Conjunction ☌ (0°), and Opposion☍ (180°).

Automatic winding. A pocket watch which is wound up by means of a weight actuated by the motion of the body. A patent was taken out in London in 1780 by Louis Recordon, but prior claim is made for Abraham Louis Perrelet, of Le Locle. The automatic wristwatch was invented by J. W. Harwood of London, in 1914.

Balance or Balance wheel. One of the first forms of oscillating control in a mechanical clock or watch. In 1675 Christiaan Huygens announced his spiral spring fitted to the balance, but Robert Hooke claimed priority. With this spring the watch could keep as good time as a pendulum clock.

Balance staff. The arbor or shaft which carries the balance wheel.

Balloon. A type of waisted clock popular in the late eighteenth and early nineteenth centuries.

Banjo clock. The recent term applied to various wall clocks somewhat resembling a banjo in shape. The earliest American example was the 'Improved Timepiece' produced by Simon Willard before 1800 and patented by him in 1802. It became one of the most popular types of clocks. Others copied and modified the original design in so many ways that an almost endless number of varieties resulted.

The banjo, in its best form, is a finely made piece. The movements used, although varying in details, were ordinarily brass, weight-driven eight-day timepieces, with a pendulum about 20–26 inches (51–66 cm) long. A few striking, as well as alarm, movements were also used. A very few Connecticut wall clocks, somewhat resembling the true banjo, were made using the 30-hour wooden movement.

Since 1800 there probably has not been a single decade when banjos have not been manufactured, so popular have they been. The clocks produced by the Willards, their apprentices, and other contemporaries until about 1830 are the most pleasing in design. Later plainer, and not so perfectly made, banjos were sold in large numbers. After about 1845 Edward Howard in Boston, alone and with others under various company names, manufactured large numbers of simple banjos in several sizes.

Because of the popularity of the banjo clock and the rarity of the best examples, a great many reproductions and rebuilt pieces have appeared. It is probably a fact that more deliberate faking has been attempted in 'making' old banjos than any other type of clock. Many old banjos have been 'improved' by adding the name of a famous maker. Such imitations or fakes are sometimes very difficult to detect. There are no consistent and positive characteristics by which genuine banjos by the Willards or other famous makers can be identified.

Banking pins. Two fixed pins which limit the motion of the lever of a lever escapement.

Barrel. A cylindrical box containing the mainspring in both clocks and watches. American clocks before 1900 often have unenclosed springs.

Basket top. A pierced metallic and roughly dome-shaped case top current at the end of the seventeenth and early in the eighteenth centuries.

Basket top, double. Two pierced metallic basket tops superimposed.

Basket top, wooden. Where a smooth wooden dome replaces the metallic bracket.

Beat. The sound made by the action of the escapement – the 'tick-tock'. A timepiece is 'in beat' when the intervals between beats are even.

Beehive clock. A form of small Connecticut shelf clock, also called 'flatiron' clock; so named because of the resemblance of the shape to an old-time beehive or flatiron. *c.* 1850–60. Common.

Bell, inverted. Similar to a bell top, except that the lower portion has a convex outline.

Bell top. The top of a clock case where the lower portion is shaped like the bell of a turret clock with concave sides.

Bezel. The metallic framing of a clock or watch glass.

Blinking-eye clocks. In which the eyes are connected to the escapement and move in harmony with it. Made in South Germany in the seventeenth and elsewhere in the late eighteenth century; a few were made in the United States in the nineteenth century.

Bob. The weight at the base of a pendulum rod. The earliest were pear-shaped or nearly spherical. Later the general form was lenticular; in some regulators and special clocks cylindrical. *See diagram under* Pendulum: bob.

Bob wire. The wire loop which passes through the bob of many American clocks. One end is threaded for the regulating nut.

Bolt and shutter. A form of maintaining power. The shutters cover the winding squares so that the clock cannot be wound without pushing them aside. This action brings into play a small subsidiary force that keeps the clock going during the period of winding.

Bow. The loop at the top of the pendant of a watch.

Box-on-box. *See* Massachusetts shelf clock.

Bracket clock. Many clocks of the seventeenth and eighteenth centuries were provided with their own brackets, usually designed to harmonize with the case. Only rarely have original brackets survived. They frequently contain a drawer to hold the winding key. Portable clocks are known as both mantel and bracket clocks.

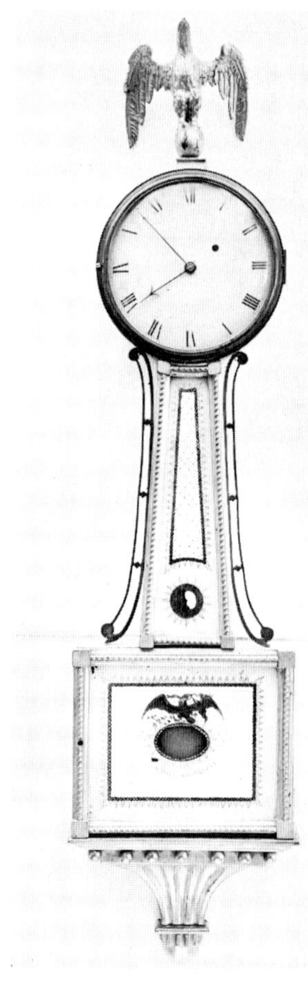

Banjo clock by Simon Willard. Courtesy of Henry Francis du Pont Winterthur Museum

Left Ebonized bracket clocks. *Left* by Jonathon Lowndes, London, *c.* 1695. *Right* by Daniel Quare, London, *c.* 1700. Spring driven and portable.

Right, below Sun and moon dialled watch (*left*) by Windmills, London, *c.* 1700, silver champleve. Pocket chronometer (*right*) by Barraud, London, the silver case hall-marked 1797

Bridge. A shaped metallic support having two terminal plates.

Broken arch. An arch terminating on either side with a horizontal projection. There are broken-arch dials and cases. If a full semicircle, they are known as deep arches; if less, and this usually applies to the earliest, as shallow arches.

Buhl. Inlay of brass or silver, usually on a base of tortoiseshell. Invented by André Charles Boulle in the latter half of the seventeenth century.

Bun feet. Small, circular, flat, 'cheese-like' feet, sometimes found on early long-case and bracket clocks.

Bushing. The filling up of worn pivot holes and their subsequent opening to size.

Calendar clock. Any clock which indicates the day, month, or year. Earliest known is that of Giovanni Dondi of Padua, Italy (1364), which showed the length of daylight for every day, and the day of the month through the year. Calendar clocks have been produced throughout the ages in all countries.

Cam. A part so shaped as to turn rotary motion into reciprocal or variable motion.

Cannon pinion. The pinion to which it is usual to fit the minute hand.

Cap (dust). A movable cap, first used early in the eighteenth century to help keep the movement clean. Only used in watches.

Cartel clock. A mural clock, usually of somewhat flamboyant design. More often found in France than in England. The English ones are usually of carved wood, whereas the French are usually of cast brass or bronze and gilt.

Cartouche. A decorative panel, sometimes applied, and framing an inscription.

Case. That which contains the clock or watch movement. Any solid material as metal, stone, or wood may be used. The variety of designs, selection of woods, and the quality of cabinet work contribute to the fascination of clocks to the collector.

Case-on-case. *See* Massachusetts shelf clock.

Case, pair. For a hundred years, beginning about the latter part of the seventeenth century, watches were usually provided with two cases, of which the outer was frequently highly ornate. In some instances a third case was provided to protect the decoration on the second.

Centre seconds. A clock or watch in which the seconds hand is placed on the same arbor as the hour and minute hands.

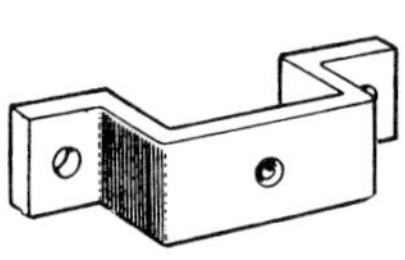

Bridge

Cam

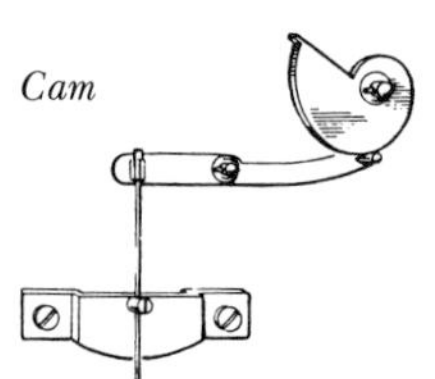

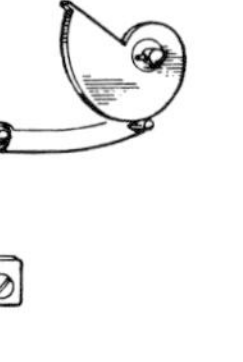

Cap

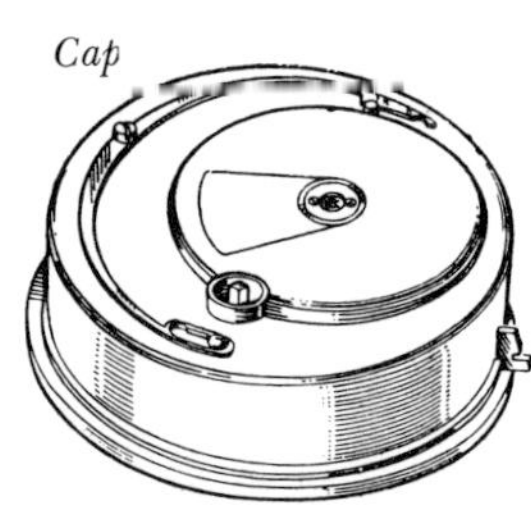

Below Cartel clock in gilt wood frame by Windmills of London, early 18th century

Champlevé. The cutting away of the dial of a watch, so that the hour numerals, minute ring, and interhorary marks remain raised.

Chapter ring. The applied circle, found in earlier clocks, upon which are engraved the hour numerals. Derives its name from the fact that hours are struck on a bell. Originally a clock served to rouse the sexton, who then struck the hour of the chapter, or religious office, on a bell.

Chiming clock. A clock which sounds at the quarters a chime on four or more bells in addition to striking the hour.

Chronograph. A watch, stop watch, the hands of which can be started, stopped, and returned to zero without stopping its motion.

Chronometer. An especially accurate portable timepiece, as a marine chronometer.

Chronometer escapement. A special type of escapement used in chronometers, also called a detent escapement.

Circular error. Christiaan Huygens, who invented the pendulum, discovered that the truly isochronous swing of a pendulum was not the true arc of a circle but on a cycloid. The course of the latter is more U-shaped than the true circle; but for a short distance at the bottom of the swing the two paths coincide. Any lack of timekeeping due to a pendulum swinging beyond this common path is said to be due to circular error.

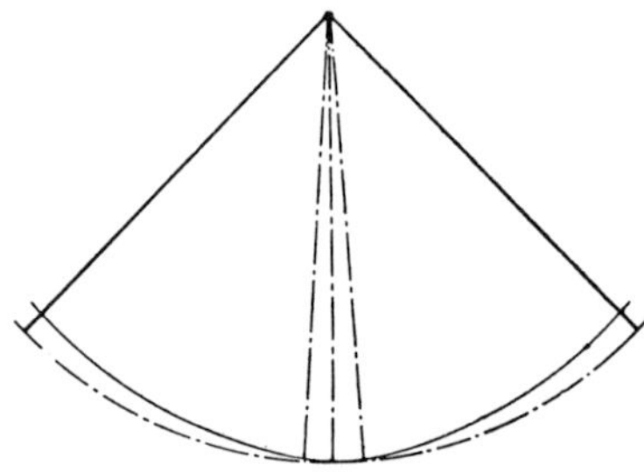

Clepsydra. A timekeeper motivated by water running either into or out from it. Water clocks are among the earliest forms known; before the discovery of the verge escapement and the weight as a motive power.

Click. The pawl that works against the ratchet wheel of the winding drum; its action causes the clicking when a timepiece is wound.

Cock (Clock). (i) The bracket that supports the pendulum; (ii) a bridge with only one terminal plate. *See diagram under* Pendulum: bob.

Cock (Watch). The bracket covering and protecting the balance, it also supports the upper end of the balance staff.

Collet. (i) A dome-shaped washer used to render firm the hands of a clock; (ii) a flange.

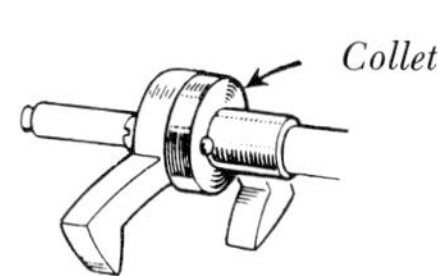

Compensation balance. A balance that corrects the influence of heat and cold upon its timekeeping. Usually of bimetallic construction.

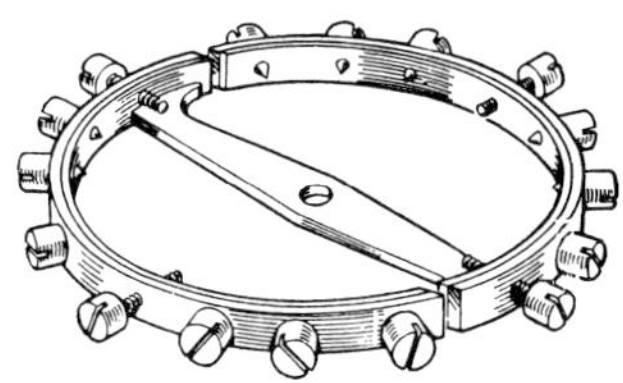

Compensation curve. A bimetallic curve in contact with one end of the balance spring. The action of temperature on the curve causes a compensating change in the effective length of the balance spring.

Contrate wheel. A wheel in which the teeth stand perpendicularly to the plane of the wheel. It is used to transmit motion from the arbor of one wheel at rightangles to the first.

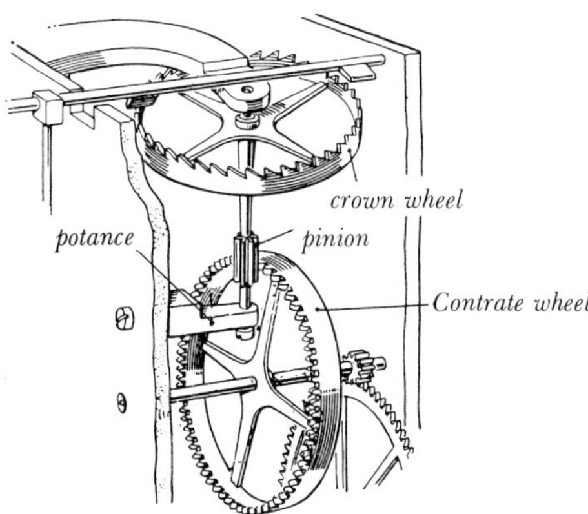

Cottage clocks. Name now given to many small Connecticut spring clocks in wood cases. *c.* 1850–1900. Common.

Crown wheel. The escape wheel of the verge escapement. *See diagram under* Contrate wheel.

Crutch. That part of the clock mechanism which, fixed to the pallet arbor, transmits the impulse to the independently supported pendulum. *See diagram under* Cycloidal cheeks.

Curb pins. Two pins astride the outer end of a balance spring. These are moved by the regulating device, and so alter the effective length of the spring.

Cycloidal cheeks. Curves fitted to a pendulum clock to overcome circular error. It was found, however, that the errors they introduced were greater than those they eliminated, so they were soon abandoned. Only found in the very earliest pendulum clocks.

Cycloidal path. Curve described by a point on the circumference of a circle rolling along a straight line.

Declination. The angular distance of a star north or south of the celestial equator. In clocks the star is usually the sun, whose declination varies between 23½° north and south of the equator.

Detent. That which detains. The term is applied to the pawl or click that takes into the ratchet wheel.

Dial. The face of a clock or watch on which are marked the hours, minutes, and seconds. The division of the circle into 360 equal parts is believed to have originated with the Sumerians about 4000 B.C. Finding that 10, the number of the fingers, was not easily divisible, they chose a unit of 6, divisible by 3 and 2. They then adopted a combination of 6 and 10 up to 6 × 10 = 60. This formed the basis for another series up to 10 × 60 = 600. This again formed a basis, but when they reached 6 × 600 = 3, 600, they considered that they had reached finality or completeness, which they symbolized as a circle.

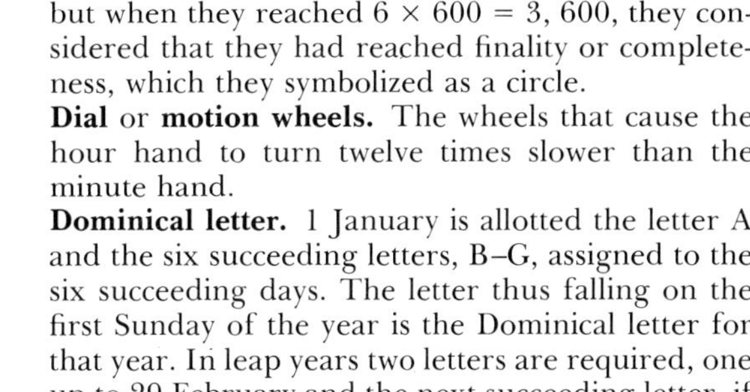

Dial or **motion wheels.** The wheels that cause the hour hand to turn twelve times slower than the minute hand.

Dominical letter. 1 January is allotted the letter A and the six succeeding letters, B–G, assigned to the six succeeding days. The letter thus falling on the first Sunday of the year is the Dominical letter for that year. In leap years two letters are required, one up to 29 February and the next succeeding letter, if necessary recommencing with A, for the rest of the year. Used in connection with the fixing of Easter Day.

Drum. The spool on to which the cord to the weight is wound.

Dutch striking. The repetition of the hour at the half-hour on a different toned bell.

Ecliptic. The apparent orbit of the sun. Total eclipses of the sun or moon are only possible when the moon is in the plane of the ecliptic. The plane of the orbit of the moon is inclined at an angle of 5° to that of the sun. Where the two intersect is termed the Nodes. They appear on clock dials as Ω.

Epact. The age of the moon on 1 January.

Epicycloid. The curve traced by a point on the circumference of a circle as it rolls around another circle. It is a curve used in the cutting of teeth for wheels.

Equation dial. A dial that records both Solar and Mean Time.

Equation kidney. A kidney-shaped cam, invented by Christiaan Huygens in 1695, which made possible the transformation of simple forward rotary motion into a backward or forward motion, varying daily, both in direction and amount, necessary to indicate the daily difference between Solar and Mean Time.

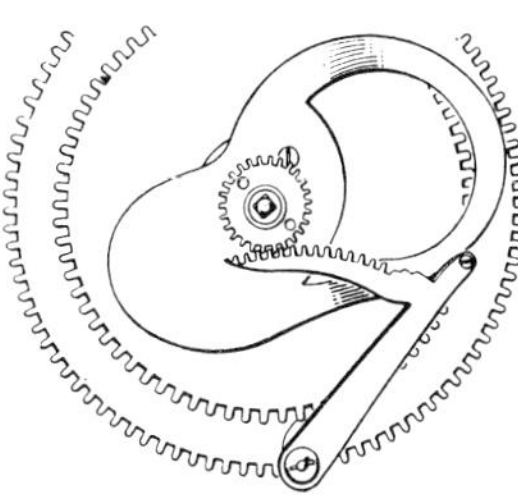
Equation Kidney

Equation of time. The solar day or time as recorded by a sundial varies each day in length; whereas Mean Time, or time shown by a clock, is exactly twenty-four hours each day. This difference, which varies irregularly daily, is known as the equation of time.

Escapement. The means by which the motion of a clock or watch is checked and the energy of the motive force, weight, or spring, is transmitted to the controller, pendulum, or balance.

Anchor. Invented about 1670 by William Clement. It revolutionized timekeeping. With it the pallets are in the same plane as the escape wheel, instead of being at rightangles to it, as in the verge escapement. It largely eliminated circular error and also made practical the use of long pendulums swinging more slowly, and thus with a lesser cumulative error. It is still used today for most domestic clocks, and particularly in long-case clocks with pendulums beating one second. It is also known as the recoil escapement, which recoil is seen in the slight shudder at each beat in the seconds hand of long-case clocks so equipped. The vastly improved timekeeping of this escapement made really practical the use of clocks for astronomical purposes. Flamsteed, the first Astronomer Royal

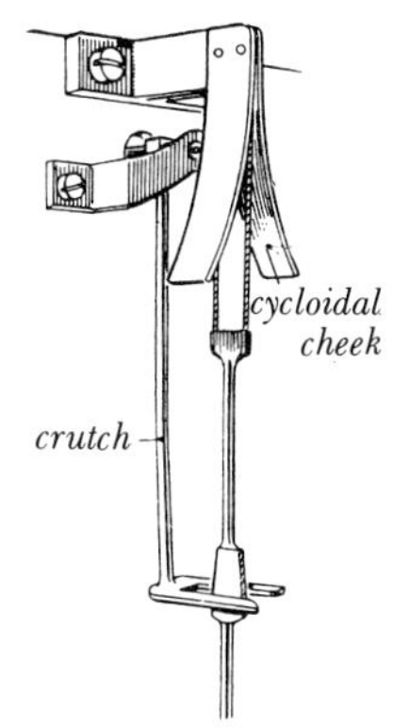

Anchor escapement

at Greenwich, in 1675, used clocks made by Thomas Tompion, equipped with the anchor escapement and with 13-foot (3.97 m) pendulums, beating two seconds, suspended above the clocks which reduced the amplitude to about 1 inch (2.5 cm), thus eliminating circular error. This largely accounted for the far greater accuracy of his observations as compared with his contemporaries. From this invention followed, directly or indirectly, practically all the subsequent improvements in timekeeping in clocks.

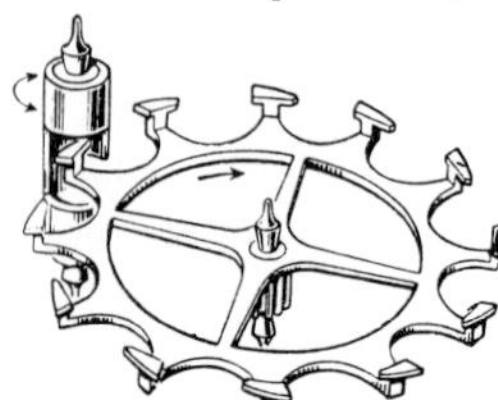
Cylinder escapement

Cylinder. A type for use in watches. A form of this escapement was patented by Tompion, Barlow, and Haughton in 1695, but it was never developed. It remained for Tompion's successor, George Graham, to perfect this escapement about 1725. Graham used it very extensively in his watches, and this greatly helped him to gain the reputation of being the best watchmaker of his day. As with the anchor escapement, the pallets are in the same plane as the escape wheel. This escapement remained the best for watches until supplanted by the duplex and the lever escapements about the end of the eighteenth century.

Deadbeat escapement

Deadbeat. Invented by George Graham about 1715. Graham was the leading astronomical instrument maker of his day, and from his close connection with astronomers was doubtless aware of their demand for still greater accuracy than could be attained with the anchor escapement. The deadbeat escapement is an improvement on the anchor in that it eliminates the recoil, and remains steady at the end of each beat. It held the field for the most accurate escape for astronomical work for nearly 200 years. It is still used today in high-grade clocks, both long-case and mantel.

Detent. In which the escapement is locked by a pin on the detent and the impulse is given every alternate vibration to a pallet on the balance staff by the escape-wheel teeth. A detent escapement goes 'tick-tick' and not 'tick-tock'. *See also* Detent.

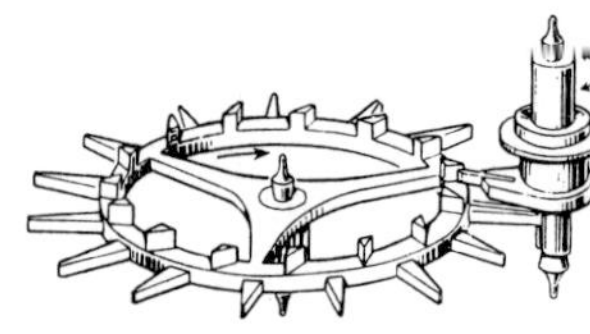
Duplex escapement

Duplex. Invention uncertain. Usually attributed to Pierre LeRoy, Paris, about 1750. The escape wheel has two sets of teeth, one long and pointed, the other short and triangular and rising from the plane of the escape wheel. The long teeth escape through a small notch in the balance staff, which also carries a long arm by which the impulse is given through the short triangular teeth.

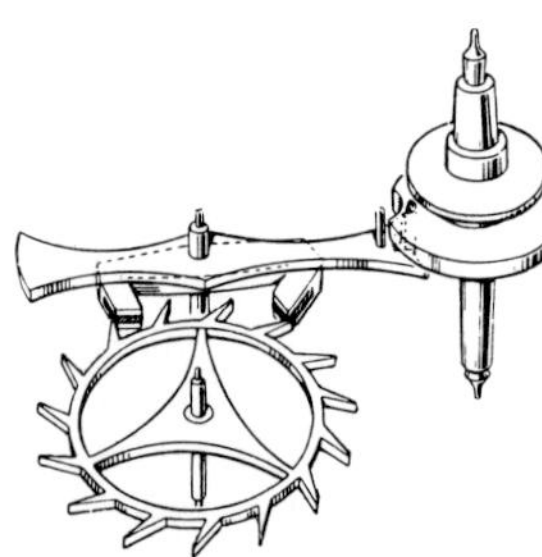
Lever escapement

Lever. First invented about 1758 by Thomas Mudge and incorporated in a watch given by King George III to Queen Charlotte. Mudge only made one or two other examples and does not seem to have realized the importance of his invention, which lies in the fact that the balance is free from interference for the greater part of its swing, thus leaving it free to perform its true function as controller. From the beginning of the second quarter of the nineteenth century the lever escapement, in one of its many forms, became the standard escapement for watches, and still is so today. Before that date, despite the appearance of the cylinder, duplex, and lever escapements, the standard watch escapement was the verge.

Pin pallet escapement

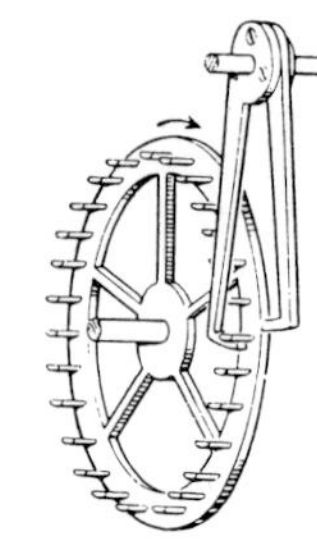

Pin pallet. Invented by Amant, Paris, about 1740. A type in which the pins stand out from the side of the escape wheel. Not much found in English clocks.

Tic-Tac. A modified form of the anchor escapement found in some early clocks. The 'anchor' embraces only two or three teeth of the escape wheel.

Verge. This was the original escapement for mechanical clocks. Date of invention unknown, possibly thirteenth century. Although it is an escapement in its worst form, in that it never leaves the pendulum or balance free for an instant, nevertheless it was in its day as revolutionary an invention as was, later, the anchor escapement. It held the field unchallenged for about 400 years; even thereafter it remained in use for clocks and watches, along with better types, for another 150 years. *See diagram under* Contrate wheel.

Escape wheel. The final wheel of the time train of a clock or watch which gives impulse to the pendulum or balance. Often shortened to 'scape wheel.

Fan. *See* Fly.

Finials. The turned, carved, or moulded ornaments, usually brass or wood, at the top of various types of clocks.

Fly. A rapidly revolving vane, the final component of the striking train, which acts as a governor for the rate of striking. Date of invention unknown, but presumably concurrent with the locking plate.

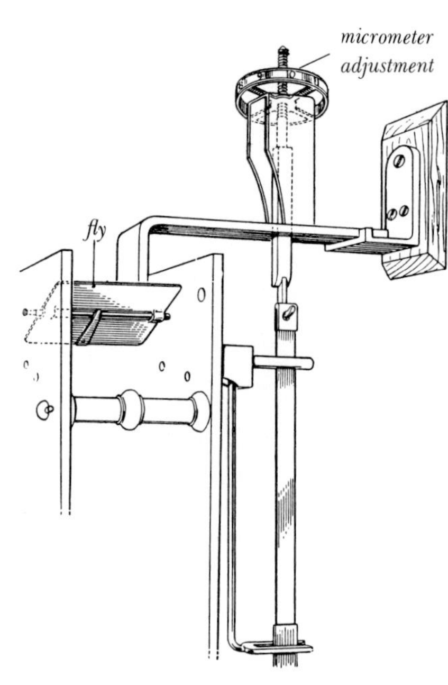

Foliot. With the balance wheel the earliest form of controller in a mechanical clock. Always found with a verge escapement. The balance wheel and, especially later, the pendulum, so improved timekeeping that it is very rare to find a clock with its original foliot. Its origin is unknown, but presumably attributable to the inventor of the verge escapement. Consists of a horizontal rod fixed to a pivoted bar carrying the verge pallets. Regulation was by moving the weights carried at each end. The word may be derived from the French *esprit follet*, a goblin associated with Puck and represented by its to-and-fro motion.

Form watch. A watch made in some form that departs from the standard of the period, e.g. book, cruciform, skull, dog, etc. These are found in the seventeenth century. Later, at the end of the eighteenth, there are lyres, mandolines, baskets of flowers, fruit, etc.

Franklin clock. A type of wooden-movement shelf clock made (1825–30) by Silas Hoadley of Plymouth, Connecticut, and called by him 'Franklin'. It is perhaps the earliest instance that a clock was given a specific (model) name by a maker. This movement is characterized by being practically an inverted form of the movement then being made by Terry and others.
Frets. Pierced metallic decorative pieces, originally used to hide the balance in lantern clocks. Later, either in wood or metal, inserted into clock cases to facilitate the elimination of sound.
Fusee. A conically shaped and spirally grooved pulley which, utilizing the principle of the lever, equalizes the pull of the mainspring of a clock or watch on the train. The inventor about 1460–70 is unknown, but the invention has not been bettered, and is still in use today in high-grade spring-driven clocks. Catgut was originally used to connect the fusee with the mainspring barrel, but from the end of the seventeenth century a chain is usually employed.
Gathering pallet. A pin or finger that revolves when the clock is striking and gathers up, at each revolution, a tooth of the striking rack.
Girandole. A type of wall clock designed by Lemuel Curtis. Considered by many to be the most beautiful American clock. *c.* 1820. Very rare.

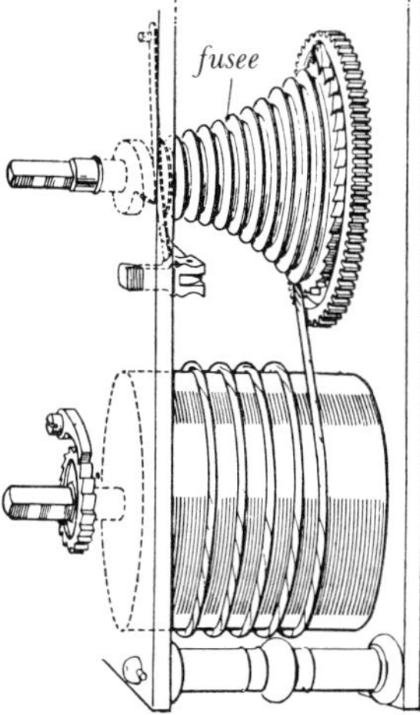

Left Girandole clock by Lemuel Curtis, American, early 19th century

Right Gothic-style cottage clock by The Waterbury Company, *c.* 1845. This timepiece could easily be adapted to alarms by fitting a separate alarm system

Gong. A piece of hardened, tempered wire wound in a volute, on which the hours are struck, instead of a bell. First used in the last quarter of the eighteenth century.

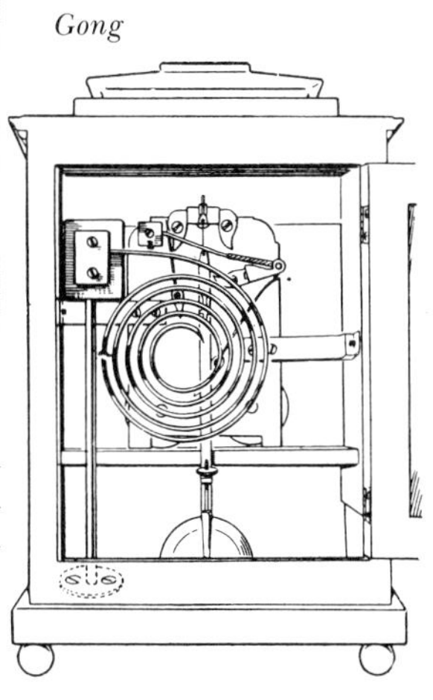

Gong

Gothic clocks. A term applied generally to all German, Swiss, or Italian clocks of the sixteenth and seventeenth centuries made on gothic lines. Pointed-topped Connecticut shelf clocks introduced about 1845. The most popular were called 'sharp gothic'; now commonly known as steeple clocks. Including round and sharp-topped gothics, variations in style and size of cases, and variations in types of movements, there are probably over 100 different forms. Most are attractive and deserve the interest of the advanced collector as well as the beginner.

Grandfather clock. Properly known as a long-case clock. Came into existence directly after the invention of the anchor escapement, 1670. The narrow arc of swing of this escapement made possible the enclosing of the weights and pendulum in a narrow trunk.
Grandmother clock. A small long-case clock, not exceeding 6 feet 6 inches (198 cm) in height.
Grand sonnerie. A system of striking whereby the hour and the quarter are struck at each quarter. The earliest is a clock about 1660 by J. G. Mayer of Munich in the locking-plate system. The next earliest known example is the movement with the silent escapement made by Tompion about 1676–80. This system of striking was rendered much more simple by the invention by Edward Barlow, in 1676, of the rack-and-snail method of striking.
Gravity escapement. An especially accurate escapement often used in tower clocks or regulators. Impulse is given to the pendulum by two weighted arms which are raised by the clock mechanism.
Gregorian calendar. The old Church calendar (based on the Julians introduced by Julius Caesar) assumed a solar year of exactly 365¼ days and that nineteen solar years contained exactly 235 lunations. Neither of these is quite accurate. By 1582 the cumulative error amounted to ten days. Pope Gregory XIII introduced the Gregorian calendar – or New Style – which brought the vernal equinox back to 21 March instead of 11 March. This change was not adopted in England till 1752, by which time the error was eleven days. In that year 2 September was followed by 14 September. The ignorant populace

rioted, saying, 'Give us back our eleven days!' This change accounted for the financial year ending on 5 April instead of 25 March in 1753, and it has so remained ever since.

Hairspring. The fine spring which regulates the motion of the balance wheel.

Half-clock. *See* Massachusetts shelf clock.

Hands. The pointers of a clock or watch. Originally clocks had no hands – they merely struck one at each hour, later the dial was made to revolve before a fixed pointer. Some time towards the end of the fourteenth century the fixed dial with a single revolving hour hand was introduced. Minute hands did not become general until the introduction of the pendulum made timekeeping sufficiently accurate to warrant their use. The study of the evolution of the design of hands will give a good guide to the date of a clock up to about 1830; after that designs are too numerous to be classified.

Hood, rising

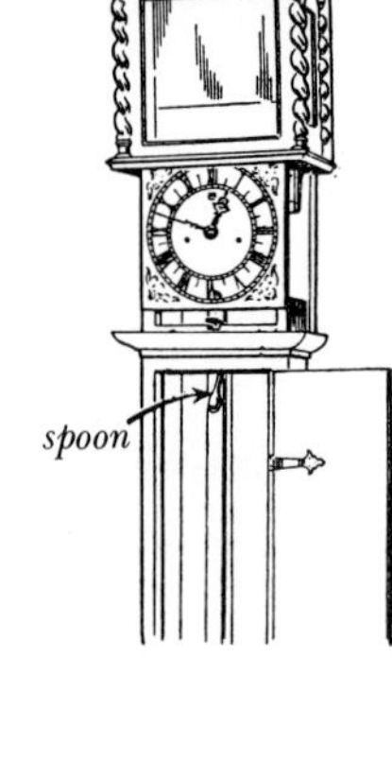

Hollow-column clocks. Weight-powered shelf clocks with free-standing hollow columns as part of the case decoration within which the weights travel. *c.* 1830–40. Rare.

Hood. The upper removable portion of a long case. In all except very early cases it draws forward.

Hood, rising. The earliest form, before the door was introduced in the front, in which the hood slides up on grooves in the backboard and is held in place by a catch, thus allowing access to the dial. As clocks increased in height, the rising hood became impracticable, and the draw-forward type with door was introduced.

Hoop wheel. A wheel, forming part of the striking train of a clock, to which is affixed a narrow band, having slots and projecting at rightangles to the plane of the wheel. This serves as a regulator between each blow of the hammer.

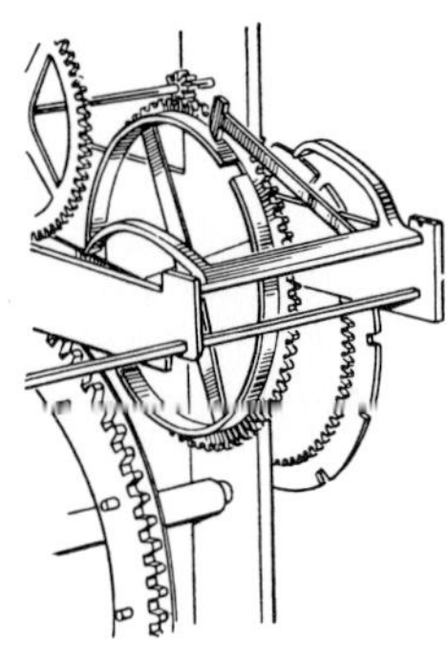

Hoop wheel

Hourglass clock. Any of several styles of Connecticut clocks in the general shape of an hourglass. *c.* 1850. Rare.

Hours, Babylonian. The Babylonians are believed to have divided the day into twenty-four hours of sixty minutes, each of sixty seconds, starting at sunrise.

Hours, canonical. Time signals were given in ancient Rome at three-hourly intervals, starting at 6 a.m. They were *mane*, *tertia*, *sextes*, *nona*, and *vespera*, and were later adopted by the Christian Church. In time other offices were added to the Church day, and the times of these offices or chapters advanced, until *nona* fell at noon. The original function of a clock was to let off an alarm every hour to warn the sexton to ring the bell for the office.

Hours, Italian. The Italians reckoned the time as twenty-four hours a day, starting from sunset. In some early Continental clocks dials were marked I to XII twice over and had a movable ring marked 1–24 in Arabic numerals, enabling the clock to be set daily at sunset for the Italian hour.

Hours, Nuremberg. In South Germany, until the early part of the seventeenth century, time was recorded as so many hours of daylight and so many hours of darkness. These varied from sixteen hours of daylight and eight of darkness in mid-summer to the converse in mid-winter. Public tables told when a hour should be transferred from one section to the other. In the town of Rothenburg this system of time recording was retained up to the early nineteenth century.

Hours, temporal. The division of the twenty-four hours into twelve of daylight and twelve of darkness, the length thus varying with the seasons. This system gradually disappeared in Europe with the coming of the mechanical clock, but persisted in Japan until 1873; clocks had to be adjusted every fourteen days.

Indiction. A period of fifteen years arising from Roman taxation laws. Used in ecclesiastical calculations. Dials marked 1–15, with a hand revolving once in fifteen years, are sometimes found on astronomical clocks.

Involute curve. The curve described by a point on a taut line unwound from a cylinder.

Involute gear teeth. Wheels having teeth cut on the principle of the involute curve.

Iron-front clocks. Small Connecticut shelf clocks with fronts of cast iron in many forms, painted and often decorated with shell inlays. *c.* 1860. Common, but interesting.

Isochronous. Performing the same motion in equal time, i.e. when the balance of a watch or the pendulum of a clock performs each vibration in the same time irrespective of the arc of vibration or swing.

Jewels. The bearings of pivots may be formed of jewels to reduce wear and friction. Jewels were first introduced by Facio de Duillier in 1704; he was a Swiss settled in London. Rubies and sapphires are usually used. Jewels are sometimes found as pallets in very high-grade regulators.

Labels. Engraved, lithographed, or printed papers are found inside many American clocks but not in European. Cabinet makers' labels, as well as those of clockmakers, are found in a few tall clock cases made about 1800 or earlier. Clock labels became a usual feature of shelf clocks from their very earliest production (*c.* 1815). These labels give the maker's name and place of business and usually the directions for setting up, regulating, and caring for the clock. Occasionally some additional useful knowledge may be given, as the equation of time, postal rates, or census figures. Such papers are of the greatest importance in identifying and valuing any clock.

Lancet clock. Design of late eighteenth and early nineteenth centuries, in which a bracket clock has a pointed 'gothic' top.

Far right Striking lantern clock signed 'Jeffrey Baylie at ye turnstyle Holborn fecit'. Brass case converted from a foliot escapement to pendulum. Clockmaker's Company Collection, London

Lantern clock. A typically English design evolved in the early part of the seventeenth century, and persisting, especially in the provinces, until well into the eighteenth century. Erroneously called a Cromwellian clock. Much copied today. All original lantern clocks are weight-driven and, with the rarest exceptions, never exceed a thirty-hour going period.

Lantern clock, wing. A type, popular for about a quarter of a century at the end of the seventeenth century, where the pendulum was placed between the going and striking trains, and took the form of an anchor, the flukes of which appeared each side of the main framework, and were protected by wings.

Lantern pinion. An early type in which the leaves are formed by wires affixed between two circular endplates.

Latched plates. The retaining plates of the movement where the distance pillars are secured at one end by swivelled catches instead of by pins passing through the head of the pillar. *See diagram under* Pendulum: bob.

Leaf, Pinion. The longitudinal teeth of a pinion are known as leaves.

Lenticle. Glass let into the door of a long-case clock to allow the motion of the pendulum bob to be seen.

Lighthouse clock. (*a*) A clock made in small numbers by Simon Willard and suggesting a lighthouse in form. *c.* 1820. Very rare; (*b*) any of several later novelty clocks resembling a lighthouse.

Locking plate. A plate with notches set at increasing intervals around its circumference, which allows the striking train to sound the correct number of blows before the locking arm falls into a notch and stops the train. Invention unknown, probably thirteenth century, concurrently with the verge escapement. *See diagram under* Pendulum: bob.

Long case. The correct horological term for a grandfather or grandmother clock.

Lunar dial. A dial which shows the lunar periods.

Lunar work. That part of the train which actuates the lunar dial.

Lunation. A period of twenty-nine days twelve hours and forty-five minutes, being the time taken by the moon to make a complete revolution round the earth and occupy the same position relative to the sun. Except in very special astronomical clocks, the period usually taken is twenty-nine-and-a-half days.

Lyre clock. Wall or shelf clocks with cases in the general shape of a lyre; the original design is attributed to Aaron Willard, Jr. Many variations in detail of cases. All of excellent quality; eight-day movements; mostly by Massachusetts makers, *c.* 182040. Rare.

Mainspring. A coiled strip of steel that provides the motive power for portable clocks. First invented about 1450. To compensate for the loss of power as the spring unwinds it is used in conjunction with a fusee, or else only a limited number of turns are used, before re-winding. Steel springs were not successfully manufactured in America for use in clocks until about 1840. Brass springs are occasionally found in small Connecticut clocks of 1840–55.

Maintaining power. A device used in weight clocks and in clocks and watches fitted with a fusee, whereby a subsidiary force is brought into play to keep the clock going while it is being wound. In early clocks the winding squares were often covered by shutters, which, when pulled aside, brought into operation the maintaining power, thus ensuring its use.

Right Eight-day long-case clock in marquetry case by Edward East, *c.* 1675. Clockmaker's Company Collection, London

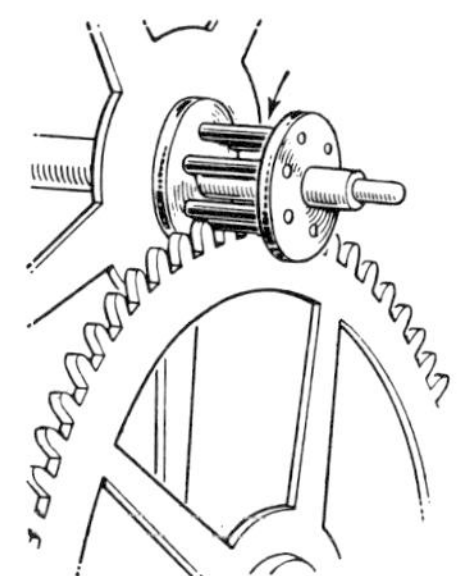

Lantern pinion

Main wheel. The first, and largest, wheel of the train; the one which first receives the power from the mainspring or weight. Also called the great wheel.

Mantel clock. Nearly synonymous with shelf or bracket clock, but used mostly in reference to modern clocks.

Massachusetts shelf clock. A type made by the Willards and others, chiefly of Massachusetts. Also called half-clock, box-on-box, or case-on-case. Eight-day brass movements, timepieces or occasionally striking clocks. *c.* 1800–30. Rare.

Above Beehive shelf clock by Brewster, *c.* 1860, with painted scene of The White House

Far right American ogee shelf clock, 1843

Below Nocturnal (night equivalent of the sun dial). Used by holding the handle downwards and viewing the Pole Star through the centre hole. The dates round the edge also show Zodiacal signs. Science Museum

Matting. A system of rendering dull the surface of the brass dial plate. The art is now lost. Usually confined to the centre of the chapter ring. In some early pendulum clocks the dials are matted all over.
Metonic cycle. The Greek astronomer Meton discovered that the days of the month on which full moon occurs constitute a cycle of nineteen years. This was considered so wonderful that the Greeks had it carved on stone in letters of gold. Clocks are to be found with a dial marked 1–19, the hand revolving in nineteen years.
Micrometer adjustment. A graduated wheel fixed to the pendulum suspension to give accurate adjustment for regulation. Early use of this was made by both Wm Clement and A. Fromanteel, but who had prior claim is uncertain. Later replaced by a subsidiary dial on the clock face, the hand of which actuated a rack and pinion or a cam connected with the pendulum suspension. *See diagram under* Fly.
Minute wheel. The wheel which is driven by the cannon pinion and of which the pinion drives the hour wheel, to which the hour hand is attached.
Mirror or **looking-glass clock.** Any clock having a mirror as a prominent part of the case. In 1825 Chauncey Jerome (Bristol, Connecticut) invented the 'looking-glass' clock to compete with the pillar-and-scroll case then being made by other manufacturers.
Mock pendulum. A swinging bob attached to the escape arbor, which shows through a slot in the dial plate. Only used in clocks with the verge escapement. Sometimes called a false bob.
Month clock. A clock that goes for a period of one month with one winding. The usual period is thirty-two days.
Movement. The 'works' of a clock or watch.
Mural clock. A clock made to hang on the wall.
Musical clock or watch. One that plays a tune at each hour or other predetermined time, as opposed to a chiming clock.
New Hampshire mirror clock. As now used refers to a distinct type of rectangular wall clock produced by several makers, mostly of New Hampshire, U.S.A. These usually are about 28–36 inches (71–91.5 cm) tall, 14–16 inches (35.6–40.6 cm) wide, and about 4 inches (10 cm) deep. The cases may be plain or with a scroll at top, or top and bottom; sometimes partly gilded; and usually have a square decorated glass over the dial. Weight-powered, eight-day brass movements. *c.* 1820–40. Rare.
Night clock. A clock that shows the time by night, usually by light shining through a pierced dial.
Nocturnal. *See illustration left.*
Nuremberg egg. A misnomer applied to early South German watches. Arose from the misreading and mistranslation of *Ührlein* into *Eierlein* (little clocks into little eggs). These early watches were usually drum-shaped.
Off-centre pendulum. A pendulum which is not hung in the centre. Specifically used in America in reference to certain early shelf clocks with wood movements by Eli Terry or Seth Thomas.
Ogee or **O. G. clock.** Technically a moulding with a reverse curve like the letter S. Used to designate the plain rectangular clocks with such an ogee moulding on the front. Probably originated in Connecticut about 1830 and made in great numbers until the first quarter of the twentieth century. The design was simple, inexpensive to make, easy to ship, and attractive. Made in numerous sizes, ranging from less than a foot (30 cm) to over 4 feet (122 cm) in height. Many types of movements, wood or brass, eight-day or thirty-hour, weight- or spring-powered, were used in these cases. They were primarily shelf clocks, but could be hung as wall clocks. Probably more O. G. clocks have been produced in Connecticut than any other type. Some are desirable on account of their rare movements or other features.

Oil sink. A shallow cup cut in the outside of a clock or watch plate concentric with a pivot hole, to retain oil.
Pallet. That part of the escapement through which the escape wheel gives impulse to the balance or pendulum. *See diagram under* Escapement: anchor.
Paperweight clocks. Small (4–6-inch (10–15 cm)) clocks with cases of moulded glass in several shapes, sizes, and colours. *c.* 1880–1910. Occasional.
Papier mâché clocks. Usually small shelf clocks, the cases of which are moulded of papier mâché; of many forms – some with shell inlays. Connecticut. *c.* 1860. Occasional.
Parquetry. A type of veneer in which the applied woods are worked into a pattern with straight-sided components – e.g. squares, diamonds, rectangles, etc.
Pendant. The small neck of metal connecting the watch case to the bow.
Pendulums.
Bob. The earliest form invented by Christiaan Huygens in 1657 and used with the verge escapement. In England the pendulum rod was usually fixed to the end of the escape pallet arbor, but on the Continent suspension was generally from a silk cord, the pendulum being actuated by a crutch. In England regulation was by means of a fine thread cut on

the lower end of the pendulum rod. The hole in the bob had a softwood core which 'took up' the threads on the rod. On the Continent regulation was by means of turning the arbor from which the silk was suspended.

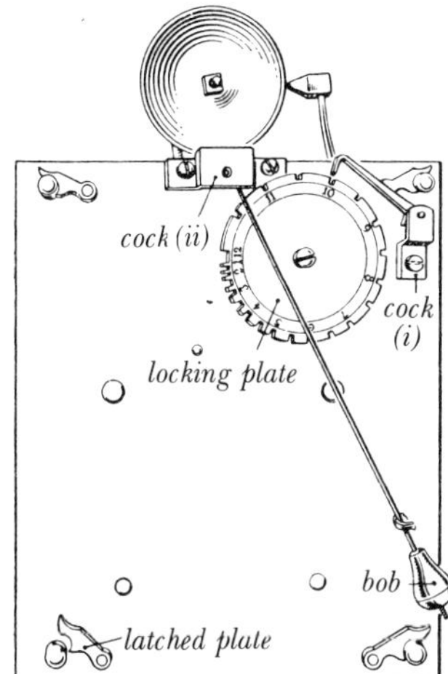

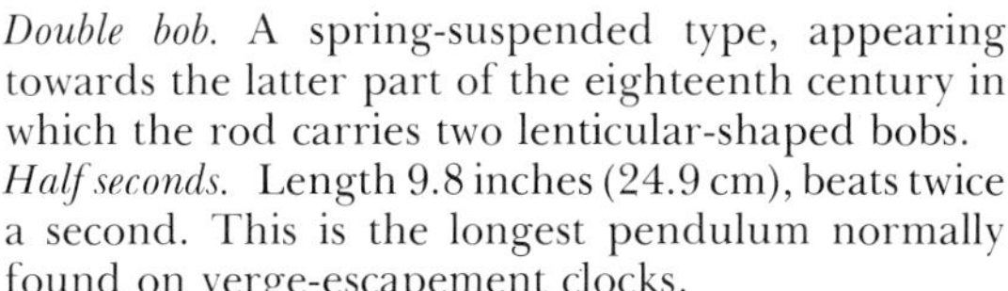

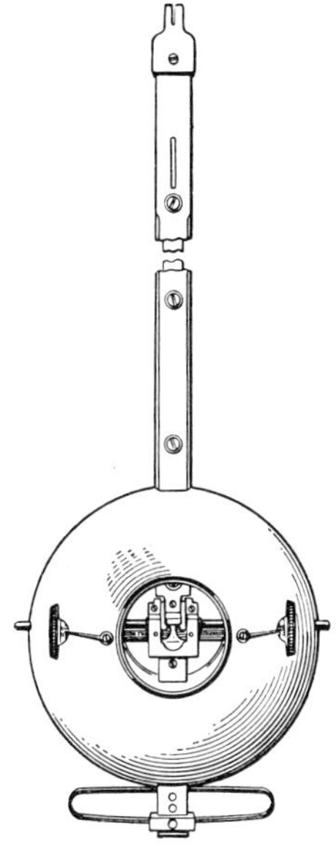

Ellicott pendulum

Double bob. A spring-suspended type, appearing towards the latter part of the eighteenth century in which the rod carries two lenticular-shaped bobs.
Half seconds. Length 9.8 inches (24.9 cm), beats twice a second. This is the longest pendulum normally found on verge-escapement clocks.
Seconds. This pendulum, 39.14 inches (99.4 cm) long, and those of greater length were made practical by the invention of the anchor escapement. The vastly improved timekeeping resulting from the adoption of the seconds pendulum and the anchor escapement in the early 1670s caused it to be called the Royal pendulum. It is the standard pendulum today for long-case clocks.
One and a quarter seconds. 5 ft 1 in. (155 cm). When the improved performance of the seconds pendulum and anchor escapement were realized, attempts were made to increase this by using longer pendulums. Wm Clement first made clocks with 1¼-second pendulums. The seconds dial of a clock originally so made should have four divisions between each 5-second interval on the seconds dial. Sometimes clocks have their escapements and pendulums altered from 1 second to 1¼ seconds in order to enhance their value. These will generally have their old seconds dials with five divisions. The base of a 1¼-second clock should have a door to allow access to the bob.
Two seconds. 13 ft 0½ in. (3.98 m). When making the first two clocks for Greenwich Observatory, in 1676, Thomas Tompion introduced 2-second pendulums and year movements, in an attempt to secure the greatest accuracy. These are thought to be the first clocks so designed in England. 2-second pendulums are now only found in some turret clocks.
Compensation. A pendulum which provides for the compensation of the effects of heat and cold.
Conical. A pendulum that rotates in a circle, the point of suspension being the apex of the cone. This was first designed by Jost Bodeker, bishop of Osnabrück in Germany, in 1578. Huygens made experiments, but it is seldom found in practice.
Ellicott. Invented in 1752, utilizing the principle of the difference in the expansion between steel and brass. The heavy bob is carried on two angular hinged supports. As the length of the pendulum rod changes with temperature, the vertical arms of the support are raised or depressed, giving a complementary movement to the horizontal arms carrying the heavy bob. Very expensive to make and not materially better than the gridiron, hence not extensively used.
Gridiron. Invented about 1725 by John Harrison, a carpenter born in Soulby in Yorks, 1693. Sometimes attributed jointly with his brother James. Harrison discovered that brass and steel have an expansion ratio of 3:2. This property is utilized in this pendulum, with its alternate rods of brass and steel. One side only is required, the other rods being put in for balance and symmetry. Still used today in high-grade clocks.

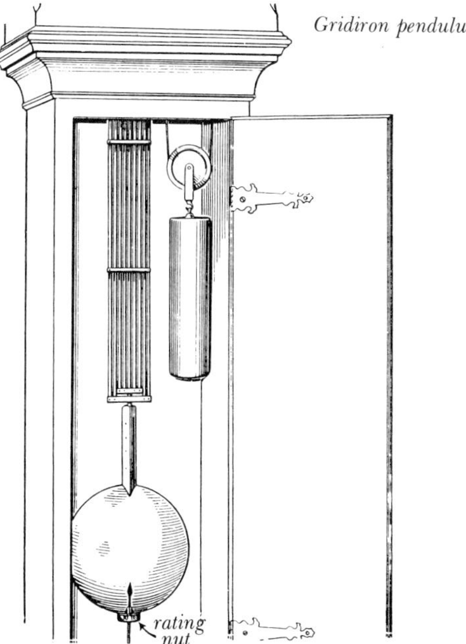

Gridiron pendulum

Mercury. Invented in 1726 by George Graham, who had previously experimented with brass and steel without conclusive results. The bob of the pendulum consists of a jar containing mercury. As the temperature changes the length of the pendulum rod, the level of the mercury in the jar alters in the inverse sense, thus keeping constant the centre of oscillation of the pendulum. Still in use today in high-grade clocks.
Simple. A theoretical conception consisting of a weight or mass suspended by a weightless thread.
Wood. A pendulum rod made of well-seasoned, straight-grained, and varnished wood is little affected by temperature or humidity. It is sometimes used in high-grade clocks and regulators.

Perpetual calendar

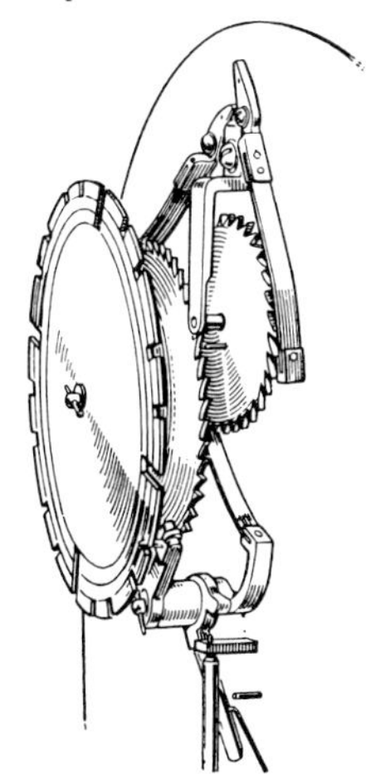

Perpetual calendar. A calendar which corrects itself for the short months, and more exceptionally for leap year. Usually consists of a slotted wheel revolving once a year (or four years) with slots of varying length which control the movement of a lever, allowing it to pass one or more teeth of the calendar wheel at a time.
Pillar and scroll. The modern name given to a style of shelf clock having delicate feet, slender pillars, and a broken arch or double scroll at the top. The design was probably an adaptation from eighteenth-century styles. Sometimes called 'Terry-type' clocks, as Eli Terry (*c.* 1816) was the first to manufacture them in

Far right Repeating gold watch by Francis Perigal, London, *c.* 1770, with gold enamel chatelaine. Fitzwilliam Museum, Cambridge

large quantities. Large numbers and several variations were made by Terry, Seth Thomas, Silas Hoadley, and other Connecticut makers until about 1830.

Thirty-hour wood movements of several types were usually used, although some fine examples are found with eight-day weight brass movements. The pillar-and-scroll clock was the first successfully mass-produced shelf clock in America. Similar clocks are found with labels of makers working (1825–40) in Pennsylvania, Massachusetts, and Nova Scotia. In addition to being so historically important, these are, perhaps, the most pleasing in appearance of all shelf clocks. Rare.

Pillars. The distance pieces separating the back and front (or top and bottom) plates of a clock or watch. Their style is a guide to the date of the piece.

Pin drum. The spiked drum of a musical or chiming clock, the spikes of which actuate the hammers as the drum revolves.

Pinion. A small-toothed wheel, in which the ratio of the axial length to diameter is greater than in a wheel. The teeth of pinions are called leaves. In clock and watch movements wheels and pinions alternate in the train. *See diagram under* Contrate wheel.

Pivot. The reduced end of an arbor, round which it revolves.

Planetarium. A representation of the chief celestial bodies, sun, moon, earth, and planets, which, when put into action, usually by turning a handle (although some are driven by clocks), shows the relative motion of these bodies. More usually called 'Orreries', after Richard Boyle, 4th Earl of Orrery, in the mistaken belief that the first of these was made for him. The first was made by Tompion and Graham for Prince Eugene, in about 1705.

Plates, back and front and top and bottom. Plates between which are pivoted the trains of a clock or watch. Early backplates in clocks were quite plain, except for the signature; later they began to be decorated, and the decoration became more and more ornate, reaching a peak in the first quarter of the eighteenth century. From this point it declined until the last decade of this century saw the return of the plain backplate. These backplates are a useful guide to the date of a clock.

Plinth. Properly speaking, the base of a clock, but more usually applied to its skirting.

Positional error. The variations in the rate of going of a watch due to change of position; pendant up, pendant down, dial up, dial down, etc.

Potance. The bracket supporting the lower pivot of the crown wheel arbor in a verge escapement. *See diagram under* Contrate wheel.

Pump across. In ting-tang quarter-striking clocks the quarters are struck on different-toned bells. Usually there are two hammers, one for each bell, and the striking action is 'pumped across' from one hammer to the other.

Quarter clock. A clock striking at the quarters as well as at the hour.

Quoins. Representations of the corner stones of a building. In almost all cases it will be found that the long cases so decorated originate in Lancashire, late eighteenth century.

Rack-and-snail striking. A system invented in 1676 by Edward Barlow which, except for turret clocks, has practically superseded the locking plate in this country. This type of striking made repeating clocks more practical.

Rack-and-snail striking

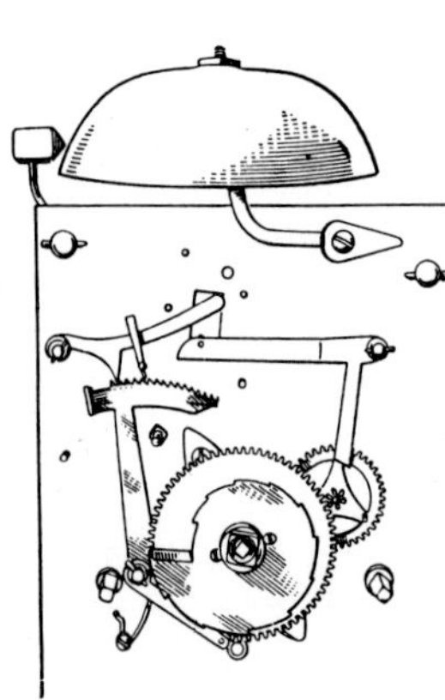

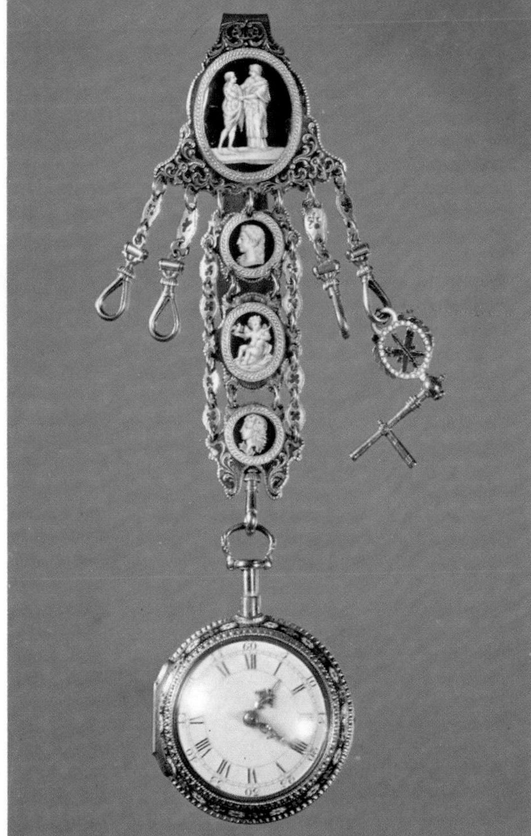

Rate. The regular amount by which a clock gains or loses in a stated period of time, usually per day.

Rating nut. The nut placed below the bob of the pendulum and used to regulate it. In some early nineteenth-century clocks the rating nut appears above the bob, in these cases movement of the rating nut is inverse. *See diagram under* Pendulums: gridiron.

Regulator. A high-grade long-case clock with compensation pendulum and possibly other refinements, such as roller bearings and jewelling. The hour is frequently read off a disc revolving behind the dial proper, and showing through an aperture.

Repeater. A clock or watch on which the hours, and generally also the quarters, and in rare cases the five minutes and even the minute, can be made to strike at will by the pulling of a cord, the pressing of a knob, etc. Repeating clocks were common until the end of the first quarter of the nineteenth century, when matches were introduced.

Repeating work. The motion work necessary to make a clock or watch repeat.

Ringing. The practice at the turn of the seventeenth and eighteenth centuries of surrounding the winding square holes, and sometimes the seconds hand arbor, with concentric decoration.

Ripple or **piecrust trim.** Wavy wood trim occasionally used to decorate the fronts of some small Connecticut clocks. Occasional.

Rise and fall. The subsidiary dial of a clock for pendulum regulation purposes.

Roman strike. A system devised by Joseph Knibb in the latter part of the seventeenth century to reduce the power needed, in spring-driven clocks especially, to drive the striking train. The hours are struck on two different-toned bells, one striking up to III and the other once for V, and twice for X. In clocks so made the IIII is usually marked IV. Sometimes found also in long-case clocks.

Saddle or **seatboard.** The wooden platform to which the movement of a tall clock is fastened. Also found in certain smaller clocks.

Sandglass or **hourglass.** An early device for measuring time consisting of two glass globes one over the other, containing fine sand which may pass from one to the other through a small opening. Their origin is unknown, but they are believed to date from the fourteenth century. Supporting frames are of wood or metal, and some from the Renaissance period, when they often appear in sets of four registering the four quarters of the hour, are very decorative. They, together with sundials, were the principal time-measuring device in the Middle Ages and in colonial America. They are usually anonymous and are frequently reproduced, but genuine ones up to the late eighteenth century are always made in two pieces and wrapped and bound round the junction.

Seconds dial. The subsidiary dial on a clock on which the seconds are marked.

Sedan clock. A large-dialled watch some 4–6 inches (10–15 cm) in diameter, with bow for hanging in a conveyance. Usually has a small watch type of movement behind the much larger dial.

Sheepshead. A lantern clock in which the chapter ring extends appreciably beyond the rectangular frame of the front dial plate.

Shelf clock. A clock, either weight- or spring-powered, designed to be placed on a shelf.

Skeleton dial. One in which the metal is cut away from the applied chapter ring, leaving only the numerals, minutes and interhorary marks.

Spandrels. Decorative cornerpieces found on clock dials for about a hundred years from 1675–80. Their design is a guide to the date of the clock.

Splat. The decorative panel, painted, veneered, or carved, placed at the top of many clocks.

Spoon. A hinged hook on the inner side of the top of the front of a long-case clock, so that when the door is closed the lower 'spoon-handled' part of the hook is pressed back and the upper hooked part pressed forward to keep the hood locked until the trunk door is opened again. Only found in early long-case clocks with rising hoods. *See diagram under* Hood, rising.

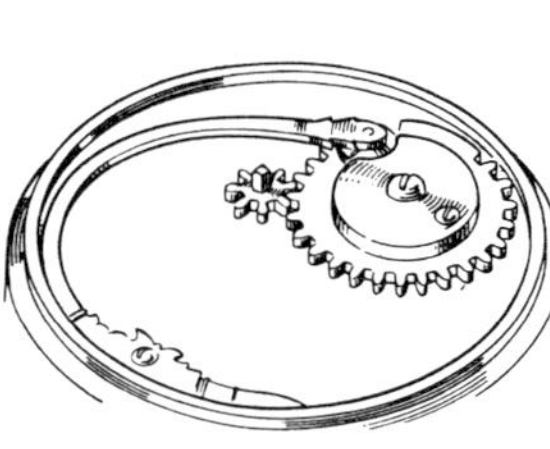

Stackfreed

Stackfreed. An early South German device of unknown origin to be found in very early watches, whereby a roller attached to a strong spring bears against a shaped snail or cam, the radius of which decreases. This cam is mounted on an incompletely cut wheel which is driven by a pinion on the mainspring arbor. The rate of uncoiling of the mainspring is checked in a diminishing degree as the roller presses against the diminishing diameter of the cam, until, after the spring has unwound about three turns, the pinion strikes the uncut part of the wheel and the watch has to be rewound, thus limiting the use of the spring to those turns of most nearly equal force. The principle of the lever underlies this as in the fusee. Both methods are found in the early sixteenth century, but tthe fusee ultimately supplanted the stackfreed everywhere.

Stencilled clocks. Name now given to many American shelf clocks which have painted and stencilled columns and splats. Also called 'Hitchcock' on account of the similarity of the decoration to that on Hitchcock chairs. Usually with wooden movements. Desirability depends on maker, type of movement, and condition of tablet and stencilling. *c.* 1825–40. Common.

Stop watch. One in which the seconds hand can be stopped or restarted at will without stopping the whole movement. In the earliest stop watches, *c.* 1680–90, the stop stopped the whole movement. They were used by doctors and were called 'pulse watches'.

Strike silent. Any mechanism that stops at will the striking or chiming of a clock. The early forms had a pin showing through the dial, attached to a lever, and had the dial marked 'N' and 'S' (Not and Strike). Later a subsidiary dial appeared for this purpose.

Sundial. Probably the earliest device to show the time of day by the shadow of a gnomon, or standard, on a base. They were the general method of recording time throughout the world until clocks became cheap enough for universal use. Multitudinous forms, both portable and static, have been produced over the ages. They were frequently provided with a compass and were adjustable for latitude. In the eighteenth century some were made to record time to the minute. The better ones in England and Europe were signed, but it is rare to find an American signature.

Sunray clock. A type developed in the late seventeenth century at the time of the cult of the *Roi Soleil*, Louis XIV. A central circular dial with carved wooden sun's rays emanating therefrom. Much copied today. Original clocks have the rays of hand-carved wood.

Suspension. Refers to the method of supporting the pendulum of a clock, spring, silk, knife edge.

Table clock. A clock with a horizontal dial, designed to be placed on a table and viewed from above.

Far right Table clock signed by John Drury but probably made by Markwick Markham, London. Tortoiseshell veneer with metal mounts, chased and gilt

English tower or turret clock. Science Museum

Tablet. The painted or otherwise decorated glass panel found in many American shelf and wall clocks. In clocks made to about 1830–5 the designs were hand-painted on the back of glasses. Scenic designs with gilt or gold-leaf borders were most common, while floral or conventional designs were also used. Most of the scenes appear to have been drawn as synthetic compositions and not from real life. Original tablets in fine condition are scarce and add much to the value of a clock. The restoration and reproduction of these reverse paintings is a specialized art, and few artists are now able to duplicate the appearance of original glasses.

The tablets in clocks since 1840 are usually printed decalcomanias, plain or coloured. Etched glasses or stencilled designs are also found in clocks of this period.

T-bridge. A type of pendulum support particularly used by Simon Willard in his banjo clocks. The suspension spring is pinned to a T-shaped unit which fits into and is held by a support on the clock movement.

Three-tier or **three-decker clock.** A variety of large weight-driven Connecticut shelf clock, the front of which usually consists of an upper and a lower door with a fixed panel between. *c.* 1828–50. Occasional.

Tidal dial. A dial that indicates daily the time of high tide at any given port. Not found on Continental clocks. The earliest English dials were made for London, and show high tide at new and full moon at 3 o'clock. Since the 24-hour cycle is completed each lunation, by having two circles, one fixed and marked 1–29½ (the days of the lunation) and the other movable, marked 1–12 twice over; if the time of high tide at any port at new moon be known, by placing that hour under 29½, the daily times of high tide for that port will be shown.

Time, Mean. Time calculated on an average basis of a day of 24 hours exactly. A year contains 365¼ mean days.

Time, Sidereal. Time as calculated by the successive passage of a selected star across the meridian. A sidereal day is 23 hours 56 minutes 4 seconds of mean time. There are 366 sidereal days in a mean year of 365¼ days.

Time, Solar. Time as calculated by the successive passages of the sun across the meridian, as shown on a sundial. This varies daily.

Ting-tang. The sounding of the quarters on two different-toned bells.

Tin-plate movement. A clock movement the plates of which are of tinned iron. Invented (patented 1859) in an attempt to save brass and reduce the cost of clocks. Small Connecticut clocks. Rare.

Torsion pendulum. A pendulum in which the bob rotates by the twisting and untwisting of a long suspension spring. Usually found on clocks designed to run a long time on one winding, as year clocks. A few eight-day, thirty-day, and year clocks with torsion pendulums were produced under one or more patents to Aaron Crane of Newark, New Jersey, and Boston, Massachusetts. *c.* 1840–60. Several styles, all rare.

Tourbillion. A watch in which the escapement is mounted on a revolving carriage, which carries it round. Invented by A. L. Breguet in 1801 to avoid positional error.

Tower clock. *See* Turret clock.

Train. A series of wheel and pinions geared together, forming the mechanism of a clock or watch. They are going, striking, chiming, musical, astronomical trains, etc.

Tropics. The interval in the celestial sphere between the parallels of latitude demarking the maximum declination of the sun north and south of the ecliptic. The Tropic of Cancer in the north and the Tropic of Capricorn in the south.

Trunk. That part of a long-case clock between the hood and the base.

Turret clock. A large clock as used in the towers of churches and other public buildings; often with two, three, or four dials. Probably the first clocks made in America were of this sort. Some in New England were made with wood movements.

Up and down. A subsidiary dial in highest-grade watches to indicate the extent to which the spring is run down.

Verge. Commonly used to designate the unit including the two pallets of the escapement; it is fixed to an arbor or directly to the crutch.

Visible escapement. An escapement which is visible or directly in front of the dial. Certain experimental models or shelf clocks by Eli Terry are rare examples.

Wagon springs. Flat-leaved springs used to power certain Connecticut shelf and wall clocks. Invented by Joseph Ives, also made by Atkins, Birge, and Fuller, and others. *c.* 1825–55. Rare.

Wag-on-the-wall. An American term applied to any wall clock in which the weights and pendulum are not enclosed in a case. Some of the earliest American clocks were of this sort. Many of the Connecticut wooden movements intended for tall clocks (*c.* 1800–25) were sold without cases and often used as wall clocks until a case might be provided. Some used in this way were provided with simple hoods to protect them from dust.

Warning. The partial unlocking of the striking train, which precedes the full release at the precise moment of striking.
Warning piece. That which arrests the warning wheel between the warning and the time to strike.
Warning wheel. A wheel in the striking train which carries a pin and which is arrested and then released by the warning piece.
Watch bow. The loop at the end of the pendant.
Watch paper. In England towards the end of the eighteenth century it was sometimes the practice to place a circular paper engraved with the maker's or repairer's name as a protection to the double case and as an advertisement. In the United States cloth was at first used, and later silk with a design or tender message. After 1800 printed papers appear.
Water clock. A contrivance used in Egyptian, Greek, and Roman times for measuring time by the regular flow of a stream of water changing the level in a container, on the surface of which floated a means of indication on a fixed scale. Water clocks in the seventeenth and eighteenth centuries were drums with internal pierced sloping divisions, causing the water to pass slowly from one to the other, making the drum revolve and its axis roll down a graduated framework. Very few genuine examples exist.
Weights. The masses used to provide motive power in fixed clocks. Usually of lead in early clocks, later cast iron. From the late seventeenth century onwards the best clocks had brass sheeting to the weights. In some primitive and country turret clocks, natural stone is used. Weights of many American grandfather clocks, especially those with wooden movements, were often cylinders of thin sheet iron (tin) filled with scrap iron or any other heavy material. These latter are called 'tin-can' weights.
Wheel, Centre. The wheel to which the cannon pinion is attached.
Wheel, Great. That which is attached to the going barrel, fusee, or, in weight-driven clocks, the gut barrel.
Year clock. A clock designed to go for one year with one winding.
Year, Sidereal. The period of one complete revolution of the earth round the sun.
Year, Tropical. The interval between two successive returns of the sun to the same tropic, or equinox.
Yorkshire clock. A broad and ill-proportioned long-case clock made for some years towards the end of the eighteenth century and early nineteenth.
Zodiac. A belt of the heavens outside which the sun, the moon, and the planets do not pass. Divided into twelve signs, each of 30 degrees, termed in astrology Celestial Houses: Aries (The Ram), Taurus (The Bull), Gemini (The Twins), Cancer (The Crab), Leo (The Lion), Virgo (The Virgin), Libra (The Balance), Scorpio (The Scorpion), Sagittarius (The Archer), Capricornus (The Goat), Aquarius (The Water Carrier), and Pisces (The Fishes).

A collection of 18th-century watch-cases. *Top* back-painted horn. *Middle two* shagreen, untanned leather or shark-skin, usually, as here dyed green. *Bottom left* plain leather. *Bottom right* tortoiseshell inlaid with silver

CARPETS AND RUGS

Ardebil carpet, Persia, 1539. Originally decorated the shrine of Shaykh Safi, ancestor of the Safavid dynasty. Victoria & Albert Museum

The covering of floors is as old as civilization. The first carpet was probably nothing more than a few rushes or straw to form the floor covering, but that at least was something upon the cold stone or earth, and better than nothing. Later the reeds were woven or plaited to make a rush matting; then came patterns and colours and, finally, weaving and embroidery to make durability and softness march with decoration and comfort, not only for floors but also for walls and furniture.

The earliest authenticated records of carpet weaving in its present form are to be found in the Assyrian and Babylonian bas reliefs, *c.* 700 B.C., but there is no doubt that a substantial carpet-making industry had existed from a much earlier period. There are many references in Greek and Roman literature to the magnificence of Eastern rugs, which the opulence and luxury of the Oriental satrap demanded. Wear and tear, combined with the comparative fragility of their constituent silks and wools, have prevented the survival of any of these products of the looms of deep antiquity.

We have, however, many examples of antique carpets and rugs four or five centuries old. These early specimens have never been surpassed in quality of fabric, design, and colour, and although Oriental carpets have kept the traditional patterns and techniques, it is sad to record a history of gradual decline in the art, albeit with many occasional flashes of brilliance and inspiration, but none, it seems, equalling the oldest pieces. During the late eighteenth and almost the whole of the nineteenth centuries the carpet industry of Asia Minor and Persia became organized for export, and large shipments were sent to Europe and America, very largely to the detriment of the general quality, which, by virtue of the painstaking nature of the hand knotting, could not be maintained under the increasing pressure of demand. Nevertheless, the discriminating collector may still find excellent pieces of a high quality if he knows what to look for, and it is among this class and age of carpet that there is great opportunity. Those older pieces of great antiquity are rarer than pearls, although during the period between the two World Wars an effort was made to revive the ancient glory of the Persian carpet industry, and many fine rugs were woven.

One of the most remarkable features of Oriental rug weaving is that the industry is so spontaneous and widespread. From Asia Minor to China; from Caucasia to India, rugs are woven by identical methods, materials, and dyes, but the patterns and colourings differ enormously and reflect the widely differing temperaments of their makers.

PERSIAN

The very finest of all the great carpets and rugs come from Persia. The Persian carpet at its best is worthy to be ranked among the great examples of creative art. Springing naturally from a luxury-loving and refined civilization, and finding at hand an unsurpassed quality of wool from the highlands of Persia, combined with a natural feeling for colour and form in all classes of its people, it is not surprising that many of these lovely pieces are so beautiful. There are secrets of dyeing: the ability to use brilliant colours impervious to strong sunlight and time alike, yet applied without damage to the sometimes delicate fabric. The apogee of Persian craftsmanship seems to have been reached during the reigns of Tashmak (1524–77) and Shah Abbas (1588–1629), and it is in this period that a number of the most famous carpets now existing were woven, usually under royal decree or patronage, and irrespective of cost.

The Persian designs can be classified as medallion, hunting, garden, vase, and prayer. These designs are the basic constituents of Persian carpet weaving, and are the inspiration of much of the Oriental textile designs. (*See* Glossary.)

Persian carpets of certain districts may be identified by the special knot which is used in a certain district and by the materials of which the carpet is woven. These basic materials are cotton, linen, wool, or silk, and often a combination of two or more. The knots are the Sehna and the Ghiordes knots. (*See* Glossary.)

CAUCASIAN

The designs of Caucasian rugs, which come from the Caucasian Mountains between the Caspian and Black Seas, show both Persian and Chinese influence, but retain strong characteristics of their own. The employment of the local highland wool, which is unsurpassed, combined with excellent weaving, has given these rugs lasting quality, and many examples of merit exist.

Among the earliest specimens are the famous Armenian dragon rugs, woven in the sixteenth century. The main motifs consist of conventional upright dragons, forming panels, flowering trees with birds, and often elephants and camels. A pleasing shade of soft rose relieved by dark blue or black is the predominant colour. The dragon design has influenced many later specimens.

The knotting is almost exclusively Ghiordes.

The most prevalent motif is of jewel shapes, both diamond and octagonal in form, with use of latch hook in white or cream. The detail is generally of conventional small flowers.

TURKISH

Turkish rugs from Anatolia and Asia Minor are probably the most numerous of antique rugs to be found in Europe, largely due to the Venetian and

Florentine Levantine trade. Large numbers were imported from the fifteenth century onwards and, owing to their distinctive designs and fine quality, were not used on floors but as wall hangings, and more often as table coverings, a custom which is still in general use in Holland. Many sixteenth- and seventeenth-century painters, notably Holbein, featured these rugs in their pictures, and they have, in fact, influenced textile design throughout Europe. These rugs come from Ladik, Kouba, Ghiordes, and Kir-Shehr, and the main design is usually what is called the Mihrab representation of the Oriental mosque arch, often embellished by a hanging lamp between pillars.

Above, left Heriz small silk carpet, Northern Iran. Christie, Manson & Woods

Left Caucasian Kouba rug, late 18th century. Christie, Manson & Woods

Above, right Turkish prayer rug, silk warp and wool weft and pile, Ghiordes knotting, *c.* 1600. Metropolitan Museum of Art

They were, of course, originally intended for and used as prayer rugs, and many, once the property of wealthy Moslems, are of incredible quality and striking beauty. During the fourteenth and fifteenth centuries the Ottoman Turks invaded Persia on several occasions, and they enriched their own carpet and rug industries by importing skilled Persian craftsmen. The influence of these carpet weavers is most marked and a tradition of design and quality was established. The greatest period was during the reigns of Selim the Great and Suliman the Magnificent, when the Persian carpet weaving was at its zenith. Contemporary specimens bear a marked resemblance to Persian rugs, but the national characteristics are clearly apparent. The flowing lines familiar in the finest products of Tabriz and Ispahan have become bold and angular. The use of stronger colours and realistic flowers are other distinguishing features.

The Persian medallion with matching cornerpieces can be seen in Ushak carpets. Kufic borders kindred to Caucasian designs were used in many rugs.

Far left, above Lotto carpet, Anatolia, late 16th century

Above 'Star' Ushak carpet, Turkey, 1585

TURKOMAN

Most rugs from Turkestan are woven in traditional variations of the same motif, the octagonal 'guls' (flowers) known as the 'elephant's foot', and generally dyed in deep, glowing Turanian red, with dark blue and black.

CHINESE TURKESTAN

The influence of Chinese Art is clearly defined in these rugs.

The plate medallion, cloud bands, and lotus, pomegranate, and peony from the motifs are all distinctly Chinese, but in subtle manner the rugs show Persian influence.

The knotting generally is not fine; the merit of these rugs is in the extremely varied and unusual colouring – yellows, lacquer red, blues in infinite variety.

The main types are from Khotan and Kashgar, and are often called Samarkand.

٠,١,٢,٣,٤,٥,٦,٧,٨,٩, سنة
0, 1, 2, 3, 4, 5, 6, 7, 8, 9, SANA (YEAR)

The Arabic numerals with the English, for identification of dates.

European

When carpets first came to Europe from the Near East in the fifteenth and sixteenth centuries they were used as covers for tables, cupboards, and chests, or were placed before the altar in church or chapel. Only kings and the higher nobility used foot carpets, and they were a mark of rank. A small number of knotted-pile carpets in imitation of Oriental ones were made in Europe. English examples date from the sixteenth and early seventeenth centuries. Some of the patterns follow Turkish models, others are like contemporary English embroideries. It was in France, at the Savonnerie, that a Western style of carpet was created which was taken up by different countries when the use of floor carpets became more general in the eighteenth century. But Oriental carpets were also imitated with the needle, working in tent and cross stitch on canvas. In the eighteenth century this was developed into a purely European type of needlework carpet, especially in England. Besides these, cheaper forms of carpeting were used in the sixteenth, seventeenth, and increasingly in the eighteenth centuries. Apart from tapestry, woollen cloth with a nap, patterned ply weaving, and moquette (woven as a velvet or plush) were used, the narrow woven strips being sewn together.

Top American rug with primitive design of a lion with birds, flowers, and beavers in the foreground, 19th century. American Museum in Britain

Centre English rug, wool on canvas with a design of lilies, *c.* 1860

Bottom French Savonnerie carpet woven for the Apollo Gallery, second half of the 17th century

American

Embroidered rugs were popular from 1800 to 1835. Rugs, braided or woven on the loom, from rags, were also used, but their exact period remains unknown. Carpets were home-woven about 1820 from multicoloured woollen yarns and were probably in use until about 1850. Double-woven carpets were being produced by the professional coverlet weavers in the 1820s and 1830s, but all large-sized floor coverings were very expensive, and the average housewife produced smaller rugs from scrap material. It is probable that at first these were scraps of cloth sewn to a fabric base and later were strips hooked through the base.

Yarn-sewn rugs are those in the bed-rug technique which are sometimes described as embroidered, needle-tufted, or reed-stitched. In this technique a homespun linen or tow ground fabric was used and the pile surface was formed of several strands of two-ply yarn. The yarn was sewn through the ground, taking a short stitch and leaving a loop on the surface. Another stitch was taken close to the first and in a line following the curves of the design. Sometimes the pile is very long and sometimes exceedingly short. Rugs with short loops made of fine yarns may have been intended for use as table rugs. This technique produces a very soft, flexible rug. The colours usually found in yarn-sewn rugs are the ones made from natural dyestuffs. Rugs in this technique were probably first made some time in the middle of the eighteenth century and continued until about 1830.

Patched rugs may be constructed in two general ways. The basic fabric may be new or used homespun linen, tow or woollen cloth, or it may be cotton sacking. The scraps of woollen cloth may be sewn to the surface of this ground material in two ways. In the first technique, which has been called button or patchwork, the pile cloth was cut into small square or circular patches ½–1 inch (1.3–2.5 cm) across. These were folded in fourths and sewn down at the folded point to the ground. When sewn close together the effect is the same as the hooked rugs which have been sheared.

The second way, sometimes called chenille or caterpillar, was to cut strips ¼–1½ inches (0.63–3.8 cm) wide which were shirred and sewn to the ground. Sometimes the wider strips, cut on the bias, were folded through the centre and shirred before being sewn on, and sometimes the strips were shirred through the centre and sewn on with the two edges standing straight up. They were also constructed by cutting the strips very narrow, on the straight of the goods, and sewing them on flat so that they form small cartridge pleats and look very much like an unclipped hooked rug. Most of the specimens seem to have originated between 1840 and 1860.

Hooked rugs form the third group in regard to technique. The background material for these rugs was homespun linen, factory-woven cotton or burlap. The cloth scraps were cut in strips and a hook was used to draw these up in loops from the back of the ground fabric. Sometimes the loops were cut when made, sometimes not; and in some rugs the loops were varied in length to give a raised or sculptured effect to parts of the design.

The best material for the pile was woollen rags,

Top Yarn sewn American rug, floral design in natural colours. Courtesy of New York State Historical Association

Above Shirred strip American wool rug, made with Caterpillar technique. Courtesy of New York State Historical Association

Below Hooked American rug, wool on linen ground, floral design with leafy scroll border, Waldoboro, Maine, 1825–50. Courtesy of Henry Francis du Pont Winterthur Museum

and the more cotton fabric that is found in a rug the later in period it may generally be presumed to be. The ones hooked through a linen foundation are usually earlier than the ones with burlap. Burlap was probably not used to any extent before 1850. Almost any colour may be found in a hooked rug. Hooked rugs in general probably date from 1840 to 1900. They come not only from New England but from Pennsylvania and other states, where the hooking is likely to be coarser and much cotton fabric included. The designs used for hooked rugs encompass almost everything known to tradition.

Among the simplest patterns, which were ideal for using up the accumulation of varicoloured scraps unsuitable for a formal design, are: block and basketweave, which consist of squares or other geometrical forms, filled with stripes running at right angles to the stripes in adjacent forms; wave or zigzag where one colour follows another in undulating rows looking like mosaic work; inch (2.5 cm) square with multicoloured squares resembling a simple quilt design from which it may well have come; log cabin which is definitely like the quilt pattern of the same name and shows the same variations of shading; shell or fish-scale design which is a very old pattern of overlapping arcs. There are also repeating geometrical forms such as circles, squares, diamonds and medallions which are often filled with stylized flowers.

In the floral designs, the flowers in vase or jar or loose sprays or bands of flowers may occupy almost the entire rug area or may be confined to a central medallion with a scrolled border surrounding it. The flowers became less stylized and more realistic as the Victorian era advanced.

Animal forms in hooked rugs may be early but are more common in the Victorian period. They include dogs, stags, parrots, lions, swans, cats with kittens, and various unnameable species. Landscape designs are also found and these may include buildings or animals. Nautical designs are more common near the seacoast where some of them were probably made by sailors.

Patriotic, fraternal, and symbolic designs are not so common and are, with the exception of the popular eagle of the 1820s, usually of rather late vintage. A common patriotic design celebrated the centennial of the Declaration of Independence in 1876. Along with these Victorian patterns go the rugs with mottoes, such as *God Bless Our Home*, *Good Luck*, etc. Many of the Victorian designs seem to be derived from the designs for Berlin work which were published in *Godey's Lady's Book* and *Peterson's Magazine*.

Commercial designs were certainly available by 1870 when one Edward Sands Frost, a tin pedlar from Biddeford, Maine, was already selling his designs. These he printed in colours on burlap by means of metal stencils.

Hooked rugs are found in all shapes and sizes. There are half-round threshold or 'Welcome' mats and round, oval, square, and rectangular rugs of all sizes from 18 inches (45.7 cm) square to large carpets and hall and stair runners.

Floorcloths or oilcloths, made of canvas or linen heavily coated with paint, were fairly common in the eighteenth century. In the first half of the century they were decorated with a design in imitation of marble-tiled floors, but later design kept pace with the times, and imitations of Wilton or Brussels carpeting are known. These floor coverings were so perishable that almost none have survived.

The Oriental 'Carpitt' in Colonial America

Rugs from the Orient have enjoyed distinction in the West from earliest times. Rome, Byzantium, Venice, France, and Flanders have in turn exerted extraordinary efforts to secure them. They came rather late to England, less than a century before the colonists brought with them to America an appreciation of the Oriental rug as an object of luxury.

Knowledge of the appearance of the early examples to reach Europe is gained from paintings. Italian frescoes of the fourteenth century depict almost exclusively simple repeat panels containing either stylized birds or animals. As the fifteenth century progressed animal styles continued, frequently more complex in execution and with such motifs as the dragon and phoenix, an early design migrant from China. At the same time, highly developed abstractions appeared in large numbers, based primarily on tree, shrub, and flower motifs in which geometric drawing becomes evident. This second type soon became predominant.

Strong evidence of rug importations into western Europe is furnished by Van Eyck and Memling, whose paintings show rugs which parallel those depicted by such fifteenth-century Italian masters as Ghirlandaio.

TUDOR ENGLAND

The insular position of England and her distance from sources of supply delayed introduction of these rugs to any extent until the sixteenth century. It was time for a distinguished collector to appear and he was at hand – Henry VIII. His new palace of Hampton Court was not a fortress, but matched in luxury the Fontainebleau of Francis I. Henry VIII had almost certainly seen a sufficient number of rugs on the Continent to excite his interest. He sought the proper connections and found that Cardinal Wolsey, through Rome and particularly through Venetian traders, could supply the needs of Hampton Court for the prized Oriental weavings.

From Holbein, court painter to the King, much can be learned regarding the colour, design, and scale of the rugs obtained. One of his portraits shows the King in characteristic stance on a Turkish rug with indented repeat medallions of a type now known as a 'Star' Ushakh, in a style which persisted into the eighteenth century. In Hans Eworth's portrayal of the royal family the floor is covered with another of Cardinal Wolsey's carpets, a well-known type with a central medallion on a rich red ground. This too is a Turkish rug from the vicinity of Ushakh, a type which has continued in more or less degenerate form almost to our own day.

In Holbein's *Ambassadors* at the National Gallery, London, two envoys stand one on either side of a table covered with a small rug differing in design from the rugs in the royal collection and almost entirely geometric in character. It probably came from an outlying village, not from one of the great weaving centres.

The English nobility were quick to follow the royal example. The Montague family have at least two rugs of the 'Star' Ushakh type, one of which has embroidered in the end selvage the date *1580*. These two rugs are in the collection of the present Duke of Buccleuch and have been published many times.

IN AMERICA

There are no seventeenth-century portraits of colonial owners of Oriental rugs, and not until the following century do these appear. It is therefore necessary to look elsewhere for some indication of their arrival in the colonies. For the time being, inventories provide us with the only information available, and as they are mentioned in inventory after inventory, it is apparent that the colonists must have valued the Oriental as much as their contemporaries in England.

Contrary to general opinion, a number of colonists were men of some property on arrival, or soon created it through superior enterprise in their new environment. This was particularly true in New England, where ships were built almost at once and ocean trade with the West Indies and Europe began to flourish. Successful merchants managed to acquire the means to supply themselves with 'Turkey carpitts' in comparatively short time. Such a one was William Clarke of Salem, the inventory of whose estate, taken after his death in 1647, just twenty-seven years after the landing of the Pilgrims at Plymouth, included the following: '1 Turkey carpitt' valued at £1, and '1 old Turkey carpitt' valued at 8*s*. These are in contrast to entries of '1 Red Rugg, 1 Greene Rugg', etc., in the same inventory. This early example is the forerunner of many as the century advanced.

It is generally stated that carpets were used as a covering for tables and not on the floor, and it is undoubtedly true that many were so used. However, it seems wrong to argue that they were never used on the floor, in the light of the following announcement from the *Boston Gazette*, 26 March 1754: 'To be sold at public vendu at the dwelling house of the late Ebenezer Holmes in King Street, Boston . . . a large Turkey carpet measuring eleven and a half by eighteen and a half feet. . . .' This could obviously have been used only on the floor and in a room of considerable size.

The acquisition of Oriental carpets could be made at that time, legally, only through England, or beyond the legal pale through smuggling. A successful raid on a Dutch or Spanish merchantman might also have yielded such a prize.

An indication of the esteem in which the Turkey carpet was held is seen in an advertisement in the *Boston News-Letter*, 20 February 1755: 'Stolen out of a house in Boston a Turkey carpet of various colors, about a yard and a half in length, and a yard in width fringed at each end. Three dollars reward.' In pre-Revolutionary America the dollars were the Spanish milled dollars which were important in the financial dealings of the day, and their value was considerable, so that the reward was actually a high one.

Colonies such as Pennsylvania and Virginia had many families of wealth and culture, but as these colonies had no such stringent laws regarding the inventories of the deceased as existed in New England, more is to be learned from New England, particularly Massachusetts, in this respect.

Up to the present time, no American family has been able to offer one shred of evidence of an existing Oriental carpet which has come down to them from their seventeenth- or eighteenth-century ancestors.

PORTRAITS SHOWING ORIENTAL RUGS

The only visual evidence of the types of Oriental rugs known in early America is found in portraits, particularly in four that are very well known. These are:

1. John Smibert's *Portrait of Bishop Berkeley and his Entourage*, done in 1729 during Berkeley's two-year sojourn in America spent chiefly in Newport, Rhode Island. This, which is now in the Yale University Art Gallery, New Haven, Connecticut, shows the group seated at a table covered with an Oriental carpet.

2. Robert Feke's *Portrait of Isaac Royall and his Family*, painted in 1741, is now owned by the Law School of Harvard University, Cambridge, Massachusetts. Isaac Royall's fine house at Medford is one of the historic New England houses open to the

public. A copy of Feke's picture hangs over the mantel where the original once hung. Feke was familiar with Smibert's picture, as he has copied the arrangement, and shows the carpet in a similar way on the table, but the carpet itself is entirely different, which argues for the actuality of the original in Royall's possession. Although of the same type, it is of later date than the rug in the Berkeley portrait.

3. John Singleton Copley's *Portrait of Colonel Jeremiah Lee*, 1768, shows the wealthy Marblehead merchant standing on a Smyrna carpet. This portrait is now in the Wadsworth Atheneum, Hartford, Connecticut.

4. Gilbert Stuart's 'Lansdowne' *Washington*, 1796, is not properly of the colonial period. It shows Washington standing on an eighteenth-century medallion 'Ushakh', definitely of a late eighteenth-century origin and lacking much of the refinement of the mid-eighteenth-century type.

TERMINOLOGY

It has become the custom to use the word rug for what our ancestors in England and America called the 'Turkey carpitt', and the word carpet is generally reserved today for the machine-made product, acquired in strips and used to cover an entire room. The carpets of the eighteenth century, and earlier, were more frequently used on the table, but as trade made them more common they were used on the floor. The advertisement of 1754 makes it clear that Boston had homes where Oriental rugs were used on the floor in mid-century. After the Revolution, when trade directly with the East and Near East was undertaken, Oriental rugs must have become still more familiar.

While carpets took their place on the floor, the 'rugg' remained what it had been, a cover for a bed. What is called today a coverlet was often recorded as a 'bed rug'. The steamer rug represents a survival of the old use of the term.

COLLECTIONS

Recognition of the importance of the Oriental rug in colonial and post-colonial decoration has advanced rapidly in recent years. Henry F. du Pont, in furnishing the matchless series of American rooms at the Winterthur Museum, Winterthur, Delaware, was a pioneer. The buildings of the restored colonial capital of Williamsburg, Virginia, show an admirable selection of authentic types in the Governor's Palace, the Wythe house, Brush-Everard house, and elsewhere. The American Wing of the Metropolitan Museum in New York will soon have rugs especially chosen to agree with the period of each room. The houses in Fairmount Park, Philadelphia, under the care of the Philadelphia Museum of Art, the houses at Old Deerfield, Massachusetts, and at the Shelburne Museum, Shelburne, Vermont, as well as interiors in the museums in most of our large cities, show the use of such rugs as were known in early America.

Glossary

Abruzzi. *See* Italy.

Afghan. Afghan rugs are coarser in texture and design, but follow tradition of the other Turkoman types, looking rather like a much coarser Bokhara (*q.v.*).

Alpujarras. *See* Spain.

Aubusson. Knotted-pile carpets were made at Aubusson from 1742 and at nearby Felletin from 1786. An upright loom was used as at the Savonnerie, but the carpets were considerably cheaper. Women, who were not allowed to work at the *basse-lisse*, and children, were employed for low wages. Eighteenth-century Aubusson carpets were designed by the Court painters and were of excellent quality. Tapestry or smooth-faced carpets were also made, especially in the nineteenth century. With the Revolution the production of moquette carpets (*q.v.*) was introduced.

Axminster. Thomas Whitty began the weaving of knotted-pile carpets, at first inspired by Turkish models and then learning from Parisot at Fulham (*q.v.*) (1750–5). In 1757–9 he won three awards from the Royal Society of Arts, submitting six carpets for the 1759 competition. His prices were more moderate than Moore or Passavant, and his industry thrived and was continued by his son. The large carpet made for Carlton House (*c.* 1790, at Buckingham Palace) and a fine carpet at Ramsbury Manor, Wiltshire, are surviving examples of his work. A little later Axminster carried out import orders for Brighton Pavilion (1810–20). Parts of these still exist. The Victoria and Albert Museum has a carpet of this period, or slightly later. Before the Axminster workshops closed down in 1835 two important carpets were made for the Goldsmiths' Hall and the Sultan of Turkey. The looms were taken over by Wilton (*q.v.*).

Beauvais. Knotted-pile carpets in the Savonnerie manner were made between 1780 and 1792 and again for a few years under Napoleon.

Belouchistan (Turkoman). Early rugs often in prayer designs, the use of blue and lustrous yarn, combining with the coppery red, giving an iridescent effect to otherwise heavy colours.

Bergama (Turkish). Bergama rugs usually have a Mihrab on each end, giving a balanced design. These rugs, woven entirely of very lustrous wool, though not fine in texture, have pleasing colours, the borders bearing a marked affinity to the Caucasian weaves.

Beshire or **Bushire** (Turkoman). Carpets actually made in Bokhara City. They provide a variation in the design strongly reminiscent of the Herat 'fish' design, but the colouring is the usual red, often on dark blue; a strong yellow outlines the design.

Bessarabia. *See* Rumania.

Bokhara or **Bokara** (Turkoman). These rugs have long been popular in England, and are, in fact, from three tribes; the Tekke is the most esteemed, the 'guls' being well balanced and the side borders following variations of the same motif. The end borders are usually latch hook in diamond formation, and conventional tree-of-life forms. The yarns are very fine, often knotted 300–400 to the square inch (6.5 sq. cm) on a weft and warp usually of wool, but sometimes of fine hair. Woven in prayer rugs and also in fine camel bags.

Brussels carpets. *See* Moquette.

Central Eastern Persian carpets. These come from Feraghan, Herat, and Khorassan (*qq.v.*). They are all very similar in design, often with conventional flowers on a dark field, generally blue.

Chichi (Caucasian). These rugs have small jewel

effects in the centre panel, with multitudinous borders.

Djoshagan (Persian). Generally of palmette or vase designs, these rugs are simpler in design than those of Ispahan or Tabriz, with blue or deep red predominating. Knot: Ghiordes.

Donegal. Alexander Morton organized the weaving of coarse-knotted carpets in Donegal at the request of the Congested Districts Board in 1898. Pile carpets are still woven there.

Ersari (Turkoman). In this type the octagonal 'gul' is usually enclosed by bands forming a distinct diamond design.

Exeter. Claude Passavant, a native of Basel, and successful wool merchant and manufacturer at Exeter, started the subsidiary enterprise of making expensive hand-knotted carpets. He bought up Parisot's equipment in 1755 and took many of his men to Exeter. In 1758 he was a competitor for the Royal Society of Arts prize and gained an award. A beautifully made and excellently designed carpet by him in the Victoria and Albert Museum is marked 'Exon 1757' and may be the prize-winning piece. Another dated 1758 is at Petworth, Sussex. Giuseppe Baretti, secretary of the Royal Academy, wrote a favourable account of his factory in 1760 and reported on his success; but his carpets, which were more expensive than Thomas Moore's of Moorfields (*q.v.*), are extremely rare.

Feraghan (Persian). Woven with a Sehna knot, it has enjoyed great popularity in this country, and varies slightly in the treatment of the traditional Herat design; the two most distinctive effects known as Guli Hinnai and Mina Khani. Knot: usually Sehna.

Finland. The Ryijy rugs of Finland are in the old Norse tradition of knotted-pile technique, which may go back to the Danish Bronze Age quite independently of Near Eastern influence. Although derived from Norway and Sweden, in the sixteenth century Finnish pile weaving already enjoyed a special reputation. Made primarily for bed coverings, sleigh rugs, or horse cloths, they have a very long knotted pile, but the ground texture of wool or linen is not thick and there are usually ten to twenty shoots of weft between the rows of knots. The knotting

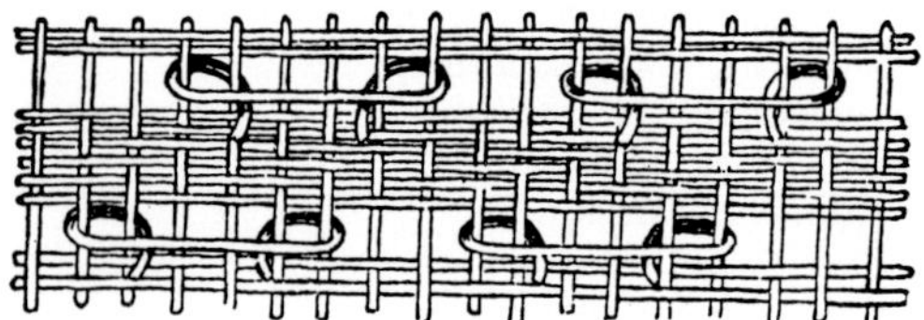

technique is also curious and varied. Made on a narrow loom, two widths were joined together, but a wide loom was also used. Patterns vary from plain-colour weavings and geometric motifs to simple floral patterns. It was customary for a girl to make a rug for her dowry, and many such pieces are dated, though few after 1860. The making of these exceptionally attractive rugs has been revived in the present century.

Frome. William Jesser, of Frome, entered (unsuccessfully) for the Royal Society of Arts prize for hand-knotted carpets in 1759, but nothing further is known about his manufacture.

Fulham. Peter Parisot, an ex-Capuchin monk from Lorraine, procured the patronage of the Duke of Cumberland for a carpet-knotting factory in Fulham. He is supposed to have employed as many as a hundred workmen, many from the Savonnerie, but owing to extravagances he was forced to sell up within five years (1755). A portrait of the Duke, dated 1755, is probably his work, and pile fire screens are occasionally found.

Garden carpets. Persian carpet design showing a formal garden with alleys, trees, and pools.

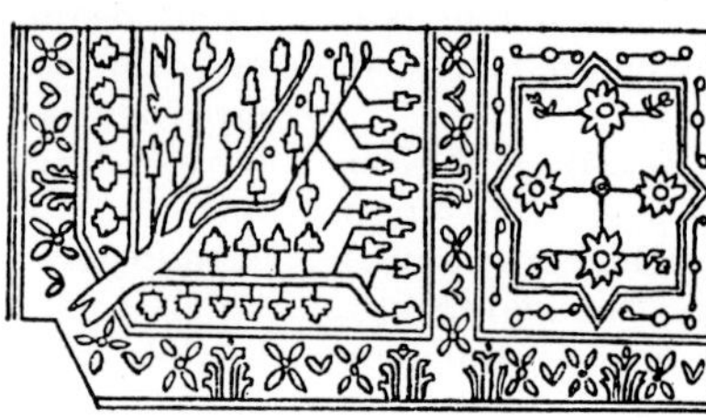

Ghiordes. These rugs are the finest of the Turkish types and represent the apex of Turkish weaving. The knot is usually Turkish; yarns are very fine, warp and weft often being of silk. The colours are very varied, while the borders usually consist of bold conventional floral designs, beautifully treated.

Ghiordes or **Turkish knot.** Used in most carpets from Turkey and some from Persia.

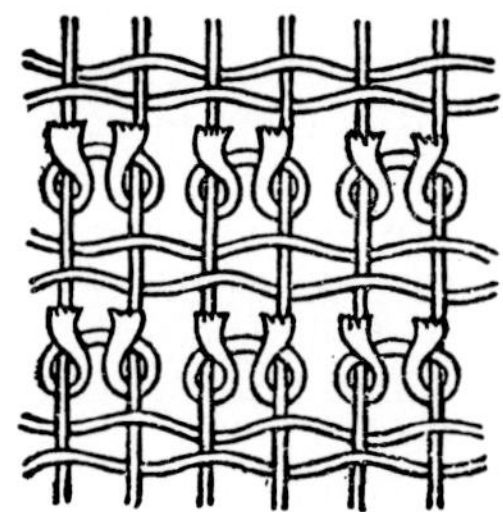

Ghiordes or Turkish Knot

Guls. *See* Turkoman 'guls'.

Hamadan (Persian). The marketing centre for Kurdish rugs (*q.v.*) which are often known by this name. Heavy, long pile of great durability, rather coarse in knotting, but well coloured, designs often embellished with animal figures. Are often found under the general 'Persian' classification.

Herat. These carpets are the aristocrats of the Central Eastern Persian group. The design most closely associated with this weave is a close conventionalized all-over effect. With a recurring leaf or 'fish' motif and small rosettes. This is copied throughout Persia, ground shade is usually dark blue, and a distinguishing feature of fine specimens is a soft green border. Knot: Ghiordes or Sehna.

Hila (Caucasian). These rugs often have a small centre medallion with matching cornerpieces, the subsidiary design being a clearly defined cone. Ice blue is the distinguishing shade of these rugs.

Hispano-Moresque. *See* Spain.

Hunting Carpets. Persian carpet design with elaborate hunting scenes, realistically depicted.

Hunting carpet

Ispahan (Persian). The great carpets so called were probably made in Herat. Medallion and vase designs were used, and a wide range of colours, the composition being very well balanced. Knot: Sehna.

Italy. Pope Clement XI founded a carpet-weaving establishment at San Michele, Rome, in the Savonnerie manner (early eighteenth century). Peasant weavers in the Abruzzi highlands and in Sardinia have continued to weave rugs which are really stout coverings for beds, marriage coffers, or carts, although knotted-pile pieces and kilims are very occasionally found. Generally they are ply or double-cloth weaves (called *Karamania*) or woven with a floated-weft pattern. The patterns have a marked geometric tendency, but derive from traditional Late Medieval and Renaissance designs, just as the better-known Perugia linen and cotton fabrics do.

Kabistan. Districts from which the principal rugs of the Caucasus come. The rugs considered the finest of the type are from the Baku district, and include the Kouba and Hila rugs.

Kasak (Caucasian). These rugs bear panelled designs of bold character and in striking colours. They are deep-pile rugs and have a masculine character entirely their own. Strong deep red, clear yellow, and blue are the predominant shades. Woven with extra weft threads, the pile lies flat and is very strong.

Kashan (Persian). Medallion and prayer designs predominate, woven in wool or silk; they are orthodox in conception, and are notable for the use of ivory as a ground shade; the most favoured colours are rich tones of red or blue. The famous Polonaise rugs, remarkable for the use of gold and silver thread as a base and the unusual colour effects in pastel greens and browns, were probably woven in Kashan. It is thought that they were woven as gifts to foreign monarchs by the order of Shah Abbas. Knot: usually Sehna.

Kerman. This Persian district has produced many rugs of merit, although they are usually of later manufacture. Medallion and tree designs are popular, introducing floral effects in graceful intertwining vines. The yarn used is rather soft. The colours are beautifully toned, and are particularly suitable for English furnishings. Knot: Sehna.

Khorassan (Persian). In these carpets the yarn is generally softer; the knotting is fine and the general effect is more splendid than Feraghan carpets (*q.v.*), but they are not so durable. Knot: usually Sehna.

Kidderminster. Probably the oldest centre of rug production in England, the early pieces were smooth-faced and without a true pile – that is to say, a cheap form of carpeting. Kidderminster carpets were often mentioned in inventories: for example, '4 carpetts of Kidderminster stuff', in the Countess of Leicester's inventory, 1634. Two-ply or double-cloth carpets were made there from 1735, when Pearsall & Brown built their factory. But in 1753 Brussels carpets or moquette (*q.v.*) were introduced by Brown in rivalry with Wilton. A thousand looms were at work in 1807, rising to 2,020 in 1838. Jacquard looms were introduced about 1825, and the use of jute rather earlier.

Kilmarnock. Double-cloth carpeting was made from 1778, and three-ply was perfected in 1824.

Kir-Shehr. These rugs show typical Turkish designs. The Mihrab is usually filled with a very angular tree, border and panel are conventional, while the colours are bright and virile, varying reds being a feature of the weave. Warp and weft are usually wool.

Kouba. The design of these rugs consists often of independent flowerheads, palmettes, and eight-pointed stars, with well-balanced borders carrying the same motifs. Some early examples show an elongated panel with interlocking tree forms.

Kula. These Turkish rugs are less varied in colour than the Ghiordes rugs (*q.v.*), and the panels of the Mihrab are usually fully patterned. Borders are popular with repeating floral miniature motifs.

Kurdish (Persian). Nomadic tribes wove these rugs. The virile designs are often bold and the colours limited. The yarns employed are generally coarse, but the effects are pleasing and the wearing quality excellent, often found in long runners. One of the outstanding types is the Bidjar, probably the heaviest of all Oriental rugs. Woven on a twofold warp, designs are diversified, but often a bold medallion and cornerpieces on a plain field and borders with Herat influence. Knot: Ghiordes.

Ladik (Turkish). These rugs follow the Ghiordes (*q.v.*) design very closely, though the use of Rhodian lily motifs is a distinguishing feature.

Medallion design. Persian designs common in all Eastern decoration. The Ardebil carpet in the Victoria and Albert Museum is considered the finest example of this type.

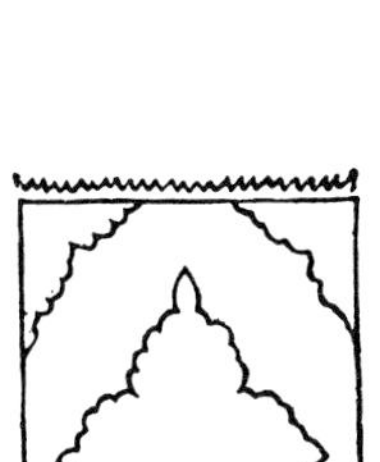
Medallion design

Moorfields. Thomas Moore, of Moorfields, successfully competed for a Royal Society of Arts award in 1757. An account of his workshop, where hand-knotted carpets of the highest quality were produced, was given by Lady Mary Coke in 1768. A carpet was then being woven for Lord Coventry, to cost 140 guineas. Moore was extensively used by the architect Robert Adam, and a number of his carpets have survived in beautiful condition, as well as Adam's designs for them at the Soane Museum. The carpet at Syon House is inscribed 'by Thos. Moore 1769'. There are two at Osterley, made about 1775 and 1778; and Chippendale recommended him to Sir Edward Knatchbull in 1778, who paid him £57 for a carpet for Mersham le Hatch. Moore's carpets in neoclassical design were sumptuous additions to the houses they furnished.

Moquette. Woven on the principle of velvet, but in coarser wool and linen materials, moquette is allied with plushes and Utrecht velvet as an upholstery or carpeting material. Tournai seems to have been its chief centre in the Middle Ages. It was much used in the sixteenth to eighteenth centuries. Abbeville was the chief centre of production in France from 1667. Antwerp, Amsterdam, Utrecht, and Leyden and Thuringia, in Germany, were other centres of production. Known as 'Brussels carpet' in England, it was made at Norwich and Bradford besides Kidderminster and Wilton. The use of the Jacquard loom greatly increased and cheapened production in the early nineteenth century.

Morris, William. His first carpets were made about 1878 at Hammersmith (mark: hammer, river, and letter M); from 1881 at Merton Abbey. The later two- and three-ply carpets were woven for Morris & Co. at Heckmondwike (Yorks).

Needlework carpets. In the sixteenth and early seventeenth centuries Oriental carpets were much copied in Europe in cross and tent stitch on canvas. This was quite suitable for use on tables and cupboards, for which they were intended. There is a good collection in the National Museum, Zürich, and some superb English examples in the Victoria and Albert Museum. In the eighteenth century they were again in favour, but the designs were now purely European, with lavish floral patterns for the floor of boudoir or drawing room. Many of these carpets have survived in England, but they are rarely found in good condition, as they wear easily. Their beauty depends as much on the brilliant dyes used as on the design. The fashion continued into the nineteenth century, but these pieces can be recognized by design and colour. Italian carpets embroidered entirely in silk are occasionally seen.

Norway. Double-cloth rugs for covers and cushions were made in the eighteenth and nineteenth centuries; a looped-pile technique is rarer.

Norwich. Norwich carpets are mentioned in seventeenth-century inventories. Possibly Turkey-

Far right Savonnerie carpet, Directoire style with medallions and pompeian figures, brown ground scattered with stars

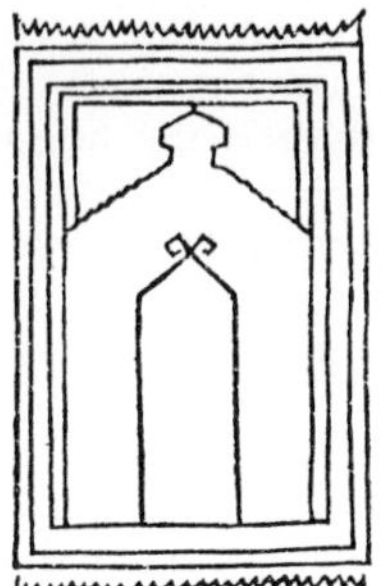

Prayer rug

Screen panel depicting a fable by Aesop, Savonnerie, mid-18th century

Savonnerie carpet knotting

work (*q.v.*) was made there as well as cloth carpeting and moquette (*q.v.*).

Poland. Peasant kilim rugs, like those of the Ukraine and Rumania, were woven in the eighteenth to nineteenth centuries. Some knotted-pile rugs of the seventeenth century are also known. They are West European in style and the quality is excellent.

Prayer rugs. Persian design, the central feature of which is the Mihrab, a design derived from the traditional form of altar of the Mohammedan mosque.

Rumania. Tapestry-woven rugs were woven in every village as covers and wall hangings, and many pieces are dated (eighteenth to nineteenth centuries). Lozenge and geometric patterns prevail in Wallachia and Moldavia, floral designs in Oltenia and Bessarabia. The floral patterns tend to be large and sprawling and the field and border are scarcely differentiated. Oltenian rugs are reputed to have the best dyes, and Turkish influence is evident in their more regular and compact designs and their firmer borders. The main tradition of Oltenian designs is supposed to derive from the period of Constantine Brancovan (late seventeenth century). Floral, tree, and bird patterns are common in Bukovina. Although apt to be garish and loud, the best Rumanian weavings are a very attractive form of peasant art. Knotted-pile rugs are occasionally found in Bessarabia.

Salor (Turkoman). These rugs are similar in texture to the Tekke rugs, but the octagonal 'gul' is more pronounced and the red is usually slightly brighter. Woven in prayer rugs and also in fine camel bags.

San Michele. *See* Italy.

Sardinia. *See* Italy.

Saruk (Persian). These carpets follow closely the tradition of the Kashan carpets, often using the Herat motifs and medallion designs. The construction is sturdy, closely knotted deep pile. Knot: Sehna.

Savonnerie. Knotted-pile carpets in the Turkish manner were first successfully made in France by Pierre Dupont, whom Henry IV installed in the Louvre in 1606. In 1627 the old soapworks on the quai de Chaillot, called the Savonnerie, were acquired and Dupont's partner, Simon Lourdet, began work there with orphan children as apprentices. The Louvre and Savonnerie workshops flourished, particularly under Louis XIV. Large carpets were made for the Grande Gallerie du Louvre and the Salle d'Apollon (pieces still preserved in the Louvre), while others were given as diplomatic presents, including one to the King of Siam, which was restored at the Gobelins in 1910. A suite of carpet and upholstery for chairs and settees was made for Mazarin. Pierre Dupont died in 1644 (he wrote a treatise on carpet making, *La Stromatourgie*) and was succeeded by his son, who removed to the Savonnerie in 1672. During the eighteenth century work continued steadily at the Savonnerie, although many of the workmen emigrated. Not till 1768 were Savonnerie carpets available to private individuals, but prices were very high and few pieces sold. Under Napoleon the looms were kept busy. The Savonnerie was amalgamated with the Gobelins in 1825, where some looms are still at work. It was the Savonnerie which set the standard for European hand-knotted carpets and created a style which was copied far afield. The Turkish knot was used.

Scotch carpets. Double-cloth or ply weavings for the floor, also known as Kidderminster or Ingrain.

Sehna or **Sennah** (Persian). The knot, generally described as Persian, is named after this weave. Finely woven in small Herat and cone designs, although lighter in colouring and general effect. These rugs are of real merit and can be distinguished by the very short, upstanding pile.

Sehna or **Persian knot.** Used in carpets from Sehna, Ispahan, Tabriz (also the Ghiordes knot, *q.v.*), Saruk, Serebend, Feraghan, Kerman, Shiraz, and Herat.

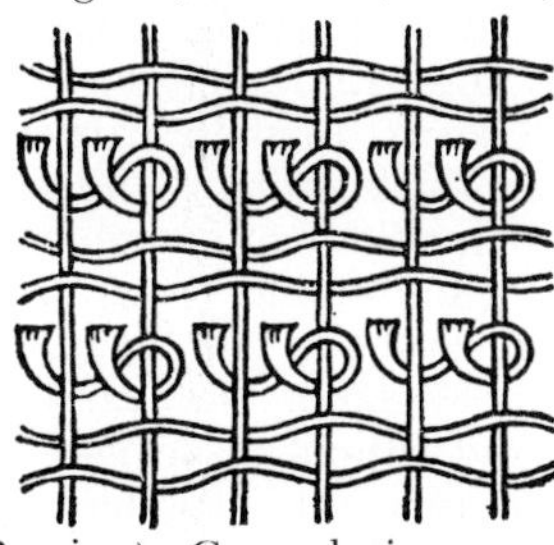

Serebend (Persian). Cone design usually on red or blue field, the border following Herat influence. Fine examples are known as Mir. Knot: Sehna.

Shiraz (Persian). Designs are of a conventional Moslem character, woven by Kashkai nomads bearing relation to Caucasian types. Diamond medallions predominate, while cone designs and latch hooks are also used. The term Mecca is often used to describe pieces of outstanding merit. Knot: Ghiordes or Sehna.

Shirvan (Caucasian). These rugs are similar in design but generally coarser in quality and lack the detail of the Hila rugs (*q.v.*). Crude animal forms are often introduced.

Soumac (Caucasian). These rugs have a smooth-faced weave with conventional designs. Large octagonal and star panels; colourings are mainly a deep copper and blue.

Spain. Hispano-Moresque carpets were woven in Spain in the early Middle Ages. Unlike Near Eastern carpets, they were generally woven with the single-warp knot. Murcia was still the centre of production in the fifteenth century, when many carpets were woven with the arms of leading Spanish families. After the defeat of the Moors, the 'Mudéjar' style, based largely on Renaissance silk patterns, developed in the sixteenth and seventeenth centuries, with important centres at Cuenca and Alcaraz. There is a fine collection of all these types at the Victoria and Albert Museum. There was a royal factory at Madrid in the eighteenth century.

The looped-pile peasant weavings, chiefly from the Alpujarras Mountains in South Spain, are the best of all European peasant rugs, and until recently were plentiful and cheap. They were made as bed covers and rugs for out-of-doors' use in a great variety of patterns, often in black and white, but also in red and green and mixed colours. Cross-stitch needlework carpets in similar style were also plentifully made. Cloth rugs or covers with floated-weft pattern in wool, like the Italian Abruzzi weavings, were also made in Spain.

Sweden. Knotted-pile rugs as in Finland (*q.v.*) were made throughout the eighteenth and nineteenth centuries as well as double-cloth weavings.

Tabriz. The capital of Ancient Persia. Rugs and carpets from here show greater realism of design than those from Spahan, and it is in Tabriz that the greatest of the hunting carpets were woven; the most famous, considered by many experts to be the greatest, example of Persian weaving, may be seen in the Österreichisches Museum für Angewandte Kunst, Vienna. The use of court figures and a wide range of animals and birds appear in the designs, although the medallion on a plain ground is common. No other district has woven such a wide range of designs or used such variety of colour. Silk is sometimes used in fine specimens, either for contrasting effect with wool or sometimes alone. Knot: Ghiordes or Sehna.

Tekke. *See* Bokhara or Bokara.

Turkeywork. This was the name generally given to carpets, cushions, and upholstery knotted in the manner of Near Eastern rugs in sixteenth- and seventeenth-century inventories. Apart from larger carpets and rugs, Turkeywork cushions appear to have been made in not inconsiderable numbers in England, though they are now rare. Examples can be dated throughout the seventeenth century, and armorial cushions are noteworthy: for example, a set at Norwich Cathedral (1651); at Pembroke College, Cambridge (1666–7); at Brasenose College, Oxford (1666). In the eighteenth century cross-stitch embroidery took the place of knotted pile for upholstery.

Turkoman 'guls' or **flowers**

Ukraine. Tapestry-woven rugs, akin to those of Rumania and Yugoslavia, were made as a peasant craft. The Turkish influence in some is clear; others have the sprawling floral patterns akin to those of Bessarabia. West European influence appears in the middle and latter nineteenth century.

Vase carpets. Persian design, with graceful interlocking palmettes and floral designs, developing from a central motif.

Wilton. Although a charter for clothiers was granted in 1701, it is doubtful whether carpets were then made there. Lord Pembroke introduced Brussels carpet or moquette (*q.v.*) looms in 1740. From that date Wilton was in keen rivalry with Kidderminster. The cutting of the looped velvet pile was probably an early speciality of Wilton, a type of carpeting subsequently called by its name. Wilton carpets, made on velvet or moquette looms in narrow strips with simple geometrical patterns, were certainly much used in eighteenth-century houses, as were the costlier knotted-pile carpets. The Brighton Pavilion accounts, for example, record orders for both. It is unlikely that knotted-pile carpets were made at Wilton until the acquisition of the Axminster looms in 1835, since when they have continued to work.

Vase carpet

Yomud (Turkish). Rugs usually having diamond-shaped motifs, often composed of latch hooks and cloud-band borders.

Yugoslavia. Kilim or tapestry-woven rugs were woven in Bosnia, Serbia, and the Banat throughout the nineteenth century; looped- or knotted-pile examples are occasionally found. Typical Slav geometric patterns of lozenges and zigzags are general, with floral and tree motifs also treated geometrically. Prayer carpets with a niche are not uncommon. These rugs have many points of similarity with Rumanian rugs.

Below Vase carpet, Persian, 16th–17th century. Victoria & Albert Museum

COINS AND MEDALS

Right Gilt bronze medal by Ottone Hamerani

Above Stater, Philip II of Macedon (359–336 B.C.), obverse and reverse. British Museum

Coins

The collecting of coins has almost as long a history as coins themselves, for we are told by Suetonius that the Roman emperor Augustus, if not actually a collector, did at least assemble some ancient pieces, presumably Greek, which he gave as gifts to his friends. The princes of the Renaissance were the first collectors proper of coins, and ever since then collections have been formed by all sorts and conditions of men.

The attractions of coin collecting are manifold. There is, initially, the fascination of handling objects that have passed through the hands of men in all the civilizations from the seventh century B.C. onwards. Coins were first used in Europe after the destruction of the Mycenean civilization in 1200 B.C. The refugees, who settled in western Asia Minor, traded money with the Greeks, and were making their own coins some 700 years before the beginning of the Christian era. Coins form, moreover, the most complete series of artistic objects that can be assembled from the pristine vigour of classical Greek art, through the formalism of Byzantinism and the strivings of the Middle Ages to the heights of the Renaissance and on to our own day. Again, in the great sweep of centuries before the invention of printing, coins provide a great, continuous series of historical documents, giving contemporary comment on events and recording the likenesses of history's great men, the details of ancient architecture and the accompaniments of the world's religions. Unlike many other antiquities, where each piece is unique, the special work of a craftsman or artist never exactly repeated, many of the most beautiful coins of all ages were produced in their thousands and exist, even today, in their hundreds; for once the artist had engraved his dies, or made the model for his mould, the limit to the number of pieces which could be produced was the physical limitation of these instruments.

To form a collection of coins is not, even in this present age, the privilege of wealth; but since the field is so vast, complete coverage can be contemplated by, say, only a national collection, formed over centuries, and the private collector will be counselled to select an artistic or historical period which appeals to him. Even within the major periods which are described below, a selected portion – one century or one state – will provide great variety and range.

Greek

The term Greek coins is loosely used to cover not only the coinage of Greece proper but also of all the places in the Mediterranean basin to which Greek civilization spread, including Egypt, the Near East and the Black Sea. Greek coinage is the earliest coinage of Western civilization, and its development from the seventh century B.C. till the extinction of its last remaining forms in the third century A.D. provides a continuous illustration of that civilization and art from which most subsequent European forms spring.

ARCHAIC (700–480 B.C.)

The earliest coins in the seventh century in Asia Minor were simply pellets of electrum with, on one side, the badge of the city, guaranteeing the piece. Croesus, King of Lydia, struck similar pieces in the sixth century, but in gold and silver, an example followed by the Persian kings with their silver shekels and gold darics. In Greece proper the earliest coins, also with a badge on one side and a rough incuse square on the other, were struck at Aegina. Other states, such as Corinth and Athens, quickly adopted the idea. Probably the earliest coinage with devices on both sides was developed at Athens in the sixth century. The early coins of Magna Graecia were round and flat, and some cities, such as Metapontum, have a curious fabric with the same device on both sides, in relief on the obverse and incuse on the reverse. The coinage of this period is somewhat angular and stiff in style, and the human eye, even when shown in profile, is drawn as if seen from the front.

CLASSICAL (480–336 B.C.)

The features of this coinage are the delicate and detailed rendering of the subjects, particularly the human body and the high relief of the experiments in portraiture, including facing heads. In the Asian cities the incuse of the Archaic period remained popular, though later two-sided types appeared. In the fifth and fourth centuries in Greece proper the coinage of Corinth, with its obverse type of Pegasus, rivalled that of Athens in its circulation. Mid-fourth century, however, saw in Greece the rise of Macedonia under Philip II to political hegemony, of which the symptom and instrument was the rich series of gold staters with head of Apollo and biga reverse. This popular coinage was copied extensively in Europe, successively in the Danube basin, Gaul, and Ancient Britain. In the West a magnificent series of coins issued from the cities of southern Italy and Sicily, particularly from Syracuse after the Athenian defeat. Of equal quality are the coins of the Phoenician merchant city Carthage.

HELLENISTIC (336–1 B.C.)

The extension of Macedonian hegemony over most of the Greek world in the East by the conquests of

PR·HENR·A·TVR
ARV·VIC·TVREN

Alexander the Great brought a reduction in independent coinages and the establishment of the first 'world' coinage with his series of gold staters and silver tetradrachms issued at mints throughout his Empire. The kingdoms into which Alexander's empire split on his death lasted till the establishment of the Roman Empire in the last century of the era. The features of the coinage of these kingdoms is the development of true and expressive portraiture as in Bactria in Northwest India and the Seleucid kingdom and in Egypt under the Ptolemies, though on much copper coinage the gods retained their place. The silver cistophoros with its Bacchic cista and snakes types, beginning in the second century B.C., was the standard coinage of western Asia Minor into Roman times.

IMPERIAL (A.D. 1–296)

Under the Roman Empire, almost the only autonomous coinages of the Greek cities were in bronze. These and the 'imperial' issues with emperor portrait from Greek cities and colonies, though of comparatively poor workmanship, provide an interesting record of local cults, ancient works of art and architecture. A continuous series of tetradrachms with an imperial portrait was issued from Alexandria in Egypt, but by the close of the third century A.D., the tetradrachm, shrunk and debased, is scarcely recognizable as the ultimate descendant of the great Greek series.

Above Tetradrachm, Demetrius Poliorcetes of Macedon (d. 283 B.C.). British Museum

Right Arsace, King of the Parthians (238–191 B.C.). British Museum

Roman

Roman coinage, beginning only in the third century B.C., combines a native Italian bronze coinage with a coinage of silver didrachms in the Greek style. This was replaced in the late third century by the silver denarius, which, with a modified bronze series and an occasional issue in gold, provided the staple coinage throughout the Republic. The features of early Roman coinage are the absence of portraiture and the prolific variety of types alluding to events in Rome's history and legends and to the family history of the moneying magistrates. The Imperial coinage, instituted by Augustus at the end of the first century B.C., added a consistent gold coinage and a new series of bronzes. Portraiture, begun during the civil wars preceding the establishment of empire, is the prime feature throughout all Imperial coinage, while the reverses provide a commentary on events, actions, and policies. Currency reforms in the third and fourth centuries A.D., though changing denominations, did not alter greatly the shape of the Roman coinage.

Denarius, obverse and reverse

Oriental

In the Near and Middle East some series of Oriental coins preserve the characteristics of the Greek and Roman coinages with which they are contemporary. The Jewish coinage, under the Jewish rulers in the last two centuries B.C., under the procurators of the Roman Empire, and during the two revolts against the Romans, normally eschewed portraiture but had types in Greek fashion with inscriptions in Hebrew.

The coinage of the Parthians from third century B.C. to third century A.D. was a portrait coinage in the Hellenistic manner but with a distinctive Assyrian flavour. The features of the Sassanian coinage from third to seventh century A.D. are the portrait types with Pahlavi inscription and an invariable fire-altar reverse.

The rise of Islam in the seventh century and the subsequent extension of its power produced in the Near and Middle East, across North Africa and into Spain, and into West and Southwest Asia a coinage mainly of gold dinars and silver dirhems, uniform but for the titles of rulers, names of mints, and religious formulae. Portraiture on Mohammedan coinage is rare, and artistic effect lies in the calligraphic designs.

In India, on the other hand, the types of coinage are as numerous as the constituent states. An outstanding medieval series was that of the Gupta kings, a rich succession of gold coins with figure types, showing still some connection with the Graeco-Bactrian coins of the northwest. In the extensive series of the Mogul emperors, as well as the calligraphic patterns, common to all Mohammedan coins, there was a rich variety of representations on some of the gold coins. In medieval Ceylon the designs on the coinage were a uniquely formal art style, of its own culture.

Coinage in China is said, traditionally, to date from the second millennium B.C. Early types were small-scale reproductions in bronze of objects exchanged in barter – knives, spades, etc. From about the middle of the first millennium B.C. these pieces were inscribed. Although this type of coinage lasted down to the beginning of the Christian era, round money in bronze, with a square hole in the centre, and inscribed with characters, was in circulation several centuries before this. Apart from varying characters, Chinese coinage retained this form till comparatively recent times. The Japanese coinage is a derivative of the Chinese, which it closely resembles apart from its distinctive characters. In the sixteenth century gold coins in the form of thin, oval plates began to be issued, and there were also small rectangular silver blocks.

British

The Ancient Britons struck a coinage of gold staters, imitating the types of the stater of Philip II of Macedon, and later, in the first century A.D., produced some silver imitating Roman types. The first Anglo-Saxon coinage was of small silver sceattas with designs elaborated from late Roman coins, but in the eighth century the silver penny, parallel to the Continental denier, began to be struck. This denomination, acquiring in time a royal portrait type, persisted, with variations of design, as the standard coin till the fourteenth century, when the fourpenny piece, or groat, was added, together with a coinage in gold. With the Renaissance and prosperity under the Tudors, larger denominations of greater intricacy of design made their appearance in both gold and silver. The introduction of mechanical means of coin production after the Restoration brought a standardization of coin types and the discarding of unusual denominations, leaving the coinage in much the form which it retains today.

Sovereign, Henry VII (1485–1509), obverse and reverse. British Museum

Medieval

Sixth–fifteenth centuries

Following the break-up of the western Roman Empire in the late fifth century, the Visigoths in Spain and the Merovingians in France produced a coinage of small gold, imitating the tremisses of the late Empire. Under the Carolingian Empire, covering a great part of Western Europe, a new coinage of silver deniers, rated at 240 to the pound, was established in the eighth century. This denier, under various names and with varying types, remained the standard coinage throughout Western Europe under the German Empire and in the great number of independent states and kingdoms which emerged through the centuries. In the early fourteenth century larger silver pieces, roughly equivalent to the groat in England, were added, while about the same time increasing trade and prosperity re-introduced coinages in gold.

The eastern Roman Empire, which held precariously together till the mid-fifteenth century, continued the Roman coinage of gold solidi and bronze coins but little silver. A new series of bronze coins was introduced in 492, and the dumpy solidus became thin and scyphate, and from the eleventh century this, the nomisma, became the sole gold coinage. This Byzantine coinage influenced the shape of coinage in the Balkans and Eastern Europe and, till the eighth century, North Africa and much of Italy.

Gold Florentine florin showing John the Baptist, issued by Boninsegni. British Museum

Modern

The later fifteenth century, when the spread of the Renaissance in art and technique began to make its effect felt, marks the beginning of modern coinage. Increasing prosperity arising from the unification of petty states into sovereign powers and the growth of commerce, making necessary a wider range of coinage, coincided with the discovery of supplies of precious metals in the New World. Larger silver pieces, such as the franc in France, the teston in Italy, and the papal giulio, were introduced, while Spain, with its control of American silver, issued her large 'pieces of eight'. In Bohemia the silver from the Joachimstal was issued as thalers, a denomination copied in many German states and the antecedent of the American dollar. Coinage in gold in a variety of denominations became more abundant, particularly in mercantile Western Europe. Demand for small change produced a coinage in copper or bronze somewhat later, while in Northern and Eastern Europe readily available supplies produced for a time a full-value copper coinage, not merely tokens. By the seventeenth century mechanical production of coins had effected a standardization of design and denomination, and with the adoption of the decimal system in most of Europe and America in the late eighteenth and early nineteenth centuries, coinage settled down into its modern shape.

American

The collector of American coins usually starts by trying to obtain a specimen of one denomination for each year. Once he has done this he will probably specialize in one of the fields to which he finds himself particularly attracted. Forming a cabinet of types is likely to prove much more ambitious than it seems at first. It is hardly possible for a collector of Americana to go far without learning much about his country's history, and coins often bring home the significance of events previously disregarded.

COLONIAL COINAGE OF MASSACHUSETTS

Until 1773 no advantage was taken of the right of coinage granted in the charter of Virginia. No such grant was made in the charter of the Massachusetts Bay Colony. The coinage struck at Boston between 1652 and 1683 is perhaps the most interesting in American history. The shortage of small change was one of the most serious handicaps which the colonists had to face. Petitions to Charles I for a colonial mint had proved fruitless. A like inadequacy of the coinage prevailed in England at this time. Granting the right to coin money was a prerogative of the King. Within a few years after the death of Charles I, whether with or without the consent of the Commonwealth is not known, a mint was set up in Boston. John Hull was placed in charge along with his partner, Robert Sanderson, both silversmiths. The earliest pieces bear merely the initial letters *NE* in script capitals (for New England) on the one side and the value in Roman numerals on the other side. With but one exception, all the subsequent coins bear the date 1652. With the return of Charles II to the throne in

Pine Tree shilling, silver, Massachusetts, 1662, obverse and reverse

1660, the colonists were in a serious predicament, and the charge of having infringed the royal prerogative was one of those alleged as a cause for the withdrawal of the charter in 1683.

Because the *NE* pieces had a large part of their field blank, it was realized that this would offer opportunity for clipping, so a design which would fill the field was ordered, namely 'a tree'. This tree type has three forms. The first of them, and the crudest, has since been dubbed the 'willow tree', to which the design bears but slight resemblance. Many of the 'willow tree' pieces have been double-struck, with the traces of the first striking interfering with the other. Their crudity must have been one of the reasons why this type is the rarest of the tree forms.

A marked improvement characterizes the succeeding type, called the 'oak tree', to which the design does bear some resemblance. In 1662 an oak-tree twopence was added to the three previous denominations, and this bears the date of its authorization; it is the only issue with a date other than 1652.

The type known as the 'pine tree' is the latest of the three. At its initiation it is on the same-sized flan as its predecessors, but about half of the known dies are constricted, from 30 to 25 mm. All of these tree forms were engraved in the die and resemble line drawings rather than modelled reliefs. This is less noticeable in the inscriptions, which are marked by interesting letter forms and variations. The spelling *Masathusets* continues unchanged (with one exception – the H is omitted), and this gives that spelling some claim to having been considered official.

Despite long-drawn-out efforts to overcome opposition, it became apparent that the colony's charter was about to be rescinded, and since the coining of money was one of the offences charged, and because any minimizing of the offence was impossible, the production seems to have been increased, for we find more than the usual number of dies being used at the same time. The thinness of these pieces permitted bending, from which one very interesting phenomenon resulted, for they were believed to be a protection from witches and were worn (bent or pierced) on the person for this purpose.

Perhaps the rarest of the Massachusetts issues, and the most ambitious artistically, is the Good Samaritan shilling, with the two figures of that parable on its obverse. It was struck from dies, but in the placing and form of the inscription it differs from all previous forms. The occasion for its production, probably unofficial, has not been discovered.

Plantation token coinage of the reign of James II, made of pewter, 1688, Virginia, obverse and reverse

MARYLAND, NEW JERSEY, CONNECTICUT

A coinage for Maryland dated 1658 was struck in England by the Proprietor, Cecil Calvert, Lord Baltimore, whose bust occupies the obverse. The reverse bears the family coat-of-arms. There were three silver denominations – the shilling, the sixpence, and the groat (fourpence) as well as a copper penny, which has a crown with two pennants for its reverse type.

In 1682, in order to relieve the shortage of small change, the General Assembly of the Province of New Jersey authorized the circulation of halfpence and farthings, which are believed to have been issued in Dublin and brought to the colony by Mark Newby the preceding year. Because of the type, representing St Patrick in ecclesiastical robes, these pieces are known by both names. The supply must have been fairly considerable, to judge from the number of dies known.

The patent granted to William Wood for making copper tokens for Ireland and the American colonies resulted in two types. Both bore on the obverse the head of George I. The former has for its reverse a beautifully conventionalized rose, and bore the inscription ROSA AMERICANA and UTILE DULCI with the date for all but the first issue. The denominations

are twopence, penny, and halfpenny; the dates are 1722, 1723, 1724, 1733 (this last for a pattern twopence only). The issue for Ireland had for its reverse a seated woman with a harp; the dates are 1722–4. When these pieces proved unpopular in Ireland they were sent to America. The denominations were halfpenny and farthing only.

A small group of coppers having a connection with Connecticut is known as the 'Higley Coppers', named after their producer, John Higley, who controlled a small copper mine near Cranby, from which came the metal for these coins. The earliest pieces had for type a stag to left with inscription *Value of Three Pence.* When refused for this equivalent in circulation a second die was prepared with the words *Value me as you please.* Later there was a second reverse die having a hatchet for its type and for legend *I cut my way through.* This last and another type (a wheel) are undated; the others show the date 1737.

LATIN AMERICA

The abundance of coined silver in Latin America explains why some collectors have been turning to the coinages of the Spanish mints in the New World. It is from these that much of the silver which circulated here came after the coining in Boston was stopped. It is these Spanish milled dollars, in which payment was promised on the Continental Congress's paper notes which, to a large extent, financed the Revolution. The paper notes of the Continental Congress were printed in large numbers and so soon counterfeited that they quickly depreciated, becoming 'not worth a Continental'. Besides Mexico City,

Copper coin minted in England by William Wood for the American colonies bearing the head of George I and the inscription Rosa Americana, 1723–4, obverse and reverse

Piece of Eight, silver, minted in Mexico, Philip V (1700–46), obverse and reverse

Santa Fé de Bogotá in Colombia and Potosí and Lima, then both in Peru, were the most prolific mints for the 'pieces of eight'. Some of the gold in circulation came from Brazilian sources, possibly by way of Jamaica. They were known as 'Joes' and 'half-Joes' because they bore the Latin form of the name of the Portuguese king (Johannes). The New Englanders brought their salted codfish to the West Indies, exchanging it there for other desirables, including hard cash. A little later, when coins in small denominations became very scarce in the West Indies, they resorted to an interesting substitute which has intrigued many collectors. The Spanish mainland coins were cut into segments or lowered in weight by having a portion cut away. Some perversions consist in having cut the 'piece of eight' into five 'quarters', with the shortage so slight that it would escape the observation of the unwary. Gold pieces were sometimes plugged with added metal to raise them to a standard required by local legislation.

OTHER PRE-REVOLUTIONARY COINAGE

Shortly before the outbreak of the American Revolution Virginia took advantage of permission given in her charter to have an issue of halfpennies struck in England. Although these bear the date 1773 the shipment did not reach its destination until 1774, and since the obverse shows the head of George III, they can scarcely have become popular.

A few specimens of a dollar bearing the date 1776 and the inscription *Continental Currency* are known. There are strikings in pewter and brass as well as in silver, and this seems an indication that it never got beyond the pattern or trial-piece stage. The interval between the signing of the Treaty of Peace in 1783 and the ratification of the Federal Constitution in 1788 found several of the states authorizing the coinage of cents, and one of these issues was by provision of the Continental Congress and bears the dates 1787 and 1788. The design, showing a sundial and the word FUGIO, had for reverse a chain of thirteen links – one for each state – a device which had been used for the earlier Continental dollar, which is thought to have been supplied by Franklin.

The devices used on issues authorized to relieve the currency shortage by the several states display wide variety and some ingenuity. One of the first to appear, that of Vermont, came from a state which was not among the first thirteen to ratify. Massachusetts issued a half cent. New York and New Jersey used a Latinized form of their names. The coinage for Connecticut was one of the heaviest. There is an unofficial issue (1783–6) bearing the inscription NOVA CONSTELLATIO. Unofficial coinings often bear the head of Washington. The absence of specific laws prohibiting such coins was taken advantage of by several goldsmiths or jewellers, such as Ephraim Brasher in New York, who fathered a very well-designed doubloon (gold) on which he counter-stamped his initials EB. In Maryland, I. Chambers of Annapolis struck silver shillings, sixpences, and threepences dated 1783, and in 1790 in Baltimore Standish Barry produced a silver threepence bearing his name. The federal mint did not come into operation until 1792.

FEDERAL MINT ESTABLISHED

The initial coinings at the mint set up in Philadelphia are an indication of the great need for smaller denominations. A few pieces were struck in 1792 – the disme and its half – traditionally believed to have been struck from silver plate supplied by Washington. These were obviously patterns, as were designs for cents prepared by Thomas Birch. By 1793 cents and half cents had been put into circulation, the former in several varieties – chain type, wreath, Liberty head. By 1796 a type with a draped bust had become established. In 1794 dollars as well as half dollars and half dimes were issued. 1795 saw the striking of gold; the half eagle ($5.00) preceded the eagle. Not until 1796 were quarter eagles minted ($2.50); the quarter dollars of this date were without indication of their value, and further strikings did not occur until 1804. Pieces of these early dates in prime condition are eagerly sought today, but it is impossible to list the many varieties. Sometimes changes are very considerable, such as that in the diameter of the cents in 1857, when the flying-eagle type appeared officially. Pieces of this type bearing the date 1856 are considered patterns; only 1,000 are believed to have been struck. Other patterns are known to have been considered but never sanctioned. Among these is the gold stella of 1879 and 1880, with the gold value of four dollars, but patterns were also struck in other metals. Three-dollar pieces in gold were struck between 1854 and 1889.

When the mint at New Orleans fell into the hands of the Southerners they found dies there for half dollars bearing the date 1861. A reverse die with the inscription *Confederate States of America* was cut, and a small number (four?) of specimens was struck. One of the coins and both dies were found in the possession of a citizen of New Orleans in 1879 and later acquired by a New York coin dealer. He obtained half dollars of the New Orleans mint for 1861, planed off their reverses and re-struck them from the Confederate die. A die for a cent was ordered but never delivered. It was used later for re-strikes by the dealer who acquired the die.

TERRITORIAL GOLD COINS

The private or territorial gold coins constitute a series from which considerable American history may be learned. Prior to the California Gold Rush in 1849 the supply of gold came from two southern states, Georgia and North Carolina. Local assayers were responsible for pieces of honest weight, and these circulated without government prohibition. The first, struck by Templeton Reid, bore the word *Georgia Gold*, his name and date 1830, along with indication of their value – ten, five, and two-and-a-half dollars. Later (1849) pieces having the value of ten and twenty-five dollars bear his name, but it is accompanied by *California Gold.* He must have gone to the west in the interval.

In Rutherford County of North Carolina a family of German metallurgists named Bechtler coined one-, two-and-a-half, and five-dollar gold pieces over a period of twenty-two years. These too were without type or symbol, merely giving name, date, and denomination.

The exigencies of the Gold Rush to California are brought out by the pieces struck there by accredited assayers while that state was still a territory, and both before and after Augustus Humbert had set up a U.S. assayer. The earliest of the fifty-dollar gold slugs coined by him are dated 1851, and the previous issues of smaller size were discredited, with a very inconvenient shortage of small change resulting. Authority for ten- and twenty-dollar coins was finally accorded in February 1852. By 1854 eagles and double eagles were being struck by the San Francisco branch mint. A state assay office provided by law in 1850 seems to have been discontinued as soon as the U.S. assay office was established. Bars and ingots, stamped with their intrinsic value and the name of the assayer, circulated as late as 1860 and are collected by some enthusiasts, although they can scarcely be classed as coins.

Five- and ten-dollar pieces struck by the Oregon Exchange Company have a beaver as type and are dated 1849. The Mormons in Salt Lake City struck pieces in 1849 with the inscription *Holiness to the Lord* and with clasped hands on the reverse. In Colorado several firms, among which that of Clark, Gruber & Company was prominent, struck gold coins dated 1860 and 1861, the largest denomination being twenty dollars. Many of these bars and slugs must have gone into the melting pot when the stabilized price for gold was less than their pure content.

TOKENS

In two periods of our history tokens played a part which entitle them to the attention of collectors. Shortly after 1837, during the presidencies of Jackson and Van Buren, a period of widespread depression, there was a considerable striking of these unofficial coins which are now called 'Hard Times Tokens'. Many are of a satirical nature and reflect the economic situation. More than 100 varieties are recorded, chiefly in the large cent size.

A second period of coinage stringency occurred during the war between the states. The mint did not strike cents in sufficient quantity to meet the needs of circulation, and substitutes were put out by commercial firms, redeemable at their establishments, to overcome the shortage. Many have a local interest because they bear the names of issuers no longer in existence. These little tokens were of the size of the small cents introduced in 1857 and were usually in bronze. The varieties run into thousands.

NEW DESIGNS

During the presidency of Theodore Roosevelt, and with his enthusiastic encouragement, an effort was made to improve the artistic standard of the coinage. Augustus Saint Gaudens (and his pupils) were entrusted with the making of new designs. His design for the twenty-dollar gold piece was of great beauty, but by the time the mint officials had modified it to meet the requirements of minting and circulation it had lost much of its initial attractiveness. The half dollar and the dime were designed by A. A. Weinmann, the quarter by H. A MacNeil and the five-cent piece (perhaps the most characteristically American of the types) by James E. Fraser. The Lincoln cent was the work of V. D. Brenner. In 1921 a Peace Dollar was authorized; the design, selected from a competition in which eight invited sculptors participated, was by Anthony de Francisci.

Florentine medal of Erasmus, 1531. British Museum

Medals

The art of the medal is patently related to that of coins, but it is a special and comparatively modern development of certain features of coin art; for the medal is no older than the Renaissance of the fifteenth century. It is true that certain large Greek coins and, to an even greater extent, the Roman Imperial medallions have a medallic character, but these pieces were primarily monetary, whereas the medal is essentially an artistic commemoration in metal of persons and events.

Medal of Filippo Maria Visconti, Duke of Milan, by Pisanello, *c.* 1441. Victoria & Albert Museum

Italian Renaissance

In Italy, in the growing interest in the civilization and art of the ancient world, one feature in ancient coinage which obviously fascinated was the great series of Roman Imperial portraits, particularly those on the large bronze sestertii. From this and similar inspirations developed the school of Italian Renaissance medallists, of whom the earliest, and possibly the greatest, was Pisanello (*fl.* 1452). The qualities of the art of this century are realism of portraiture and naturalism of design, a striking antithesis to medieval art. Of the numerous artists of this period, mention can be made of only a few such as Matteo de Pasti, Sperandio, and Niccolò Fiorentino.

Sixteenth-Century European

Although by the end of the fifteenth century medallic art had spread to most countries in western Europe, examples are rare outside Italy, but the sixteenth century saw the medal firmly established with a great variety of practitioners and styles. Already far removed from the style of Pisanello is the richly ornate English medal by Nicholas Hilliard on the defeat of the Armada in 1588. In Italy there was a more continuous development by such artists as Benvenuto Cellini (1500–71), Leone Leoni (1509–90), and Jacopo da Trezzo (*fl.* 1589). In France, where the qualities of sculptural art were being blended into the medal, two of the great masters were Germain Pilon (1539–90) and Guillaume Dupré (1574–1647). The peculiar quality of the German medal of this century, a certain rough strength, is due to the fact that the original models were carved in wood or stone, not modelled in wax as elsewhere. Prominent artists were Hans Schwarz (1493–1530), Hans Reinhardt (*fl.* 1535–49), and Cristopher Weiditz (*fl.* 1523–37), and a number of medals are regarded as being at least from the designs of Albert Dürer.

Seventeenth-Century Portrait Medals

Much of the pristine freshness and vigour of medallic art disappears in this century with the establishment of a more formal 'classical' style. The exponents of this style were principally French, medallists such as Jean Varin (1604–42), Jean Mauger (1648–1722), and his pupil Jean Dassier (1676–1763), the last of whom produced numerous series of medals of famous characters in history. This style became international and varied only according to the quality of the individual artist. A particularly successful portrait modeller was Thomas Simon in England, though he was only one of quite a school in this country. An unusual treatment of the portrait is that of the Dutch artist Jerian Pool (*fl.* 1653–67) in his three-quarter facing portrait of Admiral Tromp.

Above Portrait medal of Pope Clement XI (1700–27) by Charles-Claude Dubut, 1708. Gilt metal

Left Medal commemorating the Restoration by John Roettier showing Charles II, 1660

Italian Baroque

Surprisingly little attention has been given either by scholars or collectors to the medals of the seventeenth and eighteenth centuries which are well worth the attention of all lovers of Italian baroque art. With their portraits of crowned popes, birettaed cardinals and heavily bewigged princes, generals and artists, they present one of the fullest portrait galleries of Italian notabilities. On their reverse sides one may find representations of such buildings as the façade of S. Giovanni in Laterano or the Arco S. Gallo at Florence, boldly rendered allegories or views of harbours and ships. Fortunately such medals are valued mainly for their rarity rather than their aesthetic merits, and the discerning collector may therefore find magnificent examples of high artistic quality at a fraction of the price of a bronze statuette of the same date.

In the seventeenth and eighteenth centuries Italian noblemen, and even some visiting grand tourists (Baron Stosch and Sir Richard Molesworth among them), commissioned portrait medals of themselves. Medals were also made of important artists, writers, and mathematicians. The vast majority of the medals of this period are, however, of a more official nature.

Papal medals naturally attract most interest, since they provide a valuable portrait gallery of the popes and often show on their reverse sides the important architectural works they commissioned. A medal produced by Ottone Hamerani for Clement XII in 1732, for instance, has a portrait of the pope on the obverse and a view of the recently completed façade of S. Giovanni in Laterano on the reverse. A pope normally had a medal struck to mark his election, and Clement XI, who persisted in the *grande rifiuto* against the wishes of the conclave for three days, issued one with an image of Christ falling beneath the cross on the reverse. Several thousand brass medals were struck each year for the pope to give to pilgrims, and in the *Anno Santo* or jubilee year (1600, 1625, 1650, etc.) special medals were issued, bearing a portrait of the pope on one side and usually a view of the Holy Year door to the Lateran on the other. Medals were also issued to mark the ceremony of canonization, with images of the newly sanctified on the reverse. From 1610 to 1625 the papal medals were principally the work of Giacomo Antonio de Mori. He was succeeded by Gaspare Mola, who was chief engraver to the *Zecca* until 1640, when he was followed by his nephew, Gaspare Moroni. On Moroni's death in 1669 the post of chief engraver passed to Alberto Hamerani, whose family held it until the end of the eighteenth century.

Reverse of Jubilee medal of Pope Benedict XIII by Ermenigildo Hamerani, 1725, showing Agostino Cornacchini's statue of Charlemagne. Museo Nazionale, Florence

The official papal medals were not the only ones to be executed in Rome. Apart from the cardinals, many of whom wished to have their likenesses recorded in this way, the Queen of Sweden and, later, the Old and Young Pretenders to the English crown were among the medallists' most frequent patrons. Jacobite medals are numerous, and many of them, by members of the Hamerani family, are of great charm. They also throw some light on an aspect of English history. The earliest of them, struck at the pope's order in 1689, shows Innocent XI condoling with James II. A later medal, bearing a portrait of Prince Charles Edward with the motto *Hunc saltem everso juvenem*, was seen by Horace Walpole at Hamerani's in 1740 and convinced him that the Stuarts were planning an imminent assault on Britain. This medal had, in fact, no more political significance than the many others commissioned by the exiled family.

Outside Rome, the principal towns where medals were produced in this period were Florence, Naples,

Obverse (left) Francesco Redi by Massimiliano Soldani-Benzi, 1684. Redi was a famous Italian naturalist and poet who was personal physician to the Grand Duke of Tuscany. *Reverse* Aere Perennius

and Turin. Some of those produced at Naples in the eighteenth century, bearing portraits of the Bourbon kings, are of good quality. At Turin the Lavy family, who controlled the mint from 1749 until the mid-nineteenth century, engraved some fine medals of a somewhat Frenchified appearance. But from the artistic point of view the best Italian baroque medals are probably those designed by Massimiliano Soldani for the Grand Duke of Tuscany. His portrait medals, whether they represent writers like Francesco Redi or commemorate the *déraciné* features of the later Medici Grand Dukes, have a strangely vigorous baroque vitality. When he went to Paris to model a portrait medal of Louis XIV in the 1680s Colbert remarked that France did not possess a medallist of the same ability. Unfortunately, Soldani was unable to cut his own dies, and this work was entrusted to other craftsmen, who were seldom capable of producing work as technically accomplished as that of the Hamerani at Rome, even though the design might be far superior.

Soldani was by no means the only Italian sculptor to provide models for medals. Indeed, even G. L. Bernini has been said to have done such work. It also seems highly probable that the medallists sometimes derived their portraits from carved or painted likenesses rather than from the life. Stylistically, therefore, the Italian medal is close connected with the history of Italian sculpture. Early in the seventeenth century Italian medals showed both in their portraits and their allegorical devices the influence of Mannerism. By the 1620s, however, the early baroque style is clearly evident in the medals produced in Rome, and a complete series of papal medals reveals the gradual development of the baroque in all its exuberance. Some patrons chose to have themselves represented in a classical manner, with hair cut in the ancient Roman fashion. Before the middle of the eighteenth century the pomps and splendours of the baroque had given way to the elegancies of the rococo, and portrait heads on medals were handled with a greater delicacy and precision. It was not until the last quarter of the century, however, that the neoclassical style began to exert any very strong influence on the official medallists. Neoclassical medals are marked by the late eighteenth-century desire for simplicity and nobility. Generally they are much more deeply cut than the medals of the previous 150 years and instead of bearing a quarter-length portrait of their subject they show the head alone, sometimes surrounded by a laurel wreath, but more usually on an undecorated ground. Numerous portraits of Napoleon, the various members of his family, and Gioacchino Murat, were executed in this style, with heads treated in a manner strongly reminiscent of Canova's busts.

In the seventeenth and eighteenth centuries most Italian medals, apart from those produced by the engravers to the large mints of Rome, Florence, Naples, and Turin, were cast, though the practice of die engraving became more usual towards the end of the period. It should be remembered that those medallists who signed their works with initials normally added the letter *F* for *fecit* at the end: thus, Filippo Balugani signs F. B. or F. B. F.

Eighteenth and Nineteenth Centuries

Medallic art in this period underwent a continuous decline in standard, although medals continued to enjoy a great vogue and to be produced by artists in all countries. The best of the medals, however, seldom achieve more than a high level of technical accomplishment, and the decline in standard was possibly hastened by the introduction of the reducing machine, so that the artist no longer worked his original model on the scale of the finished product. It may suffice for this period to cite a few typical medals, such as the extremely popular series struck in England in 1739 in honour of Admiral Vernon by a variety of artists or the Nelson medal of 1805 by Conrad Kuchler. In France towards the end of the eighteenth century the Revolution injected some fresh life into the art, producing pieces such as those by Benjamin du Vivier.

American

Until the U.S. mint was established in 1792 facilities

for preparing medals were almost entirely lacking, and it was necessary to rely on English or French artists. The direct cutting of steel dies was arduous, and there were few in the colonies with experience for doing this. Later, hubs, modelled in relief, were used for portrait medals. Not until a reducing machine had been imported well after the mid-nineteenth century were medals produced in any considerable number. There is one outstanding exception to this statement, however: the Indian Peace Medals, which have exceptional antiquarian interest. Intended as marks of favour to prominent chiefs, whose aid, along with that of their tribe, it was desirable to enlist, they had been used with considerable effect by the French in Canada, and later by the English. Possession of one of these medals was a fairly clear indication, and this was sometimes needed, of the side to which the wearer belonged. Indeed, several of the French medals are known with the LUDOVICUS of their inscription erased and GEORGIUS (in one case GORGIUS) substituted to indicate a change of front on the part of the owner. In consequence the Congress was early faced with the necessity for attracting Indians they wished to draw away from their allegiance to the English forces in the north. How could this be done when no equipment for striking medals was available? During Washington's administration the situation was met by presenting large oval plaques of silver with the design engraved. As these were considerably larger than the struck English medals, they seem to have made a deeper impression and to have been more highly prized. An early recipient was the famous and rightfully distinguished leader, Red Jacket, who received the largest of the three sizes distributed; and it is by his name that these engraved medals are sometimes known. The preparation of an engraved medal was possible much more quickly than would have been the case had dies been made, and their popularity with the red warriors satisfied both parties. Such engraved medals with the dates 1789, 1792, 1793, and 1795 are known and are assumed to indicate that they were awarded during the visit of a formal nature to the capital in those years. The designs are in some instances signed with the initials *JR*, probably to be identified as those of Joseph Richardson of Philadelphia. Another countermark, *JL* or *IL*, is less certain.

A group of three Seasons Medals, 45 mm in diameter, were ordered in England by Rufus King, the American minister. They are dated 1796, and their design was entrusted to the painter John Trumbull, at that time an art student in England. His designs were rather fanciful and intended to persuade the Indians of the advantages of the pursuits of peace, such as cattle raising and agriculture. These medals in silver and copper were not received until 1798. Under Thomas Jefferson and most of the succeeding presidents, struck medals were prepared at the mint; a common reverse displayed clasped hands and the words PEACE AND FRIENDSHIP. There are three sizes for the medals of Jefferson, just as there had been three grades of the engraved pieces, and there are further variations in size or method of manufacture. A supply of Jefferson medals is known to have been taken by Lewis and Clark on their expedition to the northwest. A supplementary group consists of medals given by the American Fur Company to its Indian trappers. One, in silver, bearing the portrait of John Jacob Astor and PRESIDENT OF THE AMERICAN FUR COMPANY, is to be dated about 1834. The second (in pewter) is that of Pierre Chouteau, Jr. Both bore the customary clasped hands on the reverse; the latter is dated 1843. The privilege of distributing such medals was withdrawn by the Secretary of War in 1843.

An excellent selection of recent medals will be found in the Museum of the American Numismatic Society.

Indian Peace Medal, reverse, showing George Washington 1792. Awarded to Chief Ojagetti (Fish Carrier) of the Cayugas (Iroquois). Public Archives of Canada

Glossary

Aes. The term used for coinages in copper and bronze.

Aes grave. The heavy cast-bronze coinage of the Roman Republic in the third century B.C. The unit was the as with its fractional parts.

Aes signatum. The earliest Roman coinage. Large rectangular blocks of bronze, stamped with a design on either side.

Akce. Turkish silver coin issued between the fourteenth and seventeenth centuries with inscription types on both sides.

Albertin. Gold coin named after its issuer, Albert, Archduke of Austria, governor of Spanish Netherlands (1598–1621). Types, busts of Albert and wife Elizabeth with reverse cross and date.

Altun. Turkish gold coin introduced by Muhamad II in 1454. Obverse type, Sultan's name and mint and date; reverse, titles.

Ambrosino. (1) Gold coin of Milan of thirteenth century with type of St Ambrosius; (2) silver coin of thirteenth to fifteenth century with types, cross, and St Ambrosius.

Ange d'or. Gold coin instituted by Philip IV of France in 1341 with types of St Michael and the

dragon and an elaborate cross with four crowns. Imitated with variations in the Low Countries.
Angel. Gold coin of value 6*s* 8*d*, introduced by Edward IV in 1465 with types of St Michael slaying dragon and ship bearing shield and cross above. The angel was struck up to the reign of Charles I.
Anna. Copper subdivision of the silver rupee in India. Types, badge of East India Company and balance.
Antoninianus. The double denarius, instituted by the emperor Caracalla in A.D. 215. The obverse bears an Imperial portrait wearing a radiate crown. The piece was originally issued in silver, but through successive debasements it became by mid-third century a copper piece with a surface wash of silver, and disappeared in Diocletian's reform of A.D. 296.
Aquilino. Silver coin of gros class, struck in Tyrol and North Italy in thirteenth century with types of eagle and double cross.
Argenteus. The larger Roman silver coins issued from the reform of 296 throughout the fourth century.
As. The unit of the early Roman Republican bronze coinage with, obverse, head of Janus and, reverse, the prow of a galley and sign of value. After the reorganization of the coinage by the Emperor Augustus in 27 B.C. the as was struck as a quarter of the large bronze sestertius. On the Imperial as, which continued to be struck till the late third century A.D., the types are, on obverse, the Imperial portrait and titles and, on reverse, a personification or scene.
Augustalis. Gold coin of Frederick II of Sicily (*c.* 1231), with profile portrait type in Roman manner on obverse and eagle reverse.
Aureus. The chief Roman gold coin. Little issued in the Republic except by the contenders for power in the civil wars at the end of the first century B.C. Under the emperors the aureus became a regular issue and was struck at varying standards till its replacement by a new piece in A.D. 312.
Baiocco. Papal copper coin of eighteenth and early nineteenth centuries. Usual types, papal arms with reverse, word BAIOCCO.
Bawbee. Billon coin issued in sixteenth and seventeenth centuries in Scotland with types of thistle and cross. Later, royal portrait on obverse.
Bezant. General name given to gold coins of the Byzantine Empire and their imitations.
Bolognino. Silver coin originally issued by Bologna from twelfth century with types, Imperial title and word BONONI. Widely copied throughout Italy.
Bonnet piece. Scottish gold coin of James V with profile portrait of king wearing bonnet and Scottish arms on reverse.
Botdrager. Silver coin of double-gros class in fourteenth century in Brabant and Flanders. Name derived from obverse type of helmeted lion, colloquially termed the 'pot-carrier'.
Bracteate. Thin silver coins with type in relief on one side and incuse on other, widely issued in Germany and Switzerland from twelfth to fourteenth centuries. Types, facing portraits, buildings, and heraldic devices.
Carlino. Gold and silver coins introduced by Charles II of Naples in 1287 with types of angel greeting the Virgin and shield reverse.
Cash. Generic term for many small Oriental copper coins, particularly Chinese.
Cast. A piece produced by pouring molten metal into a previously modelled mould. The early Roman aes grave, many coins of the Greek 'imperial' period, and medals of the fifteenth and sixteenth centuries were cast. In most other series the minute roughness of a cast surface is indicative of a forgery.
Cent. Copper coin of the United States, one hundredth part of a dollar. Various types of which the most famous is the Indian head.
Chaise d'or. Large gold coins issued in France in fourteenth century with type of king enthroned.
Ch'ien. Chinese round copper coin, first introduced in twelfth century B.C. Earlier type up to sixth century B.C. has round hole in centre and characters indicating weight and source. Later types up to nineteenth century have square centre hole. Still later, characters indicating value were added.
Cistophoros. Large silver coin, issued from *c.* 200 B.C. under the kings of Pergamum and in other cities of western Asia Minor and continuing under Roman proconsuls and emperors. Types, mystic Bacchic cista and entwined snakes.
Contorniate. Roman bronze pieces with a distinctive flattened edge issued in the fourth century A.D. Types are heroes of mythology, former great emperors, and scenes alluding to sports. These were not coins but a kind of token used in connection with the public games.
Countermark. A symbol, letter, or group of letters punched into the face of a coin to extend the validity of the coin in time or space. Commonly found on bronze coins of the early Empire.
Crown. (a) Gold coin of value 5*s* struck in the reigns of Henry VIII and Edward VI with Tudor rose types, and in reigns of Edward VI, James I, and Charles I with various portrait types; (b) large silver coin of same value first struck by Edward VI with equestrian portrait. Continued in all subsequent reigns, usually with profile portrait.
Daalder. Silver coin of the thaler class in the Low Countries. Most common type is a standing mailed figure holding shield and provincial arms.
Daric. Gold coin of the Persian kings, with type of king shooting with bow – incuse reverse. Name derived from Persian King Darius.
Denarius. The standard silver coin of the Roman Republic and early Empire, first introduced in 211 B.C. Types under the Republic: first, the helmeted head of Roma on obverse with mark of value X (ten asses) and Dioscuri on reverse; later, scenes alluding to the family history of the moneying magistrates appeared on the reverse. In the first century B.C. both obverse and reverse have personal allusions, but portraiture of living persons is not found till the issue of Julius Caesar in 44 B.C. Throughout the Empire the denarius had on obverse the portrait and title of the Emperor or one of his family and on reverse a personification with well-marked attributes as a pictorial shorthand for various qualities and acts of the Emperor. The denarius was ousted by the antoninianus in mid-third century.
Denga. Russian silver coin issued from fourteenth century by Dukes of Moscow and Kiev. Often of irregular shape. Common type, figure on horseback.
Denier (denar, denaro, etc.). Silver coin similar to English penny issued from time of Charlemagne (768–814) and copied all over western Europe. Variety of types including the inscription type with monogram of Charlemagne, ecclesiastical buildings, portraits, mint names.

Sextanal as, Janus–Prow, *c.* 211 B.C., obverse and reverse

Die. The metal punch in which the design for a coin or medal is engraved in intaglio. From the die, placed on a piece of metal and struck, a coin is produced.
Dinar. Islamic gold coin. The earliest dinars in later seventh century were imitations of Byzantine solidi. From beginning of eighth century the dinar has Arabic inscription types on both sides, giving mint, date, and religious formulae. Later, ruler's name was added.
Dinara. Gold coin of the Kushan kings in Northwest India and later in fourth and fifth centuries of the Gupta kings in India. Types, commonly standing figure of the king and, reverse, a seated god with inscriptions in Sanscrit.
Dirhem. Islamic silver coins with types generally similar to those of dinar.
Dobra. Gold coin of Portugal of two, four, and eight escudos struck by John V (1706–50). Types, royal portrait and Portuguese arms.
Dollar. Large silver coin of the United States issued from 1785. Name probably derived from thaler. Types, the head of Liberty and American eagle.
Doubloon. More properly dublone, Spanish gold coin of two escudos. Introduced in later Middle Ages, but struck in quantity from gold of the New World. Types, Spanish arms with value and arms of Leon and Castille. Multiples of four and eight escudos.
Drachm. Small silver coin struck by many Greek cities and states. The didrachm, the double, is the commoner. Multiple of four, the tetradrachm, was the standard large silver coin, while the ten piece, the decadrachm, was issued only occasionally. Also the common silver coin of the Parthian and Sassanian kings. Parthian types, bust of king with, reverse, seated figure and inscription in Greek. Sassanian types, bust of king with headdress and, reverse, fire altar.
Ducat (Venetian). The gold zecchino of Venice, struck from late thirteenth century with types of Christ in oval frame and kneeling Doge receiving standard from St Mark. Name derived from part of the Latin inscription.
Ducat (European). Gold coin continued from Middle Ages. Name applied to many other similar gold coins throughout western Europe with varying types. One of the most important was that of the Netherlands with types, mailed figure and inscription reverse.
Dupondius. Roman two-as piece in aes. In the Empire it was in size and types similar to the as but was distinguished from it by the radiate crown worn by the Emperor.
Edge. On medals of all periods, usually smooth. On coins up to the introduction of mechanical striking in the sixteenth to seventeenth centuries, also smooth; thereafter, milled or ribbed to prevent clipping. Some large coins have an inscription engraved on the edge.
Electrum. Natural mixture of gold and silver found locally in Asia Minor; the metal of the earliest coins.
Escudo. Spanish gold coin originally with types of Spanish arms and cross; latterly from Charles III, royal portrait and Spanish arms. Multiples of two, four, and eight.
Exergue. The portion of a coin or medal below the ground line of the design. Often contains specific information, such as mint-mark or date.
Fabric. The metal from which a coin is made, including the characteristic surface and appearance imparted by production.

Gold Florentine florin issued by Giovanni S. Tommaso de Altoviti, 1447. British museum

Guinea, Charles II (1660–85), obverse and reverse. British Museum

Fanam. Small gold coin of southern India, Ceylon, and Malabar coast, struck with great variety of types from tenth to eighteenth centuries. Silver fanams also issued from sixteenth century.
Farthing. Struck in silver commonly from time of Edward III in England and Alexander III in Scotland, with types similar to those of the penny. Farthing tokens in copper issued by James I and Charles I. Types with obverse portrait and Britannia reverse first struck in 1672.
Fels. Islamic copper coin. Earliest were imitations of Byzantine pieces, but from beginning of eighth century have types similar to those of dinar and dirhem.
Field. The flat portion of either side of a coin not occupied by the design.
Florin. The *fiorino d'oro* struck in Florence from 1252, with types of St John the Baptist and reverse the lily, the arms of Florence. The *fiorino d'argento* of same types also issued. In England gold coin of value 6*s* struck briefly in 1344 by Edward III with obverse type of king enthroned.
Follis. The large aes coin introduced by the reform of Diocletian in A.D. 296.
Franc. French silver coin in sixteenth and early seventeenth centuries of testoon class with types, royal portrait, and floreate cross. In 1795 established as the unit of the decimal system, and issued in one-, two-, and five-franc pieces. Types, head of Liberty or royal portrait and reverse, value in laurel wreath.
Fuh. Another name for early Chinese copper cash.
Genovino. Gold coin issued in Genoa from thirteenth century with types of gateway and cross.
Giulio. Papal silver coin of gros class, originally issued by Julius II (1503–13) but continued into later centuries. Types, portrait of pope, and reverse figure of saint.
Groat. Silver coin of value 4*d.* Issued commonly from Edward III to William IV with types similar to penny and, later, royal portrait and shield. Scottish groat from time of David II.
Gros (groot, groschen, grosso). Silver multiples of the denier. Issued commonly throughout western Europe from twelfth century onwards, with great variety of types. An example is the *gros tournois* of France, with representation of Tours and cross reverse.
Guiennois. Large gold coin of Edward III and the Black Prince, issued in their French possessions in Guienne. Types, prince in armour and elaborate cross reverse.
Guilder. Silver coin of the United Provinces of the Netherlands in seventeenth and eighteenth centuries, with types, provincial arms, and personification of the Netherlands with hat on spear. Multiples of one-and-a-half, two, and three.
Guinea. Gold coin of varying value, finally settling at 21*s*. Issued from 1670 to 1813. Types, royal portrait obverse and heraldic design on reverse. Multiples of five and two guineas and fractions also issued.
Halfpenny. Silver coin with same types as penny, struck occasionally in the Saxon coinage and commonly in later Middle Ages. Copper halfpenny with royal portrait and Britannia reverse first issued in 1672 by Charles II.
Hardi. Gold coin of the Black Prince struck in the French possessions with types, half-length figure of prince and elaborate cross.

Heller. From seventeenth to nineteenth centuries a copper coin of many German states, especially Cologne and Aachen. Multiples of two, four, eight, and twelve, with variety of types.
Incuse. A design or mark sunk into a coin; the opposite of relief.
Inscription. The words which often accompany a coin design. These usually run circularly round the coin, but can occupy any position.
Koban. Thin, flat, oval gold coin of Japan issued from late sixteenth to early nineteenth century. Plain surfaces except for stamps indicating value, etc.
Kopek. In sixteenth century Russian silver coin with type of Tsar on horseback. In eighteenth century a value, not token, copper coin with types Imperial arms and monogram of ruler within wreath. Variety of multiples and divisions.
Kreuzer. Billon coin of sixteenth and seventeenth centuries and copper in eighteenth century in many German states. Name derived from its cross design. Multiples in silver in later eighteenth century in Austria, Hungary, and German states.
Larin. Thin silver bars in shape of fishhook, sometimes with stamp. Current in coastal districts from Persian Gulf to Ceylon in sixteenth and seventeenth centuries.
Laurel. Gold coin of 20*s*, issued by James I. So called from obverse portrait crowned, in the Roman manner, with a laurel wreath.
Legend. Another term for inscription.
Lion (or St Andrew). Scottish gold coin issued from Robert III to Mary. Types, arms of Scotland and St Andrew on cross.
Louis. French gold coin introduced by Louis XIV in 1640 with types, royal portrait and elaborate cross with lis in angles. Continued, with variations of type, up to the Republic.
Matapan. Silver coin of Venice issued from late twelfth century onwards with types similar to the ducat.
Maundy money. Silver coins of 4*d*, 3*d*, 2*d*, and 1*d* given by the English sovereign as alms on Maundy Thursday. In the earlier reigns these were the ordinary current coins, but from George II were special issues with royal portrait obverse and plain figure giving value on reverse.
Medallion. Large pieces of medallic type (in all three metals) issued by the Roman emperors on special occasions. Many issues in gold and silver were, from their weight, intended to be multiples of the standard coins. The larger flan – a disc of metal before stamping – provided opportunity for more elaborate portraiture and types.
Miliarense. Silver coin equal to one-thousandth of the gold pound; introduced by Constantine the Great in the early fourth century.
Mint mark. The mark, in the form of a small symbol, letter or series of letters, placed on a coin to indicate the place where it was struck.
Mohur. Gold coin of the Mogul emperors in India, introduced by Akbar in 1563 and issued into nineteenth century. Early examples were square, but remainder round. Types, names of early Caliphs and, reverse, Emperor's name and titles with date and mint. Jehangir (1605–28) struck some portrait types and designs illustrating the signs of the Zodiac.
Mouton. Gold coin of France of fourteenth and fifteenth centuries with types of Lamb of God with cross and standard, and floreate cross reverse.

Noble, Edward III (1351–77), obverse and reverse. British Museum

Widely copied with variations of design in the Low Countries.
Noble. Large gold coin first issued by Edward III in 1344 of value 6*s* 8*d* with obverse, king standing in ship and reverse an ornate cross. A Scottish noble appeared under David II.
Nomisma. The gold coin of the later Byzantine Empire. Usually scyphate in form with types of the Emperor, Christ, the Virgin, and saints.
Nummus. Generic term for coin, but commonly applied to the multiple bronze coins of the Byzantine Empire with Emperor's portrait and Greek numeral of value.
Oban. Multiple of ten of the koban with similar types.
Obol. Generally small silver coin, one-sixth of a drachm. Various multiples also issued.
Obverse. The principal side of a coin ('heads') on which the more important design appears. From Hellenistic times the obverse has usually been reserved for the ruler portrait.
Onza. Spanish gold coin of eight escudos.
Pagoda. Small gold coin issued in great number of states in south India from seventh to eighteenth century. Great variety of types, often representation of a god.
Pavillon. Gold coin issued by Philip VI of France (1328–50) with obverse type of king seated under canopy. Imitated by the Black Prince in his possessions in France.
Penny. The standard silver coin from eighth to fourteenth century. In the early Saxon kingdoms the obverse bore the king's name and the reverse that of the moneyer; types, usually, cross motif. An occasional portrait type was used for obverse and became common after the unification of the kingdom when the place of minting also appeared on the reverse. Types with variations of cross reverse continued under the Normans and Plantagenets. Similar pennies were struck in Scotland and Ireland. The familiar types of copper penny were first issued in 1797.
Peso. Spanish silver coin of four or eight reales (piece of eight) struck from late fifteenth century. Types, originally Spanish arms with value VIII and arms of Castille and Leon. From Charles III royal portrait on one side. Pillars of Hercules type on peso struck in Latin American mints.
Pistole. Spanish gold coin, a double escudo, introduced by Philip II. Type and standard copied in most west European states.
Plate money. Large flat squares of copper with mark of value in each corner and centre, issued in Sweden in seventeenth and eighteenth centuries.
Pu. Early Chinese bronze coin of the type imitating, in miniature, original objects of barter, such as knives and spades. In circulation in last half of the first millennium B.C.
Punch-marked. Flat, square silver coins of India of the last few centuries B.C. Surfaces covered with small punch marks of natural objects, animals, and symbols, probably the marks of merchants and states guaranteeing the pieces.
Quadrans. Quarter of the Roman as. In the Republican aes grave types are head of Hercules on obverse and prow on reverse with mark of value. The quadrans is found only occasionally as a small bronze coin in the early Empire
Quadrigatus. The commonest of the Roman Republican silver didrachms with types, young Janus

head on obverse and, on reverse, Jupiter in a four-horse chariot.
Quinarius. The half-denarius, a rare issue, both in the Roman Republic and Empire. Types usually identical with the denarius. Early quinarii have mark of value V.
Rappen. Small Swiss copper coin of late eighteenth and early nineteenth centuries with types of shield in wreath and value and date.
Real. Silver coin of gros class, issued in Spain from fourteenth century onwards, with types the crowned royal initial and arms of Castille and Leon.
Relief. The protrusion from the field of the design of a coin.
Reverse. The less important side of a coin ('tails').
Rider (or **rijder**). Gold coin also called the Phillipus, struck by Philip le Bon for Brabant in 1435 with obverse type of prince on horseback and reverse elaborate cross.
Rose noble (or **ryal**). Large gold coin of value 10*s* issued by Edward IV in 1465 to replace the noble. Designs similar to those of noble but with rose on ship's side. This coin with variations in design was struck by the Tudor and Stuart monarchs.
Rouble. Large Russian silver coin of thaler or crown class, issued from time of Peter the Great with types, Imperial portrait and Russian double-headed eagle.
Rupee. Indian silver coin, first commonly issued by Mogul emperor, Akbar (1556–1605) and continued to nineteenth century. Types as for mohur. Often square in shape.
Salute. Gold coin of Charles VI of France (1380–1422) and Henry V and VI in the English possessions in France. Types as carlino.
Sceatta. Small English silver coin issued in seventh and eighth centuries with developments of types and designs copied from late Roman coins.
Scudo. Large silver coin in Italy, particularly in papal states from sixteenth century onwards with types of ruler's portrait and various reverses – eagle on globe, shield, etc. Scudo d'oro with similar types.
Semis. The half-as piece of the Roman Republican aes grave with prow reverse and obverse, laureate head of Saturn with mark of value S. In the late Empire the semis was the half solidus and of similar types.
Sen. Cast copper coin of Japan from eighth to tenth century, similar to Chinese cash. Issue resumed in sixteenth century.
Sequin. Popular name, derived from Venetian zecchino, for Turkish gold altun.
Sestertius. In early Roman Republic a small silver coin, the quarter of the denarius with identical types. In the Imperial coinage the sestertius was the major bronze piece, equal to four asses. The types after the first two Emperors are, consistently, an Imperial portrait and titles on the obverse and a personification or scene on the reverse with the letters SC.
Shekel. Jewish silver coin issued in the two revolts against the Romans in 132 B.C.–A.D. 5 and A.D. 66–70. Types, chalice, screen of Tabernacle, etc.
Shilling. Silver coin first issued by Edward VI with types of profile portrait and shield on cross. With minor variations in design this remained a standard denomination.
Shu. Rectangular silver coin of Japan, issued from seventeenth to early nineteenth centuries. Types, normally Japanese characters indicating value.
Siliqua. Small Roman silver coin of the fourth and early fifth centuries. Types, diademed Imperial head on obverse and reverse commonly a seated figure of Roma.
Solidus. The lighter gold piece intrroduced by Constantine the Great about A.D. 312. Obverse type a diademed Imperial portrait. Reverse types limited to Victory types and a few personifications of Imperial qualities.
Sovereign. Large gold coin of value 20*s* introduced by Henry VII in 1489 with types of king enthroned and Tudor rose on shield. Continued under the Tudors with variations of portrait. The modern sovereign with reverse type of St George and the dragon was introduced in 1820.
Stater. Generically a piece of a given weight. Sometimes applied to the principal silver coin of each Greek city, but more commonly denotes a gold or electrum coin. The Ancient Britons of first century B.C. imitated the gold stater of Philip II of Macedon. Of original types of laureate head of Apollo and horsedrawn chariot, little survived after successive copying across Europe except the wreath on obverse and disjointed horse on reverse.
Struck. The term applied to coins produced from dies. The surface of a struck coin is characteristically smooth.
Tari. Silver coin, principally of Knights of St John in Malta. Multiples of eight, twelve, sixteen, and thirty. Types, bust of Master of the Order with reverse, shield or St John's cross.
Thaler. Large silver coin of crown class. Name derived from original coins struck from silver from Joachimstal in Bohemia in 1518. This quickly became the pattern for large silver coins throughout western Europe and was struck in most countries under variety of names and with many types, latterly with ruler's portrait obverse and armorial shield reverse.
Thrymsa. Small English gold coin struck in seventh and eighth centuries with types imitating the tremissis of the late Roman Empire, usually obverse portrait and cross motif reverse.
Tical. Silver coin of Siam. Small silver bars bent inwards in bullet shape. Plain, except for punch mark, usually on inside and outside of bend. Issued from fourteenth to nineteenth century.
Toison. Gold coin of Philip le Beau (1496–1505), issued in Brabant with obverse type crowned shield with, below, insignia of Order of the Golden Fleece. Also a silver piece of similar types.
Tremissis. Small Roman gold coin, the third of the solidus. Widely copied throughout western Europe from sixth to eighth century, particularly by the Merovingians in France. Favourite types, obverse portrait and cross reverse.
Triens. Third of the Roman Republican as. Obverse type, head of Minerva in crested helmet and mark of value.
Type. The design, whether in relief or incuse, on either side of a coin or medal.
Unite. Gold coin of value of 20*s* first struck by James I. So named from the allusion of the inscription to the Union of the Crowns. Types, a profile portrait and an heraldic design. Charles I also issued this denomination together with some triple unites struck at provincial mints during the Civil War.
Victoriate. Early Roman Republic silver coin, normally with head of Jupiter on obverse and Victory crowning a trophy on the reverse.

Shilling, Henry VII (1485–1509), obverse and reverse. British Museum

ETHNOGRAPHICA

The word 'Ethnographica' has come into wide use only recently, and is most commonly to be found as a subject heading in auctioneers' catalogues. Here it replaces the term 'Primitive Art', which is coming under attack from purists who consider the adjective 'primitive' both inaccurate and derogatory in the present instance. Let us say immediately that the objects encompassed in the terms Ethnographica or Primitive Art include works of the highest artistic achievement and the finest technical execution that man has known.

Nevertheless, the use of the word 'Ethnographica' is limited to certain forms of society and certain geographical areas of the world. A practical, accurate and frank definition of the term would be: 'The artefacts of those people throughout the world who have no indigenous form of writing.' This immediately distinguishes Ethnographica not only from the art of Greece and Rome, but also from that of the Ancient Near East, ancient Egypt, most of India, and the Far East, whose 'civilizations' have long been acknowledged, studied and respected in the West. And thus by exclusion it leaves the rest of the world as the sources of Ethnographica, namely, Africa south of the Sahara; Oceania, that is to say, the islands of the Pacific, including Australia; and the Indian cultures of North and South America. The proof of the definition is to be found in the inclusion or exclusion of the pre-Columbian American Indians, depending on whether one considers their use of glyphs a valid form of writing. In this volume their art is treated separately (*see* Antiquities).

The objects concerned vary enormously and are by no means limited to works of art even in the widest sense of that term – hence the use of the word 'artefacts'. Any man-made object from an illiterate society can be included in Ethnographica, from an adze to a cooking pot, from an African mask to a gigantic Easter Island stone statue – though the latter is unlikely ever to appear in the saleroom. But many of these objects, whatever their interest as examples of material culture or technical processes, whether they be fishhooks or rice ladles, gold ornaments or carved wooden figurines, were clearly designed or decorated with an aesthetic intent. Sometimes this can be immediately comprehended by the Western eye, so that certain works, such as the terracotta heads of Ife in Nigeria, Micronesian wooden figures from the island of Nukuoro, and the carved stools and statues of the so-called 'master of Buli' from the Congo, are considered among the world's masterpieces. But in a vast number of cases the very nature of the object (helmet mask, overmodelled skull, nail fetish), its cultural context (as initiation paraphernalia, ancestor memorial, anti-witchcraft device), and the materials from which it is manufactured (mud, blood, bone, shells, pearl buttons) are beyond Western experience. Here, the combined knowledge of the art historian and the anthropologist is required; the former not only for his aesthetic judgment and familiarity with materials and techniques, but also for his awareness of the various levels of meaning of art objects in a society; the latter, for the fruits of his fieldwork, his first-hand knowledge of the people who make and use these objects, and his ability to interpret their cultural significance. In fact, without some understanding of the cultural setting and social context it is often very difficult for a Westerner to make valuable criticisms of Ethnographica on aesthetic grounds alone.

Nevertheless, where experienced fieldworkers have carried out research into the aesthetic reactions of a particular tribe to their own art, it has generally been found that these have corresponded closely with the opinions of acknowledged Western experts. An experiment of this nature consisted of asking the men in various Dan villages in Liberia to place a number of Dan masks in order of quality, and the results not only showed a high level of agreement from village to village, but also largely concorded with the opinion of the experimenter. On the other hand, when masks were shown from other tribes with whom the Dan have no communication and whose art styles were therefore unfamiliar to them, they showed consternation and no sense of appreciation. The Westerner has a similar difficulty to overcome, but he can overcome it in time and with experience.

On the other hand, overenthusiasm and lack of experience can lead to a false appreciation of inferior works, for Primitive Art, like any other art, varies enormously in quality. Furthermore, a worldwide trade in Ethnographica has developed, especially in recent decades, and now objects are being mass-produced in New Guinea (particularly along the Sepik River), in Africa, and by the American Indians, to meet the demands of collectors. From Africa alone it is reckoned that 10,000 pieces are exported annually to Europe and America. The majority of these are obviously specially made for the export trade: others are more expertly treated and variously 'aged' to give them an air of authenticity. Yet, occasionally old pieces are to be found, or again, recent pieces made for traditional use. The problem is therefore not only to tell the good from the mediocre, but even the genuine from the fake, and this may not be easy.

Age, even where it can be proved, is not necessarily a good guide to the authenticity of Ethnographica. One of the earliest outcomes of European contact with the indigenous peoples of America, Africa and Oceania was the production of 'curios' which were specially made on commission or else produced spontaneously as objects to barter for European trade goods. A famous example is to be found in the so-called Afro-Portuguese ivories, which consist of

Mask from Oruro, Bolivia, with painted electric light bulbs for eyes. Used by the local miners in the so-called 'diablada' dance. Horniman Museum

European-type spoons, forks and salt cellars, as well as horns bearing the Portuguese royal coat of arms, produced by West African ivory carvers in the sixteenth century. These, however, are today collectors' items in their own right. On the other hand, perishable materials such as wood, hide, unfired clay, and featherwork, decay rapidly in a tropical climate, and objects made of these are often very recent, even though they may look antique. A brief survey of the areas to be discussed in detail may serve to clarify this.

Africa

There is very little woodwork outside museums that is more than 100 years old, apart from Dogon or Tellem sculptures from the Hombori Mountains in Mali, where the climate and methods of preservation have been exceptional. Some of these pieces, along with textile fragments, are being dated to the fourteenth century A.D. Metalwork and terracottas (the oldest dating back to 500 B.C.) are being found sporadically, particularly in West Africa, usually by chance, though sometimes an archaeological dig follows.

Oceania

The great explorations of the Pacific can be said to have begun with Cook's arrival in *The Endeavour* in 1769, and, large stone statues and recent archaeological finds apart, this date can be considered the *terminus a quo* for almost all surviving Polynesian Ethnographica. The Cook and other early collections were dispersed, but few objects collected before 1800 are now to be found outside museums. The vast majority of Polynesian objects are nineteenth-century, for by 1900 most of the island civilizations had been destroyed and their populations decimated, though modern imitations form part of a lively tourist trade today. In some of the larger islands of Melanesia, particularly New Guinea and New Britain, tribal societies still exist and so the production of traditional objects for ritual purposes continues.

North America

Nearly 400 pieces collected by European voyagers on the Pacific North West Coast before 1800 are known to have survived in collections throughout the world. Otherwise, apart from archaeological finds, especially from the South and South West (*see* Antiquities), barely anything has come down to us that can be dated before the nineteenth century. The first crossing of the continent was made by Lewis and Clark in 1804–6, and though Clark put together an important collection of Indian relics, this vanished mysteriously after his death in 1838 and the chances of its ever reappearing are now slim. The vast majority of Indian artefacts are post-1880. Most contemporary pieces are made for the gift shop and the tourist trade, but it should be realized that some of the finest Indian baskets were made in the 1920s and 1930s, and that there are a number of good wood carvers on the North West Coast today.

South America

Few collections of Indian material were made in the last century, and nothing appears to have survived from before 1800 apart, of course, from the considerable pre-Columbian collections to be found throughout the world. In fact, it was the interest in pre-Columbian antiquities that was largely responsible for collectors disregarding contemporary Indian material for so long. Today, tribal Indian art persists in the equatorial forests, while in the cities and mining villages cults which have varied African and European origins are still alive.

From this brief outline it can be seen that authentic Ethnographica is still being produced today, but only in those societies that have succeeded in maintaining their traditional way of life in the face of encroaching industrialism. But even the largest ethnographic collections – such as those of the British Museum, the Museum für Völkerkunde in Berlin, or the Field Museum of Natural History in Chicago – are of comparatively recent date. This is not only because the objects are usually made in perishable materials, and so those collected as early as, say, the sixteenth century, mostly disappeared or disintegrated long ago, but also because collecting examples of material culture developed on a large scale only in the nineteenth century with the formation of European colonies in Africa and Oceania and the opening up of the West in North America. With the advancement of anthropology – the increased interest in the Study of Man – the formation of ethnographic collections has grown progressively throughout the twentieth century. And with the realization that much ethnographic material has an enormous aesthetic value, Museums of Primitive Art or Ethnic Art have arisen, and many scientific expeditions are now being sent into the field for the express purpose of collecting art objects.

African

It is becoming a matter of course to divide Africa up into two contrasting areas: North Africa, and Africa south of the Sahara. And although we shall be omitting a discussion of North Africa in the present section, it is essential to realize that down to the beginning of this century, the natural trade links of West Africa with the outside world were across the Sahara to the Mediterranean. It was from the north that Islam first penetrated, as it continues to penetrate, the traditional animist institutions, and from the north likewise that new techniques, such as the art of filigree work, and decorative designs were introduced. The Sahara served not so much as a barrier as an area of cultural exchange.

Nevertheless, a distinction can be made between the relative homogeneity of the peoples of North Africa compared with the enormous fragmentation of most of the rest of the continent, as can be seen at a glance at a language map. In the whole of North Africa, four basic languages are spoken – Arabic, Berber, Egyptian and Cushitic – whereas some 200 Bantu languages are spoken in Central, East, and Southern Africa, while there exist some 800 distinct languages in West Africa. There also exists a comparable, though numerically perhaps not quite so large, variety of art styles. Indeed, there has been a recent attempt to correlate art areas with language groups, and though this has been very promising, it has not yet achieved entirely successful results, and so we are bound to return to the more conservative geographical divisions of the art-producing regions.

Seated mother and child figure of the Afo of Southern Nigeria, collected *c.* 1900. Horniman Museum

Yoruba gelede society mask from Western Nigeria. Gallery 43, London

These divisions are based on wood sculpture – largely masks and figurines – and consist of West Africa and the Congo, with Cameroon acting as a sort of stylistic hinge between the two. The Congo area can be extended to incorporate East Africa and the whole of Southern Africa, which in the past were thought to be almost devoid of art, partly due to the local administrators' lack of interest in the subject.

WEST AFRICA

This is the land of the true African Negro: dark-skinned, and tall, with kinky hair, a narrow head, wide wings to the nose, and a long jaw – features often reproduced in sculpture. The area is formed by a line running from Dakar at Cape Verde eastwards to Timbuctu at the northern limit of the Niger bend, and on to Lake Chad at the north-east corner of Nigeria, and thence south-westwards to reach the coast at Duala in Cameroon. The western and southern boundary is formed by the Atlantic.

Archaeological research and the introduction of such techniques as radio-carbon dating and thermoluminescence have considerably broadened and deepened our knowledge of West African art history, while at the same time raising new problems. The earliest Negro culture so far discovered is that known as Nok, widely distributed over the Bauchi Plateau in central and northern Nigeria. This has been dated from the ninth century B.C. to the second century A.D., and from the fifth century B.C. a number of terracottas representing men, women and animals have been associated with it. Although there are local variants, a characteristic element of these is the eye enclosed within an inverted triangle or subtended arc of a circle, with a heavy, usually semi-circular, eyebrow above. Great attention is paid to hairstyle or headdress, and the facial features are clearly negroid. The pupils of the eyes, the nostrils, the everted lips and the ears all contain holes passing to the hollow interior of the head.

It had been suggested that a line of continuity in Nigerian art history could be traced from the Nok culture, through Ife (twelfth–fourteenth century), down through Benin art (1400–1897), and continuing in the wood carving of the Yoruba of south-western Nigeria to this day. But this received a bad jolt when objects from the Igbo Hoard, previously thought to go back to about 1600, were radio-carbon dated to the ninth century A.D. This Igbo Hoard consists of a number of bronze and other objects from a royal burial, a shrine, and a disposal pit, discovered near Onitsha in the Niger Delta. These reveal not only complete mastery of the lost-wax technique of casting, at an earlier date than had previously been imagined, but also a range of highly complex decorative motifs which neither look back to Nok nor forward to Ife and Benin. This suggests that further archaeological discoveries may prove that West African bronze casting not only goes back even considerably earlier in time, but also that it had a number of individual centres, each with its own particular style.

The art of Ife – a Yoruba city in the Western Region of Nigeria – was received with incredulity by many scholars when the first examples were brought to Europe in the early years of the present century. Its 'naturalism' and 'realism' (terms never quite so accurate or meaningful as they at first appear) were considered beyond the capacities of African craftsmen, and origins around the Mediterranean were looked for, particularly among the Etruscans. Today, the African source of these terracotta and bronze heads is accepted. Other problems have arisen, however. Ife is 250 miles from Nok in space, but 1,000 years away in time. The characteristic features of Nok terracottas – the triangular or hemispherical eye, the perforations of eyes, ears and lips – are wanting in Ife art, and indeed the modelling is very different. Yet no other forerunner can be suggested for the Ife terracottas, which seem to have arrived on the scene fully developed. The bronzes cannot be considered descendants of the earlier Igbo tradition, but appear to be exact translations of the terracottas into metal. Perhaps in the present state of our knowledge we are too eager to join up related but not contiguous pieces in the jigsaw puzzle.

Oral tradition relates that about 1400 the Oni, or king, of Ife was requested to send a bronze caster to the city of Benin, a hundred miles to the south east, in order to teach the inhabitants the technique. What is certain is that when the Portuguese first reached Benin in 1485 the Bini, as the people themselves are called, had already mastered the lost-wax process, though even the earliest bronze heads that have come down to us (and which probably do not predate the Portuguese) already differ considerably from those made in Ife in many respects, though not through any defect in technique. The individuality, the look of serenity, the humanism of Ife art have been replaced by coarser, harsher expressions, almost of brutality. The eyes, which seemed sometimes on the point of closing at Ife, are here wide open, and the pupil is often an iron inlay. The wings of the nose, so finely modelled at Ife, are exaggerated at Benin until they are almost separated from the septum. However technically excellent the early work of Benin, it contains within it the seeds of that decay which was to make the nineteenth-century bronzes stiff, heavy, dull caricatures of kingship.

But Benin art is manifold. Its purpose was to glorify the king and his court, and so it includes not only the bronze heads for the shrines dedicated to former kings and queen mothers, but also representations of important court dignitaries and powerful foreign visitors, both African and European; a wide range of court regalia, from pectorals and hip masks to bells, staves, bracelets and flasks; and many hundred bronze plaques which decorated the pillars of the royal palace and commemorated in high relief important events. These last are variously dated from 1550 to 1700, when their manufacture apparently ceased.

But bronze was not the only material in use. Some of the ivory carving is exquisite, both on whole tusks which were thrust into apertures in the bronze heads and rested their points against the back wall of the royal shrines, and on the king's own regalia. Terracotta and carved wooden heads are also to be found, but these are often late work or otherwise dubious. Gold is absent, except in the form of brass gilt, presumably made by the Portuguese, which was then inlaid in some of the early ivory bracelets.

At present the presumed chronology of the surviving Benin bronze heads begins in 1500 A.D. with the thinnest castings, also recognizable by the representation of a carnelian bead choker, high but restricted to the neck. This is followed about 1550 by similar heads on a rolled carnelian base like a platter, and the so-called Queen Mother heads with tall, rather conical headdresses and no base. Thereafter, with the increasing availability of brass or bronze from European sources, the heads became progressively larger and the castings thicker. The carnelian choker rises above the chin to the level of the lower lip. In the first half of the eighteenth century, a flanged base is added to the heads of kings, while the Queen Mother heads are placed on truncated pyramids. Some time after 1816 a pair of upright 'wings' was added to the carnelian crowns. In 1897 the British Punitive Expedition which overran the City of Benin and exiled the king, brought Benin art to a sudden end. Subsequent attempts to revive bronze casting and other crafts have resulted in the production of uninspired and technically poor imitations of a dead tradition.

Further to the north east, in Cameroon just south of Lake Chad, there had long flourished another culture, that of the Sao. The earliest radio-carbon results now date this back to the fifth century B.C. (contemporary with the Nok culture), but the terracottas for which the Sao are known can be dated at present only from the eleventh to the sixteenth centuries. These seldom achieve the aesthetic quality of Nok pieces, for instead of being modelled, many of the figurines appear almost to be cut-outs in two dimensions, like gingerbread men. Occasionally heads are conceived in the round, but generally they consist of balls of clay with lips, eyes, and a medial line pinched into them, and other features, such as scarification marks, scored with a blunt instrument. Terracottas dated from 1600 (when the Sao culture came to an end) are attributed to the present occupants of the area, the Fali.

There appears at one time to have been a lively tradition of terracotta animal and human figurines stretching westward at least as far as the upper Niger. In the western Sudan, chance finds are frequent, and though they are often crude, occasionally they achieve distinction, as in the case of a fine kneeling figure of a woman, about 12 inches (30 cm) high, found near Djenné. Other terracottas from the Ségou area have been dated to the fourteenth and fifteenth centuries by means of thermoluminescence.

Finally, archaeological research in the Hombori Mountains in the Niger Bend is giving a much deeper perspective to the art of the Dogon. The Dogon are famous for their cubistic masks and figure carvings which are much sought after by collectors. They are also notorious for the manner in which carvings from their area which are rounded rather than cubistic, which are heavily patinated or covered with sacrificial material, or which give a subjective impression of great age, have been attributed to the Tellem, a people who are supposed to have preceded them in the mountains, yet whose very existence has been denied by some scholars. Ever since French anthropologists began intensive fieldwork among the Dogon in the 1930s, they have insisted on the existence of the Tellem on grounds of oral tradition, on the later arrival of the Dogon themselves in the fifteenth century, and on the antiquity of certain carvings. These were preserved in conditions that are unique for West Africa: in a dry climate, and in caves high up in the cliff face where they were protected from the elements and the ravages of termites.

The latest archaeological results show that the

mountains were inhabited by an earlier population (the Tellem?) in the ninth century; that newcomers (the Dogon) arrived in the fifteenth century; that thereafter the earlier inhabitants gradually disappeared leaving the Dogon in occupation; but that gradual cultural changes occurred throughout the whole period of 1,000 years. Fragments of textiles very similar to those woven today have been radiocarbon dated to the fifteenth century, and are thus the oldest known examples of textiles south of the Sahara. Meanwhile in America laboratory tests have also dated some museum specimens of Dogon carving to the fifteenth century. The French anthropologists have thus been vindicated.

Problems persist, however. In one case, an apparently ancient granary door was shown to have been carved by a smith who was still alive a few years ago, so that we must still rely on scientific tests for dating. On occasion an apparent Tellem piece has had the outer sacrificial matter removed to reveal a typically cubistic Dogon carving underneath. And lastly, Dogon sculpture has not only been subject to modern imitation: recently a magnificent piece was found to have been assembled from limbs cannibalized from another figure.

But most African Ethnographica, as we have already said, is far more recent than this: it is authenticity rather than age that one should be concerned with in the majority of cases.

In West Africa a useful distinction can be made between village art and court art. In those societies where there is no central government, where in fact the villages are autonomous, masks and figure sculptures abound, and the chief material used is wood. Where the political unit is the state, with a state capital and a kingship system (as, for example, in Ashanti, Dahomey or Benin), then masking societies are generally absent, art and artists are controlled by the court, and precious materials such as bronze, gold or ivory are employed. But in both the peasant hut and the royal palace are found shrines with various types of ancestor figures to whom sacrifices are made.

It is the common practice to give tribal names as attributions to examples of African art, but it must be realized that some African tribes produce works in a variety of contrasting styles, while some styles are shared by two or more tribes with minimal distinguishing features. For example, the Bambara of the Western Sudan have a number of secret societies through which, traditionally, men progress during their life time, and several of these have associated masks. The boys' society, *n'tomo*, employs a face mask with a varying number of horns rising vertically above the brow. The *komo* society uses helmet masks with a long projecting animal jaw, the whole covered with mud and sacrificial material. The *kono* society also has a helmet mask with projecting jaw, but this time counterbalanced with a pair of antelope horns behind. The *koré* society uses face masks representing various animals such as the lion and the hyena. The *tyi wara* society wears antelope carvings on top of the head, while the face is masked with fibre tresses. There is not the least unity of style among these masks, yet all are made and used by the Bambara.

On the other hand, the *kono* society helmet mask with the monstrous jaw and horns behind is very similar to the *poniugo* mask of the neighbouring Senufo, which in turn seems to have been copied by the Baule of the Ivory Coast. The type extends as far eastwards as the Niger Delta, where degenerate forms are found among the Kalabari Ijo and the Ijebu Yoruba. South and west of the Bambara it is found again among the Toma and the Baga respectively.

Mende female figure from Sierra Leone with fine hair-style, beautiful neck (hence the wrinkles), large breasts and exaggerated navel representing umbilical hernia. Horniman Museum

Some very beautiful face masks, often representing the feminine ideal (though always worn by men) were used by the all-male *poro* society of a number of tribes throughout Liberia and in western and central Ivory Coast, particularly the Dan and the Senufo. In contrast, other tribes in this area, such as the Ngéré-Wobé and Grebo, employed for very similar social purposes masks combining humanized animal features whose appearance was intended to be horrific and terrifying.

Corresponding to the men's *poro* society was the women's *sande* or *bundu* society. Among the Mende of Sierra Leone, the members of the *bundu* society themselves wear helmet masks. This is one of the very rare cases of women wearing masks in Africa.

Despite the wide variety of art styles in West Africa, there is a body of features which are common to most figure carvings. The head is disproportionately large to the rest of the body; little attention is paid to the ears, or often even to the facial features; the navel is exaggerated, and the hands come to rest on either side of it or else down towards the sex; the buttocks are enlarged; the legs are slightly flexed; the calves are stressed, but little or no attention is paid to the feet, which may even disappear into the base.

The neck may be elongated and ringed as a sign of beauty, as can be seen in Mende figures from Sierra Leone and in Ashanti dolls. Sexual characteristics may be exaggerated, or male and female features combined to show a hermaphroditic figure, as among the Dogon, where the primary sexual characteristics may be absent but the secondary ones of beard and breasts appear together. Although the majority of sculptures are unclothed, great attention is paid to headdress or hairstyle and to scarification marks on face and body, for these give the figure its identity.

The figure is generally observed frontally, the pose is static, and the conception symmetrical, but there are many notable exceptions. The *epa* and *gelede* masks of the Yoruba of Nigeria often support a superstructure incorporating one or many figures in motion or interacting, as do the carved linguist's staffs of the Ashanti. And mother-and-child figures, with the mother usually seated and the child at her breast, must of necessity be asymmetrical: the fact that the majority of these are found in areas near the coast suggests European introduction of the Madonna and Child motif, but there is no evidence to prove this.

What has been said of West Africa broadly applies to the art of Cameroon and Central Africa: it is therefore interesting to concentrate on the differences.

It is the tribes of the Grasslands of central Cameroon that provide the watershed between the art of West and Central Africa. Here powerful kingship systems prevail and most art objects form part of the royal treasury. Masking societies exist, but instead of being in opposition they tend to be controlled by the king or his courtiers. Everything surrounding royalty is conceived on a monumental scale and intended to be sumptuously decorated.

Far right So-called nail-fetish from the Kongo people on the Lower Congo River. The right hand originally held a metal lance or dagger. The piece of European trade mirror closes a cavity containing magical substances. These figures are purported to have been used both to cure disease and to cause harm, a nail or piece of iron being hammered on each occasion that the figure's help was sought. Horniman Museum

M'Bulu figure of Obamba (Gaboon). These figures, carved in wood and covered with European sheet copper, were placed in baskets containing bones of ancestors, and served to ward off evil spirits. Horniman Museum

Behind thrones stand lifesize carvings of retainers, helmet masks are made twice as large as the head of the wearer, tobacco pipes are 3 feet (100 cm) and more in length. Trade beads, which were a form of currency and therefore denoted wealth, were applied all over even the largest wood carvings. More recently, copies of the carved masks have been cast in brass or bronze since this is a more valuable material, but although some of these have been worn in ceremonies, many more have been produced for the tourist trade and export.

In view of this it is not surprising that the main feature of Grasslands art is an exuberant fullness, a roundness of form. The cubistic nature of much West African art, the restraint of the finest of Congo art, are here absent. Instead, we have sculpture conceived totally in the round, asymmetrical poses, and even figures in motion, dancing. Emblems of royalty – elephant, buffalo, panther – abound.

Fine old carvings – some of them royal portraits – are now exceedingly rare, and the majority of them have been widely published in books. Small carvings, and even miniatures, exist, with or without over-all bead decoration. But also to be admired are the richly carved house posts and doorways that once embellished every royal compound.

Much work is being done to resolve the difficult question of attribution of Grasslands pieces to the various tribes and chiefdoms – Bamileke, Bamum, Bangwa, Bekon, Bacham, etc. Much has been achieved, but due to the mobility of artists, who might work for a number of different chiefs over a wide area, and the manner in which art objects were traded or exchanged, the fact that a piece was purchased in a particular village is no sure guide to its actual provenance. Precise attribution is therefore still hazardous.

In the Gaboon one enters the realm of the art of Central Africa. Here are found the unique but highly contrasted reliquary figures of the Fang and the Kuta, or BaKota. (Ba- is a Bantu plural prefix and will be omitted in further mention of Bantu tribal names: thus BaKongo becomes Kongo.) The Fang figures known as *bieri*, are conceived in rounded forms, with swelling tubular limbs; fat, almost horizontal buttocks; flexed legs and knock knees. A peg hanging down like a shooting stick served to fix the figure in a box of ancestral bones, which it then protected against evil spirits. A similar purpose was served by the *bweté* of the Kuta, though the form the reliquary figure took was geometrical, consisting of a lozenge surmounted by a flat, sometimes truncated, oval face, this again sometimes supporting a semi-lunar coiffure. The whole was carved in wood but entirely covered with sheets or strips of copper. There are many substyles of both *bieri* and *bweté*, and they include some of the finest examples of African art.

From the south-west Gaboon come the famous white-faced masks with slanting slit eyes, which give them an oriental appearance. The generic attribution to the M'Pongwe in fact covers a number of subtribes and substyles.

As far as the art is concerned, Central Africa stretches from the Atlantic to the Great Lakes, and south to the Zambezi. Six main style areas can be distinguished: (1) Lower Congo (Kongo and Vende); (2) Stanley Pool (Teke, Yanzi); (3) Kwango (Yaka, Suku, Mbala and Pende); (4) Kasai (Kuba, Lulua and Lwalwa); (5) Eastern Kasai and Katanga (Luba, Songye, Lunda and Jokwe); and (6) North and North East (Lega, Mangbetu and Zande).

The most spectacular pieces from the Lower Congo are the nail fetishes, wooden male figures, 1–4 feet (30–120 cm) in height, whose bodies and upper limbs are studded with pieces of iron, giving the impression of something between a St Sebastian and a porcupine. The arm is often raised, and held a knife or sword, and a piece of mirror may close a cavity in the abdomen which contains magical substances.

Grave figures (*mintadi*) in unusual asymmetrical poses (hand on cheek, chin on knee) were carved in stone, possibly under the influence of local Portuguese tomb sculpture. Later, they were carved in wood, as were many mother-and-child figures. There is a wide variety of masks with human faces devoid of animal features.

The old Teke figures are recognizable by the striations down the face, and the board-like beard, wider at the extremity than at the chin. Discoid face masks painted with symbolic designs are also known, but only a handful can be considered absolutely authentic.

Many of the features of Yaka art are shared with the Suku. The most distinguishing feature is the *retroussé* nose, which appears both on figures and masks, whose small face, entirely surrounded by raffia, is surmounted by a towering pagoda of a headdress, or a human or animal figurine, or even a carved hut. The Pende depict the face with pointed chin and downcast eyes, whose sleepy eyelids also droop to a point. This is attractive not only in the masks but especially in the small, finely carved ivory amulets.

Kuba is a loose but useful name to cover a number of closely connected tribes on the left bank of the Kasai. The Kuba royal portrait statues in Tervuren and the British Museum are unique in African art. On the other hand there are countless wooden palm-wine beakers, some of them beautifully and imaginatively carved in human form, the exaggerated head serving as cup.

There are a number of mask forms, the most famous of which, *mashaam boy*, is made of basketwork covered with coloured cloth, sewn with beads and cowrie shells. From the crown of the head there rises an elephant's trunk which falls over the eyes. These were once royal masks, but today are used by entertainers, and equally made for tourists.

The beauty of the best of Luba wood carving lies in its restrained expression, the rounded smoothness of the forms, and the delicacy of the long, relaxed limbs. There are male and female standing figures, stools supported by a kneeling woman, head rests supported by caryatids, seated or kneeling women holding bowls. In the west is found the Shankadi style, which includes the figures with the 'cascade' coiffure; in the east are the Hemba, to whom are to be attributed the works of the so-called Master of Buli.

Besides a superb horned mask at Tervuren, there are a number of so-called *kifwebe* masks, carved wooden hemispheres with round closed eyes, which seem to be emitting successive ripples of fine white lines – Op art at its best and before its time! The aggressive *kifwebe* masks of the neighbouring Songye differ in having projecting eyes and rectangular mouths and a trapezoidal chin.

Above Ngumi/Thonga (South Africa/ Mozambique border) pair of standing figures. Rijksmuseum voor Volkenkunde, Leiden

Left Mask of the Yaka worn by boys during initiation. The up-turned nose is a typical feature of Yaka art. The projection under the chin is to hold the mask in place. Horniman Museum

Songye figures also display the rectangular or figure-of-eight mouth. They are squat, though they may stand 3 feet (90 cm) high, with large heads and great prognathous jaws. Head, neck and body are often covered with beads, fibres, feathers, animal pelts and brass studs, and from the top of the head there usually rises an antelope horn, pointing slightly forward.

In Jokwe art, the face is in a state of repose. Deep cavities form the orbits of the eyes, which are themselves open only slit wide, sometimes giving the whole head a cadaverous appearance, beautiful though this often is. Figures tend to be squat, with stumpy legs flexed at the knee. They may represent chiefs, who wear headgear like a floppy straw hat with wide rim pushed up over the forehead. Thrones copied the form of European chairs, but the backs and stretchers were decorated with carved figures enacting scenes of everyday life.

In the north and north east, both quality and quantity of art objects appear to be poorer than elsewhere, though there are exceptions. The Lega produced a miniature art of carved wood and ivory cult objects, and the finest of these are much sought after. Zande work in wood is more schematic, but often shows a powerful grasp of form. The best pieces are probably all now in museums. Finally, the Mangbetu are known for their anthropomorphic pots, in which the neck is surmounted by a human head whose elongation reproduces the deformation of the skull which these people practise.

In East African art, one tribe, the Makonde of Tanzania and Mozambique, predominates on account of the originality of style and the quantity of works that have survived. Traditional figures and masks generally have bloated faces, with fat, blubbery lips, and often scarifications depicted by meandering threads of beeswax. Modern Makonde sculpture, consisting of senseless monsters, formless and contorted, carved in ebony (a wood almost never used in traditional African art), were first produced for the curio shops in Dar es Salaam. They are an immemorable phenomenon.

But it is slowly becoming clear that the art of East and Southern Africa consists of very much more than the old art of the Makonde. Study of the early travellers' accounts, researches in museum collections, and field reports are now revealing the existence of masks, wood carvings, terracottas, metalwork, and stone sculptures from dozens of often little-known tribes stretching from Omdurman in the Sudan to Durban in South Africa. Their range is so wide and their styles so diverse that it is difficult to make any valid generalizations, except, perhaps, to say that pole sculpture – the elongation of the figure to accommodate the natural proportions of the piece of wood – is found throughout the entire area, and is commoner here than anywhere else in Africa.

Oceanian

The island cultures of the Pacific fall into three distinct groups. First, there is the Polynesian Triangle formed by an imaginary line running from Hawaii in the north to New Zealand in the south west, and across to Easter Island in the east, and thence back to Hawaii. All the islands falling within this triangle constitute Polynesia, a name which in fact means 'many islands'. A further imaginary line running from Fiji, halfway down the western side of the triangle, north-westwards towards Luzon in the Philippines divides the rest of the Pacific into Micronesia ('small islands') to the north, and Melanesia ('black islands', on account of the very dark skin of the majority of the inhabitants) to the south. These lines are very approximate, and must not be considered to form absolute boundaries. Fiji itself is an interesting example of contact and cultural exchanges between Melanesians and Polynesians.

Australia, often excluded from accounts of Oceanic art, is here treated separately at the end of this section.

MICRONESIA

The total land surface of all the islands of Micronesia is only just over 1,000 square miles (2,600 sq km), so that there was probably never a very large production of art objects. Nevertheless, distressingly little survives from this area, though the quality of the pieces that are to be found in museum and private collections suggests a long tradition, especially of wood carving.

Micronesian art is remarkable for its reduction of natural forms to their essentials, as in the highly refined human figurines from Nukuoro in the Carolines, in which even the facial features are dispensed with on the egg-shaped heads. (Such figures are thought to have had an influence on the work of Brancusi.)

From Mortlock come gable masks with white faces outlined in black, and with curious mini-masks or discs on the left side of the head representing a topknot. Truk is known for delightful canoe-prow ornaments of opposed bird figures, so schematized that photographs of them in books are often reproduced upside down. Applied decoration usually consists of firm, elemental designs painted in black on a plain white background.

POLYNESIA

Although there is a surprising homogeneity of language throughout the vast area of Polynesia, there is very considerable variety in the art forms of West and Central Polynesia, Hawaii, the Marquesas, Easter Island, and New Zealand.

The majority of the figure sculptures that have survived from Western and Central Polynesia were collected in the last century by missionaries. Many were sent to the London Missionary Society, and were subsequently presented to the British Museum, but it must be realized that these pieces were only preserved as typical examples of the great number of 'idols' that the missionaries were persuading the islanders to destroy. As a result, only two figure carvings are now known from Samoa, some twenty wood carvings and seven carvings in walrus or whale ivory from Fiji, perhaps fifty figures in all from the Society Islands, and from Rurutu a stone bust and the lone, glorious figure of the ancestor, A'a (in the British Museum), his discoid face and firm body covered with his miniature progeny. Nevertheless, figures from Tonga, the Cook and Society Islands do occasionally turn up. With so few authenticated pieces available attribution is often difficult, but in general these pieces have abnormally large heads; their arms may be freestanding (Tonga), or else clutched to their swollen bellies (Cook and Society Is.). The style of the Cook Islands is easily recognizable by the large eyes and thick mouth which are heavily incised. The Cook Islands style thus leapfrogs the Society Islands to associate itself with that of the Marquesas to the east. But the eyes on Marquesan figures are round, or almost completely so.

The decorated handles of Tahitian flywhisks, terminating in an adossed pair of ancestors with curious topknots, are much sought after. Clubs abound, with many strange forms and often decoration covering the entire surface, but due to their exchange, either as gifts or in trade, and also the mobility of carvers, it is often very difficult to be sure whether a particular example originates in, say, Fiji or Tonga. Stamped barkcloth (*tapa*) was made throughout the whole of Polynesia, though little was produced on Easter Island, and none has survived from New Zealand. Designs varied from island to island. There was, of course, no limit to the size the cloth could attain.

A far larger quantity of figure sculpture – and of Ethnographica in general – has survived from the Marquesas than from Western and Central Polynesia. The most significant diagnostic feature of the Marquesan style is, as was said above, the eye, which is often completely round and enclosed within a clearly defined frame in relief. The thick lips of the wide mouth are slightly parted to display the tongue. The smallest and largest figures are carved in tufa, a soft volcano rock. Many of the larger ones still lie hidden in the tropical undergrowth of the islands. Small carvings, a few inches high, sometimes of an adossed couple with a hole for passing a cord through, may have been fishing charms which were attached to the nets as weights.

The smaller carvings in wood, bone, stone and ivory tend to be stumpy, but the larger ones in wood, which may be more than lifesize, take the form of pole sculpture: the stone adze has cut away only enough to reveal the human form and the stylized facial features, but at the level of the head, shoulders, hips and knees the full width of the original tree trunk is retained. Often the entire body surface of figures carved in wood is covered with curvilinear designs in very low relief. Among all the Polynesians the Marquesans were the most notorious – in the eyes of the missionaries – for tattooing themselves from top to toe. There even exist carved wooden limbs displaying specimens of the tattooists' art to help customers select the patterns they desired.

Other wood carvings include the rare canoe-prow ornaments incorporating a very fine little figure seated on what may be a schematized bird in flight. Much more common are the stilt steps (races on stilts were a favourite Marquesan sport), supported by a little carved figure, the whole decorated with tattoo designs. The Marquesans had a special form of heavy wooden club peculiar to themselves, whose striking end was decorated with a human face with the eyes and nose represented by carved skulls. The design so attracted Gauguin that he adapted it to make a woodcut of the Crucifixion. Stilt steps and clubs vary considerably in quality.

Carvings in walrus ivory include flywhisk handles which rival the wooden ones of Tahiti; ear ornaments with a projection bearing minute human figures; and frog-like miniature figures threaded on

Above Ceremonial adze with designs based on schematized human forms, from Mangaia. Horniman Museum

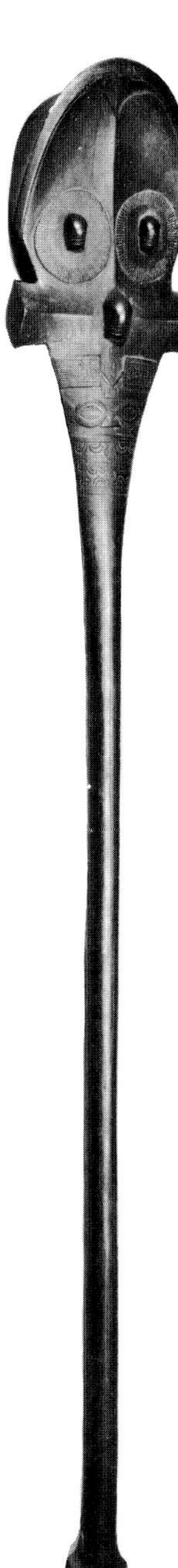

Above Club with miniature skulls forming facial features from the Marquesas. Horniman Museum

sennit for suspending coconut containers or on the more gruesome strangulation cords.

Finally, seashell and tortoiseshell plaques were cut, carved or decorated with fretwork and attached to headbands. These were worn with the shell decorations hanging downwards, like an inverted crown.

The most famous examples of Hawaiian art are probably the large, even lifesize, grimacing figures of which the best known are the two in the British Museum. Originally these stood in the sacred *heiau* or open temple area, and were even more imposing as they were supported on long posts (since cut away) planted in the ground, which gave them added height. They are commonly held to be representations of the war god Ku, but, as in the case of other attributions of carvings to particular Hawaiian deities, there is no certainty of this.

Figure carvings even on a lesser scale are now excessively rare outside museums. The human form is conceived as a number of bold, interlocking, convex masses, the breast often considered as the meeting of contrasting planes. Sex is generally indeterminate, though occasionally male and female organs are clearly depicted. On occasion, shell discs and seeds form the eyes, and human hair may be attached to the head. Besides the Ku figures mentioned, there are a number of others with tall headdresses, some of them exceeding the entire body length. A comb swooping above the head is sometimes considered the attribute of the volcano goddess Pele, but it is as likely to represent a feathered casque actually used by warriors. Figures appear in strange postures, especially as supports for drums or bowls, when they may stand on their hands or rest on their chest and knees. Hands and arms are often carved free of the body. Fat thighs are surpassed by even fatter calves.

The Hawaiians excelled in the art of featherwork, consisting of attaching feathers, taken from tens of thousands of birds, to a network foundation. Red, yellow, and rarely green, feathers were employed to make circular cloaks for chiefs, capes and helmets for great warriors, and representations of snarling gods, which are reputed to have been borne into battle on the heads of the priests in order to terrify the enemy. These last were all made before Captain Cook's discovery of the islands in 1778. Only about twenty have come down to us, and many of these have lost their feathers.

Besides examples of *tapa*, fairly common are necklaces of shells or seeds, and bracelets of turtle shell, bone, boar tusk, or seashells. Some of these, however, are of recent manufacture. The best-known Hawaiian personal ornament consists of a whale or walrus ivory carving in the shape of a fishhook with a hole in it through which were passed long loops of braided human hair. These pendants, though common, are sometimes said to have been the prerogative of princesses – in which case the royal family was exceedingly prolific!

After the gigantic stone statues the most famous examples of the arts of Easter Island are the wood carvings showing old, emaciated men, perhaps even corpses. The body is bent forward, the bearded head is bald or shaven, though it sometimes bears a bird motif in low relief, the eyes are discs of black obsidian set in white fishbone, but most important, the rib cage is depicted almost breaking through the flesh. Other similar carvings show bird men (with a bird's head or mask), double-headed men, and other grotesque types. The female figures differ in that the body, instead of being carved in the round, is treated as a flat slab with the pointed sagging breasts and the long thin arms shown in low relief. One arm crosses the stomach, while the other descends towards the sex, which is clearly female despite the existence of a short beard on the chin.

The authenticity of some of these pieces may be difficult to judge, but considerable variations in quality immediately strike the eye. An early report states that a score or more carvings might be suspended on a dancer's body, which gives some justification for the large number to be found in collections. But it is obvious that no genuine specimens were carved after 1862, when Easter Island's traditional culture came to an end due to the decimation of the population by smallpox. And it appears that already in the 1860s pieces were being specially carved for purposes of barter with visiting sailors. The finest – and apparently the oldest – of the emaciated men bear joint marks on wrists and ankles, and usually on the buttocks as well. These disappear in the poorer specimens, but this may not be a reliable means of telling traditional from tourist pieces, since this degeneration may have begun as early as the beginning of the last century. The female figures, which, on stylistic grounds, would seem to post-date the best of the emaciated males, appear never to have had joint marks.

Other wood carvings exist of lizards, birds with enormous beaks, and pectorals in the shape of a crescent with a human head looking inward at either end. A few genuine small stone heads are also known. But it must be appreciated that an export industry in all these objects has now been in existence for over a century.

The Easter Islanders had two types of club, a short one and a long one, both decorated with a human head at the handle end. The head on the long type is notable for its puffed cheeks and eyes of obsidian and fishbone. The head on the short club was simpler, and might even represent a lizard.

There were also two types of dance paddle, one in which the human face is suggested by a median line rising and breaking into two curved eyebrows, which then descend to form the outlines of ear ornaments. The other type, far less attractive, has the face painted on in red, black, and white.

Finally, as elsewhere in Polynesia fishhooks are of great interest. In particular, an ornamental double fishhook served as a delightful pendant suspended from the neck.

A large proportion of Maori wood carving is associated with the classic Maori meeting house. In this, wall posts and ridge poles, door posts, lintels and threshold boards were all highly carved. Inside, the walls consisted of carved wooden boards alternating with reed panels with geometric designs, and the rafters, too, were carved. Many a Maori figure carving has been sawn off a house ridge pole, or the top of the defensive stockade surrounding a village. This serves to explain why many of them are more than lifesize.

The majority of good Maori pieces date from the nineteenth century, when there was a florescence of Maori art, perhaps due in part to the European introduction of iron tools. A number of fine old pieces are dated to the pre-contact period, but usually on grounds of quality and style rather than any scientific evidence.

The most obvious feature of Maori art is the artist's *horror vacui* and his determination to cover the entire surface area with decorative designs. Some of these reproduce actual tattoo patterns (tattooing the human body is itself a result of *horror vacui*), but the rest consist of great circular joint marks; variations of the *manaia* design like a big-beaked bird in profile; borders of running scrolls and chevrons; and space fillers. But all-over decoration was not an essential feature of Maori art. In the early period and throughout the nineteenth century, when decorative designs became most florid and complex, figures occur which are devoid of surface decoration, even joint marks, and which, with their thickset bodies, human hair, and shell inlays for eyes, might easily be mistaken for Hawaiian were it not for the tattoo patterns round the mouth.

Finally, mention must be made of the famous *hei-tikis*, flat jade ornaments a few inches high worn suspended from the neck, and carved with a squatting figure with enlarged head hanging always to one side, either to left or right. Although very many genuine *tikis* exist, their popularity has led to recent faking, some of it carried out in Europe and the results exported to New Zealand for sale locally to visitors.

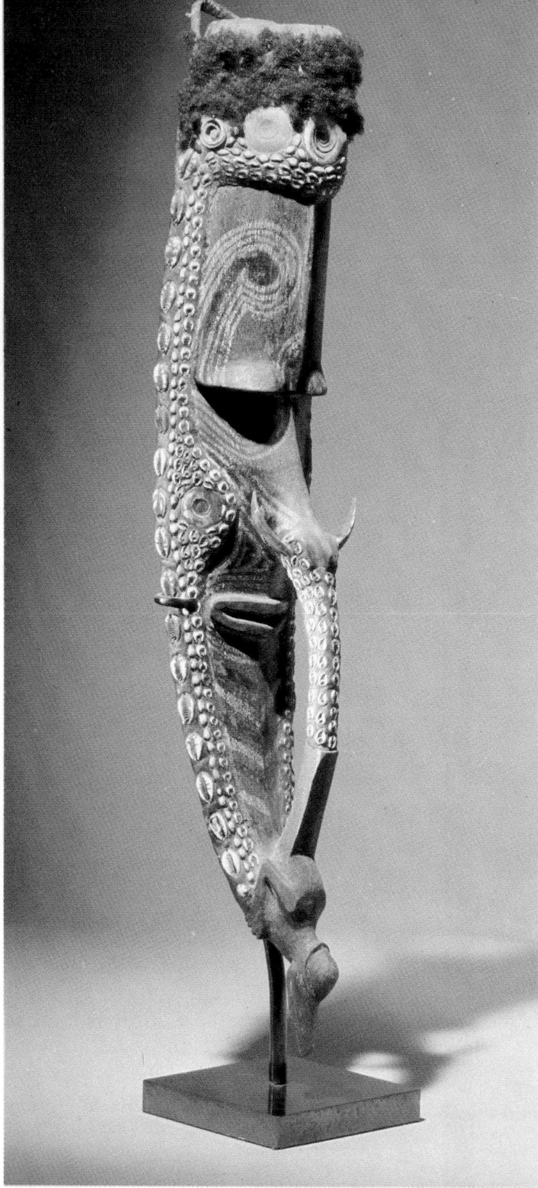

Mythical ancestor figure from Orokolo, Papuan Gulf, representing Ukaipi, wife of Ivo. Horniman Museum

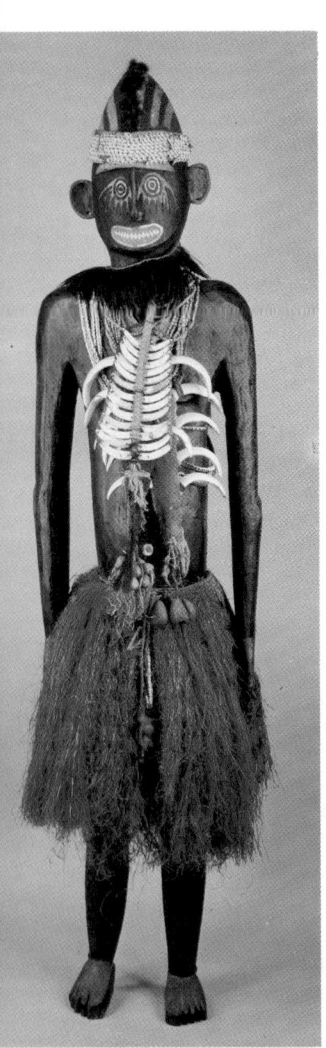

MELANESIA

The art of Melanesia differs from that of Polynesia in many respects, including the profusion of masks, the widespread use of mixed media (such as bone, shell, mud, feathers, boars' tusks, bark cloth and pigments), and the continuing production in some of the islands of objects for traditional use, alongside a flourishing tourist trade. Much of the art, particularly masks, can fairly be described as nightmarish, and it is significant to note that it appealed strongly to the French Surrealists in the 1920s, just as African sculpture had attracted the Cubists twenty years earlier.

By far the largest and most important of the Melanesian islands is New Guinea. Here there are many style areas, some first discovered early in the nineteenth century, others being explored only today. The result is that museums and private collections contain objects from areas which are now devoid of art, as a direct result of European contact, and at the same time the market is continually receiving previously unknown art forms as new areas are opened up and penetrated by dealers from Paris, London, and New York, some of whom make annual visits to the interior. For example, Duperrey brought a *korwar* skull container back from N.W. New Guinea in 1824, and though the *korwar* type is now famous, the carving of authentic *korwars* ceased after World War I. Likewise, from the 1920s onwards many of the traditional rituals, and their ritual paraphernalia, were destroyed in the Papuan Gulf as a result of cargo cults such as the Vailala Madness. On the other hand, the Korewori 'opposed hook' figures of the Hunstein Mountains south of the Sepik River were scarcely known before 1958, but since then over 100 have been brought to Europe and America. And although some examples of Asmat art from S.W. New Guinea were obtained before World War I, it has only been in the last twenty years that large collections have been formed, studied, and appreciated.

But by far and away the most prolific art-producing region of New Guinea is along the Sepik River. Here there are several different though related style areas, the Middle Sepik being the best known and the source of the great majority of pieces. These include masks, carved house posts, canoe-prow ornaments, both slit drums and hourglass drums, large carved wooden figures, and smaller figures in various media, orators' stools, painted shields, hook figures for hanging up bags of food, overmodelled skulls, and modelled and painted pots and terracotta gable ornaments from Lake Chambri. Similar objects, though not in such profusion, are being discovered in the less explored regions of the Upper Sepik and its tributaries.

Between the Middle Sepik and the coast is a range of hills where live the Abelam, whose art is often given the geographical attribution of Maprik – the two terms being interchangeable as far as provenance is concerned. The Abelam are the finest painters of New Guinea, using natural pigments of red, yellow ochre, black and white, to colour their figure carvings, which are often surmounted by a hornbill. They also paint rows of spirit faces on palm spathes stretched on a vast triangular wooden framework, which is then raised to form the façade of the enormously high men's houses.

Of the other islands, probably only New Britain still produces traditional objects today. These consist mainly of a wide variety of fantastic, surrealist masks, often rising well above the head and descending to the wearer's waist. Most of them are made of basketry, covered with painted barkcloth, to which is attached a fibre skirt reaching to the ground.

New Ireland is famous for its *malanggan*, a term applied indiscriminately to all figure carvings, carved lintels, and masks employed in funerary rites. These at their best contain bird, snake, and other animal elements, intricately carved in fretwork and beautifully coloured with red-brown, black-and-white pigments, but from even as early as the 1930s the workmanship has been sadly declining, though some fine carvings from the neighbouring Tabar Islands have recently been brought to light.

The art of the Solomon Islands is notable for the decorative use of mother-of-pearl inlaid into carved wooden bowls and figurines, and small canoe-prow ornaments of a human bust with large prognathous head and the hands often bearing a bird. Squatting figures viewed full face decorate the finely pointed, highly attractive ceremonial paddles.

In the past the New Hebrides – and particularly the island of Malekula – produced an enormous quantity of masks and puppets made of barkcloth stretched over a bamboo framework and then painted and decorated with boars' tusks. Also famous are the large tree-fern figures, but since the 1930s many of these have been made solely for export, and some of them are of very poor workmanship.

New Caledonia was also renowned for masks, carved in wood with huge hooked noses, the head surmounted by a tall pile of human hair. Genuine ones are now very rare outside museum collections.

The Australian aborigines are probably best known for their bark paintings. The bark is stripped from the eucalyptus tree, cleaned, and flattened over a fire, and then painted with natural pigments. The subjects vary from immediately recognizable representations of fish, anteaters, kangaroos, and human

Left Mvai mask from the Sepik River, New Guinea, not worn by the men but displayed in canoes. Gallery 43, London

Left New Guinea ritual stone figure representing an echidna – a kind of ant-eater. Gallery 43, London

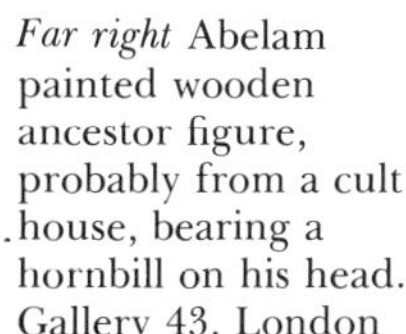

Far right Abelam painted wooden ancestor figure, probably from a cult house, bearing a hornbill on his head. Gallery 43, London

figures, to apparently abstract compositions recalling a story from the rich store of aboriginal mythology. In the latter case, it is likely that only the artist himself will be able to explain the painting.

Although some bark paintings were collected in the second half of the last century, and again at the beginning of this, the vast majority are very recent work. Quality varies enormously – as in the case of contemporary European painting – and appreciation is entirely a matter of the collector's judgment. Though some aboriginal artists are now making a personal name for themselves, prices are still remarkably low.

Although bark paintings are mainly associated with Arnhem Land and the islands off the north coast of Australia, painted wood carvings have a much wider distribution. Again their quality varies considerably, and they are likely to be of recent origin. Human heads, busts, and full-length figures are produced, as well as birds and animals. Boab nuts are carved with designs of human figures, fish and ships. These were probably traditional art forms, but today they are produced as barter goods at the Mission Stations on the Reserves, and thence find their way into the art galleries and gift shops in the cities, and are exported overseas. Old shields, either painted or carved in light relief with abstract designs, *tjuringas* – flat stones or wooden boards decorated with mnemonic devices and used in ceremonies – and ornamented boomerangs and bull roarers are unlikely to be found today except in old collections.

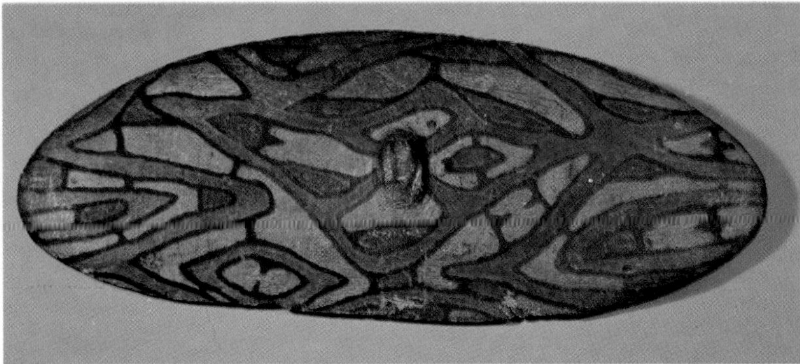

Aboriginal shield of painted wood from Queensland. Horniman Museum

American Indian and Eskimo

Though many of the art traditions of the North American Indians go back hundreds, and perhaps even thousands of years – as evidenced by archaeological finds – the art objects with which we are concerned almost all date from the nineteenth and twentieth centuries. This covers a period of great creativity, great destruction, and, in recent years, of some revival.

The continual pressure which the European settlers exerted on the Indian tribes of the eastern Woodlands, ever pushing them further westwards, suddenly escalated at the beginning of the nineteenth century when the continent was crossed from east to west by white men for the first time. Thereafter, the opening up of the West led to the dispersal of many more Indian tribes, and often their decimation as a result of fighting and disease. Though today Indians are found in reservations far from their natural and traditional homes, it is still useful to discuss the wide variety of art objects in terms of culture areas.

THE WOODLANDS

This area stretches from the eastern seaboard to the Mississippi, northwards to incorporate the Great Lakes, and north again as far as the 60th parallel, and westward to the Rockies. Here the people were small-scale farmers, hunters and fishermen, and their art reflects this. Buckskin was used for fine clothes and moccasins, and silk ribbons and especially trade beads were employed for decoration. Flower and leaf designs were typical of, but not exclusive to, the Woodlands tribes, and it is probable that these were introduced by French nuns, who taught the Indian women embroidery. A material peculiar to the Woodlands tribes is porcupine quill. The quills were flattened and dyed, and woven or embroidered on to buckskin. Sometimes they were applied to birch-bark boxes, especially by the Micmac of New Brunswick. Porcupine quill must be distinguished from the much finer moose hair, which was similarly dyed and used for decoration.

In New York State, the Iroquois used masks in their curing ceremonies. These were known as 'false faces', and the best known of them have a twisted nose, a heavily lined face, and a large mouth, sometimes twisted, sometimes in the form of a figure-of-eight, sometimes with teeth, and sometimes with a protruding tongue. The face is painted, often red, and human hair is attached. Other masks are made of cornhusks. It is interesting to note that the Iroquois still practise some of their ceremonies to this day.

Finally, an Iroquois art form that has disappeared completely is the manufacture of wampun belts. Wampun traditionally was a bead made from either the purple or the white part of the clam shell, but by as early as 1735 genuine wampun was being replaced by a type mass-produced by whites.

THE PLAINS

The Plains area is bounded in the east by the Mississippi, and in the west by the Rocky Mountains. It stretches from Texas in the south, northwards across the Canadian border to include what are now the great corn-producing areas of Alberta and Saskatchewan. Here it is referred to as the Prairies.

Plains Indian culture was revolutionized by the introduction of the horse, beginning in the sixteenth century. At first the Indians had to steal their mounts from the Spanish pushing up from Mexico, but they soon learnt to breed them themselves. The horse gave them unprecedented mobility and enabled them to hunt the buffalo on a large scale. It is not surprising, therefore, that buffalo hide was widely used for making *tipis*, for clothing, war shields, and drum heads.

Buffalo hide provided a fine surface for painting, and not only was the *tipi* decorated in this way but also men's and women's robes. The typical woman's design is known as 'box-and-border', and has the strange feature of being placed slightly off the centre of the skin. The men's robes could bear representations of men and animals, and usually depicted the owner's most famous 'coup', or success in battle. Occasionally,

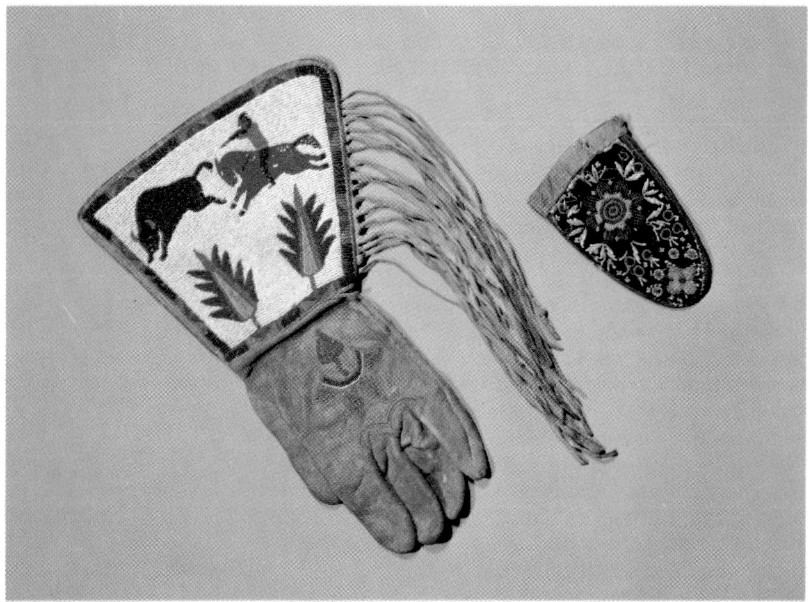

Plains Indian gauntlet (*left*) showing buffalo hunt in beadwork, and Woodlands gauntlet with beaded floral designs. John Judkyn Memorial, Bath

robes were decorated with bead or quillwork.

Shields and frame drums were also decorated with representational designs, but *parflèches* – bags of folded hide for containing food or clothing – had abstract designs symmetrically arranged.

Beadwork began to replace quillwork as the white traders moved into the Plains at the beginning of the nineteenth century. Although Plains Indian beadwork is known for its geometric and even angular designs, floral patterns are by no means unusual. Indeed, it is often not only difficult to distinguish the work of one Plains Indian tribe from that of another, but even to tell Plains work from Woodlands. This is natural enough when we realize that the Mississippi does not provide a clear-cut boundary between the two areas, and also that the Woodlands Indians themselves were being pushed further and further westwards.

Beadwork was widely used on quivers, pipe bags (for holding the pipes carved out of a red stone known as catlinite), bridle decorations, headbands, and horse collars. It was applied to cradle boards (in which a woman carried her baby on her back), and strips of it were sewn on the arms or down the front of buckskin shirts. Ghost Dance shirts, which were supposed to protect their wearers from bullets, and so signally failed to do so at Wounded Knee, were usually of buckskin brightly painted with various designs, including representations of the sun, moon, stars and birds. A strange feature of Plains Indian dress decoration was the use of seashells, *Opercula* and *Dentalia*, which were found on the Pacific North West Coast and must have been traded across the Rockies into the heart of the continent.

Kwakiutl carved wooden grave figure from the Pacific North West Coast. Horniman Museum

THE PACIFIC NORTH WEST COAST

From Yakutat in Alaska southwards through British Columbia and on to the American states of Washington and Oregon lies what is known as the Pacific North West Coast. Here, on countless islands and on a thin strip of fjord-indented coastline backed by mountains, live a number of Indian tribes who have long been renowned for their magnificent wood carvings, often conceived on a monumental scale. From north to south the best known are the Tlingit, Tsimshian, Haida, Kwakiutl, Nootka, and Coast Salish.

Of these tribes, the first four are famous for their totem poles, carved from the towering cedar, which is only one of several very tall trees found in the thick forests which cover the whole area. Totem pole is an unfortunate term, for it is rather family crests which are displayed, not 'totems' in a truly anthropological sense. Furthermore, its use has been extended to include mortuary poles, bearing a wooden coffin on their summit; house posts, for supporting the roof beams; carved doorways, with an oval hole as entrance; graveyard posts; and poles erected to record a noteworthy event.

The quantity of North West Coast art is amazing. The increased wealth accruing from the fur trade with the white man in the nineteenth century produced huge surpluses, which went to pay for the profusion of articles that were displayed, distributed, or destroyed, at the ever more lavish potlatches. Besides these were the Winter Ceremonials – dramatic cycles lasting several days during which initiations took place and myths were re-enacted. These demanded a vast range of masks, disguises, stage effects, rich clothing, regalia and musical instruments.

The various carving styles are difficult to disentangle, since sculptors copied the styles of other tribes, and masks could be actually stolen from villages often a considerable distance away. The Haida present probably the most problems in this respect, while the art of the Coast Salish, with its flat, oval faces, is easiest to recognize. The Nootka wolf mask (one example was collected around 1800) seems self-evident, yet it was closely copied by the Kwakiutl. The Kwakiutl were great lovers of stage effects at their Winter Dances, and were particularly fond of the so-called transformation mask, a great mask usually representing a bird with a long beak which opens up to reveal a second, human mask beneath.

Masks, like the totem poles and other carvings, were brightly painted, the palette consisting of black, white, vermilion, and a greeny blue. The secret of the red and blue have long been lost, and today acrylics, in a water, or better, vegetable oil medium are used. Square, watertight boxes were made by kerving, and these, and other rectangular objects such as box drums, were painted all over with human and animal forms, whose component parts were broken down to cover the surface area entirely, space fillers being added where necessary. This was a common feature of Pacific North West Coast design, and applies also to the famous Chilkat blankets of the northern Tlingit, silver bracelets, carved ladles for serving olachen oil, and conical hats made of woven spruce root.

Excellent baskets were made, but it is remarkable that north of the Fraser River, though twining and plaiting were employed, coiling was unknown. No pottery was made throughout the area. Among the decoration applied to clothing were local *Dentalia* and *Opercula*, abalone or haliotis shell (not the local variety, but a larger, brighter species brought from Monterey Bay in California), beads (including a large Russian blue and a large Chinese green variety), and Chinese coins with a hole through the middle, which served as jingles, as did deer hooves and puffin bills.

There has been a considerable revival of West Coast art in recent decades. The potlatch, which was banned for a time in Canada, has been reintroduced. The Winter Ceremonials are now held in the summer, as that is a more convenient time for people to gather together. There are a number of famous carvers, and a collector will pay $1,500 (approx. £600) or more for a really good contemporary mask. There are also successful silversmiths, some of whom have also turned to working in gold. And the Salish blanket, the manufacture of which was in danger of dying out in the 1920s, has seen a revival.

THE ESKIMO

The Eskimo are not American Indians, having arrived at a much later date, after the end of the last Ice Age, when the land bridge joining America and Asia had long sunk beneath the sea. Although their habitat stretches today from Siberia through northern Canada to Greenland, in recent times it has been the Alaskan Eskimo who have produced the minute carvings and the masks for which Eskimo art is famous. The bone carvings of the Ipiutak and Okvik cultures of Alaska, which date from the first centuries A.D., are archaeological finds and therefore strictly outside the range of Ethnographica.

From the second half of the nineteenth century onwards, walrus ivory and bone were used for carving small figures of birds, animals, and human beings, this being a leisure-time activity and purely secular. Such figures could be kept by the carver, given to friends, or bartered with white traders. A speciality for traders was the ivory pipe, a novel and non-functional form, for the Eskimo had no tobacco. While intricately carved with hunters, bears, sleighs, kayaks, ship's boats, these pipes also had fine surface engravings of similar subjects which were then outlined with soot so that they stood out against the whitish background of the ivory. More often, the tusk was not carved but used solely as a surface for depicting these enchanting scenes.

As the nineteenth century advanced, tobacco pipes and engraved tusks gave way to cruder, more realistic carvings of people in action. Since World War II a tourist trade has developed in these and they are turned out in small workshops by artists who sign their work. Finally, the Canadian Government introduced the use of soapstone (previously unknown), the old traditions of delicate workmanship in ivory on a small scale were abandoned, and the Eskimo entered the International Art market.

Another Alaskan Eskimo art form that has disappeared is the mask, of which there was a large variety. Lack of forests necessitated the use of driftwood and other materials, such as feathers and quills, so that masks were either made on a small scale or else consisted of a number of pieces pegged or even tied together, and then painted. The effect can be startling, hilarious, or even hallucinatory, but this is not surprising since the actual design of a mask was often dictated by a shaman's dream.

CALIFORNIA

The material culture of the Californian Indians, who consisted of a large number of very small tribes, was probably the most technologically unevolved in the whole of North America, and there would be little to say of their art if it were not for the magnificence of their basketry. Some Californian Indian basketry may be, both technically and artistically, the finest in the world.

Both the twining and coiling techniques are employed. The most famous baskets, and those which take up the largest proportion of most museum collections, are those of the Pomo, who specialized in overworking the baskets with different coloured glass beads, feathers and shell discs, including the bright abalone of California. These are often known

Far left Haida engraved ivory tusk (*left*) from the Pacific North West Coast and Eskimo engraved ivory spear from Alaska. Horniman Museum

Left Burden basket made by the great Washo basketmaker, Dat-So-La-Lee (1828–1925). Private collection, California

Left and below left Pair of feather-imbricated Pomo treasure baskets. Private collection, California

as 'treasure baskets', and were intended to be hung from the roof, like a chandelier. (Many have been ruined by collectors who have stored them sitting on their feather-decorated underside which was never intended for this purpose and cannot take the weight.)

The Pomo also excelled in the manufacture of miniature baskets, some of them no larger than a man's little finger nail. Their purpose was to demonstrate the skill of the woman basket maker. Usually horse hair was used for these, but in the last half century fishing gut has been employed. Such tiny examples have to be carefully conserved in a phial.

The names of basket makers are often known, and their work is not cheap. A wonderful basket by the famous Washo expert, Dat-So-La-Lee, who died in 1925, recently fetched over \$5,000 (approx. £2,100) at auction. It was 13½ inches (34 cm) in diameter and took nearly a year to make (completed 1906).

Mention should also be made of the carved paddles and elk-antler spoons of the Yurok and Hupa of northern California.

THE SOUTH WEST

Within the large Navaho Indian Reservation in Arizona lies the much smaller Hopi Reservation, with its three Mesas standing out against the sky, and at the foot of them, Oraibi, the oldest continuously inhabited site in the United States, built nearly 1,000 years ago. The Hopi, and the other Indians in the Pueblos that straddle the Rio Grande to the east, including Taos, San Ildefonso, Cochití, Jémez, Zía, and Isleta, are the indigenous inhabitants. The Navaho and their eastern neighbours, the Apache, are Plains Indians from as far north as Canada, who arrived in comparatively recent times and settled on Pueblo land and adopted many of the forms of Pueblo culture.

The Pueblos themselves consist of flat-roofed adobe structures which resemble at a distance piles of children's building bricks placed irregularly round a flat, open *plaza*. Here the annual rainmaking and solar ceremonies are performed with male dancers wearing *kachina* masks and women bearing painted and decorated boards on their heads, known as *tablitas*. The masks consist of cylinders of leather completely enclosing the head, and painted and decorated with the symbols of the particular *kachina* spirit represented. Over two hundred of these have been recorded, but twice that number may exist.

During these ceremonies, young children are given small painted and decorated *kachina* dolls as playthings, though they have the secondary purpose of instructing in the names and attributes of the different spirits. Though a ban on taking photographs of some of the actual ceremonies has been enforced since about 1915, the secular nature of the *kachina* dolls is demonstrated by the fact that for many years these have been carved mainly for tourists. Both Hopi and Zuñi make *kachinas*, and judging by museum specimens collected at the turn

Pueblo pots from the American South West. The black-on-black pot on the left is by María Martínez of San Ildefonso, who accidentally discovered this technique *c.* 1920.

of the century, the older pieces are much cruder and simpler in design, though less garish in their decoration.

The Pueblos are equally famous for their pottery. Each Pueblo tends to have its own style, which develops over the years and changes when a master potter arises and introduces innovations. For instance, María Martínez of San Ildefonso, and her husband Julian, discovered by chance in 1919 a method of producing a black-on-black ware which became popular with buyers, and thenceforth was turned out in large quantities. But they also produced many pots with black-and-red designs on a white slip. Zuñi for a time favoured the introduction of antelopes, usually within bands of geometrical design. Names are often given to different designs, such as Rainbird, Mountains, Thunderclouds, but these should not be taken too seriously as they have no ritual symbolism or ceremonial significance.

When the nomadic Navaho came and settled among the Pueblo Indians they adopted the Pueblo technique of weaving, and then completely outstripped their mentors in imaginative design and brilliance of colour. A vertical loom is used, and it is interesting to note that whereas it is the Hopi men who weave, the Navaho women weave while the men care for the sheep, an animal they also had to learn to raise from the Hopi.

The earliest fragments of Navaho weaving to have survived have been dated to the last decade of the eighteenth century, and Navaho blankets before 1850 are rare. After that date, particularly with the introduction of Spanish *bayeta* (baize) – unravelled for the brightly dyed threads, which were woven up again – and of aniline dyes, there was a rapid development of styles. The Plain Stripe was followed by the Serape style, which incorporated diamonds, zigzags and wavy lines. The Eye Dazzler is self-explanatory, but Wedge Weave was a method of changing the angle of the weft to produce a zigzag effect. Navaho blankets are woven to this day for sale in trading posts, but unlike Pueblo pottery, even a poor design can never be cheap because of the many hours of labour involved.

Navaho silverwork is of more recent origin, for the technique appears to have been introduced by a Mexican metal worker in the 1850s. The source of the metal was silver coins. The objects made were wide leather belts with heavy *conchas* (oval plaques) attached, and with silver buckles; bracelets, rings, bridle ornaments, buttons, pendants and necklaces with a typical squash-blossom design. Soon the local turquoise, which had long been used for earrings, was set in silver to make finger rings and other pieces of jewelry.

Just as the Navaho had learnt the art of weaving from the Pueblos, so now the Zuñi learnt silversmithing from the Navaho in the 1870s, to be followed at the turn of the century by the Hopi. It is difficult to generalize over differences of style, but Navaho jewelry tends to be more massive, with a use of heavier pieces of turquoise, than Zuñi or Hopi work. There are also a large number of forgeries.

Baskets were made, but only an *olla* form decorated with human, animal and bird designs, produced by the Apache, is of much interest.

CENTRAL AND SOUTH AMERICA

(*See also* Antiquities.)

Here it is often difficult to make a valid distinction between primitive art and folk art. In Central America the pre-Columbian Indian traditions were shattered by the Conquest, but the subsequent *métissage* of Spanish and Indian is reflected in the later art forms. The Indians' religious fervour found a ready outlet in Spanish Catholicism, and particularly in dramatic re-enactments of the Crucifixion during Holy Week, in colourful displays during Carnival, and the morbidly joyful celebrations of the Day of the Dead (2 November). The various Mexican tribes – often bearing names more famous in pre-Columbian times, such as Mixtec, Zapotec and Tarascan – have their own individual styles of masks. Whatever their original religious significance, these are now given a semi-Christian or secular connotation, representing, for example, a Pharisee or a bullfighter. The masks themselves are carved in wood, are generally painted, and may have hair or fur attached. Animal representations are found, and sometimes human faces are combined with animal ears and horns.

The use of masks incorporating strong Spanish influences is by no means limited to Mexico. It spread north to New Mexico and Arizona, where the Yaquí still hold a masked Easter ceremony, and south to Ecuador and Guatemala, where there is a wealth of masks today about which very little is known. At Oruro, in Bolivia, there is a devil dance in which thirty or more men take part, wearing horned masks made of plaster and brightly painted, sometimes with electric light bulbs inserted to form huge protruding eyes. Throughout the world masks have appeared to devout Christians to be 'works of the devil', and consequently to consider them as acting the part of the devil was one way of suppressing their pagan origins and absorbing them into the activities of the Church.

In contrast to Central America, many of the Indian tribes of South America have had little or no contact with white men. Consequently, their masking traditions have remained virtually untouched by the outside world, and correspondingly little is known about them. One important area, however, lies along the Upper Xingú River in Brazil. Here a cluster of tribes make both wooden and woven masks with designs painted on them. The wooden masks are generally rectangular, the flat surface of the wooden block being cut away below the brow to leave a semi-cylindrical nose in relief. Small holes are made for the eyes, from which a narrow line is generally painted running horizontally to the temple. The cheeks are painted with geometric designs. In the same area the Tapirapé make a gorgeous blue-and-red feather mask, known as 'Big Face', which is semi-circular, has tiny apertures for eyes and mouth, and wears a lip plug like an inverted matchstick. The masks come out in pairs and represent the souls of dead enemies.

On the eastern slopes of the Andes, around the border of Colombia and Brazil, are found masks of painted barkcloth. The material naturally enables an accompanying shirt to be added, sometimes with barkcloth trousers, otherwise with a fibre skirt. In some cases the mask is worn on top of the wearer's head which itself is hidden by the long barkcloth dress.

An interesting style of wood carving which is restricted to Surinam developed out of traditional West African forms introduced by the early slaves. Stools like those of Ashanti and Dahomey, paddles similar to those of the Ijaw of Southern Nigeria, drums which are completely African in shape, and ornamental combs, were all highly decorated with intricate curvilinear designs in fretwork and/or low relief. A feature peculiar to this style is the use of European brass studs to heighten the decorative motifs.

FURNITURE

Sydney Smith, writing in the early nineteenth century, said that there is 'no furniture so charming as books'. It is not necessary to be in agreement with him to admit that a finely illustrated book on furniture is the next best thing to owning the furniture, although many of us have to be content merely with the books. The aim of the Furniture section in this volume is to acquaint the reader with the basic styles which were prevalent throughout Europe and America from the Renaissance to the late nineteenth century, and also to fit into this complex picture the leading designers and cabinet makers who were instrumental in the birth of the various styles.

In many ways the study of the history of furniture seems to have been completed, but this is, in fact, far from the truth, and we are only now beginning to understand the complexity of the subject.

It has been the practice for many years to hang furniture styles on convenient pegs in the guise of the names of reigning sovereigns, leading designers, or architectural styles, many of them in fact being complete misnomers. Thus, terms such as George I or Louis XVI, Chippendale or Sheraton, the baroque or the neoclassical, are frequently used in books and auction catalogues to denote periods which are in many cases only remotely connected with the literal meaning of these phrases. Recent research has now tended to expose the fallacy of this system and, although the sovereigns' names still give some indication as to the periods, the hitherto accepted *œuvres* of the leading designers and cabinet makers are now being ruthlessly pruned, in much the same way as the works of the Great Masters are being systematically sifted from that of their pupils and followers. If Chippendale, Hepplewhite, and Sheraton had been instrumental in the production of a quarter of the pieces that have been ascribed to them by enterprising dealer and optimistic collector, then they must have run their businesses on the lines of modern mass production.

Of these three, we can only be certain that Chippendale owned a workshop and ran a cabinet maker's business and, notwithstanding this, he is primarily remembered by posterity for the publication of his *Gentleman and Cabinet-maker's Director*. Sheraton and Hepplewhite also published highly successful design books, but, as far as we know, neither of them actually made any important furniture. Many of the designs in these books were freely plagiarized from the creations of rivals and were, in their turn, shamelessly copied by cabinet makers throughout the country. Thus a pier glass, the design for which is in Chippendale's *Director*, may not necessarily have been produced in his workshop, because any of the numerous cabinet makers who subscribed to the book, or who even borrowed it, could have easily made the glass.

Therefore a piece of furniture can be proved to have been made by a certain cabinet maker only if its original account, or some contemporary description, is extant. The fact that a similar piece is illustrated in a design book is not evidence enough to who the maker was, although it is, of course, often a very good pointer. It would, therefore, appear that the essence of the true study of English furniture design is contained in contemporary bills and daybooks, and the increased study of these is enabling us to view the subject in a completely fresh light and from a new angle. The collections of the Victoria and Albert Museum include photostat copies of notable accounts, bills, and inventories of household furniture and other objects of art. Additions are constantly being made. A number of these in the charge of the Department of Woodwork, are accessible to students. The names of many cabinet makers, carvers, and designers are emerging from obscurity and, in years to come, let us hope that we may have a list of British cabinet makers, together with their histories, which may rival those long and detailed records that the French have published of their *ébénistes*.

In this section of the book the reader is given a highly erudite and comprehensive essay on French furniture and, thus, may start to enjoy the study of this complex subject in his own language.

The analysis or expertise of a piece of French furniture almost puts one in the place of a detective, for there is often so much of the false and contradictory in a piece that one needs a very level head and practised eye to separate the spurious from the original.

The importance of Italian furniture has now at last been realized, primarily because the Italians have been so intent on the tracking down of their furniture, which has for five hundred years been poured into the melting pot of Europe, owing to the series of holocausts which swept over Italy during that period. The essay devoted to its history is not solely directed to the creations of the Renaissance, as has been the tendency in earlier publications, but covers its entire history to the early nineteenth century, with special reference to Venetian lacquered furniture and Lombard *intarsia* decoration.

After the inclusion of French and Italian furniture the compilers were faced with the decision of what boundaries to set with regard to the other European countries. Spain, Portugal, Austria, Germany, Holland, and the Scandinavian countries, to mention only a few, have all produced important and individual furniture styles. These have to a great extent been moulded by national traits, historical influences, the dictates of climate, local conditions and indigenous woods, and the great general art impulse engendered by the Renaissance. The study

Desk and bookcase with chamfered corners of cherry inlaid with mahogany and light and dark woods, Connecticut or Rhode Island, 1790–1810. One of the most sophisticated examples of American cabinetmaking of the Federal period. Courtesy of the Henry Francis du Pont Winterthur Museum of the furniture of the majority of these countries in this language is still in its infancy, and the need for systematic research and scholarship is acute. A comprehensive work on the entire history of Continental furniture is badly needed in this country before the subject can be properly understood and appreciated. All these countries produced national and individual styles during, and following, the Renaissance, which thrived and blossomed until Louis XIV superimposed his artistic autocracy on France and then Europe, and thus extinguished their short-lived careers. The Grand Style which the *Roi Soleil* created for himself at Versailles, with the help of Le Brun's direction from Les Gobelins, completely shattered any vestiges that remained of national styles (with the exception of England), and the princelings of Germany and the grandees of Spain thus vied with one another in the emulation of all that was Gallic. From 1680 onwards the applied arts obeyed the dictates of Versailles and Paris, and the Louis XIV, *Régence*, Louis XV, Louis XVI, and Empire styles were freely copied and slavishly adopted throughout Europe; thus Swedish and Spanish Empire furniture appear very similar and can be differentiated only after prolonged study. However, long scrutiny is not required to distinguish them from Parisian furniture, as neither kingly neighbour nor country cousin could truly emulate the pure *style français*.

The chapter on American furniture is of great interest and is a fitting introduction to a difficult subject. The Americans, in their borrowing from English and French styles, have in many ways improved on them, and their furniture has a vigorous and unmistakable national appearance.

In this section the reader will find a useful survey of lacquered furniture, the history of which is traced in detail throughout Europe from the first importation of Oriental lacquer in the sixteenth century. The difference has clearly been shown between the European copies of Eastern lacquer, or the art of japanning as it was called, and the incorporation of Oriental lacquered panels in Occidental furniture.

The Lee Room: reconstruction of a room in a New England house with 17th-century furniture. The bed against the wall was for guests and travellers. American Museum in Britain

American

Until recent years so little was known about American antique furniture that it was widely supposed to be provincial English. Thorough study by scholars, some of them English, now tells us it has a character of its own, independent of the English furniture on which it was styled. Some connoisseurs, impartial Continental Europeans, comparing a Philadelphia 'Chippendale' highboy, a Rhode Island block-front secretary, a Duncan Phyfe sofa table (unique American types) with their nearest English parallels today, give preference to the American creations. Even when the comparison is between two of a kind, two fairly similar and equally well-made chairs or desks or chests of drawers, the choice often goes to American examples.

From the arrival of the original Pilgrims in 1620 down to the opening of the Revolutionary War in 1775, most of the early settlers in America were British although there were some settlements of Dutch, Germans, Swedes, Spanish, and French. From the first the different conditions in the two lands made for different circumstances in the lives of the peoples, their homes, and their furniture. The two countries lay in isolated hemispheres, separated by 3,000 miles of ocean. The climates were different; the requirements for survival of life were different; and so were the social, moral, intellectual, and economic environments.

As to things that the two peoples might build with their hands, such as furniture, one circumstance outweighed all others: the Americans were thrown on their own resources. They might want to model their furniture on English examples or designs, but by necessity they had to do it in their own way. In adapting their product to American use each furniture maker had to rely for the rendering upon himself. The result was variation – individuality. So marked was this variation, that today not only can we separate English from American antique furniture but we can trace most American examples to the section of the country – northern, middle, or southern – in which they were made; often to the city – Boston, Hartford, New York, Philadelphia, Baltimore, Charleston – and on occasion actually to the shop of the man who made them.

Save in local regions where the settlers were Dutch, German, etc., Americans followed the English furniture styles. Perched along the shore of a vast continent which had to be tamed by the plough, they had no time in which to work out polite modes of their own. They turned for their fashions to the country from which most of them had come. They were usually ten to twenty years behind the style, but followed in the path. It was hardly possible to follow the fashions, except in an independent way, because of the scarcity of models and the absence of guides. Only the merest scattering of families imported their furniture. Ships were few and small; furniture is bulky; and cargoes were given over to goods that could not be readily produced in the New World. Furthermore, it had been early discovered that imported furniture woefully suffered shrinking and cracking in America's drier air; also, that it offered no resistance to American insects. In short, almost every

Oak chair-table, 17th century. Smithsonian Institution

eventuality tended to make American furniture, though English in style, American in distinctive spirit and characteristics.

Much English antique furniture, when compared with American, appears to have been inspired by the desire for impressive show. No such noble grandeurs occur in American furniture, no broad and spacious sizes, no courtly elegance, no lavish luxury, no sumptuous ornamentation, no massive, monumental plainness. American furniture is unsophisticated, informal, democratically modest. Based on English originals though they be, American examples tend to be more forthright in design, more straightforward in construction, smaller in size, quieter in taste, and more utilitarian in the practicalities.

The spirit of early American furniture makers was one of buoyant vitality, of energies released by exhilarating opportunity and channelled into handicraft by freedom of choice. Some workmen might be rude in skill, some naïve, some expert, but almost never were they routine. Their spontaneity was as endlessly fresh as life itself in the New World. Added to the spontaneity was the aspect of unassuming skill. To be sure, there was pride. Early American furniture makers clearly were as proud of their work as artists are of their art, yet none, not even the most adroit, showed overweening self-assurance.

Above Colonial slat-back armchair, New England, late 17th century. Maple, ash and oak. American Museum in Britain

Sobriety, spontaneity, informality, democratic modesty, unassuming skill; there is a common denominator in these qualities of spirit, and the factor can be summed up in one word – simplicity. American antique furniture is simpler than English antique furniture. The tendency holds true not only up to the Declaration of Independence in 1776 but also from 1620 to 1820, and the reason is obvious. In America the environment, the times, and the people were simpler. This simplicity of spirit manifests itself in physical characteristics. The forthright design in American furniture becomes, in the working out, a physical characteristic. So does straightforward construction, modest approach, spontaneity, and unassuming skill. The excellence of the American handiwork often astonishes Englishmen. Skill that was rough and ready did occur – possibly too much of it – but there are surviving examples which show masterly skill, on occasion as fine, though never as formidable, as any achieved in London.

Several scholars have remarked on the generally smaller size of American furniture, and given as the reason for it the smaller size of the American home. Few, however, have as yet pointed out another physical characteristic equally central: that while English antique furniture tends to be broad and horizontal (perhaps the broader size led naturally towards the horizontal), American furniture tends to be vertical. Slender, lean, thin, tallish, these are the adjectives that generally describe it. The tendency appears in every American furniture style from Queen Anne on through Sheraton, and appears in every type of article – the height of the side chair in relation to width, of the armchair as well, and the wing chair, the highboy, the secretary, and so on. Even in post-Revolutionary forms, late forms such as the sideboard, the American accent is on vertical line, the English on horizontal. This American tendency to be tall and slender, combined as it is with less carving than the English liked – indeed, less ornament of any sort – makes for a quite distinctive and non-English character.

Comparisons aside, American antique furniture is worthy of praise for its own sake. At its best it has the vigour of direct, of functional design, the merit of harmonious proportions, the grace of slender line and outline, the charm of informal size, the beauty of richly grained wood surfaces, and the force born of lack of elaboration, simplicity.

Chief Periods and Styles

JACOBEAN

The first furniture made in North America was based on the English Jacobean style. Modelled after characteristic household pieces which the Pilgrims of 1620 and later permanent first settlers brought with them from England to the New World, the earliest examples now surviving probably date between 1650 and 1670. They are of strong, straightforward, simple design and construction, generally bulky, yet often remarkably well proportioned. From the many Jacobean examples which have been gathered into museums, we judge that the woods employed were mostly American oak, pine, and maple. Perhaps most numerous are oak chests, usually with a bottom drawer or two, and all but covered with flat carving. Handsomest are three more forceful forms: (1) Jacobean court cupboards, a kind of buffet, generally oak, adorned with applied and often ebonized wood panellings, mouldings, bosses, spindles, and bulbous or columnar supports; (2) press cupboards, very similar cupboards, in which the lower section is closed with doors or made as a chest of drawers for holding household linens, etc.; and (3) separate chests of drawers, likewise much ornamented with mouldings, bosses, and panellings. Among American Jacobean tables are dining boards on trestles or plain frames and, for other rooms, stout smaller tables on four legs generally connected by sturdy stretchers. Often the legs and stretchers are spiral-twisted for the sake of ornament, or lathe-turned in the shape of balls, knobs, etc. Similar legs and stretchers are generally found on the most popular table in seventeenth-century America, the gate leg. American chairs in the Jacobean manner may be

Far right Press cupboard of carved oak, pine and maple, New England, 1660–80

Above Colonial cradle, mid-17th-century. American Museum in Britain

Above, centre Hartford, Connecticut or Sunflower chest, made in Connecticut of oak and pine, *c.* 1670–90. American Museum in Britain

Above, far right Armchair with Carver-type back, rush seat and turned legs, New York, late 17th century. Metropolitan Museum of Art

Far right William and Mary maple wing chair with rudimentary Spanish foot, *c.* 1700, New England. Metropolitan Museum of Art

Below Walnut double gate-leg table, New England, 1675–1700. Metropolitan Museum of Art

divided into three groups: three-legged armchairs, plain or carved wainscot chairs, and 'Dutch'-type armchairs made of posts and spindles. Americans subdivide the latter kind into Carver chairs, with one row of vertical spindles in the back, and Brewster chairs, with two rows. These are names of Pilgrim Fathers who are said to have brought them over in the *Mayflower*. A later chair, quite the most luxurious made in seventeenth-century America, is the high-back cane chair, boldly turned and scroll-carved, the so-called 'Charles the Second' chair. A few day beds of this luxurious 'Carolean' type also have survived.

WILLIAM AND MARY

After Queen Mary and her Dutch husband, William of Orange, came to the throne in 1689, a Dutch-influenced style of furniture gradually began to appear in England. Examples of it reached America just before the beginning of the eighteenth century and started a new fashion there, a number of cabinet makers being skilled enough to adapt the new style admirably to American use. Americans liked this furniture in the William and Mary style. They found it less ponderously heavy and bulky than the Jacobean, and therefore better suited to their small houses. They liked its decorativeness, its pleasant inlays, its marquetry work. That they also liked the few lacquered pieces which reached them is indicated by several surviving examples of quaintly simulated American lacquering. This lacquering, then called japanning, was practised from about 1712 up to the time of the Revolution, and seems to have been done best by a group of Boston workmen. American furniture based on the William and Mary style is definitely less massive and formal than English pieces, less imposing. It is often fine furniture none the less, the finest made in America up to 1720–5, unless we except 'Charles the Second' chairs. Perhaps the most notable single development was the tall chest of drawers, evolved by setting five or six tiers of drawers on a stand high enough for the drawers to be opened without stooping down. The combination is

Left William and Mary highboy, bilsted (gumwood), on rope-twist turned legs, made for the Mitchell family of Port Washington, late 17th century. Metropolitan Museum of Art

Above Queen Anne walnut leather-covered sofa, arrow-shape stretchers, carved web feet and scrolled knee blocks, Philadelphia, 1740–50. Courtesy of Henry Francis du Pont Winterthur Museum

nowadays called a highboy, and when the stand is made as a separate piece of furniture, a sort of dressing table with drawers, it is called a lowboy. By the addition of other features, highboys and lowboys became unique American designs. Those in the style of William and Mary were mostly of walnut or walnut veneer, the stand on six tall legs with connecting stretchers and ball-shaped feet, making for an attractive silhouette, doubly so because the stretchers were curved and the six legs prettily turned in the shape of inverted cups, trumpets, or balls-and-cones. Among other developments of the William and Mary style perhaps thc most widely adopted in America was the cabriole leg.

Fan-back Windsor armchair, Pennsylvania, 1750–80. Courtesy of Art Institute of Chicago

QUEEN ANNE

The Dutch influence introduced into England by William and Mary transformed English furniture in the reign of her sister and successor, Queen Anne (1702–14). The transformation was from large to smaller furniture and from fairly stiff and formal lines to lovely curves, the happiest change in English furniture in hundreds of years. Furthering this air of grace, a touch of carving, notably the scallop shell, was added. The style of Queen Anne seems not to have reached America until after her death. However, for the next half-century, even up to 1755–60, it was the fashion and standard in good furniture. Expansion was the order of the day in America. The wilderness was being pushed back even farther from the coast; new villages and towns were being founded; cities were growing larger; trade and agriculture were increasing by leaps and bounds; many new and especially pleasant houses were being built; Queen Anne furniture was ideally suited to dress them; and cabinet making had reached a new high level of skill. In consequence, a good deal of fine furniture in the Queen Anne style was made in America. Hogarth's 'line of beauty', the wave-like, cyma curve, characterized it. Chair legs, chair seats, chair backs, chair splats, all were curved, front view and profile. Spacious wing chairs, comfortably upholstered, came into use. Also corner chairs, and those stick-and-spindle chairs, open, cool American Windsors. Even sofas in the Queen Anne style were made, though not many. On case pieces as well as on chairs and sofas the rounded Dutch or club foot was much used, its popularity continuing long after the claw-and-ball foot came in. On highboys and lowboys the six turned legs were superseded by four cabriole legs, with hints of the missing two appearing as pendant knobs, centre front. Secretaries and clothes cupboards incorporated Queen Anne style elements, such as doors with the panels arched. A few four-post bedsteads with cabriole legs and Dutch feet have survived. Tables also often had Dutch-type feet and cabriole or at least curved legs, while that most popular American table up to then, the gate leg, gradually gave way to the drop-leaf table, in which hinged leaves were propped up by swinging arms or legs without gate features. Many drop-leaf tables are squares or rectangles when open; numerous oval and circular ones also occur. A separate word about Queen Anne mirrors should be added, since they were probably the first fine mirrors made in America. Usually the glass is in two parts, quite visibly, no moulding or other covering masking the joint. The upper glass section is shaped to fit the cyma-curved and arched frame in which a cresting is sometimes carved. They continued in favour almost up to the time of the Revolution.

EARLY GEORGIAN

Since furniture based on the Queen Anne style was popular in America until 1755–60, sundry features and developments readily recognized in England as Early Georgian features are often combined with it. The term Early Georgian is, however, seldom used in describing American-made furniture. In fact, the transition from Queen Anne to Chippendale's style is far more abrupt in America than in England.

CHIPPENDALE

In 1754 Thomas Chippendale published in London his now celebrated book of English furniture designs that gathered into one volume the various new tendencies which had been appearing in English furniture since the death of Queen Anne in 1714. Chippendale's designs brought to a head the transitional furniture tendencies of Early Georgian England, a transition which may be briefly described as a turning from the Dutch towards the French style. A few American adaptations of these Early Georgian characteristics had appeared a decade or two before Chippendale's book was published. But the force of the change from Queen Anne lines was not felt in America until about 1760, when the Chippendale style burst forth with all the popular impact of a triumphant fashion. Americans from that day to this have used the term Chippendale to mean Early Georgian furniture with Dutch characteristics (shell carving, cabriole legs, claw-and-ball feet, the Cupid's bow top rail), and to include the mid-eighteenth-century Georgian Gothic, Chinese, and French Louis XV features which occur in Chippendale's drawings, as well as the flowing rococo carving and embellishment in which he loved to specialize. American furniture based on his designs reached its most elaborate development in Philadelphia between 1760 and 1776, under superb cabinet makers such as Affleck, Folwell, Randolph, and Savery. However, neither in Philadelphia nor anywhere else were American Chippendale pieces as large, as lordly, or as lavishly ornamented as in England. In fact, tending towards the functional in form, American Chippendale often offers little curvature, considerable restraint in ornament, and crisp rather than flowing forms, a far cry from his rococo flights of fancy. In Puritanical districts such as New England where adornment never had been smiled upon, Chippendale-style furniture was often so simplified as to appear succinct, so straight and strict as to seem prim. To call such furniture by Chippendale's name is out of character, and is so recognized increasingly, though a more satisfactory term has not yet turned up.

American 'Chippendale', however, did constitute a new style in America, the most elaborate and luxurious up to that time. The style continued till 1785, or thereafter, bringing in the whole series of new developments that had begun about 1750, when Queen Anne chairs with looped top rails and club feet gave way to chairs with the Cupid's bow top rail, and claw-and-ball feet, while the solid vase-shaped or fiddle-back splat gave way to the open carved, inter-

Chippendale-style mahogany lowboy with brass mounts, Philadelphia, *c.* 1770. American Museum in Britain

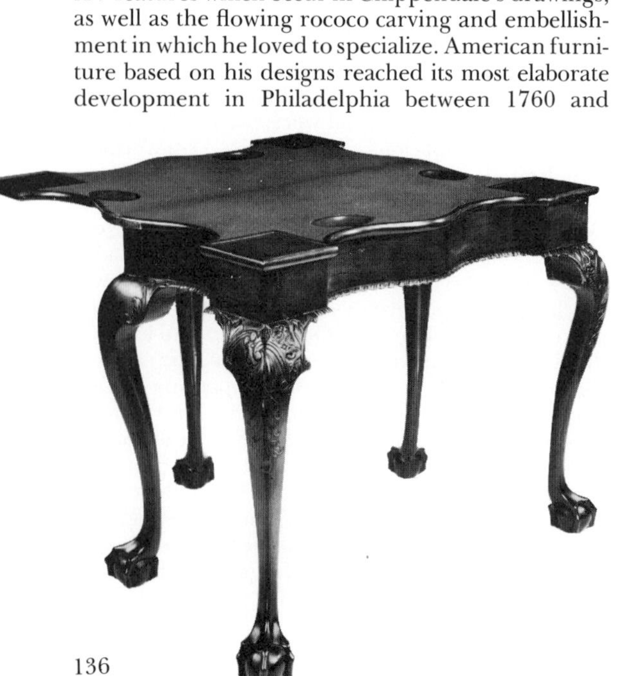

Left Massachusetts mahogany chair (*left*) in the Chippendale manner but with a Queen Anne-style kidney-shaped seat, *c.* 1765–75. One of a pair of chairs (*right*) labelled on the back with metal plates bearing the name Hopkins for the original owner, possibly made by Samuel Nickle, *c.* 1776–9. Mahogany in the Chippendale manner but with a Queen Anne style splat. American Museum in Britain

Far left New York Chippendale mahogany card table with claw and ball feet, *c.* 1760–70. Courtesy of Henry Francis du Pont Winterthur Museum

Chippendale upholstered mahogany settee, New England, third quarter of 17th century. Metropolitan Museum of Art, Sylmaris Collection

laced splat, showing Gothic, Chinese, or French motifs. Also the 'Marlborough' leg appeared, and chairs with square, straight, footless legs, generally connected by stretchers. In all these chairs the American tendency was towards smaller size, suited to a smaller chair seat than was the rule in England, American taste being modest, and American rooms not as palatially large as in fashionable English houses. Chippendale chair-back settees were made, and a few upholstered Chippendale sofas with open-rolling arms.

In England secretaries and chests of drawers with cabinet tops generally had glass doors. In America the doors were more often of wood, attractively panelled. Cabriole legs were always used on highboys and lowboys, while low-standing cabinet pieces were given either the short cabriole or a bracket foot, the bracket straight or ogee. Both cabriole and square, straight legs were used on tables, and the apron of smallish tables, like the apron of cabinet pieces, was variously treated: plain, curved, or carved with a band of ornament. Tripod tables became quite popular, elaborate examples carrying acanthus carving on the legs and pedestal. Sometimes the pedestal flaunted a surpassing luxury, a tilting top boldly shaped and carved like the notches in a piecrust. A bit of carving might also appear on the knees of bedposts with short cabriole legs. Generally, however, before the Revolution American bedpost legs were square and plain, with round, fluted footposts. The headposts, covered by draperies, were mostly plain, and headboards also tended towards the plain. Always we must remember the freedom with which American furniture craftsmen interpreted the English style, making not only for individual variation on the form but also for differences from the English style.

Connecticut block-front cherry desk signed by Benjamin Burnam of Norwich, dated 1769. Metropolitan Museum of Art

ADAM

The furniture style that superseded Chippendale's in England – the 'beautiful spirit of antiquity' which inspired the classical designs of the Adam brothers – had no following in America. The reason is that the designs were never published, and therefore were not available to Americans; that the furniture itself was made for the rich and not for export; and that in 1775, just about the time that Americans might have heard about the Adam style, the Revolutionary War broke out. When relations between the two countries opened up again in 1784 the Adam style was already on the wane in England, giving way in the next few years to the Hepplewhite and Sheraton styles. The result was that in America the style called Chippendale was followed by the styles of Hepplewhite and Sheraton, the two arriving at much the same moment and sharing the honours as to esteem. It is true that some Adamesque mirrors (probably Hepplewhite mirrors with motifs derived from Adam) were made in America; also that there were installed a few mantelpieces in the classical manner. But no American furniture in the Adam style was produced. Fittingly enough for the new republic, a revival of classical architecture, encouraged by Thomas Jefferson himself, arose in the United States immediately after the Revolution. The first Government building constructed, the Bank of the United States in Philadelphia, was designed as a Romanesque temple in 1795. Both in public and in residential architecture the classical revival swept the country for the next three-quarters of a century, streaming westward 3,000 miles across the continent to the Pacific coast, and losing favour only when set aside by untoward circumstances, notably the Civil War of 1860–5. How appropriately these houses in the new republic would have been dressed had they been furnished in an informal American version of Adam's classical style!

HEPPLEWHITE

In American furniture the style of Hepplewhite so often tends towards, or incorporates, features of Sheraton's style, that many articles called Hepplewhite are best described as combination Hepplewhite–Sheraton. This American mixture of two English furniture fashions was natural in the circumstances. The peace treaty ending the war between England and the United States had been signed in the latter part of 1783; trade between the countries had begun again in 1784; and by 1785 the type of furniture then the latest vogue in England, Hepplewhite, was being advertised in American newspapers as the latest importations. Another five years were to pass, however, before the economy of the United

States had sufficiently recovered from the war for many citizens to buy these importations or to order American-made furniture based on Hepplewhite designs. By that time, 1790, a new type of furniture, the Sheraton, had sprung into being in England, and American cabinet makers were shortly beginning to adapt it to American use. It was inevitable in these circumstances that elements of the two styles (which already had certain features in common) should often be combined.

The two styles can be differentiated, however, in a great many pieces of American furniture, though the distinction is not easy to sum up in words. American Hepplewhite chairs generally have shield-draped backs (or shield variants, such as the interlaced heart, the oval, etc.) with either openwork splats or banisters in the back. The splats may be touched with carving, such as plumes, wheat ears, or leaves. The legs on these chairs are generally square and tapered, often ending in spade feet. Such legs also generally appear on Hepplewhite wing chairs, sofas, tables, and, that new convenience in the dining room, the sideboard. In most late eighteenth-century sideboards the front was designed in a serpentine curve, and it is said that if the ends of the curve are concave the design is Hepplewhite; if convex, Sheraton. All are generally veneered in finely marked mahogany and carry a bit of inlay – satinwood or maple strings bordering the drawers, a few bellflowers dropping down the legs, etc. In the main, American sideboards are so much less ornamented than English as to be easily distinguished.

A word should be added about the new type of drawer handle introduced about 1780: a bail pull attached to an oval brass plate. Such handles, the plate often stamped with an eagle, acorn, oak leaves, grapes, or some such design, continued to be used until 1820, though small round brass knobs were sometimes used instead. Wall mirrors now began to be made in smaller sizes. These Hepplewhite mirrors seem to have been much influenced by Adam's classical (Pompeiian) mirror designs, and the influence carries over into American Hepplewhite mirrors to the extent that the frames are elegantly thin (Pompeiian), carved, gilded, often bear garlands of leaves and flowers hanging halfway down the sides, and are surmounted by a finial, usually an urn, set in a scrolling ornament as delicate as filigree work.

A major change in the dressing of American rooms was visible by the end of the eighteenth century; for sundry articles of furniture were going out of fashion – lowboys, highboys, tall chests of drawers, etc. – the replacements being chests of drawers of more moderate size, decorative types of tables, and several new furniture forms. The increased use of occasional furniture, such as card, tea, side, Pembroke, pedestal, and sofa tables, alone would have changed the appearance of rooms. Add waist-high chests of drawers (bureaux), modest-size bookcases, tambour desks, china closets, sideboards, etc., and the change becomes pronounced.

SHERATON

As in England, so in America, Sheraton's designs were so much an anthology of other men's ideas – Adam, Hepplewhite, Shearer, not to mention his debt to the French creators of *Louis Seize* furniture – that the style which bears his name is more eclectic than original. Sheraton's designs incorporate, one way or another, almost every characteristic of Hepplewhite. Nevertheless, the prevailing elements are the straight lines, rectangular forms, and vertical rhythms of classical architecture which Sheraton had got from Adam and French revivers of the classical. Sheraton-style furniture is less forceful than Hepplewhite, more delicate. Where Hepplewhite is masculine, Sheraton is feminine, even, on occasion, dainty. So much refinement charmed Americans. It was in contrast to their rugged environment and might be said to have represented to them the triumph of art over necessity, of grace over Nature. The result was that there was made in America a great deal of beautifully skilful furniture based on Sheraton's designs. Much of it survives; though many pieces nowadays have become so fragile as to be more suited to museum than to home use. Among the many American cabinet makers who produced fine furniture in the Sheraton taste, the most noted is Duncan Phyfe, of New York. Phyfe's fame has risen so high that many persons today mistakenly describe American Sheraton as 'Phyfe-style' furniture.

Above Mahogany side chair with carved eagle back splat, attributed to Duncan Phyfe, 1810–15. Museum of the City of New York

Right Lady's desk of mahogany inlaid with satinwood, closely related to Sheraton's design in Plate 50 of his 'Drawing Book'. 1795–1810. One of the most sophisticated examples of American cabinetmaking of the Federal period. Courtesy of Henry Francis du Pont Winterthur Museum

Left Mahogany butler's desk, attributed to Duncan Phyfe, 1810–20. Museum of the City of New York

The chair backs, characteristically, are square or squarish with banister backs or openwork splats combined with banisters. Chair legs are straight and tapered; sometimes square, sometimes round. When round they are often reeded. Sofas having now come into widespread use, many were made from 1795 to 1825 in the Sheraton style. Their legs resemble the chair legs. Their backs are often a horizontal D shape, but usually they have rectangular backs with narrow arms in line with the legs and connected to the legs by columnar supports, often in the form of an elongated vase. Back rail, arms, supports, legs, all are often reeded, but at times the back rail bears, instead, a bit of cameo carving. The distinctive feature of Sheraton dining, card and Pembroke tables is that the legs are generally round and reeded or, if supporting a pedestal or platform, splay-curved. Chests of drawers (bureaux) may be distinguished by reeded or ringed corner-column supports ending in round, tapering feet. These columns stand out from the body of the bureau, the top corners of which are cut almost circular in order to cover the columns. Tambour desks, moderate-size bookcases, china cabinets, and occasional furniture were increasingly

in demand. Sheraton himself designed no mirrors. His name, however, is given to the type of mirror that was most favoured during his vogue in the United States (1795–1820). The characteristics are a vertical rectangle with thin columns projecting at the sides and an overhanging cornice ornamented with a row of balls or acorns. The columns often carry delicate reeding. Between the cornice and the glass is generally found a quaint painting or an applied decoration, often of a patriotic nature.

An authority, Lockwood, has pointed out as a special feature of American Sheraton cabinet furniture, that 'it is almost devoid of mouldings', the bareness of the straight edges often 'being relieved by inlay' or some slight ornament. Inlay became much more used than hitherto, though still far less than in English Sheraton. This tendency towards embellishment was increased by the use of discreet carving such as cameo cutting on chairs and sofas, reeding, fluting, and the use of applied classical swags, festoons, and rosettes or paterae: also, the painting or stencilling of certain articles such as occasional chairs, and by exceptionally decorative, even fanciful, veneering.

DIRECTORY

Early in the nineteenth century (*c.* 1805–25) American furniture was to a certain extent inspired by the French classical *Directoire* mode. Whether this influence came direct from France or, indirectly, through England, is not quite clear. In any event, in American furniture the Directory influence is limited mostly to chairs and sofas. It is marked by concave, 'sabre-shaped' curves. The stiles of the side chair are sabre-curved; the stiles turn forward as seat rails which repeat the concave curves; these curves are repeated again in the sabre-shaped front legs; and again, at least somewhat, in the concave-curved rear legs. The back may contain a crossbar or a splat of either lyre or vase form. Every line and outline of the chair is curved except the seat. Add curving arms to this form and you have the Directory armchair, which sometimes, as in a library chair, is partly upholstered. Directory sofas are in the shape of a broad, squat lyre which rests on short, sabre-curved legs, the upper outward curves of the 'lyre' transformed into outrolling arms. The wood of these chairs and sofas is mostly mahogany. As to decora-

Top A room in the Pierce-Nichols House, Salem, Massachusetts, with furniture *c.* 1800

Above Bedroom in Pingree House, Salem, Massachusetts with early 19th-century furniture. On the cornice of the bed are symbols of Cupid

Square card table, probably made in the workshop of Duncan Phyfe, *c.* 1825. Metropolitan Museum of Art

tion, reeding is sometimes added, or a little carving, such as cameo-cut leaves, wheat ears, or 'sheaves of lightning'. The master of the Directory style in America was Duncan Phyfe, whose finely harmonious proportions and curving rhythms have been fully praised. Aronson, for example, said: 'There is little in any furniture, American or European, to excel in beauty or technique the grace of these interpretations.'

EMPIRE

When the war of 1812 between England and the United States was ended (1814) few Americans were in the mood to follow the classical Regency furniture style then the vogue in England. They turned, instead, to Napoleon's classical style – French Empire – for which they had cared little until then. This style was marked in America, as in France, by largish, bulky furniture in cube or rectangular forms, which gained a showy effect from sumptuous veneers of mahogany or rosewood. As usual, the Americans interpreted the style with much freedom, leaving out most of the Roman and Egyptian motifs so dear to Napoleon. There were no gilded bronze mountings as in France, only a little brass ornamentation, and few, if any, Egyptian sphinxes or Roman allegorical figures and military symbols, such as fasces and laurel wreaths. In brief, the adaptation followed the traditional American tendency to be simple and inornate.

While many of the chairs combined motifs borrowed from other periods – for example, sabre-curved stiles and side rails from the Directory together with reeded or ringed-and-collared straight round front legs from Sheraton – the characteristic American Empire chair has a downward-sloping, loop-like top rail, a vase-shaped splat with a hood fitted between it and the top rail; concave-curved front legs, often with projecting knees, and raked or sabre-curved rear legs. American Empire sofas also show motifs from other periods such as Directory 'roll over' arms. But as a rule the whole conception and construction of the sofa is more massive, and the squat-lyre-form outline curves tend to become swan-neck or cornucopia curves, a tendency emphasized by carving them to resemble swan necks or cornucopias. The legs of these sofas are scrolls or, later, winged legs with animal feet (representing the Egyptian griffin). Animal feet, with or without wings, are found on bureaux, wardrobes, sideboards, pier tables, etc. In many American Empire bureaux (chests of drawers) the top drawer overhangs the lower drawers, and the overhang is supported by columns, some plain, some variously ornamented with ring turnings, reeding, or carving, such as quilted or 'pineapple' designs. The columns and overhang also appear on American Empire desks, secretaries, and sideboards. In some cases, probably late examples, vertically elongated scroll supports are used instead of columns. Another feature often found on American Empire cabinet pieces is the treatment of the top drawer as a broad, convex-curved 'torus' moulding. Frequently the sides of such cabinet pieces are panelled. A type of chair and sofa not previously mentioned now made its appearance: the ancient Roman curule seat, formed by joining two half-circles back to back, X-shaped. Other singular forms such as sleigh-shaped beds and 'Grecian' sofas became popular. A new development in mirror frames also appeared. The columns at the sides became larger and heavier yet were used decoratively rather than structurally. Instead of delicate reeding, they carried broadly carved leafage, spirals, or rings; and sometimes the columns were partly gilded and partly painted black. In brief, they lose their architectural character and, consequently, are no longer wall mirrors but, rather, looking glasses to hang on a wall.

The handles in the Early Empire period were, characteristically, projecting round brass knobs often stamped with the American eagle, the head of Washington, or some other patriotic motif. The characteristic Late Empire handle was a ring pull hanging from the mouth of a brass lion's head. The tawny gleam of brass was in happy accord with the glowing red mahogany or rosewood in rich 'crotch-grained' veneers. Seldom has veneering been used with more brilliant effect. The forms of the furniture grew stiffer, colder, and more austere, but the surfacing grew more resplendent. Despite the fact that the style was in the hands of master cabinet makers, eminent among them Duncan Phyfe, the taste of the day was deteriorating. By 1830 American Empire had fallen from bad to worse, the forms becoming bulky, the proportions coarse, the rhythms heavy. Phyfe himself called it 'butcher furniture'. The decline continued until about 1840, when Americans began to turn from it and take up a new furniture style, the early Victorian.

Cabinet makers

Affleck, Thomas. Born in Aberdeen, Scotland, he learned his trade in London where, as a young man in 1763, he was chosen by John Penn, commissioned governor of Pennsylvania, to go with him to Philadelphia as resident cabinet maker. Affleck died there in 1795, a prominent citizen who counted among his friends eminent persons such as Benjamin Franklin. He is generally reckoned the most skilful cabinet maker in eighteenth-century Pennsylvania and the leader of the Philadelphia Chippendale school. Evidence indicates that he owned a copy of Chippendale's *Director*; and several of his documented chairs do closely parallel certain plates in the *Director*. Joseph Downs says that Affleck's

Philadelphia work 'brought an unparalleled urbanity of . . . Chippendale pattern to Philadelphia furniture'.

Allison, Michael (*fl.* 1800–20). New York cabinet maker. Some of his furniture is stamp-punched; many of his other pieces have been attributed to Duncan Phyfe.

Appleton, Nathaniel. Early nineteenth-century Salem, Massachusetts, cabinet maker distinguished for his furniture in the Federal styles.

Ash, Gilbert (1717–85). Much-respected New York joiner and chair maker. Some of the earliest American Chippendale chairs were from his hand. He often repeated, with attractive variations, the diamond lattice-back chair.

Burling, Thomas (*fl.* 1772, d. 1800). New York cabinet maker, whose superior skill has been established by five or six examples which still bear his label. He was selected by George Washington in 1795 to make a 'writing desk and apparatus' (price 40 guineas) for the first official residence of the President.

Chapin, Eliphalet (1741–1807). Leading member of a well-known Connecticut family of furniture makers. Chapin practised for a time in Philadelphia with the result that the Chippendale highboys and secretaries made by the Chapins incorporated Philadelphia features such as elegant pediments with delicately pierced scrolls and a fancy finial. But they are generally in Connecticut cherrywood rather than mahogany, and far simpler than Philadelphia work; indeed, show the spare ornament, narrow proportions, and slender vertical rhythms prevalent in New England.

Claggett, William H. (1716–49?). Newport, Rhode Island, master clockmaker. In youth he had a brief career in Boston, where he may have been trained.

Cogswell, John (*fl.* 1769, d. 1818). One of the most distinguished of Boston cabinet makers whose work is more elaborate than was the custom in New England. Perhaps best known for his Chippendale bookcases and *bombé* chests of drawers; also, together with his son, Junior, for Hepplewhite and Sheraton sideboards and blue-lined tambour desks.

Disbrowe, Nicholas 1612/13–83). Earliest known American furniture maker. Born in Walden, Essex, England, the son of a joiner. One of the settlers (before 1639) of Hartford, Connecticut. A signed chest made by him shows flat carving of tulips covering the entire front, and might be called the first of the so-called Hadley chests.

Dunlap, Samuel (II) (1751–1830). New Hampshire cabinet maker known for his maple highboys and secretaries with a distinctively scrolled pediment and interlaced cornice. Leading member of a New Hampshire furniture-making family that included John I, John II, and Samuel I.

Edgerton, Matthew (*fl.* 1742, d. 1787). Leading cabinet maker of New Brunswick, New Jersey. Several fine examples of his skill have been identified from existing labelled pieces.

Elfe, Thomas (*fl.* 1751–71). Perhaps the most prominent of the Charleston, South Carolina, cabinet makers. His elaborate Chippendale mahogany case pieces are much prized. He employed a dozen or more Negro slaves, trained craftsmen, whom he owned.

Elliot, John (*fl.* 1756, d. 1791). Philadelphia cabinet maker noted for his wall mirrors. After his retirement in 1776 his business was carried on by his son, Junior.

Folwell, John (*fl.* 1775). Philadelphia master cabinet maker of the Chippendale school, whose works, according to Horner, 'are unsurpassed in historic appeal and artistic significance'. Just before the Revolution, Folwell solicited subscriptions for his proposed book of American furniture drawings, titled *The Gentleman and Cabinet-maker's Assistant.* In consequence, he is sometimes called the Chippendale of America.

Frothingham, Benjamin (*fl.* 1756, d. 1809). Foremost cabinet maker of Charlestown, Massachusetts. Several soberly elegant pieces, such as a block-front chest of drawers and a reverse serpentine desk, still bear his label. Son of a Boston cabinet maker, Frothingham became a major of artillery in the Revolution and counted his commander-in-chief, General Washington, as a friend.

Gaines, John (*fl.* 1724, d. 1743). Gifted cabinet maker of Ipswich, Massachusetts, earlier of Portsmouth, New Hampshire. He may have originated

Block-front mahogany chest-on-chest, Townsend-Goddard School, Newport, Rhode Island, 1765–80. Courtesy of Henry Francis du Pont Winterthur Museum

Sheraton-type Salem mahogany sofa, the carving attributed to Samuel McIntire, *c.* 1800. Metropolitan Museum of Art

the Queen Anne chair variants which combine the solid splat with the earlier caned Flemish and banister-back chairs. His son, George, a major in the Revolution, also became a well-known cabinet maker.

Gillingham, James (1735–91). Skilful cabinet maker of Philadelphia. Several of his Gothic Chippendale chairs, with distinctive, trefoil-pierced slats, have been identified.

Goddard, John (1723/4–85). The originator perhaps together with his brother-in-law, John Townsend, of block-front and shell-carved cabinet furniture. Widely reckoned the foremost Rhode Island furniture maker of his day. Apprenticed to Job Townsend, of Newport, whose daughter he married. His sons, Stephen and Thomas Goddard, became first-class cabinet makers. (*See* Townsend, John.)

Gostelowe, Jonathan (1744–1806). Outstanding Philadelphia cabinet maker. His mahogany furniture in late Chippendale patterns is unsurpassed. He designed several patterns of his own, among them 'impossible serpentine and fluted-corner chests of drawers'.

Harland, Thomas (*fl.* 1773, d. 1807). Sometimes called the ablest Connecticut clockmaker of his day. A number of his workmen became well-known clockmakers on their own, including William Cleveland, grandfather of the twenty-second President of the United States, Grover Cleveland.

Scroll-back side chair of mahogany made in the shop of Duncan Phyfe, New York City, 1807. Courtesy of Henry Francis du Pont Winterthur Museum

Hopkins, Gerrard (*fl.* 1767–93). Baltimore cabinet maker, trained in Philadelphia. Especially remembered for his furniture in the Chippendale manner. Son of another furniture craftsman, Samuel.

Hosmer, Joseph (*fl.* 1775). Concord, Massachusetts, cabinet maker. He learned his trade from an American Frenchman, Robert Rosier. He produced skilful and distinctive works often in cherry or other New England woods. In 1775, his house, barn, and shop were burned by the British. Later that year, as a lieutenant of Minute-men, Hosmer became a historical figure. Shouting 'Will you let them burn the town down?' he led the attack on Concord bridge, in which the British suffered their first defeat in the American Revolution.

Lannuier, Charles, Honoré (*fl.* 1780–1819). New York cabinet maker. Perhaps trained in France, he produced elegant, often elaborate, furniture, and is especially remembered for his work in the Directory style. His pieces are often attributed to Phyfe.

Lemon, William (*fl.* 1796). Master cabinet maker of Salem, Massachusetts. Of peerlessly refined skill, he is noted for his superb furniture in the Hepplewhite manner.

McIntire, Samuel (1757–1811). Famous architect, woodwork designer, and carver of Salem, Massachusetts. A superior craftsman, he is by some students considered the leading American furniture carver, especially of Sheraton ornament in the Adam (classical) manner. There has been hot controversy as to whether or not he was a cabinet maker. There is no documentary proof that he was. His son, Samuel, also did furniture carving.

Moore, Robert (*fl.* 1769). Brother of Thomas and William, all cabinet makers of prominence in pre-Revolutionary Baltimore.

Nash, Thomas (*fl.* 1638–58). Earliest recorded clock-maker in America. He was a gunsmith of New Haven, Connecticut.

Phyfe, Duncan (1768–1854). New York master cabinet maker. Born in Scotland, he went in his early 'teens to Albany, New York, and there became apprenticed to a cabinet maker. In 1790, aged twenty-one, he arrived in New York City, where he set up a shop and made fine-quality furniture in the Sheraton and Directory styles. Phyfe's work possesses a grace of line, a refinement of proportions, and a delicacy of ornament – reeding, fluting, cameo carving – which lends it both elegance and a distinctive air. Among his chairs, sofas, and tables he produced so many little masterpieces incorporating the lyre motif that he is now considered its chief American exponent. Phyfe's individuality again stands out in his Empire-style furniture. He was so successful that at one time he employed a hundred workmen; eventually his work suffered from his success. He retired from business in 1847. Fine collections of Phyfe furniture are owned by the Museum of the City of New York; the Metropolitan Museum, New York; the Taft Museum, Cincinnati, Ohio; and Henry Ford's Edison Institute, Dearborn, Michigan.

Pimm, John (*fl.* 1735, d. 1773). One of the ablest Boston cabinet makers in the Queen Anne style. A handsome japanned highboy, signed by him, survives.

Prince, Samuel (d. 1778). Able and highly prosperous New York cabinet maker. He is especially identified with furniture in the Chippendale manner. Thomas Burling was apprenticed to him.

Randolph, Benjamin (*fl.* 1762, d. 1792). Shares with Thomas Affleck the reputation of being the leading exponent of the Philadelphia Chippendale school. He owned considerable property and is believed to have had the largest cabinet-making shop in Philadelphia. Of him Nagel says: 'No other American cabinet-maker mastered the true spirit of the rococo more completely or came closer to the English tradition than Randolph.' A finely carved French Chippendale wing chair attributed to him has been sold at auction to John D. Rockefeller, Jr, for $33,000.

Rittenhouse, David (1732–96). Noted American astronomer, surveyor, inventor, and clockmaker of Philadelphia. Of his grandfather clocks, already famous in his day, only a few survive. He is said to have constructed his first clock when he was only seventeen. Thomas Jefferson, third President of the United States, wrote of him: 'We have supposed Mr Rittenhouse second to no astronomer; that in genius he must be first because he is self taught.' Rittenhouse (from the original Dutch, Rittenhuisjen) was a grandson of the first Mennonite bishop in America. He became Director of the United States Mint, and succeeded Benjamin Franklin as President of the American Philosophical Society. His brother, Benjamin, was also a clockmaker.

Sanderson, Elijah (1751–1825). Able cabinet maker of Salem, Massachusetts. Together with his brother Jacob (1757–1810) he employed the finest craftsmen available, including the carver Samuel McIntire. They shipped much of their furniture to Southern states, where it is said to have been sold on the piers. They also shipped furniture to South America.

Savery, William (1721–87). Renowned cabinet maker of Philadelphia. At one time reckoned the paramount furniture craftsman in Pennsylvania, he is still considered peerlessly sound. Joseph Downs tells us that his career began in 1742, continued forty-five years, and that his work ranged from simple maple rush-bottom chairs to soberly elegant carved Chippendale mahogany highboys.

Seymour, John (*fl.* 1790–1820). Master cabinet maker of Boston. His distinctive Federal furniture interprets Hepplewhite, Sheraton, and Directory designs, often combining features of each. He is famous for his masterly satinwood inlays and tambour doors. He had a son in business with him.

Shaw, John. Exceptionally skilful cabinet maker of Annapolis, Maryland. He flourished in the late eighteenth century. There exist several labelled examples of his work in Hepplewhite and Sheraton styles.

Terry, Eli (1772–1852). Master clockmaker of Connecticut. He developed nine clocks, which he patented, the best known being the so-called 'Terry' clock, a then inexpensive shelf or mantel timepiece with wooden works running thirty hours. It is housed in a case with a scrolled-arch top, small round pillars at the sides, and delicately small feet. Early in his career Terry toured the countryside, peddling his clocks from door to door.

Thomas, Seth (1785–1859). Connecticut clockmaker, once a workman for Eli Terry. He bought up the rights to make 'Terry' clocks, but seems to have created no clock of his own. Today clocks bearing the name Seth Thomas are still being manufactured.

Townsend, John (b. 1733). Renowned cabinet maker of Newport, Rhode Island. He made excellent block-front furniture and is believed to have been associated with his brother-in-law, John Goddard, in originating it. Captured in the Revolution, he was released from a British prison ship in 1777, took up residence in Norwich and, later, Middletown, Connecticut, where groups of block-front furniture makers sprang up around him. Outstanding member of a famous furniture-making family, including his father, Job, several brothers, sons, and nephews. Some scholars think the Townsends deserve most of the credit now given to John Goddard for originating block-front furniture.

Tufft, Thomas (*fl.* 1765, d. 1793). Well-known cabinet maker of the Philadelphia Chippendale school. His identified work is not as elaborate as some, but his chairs and carved highboys and lowboys set 'a standard of exquisite detail'.

Weaver, Holmes (1769–1848). Newport, Rhode Island, cabinet maker. Produced excellent work in Hepplewhite and Sheraton styles. Was at one time clerk of the supreme court of his county.

Willard, Simon (1753–1848). Widely regarded as America's foremost clockmaker. Member of a famous family of Massachusetts clockmakers, including his father, Benjamin; three brothers (Benjamin, Jr, Ephraim, and Aaron); a son, Simon, Jr; nephews and cousins. His most famous clock – a weight-driven, accurate, eight-day movement, housed in a banjo-shaped case – he patented in 1800, having invented it several years earlier. He also made grandfather clocks of the finest workmanship. His reputation grew so great that other clockmakers are known to have put his name on their clocks.

American Victorian Furniture

The American Victorian style, in existence from 1840 until about 1910, displays strong English influence, as the name implies. Designs and design books were simultaneously published in London and New York. Basically the Victorian is an eclectic style. Many different sources were used for inspiration, with innovations introduced in construction and proportion. Most of the misunderstanding of this style comes from the fact that its originality is not accepted as anything more than lack of ability at imitating. Actually, the Victorian designers tried to remain close to their models but also wanted to create practical furniture, and they changed the scale and some of the details to suit the rooms for which the furniture was intended.

The style has been referred to by Carol Meeks as one of 'Picturesque Eclecticism'. The emphasis is on visual elements. Covering and screening new types of construction with traditional motifs is general.

New designs were always based on previous periods. At times the sources were close at hand in the various eighteenth-century styles, but occasionally the more exotic and distant models, such as Jacobean and Near Eastern, were employed.

Very important to the development of furniture production was the partial industrialization that became typical of the craft in the United States. The large workshop with the bare beginnings of mass production and specialization, gradually became common in the centre where furniture was made. This was responsible, in part, for some of the changes in what might be considered traditional forms.

By 1840 many manufacturers in American cities were known to employ from forty to one hundred men, most of whom were unskilled workers. Furniture designs were created by the shop owner, and a minimal number of skilled men were required to follow the designs. The larger shops produced inexpensive furniture that could be shipped easily. John of Cincinnati supplied many small Mississippi river towns with stylish furniture. The furniture of Hennesy of Boston was available in many smaller towns along the seacoast.

We can get some idea of the Victorian conception of styles from the writing of the American architect, A. J. Downing. In *Cottage Residences*, published in New York in 1842, he implies the use of more than one furniture style when he says: 'A person of correct architectural taste will . . . confer on each apartment by expression of purpose, a kind of individuality. Thus in a complete cottage-villa, the hall will be grave and simple in character, a few plain seats its principal furniture; the library sober and dignified . . .; the drawing room lively or brilliant, adorned with pictures. . . .'

He continues in the same vein in another book, *The Architecture of Country Houses*, one edition of which was published in 1861 (others earlier): 'Furniture in *correct taste* is characterized by its being designed in accordance with certain recognized styles and intended to accord with apartments in the same style.' Downing goes on to describe the various styles and he includes Grecian (or French) Gothic, Elizabethan, Romanesque, and a version of the Renaissance style. Each has its place. The idea of using the different styles was criticized later by Charles Eastlake, an English architect who was influential in America. In 1872 he said, 'In the early part of the present century a fashionable conceit prevailed of fitting up separate apartments in large mansions each after a style of its own. Thus we had Gothic halls, Elizabethan chambers, Louis-Quatorze drawing rooms, etc. . . .'

These various styles of the Victorian period were used at about the same time, but fashion determined when they were replaced and none lasted throughout the period.

The earliest significant style was a continuation of American Empire. This furniture was heavy in proportion and differed from the earlier models only in a few details. The wavy moulding was a border introduced late; medallions and other small details of applied carving in leaf or floral motifs reduced the simplicity and classicism characteristic of earlier furniture. In the Victorian versions drawers rarely have borders of moulding, but rather are flush with the front surface. Marble tops for small tables and bedroom chests are common. Bracket feet are a frequent support for heavy case pieces. On tall legs turning as well as heavy carving was employed. Popular as finer woods were mahogany, black walnut, and rosewood. Simpler, less expensive pieces were made of maple, butternut, or other hard woods, which are often stained quite dark in red or brown. Veneers in prominent grains were used on case pieces as well as on the skirts of sofas or chairs.

In general, there were few new forms developed. Among the new were such peculiarities as the Lazy Susan and the ottoman; however, the wardrobe and the bookcase, which were known only infrequently before, were better known in the Victorian period.

With the factory replacing the craftsman's workshop, techniques requiring less skill developed. Machine sawing and planing were used with hand-fitting and finishing. The lines were planned by someone higher in rank than the man who operated the saw or did the finishing. The larger-scale operations made competition a more important factor than ever before, with price more important than workmanship.

A Baltimore cabinet maker, John Hall, published a book of furniture designs in 1840. One of the objectives of his book he describes by saying, 'Throughout the whole of the designs in this work, particular attention has been bestowed in an economical arrangement to save labour, which being an important point, is presumed will render the collection exceedingly useful to the cabinetmaker.' The designs are Grecian, he says in his commentary and '. . . the style of the United States is blended with European taste . . .' This is the style that A. J. Downing refers to as Greek, modern, and French and 'the furniture most generally used in private houses'. Contemporary cartoons and illustrations confirm his remark by usually including this kind of furniture. A popular woman's magazine of the time, Godey's *Lady's Book*, consistently presented suggestions for furniture in the style from the late 1840s to the 1860s which was called 'cottage furniture'.

Victorian rosewood armchair, the frame pierced and carved with flowers, leaves, fruit and acorn designs, showing revival of the rococo style. Metropolitan Museum of Art

The Gothic style in Victorian furniture has two aspects. As a variation of the classical, it involves only the use of the pointed arch and related motifs in what is basically the classical style. As a more ambitious innovation, it involves the use of Gothic ornament in a more serious attempt to create a special style. The first approach was used by Chippendale, who included Gothic motifs in his rococo suggestions. Later, Sheraton included Gothic arcades in suggestions of designs, primarily neoclassical. This continued in early Victorian furniture in the Greek style. The other aspect was connected with the Gothic revival in architecture, which, although begun in the eighteenth century, had an important effect on home building after 1830. Suitable to houses in the Gothic style was furniture repeating the motifs. Large bookcases, which seem almost like architectural elements, and hall chairs, high-backed side chairs carved elaborately, are often the most spectacular examples of the style.

Some of the finest examples were designed by architects for use in their buildings. Occasionally spiral-turned columns, seventeenth-century in inspiration, are combined with elements of earlier inspiration. The characteristic feature of the style is the pointed arch of simple or complicated form used with incised or pierced spandrels and bold raised mouldings. The Gothic style is one favoured for hall decoration and used less frequently in the parlour. Sets of bedroom furniture in the style are known. Tables are extremely rare in this style.

When referring to furniture of various kinds Downing says in *The Architecture of Country Houses*: 'There is, at the present moment, almost a mania in the cities for expensive French furniture and decorations. The style of royal palaces abroad is imitated in town houses of fifty foot front. . . .' This style was often called Louis XIV, although it is a combination of various French styles from Louis XIV to Louis XVI.

Revival of rococo style had started in France as a reaction to its classicism which was dominant shortly before the Revolution. With the Restoration came a desire for the good old days and a style related to them. Napoleon's Romanism was as distasteful as his political upsets. From France the revival spread to the rest of the Continent, England, and the United States. In the Victorian home, where each room varied in style to suit its proper mood, the French style was most popular in the parlour, although bedroom furniture in the style is known.

The American Victorian pieces were smaller in proportion than the eighteenth-century models. The curving lines of the back stiles are often exaggerated so that the back is balloon-shaped. Cabriole legs are restrained in their curve. Console tables with marble tops come in scallop shapes. Curving fronts are typical for case pieces. Carving in rose, grape, or leaf motifs with elaborate details in high relief is seen on chairs and sofas. On other forms this carving is flatter. Elaborate carving was frequently used on cabriole legs.

The curve becomes all important as a contrast to the straightness of the classical. Small boudoir pieces were made in this style as well as whole matching parlour sets which include a sofa or love seat, gentleman's armchair, lady's chair, four side chairs, an ottoman, and centre table. In a drawing-room set there are additional pieces such as an extra sofa, more side chairs, and possibly a matching *étagère.* There seem to be no dining-room pieces in this style. Introduced in America about 1840, it was important until some time in the 1870s. One of the most important cabinet makers working in this manner was John Belter of New York. Born in Germany, he opened a shop in the city of New York in 1844 and continued in business until his death in 1863. Belter's work was a distinctive variation of the Louis XV style. He invented a laminating process for curing wood that he used in making the sides of case pieces and chair and sofa backs. He destroyed the means of doing this laminating shortly before his death, so that it was never used later. Solid curving pieces are characteristic of Belter's shop, as is elaborate carving in high relief and balloon-shaped chair backs. Belter's parlour sets are best known, but he also made bedroom furniture.

Philadelphia mahogany table with intarsia marble top and brass inlay, by Antoine-Gabriel Quervelle, *c.* 1830. Metropolitan Museum of Art

Below Victorian bed by John Henry Belter, showing laminated construction, *c.* 1850. Courtesy of Brooklyn Museum

The Louis XVI style was more specifically popular after 1865 when there was some reaction to the exuberance of the rococo revival evident in the Louis XV-inspired examples. The straight line and the fine detail are opposed to the heavier curving style.

Other revivals of interest occur in the early period, but to no great extent. Downing's suggestions include pieces in what he refers to as the Flemish style, but actually of William and Mary origin.

After 1870 there were several other adaptations of eighteenth-century models. The Adam and Sheraton styles served as inspiration for dining-room and parlour pieces done with greater faithfulness to the model and less for modern requirements.

The Renaissance style was introduced at the Crystal Palace exhibitions of 1851 (London) and 1853 (New York). It is a style heavy in proportion and generally straight in line. Decoration is elaborate and frequently inspired by architectural rather than furniture design. The pediment is used to top many of the forms, from chairs to large case pieces. Bold mouldings, raised cartouches, raised and shaped panels, incised linear decoration, and applied carving in garlands and medallions are all characteristic. Occasionally, animal heads and sporting trophies appear on dining-room pieces. The style was used primarily for bedroom, library, and dining-room, but also parlour furniture. This style continued to be important until about 1880.

Factory production inspired spool-turned furniture, a particular type easy to produce for the lower-priced furniture market. In the main, designs were simple and the sizes were right for easy handling in lower-middle-class interiors. This furniture was decorated by turning on a lathe the legs, arms, and supports and obtaining identical units repeated in any of a variety of motifs that include the bobbin, knob, button, sausage, and vase and ring. The lines are generally rectangular and simple. This furniture did not include every form, but rather emphasized beds and tables.

The first seeds of modernism can be traced from the reactions against bad craftsmanship in the Victorian period. As a period of mass production and keen competition, the Victorian period saw the development of truly bad design as well as some very good design that has been misunderstood. By attempting to make things cheaply without simplifying the design and method of production, some makers produced surprisingly unsuccessful results.

One of the first important reactions was the book, *Hints on Household Taste*, which had an American edition in 1872. The author was the English architect, Charles Lock Eastlake, who decried bad craftsmanship and the shams it involved. He sought to inspire simple honest work in solid woods. He disliked shoddy veneer and too elaborate work. His argument was: 'I recommend the re-adoption of no specific type of ancient furniture which is unsuited, whether in detail or general design, to the habits of modern life. It is the spirit and principles of early manufacture which I desire to see revived and not the absolute forms in which they found embodiment.'

Eastlake proposed that craftsmen follow appropriate models that would not be difficult to execute. He disliked the over-ambitious attempts of the 1850s in which the rococo was used to excess. The resultant style was simple and rectangular. Most of what he suggested was to be executed in oak, a durable but inexpensive wood. Carving could be simple, and turnings were to play an important role. This style was gradually more and more important on the American scene. Related suggestions follow in ensuing decades, and the oak furniture of the turn of the century by Gustav Stickley is probably basically of the same inspiration.

Attempts to find new and more appropriate sources of design resulted in furniture of exotic inspiration, such as that of the so-called Turkish style, seen in overstuffed pieces for parlour use.

The Victorian period is marked by variety of inspiration, stimulated by the use of different styles to suggest different moods. In the first half of the period the changes from the original to the Victorian interpretation were probably greater. After 1880 there was a more faithful adherence to the lines of the models, although the results always differed from the originals. About the same time attempts to make furniture only vaguely connected with earlier styles were evident, and there was also a search for new sources of inspiration.

In the Victorian age mass production was a key factor in the development of the kind of competition which made bad craftsmanship profitable. This resulted from cutting costs without considering the need for simplification in design.

CAST-IRON FURNITURE

The manufacture of cast-iron furniture in the United States began in the 1840s and continued until the first decade of the twentieth century. The manufacturers were firms making grille work, architectural ornaments, and building fronts. Both indoor and outdoor furniture was produced, although, with few exceptions, the indoor furniture was popular for a much shorter time than the outdoor furniture. Cast-iron furniture for interiors was introduced in the 1850s, a little later than the garden furniture. It was designed as an imitation of wooden furniture in the various Victorian styles and was painted to simulate wood. The exceptions to this characterization were the beds and hat racks in which imaginative forms were developed. These two forms continued to be popular after cast-iron furniture for interiors had become unfashionable.

Garden furniture of cast iron was used for a longer period, and the designs became standardized. The dominant influence was the romantic garden which had come into fashion at the end of the eighteenth century. It was created to appear wild, as if man had not had a hand in it. The furniture was designed to have a rustic look, to appear to be made of unhewn logs, or boughs of trees, vines, or flowers. The various patterns used seem to have been followed by many manufacturers. The same designs appear in early and late examples. The earliest catalogue known to contain an illustration of cast-iron garden furniture appeared in the 1840s in Philadelphia, but almost every American city of any size produced it some time during the nineteenth century. Often the mould contained the name of the manufacturer, and the piece can be dated by consulting city directories.

Chinese and Japanese

Both the Chinese and Japanese are highly skilled wood workers, and both nations have produced furniture of very good quality. An important difference between the two countries until very recently was that the Japanese lived much nearer to the floor, sitting on mats placed on a low raised platform, and eating from tables only a few inches in height. The Chinese, on the other hand, have used chairs and tables similar in principle to those of the West for centuries, although there are still a few survivals of the remote times when their habits resembled those of Japan. Notable among them is the platform-like *k'ang*, which is a long, wide, wooden couch or day bed with back and arms, sometimes built in and at all times massive and heavy, on which two people could recline side by side parallel with the arms, having between them a low table, known as a *k'ang* table. The couch (*ch'uang*) is basically similar to the *k'ang* in general form, but the seat is much narrower and nearer to the conventional European settee.

The wood most frequently employed for fine quality work in China is called *hua-li*, and it seems to have been a kind of rosewood (species *Dalbergia*). The Chinese lacked wood of a quality suitable for good quality furniture making within their own borders, and consequently most of their timber for this purpose was imported from the south. The woods, on the whole, were not those imported into Europe for similar purposes, and it is difficult to make exact identifications from manufactured and polished specimens when only the Chinese terms are known, since equivalents in European languages have never been fixed. Blackwood, which is not black naturally but very dark in colour, is a rosewood, the East Indian *Dalbergia latifolia*. It is sometimes called *tzŭ t'an mu*, but the same term is sometimes employed to describe any fine-grained, heavy, hardwood of the kind used for furniture making. Padouk wood, also imported into England and used by Chippendale, came from the Andaman Islands, and is more easily identified. It has dark chocolate-brown markings and a purplish or crimson background, and the Chinese used it in the eighteenth century to make furniture for export to the West. Camphorwood, which repels such insects as the clothes moth, was used to make chests in which furs and clothes were stored, and the bamboo was employed to make light summer furniture for garden use. Furniture of woven rattan cane was also made but has not survived. It is known from prints. Nearly all Japanese furniture is lacquered, and polished wood is exceptional, so the identification of the various woods employed is not only difficult but usually of no particular interest.

Very little is known about Chinese furniture made before the Ming dynasty (1368–1644), although paintings of earlier dates than this, and literary references, suggest that Ming designs were a continuation of a slow process of evolution. There are also one or two specimens of Chinese furniture in the eighth century closed collection of the Shosōin Pavilion at Nara (Japan) which belonged originally to the Emperor Shomu.

The chair was introduced towards the end of the Han dynasty (206 B.C.–A.D. 220) as a seat of honour or throne, and it was almost certainly Buddhist in

Above Rosewood armchair, Chinese, early 17th century. Victoria & Albert Museum

Far right Side table, Chinese, 17th century. Victoria & Albert Museum

origin. It arrived in Japan during the Nara period (710–94) and was employed for the same purpose, afterwards becoming the prerogative of Buddhist priests, but, unlike China, it did not come into general domestic use till modern times.

The chair is perhaps the commonest survival in China from early Ming times, and a number of specimens are known dating back to the reign of the Emperor Hsüan-te (1426–35). Early examples have a box frame and back and arm rails formed in a continuous curve as far as the seat, the centre of the back supported by a solid curved splat. The wood was usually *huang hua-li* (rosewood). The design, with the lower part replaced by four legs of the modern type (i.e. without the box frame) has been closely followed in some modern Japanese chairs. Another early type has a box frame and a straight back, and these, when the back is higher than customary, are reminiscent of a design by Rennie Mackintosh.

Right Armchair of padouk inlaid with bone, early 19th century. Victoria & Albert Museum

Chairs with arms were far outnumbered by chairs without arms and the backless stool, both of which are rarely seen in the West. The armchair was intended for the head of the household and his honoured guests. Persons of lower rank occupied armless chairs, and paintings usually show women seated on stools – a system of etiquette in seating apparently as rigid as that of Louis XIV at Versailles. Porcelain or stoneware barrel-shaped seats were sometimes used indoors; more often in the garden.

The Chinese valued comfort, and the chairs of important people were covered with furs and decorative textiles – the greater their importance, the more ample the covering. There was also an easy chair with an adjustable reclining back and an extension to support the legs which was known as 'the drunken lord's chair'.

Although tables were made in great variety the principal kinds divide readily into two classes – side tables, narrow, rectangular, and massive, and made in pairs to be placed against the walls, and dining tables, brought into the room when the meal was ready to be served and therefore light in weight. Dining tables were round or square. In restaurants catering more or less exclusively for a Chinese clientele it is not uncommon to see a circular table on a low dais at one end of the room. This is the place of honour for important parties. The table is of a size sufficient to allow diners to reach out with chopsticks and serve themselves from dishes placed in the centre of the table. For this reason, for a very large party the Chinese usually arrange a number of small square tables separately instead of putting them together.

Tables for special purposes, such as altar tables used in the ancestral hall to venerate the spirits of

the dead, lute tables made to carry the Chinese zither, gaming tables with recesses for counters, and small low tables usually intended as *k'ang* tables, were all numerous. Desks often resembled the European pedestal writing desk, with drawers on either side. Writing tables were large and flat, and since painting and calligraphy are closely allied arts, they were employed for painting as well. The implements for the writing table, employed alike for writing and painting, are a brush pot, inkstone, water dropper, brush rest, wrist rest, paperweights, and a table screen, all of which are often of porcelain or jade. Table screens of jade, porcelain, or lacquer are slotted into a heavy carved wood base, and there are instances of these stands having been converted to hold a small swing toilet mirror in the European manner. A much enlarged version of the table screen about 5 feet (1.5 m) high was sometimes employed decoratively in the Chinese interior. The base supported a painting on silk in an ornate carved or inlaid frame.

Storage cupboards were made in great variety, the doors with exterior hinges and large engraved lockplates of paktong or pewter. The Chinese preferred closed cupboards to open shelves, unlike the Japanese who used open shelving almost exclusively. When the Chinese used shelving it differed considerably from that of Japan because, even when the shelves were split level, they were always symmetrically disposed, whereas the Japanese disposition is almost invariably asymmetrical. This peculiarity is to be observed throughout the whole of the interior decoration of the two peoples. The Chinese made wardrobes and side tables in pairs; vases were made in pairs, or sets such as two and three; decoration was more or less symmetrically disposed. In the matter of porcelain decoration it may help to clarify the difference if we appreciate that the Chinese used white porcelain as a ground on which to paint, while Kakiemon at Arita employed it as an integral part of the decoration by leaving areas unpainted. It is difficult to say when this principle of asymmetricality made its appearance in Japanese art – this balanced unbalance – but it is Zen Buddhist in origin, and it had established itself by the Momoyama period (1576–1600). It is a particular feature of the highly valued gold ground screens of the period, and ultimately it without doubt played a significant part in inspiring the course taken by the rococo style of Louis XV.

Chinese wardrobes and tall cupboards are comparatively narrow for the most part. Those of lacquer tend to be wider in proportion to the height. Most of them have a small cupboard at the top intended for the storage of hats. They were made in pairs. Although lacquer wardrobes are rare, and principally were to be found in Imperial palaces, the Musée Guimet in Paris has a superb specimen decorated with gold dragons on a black ground which dates from the reign of K'ang Hsi (1662–1722), and the same museum has another of the same provenance decorated with mother-of-pearl inlay. The Victoria and Albert Museum has an equally magnificent example in brightly coloured lacquer and gold consisting of two cupboards of equal size, one on the other. In the same collection is a wardrobe of carved red lacquer. These examples serve to give an impression of the colourful magnificence of the interior decorated with lacquer furniture, although for the most part the Chinese preferred polished wood furniture of simple design in conjunction with polished wood floors.

Chests, often of camphorwood, were used for storing clothes and valuables, and most are equipped with a drawer or drawers. Pieces of furniture similar in principle to the commode with doors, i.e. with drawers in the frieze and cupboards under, or commodes with drawers in the frieze and shelves below, were used for the storage of a multiplicity of objects. Chests were much rarer in Japan, where the simple lacquer kimono rack was for storing clothes.

The general impression one gains from a study of Japanese life and art, leaving to one side the objects of poor quality exported to the West towards the end of the nineteenth century, is of a people who attached much more importance to the quality of objects than to the quantity. Unlike the West, with its comparatively recent arbitrary division between what it is pleased to call the fine arts (painting and sculpture) and the variously termed applied, industrial, or decorative arts, both China and Japan, largely under Buddhist influence, made no serious distinction between works in any medium, but laid great emphasis on the quality of craftsmanship. In a sense, before it renewed contact with the West in 1853, almost everything made in Japan, except perhaps the most utilitarian objects, deserved to be regarded as works of art. Special objects with no particular purpose except that of being ornamental were usually termed *okimono*, which means, approximately, 'an object for a special place'. These were set apart in a niche reserved for the purpose, and changed from time to time.

The Chinese, also, do not decorate their homes with large numbers of objects. They are inclined to display such things as porcelain vases on side tables, but valued pieces of porcelain which would be displayed in cabinets in the West are kept in padded boxes, to be opened one by one for the delectation and admiration of honoured guests and the owner himself.

The screen played a very important part in the Japanese interior, serving a number of functions – as decoration, as a protection from draughts, to ensure a measure of privacy, and to act as a room divider. For the latter purpose channels were provided in the floor in which it moved. The framework is of lacquered wood over which strong paper is stretched. A painting or piece of calligraphy is executed on the paper. The art of the painted screen flourished especially in the Momoyama period, when the finest work was done on a ground covered with gold leaf. Often the only decoration of a screen will be calligraphy, and this is an important art in both China and Japan, being employed as a type of ornament on many things, from screens to porcelain, in a form either painted, carved, or incised.

The principal type of Japanese screen is termed *byōbu.* It varies from two to eight panels, and will usually be about 5 feet (1.5 m) in height. The *furosaki byōbu* is a small screen of two leaves to protect the brazier used in the Tea Ceremony from draughts. The *kembyō*, derived from China, is a small table screen to protect the inkstone on the scholar's table from the dust which might otherwise be blown on it.

The Chinese employed the screen in the interior to a smaller extent, usually the six- or twelve-fold tall incised lacquer screen which dates from early in the seventeenth century. This was the type known in Europe as 'Coromandel' or 'Bantam'. The design, often quite elaborate, was incised into the lacquer ground and the incisions were then filled in with colours and gilded.

The Chinese house was illuminated by lanterns protecting lamps burning oil or a pricket candlestick. These were often suspended from lantern stands, sometimes of fairly plain construction, and sometimes decorated with carved work. The finest lanterns were those of a highly translucent porcelain painted with *famille rose* colours made during the reign of Ch'ien Lung (1736–96).

So far this discussion has been limited to furniture in native taste, made for the Chinese house. Examples have been exported to the West, and they occur in Western collections, but the more ornate carved and decorated specimens of polished wood furniture were probably made to order for a European customer. Since the Chinese were highly skilled cabinet makers they found no difficulty in copying European furniture, no matter how elaborate, and specimens exist, such as an English-style fall-front bureau-cabinet of *c.* 1725 in padouk wood, undoubtedly copied from a European model provided, even to the brass handles and lockplates.

Chinese furniture had great influence on the designs of Chippendale, although little on that of some of his contemporaries, who boasted that their Chinese ornament was their own invention. The Anglo-Japanese furniture of Godwin and others in the 1870s often owes at least as much to Chinese furniture as to Japanese. Japanese lacquer panels exerted great influence on some of the most important eighteenth-century French rococo furniture, as well as on the porcelain of the period, and the influence of Japan again occurred in the 1880s when it was among the strongest of the formative influences which led to Art Nouveau.

LACQUER

Lacquer is the product of the *rhus vernicifera* (the lacquer tree) which is tapped in the same way as the rubber tree when it exudes sap which, when dry, forms a hard, semi-transparent film.

Lacquer first appears in China as far back as the Shang dynasty (*c.* 1600–1027 B.C.). It will adhere equally well to wood or metal and is often employed over a kind of papier mâché. By applying it to leather the Japanese made a light and effective armour. The Japanese were, in fact, more versatile than the Chinese in finding uses for it, and employed

Below The throne of Emperor Ch'ien Lung (1736–95), carved red lacquer with layers of green and yellow. Victoria & Albert Museum

Bottom Early Ming palace table, carved red lacquer on wood. The dragon and phoenix designs symbolize its use by Emperor and Empress. Mark and reign of Hsüan-tê (1426–35). Victoria & Albert Museum

lacquer for such domestic utensils as plates, cups, and saké cups.

Most lacquer is decorated with painting, pigments being mixed with the substance before it hardens, but during the T'ang dynasty (618–906) the Chinese developed a method of building up thicknesses sufficient for low-relief carving by applying successive layers, allowing each to dry. This technique was used to a very limited extent in Japan soon afterwards, but was especially developed by the Chinese during the early reigns of the Ming dynasty, when several colours were sometimes superimposed one on the other and then carved through as required to form the design. An important, but fussily overdecorated example of carved lacquer is the throne of Ch'ien Lung (1736–96) in the Victoria and Albert Museum, but the best lacquer furniture dates back to the early reigns of the Ming dynasty (1368–1644), when furniture generally was of fine quality.

In the eighth century the Japanese developed a sophisticated type of portrait sculpture using lacquer over a hempen cloth foundation supported by an earthen core, afterwards removed, a type known as 'dry' lacquer (*kanshitsu*). These figures were almost lifesize. Another technique was to prepare a light wooden framework over which the details were modelled in a mixture of lacquer and fine sawdust. Both these types had fallen into disfavour soon after the close of the ninth century, and specimens are not often seen in Europe. They may also have been made in China, possibly early in the Ming dynasty, but this observation depends on two specimens of uncertain provenance and dating, and a report that 'dry' lacquer figures had been seen being carried in temple processions.

The fame of Chinese lacquer had reached Europe by the beginning of the seventeenth century, and the objects themselves, especially screens and cabinets, soon followed. The varieties imported fall into three categories: painted, carved in relief, and with incised designs, of which the first and last were the commonest. Incised lacquer, usually in the form of screens and panels for cabinets, was called Bantam work, from the port of Bantam in the Dutch East Indies, or Coromandel lacquer from the fact that these wares were transhipped on the Coromandel coast. Many of the earlier imports, such as screens, were broken down into panels and made up into cabinets by European craftsmen, but by 1670 models for the making and decoration of cabinets were being sent to China by the various East India Companies, and this practice continued at least until 1725. Imported panels from China and Japan were employed in France by the *maître ébénistes* for the manufacture of commodes and *encoignures* which are usually termed *à la pagode* in such contemporary records as the *Livre-Journal* of Lazare Duvaux. Demand so far outran supply at all periods that there were many European attempts to imitate Oriental lacquer in other materials which are discussed at length in the section headed European Lacquer Furniture. Throughout this whole period Japanese lacquer seems to have been the more highly valued in the West, and surviving correspondence with representatives in the Far East of the East India Companies often refers to the inferior quality of the Chinese product and the difficulty occasionally experienced in selling it profitably. Even so, the

Coromandel incised lacquer screen, 17th century

Japanese did not allow the finer qualities to be exported at this time.

Most sought by collectors of lacquer are the smaller works of Chinese carved lacquer from the Ming dynasty onwards, early examples being very rare, and the many decorative examples of Japanese lacquer art, such as the *inrō* (seal case). By the Fujiwara period in Japan (894–1184) objects decorated with lacquer in a variety of techniques included chests, shelves, dressers, low tables, cosmetic and writing boxes, and many other things, all of which continued to be made during the centuries which followed. The finest Japanese lacquer can be classified among the fine arts in that country, and remarkable ingenuity was exercised in devising numerous ways of decorating it – far too many for more than the most important to be mentioned here.

Colour may take the form of pigment incorporated into the lacquer itself, or dusted on to the surface while it is still sticky. The principal colours are black, scarlet, green, yellow, brown, purple, and white, a more limited palette than that of China. The Japanese excelled in the use of such metallic powders as gold, silver, and copper. The normal foundation is of light wood, but a type of papier mâché, or a fabric like hemp, are sometimes employed.

The principal basic techniques are noted below, but they represent the beginning of a vast subject which is as fascinating as it is inexhaustible. Lacquer is valued for the high quality of its craftsmanship and meticulously detailed finish. It is thus at the opposite pole to certain kinds of pottery, where accidental effects are deliberately sought and valued.

Much Japanese lacquer is inlaid with mother-of-pearl. The technique dates from the Nara period (710–93) and was originally derived from China during the T'ang dynasty. The Chinese made relatively little use of it thereafter, but it was considerably developed by the Japanese during the centuries which followed. It is termed *raden*.

The commonest basic technique of decoration is termed *maki-e* (sprinkled picture) in which the design was first painted on a prepared lacquer surface, and then, while the painting was still sticky, gold or silver powder was blown across it or sprinkled on, and it adhered to the sticky areas. It was then covered with clear lacquer. In the case of *togidashi maki-e* a coat of black lacquer was laid over the design and then rubbed down with charcoal and powdered deer's horn till the picture reappeared, yielding very delicate tonal effects. *Taka maki-e* is *maki-e* in relief, in which the design or picture is built up with a thick coat or successive coats of yellow ochre mixed with raw lacquer, which is then covered with gold *maki-e*. This dates from the Kamakura period (1185–1333), and was first combined with the more familiar *maki-e* technique during the Muromachi period (1134–1577). *Iro taka maki-e* is coloured work in a similar technique. *Todaiji maki-e* dates from the Momoyama period (1573–1614), and the term refers to a design of natural plants in *maki-e* on a black lacquer ground. *Hatsune maki-e* belongs to the Edo period (1615–1867) and is found decorating furniture. It comprises principally scenes from palaces and gardens.

Nashiji is aventurine lacquer, aventurine being a kind of brownish hardstone with gold or coppery flecks beneath its surface. In the lacquer version small flakes of gold or silver foil occur at different levels from the surface. It is frequently employed alone, especially for drawer interiors, or the interiors of boxes. It was introduced during the Fujiwara period.

Hyomon refers to the inlaying of thin cut metal sheets into the lacquer surface, usually in conjunction with other techniques. First introduced during the Nara period, it was revived during the Kamakura period. *Shunkei-nuri* is a transparent lacquer tinged with a light reddish brown which is used over natural wood when it is desired to reveal the grain. The term *Mitsuda-e* actually refers to painting in lead oxide mixed with oil (a type of oil paint) on wood, and probably dates back to the Fujiwara period. The term is used of oil painting in the same colours on a lacquer ground. Specimens are rare. *Shitsu-ga* refers to pictures painted in coloured lacquers.

Guri lacquer is a type where the work was first formed of superimposed layers of various colours. These were then carved with landscapes and figures, the coloured layers forming the different planes of the picture. Another variety has a spiral pattern engraved through the colours with a lozenge-shaped burin (engraver's tool) to give a pattern of V-shaped grooves which were polished to reveal the superimposed colours.

A certain amount of carved lacquer was made in Japan, inspired by that of China, but the quality is rarely as good as Chinese work. Wood carved in the manner of lacquer in low relief and then covered with red lacquer (*kamakuri-bori*) was made between the thirteenth and eighteenth centuries. The same technique has been used later for poor quality forgeries of Chinese carved lacquer.

The processes outlined above are, of course, intended to be sufficient to identify the main category to which a specimen belongs, and have been very much simplified and reduced to essentials. In practice all of them require a great deal of highly skilled work in preparing the surface, in executing the design, and in finishing and polishing. Often several coats of lacquer, each of which is rubbed down with mild abrasives, are applied, and the surface is polished finally with a light vegetable oil and the thumb of the workman. The makers of the wooden foundations for lacquerwork belong to a separate craft, but few who have seen the close-fitting, almost airtight, joints between the various parts of, for example, some *inrō* can fail to admire their skill.

Lacquer of interest to the collector more or less finishes about 1870, when large quantities of inferior work were made for export to the West. For all but the most expert, quality of design and craftsmanship, and an avoidance of overelaboration, remain the best guide. Most of the excessively decorated work belongs to the nineteenth century.

The subject matter of lacquer decoration is vast, and virtually everything is symbolic in one way or another. Some of the subjects come from literary sources, such as the Noh plays and novels, and these may be straightforward illustrations without any concealed meaning. But the greater part of the ornament used on such small lacquer wares as *inrō* are intended to be symbolic, although the meaning in Japan is not always the same as in China. The peach still symbolizes longevity and the prunus (imported from China) represents spring. The chrysanthemum (*kiku*) is much more important than in China, since in a stylized version it is the *mon*, or heraldic badge of the emperor. The Japanese are fond of insects, especially the 'singing' insects like the cicada, the cricket, and the grasshopper, which are put into small cages for the sake of the strident sounds they make. Colourful butterflies and dragonflies both occur as lacquer decoration, the latter symbolizing Japan itself, from the supposed resemblance of the outline of the islands to that of the insect. As in China, the crane is a longevity symbol, and the duck, peacock, and pheasant are popular subjects among birds. The badger and the fox have great supernatural powers, and the bat has been borrowed from China and has much the same meaning. The lion (*shishi*), not indigenous to Japan, was a version of China's lion of Fo, and resembles a small dog to a far greater extent than the Chinese lion. The buffalo is often depicted as a riding animal, sometimes bearing a small boy playing a flute, and sometimes Lao Tzŭ or one of the native Japanese mythological personages. The rat is a good luck symbol which is sometimes shown gnawing one corner of a bag of rice on which sits the god of riches, Daikoku.

Marine life of all kinds is a very popular subject in Japanese art generally, but especially as a decorative motif on lacquerwork. The carp is the most frequently represented, often leaping up a waterfall. The water tortoise (*minogame*, or 'raincoat' tortoise) is also popular. The dragon is very similar to the Chinese version, both in form and connotation, but it nearly always has three claws. The five-clawed dragon appears to have been depicted very occasionally, and probably had Imperial connections. The so-called phoenix (Chinese *fêng huang*) is the Japanese *ho-ho* bird, and it is a popular lacquer subject. There are many other subjects and symbols, some abstract, some representing natural objects, some purely Japanese, others of Chinese origin. The Eight Precious Things, for example (*see* the Pottery and Porcelain section glossary) occur also in Japan. Many of the subjects listed above, and in the section referred to, are also the subject of carved *netsuké* (toggles) and of such metalwork as decorative sword-guards.

Signatures are not uncommon, and the names of artists in lacquer form a very long list. Little more than the name and an approximate period is known of some, but much more is known about others, especially those working in the nineteenth century. As in the case of other Japanese works of art, which are very frequently signed, it is possible to learn to read the characters without excessive difficulty. The Japanese have devised a system of using the elements of Chinese ideograms to form a syllabary which can be romanized, and F. A. Turk, *Japanese Objets d'Art* (London, 1962), gives a very useful appendix on the reading of dates and names. Individual Chinese ideograms on the other hand represent an idea or a thing, and need a prodigious memory or a good dictionary (which in itself is not easy to learn to use) before they can be read. Like Chinese, the Japanese cursive script is virtually impossible to learn to read, except for the most devoted scholar, and seal characters (*tensho*) are also exceptionally difficult to decipher.

As with Chinese signed works it is always difficult to be certain whether a signature is a forgery, whether it is that of a pupil imitating a master, or whether it has been added by a later hand as a mark of commendation. Experience, and an acquired sensitivity to the art of the country, are the best safeguards.

Five-case *inrō* signed in gold characters by the Kajikawa family, lacquer with gold and mother-of-pearl inlay. The *netsuké* is a miniature mask from the classical *No* theatre, early 19th century

English

The Age of Oak

English furniture from the Middle Ages to the Restoration in 1660 was made almost entirely of oak. William Harrison, writing late in the sixteenth century in his *Historical Description of the Island of Britaine*, said that 'nothing but oak was any whit regarded'.

The oak, which is the most common species of tree in this country, is hard and heavy, the colour varying from white to brown. Evelyn, in 1663, writes that it was 'of much esteem in former times till the finer grain's Norway timber came amongst us which is likewise of a whiter colour'. Although the oak is a very tough tree, it was discovered at an early date that there was little difficulty in splitting it along the lines of the medullary rays, provided that this were done before the fibres hardened. However, it must always have been necessary to use a saw for wood of a great age, or for wood that had been allowed to harden after felling. These saw-cut logs were immersed in flowing water for a period of up to two years and were then stored for a further ten to twenty years, after they had been converted into planks. The timber, thus seasoned, was then considered to be ready for use.

CONSTRUCTIONS

Furniture of the oak period is generally rectangular in construction and is very strongly built. Its component parts are put together with mortise and tenon, which in turn are held in position by wooden dowels. Evelyn, describing the furniture of the early seventeenth century, writes: 'they had cupboards of ancient, useful plate, whole chests of damask for table . . . and the sturdy oaken bedstead and furniture of the house lasted the whole century'. Much of this oak furniture has, of course, lasted far longer than a century, and on account of its strength has come down to us in almost pristine condition.

Far right James I side table, carved oak, with a drawer in the frieze and turned legs. Mary Bellis Antiques, Hungerford

Right Carved oak armchair with inlaid decoration, mid-17th century. Victoria & Albert Museum

Below Caqueteuse, carved oak with turned arms and front legs, Scottish, 16th century

SURFACE DECORATION

Early Gothic furniture, which is extremely rare, was of relatively plain form and relied on colour for its decoration. Its surface was often lime-whitened, and to this ground was added a polychrome scheme of decoration executed in oils or tempera. By the middle of the sixteenth century the surface was frequently left in its natural state, and by the seventeenth century some kind of preservative such as beeswax was rubbed in, which now gives to the oak its deep and rich patination. The use of gilt and gesso, so dear to the Italians during the Renaissance, was seldom if ever used in England during the period under review.

CARVING

The Gothic style of carving and ornamentation, which had grown very flamboyant by the end of the fifteenth century, was gradually superseded during the reigns of the Early Tudors by Renaissance motifs. These were introduced from the Continent by Italian, French, and Flemish craftsmen. The earlier linenfold panelling was often combined with the new forms of decoration, such as grotesque masks, arabesques, and carved caryatids. During the Elizabethan period every kind of carved motif was employed and we find strapwork, terminal figures, bulbous supports, festoons, swags, geometric and medallion panels, lozenges, arcading, and pilasters.

There was a marked reaction against this flamboyant style by the early seventeenth century, and carving began to give way to applied decoration. Bosses, demi-balusters, and other forms of pendant decoration, often stained black in imitation of ebony, were applied to the plain or panelled surfaces, and moulded geometric panels were a favourite form of ornamentation. The sober spirit of the Commonwealth was reflected in its furniture, which was simple to an almost monotonous degree, as every form of decoration was frowned upon. The Restoration of the Monarchy, which heralded the walnut period, was a complete antithesis to the austerity of the Interregnum, and the exuberance and vivacity of the Court of Charles II were immediately attracted to the International Baroque.

Oak chest, carved with arcaded front, *c.* 1600. Victoria & Albert Museum

INLAY

The use of an elaborate pictorial marquetry of many exotic woods was a feature of Renaissance decoration and entire rooms were panelled in this extravagant form of ornamentation. It was greatly favoured on the Continent, as the panelled rooms at the Escurial outside Madrid and the Ducal Palace at Urbino bear witness, and it was also popular in the North of England. The finest extant example in Britain is the room from Sizergh Castle which has now been re-assembled in the Victoria and Albert Museum.

Pieces of Elizabethan and Jacobean oak furniture were often inlaid with a chequered design of marquetry – or parquetry, as a geometric, mosaic, or cube design inlay of woods is called – in boxwood, holly, poplar, and bog oak. The last-named was obtained from portions of trees which were found submerged in peat bogs – hence the black hue. The most elaborate form of marquetry found in oak furniture is in the so-called 'Nonsuch Chests'. The term is derived from the name of the celebrated palace which was built by Henry VIII at Cheam, and representations of it were inlaid into the front panels of coffers or chests, and occasionally smaller objects. Chests of similar design were made in Scandinavia and southern Germany, and it is probable that chests of this type originated in one of these countries, the design then being copied by craftsmen in England. Burnt pokerwork, which is employed in conjunction with floral marquetry, is another form of decoration which is sometimes found in this country. It is usually used on chests which are of a distinctly Italian appearance. However, there is evidence enough to show that some were made in this country, and the style of dress worn by the figures which are portrayed is definitely of British origin.

Shaped slivers of wood about the thickness of a piece of paper are laid on the ground which is to be inlaid, and the required design is then marked round them. This is in turn cut out from the surface and the prepared pieces of wood are inlaid and glued down. A distinctive style of inlay was evolved during the latter half of the seventeenth century in which pieces of engraved bone and mother-of-pearl were inset as a form of surface decoration. The Portuguese in India and the Moors in southern Spain both used this form of inlay, and it was probably introduced to Britain from one of these two centres.

CHIEF PERIODS AND STYLES

The history of early furniture is in many cases affiliated to the architectural styles. Oak furniture can therefore be readily divided into the Gothic, the Renaissance, and the Jacobean and Commonwealth periods. The Gothic forms of design and ornamentation, although they were firmly established, offered little resistance to the new influences of the Renaissance. The wealth which was suddenly acquired by Henry VIII and his friends from the Dissolution of the Monasteries, the stability of the country at large, and the King's and Wolsey's personal taste for grandiose building schemes were all important factors which helped towards the adoption of the new designs.

During Elizabeth I's reign wealth and prosperity were even more abundant, and this new gracious form of living was not reserved for the nobility and gentry alone, as is shown by Harrison's reference to yeomen farmers who were able to 'live wealthie, keep good houses, and travell to get riches'. They also bought 'costlie furniture', and they had learnt to 'garnish their cupboards with plate, their joined beds

Oak chest, carved and inlaid with various woods, *c.* 1600

with tapestrie and silk hangings, and their tables with carpets'.

By the mid-sixteenth century the High Renaissance style had percolated through to England via Flanders and Northern Europe. It had become rather vulgar and overelaborate and the true decorative motifs were considerably coarsened. The style was introduced by Continental craftsmen, who were either invited over to carry out special commissions or were attracted by the general prosperity of the country. Pattern books were also being published in Italy, France, and Germany, and these had a wide influence on the embryonic Elizabethan style.

Carved court cupboard of bulletwood and satinwood, early 17th century. Victoria & Albert Museum

Oak table with carved frieze and stretchers and turned supports, early 17th century

Charles I oak armchair with parquetry inlay of various woods in the design of conventional floral sprays, springing from a vase. The back is surmounted by richly carved scrolls with Brackets attached to the sides. Mary Bellis Antiques, Hungerford

Many ambitious building schemes were put in train during the early years of the seventeenth century, and of course the necessary furniture and furnishings had to be produced to decorate these new rooms and apartments. 'No kingdom in the World spent so much on building as we did in his time,' writes a diarist of James I's time. Most of the oak furniture which survives today was made in the early seventeenth century, and it must be borne in mind that much of the extant furniture of Elizabethan design was actually produced in the reigns of James I and Charles II. Craftsmen were conservative to a degree, and new ideas and designs travelled slowly to the provinces.

The Age of Walnut

There is some doubt about the exact date when the walnut tree was introduced into England, but it is certain that it was being used for furniture in the Tudor period, especially for beds. One of Henry VIII's great beds had a headpiece of walnut, and in 1587 we read of 'a bedsteed of wallnuttrye in Ladies chamber'. But as the chief wood of fashionable furniture the great period of walnut can be considered to cover the best part of the century beginning at 1660. Two main kinds of walnut were used, the European (*Juglans regia*) and the North American (*Juglans nigra*, the black or Virginia walnut). The former had many good qualities for furniture. Its attractive colouring, with beautiful figure and uniform texture, made it very suitable as a veneer, on a carcase of yellow deal. When properly seasoned (a process which might take seven to ten years) it was a solid and compact wood, hard enough to carve into delicate shapes, and, unlike oak, comparatively free from shrinkage or swelling. The burr and curl woods were particularly beautiful, the former being cut from the burrs or abnormal excrescences which grew at the base of the trunk and produced a finely mottled grain, and the latter from just below a fork in the tree. The timber's one great defect was that it was liable to worm, especially in the sap wood. In this respect the Virginia walnut was much better, as the well-seasoned timber was largely immune from worm.

Far right Writing desk, walnut with arabesque or seaweed marquetry of box or holly wood, *c.* 1690. Victoria & Albert Museum

The *Juglans regia* grew throughout most of Europe and was the chief kind used until about 1720. The English variety was considered to be somewhat coarse and featureless for high-quality work, though at times it produced some good varieties of figure. Italian walnut was rated very highly, for the timber which grew in the mountainous regions had a close-grained texture with dark streaks, ideal for decorative work. French walnut was also greatly esteemed; it was straight-grained with a lighter, quiet grey colour. The Grenoble area produced timber which became a hallmark of distinction in furniture. Spanish walnut was similar to the French, but it was liable to have more faults. The superiority of these foreign timbers over the English led to considerable imports of walnut into England, especially from France. In the three years 1700–2 inclusive, just before the Spanish Succession War (1702–13), imports of 'wallnut tree plank' from France amounted to £534 8*s*, £1,009 4*s*, and £339 respectively, and just after the outbreak of war, in 1704, walnut worth £1,330 was registered among the prize goods captured from the enemy.

There are indications that English walnut was relatively scarce in the seventeenth century. John Evelyn, in his *Sylva* (first published in 1664), wrote: 'In truth, were this timber in greater plenty amongst us, we should have far better utensils of all sorts for our houses, as chairs, stools, bedsteads, tables, wainscot, cabinets, etc., instead of the more vulgar Beech.' He praised the black walnut highly: 'The timber is much to be preferred, and we might propagate more of them if we were careful to procure them out of Virginia . . . yet those of Grenoble come in the next place and are much prized by our cabinet-makers.' Some of the black variety was grown in England in the seventeenth century, but there is little doubt that the shortage of English walnut and the cost of imported walnut had much to do with the great use of veneers. After the Spanish Succession War, during which the severe winter of 1709 had killed off many trees, the French Government prohibited the export of walnut in 1720, with the result that from that date, though supplies continued to come in from Holland and Spain, much more of the North American variety was imported. Virginia walnut was darker and of a more uniform colour than European (it is the only walnut with traces of purple), and its strength and excellent working qualities explain the bolder designs in the solid after the Queen Anne period. But after the first quarter of the eighteenth century walnut was beginning to feel the effects of competition from mahogany, and was entering on its last phase as the fashionable timber. In 1803 Sheraton wrote in his *Cabinet Dictionary* that 'the black Virginia was much in use for cabinet work about forty or fifty years since in England, but is now quite laid aside since the introduction of mahogany'.

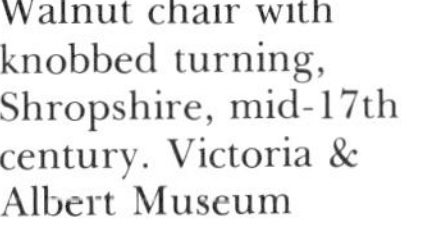

Walnut chair with knobbed turning, Shropshire, mid-17th century. Victoria & Albert Museum

CHIEF PERIODS AND STYLES

In the walnut period the styles take their names from the reigning monarchs – Charles II (1660–85, and including the short reign of James II, 1685–8); William and Mary (1689–1702); Anne (1702–14); and the early Georgian (George I, 1714–27, and George II, 1727–60). The furniture of the whole period reflected the growing standards of wealth and comfort; many new pieces were produced to satisfy social needs, and adapted to conform with improving standards of design. Two factors which helped to make the knowledge and use of good furniture widespread were the increased skill of the craftsmen and the development of London as the chief furniture-making centre of the country. This was the period when the joiner was being replaced by the cabinet maker as the supreme furniture craftsman. It will be noted that Evelyn, in the passage quoted above, was already referring to cabinet makers as early as 1664, and he frequently used this term in his various works. The English craftsmen had to learn many new techniques at first from foreigners, but on the whole it can be said that they assimilated them and interpreted them with good sense and balance; and by the end of the seventeenth century they were not only supplying the home market but had also built up a flourishing export trade in furniture to all parts of the world. London's size was meanwhile making it a focal point for the whole kingdom. By 1700 the capital had half a million inhabitants; the next largest towns had no more than 30,000. Though there were other notable furniture centres – Lancaster, for instance – there was no doubt about London's leadership in styles. The social convention of the seasonal migration of the landed gentry to London helped to spread furniture fashions throughout the country, as Defoe noted early in the eighteenth century, and for the first time it was possible to distinguish town and country pieces.

The reign of Charles II was marked by an exuberance and flamboyancy which was reflected in such things as costume and plays, as well as in furniture. The reaction to the Puritanism of Cromwell's regime and the return of Charles and the aristocracy from exile abroad opened the country to a flood of Continental fashions – French, Spanish, Portuguese, Italian, Dutch, and Flemish. Increased trade and colonization brought riches to the upper and middle classes. The Great Fire of 1666 both led to a greater output of furniture and brought it under the influence of architects like Sir Christopher Wren and of craftsmen like Grinling Gibbons. New ideas, or new twists to older ideas, were apparent in the use of glass, cane, turning, veneering, marquetry, gesso, and japanning. The reign of William and Mary saw, in general, a sobering down in furniture styles, due to William and his Dutch background, and the work of his great craftsman Daniel Marot, a Huguenot

Above, far left Queen Anne walnut bureau with bracket feet and matched veneers, the drawers and flap have ovolo moulding. Mallet & Son, London

Above, centre Card table with parquetry of contrasting veneers, cross-bandings of laburnum, *c.* 1715. Ickworth Park, Suffolk

Above Chair of carved birch with cane seat and back, *c.* 1685. Victoria & Albert Museum

refugee, who in his furniture for his royal patron interpreted Louis XIV fashions in a quieter Dutch idiom. But there was no decrease in output. The revocation of the Edict of Nantes by Louis in 1685 sent many Huguenot refugees to England, and one result was the flourishing Spitalfields silk industry and improvements in upholstery. There were developments in such things as writing-desk furniture (in which increased letter writing, due to improved postal services, was a major factor), card and tea tables, bookcases, chests of drawers, and cabinets, the last-named due to the upper-class fashion for collecting 'rarities' or curiosities of all kinds. It was in the Queen Anne period that walnut furniture reached its best phase. With its emphasis on graceful curves, and a return to veneers to bring out the beauty of figure, compared with the previous Dutch fashion of marquetry, this reign is distinguished by its simple elegance, shown in such details as the hooped-back chair, the cabriole leg, the bracket foot, and a general stress on good design. The earlier Georgian period produced a heavier and more florid baroque style, partly perhaps as a reaction to simpler fashions, but mainly due to the Palladianism of William Kent, the architect (1684–1748), who affected much elaborate gilt ornament with classical motifs, carried out in softwoods or gesso.

OTHER TIMBERS

Though walnut put the seal on fashionable furniture, many other timbers were important during the same period. The great popularity of veneers, inlay, and marquetry led to a demand for a wide range of coloured woods. Among the native timbers used for these purposes, lighter shades, white or yellow, could be obtained from apple, holly, dogwood, boxwood, maple, laburnum, sycamore, and plane, and darker colouring from olive, pear, and yew. Elm and mulberry were also prized for their burr veneers. Timbers imported from the East, South America, and the West Indies included ebony (black), fustic (yellow, turning to a dead brown), and kingwood, lignum vitae, partridge wood, rosewood, and snakewood (all giving various shades of brown and red). For carcase work, and as a ground for veneers, yellow deal was almost always used. But for clock cases wainscot oak was used. Great quantities of deal were imported from Baltic countries in the late seventeenth century. Oak and ash were used for drawer linings.

DECORATION

Gesso

Gesso work came into fashion in England just before 1700 and was a popular form of decoration until about 1740. It was a mixture of whiting and parchment size which was applied coat after coat and allowed to dry. When there was sufficient, a pattern was formed in relief by the background being cut away. The former was burnished and the latter left matt. Furniture was given a brilliant and highly ornate effect when gold leaf was used, but there was also much cheap colouring which tended to fade. Perhaps the most celebrated exponent of the use of

Left Chair of carved, gilt and gessoed beechwood, bearing the crest of Sir William Humphreys (arms granted in 1717) and upholstered in Genoa velvet. Victoria & Albert Museum

gesso during the early eighteenth century was the Royal cabinet maker, James Moore.

Japanwork
Japanned or lacquered furniture enjoyed a considerable vogue in the walnut period. As early as 1661 Pepys recorded seeing 'two very fine chests covered with gold and Indian varnish'. Lacquerwork was originally imported from the East, and was known variously as Indian, Chinese, or Japanese, but the best kind was made in Japan, and was called 'fine' or 'right' japan, to distinguish it from substitutes. Most of the genuine Japanese work was brought to England by the Dutch, but the English East India Company handled Chinese and Indian varieties, which had a ready sale in the home market and went under the general name of 'Indian' goods (and were sold in 'Indian' shops). So great was the demand for these goods that some English merchants exported patterns and models of all kinds of furniture to be copied and lacquered by native workmen, who could thus manufacture English-style furniture. The completed goods were re-imported and sold at home. But meanwhile an English japan industry had sprung up. In 1688 Stalker and Parker published their *Treatise of Japaning and Varnishing*, and in 1693 a company was formed with the title of 'The Patentees for Lacquering after the Manner of Japan'. Naturally, the home producers of japan disliked the practice of sending goods abroad to be lacquered, and so did other cabinet makers, who looked upon it as unfair competition. In 1701 the London cabinet makers, joiners, and japanners petitioned Parliament to put a stop to it, and an Act was passed imposing heavier duties on all imported lacquer (12 & 13 William III, c. 11). Thus from that date nearly all japanwork was homemade. It was very popular until about 1740, and much of it was exported. The colours used were bright ones, often scarlet, yellow, etc., and carried out Eastern designs, but English work lacked the high quality of the true Oriental variety. In fact, inferior work was merely varnished. It was usually applied on a background of deal for carcases, or of beech for chairs. Good-class work

Japanwork. Eastern design

often had a smooth-grained, veneered surface as a basis. Normally, designs were raised on the surface, but a rare form of lacquerwork, known as Bantam work, used incised designs. Cabinets, chairs, bureaux, screens, clock cases, and mirrors were among the more usual pieces for japanning. There was a revival of this fashion in the later eighteenth century.

Mouldings
Mouldings, the contours given to projecting members, were an important part of the decorative treatment of walnut furniture. On tall pieces – cabinets, tallboys, clock cases, etc. – the profiles of the straight cornices, which were popular until the Queen Anne period, were built up in architectural style, usually in layers of cross-grained wood. One characteristic feature of the later seventeenth century was the convex (torus or swell) frieze. The convex was not universal, however, for the concave (*cavetto*) frieze was used at the same time, and superseded it early in the next century. Mouldings also accentuated the arched curves and the varieties of broken pediments when these came into fashion. Towards the end of the walnut period dentil mouldings (tooth-like cubes) were often found on straight-line cornices or angular pediments.

Another moulding of convex profile, called the ovolo (or lip), was applied to the top edges of chests of drawers, stands, and tables, and on the upper sections of bureaux. Chests of drawers and bureaux sometimes had plinth mouldings, above ball, bun, or bracket feet. The general development of drawer furniture produced several kinds of smaller mouldings (sometimes called reeds) around the drawer fronts, to offset the otherwise flat surface. These were normally cross-banded veneers of walnut glued to a back of deal, and applied at first to the carcase, and later to the drawer edge. From 1660 to about 1700 the most usual kind was a convex half-round moulding on the rails between the drawers, but just before the end of the century two smaller half-round mouldings, or sometimes three reeds together, were applied to the rails, and this vogue lasted until about the end of Anne's reign. From 1710 a distinct change in method was beginning; the mouldings were now applied to the edge of the drawer, in ovolo section, and projected sufficiently (about a quarter of an inch (.63 cm)) to hide the join between opening and drawer when the latter was shut. From about 1730 cock beading, a half-round bead projecting outwards from the edge of the drawer, was introduced, and became the chief drawer moulding for mahogany furniture. Mouldings also edged the doors on clock cases and surrounded mirrors or panels on cabinet doors. On the latter, broader types of moulding were common, in astragal section, semicircular with the addition of a fillet at each side.

Turning
Until about 1700 turning was one of the outstanding features of the legs on chairs, tables, and stands, and of the uprights on chairs. It was carried out on the foot-operated pole lathe which rotated the wood while the turner's chisel cut the required shape. Twist turning, which came to England from the Continent shortly after the Restoration, and replaced the earlier bobbin turning, resulted from a mechanical device which moved the chisel continuously to produce the oblique curves. For this walnut was a much better medium than the more brittle oak. At first the Flemish 'single rope' style was used, but this was followed by the English double rope or 'barley sugar' twist, finished by hand and sometimes pierced. The design was working itself out on chairs by 1685, but it persisted on tables for some time longer. Another form, baluster turning, was produced by the turner holding the chisel himself and varying the pressure to get a number of diverse shapes. This type is connected with William and Mary furniture. There was an almost bewildering variety of such designs, but among the more popular can be distinguished the Portuguese swell, a bulb-like shape, followed by the

William and Mary walnut long-case clock, the front veneered in seaweed marquetry, *c.* 1699. Frank Partridge, London

Above Cabinet, ebony veneer carved with scenes from the stories of Diana and Endymion and other mythological subjects, and the labours of the months, mid-17th century. Victoria & Albert Museum

Above, right Cabinet on stand, decorated with floral marquetry on ebony panels, walnut oyster pieces and bandings of holly, late 17th century. Victoria & Albert Museum

mushroom, and, later still, by the inverted cup. Some legs were squared off by hand to octagonal and other patterns. *See also* Chairs.

Veneers, marquetry, and parquetry

Veneering was the chief decorative feature of walnut furniture. It originated on the Continent, and gave opportunity for flat decoration, which showed to the full the beauties of the grain. Veneers were thin layers of wood cut by handsaw, perhaps one-eighth of an inch thick, and glued to a carefully prepared surface, which was nearly always of imported yellow deal, a variety of pine or fir which was better able to take glue than oak. Not only did the veneers preserve and strengthen the wood underneath, but they were found to be the only practical way to use the rare woods like walnut burrs, which would twist if worked in the solid. The chief patterns were the 'curl' or 'crotch', a plume effect taken from the junction of a side branch with the main trunk, the 'oyster', cut from branches to show the rings in the wood and the 'burr', an intricate figuring from abnormal growths at the base of the trunk. Successive veneers from the same piece of wood, showing duplicated patterns, were often quartered, or glued in sections of four, on suitable surfaces. Besides walnut, yew, elm, and mulberry made high-quality veneers, and laburnum and olive produced excellent oyster figures.

Marquetry was an advanced form of veneering, much employed in Holland, which first came into prominence in English furniture about 1675. With infinite patience and skill veneers of various coloured woods were cut into delicate patterns and fitted together like a jigsaw puzzle. For this process walnut could be changed in colour by dyeing, scorching with hot sand, staining, bleaching, and fading, but, naturally, many other timbers of suitable colour, both native and foreign, were used (as indicated under 'Other Timbers' above). At first English marquetry followed the Flemish mode and concentrated on bird, flower, and foliage designs, sometimes with the aid of

Marquetry bird, flower and foliage design

materials other than wood, such as bone and ivory. The colours tended to tone down to quieter dark or golden shades about 1690. By 1700 arabesques were popular, together with the most intricate form of all, the seaweed or endive marquetry, which was shown to great effect on clock cases, cabinets, and table tops. Early in the eighteenth century the marquetry phase was running out, and there was a return to the plainer veneering. Parquetry was a form of marquetry which emphasized geometrical patterns, with the same skilful use of contrasting colours. It was used far more widely on the Continent.

Veneered surfaces had two characteristic decorations, cross banding, or cross grain, veneered strips bordering other veneers, and herringbone banding, two smaller rows of tiny strips of veneer applied diagonally, often in contrasting colours. Each could be used singly, or together, on drawer fronts, table tops, bureau flaps, and similar fields. The popularity of veneering introduced distinct changes in the construction of furniture as well as in its appearance. The panelling technique of oak was unable to provide the flat, smooth surfaces necessary for taking veneers. For angles on carcases and drawers the old method of dovetailing (the through or common dovetail), though the strongest form, had the great disadvantage of showing the end grain on both sides of the angle, and this was unsatisfactory for holding veneers. Shortly before 1700 it was replaced by the lap or stopped dovetail, which had the end grain on the side only, leaving the front quite clear for veneering.

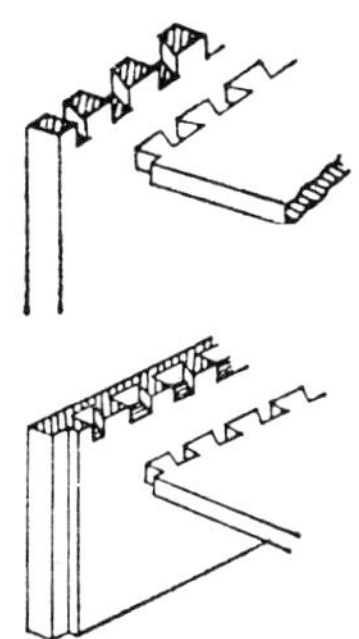

Dovetail (top) *and lap dovetail*

Bureaux, cabinets, bookcases, etc.

The bureau was one of the pieces of furniture which met the demands of the new habit of letter writing in the Restoration period. Early bureaux were mounted on stands and were nearly always of narrow width, with one or two rows of drawers under the sloping writing fall. The stands were gradually discarded and bureaux became wider and more solid. Most were now 3½ feet (106.7 cm) wide, though narrower ones (for standing between the windows of a room) continued to be made. The legs of the early stands followed contemporary side-table developments, while the more solid bureau followed the chest of drawers (*see* separate sections below).

Another piece was the writing cabinet, which developed in two main stages. The first stage was the scrutoire, a box-like structure consisting of an upper part of drawers and pigeonholes, enclosed by a hinged let-down front which made a large writing surface, and a lower part formed by either a chest of drawers or a stand with legs and stretchers. The disadvantage of having to clear away all papers before the front could be closed led to the second stage, the bureau writing cabinet or the bureau-bookcase as it is now termed. This had a shallow cupboard enclosed by two doors for the upper part and a bureau for the lower. The space in the bureau top for papers made this a more convenient piece than the scrutoire; it was also more elegant. It became fashionable in William III's reign and was either veneered with walnut or japanned.

Meanwhile, the cabinet was assuming the forms which had long been known on the Continent, and from the increasing skill required in making it was producing the first English cabinet makers. It developed from the chest, acquired a number of drawers (many of them 'secret'), cupboards, and pigeonholes, and was mounted on a tall stand or chest of drawers. At first the tops were straight, with rather heavy cornices, and two doors enclosed the front. Later the frieze was developed; the swell variety became more common, and a shorter stand was used. One type of cabinet that was mounted on a chest of drawers was copied from Chinese cabinets, and had engraved hinges and lockplate, and finely figured walnut veneers to vie with japanned pieces. Other cabinets were excellent showpieces for decorating with marquetry and parquetry, applied to the many small drawers as well as to the doors inside and out.

There was, however, from 1600 onwards considerable diversity of decoration and design in these pieces, as the cabinet could be used for various purposes. With glazed front and shelves, it was used as a bookcase or display cabinet. It now seems clear, contrary to former belief, that cabinets were not used to display china but held small curios like medals and miniatures. Other cabinet doors had mirror plates instead of clear glazing, or no glass at all, relying upon panels of finely figured walnut for effect; mirrors and panels were often enclosed in mouldings which had a graceful curving form at the top. These shapely curves were a predominant feature in the late seventeenth century and in Anne's reign, and were applied to the tops of cabinets in various ways – double and, occasionally, triple arches and broken circular pediments. They showed the application

Scriptor veneered with oyster parquetry of kingwood, turned and carved stand of the same wood, embossed silver mounts, *c.* 1675. Victoria & Albert Museum

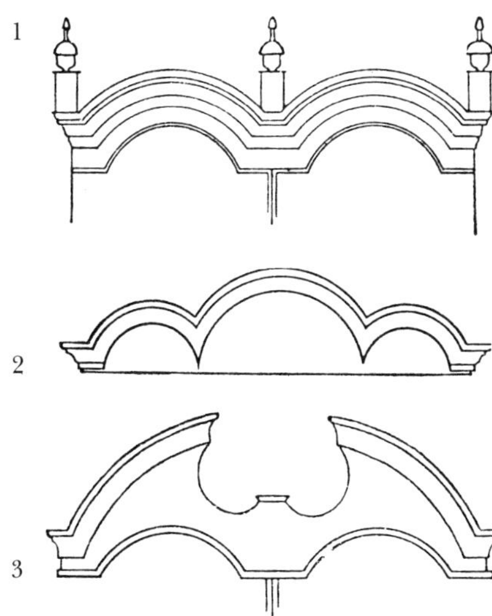

Cabinet tops: 1 Double arch; 2 Triple arch; 3 Broken circular pediment

of architectural principles to these larger pieces of furniture. But there was still a strong liking for the simple straight cornice. It is not always certain now for what purpose some cabinets were intended. Many which resemble bureaux-bookcases, with the bureau replaced by a chest of drawers, have survived. They have been used for storing clothes in the bedroom or as a cupboard in the parlour.

For larger bookcases, such as those which Pepys bought from Simpson the joiner in 1666, the doors were glazed in rectangular panes like windows. The growing popularity of glass fronts made glazing bars important. At first they were usually semicircular, veneered with cross-grained walnut, or astragals, a half-round moulding worked on the edge. In the eighteenth century another form of astragal, with a small fillet at the top of the curve, came into use. These astragals, often larger in shape, framed the mirrors or veneers on doors which did not have clear glazing.

Chairs, day beds, stools, and settees

Chairs in the Charles II period were distinguished for their elaborate carving and turning. Twist turning was at first often applied to the back and front legs and uprights, and carving was the treatment for the top rail between the uprights and for the wide stretcher set halfway up between the front legs. Another novelty, canework, was found on the seat and back, framed in a carved panel, rectangular or oval in shape, separated from the uprights and seat. After the middle of the century carving improved considerably. At first it was heavy looking, emphasizing scrolls, foliage, and crowns; later it became much lighter and pierced, and top rail and stretchers curved upwards, often ending in a crown supported by *amorini*. From about 1675 S-shaped scroll designs (the 'Flemish' scroll) were popular for front legs, and on armchairs this shape was continued in the arms which curved downwards in the centre and formed deep scrolls over the supports. By the end of Charles's reign twist turning was being replaced by baluster turning. Canework was also becoming finer in texture, and many specialist craftsmen were making large numbers of cane chairs for export as well as for home use. The back legs were splayed for steadiness. There was also a fashion for some chairs to be entirely upholstered with overstuffing, carried out in fine materials, damask, velvet, embroidery, or Mortlake tapestry.

The lightness of cane helped to popularize a pre-Restoration piece, the day bed, or couch. This had a chair back (sometimes one at each end) and a long seat carried on six or more legs joined by richly carved stretchers. It was used in the living room (which no longer had a bed in it), and had to be easily movable. Some day beds were ornately japanned.

William and Mary chairs saw distinct changes in design. The flamboyancy of the previous period tended to give way to a simpler style, though there was still much rich carving. Backs had a tall and narrow appearance, due to the fashion in women's hair styles, and took on a pronounced backward tilt. Chair legs either kept the scroll form or were decoratively turned in one of the many baluster or geometrical shapes. Prominent among these were the Portuguese bulb, mushroom, inverted cup and square. Feet were ball or bun shape, or else carved in the Spanish foot design. Another novelty was the introduction of curved stretchers under the chair, going diagonally from squares just above the feet, and either crossing directly, tied in the centre with a finial, or fixed into a central platform. Front stretchers in the older form still persisted, but the fashion now was to set them back from the front legs and fit them to the side stretchers. The upright aspect of the backs, very characteristic of this time, was accentuated by the arching of the cresting rail above the back uprights. Usually seats were upholstered, with a tasselled fringe, but backs were treated in various ways – pierced carving, canework (in thinner panels), or upholstery.

All these changes were nothing compared to the revolution in chair design in the early eighteenth century. Straight lines gave way to curves, turned legs and stretchers to cabriole legs without stretchers, and overstuffing to the drop-in seat. The back uprights took a graceful hoop form, and the centre of the back was occupied by a single solid splat, often veneered, showing a variety of smooth curves. For the first time the chair back was shaped for the sitter, giving the aptly named 'bended' back. The cabriole leg came from France about 1700. Taking its shape from an animal's leg, it had various endings, a hoof, a pad, or club (*see right*), or the celebrated ball-and-claw foot, which came in about 1720. These legs, worked from the solid by hand, were strong enough to hold the chair without stretchers. The general emphasis on curves was continued in the frame of the seat. Carved decoration was usually limited to the knees of the cabriole legs, cresting rail, and seat rail, in the form of shell or acanthus designs, or, later, a mask on the rail. A new treatment of chair arms was to set them back in a curve from the front of the chair, to allow room for the wide-hooped dresses of the time.

Another pleasant type of chair which had made its appearance by about 1700 was the upholstered wing variety. The wings at the shoulders curved down to

'Sleeping chayre', one of a pair, gilt wood with brocade upholstery; the back lets down by ratchets, *c.* 1675. Ham House, Surrey

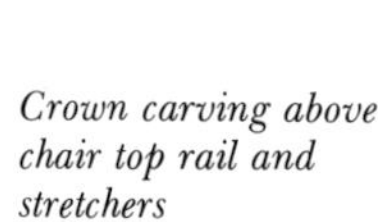

Crown carving above chair top rail and stretchers

Walnut chair with spiral stretchers, upholstered in wool and silk embroidery in cross stitch. Victoria & Albert Museum

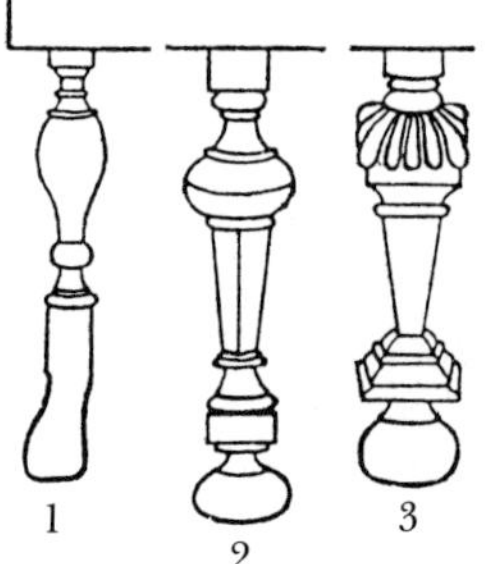

Chair legs: 1 Portuguese bulb; 2 Mushroom; 3 Inverted cup and square

Chair splat, carved and pierced with strapwork designs

well-padded arms which scrolled outwards. The legs often had cabriole shape, but the size and weight of the chair required stretchers, of the simple turned kind.

Towards the end of the walnut period some of the simple grace of the Queen Anne chairs was lost. In the early Georgian era they tended to become heavier and more squat in appearance, and carving was more ornate. The splat was not left plain, but was carved and later pierced with strapwork designs.

From 1660 stools closely followed the prevailing chair designs. They had an importance which today may be easily overlooked. In general, their form was that of chairs without backs, except that all four legs were the same shape. They were often richly upholstered. A later development was the settee, which sprang from the fusion of two armchairs, with double backs, outer arms, and five legs. In their earlier forms – later seventeenth century – they were often two cane chairs together.

Chests of drawers and tallboys

The time-honoured chest, long distinguished for its frame construction and carving in the oak period, became the more useful chest of drawers after the Restoration. Already in 1661 Pepys bought 'a fair chest of drawers' in London. The chest itself did not disappear quickly; it persisted well into the next century, made in the traditional oak, then walnut and,

Oak chest of drawers veneered with snakewood and ebony within fruitwood moulding, *c.* 1660–80. Victoria & Albert Museum

later, mahogany, or japanned, when that form of decoration was popular. But long before 1660 its future development was indicated when the bottom drawer was added to it, to form the mule chest. The chest of drawers developed along three lines: the familiar solid type, from the chest; the chest on stand; and the chest on chest, or tallboy.

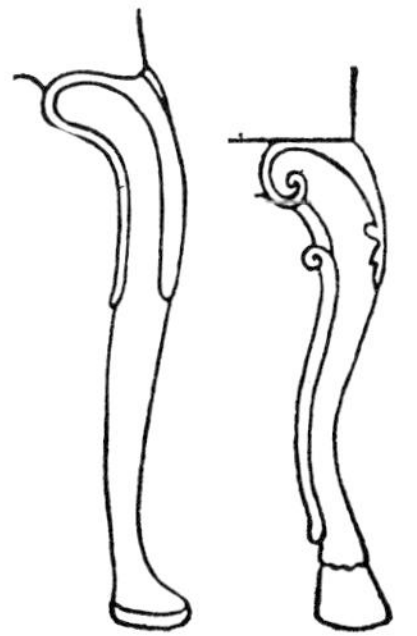

Cabriole-leg hoof and pad endings

The solid type was still being made in oak in Charles II's reign, but it was gradually replaced by walnut and incorporated all the refinements and techniques due to the new wood. Larger chests of drawers stood up to 3½ feet (106.7 cm) high, usually with five drawers, three long ones at the bottom and two smaller ones at the top. But many fine smaller ones were also made. They were admirably suited for veneers (applied to the top and sides of good pieces, as well as to drawer fronts, with cross-banding and herringbone patterns), marquetry and japan. Besides walnut, or used with it, other woods, particularly yew, fruit woods, and burr elm, made good veneers. Laburnum and walnut were used for oyster veneering. This effect, which resembled a row of oysters lying side by side, was achieved with slices of wood cut transversely from small boughs or saplings, showing a series of irregular concentric circles. To overcome the straight-line effect of the drawers, various mouldings, at first on the frame and then on the drawer edges, were applied to give decorative effect. The tops also had larger ovolo mouldings jutting out over the edges, and similar mouldings at the bottom of the carcase, above the feet. The development of the feet showed a constant search for good design. At first they were of the turned ball or bun type, but as this did not harmonize with the general appearance of the chest, they gave way to the square bracket feet, flanked by small curved pieces.

The use of stands for mounting chests of drawers was common after the Restoration, and lasted until the early eighteenth century. The chest of drawers developed on the same lines as the solid type, and the stand bore very close relationship to contemporary side tables (*see* Tables). At first the stand was low in appearance, on thick turned legs linked by a succession of arches, but by the 1690s it was higher, with twist-turned and later baluster-shaped legs joined together by curling stretchers. Drawers were added to the stand, usually a shallower central one and a deeper one at each side. The apron piece, an important decorative feature, took the form of smooth-flowing curves, which balanced the severer lines of the upper work. During the William and Mary period two other significant characteristics were the inverted-cup legs and the pronounced swell frieze below the cornice. The drawers in the stand tended to shorten the legs once more, and they took cabriole form by Anne's reign. From about 1710 there was a natural transition to the tallboy, in which the stand was replaced by another chest of drawers. Tallboys reached monumental proportions, and came in for a great deal of architectural treatment. The frieze lost its swell outline and became concave. By about 1730 the drawers had become cross-banded with ovolo mouldings. The corners of the upper section were canted to take partly fluted and partly reeded pilasters, and the feet had gone from the plain bracket to ogee form, resembling cabrioles. The tallboy had a long vogue in the eighteenth century as a cabinet maker's showpiece, until the awkward height of its top drawers led to its gradual disuse in England. It persisted longer in America, where some very fine examples were produced.

Clock cases

The long clock case (or grandfather clock) was another new piece of furniture which appeared at the time of the Restoration. Two major factors in its development were Robert Hooke's invention of the anchor escapement (which made the long pendulum possible) about 1670, and the outstanding work of great English clockmakers like Thomas Tompion and Joseph Knibb. From its beginning the case took on the familiar design of a hood for the dial and movement, a long, narrow body for the pendulum, and a pedestal base. The body became wider as the clock dial increased in size, but retained its slender waist appearance until mahogany was extensively used. Naturally, the size of the cases (up to 7 feet (213

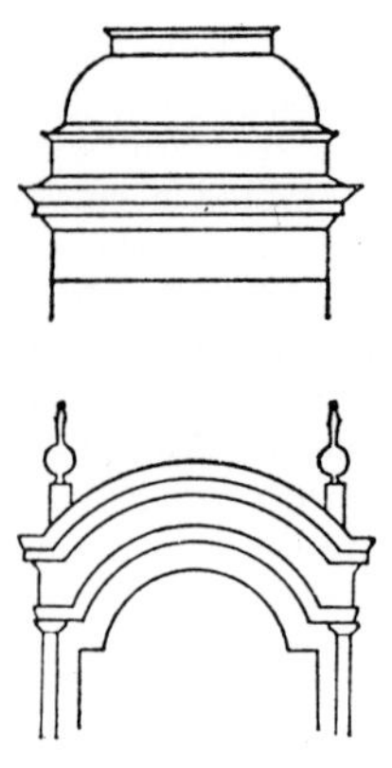

Clock-case tops: flat dome (top) *and arched*

cm) in even the earliest examples) and their prominent position in the house brought out all the case maker's skill, and the large space available was ideal for the best decorative work in veneers, marquetry, and japan. At first – about 1660 – the cornice of the hood was surmounted by a classical pediment, which was followed after 1670 by a carved and pierced cresting. The glass face of the dial was usually flanked by two columns, which were either twist-turned or plain-turned with tiny capitals and bases. Oak was the usual carcase wood, veneered with ebony and walnut and often finely decorated with the various kinds of fashionable marquetry. The door on the body was edged with half-round moulding in rectangular lines. By 1700 the hood had begun to change its appearance. A flat dome was added to the top, which was sometimes ornamented with brass or gilt wood finials at the corners and centre. From about 1715 the clock dial was arched, and the cornice above it took the same curving shape, as did the moulding over the door in the body. The clock case, in other words, underwent the same treatment of arched curves as cabinets and mirrors. English japanners had a partiality for clock cases, and hundreds were exported during this period; but walnut enjoyed a considerable vogue for cases, and retained its popularity until after 1750.

Mirrors

Note. For a fuller coverage of this subject *see* separate section on Mirrors.

Mirrors began to play an important part in interior decoration in late Stuart times, and an indication of their growing use is that while in 1660 they were still being imported (particularly Venetian glasses), by 1700 English-made glasses were being sent abroad. Between those two dates progress was largely explained by the establishment of the Duke of Buckingham's famous glassworks at Vauxhall in 1665 and the emergence, some twenty years later, of the specialist looking-glass makers. Mirror plate was expensive for some time to come, but wealthy people used it in many ways, for wall mirrors, toilet mirrors, tall ornamental glasses, and on cabinet doors. Until about 1690 wall mirrors were square in shape and the glass, with bevelled edges, was enclosed in frames up to 6 inches (15.2 cm) in width, topped by a semicircular crest in the Italian manner. They were naturally picked out for fine (especially oyster) veneers and marquetry work. By 1700 taller mirrors were becoming fashionable (of large Vauxhall plates, or smaller mirrors joined together with a moulding to cover the join) and the influence of Wren and Gibbons was shown in architectural features like pediments and pilasters, or in intricately carved limewood frames. Colourful decoration was emphasized and took several forms, bright gilding, marquetry, japan, gesso, and even silver. These forms continued into Anne's reign, but there was also a return to simpler styles. Three main trends can be distinguished among the many varieties. One attractive type of wall mirror had a frame narrow at the sides, the glass itself surrounded by a thin gilt gesso moulding, and wide flat crest and base, both carved in graceful flowing curves, veneered with walnut and holding two circular inset pieces with the shell motif. Another kind had an inch (2.5 cm)-wide frame all the way round following the top of the scalloped glass in simple arched curves. It was this design which was often found on cabinet doors, the mouldings surrounding the mirror plate taking the same curves as the top of the cabinet. A third kind was the pier glass, tall and narrow in shape, usually made in pairs to stand between windows, in elaborately carved and gilded frames, often with another mirror in the arching crest, and with pilasters at the sides. John Gumley, who opened his glassworks at Lambeth in 1705, specialized in these. Some of the mirrors that he made for Hampton Court Palace and Chatsworth are still extant and can be seen in the two Palaces. Towards the end of the walnut period gilded mirrors were common, and came under architectural influence. A typical example of this type has the frame enriched with gadrooning, drapery, and foliage; the shell decoration in the base; and the broken pediment with a central cartouche (other finials were a plume, shell, mask, or eagle). There were, however, other examples carried out with burr walnut veneers and gilt gesso ornament.

The early eighteenth century also saw the introduction of the 'chimney glass', a wide mirror above a chimneypiece, consisting of three plates, two smaller ones flanking a larger one, and all topped by flowing curves, framed in walnut or following the other decorative fashions. Another development, the toilet mirror, had the same curved top and was mounted on two uprights resting on a miniature chest of drawers. Some of these, in walnut or japan, were beautifully made and were designed for the slender dressing tables of the period. When these toilet mirrors were mounted on miniature bureaux they were called 'Union Sets'.

Tables

The walnut period inherited the gate-leg tables introduced during the preceding oak period, and these continued in use for dining, with modifications due to the new timber. Gate-leg tables retained their popularity for a long time, and in larger houses several were used together, when required. Their legs gradually took on cabriole form. But a new feature from 1660 was the variety of small tables, many of them multipurpose, the more formal side and occasional tables, and others used for specific requirements such as writing, tea drinking, dressing, and card playing. At first solid walnut was usual, but later table tops (and drawer fronts, wherever these were found) were decorated with veneer or marquetry, with cross-banded or herringbone borders and ovolo-moulded edges.

A side table, with oyster veneers, single drawer, twist-turned legs, and a waved flat stretcher, was very characteristic of the later part of Charles II's reign. The legs ended on ball or bun feet, immediately above which the stretcher terminated in small square platforms. The stretcher was noted for its curves and central shelf. Twist turning persisted on tables for some time after it had passed out of fashion on chairs. But by the William and Mary period varieties of baluster turning, or the more elaborate scroll form, were coming into use. The stretcher became more slender and had a pronounced X shape. The finial on the shelf was often matched by similar finials, inverted, on the apron piece, which became an important part of late seventeenth-century work. Tables fitted with drawers and a knee hole could be used as dressing or writing tables. There was a marked change in design by the early eighteenth

Walnut card table with cabriole legs and claw and ball feet, *c.* 1720. Mallett & Son, London

Toilet mirror

century. The slender cabriole legs and ball-and-claw feet of, for example, a Queen Anne card table did not require stretchers and gave the table a shapely line. The tops of these card tables unfolded and were supported by swinging out one of the legs; or else in some cases the whole top was pivoted sideways and opened to rest on the frame. The surface was covered with cloth or veneered. To protect it the corners were rounded to hold candlesticks (later small movable trays, hinged to the top, were used for this) and small circular depressions were made for money or counters. The wide ovolo mouldings found at the edges of the earlier table tops were now replaced by flatter, vertical mouldings. Decoration was usually limited to a carved shell or leaf on the outside of the knee and a scroll on the inside, and to a curve on the frieze. These tables emphasized the beautiful figure of walnut. Despite subsequent changes, this simple design was never entirely lost, for small tables were made in walnut, even when mahogany was becoming fashionable. But, by contrast, from about 1725 pier tables (standing between mirrors and windows) and console tables (permanently standing against the wall with bracket-shape legs) had a florid magnificence, in the Kent tradition. Made of gilded softwoods, or with the addition of gesso, they relied for effect on masks, scrolls, foliage and classical designs, and heavy marble tops.

Side table with carved and gilded base and marble top, designed by Matthias Lock, *c.* 1740. Harewood House

Small tripod tables also appeared after 1660 for use as candlestands, in the form of a tray held by a turned pillar standing on jutting-out feet. As can be expected the upright at first was often twist-turned, and the feet had scroll shapes. From about 1685 the feet began to show sharper angles where the various curves met. By the Queen Anne period the feet were beginning to show cabriole form and the ball-and-claw ending. This type of table was to have a long vogue, as candlestands were in great demand when large plate mirrors came into use and as much light as possible was called for to add brilliance to large rooms.

The Age of Mahogany and Satinwood

Mahogany was competing with walnut after the first quarter of the eighteenth century and had supplanted it for the highest-quality work about 1750. From then on its many virtues made it the premier wood in cabinet making. It had a beautiful patina which improved with age; a metallic strength which led to remarkable advances in carving and outlines; a fine figure which made it equally suitable for veneers; a range of colour from a light-reddish to a rich dark shade; and a natural durability which was resistant to decay. It also seasoned readily, and the great size of the trees produced excellent timber for table tops, wardrobe doors, and similar pieces. Altogether, for furniture of every kind, for work in the solid, for carving, inlay, or veneer, it was an excellent medium for the great cabinet makers of the Georgian era. Two main varieties of mahogany were used. One kind (*Swietenia mahogani*) came from the West Indies, mainly San Domingo, Jamaica, and Cuba. The San Domingo timber (usually known as 'Spanish', or sometimes as 'Jamaican') was prized more highly at first. It was a dense, hard wood, with little figure, and was used mainly in the solid. Then the Cuban mahogany became more popular, as it had two outstanding qualities: it was easier to work and had a fine figure for veneers. The other species (*Swietenia macrophylla*) came from Central America, particularly from Honduras (whence it obtained its other name of 'baywood'). It was lighter and softer than the Cuban, and was often used as carcases to take Cuban veneers. There was considerable overlapping in the periods when these various kinds were most in use, but it can be said that San Domingo mahogany was popular until about 1750, when it was replaced by Cuban for best work, while Honduras was found in later eighteenth-century carcase construction.

Mahogany had been used for shipbuilding since the sixteenth century, and for inlay and panelling since the seventeenth. It was known at first as cedar or cedrala. Evelyn referred to its worm-resisting qualities in his *Sylva* under its French name of *acajou* from 'the Western Indies'. The date when it came into use for furniture cannot be given exactly. The story of Dr Gibbons of Covent Garden, who is said to have had some mahogany made into furniture by his cabinet maker Wollaston about 1700, and to have thus popularized this wood, has now become a tradition. Its use was no doubt encouraged by the shortage of European walnut after the Spanish Succession

War, though supplies of Virginia walnut were to be had. Probably mahogany advertised itself well enough. An Act of 1721 allowed timber from any British plantation in America to be duty free. Another Act in 1724 mentioned mahogany by name; it had a special rate imposed upon it instead of the declared value by the importer, but if it were from British possessions it was included in the terms of the 1721 Act and allowed in duty free. From the 1720s, therefore, Jamaican mahogany had preferential treatment. This not only assured supplies from British sources but also encouraged timber dealers in the West Indies to send the popular Spanish wood to England via Jamaica and other colonies to avoid the duty. This practice went on throughout the century. In fact, the British Government connived at it, for it allowed, and later legalized, the entrepôt trade with the Spanish settlements. There was thus no lack of mahogany, once trade had got under way, as there had been with European walnut. Mahogany was certainly competing strongly with walnut for fashionable furniture by the 1730s. In 1733 the poet James Bramston, in his *Man of Taste*, written to defend the modes of his day against those who complained of lost hospitality, asked: 'Say thou that dost thy father's table praise, Was there Mahogena in former days?' By that time, also, British logwood cutters in Campeche Bay, Central America, were leaving that area to cut the more valuable mahogany in the Belize district of Honduras, thus provoking a long-drawn-out dispute with Spain. The ever-growing demand for mahogany can be judged in the rise of import values from £276 in 1722 to £77,744 in 1800. In the early nineteenth century import duties which had been imposed on mahogany during the French Wars began to affect trade figures, but Crosby's *Pocket Dictionary* of 1810 still described cabinet makers as 'workers in mahogany and other fine woods'.

CHIEF PERIODS AND STYLES

The furniture styles of the eighteenth century take their names not from the reigning monarchs but from outstanding designers, both craftsmen and architects. In the case of the craftsmen like Chippendale, Hepplewhite, and Sheraton this distinction must be recognized as doing less than justice to many contemporary cabinet makers whose work equalled or even in some cases excelled theirs. Indeed, it is not certain that Sheraton had a workshop or produced furniture of his own. Their claim to fame rests on their famous design books, which interpreted prevailing styles with a high degree of skill, and thus their names serve as a very convenient label for particular phases of development. The whole period showed a ceaseless spirit of experiment and a constant demand for novelties from the upper classes, whose needs were supplied by a succession of great cabinet makers and upholsterers; some of these cabinet makers' shops, like that of George Seddon (1727–1801), were large-scale businesses. Their products displayed a technical excellence fully equal to the work of the best Continental craftsmen. Their patrons, with wealth from land, trade, and industry, showed, in general, a high standard of taste. Much furniture was designed for the many new town and country houses, and this explains the importance of architects like Robert Adam, whose planning of a house covered every detail, inside and out.

The earlier Georgian period, to the mid-1740s, when mahogany was beginning to come in, was dominated by the Palladian revival, largely inspired by Lord Burlington, and interpreted by William Kent (1684–1748) and another contemporary architect, Henry Flitcroft. Kent was the first architect to include furniture in his schemes of work. He used mainly softwoods to take carving and gilding, but some of his pieces were in mahogany parcel (i.e. partly) gilt. His designs, somewhat modified, appeared in one of the earliest design books, *The City and Country Workmen's Treasury* by Batty and Thomas Langley (1739). But it is noteworthy that a prominent contemporary cabinet maker, Giles Grendey (1693–1780), produced mahogany furniture in a simpler style, reminiscent of the Queen Anne period.

Below Chippendale-period mahogany desk with cock-beaded drawers and gilt handles, *c.* 1750–65. Frank Partridge, London

Bottom Sideboard pedestal and urn veneered with rosewood and inlaid with satinwood, mounted with ormolu, by Thomas Chippendale, *c.* 1770. Harewood House

Palladianism went out of fashion in the mid-century, and was replaced by a diversity of styles, the rococo from France (then called the 'modern' taste), Chinese, and Gothic. This was the period of Thomas Chippendale (1718–79), whose *Gentleman and Cabinet Maker's Director* first appeared in 1754. No mention of mahogany appeared in the first edition, and only a passing reference (to six designs for hall chairs) in the third, in 1762. But much first-class furniture was made in this wood by Chippendale himself and the best contemporary craftsmen, such as John Bradburn, William Vile and John Cobb (these two in partnership) and Benjamin Goodison. Chippendale's great service was to apply the rococo style of decoration to a wide range of furniture and generally to curb its more excessive forms. He is now known to have employed on the *Director*'s plates two artists, Matthias Lock and Henry Copland, who were pioneers of the rococo in England. The taste for Chinese and Gothic furniture, the former largely inspired by the works of Sir William Chambers, and the latter by Horace Walpole, was cultivated by sections of the upper classes. While rococo relied for its effect on the use of flowing lines, Chinese work was seen in the popularity of geometrical fretwork patterns and Oriental figures and designs, and Gothic in the use of the pointed arch.

The neoclassical revival began in the 1760s, inspired by Robert Adam. His furniture, beautifully designed and made, was decorated with delicate

Adam furniture decorations

Far right Armchair in the Hepplewhite style, carved mahogany, *c.* 1780

Right Gilded armchair designed by Robert Adam and executed by Thomas Chippendale who described it in his account as 'exceedingly richly carved in the Antik manner', 1764. Victoria & Albert Museum

Below The Eating-room, Osterley Park, Middlesex, designed by Robert Adam in 1767. The pattern in the chair backs echoes that in the plaster work above

classical motifs, paterae, pendant husks, urns, fluting, etc. His liking for furniture of a more elegant appearance led to a revival of fine inlaid work, and much use of satinwood and other timbers. But mahogany, used as a veneer by itself, or with other woods, or for carving the classical motifs, was well adapted to the new mode, shown in the work of Chippendale (who worked for Adam) and Cobb in their later periods, John Linnell, William France, and others. In 1788 appeared George Hepplewhite's *Cabinet-makers' and Upholsterers' Guide*, two years after

the author's death. The great merit of this work was that it interpreted the new classical styles skilfully for all kinds of furniture. The explanations of the designs in the *Guide* constantly stress the suitability of mahogany both for small work, like cellarets and knife boxes, and for larger pieces, like tables and bookcases.

Thomas Sheraton (1751–1806) produced the *Cabinet Makers' and Upholsterers' Drawing Book* between 1791 and 1794 and bridged the gap between the neoclassical and the Regency periods. Sheraton favoured light, delicate furniture, including painted work, and for his finest pieces he recommended satinwood. He also used other tropical woods, popular about 1800, for the best apartments of the house, such as the drawing room and boudoir. His period is distinguished for the dainty, almost fragile, appearance of some of his furniture. This cannot be said of the final period, the Regency, ending about 1830. There was a renewal of classical forms inspired by the Directory and Empire styles in France, but these were carried out in a strict and narrow fashion, a 'chaste' and literal interpretation of Greek, Roman, and Egyptian examples. The designer Thomas Hope in his *Household Furniture* (1807) heralded this stress on an archaeological approach. Furniture took on a heavier appearance. One result was to re-emphasize dark, lustrous, or heavily figured woods, especially to show brightly gilt mounts in the prevailing mode. This explains the popularity of rosewood after 1800, but there was also a great demand for mahogany because of its suitable colour and grain.

OTHER TIMBERS

The popularity of satinwood from 1770 has already been mentioned, paving the way for a lighter, more delicate, aspect of furniture design. This trend, emphasized by a revival of veneers and fine inlaid work, led the cabinet makers to experiment with a wide range of exotic timbers, brought to them from all parts of the world, especially from tropical areas, by enterprising merchants. Satinwood itself, from

Secretaire inlaid with various woods and recumbent figure of ivory on an ebony ground. Attributed to Thomas Chippendale, *c.* 1770–5. Harewood House

both the East and West Indies, was yellowish in tone; so was fustic, from the West Indies, but this faded to a dead brown and was decried by Sheraton. Other woods, which showed rich shades of brown and red, varying from light to deep, included calamander, snakewood, coromandel, and rosewood from India and Ceylon, thuya from Africa, ebony from the East, kingwood, partridge wood, purplewood, and tulipwood from Central and South America, and amboyna from the West Indies. Camphor from the East Indies was also used for boxes and trunks, and red cedar from North and Central America for drawer linings, trays, and boxes. Native woods were not neglected: holly, pear, maple, and laburnum were used for inlays on first-rate pieces, and there was a demand for sycamore, which was stained a greenish-grey colour, and known as harewood, for veneers. Mahogany was used with these woods, which led to a closer study of its beautiful figure and fine range of colour, and made it appreciated more than ever. Figure and lustre were fashionable qualities after 1800, hence the importance of rosewood, large fresh supplies of which were now available from the opening up of trade with South America (particularly Brazil), calamander, coromandel, snakewood, tulipwood, and zebra wood: the last, as its name implies, having an effective dark stripe. Imported deal continued to be the favourite wood for carcase work during this period, but from 1750 red deal from North America largely replaced the former yellow variety.

DECORATION

Fretwork

This form of decorative work was popular in Chippendale's time, particularly to show Chinese patterns. Fret designs could be either open or applied. The open fret was seen on table and cabinet tops and the applied fret was found on the flat surfaces of chairs, tables, cabinets, etc.

Inlay

Robert Adam revived fine inlaid work, which in technique resembled seventeenth-century marquetry (*see* Walnut) but differed from it in the use of classical designs and figures, and of new, lighter-coloured woods. An effective form of inlay much favoured by Sheraton was stringing, or lines of inlay in contrasting woods or brass, some of the work being of extreme delicacy.

Metal mounts

These were made of brass and were fine gilt, which gave them a rich and golden appearance. They were used for work in the rococo style and decorative effect in the Regency period. The finest quality ormolu mounts were made by Matthew Boulton in his factory at Soho, outside Birmingham. His best period was 1762–76.

Veneers

Mahogany had a variety of beautiful figures or mottles. Some of the early San Domingo wood had 'roe' mottles, dark flakes running with the grain, giving attractive effects of light and shade, and at their best when the lines of figures were broken, they then varied in appearance according to the angle from which they were viewed. Cuban and Honduras mahogany, however, had a wider range of figures and were in great demand for veneers after 1750. Cuban 'curls' were highly prized. Their feather was obtained by cutting the tree where a large branch joined the trunk. This limited their size, and made them expensive and somewhat brittle ('Cross and unpliable' – Sheraton), unlike most mahogany veneers. The 'fiddle-back' came from the outer edge of the trunk and had even streaks running across the grain. The 'rain' mottle was similar but had wider and longer streaks. The 'stopped' or 'broken' mottle had irregular but brilliant flame-like markings. Dark and oval spots in the wood produced the 'plum' – or 'plum-pudding' – mottle. All these veneers were saw-cut and thick enough by modern standards to be considered more as facings than veneers.

Bureaux, cabinets, desks, bookcases, etc.

Endless varieties of writing, display, and cupboard furniture were produced in the mahogany period, many of them being directly descended from the walnut prototypes. Bureaux followed very much the same development as contemporary chests of drawers. Mahogany was a favourite medium for these until Sheraton's time, as the figure of the wood, especially Cuban curls, made a fine show on the flaps and drawers. A newer development was the desk, which had taken its place in the rich man's library by 1750. This was usually solid in appearance, with side drawers or cupboards of similar proportions to the classical pedestals of early sideboards (*see* Tables). Other kinds were serpentine-fronted and often had canted

Far left Mahogany break-front bookcase, *c.* 1775. Mallett & Son, London

corners with rococo carving. Mahogany was particularly suitable for all kinds of library furniture, and both Hepplewhite and Sheraton stressed this in their design books. Sheraton, however, gave his bureaux a lighter appearance. Many of them were intended for ladies' use, and he favoured the employment of satinwood. He also preferred the tambour or cylinder front instead of the flap.

But what especially exercised the best Georgian cabinet makers were the combined pieces – the bureau-bookcase, cabinet, press, and their variations – which demanded the highest skill in design and decoration. Their size encouraged an architectural treatment. Such pieces in the walnut period had been topped by arched curves, but these were replaced in early Georgian times by forms of broken pediments, angular or swan-neck. The open space in the centre was filled with a carved piece, or left free. Kent emphasized his pediments, and used classical pilasters on the corners of the doors, with much gilding. Many cabinet makers, however, preferred a simple straight cornice, and one effect of the wider use of mahogany was the return to a general lighter style. Pediments were retained but often their only decoration was carved dentil mouldings, also found on the cornice. Towards 1750 mirror plates on cabinet doors were going out of fashion. They gave way either to clear glazing or to panels of carefully chosen mahogany framed in applied mouldings or in stiles with curved inner edges.

The mid-century Gothic and Chinese fashions affected these pieces in several ways. The glazing bars of glass-fronted cabinets formed geometrical patterns or pointed arches. Carving or fretwork with similar designs was applied to the frieze and bottom edge of the cabinet, and to the frieze and feet of the bureau. A pagoda roof was sometimes added, and the pediment was pierced with fret-cut outlines. Rococo treatment might be found in ornate carving or fine gilt mounts. Loop handles without back plates were popular in the 1730s.

The bureau-bookcase of the late eighteenth century often had a 'pear-drop' moulding below the plain cornice. There might be a delicate key pattern at the central edge of the doors, along the top and bottom edges of the bureau, and on the uprights separating the small drawers within the flap. A curved apron piece and slender outward pointing feet are characteristic of this particular period. Octagonal handles dated from about 1785. In the Regency period a feature of the bookcases, apart from the new forms of decoration, was their low height, to leave the walls above them free for pictures.

Chairs

In the transitional period between walnut and mahogany the graceful Queen Anne hooped-back chair had become more ponderous in appearance, with an emphasis on the carving of ornament. At the same time Kent was designing his elaborate chairs for wealthy clients making use of walnut or mahogany, partly gilt, or of softwoods entirely gilt, for scroll-shaped legs, or versions of the cabriole, and a great deal of flower, fruit, and mask ornament. This vogue was passing about 1745, when mahogany really came into its own in chair design. The general effect was to re-emphasize form and proportion, and to initiate an era in which much ambitious splatwork became the fashion. Chippendale used the rococo, Chinese, and Gothic motifs in a great variety of chair backs. The typical rococo chair consisted of a back framed by two outward-curving side rails meeting in a Cupid's bow top (which had made its appearance some little time before Chippendale), usually with scrollwork on the corners, and the splat pierced with interlaced strapwork. The back legs tended to curve away noticeably. The cabriole leg was lighter in treatment than the Queen Anne variety and the ball-and-claw foot, though it was found on many chairs, was sometimes replaced by the French knurl or scroll toes. The famous 'ribband-back' chairs showed mahogany carving and rococo decoration in perhaps their most dazzling forms, the ribbons and bows forming intricate patterns which in some chairs joined up with the side rails. This was an extreme form. In general, Chippendale avoided the excessive ornament of the Continental rococo. In some of his chairs he showed the craftsman's eye for a well-balanced design. These had carefully restrained rococo carving in the splat, which tended to be narrower in shape, and straight legs, sometimes fluted, joined by plain stretchers, which were now being reintroduced on chairs of this type. The contrast between straight legs and curved backs and the use of carefully chosen upholstery for the seat (including plain leather) was pleasing. Another chair in fashion at mid-century was the mahogany Chinese chair. The characteristic features are the pagoda cresting rail, the splat pierced and carved with geometric patterns, the fretted work in similar designs on the back uprights, legs and feet, the cluster column legs, and the bracket between legs and seat. Other chairs of this type had stretchers which, together with the front legs and brackets, might be pierced and fretted with patterns, or, alternatively, applied ornament might be found on legs, stretchers, and seat front. In the case of Chinese armchairs, lattice work also filled the space between arms and seat. Gothic chairs showed interlacing pointed arches in the splats, or covering the whole of the back. Another attractive chair design was the 'ladder back', taken from a traditional country style. At its best it showed undulating curves on the cross and cresting rails, which were pierced and carved and often had a small carved emblem in the centre.

The interest of the Adam brothers in classical art

Below Mahogany chair in the manner of Thomas Chippendale, *c.* 1760

Ribband back

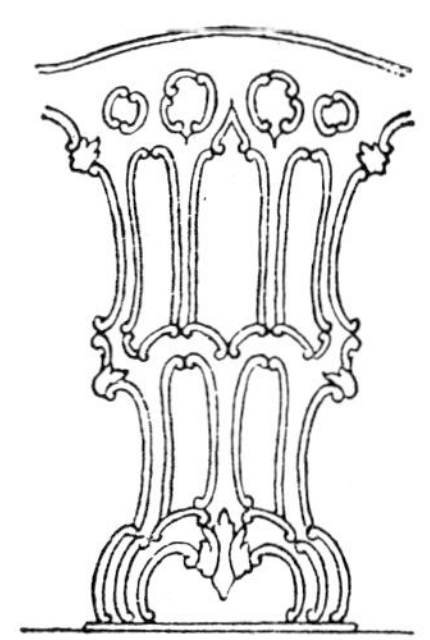

Gothic back

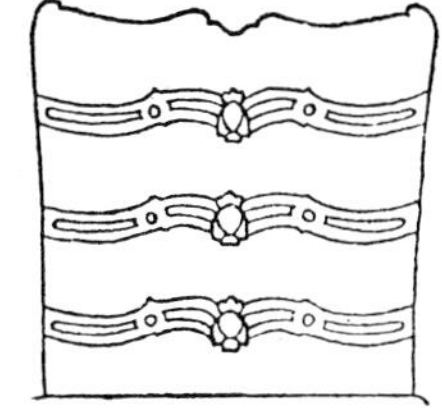

Ladder back

influenced chair design by introducing a lighter type of chair, emphasizing oval lines in the backs and using straight legs tapering from square knee blocks to feet set upon small plinths. The construction of chair backs changed, as the splat gradually lost its link with the back rail of the seat and became enclosed within the uprights. In this, again, the strength of mahogany was a definite factor. There was a sympathy for delicate fluting and channelling on the back, arms and legs and the addition of classical ornaments on the seat rail and (especially carved paterae) at the top of the front legs. But another kind of chair which enjoyed a long vogue was the 'French Adam' type. Dating from about the mid-1770s, it shows the cabriole leg in its final form, ending on scrolled feet. This chair is distinguished by the use of gentle curves, of gadrooning on the edges of the legs, arms, seat, and back, and of beautiful upholstery, all treated with the utmost refinement. Other French-style chairs had straight, tapering legs, usually fluted, and some of the backs were square in shape, with a lyre, including brass strings, for the splat. The versatility of form cannot be overstressed. Adam liked both painting and gilding; beech was used if chairs were to be gilded, and satinwood was becoming popular for fragile-looking drawing-room chairs. He also reintroduced cane seats.

As Hepplewhite's chairs are famous, it is worth noting his own directions for making them: 'Chairs in general are made of mahogany, with bars and frame sunk in hollow, or rising in a round projection, with a band or list on the inner and outer edges. Many of these designs are enriched with ornaments proper to be carved in mahogany.' His most celebrated form was the shield back (which he varied with heart or oval shapes). In a typical shield back the top rail rises in the centre over a splat consisting of narrow curving bars which terminate in a carved wheat-ear design. The bottom of the shield is just above the back of the seat. The arms add distinction to the chair, with the pronounced backward-sweeping curve from the top of the front legs straightening out at the arm rests which join the shield about halfway up. The tapering legs and plinth feet, the carefully limited carving on legs and arms, the channelling throughout, the serpentine front to the seat, overstuffed, are all typical of Hepplewhite's work. Other carved ornaments in the back included the Prince of Wales' feathers, leaves, vases, and drapery. He also used satinwood inlay on a mahogany background and, like Adam, designed some lyre backs.

The refinement in chair design reached its peak with Sheraton. He preferred rectangular shapes to emphasize lightness. The wide cresting rail over-running the uprights and shaped for the sitter's back is particularly worth noting, as this was a novelty in chairs and was found in wide use after 1800. The back has merely a single rail, and the legs are forward-splaying, with little attempt at foot design. Carving is replaced by clear, straight-lined inlay, in a contrasting coloured wood, on the cresting rail. For upholstery a striped material was popular, in keeping with the general rectangular effect of the rest of the chair. Like other designers, Sheraton did not confine himself to one pattern. On the whole he preferred to leave the back of his chairs as open as possible, and broke away from the vertical splay designs of his predecessors. He brought in a revival of painted chairs (of beech), usually decorated with bright floral devices on a black background and having plain cane seats and turned legs. He did not neglect carving by any means, but he is particularly noted for his employment of stringing as decoration. Basically, this was the same as the inlay on the cresting rail, but he carried it to extreme delicacy by using very thin lines of wood or brass. Chair arms often took a wide sweep upwards immediately above the legs, and another at the back to join the uprights at the cresting rail.

Sheraton lion's paw design for legs and arms

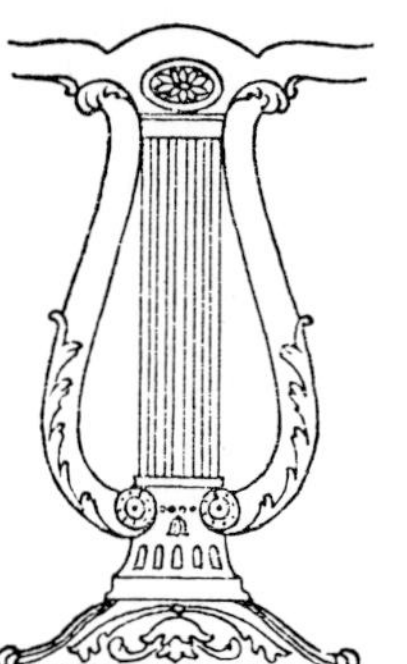

Lyre-shaped splat

Above One of a set of four Hepplewhite painted chairs, *c.* 1775. Glaisher and Nash Ltd., London

Above, right One of a set of gilt armchairs carved with Grecian ornament and covered in ottoman silk, *c.* 1769–9. Southill Park

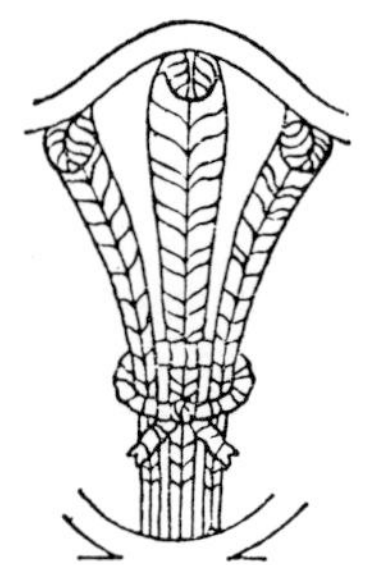

Chair-back ornament of Prince of Wales feathers

Sheraton's work already reflected many features of the so-called French Empire style, which blossomed out fully in the Regency period. Painted chairs remained popular, and the sweeping forward of the front legs, balanced by a similar outward curve on the back legs, was accentuated because of its resemblance to the chair figured on classical Greek vases. The cresting rail, in a variety of shapes, was a prominent feature, and the whole back was often given a very pronounced rake. Much of Sheraton's lightness disappeared with the extended use of lion's paw designs for legs and arms, and the addition of gilding and novelties like Egyptian motifs. A throne-like armchair, in which the whole sides – front and back legs, uprights and arms – were made in units, into which the back and seat fitted, tended to give this type a somewhat heavy and ornate appearance.

Chests of drawers, commodes, and tallboys

Until about 1750 chests of drawers were still straight-fronted, with, normally, four or five drawers, bracket or cabriole-shape feet, and ovolo or cock-bead moulding on the drawer edges. Not much change had been made in the Queen Anne design except that the front corners were usually canted and carved, as were the top edges. Classical pilaster designs were popular on the corners. From 1740 chests of drawers began to be designed with their

Right Mahogany library chair, scrolled arms supported on Egyptian heads, made by Thomas Chippendale junior, for Sir Richard Colt Hoare in 1802. Stourhead, Wiltshire

Far right Dressing table by Thomas Chippendale, rosewood and gilt, *c.* 1760. Lady Lever Art Gallery

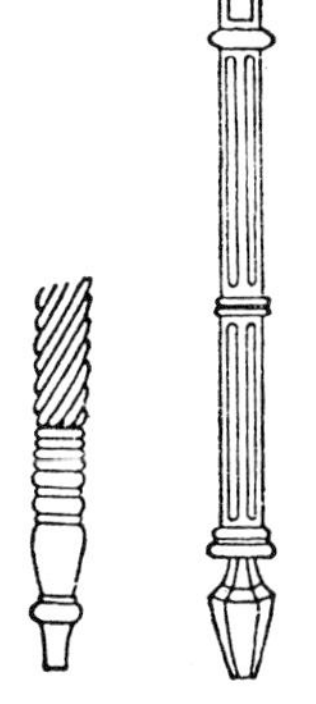

Quarter columns on front corners of bedroom chests of drawers: spiral shaped (left) *and reeded*

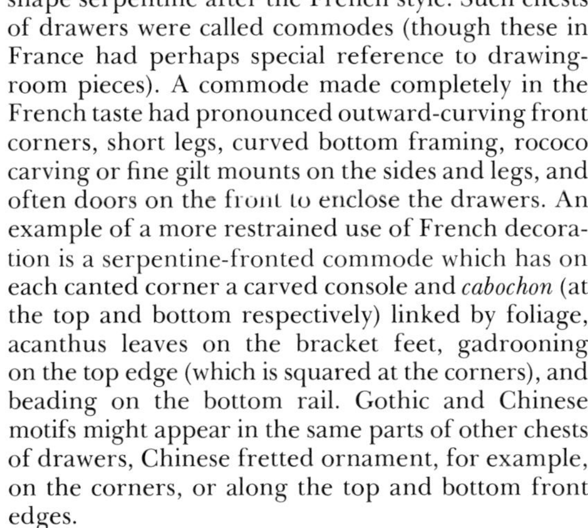

shape serpentine after the French style. Such chests of drawers were called commodes (though these in France had perhaps special reference to drawing-room pieces). A commode made completely in the French taste had pronounced outward-curving front corners, short legs, curved bottom framing, rococo carving or fine gilt mounts on the sides and legs, and often doors on the front to enclose the drawers. An example of a more restrained use of French decoration is a serpentine-fronted commode which has on each canted corner a carved console and *cabochon* (at the top and bottom respectively) linked by foliage, acanthus leaves on the bracket feet, gadrooning on the top edge (which is squared at the corners), and beading on the bottom rail. Gothic and Chinese motifs might appear in the same parts of other chests of drawers, Chinese fretted ornament, for example, on the corners, or along the top and bottom front edges.

Adam's work expressed itself principally in two ways. Where solid work persisted, the carving naturally became classical in treatment, emphasizing the corner pilasters, and making use of dentil and key patterns on the cornice moulding. On the other hand, fine inlay, in all the fashionable woods, was used eagerly by designers when drawing-room commodes were in great demand and their doors were ideal for showing first-rate work. Great patience was expended in devising ovals and circles to show figures or scenes from classical mythology, surrounded by inlaid designs. This set the taste for a lighter appearance in chests of drawers, in satinwood especially, or for painted decoration. Sheraton is connected with the bow-fronted chest of drawers, which was now used with the serpentine- and straight-fronted types. He by no means emphasized the new style, however. He designed in all shapes, including a return to the simple straight lines of early pieces. Two other innovations were the stringing (in wood or brass) on the drawer fronts and the use of an exceptionally deep frieze above the top drawer, which gave the chest of drawers a characteristic tallness. In the Regency period the decline of marquetry decoration gradually led to the replacement of the drawing-room commode by the chiffonier, a low cupboard with shelves, and often with a built-up superstructure above. Bedroom chests of drawers, tall, and either bow- or straight-fronted, had turned feet, and a distinctive feature on many were the quarter columns, spiral-shaped or reeded, on the front corners. By this time tallboys were going out of fashion, after a long vogue; they followed closely the designs for chests of drawers, and in their final period a few bow-fronted ones were made. These pieces do not require any separate description, therefore, except to stress that their great size led to special care being taken over their proportions and decoration.

Clock cases

Mahogany affected clock-case designs somewhat later than other pieces of furniture, for japanning and walnut veneers enjoyed a long vogue; indeed, figured walnut cases continued to be made until late in the eighteenth century. But by about 1760 mahogany was sufficiently in use to begin to give cases a heavier and broader appearance. At first veneering on an oak carcase was normal, followed by

Commode inlaid with medallions of Wedgwood and East Indian satinwood, the borders of hare- and tulipwood, *c.* 1775. Lady Lever Art Gallery

solid mahogany carcases for the best work, and carving. Hoods came in for elaborate treatment. As the arched dial was usual, the cornice was also strongly arched and moulded above it, and surmounted by a broken pediment, usually swan-neck, with finials as in the earlier fashion, or a simple plain pedestal in the centre. Naturally, full advantage was taken of the high case front to show the fine figure of the wood, and some very beautiful Cuban curls are found on outstandingly good work. In the mixture of styles of the Chippendale period detailed decoration was carried out in various ways; Chinese pagoda hoods and japanned cases, Gothic arches in the mouldings above the door, ornate rococo motifs; or fretwork in the frieze, across the top of the body below the hood, and around the bottom edge and sides of the base. The classicism of the latter part of the century emphasized the proportions of the case, used capitals at the sides of the hood (sometimes two at each side), and showed fluted pilasters worked in the canted front corners of the body, as on chests of drawers. The base was mounted on a solid plinth at first, but later acquired small bracket or cabriole-shape feet. Later work also included fine inlay such as satinwood inlays in classical designs on a background of mahogany. By Sheraton's time the tall clock case was going out of fashion. His period produced some fine inlaid and veneered work in many woods, but such pieces were by this period comparatively rare.

Rococo mirror frame decoration

Chinese pagoda hood

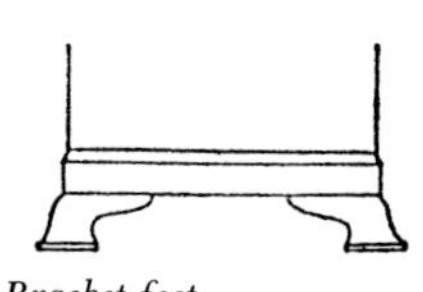
Bracket feet

Mirrors

Note. For a fuller coverage of this subject *see* separate section on Mirrors.

Mirrors were no longer a novelty in the eighteenth century. Improved methods of production led to a greater output of glass and to larger plates. Very large mirrors were still expensive, but small wall and toilet mirrors in simple styles were cheap enough for tradesmen's houses. In larger houses mirrors of all kinds adorned the best rooms, from smaller wall mirrors to pier and chimney glasses, often with wall lights (sconces and girandoles), and their conspicuous position singled them out for highly decorative treatment, especially gilding. For this reason it cannot be said that mahogany played any decisive part in their development. In the Kent period pier glasses, already reaching a height of 6 or 7 feet (183–213 cm) by the 1730s, were given brightly gilded frames and broken pediment tops, and this design affected wall mirrors in general. The pediments sometimes ended in a graceful acanthus leaf, and there was a prominent central motif in the form of a spread eagle, cartouche, or shell. The gilding was carried out on softwoods. On the other hand, the simpler kind of Queen Anne mirror with carved flowing curves on crest and apron piece continued to be made. These had mahogany frames, sometimes partly gilt, and incorporated a dominating centrepiece in the prevailing fashion.

There was a distinct change after the mid-century, when mirrors provided perhaps the best examples of the almost fantastic limits to which the new styles could go. Several designers, including Lock, Copland, and Johnson, paid particular attention to applying rococo and Chinese ornament to mirrors, and these trends were made fashionable by Chippendale, who employed the first two artists to produce designs for the *Director*. Mirror frames now avoided a symmetrical appearance and were carved and gilded in an intricate pattern of scrolls and foliage in the rococo mode, and to these were added numerous Chinese designs such as exotic birds, pagodas, mandarins, and bells, or even Gothic elements. Nowhere else were these styles so intimately united. This vogue did not last long, for Adam, and after him Hepplewhite, designed beautiful and delicately proportioned mirrors, oval or rectangular in shape, surrounded by much simpler scrollwork picked out with paterae, husks, and honeysuckle and leading up to a vase or similar classical motif. Adam favoured giltwork, usually on carved pine, and he used the mirror frames to show fluting, the key pattern, and Vitruvian scrolls.

Typical of the Sheraton and Regency periods was the circular gilt convex mirror, 1–3 feet (30.5–91.4 cm) in diameter. The gilt frame usually had an ebonized fillet on the inside edge and a reeded band on the outside; between the two was a pronounced hollow filled with small circular patterns of flowers or plain spheres. Above the frame was foliage, usually the acanthus leaf, supporting an eagle, one of the most popular designs for mirror crests during the whole of this period, or a winged creature.

Mirror crest decoration with foliage and winged creature

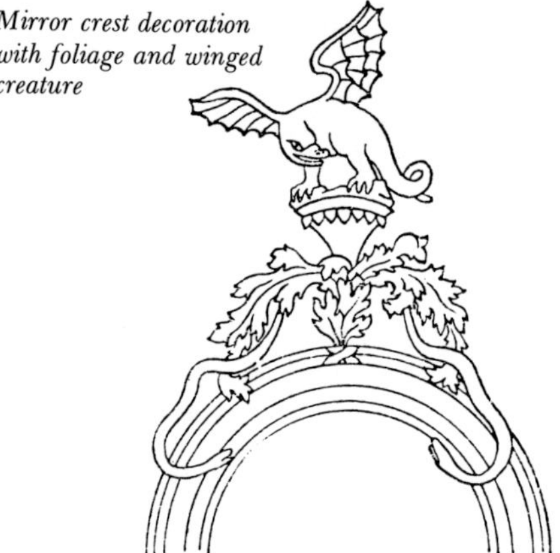

Mahogany played a much more important part in the evolution of the toilet mirror. From early in the eighteenth century many dressing tables were designed with collapsible mirrors which fitted into the tops of the tables, and the latter usually followed the design of chests of drawers, with a knee recess. But there was a great demand for the separate toilet glasses, the rectangular swing mirrors above minute drawers, made in mahogany. They preserved their simple, attractive shapes and avoided excessive decoration. In the Hepplewhite period the mahogany frames followed the design of the shield-back chair; later still, about 1800, they became flat rectangles. The tiny chests of drawers were often veneered and had serpentine or bow fronts. Sheraton devoted much skill to incorporating mirrors in dressing tables. He also popularized cheval glasses, known for some time before. These tall glasses stood between two uprights ending in outward-curving feet connected by a stretcher, and had decorative headpieces often painted, inlaid, or fretted.

Shield-back mirror frame decoration

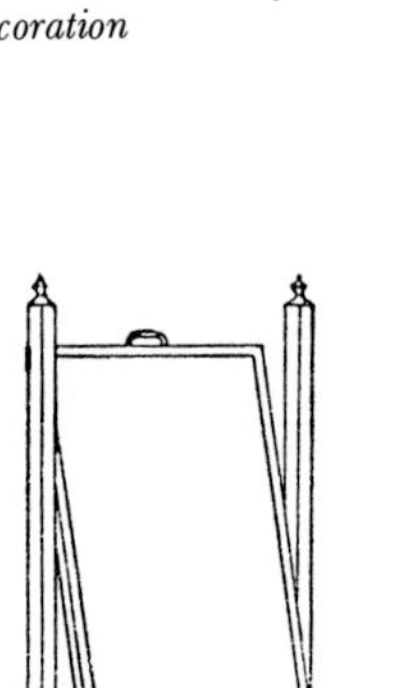

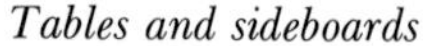
Cheval glass

Tables and sideboards

Small tables. As mahogany came into general use and the heavy side table of the Kent period went out of fashion, there was a return to the simpler style of small and occasional table which had been produced in Anne's reign. By the time of the publication of

Pair of French Hepplewhite mahogany card tables, *c.* 1785. Mallett & Son, London

Chippendale's *Director* the constantly changing needs of the upper classes were reflected in endless varieties of tea, breakfast, card, writing, and dressing tables, as well as the more formal side and pier tables. One very characteristic piece of the mid-century was the Chinese tea table. This had Chinese patterns on the frieze (usually in applied work), on tiny fretted galleries which ran round the edge of the top, and on the straight legs, which were fretted or perhaps carved in the solid. Some of these tables had fretted stretchers which crossed diagonally between the legs. Breakfast tables, made for the convenience of fashionable people who rose late and had their first meal in their bedrooms, had the same kind of decoration but a different form; they usually included flaps and drawers and a shelf, which was enclosed on three sides by trelliswork in mahogany or brass wire. A restrained French taste showed itself in slender, curved legs, sometimes with metal mounts, and curved friezes edged with gadrooning. An example of a table cabinet of about 1760 which could be used for writing, has a Chinese fret gallery at the top. The cabinet doors, displaying good figuring, are framed in curved stiles (a fashion which dated back some time before 1750), and are finished off with small foliage carving at the corners. A tea table of the same date has a hinged top, and traces of Gothic work in the legs, which are fluted in ogee section and have a tiny trefoil arch at the top. The delicate carving on the table edge and at the bottom of the frieze, and the curved bracket, as well as the veneers, show the many admirable uses to which mahogany could be put. The Adam period introduced two distinctly new trends. Besides rectangular shapes, others were appearing – oval, semicircular, kidney-shaped, and serpentine – with tapering and fluted legs or, as on some contemporary chairs, slender cabriole legs ending on knurl or scroll toes. For the daintier kinds of tables, satinwood and other exotic woods, inlays and gilding, and the choicest figured mahogany were all used, and in some of the best examples the tops were painted by Angelica Kauffmann, Pergolesi, and others. On the other hand, for the large rooms of the new town and country houses were produced many long side tables in mahogany. In these tables straight lines are emphasized. The legs are fluted, and taper to plinth feet. Carved decoration appears on the frieze in the classical moulding and the typical paterae over the legs and on the small central panel, where they are linked by husks. This kind of table represented the midway design between the dining and side table, and from it developed the sideboard, as is indicated below, as a separate piece of furniture.

This development of the sideboard seemed to redirect the designers' attention to small tables. Hepplewhite continued on Adam lines, but Sheraton designed a number of extraordinarily delicate tables, some, like his ladies' worktables, with an ingenious arrangement of drawers and sliding tops, being specially made for carrying from room to room. Neatness was indeed Sheraton's own word for this kind of work: 'These tables should be finished neat, either in satinwood or mahogany.' He also popularized the Pembroke table (though it had been known for some time before), with two semicircular flaps hinging on a rectangular centre. Usually the legs on his tables were unmistakable for their long, fragile-looking, tapering forms, but on some he showed a radical change in treatment which was to last through the Regency period. He used two solid end uprights, in the old trestle style, resting on short, outward-curving legs; or else a lighter version, with a central stretcher joining the ends.

Another kind of table which was common in the early nineteenth century was the drum or capstan kind, with a deep frieze for drawers (sometimes this was left open for books) and a central support in tripod style, the legs having the pronounced curve typical of the period. Some of these tables had a solid three-sided pedestal base or monopodium mounted

Far left Gilt card table inlaid and veneered with harewood and satinwood, attributed to Peter Langlois, *c* 1770. Syon House, Middlesex

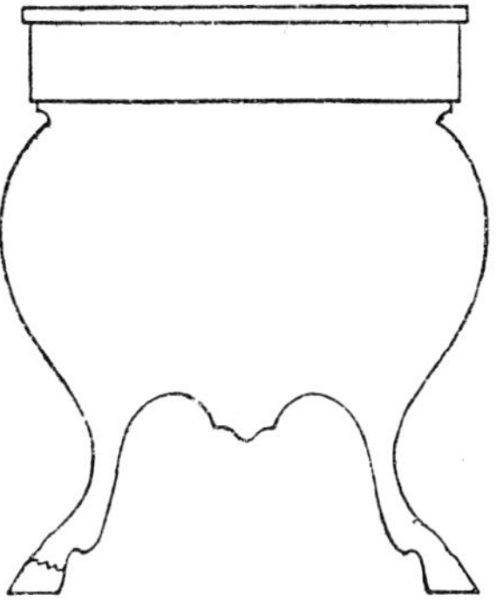

Sheraton table with solid end uprights resting on short, outward curving legs

Sheraton-style drum table, *c.* 1790–1810. H. Blairman & Sons, London

on claw feet. Rosewood or mahogany was usually the wood; some had light-coloured mahogany veneers and classical designs inlaid on the top and pedestal sides, in a contrasting colour.

Tripod tables

The application of the tripod construction to tables in general, from about 1800, indicates how popular this feature had become during the previous century. The small tripod tables developed from the candlestands of the walnut period, but by Chippendale's time they were being used for other purposes, as occasional and tea tables. Mahogany led to a considerable increase in them, as the tops could be made from one piece of wood, and, naturally, they became showpieces for the various fashionable enrichments. There were the celebrated 'piecrust' tables, named after the scalloped and slightly raised edge of the top. Some were hinged so that they could stand against the wall when not in use. Other tripod tables had elaborate carving on the top as a border to the edges. On others, again, a small fretted gallery appeared, like those on contemporary Chinese tables. Feet might be hooves, paws, or dolphins (the third copied from French tables). Later in the century the tops had often fine inlaid work when this fashion revived under Adam. About 1800 the legs had tended to become very delicate in appearance, with definite concave or convex curves finishing on thin, pointed feet. Sheraton used these on screens as well as tables. But even in Hepplewhite's work the three legs had sometimes been replaced by a solid base, and the extension of this practice, and the many varied leg forms, meant the loss of the original 'pillar and claw' principle.

Dining tables

For the better part of two centuries it has been almost a convention to associate mahogany with good dining-room tables. One of the chief uses to which the early imports of San Domingo mahogany were put was to make the spacious tops of these tables. They had remarkable weight and strength, and yet the mahogany legs were able to support them without stretchers. This gave clean lines to even the biggest tables and led to many developments in flaps and pivoted legs. In the second half of the eighteenth century large dining tables were made up of two smaller ones which were joined, when necessary, by flaps supported on gate legs. These legs at first either had cabriole form or were turned. The same construction continued in the Adam period, but very effective use was made of the size of the tables to give them figured veneers instead of solid mahogany, straight, tapering legs and classical ornament. Side tables could in every way resemble the contemporary dining table, except that the latter had ten legs, four each for the two end tables and an extra two for the flaps. The tops were of varied shapes – rectangular, semicircular, or D-shaped – but, naturally, the central flaps were rectangular. Cabinet makers produced, and in some cases patented, many ingenious devices for extending tops, such as the 'Imperial' dining tables made by Gillow of Lancaster. From about 1800 changes in design became marked. The circular table for dining – an enlarged version of the drum table referred to above – and long tables supported on two or three tripods or similar stands were Regency features. Sheraton also designed a 'universal table' with the old-fashioned draw-leaf top on four tapering legs. 'This', he wrote, 'should be made of particularly good and well-seasoned mahogany, as a great deal depends on its not being liable to cast' – a reminder that dining tables had missed much of the changing fashions in new woods and applied decoration.

Sideboards

The sideboard was a late eighteenth-century development and sprang from the table. It is said to have been originated by Adam, who introduced the custom of standing a classical pedestal mounting an urn at each end of a side table. The obvious advantage of having this storage space so close to the table led to pedestals and tables becoming one unit, and later to the replacement of the pedestals by either smaller cupboards or drawers. The cupboards were used for many purposes; some were lined with metal to keep plates warm, or to hold water or wine bottles. At first the urns which stood on the pedestals contained the cutlery, but this was transferred to a drawer when urns went out of use. Both Hepplewhite and Sheraton designed light and elegant sideboards. The former is credited with serpentine- and bow-fronted shapes and the latter paid special attention to the brass rail which often stood at the back of the table to hold plates. The serpentine-fronted sideboard is a typical example of Hepplewhite's finely proportioned work. This has the usual arrangements of legs, four in front and two at the rear, found on longer sideboards, and of a single central drawer flanked by two others (or in some cases single deep ones) on each side. The central arch (an important feature on these sideboards) has delicate inlay work, like the drawer fronts and apron piece, and there is also line inlay on the legs. The curving front makes a very effective display of figuring. Typical of the smaller Sheraton sideboard was the serpentine, break-front example with two side cupboards, a sharper curve to the arch, and stringing decoration. The legs were turned and reeded, a style for which Sheraton showed a preference in his later work (and which also appeared on his chairs). In the Regency period there was a return to the pedestal type of the early sideboards. Other versions discarded the side drawers or cupboards altogether and replaced them with two or four legs, often carved in animal forms. The deepening of the table frieze and the elaboration of the brass gallery in classical designs on these pieces deprived them of the graceful symmetry of previous examples.

Far right Serpentine break-front mahogany sideboard in the Sheraton style with inlay of holly stringing, *c.* 1790. Frank Partridge, London

Victorian Furniture

Note. For a survey of antiques in general in the later Victorian period *see* separate section on The Aesthetic Movement; The Arts and Crafts Movement; Art Nouveau; Art Deco, etc.

In the history of the decorative arts Victorian furniture occupies a strange position. Although it is probable that fifty per cent of all the furniture ever made in this country was made during the sixty-four years of Victoria's reign, and that even today perhaps twenty per cent of all surviving furniture dates from those years, it is almost a closed field to serious scholarship or collecting. Most standard works on the history of furniture stop at 1830. In the last few years dealers and collectors have begun tentatively to edge their way into the post-1830s period, usually with a limited interest in one line only (e.g. paper mâché). The main course of Victorian furniture remains, however, relatively uncharted, with the result that whereas there are thousands who can confidently date a fifteenth-century brass rubbing to within thirty years, there are few who can be equally certain about a Victorian sideboard.

The normal justification given for this curious position is that after about 1830 there was such a disastrous deterioration in standards of taste and craftsmanship that Victorian furniture does not merit the attention legitimately bestowed on earlier periods, and that in particular the eclectic enthusiasm of Victorian designers for copying the historic styles of the past deprives their productions of that degree of originality which is essential to serious connoisseurship. These arguments are not convincing. Firstly, the deterioration can be established only if the evidence is studied rather than ignored. Secondly, ugliness in the products of earlier periods has never proved a bar to serious research or enthusiasm on the part of either antiquarians or collectors. Thirdly, the accusation of unoriginal eclecticism can equally be brought against the furniture designers of the eighteenth century, and was indeed used by many nineteenth-century writers to dismiss the works of Chippendale and the Adam brothers, for example, as debased rehashes of Chinese, classical, and Renaissance elements. Finally, it is surely absurd to suppose that the vast amount of earnest and informed effort put into the design of furniture by leading architects and others, especially after 1850, could have produced nothing whatever of interest.

The real explanation for the neglect must be sought elsewhere, namely in the totally different research techniques which are required to investigate Victorian furniture by comparison with that of earlier periods. The difference arises mainly from the change in the nature of the documentary evidence available after about 1840. Research into earlier furniture has always taken actual examples as its starting point, and has, where possible, worked back from the furniture to surviving documents (family records and the like) as supporting evidence for attributions and dating. For these earlier periods the tangible evidence of the furniture itself far outweighs that of the fragmentary documentary references, and even after the appearance of pattern books in the eighteenth century the majority of surviving examples must be assessed without the aid of any contemporary visual or even verbal sources. After about 1845 the development of illustrated periodicals, trade catalogues, and exhibition catalogues rapidly transformed the situation, so that for the Victorian era the bulk of systematic contemporary day-by-day visual evidence far outweighs the quantity of authentic surviving furniture, with the result that research must necessarily take the documents as the starting point and work from them to the furniture instead of vice versa. This necessarily places collectors at a disadvantage, for it means that those who might hope to pick up interesting Victorian items at country auctions will probably find their time wasted unless they have first spent many tedious hours ploughing through trade periodicals in Shoreditch Public Library.

The clearest proof of the significance of this change in research requirements after about 1840 is the fact that the systematic research into Victorian furniture that has been undertaken has tended to be the work of experts on twentieth-century taste (who take the bulk of contemporary visual evidence for granted) pushing their researches backwards, rather than of eighteenth-century experts (who are trained in the opposite technique) pushing forwards. It is equally significant that the most substantial collection of Victorian furniture in existence – that of the Victoria and Albert Museum – has been mainly built up as a result of a systematic search for particular pieces, the original existence of which had first been established from a study of contemporary periodicals and catalogues.

It is as well that this watershed which divides pre-1840 from post-1840 research and collecting should be widely recognized as soon as possible, for otherwise there is a serious danger that the established practice of collecting without prior documentation will itself produce a cumulative distortion in the public assessment – even in informed circles – of

Above Jardinière of bog oak with elaborate carving on the stem, feet and reverse side, *c.* 1830

Far left Armchair of carved walnut and marquetry set with a porcelain plaque painted with a portrait of Prince Albert, designed and made by Henry Eyles of Bath for the Great Exhibition of 1851

Victorian design, by fostering a process of 'selective survival'. For example, in the absence of a study of the contemporary records, there was a general but erroneous belief that early Victorian furniture (in contrast to mid-Victorian) retained some of the lightness and elegance of the Regency. Once such a stereotype is established, collectors tend to be interested only in pieces whose authenticity seems to be attested by their conformity to it, and dealers come to prefer such pieces and reject others as atypical, until in the long run the only pieces which survive in quantity are those which fit into the mistaken picture, while the examples whose survival would establish its falsity are weeded out. By that time it is too late to redress the balance and all the really interesting pieces may have disappeared.

However, even after it is recognized that the prior research into and the subsequent collecting of Victorian furniture is a legitimate, indeed a praiseworthy, pastime, there still remains the problem of the type of furniture to be sought, for so much has survived, and there is documentary evidence of so many parallel levels of taste, that some choice is inevitable. The problem is aggravated by the appearance for the first time after 1850 of two separate streams: namely the *avant garde* (what would today be called the 'contemporary') furniture, consciously produced by designers from outside the ranks of the trade – often inspired by a missionary zeal to reform public taste – and appealing to a very small educated clientele; and the enormously larger bulk of trade productions designed anonymously in the studios of the large manufacturers on conservative and traditionalist lines. At first sight these two streams appear to be not only separate but entirely opposed, each contemptuous of the other; the former believed by the latter to be constantly changing in a feverish search after novelty at the whim of each individual designer, the latter believed by the former to be stolidly unchanging and impervious to any progressive influence. Both pictures are distorted, for the evidence shows that a clear logical development can be traced through the apparently unrelated twists and turns of the *avant garde* designs, and that this in its turn, and with a long time lag, is reflected in a modified form by changes in the trade designs. The length of the time lag naturally varies between London and the provinces and according to such factors as the price of the furniture and the nature of the firm, so that a comparison of trade catalogues demonstrates at any one time the whole gamut between the most advanced and the most conservative in current production side by side. Any systematic charting of the history of Victorian furniture – at least after 1850 – must therefore take constant account of this overlapping of styles, though necessarily giving prior attention to those pioneer, and indeed often rebel, designers upon whose inspiration the entire development ultimately depends. Collectors have the choice of furniture at every level of taste, though for obvious reasons it is usually only the more 'advanced' pieces, in so far as they survive, which can provide the additional interest of exact dating and documentation.

The opinions expressed in the survey which follows are necessarily personal and tentative and are based as much on an examination of contemporary documents as of actual surviving furniture. The survey concentrates on cabinet makers' furniture, and excludes upholstered furniture and those sidelines, such as metal furniture, wicker, cane, and bentwood furniture, and garden furniture, which require separate study.

EARLY VICTORIAN FURNITURE: 1837–51

The first fifteen years of Victoria's reign mark the lowest ebb ever reached in the whole history of English furniture design. Indeed, the most severe strictures so often applied indiscriminately to Victorian taste as a whole are entirely justified if only directed against the products of this initial period. It would, however, be absurd to suggest that a sudden deterioration set in as soon as the new reign had begun; the most that can be said is that a debasement which was already evident as early as the late 1820s gained steady impetus during the 1830s and 1840s. The Great Exhibition of 1851 is always taken to mark the culmination of this debasement. In a sense this is true; although it is only right to remember that by stimulating competitive ostentation among manufacturers it tended to exaggerate the most vulgar elements in early Victorian design, while the fact that, for the first time, the various illustrated catalogues of the Exhibition provide a permanent record of its horrors, unfairly weighs the evidence against the early Victorians. Had a similar exhibition been held in 1837 instead of 1851, it would hardly have demonstrated a higher average standard.

As always in such debased periods, it is impossible in retrospect to discern any logical development of design, to distinguish the personal styles and influences of the leading designers and manufacturers, or even to specify any criteria enabling one to date a surviving piece in default of documentary evidence. The pattern books of this period, such as those of R. Bridgens, R. Brown, Thomas King, and Henry Whitaker, throw no light on the matter, for each exhibits the same tepid eclecticism in which a slavish copying of past styles is accompanied by a straining after novelty in trivial details. Judgment is made more difficult by reason of the fact that no surviving examples have so far been precisely related to these patterns, with the exception of a few commonplace pieces designed by Whitaker for Osborne House in 1845, which are still there.

Mahogany work table, carved with scrolls on the sides and feet, with green leather undercarriage, *c.* 1840

Below Games table of papier mâché inlaid with mother-of-pearl, painted and gilt, 1850–60

Far right, below Fire and pole screens in gros point with mahogany frames, mid-Victorian

Below Sofa of papier-mâché, painted with flowers and inlaid with mother-of-pearl, mid-19th century. Victoria & Albert Museum

Two characteristics stand out in the general confusion: an emphasis on rich and elaborate carving, preferably with a narrative or anecdotal interest, and a delight in the numerous new substitute materials which technical progress was making available. Lacking any accepted architectural framework, the shape and outline of such items as cabinets and sideboards were frequently entirely subordinate to an over-all covering of carving, often worked not by hand carving but by new methods such as the burning techniques of the Burnwood Carving Company's 'Xylopyrography' and Harrison's Wood Carving Company (Pimlico), or the machine stamping of Jordan's Patent Wood Carving, or even produced from materials such as guttapercha, Jackson's 'cartonpierre', Bielefeld's 'Patent Siliceous Fibre', White and Parlby's 'furniture composition', or Leake's sculptured leather.

Elaborate carving became so established as the hallmark of fine furniture during this period that the furniture section of Wornum's Report on the Great Exhibition is actually headed 'Carving and Modelling', and the only artists known to have been commissioned during the years 1837–51 to design furniture from outside the trade (with the exception of Pugin, to be mentioned below) were not architects as one would expect, but sculptors, such as Sir Francis Chantrey (1781–1841), John Thomas (1813–62), and Baron Marochetti (1805–67). Inevitably the most popular examples of English furniture at the Great Exhibition were the elaborately carved cradle presented to Queen Victoria by W. G. Rogers (1792–1875) – known as the 'Victorian Grinling Gibbons'; the monstrous 'Kenilworth' buffet (now at Warwick Castle), the *chef d'œuvre* of the Warwick school of wood carvers which flourished throughout the nineteenth century; and Arthur J. Jones's ludicrous patriotic carved furniture in Irish bog oak.

The only one of the new materials which may be said to have produced something new and attractive was papier mâché, enriched after 1842 with Jennens's and Bettridge's patent jewelled effects. This plastic material, though suitable for trays, caskets, and the like, is, however, basically unsuitable for load-bearing furniture, and has no real place in the development of Victorian furniture. Owing to the natural attraction of the smaller items for collectors, it has, nevertheless, received disproportionate attention, and has helped to spread the myth that early Victorian furniture is lighter and less clumsy that mid-Victorian. In a few cases, the techniques for decorating papier mâché (e.g. lacquer painting and encrustation with shell and mother-of-pearl) were applied to a normal wooden framework, thus producing a legitimate piece of furniture; but such examples are rare.

MID-VICTORIAN FURNITURE: 1851–67

The furniture of the period 1851–67 differed very markedly from that of the preceding period. In particular, the wild eclecticism and confusion of styles was rapidly replaced after 1851 by a surprising uniformity, and a single consistent style soon imposed itself on the great bulk of fashionable productions. Victorians themselves gave no name to this style, but usually described examples of it with generalized phrases such as 'following the purest taste of the Italian Renaissance'. A careful analysis of, for example, the copious records which have survived from the vast Modern Furniture Court of the 1862 Exhibition makes its existence perfectly clear.

Its main characteristics were the use of solid wood, usually walnut or mahogany, rather than veneers or inlay, a repudiation of baroque or rococo curves in favour of more severe outlines, and a continuing emphasis on carving. The latter, however, was now no longer allowed to sprawl over the whole surface with a profusion of unrelated motifs, as in the 1840s, but was concentrated into carefully disposed and deeply cut masks, swags, and trophies (usually of 'appropriate' objects, such as dead gamebirds on sideboards), and almost invariably incorporated human figures in the form of caryatids or brackets. Indeed, this emphasis on human figures became something of an obsession with designers during this period, so that no fashionable sideboard or cabinet was considered complete without them – as large as possible and preferably free-standing. Equally indispensable was an enormous mirror, backing, and usually dwarfing, the whole piece – a direct consequence of the technical developments in the industrial section of the 1851 Exhibition.

It cannot be doubted that the best examples in this manner show a sense of style and consistency that

Above Mahogany loo table with circular top made of blue silk and silver and silver-gilt, designed and made by Henry Eyles of Bath for the Great Exhibition of 1851. Victoria & Albert Museum

Above, centre Victorian credenza, or sideboard, made of mahogany and walnut veneer with carved fretwork

Victorian Gothic bench of oak with inscribed elm seat, *c.* 1850

had been completely lost in the 1840s, and certainly justify the enthusiasm with which all writers in the 1860s refer to the great improvement in the stylistic purity of English furniture since the nadir of 1851. The improvement must be mainly attributed to the influx of French designers imported from Paris by all the leading firms after the 1851 Exhibition had so clearly exposed the general superiority of French design. Some, such as Eugène Prignot and Alfred Lormier, who acted as chief designers to Jackson and Graham throughout the 1850s and 1860s, were brought over permanently, while in other cases designs were commissioned from artists in Paris, such as Ernest Vandale and Hugues Protat. In either case, the manufacturers always emphasized that 'the piece has been entirely executed by English workers'.

Although this dominant style was pervasive enough to influence not only the productions of all the leading London houses (e.g. Gillow, Trollope, Howard, Thomas Fox, and Johnstone and Jeanes) but also the cheaper mass-production manufacturers, such as Lucraft, Smee, and Snell, and the leading provincial firms (e.g. Henry Ogden, Henry Lamb, and Bird and Hull in Manchester, John Taylor, Whytocks, and Purdie, Bonnar and Carfrae in Edinburgh, and C. and W. Trapnell in Bristol), some furniture was, of course, produced in other manners. Thus, a few firms (Charles Hindley, William Fry of Dublin, and J. G. Crace) worked in the 'Gothic taste' (*see* below); Wright and Mansfield produced an entirely atypical series of copies of original Adam designs; and Dyer and Watts had considerable success with cheap, stained bedroom furniture, an example of which was even purchased by the Empress Eugénie from the Paris Exhibition of 1867.

This nameless mid-Victorian style must be regarded as the last style to have originated within the trade. Thereafter all further developments took place under the shadow of the individual reformist artist-designers and architect-designers whose appearance on the scene so decisively changed the whole trend of English furniture design.

THE GOTHIC REVIVAL

The first conscious reformers of Victorian furniture design – A. W. N. Pugin (1812–52) and William

Burges (1827–81) – cannot be said to have had a direct or decisive influence on the general trend of trade design. Nevertheless, the developments of the late 1860s cannot be explained without a reference to their role. Though they both worked within the orbit of the Gothic Revival, their actual designs differed very radically.

The influence of Pugin on English furniture design has usually been overrated. His general influence as a propagandist, his key position in the mid-century transition from a sentimental to a scientific medievalism, and the significance of his teachings on church furnishings have tended to obscure the fact that his own domestic furniture had little influence and that his following among furni-

Victorian Gothic armchair of gilt beech, *c.* 1830. Victoria & Albert Museum

Carved and painted oak cabinet with brass fittings, designed by A. W. N. Pugin and made by J. G. Grace, and exhibited at the Great Exhibition, 1851. Victoria & Albert Museum

ture designers was always small. He himself designed a good deal of furniture in an extremely plain and unromantic Gothic style for the numerous houses which he erected in the 1840s, but as this was never published, it had no effect on the trade.

By contrast, the much more ornate and monumental furniture which he designed for the Houses of Parliament, and in particular the elaborate display piece which he designed for J. G. Crace for the Medieval Court of the 1851 Exhibition, and which was purchased by the Museum of Ornamental Art in 1852, were much publicized and copied. Consequently the trade furniture of the 1850s which was claimed by its manufacturers to be 'in the purest Gothic taste, after recognized authorities', and dismissed by its detractors as 'Puginesque', tended to repeat all those faults of overelaboration with architectural conceits in the way of finials, crockets, and the like, which Pugin himself had so trenchantly attacked in his *Contrasts* and which his own domestic work so skilfully avoided. In fact, this type of architectural Gothic furniture was far too closely associated in the public mind with Pugin's catholicism to have any wide vogue, and soon came to be the exclusive preserve of a number of specialized houses – of which the most prominent was Hardman and Cox – dealing mainly in church fittings, and generally referred to by contemporary writers as the 'Wardour Street ecclesiastical upholsterers'. It is true that in 1862 the young Norman Shaw (1831–1912) designed an elaborate bookcase in this style, which has often been quoted since, merely by virtue of having been illustrated in the official catalogue of the Exhibition, but it typified no general trend and was produced not by a furniture firm but by James Forsyth, a specialist in stone carving.

The Gothic furniture of William Burges occupies a somewhat different position. The main body of his furniture – designed largely for his own use or as part of the huge schemes of interior rebuilding which he undertook for the Marquis of Bute at Cardiff Castle and Castell Coch – involved a far too personal interpretation of thirteenth-century Gothic to have any wide influence. Its fanciful – even facetious – adaptation of medieval forms to present-day needs, and its garish polychromatic decoration, made its incorporation into a normal domestic interior quite impractical. However, two particular pieces in a rather more restrained style, which were shown in the Medieval Court – not (significantly) in the Modern Furniture Court – of the 1862 Exhibition, received a great deal of favourable attention and publicity and deserve separate consideration. They were a huge bookcase, admittedly castellated but otherwise severely unelaborated, painted by no fewer than eleven leading artists, and now in the possession of the Ashmolean Museum, Oxford, and a celebrated plain rectangular cabinet painted to Burges's specifications by E. J. Poynter (1836–1919) with scenes representing 'the Battle of the Wines and the Beers' (bought for the South Kensington Museum from the Exhibition). The main significance of these pieces is that they are both in the plainest possible shape, entirely unlike the Wardour Street architectural Gothic, and depend entirely for their appeal on the painting of their surfaces. A subsidiary significance lies in the fact that their message to the trade was simultaneously endorsed at the 1862 Medieval Court by the furniture here displayed to the public for the first time by the newly created association of Morris, Marshall, Faulkner and Co.

MORRIS FURNITURE

Several pieces exhibited by the Morris firm in the 1862 Court have survived (the most attractive example is the 'Backgammon Players' cabinet), and all are similar to Burges's exhibits in being solidly constructed, supposedly Gothic, carcases, used as surfaces for painting. They belong by rights to the history of painting rather than of furniture. However, the Morris firm also produced (though it did not exhibit in 1862) several other types of non-Gothic furniture, each of which had an influence on the general trend of furniture design. So many misconceptions are current about Morris furniture that it is necessary to examine these in some detail.

Morris himself (despite frequent statements to the contrary) never designed any furniture, nor do his writings indicate much interest in it. All the furniture produced by the firm was the work of his various collaborators. Four different types were manufactured in these early years. Firstly, Philip Webb (1831–1915), the architect, designed a number of large tables depending for their effect entirely on the use of unstained oak and on the interest of their unconcealed joinery construction, thus marking a conscious revolt against the debasement of mid-Victorian cabinet making. Though they were exaggeratedly massive and monumental, their proportions and their simple chamfered decoration reveal the hand of a sensitive architect. Their importance lies not in any immediate influence on the trade but in their delayed influence on the Arts and Crafts furniture designers of the 1890s, and they can be legitimately regarded as the original prototypes of the whole Cotswold school of joinery.

Secondly, Ford Madox Brown designed a set of cheap bedroom furniture, produced by the Morris firm in large quantities, usually in a green-stained version, of which a few examples have survived. These appealed particularly to those mid-Victorians who felt that the introduction of examples of good plain design into servants' bedrooms could not but help raise the taste, and even the morals, of the lower classes. Their success led to plagiarism by many firms in the 1880s.

Thirdly, the firm produced and sold right up to the 1920s a set of cheap rush-bottomed chairs and settle in turned ebonized wood, including seven alternatives shapes, which quickly became immensely popular with middle-class families anxious to escape from the general philistinism of contemporary decoration. These also were copied with minor modifications by numerous other firms. This set was not originally designed by the firm, but was adapted from a traditional-type country chair seen by William Morris in Sussex.

Fourthly, the firm produced with equal success a drawing-room easy chair with an adjustable bar at the back, which became so popular that in the United States the type is still known as a 'Morris' chair. Though often spoken of as designed by Morris himself, it was in fact copied directly from a chair seen in 1866 by Warington Taylor, the young manager of the firm, at the workshop of a Herstmonceux furniture maker named Ephraim Coleman.

Later in the century the firm evolved several entirely different types of furniture, which are refer-

Sofa or library table of amboyna wood, inlaid with various darker woods, *c.* 1870

red to below in connection with the Arts and Crafts movement.

BRUCE J. TALBERT AND C. L. EASTLAKE

Although neither the architectural Gothic of Pugin nor the painted-plank Gothic of Burges and the Morris firm had much direct influence on trade design, they were nevertheless responsible for providing the point of departure for the development of what ultimately became the most widespread and original of all Victorian styles – a development that was so rapid that in the decade 1868–78 it transformed the whole course of Victorian furniture design. Two stages – or rather two overlapping strands – can be traced in it: the first associated with Bruce J. Talbert (1838–81) and C. L. Eastlake (1836–1906), the second with T. E. Collcutt (1840–1924). Once again the usual Victorian confusion about labels has served to obscure the significance of these changes and the originality of the furniture which developed from them, for contemporary writers gave the style no name and referred to its products as simply Gothic, Early English, Old English, or even Jacobean.

The first stage dates from 1867, when Talbert, a prolific and neglected designer, won a silver medal for Holland and Sons at the Paris Exhibition with a so-called 'Gothic dressoir' and several smaller cabinets. The influence of this success was consolidated by the publication in the same year of Talbert's *Gothic Forms, applied to Furniture, Metalwork, etc. for Interior Purposes*, and in 1868 of Eastlake's *Hints on Household Taste*, a book which exerted an enormous influence in sophisticated middle-class circles – especially in America, where it gave rise to a so-called 'Eastlake style'.

Although Talbert's Paris Exhibition pieces were still in a heavy semi-Gothic style, not so far removed from the 'Puginesque', the more unpretentious examples in both his book and in Eastlake's, which were, of course, those which had most influence on trade production, marked a definite step away from the Gothic of both Pugin and Burges towards a style more practical and three-dimensional. Its main characteristics were a rigid avoidance of curves or florid carving, a concentration on straight lines and an elaboration of surface colour and texture (but always in the lowest possible relief) by the use of a great variety of different techniques and materials, including the insertion of painted and stained panels, tiles, stamped leather, embroidery, enamels and chased metal. Talbert produced large quantities of this furniture, not only for Hollands but also for Gillow, and for Marsh, Jones, and Cribb of Leeds. However, only two authenticated examples of his work have so far been traced (both of which have been acquired by the Victoria and Albert Museum). They are both in this modified Gothic style, and demonstrate the particular flavour of rich sobriety which characterized his work. Other examples must certainly survive, along with pieces by Eastlake himself (he designed for Heaton, Butler, and Bayne), and those designers who closely followed this style in the 1870s, such as E. J. Tarver (working for Morant Boyd) and Owen Davis, the eclectic assistant of Sir Matthew Digby Wyatt and author of *Art and Life* (1885) (working for Shoolbred).

Mahogany desk with carved decoration and stamped leather top which can be adjusted for reading, brass gallery and handles, made by Gillows

Despite the acclaim with which Talbert's book was received and the designs in it copied, he himself quickly abandoned the style, and already in the early 1870s turned towards a dull and unoriginal rehash of Jacobean motifs, with a tedious elaboration of carved strapwork and a generally baronial air. This change can be clearly traced in the designs which he exhibited at the Royal Academy over these years, and in his second book of designs, *Examples of Ancient and Modern Furniture*, published in 1876. Its influence was slight for it merely provided additional models for the large firms of traditionalist decorators, such as Gillow and Trollope, who had in any case always found in late Elizabethan and early seventeenth-century oak carving a readymade source of inspiration for their more pretentious schemes.

T. E. COLLCUTT

The second stage in these developments, though it stemmed directly from the first and rapidly followed on its heels, was due neither to Talbert nor Eastlake, but to Thomas Edward Collcutt. Though remembered as the architect of the Imperial Institute, his role as a furniture designer has been entirely forgot-

Ebonized mahogany cabinet made by Collinson and Lock and painted by Albert Moore, 1871. Victoria & Albert Museum

often divided off by little railings of turned balusters or embroidered curtains, and panels painted with floral sprays or willowy female figures, usually on a gold ground. A persistent cliché which became almost a trademark for the style was a double panel in which an inner oblong or hexagon is joined to an outer frame by ties at the four cardinal points.

At its best, the style must be regarded as the Victorian era's most individual contribution in the whole field of furniture design. Quantities of its cheaper manifestations have survived, particularly in country rectories. Overmantels, usually backed with numerous small mirrors, have tended to survive as being fixtures, and examples of a drawing-room version of the style, decorated in black and gold, can also be found. Authentic pieces from the Collinson and Lock 1872 catalogue are, however, very difficult to come by.

The surprisingly rapid spread of Talbert's original style, and Collcutt's later version of it, can only be explained if account is taken of the way in which Eastlake and the many publicists who followed him supported their influence with arguments which seemed to provide would-be connoisseurs and purchasers with certain easily remembered maxims for judging furniture, and which buttressed their own uncertain taste with apparently authoritative criteria. These all derived ultimately from the teachings of Pugin, Owen Jones, and Ruskin on 'honesty in design'. The most telling was the proposition that because wood has a straight grain it should always be used in the plank and never debased by being carved or curved into twisted shapes more appropriate to plastic or ductile materials. This argument was strengthened by simultaneous appeal to economic and nationalist considerations, for the carving or

ten. It opens in 1871, when Collcutt exhibited at the South Kensington International Exhibition a cabinet designed for Collinson and Lock, which was bought by the Commissioners of the Great Exhibition and finally found its way into the South Kensington Museum. The publication in 1872 of a large catalogue of designs by Collinson and Lock (mostly the work of Collcutt, although J. Moyr Smith, the author of *Ornamental Interiors* (1887) later claimed some credit for them) gave the style a wide currency in the trade, so that already by the time of the Paris Exhibition of 1878 firms such as Cooper and Holt, and Bell and Roper of London, and Henry Ogden of Manchester were copying it precisely. By 1880 its influence appears in the catalogues of mass-production firms such as Hewetson and Milner, Smee, and Lucraft.

In Collcutt's hands the style, though following Talbert in the emphasis on straight lines and the use of coved cornices and painted panels, was elaborated in a far more fanciful and light-hearted spirit, which marked a further stage in the evolution away from the medieval. A simultaneous emphasis on both verticals and horizontals, and a proliferation of shelves and divisions, diversifies the façade and provides variety by giving space for the display of knick-knacks. As always, the rapid spread of the style was accompanied by an equally rapid debasement, so that by the early 1880s it was responsible for a mass of elaborate but gimcrack cabinets, whatnots, corner cupboards (a particular favourite) and the like, with spindly supports, a profusion of small pigeonholes,

Satinwood cabinet with marquetry of coloured woods, gilt mouldings and Wedgwood plaques, made by Wright and Mansfield, 1867. Victoria & Albert Museum

curving of wood obviously involves the cutting-to-waste of good timber, while 'wanton curves' and 'meaningless scrolls' could be condemned as symbolizing the decadent extravagances which had so recently brought the French Second Empire to the ground.

During this period a parallel movement in favour of straight lines, a lighter and more varied colouring and texture, and a shunning of the deep carving of the 1860s can be traced even in the luxury productions of firms such as Jackson and Graham, and Wright and Mansfield. At its best it produced some very handsome pieces, such as a cabinet by Wright and Mansfield which won the highest awards at the Paris Exhibition of 1867 and was purchased for the South Kensington Museum for £800. Judging from contemporary descriptions, the elaborate inlaid furniture produced by Jackson and Graham in the early 1870s for Alfred Morrison's palace at 16 Carlton House Terrace, to the designs of Owen Jones (1809–74), must have reflected the same trend. The 1870s also saw the production of furniture designed by Norman Shaw for Lascelles and Co. Unfortunately, in the absence of surviving photographs or specimens, the wildly conflicting opinions of contemporary critics provide no clear picture of its style.

THE ANGLO-JAPANESE STYLE

Owing to the absence of furniture in the European sense in the traditional Japanese home, the revolutionary influence on Victorian designs of the displays of Japanese craftsmanship at the International Exhibitions of 1862 (London) and 1867 (Paris), following the opening-up of Japan by the West, had rather less effect in the field of furniture design than in those, for example, of wallpapers, textiles, or book illustration. Nevertheless, the impact of the new culture – providing, as it did, a heaven-sent stimulus to jaded designers in search of some authentic historical style that had not already been copied *ad nauseam* – was sufficient to inspire a vogue for so-called 'Anglo-Japanese' furniture in the 1870s and 1880s.

The first enthusiast was E. W. Godwin (1833–86), the architect and stage designer and associate of Whistler and Ellen Terry. He is said to have decorated his own house in the Japanese manner as early as 1862, and was certainly designing furniture showing a strong Japanese influence by the late 1860s. An illustrated catalogue issued by William Watt in 1877 contained many examples of his work and did much to familiarize the general public and the trade with his particular style. His best pieces, such as two fine cabinets in the Victoria and Albert Museum and a collection of furniture belonging to the Bristol Art Gallery, show a remarkable capacity for translating into European terms, and into the scale of full-size furniture, the asymmetrical elegance, the attenuated supports, and in particular the subtle three-dimensional interplay of void and solid, which are the main characteristics of the Japanese lacquer boxes and cabinets which were then being imported in large quantities. To these he added certain personal mannerisms of his own, such as the use of elbow-like struts, square in section but rounded at the angle, which serve no function but to span the spaces between the component parts of a cabinet or sideboard and thus draw the whole composition together.

Inevitably the trade version of Godwin's style, worked out in the 1880s by hack designers, produced some deplorable furniture, in which the Japanese inspiration was limited to such obvious tricks as imitation bamboo legs, and asymmetrical fretwork panels. However, a few of the better professional designers managed to design some quite pleasing pieces by grafting certain Japanese motifs on to the Talbert–Collcutt style. The most successful of these was H. W. Batley, who designed some very elaborate furniture for James Shoolbred and for Henry Ogden of Manchester. It is possible, also, that some of the 'Anglo-Japanese' furniture produced by the short-lived 'Art Furnishers' Alliance', founded in 1880 by Christopher Dresser (1834–1904), the indefatigable but eccentric designer and publicist (he was for a time Art Editor of the *Furniture Gazette* in the 1880s), may have been of interest, for Dresser had a real understanding of Japan, which he visited officially in 1876; but the only two surviving examples are too unimportant to justify an opinion.

This Anglo-Japanese vogue was accompanied in the 1880s by a revival of interest in other exotic styles, such as the Indian, Persian, and Moorish, as a result of which such features as 'Anglo-Arab lounges' and 'Hindoo smokerooms' became popular, particularly in clubs and hotels. However, this fashion was largely met by the importation and adaptation of genuine Oriental examples (Egyptian mushrabiya panels, Chinese embroidered screens, Indian mother-of-pearl and ivory tables, and the like) by firms such as Liberty's, rather than by Western manufacturers, and no serious English designers seem to have been influenced by it.

THE ARTS AND CRAFTS MOVEMENT

Late Victorian furniture design – indeed, the late Victorian decorative arts generally – was dominated by the birth of what has come to be known generically as the 'Arts and Crafts movement' (i.e. the Century Guild, 1882; the Art Workers' Guild, 1883; the Arts and Crafts Exhibition Society, 1888; the Guild of Handicraft, 1888; the Home Arts and Industries

Far right Cabinet on stand inlaid with ivory, probably designed by Ernest Gimson for Kenton & Co., *c.* 1890. Christie, Manson & Woods

Cabinet stamped Gillows 16649, made of oak inlaid with mother-of-pearl and marquetry, *c.* 1890

Association, 1889; the Wood Handicraft Society, 1892; and many others). In fact, during the last dozen years or so of the Victorian era no furniture of interest was designed outside its orbit.

In these its initial stages the movement gave rise to a bewildering variety of different styles of furniture, and it would be quite wrong to suppose that its productions were in the main limited to that particular type of austere and undecorated cottage-style joinery which, as we have already seen, had been practised by Philip Webb in the 1860s, and which has come to be associated with the Arts and Crafts movement during the twentieth century and particularly with its important Cotswold offshoot. Indeed, two equally strong tendencies were pulling in exactly contrary directions.

In the first place the movement fostered a revival of interest in the styles and craftsmanship of the eighteenth-century English cabinet makers, partly no doubt as a natural reaction against the disrepute in which they had been held by the medievalists of the 1860s, partly as a corollary to the renewed interest in eighteenth-century architecture stemming from the Queen Anne revival, and partly in continuation of that general movement towards greater lightness and elegance of detail which we have already noted in the work of both Collcutt and Godwin. In the second place, the move away from austere joinery was stimulated by the natural temptation for furniture designers to put into practice the movement's beliefs about the need for greater co-operation between the various crafts, by calling in workers in pewter, ivory, brass, stained glass, leather, and so on to adorn the efforts of the carpenter and cabinet maker.

These contrasting tendencies can be seen very clearly in almost all the furniture shown at the various Arts and Crafts Exhibitions (1888, 1889, 1890, 1893, 1896, 1899). They are certainly evident in the Morris furniture for though almost all designed by George Jack (1855–1932), Philip Webb's closest pupil, it bore little resemblance to the latter's solid-wood joinery. Most of it consisted of florid and very expensive walnut and mahogany pieces, covered all over with elaborate floral marquetry and inlay. Two particular pieces have survived in several versions, namely a free-standing escritoire and a handsome glass-fronted bookcase. The latter, as also an elegant circular mahogany tea table with shaped legs, are entirely urban pieces and as far removed as possible from any Gothic or medieval influence. The same is true of some curious furniture which the firm produced at this date to the designs of W. A. S. Benson (1854–1924), the metal worker, in which he incorporated elaborate metal panel frames, locks, handles, and hinges.

Curiously enough, it remained for Ford Madox Brown (1821–93) – now no longer associated with the Morris firm – to produce the type of furniture which would presumably have accorded better with Morris's philosophical views than did Jack's expensive projects. In 1890 he exhibited a 'Cheap Chest of Drawers for a Workman or Cottager' which created a great deal of interest. Judging from a contemporary photograph, the piece was so far in advance of its times that it could easily have passed for an example of utility design in World War II – even to the use of sunk finger holes instead of drawer handles.

The furniture of the short-lived association of

architect-designers known as Kenton and Co. (named after a street near its Bloomsbury workshop), which lasted for eighteen months in 1890–1 and exhibited at the Arts and Crafts Exhibition of 1890, throws these contradictory tendencies within the movement into even sharper relief. Reginald Blomfield (1856–1942) and Mervyn Macartney (1853–1932) used the workshop to produce eclectic walnut and mahogany pieces in adaptations of eighteenth-century styles. (R. S. Lorimer produced some similar designs at the very end of the century.) Ernest Gimson's designs (apart from some turned ash chairs which he made himself by the traditional methods which he had learnt from a Herefordshire chair turner in 1888, and one or two Windsor-type examples) were entirely original, and clearly adumbrated that combination of angularity and elegance and of austere outlines and elaborate surface decoration which he later developed so successfully in the Cotswolds. On the other hand, Sidney Barnsley's solid pieces in unstained oak acknowledge a direct debt to Philip Webb and clearly anticipated the more unsophisticated and rustic side of the Cotswold movement. The same is true of W. R. Lethaby's (1857–1931) essays in the use of a coarse type of floral marquetry using unstained woods, though, as if to emphasize the confusion of styles, Lethaby was simultaneously designing in 1890 some entirely dissimilar rosewood and mahogany drawing-room furniture in a modified Chippendale manner, executed by Marsh, Jones, and Cribb of Leeds.

When we come to consider the furniture designed by other pioneers of the Arts and Crafts movement, the picture is even more complex. On the one hand, each tended to strike out in his own individual direction, uninhibited by the existence of any accepted norms. On the other hand, the very frequency of the Arts and Crafts exhibitions, and in particular the extent to which the illustrated journals immediately

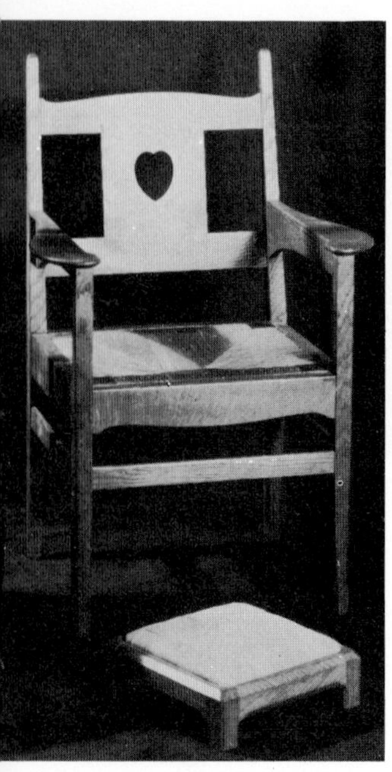

published photographs of every interesting piece as it appeared, made it quite impossible to design in isolation. As a result, the years between 1888 and 1901 witnessed a most complicated pooling of ideas and interplay of influence and counterinfluence which would require a large volume to unravel. For example, a characteristic square-cut tapering leg with an enlarged foot, first used by Mackmurdo in the 1880s, was taken up by Voysey in the 1890s; the latter's weakness for fanciful spreading hinges was immediately copied by C. R. Ashbee (1863–1942); Ashbee's use of thonged leather was plagiarized by Baillie Scott and Wickham Jarvis – and so the list could continue. In fact, so interwoven are the various strands that it is difficult to date precisely, and to pin down initial responsibility for, the introduction of even the most emphatic mannerisms of the period, such as the addition of elongated finials to the corners of cupboards and sideboards (probably first used by Walter Cave on a piano exhibited in 1893) or the decoration of chair backs with cut-out heart shapes (almost certainly due to Voysey).

Although a painstaking examination of the huge mass of contemporary periodical literature of these years is an indispensable prerequisite to any definitive unravelling of these developments, the story can only become clearer as more of the key pieces of the period are unearthed. Many have unhappily disappeared for ever, but others undoubtedly survive, as yet unrecognized and awaiting discovery by enterprising collectors. Century Guild furniture, for example, which was designed by A. H. Mackmurdo (1851–1942), is known by a small group of pieces in the William Morris Gallery at Walthamstow, and yet much more must surely survive, for a good deal was sold by Wilkinson's of Old Bond Street in the late 1880s. Examples of the work of C. R. Ashbee's Guild of Handicraft are even scarcer. Contemporary photographs exist, however, of many more examples, and it is inconceivable that they have all disappeared.

Above Oak chair with a rush seat and stool by C. F. A. Voysey

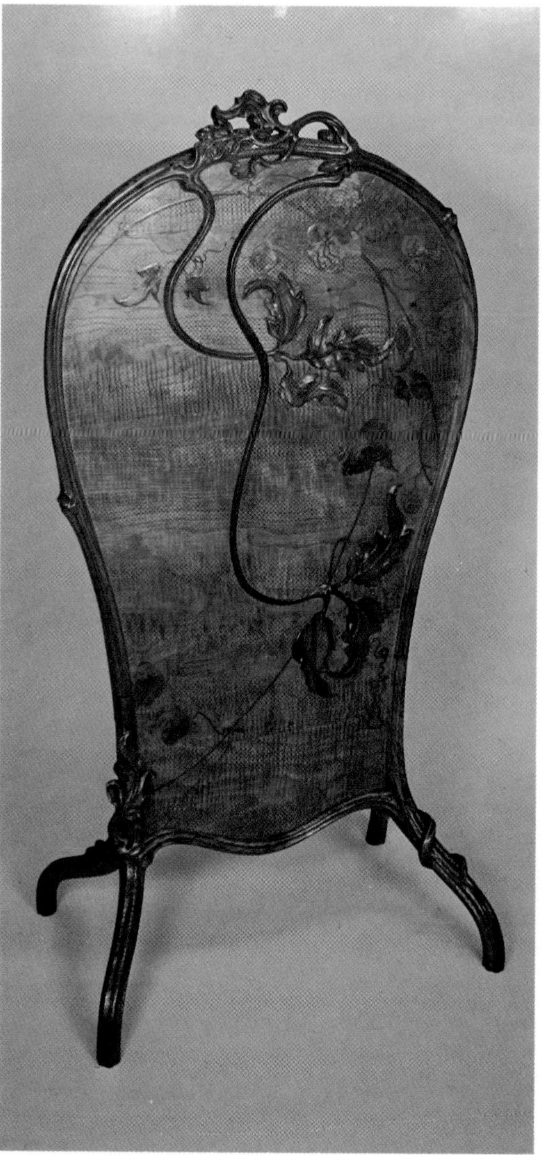

Right Ash fire-screen by Emile Gallé, 1885–1900. Bethnal Green Museum

C. F. A. Voysey (1857–1941) is rather easier, and a fair amount of his furniture has already been located. It is unlikely that many more of his elaborate – and often eccentric – individual pieces have survived untraced, but many examples of the several styles of chair which he designed for standard production must still be in use. Furniture by Charles Rennie Mackintosh (1868–1928), the Glasgow architect, is in a different category, for although considerable quantities of it survive it is almost all concentrated in the hands of the Glasgow School of Art and the Glasgow City Corporation, and therefore unavailable to the private collector. It has been fully documented in Thomas Howarth's *Charles Rennie Mackintosh and the Modern Movement* (London, 1952). There should be considerable scope for pioneer collecting in the early furniture of M. H. Baillie Scott (1865–1945), for though a number of his Edwardian pieces have survived, notably in Switzerland, nothing of his work in the Isle of Man (1887–1900) has been traced. Minor figures of the movement such as Edgar Wood, Charles Spooner, Wickham Jarvis, and Walter Cave, all of whom designed interesting if not startlingly original furniture in the last years of the century, await the attention of both research workers and collectors. Many photographs of their work exist in contemporary periodicals.

If so many different crosscurrents are discernible among the furniture of the leading late Victorian designers, it is not surprising that the changes of fashion in the run-of-the-mill trade furniture produced during the 1890s should be even more difficult to chart. The days when the trade could afford to ignore the existence of the reformers were now long past, and Arts and Crafts developments were recorded as a matter of course – and usually respectfully – in the various trade periodicals. Indeed, in 1893 the firms of Gillow, Howard and Sons, and Collinson and Lock participated in force at the Arts and Crafts Exhibition, though for some reason this experiment was not repeated.

The direct influence of the movement on the trade seems to have operated at two quite different levels. In the first place, a certain number of hack designers simply added to their repertory of styles some of the more obvious mannerisms of the Arts and Crafts designers and evolved from them a bastard concoction which they christened the 'Quaint Style'. This first appeared in 1891, and became more monstrous as the century ended, especially after 1893, when the so easily aped and misunderstood extravagances of Parisian 'Art Nouveau' were added to the mixture.

On an entirely different level was the furniture produced at the very turn of the century by a few firms, such as Heal and Son, the Bath cabinet makers, J. S. Henry, and Wylie and Lockhead, which had taken the trouble to assimilate the basic principles of the Arts and Crafts movement. Though the full fruits of this important development fall properly outside the Victorian era, some of the exhibits at the Paris Exhibition of 1900 and the Glasgow Exhibition of 1901 already herald the change.

SMALLER FURNITURE OF ALL PERIODS

A fairly wide interpretation has been given here to the term 'small furniture'. It includes, in general, those smaller pieces which are not dealt with elsewhere in this section, but for which entries are to be found in the glossary (e.g. canterbury, cellaret). It has also been assumed that readers will be familiar with the main developments of English furniture styles, to which smaller furniture, as well as the larger, conformed; with the warning that 'country' furniture might continue to be made in a style which had passed out of fashion, perhaps long previously, in London and the chief provincial towns.

The collection of small pieces of furniture can be a most fascinating pastime, not only for obvious financial reasons but also because they are a constant delight to the eye, and – a point of special weight in these days when living room is not so spacious as in times gone by – because they can be frequently used as their original makers and owners intended.

The study of the evolution of smaller articles of furniture can also be a study of social history; for they portray, as Horace Walpole wrote of the furniture in Hogarth's pictures, 'the history of the manners of the age'. One can see how they came into use as the rooms of houses began to take on their separate character and as new conventions established themselves in society. Note, for example, how at the end of the seventeenth century the two new fashions of tea drinking and displaying china produced a whole range of small pieces, among which can be included on the one hand, tea boards, kettle stands, and caddies, and, on the other, china stands, brackets, and shelves. With the coming of home manufacture of mirror glass, the development of special processes of decoration such as Tunbridge ware and straw work and the introduction of new materials like Clay's papier mâché, many new articles came into production or new forms and models of decoration were given to older ones. The great diversity of small pieces in Georgian dining rooms tells its own story of the importance placed by the upper classes in those days on eating and drinking.

With regard to the furniture which is described hereunder, one might be tempted to write, as did Sheraton in his *Cabinet Dictionary*, that 'the reader will find some terms which he will probably judge too simple in their nature to justify their insertion'. One feels, however, that this apology is unnecessary; the simplest articles are often the most useful, and their names, though no doubt very familiar, do not give what is, after all, the intention of this section, viz. their history and development. It might be added, in conclusion, that Sheraton's own period delighted in small furniture which combined, to a greater degree than at any other time, usefulness with extreme delicacy of appearance.

Detail of an English writing cabinet, Japanned red and gold on a pine carcase, *c.* 1730. Victoria & Albert Museum

European Lacquer Furniture

Great cabinets, bureaux, console tables, day beds, and chairs of green, vermilion, or jet-black lacquer added the final touch of opulent magnificence to many a late seventeenth- or early eighteenth-century salon. 'What can be more surprising than to have our chambers overlaid with varnish more glossy and reflecting than polisht marble?' asked Stalker and Parker, the authors of the first English *Treatise of Japaning and Varnishing*, in 1688. 'No amorous nymph need entertain a dialogue with her Glass, or Narcissus retire to a fountain to survey his charming countenance when the whole house is one entire speculum.' They even went so far as to declare that 'the glory of one country, Japan alone, has exceeded in beauty all the pride of the Vatican at this time and the Pantheon heretofore'. Lacquer had already been introduced into Europe, and soon there was hardly a great house in England, France, Germany, or Italy that could not boast a few pieces of lacquered furniture, if not whole rooms 'overlaid with varnish more glossy and reflecting than polisht marble'. Many such works in lacquer have survived to our own day, mellowed but hardly decayed by time, and in their shining surfaces, between the exotic birds and wispy trees, we may still catch a reflection of the brilliant world of which they were created.

Before proceeding to an account of how and when lacquer was used for the embellishment of European furniture a few words must be said about the substance of this brilliant paint or varnish. Although intended to imitate Oriental lacquer (*see* Chinese and Japanese Furniture), European lacquer was, perforce, made in a different way. Chinese and Japanese craftsmen derived the lac, the basic constituent of the varnish, from the resin of a tree, the *Rhus vernicifera*, and applied it to the wood they wished to decorate in many layers, each of which was allowed to dry before the next was applied. The surface was then highly polished and decorated with designs in gold leaf. As the resin from which true lac was obtained was unavailable in Europe and could not satisfactorily be imported from the East, craftsmen had to resort to other means to achieve the same effect, and they propounded a wide variety of different receipts. Filippo Bonanni, an Italian who wrote a treatise on lacquering in 1720, listed some ten different methods employed by English, French, German, Italian, and Polish craftsmen. Usually the wood was prepared with a mixture of whitening and size and then treated with numerous coats of a varnish composed of gum lac, seed lac, or shell lac, different preparations of the resin broken off the twigs of the tree on which it is deposited by an insect, the *coccus lacca*, and dissolved in spirits of wine. The decorations were outlined in gold size, built up with a composition made of gum arabic and sawdust, coloured, polished, and gilt with metal dust. The surface was burnished with a dog's tooth or an agate pebble. Such methods could not, of course, produce a substance as hard and glittering as Oriental lacquer, but as experiment succeeded experiment, European craftsmen gradually improved their technique and were eventually able to produce a varnish of great beauty. Some, indeed, thought they had improved upon their models and Voltaire rhapsodized over

> . . . les cabinets où Martin
> A surpassé l'art de la Chine.

By the irony of chance, time has dealt more kindly with these European imitations than with Oriental lacquer of the same period, much of which has now faded to a drab and unappetizing hue.

IMPORTATIONS OF ORIENTAL LACQUER

Although considerable quantities of Oriental porcelain had been brought to Europe before the end of the sixteenth century, importations of Chinese and Japanese lacquer had been on a much more modest scale. Two varnished boxes which were in the collection of the Queen of France in 1524 and a 'purple box of Chine' which the Emperor sent from Aachen to Elizabeth I in 1602, may have been lacquered, but we cannot be sure. There is no doubt, however, of the attention which Oriental lacquer held for sixteenth-century travellers to the East. 'The fayrest workemanshippe thereof cometh from China,' wrote Van Linschoten in 1598, in the account of his voyage. And he went on to praise the 'Desks, Targets, Tables, Cubbordes, Boxes, and a thousand such like things, that are all covered and wrought with Lac of all colours and fashions'. By 1610, indeed, one Jacques l'Hermite had sharpened his taste for lacquer to such a degree that he was able to despise a consignment sent to Holland from Bantam, declaring that it was far inferior to that which came from Japan.

Lacquer was imported into Europe in ever-increasing quantities during the first half of the seventeenth century. An inventory of 'goodes and household stuffe' belonging to the Earl of Northampton in 1614 refers to a 'China guilt cabinette upon a frame', and in the same year the East India Company's ship *Clove* returned to London, after the first English voyage to Japan, loaded with a cargo of Japanese wares which included 'Scritoires, Trunkes, Beoubes (screens), Cupps and Dishes of all sorts and of a most excellent varnish'. Lest the market should be flooded, these objects – the first of their kind to reach England in quantity – were sold off slowly to inflate their commercial value. This device had such good effect that 'small trunkes or chests of Japan guilded and inlaid with mother of pearle having sundry drawers and boxes' which fetched £4 5*s* and £5 in 1614 commanded as much as £17 apiece four years later. Lacquer was also popular in France during this period. By 1649 Mazarin had three Chinese cabinets in his collection of orientalia, besides many pieces of Eastern porcelain and embroidery, and he acquired more lacquer furniture in the next few years.

Mid-seventeenth-century travellers to China, whose *Voyages* were translated into many languages and read throughout Europe, were full of admiration for the lacquer they had seen in Peking and elsewhere. John Nieuhoff, the steward to the abortive Dutch embassy to the Emperor of China in 1655, described the process by which it was made, enlarging on the beauty and utility of lacquer: 'There is also in divers places throughout the whole Empire, a certain sort of Lime which they press from the Bark of a Tree, being tough and sticking like Pitch; of this, which I suppose I may call a Gum, they make a certain sort of Paint wherewith they colour all their Ships, Houses, and Household-stuff, which makes them shine like Glass; and this is the reason that the houses in China, and in the Isle of *Japon*, glister and shine so bright, that they dazzle the eyes of such as behold them. For this paint lays a shining colour upon Wood, which is so beautiful and lasting, that they use no Table-cloaths at their Meals; for if they spill any grease, or other liquor upon the Table, it is easily rubbed off with a little fair water, without loss or damage of colour.'

In addition to the painted lacquer – of the type described by Nieuhoff – incised Coromandel lacquer was extensively imported into Europe in the seventeenth century, mainly from the Dutch trading station at Bantam in the Malay peninsula, whence it derived the name 'Bantam work'. Cabinets and vast six-fold Coromandel screens were brought to Europe but enjoyed a somewhat wavering fashion, perhaps on account of their gaudy, if not garish, colour schemes, which have only now faded to an attractively subdued tone (fragments of Coromandel lacquer preserved inside cabinets give one an idea of its startling pristine colours). In 1688 Stalker and Parker, who were certainly prejudiced in favour of painted lacquer, declared that Bantam ware was 'almost obsolete and out of fashion' in England. 'No person is fond of it, or gives it house-room', they scornfully remarked, 'except some who have made new Cabinets out of old Skreens. And from that large old piece, by the help of a Joyner, made little ones . . . torn and hacked to joint a new fancie . . . the finest hodgpodg and medly of Men and Trees turned topsie turvie.' Without any regard for the figures of the design, strips of Coromandel were used in this way to face the drawers of cabinets or to frame looking glasses, like that which is still to be seen at Ham House. Nevertheless, Coromandel screens retained their popularity in some circles, and the Duke of Marlborough included one among the furniture he took with him on his campaigns. In Germany and Holland the vogue for Coromandel seems to have been steadier and of longer duration than in England.

THE EARLIEST EUROPEAN LACQUER

The first attempts to imitate Oriental lacquer in Europe were made in the early seventeenth century. Marie de' Medici is known to have employed a skilful cabinet maker named Étienne Sager to make 'with lacquer gum and gold decoration in the manner of the same country (China), cabinets, chests, boxes, panelling, ornaments for churches, chaplets, and other small articles of Chinese goods'. She also established a vendor of Oriental wares in the Louvre, and this shop would, no doubt, have contained articles of European lacquer as well. At about the same time imitations of lacquer were produced in Italy, and when William Smith wrote to Lord Arundell from Rome in 1616 he was able to list among his many accomplishments that he had 'been emploied for the Cardinalles and other Princes of these parts, in workes after the China fashion wch. is much affected heere'. Imitations were also made in England, as is shown by the inventory of furniture belonging to the 1st Earl of Northampton on his death in 1614. In addition to a few genuine Oriental articles, Lord Northampton owned several examples of 'china worke' (i.e. European lacquer). He had, for instance, a 'large square China worke table and frame black varnish and gold', a 'small table of China worke in gold and colours with flies and wormes upon a table suteable', and a 'Field bedstead of China worke blacke and silver branches with silver with the Armes of the Earl of Northampton upon the head piece'. These must have been European and were perhaps of English lacquer. Next year, in 1615, Lady Arundell was matching curtains to her 'bedde of Japan' which may also have been of English make. Unfortunately, none of these objects has survived, but a small group of English lacquer pieces dating from the second decade of the seventeenth century may give us some indication of what they were like. These consist of a ballot box dated 1619, in the possession of the Saddlers' Company at London, a cabinet and a box of twelve roundels in the Victoria and Albert Museum. All are of oak painted in gold and silver with a curious *mélange* of European and Eastern motifs on a thickly varnished black ground. Similar lacquer-work, though of somewhat higher quality, was also produced in Holland. The fashion for imitation lacquer appeared in Denmark in the 1620s, when a remarkable room in Rosenborg Castle at Copenhagen was decorated with panels of dark green and gold lacquer, set in imitation tortoiseshell frames and painted by Simon Clause with views of fantastic buildings and fragile little junks.

Although European craftsmen had greatly improved the technique of lacquering by the middle of the seventeenth century, they had not yet succeeded in producing wares which could vie with the genuine Oriental articles. Importations of chests and screens from China and Japan continued unabated. But Eastern cabinet makers did not produce all the

Oak cabinet decorated in arabesque and figures in Oriental costume in gold and silver on a black ground, *c.* 1620. Victoria & Albert Museum

Panel of lacquer painted by Simon Clause, in the Rosenborg Castle, Copenhagen

objects of furniture deemed necessary for a European house, and merchants therefore sent out designs of various objects to be copied in the East. Here again there was a difficulty; for although Eastern craftsmen excelled in lacquer decoration, their cabinet making was found to be of surprisingly poor quality. As Captain William Dampier remarked in 1688, 'The Joyners of this country (China) may not compare their work with that which the Europeans make; and in laying on the Lack upon good or fine joyned work, they frequently spoil the joynts, edges, or corners of Drawers and Cabinets: Besides, our fashion of Utensils differ mightily from theirs, and for that reason Captain Pool, in his second voyage to the Country, brought an ingenious Joyner with him to make fashionable Commodities to be lackered here, as also Deal boards. . . .' Very few such European carpenters seem to have been taken out to China, but unpainted furniture was occasionally shipped from Europe to the East to be lacquered and returned home for sale. This costly procedure was not practised for long, however, as European lacquerers had attained sufficient skill in their medium to satisfy all but the most fastidious connoisseurs before the end of the seventeenth century.

The great age of European lacquer begins in the late seventeenth century. French, English, Dutch, German, and Italian craftsmen had discovered a means of imitating the fine hard polish of the Oriental substance; they had, moreover, learned to decorate it in a freer style with designs which expressed the European's strange vision of the infinitely remote and exotic lands of the East. At Versailles and in some of the greater English country mansions whole rooms were lined with lacquer panels, of European or Oriental origin, and great Chinese, or Chinese-style, cabinets mounted on ponderous gilt baroque stands became an essential feature in the furnishing of any truly grand house. Towards the end of the century the art of lacquering was also practised by amateurs in France and England, where many a young lady spent her leisure hours 'japanning' any piece of furniture – large or small – on which she could lay her hands. Changing in style with the times, lacquer furniture maintained a fluctuating popularity until after the end of the eighteenth century. During this period lacquer was produced in England, France, Germany, Holland, and Italy, and the furniture made in each of these countries must be considered separately.

ENGLISH LACQUER

Great square cabinets were probably the most popular objects of Oriental lacquer to be imported into England in the late seventeenth century and seem to have been the most widely imitated. Such cabinets have two doors, with elaborate metal hinges and lock guards, which open to reveal numerous small drawers and sometimes a central cupboard. Oriental examples can be recognized not only by the style of their gilt decorations but also by their metalwork. In China such cabinets stood on the floor or on simple hardwood tables, but in England they were mounted on grandiose frames intended to set off their importance and make them harmonize with the other furniture of the rooms in which they were kept. The cabinets themselves usually had black or imitation tortoiseshell backgrounds, but red ones were also made, especially for export to Spain and Portugal, where this colour was preferred. England was indeed famous for its red lacquer, which Bonanni, in 1720, declared to be of a colour more beautiful than coral – 'si bello che vince il colore di corallo'.

The stands for these cabinets were either gilt or, more usually, silvered and varnished so that they appeared to be gilt (it seems probable that most of the surviving silver stands were originally varnished in this manner). In the 1660s and 1670s the stands normally had four legs, sometimes crowned with *putti* or blackamoors, joined by aprons which were richly carved with figures, and swags of fruit and flowers, amid a profusion of swirling baroque scrolls. Towards the end of the century the design changed and stands were often made with three or four legs along the front connected by aprons carved in a lighter style. These stands usually had stretchers which were provided with round plates on which vases of Oriental porcelain might be placed. The top of the cabinet was sometimes enriched with a cresting carved in the same style as the stand, but was more often left free to serve as a table for more Oriental vases. In the second decade of the eighteenth century the heavy baroque stand went out of fashion and was replaced by a lighter and more elegant frame with cabriole legs, but these, alas, were seldom able to support the weight of the cabinets, and relatively few have survived. At about the same time a few craftsmen departed from the traditional shape of the cabinet itself, giving it a shallow domed top.

When John Evelyn visited Mr Bohun in 1682, he noted that his 'whole house is a cabinet of all elegancies, especially Indian; in the hall are contrivances of Japan skreens instead of wainscot. . . . The landskips of these skreens represent the manner of living and Country of the Chinese.' Many other such rooms, including those at Burghley House, Hampton Court Palace, and Chatsworth, are mentioned in diaries of the period. One such room has actually survived at Drayton in Northamptonshire. It is a small closet off the State Bedroom which has been lined with ten panels cut from a Chinese Coromandel screen.

Lacquer was at this date used for decorating nearly all articles of household furniture. In 1697 a company of 'The Patentees for Lacquering after the manner of Japan' (founded in 1694) was offering for sale 'Cabinets, secretaires, tables, stands, looking-

Green lacquer commode with concave front, mid-18th century. Mallett & Son, London

One of a pair of lacquer commodes made for Uppark, Sussex, probably designed by John Linnell. Mallet & Son, London

glasses, tea-tables and chimney pieces'. Other lacquer objects made at the same time included chests of drawers, corner cupboards, clock cases, day beds, chairs, and small articles for the dressing or writing table. These pieces were usually made of deal, oak, or pear-tree wood on patterns which were identical with those of contemporary walnut furniture. The lacquer grounds were of various colours: black, vermilion, tortoiseshell, dark green (particularly popular for clock cases), yellow or blue, and the gilt decorations represented a wide variety of fanciful scenes copied from genuine Oriental objects, taken from Stalker and Parker's treatise or invented by the craftsman. Stalker and Parker claimed to have derived their designs from Oriental cabinets, somewhat ingenuously confessing that they had, perhaps, 'helped them a little in their proportions where they were lame or defective, and made them more pleasant, yet altogether as Antick'. In the later 1720s *chinoiserie* decorations suffered a temporary eclipse and were replaced by flowers painted in naturalistic colours on a light ground.

In the late seventeenth century much lacquering, or 'japanning' as it was called, was executed by amateurs who applied themselves to the difficult art with a will, and the principal book on the subject, Stalker and Parker's *Treatise of Japaning and Varnishing*, seems to have been designed mainly for a public of amateurs. By the 1680s the art of lacquering had taken its place among the genteel occupations suitable for young ladies, and in 1689 Edmund Verney permitted his daughter to take this extra subject at school, telling her: 'I find you have a desire to learn to Japan, as you call it, and I approve of it; and so I shall of anything that is good and virtuous, therefore learn in God's name all Good Things, and I will willingly be at the charge so far as I am able – though they come from Jappan and from never so farr and Looke of an Indian Hue and colour, for I admire all accomplishments that will render you considerable and Lovely in the sight of God and man. . . .' That the art of lacquering – like water-colour painting in a later age – rendered young ladies lovely in the sight of man is, perhaps, confirmed by Dryden's lines to Clarinda (1687) in which he remarks that:

> Sometimes you curious *Landskips* represent
> And arch 'em o'er with gilded *Firmament*:
> Then in *Japan* some *rural Cottage* paint.

Nothing was sacred to these eager japanners, who seized on any object that could be decorated with Chinese figures. Sometimes they may have applied themselves to specially prepared furniture, but often they were content to lacquer ordinary walnut pieces. Nor was this pastime reserved for the young. Mrs Pendarves (later Mrs Delany) declared in 1729: 'Lady Sun[derland] is very busy about japanning: I will perfect myself in the art against I make you [Mrs Anne Granville] a visit, and bring materials with me.'

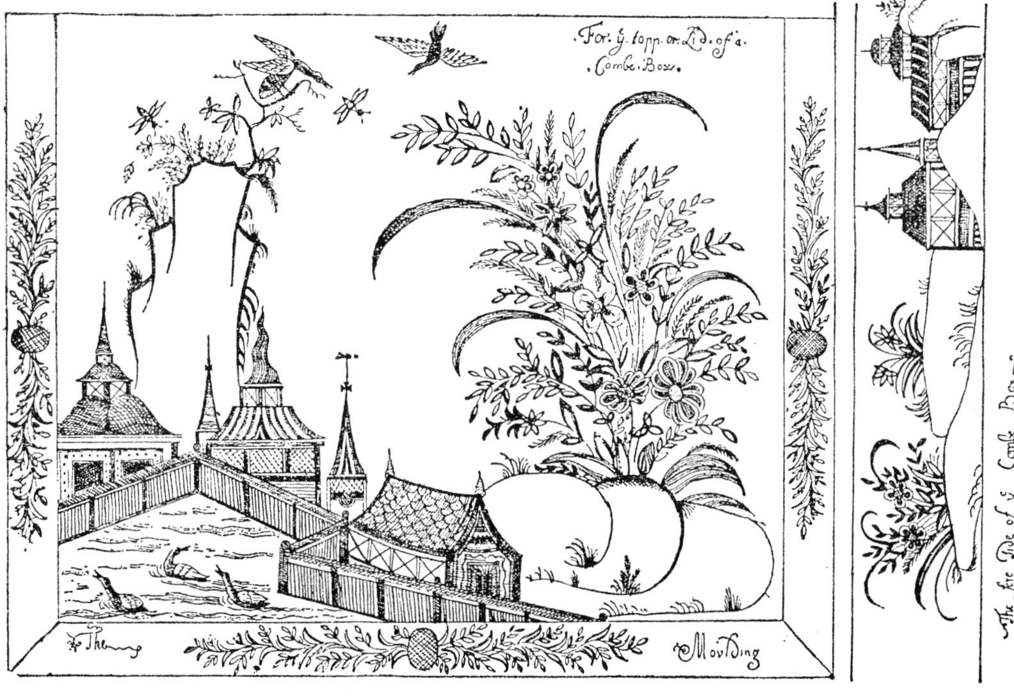

Design for a comb box from Stalker and Parkers' Treatise of Japaning and Varnishing, *1688*

'Everyone is mad about Japan work,' she later remarked. 'I hope to be a dab at it. . . .' Even the Prime Minister's wife, Lady Walpole, applied herself to the art and it was to her that John Taylor dedicated his book: *The Method of Learning to draw in perspective. . . . Likewise a new and Curious Method of Japanning . . . so as to imitate China and to make black or gilt Japan-ware as Beautiful and Light as any brought from the East Indies* (1732). Horace Walpole preserved an example of his mother's handiwork – a cabinet – at Strawberry Hill.

Amateur japanners, it may be guessed, kept alive the vogue for lacquer furniture which, after a temporary eclipse, returned to fashion in the late 1740s. In 1749 Mrs Montagu – the Queen of the Blues – remarked that 'sick of Grecian elegance and symmetry, or Gothic grandeur and magnificence, we must all seek the barbarous gaudy *gout* of the Chinese. . . . You will wonder I should condemn a taste I have complied with, but in trifles I shall always conform to the fashion.' Accordingly, three years later she ordered a suite of japanned furniture, in full conformity with the *chinoiserie* taste of the moment, from Mr (presumably William) Linnell; some of it is now at Came House, Dorset. This revived fashion for *chinoiserie* did not, however, escape the attention of critics, who poked merciless fun at the Mandarins and Mandarinesses of England. One of them, an anonymous writer in *The Connoisseur* (1755), gave a graphic description of a fop's dressing table: 'But the toilet most excited my admiration; where I found everything was intended to be agreeable to the Chinese taste. A looking-glass, inclosed in a whimsical frame of Chinese paling, stood upon a Japan table, over which was spread a coverlid of the finest Chints. I could not but observe a number of boxes of different sizes, which were all of them Japan, and lay regularly disposed on the table. I had the curiosity to examine the contents of several: in one I found lip-salve, in another a roll of pig-tail, and in another the ladies black sticking plaister. . . .'

Many of the mid-eighteenth-century examples of English lacquer furniture were wholly designed in the Chinese taste, with fretwork doors and square legs carved with a similar fretted pattern. The cabinet and table made by Linnell for Mrs Montagu were in this style. Thomas Chippendale intended many of his designs for *chinoiserie* furniture, especially the standing shelves designed for the display of Chinese porcelain, to be embellished with japanned decorations, but furniture in the current 'French' style, notably commodes and bureaux, were also decorated with panels of European or Oriental lacquer. A commode in the possession of the Shaftesbury Estates Company has a veneer of Chinese lacquer on the front and is painted with English japan on the top and sides. Many smaller articles, like those on the fop's dressing table, were prettily lacquered with gay Oriental figures. Snuffboxes and other trifles in lacquer were produced by John Taylor at Birmingham, who seems to have made a fortune out of this trade.

After about 1765 the fashion for lacquer furniture began to decline in England, though the art of japanning remained a popular amusement among amateurs, for whom such books were written as *The Ladies Amusement or the Whole art of Japanning made easy.* This valuable manual, illustrated with numerous plates after Pillement and others, advised its readers of the liberties which might be taken with Indian or Chinese designs, 'for in these is often seen a Butterfly supporting an Elephant, or things equally absurd'. Among amateur japanners of the late eighteenth century, the King's third daughter, Princess Elizabeth, was surely one of the most passionate and decorated two whole rooms at Frogmore, one with scarlet and gold and the other with black and gold lacquer. Perhaps it was from her that George IV acquired his fondness for *chinoiserie* which was largely responsible for the third revival in lacquer furniture towards the end of the century.

Pagoda cabinet in the manner of Thomas Chippendale, made for Uppark, Sussex, lacquered and japanned with some of the panels in Italian pietre dure. The upper drawers are mounted with carved ivory medallions of Homer and Brutus, mid-18th century. Uppark, Sussex

Although lacquer does not seem to have been used to furnish the famous Chinese drawing room at Carlton House, it was freely applied to furniture in the Sheraton and Hepplewhite styles during the last decades of the eighteenth century. In 1804 the Prince Regent sent Dr James Grant to collect lacquer and other orientalia in the Far East, and the panels with which he returned were probably among those used to adorn the furniture of the Royal Pavilion at Brighton. Other pieces of furniture at Brighton were painted with English lacquer, which also enjoyed a popular vogue, especially for the decoration of cabinets and bookcases. The design of such furniture conformed with the usual Regency patterns. Amateurs continued their labours for some time, and even as late as 1828 Mrs Arbuthnot, the Duke of Wellington's friend, could be found 'making up a japan cabinet I painted last year. . . . The cabinet is really excessively pretty.' Lacquer seems finally to have gone out of fashion in the late 1830s, but at the Great Exhibition of 1851 Messrs W. W. Eloure were showing various papier mâché 'imitations of japan work. Cabinet doors, and folding fire screens in imitation of India-Japan, ornamented with gold and inlaid with mother of pearl'.

Regency lacquer cabinet with gilt lion paw front feet, *c.* 1830. H. Blairman & Sons, London

DUTCH AND FLEMISH LACQUER

Of all European countries, Holland was perhaps the most closely connected with the trade in Oriental lacquer during the seventeenth century. Before the middle of the century Dutch merchants had, indeed, established a virtual monopoly in the export of lacquer from Japan. Nevertheless, a need seems to have been felt for a greater supply of lacquer than the trading ships could provide, and early in the century craftsmen set themselves to the imitation of lacquer in Holland. The style of their work, which was of much higher quality than contemporary English work, may be judged from a casket decorated with birds perching among flowering plants, in the Rijksmuseum. Dutch *Japanish Verlaker* – japanners – attained great skill in the second half of the century and produced some of the closest imitations of Oriental lacquer made in Europe. It has even been suggested, with some probability if no evidence, that Japanese lacquer workers were brought to Europe to school the Dutch craftsmen. Late seventeenth- and early eighteenth-century Dutch lacquer was usually somewhat sparsely decorated with *chinoiserie* designs in gold on a lustrous black ground. A good though miniature example is provided by the doll's house cupboard in the Rijksmuseum. Lacquer furniture decorated in colours on a cream or white ground was also popular in Holland. In style, Dutch lacquer furniture was similar to the walnut and marquetry pieces produced at the same time. Cabinets – whether Dutch or Oriental – which were as fashionable here as in England, seem usually to have been mounted on scroll-shaped legs which were also lacquered rather than on gilt baroque stands. In the early eighteenth century lacquer with *chinoiserie* decorations was most notably applied to large chests of drawers and wardrobes. Good examples are in the collection of Graf van Aldenburg-Bentinck at Schloss Amerongen.

Lacquer casket, early 17th century. Rijksmuseum, Amsterdam

Cabinet and stand by Gerald Dagly, c. *1700*

Spa, the watering place near Aix-la-Chapelle which was for centuries the Mecca of European hypochondriacs, was the principal centre for the production of lacquer in Flanders. A lacquer industry grew up here in the late seventeenth century and its products, known as *bois de Spa*, soon became famous throughout Europe. All manner of large and small objects from snuffboxes to corner cupboards were produced at Spa in the eighteenth century and purchased by those who came from far and wide to drink the famous medicinal waters or gamble in the scarcely less celebrated gaming rooms. *Bois de Spa* was usually decorated with gilt *chinoiserie* motifs on a black ground. Spa was, moreover, the birthplace of one of the foremost masters of European lacquer, Gerard Dagly (*fl.* 1665–1714), who, though he executed most of his work in Germany, may fitly find mention here.

Gerard Dagly was born at Spa some time before 1665 and went at a fairly early age to seek his fortune in Germany. In 1687 he was appointed *Kammerkünstler* to the Kurfürst of Brandenburg and in this capacity was principally employed in producing lacquerwork in the Chinese manner. In 1696 he lacquered four black and gold coin cabinets, one of which is at Berlin – a fine piece of work mounted on a stand with twist-turned legs on which small floral motifs are picked out in gold. Another cabinet, formerly in the Hohenzollernmuseum at Berlin, was painted with a lovely prospect of mountains on the outside of the doors and dancing Chinese figures on the inside. He also produced very elegant lacquer furniture decorated in gold on a white ground; a good example of this type of his work is, or was, in the Schloss Monbijou. Other works by Gerard Dagly are to be found in the Royal Palace at Stockholm and the museum at Brunswick. He attained wide renown in Germany, and when the Kurfürstin of Hanover sent her Prussian son-in-law a clock case she felt bound to remark that 'it comes from England but Dagly makes much better ones'. On the accession of Friedrich Wilhelm I to the Prussian throne in 1713 Dagly was among the many Court employees who were promptly dismissed. He seems to have returned to Spa. For a full account of Gerard Dagly see *The Connoisseur*, 1934, vol. XCV, pp. 14 ff.

FRENCH LACQUER.

In the earlier seventeenth century Oriental lacquer was imported into France from Portugal and it was to the Portuguese stalls at the Foire de Saint Germain that Scarron directed the connoisseur's attention for 'beaux ouvrages de vernis'. After the foundation of the French *Compagnie des Indes* in 1664 importations were considerably increased and the vogue for lacquer furniture reached a new height. The French attitude to lacquer at this date and during much of the eighteenth century was, however, somewhat unusual. Lacquer seems to have been prized more for its rarity and commercial value than for its style of decoration. Louis XIV evidently thought it in no way incongruous to have silver plaques engraved with the Labours of Hercules applied to a Chinese cabinet.

As we have already mentioned, lacquer was made in France early in the seventeenth century, though no examples of it are known to have survived. Nor is much known of the productions of 'Les Sieurs Langlois, père et fils', who, in 1691, were making 'cabinets et paravents façon de la Chine, d'une beauté singulière' with ormolu mounts which were expressly intended to make them harmonize with other pieces of furniture in the great salons. Like the English, the French occasionally sent furniture out to the East to be lacquered, and it seems probable that Mme de Sévigné's writing desk in the Musée Carnavalet at Paris, which is of a normal French pattern embellished with Oriental lacquer, is one such piece.

In 1713, or shortly after, the Flemish craftsman Jacques Dagly (1655–1728), brother of Gerard Dagly (see p. 189), settled in France and obtained a licence to 'establish . . . a factory to make varnish', but this paint seems to have been primarily intended for application to textiles. Not until some years later did French craftsmen succeed in producing lacquer of conspicuously high quality. Between 1733 and 1740 the Duc de Bourbon was maintaining at Chantilly an *atelier* where, according to a contemporary, lacquer furniture was produced in such close imitation of Chinese models that even the greatest connoisseurs had been deceived by it. Meanwhile, the brothers Martin – Guillaume (d. 1749), Étienne Simon (d. 1770), Julien (d. 1782), and Robert (*fl.* 1706–65) – had perfected the lacquer to which they gave their name, *vernis Martin*. Letters patent, issued in 1730 and renewed in 1744, granted them the exclusive monopoly of 'toutes sortes d'ouvrages en relief et dans le goût du japon ou de la Chine' for twenty years. They did not, however, confine themselves to decorations in the Chinese style, and many of the best examples of *vernis Martin* are either without any ornament or simply stippled with gold specks – like the sedan chair made for the Montmorency children and now in the Musée de Cluny at Paris. *Vernis Martin* was produced in several colours, of which the green was the most celebrated. Among the larger works undertaken by the Martins were the decorative paintings in several of the *petits appartements* at Versailles. They were also much patronized by Mme de Pompadour.

Lacquer was extensively used for the decoration of furniture in the Louis XV period, but, whether of French or Oriental make, was usually treated in a cavalier fashion. The curling tendrils of rococo mounts were allowed to clamber over it and obscure

Slope-fronted secretaire by Martin Carlin, ebony with black Japanese lacquer panels, marble top and ormolu mounts, 18th century

much of the pattern, while handles were screwed on without any regard for the figures on the design. On a chest of drawers in the Wallace Collection – the so-called Marriage coffer of Marie Antoinette – the exquisite panels of Japanese lacquer on the front and those of French lacquer at the sides are half hidden behind bronze fretwork grilles. Here the lacquer seems to have been considered purely as a precious substance which could add the final touch of opulence to a magnificent piece of furniture. The famous *ébéniste B. V. R. B.* (identified as Bernard van Risen Burgh) treated lacquer, which he very frequently used, in a much more respectful manner. But he, too, chose to emphasize the beauty of its glossy substance rather than the charm of its gilt decoration.

With the development of the Louis XVI style this attitude seems to have changed. The greater rigidity of the furniture produced in this period enabled *ébénistes* to show off panels of fine Japanese lacquer much more effectively. Indeed, objects like the secretaire by P. Garnier in the Louvre seem to have been conceived mainly as frames for exquisite panels of lacquer. Much of the furniture bought in Paris for George IV and now at Windsor Castle is of this type. French lacquer was applied to various types of furniture, but perhaps most notably to these pieces which could not easily have been veneered with Oriental lacquer. In the Victoria and Albert Museum there is an exceptionally fine harpsichord made by Pascal Taskin in Paris in 1786 and painted on the lid and sides with engaging little gilt Chinamen dancing on a puce ground.

The taste for lacquer does not seem to have survived the French Revolution. Lacquer furniture clearly had no place amid the Greek- and Egyptian-style objects of an Empire salon. It may perhaps have been used after the Restoration by those cabinet makers who reverted to the production of furniture in the Louis XVI style.

GERMAN LACQUER

As miniature versions of Versailles sprang up outside the capitals of nearly every German principality in the late seventeenth and early eighteenth centuries, so the taste of the French court spread throughout Germany. Lacquer consequently became an accepted, indeed an all but essential feature of palatial decoration. Rooms panelled from floor to ceiling in lacquer and provided with whole suites of furniture to match were installed in many a stately *Schloss* and *Residenz*. Small lacquer objects were also produced in Germany before the end of the seventeenth century, and a pattern book of the period gives designs for tobacco boxes and trays to be painted with Chinese scenes from the plates in John Nieuhoff's *Embassy*.

In the last two decades of the seventeenth century the Flemish craftsman Gerard Dagley (see p. 189) was producing exceptionally fine lacquer at Berlin. He attracted several imitators who were probably responsible for some of the pieces of lacquer furniture which were until World War II, in the Charlottenburg Palace. These included a table, a writing table, and a harpsichord decorated with little *chinoiserie* figures on a white ground – the harp-

Secretaire decorated with panels of Chinese lacquer by P. Garnier, *c.* 1770. Louvre

Black lacquer *secretaire-en-pente* stamped I Dubois, mid-18th century. Christie, Manson & Woods

sichord is mounted on a base painted with purely European floral motifs. Among Dagly's named followers was Martin Schnell, who worked with him from 1703 to 1709 and then returned to his native town of Dresden, where he produced some splendid examples of lacquerwork besides providing designs for porcelain during the subsequent three decades. Schnell is best known for his small lacquered trays – the finest of their kind – of which there are good specimens in the Residenzschloss at Dresden. He was also responsible for furniture and decorations in Schloss Pillnitz – the *Japanische Palais* – which contains one of his most notable works, an English-style fall-front secretaire.

Lacquer furniture was also made at Augsburg in the first half of the eighteenth century, and a notable example of it is provided by a clock now in the Bayerisches Nationalmuseum at Munich. The clock itself is of a baroque architectural pattern with columns at the corners, and stands on a low table. All the woodwork, including the columns, is decorated with *chinoiserie* motifs in colours on a white ground, and a painted mandarin squats on the stretcher of the stand. Another centre for the production of lacquer was Hamburg, where a very fine harpsichord was made in 1732.

Lacquer harpsichord case made at Hamburg in 1732. Kunstindustrimuseet, Oslo

One of the earliest of the several surviving German lacquer rooms was that built for the Kurfürst Lothar Franz von Schönborn in the Neue Residenz at Bamberg in about 1700. It is decorated with a series of panels of black and gold lacquer set amidst a profusion of carved swags, and contained a handsome lacquer cabinet, similar to those popular in England but without doors, set on very short legs to serve as a chest of drawers. Between 1714 and 1722 one Johann Jakob Saenger painted the magnificent lacquer room in Schloss Ludwigsburg, at Württemburg, with *chinoiserie* birds and dragons sporting in a garden which is decorated with baroque urns. In the Pagodenburg Pavilion in the Nymphenburg gardens there is a room decorated with red and black lacquer panels of 1718. The Residenz at Munich had a bedroom of about the same date which was adorned with large panels of lacquer each painted with three or four *chinoiserie* scenes placed inconsequentially one above another. At Schloss Brühl, near Cologne, there is an exceptionally attractive *Indianische Lackkabinet* painted for the Kurfürst Clemens August between 1720 and 1730 with gay, brightly coloured *chinoiserie* scenes on a cream ground. A later example of a lacquer room is that in Schloss Nymphenburg, decorated by J. Hörringer in 1764.

Frederick the Great, an admirer of Oriental lacquer (he gave his sister Amelia the Coromandel panels for a room which is still in the Neue Residenz at Bayreuth), also patronized European lacquer workers, acquiring them in much the same way as he gathered literary lions to adorn his court at Potsdam. In 1747 he commissioned Jean Alexandre Martin, the son of Robert Martin, to decorate the *Blumenkammer* – otherwise known as the *Voltaire Zimmer* – at Sanssouci: and some twenty years later he again lured him away from Paris, appointing him *vernisseur du Roy*. In 1765 Frederick commissioned another French lacquer worker, Sébastien Chevalier, to decorate an oval room in the Neuen Palais at Potsdam. He then encouraged Jean Guérin, the son-in-law of Johann Heinrich Stobwasser, who had for long been providing lacquered canes for Prussian army officers, to set up a lacquer industry at Berlin. Stobwasser himself remained at Brunswick, where he produced the many exquisite snuffboxes, canes, etc., which won him European renown. He also developed the art of lacquering on papier mâché in the English manner. As late as the 1790s the Stobwasser workshop at Brunswick was producing little lacquered objects and small pieces of furniture painted in lacquer with classical figures and motifs.

ITALIAN LACQUER

Venice was already famous for its lacquer in 1668 when Maximilien Misson remarked that, 'La Lacque de Venise est comme on sçait en réputation: il y en a à toute sorte de prix.' Unfortunately no examples dating from this early period can be identified, but a few later seventeenth-century pieces show that the Venetian craftsmen produced both black and vermilion lacquer decorated with gold *chinoiserie* subjects. A notable example of this style of work is the writing table formerly in the collection of the late Mr Arthur Spender of Venice and exhibited in the 1938 exhibition of Venetian lacquer. As in other parts of Europe, lacquer was applied to furniture of normal design, but the Venetian attempts to imitate the substance of Oriental lacquer were rather more perfunctory. The base of white wood or *cirmolo* (a type of pine from Cadore) was treated with successive layers of gesso, each of which was polished, gold paint was then applied to the raised decorations, which were generally reserved for the main surfaces, and other portions were painted in tempera, the whole piece was then given a coat of transparent varnish. In the early decades of the eighteenth century the Venetians excelled in the production of dark-green lacquer with gold decorations, of which the finest examples are probably those now in the Palazzo Rezzonico at Venice.

Venetian eighteenth-century lacquer was the work of the guild of *depentori*, which had, in earlier centuries, included all painters, but from which the painters of pictures (*pittori*) had split away in 1691. Iseppo Tosello, who is mentioned in a document of 1729 as a *depentor alla chinese*, was one of many who produced lacquer, but his name has survived only by chance, and we know of none of his productions. It is also possible that some of the great *settecento* painters occasion-

Venetian lacquer harpsichord case, *c.* 1750. Museo Civico, Treviso

ally worked in lacquer, and a pair of doors in the Palazzo Rezzonico has tentatively been ascribed to G. B. Tiepolo, though not, it must be admitted, with much confidence. Whether the work of modest *depentori* or of *pittori*, Venetian lacquer of the eighteenth century is distinguished for its gay colours no less than for the accomplishment and frivolity of its decorations. Early in the century *chinoiserie* figures in gold or colours on a ground of black, green, red, or yellow seem to have been the invariable rule, but a preference was later shown for floral motifs or little landscapes painted in the style of Zais or Zuccarelli. All manner of objects were thus decorated – from great *armadi* and secretaires (known as *bureaux trumeaux*) to little boxes, fans, trays, brushes, and small ornaments in the form of animals. Perhaps the most satisfying of all non-*chinoiserie* examples of Venetian lacquer is the harpsichord in the Museo Civico at Treviso, sprinkled with exquisitely painted little bunches of mid-summer flowers on a brown ground. Similar floral decorations were very happily applied to the undulating surfaces of chests of drawers. These pieces, like so many examples of later Italian furniture, show how the craftsmen concentrated their attention on the decoration rather than the structure, and their joinery is often of poor quality.

Venetian lacquer of the type already described seems to have been reserved for the grander palaces and villas. But a cheaper substitute was also made in the eighteenth century and enjoyed a very wide popularity in Venetia. Works of this type were painted all over in a uniform colour, then decorated with cut-out prints produced for this purpose by the Remondini of Bassano and others. The prints were painted or gilded and the whole surface covered with a coat of transparent varnish. Furniture decorated in this manner looks from a distance as if it were lacquered but can easily be distinguished on close inspection. Despite their somewhat rustic character, the decorations themselves are often attractive. Most of the surviving examples of furniture decorated with this *lacca contrafatta* are *armadi*, chests of drawers, or secretaires.

Although Venetian lacquer was the most famous, lacquer furniture was made in several other Italian towns in the eighteenth century. At Florence lacquer was made for Cosimo III with ingredients brought back from the Far East, and good examples of Genoese and Lucchese lacquer, little inferior to Venetian, are also recorded. During the second quarter of the eighteenth century there was a vogue for rooms wholly panelled with lacquer in Piedmont. The most notable is that designed by the great architect, Filippo Juvarra, in the Palazzo Reale at Turin. Records show that sixty of the panels in this room were bought at Rome in 1732, but the decorative scheme was not completed until 1736, when one Pietro Massia provided further panels in the same style. Painted with birds and flowers in red and gold, the panels are set within elegant gilded rococo scrolls on a vermilion wall and produce a remarkable impression of sumptuous grandeur. A somewhat simpler room executed at about the same time or a little later was in the Villa Vacchetti at Gerbido, near Turin, and is now at the Rockhill Nelson Gallery of Art at Kansas City, Missouri. Here the panels are red and gold set against walls of celadon green. The designs used for the panels of both rooms reveal an Italian interpretation of *chinoiserie*.

The use of lacquer declined in Italy towards the end of the eighteenth century. Much fake eighteenth-century lacquer was, however, produced after the revival of interest in later Italian furniture in the 1920s.

LACQUER MADE IN OTHER COUNTRIES

Lacquer furniture was produced in several other European countries during the eighteenth century. The Portuguese produced a certain amount, the most notable pieces being secretaire cabinets, usually with gold *chinoiserie* decorations on a red ground, containing shrines in their upper parts. But both Portugal and Spain imported English lacquer during the first half of the eighteenth century. Giles Grendy, the maker of a red and gold day bed now in the Victoria and Albert Museum, seems to have specialized in catering for this export trade.

Surprisingly little lacquer seems to have been produced in Austria. A few examples of Viennese lacquer are in the Museum für Angewandte Kunst at Vienna. Lacquer was also produced to a limited extent in Denmark and Sweden.

French

From 1500 to the Revolution

To collectors and connoisseurs in England, French furniture, and particularly that of the late seventeenth and eighteenth centuries, presents certain problems. Firstly, the range of materials employed on the embellishment of certain pieces extends far beyond wood; secondly, the wealth and admixture of motifs, veneers, inlays, and the profusion of metal ornament are often alien to English taste; and thirdly, the number of craftsmen to be found in Great Britain who are competent to appreciate and repair French furniture is still so small that valuable pieces are in constant danger of being badly treated with the wrong substances.

From the historical point of view, the various periods and styles have become so bound up with the reigns of the three Kings of France, Louis XIV, XV, and XVI, that it is frequently difficult to realize that these styles and fashions in designing and decorating furniture often began long before, and ended long after, the rather arbitrary dates connected with them.

Nevertheless, the regnal divisions into which the subject has been conventionally split up have their uses in indicating the approximate style and period in which a piece of furniture may have been produced, and they have therefore been retained for the purposes of this study.

THE RENAISSANCE AND SEVENTEETH CENTURY

In spite of the large amount of furniture which was made in France in the sixteenth century, not very much has come down to us, and what has is almost completely undocumented. We are thus very seldom in a position to say when a given piece of furniture was made, for whom it was made, or by whom. A great deal of research has at one time or another been devoted to distinguishing between the various provincial centres where furniture was produced in the sixteenth century – whether, for instance, at Lyons or in the *Île de France* – but the theories put forward are not very convincing, and it is safer to assume that most of the best furniture was made in Paris and probably for the Court, and that such known provincial pieces are variations on a style existing at the central point.

By far the largest number of such pieces to have survived are made of walnut, usually elaborately carved. The most common piece is the dresser (*q.v.*), but tables, chairs, beds, cabinets, and cupboards are also found. These take various forms and are often covered with carving, the dressers particularly receiving the most elaborate treatment in this respect.

The carving is usually in the Italian style, imported into France by the wars of Francis I, and the engravings of du Cerceau and others were important in

Carved walnut cabinet, *Île de France*, second half of the 16th century. Victoria & Albert Museum

Right Ebony cabinet on stand carved with scenes from the legend of Atlanta and Meleager, mid-17th century. Christie, Manson & Woods

Left Walnut cabinet, carved, partly gilt and inlaid with marble panels, second half of 16th century. Victoria & Albert Museum distributing knowledge of the motifs which were employed at Court. The absence of any local inspiration for design meant that the Court style became predominantly Italian in character, as did the architecture of the period also. Often a decorative motif on a piece of French Renaissance furniture is taken direct from a known Italian engraving or plaquette. It is also important to remember that furniture at this date was intended easily to be taken to pieces and moved about (hence the word *mobilier*), and this can almost always be done with the pieces which we are considering.

With the more secure ways of life which came in with the seventeenth century, furniture began to become more stable, and thus the opportunities for decoration more appropriate. But France sadly lacked the craftsmen to carry out the elaborate inlays which were the fashion in Italy and which were favoured at Court after the arrival of Marie de' Medici as Queen of Henri IV. Up to the foundation of the Gobelins factory in 1663, therefore, the period is one of constant infiltration of foreign craftsmen, from whom, of course, Frenchmen in the next generation were to learn much.

The engravings of Adam Bosse, however, show how sparsely furnished the rooms of the prosperous members of society were, and do not show the elaborate cabinets and bureaux which have come down to us, and which must have been not only rare luxury products but almost entirely made by foreign craftsmen. These often incorporate elaborate carving, marquetry, and also intricate mirror arrangements in the interiors. They are usually designated as French in the absence of knowledge as to who actually made them, but it seems likely that Italian and Flemish craftsmen must have been largely involved. The taste for the Italian style was further extended by the rise to power of Cardinal Mazarin, himself an Italian, whose personality dominated the French scene through the minority of Louis XIV.

THE LOUIS XIV PERIOD

The *Roi Soleil* came to the throne in 1643 at the age of five. It can be well imagined therefore that the artistic characteristics which have become associated with his name did not come into existence at once. Indeed, the changes of style in furniture did not begin to appear until the King's majority and the establishment under Colbert of that great organization for the production of objects of art, the *Manufacture Royale des Meubles de la Couronne* at Gobelins in 1663. This foundation, as much an act of policy as everything else, was intended to co-ordinate control of all the applied arts in France to the glorification of the Crown and the State, and under its brilliant first director, Charles Le Brun, achieved its aim at least for a generation. The establishment of the *Manufacture* is, in fact, the cardinal event in the history of French decoration and furnishing, for it was under its aegis that all the foreign and native talent and experience which had been employed for two generations previously was incorporated and made to serve as a foundation for the establishment of new standards of taste and craftsmanship, this time wholly French in style and intended to serve a national aim.

As is well known, the first great task awaiting the *Manufacture* soon after its foundation was the decoration and furnishing of the new palace at Versailles, which was to become the cradle of French decorative taste for the centuries to come, and to demand an output of lavish expenditure unparalleled in history. It is only the more unfortunate that almost all the furniture produced during the first years of the *Manufacture*'s existence has disappeared, and even the celebrated silver furnishings of Versailles were later all melted down to provide bullion to support the various wars of the later years of the reign.

Boulle dressing table, pine veneered with marquetry of brass, ebony and ivory with tortoiseshell, *c.* 1700. Victoria & Albert Museum

What remains, then, must be regarded as only a fraction of what once existed, and by far the most important series of furnishings which have come down to us are the productions of the workshop of André Charles Boulle (1642–1732), the most celebrated cabinet maker of the whole period, and the great exponent of the marquetry which bears his name. Boulle was trained under foreign influences, and his achievement lies in his adaptation of foreign techniques to his own original ideas, and to the combination of a new monumentality and elegance of design with a perfection of craftsmanship in a very complicated and elaborate technique.

In his early years he almost certainly worked in wood marquetry, following designs similar to those produced in Italy and Flanders, and to this was sometimes added the use of small amounts of metal for decorative purposes; but the intricate marquetry of tortoiseshell and brass with which we associate his name is, to all intents and purposes, an individual creation.

The principal innovations in furniture design during the period were first of all in the chest of drawers, or *commode*. It can be said to date from about 1700, though it probably did not come into general use

One of a pair of Louis XV marquetry commodes by Bernard van Riesenburgh, mid-18th century. Christie, Manson & Woods

until rather later. The other main type to be evolved was that of the writing table, or *bureau*. This first begins to appear before the turn of the century in the form of a table top with two sets of drawers beneath, flanking a knee hole, and later took on its more usual form of a flat table with shallow drawers under the top.

The demand for Boulle furniture diminished in the middle years of Louis XV's reign, but returned in full force in the last quarter of the eighteenth century, when the neoclassical style came into its own. Often the same designs, motifs, and techniques were used, and it is sometimes extremely difficult to be certain in which period a piece was made when the quality of marquetry and bronze are the same.

It must be remembered that all furniture at this time, and indeed later, was made in order to harmonize with the rich carving and painted decoration of the setting for which it was intended, and designs which may appear overelaborate when isolated would often seem at home in their original positions.

THE LOUIS XV PERIOD

When considering the characteristics of anything connected with what has become known as the Louis XV or rococo styles in France, it is important to remember that their evolution was gradual, and indeed began some years before the date when the *Grand Monarque* actually died. The genesis of rococo design can, in fact, be traced back to the last years of the seventeenth century, and the engraved compositions of an artist such as Jean Bérain provide ample evidence of the new feeling which finally usurped the classicism, formality, and monumentality exemplified by the creation of Versailles.

It was, however, the removal in 1715 of the central personality in the formal and centralized Court and Government, and the succession of a small boy, with the consequent reign of a pleasure-loving Regent, which provided the circumstances for the change in taste which can be so readily observed in the years which immediately followed. It is, however, a mistake to isolate the style of the Regency with what followed and to try to identify objects as belonging to the *Style Régence* unless they can be proved to have been created within the years 1715–25. It is much more sensible to regard the products of these years as the first fruits of what was to become the *Style Louis Quinze* proper, and the absence of documentary evidence providing the necessary dating makes this course more prudent.

The new style inevitably, however, received its first impetus from the Court of the Regent Orléans at the Palais Royal, and almost at once there is a lightness to be observed in interior decoration and furniture. The relaxation of the rigid etiquette of the Louis XIV Court, caused apartments, and therefore furnishings, to be smaller and less formal, and gave opportunities for lightness, fantasy, and colour impossible twenty years before. Gradually, therefore, the heavy monumental furnishings made for Versailles at the Gobelins gave place to smaller, more elegantly contrived pieces suited to the lighter and more informal atmosphere of the new type of interior decoration.

More and more, furniture was adapted and decorated to harmonize with wall decoration, which, being also almost exclusively of wood, created a harmony of design and craftsmanship never equalled outside France. The Boulle technique passed temporarily out of fashion, though the *atelier* continued to produce furniture throughout the eighteenth century and Boulle himself did not die until 1732. The new taste favoured elaborate wood marquetry overlaid with delicate gilt-bronze (ormolu) mounts, and during the period the combination of these types of decoration reached a perfection of design and execution only surpassed by the subsequent period. The opening up of trade routes with the Far East brought a large number of Oriental goods on to the home market, with the result that a taste for lacquer was created, both applied in the original from China or Japan, or imitated in France and applied locally. The most celebrated imitation of lacquer was produced by the four Martin brothers, who patented their *vernis Martin* in 1730 and again in 1744. A number of Oriental woods useful for marquetry were also imported, notably kingwood and, later, purplewood, which was used very widely. Other woods used for veneering and inlaying were tulipwood, hazelwood, satinwood, casuarina, and sycamore, often mixed in elaborate floral, pictorial, or geometrical designs, framed with fillets of box and holly. The range of design was very wide and soon began to be used with remarkable skill.

Apart from relaxation in formality, the earlier part of the reign did not witness any very startling change in the actual types of furniture used, and the forms prevalent under Louis XIV still lingered on, particularly the wardrobe, or *armoire*, and the chest of drawers. The former, however, while keeping its monumental proportions, was often constructed of plain wood undecorated except for carving; while the latter underwent a number of changes in design. The main tendency was for straight lines and flat surfaces to become curved and *bombé*, and for the functional purposes of the piece to be concealed beneath the general scheme of decoration. Two commodes in the Wallace Collection, London (one by Gaudreau and Caffiéri, the other by Cressent), show these characteristics well, the divisions between the drawers being invisible beneath the designs of the marquetry and mounts. There is, however, not one straight line to be

Louis XV *bureau plat*, known as the table of Catherine II, oak carcase veneered with contrasting strips of kingwood, the top lined in black tooled leather, mid-18th century

found on either piece. The extreme rococo tendency towards asymmetry did affect mounts and *bronzes d'ameublement*, though not for very long.

The latter part of the reign, with its increase of luxury expenditure, saw the creation of a large number of new types of furniture, mainly small, and nearly always intended for female use. The *secrétaire à abattant* began to appear in the 1750s, also the *bonheur du jour*, the *bureau-toilette*, worktables and other pieces, while commodes, chairs, sofas, and *bronzes d'ameublement* of all kinds were produced in large quantities. This is the period also of the greatest *ébénistes*, including Oeben, Riesener, Leleu, Dubois (*qq.v.*), and others, and it is in the 1760s that foreign craftsmen, particularly Germans, began to arrive in Paris to seek their fortunes, usually finding them, in the profusion of demands for furniture. Madame de Pompadour played a large part in forming the taste of her time by her constant purchases of objects of all kinds and the *Livre-Journal* of Lazare Duvaux, from whom she bought so much, gives a very clear picture of how much money was spent. She was not responsible for the introduction of the neoclassical Louis XVI style, however, as she died in 1764, and many of the portraits of her, even just before her death, show her surrounded by furniture, particularly in the advanced Louis XV style.

A word should be said here about the actual creation of a piece of eighteenth-century French furniture. First of all a designer, sometimes the *ébéniste* himself, though sometimes equally a decorator, produced a drawing of the piece. This was then made by an *ébéniste* in wood, veneered and inlayed if necessary. Mounts and fittings were then produced by a sculptor and a *fondeur*, and if required were gilded by a *doreur*, thus often involving members of three craft guilds and two artist-designers. Occasionally painters were also involved, thus bringing in yet another guild. When one considers the number of different craftsmen employed on a single piece of furniture, the harmony and perfection so often achieved are the more remarkable.

Louis XVI *bonheur-du-jour* with marquetry inlay. The *bonheur-du-jour* first appeared in about 1760 and is a small writing-table, usually fitted also with toilet accessories and often surmounted by a cupboard of some sort. Christie, Manson & Woods

THE LOUIS XVI PERIOD

As is well known, the main characteristic of the Louis XVI style is the return to classical forms and motifs after the exuberance and fantasy of the rococo. This tendency begins to make itself felt at least twenty years before Louis XV died, and it is indeed this particular regnal division which is so misleading. Between 1750 and 1774 a very large amount of furniture was made incorporating classical tendencies, and it is most important to realize this when attempting in any way to date a given piece of furniture from stylistic evidence. The change of taste was very gradual, as the artistic writings of the time show, and, as elsewhere in Europe, was motivated very largely by the discovery of the Roman remains in the old Kingdom of Naples, at Pompeii and Herculaneum. The subsequent interest in classical subjects aroused by such writers as de Caylus, and the contempt poured on the rococo also played its part. From a purely stylistic point of view it can be said that the Louis XV style proper had worked itself out, and the return to classicism came therefore as a necessary reaction, and antidote. In spite of the enormous expenditure on furniture in the 1770s, both by the Court and private patrons, no very striking innovations took place in actual furniture design. The main feature of the reign was, however, the perfecting of processes used hitherto to an unprecedented degree. This is particularly the case with ormolu, which has never attained before or since such refinement as it did at the hands of Gouthière, Thomire, Forestier (*qq.v.*), and others. Apart from the elaboration and refinement of marquetry, plain woods, and particularly mahogany, begin to be used as veneers, and the rather controversial embellishment of furniture with porcelain begins to make its appearance. The large number of German *ébénistes* increased, of which Weisweiler and Beneman (*qq.v.*) were the most celebrated. The work of Georges

Jacob (*q.v.*) in making chairs also reached its highest peak, and Boulle furniture became fashionable again and was produced in large quantities.

The influence of Queen Marie Antoinette on the taste and craftsmanship of her time, with particular reference to furniture, has often been stressed. It is true that she employed extensively and lavishly the incomparable craftsmen whom she found in Paris on her arrival as Dauphine, but, apart from this expenditure and a liking for beautiful objects, it is doubtful if she possessed any real understanding of the visual arts, and she certainly was no rival of Madame de Pompadour in this respect. It has also been suggested that her nationality attracted many German-born craftsmen to Paris, but, in fact, the influx of foreign workmen had started and become an established fact long before there was any question of her being Queen of France. She undoubtedly did employ Riesener, Weisweiler, and Beneman very extensively, but chiefly because of their qualities as craftsmen, and only then on the advice of the *Garde Meuble*.

CABINET MAKERS AND CRAFTSMEN

Beneman, Jean Guillaume. German by birth. Came to Paris *c.* 1784, but seems to have been trained prior to this date, when he is first mentioned as being employed by the *Garde Meuble de la Couronne*. In 1785 he became a *maître-ébéniste* but without going through the normal formalities. His employment by the Crown coincides with the disfavour into which Riesener fell owing to his high charges. Beneman made a large amount of furniture for Queen Marie Antoinette and the Court, and was employed also to repair earlier furniture in the possession of the Crown. He collaborated with all the leading craftsmen of the time, including Boizot and Thomire, but his furniture retains usually a rather heavy Teutonic appearance. He seems to have specialized in making commodes and *meubles d'entre deux*. He was officially employed under the *Directoire* and Consulate, but his name disappears about 1804. He used the stamp:

G • BENEMAN

Boulle, André Charles (1642–1732). Born in Paris, the son of a carpenter, and died there. His training was very varied, and he appears to have worked at different times as a painter, architect, engraver, and bronze worker, as well as an *ébéniste* of importance. He worked as an *artisan libre* from 1664 onwards, but in 1672 he was appointed *ébéniste du Roi* through the intervention of Colbert. From this time he worked continually for the Crown and established a workshop in which he employed about twenty assistants, who were constantly at work providing furniture for the new palace at Versailles.

Boulle did not invent the marquetry which has become associated with his name, the combination of metal and tortoiseshell in the form of an inlay being used since the sixteenth century in Italy and Flanders; but he did evolve a particular type which he adapted to the taste and requirements of the time.

He possessed a large collection of Old Master drawings from which he may easily have drawn inspiration for his mounts. His ingenuity as a designer was very great, as can be seen from a series of engravings which he published, and from a number of his drawings which still exist. But throughout his career his actual style changed very little. He never signed his work and his authenticated productions are very rare. The only pieces which can be said definitely to be by him are two commodes originally made for the Grand Trianon and now in the palace at Versailles.

Caffiéri, Jacques (1678–1755). Son of Philippe Caffiéri, and came from a large family of sculptors. Became one of the chief exponents of the rococo style in France and was employed extensively by the Crown at Versailles, Fontainebleau, and elsewhere. He also occasionally worked as a portrait sculptor. He often signed his bronzes with his surname only, and his chief works are to be found at Versailles, the Louvre, the Wallace Collection, and elsewhere.

His son, Philippe Caffiéri, was also a sculptor of note, and occasionally collaborated with his father in bronzework.

Carlin, Martin. Very little is known about the life of Carlin. His place and date of birth are unknown. He died in Paris in 1785. He is first mentioned in 1763 and became a *maître-ébéniste* in 1766. He worked for Queen Marie Antoinette and the Royal Family, but it is uncertain whether he received an official appointment with the *Garde Meuble*. He supplied a large amount of furniture through the dealer Darnault.

Carlin was a most refined and delicate craftsman. He worked particularly in lacquer and with plaques of Sèvres porcelain.

Left Games table of tulipwood with ebony and ivory insets and twenty-six Sèvres porcelain plaques, by Martin Carlin, 1775

Below Louis XVI *bureau plat* with pale tulipwood veneer and shaped ormolu gallery, attributed to Martin Carlin. Sèvres porcelain inkstand on top

Cressent, Charles (1685–1768). Born at Amiens, the son of François Cressent, a sculptor, and grandson of a cabinet maker. He was apprenticed to his father, but probably learned cabinet making from his grandfather. He became a member of the *Académie de Saint Luc* in Paris in 1714, and in 1719 married the daughter of Joseph Poitou, an *ébéniste* working for the Duc d'Orléans, and he also at this time was given commissions by the Regent. After this he seems officially to have abandoned sculpture for *ébénisterie*, but he was several times prosecuted by the *Corporations des Fondeurs* and *Doreurs* for casting and gilding his own mounts. In 1723 he was actually forbidden by law to produce mounts not made by a qualified *fondeur*. This type of litigation was repeated from time to time throughout his life.

The Regent died in 1723, but Cressent continued service with his son Louis, Duc d'Orléans, as late as 1743, on the Duc's retirement from public life. He also worked for important private patrons in France, and carried out important commissions for King John V of Portugal and the Elector Karl Albert of Bavaria. With the profits from the sale of his furniture Cressent formed an impressive collection of works of art, which he three times tried unsuccessfully to sell owing to financial difficulties. The first sale in 1748 was, in fact, withdrawn owing to fresh orders received for work.

His best work is never stamped. Towards the end of his life he did use the stamp: C. CRESSENT, but it never appears on pieces of very great quality, and should always be treated with suspicion in view of his fame in his lifetime and later. The identification of his work therefore depends almost entirely on documents and tradition.

Dubois, Jacques and René. Jacques Dubois (*c.* 1693–1763) was born in Paris. He became a *maître-ébéniste* in 1742, and was elected a *juré* of the guild in 1752. He specialized in the use of lacquer both Oriental and European, and died the same year as Oeben, whose stock he helped to value. He used the stamp:

IDUBOIS

After his death his widow carried on the business with the help of her sons, the most celebrated of which was René (1757–99), who always used his father's stamp. He became a *maître* in 1754, was much patronized by Marie Antoinette, both before and after she became Queen, and also by the Court and nobility. He worked mainly in the Louis XVI style and eventually abandoned cabinet making for selling furniture.

Forestier, Étienne Jean and Pierre Auguste (1755–1838). Two brothers, the sons of Étienne Forestier (*c.* 1712–68). All three were *fondeurs-ciseleurs*, and after the father's death his widow carried on the business with her two sons. Their names constantly occur in the Royal accounts, and they are known to have worked at Versailles and Compiègne, and for the Prince de Condé. After the Revolution, Pierre Auguste established a successful workshop, supplying furniture, *bronzes d'ameublement*, etc.

Gaudreau, Antoine Robert (*c.* 1680–1751). One of the most celebrated of the known *ébénistes* of the Louis XV period. He was in the Royal Service from 1726. He became a *syndic* of the *ébénistes* guild in 1744, and worked for the Crown and also later for Madame de Pompadour. Among his most important works are a medal cabinet and a commode, which were made for the King's private apartments at Versailles. On the latter he collaborated with J. Caffiéri, who signed the bronzes. It is now in the Wallace Collection, London.

Gouthière, Pierre (1732–1813). The most celebrated of the late eighteenth-century *fondeurs-ciseleurs-doreurs*. Born at Bar-sur-Aube, the son of a saddler. He is known to have been in Paris by 1758, where he became a *maître-doreur*. He was employed by the Crown between 1769 and 1777, but after the latter date his name disappears from the Royal accounts. He had, however, a large number of private patrons, including the Duc d'Aumont and the Duchesse de Mazarin. He also worked for Madame du Barry at Louveciennes. He was constantly in difficulties financially, and his patrons were almost always behind with their payments. In 1788 he was declared bankrupt, and he never completely recovered, although he lived on until 1813, and died in poverty. Gouthière's signed works are exceedingly

Top Commode, veneered on oak with kingwood and mahogany with chased and gilt bronze rococo mounts, made by Antoine Gaudreau and Jacques Caffieri in 1739 for the bedroom of Louis XV at Versailles. Wallace Collection, London

Above Commode à la Regence, by Antoine Gaudreau, *c.* 1740. Of the type called *en tombeau* because it is modelled on an ancient sarcophagus, or tomb

rare and can be supplemented by a few which are able to be identified by documents. Almost all bronzes of any quality of the Louis XVI period have been attributed to him, and only the increased study of the Royal accounts has revealed the names of other *ciseleurs-doreurs*, who seem to have been his equals in many cases, even though we know little more than their names.

The attributions of bronzes to Gouthière on grounds of style alone should be made with great caution.

Above Two from a set of six armchairs and a sofa, gilt birch carved with rope beading and upholstered with Beauvais tapestry, by Georges Jacob. Stamped G. Jacob. Wallace Collection, London

Right Cupboard by the Jacob Frères (sons of Georges Jacob) with mounts by Pierre Philippe Thomire. Victoria & Albert Museum

Jacob, Georges (1739–1814). Born in Burgundy, died in Paris. Little is known of his early life, but he was the founder of a long line of makers of furniture who specialized in the production of chairs. He is thus usually thought of as *menuisier*, although he did carry out some works in the *ébéniste*'s technique. He was made a *maître-ébéniste* in 1765 and carried on his business in his own name until 1796, when he sold it to his two sons, Georges II and François Honoré. On the former's death in 1803 the latter took the name of Jacob-Desmalter and joined with his father until the latter's death in 1814. He then carried on the business himself until 1824, and his son continued it up to 1847. The first Jacob was a craftsman with an extraordinary wealth of invention, and his designs for chairs are of the utmost elegance, but are also pleasantly varied so that they do not often repeat themselves. He also made a number of beds, which show the same qualities. He worked extensively for the Crown and in consequence was denounced at the Revolution, in spite of his friendship with the painter Jacques Louis David. His own work is usually stamped:

J·F·LELEU

Leleu, Jean François (1729–1807). Born and died in Paris. Trained under J. F. Oeben (*q.v.*), after whose death in 1763 he hoped to be chosen to take over the direction of the workshop. Oeben's widow's choice, however, fell on Riesener, whom she married, and Leleu never became reconciled to this. He became a *maître-ébéniste* in 1764, and worked both for the Court and for private patrons. He was also employed by Queen Marie Antoinette, Madame du Barry, and the Prince de Condé. He became successively *juré* and *député* of the *ébénistes* guild, and in 1780 went into partnership with his son-in-law, C. A. Stadler, who succeeded to the business in 1792.

Leleu was a very versatile craftsman and worked in a number of styles; he seems to have been as equally at home in the advanced rococo as with the most severe neoclassic, and he also used Boulle marquetry and Sèvres porcelain to decorate his furniture. He used the stamp:

G ♦ IACOB

Oeben, Jean François (*c.* 1720–63). The son of a postmaster at Ebern in Franconia. He married in Paris in 1749, but we do not know the date of his arrival there from Germany. He entered the workshop of C. J. Boulle in 1751, and on the latter's death in 1754 Oeben succeeded him as *ébéniste du Roi* and was granted lodgings at the Gobelins, whence he moved in 1756 to the Arsenal. While working for Boulle, he was also employed by Madame de Pompadour and others, and after his move to the Gobelins he began in 1760 his most celebrated work – the monumental *Bureau du Roi Louis XV*, which, however, was not completed until after his death. Riesener, who was one of his assistants, succeeded him at the Arsenal, together with Leleu. Oeben also collaborated with Carlin and with P. Caffiéri. He died bankrupt in Paris and his widow carried on the business until 1767, when she married Riesener, who then carried on the business in his own name.

Oeben only became a *maître-ébéniste* in 1761 under special circumstances, having worked for the Crown for so long. His stamp on furniture is therefore rare, and when found it is more probable that the piece was made by Riesener before he took over the business, as Madame Oeben continued to use her husband's stamp while running the workshop herself.

After Cressent and Gaudreau, Oeben is the most celebrated *ébéniste* of Louis XV's reign. He specialized in elaborately planned pieces, fitted with secret drawers and complicated locking devices, but, owing to the amount of furniture which must necessarily have left his workshop unstamped, his work cannot easily be identified. He made extensive use of elaborate marquetry and parquetry.

Above Roll-top desk known as the *Bureau du Roi*, made for Louis XV by J. F. Oeben and completed after his death by J. H. Riesener, 1760–9. Château de Versailles

Riesener, Jean Henri (1734–1806). The most famous *ébéniste* of the eighteenth century in France. Born at Gladbeck, near Essen, but it is not known when he came to Paris. He entered Oeben's workshop at the Gobelins about 1754, and moved with him to the Arsenal. At Oeben's death he was selected by the widow to take over the workshop, and he married her in 1768, the year when he became a *maître-ébéniste*. In 1769 Riesener completed the great *Bureau du Roi Louis XV*, which his predecessor had left unfinished (*see under* Oeben). In 1774 he succeeded Joubert as *ébéniste du Roi*, and for ten years enjoyed the patronage of the Crown to a hitherto unprecedented degree, as expenditure during that decade was higher than it had ever been. His wife died in 1776, and seven years later he remarried, but unhappily.

After 1784 his prosperity began to decline and he was made drastically to reduce his prices by the Treasury. It was at this time that Beneman to a certain extent succeeded him in the favour of the Court. Queen Marie Antoinette, however, seems to have remained faithful to Riesener throughout, for she continued to order furniture from him right up to the Revolution.

He continued in business during and after the Revolution, but never actually reinstated himself. He seems to have retired in 1801 and died in Paris in 1806.

Riesener's stamp appears frequently on furniture of all kinds in the Louis XVI period, but it is probable that works bearing Oeben's stamp may also be by him, and made while he was working for Madame Oeben before their marriage (*see* Oeben).

J•H•RIESENER

He was the most versatile, and became the most accomplished, *ébéniste* of the time, and certainly deserved the success he obtained. His work covers nearly all types of furniture in use, and he specialized in highly elaborate marquetry, mostly in geometrical designs.

Roentgen, David (1743–1807). Born near Frankfurt, the son of the cabinet maker Abraham Roentgen, whose workshop at Neuwied on the Rhine he took over in 1772 and developed considerably. He first came to Paris in 1774 and received patronage from Queen Marie Antoinette. This established his reputation, which, by the time of his second visit in 1779, had increased considerably, and he established a depot in Paris for selling furniture, as he did also in Berlin and Vienna. He travelled widely and visited Italy, Flanders, and Russia, where he sold a great deal of furniture to the Empress Catherine II.

In 1780 he was compelled to become a *maître-ébéniste* in Paris, using the stamp: DAVID, and in 1791 was made Court furnisher to Friedrich Wilhelm II at Berlin. He was ruined by the Revolution, and his depot in Paris was confiscated. His workshop at Neuwied was also overrun by Republican troops. He returned there in 1802, however, and died in 1807.

Roentgen specialized in furniture veneered with extremely elaborate pictorial marquetry and fitted with complicated mechanical devices, concealing secret drawers and multiple locks. His furniture was mostly made outside France and is seldom stamped.

Far right Ormolu mantel clock probably by Pierre Philippe Thomire, the movement by Jean André Lepaute

Commode, veneered on oak with mahogany, with chased and gilt bronze mounts, stamped by J. H. Riesener. Wallace Collection, London

Thomire, Pierre Philippe (1751–1843). The son of a *ciseleur*. Worked under the sculptors Pajou and Houdon. In 1783 entered the service of the Sèvres porcelain factory. From 1784 onwards he was frequently employed by the Crown to make mounts for furniture, and often collaborated with G. Beneman. In 1785 he was commissioned by the City of Paris to make a candelabra celebrating the American Declaration of Independence for presentation to General Lafayette (now in the Louvre).

He built up a large workshop, which is said to have employed as many as 800 workmen. He worked extensively under the Empire and received a number of important commissions from the Emperor himself. The firm was known as *Thomire-Dutherne et Cie*, and Thomire himself retired from business in 1823. It by no means always follows that bronzes stamped with the name Thomire are by Pierre Philippe himself. More probably they are products of the workshop.

Weisweiler, Adam. Born *c.* 1750 at Neuwied and trained in the workshop of Roentgen (*q.v.*). Established in Paris before 1777. Became a *maître-ébéniste* in 1778. He worked for the dealer Daguerre and, through him, supplied a large amount of furniture for the Royal palaces, and particularly for Queen Marie Antoinette at St Cloud. He was a good businessman, and in consequence survived the Revolution safely, and was employed under the Empire, during which time he executed commissions for Queen Hortense. He was still in business in 1810. He used the stamp:

A·WEISWEILER

Italian

When collectors turn their attention to Italian furniture they must be prepared to look for qualities different from those they see in the work of the great French and English cabinet makers. At first they may well be disappointed to find that relatively few pieces show the delicacy and lightness or the superb standards of finished craftsmanship of a Riesener or a Chippendale. Charming boudoir pieces were made in northern Italy, and especially in Venice, during the late eighteenth and early nineteenth centuries, but the Italian craftsman's talents were shown less in the creation of such intimate little objects than in furnishing the sumptuous saloons of great palaces in Rome, Naples, Florence, Genoa, and Turin. Richly carved, lavishly gilded, and upholstered in the most opulent Lucchese silks and Genoese cut velvets, the furniture which stands beneath the vast frescoed ceilings of Italian *palazzi* is outstanding for its air of grandiose magnificence and princely splendour.

It must be admitted that Italian furniture does not show the consistently high finish of French or English work. In fact, its construction is sometimes distinctly shoddy. Yet this is not to deny it high quality in other respects. Generally speaking, the Italian cabinet maker seems to have been more interested in the design and decoration than the finish of his work, and he seldom bestowed much attention on those parts which were not intended to be seen – the backs of cupboards or the insides of drawers, for example. But such slipshod methods did not always, or everywhere, prevail. In the Renaissance period painters gave as much care to the decoration of a *cassone* as to a great fresco, and in the seventeenth and eighteenth centuries several sculptors carved chairs, console tables, and frames with the same accomplished freedom of hand as they lavished on independent statues. Fantastic armchairs by Brustolon, inlaid tables and cabinets by Piffetti, and lacquer furniture exquisitely painted by a host of anonymous Venetian artists, reveal impeccable standards of craftsmanship in their design and decoration, even if they occasionally appear somewhat rough and ready in their carpentry.

To speak of Italian furniture as we speak of English or French furniture is, however, somewhat rash. The regional differences which are familiar to every student of Italian painting and sculpture are no less marked in the minor arts and crafts. Although Venice is but ninety miles from Bologna and Bologna no more than sixty miles from Florence, radical differences of style distinguish the furniture produced in these three centres until well into the eighteenth century. The Renaissance which was born in Florence did not affect the Venetian painter, let alone the cabinet maker, for some fifty years. Similarly, the neoclassical style appeared in Venice long after it had been accepted in Rome and Turin. Moreover, different types of wood requiring different treatment were available in the various districts and helped to produce regional styles. In the south olivewood was often used. In Lombardy and Tuscany, where a rich variety of nut- and fruit-tree woods were available, much inlaid furniture was made, while at Venice, where the finer types of wood seem to have been difficult to obtain, a considerable proportion of the furniture was lacquered. We also find that much of the furniture made at Lucca and Genoa was designed mainly to show off the magnificent textiles those cities produced. In general, however, walnut was the wood most widely used in all districts from the middle of the sixteenth century until the late eighteenth century. Mahogany never achieved the same popularity in Italy as in England or France, probably for economic reasons.

The foreign influences which played an important part in Italian furniture designed after the middle of the seventeenth century were felt more forcibly in some regions than in others. French influence was, of course, exerted throughout the peninsula as in the rest of Europe, but was at its strongest in Liguria and Piedmont. Venice was subject to a limited German and Austrian influence, while the Kingdom of the Two Sicilies produced furniture which owes a certain debt to Spain. After the middle of the eighteenth century the English pattern books of Thomas Chippendale and later of Sheraton and Hepplewhite circulated in Italy and seem to have been copied by cabinet makers in many districts. With the Napoleonic conquests the Empire style became generally accepted and, for the first time in history, a general pattern was imposed on the furniture production of the whole country.

In view of the considerable local differences in style, it is hardly surprising that no wholly satisfactory comprehensive account of Italian furniture has ever been written. Books have appeared on the furniture of various districts and periods, but Italian furniture as a whole awaits a historian. Bearing local variations of style in mind, it is, however, possible to sketch the broad outlines of this fascinating and neglected subject.

RENAISSANCE FURNITURE

Very few examples of Italian furniture can securely be dated before the beginning of the fifteenth century, the most important exceptions being two thirteenth-century X stools in the Cathedral at Perugia and the Austrian Museum at Vienna. Similar X chairs and some three-legged stools of a type used in the fourteenth century are also known, but as these objects retained their popularity until well into the sixteenth century, it is seldom possible to date them with any precision. A few *cassoni* and *armadi* decorated with somewhat primitive paintings or flamboyant Gothic carving have been preserved, but most of them derive from northern districts, where the Gothic style lingered on after it had given way to the Renaissance in Tuscany. The history of Italian furniture therefore begins with the Renaissance. Yet to study the furniture even of this period we must supplement our knowledge of existing pieces by reference to paintings. The *prie-dieu* at which the Virgin kneels or the desk at which St Jerome studies in *quattrocento* paintings give us a better idea of the furniture of the period than any surviving examples. And it should be pointed out that the furniture which appears in these pictures acquired a sentimental charm which appealed very strongly to late nineteenth-century collectors, for whom unscrupulous craftsmen produced a large number of similar works.

To judge from paintings, the majority of *quattrocento* furniture was very unpretentious and much of it was usually covered with linen or glowing

Chestnut wood folding armchair inlaid with ivory and light coloured wood. In the centre back is the escutcheon of Guidobaldo II, Duke of Urbino, *c.* 1550. Victoria & Albert Museum

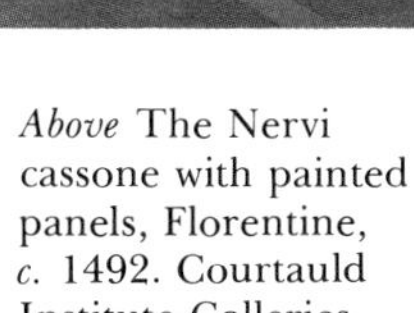

Above The Nervi cassone with painted panels, Florentine, *c.* 1492. Courtauld Institute Galleries

Venetian throne, carved and gilt, late 17th century-early 18th century. Palazzo Rezzonico, Venice

Turkish carpets. It is, perhaps, significant that the most notable pieces of furniture to survive from this period are *cassoni* and *armadi*, which were seldom muffled in drapery and were thus more richly decorated than the simple tables and *credenze*. *Cassoni* were often painted by the leading artists of the time, while *armadi* were treated in an architecturally monumental fashion. Indeed, these magnificent cupboards often have the same harmonious proportions and noble simplicity of decoration as the façades and interiors of early Renaissance palaces and churches. As the early Renaissance developed into the high Renaissance and, finally, the mannerist style, so furniture makers enriched their designs, making greater use of figurative carving. Mid-sixteenth-century refectory tables have their legs carved with mythological and human figures, and the *armadio* is often provided with a broken pediment and low relief panels on its doors. At about the same time Bolognese craftsmen began to apply brass handles in the form of cherub or satyr heads to their furniture and maintained this style of decoration throughout the first half of the seventeenth century.

Roman baroque carved giltwood vitrine in two parts, early 18th century. Christie, Manson & Woods

BAROQUE AND ROCOCO FURNITURE

Early in the seventeenth century the nervous angular mannerist line broke into the easy baroque flame in painting, sculpture, and architecture. The baroque style also affected the cabinet maker, who now developed a greater feeling for three-dimensional form. The top line of the *armadio* swells into a ponderous curve and the front occasionally bellies out in the centre. Richness is supplied by the free use of bulging balusters, by inlays of rare woods, or, on the most sumptuously palatial furniture, by panels of semi-precious stones. At the same time chairs began to take on a more grandiose appearance, with carved and gilded backs which sometimes erupted into a profusion of scrolls at the sides; they were often upholstered in rich velvets or damasks and were made more comfortable. As the century advanced the use of gilding on all articles of furniture increased, and further tones of opulence were added to the palace interior by the introduction of objects of mainly decorative value, such as console tables and *reggivasi*. The consoles were particularly magnificent, with vast slabs of rare and brilliantly coloured marble supported by human figures, mythological creatures, or gigantic seashells. Furniture made in England to the designs of William Kent in the early eighteenth century reveals the influence of these works.

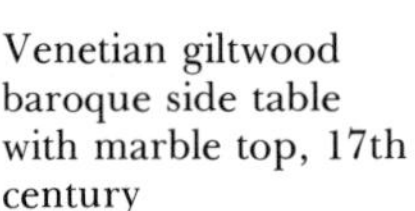

Venetian giltwood baroque side table with marble top, 17th century

Whereas Italian furniture had influenced the rest of Europe in the sixteenth and, to a less marked degree, the seventeenth centuries, it began to succumb to French influence before the beginning of the eighteenth century. Indeed, French models were so widely copied in Italy that one is tempted to classify Italian furniture in French periods from *Régence* to *Empire*. Eighteenth-century Italian furniture was also affected by a change in the manner of living; for now the daily life of the palace moved from the great saloons on the *piano nobile* to the smaller rooms on the mezzanine floor, which demanded more delicate furnishings, usually derived from French models.

As the rococo style won general acceptance in the second quarter of the eighteenth century, broken *rocaille* decorations took the place of the great sweeping baroque scrolls, and figures vanished from all furniture except the *giridoni* and *reggivasi*. The new patterns which came from France were not slavishly copied, however. Venetian craftsmen, who were surely the most accomplished furniture makers in early eighteenth-century Italy, indulged their flair for fantasy by exaggerating the French designs, giving *bombé* commodes more absurdly bellying fronts, extending the sofa to an inordinate length and applying a greater profusion of rococo twists and turns to the woodwork. Elsewhere, especially in Rome and Naples, French patterns seem to have been toned down and made more rigid.

NEOCLASSICAL AND EMPIRE FURNITURE

The neoclassical style which began to influence painters and sculptors in Rome soon after the middle of the eighteenth century hardly affected the cabinet maker until the 1770s; though some furniture made in the 1760s reveals a greater simplicity of line and severity of decoration. In Rome classical term figures and winged lions began to reappear as the supports of console tables, but the force of the new style was most strongly felt in Piedmont, where it was employed by G. M. Bonzanigo. Only the Venetians remained obstinately rococo, treating the new patterns from France in a distinctly frivolous fashion. But France was not the only country to influence the Italian cabinet maker, for in the second half of the eighteenth century English designs were also copied, and the *salone* might include examples of Italian Chippendale and Sheraton furniture jostling Italian Louis XV and Louis XVI pieces.

The greater rigidity of Louis XVI designs paved the way for the acceptance of the Empire style, which spread over Italy almost as fast and inexorably as the advance of Napoleon's armies. In the early 1800s the slender columns, the Egyptian heads, and the elegant ormolu mounts which had overrun the salons of Paris began to appear also in the great Italian *palazzi*. Much of this furniture was imported from France, but many pieces of high quality were made in Florence and Lucca under the guidance of French *ébénistes*. Moreover, the Empire style long outlived the Napoleonic regime in Italy. It was very successfully used by Pelagio Pelagi to decorate the throne room of the Palazzo Reale in Turin in the late 1830s: and, even in the 1840s, one Peters, an English cabinet maker, was producing somewhat ponderous Empire furniture at Genoa. In Naples palatial furniture of the late Empire character, in what may be termed the Bourbon style, was made to fill the vast apartments of Capodimonte and Caserta in the late 1830s and early 1840s. The revival of old patterns had, however, begun, and soon cabinet makers were everywhere busy producing solid *credenze*, *armadi*, and *cassoni* to furnish houses in the 'Dantesque' fashion. Italy still rejoices in numerous craftsmen of great ability who work in a tradition which has been handed on from master to *garzone* for generations. The collector should, perhaps, be warned that many of them devote themselves to making furniture on old designs and with old materials.

Chair, carved and gilt, probably Florentine, *c.* 1820. Palazzo Pitti, Florence

Cabinet Makers

Relatively few pieces of Italian furniture can be attributed to named cabinet makers or designers. Household accounts of many great palaces record payments to the *intagliatori*, or wood carvers, and the same palaces are filled with furniture. But the task of associating the names of the craftsmen with the works they produced still remains to be done. Indeed, it is not until we reach the last years of the seventeenth century that it becomes possible to ascribe any individual pieces of Italian furniture to known craftsmen. Of these the most notable was probably the Venetian Andrea Brustolon (1662–1732), a highly accomplished sculptor in wood who executed the superbly fantastic chairs, *reggivasi*, and *giridoni* supported by blackamoors, carved out of ebony and boxwood, now in the Palazzo Rezzonico at Venice. Chairs decorated with *putti*, and a grandiose looking-glass frame in the Palazzo Rezzonico have been attributed to Antonio Corradini (1668–1752), a Venetian sculptor who otherwise worked in marble. The notable Genoese wood sculptor Anton Maria Maragliano (1664–1739) may well have been responsible for some of the finely carved console tables supported by mythological creations in the palaces of his native city. Another Genoese sculptor, Domenico Parodi (1668–1740), carved a magnificent looking-glass frame for the Palazzo Balbi, now Reale, at Genoa and may also have produced console tables. All these artists were, however, *intagliatori* rather than cabinet makers, and their works are distinguished primarily for the quality of the carving. Moreover, they are all, with the exception of Brustolon, better known for their statues than for their furniture.

Early in the eighteenth century the architect to the court of Savoy, Filippo Juvarra (1676–1736), designed furniture for the great palaces he built in

Design by Filippo Juvarra for a console table for the King of Savoy

Writing desk by Pietro Piffetti (*c.* 1700–77), inlaid with precious woods and ivory, signed and dated 1741. Museo Correr, Venice

and near Turin (see *The Connoisseur*, November 1957). A little later the same court was served by Pietro Piffetti (*c.* 1700–77), the first Italian to merit the title of *ébéniste.* He was a brilliant craftsman, but his furniture looks fussy and overelaborate, as he tended to sacrifice the general design to the details, concentrating on the exquisite panels of inlaid ebony, ivory, and mother-of-pearl with which they were embellished. Francesco Ladatte (1706–87), a notable sculptor in bronze, supplied the fine mounts for some of Piffetti's furniture. In Lombardy Giuseppe Maggiolini (1738–1814) produced furniture in the Louis XVI style, decorated with *intarsia* panels representing portraits, bunches of flowers, and ruins. At about the same time, in Turin, Giuseppe Maria Bonzanigo (1744–1820) was producing a few exceptionally fine works in the same style, notably a secretaire and a fire screen, which are carved with a delicacy and precision seldom equalled even in France. In 1782 the Lombard architect, Giocondo Albertolli (1742–1839), published the only important Italian pattern book of furniture designs which shows, perhaps, too strict a regard for archaeological accuracy. During the Empire period fine furniture was produced at Lucca under the French *maître-ébéniste*, Youf, and at Florence by the Italian Giovanni Socchi, many of whose works are still in the Palazzo Pitti.

Glossary

Acanthus. The leaf used in classical and Renaissance architectural design, particularly on Corinthian capitals. Adapted later as a motif in furniture design. Most important in Chippendale furniture as decorative motif on the knees of cabriole legs.

Acanthus

Acorn clock. American shelf or mantel clock, generally about 2 feet (61 cm) high, with the upper portion shaped somewhat like an acorn. Popular in New England about 1825.

Ambry (aumbry, almery; *Fr.* **armoire).** Enclosed compartment or recess in a wall or in a piece of furniture, the original sense of the term having been usurped by cupboard, which originally had a different connotation. 'Cuppbordes wyth ambries' are mentioned in inventories of Henry VIII's furniture. Today ambry, etc., is principally used architecturally and ecclesiastically, as of the doored compartments or recesses for the Reservation of the Blessed Sacrament, this usage perpetuating the original sense. The French form *armoire* is often applied to large presses or press cupboards.

Apple. A fruitwood much used in America for turnings, also often in case pieces, such as slant-front desks, etc., to show off the rich-coloured pink-brown wood.

Apron work. Prolongation downwards, beyond what is essential to construction, of the lower edge of a member, such as the shaped lower edge of the front of certain boarded chests, or the lower frontal framework, below the drawers, of certain dressers. In such cases an apron is purely ornamental; in others, e.g. the seating of close chairs, its purpose is that of concealment.

Ark. Term frequently encountered in medieval inventories, seemingly meaning: (*a*) a chest with a coped or gabled lid; (*b*) perhaps a structure resembling a reliquary (*Fr. chasse*), as exemplified by the sixteenth-century ambry in Coity Church, Glamorganshire. That ark was a distinct term is shown by such entries as the following from an inventory of the contents of St Mary's, Warwick, 1464:

> 'It: in the Vestrye i gret olde arke to put in vestyments etc.
>
> 'It: in the Sextry above the Vestrye, i olde arke at the auters ende, i olde coofre irebonde having a long lok of the olde facion, and i lasse new coofre having iii loks called the tresory cofre and certeyn almaries.' (Quoted by Philip Mainwaring Johnston, F.R.I.B.A.: *Church Chests of the Twelfth and Thirteenth Centuries in England*; 1908, p. 60.)

Armadio. The French *armoire*, a large cupboard, usually of a somewhat monumental character, which seems first to have been used to supplement the *cassoni* in the furnishing of Italian houses in the late fourteenth century. Early examples are usually about 4 feet (122 cm) in height, and some are decorated with flamboyant Gothic carving in low relief. An early fifteenth-century example (in the Museo Bardini at Florence) is in the form of a long, low cupboard with several very simply decorated doors and a panelled backboard of the same height as the cupboard. In the sixteenth century two-storey *armadi* became popular. They were often decorated with two orders of pilasters or pilasters above elongated consoles (there is a good Tuscan example of this type in the museum at Berlin). Sometimes the two storeys were separated by a projecting drawer. This pattern was superseded in the seventeenth century by a still more massive type, with pilasters some 6 feet (183 cm) tall at either end, and sometimes with a pair of drawers in the plinth. When a less ponderous effect was desired the cupboard was mounted on turned legs.

The tops of seventeenth-century *armadi* are often shaped in baroque curves. In the eighteenth century the *armadio* was usually made on a lighter and more elegant pattern and was often designed to stand in a corner. But with the introduction of the chest of drawers the *armadio* lost much of its former popularity in the house.

Many of the early surviving *armadi* were intended originally for the sacristies of churches, where they were used for the storage of vestments, and it is often difficult to distinguish these from domestic examples except when they have specifically religious motifs in their decoration. After the sixteenth century such *armadi* were usually built-in furnishings of the sacristy. Sometimes they were richly carved or decorated with *intarsia* panels.

Arming chest. Chest for the housing of armours and weapons. Arming chests might be fitted with compartments of varying size to accommodate breastplate, etc. (*see* Chest). (In navigation an arming box contains tallow for the 'lead'.)

Armoires. *See under* Wardrobes.

Artisans libres. The name given to French craftsmen who chose to work outside the guild jurisdiction and who sought refuge in what were known as *lieux privilégiés* in Paris. Being exempt from guild charges and regulations, they were a continual source of irritation to the guilds, particularly as they included a large number of foreign *ébénistes* who came to Paris in the mid-eighteenth century. These included some of the finest craftsmen of the time, a number of whom later became *maître-ébénistes.*

Ash. The American ash, a cream-coloured hardwood with oak-like graining; much used for furniture parts, such as upholstery frames, where strong, but not heavy, wood was desired. In England it was used in eighteenth-century furniture, particularly for the hooped backs of Windsor chairs.

Athénienne. A form of candelabrum consisting of an urn supported on a classical tripod, invented in 1773 by J. H. Eberts, editor of the famous *Monument de Costume.* The name derives from a painting by J. B. Vien entitled *La Vertueuse Athénienne*, which shows a priestess burning incense at a tripod of this type. They were made of patinated bronze with ormolu mounts or in carved giltwood, but not many survive. They are, however, typical of the classicizing tendencies of the last quarter of the eighteenth century.

Bail. Half-loop metal pull, usually brass, hanging from metal bolts. First used in America about 1700; slowly grew into use for drawers of William and Mary pieces. The reigning fashion from 1720 to 1780 for drawers of Queen Anne and Chippendale pieces.

Ball-and-claw foot. *See* Claw-and-ball foot.

Balloon seat. *See* Bell seat.

Banister-back chair. Probably simplified from the cane chair (*q.v.*) but with vertical split banisters in the back. Generally maple, often ebonized. Widely used in rural America, 1700–25 until the end of the century.

Banjo. Modern name for the American wall clock with a longish pendulum, the whole housed in a case shaped somewhat like a banjo. Invented in the 1790s by Simon Willard, and patented by him about 1800. Decoratively attractive, its popularity spread from 1800 through the next half-century.

Bargueño (or **Vargueño**). Spanish cabinet with fall front enclosing drawers and often mounted on a stand. Mixed materials are found.

Barley sugar. *See* Twist turning.

Baroque. The late Renaissance style of vigorously elaborate furniture with sweeping curves and resplendent ornament. It originated in sixteenth-century Italy, spread through Europe, but was little practised in England, and known in America only in *bombé* case pieces and in greatly simplified forms of some William and Mary and Queen Anne furniture (*see* Rococo).

Basin stand. *See* Washing stand.

Bedstead. So far as practical collecting is concerned, main basic types are the box (or enclosed) bedstead, wainscot (including bedsteads panelled at head and foot), post (with two or four posts supporting the tester), stump (or low type), and the truckle or trundle (with wooden wheels at base of uprights). These are not hard-and-fast definitions; one type may well overlap another (e.g. box and wainscot). Parts of bedsteads have been re-used for other purposes of a decorative nature, such as overmantels. We know little of the shape of Italian beds before the sixteenth century, save from those which appear in such paintings as Carpaccio's *St Ursula* or Ghirlandaio's *Birth of the Virgin.* One of the earliest is that formerly in the Palazzo Davanzati at Florence, a handsome piece of furniture mounted on a wide plinth. Sixteenth-century examples often have rich carving on head and foot and are without the plinth. In Sicily iron bedsteads with four posts supporting a canopy were popular from the late sixteenth century. The use of four posts was, however, unusual on later Italian beds, which sometimes have stumps at the corners and are covered by canopies supported from the wall. Lucchese examples are often richly covered with fabric which is matched on the bedspread.

Beech. A smooth, close-grained wood of light colour less frequently used in America than England. Found in the underframes of New York Chippendale pieces and occasionally in New England Chippendale as well as early turned pieces.

Beer wagon. *See* Coaster.

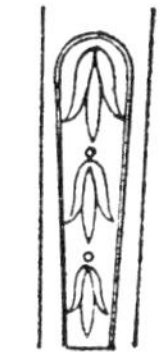

Bellflower

Bellflower. Conventionalized hanging ('belle') flower-bud of three, occasionally five, petals carved or, more often, inlaid one below the other in strings dropping down the legs of a table or chair or, sometimes, a chair splat. Seen in American Hepplewhite and Sheraton, notably Maryland furniture. It is practically the same as the English 'husk' motif.

Bell seat. The rounded, somewhat bell-shaped, seat often found in late Philadelphia Queen Anne side chairs. Nowadays often called balloon seat. Mostly about 1740–55.

Bench. A long seat, backed or backless, fitted or movable (*see* Form, Settle, Table bench).

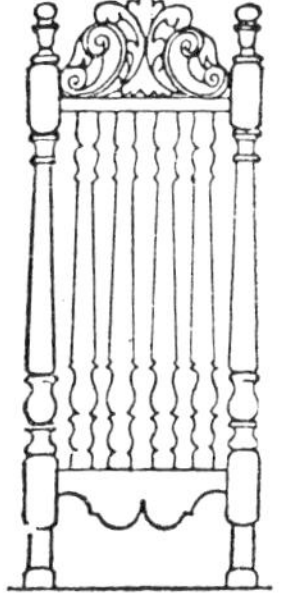

Banister-back chair

Bible box. Popular term for a variety of box, generally of small size. That some such boxes were used to hold the family Bible, or average meagre domestic library, is probable, though they doubtless served other purposes. Lace boxes enter this category.

Bibliothèque-basse. A low cupboard fitted with shelves for books, and doors often of glass but sometimes fitted with grilles.

Bilbao or **'Bilboa'.** U.S. wall mirror framed in coloured marbles or marble and wood with scrollwork headpiece and gilded mouldings. Adam or Hepplewhite followers might have designed them, yet they are believed to have originated in the Spanish seaport Bilbao. Stylish in New England seaport towns 1780–1800.

Bilsted. Word used in colonial New York for sweet-gum wood.

Birch. Hard, close-grained wood. Stained to substitute for mahogany in country furniture. Resembles satinwood in certain cuts. The American variety, *betula lenta*, was exported to England in the second half of the eighteenth century.

Bird's eye. A marking of small spots, supposed to resemble birds' eyes, often found in the wood of the sugar maple. Used and much prized from the earliest to present times.

Blister. A marking, thought to resemble a blister, found in various woods – cedar, mahogany, poplar, pine, and, especially, maple.

Block front. A whole range of forms – chests of drawers, chests-on-chests, knee-hole dressing tables, slant-front desks, secretaries, etc. – in which thick boards, usually mahogany, for the fronts of the drawers and cabinets are cut so that the centres recede in a flattened curve while the ends curve outwards in a flattened bulge. At the top of the three curves, one concave and two convex, a shell is often carved or glued on. Should the piece be in two sections, often only the lower section is block-fronted. The origin of block fronting is unknown; the development is believed to be American, evolved about 1760–80, by John Goddard of Newport, Rhode Island, perhaps with the aid of his associate, John Townsend. They may have arrived at it by straightening the curves of the Dutch cabinet. The late American authority Wallace Nutting called block fronts 'the aristocrats of furniture'. The English antique furniture authority, Cescinsky, described them, especially the secretaries, as 'the finest examples of American furniture'. They are much sought after.

Boat bed. American Empire-style bed shaped somewhat like a gondola. A variant of the sleigh bed.

Bombé. Lit. 'inflated, blown out', i.e. of convex form generally on more than one axis.

Bonheur-du-jour. A small writing table usually on tall legs, and sometimes fitted to hold toilet accessories and *bibelots.* It first appeared in France *c.* 1760, but remained in fashion for a comparatively short time.

Bonnet top. When the broken-arch pediment of tall case furniture covers the entire top from front to back, this hood is called a bonnet top. It is usually cut in the same curves as the arch, but is sometimes left uncut, a solid block of wood behind the arched fronting. 1730–85. Same as 'Hood'.

Writing table of inlaid rosewood, in the manner of a Louis XVI *Bonheur-du-jour*, *c.* 1780

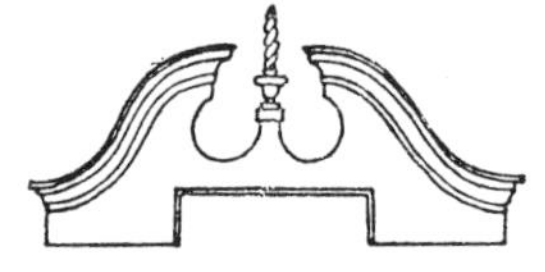

Bonnet top

Bookcase after a Sheraton design of 1806 with carved ebonized ornament

Bookcase. In England bookcases, either fitted or, in some cases, contained in other furniture, were known medievally, but the domestic bookcase mainly derives from the period of Charles II (1660–85). In Italy bookcases were less frequently made individually than as part of the built-in decorations of a library. In Venice there is an excellent example of a late seventeenth-century library with cases carved by German craftsmen in the monastery of S. Giorgio Maggiore (now *Fondazione Cini*) and an exquisite small, early eighteenth-century library, with painted cases, in the Ca' Sagredo. Both of these have two tiers of bookcases which fill the walls. In houses that could not afford to give up a whole room to the library the books were probably kept in an ordinary *armadio.* Eighteenth-century bookcases resemble either a section of a complete library or, more usually, an *armadio* with wire grilles in place of panels in the doors. Although a few enormous early bookcases exist, bookcases were seldom made in America as an article of furniture before 1785–90, the average family before then keeping their books in locked chests, cupboards, and the tops of secretaries. Bookcases are generally large and heavy until about 1880, when the smaller type came in (*see* China cabinet).

Book rest. A stand used in Georgian libraries to support large books, consisting of a square or rectangular framework with crossbars, the upper bar being supported by a strut which was adjusted on a grooved base. This kind of stand was sometimes fitted into the top of a table.

Bookshelf. *See* Shelves.

Boston rocker. In America the most popular of all rocking chairs. Apparently evolved from the Windsor rocker (*q.v.*). Usually painted, it has curved arms, a tall spindle back, broad top rail generally showing stencilled designs – a kind of ornamental panel – and a 'rolling' seat, curved up at the back and down at the front. When standardized and mass-produced (after 1840) it is not a true antique.

Boulle marquetry. The name given to the type of inlay evolved for use on furniture in the late seventeenth century by André Charles Boulle (1642–1732) (*see under* French furniture).

Detail of Boulle marquetry dressing table, 1700. Pine veneered with marquetry of brass, ebony, ivory and clear tortoiseshell. Victoria & Albert Museum

The process involves the glueing of one or more thin layers of tortoiseshell to a similar number of brass layers. The design of the marquetry is set out on paper, and this is pasted on to the surface. The pattern is then cut out by means of a saw. After this, the layers of brass and tortoiseshell are separated and can be made to form two distinct marquetries by combining the materials in opposite ways: either with the design formed by the brass on a ground of shell, known as *première partie* or first part, or the exact opposite, known as *contre-partie* or counterpart, with the design in shell on a ground of brass. These two types of inlay can then be glued on to a carcase in the form of a veneer. Often the two types are found side by side as part of the same design, in order to give contrast. Again, when pieces are made in pairs one is often veneered with *première partie* and the other with *contre-partie* marquetry.

The brass in the *première partie* marquetry was often engraved naturalistically, frequently very finely, and was sometimes combined with other substances, such as pewter, copper, mother-of-pearl, and stained horn, again usually to give contrasts and naturalistic effects to the design. Additional colour was also given occasionally by veneering the shell over coloured foil, usually red or green.

The carcases on to which Boulle marquetry is veneered are usually found to be of oak or deal, and the parts which are not covered by the inlay are veneered with ebony, Coromandel wood, or purplewood, in order to tone with the shell of the inlay.

Finally, Boulle furniture is usually lavishly mounted with ormolu, so as to protect the corners and the more vulnerable parts of the inlay, but the mounts are frequently also adapted in a decorative manner to form hinges, lockplates, and handles. It will be noticed that the ormolu is sometimes fully gilt, which provides a strong decorative contrast with the inlaid brass; equally, the bronze is sometimes left ungilt, and therefore harmonizes with the metal inlay to a greater extent.

Boulle furniture, so much in demand in the reign of Louis XIV, went out of fashion during most of that of his successor, but it did not cease to be made, and the Boulle *atelier* continued to turn out pieces from time to time. They were therefore ready when, under Louis XVI and the classical revival, the taste for this type of furniture returned, and at this period a very large number of pieces were made, often using the original designs, mounts, and processes as in the former period. It is thus often extremely difficult to tell whether a piece was made in one period or another, and it is better not to be too dogmatic about this, as there are very few distinguishing characteristics. Two may perhaps be mentioned: the engraving of the brass inlay is less common in the Louis XVI period and, when it does appear, of inferior quality; secondly, the use of other metals than brass and freer designs are slightly more common.

In the earlier period a large number of designs for Boulle marquetry are derived from the engravings of Jean Bérain, who was, like Boulle, also employed by the Crown.

Boulle marquetry is sometimes erroneously referred to as Buhl. This is a Teutonic adaptation of Boulle's name for which there is no justification.

Bow back. *See* Windsor chair.

Bow front. A curving front used on case pieces in New England during the Chippendale period.

Box and casket. Boxes were among the most attractive of the smaller pieces of furniture, and were used from medieval times for a multitude of purposes – personal effects, toilet and writing materials, valuables, documents, etc. Tudor and early Stuart boxes were usually square in shape and made of oak, carved, inlaid, or painted, and occasionally stood upon stands, few of which have survived. In the later seventeenth century walnut was commonly used (sometimes decorated with marquetry or parquetry), but other materials included parchment, tortoiseshell, and stumpwork, the latter particularly on the boxes kept by ladies for their cosmetics, etc. The interiors were often ingeniously fitted with compartments and drawers. In the eighteenth century some beautiful mahogany and satinwood boxes were made, until they were gradually replaced by small worktables, though boxes on stands, conforming to the prevailing decorative fashions, were to be found. Among other examples were Tunbridge-ware (*q.v.*) boxes, and travelling boxes fitted with spaces for writing, working, and toilet requisites. About 1800 work and toilet boxes covered with tooled leather were in vogue.

Boxwood (*buis*). A very closely grained wood of a yellow colour found frequently in Europe and elsewhere. Extensively used in France for fillets to frame panels of marquetry.

Boys and crowns. Old term for a type of carved ornament on the cresting of late seventeenth- and quite early eighteenth-century chairs, day beds, etc. (*see under* Restoration). The motif, a crown, usually, though not necessarily, arched, supported by two flying or sprawling naked boys, derives ultimately from the flying *putti* frequently found in Renaissance design. In England, the idea was familiar long before it achieved (*temp.* Charles II) a vogue on chair backs.

Bracket. The detachable wall bracket, as distinct from the fixed architectural feature, appeared towards the end of the seventeenth century, and seems to have been used at first for displaying china. Its prominent position in the room singled it out for special decorative treatment in carving or gilding. In the early Georgian period the bracket was often used to support a bust or vase, and as a result it tended to become larger in size and more heavily ornamented; but with the return of the fashion for displaying china about 1750 and the growing use of the bracket for supporting lights, it became altogether more delicate in appearance, and was adapted to the various styles of the Chippendale and Adam periods. The wall bracket supporting a clock was a popular form of decoration in the later eighteenth century.
Bracket foot. A foot supporting a case piece and attached directly to the underframing. It consists of two pieces of wood, joined at the corner. The open side is generally cut out in a simple pattern. The corner end is sometimes straight, at other times curved in an ogee pattern.
Bras de lumière. *See under* Wall lights.
Brazier. A portable metal container used from Tudor times for burning coal or charcoal; with handle and feet, or sometimes mounted on a stand.
Breakfast table. A small table with hinged side leaves that can be used by one or two people. After the Chippendale period the name Pembroke (*q.v.*) is often applied to the type.
Brewster chair. A seventeenth-century American armchair of turned spindles and posts with rush seat. The back has two tiers of spindles. There is a tier under the arms and one under the seat. The chair is usually of ash or maple. Named after William Brewster, elder of Plymouth Plantation, whose chair is preserved at Pilgrim Hall, Plymouth, Massachusetts. Similar to the Carver chair (*q.v.*).

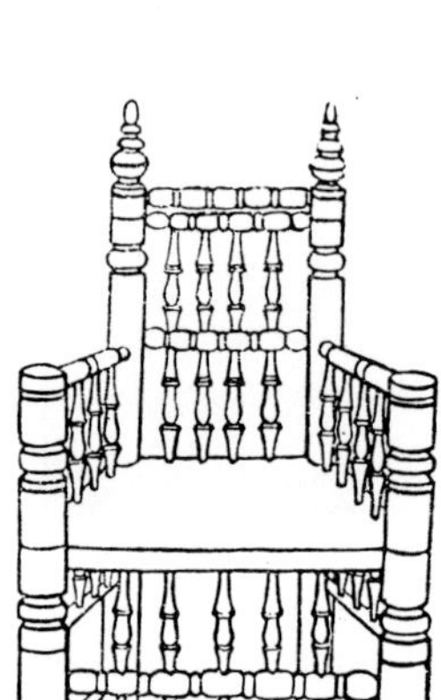
Brewster chair

Broken arch. *See* Scroll top.
Bronzes d'ameublement. A term with no exact English equivalent covering all furniture, practical or decorative, made of bronze, patinated or gilt. It embraces such items as candelabra, candlesticks, wall lights, chandeliers, firedogs, clock cases, mounts for furniture and porcelain, etc. Their manufacture was the particular province of the *fondeurs*, *ciseleurs*, and *doreurs*.
Buffet. Term variously applied to open, doorless structures, of more than one tier (*see also* Court cupboard, Livery cupboard (*under* Cupboard)).
Bull's eye. A popular term for the small round mirror with convex or concave glass and an ornate gilt frame. The type was fashionable 1800–20, and often of English or French manufacture. An alternative meaning is the reference to clear glass with a large centre drop or gather employed as window glass and in cabinets.
Bureau. In America, ever since the eighteenth century, the word bureau means a chest of drawers, with or without a mirror, and regularly used in the bedroom. Originally, and still in England, a desk. Examples were made in the William and Mary style, dating 1700–10, but the form dropped completely out of use until revived about 1750. They are found in the Chippendale and every style thereafter, the revival probably springing not from the earlier form but from Chippendale's designs. Many authorities describe bureaux according to the shape of the front – serpentine, reverse serpentine, bow or swell, and straight front – but that is mere grouping, not classification proper. In England the word denotes a writing desk with a fall, a cylinder, or a tambour front.

Bureau (American)

Bureau-plat. A writing table supported on tall legs with a flat top with drawers beneath. Began to appear in France towards the end of the seventeenth century.
Bureau table. A dressing table with drawers on short legs and a knee-hole recess.
Bureau-toilette. A piece of furniture for female use combining the functions of a toilet and writing table.
Burl. A tree knot or protruding growth which shows beautifully patterned grainings when sliced. Used for inlay or veneer. Found in some late seventeenth- and much eighteenth-century American furniture, and chiefly in walnut and maple burls.
Butler's tray. A tray mounted on legs or on a folding stand, in use throughout the eighteenth century. The X-shaped folding stand was in general use from about 1750, the tray normally being rectangular and fitted with a gallery. Oval trays were sometimes made in the later part of the century.
Butterfly table. A William and Mary style drop-leaf table with solid swinging supports shaped a little like butterfly wings. The supports are pivoted on the stretchers joining the legs. Assumption that the type is of American origin is probably incorrect.

Cabinet. The glass-fronted cabinet intended for the display of a collection of porcelain or other *objets d'art* is an eighteenth-century invention. Such cabinets were made in Italy in conformity with the rococo and neoclassical styles.
Cabriole leg. The curving tall furniture leg used in American Queen Anne and Chippendale furniture, and almost universally used in the eighteenth century. The adjective is from the French noun, which is a dancing term meaning a goat leap, and is used in the idiom *faire le cabriole* to refer to the agility and grace of a person. The leg is inspired by an animal form, unlike the earlier scroll and turned shapes and is terminated in the claw-and-ball foot, the hairy paw, or the scroll in the Chippendale period and earlier the claw-and-ball, the pad, trifid, or slipper foot.

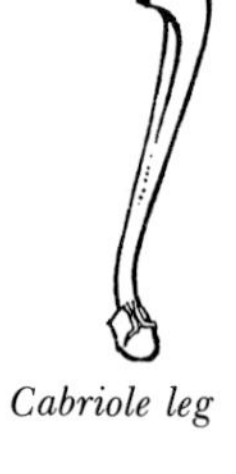
Cabriole leg

Camel back. Colloquial term for a chair or sofa, such as Hepplewhite, with the top curved somewhat like the hump of a dromedary.

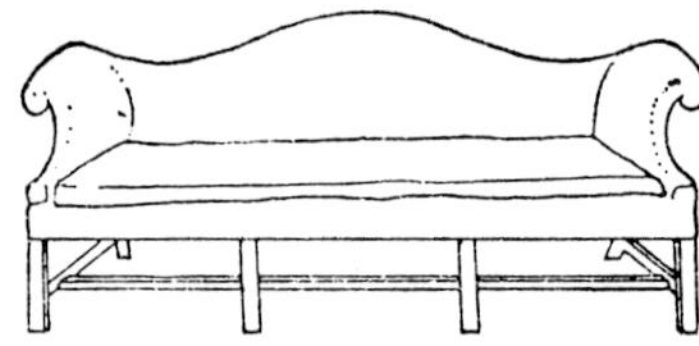

Canapé. The ordinary French word for a sofa. Evolved in many forms during the Louis XV period.

Torchère or candle-stand, gilt wood and gesso, *c.* 1690–1700. Glaisher & Nash, London

Candelabrum. A lighting appliance with branches supporting sockets for more than one light. They took many forms, but are usually made of ormolu, sometimes with figures in patinated bronze. They were often made in pairs or sets of four.

Candle box. A cylindrical or square box, of metal or wood, widely used in the Georgian period for storing candles.

Candlestand. A portable stand (known also as a lampstand, *guéridon*, and *torchère*) for a candlestick, candelabrum, or lamp. After 1660 the fashion arose of having two candlestands flanking a side table with a mirror on the wall above; the stands usually took the form of a baluster or twist-turned shaft, with a circular or octagonal top and a tripod base. At the end of the century more elaborate kinds, copying French stands, became fashionable, with vase-shaped tops and scrolled feet, all carved and gilded. Other examples were of simpler design, but had rich decoration in gesso or marquetry. In the early Georgian period, when gilt stands followed architectural forms, the vase-shaped tops and baluster shafts were larger, and the feet curved outwards, replacing the scrolled French style. About 1750 stands became lighter and more delicate, many of them being enriched with rococo decoration. There was a distinct change in design in the later eighteenth century: the traditional tripod continued, often in mahogany, with turned shaft and a bowl or vase top in the classical taste; but a new type, which was originated by Adam, consisted of three uprights, mounted on feet or a plinth, supporting usually a candelabrum, or with a flat top. Smaller examples of the latter type were made to stand on tables. A much smaller version of candlestand was also popular after 1750 – with a circular base and top, and sometimes an adjustable shaft.

Candlesticks (*flambeaux*). A portable lighting appliance with one socket for a single light or candle. Large numbers were made almost exclusively of ormolu in the late seventeenth and eighteenth centuries, usually in pairs or sets of four, but sometimes in larger quantities.

William and Mary caned maple side chair, probably New England, *c.* 1700. Metropolitan Museum of Art

Cane chair. First produced in England in Charles II's reign, it was very popular in London because it was cheap, light, and durable. It was used in America first in about 1690, in William and Mary tall-backed chairs. The type occasionally occurred in Queen Anne, but was revived in the classical style. Duncan Phyfe used it. Caning was introduced from the Orient through the Netherlands.

Canted. Sloping, at an angle.

Canterbury. (1) A small music stand with partitions for music books, usually mounted on castors, and sometimes with small drawers, much used in the early nineteenth century; and (2) a plate and cutlery stand particularly designed for supper parties in the later eighteenth century, with divisions for cutlery and a semicircular end, on four turned legs. 'The name "Canterbury" arose', wrote Sheraton, 'because the bishop of that See first gave orders for these pieces.'

Carolean. Term of convenience strictly applicable to pieces made in the reign of Charles I (1625–49), those made under Charles II (1660–85) usually being dissociated. Actually the Carolean style is as much an extension of the Jacobean as the latter was of the later Elizabethan.

Cartonnier. A piece of furniture which took various forms. Usually it stood at one end of a writing table (*bureau-plat*) and was intended to hold papers. It was sometimes surmounted by a clock. Also sometimes called a *serre-papier.*

Cartouche. A fanciful scroll; used in America mostly as a central finial for the tops of Philadelphia Chippendale highboys, clocks, and, occasionally, mirrors.

Carver chair. Modern term for an early seventeenth-century 'Dutch'-type armchair made of turned posts and spindles. It has three rails and three spindles in the back. Such chairs may be seen in

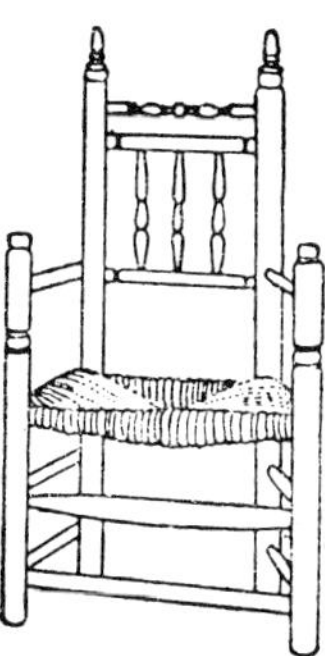

seventeenth-century paints of humbler Dutch interiors, though the source of the American ones was probably an English model. Usually of ash or maple, with rush seats. Named after John Carver, first governor of the Plymouth colony, who is said to have brought one to America with him in the *Mayflower*. Made until the end of the century. Many examples survive, the earliest dating perhaps about 1650. (*See* its variant, Brewster chair.)

Caryatid. Upright carved in semblance of a human figure or, more frequently, a demi-figure on a terminal base. Strictly, Caryatid implies a female, Atlanta or Atlas figure a male figure, though Caryatid is used for either. The term derives from the legend of the women of Carya, enslaved and immured for their betrayal of the Greeks to the Persians. Atlanta refers to the myth of Atlas upholding the heavens.

Cassapanca. A wooden bench with a built-in chest under the seat. Early *cassapanche*, like that of the fifteenth century in the Ca' D'Oro at Venice or the magnificent sixteenth-century example in the Bargello at Florence, are in the form of a *cassone* (*q.v.*) with back and arms. After the *cassone* went out of fashion in the early seventeenth century the *cassapanca* survived as a useful piece of entrance-hall furniture. Seventeenth- and eighteenth-century examples often have immensely high backs of thin wood painted with mythological beings or a coat-of-arms amid a profusion of scrolls.

Cassone. The *cassone*, or chest, was clearly one of the most popular pieces of furniture in fifteenth- and sixteenth-century Italy. It was also the most richly decorated, and, for this reason, perhaps, numerous examples have survived. It was used to hold linen or clothes and might also serve as a seat – with or without the upright back which made it into a *cassapanca* (*q.v.*). *Cassoni* are frequently referred to as dower chests, and although they were often made to hold the supply of linen which a bride took to her new home, there is no reason to suppose that the majority were intended for this purpose. The *cassone nuziale*, or dower chest, can be recognized as such only if it bears the coats-of-arms of two families between whom a marriage took place.

Left Cassone, carved walnut, Italian, 16th century. Christie, Manson & Woods

Right Oak chair covered in 'Turkey-work', dated 1649. Victoria & Albert Museum

The earliest *cassoni* were probably very unpretentious affairs, but a few of the early fifteenth-century examples which have survived are decorated with Gothic curvilinear carving or rough paintings of heraldic achievements. In the Renaissance period great ingenuity was expended on their design and adornment. Some were decorated with gesso friezes of *putti* sporting on the front and sides and others were fashioned like antique sarcophagi, but most seem to have been painted on the front (some were also painted inside the lid). Several highly able Florentine *quattrocento* painters, like the famous Master of the Jarves *cassoni*, seem to have specialized almost exclusively in the decoration of furniture of this type: and some more important artists, like Bartolomeo Montagna, occasionally turned their hands to this decorative work. In Florence paintings of battles and the triumphs of Roman generals were in particular demand, elsewhere religious and mythological scenes seem to have enjoyed great popularity, but in Venice patterns of ornamental motifs were generally preferred. *Intarsia* views of real or imaginery architecture were also employed to decorate *cassoni*. In the sixteenth century the painted *cassone* seems to have gone out of fashion, and most surviving examples from this period are simply carved with abstract decorations. A few later sixteenth-century *cassoni* are adorned with mannerist term figures at the corners and low reliefs in the same style on the front. The *cassone* survived the sixteenth century only in the form of the *cassapanca* or of a simple unembellished utilitarian travelling chest.

Cat. A stand used after about 1750 to warm plates in front of the fire; it had three arms and three feet of turned wood (or three legs of cabriole form). The turning was well ringed to provide sockets for plates of various sizes.

Causeuse. A large chair or small sofa to accommodate two persons. Roughly corresponds to the small English settee. Sometimes referred to colloquially as a love-seat.

Cedar. Handsome pieces of furniture were occasionally made of colourful red cedarwood, though cedar – both the red and the white – was usually set aside for drawers, chests, linings, etc.

Cellaret. The name given generally after 1750 to a case on legs or stand for wine bottles; prior to that date, from the end of the seventeenth century, the same kind of case was called a cellar. In the early eighteenth century cellarets, lined with lead and containing compartments for bottles, stood under side tables, and they were still made later in the century when sideboards, which had drawers fitted up to hold bottles, came into general use. Sheraton classified the cellaret with the wine cistern (*q.v.*) and sarcophagus, and distinguished them from the bottle case, which was for square bottles only.

Box-shaped armchair with linen-fold carving, first half of the 16th century, oak

Mahogany cellaret on pillar base by Sheraton, *c.* 1790

Chair. In its old sense chair meant, as like as not, an armchair, what is now called a single or side chair being a backstool (stool with a back).[1] To what extent the chair originated from such box forms as the chest is suggested by early surviving examples of box-like structure. Development from the wainscot chair to the open-framed variety with panelled back belongs in general to the late sixteenth century. Folding or rack chairs and X chairs (so called from their shape) have also a long history. Certain sixteenth-century chairs with narrow backs and widely splayed arms are known as *caqueteuses* or *caquetoires*. The so-called farthingale chair (a term freely applied to many pieces, mostly of the earlier seventeenth century) has its back support raised clear of the seat. Upholstery (not unknown earlier) had arrived, seats and back pads being covered in velvet or in 'Turkeywork'. Leather was used, especially on Cromwellian chairs, some of which date from the Interregnum, though the type endured until relatively late in the seventeenth century. Leather or Russia chair are old terms for such items. About the middle of the seventeenth century are found what are often termed 'mortuary' chairs, a term of doubtful origin for chairs with a small moustachioed and bearded head (supposedly allusive to Charles I) in the centre of the shaped and scrolled back rails. Similar chairs occur without the masks, and the type is a variation of Yorkshire or Derbyshire chair, the geographical distribution of which is undefined.

Cane chairs (*q.v.*) achieved main popularity in the second half of the seventeenth century, their backs and seats being caned. Scrolling, curlicues, boys and crowns, etc., were favoured as carved ornament. Backs lengthen, assuming the form of a narrow panel or centre (often caned or stuffed) flanked by uprights. Already had been reached the period of barley-sugar turning (*see* Twist turning).

[1] 'Back chaier' occurs (e.g. Unton Inventory, 1620).

Corner chairs, some of triangular formation, and sundry related types, were already in being. A later variety has the seat disposed diagonally to the low, rounded back. Elbow chair and roundabout chair are synonyms in use. An allied type is the circular chair (with circular seat), often Dutch, and known as burgomaster or (again) roundabout chair, such terms being jargon. Thrown chairs of various shapes, with much turnery, have been often assigned to the sixteenth century, though many are certainly later. Though scarcely belonging to the Age of Oak, the Windsor chair (*q.v.*) may have owed something to older types. The basic characteristic of Windsors is not the bow or hoop back, but the detail that back and underframing are all mortised into the wooden seat, itself frequently saddle-shaped and 'dished', but sometimes circular, etc. The bow-back type (late eighteenth century and later), preceded by the comb or fan back (early eighteenth century and later), was itself followed by other formations on more or less 'Regency' lines. Types are many with much overlapping; woods are mixed. Scole or Mendlesham chairs are East Anglian types on Windsor lines. Yorkshire and Lancashire Windsors usually show 'frilly' splats and developed turnery, but the type was not confined to the North of England. In America, Windsors were made from the early eighteenth century, and include some fine types. Lancashire chair is also applied to an extensively made type of bobbin back, much favoured in the eighteenth and early nineteenth centuries, but, here again, as with Yorkshire and Derbyshire chairs in general, the geographical location has been overstressed (*see* Close chair and stool; *also* Restoration).

In the Renaissance period those made in France were on the whole very simple, constructed of plain wood, usually walnut, and carved with conventional motifs in the Italian style. Often they are of the

Carved oak armchair, early 17th century

ecclesiastical type with high backs carved in relief. Others have carved arms and stretchers. These types continued into the early seventeenth century, usually accompanied by some upholstery.

Such chairs of the Louis XIV period as have come down to us are also almost always of plain wood, carved in the classical manner. The backs are high, often with elaborately carved cornices. The legs are also elaborately carved and are often joined with stretchers. The chairs are upholstered on seats and back, either with embroidery, velvet, or with cane. Tapestry does not appear until later in the eighteenth century.

In the Louis XV period the design of chairs became less formal and the carving soon began to be carried out in the rococo manner. The outlines of the upholstered backs and seats, and the legs, gradually became curved and bowed until there is not a straight line in the whole design. Often chairs of the Louis XV period are of considerable size and of rather a heavy appearance. They are upholstered usually with silk, velvet, or brocade, but sometimes with tapestry, which begins to make its appearance at this time.

In the Louis XVI period chairs, in particular, take up the prevailing neoclassical style, the change being noticeable soon after 1755. Legs gradually become straighter, as do the outlines of backs, seats, and arms, and the motifs employed in the carving derive from classical sources, the most commonly found being the acanthus leaf in various forms, the wave-like band and the Ionic capital, as well as symmetrical garlands of flowers. It was at this time that the carving of chairs, particularly those produced by G. Jacob, reached the very greatest refinement, both of design and detail.

The frames of chairs of the Louis XV and Louis XVI periods are usually made of beech, birch, or walnut, and they are often gilt. It is important to remember, however, that they may not originally have been so. Sometimes the wood forming the frames was left plain and unadorned, more often they were painted white, or white and partly gilt. Equally, a chair may have been originally plain or painted, and then gilt before the end of the eighteenth century. More often gilding or regilding was carried out in the nineteenth century, and often very coarsely. Collectors should bear this in mind when judging both the style and condition of French chairs.

The earliest Italian chairs were probably no more than square stools to which a back and arms had been added, but they do not seem to have been in general use until the fifteenth century. Folding chairs (*sedie pieghevoli*) were made before the beginning of the fourteenth century, however, and one or two fourteenth-century examples have survived. The most popular form of chair in the fifteenth century seems to have been the so-called 'Dantesque' or X chair which might also, if necessary, be folded for travelling. Two thirteenth-century wooden X chairs are known, but most chairs of this type seem to have been made of metal rods. At first the X chair was without any form of back but this was added in the sixteenth century, and many examples survive from this period. The so-called Savonarola chair was a development of the simple X chair with a number of struts following the curve of the design. Chairs of both these types were made throughout Italy in both the fifteenth and sixteenth centuries. Wooden tub

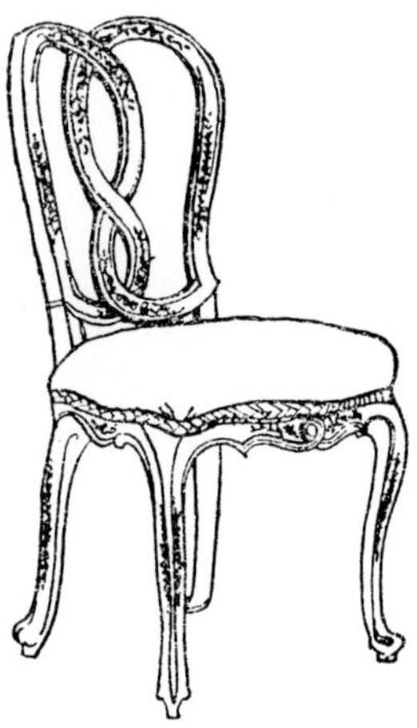

Mid-18th-century Venetian chair with figure-of-eight back

chairs seem to have enjoyed a limited popularity in the fourteenth and fifteenth centuries (a good example is in the Horne Museum at Florence). The 'Andrea del Sarto' chair, which has a semicircular seat above which a thin strip of wood supported on balusters serves as both back and arms, was introduced into Tuscany in the early sixteenth century.

In the course of the sixteenth century the upright chair with straight back and arms was developed and ornamented, eventually becoming the standard pattern. Seventeenth-century craftsmen used it as the basis for their richly carved and gilded thrones, such as the one in the Palazzo Rezzonico at Venice. The easy chair (*poltrona*) does not appear in Italy until the late seventeenth century. During the eighteenth century Italian chairs differed little from those made elsewhere in Europe. In Venice, however, chairs with backs in the form of a figure of eight enjoyed great popularity.

Chamfer. Bevelled edge, as when the sharp edges of a beam are bevelled off. A dust chamfer (i.e. to throw off dust) is a smooth bevel at the lower edge of the framework of a panel, the other edges being moulded, or part moulded and part of rectangular cut. Of stop chamfer there is no better simple definition than Walter Rose's in *The Village Carpenter*: 'where slope finishes and square begins' [to arise].

Chandeliers. A branched lighting appliance consisting usually of several lights which can be suspended from a ceiling. Large quantities were made in France in the seventeenth and eighteenth centuries, but not many have survived. They were made of various materials: ormolu, wood, crystal, glass, and occasionally porcelain.

Cherry. A hard, close-grained, reddish- or pinkish-brown wood, it was used in England for chairs and panels in the seventeenth and eighteenth centuries, though few examples remain. It was often used in America for furniture of the finest design and workmanship. In use as early as 1680. Joseph Downs says cherry was a favourite wood among New York cabinet makers; was more often used than mahogany in Connecticut, and quite often used in Pennsylvania, Virginia, and Kentucky furniture.

Chest (*see also* Coffer). One primitive form of chest is the dug-out or trunk, its interior gouged in the solid. Some dug-outs are of considerable antiquity; others may be of more recent date than their appearance suggests. In name and rounded lid the travelling trunk, as it is still known, recalls the ancient use of a tree trunk. Framed chests are also ancient, the earliest surviving medieval examples being formed of great planks so disposed as to present an almost or wholly flush surface at front and back. Panelled chests were being made in the fifteenth century, later becoming very popular. The earlier 'flush' construction was, however, to some extent perpetuated until a very late period in the boarded chest, made entirely of boards, including the ends, which also form the uprights (*cf.* Wainscot). Unusually long examples are sometimes, but not necessarily correctly, called rapier chests. The validity of the term is uncertain. Popularly called 'non(e)such' chests, mainly of the latter part of the sixteenth century, are inlaid with formalized architectural designs, thought possibly to represent the Palace of Nonsuch, or Nonesuch, at Ewell, Surrey. Such architectural motifs are, however, exploitations of a Renaissance design favoured on the Continent, though a possible affinity exists between them and the crowded towns in Gothic art. Mule chest (implying a hybrid) is collectors' jargon of no validity for a chest *with* drawers.

Chest of drawers. This derives in name, and to a considerable extent in principle, from the chest, a link being the chest with drawers, with a single range of drawers beneath the box. Such pieces were in being by the latter part of the sixteenth century, a gradual tendency to increase the drawer-space at the expense of the box resulting in the chest of drawers. At the same time various structures enclosing a quantity of drawers were also in being, on the Continent and in England, as with the 'new cubborde of boxes' made by Lawrence Abelle in 1595 for Stratford-upon-Avon or the 'cubborde with drawing boxes' of the Unton Inventory, 1596. 'Nests of boxes' is another old term (*see also* Bargueño, Writing cabinet). The chest of drawers was introduced into Italy, probably from France, in the late seventeenth century. An early example in the Palazzo dei Conservatori at Rome is of a square pattern adorned with pilasters at the corners, but the French *bombé* shape was generally preferred. In some mid-eighteenth-century Venetian examples the curve of the belly has been ridiculously exaggerated and the top made considerably larger than the base. In Rome and Naples

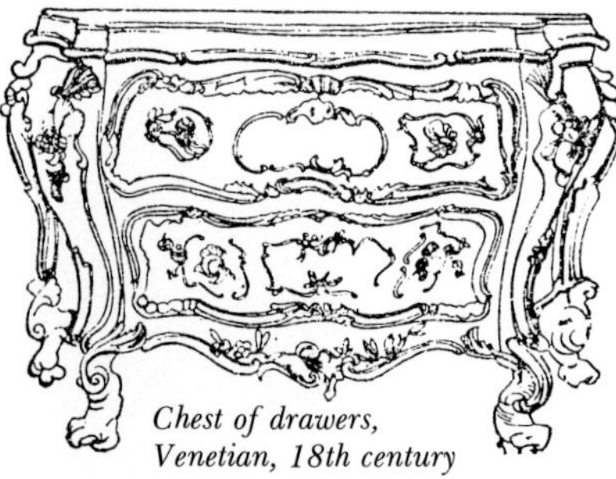

Chest of drawers, Venetian, 18th century

rather more reticent designs were adopted. In Venice and Genoa chests of drawers were frequently lacquered or painted, while Lombard examples were often decorated with *intarsia*. Elaborate bronze mounts in the French style are rare on *cassettoni* made outside Piedmont. In the United States it was not common in the Queen Anne period, but was revived,

Right Oak chest, decorated with iron scroll work, second half of the 13th century. Victoria & Albert Museum

Panel of 'non(e)such' chest

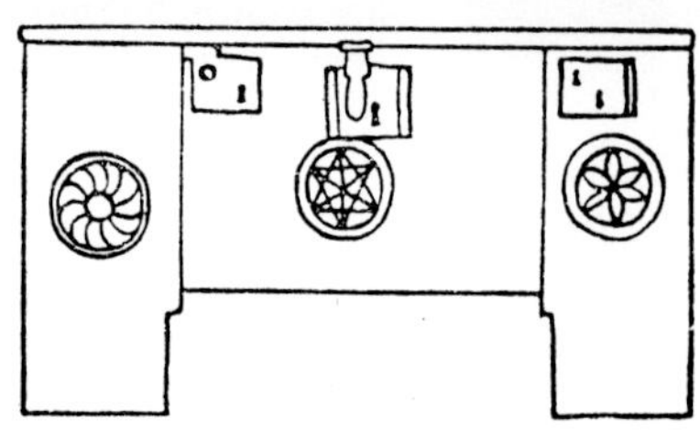

Chest of 13th-century construction

especially in New England, during the Chippendale period. Serpentine, oxbow, and block-front shapes are found on New England Chippendale chests.
Cheval glass. A larger type of toilet mirror in a frame with four legs; also known as a horse dressing glass; dating from the end of the eighteenth century. The rectangular mirror either pivoted on screws set in the uprights or moved up and down by means of a weight within the frame ('the same as a sash-window' – Sheraton). Turned uprights and stretchers were often found on these pieces about 1800.
Cheveret. *See* Secretaire.
Chiffonier. A piece of furniture which has given rise to a certain amount of confusion. The French chiffonier was a tall chest of drawers, but the *chiffonière*, a quite different piece, was a small set of drawers on legs. It was the latter which seems to have been copied in England in the later eighteenth century. Another form of chiffonier was popular in the Regency period – a low cupboard with shelves for books. As this was similar to contemporary commodes, it can be taken that the English version of the *chiffonière* was the only true small piece of furniture.
Child's furniture. Mostly small-scale furniture for children's usage, distinct from toy furniture. Some confusion exists between tables and the square joined stool (with unsplayed legs) which certainly existed as such. Chairs follow full-scale design, or are high-chair pattern, some of enclosed or wainscot fashion, others elevated on tall legs. A framework on wheels to support a toddler has been given various names, e.g. baby cage or go cart.
China cabinet. Seldom, if ever, found in America as a separate piece of furniture before 1790–1800. Even then it is perhaps a 'bookcase' (*q.v.*) used for displaying china. In early examples the lower portion is often a shallow cupboard on legs. Most American china cabinets date after 1800 and are in the Sheraton or a later style.
China stand. An ornamental stand for displaying china or flowers, introduced at the end of the seventeenth century and at first taking the form of a low pedestal on carved and scrolled feet, or of a vase on a plinth. In the early eighteenth century the form was sometimes that of a stool with cabriole legs, in mahogany. More fanciful designs, in the rococo taste, were evident after 1750, as in the 'Stands for China Jarrs' presented in Chippendale's *Director*. In the Adam period some attractive stands for flower bowls resembled the contemporary candlestands with three uprights. Little four-legged stands with shelves were also made at this time for flowerpots.
Chip carving. Lightly cut ('chipped') surface ornament, mostly of formal character and including whorls, roundels (*qq.v.*), etc. Such work, known medievally, persisted on items of much later date.
Classical style. Basically any humanistic style emphasizing ancient Greek ideals, and in the arts a style inspired by Greek and Roman art and architecture. In American furniture the style reflected the innovations of Robert Adam, the British architect who was inspired by ancient Roman design. The design books of Hepplewhite and Sheraton helped communicate the style to America, where it has been called after them by dividing the style into two tendencies, the Hepplewhite and Sheraton. This is a difficult distinction to make.
Claw-and-ball foot. An adaptation, probably from the Chinese, of a dragon's claw grasping a pearl. Perhaps first adapted in Europe by the Dutch, it spread to England, from whence it was introduced into America about 1735. Enormously popular as the foot of American cabriole leg furniture in the Queen Anne and Chippendale styles. It remained much in fashion as late as the 1790s. In America a bird's claw was generally used, mostly the eagle's.
Clock cases. Elaborate clock cases made their appearance in France in the Louis XIV period and were often treated in the most monumental manner. They became a special product of the Boulle *atelier*, as they did of the workshop of Cressent later. In the Louis XV and Louis XVI periods they took almost any form which appealed to their creators, and a great deal of ingenuity, both of design and craftsmanship, went into their production. Roughly, they divided themselves into five main types: wall or cartel clocks, mantel clocks, pedestal clocks, *régulateurs*, and bracket clocks, the names of which are self-explanatory.

Bracket clock by A. Brocot Delettrez, Paris, enamel dial contained in waisted gilt metal-mounted cage decorated with brass scrolls on red tortoiseshell, French, late 19th century

If the movement or make of a clock is known and the date is established the collector should remember that it may have originally been placed in another case. This is not uncommon.
Close chairs and **close** or **night stools.** Were sometimes chair-shaped, sometimes rectangular or drum-shaped boxes (possibly covered and padded), and sometimes rectangular boxes on legs. A type of joined stool with a box top was so usable, though it does not follow that all stools with this feature were for sanitary usage.
Coaster. A receptacle which came into use before 1750 for moving wine, beer, and food on the dining table; also variously known as a slider, decanter

stand, and beer wagon. For ease of movement, the coaster was normally fitted either with small wheels or with a baize-covered base, and the materials used in good examples included mahogany, papier mâché, and silver. Beer wagons were sometimes made with special places for the jug and drinking vessels.

Cock's head. Twin-plate hinge of curvilinear shape, the finials formed (more or less) as a cock's head. Frequently found on woodwork of the late sixteenth and first half of the seventeenth centuries.

Coffer. Term freely confused with chest. In strict definition a coffer was a chest or box covered in leather or some other material and banded with metalwork, but it seems likely that the term was not always precisely used. It may not be wrong to class as coffers various stoutly built and/or heavily ironed strong chests and boxes, even though they do not fulfil all the above requirements. Trussing coffers were furnished with lifting rings and shackles or other devices for transportation; but chests and coffers not intended for transport might be chained to the wall for security.

Comb back. *See* Windsor.

Commode. The normal French word for a chest of drawers, which seems to date from the early eighteenth century.

Louis XV commode by J. Schmitz, the front veneered with flared and contrasting panels of tulipwood, bombe shape, cabriole legs, ormolu mounts, mid-18th century

Concertina action. A device on card and gaming tables for extending the frame to support the table top when it is opened. The back half of the frame is made up of two hinged sections that fold in to reduce the frame size when the top is closed.

Connecticut chest

Connecticut chest. So named because chiefly made in seventeenth- and eighteenth-century Connecticut. Decorative chest with or without a bottom drawer or two. Ornamented with applied bosses and split spindles which set off three front panels carved, low relief, in conventionalized flowers – centre panel, sunflowers; other panels, tulips.

Constitution mirror

Constitution mirror. A term of obscure origin, perhaps a misnomer, widely used in America when referring to a Chippendale-style wall mirror with strings of leaves or flowers at the sides, a scrolled-arch top, and a fanciful finial, generally a bird. The frame is usually in walnut or mahogany and partly gilded. (*See also* Martha Washington mirror).

Corner chair. A square or squarish seat supported by two side posts and a back post, the three extending above the seat to a low, strong, semicircular top rail. The fourth support, a leg, is added centre front. Made in America from about 1700 to 1775, it is found in three styles – Dutch–Queen Anne transitional, Queen Anne, and Chippendale. Also called roundabout and writing chair. Some authorities say the American Windsor chair (*q.v.*) may have been evolved from it.

Corner cupboard. This type of furniture consists of a triangular cupboard containing shelves and closed by a door, which is sometimes curved. It is made to fit into the rightangled corner of a room. *Encoignures* begin to appear in France during the Louis XV period, and are usually made in pairs, often *en suite* with a secretaire or chest of drawers. They continued to be made right up to the Revolution.

Coromandel or **zebra wood.** A form of ebony with light-coloured striped markings found on the Coromandel coast (*see also under* Ebony).

Couch. A seventeenth- and eighteenth-century term for day bed; not used as synonym for sofa or settee until recent times.

Counter. Hutch-like structure, sometimes approximating to a table with an undercompartment. The name (surviving in shop counter, etc.) derives from the top being employed for reckoning accounts with counters or jettons disposed on a marked scale. When not so used the counter was available for a variety of other purposes.

Court cupboard. The earliest fine cupboard in America. A kind of Jacobean buffet (and called a buffet in England), with the upper portion enclosed, the lower open. Sometimes, however, the upper portion is partly open – that is, contains a closed central cupboard with splayed sides. When the bottom portion is also closed, whether with doors or as a chest of drawers, it is in America called a press cupboard (*see under* Cupboard). Early ones are generally of oak, with much sturdy Jacobean ornament, and seldom, if ever, ornamented alike (*c.* 1650–70).

Courting mirror. Small mirror framed with mouldings and a cresting, the crested area often containing a painted picture or design. They were traditionally a

Far right Oak splay-fronted court cupboard with carved bulbous supports. Mary Bellis Antiques, Hungerford

courting gift in eighteenth-century New England. Lockwood says their source was a similar mirror made in China for the export trade.

Cradle. The cradle, which had hitherto been a fairly simple piece of furniture occasionally carved but otherwise of a type that might be found in any other European country, was developed into an object of extravagant fantasy in mid-eighteenth-century Venice. Here cradles were made with rippling rococo rims and lacquered with floral motifs or heavily carved with *putti* and gilded. The most fantastic of all is that formerly in the *Donà dalle Rose* Collection at Venice, in which the cradle itself is swung between two branches of a naturalistically carved tree, with a stork gazing at the occupant from the foot and a *chinoiserie* parasol suspended over its head.

Credence. Side table as used ecclesiastically for the Elements prior to Consecration, and for the Cruets, etc., therewith associated. Such tables were sometimes of hutch-like formation, and the term credence has been loosely extended to cover other furniture of more or less similar construction.

Credenza. An Italian sideboard or buffet used as a serving table on which silver might also be displayed. Fifteenth- and sixteenth-century *credenze* were either simple tables designed to stand by a wall or else long cupboards, sometimes with canted corners, the

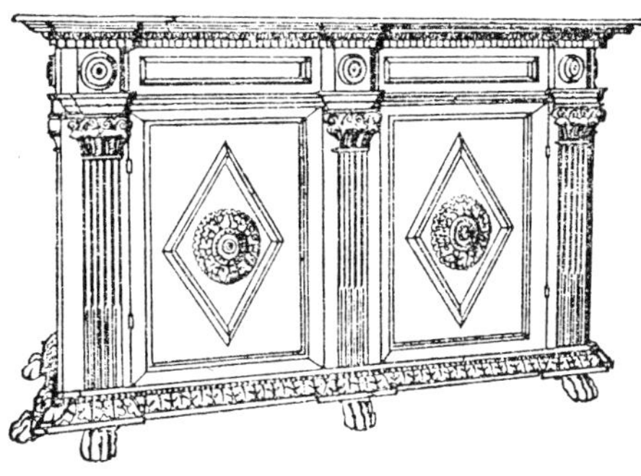

Left Court cupboard, oak; English, early 17th century. Victoria & Albert Museum

height of an ordinary dining table. As they were normally covered with linen, they were very simple in design and decoration. A recessed top storey containing a cupboard was added to many *credenze* in the sixteenth century, and this was usual in subsequent periods.

Cresting. Shaped and sometimes perforated ornament on the top of a structure, as in the cresting of a chair.

Croft. A small filing cabinet of the late eighteenth century (named after its inventor), specially designed to be moved about easily in the library; it had many small drawers and a writing top.

Cromwellian. Term of convenience applied to English furniture of austere character, actually or supposedly made about the time of the Commonwealth or Interregnum (1649–60), but also used loosely of related types.

Cromwellian chair. Spanish-type chair with strips of leather for the seat and back; turned legs and stretchers, occasionally spiral-turned. Generally ornamented with brass-headed tacks. A mid seventeenth-century 'Puritan' chair. Very few have been found.

Cross stretcher. X-shaped stretcher in straight or curved lines. Sometimes found on occasional tables, a few chairs, and in America on highboys and lowboys.

Cupboard. Originally cup-board, a species of sideboard for the display and service of plate, etc., and having no essential connection with enclosed and doored structures. When equipped with such features, these might be noted (*see* Ambry). The modern sense of cupboard, as an enclosed structure, is a long-standing usurpation, such items being mostly descended from the press, press cupboard, etc. Livery cupboard (a much-abused term from Fr. *livrer*, to deliver) was a *doorless* structure, as is clearly stated in the Hengrave Hall contracts, 1537–8. That it was distinguished from the court cupboard is shown by such an entry as 'ij court cubbordes, and one liverye cubborde', in Unton Inventory, 1596 ('Liverie table' is also listed). Court cupboard was likewise an open structure, or with a small enclosed compartment in the upper part (*see* R. W. Symonds, 'The Evolution of the Cupboard', in *The Connoisseur*, December 1943, and 'The Dynyng Parlor and its Furniture', op. cit., January 1944). The tendency to compartment such furniture eventually resulted in enclosed pieces of similar outline being called court cupboard, though press cupboard is preferable. Welsh varieties of the press cupboard are the cwpwrdd deuddarn (two-tiered) and the cwpwrdd tridarn (three-tiered, the top stage often more or less open). Dole cupboard strictly applies to hanging or other structures open-shelved, or doored and railed, used in the charitable dispensation of bread, etc., in churches and other institutions. The term is often wrongly applied to food cupboard, or, better, food hutch. Spice cupboard is a hanging 'cupboard', usually of small dimensions, internally fitted with shelves or compartments and drawers, and fronted with a door. Doubtless many were used to hold spices, herbs, and medicaments, though they could have served various purposes. Corner cupboard is a triangular structure, doored or open, independent or fitted, and normally furnished with shelving.

Cupid's bow. A term used to describe the typical top rail of a Chippendale chair back which curves up at

the ends and dips slightly in the centre.
Curly. The grainings of some woods – maple, walnut, birch, etc. – sometimes show feather-like, curly or tiger-stripe markings, which are much prized. Not to be confused with other markings, such as bird's eye, wavy, blister, and quilted.
Cutlery stand. *See* Canterbury (2).
Cylinder-top desk. A writing table, incorporating drawers and writing accessories, the functional part of which is closed by means of a curved panel fastened with a lock. It is usually supported on tall legs and differs from a roll-top desk (*q.v.*) in that the curved panel is in one piece and not slatted.
Cypress. Fine furniture was sometimes made of the pale to dark brown (swamp) cypress, especially in South Carolina, Georgia, and other southern American states. More often used for drawers and linings, and for utility-type furniture. It is noted for its resistance to decay.
Daventry. A small chest of drawers with a sloping top for writing; said to be named after a client of the firm of Gillow who claimed to have invented it.
Day bed. Known in England from the sixteenth century, though authentic examples are mostly of much later date. The original form approximated to a stump bed with a sloped back at one end. In the period of Charles II, and later, day beds were caned, their frames often being elaborately carved, quite likely *en suite* with cane chairs.
Decanter stand. *See* Coaster.
Desk. A term of varied meaning, but taken here to refer to two portable pieces. (1) The commonest meaning was that of a box (originating in medieval times) with a sloping top for reading and writing. Early examples in oak in the Tudor and Stuart periods had carving and inlay, and sometimes the owner's initials and date. When bureaux came into use at the end of the seventeenth century these small desks were too useful to discard, and were fitted with drawers and pigeonholes; many were veneered with walnut, or japanned, and some were mounted on stands. In the Georgian period they became less decorative, and were usually of plain mahogany, few were made after 1800. (2) In the later eighteenth century 'desk' was the current term for what would now be called a music stand (which was also used for reading); it generally took the form of a tripod base supporting a shaft and a sloping, adjustable top.

Baltimore Hepplewhite inlaid mahogany card table, 1790–1800. Courtesy of Museum of Fine Arts, Boston

Desk box. A rectangular box with sloping lid for the storage of books and writing materials; more popularly known in America as a Bible box.
Deuddarn. *See* Cupboard.
Document drawer. A thin narrow drawer in a desk for important papers.
Doreurs, Corporation des. The craft guild responsible for gilding in all its forms in France. The organization was similar to that of the *menuisiers-ébénistes*, except that the apprenticeship lasted five instead of six years. There were 370 *maîtres-doreurs* at the end of the eighteenth century (*see also* Ormolu).
Dowel. Headless pin used in construction. Though, architecturally, dowels may be of other materials, wood is understood when speaking of furniture. Trenail (i.e. tree-nail) is another term for a wooden dowel (*see Nails).*
Dower chest or **dowry chest.** Is one made to store the trousseau of a prospective bride. Outstanding among American examples are the Hadley chest (*q.v.*), the Connecticut chest, and the painted Pennsylvania-German chest.
Drake foot. *See* Duck foot.
Drawer. Box in a framework from which it can be drawn. In some simple or traditional constructions drawers merely rest on the framework, but a typical feature of the late sixteenth to seventeenth century was a groove on each side of a drawer, accommodating projecting runners on the framework. This gave way, in later furniture, to runner strips at the base of the drawer itself, and the encasing of the interior framing with dustboards.
Dresser. On which food was dressed; a species of sideboard with or without a superimposed 'back'; also for service of food, and/or storage of plates, dishes, etc. Some backless dressers are closely allied to the side table. Dressers are wontedly furnished with storage accommodation (such as ambries, shelving, drawers, etc., or combinations of such). Welsh dresser is used of local varieties of the tall-back dresser found virtually everywhere. North Wales and South Wales types are differentiated.
Drop or **tear-drop handle.** The characteristic pull used on furniture with drawers, 1690–1720. Of brass, solid or hollow, this pendant hangs from a brass plate and is attached to the drawer by wire pins. Also called tear drop and pear drop, which picturesquely suggest its shape.
Drop leaf. A table with one or two hinged leaves which can be raised or dropped by bringing swinging legs or supports into use. Many kinds of drop-leaf tables have special names – butterfly, corner, gate leg, library, Pembroke, sofa, etc.
Drum table. A circular top table on a tripod base with a deep skirt that may contain drawers. The type exists only in the classical style, and American examples appear late.
Duck foot. Colloquial American term for the three-toed club or Dutch foot, mostly found in Delaware River Valley furniture. Also called drake foot and web foot. For some reason the pad foot is often mistakenly called a duck foot.
Dumb waiter. A dining-room stand, an English invention of the early eighteenth century, with normally three circular trays, increasing in size towards the bottom, on a shaft with tripod base. This established design gave way to more elaborate versions at the end of the century; four-legged supports and

rectangular trays were found; and quite different kinds were square or circular tables with special compartments for bottles, plates, etc.

Eagle, American. The Seal of the United States, adopted 1786, emblematizes the American bald eagle with wings outspread. This emblem promptly became popular as furniture ornament in America – carved (free or engaged), inlaid or painted – replacing the fanciful phoenix which had been used since the mid-eighteenth century.

Ébéniste. The ordinary French term for a cabinet maker concerned in making veneered furniture as distinct from a *menuisier* (*q.v.*). The word derived from the ebony (*ébène*) to be found on the earliest veneered furniture in France. It is not found, nor are *ébénistes* associated by name with the *menuisiers* guild, until 1743, by which time the use of ebony was more or less confined to pieces in the Boulle technique. Although permitted by guild regulations to work in plain wood like the *menuisiers*, an *ébéniste* usually confined his activities to techniques requiring veneer or inlay (*see also under* Menuisiers-Ébénistes).

Ebonize. To stain wood to look like ebony. This was often done in the seventeenth century for the applied ornaments on oak furniture. Also used in William and Mary period when contrasting colours in wood were sought.

Ebony. A hard wood, black and finely grained, sometimes found with brown or purple streaks. Found commonly in tropical climates in Asia, Africa, and America. Extensively used in France for veneering furniture, particularly in combination with Boulle marquetry (*see also under* Coromandel or zebra wood and Boulle marquetry). Grandfather and other clock cases were veneered with ebony in England in the seventeenth century.

Egg-and-tongue (egg-and-dart). Repeat ornament of alternated ovolo and dart-like motifs; as much other ornament of classical origin, transmitted through Renaissance channels.

Elizabethan. Term of convenience, strictly applicable to furniture, etc., made in the reign of Elizabeth I (1558–1603), though loosely used of pieces of later date displaying Elizabethan characteristics. The reign was long; just as early Elizabethan furniture shows influences from previous reigns, so late Elizabethan merges easily into Jacobean.

En arbelette. An expression used for shapes and forms which have a double curve similar to that of a crossbow.

Encoignures. *See under* Corner cupboard.

Espagnolette. A decorative motif popularized by the engravings of Gillot and Watteau and consisting of a female head surrounded by a large stiff collar of a type worn in Spain in the seventeenth century. It was used frequently in the early eighteenth century as a mounted decoration for furniture.

Étagère. A small worktable consisting usually of shelves or trays set one above the other. The word is of nineteenth-century origin, the ordinary term used earlier being *table à ouvrage*.

Fake or forgery. Furniture (or other objects) made or assembled in simulation of authentic antiquities, with deceptive intent, Fakes are of several kinds, of which a few may be listed: (*a*) the wholly modern fake, though quite possibly made of old wood; (*b*) the fake incorporating old and in themselves authentic parts; (*c*) the 'carved-up' fake, as, for instance, a plain chest (itself antique) with modern carving added; (*d*) the 'married' piece, of which all, or considerable portions, may be authentic, but which has been 'made up' from more than one source. Difficult of classification are certain items which have been liberally restored (*see* Restoration), each case demanding judgment on its own merits. Though over-restoration is reprehensible, cases occur of pieces reconditioned with innocent intent. An ordinary repair to a genuine antique need not disqualify it. At the same time a watchful eye should be kept for an old faking trick of inserting an obvious 'repair' for the sole purpose of making the rest of a spurious piece look older by contrast.

Egg-and-tongue

Mahogany tripod pole screen with needlework panel, *c.* 1750. Frank Partridge, London

Fan back. *See* Windsor chair.

Fancy chair. Almost any variety of decorative occasional chair, generally light in weight, painted, and with a cane seat. The source was probably the late Sheraton occasional chair. Popular in all styles from 1800 to 1850.

Fan pattern. Description of the back of a chair when filled with ribs somewhat resembling the stalks of a half-open fan. Also said of any fan-shaped carving, inlay, or painted decoration. (*See* Rising sun).

Federal style. A term often used in America to describe furniture made in the United States between 1785 and 1830, the early days of the Republic. It includes works showing Hepplewhite, Sheraton, Directory, and early Empire influence. An inexact, therefore unsatisfactory, term – though at times highly convenient.

Firedogs. An appliance, popular in France for use in a fireplace to support the logs of a fire. These were usually made in pairs of iron with bronze ends or finials, sometimes patinated and sometimes gilt. They took various forms during the Louis XV and XVI periods, when the ornamental parts are usually made of ormolu and are often of the finest quality.

Fire screen. An adjustable screen made from the end of the seventeenth century to give protection from the intense heat of large open fires. Two main kinds were used. (1) Pole screen: with the screen on an upright supported on a tripod base; known as a 'screen stick' in the late seventeenth century; and in very general use in the eighteenth. The screen, often of needlework, was at first rectangular, but oval and shield shapes were fashionable in the late eighteenth century. In the Regency period the tripod was replaced by a solid base, and the screen was a banner hung from a bar on the upright. (2) Horse or cheval screen – two uprights, each on two legs, enclosing a panel. Elaborate carving and gilding of the crests was often found until the end of the eighteenth century, when lighter and simpler screens were in vogue. Needlework was the popular material for the panel.

Fish tail. The carving, somewhat resembling a fish tail, on the top rail of a banister-back chair.

Flag seat. Colloquial term sometimes used for a seat woven of rush-like material.

Flambeaux. *See under* Candlesticks.

Flame carving. A cone-like finial carved to represent flames, either straight or spiralling. Used on highboys, secretaries, grandfather clocks, etc.

Flemish scroll. A curving double scroll used on William and Mary style legs; also on the wide stretcher connecting the front legs.

Flower stand. *See* China stand.

Fluting. Narrow vertical groovings used in classical architecture on columns and pilasters. In furniture fluting is employed where pilasters or columns are

Fluting

suggested and on straight legs. It is of particular importance in the classical style, but is encountered in earlier work as well.

Folding table. *See* Gate leg.

Fondeurs, Corporation des. The craft guild responsible for casting and chasing metal, either for sculpture, furniture, or *bronzes d'ameublement* in France. It was organized similarly to those of the *menuisiers-ébénistes* and *doreurs*.

Form. Long, backless seat, with any number of supports from two upwards. Of ancient lineage, the form is simply a long stool. 'Longe stoole' occurs in old inventories.

Four-poster. Colloquial term widely used for a bedstead with four posts.

Frame. The style of picture frames altered with the style of painting. The earliest to be found in private houses were very simple, of painted or gilt wood. Late sixteenth-century artists seem sometimes to have designed and painted allegorical frames for their own works. Not until the seventeenth century did the richly carved and gilded frame come into its own. Some late seventeenth- and early eighteenth-century frames are, indeed, better and more elaborate works of art than the pictures they enshrine. Later, eighteenth-century frames are usually more discreet and simple.

Gadrooning. A carved ornamental edging of a repeated pattern which, on Chippendale furniture, is often no more than curving, alternating convex and concave sections. Particularly popular in New York and Philadelphia in the Chippendale period.

Carved oak chest with arcaded front and gadrooned drawer at base, late 17th century. Mary Bellis Antiques, Hungerford

Garde Meuble de la Couronne. The department which dealt with all matters connected with the furnishing of the royal palaces in France. It was established by Louis XIV in 1663, and survived until the end of the monarchy. Very fortunately, its records survive more or less intact.

The first inventory of furniture belonging to the Crown was complete in 1673 and has been published in full by M. Émile Molinier (*see* Bibliography), but the most important item among the records is the *Journal*, instituted in 1685 and continuing until 1784. In it every piece acquired for the Crown was scrupulously entered and given a number, with dates of delivery, the name of the maker, costs and measurements, its eventual destination in the royal palaces, and a full description. The numbers often correspond with those painted in the backs of existing pieces (*see* Inventory numbers), and these can be thus identified fairly closely from the descriptions and measurements.

The *Journal* consists in all of eighteen volumes and 3,600 pages, of which only a small proportion are missing, and is preserved in the *Archives Nationales* in Paris. After 1784 a new system of recording was introduced, but the same numbers were preserved, and these, in fact, continued to be used until well into the nineteenth century.

Gate leg. A form of drop-leaf table with swinging supports that are legs joined to the main frame of the table by upper and lower stretchers which make a gate. First used in the late seventeenth and early eighteenth centuries.

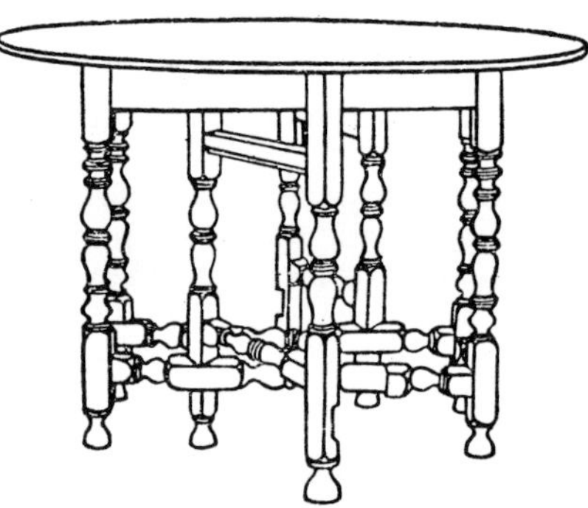

Gesso. Composition of plaster of Paris or whiting and size for making bas reliefs and other ornaments. It came into fashion in England just before 1700 and was a popular form of decoration until about 1740.

Giridon. *See* Guéridon.

Glastonbury chair. Is collectors' jargon for a type of chair with X supports and elbowed arms linking seat and top of back. The name derives from an example at Wells, supposedly associated with the last Abbot of Glastonbury. Examples of like construction have been made or embellished at various, including modern, periods.

Gobelins, Manufacture Royale des. The State-supported organization founded by Letters Patent at Gobelins in 1667 through the inspiration of Colbert, Louis XIV's finance minister. It was designed to provide, apart from tapestry, all products of the luxury art, including furniture, and its first great task was the equipment of the interior of the Palaces of Versailles. It owed its success and great reputation to the energies of its first director, Charles Le Brun, who made it into the foundation stone of the organized applied arts in France.

Goose neck. *See* Scroll top.

Gothic. A twelfth- to fifteenth-century style revived superficially in the eighteenth century. Chippendale offered designs in the 'Gothick Taste', occasionally followed by American craftsmen. These consisted of arcades of pointed arches and quatrefoils on chair backs. In the classical period there are also occasional designs employing Gothic motifs.

Guéridon or **guéridon table.** A small piece of furniture, usually circular, intended to support some form

of light. In the seventeenth century it sometimes took the form of a Negro figure holding a tray, and the name derives from that of a well-known Moorish galley slave called Guéridon. Subsequently the term was extended to cover almost any form of small table on which candelabra, etc., might be placed.
Guilloche. Band of curvilinear ornament suggesting entwined ribbons.
Hadley chest. So called because mostly found in and around Hadley, Massachusetts. A characteristic New England dower chest of 1690–1710. Its distinctive feature is the incised carving of tulips, vines, and leaves which cover the entire front.

Handkerchief table. A single-leaf table with leaf and top triangular in shape. Closed, the table fits in a corner, opened, it is a small square.
Hickory. Oak-like American wood often used for furniture parts needing strength without heaviness; also for bent parts; and almost always for spindles of Windsor chairs.
Highboy. Uniquely American tall chest of drawers mounted on a commode or lowboy (*q.v.*) and topped with a broken-arch pediment usually heightened with finials. Characteristically plain in New England; richly carved and ornamented in Philadelphia. It was made in three styles – William and Mary, Queen Anne, and Chippendale. The Philadelphia Chippendale highboy is sometimes thought to be the most remarkable creative achievement in American antique furniture design. The late authority on English antique furniture, Herbert Cescincky, wrote: '. . . there is little or no kinship between a Philadelphia highboy and anything ever made in England'.

Above Ormolu and Sèvres mounted *gueridon*, by Martin Carlin, stamped M. Carlin J.M.E. Christie, Manson & Woods

Left Philadelphia highboy of white cedar, oak, mahogany, tulip and yellow pine, 1765–80, known as the Van Pelt highboy. Courtesy of Francis du Pont Winterthur Museum

Hitchcock chair. American adaptation of the late Sheraton-style painted and stencilled chair. It has round-turned legs, raked, and an oval-turned 'pillow-back' top rail. Almost always painted black with stencillings of fruits and flowers in gold or colours. Named for Lambert Hitchcock, of Hitchcockville, Connecticut, who made them in quantity from 1820 to 1850.
Holly. A hard wood with a fine close grain. White or greenish white in colour. Found commonly in Europe and western Asia. Used extensively for fillets to frame marquetry (*see also* Boxwood).
Hood. *See* Bonnet top.
Hoop back. *See* Windsor chair.
Hope chest. Colloquial American term, widely used for dower chest, which itself is a misnomer, since a chest normally serves more purposes across the years than holding a trousseau (*see* Dower chest).
Horse glass and **horse screen.** *See* Cheval glass and Fire screen.
Horseshoe back. *See* Windsor chair.
Hutch. Enclosed structure, often raised on uprights, or an enclosed structure of more than one tier. The name derives from Fr. *huche*, a kneading trough or meal tub, but the significance of hutch was much wider. Food hutch, often confused with dole cupboard, is a name given to a hutch with perforated panels.
Inlay. Surface ornament formed by insetting separate pieces of differently coloured woods, or bone, ivory, shell, etc., in a recessed ground.
Inventory numbers. These are often found usually painted or branded on furniture made for the Crown or Royal Family of France. They often refer to the *Journal du Garde Meuble de la Couronne*, which has survived intact for some periods between the late seventeenth century and the Revolution. When accompanied by a palace letter (*q.v.*), the numbers may refer to the inventories made of that particular royal residence which may or may not still be extant. Considering everything, the documents of furniture made for the French Crown have survived in an extraordinary number of cases.

The discovery of an inventory number of any kind on a piece of French furniture of whatever date is always worth the closest investigation, as it may be possible to identify it.
Jacobean. Term of convenience usually applicable to furniture made in the reign of James I (1603–25), and perhaps, though unusually, to that of James II (1685–8). In general, loosely applied to furniture styles in direct descent from the Elizabethan tradition. It is thus employed of certain types of furniture covering virtually the whole of the seventeenth century and even later, though from the time of Charles II it is generally restricted to pieces of unmodish or traditional character. Jacobean is not now favoured as a descriptive label by scholarly writers, except in

cases of uncertain dating, preference being given to a more precise system involving such approximations as '*c.* 1620' or 'first quarter of the seventeenth century', etc.

Japanning. European and American version of Oriental lacquering often substituting paint for the layers of varnish on lacquered wares. Raised *chinoiserie* in plaster is generally the added decoration. The technique became popular in England late in the seventeenth century; a book of instructions, *Treatise of Japaning and Varnishing*, by Stalker and Parker, was published in 1688 in London. In America the technique was practised before 1715 and continued to be used throughout the century.

Jewel. Ornament with raised devices distantly suggestive of gem stones, often combined with systems of reeding (*q.v.*).

Joined. Term used in describing furniture made by a joiner.

Kas. The Dutch word, *kast*, for wardrobe incorrectly spelled. Used to refer to the wardrobes made by Dutch settlers in America. They are generally large, with wide mouldings, heavy cornice, and on ball feet. Their style is of the seventeenth century, but they were made for a great part of the eighteenth.

Kettle stand (also **urn** and **tea-pot stand).** A special stand which was introduced with tea drinking in the later seventeenth century, of two main kinds. (1) A small table, tripod or four-legged, with a gallery or raised edge round the top. Slender four-legged tables were common in the later part of the eighteenth century, nearly always with a slide for the tea pot. (2) A box-like arrangement set on four legs; the box was usually lined with metal, and had an opening in one side for the kettle spout, as well as a slide for the tea pot. Another version of the box type had a three-sided enclosure with a metal-lined drawer. The two main types of kettle stand persisted until the end of the eighteenth century, when they were superseded by occasional tables.

Kingwood. *See under* Rosewood.

Knife case. A container for knives (and other cutlery) introduced in the seventeenth century for use in dining rooms. Two distinct varieties appeared. (1) Until the later eighteenth century the usual shape was a box with a sloping top and convex front; the interior had divisions for the cutlery. Walnut, shagreen (untanned leather with a roughened surface), also made from shark skin, and later mahogany, sometimes inlaid, were the main materials. (2) This was succeeded by the graceful vase-shaped case, the top of which was raised and lowered on a central stem, around which the knife partitions were arranged; this type was designed to stand on a pedestal or at each end of the sideboard. Straight-sided cases were favoured in the early nineteenth century.

Knop. Swelling member on an upright, etc., a knob. Thus a knopped post.

Knotted pine. Originally a second-best plank of pine with the rough knot showing in the wood and therefore used only when covered with paint. Today the paint is removed, the knot design being liked by enough collectors to make old knotty pine sought after.

Labelled furniture. Mid-eighteenth-century American and British chair and cabinet makers often pasted small paper labels, advertising their wares, on furniture leaving their shops. A number of these labels remain to this day on the furniture and, when genuine, help establish characteristics of a particular shop.

Lacche. The word *lacche* is used in Italian to cover all painted decoration applied to furniture, whether or not it has the hard gloss of Oriental lacquer (see p. 149). Painted furniture (*mobilia laccata*) was produced in most districts of Italy in the eighteenth century, but the most celebrated centre for it was Venice. Earlier examples were normally decorated with *chinoiseries*, but in the middle of the eighteenth century floral motifs were more popular and some *armadi* were painted with landscapes in their panels. Desks were occasionally painted with *trompe l'œil* prints which appear to be pinned to them.

Lacquer. A form of resinous varnish capable of taking a high polish. Its chief application to furniture in France dates from the early eighteenth century, when it was imported for this purpose from China and Japan. The Oriental lacquer was also often imitated in France and then applied to furniture locally (*see also under* Vernis Martin).

Ladder back. A chair back with the vertical centre splat replaced by a series of horizontal bars cut in curving lines. Usually this type of chair has straight legs. It originated in the Chippendale period, but persisted until the end of the eighteenth century.

Lambrequin. A short piece of hanging drapery, often imitated in metal or wood for decorative purposes.

Lantern. A container for a candle or candles; portable, fixed to the wall or hung from the ceiling; especially useful for lighting the draughty parts of the house. Early lanterns (*c.* 1500–1700) were made of wood, iron, latten (a yellow alloy of copper and zinc), and brass, the most common filling being horn (whence the Shakespearean 'lanthorn'). After 1700, when glass become more plentiful, lanterns were increasingly fashionable, particularly as they prevented candle grease from falling about, and their frames, of metal, walnut, and mahogany, followed the main decorative modes of the times. In addition to these more elaborate kinds, simpler lanterns of glass shades, in a variety of forms, were in wide use in the eighteenth century.

Lazy Susan. *See* Dumb waiter.

Library steps. Found in libraries of large houses after about the middle of the eighteenth century, and of two main kinds: (1) the fixed pair of steps, some with hand rails, and (2) the folding steps, sometimes ingeniously fitted into other pieces of furniture, such as chairs, stools, and tables.

Linenfold. Carved ornament suggested by folded linen, first found late in the fifteenth century, very popular in the first half of the sixteenth, and continuing in diminishing quantity for many years.

Attempts to distinguish 'true' (realistic) from 'mock' (formalized) linenfold need not be taken too seriously. Some of the single-fold types (often cusped and foliated) have been differentiated as parchemin (Fr.), from a supposed resemblance to cut parchment. Apart from its obvious decorativeness, no satisfactory explanation of the origin of linenfold has been adduced. An attractive suggestion is that it was inspired by the Veil of the Chalice, though it could have arisen in other ways.

Linen press. A frame with a wooden spiral screw for pressing linen between two boards, dating from the seventeenth century.

Livery cupboard. *See* Cupboard.
Lobby chest. Defined by Sheraton as 'a kind of half chest of drawers, adapted for the use of a small study, lobby, etc.'.
Lockplate (or **scutcheon).** Front plate of a lock, or the plate protecting a keyhole.
Looking glass. In the sixteenth and seventeenth centuries looking-glass frames were similar to picture frames, though seldom as ornate as the richest examples. During the eighteenth century they were made with delicate mouldings in the wide diversity of shapes which the rococo taste approved and the mirror – unlike the painting – permitted. Large mirrors, or pier glasses, in elaborately carved frames were used in palatial decoration in the early eighteenth century. Small wall mirrors, framed in wood or pottery, and with designs engraved on the glass were popular in the mid-eighteenth century, especially in Venice. They were sometimes designed to serve as *girandoles*. Toilet mirrors with lacquered, gilt, or simple polished wood frames, similar to French and English examples, were made throughout Italy in the eighteenth century.
Loop back. *See* Windsor chair.
Love-seat. *See* Causeuse.
Lowboy. Modern name for an American creation inspired by the English flat-top dressing table with drawers, yet in its final development closer to the French commode. Attractively plain in New England, much carved and ornamented in Philadelphia. It occurs in three styles – William and Mary, Queen Anne, and Chippendale. Often made as a companion piece to the highboy (*q.v.*). Dressing table, chamber table, low chest of drawers were eighteenth-century names for it.
Lunette ornament. Formal carving composed of a horizontal system of semicircles, variously filled and embellished, frequently disposed in a repeat band.

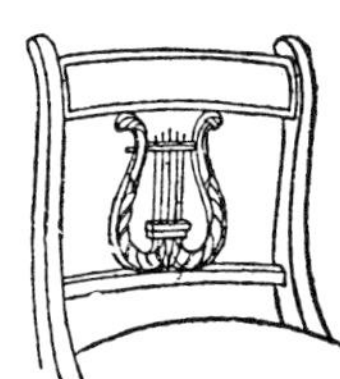

Chair back with lyre-shaped splat

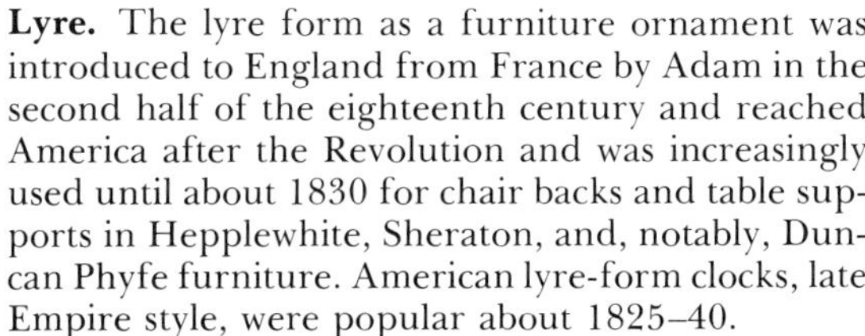

Lyre. The lyre form as a furniture ornament was introduced to England from France by Adam in the second half of the eighteenth century and reached America after the Revolution and was increasingly used until about 1830 for chair backs and table supports in Hepplewhite, Sheraton, and, notably, Duncan Phyfe furniture. American lyre-form clocks, late Empire style, were popular about 1825–40.
Mahogany. A dense, dark, heavy wood which in the eighteenth century was known in two varieties, the Spanish and the Honduras. The Spanish from Cuba, San Domingo, and Puerto Rico was darker and harder than the variety from Honduras. By 1750 it had supplanted walnut for the highest quality work in England, and at about the same time it became important in America.
Maple. A handsome, pale, satiny hardwood of close grain, plentiful in the northern part of America. Much used for furniture, especially in New England, ever since earliest times. Often it was the inexpensive substitute for walnut or mahogany, also for satinwood inlay, etc. Old maple takes on a rich honey colour. Its regular or plain graining is subject to several very attractive markings – curly (a tiger striping), bird's eye, blister, and quilted. Many pieces of furniture have been established as American because the underframing or secondary wood is maple.
Marlborough leg. Of obscure origin, perhaps originating in England as the trade term for a bed with square or square tapering (pillar) legs and block (plinth) feet. In America, by extension, a whole range of elegant furniture, mostly mid-eighteenth-century Philadelphian, with legs as described, generally with the inside edge chamfered to lighten the appearance. The authority, Horner, says: 'A refinement and rival of the cabriole. . . . There were but few pieces of the Chinese-Chippendale ever made in Philadelphia, so that nearly all Pembroke tables and similar articles should be classified as Marlborough. . . .'

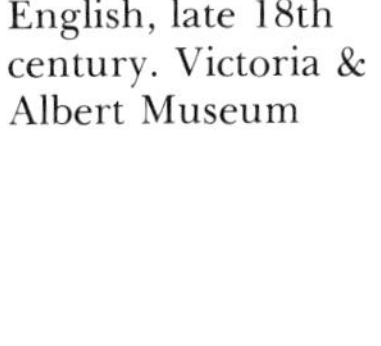

Far right Marquetry decoration of floral wreaths on a Pembroke table top, English, late 18th century. Victoria & Albert Museum

Marquetry. The ordinary word for a design formed of substances inlaid on a carcase in the form of a veneer. It can consist of various types of wood, combined with such materials as tortoiseshell, brass, pewter, copper, mother-of-pearl, etc. It first came into prominence in English furniture in about 1675. It is found in Italy in the sixteenth century and in Flanders in the seventeenth century. It was from these sources that it came to be imported into France mainly by the foreign craftsmen working at the courts of Henri IV and Louis XIII. After the majority of Louis XIV, Boulle marquetry (*q.v.*) came to be used extensively. In the eighteenth century the possibilities of wood marquetry were developed until they reached their ultimate perfection in works of J. H. Riesener (*q.v.*).
Martha Washington chair. Slender Chippendale-Hepplewhite armchair with tapered outlines; a 'lady's chair', with upholstered, low, shallow seat and high back, which usually ends in a serpentine curve. So named because Martha Washington is supposed to have used one at Mount Vernon.

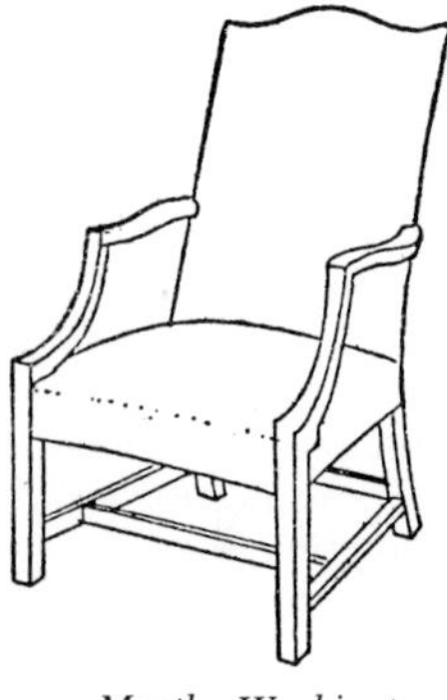

Martha Washington chair

Melon bulb

Martha Washington mirror. Walnut or mahogany wall mirror, Georgian style, with handsome gilded mouldings, strings of leaves, fruits, or flowers down the sides, a scroll top, and a bird finial. The base is cut in a series of bold curves. Made in America from about 1760 to 1800. So named because Martha Washington is supposed to have used one at Mount Vernon. (Same as Constitution mirror.)

Martha Washington sewing table. Oval box-form sewing table with rounded ends and hinged top. Fitted with drawers and sewing material compartments. The general style is Sheraton, but the particular type seems to be an American variant. It was so named because Martha Washington is supposed to have used one at Mount Vernon.

Melon bulb. Jargon and comparatively modern term for the swollen member on legs or posts of furniture. An exaggeration of the knop, it attained full development in the Elizabethan period, thereafter dwindling away.

Menuisier. The term corresponds roughly to the English 'carpenter' or 'joiner'. In France, as far as furniture was concerned, the *menuisiers* were responsible for making chairs, beds, and other furniture made from plain or carved woods, as distinct from veneered pieces, which were the province of the *ébénistes* (*q.v.*). Although permitted by guild regulations to work in both techniques, they seldom did so (*see also* Menuisiers-Ébénistes, Corporation des).

Menuisiers-Ébénistes, Corporation des. The craft guild which embraced all craftsmen engaged in making wood furniture in France.

An apprentice began his training with a *maître-ébéniste* or *maître-menuisier* at the age of fourteen, and it lasted for six years, after which he entered on his next stage, known as *compagnonage*. This lasted for three to six years, according to whether the craftsman had served his apprenticeship in Paris or elsewhere. During this time the *compagnon* was paid for the work he did. After his *compagnonage* the craftsman was ready to become a *maître* of the guild, but often the period was extended because of lack of vacancies or because of his inability to pay the fees required. These were fairly large and were devoted to the running expenses of the guild. The number of *maîtres* was limited. In 1723 there were 985, and in 1790 this figure had not increased. The King, moreover, had the right to create *maîtres* on his own authority.

A *compagnon* had to submit a specimen of his work before receiving the *maîtrise*, but once a *maître*, he was permitted to open a shop in his own name, in which he could employ some *compagnons*, and was required to take in one apprentice at least. At his death his widow could continue to direct his business, provided that she had qualified *compagnons* to assist her.

After 1751 a *maître* was also required to stamp the furniture he put on sale (*see* Stamps).

In addition the apprentices, *compagnons*, and *maîtres*, there were two other types of craftsmen involved in the guild organization. Firstly, the maintenance of standards was in the hands of a *syndic* and six *jurés*, elected once a year from among the *maîtres*, whose duty it was to examine the specimens submitted by aspiring *maîtres* and also to inspect all workshops in Paris four times a year and examine work in hand. All pieces of furniture approved by the *jurés* were stamped with the monogram JME (*juré* or *jurande des menuisiers-ébénistes*) (*see also* Stamps).

Meuble à hauteur d'appui. A term used extensively in France at all periods for any low bookcase or cupboard, usually between 3 and 4 feet (91.4–122 cm) high.

Meuble d'entre deux. A term used in France in the eighteenth century for a type of furniture which usually consists of a cupboard or chest of drawers flanked at each side by a set of shelves. Often these are open, but sometimes are enclosed by a curved door forming a small cupboard with shelves.

Mirror stand. An adjustable mirror mounted on a shaft and tripod base, resembling a pole screen; popular at the end of the eighteenth century.

Misericord. In ecclesiastical woodwork, bracket on underside of hinged seat of a stall, to support an occupant when nominally standing during certain offices. From a 'monastic' usage of L. *misericordia* (pity, compassion), in sense of 'an indulgence or relaxation of the rule' (O.E.D.). Miserere is an incorrect alternative.

Mortise and tenon. For joining two pieces of wood. The mortise is a cavity, usually rectangular; the tenon, an end shaped to fill the cavity exactly; characteristic of Philadelphia chairs, where seat rail joins the stiles.

Mother-of-pearl. Inlay of nacreous shell slices, often used on early nineteenth-century American fancy chairs, tables, etc.

Moulding. Shaped member, such as used to enclose panels; or the shaped edge of a lid, cornice, etc.

Muntin. Upright (other than an outermost upright) connecting the upper and lower stretchers of a framework. An instance is the bearer between the doors of the lower stage of a press cupboard; but the number of muntins depends on the nature of the structure. (*See also* Stile.)

Music stand. *See* Canterbury (1) and Desk (2).

Nails. A popular notion that iron nails are never found in antique furniture construction is fallacious. In fact, metal nails have been known for centuries, though the use of the wooden dowel (*q.v.*) must not be minimized by implication. Old handmade nails are very different from the modern, mass-produced variety; but the manufacture of handmade nails (and screws) has been revived.

Name chests. Colloquial term for chests that bear the decoratively carved or painted name of the original owner.

Neo-Greek. Alternative term for furniture of the brief classical revival in early nineteenth-century America. Mostly said of the late Empire style, 1815–40.

Night table. A pot cupboard which replaced the close stool after 1750; sometimes also fitted as a washing stand (*q.v.*). Among the features commonly found on these pieces may be noted a drawer under the cupboard, a tambour front, and a tray top. Some night tables were given a triangular shape to fit into a corner.

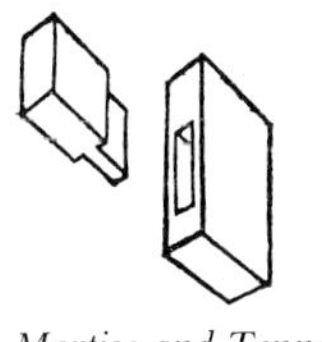

Mortise and Tennon

Oak. A hard wood with coarse grain used almost exclusively up to the seventeenth century and as a secondary wood later. Its hardness made it difficult to carve but quite durable.

Occasional table. Any light table easily moved here or there to meet the occasion. Much used in America ever since early eighteenth-century times.

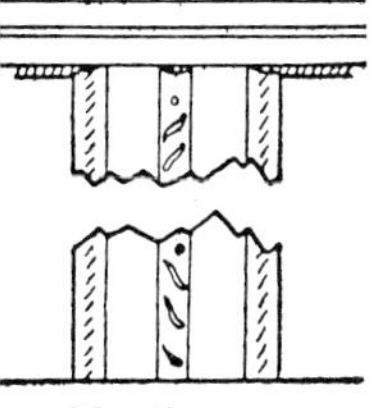

Muntin

Ormolu. An English word in use from about the middle of the eighteenth century, derived from the French term *bronze dorée d'or moulu*. Its most accurate equivalents are *bronze dorée* or gilt bronze. It was a French speciality, and when found on English furniture it is likely that it was done by French craftsmen. Ormolu is the substance from which all objects covered by the term *bronzes d'ameublement* are made, e.g. lighting fixtures, including candelabra and candlesticks, clock cases, appliances for doors and fireplaces, as well as mounts for furniture. Its manufacture was the function of two craft guilds; the *fondeurs* (*q.v.*) and the *doreurs* (*q.v.*). Its preparation consisted of a model in wood or wax being produced by a sculptor, often of some note; this was then cast in bronze by a *fondeur*, usually by the *cire perdue* method, but sometimes from a mould of clay or sand (*see* article on Bronzes). The casting was then tooled and chased until the required degree of finish had been achieved. This last process (known as *ciselure*) was carried to an extraordinary degree of refinement in France in the eighteenth century, and the tools which the *ciseleurs* used are illustrated in the *Encyclopédie*, showing the precision which could be obtained. The bronzes when finished were often merely dipped in acid and then lacquered, and this often needed to be done more than once, when the surface became dirty.

If they were required to be gilded, this was usually done by the mercury process, of which detailed particulars are also given in the *Encyclopédie*. It consisted of coating the bronze with a paste formed by dissolving gold in heated mercury. The bronze thus coated was then itself heated, and the mercury driven off, when the gold was left adhering to the surface of the metal. The fumes of the mercury vapour produced at this stage were very dangerous and the heating had to be carried out in a furnace with a strong draught. Finally, when the process was completed the gold was either burnished or given a matt finish, according to requirements, but sometimes both types of finish were used on the same piece for purposes of contrast.

During the Louis XIV period the leaf gilding of bronzes was sometimes employed, and occasionally bronzes were silvered (which is rare at any time).

It is important to remember that only the finest bronzes were gilded in the manners described, the remainder being merely dipped and lacquered. The owners of furniture and *bronzes d'ameublement* in the eighteenth century were also not averse from having their ormolu regilded by the mercury process in order to keep it in a bright condition. So far as one can judge from contemporary accounts, ormolu was never allowed to become as dull or dirty as it often is today, and there seems to have been no taste for patina for its own sake.

The craft of making ormolu reached its height towards the middle of Louis XVI's reign, the chief exponents being Pierre Philippe Thomire, E. Forestier, and others. During the Napoleonic period the quality of ormolu declined, mainly owing to the cost of gilding by the mercury process. Later in the nineteenth century, however, with the advent of machinery and mass-production methods, fine ormolu was produced, and although it often lacks the personal perfection which the earlier craftsmen gave it, it is sometimes very difficult to distinguish between a piece produced in 1770 and another made in the same style in 1860. Connoisseurs and collectors should always keep an open mind about this.

Oxbow, oxbow front. The reverse serpentine curve, somewhat resembling the curve of an oxbow. Often employed in the finest eighteenth-century New England, especially Boston case furniture such as chests of drawers, secretaries, etc.

Palace letters. These, with inventory numbers (*q.v.*), are often painted or branded on furniture and occasionally stamped on *bronzes d'ameublement*, made for the French Crown. On veneered furniture they are usually to be found on the carcase at the back or under marble slabs, but in the case of chairs and *menuiserie* generally, they are often in the underparts and sometimes on the bottom of the upholstered seats. They almost always take the form of the intial letter or letters of the palace concerned beneath a crown. Thus F = Fontainebleau; C.T. = Château de Trianon; W (two Vs) = Versailles; S.C. = St Cloud, etc. Like inventory numbers, their existence on furniture of any date is worth careful investigation.

Panel. Compartment usually rectangular, and sunk or raised from the surface of its framework. Panel is the filling of such framework, whereas panelling refers to the framework and its filling (*see* Wainscot).

Papier mâché. Moulded paper pulp used for many small articles and particularly suitable for japanning and polishing; the original process came to England via France from the East as early as the seventeenth century. Considerable stimulus was given to this kind of work in 1772, when Henry Clay of Birmingham, and later London, patented a similar material and manufactured various pieces, among which trays, boxes, tea caddies, and coasters were prominent.

Parquetry. A word connected, as its French equivalent implies, with the laying of floors. It is sometimes used in connection with furniture inlaid with geometrical cube designs in the manner of a parquet floor. It should be used with caution and is not really applicable to furniture at all.

Detail of mother-of-pearl inlay on oak cupboard, English, 17th century. Victoria & Albert Museum

Patina (and colour). Of furniture and woodwork, patina is the undisturbed surface, heightened by centuries of polishing and usage. Contrary to popular belief, some old oak furniture shows clear signs of having been originally varnished; some was also polychromed. Patination and colour pose problems to a faker. To some extent they can be simulated, but, when artificially produced, deteriorate (*see* Fake and Stripping).
Pear drop. *See* Drop handle.
Pedestal table. A table on a round centre support.
Pembroke table. A small table with short drop leaves supported on swinging wooden brackets. The term Pembroke is used in England first in the 1760s. Although Chippendale lists tables of this description as 'breakfast tables' in the *Director*, he used the term on bills. Sheraton said this type of table was named after the lady who first ordered it. It was particularly popular in the classical period, and both Hepplewhite and Sheraton suggested designs for it.
Pennsylvania Dutch. The name applied to German settlers in Pennsylvania. Their furniture has many distinctive qualities, since it assimilates English and German peasant styles. Their cabinet makers worked in soft woods, which they painted and often decorated with floral patterns and other motifs from the vocabulary of peasant design.
Piecrust table. A round tilt-top tea table on a tripod base. The top has a scalloped edge finished with a carved moulding which is suggestive of the notched rim of a piecrust; tables in the Chippendale style have pedestals elaborately carved. The tripod consists of three cabriole legs terminating generally in claw-and-ball feet.

Tripod tea-table with piecrust edge and tilting top, Philadelphia, 1760–75. Courtesy of Museum of Fine Arts, Boston

Pier table. A table designed to stand against the pier, the part of the wall between the windows. In America the term is used loosely to refer to a table designed for use against a wall, a side table.
Pilgrim furniture. Term used to describe American seventeenth-century furniture.
Pine. Often used for panelling rooms in eighteenth-century England. It was also used for the carcases of veneered furniture. From the time of the Pilgrims down to the present, much of the everyday utility furniture in America has been made of pine, especially the soft white pine of New England. Antique examples of it are much prized today for countrified settings. White pine was also much used for the unseen parts of furniture and other secondary purposes, as well as for overlaying with veneer. Its presence often identifies the furniture as American. Short-leaf, yellow, hard pine is often used as the secondary wood in New Jersey, Pennsylvania, and Virginia furniture. The long-leaf, yellow, hard pine, so plentiful in the south, does not make good furniture.
Pin hinge. Method of hinging, as found on thirteenth-century chests, the lid being pinned through the rear stiles and pendent side rails of the lid.
Pipe rack. A stand for clay pipes. Of the various wooden kinds in use in the eighteenth century one can distinguish: (1) the stand of candlestick form with a tiny circular tray on the stem, pierced with holes for holding the pipes, and (2) the wall rack, either an open frame with notched sides so that the pipes could lie across or a board with shelves from which the pipes hung down (cf. spoon rack). In addition to these, metal pipe kilns were widely used from the seventeenth century – iron frames on which the pipes rested, deriving their name from the fact that they could be baked in an oven to clean the pipes.
Pipe tray. A long and narrow wooden tray with partitions for churchwardens, in use throughout the Georgian period.
Plate pail. A mahogany container with handle for carrying plates from kitchen to dining room (often a long journey) in large houses in the eighteenth century; of various shapes, generally circular with one section left open for ease of access.
Pole screen. *See* Fire screen (1).
Poplar. *See* Tulipwood.
Poppy (popey) head. Decorative finial of a bench or desk end, as in ecclesiastical woodwork. Plant and floral forms are numerous; human heads, figures, birds, beasts, and other devices are found. Derivation of term is uncertain, one suggestion (rejected by some writers) being from Fr. *poupée* (baby doll), or from poppet, puppet.
Porcelain. In the Louis XV and Louis XVI periods there were two important uses of porcelain in connection with furniture. First, for purely decorative purposes, actual pieces of porcelain were mounted with ormolu, often of very high quality. This is what became known as 'mounted porcelain', and the pieces so embellished came not only from the French factories of Vincennes and Sèvres but also from Meissen, and particularly from the Far East, *celadon* and *famille rose* being specially favoured. The ormolu decoration is usually confined to ornamental bases and bands for the necks of vases, but is sometimes extended to form handles, knobs for lids, etc. It is screwed on to the porcelain by means of a hole bored in the latter. The types of porcelain chosen are usually vases of various shapes, shallow bowls, ewers, and particularly the famous bunches of flowers from the Meissen factory, which were imitated at Vincennes. Sometimes groups of *biscuit de Sèvres* were similarly mounted. The demand for all these types was very high and extended right up to the Revolution, the usual changes in style being noticeable.

The other principal use to which porcelain was put did not come into fashion until the latter part of Louis XVI's reign. This consisted of the inlaying of plaques of porcelain into the veneered surfaces of pieces of furniture. This method of decoration, although it sometimes produces an extremely sumptuous effect, is often criticized on the grounds that it lies outside the scope of practical cabinet making, and it has always been foreign to English taste. The covering of parts of furniture with porcelain does certainly make the pieces much more fragile, and there is evidence to show that a number of the plaques adorning extant pieces are not in fact the originals.

The porcelain so used almost always came from the Sèvres manufactory and often, therefore, has the royal monogram with or without date letters or painters' marks. If a date letter is found and is genuine it may help to date the piece of furniture fairly exactly, but it is always possible that the plaque is not the original, and may have replaced another, in which case the date letter may bear no relation to the year in which the furniture was made.

The porcelain is let into cavities in the carcase and kept in position originally by means of ormolu fillets. Martin Carlin and Adam Weisweiler were two *ébénistes* who appear to have specialized to some extent in making furniture of this kind, and the custom of mounting porcelain of any date on furniture was particularly prevalent in the nineteenth century, during the Restoration and reign of Louis Philippe. Collectors should always bear in mind that the porcelain on furniture may be a later addition or replacement, and this is particularly to be suspected if there is any lack of harmony between the furniture and the plaques, or any confusion of dating.

Press. Broadly, a tall, enclosed, and doored structure comparable to the modern wardrobe or hanging cupboard. Not to be confused with linen press, in the sense of a framework with a screw-down smoother. (For press cupboard *see under* Cupboard.)

Prie-dieu. The earliest surviving examples of the *prie-dieu* in Italy date from the sixteenth century and are simple contrivances with a step for the knees, an upright panel or shallow cupboard, and a shelf on top. Two or three drawers occasionally replaced the cupboard in the seventeenth century and the whole object was treated more decoratively. A magnificent early eighteenth-century example in the Palazzo Pitti at Florence is enriched with swags of fruit in *pietre dure*. Later in the eighteenth century the *prie-dieu* was made in conformity with rococo taste, usually with a single curving column supporting the shelf. Other more substantial examples were made to fold up into chairs.

Puritan. A term applied to simpler seventeenth-century American furniture.

Purplewood. A wood with an open grain which is fairly hard. It is brown in its natural state, but turns purple on exposure to the air. Found chiefly in Brazil and French Guinea. Very extensively used for marquetry in France in the eighteenth century.

Rail. The horizontal piece in framing or panelling. In a chair back the top member supported on the stiles.

Reeding. Similar to fluting but with the ornament in relief.

Reggivaso. A vase stand, a purely decorative piece of furniture which enjoyed widespread popularity in Italy in the eighteenth century. *Reggivasi* were made in the form of *putti*, satyrs, chained Negro slaves, or blackamoor page boys and are often minor works of sculpture of great charm. A superb example by Andrea Brustolon in the Palazzo Rezzonico at Venice is made in the form of a group of river gods holding trays for the porcelain vases.

Renaissance (Fr. for rebirth). Applied to the effects of the revival of learning and embracing the use (often very freely interpreted) of classical as opposed to Gothic motifs. Originating in Italy in the fifteenth century, Renaissance design spread throughout Europe, beginning to make itself felt in England in the early sixteenth century.

Restoration. (1) A proper renewal of a piece by a candid replacement of hopelessly damaged or missing parts; (2) restored is sometimes used to indicate either that a piece has been over-restored or that the extent of its restoration is dubious.

Restoration furniture. Term applied to certain elaborately carved and scrolled chairs, etc., their backs surmounted by crowns or boys and crowns. It was said that such pieces recorded the restoration of King Charles II (1660), but many so-called Restoration chairs are now known to date from late in his reign when not from a subsequent period. Such chairs may be of mixed woods, and other than oak.

Rising sun. When a fan-shaped ornament is carved half-circle, and the resulting spray of stalks suggests sun rays it is picturesquely called a rising sun. 'Setting sun' is sometimes used. It was so often the only decoration on New England highboys that its presence generally indicates the New England origin of the piece. James (later President) Madison recalled that when the Constitution of the United States was finally adopted after much contention, Benjamin Franklin pointed to a decoration of this type painted on the back of the chairman's chair and said he had looked at it many times during the sessions 'without being able to tell whether it was rising or setting, but now I . . . know that it is a rising . . . sun'.

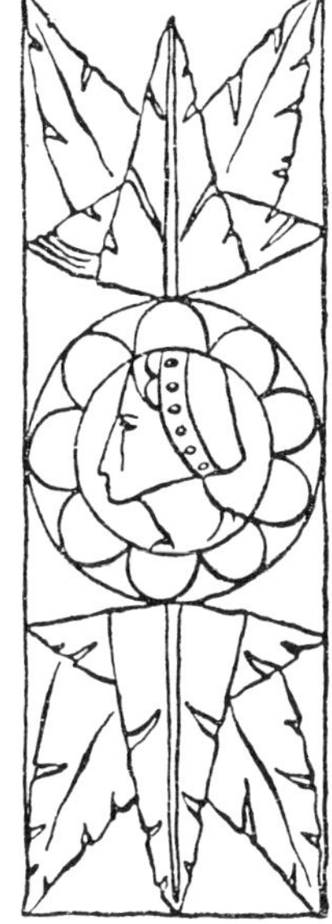

Romayne work with head in roundel

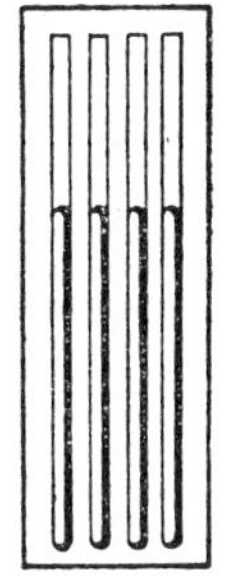

Combined reeding and fluting

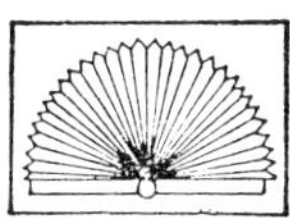

Rising Sun

Rocking chair. A chair of almost any simple type mounted on bends, rockers. An American invention. Authentic 'slat-back' examples are said to date as early as 1650–1700, though 1800 would seem to be safer. Special types were developed (*see* Boston rocker, Salem rocker, Windsor).

Rococo. An ornate style developed in France from the Chinese forms. It came to England in the Chippendale period. It appeared in its most characteristic forms on sconces, mirror frames, and console tables, all elaborately carved and gilded by special craftsmen. The American version only barely suggests the exuberance of the Continental rococo style. Ornament rococo in spirit is used on American Chippendale furniture, particularly in Philadelphia, but the lines of the furniture are more conservative.

Roll-top desk. Similar to a cylinder-top desk (*q.v.*), but the writing table and fittings are enclosed by a curved slatted panel.

Romayne work. Old term for Renaissance carving with heads in roundels, scrollwork, vases, etc., some few heads being portraits, but most purely formal. The taste was widespread in Europe, and traditional traces survived in Brittany until quite a late period. The vogue for romayne work in England was under Henry VIII (1509–47), thereafter dwindling.

Rosette. A round ornament in a floral design.

Rosewood or **kingwood.** A coarse-grained wood, dark purplish brown or black in colour, varying considerably in hardness. Found in India, Brazil, and the West Indies.

Roundabout. *See* Corner chair.

Rounded ends. The top rail of early Chippendale chairs is sometimes made with rounded ends, somewhat in the style of a Queen Anne chair (*see* Cupid's bow).

Roundel. Circular ornament enclosing sundry formal devices on medieval and later woodwork; also human heads as in romayne work (*see also* Whorl).

Runner. Alternative term for the rocker of a rocking chair.

Rush seat. A seat woven of rushes. Used in America from the earliest times, generally with simple furniture. Still popular for country chairs (*see* Splint seat).

Sabre leg. A term used to describe a sharply curving leg in the classical style which has also been called scroll-shaped and even likened to the shape of a cornucopia. It is generally reeded. This leg is found on small sofas attributed to Duncan Phyfe.

Saddle seat. When the seat of a Windsor chair is cut away from the centre in a downward slope to the sides the shape somewhat resembles the seat of a saddle, and is picturesquely so named.

Salem rocker. Salem, Massachusetts, variant of the Windsor rocker (*q.v.*) and with a lower back than the Boston rocker (*q.v.*), early nineteenth century.

Salem secretary. Salem, Massachusetts, variant of

Sheraton's secretary with a china cabinet top; also, by extension, a Salem sideboard with a china cabinet top (*c.* 1800–20).

Salem snowflake. A six-pointed punched decoration resembling a star or a snowflake found as a background in the carved areas of Salem, Massachusetts, furniture.

Sample chairs. A group of six chairs thought to have been made by Benjamin Randolph, a Philadelphia cabinet maker, as samples of his skill. The group of chairs (one wing and five side chairs) is in the most elegant Philadelphia Chippendale style.

Satinwood. A fairly hard wood, with a very close grain. It is yellow or light brown in colour and has a lustrous surface somewhat like that of satin. It is found in central and southern India, Coromandel, Sri Lanka, and in the West Indies.

Sawbuck table. A table with an X-shaped frame either plain or scrolled. Frequently found in rural New England and in Pennsylvania-German examples.

Sconce. A general name for a wall light consisting of a back plate and either a tray or branched candleholders. Metal seems to have been the chief material from later medieval times until the end of the seventeenth century when looking glass became fashionable for back plates (and when 'girandole' was another name for these pieces). The use of looking glass meant that sconces tended to follow the same decorative trends as contemporary mirrors, but metal back plates continued to be made, and for a period after 1725 there was a preference for carved and gilt wood and gesso work, often without looking glass. About 1750 sconces provided some of the freest interpretation of the asymmetrical rococo mode, either with looking glass in a scrolled frame or in carved and gilt wood only; Chinese features were often blended with the rococo. In contrast, the sconces of the Adam period had delicate classical ornament in gilt wood or in composition built up round a wire frame. Cut-glass sconces were in vogue at the end of the century.

Scoop pattern. Popular term for a band or other disposition of fluted ornament, gouged in the wood, the flute having a rounded top and, sometimes, base. A motif of Renaissance origin, its use was widespread (*see* Fluting).

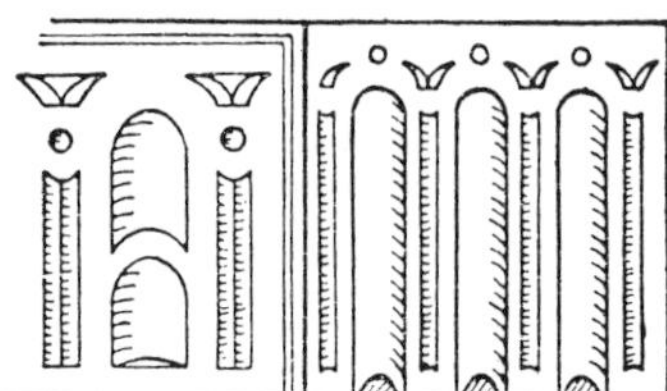

Double scoop and fluting (left)*; reeding and fluting* (right). *17th century*

Screen. Although frequently used in the church, screens do not seem to have been introduced into the house until the late seventeenth century. In Italy, as in England, Coromandel screens imported from the East were very popular, but screens, either hung with silk or painted with floral motifs, standing figures, etc., enjoyed a considerable vogue. The fire screen was more widely used. An excellent example carved by G. M. Bonzanigo, is in the Castello di Stupinigi at Turin.

Scroll top. A curved broken-arch pediment used on case pieces. Also called goose neck, swan neck, etc.

'Scrutoire, escritoire. Eighteenth-century American term for an enclosed writing desk, often with a

Piedmontese fire screen by Giuseppe Maria Bonzanigo, carved and gilt walnut, *c.* 1775

Secretaire bookcase in the style of George Hepplewhite, satinwood. Made for Mrs Fitzherbert, wife of the Prince of Wales, *c.* 1788. Royal Pavilion, Brighton

cabinet top. Lockwood differentiates three varieties: fall-front, slant-top with ball feet, and slant-top with turned legs. In England called a bureau or bureau-bookcase.

Scutcheon. Shield on which are armorial bearings or other devices, and, by extension, sundry shield-shaped ornaments and fitments (*see* Lockplate).

Secretaire (or **secretary).** The name somewhat loosely applied to different kinds of writing furniture, of which two small varieties call for mention here. (1) At the end of the seventeenth century appeared the small bureau mounted on legs or stand, very similar to the contemporary desk on stand (*q.v.*). This kind seems to have been designed for ladies' use, and sometimes had a looking glass at the top. (2) In the late eighteenth century large numbers of light and graceful secretaires were made, one popular kind taking the form of a small table with tapering legs enclosing a drawer and supporting a little stand with drawers and shelf. The stand, which was used as a small bookshelf, was often provided with a handle so that it could be lifted off. This type of table was also known as a cheveret.

Serre-papier. *See under* Cartonnier.

Victorian settee of satinwood, painted with wreaths and cameos, revival of the neoclassical style of the late 18th century

Settee. A low, long seat with upholstered back and arms, which developed along the same lines as the armchair.

Settle. Long, backed seat with boxed base, or on legs, and at each end side pieces or arms. Fixed or movable, the settle represents a stage preceding the settee, a derivative of the chair. Some quite late settles have one end scrolled like a sofa head. Some, mostly country-made, settles have a storage press in the back, such being loosely known as bacon cupboard.

Sewing tables. *See* Worktable.

Shaker furniture. A whole range of furniture – chairs, tables, chests of drawers – made by early nineteenth-century Shakers, a celibate American sect. This furniture, while provincial, is of such sheer simplicity, so pure in line, so lean and functional in form, so well proportioned and soundly constructed, that it is much prized today. Usually in pine, maple, walnut, or fruitwoods.

Shearer, Thomas. English furniture designer whose drawings, first published in the *Cabinet-Maker's London Book of Prices*, 1788, influenced many American cabinet makers from 1790 to 1810, though the credit has to this day gone to his contemporaries, Hepplewhite and Sheraton, both of whom took many a leaf from Shearer's book.

Shelves. Taken here to refer to hanging or standing shelves without doors, for books, plate, and china. Small oak shelves of the Tudor period were square in shape; while arcaded tops appeared in the early seventeenth century. Carving was the chief decoration, and this became more ornate after 1660. It is probable that many walnut shelves were made, but few of these seem to have survived. It was at this time that shelves were used for displaying china; a fashion which continued into the early eighteenth century, but was then replaced by that of keeping china in cabinets and cupboards. Open shelves, however, returned to favour in the Chippendale period, when they were often decorated in the Chinese taste, and had fretted sides and galleries. Simple, light shelves were generally in vogue in the later eighteenth century, for books or china; Sheraton emphasized that shelves should be light enough for ladies to move about and to contain their 'books under present reading'.

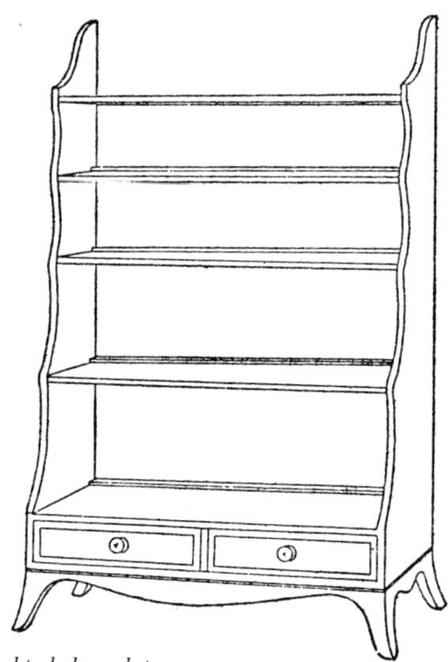

Simple, light shelves, late 18th century

Shibayama work. Incrustations or inlays, usually on a lacquer ground, but occasionally on ivory, wood, or metal, called after the Japanese Shibayama Dosho, first of a family of artists, who founded the school towards the end of the eighteenth century. The best work is small (usually *inrō q.v.*) and was done between this time and the early decades of the nineteenth century. Among the materials employed for inlaying may be numbered ivory, mother-of-pearl, coral, soapstone, and metals like gold and silver. Inferior work of this kind, including screens, was done towards the end of the nineteenth century for export, but genuine examples of the Shibayama school are comparatively rare in the West.

Sideboard. Literally a side-board (as a cupboard was a cup-board); a side table or other structure convenient for the display and service of plate, foodstuffs, etc., and possibly including storage facilities such as ambries, drawers, etc. A near relative of the dresser, and in some cases indistinguishable from such.

Slant-front desk. A frame or chest of drawers with a top section as an enclosed desk for writing, the hinged lid sloping at a 45 degrees angle when closed. Called in England a bureau.

Slat back. A seventeenth-century style chair made of turned posts connected by horizontal slats across the back. Persisted in rural areas to the twentieth century.

Sleigh bed. American French Empire bed somewhat resembling a sleigh.

Slider. *See* Coaster.

Sofa. The sofa as we know it developed in the Louis XIV period out of the day bed (or *lit de repos*). It became established more or less in its present form in the Louis XV period as a regular part of a *mobilier de salon*, and was often made to match a set of chairs and *causeuses*, in which case it was upholstered similarly. The sofa was first introduced into Italy in the late seventeenth century. Its stylistic history follows that of the chair: indeed, many Italian sofas resemble a row of chairs joined together. Extraordinarily long sofas with carved wooden backs and, usually, rush seats, were much favoured for the furnishing of eighteenth-century ballrooms. Padded sofas with outcurving arms were popular in Venice in the eighteenth century, and some were made in the form of folding beds.

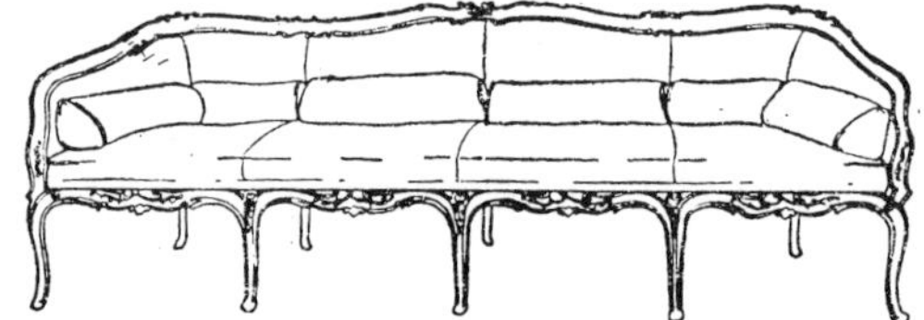

Sofa, Venetian, mid-18th-century

Sofa table. Small, narrow, rectangular table with two front drawers in the apron and hinged leaves at each end; the underframe of two legs at each end, or graceful bracket supports connected by a stretcher. First made in America about 1800 from Sheraton's designs. Duncan Phyfe developed several fine variants. Popular until the passing of the Empire fashion about 1840. Rare today in America but common in England.

Sofa table with harp legs, veneered rosewood with satinwood bandings. Made by Thomas Chippendale the Younger, 1802

Spanish foot

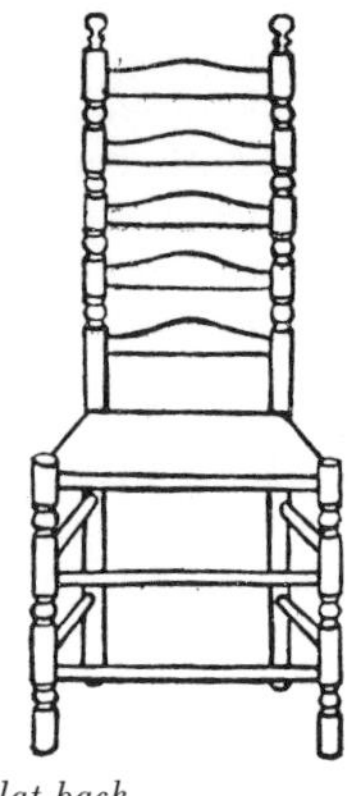

Slat back

Spanish foot. William and Mary, also early Queen Anne, chair or table foot, with vertical ribs somewhat like a hand resting on its finger knuckles. An important detail of elegance in American furniture (*c.* 1700–25).

Spinning wheel. A machine for making yarn or thread, employing foot or hand power. As a piece for the home, it was generally made of turned parts. Used through the nineteenth century in rural areas.

Splint seat. A seat made of oak or hickory strips interlaced. Used in country furniture through the eighteenth century.

Spool. A turning in the shape of a row of spools which was employed for long, thin members such as legs. Introduced after 1820 and continued through the Victorian period in rural work.

Spoon back. Colloquially used of a Queen Anne chair with a back, curved like a spoon, conforming to the human back.

Spoon rack. A stand for hanging spoons, dating from late Tudor times when metal spoons came into general use. The usual form, until the end of the eighteenth century, resembled a miniature dresser – a wooden board with small slotted shelves for spoons, and, attached to it at the bottom, a box for knives and forks.

Stamps. Various names and letters are often found stamped on French furniture made in the eighteenth century or later. The principal and most important of these is the stamp (*estampille*), giving the name and often the initials of the *ébéniste* who made the piece of furniture concerned, which, after 1751, he was compelled by guild regulations to strike on all his work, unless he happened to be a privileged craftsman working for the Crown. Before 1751 *estampilles* are very rarely found.

These stamps are a most important means of identifying the makers of individual pieces of furniture, but it must be borne in mind that sometimes they refer only to the repairer of a piece as distinct from its original maker. Thus some pieces bear more than one *estampille*, and it is often doubtful which *ébéniste* was the actual maker. The importance of the stamps, however, was only rediscovered in 1882, as a result of an exhibition held in Paris under the auspices of the *Union Centrale des Arts Décoratifs*, and as an unfortunate consequence, a number of false signatures have been applied to furniture since that date by unscrupulous dealers. Connoisseurs and collectors should be on their guard against this and also against the attribution of unstamped pieces to individual *ébénistes* on grounds of style alone.

The *estampille* is of roughly uniform size and format, usually incorporating the *ébéniste*'s name and initials, but sometimes the surname only (*see* pp. 198–202). They are usually found in an inconspicuous place on the carcase of the piece, often on the bottom or top rails, front or back, under marble tops, etc. Very occasionally they appear on the surface of the veneer itself, and sometimes panels of marquetry are signed in full by their makers.

Another important stamp to be found on furniture after 1751 is that of the *jurés*. It consists of a monogram incorporating the letters JME (*juré* or *jurande des menuisiers-ébénistes*), and its presence implies that the piece concerned has passed the standard required by the *jurés* of the guild (*see* Menuisiers-Ébénistes, Corporation des).

In addition to the *estampille* and the *juré*'s stamp,

furniture made for the Crown sometimes, though by no means always, bears the stamp of the *Garde Meuble de la Couronne* (*q.v.*). Inventory numbers and palace letters (*qq.v.*) are usually painted or branded, but seldom stamped, on furniture.

In the eighteenth century *bronzes d'ameublement* are very rarely stamped, but sometimes they do bear signatures. Jacques Caffiéri frequently signed his work with his surname. Inventory numbers and palace letters are even rarer, but they do occasionally occur on bronzes, and where they can be checked with existing documents they are found to be of eighteenth-century origin.

Stars. American ornaments often inlaid or painted on clocks, mirrors, tables, desk tops, etc., usually celebrating the number of states in the Union. The date of the article is sometimes traceable to the number of stars thus employed: the thirteenth state, Rhode Island, being admitted in 1790; the fourteenth, Vermont, in 1791, etc.

Stile. In construction an outermost upright, as a muntin is an inner one.

Stool. Small, backless seat. Apart from rack or folding stools, the main basic types are trestle and legged. Trestle, with two uprights out from the solid, on the same principle as the ends of a boarded chest, may be included among stools of wainscot. Stools with legs may have three or four supports, and some quite common, and indeed modern, stools of traditional form are of very ancient lineage.

Joined stool (joint is a corruption) is proper to stools made by joinery. The term coffin stool invariably used by beginners is only correct when the use of joined stools as a coffin bier (as in some old churches) is known. It is incorrect for the domestic article. For close stool see that section. An old term for a box-top stool was 'stool with a lock'.

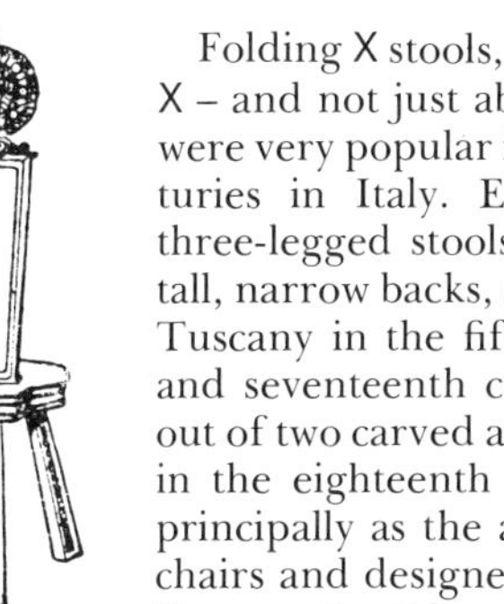

Strozzi stool, Tuscan, 15th century

Folding X stools, with the seat placed on top of the X – and not just above the crossing as in X chairs – were very popular in the fifteenth and sixteenth centuries in Italy. Elegant but very uncomfortable three-legged stools with small octagonal seats and tall, narrow backs, called Strozzi stools were made in Tuscany in the fifteenth century. In the sixteenth and seventeenth centuries stools with legs formed out of two carved and shaped planks were usual, but in the eighteenth century the stool was regarded principally as the appendage of a chair or suite of chairs and designed in conformity.

Strapwork. Of carving, band of ornament more or less suggestive of plaited straps, often highly formalized; distinct from guilloche.

Elizabethan carved oak joint stool, the legs of fluted baluster form. Mary Bellis Antiques, Hungerford

Straw work. A method of decorating furniture, particularly smaller pieces, with tiny strips of bleached and coloured straws to form landscapes, geometrical patterns, etc. This craft came to England from the Continent towards the end of the seventeenth century and was centred at Dunstable. There was a big increase in output during the Napoleonic Wars, when French prisoners, many of whom were craftsmen who had been conscripted into the French Navy, decorated articles in this way during their captivity in England. Among the chief pieces thus decorated were tea caddies, desks, and boxes.

Stretcher. A horizontal member connecting uprights.

Stripping. Furniture, the old surface of which has been removed and reduced to the wood, is said to have been stripped. Though stripping can be properly used, it should never be lightly indulged, as for a supposedly aesthetic advantage (*see* Patina).

Stump feet. A plain turned foot – the 'stump' of the leg – much used on the back legs of American Queen Anne and Chippendale chairs, etc., with cabriole front supports, particularly in Philadelphia.

Stump leg. A simple, thick rear leg curved at the corners; used on Queen Anne and Chippendale chairs.

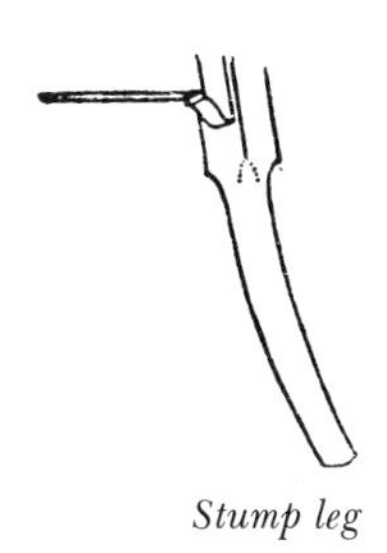

Stump leg

Sunburst. English source of the American rising sun ornament (*q.v.*).

Sunflower. From earliest American times the conventionalized sunflower was a popular carved ornament on Connecticut desks and chests (*q.v.*).

Swan neck. *See* Scroll top.

Sweet gum. Close-grained, silky, red-brown American wood easily stained to look like mahogany and sometimes used as a substitute for it in less-expensive furniture. Miller says that during the Revolution, when mahogany was not obtainable, American sweet-gum wood, then called 'Bilsted', was often used.

Swing-leg table. A hinged-leaf table with a swinging rather than a gate leg. Handsome examples, some of them cabriole, survive.

Table. Primarily, board forming the top only of such furniture, and by later extension the whole structure. *Table tretteau* (table trestles) in the famous

Side table by Robert Adam, 1765

Épitaphe of François Villon is thus a precise, as well as a poetic, statement. The trestle table is a very old form, an advantage being in its ease of clearance and storage, but trestle supports are often ponderous. The other main basic type of table is that supported by a developed framework with a leg at each corner and possibly others along the sides. Of about the early sixteenth century frame tables constructionally ancestral to later types are in evidence, though authentic examples are all but unprocurable in the market. By the end of the same century tables with a developed underframing and fixed legs were usual. The term refectory table is popular jargon, better replaced by long table or other suitable description. Dining or parlour table is used of less extensive items. Drawing or draw table had movable extensions of the top, pushed in below it and drawn when needed. Various kinds of side table include what is now called occasional table. Some small examples are known, correctly or otherwise, as games or gaming tables. Certain table constructions are now reclassified as counter. Billiard tables were known in the sixteenth and seventeenth centuries. As apart from the draw table, the folding, falling (or flap) table, its top with one or more hinged sections, was in more or less general usage by the early seventeenth century. Various forms include bow and bay front (also found minus flaps). Flaps were supported by a movable bracket or leg. A development of the principle resulted in the gate or gate-leg table, with oval or circular top, the developed underframing of legs and stretchers including movable sections or gates. Gate tables made to fold completely flat are known, but the usual construction involved a rigid centre section.

In churches the post-Reformation communion table, replacing the medieval altar, is essentially similar to the domestic long, parlour, or side table previously mentioned, though some examples have special features.

Table chair or **bench.** Correct term for the absurdly misnamed monk's chair or bench. Chair table is also used. Convertible chair, the back pivoted to form a table top when dropped across the uprights. Though the type existed in pre-Reformation times, most surviving examples are so much later in date (say seventeenth-century) as to obviate any monastic association in England.

Tarsia. A form of wood inlay or marquetry widely used in Italy but most notably in Lombardy and Tuscany. Tarsia decoration *alla certosina* made up of polygonal *tessere* of wood, bone, metal, and mother-of-pearl arranged in geometrical patterns was very popular in Lombardy and Venetia in the fifteenth century and much used for the decoration of *cassoni*. The art of pictorial *tarsia* was brought to a high level of excellence at Florence in the fifteenth century by a number of craftsmen, of whom Francesco di Giovanni called il Francione was, according to Vasari, the most highly esteemed. In the fifteenth and subsequent centuries *tarsia* was much used for the decoration of both ecclesiastical and domestic furniture. Panels representing views of real or imaginary architecture were popular on *cassoni* in the late fifteenth and sixteenth centuries, but during the seventeenth century abstract designs seem to have been preferred. In the eighteenth century *tarsia* was applied to tables and chests of drawers, usually in patterns of flowers and ribbons. The last great artist in *tarsia* was the Lombard Giuseppe Maggiolini.

Tavern table. Small, sturdy, rectangular table on four legs, usually braced with stretchers. Generally

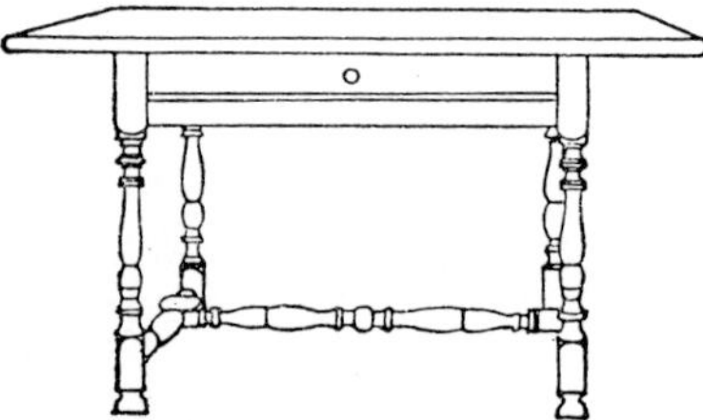

with a drawer or two in the apron. Much used in eighteenth-century taverns for serving a customer where he was seated.

Tea caddy and **tea chest.** A small box for storing tea. 'Tea chest' was the common name for this piece from the end of the seventeenth century, when tea drinking was introduced, until the second half of the eighteenth century, when 'caddy', a corruption of 'kati', a Malay measure of weight of just over one pound, came into general use. The custom of locking up the family's tea in a box continued long after tea had ceased to be an expensive luxury; caddies, therefore, were invariably provided with locks and were either divided into small compartments or were fitted with tea canisters (*q.v.*) for the different kinds of tea. A great variety of materials was used in their construction, including woods of all kinds – carved, inlaid,

Oak gate-leg table with knob-turned legs and semicircular folding top and carved frieze, *c.* 1660. Mary Bellis Antiques, Hungerford veneered, painted, or decorated with tortoiseshell, ivory, rk (*q.v.*), Tunbridge ware (*q.v.*), etc. – metal (silver in the best examples) and papier mâché (*q.v.*). There was also considerable diversity in shape, from rectangular to square and octagonal; while vase and pear forms were introduced after 1750.

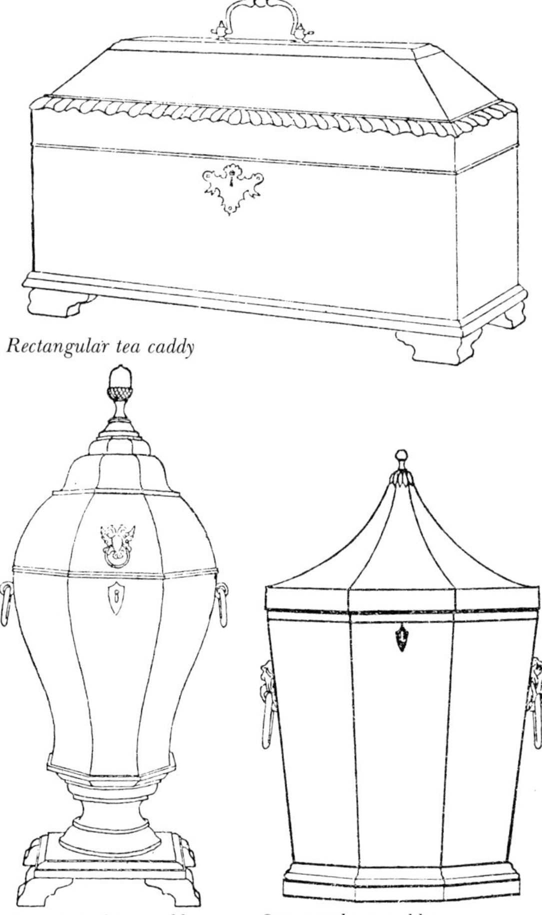

Rectangular tea caddy

Pear shaped tea caddy *Octagonal tea caddy*

Tea canister. The container for tea in the caddy (if the latter were not already divided into compartments); made of glass, metal, or earthenware; usually bottle-shaped until *c.* 1750, and vase-shaped later.
Tea-pot stand. *See* Kettle stand.
Tear drop. *See* Drop handle.
Toilet mirror (or **dressing glass**). A small mirror designed to stand on a table or, in early examples, to hang on the wall. This kind of mirror was a luxury in the medieval and Tudor periods, and did not begin to come into wider use until the late seventeenth century. Post-Restoration mirrors were usually square in shape, and frequently had their frames decorated with stumpwork; they stood by means of a strut or hung by a ring. By about 1700 oblong mirrors with arched tops, in narrower moulded frames, veneered or japanned, had begun to replace the square shape. In the eighteenth century several changes occurred. Shortly after 1700 appeared the mirror supported by screws in uprights mounted on a box stand; the box was often in the form of a flap or desk above a drawer which contained the many toilet requisites of the time; the mirror had a pronounced arched heading at first, and the front of the box was sometimes serpentine in form. The older type of strut support, without the box stand, continued to be made, however, and occasionally a stand with small trestle feet was found. By 1750 mahogany was in general use for toilet mirrors, though some in the Chinese style were gilt or japanned. Similar designs were introduced in the neoclassical period; mirror frames, in mahogany or satinwood, were often of oval or shield shape, and the uprights were curved to correspond. The stand was also a simpler arrangement, as toilet articles were now placed in the table on which the mirror stood. At the very end of the century and later, a wide oblong mirror was fashionable, and was usually swung on turned uprights. Mahogany and rosewood, often decorated with stringing, were the chief woods for such mirrors at this time.

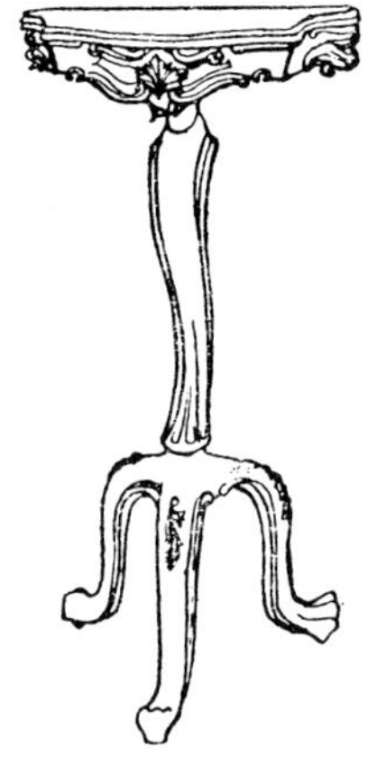

Trespolo

Torchère. *See* Candlestand.
Toy furniture. Though toy furniture authentically of the Age of Oak exists, it is rare, and there are many copies or imitations. Toy is here used in its sense of knick-knack. Some such pieces were children's toys, or dolls' furniture, others were made as models to satisfy the adult love of 'miniatures'. Yet others are said to have been fashioned as trade samples, or as 'prentices' pieces' to demonstrate an apprentice's skill. In practice, it is not always possible to differentiate between these various subdivisions.
Trail. Undulating band of formalized leaf, berry, or floral pattern. Thus vine trail.

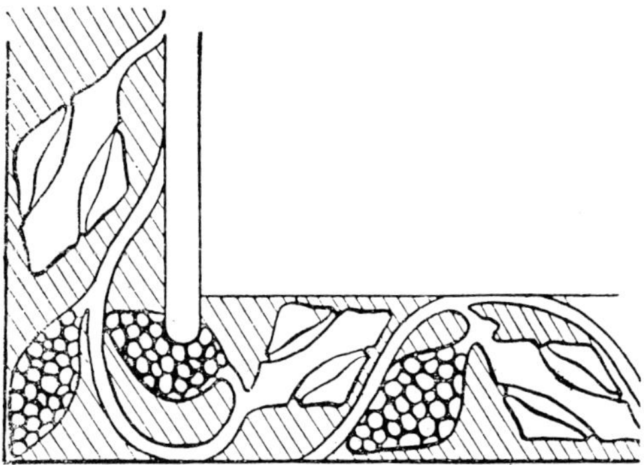

Tray. For food, tea things, plates, etc.; also known as a voider (the medieval term for a tray which was still in use in late Georgian times). Tea trays (or 'tea boards') were introduced in the late seventeenth century, and most of them were japanned; none, however, seems to have survived. Japanned trays were still popular in the middle of the eighteenth century, though by then ornamental mahogany trays with fretted borders were being made. Later, oval trays decorated with fine inlay were in vogue. About 1800 there was a considerable production of trays in japanned metal and papier mâché.
Treen. Old adjectival form of tree; wooden. Now used of an extensive array of articles, mainly small and of almost any period, such as bowls, Welsh love spoons, stay busks, etc., and not excluding furniture.
Trespolo. Elegant three-legged tables known as *trespoli*, usually designed to stand against a wall and to carry a small *objet d'art* or candlestick, were very popular in the eighteenth century, especially in Venice. Sometimes the supporting column was made in the form of a term figure, but it was more usually carved in a graceful curve.
Tricoteuse. A term probably of nineteenth-century origin, applied to a small worktable surrounded by a gallery, part of which can be lowered to contain sewing materials.

Tridarn. *See* Cupboard.

Tuckaway table. A hinged-leaf gate-leg table with cross legs which fold into each other as compactly as if tucked away.

Tudor. The Tudor dynasty reigned from 1485 to 1603; Tudor is loosely used of furniture emerging from the Gothic or not fully developed as characteristic Elizabethan. The periods of Henry VIII (1509–47) and Elizabeth (1558–1603) are usually given their own names.

Tulip ornament. Formalized ornament of tulip-like form, influenced by the tulip mania in Holland, when huge sums were paid for rare bulbs. On English furniture the vogue for tulip ornament continued from about the middle to the end of the seventeenth century.

Tulipwood (or **tulip poplar**). A soft, light wood used as a secondary wood and in painted furniture.

Tunbridge ware. A special form of inlay which developed at Tunbridge Wells *c.* 1650, employing minute strips of wood, in a great variety of natural colours, to build up geometrical patterns and, later, floral decoration, landscape scenes, etc.; used for boxes, trays, desks, tea caddies, etc.

Turtle back. A type of ornamental boss, shaped somewhat like a turtle's back, often applied to Jacobean-style cupboards, etc.

Twist turning. Form of turning derived from the twisted columns of Romanesque via Renaissance architecture. In England its main vogue on furniture (as apart from later, including romantic antiquarian revivals) was in the mid/latter half of the seventeenth century. R. W. Symonds had differentiated the single-roped twist (Dutch-Flemish type) from the English double-roped or barley-sugar twist (*see English Furniture from Charles II to George II*).

Urn stand. *See* Kettle stand.

Veneer. Thin sheets of wood applied to surface for decorative effect or to improve appearance of furniture. Though veneering arrived in the second half of the seventeenth century, at the end of the oak period, it is sometimes found as a limited enhancement of pieces which would be classed as oak by collectors.

Vernis Martin. A term applied generically to all varnishes and lacquers used for furniture and interior decoration in France during the eighteenth century. It derives from the brothers Martin, who in 1730 were granted a monopoly to copy Chinese and Japanese lacquer. They also evolved a special kind of coloured varnish, which was applied in a large number of coats and then rubbed down to give it lustre. It was available in a number of colours, including grey, lilac, yellow, and blue, but the most famous was the green, which was often applied to furniture. *Vernis Martin* was also used to decorate *boiseries*, carriages, fans, and small boxes. The Martin family were much patronized by the Court and by Madame de Pompadour (*see also under* Lacquer).

Wagon seat. An American double seat, generally with a two-chair back of slat-back or Windsor variety, usable both as a farm porch settee and a wagon seat.

Wainscot. Now mainly used of wall panelling, but anciently of wider significance, its derivation from MLG. *Wagenschot*, perhaps meaning wagon boarding, referring rather to the planking itself, and thence to a wall lining as well as to other forms of woodwork. Bedstead, chair, stool, etc., are frequently listed as being 'of wainscot'. Though this term in some cases implied that their construction involved a noticeable amount of panelled work, furniture stoutly built of slabs or planks of wood was perhaps 'of wainscot', involving various forms of boarded furniture with 'slab ends'. As a term, wainscot may have been loosely as well as precisely used (*cf.* definition of coffer).

Wall lights. A lighting appliance usually of more than one light which can be fixed flat to the surface of a wall. They were very popular in France during the Louis XV and Louis XVI periods, and large numbers were made, usually of ormolu and often in pairs or sets of four to six. The *ciselure* and gilding on many of them are often of very high quality.

Walnut. Finely figured hard wood good for carving, veneering, and turning. Black walnut was used particularly in the William and Mary and Queen Anne periods for elegant furniture, and replaced by mahogany when importations increased. In America it retained popularity in Pennsylvania and the south. White walnut, known better as butternut, grows between New England and Maryland. It is open-grained and light-brown, and used mainly in country furniture.

Wardrobes. The wardrobe developed out of the cupboard and the cabinet in the late seventeenth century and was treated monumentally by Boulle and his *atelier*, many being made for the Crown and very sumptuously decorated. From the constructional point of view it consists of a straight, upright cupboard closed by two doors and with one or more shelves on the undecorated interior. It survived into the early Regency, sometimes of plain carved wood, but as rooms became smaller it seems to have disappeared. A number, however, were made in the Boulle technique in the Louis XVI period from earlier designs. Some were also made of plain wood under the Empire.

Armoire, veneered on oak with ebony and Boulle marquetry of brass, partly engraved, and tortoiseshell. Bronze mounts, chased and gilt. The groups on the doors represent: *left* Apollo and Daphne, *right* The Flaying of Marsyas. Attributed to Andre Charles Boulle. Wallace Collection, London

Washing stand (or **basin stand**). Specially adapted for bedroom use after 1750, and of two main kinds. (1) A tripod stand with three uprights, a circular top fitted with a basin, and a central triangular shelf with a drawer (or drawers) and receptacle for soap. A four-legged version of this type was also made. (2) A cupboard or chest of drawers on four legs with a basin sunk in the top, covered by a lid or flaps.
Water leaf. A carved ornamental motif of narrow leaf with regular horizontal undulations divided by a stem going down the centre. Used in classical style and much favoured by Duncan Phyfe as a leg decoration. In many ways it is the classical-style counterpart of the acanthus leaf of the Chippendale period.
Web foot. *See* Duck foot.
Whatnot. A portable stand with four uprights enclosing shelves, in use after about 1800 for books, ornaments, etc.
Wheat ears. Hepplewhite-carved ornament of wheat ears, used in America by McIntire, Phyfe, and others as low-relief decoration on bedposts, chair and sofa backs, etc.
Whorl. Circular ornament on medieval (and later) furniture, the enclosed carving raying from the centre of the circle, or in certain other, including geometrical, dispositions. The general sense of the term seems to approximate whirl. Whorl is freely used, though in doubtful or obviously inapplicable cases roundel is employable.
Windsor chair. Developed from the buffet chair, made of turned members with a saddle seat. Until recently the English Windsor chair was made only around High Wycombe, Bucks. Whether the American Windsor chair was evolved from the English Windsor or the English corner chair, or both, is not yet certain. In any event, the American development is unique. In the American Windsor the back has no splat and is formed entirely of spindles socketed into a top rail. There are two main types – comb back, in which the top rail is shaped like the head of a comb; and hoop or bow back, the top rail bent like half a hoop. Four other types are differentiated – low back, a semi-circular horizontal top rail somewhat like that of a corner chair; New England arm, a simpler form of the hoop back; fan back (which some authorities think may have been the side chair to the comb back armchair); and loop or balloon back, the top rail loop-shaped. American Windsors have saddle-shaped seats of solid wood or, occasionally, rush seats. The legs, simple turned, are pegged into the seat at a rakish angle, adding a final charm to the stick-and-spindle lines. Windsors were first made in or near Philadelphia about 1725, and were found so comfortable that by 1760 they had become the most popular chairs in everyday use. A type fitted with rockers, called the Windsor rocker, is often found.
Wine cistern (or **cooler**). A case for wine bottles, very similar to a cellaret (*q.v.*), but normally larger, without a lid and designed to contain ice or water for cooling the wine. Bowl-shaped wooden cisterns on feet or stand were lined with lead and came into wide use after *c.* 1730; stone and metal (especially silver) cisterns were also found. At the end of the century the tub form, with hoops of brass, was general.
Wing chair. An upholstered chair with high back, stuffed arms, and wing-shaped protectors at head level protruding from the back over the arms. Known in England during the seventeenth century and probably introduced in America before 1725.

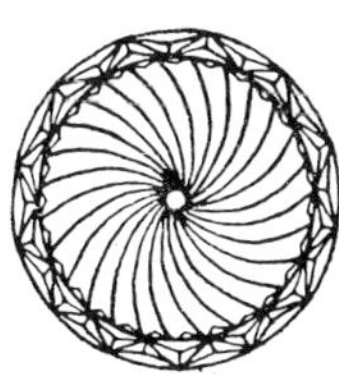

Whorl (top) *and roundel*

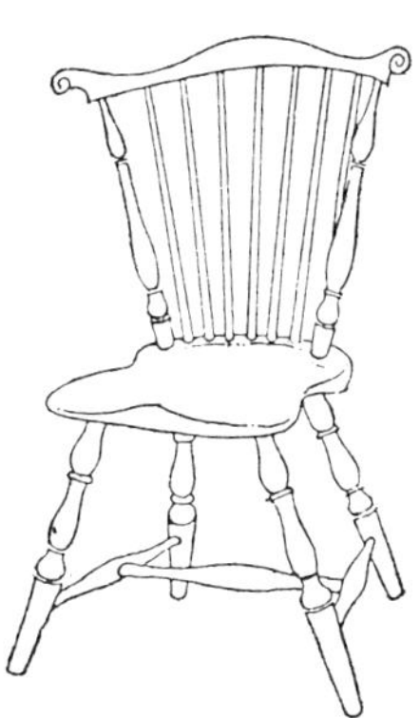

Comb-back Windsor chair

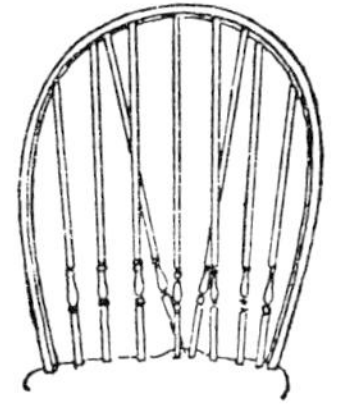

Hoop-back Windsor chair

Winthrop desk. A Chippendale slant-top desk mistakenly named for one of the seventeenth-century governors of Massachusetts.
Worktable. The name usually applied to the special table made in the second half of the eighteenth century for ladies' needlework, etc. In Sheraton's time these tables were of several kinds; some, mounted on four tapered and reeded legs or on trestle feet, might include, in addition to a drawer, such fittings as a pouch for the work materials, an adjustable fire screen, and a writing board or slide. Another type, the 'French worktable', was a tray on trestle feet with a shelf or shelves below.
Worm hole. Tunnel bored in woodwork by various types of beetle, collectively and popularly called 'the worm'. Worm holes are not *per se* evidence of antiquity, though they *have* been artificially simulated. 'Worm' is, however, a condition demanding attention to destroy infection. New worm holes usually show a light-coloured interior, whereas old ones may be discoloured. A simple, though not final, test for possible activity is to tap the suspected piece and watch for a fall of wood dust. If the mischief is superficial, furniture may be cured by repeated applications of one of the proprietary fluids sold for this purpose; but more heavily infested articles may need expert attention. In some furniture worm may have been extinct for centuries. When worm holes are laterally exposed to any noticeable extent, it may be inferred (*a*) that the wood has been recut after infestation; or (*b*) that the surface was formerly painted or otherwise covered with some since-vanished substance which formed a side wall to the channel. Exposed channels occur on some fakes (*q.v.*), but are not *per se* condemnatory, though, in many cases, suspicious.
Writing cabinet. Fall-front cabinets, enclosing a system of small drawers, became prominent in the latter part of the sixteenth century, especially in Italy and Spain (*see* Bargueño), some of them serving as writing cabinets. Such cabinets were sometimes furnished with stands, though others were stand-less, placed on top of a table or chest as needed. Certain of the latter were supplied with stands at a later period.

Such pieces are ancestral to the fall-front scrutoire, secretaire (*qq.v.*) (from Fr. *secrétaire*) of later times, the slope-front variety being at least in part a development of the writing desk.
Writing table. Many varieties of small writing tables can be found dating from the end of the seventeenth century, when they were first introduced. Early examples were made with turned baluster legs and folding tops, and were frequently used also as side and card tables. Gate legs were usual and some tables were fitted with a drawer. Decoration with marquetry was often found on them. In the early eighteenth century small knee-hole writing tables were popular, with tiers of narrow drawers on each side of the central recess. Similar tables, it may be noted, were also used as dressing tables, and it is not always possible to determine their exact purpose. After the introduction of mahogany, when the fashion arose for larger pedestal tables in libraries, many versions of the convenient lighter table continued to be made. It was at the end of the century that perhaps the most elegant kinds of these smaller tables were seen, frequently of satinwood. Some closely resembled contemporary secretaires and cheverets; others were fitted with an adjustable writing board and a screen.

HOLA·WO·HEE
MIT·DER·LEIM·STA
NGEN·ICH·MEINDT·DV·WOL
ST·AVCH·VOGEL·FANGEN.
SICH·LIEBER·SICH·WIE·EIN·FEIN·LEIM
KNECHT·BIN·ICH·MIT·MEINER·GE
SCH VCRTEN·LEIM·STANGEN·
HABICH·VOGEL·VND·HASEN·
GEFAGEN..

GLASS

A small goblet still testifies to the fact that Egyptians had mastered the fundamentals of glass making more than 3,500 years ago. Collectors today, looking back over the intervening centuries, can trace a fascinating story. The Egyptians shaped their hollow vessels round cores of sand and pressed molten glass into open moulds. Some 2,000 years ago came the fundamental discovery that the hot glass could be shaped on a hollow rod by blowing, and Syria and Egypt thus produced great quantities of domestic vessels under the power of Imperial Rome.

From Rome in the first four centuries A.D. glass makers penetrated to the Roman colonies, and by the time the empire crumbled the craft had gained footholds in the Rhône valley and along the Rhine and the Seine. It is probable that the Chinese acquired their knowledge of glass making and the pottery glaze first used during the Han dynasty (206 B.C.–A.D. 220) from the Romans. In the first century A.D. the Romans referred to China (the source of silk) as Seres, and the end of the overland caravan route was probably the Syrian coast, famous for its glass manufactures. But the Chinese made relatively little use of glass for important work, preferring to concentrate their attention on ceramics and jade carving. Little remains from the dark ages that followed the rise and fall of the Roman empire, but in the following pages the story is taken up again with the Venetian triumph of clear 'crystal' glass, and the result of this may be observed in the account of Bohemian glass.

England assumed the lead in domestic glassware in the late seventeenth century with Ravenscroft's incomparable flint glass, and the story of the eighteenth and nineteenth centuries embraces the contrasting purposes and rival techniques of Britain and America, of Scandinavia and France. In particular, the nineteenth century's technical triumphs emphasize that glass making is still a craft and an art, living, expanding, essential to mankind.

American

'We sent home ample proofs of pitch, tar, glass . . .' wrote Captain John Smith in his *Historie of Virginia*. Whatever the forms given to those 1609 proofs of glass, it is certain they were neither omens of a new national style nor of a New World contribution to glass as an art. And they never expanded into profitable production of this indispensable man-made substance. As to the glass blown and the articles fashioned during the abortive struggles of the four or five subsequent seventeenth-century attempts to root glass making, they can only be guessed at.

With but few exceptions, all this is true of the ten or eleven eighteenth-century houses in which hopeful colonial businessmen sank their capital. One was sufficiently successful making window glass and blowing bottles and jars to operate for nearly forty years: Wistar's, whose small glasshouse community, near Salem in southern Jersey, was called Wistarburg (*c.* 1739–75). Similar utility wares, mainly green glass and inevitably counterparts of European prototypes, were made at the New York and New Windsor (*c.* 1752–67) works of the Glass House Company of New York, and at the Germantown works near Boston (1753–68). Bottles and window glass were to be the financial backbone of glass making for well over a century.

Only two pre-Revolutionary enterprises (so present evidence indicates) attempted to specialize in tablewares: Henry William Stiegel's second glasshouse (1769–74) at Manheim, Pennsylvania, and the Philadelphia Glass Works at Kensington. But both Stiegel and the proprietors at Kensington produced window glass and bottles also. In fact, these necessities of life were the paying output of Stiegel's Elizabeth Furnace Works (1763) and the principal products of his first at Manheim (1765). However, tableware production was intensive from 1769 into 1774 at Manheim, and from about 1772 into 1777 at Kensington. Each claimed to be the first flint-glass manufacturer in the country, but Stiegel, at least, made non-lead glass as well. Though flint glass was the popular name for lead glass, it seems likely that in the eighteenth as well as the nineteenth century non-lead-glass tablewares were often called flint because it implied quality.

At Manheim, Continental and English styles met, but apparently did not blend. Actually Continental casually and shallowly engraved glass of the type today called peasant glass was followed so closely that few students consider physical characteristics alone a safe basis for attribution. The same, unfortunately, is true of English pattern-moulded types. Articles listed in Stiegel's account books and his advertisements indicate that the range of articles was wide and followed imports. In 1771 the American Philosophical Society in Philadelphia pronounced the specimens exhibited to its members 'equal in beauty and quality to the generality of Flint Glass imported from England'. As for Kensington wares, advertisements and owners' nationality indicate they were English. They represented the last effort to make fine glassware until after the Revolution.

In the first forty-two years – from 1783 to 1824 – of the United States as a sovereign nation, about ninety-four glasshouses were built in spite of turbulent, unfavourable economic conditions. The depressed state of trade and commerce following

Humpen (tall beaker) with enamelled decoration of a hunter and a woman, Bohemian, *c.* 1594

Above, left Covered sugar bowl with chicken finial, German, last half of 18th century. Casper Wistar imported many of his glass blowers from Holland and Germany and with them they brought their old traditions. *Centre and right* Covered sugar bowl and candlestick, olive green and aquamarine glass. South Jersey, possibly Wistarburg or Glassboro, *c.* 1740–80. Corning Museum of Glass

the Revolution could not dampen optimism for various domestic manufactures. Shortly before 1800 westward migrations encouraged the establishment of glass making in the Midwest, where the Pittsburgh Glass Works erected America's first coal-burning furnace (1797) – immediately sealing the doom of many as yet unplanned eastern wood-burning houses and determining the future hub of the glass industry. Optimism ran higher still with President Jefferson's embargo on trade with Britain (1806–7) and the Non Importation Act (1811). It climbed to greater heights during the war of 1812. With each encouraging event or condition, a graph of glass-houses would rise to ever higher peaks and, between them, their failures drop to greater depths. New houses were built; some old ones were abandoned; others were taken over by new firms. In the whole period at least three times as many firms were formed by an even larger number of glassmen, merchants, brewers, and other businessmen. The few houses planned for tableware production either failed, or became green-glass houses, or added its production in order to survive. Not until 1824 did Congress pass a tariff ensuring survival with profit of flint-glass manufacturing as well as window glass and bottles. Fought unsuccessfully by importers and independent glass-cutting shops, the 1828 and 1832 tariffs doubled the insurance.

Among the post-Revolutionary tableware houses important from the collector's viewpoint only one was eighteenth-century: the New Bremen Glass manufactory (1785–95) of John Frederick Amelung & Company, near Frederick, Maryland; an over-ambitious project misreading desires of the fashionable and overestimating demand for domestic glassware, luxury or ordinary. The New Bremen commercial tablewares presumably followed prevailing fashions, especially some of the finer Continental cut

Left Two blown and enamelled tumblers, possibly Manheim, Pennsylvania glasshouse of Henry William Stiegel, *c.* 1770. Corning Museum of Glass

and engraved glass, and were non-lead, as are the authenticated pieces which have been tested for lead content. These latter are mainly so-called 'presentation pieces' or gifts. Their shapes, engraving technique, decoration by individual combinations of mainly Continental motifs and metal are Amelung earmarks. Similarity to their stylistic and physical characteristics has been the basis for attributing other pieces to New Bremen. The decorative techniques practised in addition to engraving were pattern moulding, applied and tooled decoration, and, to a limited degree, enamelling and gilding.

In the early nineteenth century there were several important houses. Bakewells' (1809–80) was prominent in the Pittsburgh area. This first successful flint-glass manufactory in the country (even so, green glass was added to the output in 1811) was without effective rival among the few other Midwestern houses before John Robinson's Stourbridge Flint Glass Works (1823–45). By then demand and other favourable conditions were sufficient to support several houses. In the east, flint-glass production was rooted firmly by Thomas Cains, to whom the Boston Glass Company gave permission to erect a small flint-glass furnace in its South Boston works. Briefly (*c.* 1815–22) at Keene, New Hampshire, the Flint Glass Works on Marlboro Street made lead-glass bottles, flasks, and tablewares before becoming just a 'bottle' house. At Cambridge, across the Charles River from Boston, the New England Glass Company, for over half a century probably the east's largest producer of fine glasswares (1818–80), took over a postwar casualty, the Boston Porcelain and Glass Company, organized in 1814. In New York, there were the Fisher Brothers' Bloomingdale Flint Glass Works (1822–45) and the Brooklyn Flint Glass Works founded by John L. Gilliland & Company (1823–68, moved to Corning, N.Y.), which won the prize for the best flint-glass metal at the London Crystal Palace, 1851. The Jersey Glass Company (1824–*c.* 1862), one of the improvers of mechanical pressing, built its works on Paulus Hook, across the Hudson from New York. That all, including the Midwestern, had ready access to water carriage is significant. Their production included pattern-moulded and free-blown wares, new commercial types as they evolved and, naturally, cut and engraved like popular imports. Also, by 1823, export of American glass, particularly to the West Indies and South America, had started.

Vast reaches of country, continual westward expansion, inadequate and slow transportation – by land or water – were among the factors determining locations and quantities of glasshouses. Scattering was logical if the country was to be independent of imports, as its glass makers so vainly hoped. The increase, checked briefly by the 1830s' depression, continued so that at least ninety new works were erected from 1825 to 1850. More than ever before were dedicated to flint-glass wares. For collectors the foremost among them were the Boston and Sandwich Glass Works, Sandwich, Massachusetts (1825–88), the Union Glass Works, Kensington, Philadelphia (1826–?), the Providence Flint Glass Works, Rhode Island (1831–5) (short lived but leaving marked pressed salts), the Curlings' Fort Pitt Glass Works, Pittsburgh (1826–*c.* 1900), and the Sweenys' (1831–67) and the Richies' (1829–?) works, Wheeling, West Virginia. However, as always, the majority were bottle and/or window-glass houses. Not all the new houses survived; many old ones drew their fires; the inevitable westward shift accelerated. Most eastern houses, especially in New England and western and northern New York, depended upon wood for fuel. For many exhaustion of wood holdings and prohibitive cost of transporting fuel, even if furnaces were converted to coal, meant extinction. Also canals and improved roads, by enabling some houses to transport materials and wares more efficiently and cheaply, contributed to the failure of less fortunately situated works.

During this period glass making was ineradicably rooted in the United States. Future pioneering was to be in glass technology and production. Experiments with blowing glass by machine had already begun, and even more immediately fateful to glass blowing as an art, John P. Bakewell of Pittsburgh obtained a patent on machine pressing in 1825. By the mid-century, the machine had made mass production possible. Experiments in colour and composition bore strange and sometimes lovely fruits, forerunners of the later remarkable art glasses. The conscious effort to create the novel, symptomatic of an indus-

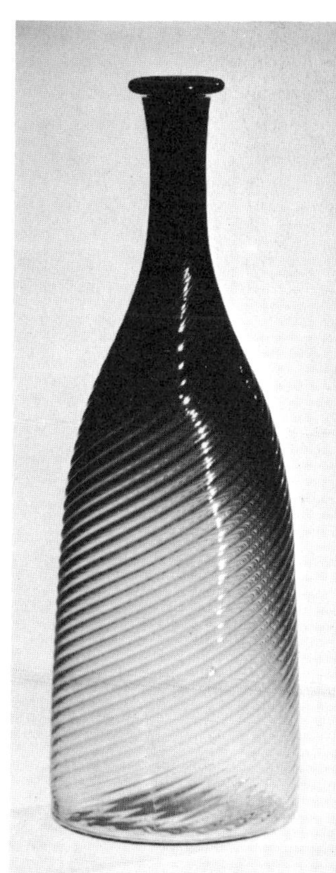

Above Amberina decanter, New England Glass Co., 1883–8. Corning Museum of Glass

Far left Covered tumbler, John Frederick Amelung's New Bremen Glass Manufactory, dated 1788. Corning Museum of Glass

Below Amethyst vase, probably Boston and Sandwich Glass Company, 19th century. New York Historical Society

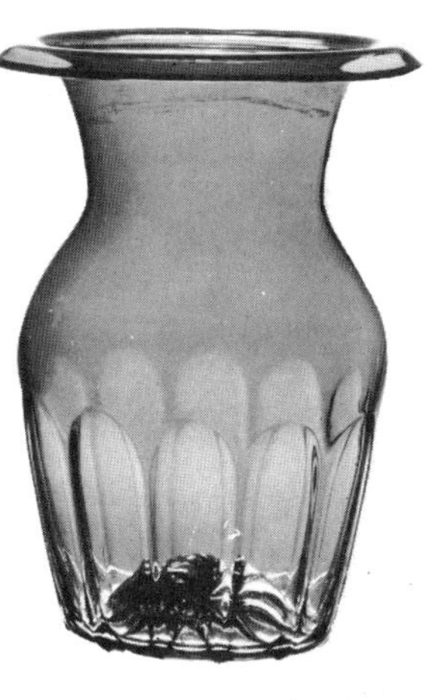

Amethyst salt, Stiegel Midwestern type, pattern moulded and expanded in diamond design with petalled foot, early 19th century. New York Historical Society

trial society, became habit. Then, too, the term glasshouse, with its aura of craftsmanship and the art of glass blowing, no longer fitted most establishments, but rather factory, with all its twentieth-century connotations.

In all these years neither social, economic, nor psychological conditions were favourable for the emergence of a national style in blown tablewares. Glassmen, manufacturers, merchants, and customers were too fixed in their orientation to Europe's fashions and traditions. The glassmen enticed across the Atlantic brought inherited traditions and techniques practised in European houses. Almost without exception they were Continentals until Stiegel persuaded English blowers and decorators to Manheim. Afterward the numbers from Britain increased, especially for flint-glass manufacture, familiar far longer and to more British glassmen than to Continentals. If they remained in their crafts, their techniques and traditions were taught to native-born boys. Still, since defection to easier occupations or to the land was constant, thinned ranks had to be refilled from Europe. Thus, unless deliberately diverted, the stream of European traditions in glass blowing and ornamentation – Continental and British – played continuously upon American-made glass.

Decanters, 19th century, that on the right is attributed to Dummer's Jersey City Works or Gilliland's Brooklyn Flint Glass Works, *c.* 1845. New York Historical Society

The men who started the glasshouses were necessarily more concerned with finances than aesthetics. Many were merchants and importers familiar with the glassware demand, and well aware that competition entailed imitating imports, of which English were considered best. Consequently style and design of commercial glasswares were determined mainly by imports. Nevertheless, along with glass cut or engraved to the 'latest London pattern' but within an accepted style, there were inevitable deviations, differing details and features. Though as yet this field of American glass had received limited scrutiny, it seems proved that idiosyncracies and types peculiar to certain houses and area developed, more Midwestern than eastern. In houses removed geographically and socially from the more European-style-conscious East, conditions were more favourable for the emergence of local features and types. The salt, with its combination of broken-swirl ribbing, double-ogee bowl, and ribbed drawn knop, illustrates one such type.

Actually, if flint-glass makers had depended solely upon the carriage trade – and in a free market – few would have survived. Fortunately a sizeable pedestrian trade developed and expanded rapidly. Its needs could be met by new commercial wares such as blown-three-mould, early pressed, and lacy glass, and a new type of bottle packaging too – historical, pictorial, and decorative flasks and bottles. These categories contain distinctive United States designs. While they do not represent art in glass, many, especially among the flasks, may be called popular art in glass. The inexpensive blown-three-mould and early pressed wares enjoyed a comparatively brief reign; the flasks, with their blown-moulded designs, such as portraits of presidential candidates, emblems and slogans, monuments and heroes – even George Washington – were popular for nearly three-quarters of a century. They were a national style in packaging potables.

As a type of tableware, blown-three-mould may have originated in the United States shortly after 1812, perhaps at South Boston under Thomas Cains. It was a sort of poor man's cut glass created by using a full-size mould having its inner surface the size and shape of an article and with an intaglio pattern. The patterns, an earmark, are classified as arch, baroque, and geometric. Of over 150 examples recorded, the majority are geometric, inspired by and in some instances identical with cut glass. Also the majority are apparently peculiar to the United States. British production seems to have been limited to a few articles and a few geometric patterns, composed mainly of ribbings and diamond diapering in bands and blocks. The arch and baroque patterns have no known foreign counterparts.

The number of different articles in which each pattern appears and the number of moulds bearing each pattern varies widely. In the most common, McK GII-18 – band of diamond diapering between bands of vertical ribbing – over twenty articles have been recorded, over fifty individual moulds determined. While 400 moulds have been determined by analysis of actual pieces, they were for few articles, principally decanters and tumblers of many sizes and several shapes, castor bottles and inkwells. However, these were used to pattern gathers of glass to be fashioned, partially or entirely, by blowing and manipulation into other articles. For instance, a pitcher would frequently be patterned in a decanter mould, the body form retained but the neck expanded and lipped, and the handle, of course, applied. Bowls and dishes were fashioned freehand from the gather after it had been patterned in either a tumbler or a decanter mould.

By 1830 the popular demand for blown-three-mould was shrinking and had focused on the early pressed glasses. From 1825, when Bakewell patented mechanical pressing of knobs, the process developed and improved so rapidly that by 1828 creamers could be pressed with handles and bodies in one piece. The invention of mechanical pressing and development of this revolutionary production method has been charged to America. Apsley Pellatt's 1831 specifications (British Patent No. 6091) for his press and mould referred to the 'mode' as 'lately introduced from America'. By 1852, to paraphrase Deming Jarvis, founder of the Boston and Sandwich Glass Works, the American invention had so reduced cost of production, thus lowering retail prices of glasswares, that consumption had increased tenfold. It was undoubtedly a factor also in any successful competition with European glass in the export markets.

By then there had been several phases in pressed-glass design. As in the case of blown-three-mould, the earliest patterns were inspired by cut glass and adopted its motifs, especially the strawberry and fine-cut diamonds and, for rims, the fan escallop. However, about 1828 lacy glass, which was to be typically American for well over a decade, was evolving. With limitless variety made possible by mechanics, decorative design quickly passed beyond the close confines of contemporary cut glass, with its simple geometric motifs regimented in stiff bands and into both simple and intricate variety of motifs on a stippled background. The stippling, tiny relief dots, was a glitter-producing device new in glass making and the earmark of lacy. The patterned surface of the glass was lustreless; the smooth, through which the innumerable facets and angled planes refracted light, brilliant and sparkling.

Lacy designs reveal a catholicity in taste and free use of many sources in the arts and crafts. They adapted motifs and treatments popularized by the classical and Gothic revivals, from architectural ornament, ceramics; turned to conventionalized and naturalistic flowers and leaves; used local and national emblems, symbols, national heroes' portraits; favoured geometric figures; never completely discarded the various diamond motifs. Many designs were well realized, with motifs in sound balance and accent; many were overelaborate and poorly composed. Some eastern lacy glass was very similar to some manufactured abroad, and other lacy-glass designs have their counterparts in Meissen porcelain forms and decoration. Most designs, however, are exclusive to American lacy glass, and the Midwestern designs are easily distinguishable from their eastern counterparts.

During the depression starting in 1837, apparently another design phase appeared. As lacy moulds with stippling and many-planed patterns were expensive, their cost, as well as general economic conditions, doubtless contributed to the decline of lacy production and the rise of a simpler style. The new designs emphasized form and simple geometric motifs, unquestionably influenced by cut glass of that period. They were ideal for the pressed-pattern glass, as the table and bar glass popular from around 1840 were called. In many patterns table sets were quite complete, including, as American lacy did not, various types of drinking glasses. The new style found expression also in innumerable lamps, candlesticks, and vases, produced in all the old and many new tints and tones of greens, blues, amethyst, and yellows, transparent, translucent, and opaque. However, in pressed glass, early or late, good or bad designs, American or derivative, art had passed to the mould maker.

But even as the machine was dominating commercial glasswares, wherever there were bottle- and window-glass houses the art of glass blowing was being practised freely and unhampered by fashion or a designer's specifications. So it must always have been in such glasshouses. In the Midwest until about 1835, and in the east into the late nineteenth century, distinctively American glass was fashioned for local custom in the early years and in isolated communities, always for friend and family. Vessels for use in pantry, kitchen, and on the table – they were individual, functional, and honestly sturdy, free-blown from window and bottle glass, mainly in natural colours. In general, the Midwestern colour range outstripped the eastern in quality of vibrant brilliance, subtle nuances of colour tone, and use of artificial colours. Many were plain or simply ornamented – perhaps a folded rim, threading, or a scalloped foot, the last rare in the east. The Midwestern tended to be thinner walled than the eastern, and in other aspects were quite different.

Major differences lay largely in shape, proportions, and decorative techniques. In Midwestern houses, shapes evolved which were peculiar to the region; for instance, the sugar-bowl, with its wide galleried rim, high, short, sharply angled shoulder, straight sides sloping abruptly to the base, and the type of double-domed cover. Eastern shapes conformed more closely with commercial wares, and more seldom included an eighteenth-century feature or treatment. For bottles and flasks as well as hollow ware, the preferred Midwestern decorative technique was pattern moulding, mainly ribbing, fluting, the broken swirl, and various expanded diamonds. The broken swirl was tight 'popcorn', or widely expanded resembling feathery diamond-on-the-diagonal. Though far from frail in appearance, this Midwestern glass seems to derive lightness and poised strength from its patterned surface and brilliance of metal.

Left to right Goblet, blown with applied pattern-moulded decoration, possibly New Geneva, Glass Works of Albert Gallatin, *c.* 1798–1810; sugar bowl with cover, chicken finial and applied lily pad decoration, New York, Redford or Redwood Glass Works, *c.* 1835–50; pitcher, dark amber with opaque white decoration, attributed to South Jersey, Bridgeton Glass Works, *c.* 1836–50. Corning Museum of Glass

Blowers in New Jersey, New York, and New England bottle- and window-glass houses rarely used the pattern mould: they practised the centuries-old arts of glass blowing and decorating, applying glass to itself and tooling it into ornamentation. Of many devices, perhaps the favourites were threading, prunts, quilling, crimping, also swagging, gadrooning, and (nineteenth century) the so called lily pads fashioned from a superimposed layer, and embedded loopings. Though the devices were traditional or variations of ancient devices, it is unlikely the blowers, especially in the nineteeenth century, realized their vessels' close kinship with Continental 'forest glass' and more remote ancestors. In fact, many expressions, the lily pads in particular, probably were independent inventions. All these individual pieces, plain and decorated, are called South Jersey type; the first of their kind unquestionably were from Wistar's eighteenth-century glassworks, southern Jersey. They are called folk art in American glass, largely because they are individual within a traditional stream and independent of sophisticated commercial style.

Folk art in American glass is a comparatively new term in the American collectors' glossary, which, as in trades, professions, and other hobbies, contains many words unintelligible to the uninitiated. It is a compilation of the glassman's obsolete and modern technical terms, English and Anglo-Irish glass terms, and terms coined by American collectors and writers to meet descriptive needs and afford identification of forms, types, and decoration. Many of those in common usage can be found in the glossary.

Pitcher with lily pad decoration, New York, Lockport or Lancaster glassworks, *c.* 1840–60. Corning Museum of Glass

Bohemian

Bohemian glass is the generic term for the ornamental glass made in and near the mountains covering the borders of Bohemia and Silesia. Glasshouses were established there because the country was rich in natural resources: pine and beech forests provided furnace fuel and potash: pure white sand was plentiful in the hillsides. Forest-glass domestic ware, tinged green, yellow, or brown, was made there as early as the fourteenth century. In the sixteenth century a fine soda glass was evolved, faintly tinged topaz yellow; this was decorated with bright enamels. Thus Bohemia became the first country to enter into direct competition with Murano.

During the reign of the Emperor Rudolph II the medieval art of decorating glass with designs cut on the lapidary's wheel was revived by Caspar Lehmann (1570–1622). At the age of eighteen he was appointed lapidary and glass cutter to the emperor and given a life patent of monopoly. He was the first of Bohemia's master decorators and operated extensive workshops at Prague, far from the glasshouses. After Lehmann's death the monopoly was granted to his assistant Zacharias Belzer and a scholar George Schwanhard. The latter's sons, George (d. 1676) and Henry (d. 1696) worked on the wheel engraving incavo, and were also skilled with the diamond point. In about 1670 Henry perfected a method of etching glass with fluoric acid, the ground being eaten away and dulled, so that the ornament showed smooth and clear in its original surface against a dull ground. Later in the decade the famous Bohemian ruby glass was perfected by Johann Kunkel, director of glasshouses at Potsdam. This intensely strong colour was obtained by using the recently invented purple of cassius or gold chloride. This ruby glass and the emerald glass, also evolved by Kunkel, rarely come within the reach of the collector.

Then, in 1680, a now forgotten glassman in northern Bohemia produced a glass of greater clarity by replacing soda with potash and adding chalk. This crystal glass, quickly copied by other Bohemian glassmen, was thicker, heavier, and more resistant to wear than the former ware, and Henry Schwanhard applied to it the methods used for cutting rock crystal. Although cutting produced a hard glitter, this glass did not possess the power of dispersing light as did the English flint glass. Every kind of picture was cut and engraved, including landscapes, sporting scenes, flowers, animals, coats-of-arms. A stag bounding through the forest was characteristic.

Bohemian glass, engraved, etched, or enamelled by master decorators working to commission in the cities, was for long considered the finest glass in Europe until the 1730s, when tough English flint glass, produced on a vastly increased scale, superseded it for plain domestic ware. The Bohemian glass when cut lacked prismatic sparkle. Dr Pococke recorded in his *Travels*, Vol. II, that in 1736 he visited the glasshouse at Rispen, Bohemia. Their glass, he says, was thick and strong and almost as good as English flint glass. The blanks were sent to Breslau for engraving, and he saw a glass which was cut at a cost of £20. Some of the large drinking goblets were so finely cut as to sell for £100 to £150.

Bohemian crystal glass was manufactured on a commercial scale and widely exported, its low price competing successfully against flint glass. Fine examples by master decorators remained supreme. Then, after the close of the Napoleonic wars in 1815, came a demand for coloured glass, hitherto made only in small quantities. In addition to the celebrated ruby-red, tones of green, blue, and amethyst were perfected. Josef Riedel of Iserberg introduced greenish and yellowish green derived from uranium. Topaz and amber tones were produced from combinations of uranium and antimony.

In the Gratzen district of Bohemia several glasshouses were operated by Count von Buquoy, who specialized in glass coloured sealing-wax red, catalogued as red hydralite. From about 1820 he made jet-black glass in shapes adapted from Wedgwood's black basalts and enriched by painted motifs in gold and silver. At Zechline black glass had been in production from 1804, also in imitation of Wedgwood ware. Friedrich Egerman, specializing in coloured glass, patented in the late 1830s an almost opaque glass marbled in strong colours which he marketed under the name of lithyalin.

Cased or overlay glass began to be made from 1815 in commercial quantities, by a technique nearly two thousand years old. A thick layer of opaque white enamel was laid over a base of clear glass, and over this were laid films of molten glass in two or three colours, rarely as many as four or five, each applied at a progressively lower temperature. The piece was then cut with facets and geometrical patterns in various colours made by grinding away some of the outer films of colour as required. Further enrichment might be added in the form of engraving, deep cutting, or acid etching.

Scent bottle and stopper, Lithyalin glass, factory of F. Egerman, Blottendorf, *c.* 1830

Scent flask, stopper and cover. Blue and colourless opal glass with enamelled and gilt decoration, *c.* 1830–40. Victoria & Albert Museum

Cased glass exported from Bohemia included tall, slim decanters, wine glasses, wine-glass coolers, finger bowls, fruit dishes and dessert plates, toilet bottles, powder boxes, and vases.

The much less expensive and not so attractive flashed glass appeared on a similar range of articles at the same period. In this a thin surface layer of coloured glass sufficient to give full colour was applied direct to the clear glass without the enamel underlay. In many instances the wheel was used to cut through the colour into the clear glass. In this way the film of colour was irradiated by the light striking on the cut facets. The Bohemians manufactured stained table glass from the 1830s. Blown-moulded and, later, pressed glass, could be stained. Coloured designs were stained on clear glass with the aid of stencils.

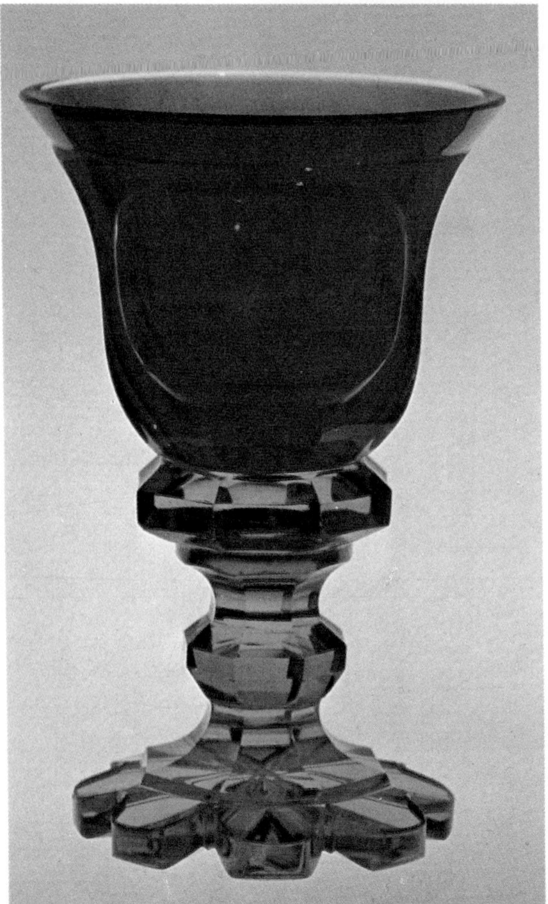

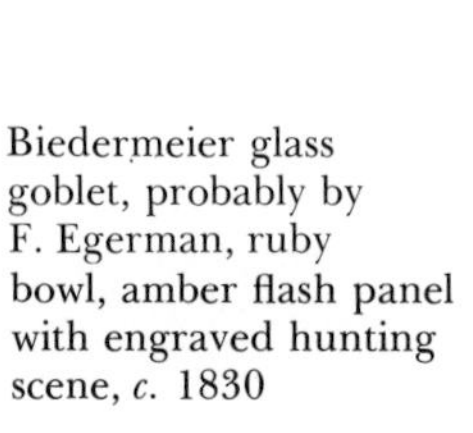

Biedermeier glass goblet, probably by F. Egerman, ruby bowl, amber flash panel with engraved hunting scene, *c.* 1830

Decorative glass manufactured on a commercial scale encouraged the establishment of more glass-houses. In 1847 Bohemia was operating 160 glass-houses, four times as many as Britain, and exported 21,000 tons of glass, much of it in colour. Twenty-six Bohemian glass manufacturers exhibited at the Great Exhibition, 1851, and gold medals were awarded to three. The Jury recorded that the Venetian origin of their decorative glass was conspicuous in Eastern forms, reticulated patterns, taper stems, and wide range of colours. The Bohemian exhibits included many millefiori paperweights.

Right Glass bottle, opaque white glass cased with blue, engraved on the wheel, mark and reign of Ch'ien Lung (1736–95). Victoria & Albert Museum

Chinese

Glass was known in China from the Han dynasty (206 B.C.–A.D. 220) onwards, but it is uncertain whether the Chinese made any before the fifth century A.D., although they were acquainted with Roman and Syrian glass and were using a lead silicate glaze in the making of pottery. They appear to have regarded glass as an inferior type of jade and carved it in the same way. A *pi* and a cicada-shaped tongue amulet in the Victoria and Albert Museum may date from the Han dynasty. The Chinese were very slow to adopt such European techniques as glass-blowing, and Father Ricci refers to glass-blowing in his day (1583–1610) by saying that it fell far short of European workmanship. By the reign of K'ang Hsi (1622–1722) the technique had been largely mastered, but the metal was defective and crisselling a common fault.

There was a Dutch Jesuit in charge of the mission during the reign of K'ang Hsi who may have interested himself in the glass industry, since specimens at the Victoria and Albert Museum have both Dutch and Venetian influence, but the initial technical difficulties seem never entirely to have been overcome, and by the reign of Ch'ien Lung (1736–96) glass was once more being decorated in the manner of jade and other hardstones. Glass of one colour cased with that of another was employed in this way, and some fine examples exist which, but for the material, would be much better classified as hardstone carving. Glass snuff-bottles for the most part imitate those of hardstone. Some rare enamelling on opaque white glass is the Ku Yüeh Hsüan technique discussed under the heading of Pottery and Porcelain. Although painting on glass was the earlier, it seems that opaque white glass was being used for the same purpose as it was so often used in eighteenth-century Europe, as a porcelain substitute, probably at the suggestion of a Western merchant who may have imported some European glass of the kind.

Sheet glass for mirror- and glass-painting was imported from France and England, and attempts to make it in Canton were unsuccessful.

Chinese glass is represented at the Victoria and Albert Museum, and the Ku Yüeh Hsüan technique in the Percival David Foundation, Gordon Square, London.

English

English tableware of fine quality was first made in England by Jean Carré (*q.v.*), who in 1570 established a glasshouse in the Crutched Friars, London, for the purpose of producing glass resembling the Venetian. Imported Venetian glass was highly fashionable, more than fifty families in London being supported by the sale of such glass. After Carré's death in 1572 Giacomo Verzelini (*q.v.*) acquired the glasshouse and commercialized the manufacture of this fragile Anglo-Venetian soda glass, which was clouded by microscopic air bubbles and discoloured in various hues. He was granted a monopoly to make 'Venetian glass'. About a dozen of his goblets, elaborately engraved by the diamond point, are known to remain. Venetian traditions dominated fine glass making for the next hundred years.

Sir Jerome Bowes (*q.v.*) acquired the monopoly from Verzelini in 1592. In 1614 James I extended the monopoly to cover all branches of glass making, and granted it to a group of financiers in return for a payment of £1,000 a year. From 1618 until the King Charles I's death in 1649, when monopolies were ended, the monopoly was under the control of Sir Robert Mansell (*q.v.*).

Little improvement was made in the quality of Anglo-Venetian glass during the reign of Charles II, and within a decade of George Ravenscroft's (*q.v.*) introduction of flint glass in 1674 (see below) its manufacture had virtually ceased. Early flint glass was, naturally, influenced by Venetian design, and the new metal was blown thinly. By 1682 it was found

Posset pot made by George Ravenscroft at Savoy or Henley-on-Thames Glasshouse, *c.* 1677. Pilkington Glass Museum

that by doubling the gather of metal taken from the pot a far more substantial ware was produced without loss of translucency. New forms in tableware now appeared, ponderous and heavy, purely English in character.

Noble goblets, known as tallboys, with sturdy baluster stems supporting thick-walled, heavy-based bowls of the round funnel or conical type, became fashionable. Other ware was made on similar massive lines. In 1695, when twenty-seven flint-glass houses were operating in England, it was recorded that 'the makers of Flint Glasses have long since beaten out all foreigners by making a better glass and underselling them'.

Glass collectors must possess a background knowledge of the improvements made in flint-glass manufacture between then and 1820. Each influenced the quality of fine metal, making it possible for specimens to be grouped chronologically, due consideration also being given to form.

Early flint glass varied considerably in weight and clarity; formulae were not standardized, ingredients were impure, and furnace heat was irregular and could not be raised to a temperature adequate for efficient fusing of the materials. Flint glass made in these circumstances was highly brittle and its fabric unable to withstand without fracture the stresses caused by sudden changes of atmospheric temperature or slight surface shocks, even though it had been

Green glass bottle, sealed with merchant's mark and date, 1698

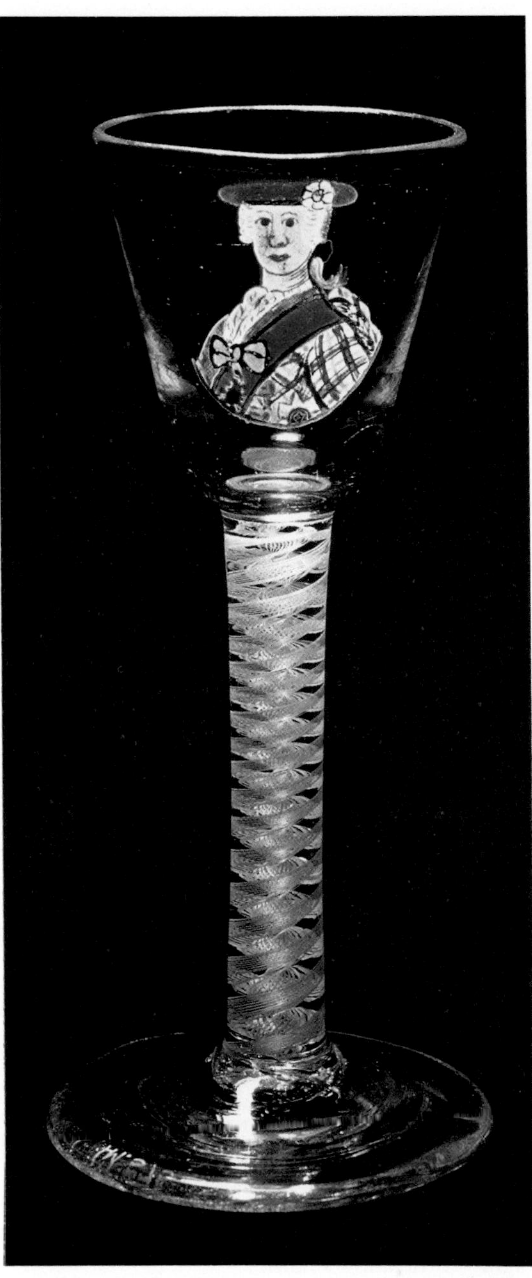

Wine glass, enamelled with a portrait of the Young Pretender, *c.* 1745, possibly by the Beilbys

annealed in an oven above the furnace. Improvements in this toughening process were made in about 1740 and again in about 1780. It was found in about 1745 that double annealing produced a stronger and more brilliant glass.

The introduction of the Perrot furnace in about 1734 provided a vastly increased and more uniform temperature than had previously been deemed possible. The capacity of melting pots until now had been little more than that of a large bucket: now they might contain as much as 1,500 lbs of glass. The quality of the glass was itself improved by these means, and by 1740 glass from such furnaces lacked the dark tinge usually associated with early glass and displayed greater clarity and brilliance. The manipulative capabilities were improved, enabling more pieces to be made per pound weight of molten glass. As the eighteenth century progressed the clarity of fine flint glass was somewhat enhanced.

So prosperous became the glass trade that in 1745, and again in 1777, excise taxes were levied upon glass. Illegal glass makers working old-style furnaces and not operating a tunnel leer (*see* Annealing) perforce continued making dark, heavy flint glass in forms similar to those fashionable early in the century.

Manufacturers of the new metal did not rely upon pure form for ornament, and it rapidly became a field for applied decoration. Toughness resulting from the introduction of the tunnel leer in *c.* 1740 permitted shallow cutting to be commercialized: the improved leer of 1780 made possible such annealing of the glass that deep-relief cutting could then be carried out on a commercial scale.

Until about 1802 flint glass was melted in pots 'set in a furnace and directly heated', adversely affecting clarity. The new furnace evolved at this time reduced fuel consumption by two-thirds, provided such intense heat that the materials fused in half the time, and produced the more crystalline glass associated with early nineteenth-century deep-relief cutting.

Glasshouses were in existence in the city and port of Bristol in the seventeenth century, and it is recorded that about 1651 'Edward Dagney (or Dagnia), an ingenious Italian, had a glasshouse at which the master was John Williams'. By the end of the

Tea canister of opaque white glass with cap of painted enamel on copper, probably of South Staffordshire origin, *c.* 1755–60

century there were ten glassworks in Bristol, and in 1722 the number had increased to fifteen. Most of them made only window glass (known as 'crown glass') or bottles, for both of which there were good markets locally and overseas.

It was not until the middle years of the eighteenth century that more sophisticated articles of good quality began to be made in quantity, and in pattern similar to the productions of other glass-making centres. The trade card of the Phoenix Glasshouse of Messrs Ricketts, Evans and Co. (in the City Art Gallery, Bristol) is engraved with typical pieces that were in fashion at the end of the eighteenth century, and these are no different in appearance from wares that emanated from Stourbridge, Newcastle, or Waterford.

In 1745 the Glass Excise Act laid a duty on glass, which was levied by weight and which seriously hampered the trade. In order to recoup themselves for their lowered turnover from making articles of lighter forms, the manufacturers introduced decoration wherever possible. This took the form of engraving, cutting, gilding, and enamelling, all of which began to flourish shortly after that date. It has been suggested that these same circumstances caused the Bristol makers to produce coloured glass; a material with which their name has been linked inescapably, rightly or wrongly, ever since. In particular, glass of a rich, deep blue colour is termed 'Bristol', and the same name is applied to glass in tints of purple, green, and red.

Although coloured window glass had been made for centuries, particularly for stained-glass windows, it was not until more recent times that colouring was employed in England for domestic articles made of good-quality glass. Certainly, in the case of blue glass there is proof that this was made in Bristol; for pieces are known signed with the name of the maker, Isaac Jacobs, and that of the city in addition. The same manufacturer advertised that he made purple glass.

There is less reason for being certain about the west-country origin of glass in colours other than blue and purple. Articles of green glass had been made in England as early as 1700, and by 1751 it was noted by a traveller that Stourbridge was making glass 'in all the capital colours'. There is no doubt that similar pieces were made by then, or soon afterwards, not only at Bristol but elsewhere.

Of greater artistic importance and more positively indentifiable, is the opaque white glass for which Bristol is also famous. As this is very rare, it is known only to a restricted circle of collectors, students, and dealers, and is generally unrecognized by the devotees of the flamboyant coloured pieces.

White enamel glass was made in several factories on the Continent as well as in England, but that of Bristol was particularly satisfactory and individual. Whereas much eighteenth-century white glass is only just opaque and mostly has a pronounced pink tinge, the Bristol variety is completely opaque, was made very thinly in pleasing shapes, and is of a distinctive creamy colour. It seems probable that it became popular at the time because it was not liable for duty under the Act of 1745. This loophole was, however, closed by the Act of 1777, and it is doubtful if much was made after that date. Unquestionably, it was made also to rival the porcelain then being made, and

Right Pair of blue glass decanters with gilt decoration by James Giles, *c.* 1770

Below Pedestal sweetmeat glasses: *Left to right* quilted ogee bowl, 1740; double ogee bowl flared into eight panels, 1730; double ogee bowl with an everted dentil rim, 1750; flared double ogee bowl with Silesian stem, 1730; saucer bowl with Silesian stem, 1740; double ogee bowl, 1740; double ogee bowl, 1740

Bottom Tea canisters of opaque white glass enamelled in colour, Bristol, second half of 18th century. Victoria & Albert Museum

Gilt and enamelled glasses: *Left to right* gilt cider glass from the atelier of Giles of London, 1775; white enamelled wine glass by Beilby, 1775; gilt wine glass by Giles, 1780; white enamelled wine glass by Beilby, 1775; armorial masonic firing glass with the arms of the Grand Lodge of England by Beilby, 1765; white enamelled wine glass by Beilby, 1770; gilt wine glass by Giles, 1780

most of the painting on both glass and china was in parallel styles.

Among the many artists who must have been employed in decorating Bristol white glass, only the name of Michael Edkins is known. At one time both the glass itself and the name of its only recorded painter were forgotten completely; but a century ago, William Edkins, grandson of the painter and a well-known collector of china, made public the fact that he possessed several pieces of this scarce glass, and that these had been painted by his grandfather.

As further proof of the activities of Michael Edkins, his notebooks have survived and are preserved in the Bristol Museum. These record briefly much of the work he did between 1762 and 1787, and although the majority of it cannot now be identified, there is no doubt that he did paint a quantity of the white glass, as well as gild some of the blue.

A glassworks was opened at Nailsea, a few miles west of Bristol, in 1788 by John Robert Lucas, a Bristol bottle maker. The factory was taken over during 1810 to 1815 by R. L. Chance, and under various proprietors continued in production until 1873. It has been assumed that J. R. Lucas took advantage of the fact that there was a lower duty on common bottle glass than on the normal glass used for domestic wares, and decided to make a wide range of articles from the cheaper material.

None of the glass made during the eighty-five years in which the factory was at work bears a mark to indicate its provenance, and for this reason both mystery and argument surround the glassworks itself and the articles that were made there.

A brownish-green glass speckled with splashes of white is said to have been the earliest and most characteristic type made at Nailsea. It is no more than a standard bottle glass with surface decoration of fragments of opaque white glass scattered on it and melted. An unusual wine bottle inscribed *J. S. J. M. Stirling* 1827 is of the same material as the foregoing. However, in view of the fact that it bears a Scottish place name and similar glassware is known to have been made at that date in many places far nearer to Scotland than Nailsea, it is not improbable that this bottle, and many other pieces, came from a more northerly factory.

Below Nailsea jug of clear green glass with waves of white, late 18th or early 19th century. Victoria & Albert Museum

Left Candy-striped Nailsea bell, 19th century. Victoria & Albert Museum

Other articles ascribed to Nailsea are made with coloured or white stripes in clear glass, and are said to have been made by a group of French workmen introduced by R. L. Chance. It is recorded that a row of cottages named 'French Rank' was built in Nailsea, and it was there that this colony of craftsmen resided.

The variety of articles made at Nailsea was probably wide, but certain of them are supposed to have been invented there and to have been a monopoly of the factory. These include such popular 'bygones' and 'friggers' as inscribed or plain glass rolling pins, witch balls, fancy (and usable) glass tobacco pipes, 'yards of ale', walking sticks (solid or filled with coloured sweets), and, more conventionally, cream jugs and pocket flasks.

It is agreed generally that the output comprised pleasing, but simple, articles for everyday use to be sold at country markets and fairs. It is highly probable that much of the production was exported to America by way of Bristol, and that many of the pieces served as models for the glass manufacturers there. This is especially probable in the case of those in New Jersey, Pennsylvania, and the Middle West, for, as W. B. Honey pointed out: 'Much glass preserved in American collections as the work of these makers is indistinguishable from English country-market glasses.'

Altogether there has been a tendency to attribute both to the Nailsea and the Bristol glassworks a very large amount of glass that was almost certainly made elsewhere. No doubt in time more thorough research will be carried out and result in the clear definition of just what was made at either place, but in the meantime it is only possible to follow what are thought to be established attributions.

Finally, it should be mentioned that almost all the accepted Bristol and Nailsea types have received careful and ample attention from copyists, and collectors should be on their guard against the numerous reproductions on the market. In particular, Czechoslovakian blue glass is frequently labelled *BRISTOL*, and bought as such by the inexperienced; an occurrence that is the more irritating when the price was possibly that usually paid for an English piece.

French

NINETEENTH CENTURY

In the history of French glass vessels the nineteenth century is *le grand siècle*. During the Middle Ages the French created, in stained glass, an art which has never been surpassed: and from the late seventeenth century they were the leading mirror makers in Europe. But for vessels glass had been considered a secondary material, well enough suited for the production of utilitarian types like drinking glasses and bottles, but unworthy of being treated as a serious artistic medium. Apart from the great technical inventor Bernard Perrot, who during the seventeenth century received royal privileges, no glass artist was patronized by the Court as were craftsmen working in so many other materials. Charming as is French glass of the sixteenth and seventeenth centuries, it has the character of folk art compared with the English and German glass of the period and with the tasteful and sophisticated French achievements in other branches of the applied arts.

Vase of transparent cut glass with bronze mounts, Baccarat, 1810–20. Kunstindustrimuseet, Oslo

The reasons for the great expansion during the nineteenth century can be at least partly explained. Early in the century the industry grew rapidly, and as firing methods were changed from wood to coal it was reorganized geographically. Many of the factories moved nearer to the big towns and became part of French urban life. As will be seen, several of the factories in and near Paris are among the pioneers in the new French art of glass. During the early part of the century the glass industry was protected from foreign competition by a strict customs barrier. French art glass between 1830 and 1870 has a definitely experimental character, with technical invention and ingenuity as the main inspiring forces. The long and detailed technical descriptions, which accompany the glass shown at French nineteenth-century exhibitions bear witness to the pride and satisfaction on the part of technicians and directors at difficulties successfully overcome.

The important new feature in nineteenth-century decorative glass is the prevalence of rich and exotic colour. Love of colour is, of course, a general characteristic of the Romantic Age, and can be seen reflected in almost all products of the period, from the canvases of Delacroix to the upholstery of furniture and in ladies' dresses. During the neoclassical period at the end of the eighteenth century the French, like most European glass makers, had felt

Vase of opal glass with a clinging green wreath, Cristalleries de Saint-Louis, *c.* 1850. Musée des Techniques, Conservatoire National des Arts et Métiers

the need for more solid material effects than those found in transparent crystal, which had dominated the artistic scene for more than a hundred years. The first expression of this tendency in France was the making of opal glass, begun some time before 1800. Most coloured glass of the nineteenth century in France is made on a basis of opal glass (*see* Opaline).

The 1830s seem to have been the time when colour experiments on a large scale began in the French *cristalleries* (*q.v.*) and they were first carried out in imitation of Bohemian and Venetian glass. The new style of cased and flushed glass in bright colours, and with cut and engraved decorations, developed in Bohemian factories during the 1820s and 30s, was just catching the fancy of a wide public everywhere. In 1836 *La Société d'Encouragement pour l'Industrie Française* offered prizes for coloured and decorated glass in the Bohemian style, and directors from French factories visited Bohemian and German glassworks to study their methods. At the same time the highly complicated colour techniques employed by the Venetians during the Renaissance and baroque periods were being revived in Murano on an antiquarian basis, and among glass makers north of the Alps it became an ambition to re-create latticino and millefiori glass. In France these techniques were the objects of fruitful experiments during the 1830s and 40s.

The history of French nineteenth-century glass can be divided into three main periods: (1) During the first two decades the old eighteenth-century tradition stands more or less unchallenged, with transparent crystal with cut or engraved decoration as the main luxury product. Glass in this genre continued to be made right through the century, and the factory of Baccarat (*q.v.*) was the chief producer of glass in this style. (2) The period from 1830 to 1870 is the exciting time of experiment and discovery in the field of coloured glass, carried on at Baccarat and St Louis, and a group of smaller factories in and near Paris, with Georges Bontemps (*q.v.*) as the central

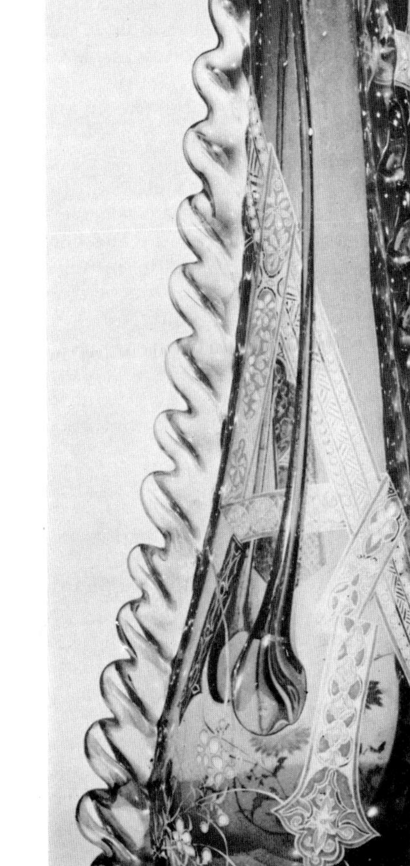

Vase of red glass with enamelled and trailed decoration by A. Jean, Paris, *c.* 1880. Musée des Techniques, Conservatoire National des Arts et Métiers

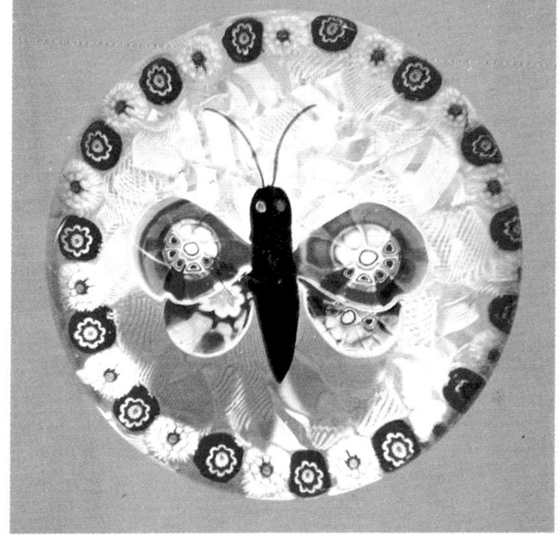

Left Millefiori paperweight, Baccarat, with butterfly hovering over white lace edged with circle of canes

figure. A main product of this time was the paperweight with inlaid colour patterns. Originating in Venice, but perfected at the St Louis glassworks, it very soon found many imitators, both in that country and elsewhere. But it is conceded generally that few can vie with the French productions, whether from St Louis or from its contemporaries at Baccarat and Clichy. Not only in the past have these attractive objects suffered the close attention of copyists, but today they are equally carefully imitated. Much of the fine coloured glass of the mid-century received its final shape through moulding. (3) During the latter part of the century the technical achievements in the use of colour are subordinated to the new stylistic development of the time, inspired in its ideas by the Arts and Crafts Movement in Britain and in its forms by the art of Japan. It culminates in the creation of the *Art Nouveau* about 1890, and the art glass of Émile Gallé (*q.v.*) was a characteristic and original expression of the style.

The history of French nineteenth-century glass has not yet been fully investigated. Consequently there are still considerable gaps in our knowledge of it.

Left Perfume bottle and stopper, 1889, by Émile Gallé, Nancy. Pilkington Glass Museum

Irish

Ireland's earliest flint-glass house was established in Dublin during the early 1960s by Captain Philip Roche. This was known as the Round Glass House, and under various proprietorships continued operating until 1755. Productions by the mid-century, according to an advertisement in *Faulkner's Dublin Journal* quoted by Westropp, included 'all sorts of the newest fashioned drinking glasses, water bottles, claret and burgundy bottles, decanters, jugs, water glasses with and without feet and saucers, plain, ribbed, and diamond moulded jelly glasses of all sorts and sizes, sillybub glasses, comfit and sweetmeat glasses for desserts, salvers, glass plates for china dishes, toort covers, pine and orange glasses, hall lanthorns for one to four candles, glass branches, cut and plain barrel lanthorns, glove lamps, etc, all in the most elegant and newest fashioned mounting now used in London. . . . All sorts of cut and flowered glasses may be had of any kind to any pattern, viz.: wine glasses with a vine border, toasts, or any flourish whatsoever; beer ditto with the same, salts with and without feet, sweetmeat glasses and stands, cruits for silver and other frames all in squares and diamond cut, tea cannisters, jars and beakers of mock china, mustard pots, crests and coats of arms, sweetmeat

Above Chandelier of clear glass with cut decoration, Waterford, late 18th century. Victoria & Albert Museum

Above Boat-shaped bowl, blown and cut with large diamonds, a trefoil scalloped rim, and pressed pillar-ribbed foot, *c.* 1785. Corning Museum of Glass

Wine urn with shallow-cut flutes and pewter spigot, *c.* 1785. Corning Museum of Glass

bowls and covers.' It is doubtful if any English glasshouse could exceed the scope of productions shown on this list.

The Round House was no doubt a highly flourishing business until the export of glass from Ireland was prohibited under the Excise Act of 1745, which at the same time levied a duty of one penny a pound on English flint glass. This prohibition was directly responsible for the glasshouse closing down ten years later, and from then until 1764 no fine flint glass appears to have been made in Ireland. Then an already existing bottle house at Marlborough Green, Dublin, was enlarged to produce flint glass. By 1770 this glasshouse was under the control of Richard Williams & Company, who then announced in the *Limerick Chronicle* that their productions included 'all the newest fashioned enamelled, flowered, cut and plain wine, beer and cyder glasses, common wines and drams, rummers, decanters, water-glasses and plates, epergnes and epergne saucers, cruets, casters, cans, jugs, salvers, jellies, sweetmeat glasses, salts, salt linings' in flint glass. This firm must have operated on a large scale, for in addition to flint glass and bottles they made and ground looking-glass plates. There is no doubt that Williams made virtually all the flint glass sold in Ireland during the 1770s.

When in 1780 import restrictions were removed, several well-equipped glasshouses were established in Ireland, notably at Waterford, Belfast, Dublin, and Cork. Orders poured into Ireland from the Continent and America, for prices, and quality, were much lower than English flint glass. In 1785 Lord Sheffield observes that 'nine glass houses have suddenly arisen in Ireland, and the best drinking glasses are sold at three to four shillings a dozen less than the English'.

Although English executives and leading glass workers and decorators were employed and much of the material obtained from England, it was long before the industry became self-supporting, although still free from paying excise duty. The Dublin Society subsidized several firms: the Williams glasshouse, for instance, received £28,145 from this source between 1784 and 1794.

Irish glass of the 1780s and 1790s for the most part displayed a slightly dusky tint. From about 1800 more efficient furnaces were installed by the larger glasshouses and a clearer metal produced. This glass proved ideal for the cutting in deep relief, which now became overwhelmingly popular. Every potful of metal produced two qualities – tale and fine glass. During this period, too, some glass was issued with a faintly blue tint.

The nineteenth century also introduced a new era in blown-moulded glass, new techniques producing a wholly new range of designs, shapes, and decorations at prices lower than formerly. Moulded glass was produced in a fraction of the time possible with handwork. Blown-moulded table glass was made in shapes and designs approximating to those of free-blown and handcut glass. To distinguish it from English pressed work the following three differences should be noted:

(*a*) Mould marks are no more than slightly convex swellings on the surface of the glass in no way resembling the hair lines or threads on pressed glass, which are so sharply defined that they appear to have been applied. The number of mould marks indicates the number of pieces forming the mould. From 1835 blown-moulded glass was finished by fire polishing.

(*b*) The concave–convex relation of inner and outer surfaces of blown-moulded glass increased its refractive properties, thus accounting for its typical brilliance. The inflation of the gather of molten glass within a full-sized mould not only caused the air within the gather to force the glass into the sunk pattern, producing relief ornament on the outer surface, but also made corresponding hollows on the inner surface. A smooth inner surface indicates that the glass has been either freeblown or pressed; a slightly rippled surface proves the glass to have been moulded for pattern only and then expanded.

(*c*) The impression received on the surface of blown-moulded glass differs from that of pressed glass. Decoration motifs of the former appear to merge into each other instead of displaying the sharp, almost photographic definition of pressed glass.

The decline in the Irish flint-glass trade was brought about first by the imposition of an excise duty from 1825, such as had existed in England from 1745, and was hastened from the early 1830s by the introduction in England of glass-pressing machines capable of producing handled hollow ware at a single operation. Such a machine was first installed by W. Richardson, of Wordsley, who sold pressed glass as intagliated tableware. Other firms quickly followed, but not a single machine is known to have been acquired by an Irish glasshouse. Because of vastly lowered prices, the Irish handblown trade languished and died soon after removal of the excise duty in 1845.

Even the celebrated Waterford (*q.v.*) firm failed to survive English competition at the Great Exhibition, 1851, and closed immediately afterwards. The only Irish-made exhibit in the glass section at the Dublin Industrial Exhibition, 1853, was some 'richly cut flint glass manufactured by the Dublin Flint Glass Works'. At a further exhibition in 1865, Irish flint glass was not represented.

No Irish glass unless marked or pedigreed, or closely resembling a marked example in metal and in design, can be definitely attributed to any one glasshouse. Most designs were copied from the cut-glass men of London and Glasgow.

Scandinavian

The oldest existing glass of Scandinavian make dates from the late seventeenth century and is of Swedish origin. Glass has been made in Sweden ever since. Norway's production of glass began in 1741, and during the latter part of the eighteenth century, when Denmark and Norway were united under one crown, Denmark received all its glassware from Norway. Denmark's own glass production did not start until 1810 with the foundation of Holmegaards Glasvaerk, and it is only in comparatively recent times that Danish glass products have become of interest artistically. The same can be said for Finnish glass. The story of Scandinavian glass in the eighteenth century is really the story of Swedish and Norwegian glass.

The earliest preserved Swedish glass was made at Kungsholm Glasbruk (*q.v.*) in Stockholm. The early Kungsholm glass has a distinct Venetian flavour. The metal is thin and frequently in a bad state of glass disease, and the shapes are decorated in elaborate furnace-work. Picturesque are the goblets where the stems are formed into royal initials. Royal crowns are frequently used as handles to the covers of goblets, the ornament being a compliment to royalty and an allusion to the factory's name at the same time.

In the early part of the eighteenth century the Kungsholm goblets began to take their cue from Bohemia. The metal becomes more solid, the stem shorter in relation to the bowl, the general effect is solid and sturdy. Venetian reminiscences are the foot that is folded over from below and the 'pressed tomato' member of the stem, which remains a characteristic feature on Kungsholm goblets until about 1750. Otherwise the elaborate furnacework has been discarded and what decoration there is has been carried out on the wheel. Engraving was introduced into Sweden by one Kristoffer Elstermann (*q.v.*) who first appears at Kungsholm in 1698. The engraved patterns are mostly coats-of-arms in a dignified style; a

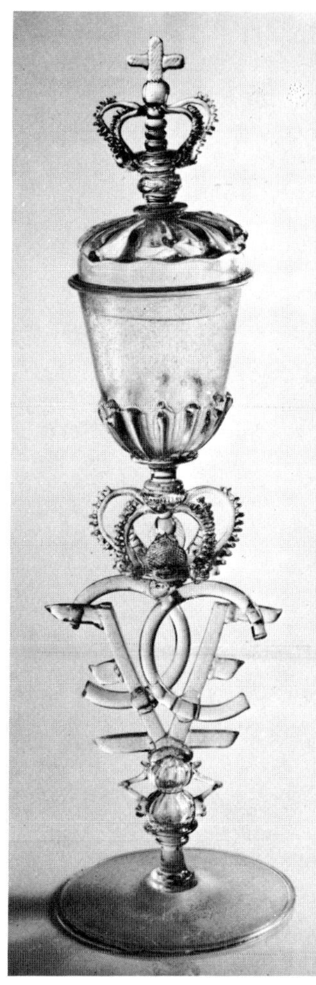

Above Goblet from Kungsholm Glasbruk, the stem formed into royal initials, early 17th century. Nationalmuseum, Stockholm

Goblet with folded foot, Kungsholm Glasbruk, 18th century. Nationalmuseum, Stockholm

sun and a radiant Northern Star being frequent accompaniments to the royal arms and the monogram of Charles XII. About the middle of the century cutting was occasionally used for stems.

The handsome, but somewhat impersonal baroque style, which was established at Kungsholm early in the eighteenth century, persisted in the products of the factory to the end of its working period, and the engraving continued more or less on the lines laid down by Elstermann, with only the smallest allowances for changes in style and fashion. Rococo and classicism seem both to have bypassed Kungsholm completely. The few more modest products that can be identified as of Kungsholm origin – beakers, decanters, wine glasses – show the same conservatism in form and decoration.

Decanter from Skånska Glasbruket, 1761. Nordiska Museet, Stockholm

During the creative period at Kungsholm (*c.* 1700) some types were made which did not survive beyond their period. Most remarkable among them are: a large Römer with a cover and prunts on the stem; a beaker on three feet with cover (clearly copied after a silver model); a tall, slim beaker with a high domed cover; a decanter with conical body, a narrow neck; a widely turned-out collar, and no stopper. They are all found with good-quality engraved decoration in the Elstermann style.

Kungsholm was always an aristocratic establishment, situated in the capital and patronized by the King. Sweden's other seventeenth-century glass foundation had a different social background, a fact which is clearly reflected in the products. Skånska Glasbruket (*q.v.*) began by making purely utilitarian glass, but in 1715 production of decorative glass was taken up.

Occasionally efforts were made, not always successfully, to copy Kungsholm models, but the majority of the products were of a less ambitious kind: tumblers, beakers, decanters, and jugs for the local market, some of them decorated with engraving. Skånska Glasbruket's engravers sometimes used the same motifs as their colleagues at Kungsholm, but their cut was broad and shallow, the motifs were simplified and the general effect unsophisticated. No great development can be distinguished in the engraving during the forty-seven years it was practised at the factory.

In spite of being simple and unsophisticated, glass from Skånska Glasbruket has its very distinct character, and in many ways it has a stronger appeal to the modern collector than the products from Kungsholm. The metal is fairly thick and clear and shiny, and the forms have a pleasant robustness which is very charming, while the engraving, in spite of the heraldic motifs of crowned cartouches and branches of palm and laurel, has almost the character of folk art. The royal monogram is often used as patriotic ornamentation on glass for ordinary customers.

The third of Sweden's old glass factories is Kosta (*q.v.*). The products of the eighteenth and nineteenth centuries were mostly unpretentious things made for daily use by the people of the districts. Of special interest are the charming little chandeliers, rustic versions of Continental types, still to be seen in some Småland churches. Over the years workers from Kosta broke away from the mother factory and founded works of their own in the neighbourhood. Most of these smaller factories were short-lived, and none of them produced anything but the simplest utilitarian glass. But this intensive glass production in Småland, which has gone on from the middle of the eighteenth century until today, has established a solid tradition of craftsmanship and a general *milieu*, which in due course has become the basis for the greater achievements of modern times. The most famous producers of modern Swedish art glass, Orrefors and Strômbergshyttan, are both situated a few miles from Kosta, which is itself one of the finest manufactories of modern glass. Småland is, in fact, one of the famous glass districts of Europe like Lorraine, Bohemia, and Venice. In the 'capital' of Småland, the city of Växjö, is the only museum in northern Europe devoted entirely to glass.

The Gothenburg factory (1769–1803) is referred to in connection with the production at Gjövik in Norway.

The Victoria and Albert Museum possesses a few pieces of Kungsholm glass, but otherwise old Swedish glass is rarely seen in England.

The Norwegian glass industry was founded by royal command and under the personal patronage of King Christian VI of Denmark and Norway and his Court in Copenhagen. Work began in 1741 at Nöstetangen (*q.v.*) near Drammen. Experiments were made in all branches of glass making, with window glass, bottles, table glass, and decorative pieces. The glass blowers came from Thuringia, and the earliest glasses that can be identified as of Nöstetangen origin are goblets in a simplified, German style, large in size, with a royal crown as handle to the cover, but otherwise without decoration. Some of them were engraved in Copenhagen to commemorate royal occasions. The pair of coronation goblets made for King Frederik V and his much-beloved English wife, Queen Louise, can still be seen in the Rosenborg Collection in Copenhagen. A few goblets made for the rich bourgeoisie in Norway have also survived from these early days. Some of them have been engraved by itinerant German glass sellers. The production of table glass was still on a small scale, and the few existing pieces show little distinctive character.

In 1753 the Norwegian glass industry was reorganized. The deciding personalities in the undertaking were Count Adam Gottlob Moltke, Frederik V's powerful minister, and Caspar Herman von Storm, a Norwegian officer and landowner and the richest man in Christiania.

The purpose of the reorganization was to make the Norwegian glass industry capable of satisfying the need for glass of all kinds in Denmark and Norway. To this end new factories were built, while the production of tableware and ornamental glass was concentrated at Nöstetangen. The factory was enlarged and modernized, some first-class German glass blowers were engaged; and, most important of all, contact was sought with the English glass-making industry. By honest and dishonest means Storm managed to gather information about, and get samples of, the much admired English lead crystal and even to lure a Newcastle crystal blower to Nöstetangen. In August 1755 James Keith (*q.v.*) arrived at the factory, accompanied by an assistant, William Brown, and a few days later Storm reported in a letter: 'I have seen the English glassmakers at work. In London itself you would not find them more able.'

Another innovation at Nöstetangen was the establishment of a cutters' and engravers' workshop. Head engraver and general artistic manager of the factory was Heinrich Gottlieb Köhler (*q.v.*). During his Copenhagen years Köhler had engraved many Norwegian goblets, and his signature can be seen, or his style recognized, on many of the great royal goblets now at Rosenberg. Köhler was not only a first-class practitioner of the art of engraving but also an original and imaginative designer, both of patterns for engraving and of glass shapes. It is probably to a large extent due to him that the German and English styles in glass making, which converged at Nöstetangen about 1755, were harmoniously merged into a unified style of distinct individual character.

In 1760 the Norwegian glass factories were staffed and fitted out for a large-scale production on modern lines and a royal monopoly for Denmark and Norway was granted. Not until 1803 was it again permitted to import foreign glass into the two countries.

The decade 1760–70 is Nöstetangen's best period, and it is perhaps the most interesting decade in the history of old Scandinavian glass altogether. During this period two different qualities of glass were made: a comparatively cheap soda-lime composition of German type, and a more expensive crystal, which was an adaptation of English lead glass. The soda-lime glass from Nöstetangen is sometimes very rough, light in weight, full of bubbles and imperfections, and with a very distinct pinkish-purple tone. The lead-glass products are usually of a very fine quality, transparent, heavy in weight, and with a deep, ringing tone. All the factory's table-glass models were copied after German and English types. The cheaper glasses for everyday use were mostly based on German models, while the more expensive glasses and decanters were derived from the English types. Baluster stems of Newcastle type and air-twist stems were particularly popular. For the larger and more elaborate articles, such as chandeliers, *épergnes*, goblets and the like, the glass blowers at Nöstetangen, developed a style of their own. Its main elements were borrowed from late seventeenth- and early eighteenth-century English glass and can be traced farther back to Venice. These elements are mostly furnace-made surface decorations like trailed threads and chains of glass, prunts, 'nipt diamond waies', flammiform fringes, or moulded surface effects, a style that was fashionable in London about the turn of the century; in 1775 it must still have been part of a Newcastle glass blower's skill. Other elements of the Nöstetangen style were inlaid decoration such as air twists and 'tears'. Complicated baluster stems of Newcastle type were also much used. These decorations were adapted no non-English forms which were popular among Danes and Norwegians from the early part of the eighteenth century. Most famous among them is the goblet, and the royal crown on the handle of the cover, which had been used at Nöstetangen (*q.v.*) before 1753, was integrated into the Nöstetangen style.

The new decoration became popular among Nöstetangen's customers, especially the rich merchants in Christiania and the surrounding country, who traded with England and were familiar with English taste and fashions. The Court in Copenhagen was more conservative, and few of the goblets made for royalty after 1753 are in developed Nöstetangen style. After the death of Frederik V in 1766 and the subsequent fall of Count Moltke, royal patronage seems to have been withdrawn from Nöstetangen. The merchants of Bergen also preferred their glass to be in the well-known German style, and for them cut-glass goblets were made at Nöstetangen. These are, however, without originality and of poor quality. Cutting was never practised with much skill at Nöstetangen.

Most famous among the products from Nöstetangen is the set of three chandeliers, made for the church in the town of Kongsberg, where they can still be admired *in situ*. They were made to designs by Köhler between 1759 and 1766. They are in clear glass, with some ornaments in purple and a few in blue. In general style they combine features from Venetian and German chandeliers, but each of the hundreds of standing or hanging ornaments is in rich Nöstetangen style. They must certainly have been made in close collaboration between Köhler and James Keith. Punch bowls, posset pots, candlesticks, tobacco jars, *épergnes*, salt cellars, sugar casters, etc., were also made in Nöstetangen style. But the most typical Nöstetangen product is the goblet with a royal crown on the cover and a stem with many members and fine inlaid or moulded decorations. Many of them are finely engraved by Köhler.

As an engraver Köhler mastered a dignified allegorical style in the Le Brun tradition, used mainly for royal orders, and a more realistic style based on close observation which he created for his Norwegian customers. Engravings from his hand in this manner give amusing and informative pictures of contemporary life. Most important among his assistants was Villas Vinter (*q.v.*). Both engravers have left a number of signed works which enable us to distinguish Köhler's quick and fluid hand from Vinter's somewhat stiff, linear manner.

In 1777 Nöstetangen was shut down and the crystal production transferred to Hurdals Verk (*q.v.*). Most of the glass blowers from Nöstetangen went on to Hurdals Verk, among them James Keith.

While a gay and gracious rococo had been the dominant style at Nöstetangen, a gentle classicism is typical of the products from Hurdals Verk (*q.v.*). Enamel twist stems are used increasingly for wine glasses, goblets, and candlesticks, and the shapes become more austere. The technical quality of the

Ewer, Nostetangen, 1760–70. Kunstindustrimuseet, Oslo

glass is higher than in Nöstetangen products; lead glass is used more extensively. In the cool stylishness of the products from Hurdals Verk one misses the gay exuberance in the glass from Nöstetangen.

As for engraving. Villas Vinter embraces the classical style for his larger compositions from about 1780, but in less ambitious things rococo remains predominant until after 1800. Köhler, the founder of the tradition, was himself exclusively a rococo artist, and even the Nöstetangen style in glass blowing, with all its baroque elements, has a rococo character, undoubtedly due to Köhler's influence.

A particular kind of cartouche is frequently to be seen on Norwegian drinking glasses from about 1770 onwards, used as a frame for initials, occasionally with gilt lines. It can be very rich or very simple, and its details can vary quite a lot – a wreath of flowers, some fine trelliswork, an open crown,[1] or a shell can be used to fill in on top or at the sides. But its main line and rhythm remained unchanged for more than a generation. Most of these 'Norwegian cartouches' were made in the workshop of Johan Albrecht Becker (*q.v.*).

A novelty at Hurdals Verk was the wide use made of coloured glass. Cobalt blue and manganese purple had been used at Nöstetangen, but, from about 1780 onwards especially, blue grass was used at Hurdals Verk to an extent unknown at Nöstetangen. The colours were used as artistic effects. The dark deep tones which camouflaged the transparency of the metal suited the austere classical shapes of Hurdals glass very well. The most important type to be made in this 'blue style' is the potpourri urn (*q.v.*). It was first made about 1780. The earliest examples are made in fairly light blue glass and in pleasant rococo shapes. Later the colour becomes deeper and the shape more classical, and about 1800 the urn has a perfect classical shape and is a deep purple blue. Candlesticks, sugar casters, salt cellars, and other objects were also made in blue style at Hurdals Verk. Simple engraved ornaments were occasionally added and embellished with gilding.

In 1809 Hurdals Verk closed down, and the production of table glass and ornamental pieces was transferred to Gjövik Verk (*q.v.*). The later production at Hurdals Verk and the early products of Gjövik Verk are practically identical with those made in Sweden at the same time. Both Gjövik and Kosta made simple little wine glasses, identical in shape and decorated with the same simple borders of stylized leaves, checkerboard patterns, etc. Glass in blue style from Gjövik can hardly be distinguished from that made at Gothenburg about the turn of the century (1796–1803). But since Gjövik Verk worked over a longer period, a greater variety of products can be traced to the Norwegian factory. The origins of the blue style, common to both Norway and Sweden, must be sought on the Continent.

Particularly attractive is the opaque glass in a light-blue shade with white borders, which seems to have been made at Gjövik during the first ten years. The classical style prevailed all through the factory's history, but after about 1830 the genuine classical feeling is lost, and the later Gjövik products are less harmonious and balanced in shape than the earlier ones.

[1] Crowns in Norwegian engraving have not necessarily a noble or royal significance. The royal initials are also used, not only on glass engraved for the royal family but on products for patriotic citizens as well.

Old Norwegian glass does occasionally appear in Great Britain. The Victorian and Albert Museum possesses two interesting eighteenth-century goblets, one in typical Nöstetangen style, the other lavishly engraved with masonic emblems by Köhler. The Bristol Museum and Art Gallery has a potpourri urn and wine glasses, and decanters often appear in the antique shops.

The technical modernization of the Swedish glass factories began early in the nineteenth century, and in Norway about 1850. With the increasing industrialization of methods and trade, national characteristics were lost and it was not until the period of World War I that Swedish glass, and to some extent Norwegian glass, became of artistic interest again.

Far right Ewer, the glass figured in imitation of agate (chalcedony), *c.* 1500. Victoria & Albert Museum

Left Engraved glasses by H. G. Kohler, 1771. Kunstindustrimuseet, Oslo

Goblets with covers, that on the right with an enamel twist stem, Hurdals Verk, *c.* 1780. Kunstindustrimuseet, Oslo

Venetian

The origins of the Venetian glass industry are obscure. In late classical times glass was probably made at Aquilea (midway between Venice and Trieste), where so many exquisite specimens of Roman glass have been dug up. Tradition has it that some glass workers from this town were among the refugees who fled before the Gothic invaders of the fifth and sixth centuries to found the city of Venice on the barren marshy islands of the lagoons. But even if they were, they could hardly have practised their craft in the isolation of the new community. The first Venetian glass maker to figure in documentary records is one Domenico, who, in 982, was described as a *fiolario*: a maker of phials. Further members of this trade are mentioned in the next two centuries, and by 1255 there were enough glass craftsmen in Venice to form a guild. Indeed, the city authorities became concerned at the risk of fire occasioned by numerous furnaces, and in 1291 gave orders that the glass factories should be transferred to the island of Murano, where they have remained ever since. Early in sixteenth century, the then Sir Richard Guildford passed through Venice on his way to the Holy Land, he made a visit to Murano to inspect the factories, which were already numbered among the tourists 'sights' of the lagoon.

In the fourteenth century the Murano glass factories are known to have been producing enamelled glass, blown glass, and even spectacle lenses. But very few objects dating from this period have survived. Among fifteenth-century works one of the most notable is a marriage cup of enamelled blue glass, which has by tradition been associated with a family of glass craftsmen named Barovier mentioned by Filarete in his treatise *De Architetura* (written between 1451 and 1464). Other cups and beakers of the same type are in the Museums of Bologna, Florence, Trento, Berlin, Cologne, the British Museum, and the Victoria and Albert Museum. All are of dark-coloured glass delicately painted with mythological figures, portrait heads, coats-of-arms, or abstract designs of dots and semicircles, in bright enamel. The forms are not unlike those of contemporary silver vessels. At this time the Murano factories seem to have begun the production of looking glasses which soon replaced the polished metal mirrors in use since classical times. They also began to imitate in glass the precious and semi-precious hard stones of which vessels were occasionally wrought by court jewellers throughout Europe in the renaissance period. Most successful of these was the imitation of chalcedony, and a fine ewer in this glass, called *vetro di calcedonia*, is in the Museo Nazionale, Florence.

The golden age of Venetian glass, both commercially and artistically, began in the early sixteenth century, when the art of making clear 'crystal' glass was discovered. The factories quickly exploited this new process, and soon Venice was exporting to all parts of Europe, cups, bowls, and dishes of a transparency which was then to be rivalled only by rock crystal. An inventory of 1547 reveals that among the six hundred or more objects in Henry VIII's 'Glasse Housse' at Westminster there were numerous goblets, jugs, and ornamental cups of Venetian origin. The fashion for this beautiful substance quickly spread, and in 1577 William Harrison remarked, in his *Description of England*: 'It is a world to see in these our days, wherein gold and silver most aboundeth, how that our gentility, as loathing those metals (because of the plenty) do now generally choose rather the Venice glasses, both for our wine and beer, than any of those metals or stone wherein before time we have been accustomed to drink; . . . and such is the estimation of this stuff that many become rich only with their new trade unto Murana (a town near Venice situate on the Adriatic Sea) from whence the very best are daily to be had . . . And as this is seen in the gentility, so in the wealthy communality the like desire of glass is not neglected, whereby the gain gotten by their purchase is yet much more increased to the benefit of the merchant. The poorest also will have glass if they may; but, sith the Venetian is somewhat too dear for them, they content themselves with such as are made at home of fern and burned stone . . .' Not all the glass made in England at this time was the coarse material Harrison describes, however, for one Jacob Verzelini, a Venetian, had begun to manufacture clear glass of the Murano type in London in the 1570s. The secret of crystal or 'white' glass had leaked out and Venice had already lost her monopoly.

The vessels of crystal glass made in Venice in the sixteenth century were of elegant form, perfectly adapted to the light weight of their substance and much less dependent on silver patterns than hitherto. Most of the clear glass – valued on account of its clarity – seems to have been left undecorated, but some examples were engraved either by wheel or with a diamond point. The Venetian factories did not, however, give up the production of coloured opaque glass. They continued to produce glass made in imitation of hard stones and indeed developed a new milky-white glass called *lattimo*, which provided an excellent background for enamel decorations. This white glass seems to have been valued abroad, and there is a mug of it, mounted in silver gilt in London in 1548, in the British Museum. They also began the production of the *reticello*, *vetro di trina*, or filigree glass, decorated with a pattern of criss-crossing white threads for which Murano has ever since been famous.

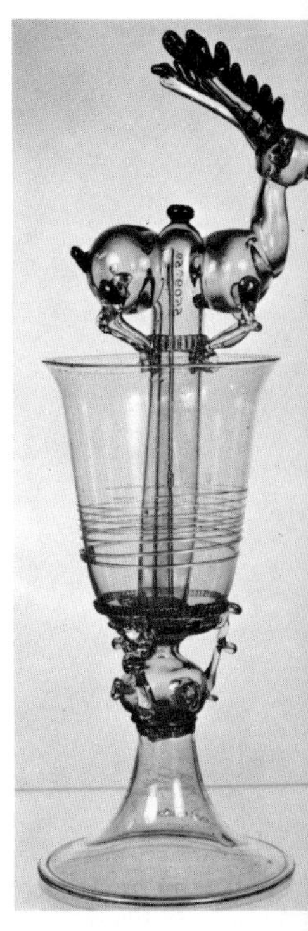

Above left Nef, or boat-shaped ewer attributed to Armenia Vivarini. Opaque glass with turquoise medallions along the side

Above Goblet with syphon apparatus in the form of a stag, 16th or 17th century. Victoria & Albert Museum

Left Murano glass chandelier with coloured glass flowers, 17th century

Far left Stand in latticinio glass, early 17th century

The decorations applied to Venetian glass in the sixteenth century reflect the current development from pure Renaissance to Mannerist ornament. Many of them are, indeed, close in style to those found on contemporary maiolica. The forms remained comparatively simple until the end of the century, when a greater sense of fantasy was employed in devising stems for goblets – in the form of dragons, serpents, or sea horses. In the seventeenth century objects still more fantastic were produced: lamps in the form of horses, jugs fashioned like ships with reticulated glass rigging, bottles with preposterously attenuated necks; while the greatest ingenuity was applied to varying the stems of cups and reli-

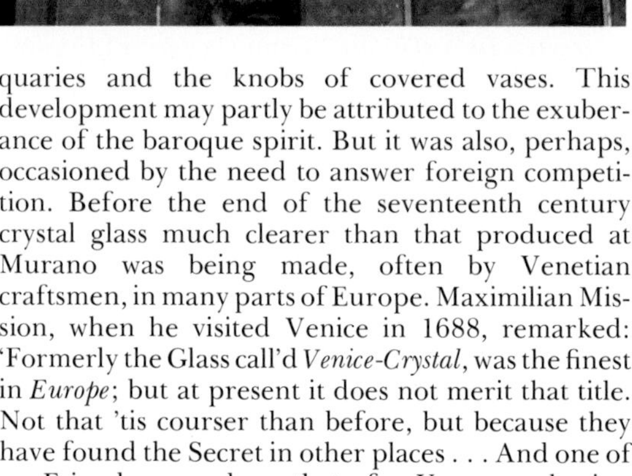

quaries and the knobs of covered vases. This development may partly be attributed to the exuberance of the baroque spirit. But it was also, perhaps, occasioned by the need to answer foreign competition. Before the end of the seventeenth century crystal glass much clearer than that produced at Murano was being made, often by Venetian craftsmen, in many parts of Europe. Maximilian Mission, when he visited Venice in 1688, remarked: 'Formerly the Glass call'd *Venice-Crystal*, was the finest in *Europe*; but at present it does not merit that title. Not that 'tis courser than before, but because they have found the Secret in other places . . . And one of my Friends assured me, that a few Years ago, having carry'd a Vial of the finest crystal of *Murano* to *London*, the workmen were so far from looking upon it as extraordinary or inimitible, that they said they cou'd and sometimes did, make finer Work. The Skill they have acquired in other Countries, and the Manufactures they have erected, have almost ruin'd the Trade of *Murano*.' If the Venetians could not make glass as clear as that produced in England, France, and Bohemia, they could, and often did, produce objects of a form far more exuberant and fantastic.

Venetian glass of the eighteenth century is principally distinguished for the bravura of its design and for sparkling gaiety of its painted decorations which reflect the styles of the great masters of the *settecento*. J. G. de Keysler, who visited Venice in the late 1730s, remarked: 'The *Venetian* glass is very pure and ductile when it is fusion; on which account it is more easily melted, and answers much better than any others for works of fantasy.' He commented with admiration on the mirrors, though, he said, those 'of any considerable size are extremely dear, when other looking glasses at present are so cheap', mainly because they were blown and not, like those made in France, cast and ground. The writer also mentions the necklaces and rosaries made of glass beads, sometimes of the form and colour of pearls (*margaritini*). Prominent among the other objects made of glass in Venice at this time are the great chandeliers, often ornamented with opaque glass flowers, bunches of grapes, and other fruit which still decorate many a Venetian salon, where they form an excellent accompaniment to the painted ceilings, from which they hang, and the exuberant rococo furniture.

Having produced so many bizarre splendours in the eighteenth century, Venetian craftsmen seem to have been unable, or unwilling, to keep pace with the change in taste from rococo to neoclassicism. Partly as a result of this, partly on account of the dwindling status of the once Serene Republic (now an Austrian possession), the glass factories of Murano fell on hard times in the early nineteenth century. In about 1820 Lady Morgan commented that the Venetian glass pearl was then 'almost all that remains of that superb *arte vitraria* which first rendered Europe independent of the sands of Tyre, and established at Venice a manufacture which, in spite of Nature had supplied the world with one of its most brilliant luxuries. The Venetian shops no longer sparkle with girandoles of seeming diamonds, with flowers more brilliant and frail than the blossoms of a Spring shower, which they imitated; and with mirrors, which first replaced the dimness of metal with the reflecting lustre of crystal.' A few years later Lady Blessington was rowed out of Murano and mused on the decadence of the factories. 'It is melancholy to see an art, once arrived at perfection, retrograde,' she wrote, 'as the trifling, though brilliant ornaments shown to us, are the only portion of the trade which now flourishes.' But in addition to the beads, which seem to have been their most numerous productions at this period, the factories still appear to have been making ornaments, vases, and goblets of a gay rococo design.

The revival of the Murano glass factories dates from the middle of the nineteenth century, and was largely due to the owner of a glassworks, Pietro Bigaglia. In his factory two craftsmen, Liberale and Angelo Angaro, applied the lessons learned from the study of old glass, which they repaired for Venetian dealers, to the design of new objects. More factories were founded, and soon Murano was once again among the leading centres of glass production in Europe. Many of the objects produced were imitations or adaptations of earlier wares, for which there is a steady market even today. Others, such as the gigantic chandeliers six or seven feet in height, were in a more markedly nineteenth-century style. These nineteenth-century wares are by no means to be despised; for although they are unlikely to win the wholehearted commendation of collectors of old glass, the vases and cups and bowls have many of the merits of seventeenth- and eighteenth-century Venetian products – so much so, indeed, that numerous connoisseurs have been deceived by them. In the present century several factories have begun to produce wares which unite the best qualities of old Venetian glass – its lightness of weight, its gay brilliance of colour, and fantasy of form – with designs which satisfy the most exacting pundits of industrial art. But these objects fall outside the present chapter.

Vase of Schmelzglass, made in imitation of Russian malachite, mounted in ormolu, by Salviati of Venice. Exhibited in 1862. Victoria & Albert Museum

Air-twist stems: *Left to right* ale glass engraved with hops and barley, 1760; cordial glass with two thick mercurial air-twist corkscrews, 1750; wine glass with double knopped air-twist stem, 1750; ale glass engraved with hops and barley and with air-twist stem, 1750; ale glass, 1750; ale glass engraved with hops and barley set on a knopped multi-ply air-twist stem, 1750

Glossary

Agata. Mottled finish used chiefly on Amberina glass, in which the article is coated with a metallic stain or mineral colour, then spattered with a quickly evaporating liquid such as alcohol. Made by New England Glass Co., 1886.

Air twist

Air twist. Spiral veins of air formed by extension of tears (air bubbles), usually in stems of drinking vessels and shafts of candlesticks; in the United States found occasionally in individual non-commercial pieces of South Jersey Type.

Ale glass. Long, narrow flute for serving strong ale, a highly alcoholic drink; from 1740 might be engraved with the hop and barley motif.

Amberina. Made from a gold-ruby compound, an amber glass mixture containing the metal gold; colours shade from yellow-amber to dark red. New England Glass Co., U.S.A., 1883.

Anglo-Venetian glass. Tableware in fine soda glass made in London from 1570 until about 1680.

Annealing. Toughening flint glass by raising it to a high temperature and then cooling it gradually. (*a*) Annealing oven: an oven known as the tower, built above the melting chamber and operated on waste heat from below; (*b*) annealing tunnel, or leer: a tunnel 5 or 6 yards (4.6–5.5 m) in length through which newly made glass passes slowly to cool, toughen, and acquire increased brilliance.

Applied decoration, finial, foot, stem. Ornament and parts formed from separate gather of metal and tooled into form. *See* Finials, Foot.

Arabesques. Engraved scrollwork of flowers and foliage on hollow ware.

Arch patterns. (1) Blown-three-mould patterns classified as arch, having an arch, Gothic or Roman, as a predominating or conspicuous motif from 1823; (2) pressed-glass patterns also.

Art glass. Late nineteenth-century U.S. glass showing use of new materials and techniques; includes Peachblow, Burmese, Satin, Tiffany, etc.

Aurene. Gold ruby glass heated to different degrees resulting in iridescent shades of yellow, violet, and pink. Stourbridge Steuben Glass Works, U.S.A.

Aventurine. A dark-brown glass with gold specks, so called from its accidental discovery at Murano, Italy. It was made by mixing copper crystals with the molten vitreous material. In the eighteenth century the Miotti factory specialized in its production.

Baccarat. Together with Cristalleries de Saint-Louis (*q.v.*) the greatest large-scale producer of fine glass in France all through the nineteenth century. It was founded in 1778. The first furnace for lead crystal of the English type was installed in 1819. From 1822 to 1858 it was under the inspiring directorship of Jean Baptiste Toussaint, to whom must go the credit for the very high quality of the products and the progressive technical and artistic style of the colour glass about the middle of the century. From about

1850 opal glass was produced in a variety of exquisite colours and elegant shapes, many of them produced by moulding. This production goes on until *c.* 1870. All through the period cut crystal glass in a rich and dignified style remained a main product of the factory.

Baluster. *See* Stems.

Baroque patterns. Blown-three-mould patterns classified as baroque, composed of bold motifs in relief; chosen instead of rococo to distinguish typical English and American designs from contemporary French glass related in design but tighter in composition and lower in relief.

Barovier, Angelo. The name of a craftsman or factory owner, of Murano, Italy, praised by Filarete in his treatise *De Architetura* (1451–64). None of his productions can with certainty be identified, though a marriage goblet in the museum at Murano is traditionally associated with him.

Batch. Mixture of raw materials ready for melting.

Beads. Called *conterie* of brightly coloured glass imitative of semi-precious and precious stones were made in Venice from a very early period. J. G. de Keysler, who visited Venice in the 1730s, noted that several streets were entirely inhabited by people making and stringing these beads which, he said, 'the women of the lower class wear about their necks and arms for ornament. The larger sort are used for making rosaries.' They were exported to the East together with *margariti* (*q.v.*) or imitation pearls.

Beakers. Stemless drinking glasses, or beakers, are among the earliest specimens of Venetian glass. A fine enamelled example is in the Victoria and Albert Museum. They were particularly popular in the eighteenth century, and many of this date are decorated either with engraving or enamelled figures.

Becker, Johann Albrecht. A Saxon glass decorator who worked at Nöstetangen, Norway, from 1767 to 1773 and later opened his own workshop in Drammen. It was active until 1807, perhaps later, and at times Villas Vinter was attached to it. Most of the engravings, however, seem to have been of an unpretentious nature.

Beilby, William (1740–1819). A celebrated enameller of flint glass who worked in Newcastle-upon-Tyne from about 1760 to 1776, signing his best work by name and with a lifelike butterfly.

Belfast (Benjamin Edwards). The earliest reference discovered by Westropp was an advertisement dated 1781. The wording suggests that the costly Perot furnace was in use and 'enamelled, cut and plain wine glasses' made as well as cheaper table glass. From 1783 Edwards was making all kinds of glass-making machinery and hollow-ware moulds, some fluted, which he sold to the newly established Irish glasshouses. By 1805 Edwards was issuing a wide variety of cut table glass and blown-moulded decanters, as well as lustres and girandoles. The glasshouse continued with varying degrees of prosperity until 1829.

Above Beaker of semi-opaque turquoise glass, painted in enamel colours and gilt with scenes from the Pyramus and Thisbe story, Venetian, *c.* 1480. Victoria & Albert Museum

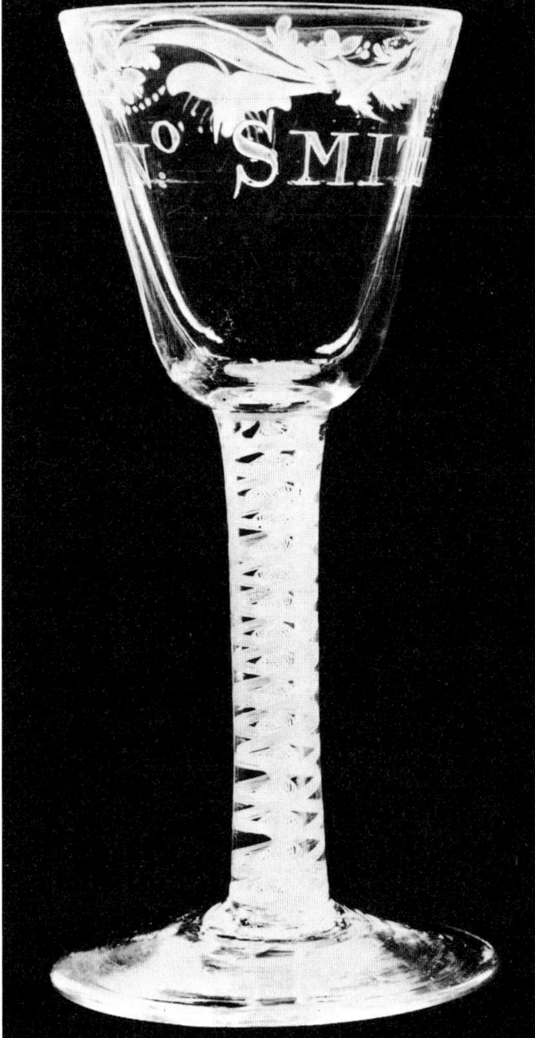

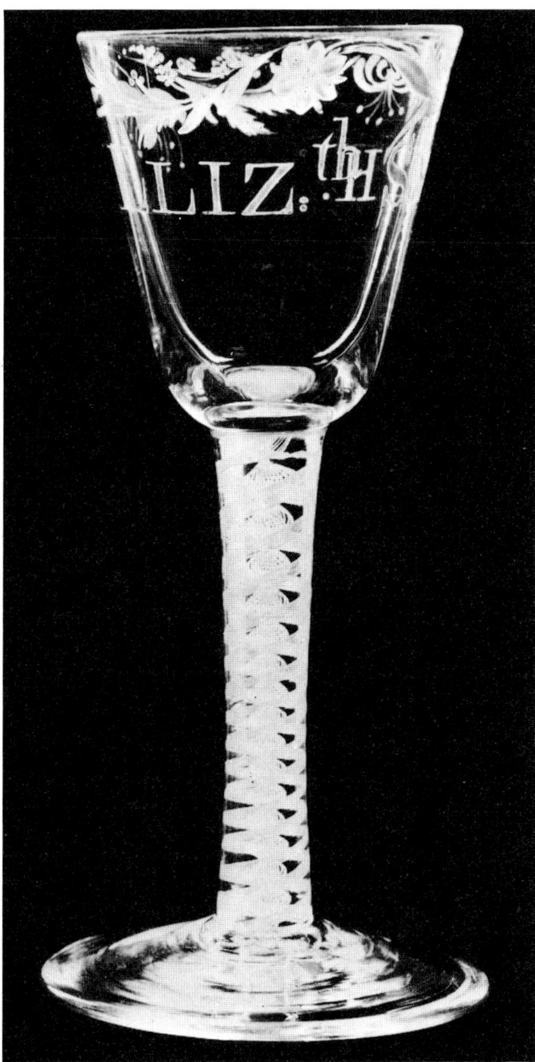

Pair of wine glasses with straight-sided bowls and straight opaque white twist stems, enamelled in white with scroll foliage and flowers and the names Elizth Smith & Jno Smith, by the Beilbys of Newcastle-on-Tyne, *c.* 1770

Blank. Uncut vessel before it is decorated.

Bloom. An all-over film of opaque dullness occasionally found on the surface of flint glass, English and Irish alike, although usually associated with Irish. It has been described by Mrs Graydon-Stannus as 'rather like the bloom of grapes and if cleaned off it will return'. This effect is caused by the use of high-sulphur fuels in the leer. Bands of bloom may be found encircling hollow ware a little distance below the rim; these are the result of reheating at the furnace mouth. This bloom is not to be confused with the milkiness found inside old decanters.

Blown mouldings. (*a*) One-piece moulds were first used in which inexpensive hollow ware was blown and shaped. Molten flint glass solidified quickly on the surface in contact with the mould; a quick-setting flint glass was therefore evolved, not possessing the high brilliancy of metal used for freeblown glass. A gather of this molten metal was taken and blown into a mould smaller than the finished glass vessel; the semi-molten glass was then expanded by further blowing. Such a mould had always to be made slightly greater in diameter at the top than at the base to permit easy withdrawal. Glass shaped by this process may be recognized by its slightly pebbled appearance caused by contact with the mould. The lower part of the mould interior might be intaglio-cut with a circuit of slender flutes rising vertically from the base. Inflation forced the glass closely against the inner surface, forming a clean impression. The quick-setting glass ensured that the section of the metal remained constant so that the flutes on the outer surface appeared as corresponding depressions within.

(*b*) The two-piece open-and-shut mould was invented in 1802 by Charles Chubsee of Stourbridge. Glass blown into such a mould was both shaped and decorated with diamond and other motifs in deep relief. Patterns followed those worked on free blown glass by the wheel cutters. From 1825 the long-accepted geometrical designs met active competition in the form of baroque scrolls, fan patterns and arch patterns. The gunmetal mould with an intaglio design sunk into the inner surface was the same size as the finished article, which was fully inflated in a single operation.

(*c*) The three-piece mould, with one fixed and two hinged sections each cut with an intaglio pattern, dates from about 1830. When the glass was inflated within the mould the blowing force caused the joints to open infinitesimally, thus producing slight ridges on the surface of the glass or a slight break in the pattern.

Blown-three-mould glass. Collector's name for a category of inexpensive blown-moulded ware, popular from about 1815 to 1835; blown in full-size piece moulds for: (1) shape and decoration; (2) decoration and partial shape; (3) for decoration only, thus using the full-size mould as a pattern mould; transitional between pattern-moulded and fully moulded; characterized by patterns classified in three categories, according to predominating or most conspicuous motifs, arch, baroque, and geometric (the last, the earliest, and simulating cut glass), concavo–convex surfaces, an identifying characteristic. It was outmoded by pressed glass.

Blowpipe. Long, hollow, iron tube used to hold a gather of molten glass.

Blue glass. The leading Irish glasshouses produced a blue glass resembling the English Bristol blue flint glass coloured by the addition of smalt. A recipe for such glass was found among the Waterford papers dated 1786. The finer-quality blue glass was prepared in small covered pots, known as piling pots, placed on the ordinary pots. The quality of the glass was improved by keeping the pot in the furnace long after completion of vitrification, thus making it harder and freer from specks and bubbles. In the early nineteenth century a less gorgeous blue was acquired by using less-expensive ultramarine. A wide variety of domestic ware was made. A set of six dark-blue wine-glass coolers has been noted marked 'Penrose Waterford'.

Blue tint. The faintly bluish hue present in the texture of some late Georgian flint glass. For more than half a century collectors deemed this to be solely a Waterford characteristic, and as such was sold at greatly enhanced prices. This claim for Waterford cannot be substantiated. True, such blue-tinted glass was issued by Waterford, for Mrs Graydon-Stannus exhibited marked examples to the Royal Society of Arts in 1925, but it is found in other Irish glass, as well as among the productions of Stourbridge, Birmingham, Bristol, Scotland, and elsewhere.

This peculiar depth of tone shows the glass to contain lead oxide prepared from Derbyshire mined lead, preferred at many glasshouses because of the superior manipulative properties it gave to the molten metal. Unfortunately the Derbyshire lead contained an impurity which caused this bluish tint, recognized as a defect by the late Georgian glassmen and which they endeavoured to eliminate.

The Irish glasshouses for the most part used lead oxide made by Wilson Patten, Bank Quay, Warrington, from Derbyshire lead. Not every consignment contained the blue-tingeing impurity, then known to glassmen as Derby blue. There was, therefore, no consistency in the presence of Derby blue in flint glass during the period concerned, and depth and tone of tint varied.

In 1810 Blair Stephenson, Tipton, Staffordshire, invented a process by which this tint could be eliminated. By 1816 most English and Irish glasshouses were using Stephenson's purified lead oxide, its manufacture proving a profitable monopoly until his manager joined another firm as a competitor. It is doubtful if the Derby blue tint is to be found in Irish glass made later than 1815.

Recent efforts to reproduce the genuine Derby blue tint have failed, but a bogus 'Waterford Blue' has been in production for more than thirty years.

Bontemps, Georges (1799–1884). Director of the Choisy-le-Roi (*q.v.*) factory from 1823 to 1848. The son of an officer, who was descended from one of Louis XIV's valets, he became an enterprising industrialist, an inventive technician, and a learned scholar. He was the real pioneer in France in the discovery and exploitation of coloured glass on a high artistic level. In 1827 he began the production of opal glass, and in 1839 was making filigree glass in the Venetian style. In 1844 he made millefiori glass. He installed a stained-glass workshop at Choisy with an Englishman, Edouard Jones, to direct it, and there also was a painters' studio. The political developments in 1848 forced him to leave the country, and he became attached to the firm of Chance Brothers in Smethwick near Birmingham. His famous handbook on glass making, *Guide du Verrier* (Paris, 1868), remained a standard work of its kind until quite recent times. By succeeding generations of French glass makers Bontemps was considered 'notre maître à tous' (Appert & Henrivaux).

Bottle glass. *See* Green glass.

Bottles. In the United States, with window glass, the commercial product of glasshouses of eighteenth and early nineteenth centuries; of dark olive-green or olive-amber metal, blown in full-size two-piece moulds. In England the use of bottles became widespread in the middle of the seventeenth century. Many were manufactured in Bristol and Nailsea. Shapes and types of English and U.S. bottles are listed below.

Calabash

Calabash (U.S.A.). Ovoid body tapering into cylindrical neck with collared lip; blown in full-size two-piece mould with intaglio designs falling in the pictorial, decorative, and historical categories; *c.* 1850–70.

Carboy (U.S.A.). Large demijohn; usually set in wooden tub; used mainly for corrosive liquids, such as *aqua fortis*.

Carboy (England). A large vessel made of green bottle glass to carry corrosive acids for industrial purposes. They date from the late eighteenth century and were packed originally in wicker containers and more recently in steel frames stuffed with straw.

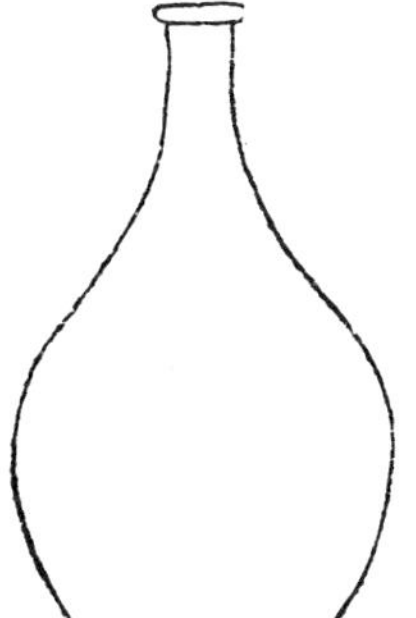
Chestnut

Chestnut (U.S.A.). Somewhat carelessly freeblown bottles with long neck and fat chestnut-shaped body, frequently full of bubbles and asymmetrical; without uniformity of size, ranging from a few ounces to a gallon or more in capacity; ranging, in natural bottle-glass colours, from ambers through olive ambers to greens; called also Ludlow because of a tradition of having been made in a Ludlow, Massachusetts, glasshouse, and junk; made generally, eighteenth–early nineteenth centuries.

Cylinder (England). Date from the late 1730s, shaped in earthenware moulds. By 1750 one-piece gunmetal moulds had been introduced. These bottles measured 5 inches (12.7 cm) in diameter, reduced to about 4 inches (10.2 cm) in the 1770s. In cylindrical bottles until the 1790s a distinct bulge encircled the base of the body. By the early 1790s bottle glass could be blown to a thinner section in the mould without loss of strength and diameter and was reduced to 3 inches (7.6 cm), with the shoulder high and less pronounced than formerly. From 1820 shoulders were still further accentuated. Mechanically moulded bottles date from the 1840s.

Demijohn (U.S.A.). Mainly a storage and shipping bottle, often with wicker jacket; freeblown or moulded for symmetrical, globular, or oval form, with long neck and lip usually collared; quart to twenty-gallon sizes. In Britain capacity not less than 3 gallons and not more than 10 gallons.

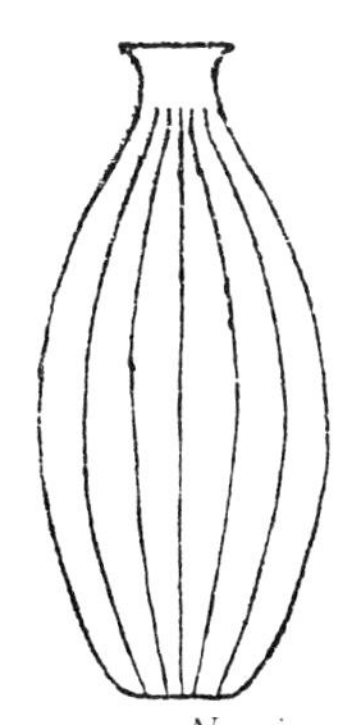
Nursing

Nursing (*sucking*) (U.S.A.). Flattened ovoid flask rounded at end, short neck with sheared, sometimes flaring, lip; plain and pattern-moulded in ribs, flutes, and diamonds; eighteenth–early nineteenth centuries.

Onion (England).

Pocket bottle (U.S.A.). Flask of about half-pint to pint capacity. *See* Flasks.

Shaft and globe (England). Sealed and dated examples show that they developed in four main chronological groups from about 1620 to 1730: (*a*) 1620–60, bulbous body, low kick and long neck encircled half an inch below the smooth, flat-surfaced lip with a thin, sharp-edged string ring. (*b*) 1650–85, the shoulder angle more pronounced, the sides of the body sloping more steeply inward towards the base, making the kick narrower. The knife edge was retained on the string ring. (*c*) 1680–1715, the body was progressively widened and became more squat, with a high kick. The neck, shorter and tapering, joined the body in a smooth curve harmonizing with the more rounded shape of the body. (*d*) 1710–40, the sides of the body became perpendicular or with a slight outward slant, curving into the neck with a shoulder more square and pronounced than formerly. The neck was wide at the shoulder junction and the string rim raised to a position immediately beneath the mouth. These forms were abandoned from the late 1730s in favour of cylindrical bodies.

Stiegel-type pocket or perfume (U.S.A.). Chunky, bulbous form, slightly flattened wide sides; pattern-moulded designs.

Swirl (U.S.A.). A Midwestern type, pattern-moulded in vertical ribs or flutes, swirled usually to right, occasionally to left; wide colour range, from aquamarines to deep greens, olive greens, citron, ambers, and blues; including two distinctive shapes: (*a*) globular, nearly spherical body, slender neck, slightly tapering or straight, collared lip; (*b*) short cylindrical body, sides often tapering slightly, sloping shoulder, short neck, collared lip; proportions, distinguishing features; some forms also with vertical and broken-swirl ribbing or fluting.

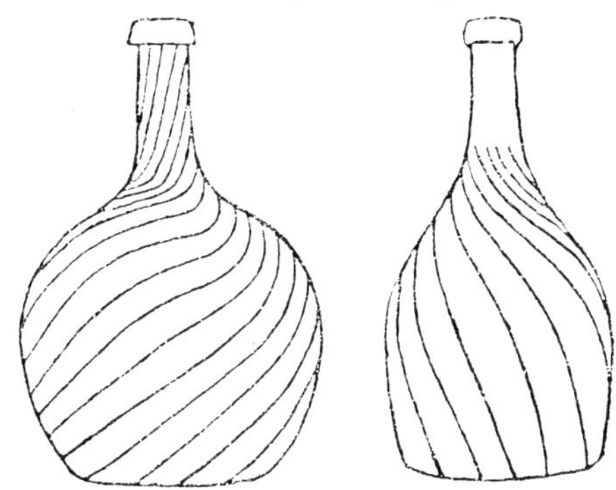

Bowes, Sir Jerome. In 1592 Bowes acquired the 'Venetian glass' monopoly in England from Verzelini (*q.v.*), paying Elizabeth I an annual rental of 200 marks (£133 6*s* 8*d*) for the privilege.

Bowl forms. (*a*) Bell, 1715–80: a deep, waisted bowl with incurved profile and wide mouth derived from the funnel bowl. The base, until 1740, might be a solid mass of glass and welded to the stem; (*b*) bucket, 1730–70: with sides almost vertical and horizontal base. Some late eighteenth-century bucket bowls are lipped. The waisted bucket and incurved bucket are also found; (*c*) double ogee, 1700–20: expansive shallow examples of thick section; from 1750, smaller and with thin walls. Ogee and waisted ogee are also found; (*d*) round funnel, characteristic of the seventeenth century, when rarely with a collar at stem and bowl junction. Until 1690 the bowl was long in proportion to the stem; as the bowl lost depth it became wider at the rim: less massive from 1710; (*e*) straight funnel or conical; a straight-sided bowl shaped like the frustum of an inverted cone; (*f*) thistle, from 1715: in several profiles in which the lower part is a solid or hollow sphere of glass; (*g*) trumpet: a waisted bowl of incurving profile merging into a drawn stem.

Engraved wine glasses. *Left to right*: waisted trumpet bowl with engraved Jacobite emblems, 1750; funnel bowl bearing Jacobite emblems, 1765; waisted bell bowl with a carnation and a bee, both of Jacobite significance, 1765; Hanoverian funnel bowl engraved with 'The White Horse of Hannover' beneath a ribbon inscribed 'Liberty'; bell bowl engraved with an oak leaf and a rose, Jacobite emblems, 1750; Jacobite flared bucket bowl with a sunflower and a butterfly, 1760; trumpet bowl engraved with buds and an oak leaf and the word 'Fiat' – Let it be done – the Jacobite motto, 1745

Bowls, drinking-glass. (*a*) Thick-walled type until the 1740s. The stem may be drawn from the base of the bowl, drawn into a short neck to which the stem is attached, or the bowl may be attached to the top moulding of the stem, traces of the weld being visible: (*b*) from 1740, light, thin-walled; (*c*) from 1790, thick-walled with cutting in deep relief.

Briati, Giuseppe (1686–1772). A craftsman who inherited, or founded, a glassworks at Murano, Italy, in the early eighteenth century. He specialized in making glass of Bohemian type and is sometimes said to have worked in Bohemia. In 1739 he transferred his premises to Venice itself, establishing a factory in the parish of S. Angelo Raffaele, where he produced, among other wares, mirrors, picture frames, bizarre table centres, panels for the decoration of furniture, and large chandeliers.

Bristol blue. Made at most glass-making centres, may be grouped into five basic qualities of glass: (*a*) 1760–90, intense dark blue with a faintly purplish hue; (*b*) 1790–1805, harsh dark blue, less intense than (*a*); (*c*) 1804–20s as (*a*) but without the faintly purplish tint; (*d*) 1821–40s, a costly near-royal blue known as king's blue; (*e*) as (*a*) but in decorative forms and not flawed. These may be subdivided into qualities varying with the technical facilties available at individual glasshouses.

Left Tazza with enamelled pattern underneath the bowl. Signed Brocard, 23 R. Bertran, Paris. Royal Scottish Museum

Brocard, Joseph. Enamel painter and decorator of glass, working in a studio in Paris during the latter part of the nineteenth century. His exquisite pastiches of Islamic enamelled glass decoration were highly praised by critics at the Paris Exhibition in 1878. Later he liberated himself somewhat from these models, and used Chinese or naturalistic flowers for his designs. He always preserved a stylization of patterns and a coolness of colour, which is reminiscent of Oriental art, and rare and refreshing in the France of the *art nouveau*. In some instances he must have collaborated with the factory which made his glass, as the decorative pattern has been embedded in the glass itself and later picked out in enamels.

Broken swirl. Pattern-moulded ribbed design obtained by twice moulding a gather in ribbed or fluted dip mould; first impression of vertical ribs, twisted or swirled, gather reinserted in mould impressing vertical ribs upon the swirled; occurring

Far left Blue mug with gilt decoration 'Friendship', Bristol, late 18th century most frequently in the U.S. on Pitkin bottles, jars and flasks having two-layered body (half-post) and on Midwestern bottles, flasks and hollow ware blown from single gather; ribs varying in closeness.

Brussa, Osvaldo. An eighteenth-century Italian glass painter. In the museum at Murano there is a portrait which shows him holding a beaker on which birds are painted.

Buckets. Either for holy water or for domestic use, these were occasionally made at Murano, Italy, in the sixteenth century and later. Their shapes are derived from silver vessels of the same type.

Burmese glass. *See* Uranium glass.

Butterfly. A coloured butterfly often occupies the centre of a paperweight. Sometimes the insect is poised over a flower, sometimes above a *latticinio*, or other filigree, ground. Also an emblem engraved on Jacobite glass, over the signature of William Beilby (*q.v.*).

Calcedonia. A type of glass which imitates the colour and veining of chalcedony, first produced at Murano, Italy, in the fifteenth century. It appears to have enjoyed great popularity throughout the Renaissance period and again in the eighteenth century. In the nineteenth century made in Bohemia and England.

Cameos. *See* Sulphides.

Camphor glass. White, cloudy appearance; known in U.S. blown-mould and pressed glass.

Candlesticks. Made at Murano, Italy, in the eighteenth century, usually copied from silver patterns.

Cane. Familiar name for the rods of coloured glass from which the patterns were formed in many types of paperweights (*see* Paperweights).

Carré, Jean. In 1570 Jean Carré of Arras established a glasshouse in the Crutched Friars, London, bringing over several glass-making families from Lorraine. After Jean Carré's death in 1572 the glasshouse was acquired by Giacomo Verzelini, until then his chief assistant.

Cased glass. Two or more layers of glass differing in colour; called overlay when design is cut through to body colour; popular Bohemian glass technique.

Caster. (1) Bottle form with perforated cap, usually metal; called also shaker; (2) frame for condiment bottles or containers such as casters (shakers), cruets, and mustard pots.

Caster bottles. Bottles to set in caster or cruet frame – shakers, cruets, mustard pots.

Chain. U.S. name for applied, tooled decoration; links formed by drawing together at regular intervals two threads of glass laid-on around a parison or body of partially formed object, called also *guilloche*; in England, trailed circuit or ornament.

Champagne glasses. English shapes: (*a*) 1678–1715: tall flute with short stem or button; (*b*) 1715 to mid-1730s: *tazza*-shaped bowl, often ogee in form, usually on moulded pedestal stem; (*c*) 1730–45: drawn flute; (*d*) 1745–1830: long-stemmed flute; (*e*) from 1830: the hemispherical bowl or coupe.

Chance, W. and **R. L.** In 1793 William Chance became a partner in the Nailsea, England, glassworks founded five years earlier by John Robert Lucas (*q.v.*). Chance's son, Robert Lucas Chance, was manager of the Nailsea factory in 1810, but in 1815 he left the west, sold his share in the glasshouse, and went to London. By 1824 he had founded the Spon Lane glassworks in Birmingham, a concern that became exceedingly prosperous and in 1870 bought up the

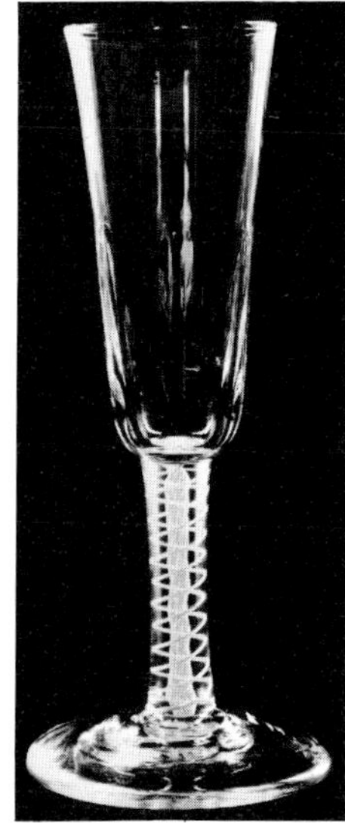

Ale glass with tall straight-sided bowl and compound opaque white twist stem, English, *c.* 1760. Victoria & Albert Museum

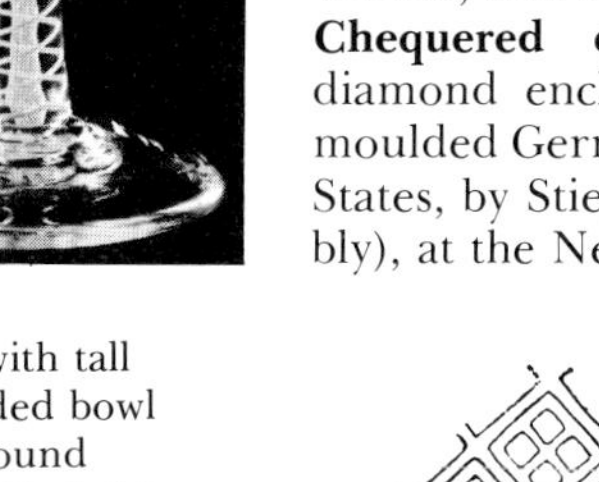

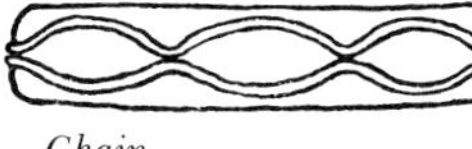

Chain

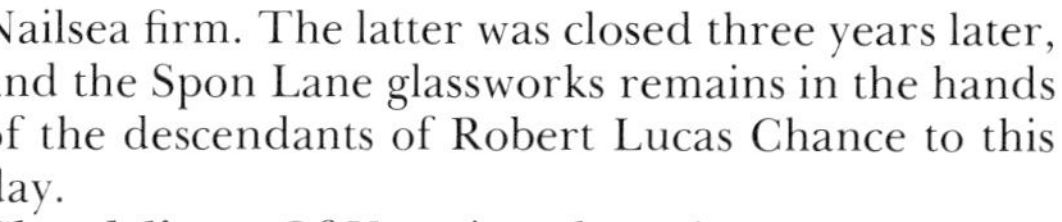

Nailsea firm. The latter was closed three years later, and the Spon Lane glassworks remains in the hands of the descendants of Robert Lucas Chance to this day.

Chandeliers. Of Venetian glass, these seem first to have been made by G. Briati (*q.v.*), who won praise from Carlo Gozzi for his 'magnificent clusters for illuminating the rooms of great Lords, Theatres or the streets on festive occasions'. They enjoyed great popularity throughout the eighteenth and nineteenth centuries. Eighteenth-century examples are among the finest objects in Venetian glass, very elaborate and richly decorated with polychrome flowers, but few have survived intact. Good examples may be seen in the museum at Murano, the Ca' Rezzonico Venice, and the Pinacoteca Querini Stampalia.

Chequered diamond. Decorative motif, large diamond enclosing four small ones: (1) pattern-moulded German diaper design; used in the United States, by Stiegel at Manheim, Pennsylvania (possibly), at the New Bremen Glass-manufactory and in

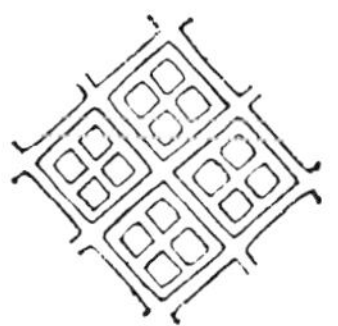

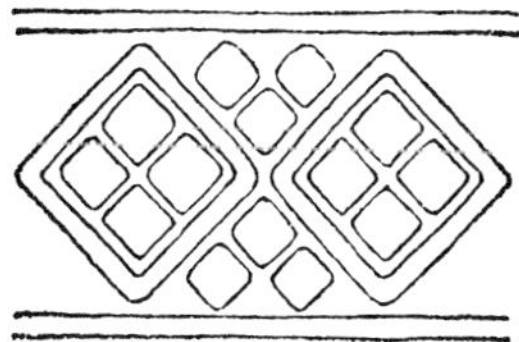

one or more early nineteenth-century Midwestern bottle houses, principally for flasks and salts of type having slender double-ogee bowl and applied circular foot; (2) full-size, piece-moulded, blown-three-mould motif in geometric pattern (McK. GII-29).

Chestnut bottle. *See* Bottles.

Choisy-le-Roi. Factory in Paris, founded in 1821 by M. Grimbolt and closed down in 1851. Between 1823 and 1848 the factory was under the inspiring directorship of Georges Bontemps (*q.v.*) and became the pioneering establishment in the country in the making of coloured glass and the exploitation of its artistic possiblities.

Clichy. Factory founded in 1837 by MM. Rouyer and Maës at Billancourt near Pont de Sèvres in Paris for the production of cheap glass for export. By 1844 the factory had moved to Clichy-la-Garenne and had begun producing coloured glass, a two-layer cased-glass technique with a fine yellow colour being a special achievement. By 1849 the factory's mastery of colour techniques must have been greatly extended, for by that time it seems to have taken over the role, previously held by St Louis, of the finest producer of paper-weights. At the Great Exhibition in London in 1851, Clichy was the only French *cristallerie* to be represented. The display consisted of much elaborate colour glass, cased glass in a great variety of shades, filigree and millefiori glass (a fine pair of signed vases are in the Corning Museum of Glass, New York), and coloured and painted opal glass. At the International Exhibition in London in 1862 an engraved cup from Clichy was acquired by Felix Slade 'as one of the best examples of engraving on glass in the Exhibition'. Slade usually collected only antique glass. In 1868 Bontemps mentions that aventurine glass has been made at Clichy. The high level of craftsmanship and artistry seems to have been kept up until *c.* 1875. About ten years later the factory was absorbed into the Verrerie de Sèvres.

Vase on a twisted stem with vine leaves cut out of a pink casing, Choisy-le-Roi, *c.* 1840. Musée des Techniques, Conservatoire National des Arts et Métiers

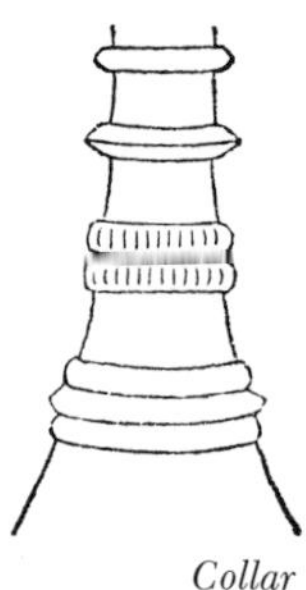

Collar

Although glass was made at Clichy for almost fifty years, and in spite of the leading position it held among the producers of fashionable glass of its time, very few pieces of the factory's products can today be identified as such.

Collar rib. Moulded rib simulating round plain collar; mainly on blown-three-mould decanters and toilet bottles.

Collars. U.S. term synonymous with neck rings. Heavy applied thread or ribbon, plain or tooled, laid on around: (1) lips of bottles and flasks; (2) necks of decanters (*a*) plain round, single or double, (*b*) rigaree, single or double, (*c*) triangular, usually single, rarely double, (*d*) triple ring (wide single with medial rib), (*e*) chain, rare; (3) around stem or shaft, also part of composite stem or shaft; vermicular (wavy), rare in American glass.

Compote. Bowl on standard (stem and foot); also on domed or pedestal foot.

Cordial glasses

Cordial glasses. During the seventeenth century cordials were taken from miniature wine glasses measuring 4–6 inches (10.2–15.3 cm) in height. A distinct type of glass, its bowl shorter, squarer, and of smaller rim diameter than a wine-glass bowl, became fashionable from about 1720; (*a*) 1720–40: straight stem of normal length and diameter; (*b*) from 1735: the stem was lengthened, of extra thick diameter, and might be centrally knopped; (*c*) from 1740: the bowl was less capacious; (*d*) 1740–70: the flute cordial, often termed a ratafia glass.

Cords. Slight striae discernible to the fingers on the surface of the glass.

Cork Glass-house, later **Cork Glass-house Company.** Established in Hanover Street, Cork, Ireland, 1793, as makers of plain and cut flint glass and black bottles. The firm specialized in light-weight blown-moulded hollow ware. Although heavily subsidized by the Dublin Society, such as £1,600 in 1787 and £2,304 in 1793, throughout its existence the Cork Glass-house appears to have laboured under financial instability and ever-changing proprietorship. A newly patented Donaldson furnace was installed under a new proprietorship. This gave flint glass a clarity and brilliance never before achieved, and some outstanding handcut work was produced. The number of handcutters employed was such that they founded the Cork Glasscutters' Union.

In 1812 the firm, under the proprietorship of William Smith & Company, became the Cork Glass-house Company. Pieces marked 'Cork Glass Co.' date no earlier than this. In 1817 steam power was installed in a final effort to survive against competition from the newly established Waterloo Glass-house. A year later, however, the glasshouse was closed.

Cork Terrace Glass-house. Established in Cork, Ireland, in 1819 by Edward and Richard Ronayne. Their productive capacity was equal to Waterford, for when the firm closed in 1841 it was announced that they possessed tools and machines for forty glass cutters. They made all kinds of table glass as well as lustres and Grecian lamps, and were specialists in cut and engraved dessert services.

Corrugated handle. *See* Handles.

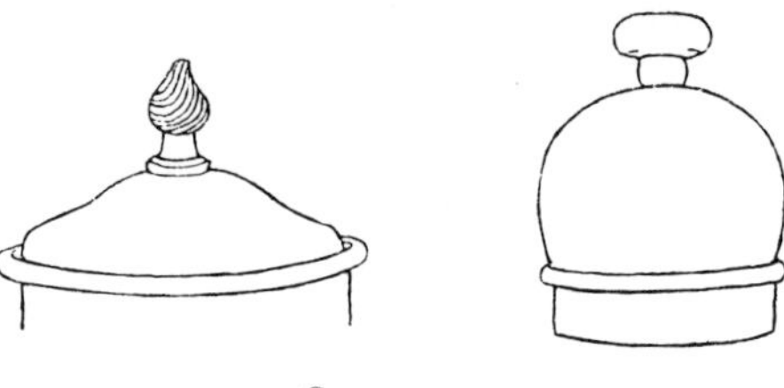

Covers

Covers. Made principally for compotes and bowls. (1) Domed: (*a*) low flattened usually on eighteenth-century set-in type, occasionally individual pieces blown mainly in early nineteenth-century U.S. Midwestern bottle-glass houses; (*b*) low or high round, flaring rim, plain or folded edge; (*c*) low or high conical (sloping), flaring rim, plain or folded edge; (*d*) double, proportions of upper and lower dome varying; (2) set-in, flanged, with short, straight neck fitting inside bowl's rim so flange rests on bowl's rim; (3) set-over, rare type, domed with straight-sided neck fitting over short neck of bowl and resting on moulding applied on bowl.

Cresting. Also termed bridge fluting, *c.* 1748–1800: an extension of faceting from the stem to bridge the junction of bowl and stem; (*a*) until about 1760 merely bridging the junction; (*b*) 1760–80 extending over the bowl base in simple designs; (*c*) from 1780 might extend halfway up the bowl.

Crimping. Dents or flutes impressed by a tool, usually diagonal, used on the foot or tip of handle.

Crisselling. Term applied to a process of deterioration which begins as a fine network of surface cracks. The cause is, apparently, the condensation of water on the surface of an unstable metal which dissolves some of the silicates. Were it allowed to continue, the object would eventually be destroyed, but under ordinary conditions of preservation this would take an exceedingly long time. The only way to arrest the process completely is to keep the object in an air-tight, moisture-proof case, which is the course adopted by museums. Crisselling is most frequent on rare specimens of Ravenscroft glass (*q.v.*) made before 1676, (and probably occurs on occasional specimens thereafter), and on some Chinese glass made around 1700. In both cases the defect showed itself fairly soon after manufacture, and was overcome by modifications in the constituents of the metal employed.

Cristal – cristallerie. The word *cristal* does not mean only lead glass of the English type (though at times it means that), but describes fine table glass and decorative glass of all kinds. Correspondingly, *cristallerie* is a factory where any kind of fine and decorative glass is made.

Cristallo. The name given in Italy to clear uncoloured glass, known in England as white glass. Since the earliest times it had been the aim of glass makers to produce a glass as clear as rock crystal. Clear glass,

Bi-conical cruet-bottle with spire stopper of gilt blue glass, probably decorated by the workshop of James Giles in Berwick Street, Soho, London, *c.* 1765–70

cristallo, produced at Murano in the early sixteenth century – though somewhat grey and cloudy by modern standards – secured the fame of its factories throughout Europe. The decline of the Venetian glass industry dates from the time when factories in other parts of Europe, usually with the aid of Venetian craftsmen, produced a glass as clear, if not clearer.

Crown. Familiar name for a paperweight composed of coloured canes radiating in straight lines from the top.

Crown glass. Early form of window glass; commercial product with bottles of early glasshouses.

Cruet. (1) Lipped bottle with or without handle; (2) caster bottle.

Cruet frame. *See* Caster (2).

Crystal. Refers to finest colourless or clear flint glass.

Cullet. Cleaned, broken glass used in all new mixtures to promote fusion and improve quality of the metal.

Cup plate. Small plate from about 2⅝ to 4⅝ inches (6.7–11.8 cm) in diameter; used as saucer for cup; also used when beverage was drunk from saucer, a custom among some groups, not sanctioned by fashionable society; found mainly in inexpensive glasswares such as pressed; nineteenth century, mainly second quarter.

Cups and saucers. Made at Murano, Italy, in the eighteenth century, of opaque glass imitating porcelain and usually enamelled with little figures.

Cut corners. Chamfered; formed by bevelling the corners formed by the meeting of two sides, making eight planes, narrow at corners; term usually applied to square and rectangular bottles shaped in full-size piece moulds.

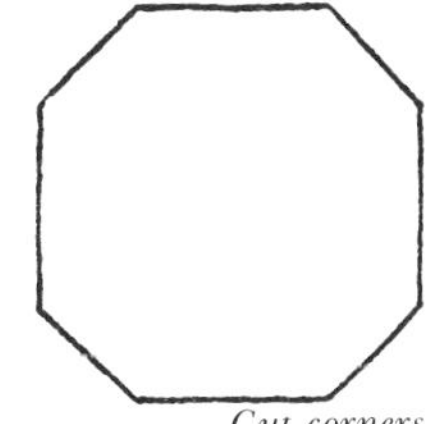

Cut corners

Cut motifs.

Diamond cutting. (*a*) Relief, convex, deepcut, and raised are various terms given to diamonds made by deeply incising V-shaped grooves or mitres crossing each other at right angles and at such a distance apart that they produce a series of four-sided pyramids, each with a sharp apex. These were at first shallow-cut in plain bands, but from the 1790s were usually deep, invariably so after about 1805.

(*b*) Cross-cut diamonds were simple relief diamonds with a tiny four-pointed star cut into the apex of each, the star points bisecting each flat surface. Such cutting was difficult to work and is seldom found on large objects.

(*c*) Strawberry diamonds were simple relief diamonds with flat tops produced by cutting the mitred lines farther apart than in (*a*). Upon each flat apex was cut a small relief diamond. In fine-quality work the centre of every tiny diamond rises to a sharp point.

(*d*) Hobnail diamonds were flat-topped diamonds cut with a simple cross or star.

(*e*) Chequered diamonds were large, flat-topped diamonds cut with four minor diamonds.

Fan or escallop shell borders. The rim of the glass was cut into a series of deep arcs, each following the outline of an escallop shell. A fan was then cut with ten, eleven, or twelve flutes radiating to each arc. The extremity of each cut was notched.

Fluting. (*a*) Hollowed or slightly concave is found either above or in association with diamond motifs. The crest might be notched until early in the nineteenth century.

(*b*) Pillared fluting consists of half-sections of cylindrical columns used in broad bands. This was a favourite Irish motif, dating from *c.* 1790 until the early 1800s, although costly to work.

(*c*) Comb fluting consists of thin hollow flutes closely spaced and encircling the base of a decanter, finger bowl or other hollow ware.

Herring-bone or Blaze. Lightly cut upright or slanting lines in graduated lengths forming alterations of crests and troughs.

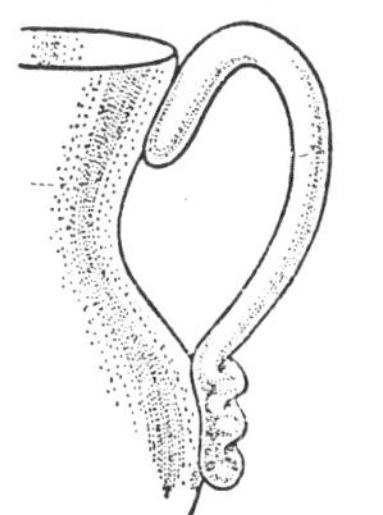

Crimping

Cut-glass decanters showing various cut motifs, *c.* 1800–30: *Left to right, top row* (1) cut strawberry diamonds; (2 and 3) cut band of diamonds and flutes; (4) step-cut neck band of diamonds and panels of fine diamonds; (5) arcaded panels; (6) band and panels of diamonds; (7) flutes and blazes; *bottom row* (1) bands of diamonds and panels of strawberry diamonds; (2–6) band of diamonds and flutes; (7) strawberry diamonds and flutes. Delomosne & Son, London

Wine cooler with step cutting and strawberry diamonds, English or Irish, *c.* 1815–20. Victoria & Albert Museum

Notching. An intermittent series of nicks cut into the sharp crests of flutes.
Printies. Circular or oval concavities cut into hollow ware. These might cover the entire surface; two or three rows encircle the body of a decanter, jug, rummer, or bowl; or a single row might encircle a bowl rim.
Prismatic cutting. Horizontal parallel grooves cut in deep, sharp prisms and requiring metal of thick section for its perfect display. Fashionable 1800–20 and revived during the 1830s. Sometimes termed step cutting.
Slice or edge-flute. Flat cutting carried out by holding the glass at an incline against a rotating mitred wheel and removing a film of glass.
Split. A small angular groove.
Sprig. Three angular grooves placed to resemble a conventional arrowhead, usually found at the angles of other motifs. Late sprigs were cut more deeply than early examples.
Stars. The early radiating stars were cut with six or eight points: by the nineteenth century, twelve-, sixteen-, or twenty-four-pointed stars were becoming fashionable. The Brunswick star had a considerable vogue on expensive glass: this was based on a sixteen-point radiating star with every seventh point joined. To produce this star twenty-four cuts were required; as many as seventy-two have been noted.
Step cutting. See Prismatic cutting.
Sunburst. A motif composed of closely spaced cut lines radiating from a printie or other plain hollow. Associated chiefly with Cork productions.
Vesica. A plain incised oval with pointed ends often containing an eight-pointed star. Where they join, sprigs are cut above and below. The vesica is usually cut, but is also found engraved and the oval filled with trelliswork. Associated chiefly with Cork productions.

Cutting. Depressions ground into the surface of glass by revolving wheels. Three fundamental types of cutting – hollow, mitre, and panel cutting – are capable of producing some fifty variants of design; (*a*) pre-1740: edge cutting and scalloping; almost-flat cutting in geometric patterns; giant diamonds and triangles in low relief; shallow slices; (*b*) 1740–1805: similar types of cutting with the addition of the sprig motif, fluting, stem faceting, incised zigzag, sliced motifs, and, from 1750, large diamonds double cut; (*c*) 1790–1830, more especially from 1805: cutting in deep relief (*see below*).

Cutting in deep relief. Some of the more frequent types are: (*a*) chequered diamond – the flat surface of a diamond in relief cut with four small diamonds; (*b*) crosscut diamonds or hobnail cutting – large relief diamonds each with a flat point incised with a simple cross; (*c*) herring-bone fringe, or blazes – a row of upright or slanting lines cut in an alternation of crest and trough; (*d*) printies – circular concavities ground into the surface of hollow ware; (*e*) prismatic or step cutting, 1800–20 and 1830–40 – deep, horizontal prisms adapted to curved surfaces; (*f*) splits: formally arranged upright grooves; (*g*) strawberry diamonds from *c.* 1805 – the flattened point of each large relief diamond cut with numerous very fine relief diamonds.

Cyst. A round protuberance in the base of a wine-glass bowl.

Daisy-in-hexagon. Daisy-like flower within hexagon, in pattern-moulded diaper design; believed to be a Stiegel original; found mainly on pocket bottles.

Decanters.

American

English terminology generally used for shapes, but sugar loaf synonymous with mallet and semi-barrel instead of Prussian (*see below*). Labelled decanters were made *c.* 1825–50: (*a*) occasionally engraved *wine* or with name of a spirit; (*b*) blown-three-mould with moulded labels in four geometric patterns and one arch. These include WINE, BRANDY, RUM, GIN, H. GIN, CHERRY and WHISKY.

English

(*a*) 1677–1700: with loop handle and mouth expanded into an almost hemispherical funnel with spout lip and loose stopper; (*b*) 1677–1760 and after 1804: shaft-and-globe, near replica of the long-neck wine bottle. With a high kick to 1740; (*c*) 1705–30: straight-sided mallet shape; (*d*) 1725–50: quatrefoil body; (*e*) 1740–1800: shouldered decanter in two forms: narrow-shouldered with outward sloping sides, or broad shoulders narrowing towards the base: more slender of body after 1750 (1 and 2); (*f*) 1755–80 and 1810–20: labelled with engraved, enamelled, or gilded inscriptions on the body (1 and 2); (*g*) 1765–80: tapered body (3); (*h*) 1755–1800: barrel-shaped body with shoulder and base of equal diameter, cut with vertical lines to represent staves and incised rings to suggest hoops: sometimes termed Indian club or oviform (4); (*i*) 1775–1830: Prussian type, often mistermed barrel: a broad-shouldered type, sides having a greater inward slope than formerly, the lower portion encircled with narrow flutes extending halfway up the body (5). Diamond-cut in relief from about 1790 (6); (*j*) 1790–1830s: cylindrical body, cut in deep relief. Decanters of dark-blue glass were made at Bristol,

See text, English decanters

and some of them have survived. These survivors are remarkable for the fact that each of them is decorated in gold with a simulated wine label suspended from its neck, and some are signed with the name of the maker: Isaac Jacobs (*q.v.*). The decanters are of a slender form and the stoppers lozenge-shaped, which leads many people to attribute to Bristol (and to the Jacobs manufactory in particular) other decanters that are unsigned but of a comparably pleasing outline. This is understandable and convenient, but it is most probable that this style of decanter was copied in other parts of the country as soon as it became popular. Apart from the signed ones, it is extremely difficult to allocate coloured glass decanters to specific makers or even to specific localities.

Irish

The majority of Irish decanters were blown-moulded, the usual size being a quart. In lightweight metal a dozen might cost as little as nine shillings, but those of average thickness with neck rings were much more costly. The features on some marked examples are as follows:

Collins, Dublin. Have bases on which radiate carefully moulded V-shaped flutes extending to the edge. The vertical sides are encircled with narrow flutes extending halfway up the body, and the punty mark is larger than noted on other marked decanters.

Cork Glass-house Company. Prussian-shaped and mallet-shaped decanters were made by pure blowing and cut with all fashionable motifs of the period. Blown-moulded types were also made. Probably because of its bottle-making activities, decanters are characterized by their long, slender necks. Neck rings were mainly of the double-feather type, although plain triple rings, square-cut rings, and facet-cut rings were made. Stoppers of the shallow mushroom type pinched with radial gadroons were in the majority, but pinched target stoppers and a conical type encircled with several ridges are found.

Blown-moulded decanters have sides only slightly off vertical. The flutes start a little above the lower rim and extend about two-thirds up the body. The shoulder is often decorated with vesica pattern.

Benjamin Edwards, Belfast. Pyriform blown-moulded decanters, bearing the name of this firm encircling the punty mark, have basal corrugations radiating to the rim, a pair of triangular neck rings, mouth slightly everted, and finished with a narrow, flat rim. The pinched stoppers are vertical, flat-sided, and impressed with trelliswork, or target type cut with a six-pointed star. Engraving encircling the shoulders consists of scrolls, swags, and stars, carefully executed. The shoulder from the lower neck ring might be encircled with wide-cut flutes.

Waterford. Those by Penrose are usually of squat Prussian shape, with three neck rings, a wide, flat mouth rim, and a mushroom stopper pinched with radial fluting and a knop below raising it above the lip. The mark is more neatly moulded than on other decanters.

Waterloo Glasshouse Company. Decanter shapes and decorations closely followed those or contemporary Waterford. The majority of marked specimens are perceptibly wider at the shoulder than the base. Flutes are longer than those of the Cork Glass-house Company. The vesica pattern was frequent: an engraved band of stars between two pairs of feathered lines and ribbon scroll engraving encircling the shoulders. It is thought that engraved circles and loops encircling the body are a characteristic feature. Neck rings usually consist of three of the plain triple variety. Stoppers were low-domed mushroom-shape pinched with radial gadrooning, often with a ball knop immediately below. Pinched target stoppers were also used.

Four decanters made by the Cork Glass Company with the factory mark impressed on the bottom of each, *c.* 1815–20, and a wine-glass cooler by Francis Collins of Dublin with a pouring lid on either side, *c.* 1815–20. Delomosne & Son, London

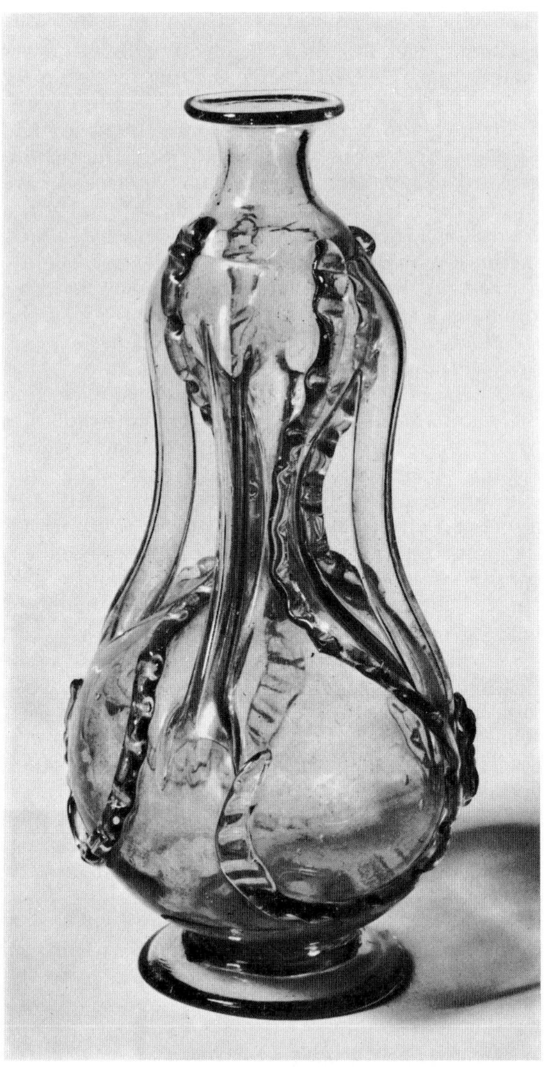

Waisted decanter with trailed decoration, Swedish, first half of 19th century. Nordiska Museet, Stockholm

Scandinavian
A very usual type of Swedish and Norwegian glass in the 1830s and 1840s is the rectangular decanter with a short, inset neck. This was the popular brandy decanter in a period of drinking unequalled in intensity before or since in either country. Another type of Norwegian decanter is the *Zirat Fladske*, an ornamental decanter made at Gjövik in the 1830s, in three different shapes: (*a*) simple bulb-shape; (*b*) rectangular, with cut corners and a long neck; (*c*) waisted. All three models are decorated with trailing prunts and flammiform fringes in naïve profusion. The waisted type has parallels in Sweden and the bulb-shaped one in England, but the origins and dates of the English versions are obscure and the connection cannot be traced.

Decanter stoppers. Rarely ground until 1745. Afterwards ground as a routine process.

Diamond. (1) Diamond diaper, blown-three-mould motif, used either in square or in band; (2) expanded diamond, pattern-moulded and expanded in process of fashioning an unformed but patterned gather into an object; in the United States three principal varieties: (*a*) diamond diaper (units varying in size and number in different moulds); (*b*) rows of diamonds above flutes. *See also* Chequered diamond; (*c*) strawberry diamond (cross-hatched relief diamond), pressed, and cut-glass motif.

Diamond daisy. U.S. design: daisy-like flower within square diamond, in pattern-moulded diaper design; believed to be a Stiegel original; found mainly on pocket or 'perfume' bottles.

Dip mould. One-piece open-top fluted or ribbed mould, varying sizes and depths.

Dishes. In Ireland date from early in the nineteenth century, and might be circular, oval, or octagonal. Early dishes were cut with shallow patterns in relief and later with deep diamonds. Sections are usually variable; sometimes one edge will be considerably thicker than the other.

Double-ogee bowl. In U.S., bowls with sides rising in distorted S, varying widely in proportions and lengths of curves; some like Haynes's pan-topped, others like his cut-topped (*Glass Through the Ages*); in so-called Stiegel-type salts, often an attenuated S.

Dram glasses. Known also as nips, joeys, ginettes, and gin glasses; (*a*) seventeenth century: small tumbler with four tiny feet; (*b*) 1675–1750: cup-shaped bowl with short, heavy knop or moulded baluster; (*c*) 1690–1710: straight-sided bowl of thick section on flattened spherical knop; (*d*) 1710–50: short, plain stem on foot attached directly to bowl; (*e*) 1720–1850: short, drawn-stemmed, trumpet-bowled: some early examples have folded feet.

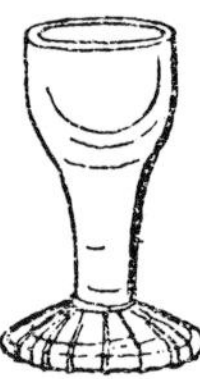

Drinking glasses. Westropp found the following named in the Waterford papers in his possession: 'Regents, Nelsons, Masons, Rummers, Hobnobs, Flutes, Draws, Thumbs, and Dandies.' To these may be added Rodneys, Coburgs, and Thistles. These names used also in England and Scotland.

Dublin – Chebsy and Company. An Irish company which made fine table glass, at a glasshouse known as Venice, from 1784 to 1798. Between 1787 and 1793 they sold glass to the value of £37,849, receiving meanwhile premiums from the Dublin Society (Westropp). They made the magnificent lustres for Dublin Castle in 1789.

Eagle, American. Like or derived from (1) seal of the United States; (2) U.S. coins; most common historical motif in pressed lacy glass and historical flasks, occasionally engraved on blown glass.

Edkins, Michael. Michael Edkins was a painter of pottery and of white and coloured glass. He received the freedom of the city of Bristol on 21 February 1756, but prior to that time is said to have served an apprenticeship in Birmingham. In 1755 he married Elizabeth, daughter of William James, a glass maker, and it is not unexpected that he should have turned his hand to decorating that ware. He would seem to have started to paint glass soon after 1760, and to have continued at least until 1787.

Edkins's business ledger, now in the Bristol Museum, records that he was employed by the following firms, no doubt in the capacity of a freelance worker:

1763–7	Little and Longman
1767–87	Longman and Vigor, and successors

1765	William Dunbar and Co.
1775–87	Vigor and Stephens
1785–7	Lazarus Jacobs

In the same volume are noted the low payments he received for his work, of which these examples are typical:

1762	Jan. 19	To 1 Sett of Jars and Beakers 5 in a Sett	2.6.
	July 26	To 1 Pint Blue can ornamented with Gold and Letters	0.8.
1764	Oct. 1	To 4 Enamell Cannisters	1.0.
1770	Nov. 6	To 12 Hyacinth glasses blue gilded	2.0.

Michael Edkins was said by his son, William Edkins, senior, to have been 'a very good musician and charming counter-tenor singer', and to have performed on the stage both in Bristol and in London. He had a family of thirty-three children, and died about the year 1813. His grandson, also named William, formed a fine collection of pottery and porcelain, which was sold by auction in London in 1874.

The glass decorated by Michael Edkins is unsigned, and much that is claimed as his is the subject of dispute. W. A. Thorpe wrote (*English Glass*, 1949, p. 206) that 'Edkins is known for his characteristic perched birds and his intense curly flower-bunches'. A tea caddy in the Victoria and Albert Museum was once owned by William Edkins, junior, and is stated to have been painted by his grandfather. One of a set of Bristol Delft plates, from the same source, also in the Victoria and Albert Museum, is initialled on the back *MEB* (for Michael and Betty Edkins) and dated 1760.

Elstermann, Kristoffer. Of German origin, Elstermann introduced engraving into Sweden. He first appears at Kungsholm in 1698 and is mentioned in the factory records up to 1715. He died in 1721.

Covered vase of Chinese potiche form, opaque white glass enamelled with flower motifs, English, *c.* 1760

Enamelling. In England, white, 1720–1800; coloured, 1760–1820: (*a*) advertised as 'white japanned flint-glass' in late 1720s: a thinly applied wash enamel in white; (*b*) from *c.* 1750, a dense, full enamel thickly applied (*see* Beilby, William).

End-of-day glass. Misnomer for marble glass (*q.v.*).

Engraving. This seems first to have been used for the decoration of glass in the sixteenth century (first recorded 1530–50). Two methods were used (*a*) diamond point: patterns hand-inscribed, using the point of a diamond or graver. In England armorial work during 1720s; arabesques and scroll patterns 1725–40; spontaneous efforts of amateurs throughout eighteenth century; early Victorian revival with sporting and coaching scenes. Rare usage in the United States. (*b*) Wheel engraving: patterns cut into the glass surface by pressing it against the edge of a thin rapidly revolving wheel. Early wheel engraving was left matt; from 1740 it might be partially polished, the tendency to polish increasing as the eighteenth century progressed. Wheel-engraved rim borders popular from late 1730s to the end of the century: at first simple designs of intertwined scrollwork and leaf arabesques; from 1740 wider borders of flowers and foliage, daisies predominating and, from 1750, individual motifs sometimes extending the full length of the border.

Etched glass. Glass decorated by biting out designs or motifs by means of acid applied to unprotected surfaces.

Ewers. These, and jugs, of Venetian glass were first made in the fifteenth century and a few survive from this period. Sixteenth-century examples are often very elaborate. A delightful ewer in the form of a ship is in the museum at Murano. Polychrome glass flowers were occasionally applied to them in the eighteenth century. Made in English flint glass from the late 1670s.

Excise Duty. The duties levied on British glass during the eighteenth century caused much concern to the glass trade, and are supposed to have driven the makers to ornament their wares with engraving, cutting, gilding, and painting to compensate for the use of less glass in the making of any one article. A further result was the widespread introduction of the coloured glass, with which the names of Bristol and Nailsea are linked.

The Act of 1745 laid down that from March 25, 1746, flint glass should pay a duty of 9*s* 4*d* per hundredweight (112 lbs), and bottle glass 2*s* 4*d* per hundredweight. Ireland was excluded from this, but more devastatingly the export of glass from Ireland was prohibited. In 1780, when the American War of Independence was harassing the British Government, Ireland asserted herself and was granted free trade: all export restrictions were abolished. Within five years glasshouses were established at Dublin, Belfast, Waterford, Cork, and Newry, all operating on a large scale and underselling English flint glass tableware, upon which excise duty had been doubled in 1777. In England, as from July 5, 1777, '. . . upon the material or metal of all Plate or Flint Glass, and of all Enamel Stained or Paste Glass 18/8d. for every hundredweight'. From May 10, 1787, the rate was raised to 21*s* 5½*d*, but bottle glass paid about a fifth of this: 4*s* ¼*d* per hundredweight.

Irish glass making continued as a prosperous industry for forty-five years. Then in 1825, under pressure from English competitors labouring under a heavy excise duty of 10½*d* a pound, the Government laid the impost on Irish glass too. Each furnace in a glasshouse was also required to be licensed at an annual cost of £20.

The duty was reduced in 1835, and finally repealed in 1845. The Irish glass trade had meanwhile rapidly declined, competing unavailingly with the glass presses installed by the English glassmen from the mid-1830s.

Eye-and-scale. Cut, blown-moulded, and pressed U.S. motif having round or oval disc or boss, plain or ornamental, at top of relief scales in vertical or swirled line, usually forming band; called horn-of-plenty in blown-three-mould glass.

Eye-and-scale

Favrile glass. Name meaning 'hand-wrought' used for U.S. art glass made by Louis Comfort Tiffany (1848–1933). *See* Tiffany glass.

Figures. Of Venetian glass, usually intended for table decorations and resembling *verre de Nevers*, were made in the eighteenth and nineteenth centuries. Those of religious subjects were probably intended for private chapels.

Filigree glass. Described as *filiganati* or *a retorti*: an improved and elaborated version of *reticello* (*q.v.*), is decorated with interweaved spirals of white, coloured, and gold threads. Glass of this type was first produced in Murano, Italy, in the sixteenth century, and seems to have remained popular ever since.

Finials

1

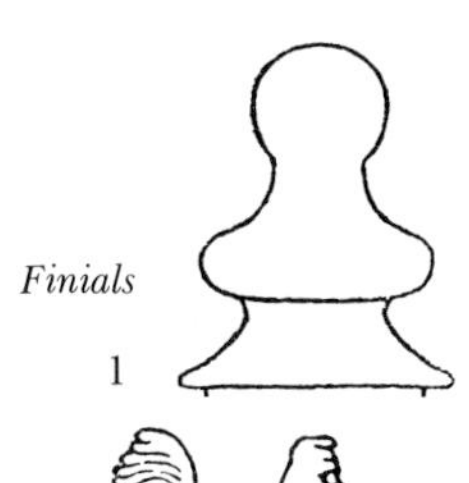

2

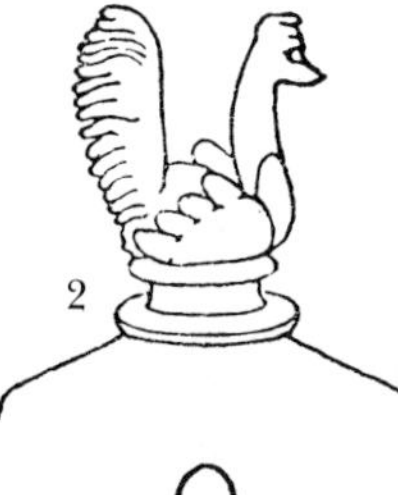

3

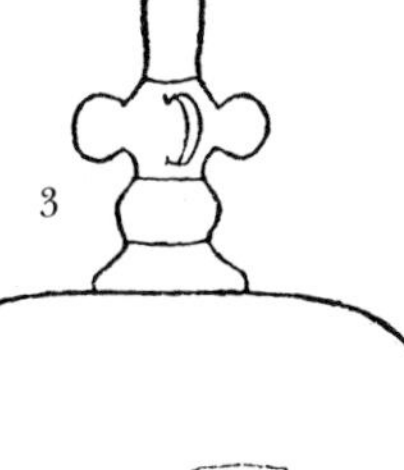

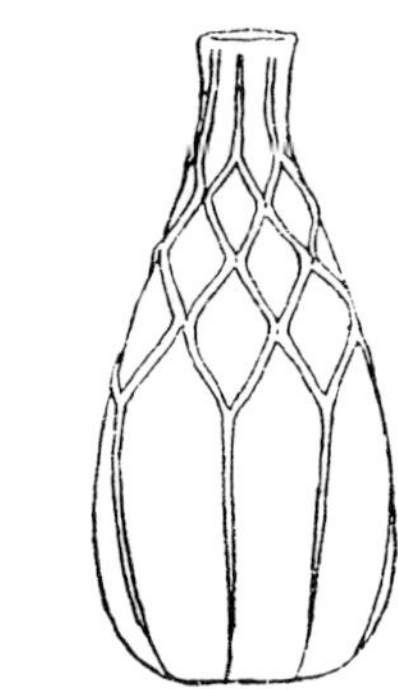

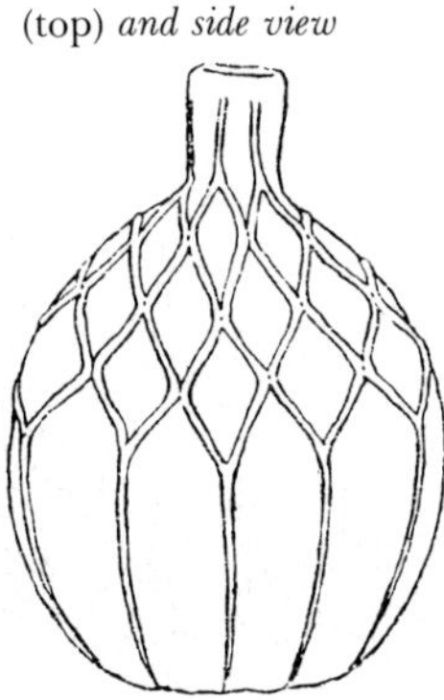

Chestnut flask: end view (top) *and side view*

Finger bowls. In England from *c.* 1760: known variously as wash-hand glasses, finger cups, finger glasses until 1840. Not to be confused with wine-glass coolers. In Ireland large numbers of blown-moulded finger bowls and two-lipped wine-glass coolers were made. They are usually in clear flint glass, English examples are found in blue, purple, amethyst, red, and green. The finest were in heavy cut glass.

Finials. Cover knob, drawn or applied, usually with short stem: (*a*) ball; (*b*) ball and button (1); (*c*) button; (*d*) mushroom, (*e*) pointed globular (spire), plain and ribbed. Or decorative finish of plain cover knob, including (*a*) chicken, nineteenth-century hen-like bird into which the eighteenth-century 'swan' degenerated, used on nineteenth-century pieces of U.S. South Jersey Type; (*b*) swan, unswan-like in having crest, in the United States similar to Continental forms, found occasionally on late eighteenth- and early nineteenth-century glass (2); (*c*) turned with or without ornamental fins (wings) (3).

Fire polishing. A method of processing blown-moulded ware to obliterate tool marks and produce a smooth, even surface. This gave to moulded diamonds, flutes, scrolls, arches, and other motifs smoothly defined edges easily mistaken for cut glass.

Firing glasses, also known as hammering glasses. Used for thumping the table as form of acclamation. Stumpy glass with drawn bowl on thick stem and heavy, flat foot.

Flashed glass. Thin coating of coloured glass over clear glass; a ruby stain in imitation of Bohemian glass, the most popular.

Flasks.

American

(1) *Chestnut.* Freeblown and pattern-moulded, rarely blown-three-mould, of the timeless and universal shape resembling a slender chestnut; without uniformity of size, ranging from a few ounces to over a quart capacity, majority of pocket-bottle size; mainly late eighteenth century to early nineteenth century.

(2) *Decorative.* Blown in full-size two-piece moulds bearing intaglio devices such as the sunburst, urn of fruit, and cornucopia; mainly half-pint and pint sizes; *c.* 1815–40.

(3) *Grandfather.* Midwestern chestnut flask of quart or more capacity; pattern-moulded in ribbed designs.

(4) *Historical.* Moulded like (2); designs of historical import; commemorative of events and public figures, emblems, slogans, candidates in presidential campaigns; emblems and designs related to economic life; also national and other symbolical emblems; *c.* 1815–late nineteenth century, majority before 1870.

(5) *Masonic.* Moulded like (2); designs with (*a*) Masonic emblems each side, (*b*) Masonic emblems one side; reverse, different design, American Eagle most common; *c.* 1815–30.

(6) *Pictorial.* Moulded like (2); designs depicting people and/or flora and fauna; *c.* 1815–70.

(7) *Pitkin.* Generic term for pocket bottles or flasks, blown by German half-post method and pattern-moulded in ribbed designs – vertical, swirled, and broken swirl; eighteenth–early nineteenth century; first identified by tradition with the Pitkins' glassworks, East Hartford, Connecticut, *c.* 1790–1830.

American decorative flasks

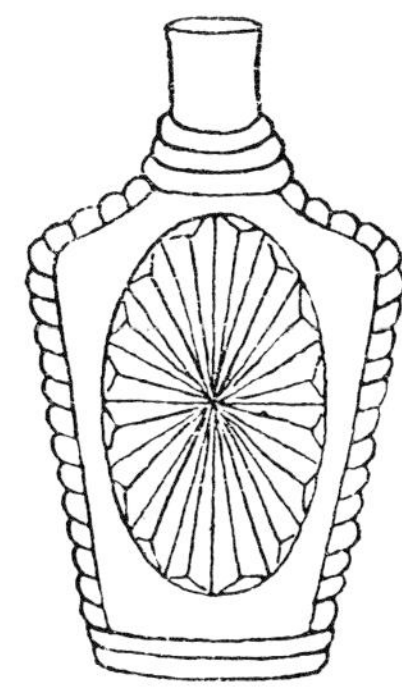

Sunburst

Urn of fruit

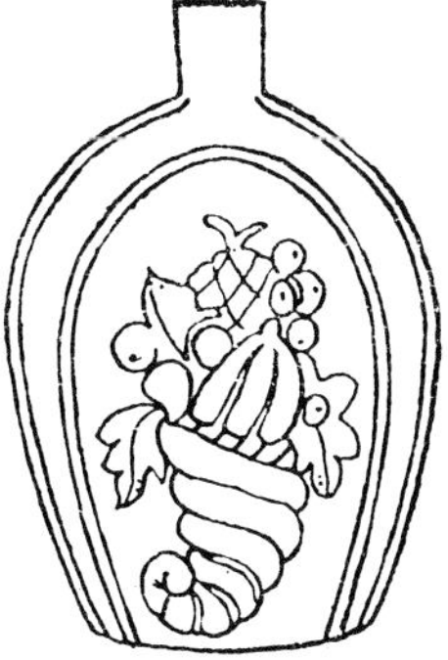

Cornucopia

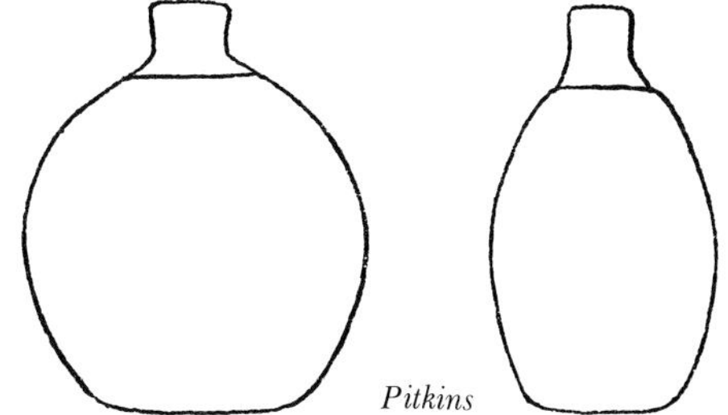

Pitkins

English
In flattened baluster or pear shape of white or coloured glass ornamented with loopings or quillings, these date from early in the nineteenth century and were made at Nailsea, Birmingham, Stonebridge, and elsewhere. Most of them were sold as vessels for toilet water. The twin flasks with two spouts pointing in opposite directions, known as a gimmel flask, was made in flint glass throughout the eighteenth century and used as a holster flask. It was made in colour from about 1820, and in some a circular crimped or petal foot was added. Flasks were also made in the shape of hand bellows.

Above, right Nailsea type double flask with white loop decoration and blue mouth rims, early 19th century

Far left Tazza with filigree decoration, Venetian, 16th century. Corning Museum of Glass

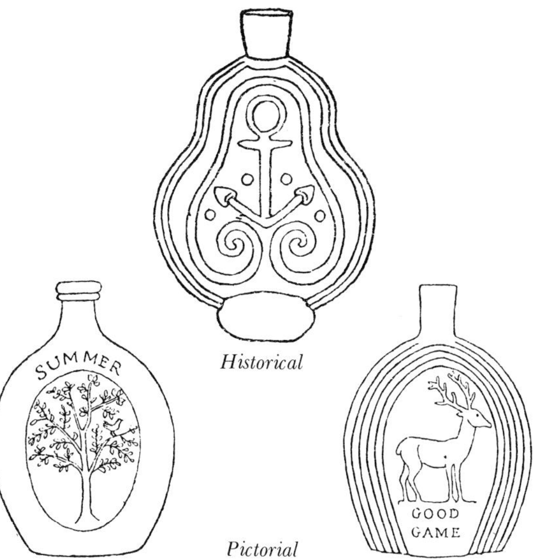

Historical

Pictorial

Venetian
In the form of pilgrim bottles, copied from silver patterns, flasks were made in the sixteenth century occasionally of *lattimo* glass decorated with enamelling.

Flint glass. Now termed lead crystal, developed by George Ravenscroft (1618–81), in England, who was granted a seven-year patent (No. 176) in May 1674 to make a glass in which the silica was derived from calcined flints. In 1675 he first used lead oxide as a flux in place of vegetable potash. This produced a glass denser, heavier, softer, and with greater refractive brilliance than anything previously made. Hollow ware, if flicked with thumb and finger, emits a resonant tone. After improvements to the process had been made during the 1680s, world glass trade became an English monopoly for more than a century and a half. In the United States a trade name for fine glassware, after 1864, including lime glass of William Leighton, Hobbs, Brockunier & Co., Wheeling, West Virginia.

Flip or **flip glass.** U.S. collector's term for tumblers, usually of pint or more capacity; something of a misnomer, as it was probably rarely used to serve the beverage called flip.

Flowered glasses (1740–80s). Trade name for tableware engraved with naturalistic flowers on the bowl; (*a*) 1740, a single flower ornamented one side of the bowl; (*b*) from early 1750s reverse side of bowl might also be engraved with a bird, butterfly, moth, bee, or other insect.

Flute. A drinking glass with a tall, deep conical bowl. Also a vertical groove cut into a stem or bowl.

Fluting. Used when wider unit of ridged design is concave; fan fluting, short tapering flutes or panels, blown-three-mould motif.

Folded Rim. *See* Rims.

Folk art in American glass. *See* South Jersey type.

Foot
American
On blown and blown-moulded glass. Applied: occasionally square; mainly circular (*a*) short-stemmed, eighteenth-century type (1); (*b*) flat; (*c*) sloping; (*d*) petalled (scalloped); (*e*) domed, high and hollow, conical (sloping) or round with flaring plain or folded rim, eighteenth–early nineteenth century; (*f*) pedestal, high and hollow, cylindrical (eighteenth-century type) or truncated cone flaring at rim (late eighteenth and nineteenth centuries) (2 and 3); (*g*) flaring (low pedestal), found also pressed. Drawn: drawn from the bottom of vessel's body and fashioned by tooling.

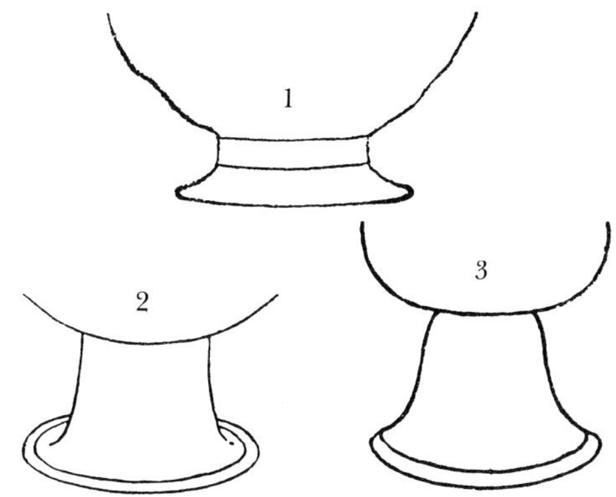

Champagne or sweatmeat glasses with Silesian (2 and 5 from left), air- (4) or opaque-twist (1 and 3) stems, between 1730 and 1760

English
(*a*) Folded, to about 1750: the rim was folded underneath while hot, forming a selvage, giving extra strength to a part most likely to become chipped in use. Pre-1690 the fold was very narrow: (*b*) domed, to about 1800: with hemispherical, sloping, or square instep, often surface-moulded from about 1705. Expansive with folded rim until 1750, then smaller and plain-edged, except on sweetmeat and allied glasses. Domed and terraced: the foot tooled in concentric circles rising one above the other; (*c*) plain, conical foot tapering up towards stem junction, to about 1780: rare in seventeenth century and infrequent until about 1740. Early examples almost flat beneath; by 1735 concave beneath, resting upon extreme rim. From 1750 instep height gradually decreased, until by 1780 had become almost flat beneath with punty mark ground away; (*d*) solid square, 1770 to end of period: might be stepped, terrace-domed, or domed.

Frigger: model of a three-masted sailing ship, complete with rigging, made of clear and blue glass, Bristol, first half of 19th century. Victoria & Albert Museum

Freeblown. Glass formed by blowing and manipulation with hand tools, without aid of moulds; called also handblown and off-handblown.

Friggers. A colloquialism used to describe the innumerable minor articles made of glass, of which the principal purposes were to delight and surprise the recipient and beholder, and to exhibit the prowess of the maker. Into this category fall such objects as hand bells, flasks, rolling pins, walking sticks, tobacco pipes, swords, sceptres, crowns, and hats, which are dealt with under the appropriate headings.

Less common than the above are model ships with rigging and crew, birds on perches, fox hunts with hounds in full cry, and similar *tours de force*. The latter were perhaps made as suitable table decorations at hunt breakfasts.

It is stated that the glass makers of Nailsea had poleheads of glass in place of the more usual ones of polished brass. These poleheads were used by the village clubs of Somerset, and are fairly common when made of brass, rare in wood, and very scarce indeed in glass.

Friggers were made both at Bristol and at Nailsea, as they were at all the other glassworks in England. Unless such pieces bear a signature or other mark of identification, there is seldom any way by which the productions of one place can be distinguished from those of another. Nor is it usually possible to tell the difference between factory-made articles of these types and those that were made by apprentices to test their skill, or those made by trained craftsmen in their spare time either for their own amusement or for sale on their own behalf.

Frit. A flux of low-temperature melting silicates used in the manufacture of glass before the invention of the high-temperature furnace in 1734. The ingredients forming the frit were fused together, ground to powder when cold, and added to the pot with the remaining ingredients before final melting.

Frosted glass or **vetro a ghiaccio.** Imitating the texture of ice more nearly than its modern namesake, was produced in Murano, Italy, in the sixteenth century. A handsome bucket of this substance is in the museum at Murano.

Fruit. Of opaque coloured glass, this was made in

Frigger: group of wrought and spun clear and coloured glass, representing a fountain ornamented with coloured birds, English, *c.* 1850. Victoria & Albert Museum

Marqueterie-de-verre vase by Émile Gallé, 1900

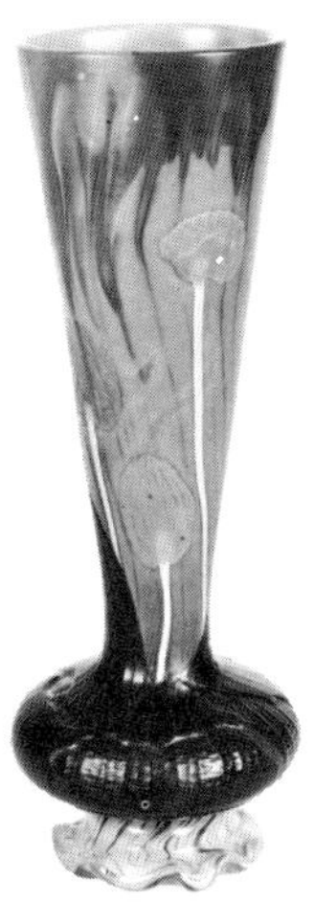

the Murano, Italy, factories in the eighteenth century and has frequently been copied.

Full-size mould. Mould composed of two or more hinged pieces (leaves), having inner surface with or without decorative design, and the size and form of an article; glass thus moulded characterized by concavo–convex surfaces.

Furniture. Occasionally decorated with panels of coloured glass in the eighteenth century. In 1777 Lady Anna Riggs Miller noted at Murano, Italy, a suite of furniture inlaid with pieces of blue glass and looking glass, commissioned by the Sultan of Turkey for his seraglio. Glass imitating marble for inlaying in furniture was patented in the 1840s by G. Newberry, London: the furniture was made by George Shove, Deptford, London. At the Great Exhibition, 1851, Zebedee Jones, Clifton, near Bristol, displayed furniture inlaid with a new style of ornamental glass known as 'vitrilapis'. Stools made entirely of flint glass from gas-fired furnaces were made in the 1860s, and some still exist.

Gadroon or **gadrooning.** Heavy rounded ribs or flutes: (1) tooled on layer if glass formed from a pearl (round gather of metal) attached to end of parison and pulled up over it; (2) dip-moulded on cup-like layer; (3) full-size moulded convex ribs, high relief, tapering from rounded end, forming band.

Gallé, Émile (1846–1904). The most famous producer of art glass of the nineteenth century. During the 1870s he took over the tableglass works owned by his father in Nancy and turned it into an art-glass factory. His early products were free variations of historic styles of Europe and the Orient, mostly in transparent glass decorated with engraving or enamel-painting. At the Paris Exhibition of 1889 his representation showed the powerful impact of Japanese art. The shapes were simple in outline, and much of the glass was massive and coloured throughout. The cased-glass technique was employed with great mastery, and the decorative patterns showed naturalistic pictures of flowers and insects. Soon after, he must have developed that style of cased glass, which more than anything gave him fame: vases made of differently coloured glass in many layers, cut away into varying thicknesses to naturalistic pictures of flowers and insects. The shapes are often irregular and suggestive of natural forms such as trees and branches, and the flowers cling to the forms in curving lines. The general impression is one of gentle lyricism. Sometimes lines from famous French poets are found written on the vases in ornamental lettering, having allegedly inspired Gallé to the particular piece. His own name and 'Nancy', also in ornamental lettering, are frequently integrated into the composition. Glasses in this style were instrumental in the development of the *art nouveau*, and the mature examples are among the most typical of the style's manifestations.

Because of their beauty, their novelty and modernity, and to some extent because of Gallé's great talent for publicity (displayed with real genius at the Paris Exhibition in 1900), Gallé's *verreries parlantes* became fashionable all over the world. In order to answer the enormous new demands for his glasses, he enlarged the factory and engaged a numerous staff of decorators who worked under his supervision. From the 1890s it was really a 'mass-production of individual glasses' that was carried on. Gallé's later years were spent in a constant search for new designs and new technical tricks. The glasses from this period are sometimes very beautiful, though sometimes forced and affected. When he died in 1904 the factory carried on until 1914 in Gallé's spirit and at a respectable level of quality under the artistic leadership of his old friend and associate, the painter Victor Prouvé. The products of this period are signed with Gallé's name preceded by a star. After World War I the production was carried on at Épinay. In 1921 it changed hands, and later products were rather debased.

Great quantities of Gallé's glass still exist. Public collections all over Europe tried to acquire examples of his art at the exhibitions in Paris in 1889 and 1900, and private international patrons also acquired his products. A survey of this vast material is not easy and the individual pieces certainly vary greatly in artistic quality. The early pieces have a genuine charm and exuberance, and the products from about 1890 are particularly fine, original, and of great beauty. The glasses of the last period are sometimes of a staggering technical complexity, but frequently lacking in balance and taste. Cased-glass vases with purple flowers on a grey background must have been made over a fairly long period to satisfy numerous customers everywhere. They exist in great numbers and vary little, though no two pieces are exactly alike. The type may appropriately be labelled 'standard Gallé'.

Much research is still needed on Gallé's complex personality and varied activities. Apart from being a glass maker he had a factory for decorated faïence and one for luxury furniture. He was a learned horticulturalist and botanist, a theorist and writer on art, and an enthusiastic champion for the new styles of the day. The uncritical attitude of his contemporaries is apt to obscure our view of him. He was certainly a great and original glass maker and an influential personality in the cultural milieu of the 1890s. Through the great fame he gained for his creations he laid the foundation for the modern conception of glass as a serious artistic medium.

His glass was widely imitated, in France and elsewhere. But as his habit of signing his works was emulated as eagerly as his lyrical flower decorations, problems of identification are comparatively simple. The only factory working in his style, whose glass could compete with the real Gallé pieces in beauty of texture and design, was Daum in Nancy.

Galleried Rim. *See* Rims.

Gather. Uninflated and unformed blob of metal taken from the pot on end of blowpipe.

Gauffered Rim. *See* Rims.

Geometric patterns. (1) Category of blown-three-mould patterns composed of motifs such as ribs, flutes, diamonds, sunburst, circles, ovals; (2) cut-glass patterns composed of ribs, diamonds, and fans on thick blown-moulded glass, called 'imitation cut glass'; (3) cut-glass motifs, strawberry diamond in particular, on mechanically pressed glass.

Gilding. Traces are visible on existing Elizabethan Anglo–Venetian drinking glasses; fashionable as rim decoration 1715–90, the finest bowl ornament in this medium 1760–90; (*a*) early eighteenth-century gilding fixed beneath a film of flint glass by a process akin to enamelling; (*b*) 1715–60: japanned gilding, burnished; (*c*) 1755–65; honey gilding: the rich brilliance of the gold was destroyed and could not be burnished; (*d*) 1760–1820: amber-varnish gilding, burnished; (*e*) 1780 onward: mercury gilding; (*f*) from 1850: liquid gold of sparkling brilliance.

Little Irish glass is known to have been gilded. That such glass was so decorated is shown by the fact that in 1786 the Dublin Society paid John Grahl thirty-five guineas for disclosing glass-gilding secrets, which were then placed at the disposal of the industry. Such gilding appears to have been impermanent, however, and has worn away, leaving the surface beneath pitted and rough. Careful examination of a lavishly cut piece will sometimes reveal traces of gilding.

Gjövik Verk (1809–47). Norwegian glass manufactory, started when Hurdals Verk (*q.v.*) closed down. Gjövik was a much smaller and less ambitious establishment, but some of the glass blowers from Hurdal came on and the tradition was continued.

Goblet. A drinking glass with the bowl large in relation to stem height and holding a gill or more of liquor. Since the fifteenth century they have been among the most popular products of the Venetian factories. The earliest are based on silver patterns. Those of the earlier sixteenth century are of clear glass with simple baluster stems and usually very shallow bowls, like those held by the banquetters in Paolo Veronese's *Feast in the House of Levi* (Accademia, Venice). Later in the century deeper conic bowls became popular and were often supported on elaborately wrought stems.

Far right Three green glass flat sided case bottles, English, *c.* 1750

Green glass. Glass in its natural colour, neither rendered colourless nor artificially coloured; generally made from coarser and less pure materials than those used for fine wares; soda, potash, or lime the principal alkaline base; many bottles and window glass made from this glass.

Guilloche. *See* Chain.

Half-post. Second gather forming two-layered body, giving added strength through double wall and terminating below neck of vessel; the post (first gather) given a half-post (second gather) by redipping in pot of metal; in the United States associated with Continental and American case bottles and Pitkin flasks and bottles.

Handbells. Coloured glass handbells were made between 1820 and 1860 at Bristol, Newcastle, Warrington, Stourbridge, and by John Davenport, Longport, Staffordshire. Authentic bells measure from 9 to 18 inches (22.9–45.8 cm) in height and have clappers of fine flint glass. Colour combinations are: blue-tinted bell, spirally ribbed handle in pale yellow with opalescent triple-knotted finial; bell with pink strands on an opaque white ground, with moulded opaque-white hand as a handle; bell with white stripes on a translucent red ground, opalescent blue handle; red bell with colour-twist spiral handle; green bell with opaque-white twist handle; opaque white throughout and may be ribbed; translucent bell with clear handle; red throughout. Glass bells are still in production.

Handblown. Freeblown; used in contra-distinction to machine-blown.

Handles. On blown glass, applied: (1) Either round in section or strap (flattened), hollow or solid, ending in (*a*) turned-back- tip, (*b*) curled tip, (*c*) crimped end with *a* or *b*, (*d*) leaf (tooled diagonal lines) with *a* or *b*, probably after 1825: 1, hollow strap, *d*; 1, round hollow, *c*. (2) Principal shapes: (*a*) 'D', rarely found on nineteenth-century glass, (*b*) loop, (*c*) semi-ear shaped, (*d*) swan: long and arching above rim.

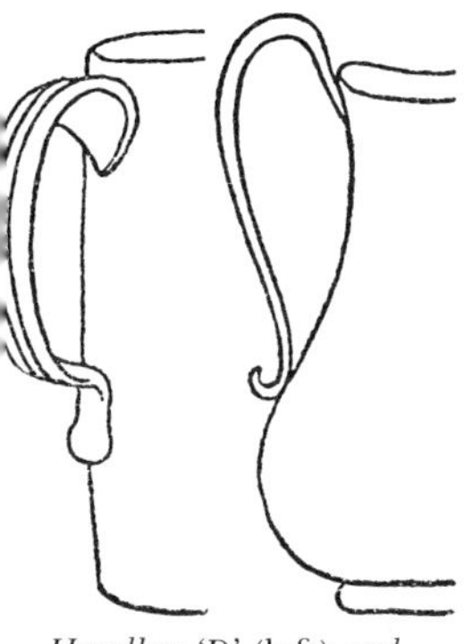

Handles: 'D' (left) *and swan*

Commonest, *b* and *c*. (3) Principal decoration: (*a*) medial rib: a centre rib, often on round, occasionally on strap, the English *trailed*; (*b*) corrugated, ridged, or ribbed strap; (*c*) double; paralleled contiguous sections, occasionally round, usually strap; (*d*) ribbed: hollow handle formed from ribbed or fluted (pattern-moulded) gather, drawn out into a tube, English incised and reeded.

Historical glass. Glass bearing decoration associated with national or local events, heroes, public figures; emblems of agriculture, trade, commerce, transportation, etc.; engraved, rare; in the United States mainly moulded in flasks and pressed in lacy glass.

Horn of plenty. (1) Cornucopia of fruit or produce; common motif on decorative flasks; occasionally in lacy glass; (2) in pressed pattern ware, stylized cornucopia-shaped motif with waffled disc at top, 'horn' with round bosses or vice versa; similar to the peacock eye in lacy glass. *See* Eye-and-scale.

Hurdals Verk glass

Hurdals Verk. Norwegian glass manufactory. When, in 1777, Nöstetangen was shut down, the crystal production and most of the glass blowers were moved to Hurdals Verk, farther up in the country, where wood for fuel was more plentiful. In 1809 Hurdals Verk closed down.

Jacobite glasses. Propaganda glasses bearing emblems and mottoes of a cryptic character associated with the Jacobite cause. Most common is the six-petalled Jacobite rose with one or two buds: the rose represents the House of Stuart, the small bud the Old Pretender, the large bud on the right being added later, either in honour of Prince Charles Edward's arrival in Scotland or after James's proposal to 'abdicate' in favour of his son. Other Jacobite emblems include a stricken and burgeoning oak, oak leaf, bee, butterfly, jay, Jacob's ladder foliage, carnation, daffodil, fritillary, triple ostrich plumes, and thistle.

Hand bell

Right Hanoverian glass (*left*) inscribed 'To the glorious memory of King William. Battle of the Boyne, 1690'. Jacobite glass (*right*) engraved with a picture of Bonnie Prince Charlie, the Young Pretender, and the inscription, 'Hic Vir Hic Est' – This is the man

Jacobs, Lazarus and Isaac. Lazarus Jacobs was in business as a glass cutter in Bristol in 1771, and died in 1796. His son, Isaac, styled himself 'Glass Manufacturer to His Majesty' (George III). Specimens of dark-blue glass with gilt decoration are recorded with the written mark in gold.

Among other pieces, Isaac Jacobs made distinctive blue glass decanters (*q.v.*) Michael Edkins was em-

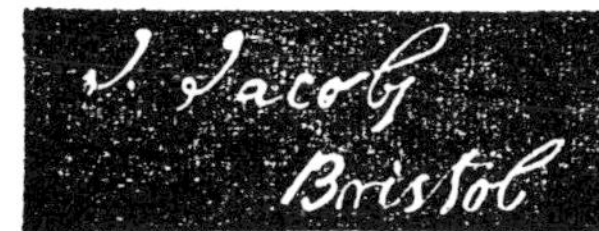

ployed by the Jacobs between 1785 and 1787, and it is not improbable that he did work for them like the gilding on these decanters.

An advertisement of 1806 referred to: '. . . Specimens of the Dessert set, which I. Jacobs had the honour of sending to her Majesty in burnished Gold, upon Royal purple colored Glass to be seen at his Manufactory, where several Dessert sets of the same kind are now completed from Fifteen Guineas per set to any amount.'

Jean, A. Originally a potter, but during the 1880s a glass maker in Paris. A small group of audacious and highly original individual pieces are known from his hand.

Jugs. In Ireland were made in large numbers in the nineteenth century. At first they were tall and narrow on a hollow foot, or, more usually, short and wide, thus giving a more shapely field for cutting in diamonds, flutes, leaf designs, prisms, and so on. These at first had the base ground flat; from about 1820 a flanged foot extending outwards was usual. Some jugs were free blown and engraved. In the United States the term is not used synonymously with pitcher.

Far right Claret jug of clear cut glass with silver mount made by Benjamin Smith Jr, Duke Street, Lincoln's Inn Fields, London, and hallmarked London 1841–2

English wine glasses with opaque-twist stems: *Left to right* four knopped, 1775; triple knop, 1770; double knop, 1770; swelling knop, 1775; 'Captain' wine glass, 1760; pan-topped bowl, 1770; double ogee bowl, 1760; ale glass with flared bowl, 1770

Keith, James. Newcastle crystal blower who was lured to Nöstetangen, Norway (*q.v.*) in August 1755. When Nöstetangen was shut down he went on to Hurdals Verk (*q.v.*), where he was pensioned off in 1787. He left a numerous family, and the name of Keith (Kith, Keth, and other variations) appears in the records of Norwegian and Swedish glass factories right up to the end of the nineteenth century.

Kewblas. Coloured glass over milk glass with coat of clear on top. Union Glass Works, Somerville, Massachusetts, 1890s.

Kick. The conical indentation to be found in the base of an early bottle or decanter. This was essential for proper annealing when glass makers had only limited means of toughening their vessels. Continued in small glass houses to about 1790.

Knob. *See* Finial.

Knop. A protuberance, other than a baluster, either solid or hollow, breaking the line of a drinking glass or other stem. (*a*) acorn: a tooled motif in the form of an acorn, sometimes inverted; used also as a lid finial; (*b*) angular: a rounded-edge, flattened knop, placed horizontally; (*c*) annulated: a flattened knop sandwiched between two, four, or six thinner flattened knops, each pair progressively less in size; (*d*) ball: a large, spherical motif often found immediately above a shouldered stem; (*e*) bladed: a thin, sharp-edged, flattened knop placed horizontally; (*f*) bullet: a small, spherical knop, sometimes termed the olive button; (*g*) collar: *see* merese; (*h*) cushion: a large, spherical knop flattened top and bottom; (*i*) cylinder: a knop in the form of a cylinder, often containing a tear; (*j*) drop: resembling in shape the frustum of an inverted cone, and usually placed half an inch to an inch above the foot; (*k*) merese: a sharp-edged, flattened glass button connecting bowl and stem, or between foot and stem of a stemmed vessel; (*l*) multiple: knops of a single shape repeated in a stem; (*m*) mushroom: usually associated with incurved and funnel bowls; (*n*) quatrefoil: a short knop pressed into four wings by vertical depressions, the metal being drawn out with pincers. The wings may be upright or twisted; (*o*) swelling: a slight stem protuberance containing an air tear.

Köhler, Heinrich Gottlieb. German chief engraver and general artistic manager of Nöstetangen, Norway. To judge from his style Köhler had been trained in the Silesian tradition. He came to Copenhagen in 1746, where he became court engraver. He settled at Nöstetangen from 1756–57 to 1770, after which he worked as a freelance in Christiania for a time and returned to Copenhagen about 1780, where he seems to have died soon after.

Kosta. Swedish glass manufactory, founded in 1742 and still in operation. Kosta lies in the district of Småland, and was founded by a member of the local nobility.

Kungsholm Glasbruk (1676–1815). Swedish glass manufactory founded by an Italian, Giacomo Bernadini Scapitta, in Stockholm. In 1678, however, Scapitta was exposed as an imposter and fled to England, and the factory was carried on under the administration of Swedish noblemen and leading civil servants.

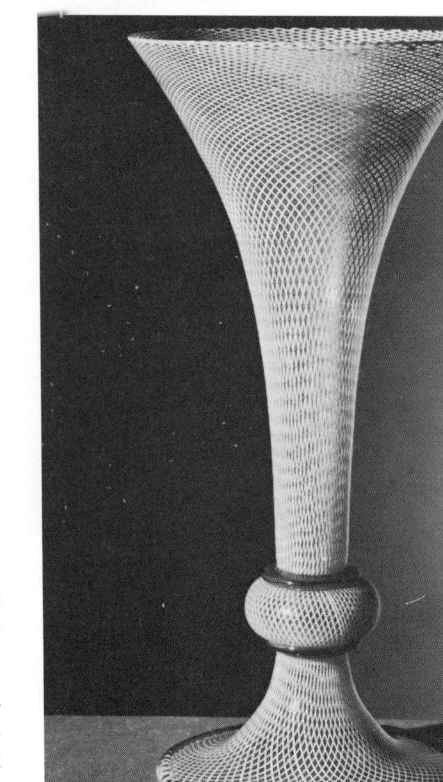

Far right Wine glass decorated in latticinio, Venetian, 16th century. Victoria & Albert Museum

Lacy glass. Type of U.S. pressed glass made *c.* 1828–40; intricate relief designs on finely stippled, lace-like background; characteristically brilliant and sparkling; mainly cup plates and salts with some dishes and plates, and more rarely, bases of lamps and candlesticks.

Lamps. Hanging oil lamps of a tubular shape with a knopped base were made in Venice in the fifteenth century if not earlier. They were occasionally decorated with enamel. Table lamps, some of fantastic form, others based on metal prototypes, were made throughout the sixteenth, seventeenth, and eighteenth centuries.

In England and America open-flame float-wick lamps were used for centuries under the name of mortars. These were small bowls of poor-quality glass, measuring 2 or 3 inches (5–8 cm) in height. Late in the seventeenth century the vessel was usually of flint glass and raised on a short stem and circular foot. From the mid-1780s it might have a thick square plinth beneath the foot.

Open-flame lamps with fixed central wicks date from the 1690s, the bowl being a small, open-topped container covered by a metal disc through which passed a short tube containing wick. These, like mortars, continued in use until the introduction of paraffin in the 1860s. Central-wick lamps were made in numerous forms, including the wine-glass lamp, peg lamp, handled lamps with stems, chamber lamps, and the lamp with a vase-shaped body from which extended three or four hollow branches. After 1820 they might be pattern moulded.

Latticinio. Familiar name for the filigree glass of Venetian origin, composed of crossing and interlacing strips of opaque and clear glass.

Lattimo. The name given to the milky-white glass made with lead, first produced at Murano, Italy, in the early sixteenth century.

Lava glass. Type of glass made in imitation of mosaic lava-ware pottery. Mount Washington Glass Works, South Boston, Massachusetts, 1878.

Lazy-susan caster. Footed caster, usually metal, with shaft terminating in handle and, at top of foot, movable circular frame with rings in which to suspend condiment containers; probably after 1830.

Lazy-susan shape. Caster (cruet) bottle formed with shoulder projecting beyond sides to rest on ring of lazy-susan caster or cruet frame.

Lead glass. Glass containing lead oxide as a flux; called flint glass (*q.v.*).

Leveillé, E. Continued the production of art glass in Eugène Rousseau's (*q.v.*) establishment in Paris from 1885 until some time after 1900. He produced massive glass, frequently crackled, with inlaid colour streaks in Rousseau tradition and a few cased-glass pieces with cut-away decoration. Leveillé's glass was eagerly bought by public collections in many countries at the Paris Exhibition in 1900 and is more frequently seen today than the real Rousseau pieces. Many of them are of fine quality and in good taste, but they lack the magnificence of Rousseau's own products. Sculptural effects such as dents, incised spirals, and twisted knots seem to have been Leveillé's personal contribution to the style.

Lily pad. Decoration formed from a superimposed layer of glass, that is, a rounded gather (pearl) attached to the bottom of a parison, pulled up over it, and tooled into the so-called lily pad; three principal types: (1) slender stem, bead-like pad; (2) wider and more valleyed stem, blobbly or small flattened pad; (3) long, curving stem, flattened ovoid pad, probably type giving rise to the term.

Vase of crackled glass with oriental scene cut out of a lacquer red casing by Leveillé, Paris, *c.* 1889. Musée des Techniques, Conservatoire National des Arts et Métiers

Lime glass. Glass containing lime; first produced by William Leighton, Birmingham, in 1864; the metal is as clear as lead glass and cheaper, but not so resonant or heavy.

Looking glasses. Documents reveal that looking glasses were made at Murano and silvered in Venice during the sixteenth century, but no examples from this period are known to survive. The earliest survivors date from the eighteenth century, when the Venetians had been surpassed by the French in the art of making such wares. Eighteenth-century mirrors were often decorated with engraved figures and set in elaborate frames of clear and coloured looking glass. Sometimes candleholders wete attached to their bases.

In England mirror plates were made by the cylinder process at Sir Robert Mansell's London glasshouse in 1625 and by the Duke of Buckingham at Vauxhall from 1663. Cast mirror plate was invented in 1688, and most early examples are wheel-engraved. From 1773 finer and larger mirror plates were in production at Ravenhead, St Helens.

Loopings or draggings. Decorative device achieved by applying threads of contrasting colours to body or parison, which are then dragged upward by a tool and rolled on marver to embed in body; used since ancient times; used at Nailsea, Birmingham, and elsewhere and in American glass on pieces of South Jersey type.

Loopings or draggings

Lucas, John Robert. John Robert Lucas was a partner in a Bristol bottle-making glassworks. In 1788 he removed to Nailsea, and there founded a factory where it is said he made articles for everyday use from common bottle glass. In 1793 Lucas acquired three partners: William Coathupe, Edward Homer, and William Chance. The latter's son, Robert Lucas Chance, founded the Spon Lane, Birmingham, glassworks, which became sufficiently prosperous to buy up the Nailsea works in 1870.

Mansell, Sir Robert. Gained control of the English glass monopoly in 1618. He reorganized the industry on a rational basis with more than four thousand workers under his authority. Charles I demanded £1,500 a year from Mansell and his associates, this being paid until the King's death in 1649, when monopolies were ended.

Marble glass. Pressed glass in variegated tints of purple and milk white made during the mid-Victorian period under the name of vitro-porcelain and now known to collectors as purple slag or marble glass. The makers were J. G. Sowerby, Gateshead, and the Kilner firm of Thornhill Lees, Wakefield. The waste or slag floating on the top of molten steel was normally tapped off into moulds and, when cold, was broken into chunks and thrown on to slag heaps. The first slag to be tapped resembled purple marbled glass. This was acquired by the two glasshouses – and probably others – suitably tempered with flint glass and pressed into ornamental ware. The Kilner firm impressed their productions with the mark of a griffin from the early 1860s. Challinor, Taylor & Co., Tarentum, Pennsylvania, made purple slag during the 1870s and 1880s.

Margariti. Imitation pearls, sometimes of prodigious size (called *paternostri*), have been made at Venice since the thirteenth century. They were exported in the fourteenth and fifteenth centuries, and when Vasco da Gama reached Calicut in 1497 he found them in use as currency there.

Marks. A considerable amount of Irish blown-moulded hollow ware – decanters, finger bowls, jugs – bears the name of the glasshouse in raised letters on a flat ring encircling the punty mark. Such marks are unknown on English glass. Nine such marks are known: Penrose Waterford; Cork Glass Co; Waterloo C° Cork; B. Edwards Belfast; Francis Collins Dublin; Mary Carter & Son Dublin; Armstrong Ormond Quay; C M C° (Charles Mulvany & Co., Dublin); J. D. Ayckbowm, Dublin. The last five were wholesale glass sellers whose sales were sufficient to warrant the manufacture of special moulds.

Marriage cups. Venetian glass cups, made to commemorate marriages, and decorated with portraits of the bride and groom, seem to have been produced only in the fifteenth and early sixteenth centuries. The most celebrated example is the so-called Barovier cup at Murano, Italy.

Marver. Polished marble slab supported by frame on which gather of metal is rolled.

Masonic flasks. *See* Flasks.

Merese. Glass wafer or button joining bowl and stem of a vessel or connecting parts of stem or shaft.

Metal. Glass either in the molten or hardened state.

Midwestern. Collector's term for U.S. glass made from about 1790 in glasshouses between the Allegheny Mountains and the Mississippi, principally the Pittsburgh–Monongehela area, Pennsylvania, Ohio, and the Wellsburg–Wheeling area, West Virginia.

Milk glass or **milk-white glass.** Opaque white glass made in imitation of Chinese porcelain, produced by mixing oxide of tin with clear glass; freeblown or, in late nineteenth century, pressed in a variety of objects.

Millefiori. The first millefiori (Italian: thousand flowers) paperweights were made in Venice. St Louis made them in 1845. In the next year they were made at Baccarat, and before long they were produced at Clichy. Also made in England at Birmingham, Stourbridge, and London.

Monteith. (1) A bowl with a scalloped rim to allow ten or twelve drinking glasses to hang by the foot into iced water for chilling. Late seventeenth century to 1790s. (2) Individual wine-glass coolers resembling finger bowls, but with one or two lips in the rim. Catalogued in early nineteenth century as 'montiffs', 1760s to 1860s.

Milk glass covered dish in design of chicken with eggs with open edge, The Atterbury Company, Pittsburgh, Pennsylvania, 1880s. New York Historical Society

Miniature inkwell and stopper, the base and stopper set with rows of millefiori canes, Stourbridge, dated 1848. Alan Tillman Antiques, London

Monteith

Mother-of-pearl or **satin glass.** This was perfected in 1880 by Thomas Webb of Stourbridge. This purely ornamental glass was produced by blowing a core of white opaque glass in a pattern mould. While the glass was still hot the outer surface was dipped into transparent coloured pot metal. A transparent crystal glazing was applied over this. After annealing, the piece was placed in a tank, where acid vapour acted on the surface and produced a satin-like finish. Several colour combinations might be applied on a single piece. Made from 1885 by the Phoenix Glass Company, Pittsburgh, Pennsylvania.

Mould-blown. *See* Blown mouldings.

Moulded glass. Glass ornamented and/or given partial or final body shape by use of a mould; applicable to pressed glass, but reserved generally for blown-moulded.

Murrini. Otherwise called mosaic glass or millefiori. *Vetri murrini* are decorated with brightly coloured discs within the glass, composed of sections of the *canna vitrea*. This process of decoration used by the Romans was rediscovered at Murano, Italy, in the sixteenth century.

Mushroom. A paperweight in which the canes are bunched together and raised in a sheaf from the bottom. Usually surrounded by a ring of lacework at the foot.

Neck rings on decanters. Seven types are found: plain-round, plain-double, plain-triple, feathered, triangular, square, and diamond-cut. The feathered ring is a double ring impressed with transverse lines. Occasionally the rings – there are usually three – do not match. Neck rings were applied by rotating the red-hot decanter and dropping a thread of hot glass around the neck. This became welded by contact, and the surplus was tapered and torn suddenly away. The whole was reheated and a tool pressed upon the ring, giving it shape and width. Joints are always faulty, and visible as hairlines having the appearance of flaws.

Newry Flint-glass Manufactory. A small glasshouse was established in the early 1780s advertising both cut and plain flint glass, and closed 1801. A new glasshouse was opened in 1824, closing in 1847.

Nöstetangen. Norwegian glass manufactory situated near Drammen. Nöstetangen was founded by royal command and under the personal patronage of King Christian VI of Denmark and Norway in 1741. When the Norwegian glass industry was reorganized in 1753 the production of tableware and ornamental glass was concentrated at Nöstetangen and German and English glass blowers were engaged. In 1777 the factory was shut down.

Nursing bottles. *See* Bottles.

Off-handblown. Freeblown.

Ogival. U.S. design expanded diamond, pattern-moulded diaper in diamond-like formation reminiscent of English nipt-diamond-waies formed by tooling applied threads; usually loosely formed diamonds above flutes.

Opalescent dewdrop (later called Hobnail). Pressed in full-size moulds; tips of nodules made of opalescent glass; made in various colours. Hobbs, Brockunier & Company, Wheeling, West Virginia, 1886.

Opaline. A word created by modern French collectors and connoisseurs to describe fine colour glass, made during the nineteenth century mainly on a basis of opal glass. The French glass makers of the period called the glass *opale* or *en couleurs opale*.

Open-top mould. *See* Dip mould.

Orrefors. Modern Swedish art-glass manufactory situated in Småland.

Overlay. *See* Cased glass.

Painted decorations. On Venetian glass these were usually carried out in enamel. For a brief period in the mid-sixteenth century, however, paintings similar to those on contemporary maiolica were applied to the backs of large plates in oil colours. Such plates must have been made solely for decorative use, since the paint was not resistant to water as it was not muffle-fired. Two methods of painting were used in England: oil or japan colours hardened by heat but not burnt in, and enamels muffle-fired and permanent. The japanned decoration is rare and pre-dates 1760, naturalistic bird, flower, and vine motifs being usual. Enamelling was at first in two styles of white: a thinly applied wash enamel and a dense full white thickly applied. Motifs between 1750 and 1780 include sporting subjects, conventional scenes, and *chinoiseries*. Armorial work in vivid colours was fashionable until the 1820s. Colours in a wider range than formerly were used from the 1830s, and included figures, ornaments, flowers, birds, landscapes, and marine views.

Nöstetangen

Panelling. Moulded contiguous round- or oval-topped arches with: (1) narrow flattened upright in bold relief, mainly eighteenth century; (2) thread-like upright and arch top, often tapering at bottom, like Haynes's 'moulded wide fluting', late eighteenth–early nineteenth century. Both often called sunken panel.

Pantin. A factory in northeast Paris, founded at La Villette in 1851 by E. S. Monot, and moved to Pantin in 1855. From the first the factory concentrated on elaborate coloured and decorated glass, and, especially between 1865 and 1900, much fine glass in a magnificent and expensive style was produced there. In 1868 Bontemps (*q.v.*) mentions that fine copies of Venetian aventurine glass was being made at Pantin. In 1878 Monot *fils* and a certain M. Stumpf joined E. S. Monot as directors of the factory, and in 1889 they seem to have taken over. By 1900 the owners were Stumpf, Touvier, Viollet & Cie.

Paperweights. The processes involved in making glass paperweights call for great skill. The final correct placing of the pattern within the clear glass calls for a high degree of craftsmanship. This is even more apparent when it is realized that the operations are performed with the glass in a molten, or near-molten, state. Only a general description of the complicated manufacturing process is given here; details vary with the different types of paperweights, and no doubt each factory had its secrets.

The canes to make the pattern are formed by several methods. In one, lengths of coloured glass are heated until they adhere together and form a solid mass. Alternatively, a rod of a chosen colour is dipped repeatedly in molten glass of other colours until a pattern is completed. In both cases, while still hot, the newly made varicoloured rod is drawn out until the section of it is of the required diameter.

The necessary canes are selected and sufficient thin slices cut from them and polished. The pattern is arranged on a piece of thin glass, a mould is placed over this, and molten glass is poured in. The half-formed paperweight is picked up on a pontil, dipped into molten glass, and shaped to the form of the finished article. Fruit and other subjects are made of coloured glass, but the process followed for making the paperweight is similar.

Great care is needed to maintain the temperature of the components throughout the manufacture, or cracking will result. The final operation is annealing: a slow cooling. When it is cold the mark of the pontil is removed by grinding.

In America the successful sale of French paperweights imported into the United States induced manufacturers there to imitate them with some success. Notably the factories of Deeming Jarves at Sandwich, Cape Cod, opened in 1825, and at East Cambridge and South Boston, in Massachusetts, opened in 1818 and in 1837. Not only were the French designs copied but original models evolved.

French paperweights. *Top* Baccarat; *left* St Louis; *right* Clichy. Alan Tillman Antiques, London

French paperweights were copied widely in England, but it is doubtful whether any were made until quite a few years after the first appearance of the French ones. The glass-making centres of Stourbridge in Worcester and Bristol in Somerset both attempted to produce imitations of the imported article. The Whitefriars Glassworks in London and George Bacchus and Sons in Birmingham also made paperweights in the style of those from Baccarat and elsewhere.

The shapes of the English glass paperweights are usually different from the French ones, and the colour of the glass and of the canes embedded in it is seldom comparable.

The encrusted cameos (sulphides) made by Apsley Pellatt (1791–1863) are, however, a notable exception, and are difficult to distinguish in many cases from the French.

Three glassworks in France were concerned in the production of glass paperweights. They were the *Compagnie des Cristalleries de Baccarat* and the *Compagnie des Verreries et Cristalleries de St Louis*, both situated in the Vosges to the southeast of Paris; and the Clichy glassworks, which stood in the suburb of Clichy in Paris itself.

All three manufactories produced similar work. But there is enough evidence from specimens presented by the manufacturers to the French museums on which to base identifications, in most cases, as to exactly which factory was responsible for certain noticeable differences. Dated paperweights from the Baccarat factory are known for the years 1846–9. The St Louis weights start a year earlier, and also continue until 1849. The dates are often on millefiori weights, are not usually noticeable, and are never set centrally. Any paperweight in which the date is in the dead centre should be regarded with great suspicion.

Parison. Inflated, unformed gather of metal.

Part-size mould. Small two-piece hinged mould; long handle usually attached to each piece to open and close mould; used to impress design on gather.

Pattern-moulded. Term designating glass moulded for decorative pattern or design only, in dip and part-size moulds and expanded; coined to differentiate glass so patterned from that blown in full-size moulds.

Peach glass or **peachblow.** Peach-like tints shading from cream to rose, red to yellow, or blue to pink, made in imitation of a Chinese porcelain. Made by the New England Glass Company, U.S.A., in 1885, but became very popular when Hobbs, Brockunier & Company of Wheeling brought out a copy of the Mary J. Morgan collection Chinese porcelain vase which brought $18,000 at auction in 1886. Their product was a cased glass with milk-white lining, whereas the Peachblow made by the New England Glass Company and by the Mount Washington Glassworks was the same composition throughout.

Peacock eye. Pressed lacy-glass motif similar to stylized horn of plenty in pressed-pattern ware (*see* Horn of plenty); 'eye' usually a large circular dot within beaded ring and 'horn' either stippled or fine-diamonded; called also peacock feather.

Peasant glass. *See* Stiegel type (2).

Pedestal foot. *See* Foot (U.S. 1, *f*).

Petalled foot. *See* Foot (U.S. 1, *d*).

Picot. Tooled decorative device, usually forming crest of wavy decoration or swagging, found mainly on U.S. South Jersey Type glass; sometimes called aborted or vestigal lily pad.

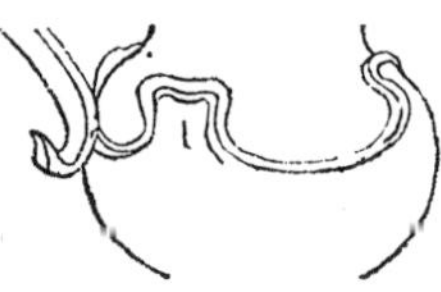

Piece mould. Part-size and full-size moulds composed of two or more pieces (leaves); necessary for motifs and designs with crossed lines, such as diamond diapering. *See* Part-size and Full-size.

Pillar moulding. A variant of the blown-moulded process by which ornamental domestic ware could be made cheaply was patented in 1835, by Thomas Green, who gave it the name of Roman pillar moulding. The exterior was corrugated vertically or swirled, while the interior remained smooth. This patent was licensed to others, and a price list issued by Apsley Pellatt illustrates several examples. This was made in colour, too.

Pillar moulding in the United States is associated mainly with a Midwestern commercial glass from the Pittsburgh and Wheeling areas and has widely spaced pillars.

Pillar rib. (1) Pronounced relief, pillar-moulded, rib; (2) wide, short, heavy ribs forming band in a geometric pattern.

Pinched trailing. English term; *see* Quilling.

Pitkin. *See* Flasks (7).

Pocket bottle. *See* Bottles.

Pomona glass. Stippled body achieved with acid combined with unstippled portion stained a straw colour; frequently decorated with an applied garland of flowers; New England Glass Company, U.S.A., 1884.

Pontil. *See* Punty.

Pontil mark. *See* Punty mark.

Portrait flasks. Group of historical flasks bearing

portraits of public figures and heroes None of those which have been identified seems to be earlier than the 1830s, and many of them fall in the third quarter of the century.

Pot-pourri urn. A speciality of Gjövik Verk, Norway, in the early nineteenth century. Their development can be followed in the diagrams. They were mostly made in cobalt blue, the shades of which differ from an ink-green tinge to a soft deep blue. Many of them have borders in white. They were also made in opaque white glass made from bone ash, with dark borders.

Pressed glass. Glass pressed manually or mechanically in moulds; molten glass is dropped into a patterned mould, a plunger is rammed into the mould, forcing glass into all parts of the mould and impressing the pattern on it; plunger or core has a smooth surface so that inside of piece being pressed is smooth in contrast to blown-moulded or blown-three-mould glass. Method said to have originated in the United States. It is wrongly called 'Sandwich Glass' from the famous factory at Sandwich, Massachusetts, where it was first produced on a large commercial scale. By 1829 at least six eastern and four Midwestern glasshouses were producing pressed glass. In England mechanical presses for making hollow ware by a single process were installed in glasshouses from 1833. Specialized workers known as 'pinchers' used hand-operated presses for making square feet in a piece with a pedestal or double stem. Target and mushroom decanter stoppers were also made in this way.

Pressed-pattern ware. Pressed-glass sets for table, bar, etc.; articles matching in pattern; earliest, about 1840.

Prunts. Applied blobs of glass tooled or moulded into various forms.

Punties. Concave shaping cut on the surfaces of a paperweight. Overlay paperweights are often cut with punties.

Punty or pontil. A long iron rod attached to one end of blown glass during the finishing processes after removal from the blowpipe.

Punty mark or pontil mark. A scar left on blown glass when the punty is broken off. Generally found on the base of a glass. Ground and polished into a smooth depression, usually from about 1750, and invariably so on fine glass from about 1780. Seemingly less frequently ground off and polished on early U.S. ordinary wares than on British.

Purled ornament. All-over diaper moulding with small round or oval compartments.

Purple slag. *See* Marble glass.

Quilling. Ribbon of glass applied and pinched into pleats. U.S. term, synonymous with English pinched trailing.

Ravenscroft, George (1618–81). Was granted a patent for manufacturing flint glass (No. 176, 16 May 1674), the entire output of which the Glass-sellers' Company undertook to market, provided he worked to their standard designs. Ravenscroft introduced lead oxide to his glass in the autumn of 1675.

Reliquaries. In Venetian glass sometimes in the form of covered cups, but more usually simple cylindrical vessels on knopped baluster stems, made of clear glass in the sixteenth century and later periods. Also made by Apsley Pellatt, London, during second quarter of the nineteenth century.

Reticello (literally network). The name usually given to glass decorated with a mesh of opaque white threads beneath its surface, otherwise called *vetro di trina* or lace glass. It was first made in Venice in the fifteenth century and in 1547 Henry VIII's 'Glasse Housse' boasted a specimen of it. Although the process was soon developed to produce many-coloured filigree glass (*q.v.*), *reticello* has held its popularity into the present century.

Prunt

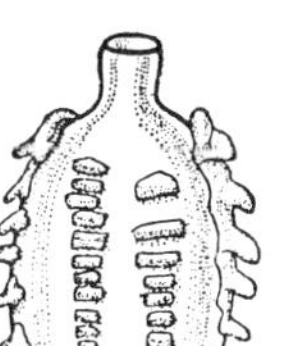

Quilling

Above Goblet with applied raspberry prunts and raven's head seal on stem, made by the Savoy Glasshouse of George Ravenscroft, *c.* 1676–8. Corning Museum of Glass

Left Two handled casket in rose-tinted glass decorated with a net pattern of white threads (*vetro di trina*)

Far left Opalescent pressed glass sauce dish, American, 19th century. Victoria & Albert Museum

Reticulated. A moulded pattern in diamond-like formation; also called expanded diamond.
Ribbing. Used when ridged design's wider unit is convex; gadroon ribbing. *See* Gadroon (3).
Rib or **diamond moulding.** Straight or twisted lines forming diamonds or other patterns impressed upon the surface of a bowl.
Ricketts glassworks. Wine bottles with seals are sometimes found bearing the mark shown here, that is to say in raised letters round the base. The name seal bearing the words *Saml. Archer* is from a bottle made in the first quarter of the nineteenth century.

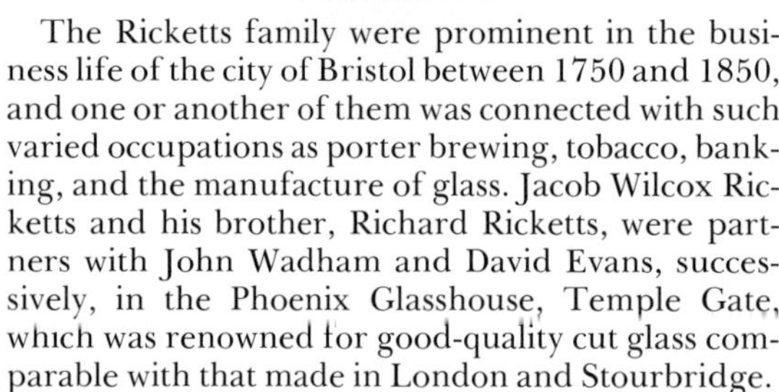

The Ricketts family were prominent in the business life of the city of Bristol between 1750 and 1850, and one or another of them was connected with such varied occupations as porter brewing, tobacco, banking, and the manufacture of glass. Jacob Wilcox Ricketts and his brother, Richard Ricketts, were partners with John Wadham and David Evans, successively, in the Phoenix Glasshouse, Temple Gate, which was renowned for good-quality cut glass comparable with that made in London and Stourbridge.

In 1811 Jacob Wilcox Ricketts and his third son, Henry, together with two partners, purchased a glassworks known as the Soapboilers' Glasshouse, in Cheese Lane, St Philip's, Bristol. They continued to make cut glass at the Phoenix factory, and made bottles in their newly acquired premises, both trading under the name of Henry Ricketts and Co. After various changes in the structure of the business it was closed finally in 1923.

Rigaree marks. Applied bands of glass tooled in parallel vertical lines to form tiny contiguous ribs; produced by the edge of small metal wheel.
Rims. (1) Folded: edge finish of foot or bowl top, sheared edge folded back forming double wall; called also welted; (2) galleried, nineteenth-century bowl-top finish; flaring rim having short, straight side and flattened plane at right angles to body, thus forming cover support; (3) gauffered, on vases and occasionally pitchers; flaring with wide-scallop edge; called also ruffled; mainly nineteenth century; (4) sheared or plain, excess glass cut away evenly and edge smoothed by reheating.
Rolling pins. Were originally made as salt containers during the Napoleonic wars when the salt tax was thirty times greater than the cost of the salt itself, which was sold by the bottle. The first of these rollers, produced in about 1800, were of thick bottle glass, the open end being tightly stoppered. Each end was provided with a solid knob so that it could be safely hung in a dry place. By 1820 salt bottles were being made of coloured glass, purple, blue, mottled, and

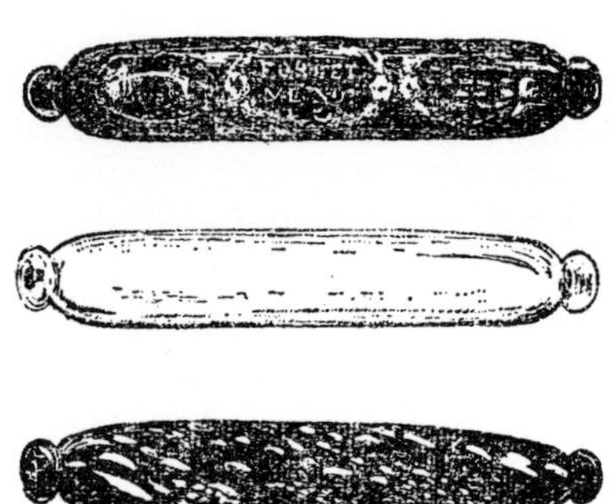

striped. The cold glass tube weighted with salt proved an excellent rolling pin for pastry. Hanging conspicuously on the kitchen wall, the rolling pin became a field for homely decoration, such as a text painted on a background of opaque white glass, and during the 1820s it tended to lose its purely utilitarian purpose and became regarded as a lucky mascot, its filling chosen to suit the occasion. Gilded, painted, and enamelled, they were inscribed with mottoes and good wishes, Biblical quotations, name of the recipient, and a date; others were decorated with seafaring subjects. Some were ornamented with the sharpened end of a specially hardened steel tool, the design being portrayed by means of small, closely spaced dots. Decorations included hounds chasing a hare, ploughing, and paddle steamers.

They were made at the glass-making centres of Bristol, Birmingham, Sunderland, and Stourbridge: reproductions have been made in tens of thousands since 1910.
Romer, 1675–1825. A drinking vessel usually of pale-green glass, consisting of a bowl more or less spherical with a slice taken off the top. The bowl opened into a hollow, cylindrical stem studded with prunts and supported by a hollow, conical foot.
Rousseau, Eugène. The greatest French glass artist of the nineteenth century. He began as a dealer in decorative ceramics and appears to have devoted himself to glass from *c.* 1875. His ideas were realized by Appert Frères, one of the most progressive and well-equipped factories in Paris at the time.

Rousseau's glasses are usually made of a heavy transparent metal, tinted into a light champagne colour. Decoration is achieved through cutting, engraving, or enamel painting, and cased and flushed glass, with cut-away patterns, can also be found. The shapes are borrowed from historical sources, German or Italian Renaissance pottery or French Baroque ornament. The Japanese fashion seems to have made a great impression on Rousseau. He reproduced Japanese ornaments and imitated the ceramic technique of running glazes, and seems even to have absorbed the subtler sides of the Japanese message, the preference for simple outlines, and the dislike of rigid symmetry and hard precision. His most famous creation is massive, sometimes crackled glass with streaks of colours, preferably purples and reds, embedded between transparent casings. The effect is obtained by the use of metal oxides. The grandeur of the execution, the boldness of the colour, and the originality and taste in the décor place Rousseau's glass in a class apart among contemporary art glass.

His works were sold in his shop at 74 boulevard Haussmann. A few are signed on the base with his name and address. At the Paris Exhibitions in 1878

Four salts and a caddy of blue glass, Irish, *c.* 1785–1800

and 1884 Rousseau's glass was highly admired, and his techniques were imitated, more or less successfully, in France and in other countries. In 1885 he handed over his establishment to E. Leveillé (*q.v.*), who carried on his work.

Rummer, 1760–1850. Short-stemmed drinking glass with capacious thinly blown ovoid bowl and

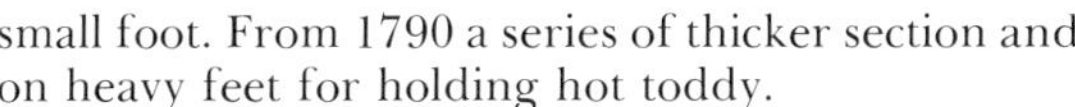

small foot. From 1790 a series of thicker section and on heavy feet for holding hot toddy.

St Louis, Cristalleries de. Together with Baccarat the greatest large-scale producer of fine glass in France all through the period. Founded in 1767 as Verrerie Royale de St Louis. In 1781 the first French production of lead crystal of the English type was started there, and from 1782 it was carried on on a commercial basis. The archives of the factory were to a large extent destroyed during World War II, and its history until 1834 is obscure. From 1839 the factory is known to have made excellent coloured glass, the earliest dated examples being from 1844. The colour products of the middle of the century are distinguished by the brightness of their colour and the simplicity and grace of the shapes. Fresh and unpompous and astoundingly modern in appearance, they are among the finest examples of glass made anywhere at the time.

All through the nineteenth century Cristalleries de St Louis were the main producer of fine table glass in France.

Romer

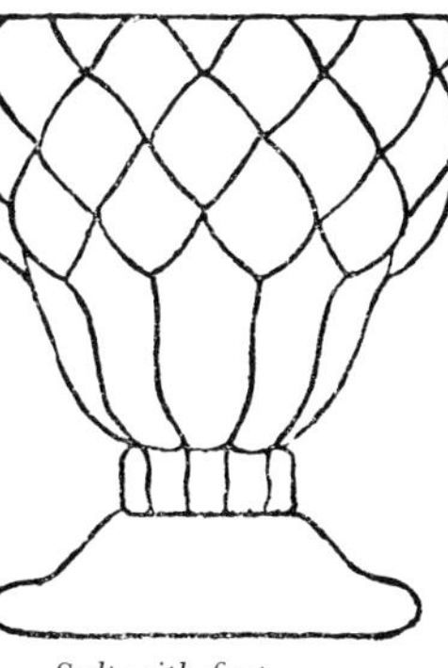
Salt with foot

Salts with feet. Small vessel with double ogee bowls, flattened knops, and applied circular feet usually slightly sloping and sometimes scalloped. 1790s to 1850s in English flint glass.

Scalloped foot. *See* Foot (U.S.).

Scalloping. A rim outline formed by a series of semicircles with edges ground sharply until about 1750. Castellated rims date from about 1770.

Scent bottles. In England scent bottles made of coloured and of opaque white glass are not uncommon. Some of the latter can be attributed to Bristol manufactories because of their creamy colour and their complete opacity, and because the painting on them is related to that on more important specimens of white glass. Of coloured glass scent bottles, it is not possible to say more than that they were probably made at Bristol. Many of the surviving examples resemble closely in their decoration the work to be seen on watch cases and other articles known to have been made in London. As it is known that glass 'smelling bottles' were being made there as early as 1752, perhaps a London origin was common to them all. Scent bottles continued to be made in the prevailing types of glass until the 1830s, when, for half a century, they were made in huge numbers and every conceivable shape and colour.

Sealed glasses. Early English flint-glass tableware to which were applied small glass discs impressed with the maker's mark: raven's head, George Ravenscroft, September 1675–1681; the King's arms, Henry Holden, glass maker to the King from 1683; Lion and coronet, Duke of Buckingham.

Seals. The circular glass seals were almost certainly impressed with an original intaglio made of brass. This was made either by a professional engraver working on his own behalf or, in the case of a glass-works specializing in sealed bottles, by one on the staff of the manufactory. No name of any craftsman connected with this particular branch of the art of die sinking has been recorded, and the makers of these seals, as most of the makers of more elaborate desk seals, have remained anonymous.

Glass bottle seals fall into three categories, whether they bear dates or not, and may be conveniently classified as: armorial, name or initial, and 'others', the last including merchant's marks, Masonic signs, and the names of houses.

Seeds. Minute air bubbles in the metal, indication that the glasshouse could not raise furnace temperature high enough to eliminate all air bubbles trapped among the raw materials.

Set-in and set-over covers. *See* Covers.

Shaft. Usually applied to section between socket or font and base of candlestick or lamp; in blown glass, applied forms similar to stems; in early pressed glass, in two sections – one with base and one with socket, joined by a merese; in later pressed glass, in one with socket and base.

Shakers. Term usually preceded by salt or pepper; casters.

Sheared lip. Plain; *see* Rims (4).

Skånska Glasbruket, 1691–1762. Swedish glass manufactory situated in Northern Scania. Skånska Glasbruket was founded by a certain Göran Adlersten, an enterprising civil servant of the locality. The factory began by making purely utilitarian glass, but in 1715 production of decorative glass was taken up. It lasted until 1762, when the works were destroyed by fire.

South Jersey tradition. Tradition of glass blowing and decorating presumed to have had its American beginnings in Wistar's and other South Jersey houses; *see* South Jersey type.

South Jersey types. Generic term for individual pieces blown from bottle and window glass in natural colours, occasionally artificial, fashioned by free blowing and manipulation, plain and decorated by glass applied to itself and tooled, very rarely pattern-moulded; first associated with the Wistar's eighteenth-century glassworks, southern Jersey, U.S.A.; then later houses in the area; now known to have been blown in most Eastern bottle- and window-glass houses into the late nineteenth century; called folk art in American glass, largely because of individual rendering and centuries-old traditional techniques in blowing and decorating include the lily pad, prunts, quilling, swagging, picots, bird finials, threading, and crimping.

Spangled glass. Molten glass rolled over flakes of mica or metal particles which fused when heated. Made by Hobbs, Brockunier & Company, Wheeling, West Virginia, 1883; called 'Vasa Murrhina'; blue flecked with silver and gold and other combinations are known. Made also in England and Bohemia.

Stems.

Dates apply to English glass.

Air-twist, 1740–65. (*a*) Single-twist air spirals in a drawn stem formed by the extension of air bubbles: multiple spirals throughout the period, from 1745 two or four corkscrews; not until about 1750 were threads of uniform thickness and spaced regularly; (*b*) single-twist in a three-piece glass: 1740–65 the shank cut from long lengths made by extension of air bubbles; from 1750 spirals made by a mould process, filaments finely drawn and coiled with precision in some thirty variations; (*c*) compound-twist in three-piece glass: 1760–5 in a dozen variations.

Baluster, 1685–1760. Stem consisting of a pure baluster form which might be inverted: also a baluster associated with various knopped motifs; (*a*) 1685–1725: heavy inverted baluster with solid bowl base and interior bowl depth almost invariably less than stem length; (*b*) 1700–25: simple knop such as angular, annulated, cushioned, or drop knop, with or without a baluster; from 1710 acorn, cylinder, or mushroom knops; from 1715 true baluster alone or with various knops and a pair of balusters placed head to head between a pair of knops; (*c*) 1725–65: light balusters, true or inverted, supporting bowls with thin bases; illustrated on trade cards of the 1760s. Between 1725 and 1740 the stem and collar baluster in which a merese separated bowl from stem.

Two wine glasses with colour-twist stems, English, *c.* 1765

Colour twist, 1755–75. Spirals of glass, opaque or transparent, singly or in combination: commonly in blue, green, or ruby, less frequently in red, yellow, sapphire, black, and greyish blue.

Composite. Built up of two or more parts welded together; found on U.S. drinking vessels, compotes, candlesticks, occasionally on covered sweetmeat dishes, sugar bowls, pitchers.

Compound-twist, 1760–1800. A pair of air or enamel spiral formations, one within the other: a central spiral or (in enamel) a closely knotted central cable with another formation spiralling around it. In straight stems only.

Drawn, from 1682. A plain knopped or baluster stem drawn directly from a gathering of metal at the base of the bowl; (*a*) to 1725 in large, heavy forms; (*b*) 1720–45 with waisted thick-based bowl; (*c*) from 1735 the standard pattern was a straw shank drawn from a trumpet-shaped bowl; by 1770 had degenerated into a thin-stemmed tavern glass.

Facet-cut, *c.* 1748–1800. Almost invariably drawn stems; (*a*) elongated diamond facets, two or three times longer than width with angles of 120 degrees and 60 degrees: found throughout the period; (*b*) 1755–80, elongated hexagonal facets; (*c*) 1760–80, shouldered and centrally knopped stems; (*d*) 1760–75, scale facets; (*e*) 1770–1800, facets cut deeper than formerly; (*f*) 1790–1800, stems shorter than formerly.

Hollow, early 1760s to late 1780s. Stem in the form of a hollow cylinder, sometimes, though rarely, knopped.

Incised, 1678–1780. Alternating ridges and grooves spiralling around the stem surface; (*a*) 1678–1720, incised balusters; (*b*) 1740–60, closely spaced medium to coarse spirals with almost imperceptible reduction of stem diameter at centre; (*c*) 1660–1780, finer, more uniform, incisions on stem of unvarying diameter.

Knopped, 1700–55. Stem composed of four to six knops, none sufficiently large to dominate its fellows; (*a*) to 1740 heavy knops, well-modelled until 1735; (*b*) from 1740 light knops.

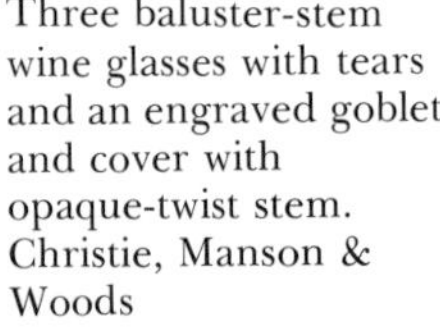

Three baluster-stem wine glasses with tears and an engraved goblet and cover with opaque-twist stem. Christie, Manson & Woods

Mercury-twist, 1745–65. Air twists of exceptionally large diameter spiralling down the centre of a stem in close coils, or a pair of corkscrew threads.

Mixed-twist, 1750–70. A combination of air twist and opaque-white twist in a single stem.

Moulded pedestal, 1705–85. Known also as Silesian and shouldered stem; on good-quality ware until about 1730; (*a*) 1705–20, four-sided moulded stem, never collared at the base; by 1710 the shoulders were being shaped in the form of four arches; (*b*) 1720–40, sides moulded with deep, vertical reeds; (*c*) 1727–35, six-sided pedestal; (*d*) 1730–50, eight-sided pedestal lacking precision and definition; (*e*) 1750–80, thin, coarse-ribbed versions of the earlier types; (*f*) 1765–85, well-designed pedestal stem with four or six sides enriched with cutting.

Opaque-twist, mid-1740s to end of eighteenth century. Spirals of dense-textured white enamel, varying from fine hairs to bread solid tapes; single or compound in more than a hundred variations; (*a*) straight stem with single twist; (*b*) with shoulder or central knop and single twist, usually multiple spiral; (*c*) straight stem with compound twist – the most common type – from 1760; (*d*) with knops in various positions, shoulder, central, base, or any two or all three, with compound twist, from 1760.

Opaque twist stems: *Left to right* large goblet with a double series opaque-twist stem consisting of two massive spiral cords, 1760; miniature sample glass with round funnel bowl on a triple series opaque-twist stem, 1770; engraved goblet with single series multi-ply opaque-twist stem, 1770; Lynn wine glass, ogee bowl on a double series opaque-twist stem, 1765; double-ended Gin measure with two ogee bowls joined by a double-series opaque-twist section, 1770; Mead glass with double-series opaque-twist stem, 1760

Rib-twist. *See* Incised.

Silesian. *See* Moulded Pedestal.

Single-twist, late 1740s to early 1800s. One formation of air, enamel, or coloured threads spiralling around a clear glass centre, or a pair of reciprocal spirals.

Straight, plain, 1725 to nineteenth century. On three-piece glasses; after 1748 tended to be thinner than formerly.

Stuck shank. A stem made from a separate gather of metal welded to the base of the bowl.

Vertical flute cutting, mid-1780s–1800. (*a*) To 1790, stem fluted above and below a central diamond-cut knop; (*b*) 1790–1800, long, straight flutes from foot to bowl, either notched on alternate angles, horizontally grooved, or sliced.

Wormed. *See* Air-twist.

Wrythen. *See* Incised.

Step. A flattened glass button connecting the stem of a rummer with its foot.

Stiegel tradition. Tradition of glass blowing and decorating by use of pattern moulds, presumed to have had its American beginnings in Stiegel's second Manheim glassworks (1769–74). *See* Stiegel type (3).

Stiegel type. Term applied to main types of ware produced in Stiegel's Manheim, Pennsylvania, glass-houses, *c.* 1765–74. (1) Engraved (shallow copper wheel) and (2) enamelled glass like common Continental commercial wares of mid-eighteenth–early nineteenth century, today called peasant glass in Europe. (3) Pattern-moulded glass, usually flint glass, like the British ware produced in the early nineteenth century; coloured (mainly blues, greens, and amethysts) and colourless. *See also* Diamond daisy and Daisy-in-hexagon.

Stiegel-type salt. *See* Salts with feet.

Stippling. Minute raised dots forming the background in lacy glass, glitter-producing device never used in glass making until made possible by mechanical pressing; an earmark of lacy glass (*q.v.*).

Stones. Red and black specks within the fabric of early flint glass, the result of imperfect fusion between oxide of lead and silica.

Strap handle. *See* Handles.

Straw shank. *See* Stems, drawn.

Striae. Apparent undulating markings within the metal, perfectly vitrified and transparent, show the metal to be of uneven composition because insufficiently molten before working.

String course or **string rim.** The raised band near the top of the neck of a bottle, which provided a grip under which the string for securing a cork or other cover might be fastened. In seventeenth-century bottles this took the form of a single band of glass about a quarter of an inch below the orifice, and it remains a feature of subsequent bottles.

Strömbergshyttan. Modern Swedish art-glass manufactory situated in Småland.

Stuck shank. *See* Stems.

Sugar basins. Have a boldly concave outline and a flat base, and are for the most part boldly cut with diamond patterns or moulded with thick gadroons.

Sulphides. Known contemporaneously as *crystallo ceramie* and by some collectors as sulphides or glass-encrusted cameos. The process was patented (No. 4424, 1819) by Apsley Pellatt, London. A pressed bas relief of unglazed white stoneware was embedded in

Sulphide. One of a pair of dessert plates, blown and cut, encrusted opaque white cameo with stag's head crest, attributed to Falcon Glass Works of Apsley Pellatt, *c.* 1821. Corning Museum of Glass

flawless flint glass, assuming the glowing loveliness of silver. Many of these reliefs were embedded in paperweights, but others enriched tableware and jewlry. Most commonly the sulphide was a profile portrait of a contemporary celebrity: profile portraits were also made to the commission of sitters now unknown.

Earlier crude examples, greyish in tint, had been made in Bohemia and France: later the French glass-houses at Baccarat, St Louis, and Clichy copied Pellatt's invention with success.

Sunken panel. *See* Panelling.

Superimposed decoration. Any decoration or device fashioned by tooling layer of glass formed from a pearl. *See* Lily pad.

Swagging. Superimposed layer tooled into wavy formation, usually crested by a picot.

Swirl. Familiar name for a paperweight composed of coloured canes radiating spirally from the top.

Swirled ribbing. Pattern-moulded design formed by twisting vertical ribs impressed in a gather inserted in ribbed or fluted dip mould; English, wrythen ornamentation.

Swords, sceptres, crowns, and hats. In England examples of these articles made from glass are occasionally seen. Their original purpose is made clear by the following paragraph from the *Daily Post*, 14 November 1738: 'Bristol, Nov. 11. – Yesterday the Prince and Princess of Wales paid their promised visit to this City. . . . The Companies of the City made a magnificent appearance in their formalities, marching two by two, preceding the Corporation and the Royal Guests. The Company of Glassmen went first dressed in white Holland shorts on horseback, some with swords, others with crowns and sceptres in their hands, made of glass.' It should be pointed out, however, that few (if any) of the surviving examples of these friggers are of such an early date as 1738, as these items continued to be made and used for a long time afterwards.

Glass hats were made for similar purposes to the above; it is said that they were very uncomfortable to wear.

Table centres. These usually consisted of numerous glass figures, and were made in the eighteenth century. An unusually large, and very fine example, in the museum at Murano, Italy, is in the form of a model garden with balustrades, urns, hedges, and a central fountain, all made of glass. Birmingham glassmen during the mid-nineteenth century made large numbers of lavishly designed table centres, particularly George Bacchus & Sons.

Tale glass. A second-quality metal taken from the top of the pot, and sold more cheaply than the lower, finer metal.

Tears. Bubbles of air enclosed within the metal for decorative purposes: first appeared in stems; from 1715 to about 1760 clusters or spherical or comma-shaped tears appeared in bowl base, knop, and finial.

Thread circuit. A thin trail of applied glass encircling a bowl rim or decorating the neck of a vessel.

Three-piece glasses. Bowl, stem, and foot made separately and welded together.

Tiffany glass. A type of U.S. art glass; made by Louis Comfort Tiffany (1848–1933) in New York in the late 1890s; many pieces marked *Favrile*. Process fused various colours by heat, then exposed the piece to fumes of vaporized metals; pieces were handblown in fanciful forms; spinning and twisting during blowing process produced wavy lines suggestive of leaves, waves, or peacock feathers; bluish green and gold, light mother-of-pearl, red, and other more unusual colours; is characteristically iridescent with a satiny finish in imitation of ancient glass.

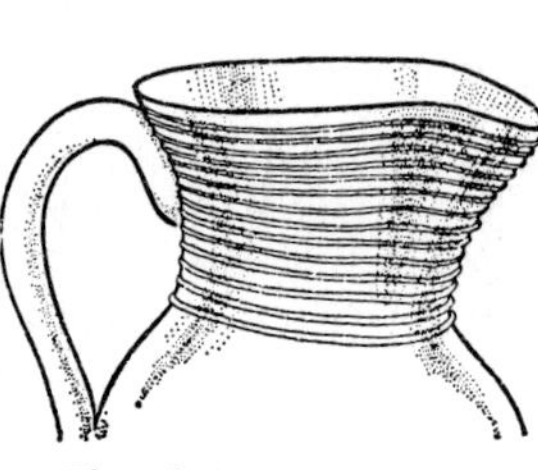

Thread circuit

Tiffany wisteria lamp of leaded marble glass with verdigris, *c.* 1900

Tint. A residual colour tinge inherent in the ingredients from which the metal is composed.

Toasting glass. A flute of fine metal with tall stem drawn to a diameter of one-eighth to one-quarter of an inch.

Toastmaster's glass. A thick bowl designed to magnify its capacity, on a tall stem. Short, deceptive glasses, known as sham drams, were used by tavern keepers, 1775–1850.

Tobacco pipes. Were made at all the glass centres in England, at first with small bowls and solid stems of transparent colour often enriched with spiralling threads of coloured or opaque white enamel. They lack the affluent air of the later pipes blown from high-quality glass. From the mid-1840s their bowls followed the designs of the new pipe bowls of porcelain with long, slender mouthpieces. Others may be found imitating early Victorian briar pipes. Measurements range from 10 to 25 inches (25.4–63.5 cm) overall with occasional giants more than a yard (91.4 cm) long. They were in considerable demand as wall decorations for small homes.

The most common form has a large bowl with a flared and welted rim, the mouthpiece with its curved stem widening as it approaches the bowl, but reduced to a very narrow tube at the bowl junction. These are to be found in all combinations of colour, *latticinio* work in milk white and pink being common. Red glass was popular and is found in qualities varying from brilliant unflawed ruby with opaque horizontal lines on bowl and bobbin stem to poor-quality colour with striations and other flaws in the glass.

Toddy lifter. A pipette with bulbous or decanter-shaped body for lifting hot toddy from bowl to drinking glass, *c.* 1800–40.

Tortoiseshell. Pale brownish-amber glass with

darker splotches; another glass made in imitation of other ware which was popular in the late nineteenth century; attributed to the Sandwich Glass Company, U.S.A.

Trailed ornament. Looped threads of glass applied to the surface of a bowl or foot.

Trailing, pinched. Applied bands of glass pinched into wavy formation.

Tumblers. Were exported from Murano in fine glass and made in most European countries in poor quality throughout the seventeenth century. By the end of the century they were made in flint glass with vertical sides and a slightly rounded base with a medium kick. From about 1710 they might be lightly touched with shallow-cut diamond facets or large diamonds and triangles. Pint, half-pint, and quarter-pint tumblers were advertised.

Not until the early 1740s were glass tumblers designed with outward-sloping sides and a height about double the base diameter. The heavy-based waisted tumbler had come into use. From the late 1750s they were made without a kick, and all-over shallow cutting became slightly deeper and a wider variety of motifs used. Finger fluting encircling the lower half of tumblers dates from the same period, at first flat and broad, little more than the surface of the glass being removed. As the century progressed flutes were cut deeper and in varying widths, and between 1790 and 1820 the crests might be notched. Deep relief cutting is found on heavy tumblers from 1790, some fifty varieties and combinations being found after 1805.

Twisted ribbing. Swirled ribs or flutes; on solid canes, used as stems, sometimes handles; English, incised or reeded, *see* Stems.

Two-piece glasses. Stem drawn in a piece from the bowl and a foot added.

Uranium glass. First produced, from the metallic element uranium, in 1857 by Lloyd and Summerfield, Birmingham, using the first gas-regenerating furnace to be built. Early uranium glass was green; it was later made in shades ranging from rose pink to pale yellow and known as Burmese glass. It can have a dull or glossy finish.

Venetian glass. Thinly blown soda glass, worked at a low temperature, cooling quickly, and requiring great speed of manipulation. Lacks the brilliance and toughness of flint glass.

Vermicular collar. A wavy trail of glass encircling a stem or decanter neck.

Verzelini, Giacomo (1522–1606). Verzelini acquired the Crutched Friars Glasshouse, London, on the death of Jean Carré, whose chief assistant he was. In 1575 he was appointed glass maker to Elizabeth I and granted a monopoly to make 'Venetian glass'.

Vinter, Villas. Danish or Norwegian born glass engraver at Nöstetangen, Norway. He was assistant to Köhler, who appears to have taught him the craft. He worked as a freelance after 1777, and signed engravings from his hand are known as late as 1797.

Walking sticks. Glass walking sticks were made in England during the nineteenth century, and some of these no doubt came from the glassworks at Bristol and Nailsea. They were of various types, and were made solid or hollow. The former were occasionally made with lengths of twisted coloured glass within the clear glass stick. The hollow ones were often filled with coloured sweets and are sometimes to be found with their contents intact.

Decanter of clear glass, engraved on the wheel, Waterford, dated 1782. Victoria & Albert Museum

Waterford. The earliest record of flint-glass making at Waterford was discovered by Westropp in *The Dublin Journal*, 1729: 'a glasshouse near Waterford now producing all sorts of flint glass, double and single . . . sold at reasonable rates by Joseph Harris at Waterford, merchant'. This glasshouse was at Gurteens, three miles from the city, and operated until 1739, producing a negligible quantity of glass.

The now celebrated Waterford glasshouse started production in 1784, financed with a capital of £10,000 by George and William Penrose, merchants. The Irish Parliament, however, granted the Penroses a subsidy to cover the expense of building and equipping their glasshouse. As works manager they employed John Hill, member of a family operating the important Coalbournhill Glasshouse near Stourbridge. In evidence given before a committee examining commercial relations between Great Britain and Ireland in 1785, John Blades, a leading cut-glass manufacturer in London, stated that, 'Mr Hill, a great manufacturer of Stourbridge, has lately gone to Waterford, and has taken the best set of Workmen he could get in the County of Worcester.' There is no doubt that the Penroses installed a furance of the Perrott type costing more than £3,000, such as were already in use at Stourbridge. The Penroses sold flint glass on a ready-money basis only.

The Penrose glasshouse was bought in 1799 by Ramsay, Gatchell, and Barcroft, who built a new factory in Old Tan Yard, advertising the old premises to be let. It is to be assumed that the most modern innovations were included in the new furnace, and that cutting was carried out by means of annealed cast-iron tools, harder and longer wearing than anything formerly available. With these were produced the lavishly decorated cut glass now inevitably associated with Waterford. Not until 1817 was a steam-driven cutting machine installed.

Gatchell had become sole proprietor by 1811, and with successive partners the firm remained in the family. At an exhibition in Dublin, 1850, George Gatchell displayed table glass 'all of opaque blue, and white or crystal'. At the Great Exhibition, 1851, he exhibited a magnificent 'etagere or ornamental centre for a banqueting table, consisting of forty pieces of cut glass, so fitted to each other as to require no connecting sockets of other material; quart and pint decanters cut in hollow prisms. Centre vase or bowl on detached tripod stand. Vases and covers. Designed and executed at the Waterford Glass Works.' This was Gatchell's swansong; his final effort to compete with England was a failure, and he closed the glasshouse later in the same year.

Few collectors realize that Waterford imported glass from England for merchanting purposes; Belfast and Cork were also supplied with Waterford glass.

Waterford blue. *See* Blue tint.

Decanter, dip-moulded, blown and cut, with three applied collars and pressed wheel stopper, Irish, *c.* 1800. Corning Museum of Glass

Waterloo Glasshouse Company, Cork. Established in 1815 by Daniel Foley, a glass and china seller of Hanover Street, who set up as a specialist in extensive table services in cut glass for military messes, particularly for regiments occupying France. By the end of 1816 he employed about a hundred men and women, many experienced workers deserting from the Cork Glasshouse Company under the lure of higher wages. On Christmas Eve, 1816, an editorial in the *Cork Overseer* recorded that 'Foley's workmen are well selected, from whose superior skill the most beautiful glass will shortly make its appearance to dazzle the eyes of the public, and to outshine those of any other competitor. He is to treat his men at Christmas with a whole roasted ox and everything adequate. They have a new band of music with glass instruments with bassoon serpents, horns, trumpets, etc, and they have a glass pleasure boat, a cot and a glass set which when seen will astonish the world.' Glass trumpets were made for sale. A steam engine was installed to operate the cutting wheels and other machinery, thus drastically reducing costs.

Geoffrey O'Connell was taken into partnership during 1825, the firm operating as Foley and O'Connell, Waterloo Glassworks Company. They advertised that they had introduced a new annealing process which enabled them to guarantee their flint glass to withstand hot water without breaking. The excise duty was too heavy a burden, and in mid-1830 the firm ceased operating. Fifteen months or so later it was reopened by O'Connell, who introduced up-to-date methods of blown moulding and advertised that he had 'restored one hundred families to employment'. An advertisement in the *Cork Comet* four months later announced that the Waterloo Glassworks continued to enjoy military patronage.

The venture could not compete with English prices, however, and in 1835 he was made bankrupt owing to his failure to pay excise duties. The *Cork Constitution* contained an auctioneer's advertisement regarding the sale of plant and stock 'of splendid cut and plain glass at the Waterloo Glassworks until the entire splendid stock is disposed of, consisting of rich decanters, jugs, salad bowls, celery and pickle glasses, dessert plates and dishes, tumblers and wine-glasses of every description, hall and staircase globes, side lights, water crafts and tumblers'.

Welted rim. *See* Rims.

Whimsey. U.S. term used for odd or unusual pieces, such as hats, slippers, buttonhooks, made by individual workmen for themselves or their families; or the adaptation of a conventional form to some odd or unusual shape or use.

Wine-glass coolers, 1750s–1860s. *See* Monteiths.

Witch balls and **reflecting globes.** From late in the seventeenth century glass makers blew short-necked spherical bottles of clear flint glass or thick, dark bottle glass. Their shape was inspired by reflecting globes, but they were intended as containers for holy water. Such a bottle was hung in the living room or elsewhere as protection against the malign influence of witches. Eventually it became an emblem of good luck.

Late in the eighteenth century spherical bottles of green and blue glass were made for this purpose, sometimes inscribed with scriptural texts in gold. Early in the nineteenth century Nailsea made coloured balls in a variety of tints, such as green, crimson, gold, and deep blue. Soon these were enlivened with various forms of decoration: some are spotted; some show either opaque-white or air-thread spirals in the thickness of the glass. Another type has four or more loops of coloured glass festooning the surface of the ball. From about 1830 transfer pictures might be applied to the interior surface. As a background to these the interior was coated white, marbled with various vivid colours. Many were made without any opening and intended as jug covers. These colourful balls were made from about 1780 until 1865.

Glass spheres, lustred to resemble shining silver and capable of mirroring a whole room in miniature, were originally Continental products of fragile soda glass, but from about 1690 English glassmen made them in flint glass. Their interior surfaces were silvered with a preparation composed of two parts bismuth, one part lead, one part tin, and four parts mercury. The lead, tin, and bismuth were melted together and the mercury added when the mixture was almost cold. It was then poured into the sphere by means of a paper funnel reaching almost to the bottom. By slowly rotating the ball, the liquid amalgam was spread in a thin film over the glass, to which it adhered.

In these early balls there was considerable distortion in the reflection. In 1843 a method was discovered of coating the interior surface with real silver. Reflecting globes have a slightly yellow tint. An improved method was patented in 1848 and 'so great was their power of reflection that the entire details of a large apartment are caught upon them with surprising minuteness and clearness of definition and in amusing perspective'. Such glass balls were made in a wide range of metallic hues and in sizes varying from 3 to 30 inches (7.6–76 cm). Originally termed watch balls, this name became corrupted to witch balls.

Writhing. Surface twisting or swirled ribbing or fluting on bowl or stem.

Yard-of-ale. A yard-of-ale is a drinking glass measuring some 3 feet (91.4 cm) or so in length. There is a record of one dating from as early as the year 1685, when John Evelyn noted in his Diary on 10 February: 'Being sent to by the Sheriff of the County to appeare, and assist in proclayming the King [James II], I went the next day to Bromely [Bromley, Kent], where I met the Sheriff and the Commander of the Kentish Troop, with an appearance, I suppose, of above 500 horse, and innumerable people, two of his Majesty's trumpets and a Serjeant with other officers, who having drawn up the horse in a large field neere the towne, march'd thence, with swords drawne, to the market-place, where making a ring, after sound of trumpets and silence made, the High Sheriff read the proclaiming titles to his bailiffe, who repeated them aloud, and then after many shouts of the people, his Majesty's health being drunk in a flint glasse of a yard long, by the Sheriff, Commander, Officers and cheife Gentlemen, they all dispers'd, and I return'd.' From which it would appear that, at any rate during the late seventeenth century, such feats of glass making and of drinking were reserved for special public occasions.

Yard-of-ale

Considering their fragile nature, it is not surprising that surviving yards-of-ale are seldom above a century old. The greater number of such survivors are not straightforward drinking vessels, but trick glasses. In them the flared mouth tapers at length to a bulb at the foot, which ensures that the drinker cannot rest the vessel, and once started the glass must be drained completely or the contents will be spilled. The trick about these glasses is that when the liquid has been nearly all consumed and the glass is raised above the horizontal to finish the remainder, the air trapped in the bulb by the action of lifting the glass forces the residuum violently into the face of the unlucky victim.

Quite a number of the glasses must have been produced in the glasshouses of Bristol and Nailsea, but here again it is not possible to distinguish them from others that were made elsewhere.

Zirat Fladske. *See* Decanters, Scandinavian.

JEWELRY

Medieval jewelry is less well known than classical Greek and Roman work, since the custom of burying valuables with their owner was discontinued in the Christian era. Few jewels survived the ravages of time. Their very nature made them easily convertible into ready cash at moments of financial stress, when precious stones were broken out of settings consigned to the melting pot. Literary descriptions and pictorial records, such as illuminations and monumental effigies, help at times to show how jewelry was applied to contemporary costume. Fortunately, much medieval goldwork survived in the sanctuary of church treasures, forming part of liturgical objects. There are reliquaries, portable altars, and altar crosses studded with jewels, statues of saints and of the Virgin wearing jewelled crowns and pectoral ornaments.

Some techniques, known from antiquity, continued in use throughout the Middle Ages. Among these were filigree and granulation work, consisting of small pellets of gold surrounding stones in high box settings, often antique gems: cameos and intaglios. Stones were rarely cut in medieval times, but usually left in their natural *cabochon* shape, which is oval; they were always polished and backed with metal foil to intensify and reflect colour. Among the personal jewelry of this early period are rings, earrings, brooches, necklaces, and pendants, often invested with symbolic, magic, protective, or religious significance. The wearing of images of patron saints was particularly popular.

During the Renaissance, pagan and Christian art begin to harmonize, and therewith the history of religious jewelry comes to an end. The magic aspect, however, was not forgotten, and the belief in specific virtues of precious stones remained as strong as ever. Hence the custom of mounting toad stones or dragons' teeth in rings, serpents' tongues and fragments of narwhal horn in pendants. Great importance was attributed to their inherent prophylactic qualities, which legends supported. Gradually, during the early sixteenth century the jeweller emerged from the goldsmiths' guild, an organization which had previously directed his efforts to the service of the Church. This emancipation coincided with the development of a prosperous bourgeoisie and the raising of the respectable matron and housewife to a socially important figure, who extended her patronage to the goldsmith. Henceforth jewelry becomes an integral part of costume, dependent upon changing fashions, which, in turn, reflect the taste and aspirations of a splendour-loving society. Painter-engravers began to design pattern books for jewellers, and it is well to remember that many Renaissance painters were sons or pupils of goldsmiths, Verrocchio, Holbein, and Dürer among them. For the first time in the history of jewel making the influence of individual artists was felt.

Far right The Cheapside Hoard, contents of a London jeweller's shop that had probably been buried before the fire of 1666, discovered in the River Thames. London Museum

Hans Holbein the Younger was foremost among those who determined the new pictorial style of Renaissance jewelry. In his drawings and engravings for the goldsmith, and in portraits of ladies and gentlemen, richly attired with rings, necklaces, and pendants of latest design, Holbein contributed much towards the creation of a new type of jewelry, centred around the human figure. Scrollwork cartouches supersede the once ubiquitous Gothic thistle leaf, tracery, and pinnacle, while the sparkle of precious stones rivals with bright enamel colours and opalescent pearls.

The hat badge or *enseigne*, as it was then called, is among the most original creations of the period. Contemporary portraits by Bartolomeo Veneto of Italy, François Clouet of France, and Hans Holbein of Germany and England illustrate how men of fashion wore these badges in their berets. Originally derived from the medieval pilgrim sign, the hat badge revealed the wearer's personality in the choice of subject matter. Humanist interests, based upon classical education, account for the noticeable preference for antique cameos, mounted in contemporary setting, with loops provided for attachment to the hat. Mythological themes, with incidents from the happy lives and adventures of Greek gods on earth, abound. Religious subjects become rare, they usually include the figure of a patron saint, to confirm the bond between wearer and protector. Some hat badges have frames of black-and-white *champlevé* enamel arabesques of a kind believed to have been first introduced in Venice by Oriental goldsmiths.

Finger rings of the Renaissance period show great variety. The signet ring, related to the hat badge inasmuch as it also defines the owner's personality, often contains an antique or contemporary intaglio, a personal cipher, device, or initials, which served as seal. Purely ornamental rings are richly enamelled, the centre stone flat or table cut, supported by caryatid figures extending to either side of the band. Some rings are provided with secret compartments, to serve specific purposes, such as the possible concealing of poison, a practice always exaggerated in novels. *Memento mori*, or mourning rings, reveal a white-enamelled skeleton beneath the hinged cover of a black-enamelled coffin, and are usually inscribed with the name and date of the deceased. Other types include the fede ring, also used for weddings, made of a band terminating in joined hands, which often hold a heart or a precious stone. Religious rings, engraved with a crucifix or the instruments of the Passion of Christ, are never quite absent, but they are at times outnumbered by those invoking magic through cabalistic signs, or those set with a toad stone, actually the tooth of a fossil, worn as a charm against evil. Towards the end of the century, especially in England, rings and pendants containing a portrait miniature gained great popularity.

The Renaissance pendant, in all its magnificence, is the most representative jewel of the period. Goldsmith and painter-engraver combine efforts as never before to lend pictorial qualities to the jewel and to introduce new story-telling elements of individual interest. Human figures, enamelled in white, form the centre of elaborate architectural and ornamental stage settings, composed of several layers of pierced and enamelled goldwork, held together by diminutive bolts and nuts. The reverse of the pendants is usually decorated with arabesques and grotesques in translucent or opaque enamel, following the designs of well-known engravers, such as Androuet Ducerceau, Daniel Mignot, Étienne Delaune, and Theodore de Bry. Favourite mythological themes were Diana with her hounds, Venus and Cupid, the Judgment of Paris, and Jupiter pursuing amorous adventures. Symbolic figures include Charity, Faith and Fortitude, and the Pelican in her Piety, while the most popular religious subjects were the Virgin Mary or St George. Baroque pearls form the bodies of birds and animals, or of more fantastic creatures: dragons, hippo-camps, mermen and mermaids, tritons and nereids. Other pendants, from the region of the Adriatic Sea, are shaped as ships with full sails, outlined by strings of tiny seed pearls; these last continued to be made until the nineteenth century. Yet another kind, worn on a heavy chain, incorporated coins, medals, or a badge, their weighty character in keeping with the dignity of office.

Pendants combining the useful with the ornamental were worn at the end of long belts. They include small prayerbooks in jewelled bindings (girdle books), and pomanders, or containers for spices and scent, opening into compartments like the sections of an orange. Occasionally toothpicks were worn suspended around the neck as jewels, as were also various charms.

Renaissance necklaces are of extravagant length, encircling the neck repeatedly and reaching down to the waist. Composed of pierced and enamelled links with precious stones, frequently interspersed with pearls, these chains form an integral part of costume, and are, more often than not, matched by earrings, bracelets, belts, and buttons. A central pendant, attached to necklace and dress, stresses the contrast between the static qualities of a pictorial jewel and the flexibility of chain links. Their basic design is formed by conventional scrollwork, which continues in countless variations until floral motifs take their place during the seventeenth century. The dainty enamelled chains, found at Cheapside in London, exhibited at the British and the London Museums, give an excellent example of this new style, composed as they are of daisies and other soft-petalled blossoms. Their lightness of touch and texture brings to mind the garden poems of Robert Herrick, whose father was court jeweller to Elizabeth I.

With the invention of the rose diamond cut in Holland shortly after 1640 the whole character of jewelry begins to change. The interest shifts from the pictorial to a display of precious stones in settings designed to complement them. Preceded by the table cut, which gave the diamond a mirror-like surface, and, more rarely, by the sharply-pointed stone which could serve for engraving and incising, the rose cut allowed the all-over faceting of diamonds, a method by which their fire and sparkle increased through additional reflection of light. From then on the value of most jewels becomes dependent upon the quality of diamonds and precious stones rather than the finer points of enamel and goldsmiths' work, which tradition connected only too readily with the name of the most representative goldsmith of the Renaissance, Benvenuto Cellini.

Jewels of the seventeenth century reveal a growing taste for precious stones rather than for elaborate goldwork, with special emphasis upon the diamond. Opaque enamel painted on white ground begins to supersede the translucent kind on gold, characteristic of earlier pieces. Such painted enamel is found on all types of jewellers' work, including watch and miniature cases and mounts for vessels carved of semi-precious stones. Jewels of this period are now exceedingly rare, and fine seventeenth-century enamelling is most likely to be found on watch cases and lockets; outstanding are those painted by the Toutin family at Blois and the Huet family of Geneva, both active during the second half of the seventeenth century. If one turns over one of these enamelled jewels to examine the back it will probably reveal a miniature-like application of enamel on white ground, forming floral patterns in natural colours, especially tulips and fritillaries, a fashion originating in Holland.

The most characteristic jewels of the late seventeenth and early eighteenth centuries were two types of brooch, worn at the centre of the bodice; they are to be seen in countless portraits of the period, in particular those of the Dutch school. The first was of girandole design, with a large centre stone around which smaller stones were grouped, and with three large pendant pearls. The second type consisted of a large openwork 'Sévigné' bow, from which hung a cross usually with one or more intervening links between. Settings, of silver or gold, were finely carved to resemble foliage. The diamond became increasingly fashionable and was soon set almost exclusively in silver, gold being reserved for coloured stones, particularly the emerald, which Spanish jewellers incorporated so attractively in brooches, pendants, and pendant crosses of openwork design. Silver was greatly favoured for the setting of diamonds; being colourless, it was less obtrusive than the brighter

Far left Pendant in the form of a turkey, enamelled gold, ruby and baroque pearl, German, *c.* 1580. S. J. Phillips, London

Right: *top left* oval portrait of Charles II, perhaps by des Granges, the reverse enamelled with the Royal Cyphon in white on turquoise ground, with drop pearl pendant. *Top centre* jewelled gold pendant set with a portrait of Charles I, *c.* 1670. *Top right* oval gold pendant set with a profile portrait of Charles I within ten rose diamonds, *c.* 1680. *Centre left* miniature portrait of William III, gold silver-gilt frame, *c.* 1710. *Centre* silver pendant jewel set with a portrait of Charles II, the border pierced with foliage and set with rose diamonds and other stones, pearl below, *c.* 1680. *Centre right* oval silver medallion of Charles I, chased in high relief by Thomas Rawlins. *Bottom left* oval grisaille portrait of Charles I in gold slide frame. *Bottom centre* oval enamel miniature of Charles II, perhaps an early work of Boit after Dixon, silver-gilt frame with engraved foliage border. *Bottom right* oval gold pendant containing a portrait of Charles I, the case in high relief with twist border embellished with white enamel. All English. Christie, Manson & Woods

Ring of rubies and diamonds in the shape of a bow, English, *c.* 1760

gold. Finally, with the introduction of the brilliant cut early in the eighteenth century, the effectiveness of the stone could be exploited to fullest advantage. The rose diamond, with its twenty-four or, at the most, thirty-six facets, seemed subdued and dull in comparison with the brilliant, which has fifty-eight facets. Today rose-diamond jewelry in original eighteenth-century settings, however, outnumbers by far any similar ornaments enriched by brilliants. The reason is that rose diamonds were no longer considered worth resetting, whereas brilliants have been transferred to jewels of later design.

Floral designs remained popular throughout the century, at first set in diamonds and of rather heavy and dignified character. About the middle of the century coloured stones returned to favour, composed as flower sprays, in which the settings are almost invisible. Until then each stone had its individual place within the composition, but now smaller stones, grouped together, formed the design, while the metal setting was concealed as completely as possible. Rococo decoration, though most successfully applied to snuffboxes, étuis, and all the favourite toys of the lady of fashion, had little effect upon jewelry design beyond lending impetus to the already apparent trend towards lighter designs.

Flower sprays composed entirely of diamonds continued to be made, with little variation of design, during the nineteenth century. However, the setting of precious stones underwent certain changes. Until about the close of the eighteenth century all stones were enclosed in collets or boxes, foiled at the back to intensify their colour. During the nineteenth century settings were left open at the back and the stone held in position by means of claws. Thus more light could surround the stone, though excluding at once all possibilities of improving their colour artificially. Therefore it would be true to state that most stones now used are of finer quality. During the nineteenth century the back of the open silver setting of diamonds was lined with a thin layer of gold. These open settings were adopted for all except 'peasant' jewelry, and their presence or absence is a fairly decisive indication of date.

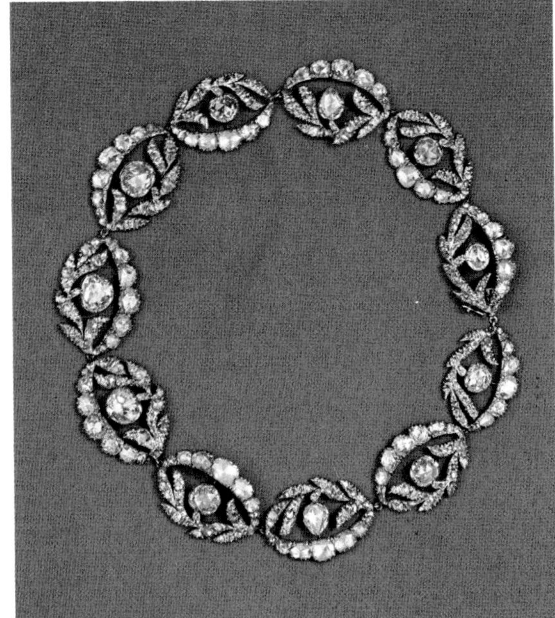

Right Diamond necklace in a stylized flower and leaf motif, English, *c.* 1760

Far right Brooch of pink topazes and diamonds in the shape of a flower, English, *c.* 1780

Far left Pendant of diamonds and turquoises in the shape of a cross, English, *c.* 1780

Left Pendant and chain in silver, the pendant partly gilt, set with emeralds and semi-precious stones, English, late 19th century

Standards of workmanship remained high until the end of the eighteenth century; though the decoration of the reverse of jewels with engraving or enamelling was discontinued. Cheap jewelry was not by any means unknown; glass pastes were used instead of stones, crystal or marcasite instead of diamonds. Porcelain, Wedgwood ware, and cut steel all enjoyed periods of popularity as inexpensive substitutes for precious stones. But about the end of the eighteenth century production of jewelry by mechanical means began, with the inevitable consequence of a decline in standards of execution and design. Cheap fancy stones were set in mounts of thin stamped gold and wire filigree. The results are flashy, but owing to the thinness of the metal used the jewels are extremely flimsy. This same criticism may be made of much of the jewelry of the nineteenth century, of which vast quantities survive. Such was the enthusiasm of the manufacturers for experiment and variety that it is difficult to define its character succinctly. The eclecticism which is so marked a feature of Victorian art is just as strongly manifested in its jewelry. There are borrowings from all the expected historical sources and from many less likely ones as well; to the Romanesque, Gothic, and Renaissance style which formed the main sources of Victorian art we may add Indian and North African designs, copied from objects shown at the international exhibitions, and Egyptian, Assyrian, Etruscan, and Scythian designs derived from objects discovered in the course of nineteenth-century excavations. Outstanding among nineteenth-century jewellers was a small group of Italian craftsmen who produced work of the highest quality and technical perfection, though strongly leaning upon ancient designs. These include Castellani, a Roman jeweller who rediscovered the Etruscan secret of applying minute grains of gold to a gold base; Carlo Giuliano, who emigrated from Naples to London; and his two sons, who carried on the business in London towards the end of the century. Even as late as the nineteenth century some of the traditional forms of jewelry were still being made in Europe: and it is these which will probably appeal most to the collector.

Left Victorian mourning jewelry: brooch and snake ring, *c.* 1850

Glossary

Aigrette. Jewel supporting a feather or imitating it in form, worn in hair or cap since the end of the sixteenth century.

Cabochon. Stone of rounded, natural form, polished but not cut.

Chatelaine. Useful ornament of silver, pinchbeck, or gilt metal, supporting watches, watch keys, seals, thimble cases, and other étuis, worn hanging from a belt.

Diamond cutting. During the Renaissance diamonds were either cut to a fine point like a pyramid, or given a flat surface, called table or mirror cut. The rose cut, invented in Holland about 1640, gives the stone up to twenty-four facets all over its surface, whereas the brilliant cut, introduced later during that century, is applied to deeper stones, ending in points at front and back and provided with up to fifty-eight facets, visible in open-claw settings.

Right A collection of gold and enamel brooches and pendants by Giuliano and Castellani, early 19th century. Christie, Manson & Woods

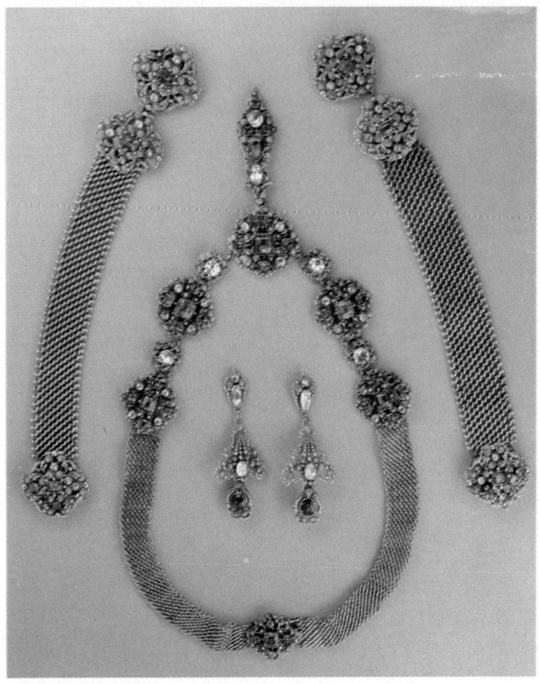

Gold filigree, emerald and aquamarine suite, English, *c.* 1820. S. J. Phillips, London

Enamel. Powdered glass, fused on to a metal base by heat, applied in opaque or translucent colours in various technical processes. During the Renaissance *champlevé* enamel was popular, consisting of a metal (gold) base, hollowed out to receive the enamel, which formed the design. Enamel *en ronde bosse* covers figures modelled in the round, usually in white. Painted enamel, as the name indicates, is enamel painted upon enamelled ground (copper), much like a miniature, usually with 'counter enamel', a thin coating of enamel at the back of the metal recipient, to prevent excessive expanding and shrinkage after the firing process.

Filigree. Gold wire or pellets, applied to a gold base in ornamental pattern.

Gems. Cut or engraved stones. Intaglios, for sealing, are usually cut with the design in reverse, to be seen in the impression. Cameos are cut in relief, the varied strata of stone or shell forming part of the design. Subjects, in great part derived from the antique, include ideal portraits and mythological scenes, the stones preferred for gem cutting include semi-precious stones, agates and cornelians for preference, and a variety of shells.

Girandole. Clasp of alternating ribbon and bow design in openwork, set with stones.

Hair jewelry. Memorial jewels, containing plaited hair in lockets, clasps, or rings, usually together with the initials and dates of the defunct, in black and white enamel.

Marcasite. Iron pyrites, faceted in the manner of precious stones, made by mechanical process.

Paste. Coloured glass, used to reproduce precious stones since Roman times, usually with coloured foil placed beneath in order to enhance their appearance. Colourless paste is practically a modern invention, worn as a substitute rather than an imitation of precious stones.

Pinchbeck. Alloy of copper and zinc, sometimes washed with gold, named after the inventor Christopher Pinchbeck, a well-known watchmaker, active in London about the mid-eighteenth century.

Sévigné bow. Graduated bow brooch, worn in front of the bodice.

Strass. Paste called after the inventor, Joseph Strass, a Viennese, who came to Paris as a jeweller in the middle of the eighteenth century. It contains a high percentage of lead, hence more closely resembling a natural diamond when faceted.

Tassies. Replicas of intaglios or glass paste impressions, named after James Tassie, who settled in London in 1766, where he became famous for these cast gems.

Engraved Gems of the Eighteenth Century

Greek and Roman engraved gems, originally intended for use as seals but later as objects of jewelry, began to attract the attention of connoisseurs in the Renaissance period. Pope Paul II was among the first collectors to acquire them, and appears to have been the first martyr to their fashion, for he is said to have died from a chill caught by exposing too many cold gems on his fingers. The taste for gems grew, however, and early in the sixteenth century the art of engraving precious and semi-precious stones was revived by numerous Italian craftsmen, many of whom produced work which is difficult to distinguish from the antique. These craftsmen also carved cameo portraits which won great popularity. By the early eighteenth century the fashion for both antique and modern gems had become a rage, and no collection of *virtù* was considered complete without its cabinet of them.

Two main types of gem were produced in the first half of the eighteenth century: more or less fraudulent copies after antique specimens, and frankly modern works which included both portraits and historical scenes. With the growth of the neoclassical movement in the 1750s, gem engravers began to imitate the style of antique specimens without basing their designs on particular prototypes. This occasioned a revival in the art of gem engraving, led by Edward Burch and Nathaniel Marchant in England, and by the Pichler family at Rome. Students of Greek and Roman art tend to regard the gems produced by these artists in the antique style as fakes. This is misguided, for they are no more fraudulent than the sculptures of Canova and the paintings of Mengs and J. L. David, who, like the engravers, sought to revive the true classical taste. Indeed, at the end of the century engravers were copying the statues of Canova even as their Greek forerunners had represented the works of Phidias and Praxitiles. As evidence of their good faith, the most notable engravers usually signed their work, inscribing their names, however barbaric, in Greek letters to avoid introducing a jarring note.

The practice of faking antique gems persisted throughout the century, however, and if their creators inscribed them, they naturally did so with fictitious Greek signatures. These works were generally copies of genuine antiques with slight, but revealing, variations. The vast number that survive provides some indication of the extent of the fashion for gems in the eighteenth century. Many of them were by artists who also produced original work. J. L.

Natter, for example, blandly remarked: 'I am not ashamed to own that I continue to make copies (with Greek inscriptions and masters' names) at all times when I receive orders: but I defy the whole world to prove that I have ever sold one for antique.' Dealers were less scrupulous than Natter claimed to be, and employed engravers to produce fakes. According to Nollekens, the notorious Thomas Jenkins, an English art dealer in Rome, 'followed the trade of supplying the foreign visitors with intaglios and cameos made by his own people, that he kept in a part of the ruins of the Coliseum, fitted up for 'em to work in slyly by themselves. I saw 'em at work though, and Jenkins gave a whole handful of 'em to me to say nothing about the matter to anybody else but myself. Bless your heart! he sold 'em as fast as they made 'em.' Many and various were the devices employed for imparting an ageless patina to modern gems. The smooth surfaces of intaglios were carefully scratched and their edges chipped. Cameos were stuffed down the necks of turkey fowls to acquire, in their gizzards, the dull, chalky appearance characteristic of antiques.

The majority of eighteenth-century gems are engraved with classical subjects. But portrait cameos and intaglios were also popular throughout the century, while a few engravers, notably Jacques Guay, carved modern historical, allegorical, and sentimental subjects. These gems follow the stylistic development from late baroque to rococo and finally neo-classicism. The best are those carved in the second half of the century showing their subjects in antique guise.

TECHNICAL TERMS AND MATERIALS

There are two types of engraved gem: the intaglio, on which the design is sunk into the stone, and the cameo, on which it is shown in relief. The intaglio may be used as a seal, though it was not necessarily intended for that purpose. The material normally used for gems of both types was a semi-precious stone, sardonyx, cornelian, agate, or onyx. Sometimes precious stones were used, including emeralds, amethysts, and even diamonds, though these were, of course, much more difficult to work. Normally the method of engraving was by a wheel, or minute copper disc, driven in the manner of a lathe moistened with olive oil mixed with emery and diamond dust. A diamond-point engraver, such as was used in classical times, was employed by a few artists.

Shell cameos were carved from the shells of various exotic crustaceans. The shells normally used were those of the *Cassis rufa* found in East Indian seas, the *Cassis cornuta* found off Madagascar, and the *Cassis tuberca* and *Strombus gigas* of the West Indies. The subjects carved are similar to those on hard-stone cameos, but the workmanship is rarely as fine. Shell cameos are hardly ever signed.

REPRODUCTIONS

Two methods were used in the eighteenth century for reproducing antique and modern gems. Most numerous are the casts or impressions of intaglios known as sulphurs, made from a composition of sulphur and wax, and showing the engraving in reverse. Many such sulphurs were taken from antique gems, but towards the end of the century engravers began to sell casts of their own work. Nathaniel Marchant, for instance, published a catalogue to accompany a collection of casts from his gems. Sulphurs were often arranged in boxes in the shape of books or gem cabinets. The other type of reproduction was made of a vitreous substance and known as a paste. Unlike the sulphur, the paste reproduced the shape of the original gem and was, in fact, taken from a cast. Most famous of these pastes, which were made according to various receipts, are those produced by James and William Tassie (see biographical notes below). Readers of Keats's letters will recall the poet's several references to Tassie's gems, which he used as seals and gave to his sister Fanny. To provide cameo portraits of celebrities the Tassies sometimes took their pastes from wax models instead of engraved gems.

SOME NOTABLE GEM ENGRAVERS OF THE EIGHTEENTH CENTURY

Amastini, Angelo (1754–1815). Born at Fossombrone and went to Rome before 1778. A fine agate cameo by him is in a private collection in Rome. His son, Nicolo Amastini (1780–1851), was also a gem engraver and is represented by a cameo in the Metropolitan Museum, New York.

Barier, François-Jules (1680–1746). Born at Laval in France and became the official gem engraver to Louis XV. His works, which included portraits of the Marchese Rangoni and Fontenelle, agate vases, and minute figures in cornelian, won the praise of Voltaire.

Becker, Philipp Christoph (1674–1743). Born at Coblenz and worked in Vienna as a medallist and gem engraver. According to Mariette, he was the best engraver of gems in Germany. His works include a portrait of Charles VI (*c.* 1711) and numerous seals cut for German princes.

Berini, Antonio (*c.* 1770–1830). Born at Rome and studied under Giovanni Pichler. In about 1802 he appears to have moved to Milan, where he cut several gems, including a notorious cameo of Napoleon (by an unhappy chance a red vein in the stone encircled the Emperor's neck, and Berini was consequently imprisoned as a suspected assassin). Most of his gems are of classical subjects, but at Windsor Castle there is an intaglio of St George and the dragon signed by him.

Burch, Edward (1730–1814). One of the most famous English gem engravers, began his career as a wherryman. In 1796 he entered the Royal Academy Schools, became an A.R.A. in 1770 and an R.A. in 1771. In 1788 he was appointed medal engraver to the King and Duke of York. He engraved numerous gems and also worked as a wax modeller.

Cades, Alessandro (1734–1809). A Roman gem engraver who worked in a style similar to that of Giovanni Pichler. He is mentioned in Goethe's biography of Hackert. His gems are signed with his full name, sometimes in Greek characters.

Calandrelli, Giovanni (1784–1852). A Roman who moved in 1832 to Berlin. He executed some gems of religious subjects but was notorious as a faker. Many of his works were bought, as antiques, by the Berlin Museum.

Costanzi, Giovanni (1674–1754). A gem engraver who worked in Rome and Naples. Two of his sons followed his craft: Tommaso (1700–47) and Carlo (1703–81). Carlo became famous for his work on precious stones, especially diamonds. He carved a diamond intaglio of Leda for the King of Portugal, a sapphire cameo of Maria Theresa, and an emerald

Head of a girl, sardonyx intaglio, by Edward Burch. British Museum

Cupid and Psyche, onyx cameo, by Alessandro or Tommaso Cades. British Museum

cameo of Benedict XIV, which took him two and a half years. In less precious and hard materials he executed portrait cameos of several grand tourists, including Sir John Frederick, J. Hamilton, and Lord Duncannon. Most of his works were, however, of antique subjects.

Dorsch, Johann Christoph (1676–1732). Said to have inundated Germany with cameo and intaglio portraits of Popes, Emperors, Kings of France, etc., and unfaithful copies of famous antique gems. His daughter, Suzan, was also a gem engraver and carved a copy of 'Solon's' head of Medusa, now in the British Museum.

Ghinghi or **Ginghaio, Francesco** (1689–1766). Born at Florence and became gem engraver first to Gian Gastone dei Medici and then Francesco III of Lorraine. In 1737 he moved to Naples. Many of his works are in the Uffizi, Florence, including a cameo of Gian Gastone dei Medici.

Above Head of a boy, onyx cameo, by Giuseppe Girometti. British Museum

Far right Bacchus and a nymph, sardonyx intaglio, by Nathaniel Marchant. British Museum

Girometti, Giuseppe (1780–1851). Began his career as a sculptor and a pupil of Vincenzo Pacetti, under whom he executed stuccoes for the cathedral of Foligno. He was also a medallist. His cameos include reproductions of antique gems, portraits of famous men (including Leonardo da Vinci, George Washington, and Napoleon), and neoclassical subjects based either on his own designs or the statues of Tenerani and Canova. He is represented in the British Museum by a fine cameo of Diomede with the Palladium.

Guay, Jacques (1711–93). The most exquisite of French gem engravers, was born at Marseilles. He studied painting in Paris under Boucher, through whom he probably met Pierre Crozat, who persuaded him to take up gem engraving. He set off on a tour of Italy, and after studying the antique gems in the Grand Ducal collection at Florence passed to Rome, where he executed some copies after the antique. After his return to Paris he came to the notice of Mme de Pompadour, who became both his patron and pupil. She also secured for him apartments at Versailles. In 1745 he succeeded Barier as official gem engraver to the King, carving a cornelian intaglio of the Victory of Fontenoy after Bouchardon (now lost) on taking office. He carved many historical scenes in cameo and intaglio, some allegorical subjects – Mme de Pompadour protecting the art of gem engraving, for example – and such characteristically rococo subjects as 'Cupid as a Gardener' and 'Cupid as a Musician'. His best works were his portrait cameos of Louis XV, Mme de Pompadour, Louis XVI, Marie Antoinette, Cardinal de Rohan, etc. C. W. King, author of the British Museum catalogue of gems, thought his imitations of the Greek style 'perfect', but they do not seem to have satisfied neoclassical taste. In 1784 the director of the French Academy in Rome suggested that his place as court engraver might be given to the Englishman Nathaniel Marchant. The best collection of his works is in the Bibliothèque Nationale, Paris.

The Birth of the Duke of Burgundy, sardonyx cameo, by Jacques Guay, 1751. Bibliothèque Nationale, Paris

Jouffroy, Romain-Vincent (1749–1826). Born in Rouen, went to Naples in 1770 and settled at Paris in 1780. From 1790 to 1805 he worked for Prince Lubomirsky at Warsaw. In 1777 he engraved an amethyst head of Medusa after the Renaissance 'Solon' cameo. He executed a large number of antique-style cameos and intaglios, three of which are in the Bibliothèque Nationale. He also carved a number of portraits, including those of Napoleon (1801) and Maria Cosway in cameo, and the architect Charles de Wailly in intaglio.

Marchant, Nathaniel (1739–1816). One of the artists principally responsible for the neoclassical revival in the art of gem engraving. He was born in Sussex, studied under Burch, became a member of the Incorporated Society of Artists in 1766, went to Italy in 1772, and worked in Rome for the next sixteen years. He was elected an A.R.A. in 1781 and an R.A. in 1809, and was official gem engraver to the Prince Regent. Marchant's gems, which were highly prized in their day, and of which he published a catalogue to accompany a selection of casts, were all carved in intaglio. Most of them were of classical subjects, but he also carved numerous portraits, including those of William Pitt, Garrick, Prince Lubomirsky, Lord and Lady Lucan, Sir William Molesworth, Major Pearson, Mrs Hartley the actress, Lord Mulgrave, and Pius VI. He was much patronized by the Duke of Marlborough, who sent gems out to be carved by him in Rome. Writing of his intaglio of the death of General Wolfe, then in the collection of Sir Richard Worsley, the notable Roman antiquarian H. Q. Visconti remarked that Marchant was without rival in his profession. Modern connoisseurs have, however, generally found his work too exquisitely fine and finicky.

Natter, Johann Lorenz (1705–63). Probably the most celebrated German gem engraver of the eighteenth century. He was originally trained as a goldsmith, but in 1732 he visited Italy to study gem engraving in Venice and Florence. In 1735 he went to Rome, where he won immediate fame by his portrait of Cardinal Albani. He went to England in 1740, but three years later left for Denmark, where he was patronized by the King, for whom he engraved gems and medals. After a visit to Sweden and St Petersburg he returned to London in 1751 and published there his *Traité de la méthode antique de graver en pierres fines, comparée avec la méthode moderne* . . . in 1754. Three years later he was appointed engraver to the mint at Utrecht, but went back to London in 1761 and secured a post as assistant engraver to the Royal Mint. Next year he was off again, travelling by way of Copenhagen to St Petersburg, where he died. He produced numerous copies after the antique, sometimes with fake inscriptions, and also carved portraits, including those of George I, George II, Lord and Lady Duncannon, Dr Mead, Baron Stosch, and the Marquess of Rockingham. His charge for engrav-

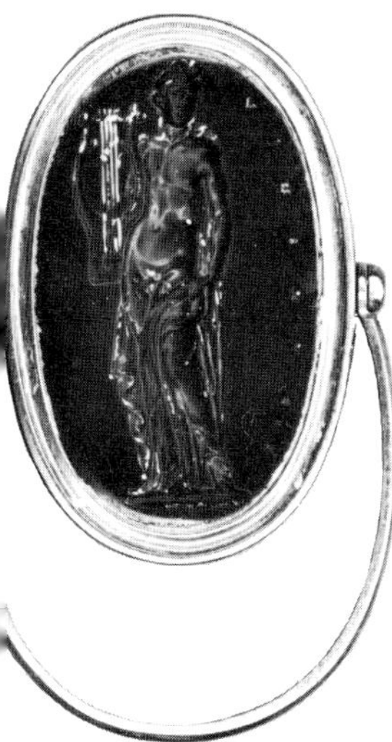

Above Apollo, sardonyx intaglio, by Luigi Pichler. British Museum

Far right A nereid, beryl intaglio, by Filippo Rega. British Museum

ing a portrait varied between 10 and 25 guineas.

Pazzaglia, Antonio (*c.* 1736–1815). A lieutenant in the Papal Guard who became a gem engraver. He was adept at imitating antique gems, which he sometimes signed with his name in Greek characters.

Pichler, Johann Anton. Usually known as Antonio (1697–1779), the founder of a very important family of gem engravers who worked at Rome. He was born at Bressanone and began his career by working for a rich uncle who was a merchant at Nice. In the 1730s he visited Italy, took employment at Naples with a goldsmith, and finally settled at Rome in 1743. He excelled in the imitation of antique subjects, but also carved intaglios and cameos from his own designs – and on one occasion at least from a drawing by Mengs – signing them with adaptations of his name, written in Greek characters. Three of his sons, Giovanni (1734–91), Giuseppe (1770–1819), and Luigi (1773–1854), became notable gem engravers. Giovanni Pichler was perhaps the most distinguished. He was trained under his father and the painter Domenico Corvi and became a prominent member of the circle of neoclassical artists in Rome. His gems were highly esteemed, and many stories were told of those that had been passed off as antiques to collectors who brought them unknowingly to their creator and asked him to copy them. Such was his reputation that his own signature was forged by contemporaries. He excelled in the representation of female figures, which he usually endowed with a slightly sentimental look characteristic of the time. His trade card shows that in 1783 he was charging 40 zecchini (about £20) for a portrait, the same for a cameo figure, and 20 for a head in cameo or intaglio. He made paste reproductions of 220 of his works. His son, Gian Giacomo (1778–1829), became a gem engraver and worked principally in Milan. Luigi Pichler, who succeeded to Giovanni's workshop in 1791, secured for himself a European reputation, became a member of the Florentine, Milanese, and Venetian academies, and was knighted by Gregory XIV. The Empress Josephine commissioned him to carve a gem of an 'Offering to the God Terminus' which she gave to Napoleon. He executed gems of antique subjects and also gems representing the statues of Canova. Among his portraits, for which he was celebrated, were those of Canova, the Cardinal de Bernis, Raphael Morgan, and Metternich.

Pompadour, Jeanne-Antoinette Poisson, Marquise de (1721–64). Said to have been an apt pupil of Jacques Guay, under whose tuition and with whose help she engraved several cameos and intaglios. Her work is represented in the Bibliothèque Nationale, Paris.

Rega, Filippo (1761–1833). Born at Chieti. His family moved to Naples in 1767 and later to Rome, where, from 1776 to 1787, the young Rega studied under Antonio and Giovanni Pichler. In 1787 he returned to Naples, where he worked for the rest of his career. He was patronized by the British ambassador, Sir William Hamilton, for whom he cut a portrait of the notorious Emma. Replicas of this work were ordered from him by Lord Bristol (the Earl-Bishop) and Nelson. Among his other portraits were those of Sir William Hamilton himself, the King and Queen of Naples, Joseph Bonaparte, and Gioacchino Murat. His numerous intaglios after the antique, signed with his name in Greek characters, are more lively and less precise than those of his principal contemporary rival, N. Marchant.

Right Minerva, onyx cameo, by Giovanni Pichler. British Museum

Far right Hercules, onyx cameo, by G. A. Santarelli. British Museum

Santarelli, Giovanni Antonio (1758–1826). Born at Manoppelle in the Abruzzi, and in 1785 went to Rome, where he worked under the Pichlers. In 1797 he moved to Florence, where he spent the rest of his life. Together with Cades and Odelli he carved numerous gems for Prince Poniatowski.

Siries, Louis (*c.* 1686–1757). Appears to have been born at Florence, where he was living in 1709, he went to Paris and in 1726 was appointed goldsmith to Louis XV. After six years he returned to Florence, and in 1732 went to Rome. In 1740 he was appointed director of the *Opificio delle Pietre Dure* at Florence. He published in 1757 a catalogue of 168 gems he had engraved. Many of his cameos were bought by Maria Theresa. He specialized in work on a microscopic scale, and according to Mariette his talent lay in achieving supposed impossibilities, dreading being thought an imitator of the ancients. Some of his works were reproduced by Tassie. He was also a medallist.

Sirletti, Flavio (1683–1737). Born in Rome. At the suggestion of Baron Stosch he revived the ancient practice of working with a diamond point. He excelled in portraits, the best of which is said to be a cameo of Carlo Maratta. He also reproduced the most notable antique statues and busts on gems. But much of his time was devoted to reworking ancient gems, to many of which he applied bogus Greek inscriptions. Some of his works were reproduced by Tassie. His son, Francesco (1713–88), was also a gem engraver.

Tassie, James (1735–99). Together with Henry Quinn, a physician and amateur of gems, Tassie invented in 1763 a vitreous paste suitable for reproducing gems. This material, the secret of which was jealously kept, was an easily fusible glass which could be made to imitate the varied layers of a chalcedony cameo. In 1766 he settled in London, and three years later was supplying casts of gems to Wedgwood. He published in 1775 *A Catalogue of Impressions in Sulphur of Antique and Modern Gems*. Pastes were made from these sulphur casts and sold in great quantity – intaglios costing from 1*s* 6*d* to 2*s* 6*d*, while he asked from half a guinea to two guineas for cameos. In 1791 Rudolph Eric Raspe, the creator of Baron Munchausen, issued a further catalogue of Tassie's collection of casts, which now numbered 15,800. His original works, all of which are portraits, were derived from waxes and not gems. James Tassie was succeeded in 1799 by his nephew William (1777–1860), who added to the collection of reproductions, of which he issued three catalogues. The last (1830) accounts for 20,000 antique and modern gems.

Torricelli, Giuseppe Antonio (1639–1719). Mainly famous for his large works in *pietre dure*, also engraved gems. In 1714 he wrote a treatise on jewels and semi-precious stones. His son Gaetano (*c.* 1691–1752) studied drawing under Tommaso Redi and sculpture under G. B. Foggini and also became a gem engraver, specializing in classical subjects. He is represented in the Kunsthistorisches Museum, Vienna, by a chalcedony head of Laocoon. The family tradition was carried on by his son Giuseppe who worked at Florence and Vienna.

Above Designs from 'A Descriptive catalogue of a general collection of ancient and modern engraved gems, cameos as well as intaglios taken from the most celebrated cabinets in Europe, and cast in coloured pastes, white enamel and sulphur by James Tassie, with copper plates', engraved by David Allan, 1791

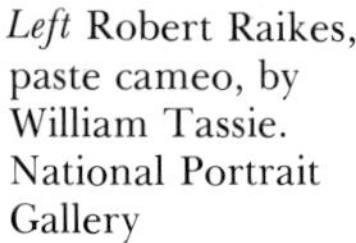
Left Robert Raikes, paste cameo, by William Tassie. National Portrait Gallery

Pietre Dure

Surprising as it may seem to present-day collectors and connoisseurs, the Grand Duke of Tuscany's *Opificio delle Pietre Dure*, or workshop of semi-precious stones, was once thought to be among the major artistic attractions of Italy. Throughout the seventeenth and eighteenth centuries sophisticated and elegant Grand Tourists vied with each other in praising its products – those smooth, glittering panels and inlaid table tops of 'Florentine Mosaic' as it was then called, choice examples of which still adorn many English country houses. Only the severest and most classically minded of *virtuosi* could resist the charms of *pietre dure*. During the nineteenth century, however, it fell into disrepute, and since then has found few admirers, even among confirmed addicts of Italian art. The charms of *pietre dure* are, it must be confessed, of the same gaudy, extravagant, and, to some eyes, rather meretricious variety as captivated the millionaire patrons of Fabergé. Indeed, it is of the great Russian jeweller's more ingenious confections that one is instantly reminded on entering the Pietre Dure Museum at Florence. As Sir Osbert Sitwell remarked, Florentine mosaic will have little appeal for the lover of old oak. But though modern aesthetes may scorn and art historians neglect them, these strange manifestations of princely taste will continue to fascinate the discerning collector who values high quality in craftsmanship, and is not too squeamishly puritan to acknowledge the attraction of jewels and precious stones. The designs employed by the artists of the Grand Duke's *Opificio* were by no means unworthy of the rare materials and laborious craftsmanship lavished upon them; but it is, of course, the pure and brilliant colours of the stones themselves – of lapis lazuli, onyx, jasper, sardonyx, chalcedony, coral, agate, rock crystal, and many others – which lend these *objets de luxe* so strange and unique a beauty.

The rise and fall of the reputation of *pietre dure* provides an interesting sidelight on the history of taste, and the comments of one or two of its more eminent admirers and detractors may not be out of place even in so brief a chapter as this one. John Evelyn, for example, after visiting the Uffizi Gallery, Florence, in 1644, declared himself to have been much impressed by 'divers incomparable tables of Pietra Commessa, which is a marble ground inlayd with severall sorts of marbles and stones of divers colours, in the shapes of flowers, trees, beasts, birds & landskips like the natural'. Especially wonderful, he thought, was a *pietre dure* tabernacle, intended for the Cappella dei Principi in S. Lorenzo, to which an entire room of the Uffizi was given up. He wrote that it was 'certainly one of the most curious and rare things in the world'. And as for the sumptuous Cappella dei Principi itself, whose walls were encrusted with vast areas of rare marbles and semi-precious stones, his admiration knew no bounds. It was 'the third heaven if any be on Earth'. Six very large columns of rock crystal were eagerly noted down by Evelyn in his diary, together with '8 figures of precious stones of several colours, inlay'd in natural figures, not inferior to ye best paintings, amongst which are many pearls, diamonds, amethysts, topazes, sumptuous and sparkling beyond description'. So taken was he with these flamboyant displays of technical virtuosity that, like many later visitors to Florence, he purchased nineteen panels of *commesso di pietre dure* and, on his return to England, had them made up into a cabinet which is still at Wotton, his country house in Surrey.

But the taste for *pietre dure* reached its height during the next century when few English travellers could resist the fascination of its ingenious craftsmanship and the startlingly realistic *trompe l'oeil* effects obtained in so difficult a medium. John, 5th Earl of Cork and Orrery, who was in Florence in 1754, remarked, in words that may easily be paralleled in many another Grand Tour correspondence or diary, that the Florentine mosaic tables in the Uffizi 'consist of jasper, topazes, agates, and all kinds of coloured marble so nicely put together, as to form the most beautiful figures and the most natural representations of towns, woods, rocks, rivers, cattle, and people; not to mention a certain pearl necklace the beads of which my daughter tried in vain to take up in her hand'.

It is interesting to compare such comments with those of a later visitor to Florence, the poet Walter Savage Landor. Writing in 1851, the year of the Great Exhibition in London, Landor dubbed the *Opificio delle Pietre Dure* a mere school for fashioning 'piebald mineralogical specimens into a greater or less resemblance of fruits, flowers and landscapes'; and he deplored the decline in taste, as he thought it, which had 'dared at last to rear, by the very side of the tombs of Giuliano and Lorenzo, the so-named (and well-named) Chapel of the Princes'. This masterpiece of the *Opificio*, so much admired by Evelyn, was in Landor's opinion, the product of 'Chinese industry and Turkish taste'. As for the *objet d'art* which had been sent to represent the birthplace of Michelangelo at the 1851 Exhibition, this, Landor remarked, was 'neither more nor less than a table in pietre dure that had cost a hundred thousand francesconi, or, in other words, a day's work of four hundred thousand Tuscans'. He considered it 'stolid impertinence' to send such an object to London instead of some sublime painting or sculpture which would have shown how 'genius and sentiment can convert all stone to precious stone; while the obscure diligence of years, uninformed by art, makes but a monument of laborious idleness'. So much for the esteem in which Florentine mosaic was held by an eminent Victorian.

HISTORY OF THE OPIFICIO DELLE PIETRE DURE

Pietre dure, or semi-precious stones, had been employed in the manufacture of *objets de luxe* long before the Medici founded their *Opificio* at Florence in the late sixteenth century. Indeed, an exhaustive account of *pietre dure* and their various uses would take us back into classical antiquity. Suffice it here to mention the lavish use made of porphyry by Roman architects and sculptors, and the popularity of other more exotic and brilliantly coloured stones among the anonymous artists of Byzantium. Wherever early records of Italian churches or palaces have survived they generally include several vessels in *pietre dure*, such as those of agate and jasper mentioned in the great inventory of the Papal Treasury made by Boniface VIII in 1295, or the early chalices and incense boats which are still preserved in the Treasury of St Mark's, Venice.

During the fourteenth and fifteenth centuries the manufacture of such costly wares gradually spread throughout the artistic centres of Italy, but by the mid-sixteenth century the Milanese school of artists in *pietre dure* had established their pre-eminence and Milanese craftsmen could be found all over Europe – in Madrid, Prague, and Vienna, as well as in most Italian cities, including Florence. Among the Milanese craftsmen in Florence were the Carrioni and Giovanni Antonio Miseroni, who were taken into the service of the Grand Duke Francesco I de' Medici in the 1570s. At about this date also a native Florentine school of *pietre dure* artists began to emerge, at first under the tutelage of these imported Milanese craftsmen. The earliest recorded Florentine craftsmen are Francesco del Tadda, who died in 1576, and his son Romolo, who was active until 1620. Francesco del Tadda worked mainly in porphyry, executing many portrait medallions and a few figures in the round, such as that symbolizing Justice which surmounts the columns in the Piazza di S. Trinità at Florence.

The Florentine *Opificio* may be said to date from about 1580, when the Grand Duke Francesco I established a special workshop in his palace, the Casino di S. Marco, for the Milanese and local Tuscan craftsmen in semi-precious stones. Some twenty years later, in 1599, Francesco's brother and successor the Grand Duke Ferdinando I de' Medici issued a decree establishing the *Opificio* as part of the Grand Ducal Gallery of Works and transferring it to the first floor of the Uffizi. There the *Opificio* remained until 1769, when the Grand Duke Pietro Leopoldo of Habsburg-Lorraine, which family had succeeded the extinct house of Medici, separated the *Opificio* from the rest of the Gallery of Works, and since that date it has remained an autonomous institution, depending directly from the State. The *Opificio* continued to reside in the Uffizi for several more years, however, and it was not until 1796 that it moved to its present location in the former Convent of S. Nicolo in the Via degli Alfani, Florence.

The *Opificio* was founded in order to provide the Medici family and its court with a steady supply of vases, jewelry, ornaments, and mosaic panels in semi-precious stones. But, although the output of the factory was restricted to the Tuscan Court, examples soon found their way abroad in the form of Grand Ducal presents to foreign potentates. A table with an inlaid top of *pietre dure*, for example, was sent to England in the late sixteenth century, presumably as a gift to Elizabeth I. Unfortunately this table cannot now be traced in the English Royal Collections. Before the end of the sixteenth century, however, a new and infinitely greater task was entrusted to the craftsmen of the *Opificio* – the decoration of the vast mausoleum of the Medici princes with mosaic wall decoration, an immense altar, gargantuan sarcophagi, and heroic-scale statues of the Grand Dukes, all in *pietre dure* and the rarest marbles.

The Cappella dei Principi in S. Lorenzo, which contains nearly an acre of wall space entirely encrusted with semi-precious stones, provides ample testimony to the skill of the *Opificio* craftsmen no less than to the wealth and grandeur of the Medici. This fantastic project – the erection of a mausoleum more grandiose than any other in the whole of Europe to a family whose fortunes were already in decline – seems to have been initiated in about 1597. In that year the Grand Duke Ferdinando I brought back from Rome some 350 porphyry fragments of antique sculpture which were to form the basis of the decorative scheme (one of them being the figure of a wolf, now in the Uffizi, which happily escaped destruction).

Work on the chapel began in 1604, under Matteo Nigetti to a design by Giovanni de' Medici, a natural son of Cosimo I, and proceeded by fits and starts over the next two hundred years. It was not, of course, possible to carry out the entire decorative scheme in *pietre dure*, as originally intended. Yet much wall space was eventually covered with mosaic panels, the finest of which depict the coats-of-arms of the principal cities of the Grand Duchy in lapis lazuli, coral, mother of pearl, jasper, cornelian, and other brilliant stones. Six great sarcophagi were hewn out of porphyry and a start was made on the altar, though gilt bronze had to be substituted for *pietre dure* in certain parts, notably for the statues.

During the first few decades of the seventeenth century the *Opificio* was mainly occupied with this chapel, but as the Medici wealth dwindled away work came gradually to a halt and the craftsmen turned their hands to smaller and more profitable work. Various unsuccessful attempts were later made to finish the chapel on more modest lines than those intended by Ferdinando I, but even in its uncompleted state the vast, glittering chamber of princely tombs was sufficiently sumptuous to strike the fancy of most Grand Tourists. They regarded it as one of the principal wonders of modern Italy if not – like John Evelyn – as 'the third heaven if any be on earth'.

When the Medici finances began to falter the *Opificio* was slowly converted from an extravagant drain into a source of profit. The Grand Dukes, who had never been too proud to sell the produce from their estates, even at the palace door, set up a brisk trade in *pietre dure* aimed expressly at the grandest of 'Grand Tourists'. Cunningly, they displayed in the Uffizi Gallery the exquisite panels and figures intended for the great Cappella dei Principi altar, together with other works made specially for the purpose. These gaudy panels attracted as much attention as the masterpieces of Renaissance painting and sculpture with which they were surrounded.

After the middle of the seventeenth century the *Opificio* seems to have been mainly occupied in catering for this tourist trade. The Habsburg-Lorraine Grand Dukes who succeeded the Medici in 1737 continued this businesslike policy towards the workshop, save for an occasional commission for the decoration of their palaces in Austria. In the mid-nineteenth century the trade was further developed and the *Museo dell'Opificio delle Pietre Dure* was opened in the Via degli Alfani, Florence, as a shop window for the workshop. Behind the museum the courtyard still resounds with the noise of cutting and grinding as the craftsmen shape and fit together mosaic panels of semi-precious stones, working in much the same way as their predecessors of 350 years ago. Only the designs have changed. Now they reproduce in *pietre dure* the more popular pictures in the Florentine galleries or – with rather greater facility – abstract paintings in the manner of Mondrian.

TABLE TOPS

Of all the various categories of work produced by the *Opificio delle Pietre Dure* the table tops are probably the

tral motif was provided by Bernardino Poccetti, while Jacopo Ligozzi was responsible for the surround. Like many other works of its period, this design was largely symbolic, incorporating Florentine lilies, the oak leaves of the Della Rovere family, dragons for the Grand Duke, shells with pearls in them for the Grand Duchess, and, in the centre, the shield of the Medici family.

Later seventeenth- and early eighteenth-century tables, of which there are several fine specimens in the Palazzo Pitti at Florence, are rather more simply decorated with arabesques and occasional *trompe l'oeil* devices such as the broken necklaces so much admired by the Earl of Cork and Orrery. Pictorial designs used in the seventeenth century frequently included a view of the harbour at Leghorn. In the mid-eighteenth century similar, though rather more elegant, pictorial designs became increasingly popular and held their appeal until the 1790s. The Empire style, however, demanded table tops of a different type. These were less closely ornamented and relied for their decorative effect on a simple still-life group on a background of porphyry or black marble. Many such tables were ornamented with groups of sea shells, but groups of blue-and-white Chinese porcelain vessels, 'Etruscan' or Greek vases, and musical

most numerous and successful. The best of these were made in *commesso di pietre dure* or true Florentine Mosaic, a species of *opus sectile* similar to wood *intarsia*. The thin *laminae* of the different stones were cut to take their places in a design which might be either geometrical, arabesque, or pictorial. Perhaps the most notable example of this type of work is the great octagonal table which once stood in the Tribune of the Uffizi and is now in the museum of the *Opificio*. Ordered in 1633 by the Grand Duke Ferdinando II, this table took sixteen years to complete and is entirely composed of agates, jaspers, lapis lazuli, and chalcedonies inlaid on a background of black Flanders marble. Numerous craftsmen were needed to produce so grandiose a performance. They included Giovanni Merlini, Giovanni Giachetti, Giovanni Francesco and Lorenzo Bottini, Giovanni Bianchi the younger, Cosimo Chermer, Giovanni Giorgi, Carlo Centelli, Pietro Chiarai, and Andrea Merlini, who worked under the direction of Jacopo Autelli, called 'il Monnicca'. The design for the cen-

Above Pietre dure panel in *scagliola* table top, lapis lazuli, agates, cornelians and marbles. L. Scott Antiques, London

Table top of porphyry inlaid with *pietre dure*, early 19th century. Palazzo Pitti, Florence

Far right Florentine mosaic panel designed by Giuseppe Zocchi, mid-18th century

instruments were also popular. The simplest were decorated with no more than a wreath of laurel leaves executed with *trompe l'oeil* precision, even to the shadows cast on the background. In the later nineteenth century floral motifs, sometimes combined with shells, returned to favour. In the museum of the *Opificio* there is a particularly fine black table top decorated with a chaplet of white magnolias, made by Edoardo Marchionni in 1881.

Table tops in Florentine mosaic were always an expensive luxury, and it was not long before a cheap and convenient substitute was devised by means of *scagliola*. This material, composed mainly of coloured plaster, had long been used for an imitation marble. But during the early eighteenth century several enterprising craftsmen, notably the Anglo-Florentine Enrico Hugford, adapted it as a medium for painting. Two techniques were developed. The first consisted in painting with *scagliola* plaster of the required colours on a wet gesso ground and firing when dry so that the finished panel could be given a high polish. The second technique involved the inlay of different coloured sections of plaster into cavities prepared in the gesso ground. Landscapes, still life, and figure subjects could be depicted by these techniques with an astonishing degree of realism. Indeed, effects of greater delicacy and subtlety could be attained in *scagliola* than in Florentine mosaic, especially by such skilled craftsmen as Enrico Hugford and his pupil Lamberto Gori. Not unnaturally, *scagliola* table tops were much in demand among visiting milords; and Sir Horace Mann, the British Resident at Florence for most of the eighteenth century, was frequently asked by English friends to obtain such articles for them.

PIETRE DURE PICTURES

Portrait of Cosimo I by Francesco Ferrucci after a painting by Domenico Cresti, 1598

Closely connected with table tops were the pictures in *pietre dure* – portraits, landscapes, and architectural views for the most part – which were also produced in large quantities by the *Opificio* during the seventeenth and eighteenth centuries. The first masterpiece in this genre is the portrait of Cosimo I de' Medici executed by Francesco Ferrucci in 1598 after a painting by Domenico Cresti called *Il Passignano*. Although less realistic than the painting, this mosaic derives from the hardness and brilliance of its medium a magnificent hierarchical effect. The most notable of all pictures in *pietre dure* are, however, those made between 1737 and 1765 for the Grand Duke Francis of Lorraine to line a room in the Hofburg at Vienna. These fifty pictures represent such subjects as *The Five Moments in the Day of a Lady*, *The Five Senses*, *The Five Seasons*, *Views of Leghorn*, *Scenes from Military Life*, the *Four Quarters of the Globe*, and the *Six Ages of Man*. This series is closely connected with another entitled the *Four Liberal Arts*, which is preserved in the Museum of the *Opificio* at Florence.

The fifty paintings for the Pietradura-Zimmer in the Hofburg at Vienna were all executed after designs by Giuseppe Zocchi the landscape painter, who is best known for his engraved views of Florentine villas, and who may perhaps be called the Canaletto of Florence. The panels reproduce his paintings with remarkable fidelity and are indeed most skilfully made to simulate the gentle gradations of tone in an oil painting. In 1794 the director of the *Opificio*, Luigi Siries, began work on a series of mosaic pictures with which it was intended to decorate a

room in the Palazzo Pitti in emulation of the Pietradura-Zimmer in the Hofburg. Only five panels of views of Roman ruins after paintings by Ferdinando Partini were, however, completed. In these works variations in the colour of the semi-precious stones were cunningly employed to suggest the effect of weathering on the marble of the ancient monuments depicted.

Small *pietre dure* pictures, intended for insertion in altars or cabinets, were, of course, made in greater quantities than the elaborate series described above. The earliest of these were made for the decoration of the great altar intended for the Cappella dei Principi, and several of them are now in the Museum of the *Opificio*. They represent such Old Testament subjects as *Jonah and the Whale*, *Samson and the Lion*, the *Dream of Jacob*, and *Abraham and the Angels*. Ludovico Cigoli and Giovanni Bilivert, two of the more notable painters working in Florence at the end of the sixteenth century, were among the artists who provided the designs for these panels. Two landscape panels, intended for the same altar, were made by Maestro Fabian, a German, and two others by Maestro Battista of Milan. Panels designed for other altars, dating from the seventeenth century, represented subjects from the New Testament, angels, and flowers. Many other small panels – such as those bought by John Evelyn – were intended to be mounted in cabinets and were usually decorated with floral motifs or groups of birds whose gay plumage might well defy the ornithologist. In the eighteenth century landscape panels became more popular. A good example of this type is the group of panels made by Baccio Cappelli at Florence in 1709 and later incorporated into a cabinet designed by Robert Adam for the Duchess of Manchester in the 1770s.

To avoid the laborious process of cutting numerous small stones into intricate shapes to make a *pietre dure* picture the *Opificio* craftsmen devised an ingenious though seldom very satisfactory compromise between *pietre dure* painting and oil painting. This method consisted of painting, in oil colours, on panels inlaid with a few large pieces of *pietre dure*, much of which could be left to represent the background. Lapis lazuli, for example, was used in this way to represent water or sky in a landscape panel, while the detail of trees, figures, buildings, etc., were added in oil colours, as in the painting of *Latona and the Shepherds* in the *Opificio* Museum. A streaky stone found in the Arno valley (called *lineato dell'Arno*) was also used as a basis for such paintings. The markings of this stone could be used to suggest the waves of the sea or the undulations of a sandy shore, as in the charming painting of *The Vision of St Augustine* (Museum of the *Opificio*), where the figures are overpainted in oil colours.

SCULPTURE IN PIETRE DURE

This section of the *Opificio*'s output was naturally the most limited, and very few examples of it have survived. The most remarkable is a portrait bust of the Grand Duchess Vittoria della Rovere, the wife of Ferdinando II de' Medici, which was executed by Giuseppe Antonio Torricelli (1662–1719), the author of an important treatise on *pietre dure*. By the most skilful use of black Flanders marble, chalcedony, and various agates, Torricelli achieved an extraordinarily realistic and powerful representation of this imposing Grand Duchess dressed in the habit of the Montalvan Order. It is both a technical *tour de force* and a convincing work of art which would deserve a place in any history of Italian sculpture. Hardly less accomplished than this bust is a low-relief portrait of Cosimo II de' Medici, now in the Museo degli Argenti (Palazzo Pitti) at Florence. This exotic creation, executed by Orazio Mocchi in 1619 after designs by Giovanni Bilivert, is composed of both *pietre dure* and jewels.

At this period also *pietre dure* ornaments, carved in high relief or in the round, were produced for the decoration of furniture as, for example, on the gorgeous *prie-dieu* in the Palazzo Pitti, Florence. Similar ornaments, slightly more restrained in style, were later exported to France for use on furniture. German *ébénistes* working in Paris during the latter part of Louis XVI's reign were particularly fond of *pietre dure*, and there are splendid examples of their use on a lavish scale by Weisweiler and others in the English Royal Collections.

Statuettes in *pietre dure* were sometimes made by the *Opificio*, but the finest examples of this category of their output were made for the tabernacle of the altar in the Cappella dei Principi in S. Lorenzo. Similar statuettes were produced for the decoration of reliquaries, notably that of S. Stanislas in the Treasury of S. Lorenzo. This difficult art was revived in the late nineteenth century, when statuettes of Cimabue and Dante were carved by Paolo Ricco.

Glossary

Commesso di pietre dure. This may be translated, literally, as 'placing together of hard stones' and is the Italian term for the process known in English as Florentine mosaic. This unique form of mosaic *intarsia* is distinguished by its use of semi-precious stones (jasper, agate, amethyst, chalcedony, cornelian, bloodstone, lapis lazuli, rock crystal, etc.). The process corresponds in technique to that of wood *intarsia*, thin *laminae* of different-coloured stones being cut to appropriate shapes and then affixed to panels in ornamental patterns or arranged pictorially so as to form landscape or figure subjects.

Mosaic. This term is usually applied to the decoration of a wall or panel with a design made up of small fragments of stones or coloured glass fixed to the surface with cement or special adhesive. The best-known form of mosaic, usually called Roman or Byzantine mosaic, is formed of small cubes or *tessere* of coloured stone and glass. The Romans also developed a second technique of mosaic, using, instead of cubes, various-sized segments cut into shapes so as to form a design or picture when joined together. This technique may be regarded as the forerunner of Florentine mosaic.

Pietre dure. This is the Italian term for those stones (literally 'hard stones') which are roughly classed as semi-precious in English, i.e. such stones as are composed mainly of silicates in contrasts to 'soft' stones, such as limestone and most marbles, which have a large proportion of calcium in their composition.

Scagliola. A technique used for the imitation of marble and especially of Florentine mosaic. The term *scagliola* derives from the name of the special plaster or gesso, made of pulverized selenite, which is of extremely fine quality, and takes a very high polish. Two processes were developed for the imitation of Florentine mosaic. The first consisted in painting on the wet gesso ground, fixing the colours by heat, and then polishing the surface until it resembled a mosaic of *pietre dure*. The second consisted in inlaying coloured plasters in the surface of the *scagliola* panel. This latter process was first developed in Northern Italy during the sixteenth century, and reaches its apogee at Florence in the mid-eighteenth century.

Stone intarsia. A mosaic technique similar to *commesso di pietre dure*, the required design being cut out of the stone surface and pieces of coloured stone, cut into the appropriate shapes, being fitted into the cavities. It differs from Florentine mosaic both in the quality of the stones used and in the less refined methods of applying the stones and joining them together.

METALWORK

Only from fragments of metal can many details be elucidated concerning the pre-history existence of mankind, and within recorded ages bronze, iron, copper, tin enriched the ancient civilizations, Asiatic, Phoenician, Greek, Roman. Copper and tin, often found together, were probably first combined accidentally – perhaps 2,000 years B.C. – to produce the splendid alloy bronze; and at least as early as 1,000 B.C. iron was smelted in Central Europe and Assyria. Tin and lead brought fame and Phoenician trade to pre-Roman Britain, and iron smelting had reached this country before Julius Caesar came to Britain.

In medieval Britain as elsewhere the copper alloys were essential for armour and cannon; from Flanders came the fashion for the church effigy brasses invaluable to later historians, and from Germany the encouragement of copper mining and brass manufacture.

Collectors must possess a clear understanding of the metals involved, the natural elements, such as iron, copper, tin, lead, and the amalgamations into alloys. Wrought iron at its finest is almost a hundred per cent true iron. By antique bronze is implied a combination of copper and tin. Antique brass consists of the cast alloy of copper and calamine, not to be confused with latten, which is the old term for hammered brass plate. Pewter, in decreasing quality, consisted of tin and copper, tin and antimony, tin and lead. Such analysis, however, suggests nothing of the fascination of these inadequately named base metals. It may be difficult today even to envisage, say, the itinerant bell founder ranging the countryside, but a trace of the ancient magic still clings to the iron horseshoe hung above the door.

American

THE METALS

A study of American tin, copper, and brass should be prefaced with some information about the physical qualities of these metals, for knowledge of their properties will assist the reader in understanding why different metals were selected for different objects. Because tin was cheap, it was used to make inexpensive 'pieced ware' such as coffee pots; the malleability of copper rendered it suitable for making hand-hammered tea kettles; and brass, the only metal of the three that can be cast satisfactorily, was used for such objects as cast jelly kettles. Each metal has unique qualities. Tin is silvery white, malleable, and easily fused, and closely resembles pewter, for pewter is 80–90 per cent tin. Tin was used in ancient times, but production of tin plate was deferred until a way to produce a thin sheet of iron was invented.

In the seventeenth century a small ingot of iron was hammered into a sheet by a man called a 'beater', but in the eighteenth century a machine was invented that rolled thin, uniform sheets. These sheets were cleaned and dipped into a vat of molten tin, so that a thin coating of tin rust-proofed the iron. This procedure produced a sheet that had the qualities of iron and some of the qualities of tin. Like iron, it was strong and rigid, and yet could be bent into many useful shapes. Like tin it was rust-proof, white, and easily joined with solder. This useful and inexpensive medium was very popular with colonial craftsmen, and was equally useful when the machine took over the production of stamped tinware.

Copper was widely used in both Europe and America in the seventeenth, eighteenth, and nineteenth centuries. Its principal assets are its resistance to rust, efficient conduction of heat, excellent malleability, and attractive red-orange colour. It was particularly well adapted to making such articles as warming pans and saucepans, where all of its qualities could be used to the satisfaction of the craftsman and his customer. The major objection to using copper for the making of cooking utensils was the disagreeable taste (perhaps poisonous effect) which foods acquired from it. Because of this reason the inside of copper culinary vessels was covered with a thin protective coating of tin. The tinning was preceded by a thorough scraping and cleaning, then sal ammoniac was applied to prevent oxidation during the application of the tin. When the tin coating was worn away in spots the entire vessel had to be re-tinned.

An alloy is a metal compounded of two or more metals to secure properties which one alone cannot provide. Such an alloy is brass, made of copper and zinc, the most frequent ratio being two parts of copper to one part of zinc. In early times brass was made by combining granules of copper with calcined calamine (impure zinc) in a crucible. The zinc, reduced to a metallic state by intense heat, combined with the copper and formed a lump in the bottom of the crucible. Several of these lumps were combined into a small ingot and sold to the craftsman or merchant. In 1781 James Emerson patented the process of directly fusing copper with zinc to make brass. The two-to-one ratio produces bright gold-coloured metal that is soft to the hammer but hardens quickly and must be frequently annealed or softened. It also produces (with some small changes in its contents) a metal which is free-flowing when molten and can be cast in thin sections, required in the making of furniture brasses, or intricate shapes such as candlesticks. Brass is one of the most valuable alloys known to man and has a number of desirable qualities. It is harder than copper; it is ductile and malleable; it takes a high polish; it is easily joined; and it does not disintegrate

Chestnut urn decorated with a landscape scene, early 19th century. Loot, London rapidly when exposed to the atmosphere. These qualities made it an attractive metal to the colonial artisans, who used it extensively for objects of utility and beauty.

THE CRAFTSMEN

Evidence of overlapping on the trades of the different metal workers can be found in the newspaper advertisement of E. Brotherton of Lancaster, Pennsylvania, obviously a manufacturer of objects made of sheet tin, copper, and brass:

> '*E. Brotherton, Coppersmith, Brazier, and Tin-plate Worker, Lately from England, Begs leave to inform the public . . .*'

Probably the most obscure craftsman involved in this study is the brass founder.

In order to follow his craft, the brass founder had to have a melting furnace, a large supply of dampened sand, and a pattern of the object which he planned to reproduce. Sand was rammed around the pattern in a box called a flask, which could be opened for the removal of the pattern without disturbing the sand. After several flasks were prepared the molten metal was dipped from a crucible or a furnace and poured into the cavity in the sand. The casting of heavy objects like bells and cannons was done below ground level so that the molten metal could run directly from the furnace into the mould. Many objects were cast in bronze in essentially the same manner.

Perhaps the most specialized skill connected with the brass industry was metal spinning. The procedure is to rotate a disc of brass on a lathe between a previously formed die on the headstock and a rotating device on the tailstock. A tool is pressed against the rotating disc until the disc conforms to the shape of the die. A large number of concentric circles is the usual evidence that an object has been spun.

PLAIN TINWARE

Decorated and plain tinware were the two types made by American craftsmen. That a larger proportion of the decorated has survived may be due to the fact that the paint gave added protection, and being largely ornamental, it was less used and better cared for.

The question as to what forms of plain tinware were made is answered by early newspaper advertisements and business catalogues. It did not cater only for city trade, for most of the advertisements mentioned that country merchants could be supplied on short notice and on good terms for cash. An interesting listing is that of Thomas Passmore, who had a wholesale and retail tin manufactory in Philadelphia. His advertisement appearing in the *Federal Gazette* on 30 November 1793 lists seventy-six specific items which he manufactured, and concludes by saying that there were other items too numerous to mention.

These objects were usually round, square, or rectangular in form, with wire inserted in the edges to make them strong and rigid. There were large articles such as tin ovens and bathing machines, and small objects such as nursing bottles and funnels. In the early period large objects were often made of several pieces of tin plate, for pieces of sufficient size were not easily obtainable. Unless an early piece was unusually well cared for, it should show some sign of

Tin weathervane in the form of a rooster, 19th century. New York State Historical Association

disintegration, such as rust. Distortion and poor soldering, however are not necessarily evidences of great age.

Because tin plate was a cheap and flexible medium there was rapid change of style, and the variety of shapes and joints indicates that the craftsmen were quick to grasp new ideas. Early pieces do not have factory-made spouts and handles like those of the 1850s and 1860s. Because he produced a custom-made object involving machine-made parts, the tinsmith stayed in business a long time. Many tin shops were still operating at the beginning of the twentieth century, and even today a few can be found in rural areas.

It is obvious that a great many of the objects made of tin plate were used in the home, more specifically in the kitchen. One of the most interesting accessories was the tin oven or roaster, which stood before the fireplace with a large roast mounted on a spit.

The making of candles was an important project for the pioneer family, and candle moulds made of tin plate facilitated the operation. That they must have been very widely used is attested by the fact that there were few attics on the eastern seaboard which

Tin candle box with hangers reinforced with wire, tinder box, candlestick and snuffer tray. Essex Institute, Salem, Massachusetts

could not boast of a few even in the late nineteenth century. Passmore made them in the eighteenth century, and the tin merchants, Hall & Carpenter of Philadelphia, sold machinery to make them as late as 1886. They were made in a variety of heights and unit combinations from two to fifty, units of two, four, six, eight, and twelve being the most common.

The candle box was also made of tin plate and hung in the kitchen to provide a small supply of candles within easy reach. The boxes were 12–14 inches (30.5–35.6 cm) long and usually about 4 inches (10 cm) in diameter; though a few have punched designs in stars and other motifs, the functional use of wire and beading is all that decorates some of them.

Some of the early tinsmiths also made gingerbread cutters. To the indigenous designs of birds, tulips, hearts, etc., were added eagles, log cabins, Uncle Sams, and Indians. The popularity of the cooky cutter continued late in the nineteenth century. The animal shapes retained the primitive feeling of the earlier designs, but the geometric patterns are uninteresting.

Museums such as Old Sturbridge Village, Sturbridge, Massachusetts, and the Landis Valley Museum near Lancaster, Pennsylvania, have displays of tinware used on the farms and in small villages during the nineteenth century. Regarded by many people today as a metal of little value, tin plate was a commodity precious to our ancestors.

SHEET BRASS AND COPPER

The survival of many objects made of sheet brass and copper can be attributed to a number of reasons. The inherent quality and beauty of the metals influenced craftsmen to use them for the making of objects of importance. These items served a long time; they were well cared for, and did not disintegrate rapidly when they were discarded for a later and more fashionable object. Generally speaking, the malleability, the colour, and the permanence of sheet brass and copper gave them a favoured position over tin. Silver was the only superior metal available to make comparable objects.

The copper weathervane of early date, of great interest to collectors, combines functionalism and good design. This is an object in which the malleability and permanence of copper are important. After years of exposure the copper turns a fine verdigris green. The earliest vanes were made of two convex pieces of copper, soldered together at the edges, forming a figure in low relief. The early ones, like Shem Drowne's *Indian*, belonging to the Massachusetts Historical Society, were probably knocked out with a mallet on a plank or a piece of lead. In the middle of the nineteenth century, however, such vanes were made by shaping a piece of sheet copper in a mould of cast iron, the mould having been cast from a pattern of wood which had been carved in full detail. The later vanes were in higher relief and more detailed than the earlier type. A variety of forms were produced, such as cocks, horses, ships, fish, grasshoppers, and horse-drawn sulkies.

The copper tea kettle deserves some consideration, for despite a long European tradition in the making of utensils, the coppersmiths of Pennsylvania and New York produced a flaring goose-neck type with a swinging handle that is peculiar to the area. Many of them can be identified because the makers stamped them with an intaglio stamp.

Weathervane in the form of an American Indian, gold-leafed repoussé, *c.* 1820. American Museum in Britain

Another significant item produced in quantity was the liquor still, for which there was a brisk demand throughout the grain-growing areas of Pennsylvania. It was easier and more lucrative to carry liquor to the Philadelphia market than cumbersome bags of grain. If the farmers were too poor to own a still for their individual use a number pooled their resources and bought one for a community. Most of the stills show evidence of fine workmanship in the riveting and planished surfaces.

The most common article made of sheet brass was undoubtedly the spun-brass kettle from Connecticut, produced in large quantities from 1851 and sold by pedlars on the eastern seaboard. Other objects besides kettles were spun, for in the collection of Old Sturbridge Village at Sturbridge, Massachusetts, can be found a basin that has the typical concentric circles, and on the bottom the stamp usually found on spun kettles. A hammered-brass kettle bears the name of William Heyser, a coppersmith from Chambersburg, Pennsylvania.

Many other objects such as braziers, coal hods, oil-lamp fillers, measures, funnels, fish kettles, chocolate pots, frying pans, house pouting, butter churns, footwarmers, and many specialized objects for the hatting and dyeing trades were made of sheet brass and copper. There were objects for marine use, and a number of copper dry measures were used by official sealers of weights and measures.

CAST BRASS

It is doubtful if any product of the American craftsman is more difficult to identify as to origin than the object of cast brass. Despite the fact that many skilled men were engaged in the craft, the names of only a few are known, and extremely few of their products can be identified, an obscurity difficult to understand, yet existing.

Early costumes and contemporary newspaper advertisements indicate that brass buttons and buckles were in wide use in the eighteenth century.

Caspar Wistar (who came to Philadelphia in 1717) was one of the first craftsmen known to have engaged in the business of brass casting, and he seems to have made just buttons. His son, Richard, continued the manufacture of brass buttons.

Most plentiful among objects of cast brass, are furniture mounts, whose places of origin are almost impossible to identify. The many English trade catalogues indicate a brisk exporting business, but there is proof that these pieces were made in America also. In 1795 Bolton & Grew of Boston advertised *Cabinet Brass Foundry Goods* and enumerated articles such as pulls, hinges, pendants, etc.

Early cast-brass andirons of American manufacture are quite rare, but in recent years a number of these have been found bearing names of American craftsmen. Andirons of iron, from which the name obviously originates were enhanced by adding a finial and plate of brass as interiors of houses became richer. Into this category fall the attractive knife-blade andirons with penny feet and brass urn finials. Late in the eighteenth century andirons of cast brass were popular and are appropriately used in a Georgian setting with Chippendale furniture. These have tall, intricately patterned columns terminating in a variety of finials, such as the urn, ball, steeple, lemon, and double-lemon pattern. They have a modified cabriole leg with a simple ball, snake, or ball-and-claw foot. The most extravagant style had a twisted baluster and diamond-and-flame finial; a pair signed by Paul Revere is now in the Metropolitan Museum, New York.

Another important product of the brass-founder was the brass doorknocker. Popular in the eighteenth century was the modified S-type, while the urn and eagle patterns were popular in the early nineteenth century. Newspaper advertisements indicate they were made in America, but a signed one has not appeared.

A number of brass founders made mathematical or surveying instruments, lancets, and the famous clockmaking Chandlees of Nottingham, Maryland, made a sundial that is signed. A few cast-brass (or bronze) skillets are known to have been made in America. The origins of the many cast kettles, and the button and bullet moulds, remain a mystery.

Objects of cast brass can be easily reproduced, and it is difficult for a novice to tell the old from the new. The absence of makers' marks and of other identifying evidence, such as patina on pewter, forces the buyer to depend chiefly on the integrity of the dealer.

British and European

The number of small objects made of metal and used about the house that were treated in a sufficiently attractive or imaginative way to interest the collector is enormous. With the exception of such 'big game' as medieval aquamaniles or Limoges enamels, out of reach of the average collector, all the articles referred to are to be found, if not in the more modest antique shops, at least in those specializing in the base metals.

The term 'base metal' is an unfortunate one, since it inevitably suggests a certain inferiority of quality. In fact, many of these articles were treated with no less exquisiteness of detail and delicacy of touch than the precious metals. Most suitable for the rendering of delicate ornament is steel, which, by reason of its hardness, could be sawn, filed, or chiselled to a lace-like fineness, such as can be found in the snuffboxes, étuis, scissors, and chains made at Brescia in the seventeenth century or in England in the eighteenth century. By reason of the enormous labour involved, steel was not used where high relief was required. In this case bronze was the most suitable material, cast, chased, and finally gilt. The reddish colour of the bronze provided a particularly well-suited base for gilding, and a very rich effect was obtained. Among the finest work achieved in this medium are the caskets and clock cases produced in South Germany in the second half of the sixteenth century. But more remarkable still are the furniture mounts and ornamental articles made by the Parisian *ciseleurs-doreurs* in the second half of the eighteenth century. The quality of the finish on the finest Louis XVI mounts is unsurpassed in the whole history of metal working. On the Continent these mounts have long been collected for their own sake, but in England it is only recently that even the excellent work in ormolu produced at Matthew Boulton's Birmingham factory in the late eighteenth century has been recognized.

Not only did the workers in the base metals achieve an excellence of quality which rivalled that of the contemporary goldsmiths, they frequently made use of the precious metals in order to enrich their own productions. The various techniques of inlaying and encrusting the surface of base metal with gold, silver, or another base metal were extensively used by the metal craftsmen throughout the history of the craft. The most ambitious and imaginative use of damascening was made by Italian craftsmen in the sixteenth century, probably inspired by the examples they saw from the Near East. The most elaborate damascened ornament was applied to armour and weapons, but the same craftsmen who decorated Milanese armour also executed the damascened enrichment on caskets and furniture mounts, and these latter can be obtained at a price far below that commanded by armour. The Milanese technique of enriching iron with gold and silver was paralleled by the Venetian technique of damascening brass with precious metal. Their manner was strongly influenced by the Orient, and the earlier brass vessels decorated in Venice are not easily distinguishable from those of Near Eastern origin.

Here we are concerned only with those pieces which have some pretensions to artistic merit. But alongside them, in the limitless field of folk art, innumerable unassuming objects, well designed for their simple domestic function, await the collector.

ANDIRONS

The iron firedog or andiron dates back to Roman times, but the earliest known examples date from the fifteenth century. As long as the fireplace occupied the central position in the hall, the firedog was of purely utilitarian design, but when the former was transferred to a side wall, becoming an important decorative feature, the firedog also received ornamental treatment. The earliest surviving firedogs conform to a standard type, whether of English, French, German, or Flemish origin, namely an arched base enriched with Gothic cusping, supporting a pilaster, the front of which is decorated with running scrolls. Sixteenth- and seventeenth-century firedogs were made to the same design but with Renaissance instead of Gothic ornament. Firedogs of this type were made of cast iron, the English ones being produced by the Sussex iron masters. There seems from an early date to have been a distinction between andirons and firedogs. The former term was used for the large dogs, standing 3 feet (91.4 cm) or more high, which were intended to decorate the fireplace. Though these andirons could also be put to use, they were usually accompanied by a smaller pair of firedogs proper, which stood closer into the hearth and supported the burning logs.

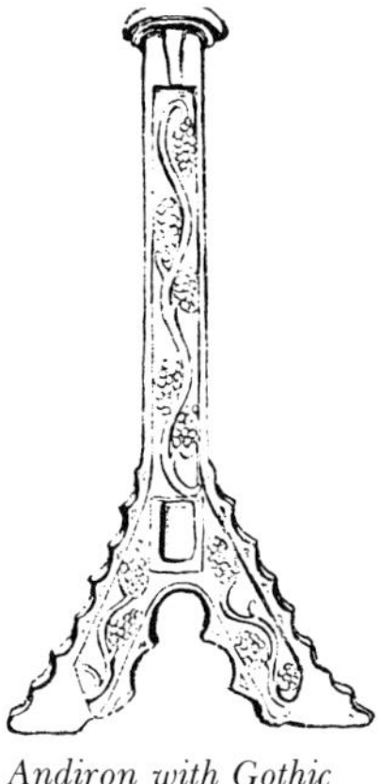

Andiron with Gothic ornament

Andiron with Renaissance ornament

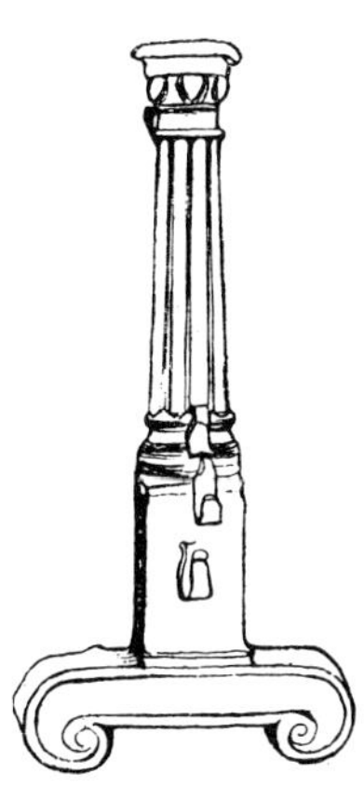

Left Pair of brass firedogs, English, late 17th century. Victoria & Albert Museum

Gilt-brass Restoration andiron

The earlier andirons were of wrought iron, but as early as the sixteenth century they were garnished with silver. In the seventeenth century andirons entirely of silver were produced, and there was a fashion for them in England after the Restoration. Numbers have survived from this date not only in the royal palaces but also in many country houses, and are not out of reach of the wealthy collector. The Restoration andiron had a particularly handsome baroque form, consisting of a pedestal on volute or claw feet supporting either a flaming vase or a figure. The finest examples, in silver, are of great magnificence and weight. Similar designs were also produced for the less wealthy in gilt brass. The introduction of the grate in the eighteenth century rendered the firedog superfluous.

In contrast to those used in drawing room and parlour, the various implements for tending the cottage fire remained unchanged and simple. Of purely functional character, they usually bore little in the way of ornamentation. As coal came into use, the poker and the shovel replaced the firefork.

Of the Continental andirons by far the most handsome type are the North Italian ones of the sixteenth and seventeenth centuries. These were cast in bronze and take the form of an elaborately worked pedestal supporting a figure of a warrior or a goddess.

AQUAMANILE

This term is used to describe the bronze ewers used in the Middle Ages for pouring water over the hands of guests after each course of a meal. As forks were not normally employed for conveying food to the mouth, frequent washing of the hands was necessary. The term is now confined to a particular type of medieval ewer of naturalistic form, the most popular being a lion on whose back crouched a dragon, serving as a handle. Other forms include a monster, a knight on horseback wearing a great helm, etc. Medieval aquamaniles of this type were cast by the *cire-perdu* process, and no two were exactly alike; many reproductions have, however, been cast from moulds in recent times. The earliest examples date from the thirteenth century, but they continued in use until the sixteenth century, when they were replaced by the more convenient ewer of helmet shape. They are now objects of extreme rarity, and few authentic examples are to be found in private ownership.

BRASS CANDLESTICKS

European candlesticks as early as the twelfth century are known but are not likely to be seen outside museums or cathedral treasuries. The earliest examples obtainable by the collector are the pricket candlesticks of enamelled copper made at Limoges in the thirteenth century. These are exceedingly rare and are pieces of high price. The only medieval candlesticks within the reach of the ordinary collector are the various fifteenth-century types produced in the Low Countries in one or other of the towns in the valley of the Meuse.

The earliest form of candlestick was the pricket, in which the candle was stuck on a metal, usually iron, spike projecting from the wax pan. The socket type, in which the candle was held in a cup or socket, did not come into common use until the fourteenth century, though it was certainly known much earlier.

The Mosan candlesticks were, until 1466, mostly

produced in the town of Dinant, and from there they were exported all over western Europe. Though the brass workers became dispersed during the latter part of the fifteenth century, they continued to work in just the same style that they had developed at Dinant. This is indicated by the remarkable uniformity of design of sixteenth-century, and earlier, candlesticks found in different European countries. From the thirteenth century onwards a large range of types were made, beginning with the rare figures of animals or monsters supporting a pricket, continuing with the fourteenth-century tripod prickets decorated with octagonal mouldings, and evolving in the fifteenth century into two main types: firstly, the pricket with tall, domed base, moulded stem, and large grease pan immediately below the pricket. The second type, which probably reached western Europe from the Near East, has a tall base of trumpet form, to the top of which is attached a wide rim or flange serving as a grease pan. The stem is decorated with lenticular mouldings and the socket is provided with a vertical opening resembling in shape a Gothic window, through which a spike could be inserted to eject the candle stub. As the sixteenth century advances the mouldings applied to the stem became more numerous, some four or five in number.

Far right Candlestick of cast brass with engraved decoration, English, *c.* 1880. Victoria & Albert Museum

Above Altar candlestick of hammered brass, English, late 17th century. Victoria & Albert Museum

In the course of the late sixteenth and early seventeenth centuries the grease pan, instead of being formed from the upper surface of the base, became independent and was set on the stem just above the base. About the middle of the century it moved up farther, reaching a position about halfway up the stem, as in the typical English candlesticks of this epoch. They are very simply constructed of a hollow tube of trumpet form decorated with a series of grooves running horizontally around the stem at regular intervals. The contemporary Continental candlestick is usually of more sophisticated form with finely proportioned baluster stem. Towards the end of the seventeenth century the grease pan completed its upwards move and reached a position just under the socket. Finally, at the end of the century the lip of the socket was turned over to give a small grease pan, the grease pan proper abandoned, and instead a depression cut in the top of the base.

The eighteenth-century candlestick went through the variations of style familiar in the evolution of silver, that is, octagonal baluster in the first quarter, shell base and vase-shaped baluster in the middle of the century, and, finally, the square base and section of the neoclassical style in the latter years of the century.

Some idea of date can often be gained from the method of construction of brass candlesticks. Until the late seventeenth century the stem and socket were cast solid in one piece and attached to the base by means of a screw thread or a tenon which projected through a hole in the centre of the base and was then burred over to hold it in place. About 1670 a new method was introduced by which stem and socket were hollow-cast in two pieces and then brazed together, thus saving much metal. In the nineteenth century there was a return to solid casting in one piece.

BRASS CHANDELIERS

Chandeliers were made in three main materials. There are those of wood and glass, which by reason of their delicacy are most suitable for reception rooms, and there are the ones of brass with which we are here concerned.

It used to be thought that all the brass chandeliers which are found in England were made in the Netherlands. Documentary and other evidence shows conclusively that this is not so and that many were made in England.

Right Pair of brass candlesticks by George Grove, English, mid-18th century. William Job, London

Far right Brass chandelier, possibly French, *c.* 1770. William Job, London

Chandeliers of English manufacture

In England there was no difference necessarily between secular chandeliers and ecclesiastical ones. The examples in the House of Commons and in the House of Lords were of brass, and so were those in the Livery Halls of some London Companies. It might be thought that the ones intended for public buildings are never available for collection. This is not so, because many were taken down when gas lighting was introduced in the nineteenth century and those that escaped the furnace were often rehung in private houses.

The earliest chandelier of those thought to have been made in England is in the church at Sonning, Berkshire. It is dated 1675. The form of construction which it and the one at Langley Marish, Buckinghamshire, and that in the nave of St Helen, Abingdon, Berkshire, exemplify was the typical one until *c.* 1740. The various parts are normally cast. The candle sockets are screwed to the end of the branches; the grease pans are wedged between; the body incorporates trays pierced with holes into which are hooked the branches; at the bottom it ends in a globe and pendant, and at the top is an ornamental finial and a suspension ring. The globe and the parts between it and the finial, exclusive of the trays, are hollow, and the whole of the body is held together by an iron rod with the pendant at one end and a hole to receive a pin at the other. The only departures from this form of construction are caused by different methods of attaching the branches. In some examples they hook into bosses which project from a plain vertical band. In others there are castings that have a top surface which is pierced and serves the function of a tray.

The branches of most early examples are of circular section; they consist simply of two opposed curves with perhaps a moulding where they join. The inner end is an open spiral, and the outer end is everted so that the screw of the candle socket passes through it at right angles. They droop heavily. After *c.* 1710, branches become more elaborate: they are often of hexagonal or octagonal section and the inner end consists of multiple scrolls while the outer end is no longer everted but thickened instead.

If there are wide spaces between the branches, these are filled by ornaments fitting into holes or dovetailing into slots. The ornaments take various forms. They may be pins, or they may be branches, each ending in a bud or a flower, or a silhouette representation of three tulips, as at Whitchurch, Shropshire. At Aston Hall, Birmingham, there are

Brass chandelier, formerly in St Mary's Church, Newmarket, English, early 18th century. Victoria & Albert Museum

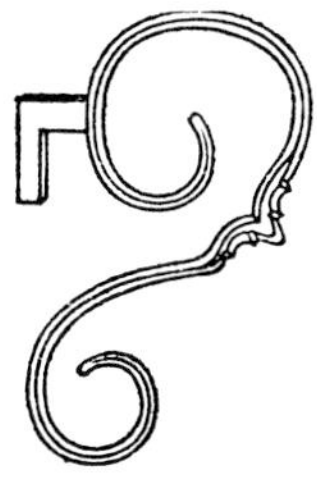

Chandelier ornaments from St Martin-at-Palace, Norwich (top) *and Llanasa, Flint*

Finials from Harlow, Essex (top) *and Langley Marish, Buckinghamshire*

Chandelier ornaments from St Helen, Abingdon, Berkshire (left) *and Wickwar, Gloucestershire*

cherubs which formerly held objects aloft, and there is the rose and thistle badge of Queen Anne at Tiverton, Devon, and Stratton Strawless, Norfolk. Similar ornaments to these may occur between the tiers of branches, in which case special trays are provided for them. Usually, they consist of S-scrolls, but sometimes there are branches, which at Deane, Lancashire, end in flying cherubs with roses and crowns, and at Llanasa, Flint, and Upholland, Lancashire, in silhouette patterns.

The purpose of the globe is to reflect the candlelight and, by its weight, to prevent the tendency to swing. It is usually spherical. When it is polygonal the candle sockets and remainder of the body are partly polygonal also. The main development that takes place in the globe is that it acquires a central collar *c.* 1715 and becomes flattened after 1725.

The finial is a feature of most chandeliers. The form which was at first most popular on account of its being a symbol of immortality was the cherub head, but after *c.* 1700 it took second place to the dove, whose justification for use was that it is the symbol of the Holy Spirit. The dove, with an olive spray in its beak, became by far the commonest form of finial. The only other regularly used was the bishop's mitre.

The construction of chandeliers underwent a noticeable change *c.* 1745. Now, the branches, instead of hooking into trays, are attached to the globe, and, for this to be possible, the halves of the globe and the collar are three separate castings and the branches are bolted to the collar. The change was not immediate, and there was a period of transition when the branches fitted by means of tenons or hooks into eyes forming a continuation of the collar. The new construction meant that there had to be as many globes as there were tiers of branches, and the result was that all details assume heavier proportions, and mouldings are correspondingly bolder. The body often incorporates sections of gadrooning; so does the pendant, which consists of several parts instead of just one. It may end in a floral motif or in a handle or ring, which is primarily an ornament but was also useful at the lowering and raising of a chandelier whenever the provision of pulley and counterweight made this possible. Branches now are of circular section and droop only slightly. The curves are ornamented with scrolls, where they join is a moulding lozenge-shaped or hexagonal in plan, and the inner end is a closed spiral. The candle sockets now have separate nozzles. Such nozzles at first are closed at the bottom. Every form of finial is virtually abandoned in favour of the flame. It is, like the cherub head, a symbol of immortality and has the merit of hiding the device for suspension.

Heavy chandeliers with flame finials continued to be made until *c.* 1770, when a reaction set in. The use of the dove as a finial was resumed, and proportions become more graceful again. The example at Eynsham, Oxfordshire, is typical of what was being designed. The flame still appears as a finial, and it frequently issues from an urn. Candle sockets of the latest chandeliers are characteristically urn-shaped, and the place of the moulding where the curves of the branches join may be taken by a pair of acanthus leaves. There were no further changes before 1830, and then the introduction of gas lighting was bringing the manufacture of chandeliers almost to an end. After this, only country dwellers and antiquarians still had a use for them.

Brass chandelier, 18th century, English. Victoria & Albert Museum

This typological study is based almost entirely on the evidence of the chandeliers made in London. The London makers were more progressive than those in the provinces. They were responsible for most of the chandeliers made in England and were the only ones until the nineteenth century to distribute their products throughout the country. There are no obvious characteristics of London work. It has to be recognized by its high quality and by the use of certain castings. Finials are the most significant because they recur with greatest frequency, and one which does so particularly is a dove which appears in 1704 and which survived as a copy into the nineteenth century. Any chandelier that has this dove as its finial is likely to have been made in London.

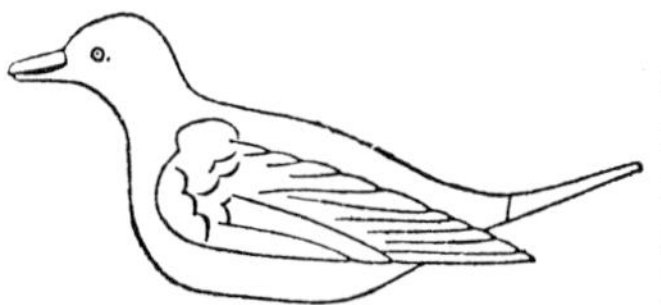

Dove finial from Marshfield, Gloucestershire

The chandeliers made at the various provincial centres have each their own characteristics. The finial is the part to look at first. Early chandeliers made in Bristol have a dove finial, made distinct by its shape and the absence of feathering on the body. Late ones have a crown of leaf-like flames. Thomas Bayley and his successors at Bridgwater used a biconical flame finial. At Chester the finial was normally a dove: with tilted tail and prominent rump, if it is early; with fantail, if late. The Cock's of Birmingham preferred a finial consisting of separate flames of sheet metal, but they shared this preference with some London makers, and their work is best identified by the form of the branches.

Chandeliers of Dutch manufacture

It is in the Netherlands that the brass chandelier has its traditional home. There, they were used for private houses as well as for public buildings. The *tableaux de modes* suggest that in the seventeenth century they were an established part of the domestic scene.

The Netherlands is probably where most, if not all, of the earliest chandeliers were made. These are the medieval ecclesiastical ones. Their central feature is the figure of a saint, which shows that they were looked on as receptacles for candles to be burnt as symbols of devotion rather than as a means of lighting. In view of the purpose which they served, most of the chandeliers were destroyed at the Reformation. If the few that survive are typical, generally the branches were ornamented with vine leaves, and an animal head with a ring through its mouth was the form of pendant terminal.

After the Reformation Dutch chandeliers were constructed in the same way as the earliest ones of English make. The former may be recognized because designs – at least in the seventeenth century – are normally more intricate and heavier and there is often a double-headed eagle finial. Branches sometimes have a foliage motif or a fish head where the curves join and a human head at the inner end. Ornaments between branches are more elaborate than those on English chandeliers. There are trumpeters and cherub heads at Cirencester, Gloucestershire, and scrolls to which are screwed finials at Sherbone, Dorset, and Woodbridge, Suffolk. The form of chandelier normal in England after 1745 does not seem to have been made in the Netherlands. There the tendency during the eighteenth century was towards plainness. Finials and other ornaments are entirely dispensed with. Branches are simply scrolled and the fish heads which they may incorporate are vestigial. They are usually provided with tenons instead of hooks. These fit into holes in the edges of hollow trays and are held in position by pins that pass through them and through the tops and bottoms of the trays. This method of attaching the branches was never adopted by English makers.

There are other chandeliers besides the ones made in England and the Netherlands. But the collector who studies their products alone will not want further evidence to convince him that chandeliers are among the finest and most spectacular achievements of the brass founder's craft.

CASKETS

The earliest caskets likely to come the way of the collector are those made in Sicily during the thirteenth and fourteenth centuries. They are constructed of ivory with brass mounts, and are believed to have been the work of Arabic craftsmen. The Near Eastern element in them can be seen, not in any constructional detail but in the painted ornament with which the finer examples were enriched. This ornament often introduces Cufic characters or amorphous scrollwork of Saracenic origin. Caskets or small coffers of the fifteenth century are far less rare than the earlier examples; there were two main types, those constructed entirely of iron and those of wood, sometimes covered with leather and always furnished with more or less elaborate bands of iron. Such caskets were made in France, the Low Countries, Germany, and Spain, and it is often difficult to be certain of the country of origin, especially of the earlier types. Subsequently, recognized national types emerge. One French type is entirely of iron with arched lid. The earlier examples have applied Gothic tracery ornamentation, the later ones have a

French casket, blue iron damascened with grotesques in gold

German iron casket showing locking mechanism on lid, 16th century. Mary Bellis Antiques, Hungerford

plain surface with either etched or damascened ornament. The Spanish type is of almost rectangular section with only slightly curved walls. It is of wood covered with one or more layers of tinned sheet iron, pierced with reticulated ornament. This type is provided with stout bands and an elaborate lock decorated with Gothic pinnacles.

South German casket, iron with mounts of gilt brass, late 16th century

The most common German type dates from the second half of the sixteenth century and shows no trace of the Gothic ornament which persisted so long into the sixteenth century in the locksmiths' workshops. It is rectangular in plan and is constructed of iron sheet sometimes enriched with mounts of gilt brass. The whole of the exterior surface is etched with floral scrolls or with hunting or allegorical subjects. The lock, which is accommodated on the underside of the lid, is of great elaboration, shooting as many as a dozen bolts. These coffers were made in Nuremberg and Augsburg, but are never signed. On the other hand, the miniature caskets of gilt brass, sometimes enriched with silver and even enamel, and engraved instead of etched, are usually known as Michael Mann boxes because so many of them bear the signature of a Nuremberg locksmith of that name.

Miniature casket, South German, c. *1600*

Snuff boxes, Brescian, late 17th century, the top one dated 1694

Fine coffers of English manufacture do not appear before the second half of the seventeenth century, when we find the very rare but incomparable works of the Bickfords (e.g. the jewel casket of Queen Mary II in the Victoria and Albert Museum) and the fairly common but extremely attractive caskets with fall fronts veneered with oyster marquetry and furnished with elaborate gilt brass hingework.

CHISELLED AND CUT STEEL

The art of steel chiselling is a byproduct of the locksmith's and gunsmith's trade. Small articles have been chiselled from iron or steel since the Middle Ages, but from the collector's point of view, four main groups can be recognized. Firstly, the articles made in the northern Italian city of Brescia in the seventeenth and eighteenth centuries. These include snuffboxes, scissors, tweezers, and thimbles, usually chiselled and pierced with floral scrollwork interspersed with monsters, similar in design to the ornament familiar on Brescian-made firearms (1). The most distinguished Brescian artist, who usually signed his works, was Matteo Acqua Fresca (2). The second group was produced in Paris by the same chisellers who decorated sword and gun furniture of the period of Louis XIV and Louis XV. Characteristic of their work are the chatelaines, étuis, shuttles, and more rarely, snuffboxes, usually chiselled with classical figure subjects against a gilt stippled ground. Similar but somewhat coarser work was also produced in Germany. The third group was produced by the artists of the Imperial Russian small arms factory at Tula. The factory was founded by Peter the Great, and their work dates from the eighteenth century. The artisans mastered not only the art of chiselling iron but also of encrusting it with various softer metals and of faceting it (cut steel). Besides smaller objects, such as candlesticks and caskets, the Tula factory also turned out large pieces of furniture and even mantelpieces entirely constructed of cut and faceted steel. The last group is English and flourished at first about the middle of the eighteenth century in Woodstock in Oxfordshire and subsequently at Birmingham in the Soho works set up by Matthew Boulton. The Woodstock cottage industry produced both chiselled and faceted steel, but the Birmingham factory, which eventually put Woodstock out of business, concentrated on cut steel. They made sword hilts, buttons, chatelaines, buckles, and

The Medici jewel casket, Italian steel, 17th century. Victoria & Albert Museum

Set of fourteen table knives with ivory handles depicting figures of kings, *c.* 1604. Victoria & Albert Museum

cheap jewelry. Cut steel was used as a more durable alternative to marcasite in the late eighteenth and early nineteenth century.

COPPER WORK

Owing to the difficulty of working copper in its pure form, it has not been extensively used by the metal worker. In the sixteenth and early seventeenth centuries caskets, clock cases, and scientific instruments were frequently made of copper, which was subsequently engraved and gilt. Those parts of the case or instrument which were cast were, however, made of brass or bronze. Owing to its suitability for engraving, it was much used for flat surfaces which were to be decorated in this way. The only other significant European use of copper was by the Italian coppersmiths, who made ewers, basins, and other vessels. The earlier examples were decorated with fine engraving, and in the seventeenth century embossed with bold floral ornament of baroque character, but vessels in this last group do not as a rule rise above the level of peasant art.

CUTLERY

The history of eating-knives goes back to remote antiquity, but for the collector it may be said to commence in the fifteenth century. Knives dating from the Romano–British period have been excavated in considerable numbers, but the condition of these is usually such that they are more likely to attract the archaeologist than the collector. Until well into the sixteenth century the history of cutlery is that of the knife only. Forks were known in the Middle Ages, but were normally used only for carving the joint of meat. An extremely rare type of fork was also used in noble households for eating certain kinds of fruit, the juice of which might stain the fingers.

The ordinary eating knife of the fifteenth century was of too simple a character to be considered worth preserving, and the only examples which have come to light have been discovered in the course of excavations. On the other hand, knives with handles of precious materials, either hardstone, gold, or silver, have been valued on account of their beauty, and a few have survived through the ages (1 and 2). The most beautiful medieval knives are those made for members of the Burgundian Court; a number of these exist, all in museums. Their handles are of silver gilt enriched with the heraldic bearings of the original owner in translucent enamel.

The inventories of the property of the Tudor monarchs show that they possessed many sets of fine cutlery contained in cases of leather or wood, and mounted in handles of hardstone or ivory. None of these pieces can now be identified, if indeed they still exist, but there are a number of sixteenth-century types of cutlery that may still be found. These include the Flemish type with handle of brass or latten fur-

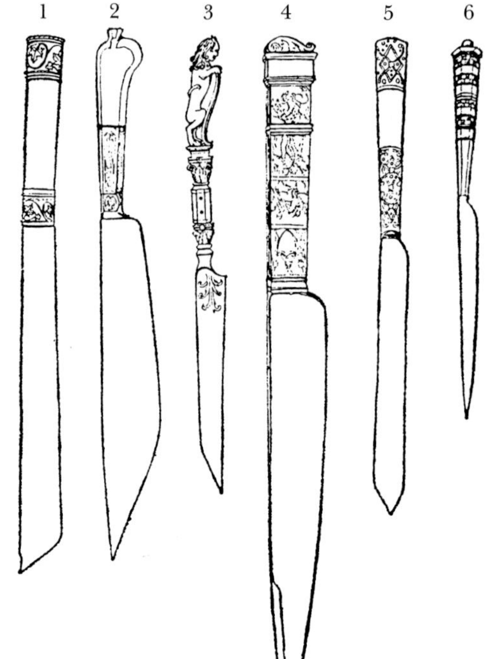

1. *Carving-knife, ivory handle with silver-gilt mounts, 14th century*
2. *Carving-knife, ivory handle with enamelled silver shoulder, Italian, late 15th century*
3. *French, 16th century*
4. *Italian, late 16th century*
5 and 6. *London-made knives of the early 17th century*
7. *Ivory handles, gilt brass terminals, German, early 17th century*
8. *Carved ivory handle, English,* c. *1680*
9. *Ivory handles, piqué with silver, English,* c. *1690*
10. *Carved ivory, Dutch, end of 17th century*
11. *Dutch, first half of 17th century*
12. *Handle of Venetian millefiori glass, late 17th century*
13. *Handle of bow porcelain, mid-18th century*

nished with wooden scales. The finials of the handles are often formed as horses' hooves, and the rivets holding the scales as horse bells, but the finest examples are engraved with minute religious subjects. These Flemish knives were exported to England in quantity, and many have been dug up in London.

The French sixteenth-century type has a handle of gilt iron, the finial chiselled in the form of an animal or monster, the scales being of ivory or mother-of-pearl (3). The most beautiful is undoubtedly the Italian form, which has a flat, pilaster-like handle of silver, sometimes enriched with niello, surmounted by a gilt bronze finial in the form of a capital (4).

Although forks had not yet entered into general use in northern Europe, a single fork is usually found along with a set of knives by the latter part of the sixteenth century. It was probably intended for carving and for serving. The true serving knife, sometimes known as a *présentoir*, which appears in the fifteenth century, has a thin, broad blade, with the edges either parallel or widening slightly towards the point, which was either cut off square or slightly rounded.

Little is known of English knives made before the seventeenth century, and it is difficult to distinguish them from imported Flemish knives. No sixteenth-century English knives of fine quality are known to exist. By the early seventeenth century, however, the English cutlers were making cutlery as fine as that of any other country. The work of the London cutlers can be recognized by the daggermark which was struck on all blades made by members of the Cutlers' Company, in addition to the maker's mark. A characteristic feature of London knives of the first half of the seventeenth century was the decorative treatment of the shoulders, which were either damascened with gold or encrusted with silver (5 and 6).

The main source of knife blades in western Europe was the German town of Solingen, whence blades were exported all over Europe, being fitted with handles in the locality to which they had been sent. A Solingen stamp on a blade does not necessarily signify that the handle was also made there.

In the seventeenth century the usual materials for handles were ivory, silver, and various kinds of hardstone, especially agate. Of the great variety of types of handle made, the most attractive are the Dutch wedding knives, made in pairs with handles entirely of silver finely engraved with Biblical subjects and grotesques, often after the designs of the Liège-born engraver Johann Theodor de Bry (11).

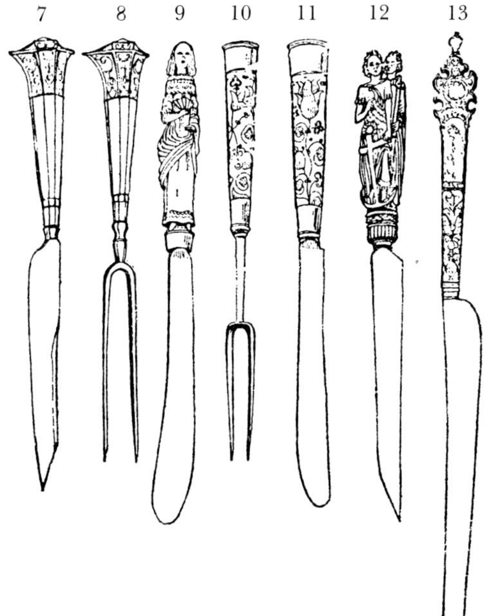

In the eighteenth century ivory and agate gave way to porcelain or stoneware as a fashionable material for handles (14 and 15), but silver remained usual for all except the cheaper grades made of horn or wood. The characteristic eighteenth-century knife has a handle of pistol shape in which is mounted a curved blade of so-called 'scimitar' form. Since the late seventeenth century the fork had become a normal feature of the dining table in northern as well as southern Europe. Though forks had been familiar objects since early in the seventeenth century, they were long used by preference for holding the meat while it was being cut, not for conveying it to the mouth. The extreme sharpness of the prongs of the early two-pronged forks may account for this delay in their exploitation. In Italy, where forks were in use in the sixteenth century, they were made of silver, which did not take so sharp a point.

Cutlery ceases to be of interest to the collector by the early nineteenth century. The last sets of cutlery worthy of notice are the travelling sets composed of knife, fork, spoon, beaker, etc., which were still produced until well into the nineteenth century, and were often mounted in gold or silver.

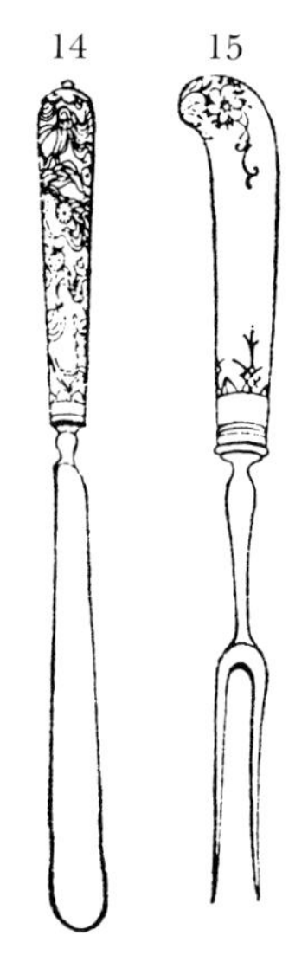

14 and 15. *Handles of ivory and agate, 18th century*

DAMASCENING

The art of encrusting the surface of iron, steel, brass, or copper with gold or/and silver has been known and practised since antiquity, especially in the Near East, but at no time in Europe has it flourished more than in Milan during the middle and second half of the sixteenth century, where it was a byproduct of the thriving armourers' trade. Thin iron sheets were embossed, often in a rather summary manner, with subjects from Roman history or mythology against landscape backgrounds and damascened with gold and silver. The Milanese damascening of this period is of fine quality and bears comparison with the best Saracenic work. Damascened plaques were made in quantity to more or less standard shapes and were sold to cabinet makers, who mounted them on ebony caskets, chest of drawers, and even large pieces such as tables and mirrors. Though the majority of the damascened ironwork encountered by the collector is likely to be of Milanese origin, there were highly competent damasceners at work elsewhere in Europe, in Augsburg and Nuremberg, in Paris, and in other Italian cities. In the seventeenth century some fine damascening was done on English sword and knife handles, probably by immigrant Italian artists. The detailed ornament that could be achieved by damascening was not appreciated in the age of baroque, when a rather more vigorous spirit was admired, and the art did not survive the sixteenth century in Italy.

DINANDERIE

Small brassware made in or around the Flemish town of Dinant, near Liège. Whereas elsewhere bronze was mostly employed for the manufacture of domestic vessels, the presence of zinc deposits around Liège led the founders of the valley of the Meuse to adopt brass in preference. The town of Dinant became by the late Middle Ages so famous for its brassware than the name *Dinanderie* was used to describe the production of the whole region. Typical articles made were aquamaniles, basins, jugs, cooking vessels, and candlesticks, many of them quite simple objects for domestic purposes. Among the more splendid achievements of the Mosan craftsmen may be mentioned lecterns and fonts. In 1466 the town of Dinant was sacked by Philippe le Bon, and as a result the brass founders emigrated, partly to other towns in the valley of the Meuse, but partly to France and England.

ENAMELLED BRASSWARE

Copper was used for preference rather than brass for enamelling in the Middle Ages, and apart from a few harness ornaments and the Garter stall plates preserved in St George's Chapel, Windsor Castle, medieval enamelled brassware does not exist. During the seventeenth century a cheap form of enamelling was introduced in England and on the Continent, in which brass was used as a base. The enamel was of the *champlevé* type, but instead of the depressions for the enamel being cut out by hand, they were cast in one with the object. Such a method was unsuited for the production of small or fine objects, but it was applied to quite a variety of brassware, including andirons, candlesticks, stirrups and horse harness, and sword hilts.

Enamelled brass objects of particularly crude quality were produced in Russia until comparatively recent times; coarsely enamelled brass icons, mostly dating from the nineteenth century, survive in such large numbers that one suspects they must have been made for export. The colour range of all this enamelled brass is restricted: blue, red, green, yellow, and white are most usual.

Far right Jewel casket, etched copper with mounts of gilt metal, German (Augsburg), 16th century. Victoria & Albert Museum

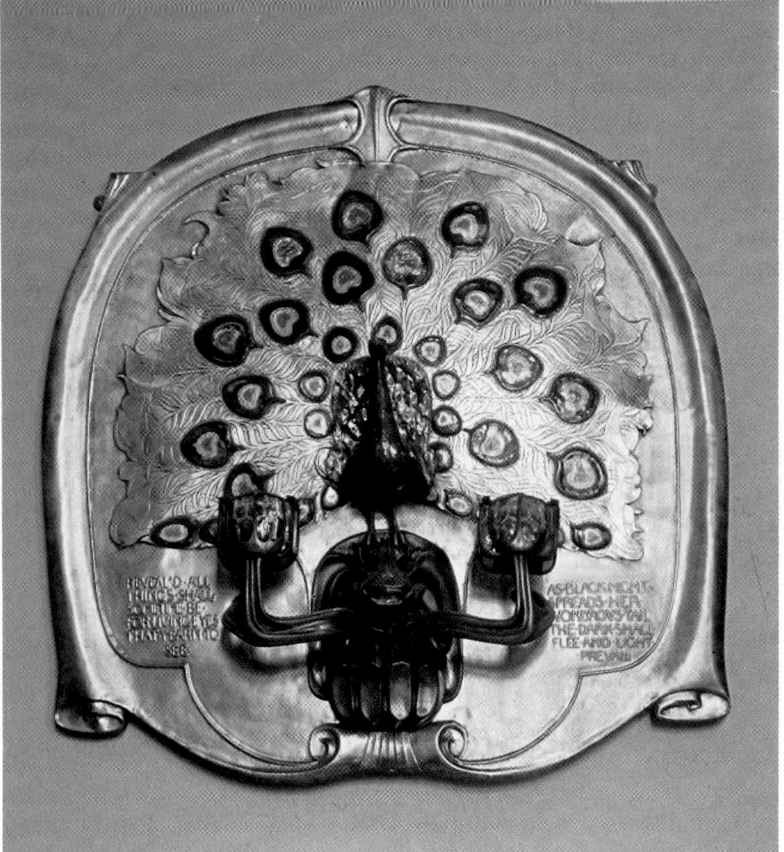

Peacock sconce made of steel, bronze, enamelled brass and silver, designed by Alex Fisher and first shown at the Arts and Crafts Exhibition of 1899. Victoria & Albert Museum

ETCHED METALWORK

The art of etching is believed to have originated in the process of ornamenting armour with acid etching first introduced in the second half of the fifteenth century. In the sixteenth century small objects of iron, brass, copper, and even silver were commonly decorated with etched ornament. This technique of ornament was particularly popular in Germany in the second half of the sixteenth century, and was applied to a great variety of objects. In the case of small articles, such as cutlery, tools, watch cases, locks, and scientific instruments, panels of mauresque ornament were used, the larger surfaces available on caskets or clock cases were decorated with figure subjects. The finest etched ornament is to be found on the various tools, instruments, and articles of military equipment made for the Saxon Court. Whether these were produced in Dresden or obtained from Nuremberg or Augsburg is uncertain. The etched ironwork of Nuremberg and Augsburg had an importance comparable with that of the damascened panels made in Milan. Etched ornament is found on French and Italian locksmiths' work, but it is not of the quality achieved by the German craftsmen.

GEMELLION

This term describes a basin provided with a spout at the base and used for the liturgical washing of the hands at the Mass. Though the ornament found on them is in most cases of secular character, their use seems to have been mainly ecclesiastical. The spout at the side indicates that they were intended to serve as ewers for pouring water rather than as basins for receiving it. The gemellion was one of the standard productions of the enamelling shops at Limoges, and the majority of those known are decorated with Limoges enamel. They date from the thirteenth and fourteenth centuries.

HORSE BRASSES

Horse brasses in gleaming, glowing tones ranging from orange to madder, lemon, and amber are now collected to ornament the fireside or hang upon the wall. Although they have a two-thousand-year-old history in England, it was not until the 1840s that it became customary to enrich the harness of a driven horse with more than a single brass known as a face piece. For the most part Georgian horse brasses were in the design known as the sunflash, with a highly burnished dome radiating beams of sunlight with the horse's every movement.

Selection of martingales with horse brasses showing typical patterns and types

Collectors now delight in ascribing their introduction to a belief in their power of quelling the evil eye, but there is no evidence to show that they were intended to serve more than an ornamental purpose.

In the saddlers', brass founders', and other pattern books of the early nineteenth century no reference is made to horse brasses. By the 1860s, however, full ranges of cart-horse harness brasses were illustrated, more than 330 different pieces composing the enrichment for a single set of harness. Fifteen or twenty of these were pendant horse brasses: there was a face piece for the forehead; a pair of ear brasses for hanging behind the ears; three for hanging on each side of the runners at the shoulders, and as many as ten hanging from the martingale.

The early and mid-Victorian makers of brass horse furniture devised many horse brasses that would have some personal association with the purchaser's trade or district. The Staffordshire knot obviously was at home in Staffordshire; the wool merchant's symbol was always stocked by saddlers in the sheep-rearing districts; the windmill was for the Lincolnshire millers; the dolphin sold well in Wiltshire. Towards the end of the nineteenth century this aspect of horse-brass salesmanship was virtually abandoned in favour of motifs in no way associated with the driven horses of specific trades or regions.

Horse brasses may be collated into nine chronological groups based on manufacturing processes.

(1) *1750s to about 1800*
Handworked from hard-textured latten, chiefly used for Georgian sunflashes. Very rare.

(2) *Until about 1860*
Cast in brass containing calamine. This polishes with far less radiance than latten or later brasses. Its surface is flawed with shallow pitting caused by the impossibility of removing all air bubbles from the molten metal. Rare.

(3) *Early 1800s to 1850*
Handworked from rolled calamine brass, soft-textured and dull in appearance, and marred with a few surface pittings. From this metal were made sunflashes – the dome burnished to brilliance – and a crescent design with incurved horns and a rectangular strap loop, a pair of wings extending outward from the loop-plate junction. Uncommon.

(4) *Late 1830s to 1860*
Cast in fine brass alloy of the pinchbeck type, composed of about equal weights of finest quality copper and zinc. This metal, much more costly than ordinary brass, could be cast in sharper relief. Horse brasses in this metal were chased, then tinged to a beautiful reddish-golden hue by heat-and-acid processes. The high lights were then burnished. From this metal were made heraldic brasses which might be gilded. Rare.

(5) *Late 1830s and 1860*
Cast from a copper-spelter metal, known as Emerson's brass, smooth-surfaced and brilliant gold in colour. It is easily distinguished from the pinchbeck metal although coloured by the same process. Uncommon.

(6) *1860 to early 1900s*
Obsolete brass-casting methods had by now been abandoned, and various alloys of commercial copper and zinc were used. The Walsall trade evolved a special alloy displaying a high brilliance when polished. The rough casting was file-finished, pierced by drilling, its relief work carefully modelled, then smoothed and polished. At the back of each brass, when it left the mould, were a pair of small projections known as 'gets'. In early examples of this period, and in all former cast brasses, these were carefully removed, every sign of their presence being made invisible. Later 'gets' were crudely removed with the file, distinct rings remaining as evidence of their presence. In some brasses the 'gets' were on the upper edge of the strap loop: sometimes these were removed by grinding. 'Gets' on all souvenirs (group 8) noted remain as ugly blemishes which would not have been tolerated by any saddler.

(7) *1866 to 1900s*
Stamped from malleable rolled spelter brass and made almost exclusively at Walsall and Birmingham. The backs of early examples were filled with lead, and they are now very rare. Stamped brasses weighed no more than 2 oz., less than half the weight of their cast equivalents, and were cheaper to produce in long runs. The metal is smooth on both sides, the relief pattern showing in reverse at the back. Stamped horse brasses may be perforated, and designs bear a close resemblance to earlier cast examples. Surrounds are usually flat, but the inner edge may be raised to form a rim in low relief. Rims and perforations were carefully finished by filing until the 1890s.

(8) *From about 1920*
Souvenirs made from contemporary designs. These are not reproductions of earlier horse brasses, but were and are made for purposes of interior decoration. The collector avoids these. They are usually sold exactly as they leave the foundry, where the removal of sand and smoothing of the surface is carried out by tumbling in an iron barrel. Some dealers hand-finish them, and so treat them that they superficially resemble genuine horse brasses, perhaps unaware that the patterns are new and the metal displays little resemblance to the Walsall alloy.

(9) *From the early 1920s*
This is the period when many fakes were made; that is to say exact copies of genuine horse brasses, intended to deceive the serious collector and abounding in great numbers. Handmade horse brasses from rolled sheet brass are still being marketed. The metal is of a quality easily distinguishable from the early alloy. Fakes are usually cast, however, and even though handwork and acids may give them an old appearance, close inspection of inner corners of the strap loop will demonstrate the presence of the faker's hand which fails to simulate exactly the effect of surfaces smoothed with years of wear by rubbing against leather. These fakes omit, too, the rubbing and consequent wear which occurred on the back of the lower edge of the brass, making it appreciably thinner. Much hand polishing in the course of years resulted in a silky texture: no amount of mechanical polishing will produce precisely this effect. Otherwise, when given a well-worn appearance it is difficult to distinguish a fake from a genuine example if the alloy has been carefully selected, which is seldom.

When a collector becomes familiar with the appearance, feel, and patterns of undoubtedly genuine horse brasses little difficulty will be experienced in distinguishing between each of the nine groups.

KEYS

The key collector can hope to include not only medieval but even Roman keys in his collection, for these have survived, though almost invariably in excavated state, in considerable numbers. With a very few exceptions that are hardly likely to come within the reach of the collector, the medieval key was devoid of ornament. It had, nevertheless, qualities beyond those of mere function, since the form of the bow and the proportion between bow, shank, and bit shows the sense of design that is natural to the craftsman. The bow usually took some simple Gothic form, such as a trefoil or quatrefoil, the shank was plain and the bit was thin with parallel sides. Gothic keys showing great elaboration of ornament should be regarded with suspicion.

It was not till the mid-sixteenth century that keys became the object of elaborate decorative treatment. The hundred years from about 1550 to 1650 were dominated by the French locksmiths, and in no other country was the beauty of their fine steelwork even approached. The finest French keys of the Renaissance were elaborate creations; the bow was composed of addorsed winged figures supported by an Ionic or Corinthian capital (4). The shank was hollow and of complex section, triangular with incurved sides, square-, heart-, or cloverleaf-shaped. Instead of the thin bit of the fifteenth century, the bit was stoutly built, splaying outwards from the shank. These finely wrought French Renaissance keys were much sought after by collectors during the latter years of the nineteenth century, and numbers of them were faked to meet this demand.

With the French masterpiece lock went a characteristic form of key with a very large bow of pyramidal design. The sides of the pyramid were filled with pierced tracery, and it was supported by a ring, the axis of which was at right angles to the axis of the shank. The ring was filled with tracery of Gothic design. Keys of this type continued to be made according to the regulations of the French locksmiths' guilds right up till the Revolution (5).

At the same time as English locks began to achieve a high standard, so also did English keys. Among the most attractive English keys are those with the bows pierced with the royal cipher or with the arms of some noble family (6–8). Characteristic of the eight-

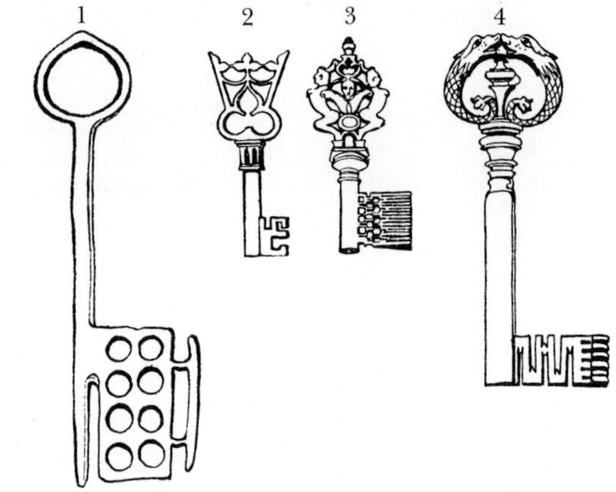

1. *14th century*
2. *French, 15th century*
3. *French, 16th century*
4. *French second half of 16th century*

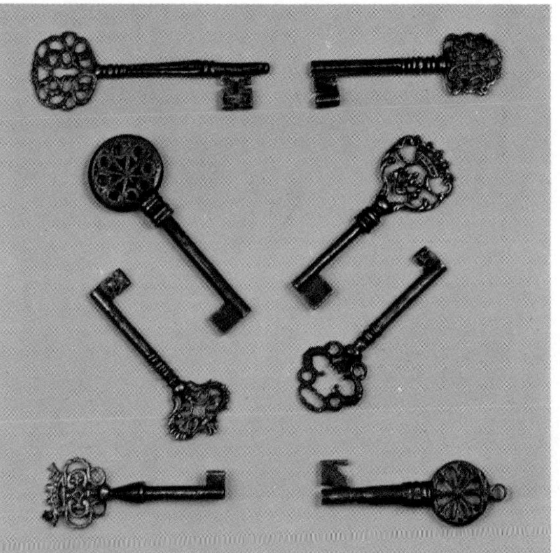

Selection of eight steel keys, French and German, late 17th century. Arthur Davidson, London

Right Rim lock with key and pair of matching hinges of pierced and engraved brass over blue steel plates. The lock signed 'Johannes Wilkes de Birmingham Fecit', English, second half of the 17th century. Victoria & Albert Museum

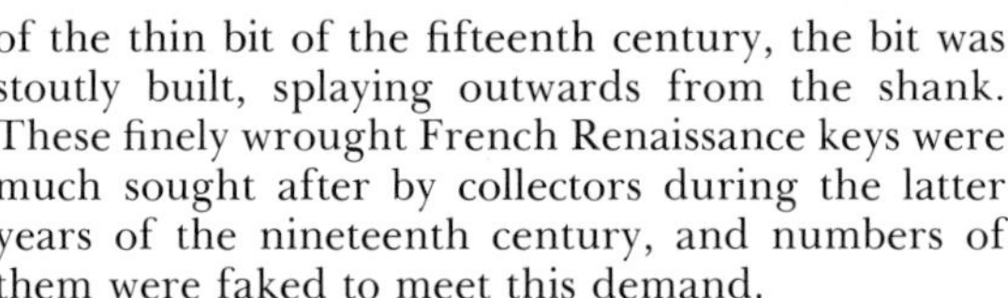

5

5. *French 'masterpiece' key, 17th century*

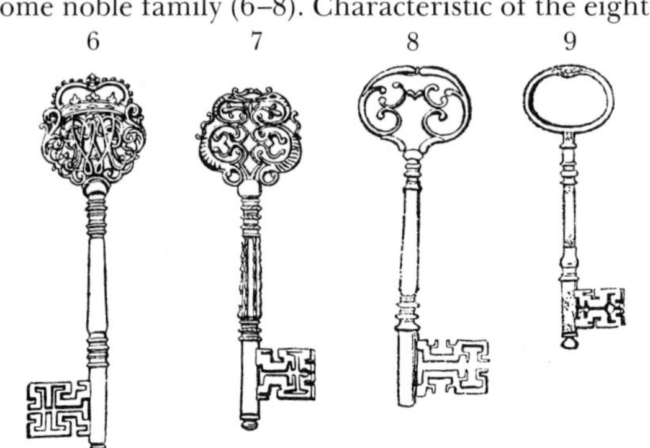

6. *English, crowned cipher of William III*
7. *English, c. 1700*
8. *English, early 18th century*
9. *English, early 19th century*

eenth century, both in England and on the Continent, are the Chamberlains' keys, made of gilt brass and worn attached to a silk rosette as a badge of office. Numbers of these survive, especially those of the smaller German princedoms. Neither German nor Italian keys achieved great artistic quality; the latter conformed to one type with a circular bow filled with roughly executed debased Gothic tracery.

LOCKS

Ancient Britons living on the coast of Cornwall nearly three thousand years ago were intrigued by the pin locks in hard wood introduced to them as objects of barter by the Phoenician merchants. The Britons were soon copying them in fine oak, creating a craft that continued unceasingly until early Victorian times, when precisely similar locks were in everyday use in Cornwall, Devon, and Scotland.

The first metal locks are attributed to English locksmiths in the reign of King Alfred: the craft had become well established in London by the twelfth century. The two principles of bolt action then in use remained unaltered until late in the eighteenth century. The majority were of warded construction: others included a tumbler in the mechanism.

Plate locks secured doors until late in the fifteenth century: their manufacture continued uninterrupted until early Victorian days. Plate locks let into rectangular blocks of oak were known as stock locks.

Rim locks, in which the mechanism was entirely enclosed with a metal case and fixed on the inner face of the door stile, became an important feature in the English home from late in the fifteenth century.

Constructional details and the decoration of English locks progressively improved between the fourteenth century and 1660, but the wearing quality of the steel was poor. Complex mechanism was the rule in fine locks, but the majority of rim locks were plainly practical and remarkably secure. By the fifteenth century locks were being made to harmonize with the character of the room into which they were fitted.

Masterpieces of ornamental locks were made by monastic locksmiths, to whom time and cost were of little consequence, cases being raised from silver plate and embossed. Lay locksmiths meanwhile were displaying fine craftsmanship in wrought-iron mouldings, quatrefoils, and floreations. In some instances the lock decoration told the story of the house and its founder. These early locks of iron and steel were enriched with gilding and brightly hued paints.

There was an early Victorian vogue for locks in this style sold under the names of Gothic and Elizabethan. Collectors distinguished these by the punch-and-bed decoration, a purely mechanical process displaying none of the infinite variety of pattern obtained by handworked saw piercing. The concealed movement is also different. Medieval plate locks were also reproduced, the mechanism riveted to rolled or cast-iron plates.

Fine locks until early Georgian days were costly: the *City and County Purchaser*, 1703, quoted prices ranging from £50 to £100. They counted as works of art and were treated as tenants' fixtures to be taken away upon their removal. The quarrel between Queen Anne and the Duchess of Marlborough was intensified when it was discovered that the duchess, upon removal from her 'grace and favour' residence in St James's Palace, took with her the brass door locks made by Joseph Key, a celebrated locksmith whose name is found on some of the magnificent locks made between 1700 and 1720. Some of these are still in use. He made the finest locks at Hampton Court at a cost of £800 and retained the royal appointment of locksmith until 1720.

Solid mahogany doors of imposing dimensions and about 2 inches (5 cm) in thickness came into use early in the eighteenth century. This resulted in the introduction of the mortice lock.

The majority of locks were made by master men working in tiny workshops adjoining their homes. The *London Tradesman*, 1747, described such a locksmith as requiring 'no Education but Writing and Reading. He earns at his first setting out of his Time, perhaps, Nine Shillings a Week, and as he increases in Strength and Experience, he arrives at Fourteen or Fifteen Shillings a Week, and is pretty constantly employed. . . . This is a species of the Smith Trade; abundantly ingenious; the Keys, Wards, Springs, and the Plates he makes himself; and he employs the Founder to cast his Cases, if in Brass. The nicest branch of this Art is tempering Springs; which almost every different Master performs in a way peculiar to himself.'

Locks with brass cases date from late in the sixteenth century, their movements being of steel. Improvements in brass-making technique in the early Georgian period enabled locksmiths to make lock cases from rolled plates of unflawed metal. This was smooth on both sides, of unvarying thickness, and softer than the outmoded latten. These qualities enabled the engraver to work more speedily. At about the same time cases for rim locks began to be produced by the brass founders and were issued with plain square or moulded edges. Towards the end of the eighteenth century Birmingham brassmen were shaping their rim-lock cases in a single piece by means of drop hammers.

Until the end of the eighteenth century emphasis on security was dependent upon wards, which had become more and more intricate as generation followed generation of locksmiths. The weakness of such movements lay in the fact that removal of much of the centre of the key bit allowed the key to pass the wards and throw back the bolt. The skeleton key reduced the security of warded locks, and the complicated box of wards become less and less in demand as the lever lock was improved from about 1800.

Expensive locks of intricate mechanism, accompanied by keys of comparable strength, continued to be made during the first half of the nineteenth century. The Jury of the Great Exhibition voiced the opinion that this was a serious defect in English locks, 'notwithstanding their ingenuity and security that keys should be so ponderous and bulky as to require for themselves special places for deposit and safe-keeping'.

ORMOLU

The term 'ormolu' (from the French *or moulu*) is used to describe decorative objects and furniture mounts of the eighteenth and nineteenth centuries, cast in bronze or brass and gilt. Though cast and gilt bronze was by no means an innovation in the eighteenth century, it was used in France to an extent that could not be paralleled in previous epochs. Ormolu was not by any means an exclusively French production, similar work was done in Germany, England, and elsewhere, but the fineness of design and perfection of finish of the French artists was never equalled. While the main volume of production was of furniture mounts, vases, candlesticks, chandeliers, andirons, inkstands, and clock cases were also made.

These objects were cast, chiselled, and finally fire-gilded. True ormolu should be distinguished from cheaper objects cast in the same moulds and from the same metal, which were roughly finished and lacquered instead of being chiselled and fire-gilded. Ormolu of the *Régence* and Louis XV periods was never so finely finished as that of the Louis XVI and Empire periods. During the first half of the century French furniture was very lavishly decorated with ormolu, and the effect was achieved by mass of ornament rather than by detail. Later, when marquetry and parquetry were going out of fashion, we find less florid mounts against a background of figured mahogany, a setting which showed them off to the maximum advantage. In the Empire period the ormolu mounts played, if possible, an even more important role, and furniture was constructed as a vehicle for the display of fine ormolu. Such was the detail of the chiselling put into good work that it was hardly less expensive than similar articles made of silver gilt.

After the Restoration in France we find a deterioration in standards of production, and the large-scale

Vase and perfume burner in white marble and ormolu by Boulton and Fothergill, Birmingham, English, *c.* 1777–8. Temple Newsam House, Leeds

Perfume burner of cast and chased ormolu by Boulton and Fothergill, Birmingham, *c.* 1770. Victoria & Albert Museum

reproduction of earlier styles, but throughout the nineteenth century there were still craftsmen who could turn out very fine work in this medium, and it is extremely difficult to distinguish between eighteenth-century ormolu and the best of the nineteenth-century reproductions.

In England the Birmingham firm of Boulton & Fothergill produced ormolu vases, candlesticks, and perfume burners during the 1760s and 1770s. The finish was never up to the highest French standards, but the designs, furnished by the Adam Brothers, were of great elegance and fitness for purpose. Many houses of the second half of the eighteenth century still retain their ormolu door furniture made by Boulton after Adam designs.

Venus clock-case by Matthew Boulton, Birmingham, marble and ormolu, *c.* 1771

PILGRIMS' SIGNS

Cast from lead, these badges were distributed at the shrines of medieval Europe to pilgrims, and were worn in the hat or on the person as evidence that the pilgrimage had been completed. These little objects, worthless in themselves, usually bore some allusion to the saint at whose shrine they were received. The best-known pilgrims' sign is the shell of St John of Compostella in Spain. The most popular English shrine was that of St Thomas at Canterbury. Pilgrims' signs, being made of lead, bear a superficial resemblance to the notorious class of fake lead medallions and amulets of the Middle Ages, made in London about the end of the nineteenth century, and commonly known after their inventors as 'Billies and Charlies'. The lettering of any inscription on a putative pilgrims' sign should therefore be examined with care, as it is in this feature that the fakers betrayed themselves.

VENETIAN–SARACENIC BRASSWARE

Among the numerous craftsmen from the Near East who settled in Venice during the later Middle Ages were metal workers and damasceners. The earlier productions of the Arabic craftsmen in Venice are hardly to be distinguished from those they had made in their native countries, but towards the end of the fifteenth century and in the sixteenth century European elements became more apparent. The brasswares made by these immigrant Saracenic smiths included ewers, dishes, bowls, candlesticks, and perfume burners or handwarmers. The earliest examples were engraved with pure, that is completely abstract, arabesques, and damascened with gold and silver, but their Western origin is often shown by the presence of an Italian coat-of-arms introduced into the ornament. By the mid-sixteenth century Italian-born craftsmen using Renaissance ornament had replaced the Saracenic smiths. On these later pieces not only is the ornament derived from contemporary pattern books but it introduces figure subjects. At the same time the damascening, which on the earlier pieces had been of exquisite quality and refinement, was restricted to a few summary details. The craft survived the sixteenth century only in a degenerate form.

Japanned Tin Plate

American

There were several tin centres in New England by the end of the eighteenth century which depended on England for their supply of tin plate. The Revolution halted the supply, but at the close of hostilities imports were again available.

The tin shops at first had no machinery. The utensils were made by hammering the metal over a hardwood mould with mallets. They were polished with wood ashes to brighten the plain tin. The shiny new pans and pails appealed to the housewife because they were light in weight. Iron was heavy and hard to clean and brass was expensive.

The size of the tin sheets naturally limited the size of the articles. The cutter had to measure accordingly and use the scrap for pepper and pill boxes or other small items. The octagonal or 'coffin' trays seem to have been the only trays made as long as sheet tin remained small. They were made in three sizes; half sheet, one sheet, and two sheets. The latter was made with a centre seam which was a clever way of producing a larger tray. The narrow gallery was a continuation of the floor of the tray and turned up five-eighths to one inch (1.6–2.5 cm). Other articles were sugar boxes and sugar bowls, trinket and deed boxes, cylindrical and oval tea caddies, bread trays, pap warmers, tea and coffee pots, the popular American apple dish, knitting-needle cases, banks and miniature domestic utensils for toys, and many other objects.

Japanning was introduced into America about the end of the eighteenth century, which furthered the development of the industry. The articles were coated with asphaltum varnish, heat dried, then decorated. After reaching a peak in popularity about 1850, production waned, and japanners wishing to remain in the craft turned to decorating sewing machines, carpet sweepers, typewriters, and other household items.

The tin centres employed pedlars who at first travelled on foot, then on horseback. Baskets for holding the tin were fastened to the saddle. Cash was scarce, so the barter and trade system was used. Many tinsmiths became prosperous through the clever bartering of their pedlars.

Of the many tin establishments, the best known are those of the Pattisons, Stevens, Filleys, and Butlers.

The Pattisons are said to have started the American industry in 1740. They came from Ireland and settled in the Connecticut River Valley in what is now the town of Berlin. Edward and his brother William were English-trained tinsmiths who, when their business prospered, trained local men in the craft. In time these men established their own shops, some in other communities, and Connecticut became the largest producer of plain and japanned tinware in America.

The Berlin pieces (1825–50) most easily recognized are stencilled. A privately owned collection of stencils has established the identity of apple dishes, coffin trays, large and small flat-top boxes, and banks. Backgrounds for such items were often transparent red, blue, green, and asphaltum. The bright tin under the transparent varnish made a rich translucent background. Opaque brown, yellow, green, white, and red were used as well. Berlin workers liked a vermilion stripe as a change from the commonplace yellow.

Not as easily recognized are the Berlin painted designs, with the exception of those attributed to Oliver Buckley. He is identified by the use of a central round spot of colour, usually chrome orange, with smaller satellite spots encircling the centre one. Brush strokes are superimposed on each spot, with heart-shaped leaves and beautiful brush strokes growing out of the centre; they fill and soften the area between spots. The complete design retains an over-all circular pattern. Also attributed to Connecticut are running borders in red, green, and black on bands of white.

Pennsylvania-German tinware, 19th century. American Museum in Britain

The American tin painters developed a forthright style that required little time for execution. It is marked by facile brush strokes and primary colours of pigment and varnish. Quick, shaded effects were cleverly done on fruits, flowers, and leaves by applying light strokes on one half and dark on the other half of a motif. The base motif was often a round, oval, or scalloped form put on with vermilion or yellow. They left to the English-trained japanner the use of gold leaf and work demanding high technical skill.

American japanned ware was almost entirely painted by girls. Some were daughters or relatives of the tinsmith or japanner. The designs in all the communities were similar in their unsophisticated quality. The colour was fresh, bright, and lasting, as has been proven by time. The homespun look of the articles and their use in rural areas has caused them to be called 'country tin'.

Zachariah Stevens abandoned the paternal blacksmith craft and became a tinsmith. His shop was in Stevens Plains, near Portland, Maine, until it was destroyed by fire in 1842.

While the Connecticut influence can be seen in some Maine work, the Stevens designs were more realistic in form and softer in colour, the result of adding white to the colours and more top detail on the flowers. Two overlapping large vermilion cherries were a speciality of Stevens Plains. The borders were original and full where space permitted, otherwise rickrack and cable borders were used. Many of the finer articles had yellow and cream white backgrounds.

Zachariah's great-great-granddaughter, Esther Stevens Brazer, 1898–1945, successfully revived the old methods of japanning and decorating. By her teaching, research, and collections of patterns and tinware, others are now able to continue further research and to perpetuate the craft.

Oliver Filley had been a pedlar when he started what was eventually to be an extensive business. In 1800 he began the manufacture and sale of tinware, selling mostly in Vermont until 1809. Subsequently he had a branch in Philadelphia and one in Lansingburgh, New York. It was a family affair with a brother in the former and a cousin in the latter. Workers and painters were exchanged between the three shops as the need arose.

The Butler family settled in East Greenville, New York, after they moved from Connecticut. A son, Aaron, was sent back to Berlin to learn the tin trade. Upon finishing his apprenticeship, he returned to Greenville and opened a shop. His oldest daughter, Ann, learned to paint tin, using a rather individual style and signature. Ann taught her two younger sisters Minerva and Marilla. Ann's work is tight, crowded, and covers most of the surface area. She liked dots as fillers and to sign her work with her name or initials, framed by heart-shaped borders.

Another firm was the Litchfield Manufacturing Company, 1850–4, makers of papier mâché. Japanners were brought from Wolverhampton and Oxfordshire to ornament daguerreotype cases, boxes, and furniture. Clock cases became their chief product. All were decorated with paint, pearl shell, and metal leaf in the English style of the mid-Victorian period. Trays were not produced.

Hull & Stafford of Clinton, Connecticut, 1850–70, were producing japanned toys.

From about 1820 English-trained stencillers were putting the finest decoration by that method on pianos and Empire furniture. As stencilling became more popular the fashion spread to the tin industry.

But it was not until the mid-nineteenth century, when factories had replaced the small tin shops, that stencilling was widely used on japanned tinware. The stencils were designed by English-trained japanners; one had his own shop in Massachusetts, and another was employed by Goodrich, Ives & Co., of Meriden, Connecticut. At this period, the machine-made japanned tinware was offered in the catalogues of wholesalers located in New England.

British

Japanned ware's beauty was combined with intriguing inventiveness to serve a host of household needs and customs throughout the reigns of the four Georges and well into Victorian days. The craft of japanning was first practised in England during the reign of Charles II (1660–85), when the ever-increasing demand for Oriental lacquerware stimulated efforts at imitation, at first on wood, then on metal. In Bilston, Staffordshire, japanners on metal were working in the late 1690s, specialists in making and decorating snuffboxes with pull-off lids.

The trade spread to nearby Wolverhampton, where a japanner of ironwork is known to have been operating in 1720, ten years before Edward Allgood founded his celebrated japan workshops at Pontypool, Monmouthshire. Little is known of Allgood productions until 1756, when Bishop Pocock visited the Allgood workshops and wrote in his diary: 'Of a thicker kind of plate they make salvers and candlesticks and many other things which they japan. I am told the light parts in this imitation tortoiseshell is done with silver leaf. They adorn them with Chinese landscapes and figures in gold only, and not with colouring as at Birmingham. This work is very much better than the Birmingham, but it is dear, there being only two brothers and their children who make it and keep it as a secret. They will also japan copper boxes, or anything made in copper which they cannot work well in iron.'

Argyll with straight spout in a form found in silver of the 1780s and 1790s, chocolate japan ground with a border of fringed festoons in silver, tinged gold by the varnish. On each side is a view of Raglan Castle. National Museum of Wales

The secret of the exquisite lustre, silky smooth to the touch and granite-hard, peculiar to Pontypool work, lay in the use of tin plate and repeated stoving at a low temperature. A single firing might be continued for as long as three weeks, and each coating of japan was smoothed down by hand. This treatment gave the japan a unique durability and made it resistant to heat. Undecorated Pontypool japanned work could be placed in the heart of a charcoal fire and later removed with a pair of tongs without visible signs of injury. This was a notable achievement for ware largely developed for the manufacture of tea and coffee urns, kettle and charcoal brazier sets, smokers' charcoal burners, candlesticks, snuffers, and their dishes.

Allgood's success was assured by his use of iron plates rolled into smooth, thin sheets of even thickness and tinned. Such tin plates became possible in 1728, when John Cooke of the Pontypool Ironworks patented an improved rolling machine, adding compressing springs to the upper part of the heavy revolving cylinders. The ductile iron associated with the Forest of Dean was flattened gradually into sheets with both surfaces free from undulations. These small plates measuring about 13¾ inches by 10 inches (35 × 25.4 cm) and not more than 16¾ inches by 12½ inches (42.5 × 31.8 cm), were tinned by dipping them into molten tin. This penetrated completely into iron, giving it a white colour throughout its texture. These tin-soaked plates were fabricated into domestic equipment, japanned, and decorated. Such methods, in which unlimited time was an important factor, earned for Pontypool a reputation for fine and costly japanning that has endured to this day.

The quality of Allgood's japanned ware was such that when the Corporation of Cardiff wished 'to present the Hon. William Pitt and the Hon. Henry Bilson Legge, Esqre., with the Freedom of that Town' in 1757, the parchments were enclosed in 'two Pont-y-Pool Boxes, with the Arms of the Town neatly engraved thereon' (*London Chronicle*, 10 May 1757).

Japanning on tinned plate had been a London craft before Allgood established his workshops. Gumley and Turing in 1728 sent George II an account for 'Japanning four fine large tin (tinned) plate receivers in Red with neat drawing in silver'. By the mid-eighteenth century there were numerous metal japanners in London; for in 1757 Daniel Mills, Vine Street, near Hatton Garden, advertised in the *London Chronicle* that he not only 'Japanned upon all Sorts of Goods made of Copper, Brass, Tin, Lead', but that he sold all sorts of materials for japanners.

Edward Allgood made a competence and retired in 1760, making over the business to his three sons. They failed to agree on matters of policy, however, and the partnerships were dissolved a year later. Thomas, the eldest, retained the Pontypool business, his brothers establishing themselves in opposition at Usk, seven miles away. Each factory developed individual characteristics, Pontypool continuing its reputation for the limited production of superb-quality japanning for the nobility and gentry. Under William Allgood, who succeeded Thomas in 1776, the business was expanded. In 1781 the Hon. John Byng wrote in his diary, 'Chepstow, I bought a Pontypool snuff-box, a beautiful and dear ware, and much to be admired.'

Archdeacon Coxe in 1799 reported that the Pontypool japanning works was a flourishing concern, but when William Allgood died in 1813 it was described as 'declining', and by 1820 had closed. One member of the family, Ann Allgood, moved to Birmingham and founded a japanning business in Lower Hospital Street.

The Allgood factory at Usk, it is assumed, continued the Pontypool processes. The favourite ground colours were deep chocolate brightened with a hard, golden-hued varnish, and crimson applied directly to the tin plate, giving a translucent appearance. The factory passed out of the family early in the

Right Coffee urn with cylindrical body and square box with perforated sides for containing the charcoal brazier. Decorated in shaded gold and silver with flowers and foliage in the Anglo-Chinese style, with butterflies. Pontypool. National Museum of Wales

Left Levno coffee urn with oval body, heated with a charcoal brazier in the perforated box below. Black japan decorated with Chinese scenes in gold. Pontypool. National Museum of Wales

Left Teapot on rectangular foot. Crimson japan decorated with bands of fine gilded ornament, Usk. National Museum of Wales

nineteenth century. The new proprietors, observing the decline of Pontypool, introduced Staffordshire processes and materials, including tin iron, and a new japan maturing with less stoving. The factory closed in 1860.

The japanners of Birmingham, Wolverhampton, Bilston, London, and elsewhere produced less costly decorated ware which they eventually named 'Pontypool', none of which is known to have been comparable with genuine Pontypool ware. England's first large japanning factories were set up in Birmingham during the 1730s by John Taylor, a journeyman cabinet maker, and Obadiah Ryton, already established as japanners at Tinshop Yard, Wolverhampton. They eventually named their factory the Old Hall Works.

This factory for more than three-quarters of a century was the centre of the japan and papier mâché trade in Wolverhampton. When Obadiah Ryton died in 1810 his brother was joined by Benjamin Walton and more efficient methods were introduced, affecting the entire japan trade. Between 1820 and the late 1830s continual employment was given to more than 800 people. In 1847 Walton died and was succeeded by his son Frederick, who traded as Frederick Walton and Co.

An industrial dispute at the Ryton establishment in 1800 prompted several of the more skilled operatives and decorators to establish themselves as master japanners. Without exception all prospered, and by 1820 Birmingham, Wolverhampton, and Bilston formed the world centre of the japanning trade. The directory for 1839 entered 57 master japanners in Birmingham, 15 in Wolverhampton, and 11 in Bilston. By 1851 the numbers had increased; Birmingham 72, Wolverhampton 19, and Bilston 22.

The range of japanned ware now of interest to collectors includes equipment for the tea table, such as tea trays and waiters, tea canisters, tea and coffee urns, bread and cake baskets, cheese cradles, plate-warming cabinets, smokers' charcoal brazier sets, toilet-table boxes, snuffboxes, knife cases, candlesticks, snuffers, and dishes. In style they range through mid-eighteenth-century rococo and Chinese fantasy, the chaste classicism of the Adams' day, the solemn pomp of the Regency, and the inexpensive forms of the 1830s and 1840s. These were followed by masses of so-called Elizabethan and classical forms and ornament which did much to destroy the trade when confronted with the clear-cut designs in electroplate.

American Pewter

Compared with the centuries-old history of pewter in all parts of the world, the history of pewter in America is a rather short one of only about two hundred years.

The record of Richard Graves, who opened a pewterer's shop in Salem, Massachusetts, in 1635, is the earliest reference to a pewterer in the American colonies. Fewer than ten pewterers plied their trade in the colonies before 1700, so far as is known today. For many years no tangible evidence of the handiwork of the early colonial pewterers was found. Excavations at Jamestown, Virginia, eventually brought forth the remnants of a pewter spoon that

Pewter teapot made by William Kirby, New York, *c.* 1770–80. Metropolitan Museum of Art

not only bore a name in its maker's touch, but also, by an unbelievable stroke of luck, the locality where he worked. The pewterer, Joseph Copeland, worked during the years 1675–91 in Chuckatuck as well as in Jamestown, both in Virginia. This artefact (now in the museum at Jamestown) is still the only definitely ascertainable pewter specimen of seventeenth-century America. The first definitely attributable pieces may be assigned to about 1725.

The average colonist owned only the most necessary pewterware. Being well aware of the vast, unsettled territory which was open to him, he brought only the things which could be carried easily. Instead of the breakable crockery, the hardier pewter, in the shapes of plates, bowls, beakers, spoons, was selected.

It could not have taken over-long before many of the plates and bowls were battered, or, being left too close to the open hearth, damaged beyond restoration by their owners. The need for trained pewterers became apparent the more pewter utensils suffered by careless handling. Before long English pewterers became aware of the opportunities to themselves which the colonies offered, ownership of land and house and the free excercise of their craft. Free from any restrictive supervision, they could ingeniously use their few moulds for any purpose to which they could be adapted. With the moulds they had, they fashioned pewter objects for which their English or Continental contemporaries would have required still others. Since they could not compete with the multitude of forms and the variations of styles imported from England, the colonial pewterers concentrated on a few forms. Against the many different rim types of the English plates and the still more numerous rim types of other European countries, they offered only two types, the earlier smooth-rim plate and the later single-reed plate.

Another compelling reason for the limitation of forms and production was the fact that the colonies, in spite of great natural resources, were entirely lacking in the most important item of the pewterer's trade, tin ore.

Under pressure exerted by the highly organized English pewterers' guilds, and in anticipation of additional revenue, the English authorities soon imposed an *ad valorem* custom duty of five per cent

Pewter communion service by Johann Christoph Heyne, Lancaster, Pennsylvania, dated 1765, made for the Canadockly Lutheran Church, York County, Pennsylvania. Collections of Greenfield Village and the Henry Ford Museum

upon imported raw tin bars, leaving the finished pewterware duty free. The disadvantages of this arbitrary rule were impossible to overcome.

The American craftsmen were forced largely to rework and recast the old pewter that was taken in trade or brought to them by merchants who dealt in new pewter.

In the reworking of old pewter the pewterer proved himself to be very often an able craftsman. His wares were generally of good quality, and while the quality or workmanship does not compare in general with the product of English or Continental pewterers, many American specimens disclose excellent workmanship and the capabilities and ingenuity of their makers.

The larger towns being centres of trade, the majority of pewterers gravitated towards them, while rural areas depended upon an occasional pewterer working there for a limited time, and on the hawkers and pedlars who in later years were able to supply the needs for pewterware from the larger towns. With incomes curtailed by the restrictions, most pewterers were compelled to apply their skill to other trades as well. Only a few were able to devote their entire time to their craft, and still fewer were comparatively well-to-do.

But the American pewterer was independent. He could work as he pleased; there were no dictates as to form or design, nor any objections to the number of apprentices or journeymen he engaged. If his pewter were of inferior quality, or his workmanship poor, only his customers could object. In spite of, or perhaps because of, this freedom from supervision and restrictions, the American pewterer generally lived up to the best traditions of the craft. He did not need to be afraid to mark his products with his touch, and when we find American pewter unmarked, but definitely identifiable as American, it compares favourably in quality and workmanship with similar European pieces. It may be stated at this point that there is no truth in the belief that unmarked pewter can always be classified as American. If this were the case, the production of our colonial pewterers would have been so large that their need to work at other trades would have been unnecessary.

EUROPEAN INFLUENCES

The early impact of English-trained pewterers and the monopoly of English-made pewterware were largely responsible for the adoption of English styles and forms, modified by the limitations in moulds and material. These limitations were frequently responsible for the clean and unpretentious lines of American pewter which the collector today appreciates. So dominant was English influence that American pewterers who trained in other European countries gradually submitted to it. The pewter of the transitional period, in which the Continental and English characteristics were united, is of great interest to the student and collector.

There are evidences in a pewterer's technique which indicate his probable origin, lacking other biographical data. If no other information had been found, the hammermarks on Simon Edgell's pewter would point him out as an English-trained 'hammerman'. The practice of strengthening pewter by light hammerblows, producing the innumerable small indentations which give light to the surface with brilliant effect, had reached such heights in England that hammermen were considered the aristocracy of the craft. Examples of American work by pewterers not trained in England show us, by comparison, the proficiency of the English in this art. The all-over hammered plates and dishes of Edgell, the hammered tankard by Benjamin Day of Newport, are outstanding examples of the tradition. Also excellent, if to a slightly less degree, are the hammered booges on the flatware of the Bassetts, Wills, Danforths, and others, representations of excellent craftsmanship which they in turn taught their apprentices. The art of the hammerman dwindled in the Federal period, so it would seem this time-consuming art was sacrificed to speedier production.

While the New England and southern colonies were settled predominantly by the English, other colonies attracted settlers from Central Europe. In continuing their Old World customs these groups influenced later generations. Central European trained pewterers were able to furnish their compatriots in the new country with pewterware that perhaps was not identical to, but approximated, familiar forms and designs. The accustomed forms prevailed until about the beginning of the nineteenth century. The steady anglicization of the population, the ascendancy of English pewter, and finally the gradual decline of pewter making extinguished the last traces of Continental influences on American pewter.

Nevertheless, the influence of the past was long discernible. The Dutch settlers of New Netherland retained the ingrained habits and customs of their original homeland. Traces of this are found for many generations in the working methods and ideas of New York artisans. The evidence of Dutch influence as to style prevailed long after New Amsterdam became New York. The roundness of the bowls of spoons, the sturdiness of hollow ware, and solidity of workmanship in general were not greatly changed by English influence.

FUSION OF STYLES

Thomas Paschall, an English-trained pewterer, opened his shop in Philadelphia in 1682; he was followed by other, also English-trained, pewterers;

Quart covered pitcher made by Parks Boyd, Philadelphia, 1795–1819. Brooklyn Museum

among them was the excellent hammerman, Simon Edgell. Their pewter, in the English manner, suited well the demands of their fellow citizens, most of them of English origin. With the increasing arrival of Continental immigrants a change of taste took place. While the English type of pewter probably never wanted for buyers. Continental immigrants were able to supply their customers with pewterware adhering to other European forms. This resulted in the creation of so many varieties of shapes, designs, and special features that the study of Pennsylvania pewter is often bewildering. There is the highly desirable English style of Cornelius Bradford and Simon Edgell; the transitional features of the pewter of Andrew Brunstrom and Parks Boyd; the astonishing versatility of Heyne, showing German–Swedish influences; the highly individual work of William Will; not to forget the mysterious maker whose pieces are marked *Love*.

TYPES

The American pewterer offered a wide range of styles in the different vessels and utensils demanded of him, although he could not match European pewter in variety. As far as the colonial pewterer was concerned, the rococo period never existed. Accepted established forms of the early eighteenth century persisted, often long after they went out of fashion in other countries.

The popularity of the porringer, a small, multi-purpose vessel that apparently made its way from New York to all parts of colonial America, increased steadily and endured far into the nineteenth century, after it had ceased to be a favourite in England and Continental Europe. Whatever ambition to decorate the American pewterer had was apparently lavished on the execution of the porringer handle. With the shape of the body remaining fairly constant, the handle was fashioned in two distinct types, the pierced or open work, and the solid or tab handle. The former was derived from English prototypes; the latter bore definite Continental characteristics. In the ornamental features of the handles great variety of treatment was exhibited, limited only by the great expense of new moulds. Generally a pewterer made porringers according to the preferences of his customers, one exception being the pewterers of Rhode Island, who, probably because of additional trade outlets, cast both types. Another exception was Thomas Danforth III of Connecticut, who, understandably, gave up his English-type porringer for the tab-handled upon setting up shop in Philadelphia.

Pre-Revolutionary touches

THE TOUCH

The English or Continental pewterer was free to choose his own design for his trademark or touch. He followed certain patterns, dependent upon the style of the period, on national preferences, and on ordinances issued by governing authorities. Frequently his touch had to contain the numerals of the year in which he was admitted to mastership, or a design denoting the quality of his pewter. The American pewterer was not bound by these rules. While it was important to advertise his work, he was not compelled to strike his touch nor any quality mark, although the legend *London* was frequently struck to show that his pewter compared with the best of England's products or to let the unwary buyer accept the native pewterware as English made. Outside the American colonies only a master pewterer was permitted a registered touch, a precious possession that he would include in the necessities which he brought to the colonies. Once in a land where no questions of his status were asked and where no proofs of official qualifications were demanded, he could use his touch or change it as he saw fit. The use of a touch was equally free to anyone else turning to pewtering. There is every indication that many a journeyman pewterer set himself up in business and marked his products as if he had qualified before his peers. Many of them became outstanding makers of American pewter.

In the choice of their touches the pewterers evidently followed the traditional patterns of their native countries. We find that the pre-Revolutionary touches closely resemble English and Continental devices, such as the rose and crown; the lamb and dove motif; the golden fleece. There are lions in circles and ovals, in or out of columns; shields, urns, hallmarks, plain initials, and many other symbols. John Will's angel touch, signifying first-quality pewter, was apparently identical to his touch as a master pewterer of his native Germany, except that now his die was American-made, since his German touch must have shown his given name *Johannes* instead of the anglicized *John*. After the Revolution the designs of the American touches lost their interesting individuality. Apparently, it was found patriotic as well as

Porringer handles

Post-Revolutionary touches

opportune to employ a device emphasizing the newly won freedom. The eagle of the Great Seal of the United States became a popular motif. Dies changed upon the admission of a new state, the numbers of stars or dots in the frame surrounding the eagle signifying that another state had ratified the Constitution. This aids in the dating of pewter except where the stars form a continuous circle surrounding the eagle, as they were then meant for decoration only.

Not long after the turn of the nineteenth century another drastic change in the type of touch took place. The symbolic and heraldic motifs were completely cast aside to be replaced by the simple intials or name of the pewterer, at times surrounded by circular or rectangular frames. The age of mass production had arrived, permitting no frills.

19th century touches

Left Pewter plate, dish and jug, mid-19th century. American Museum in Britain

BRITANNIA METAL

A steady increase in the amount of ceramics, glass-, and tinware, produced at reasonable prices in great quantities, had begun for a long time to affect pewterers everywhere. To meet this competition, pewterers intensified their search for methods to increase their output at competitive prices. Early in the eighteenth century English pewterers developed a pewter composition of tin, antimony, and copper that proved to be exceptionally durable and workable; it was generally advertised as 'hard metal'. Further experiments created an alloy that could be cast and rolled into thin sheets without cracking. When it was subsequently discovered that this metal could be cold-formed over wooden moulds on a spinning lathe, costly bronze moulds and expensive hand finishing were eliminated, and semi-skilled labourers could be employed for the simple operations of mass fabrication. When in 1825 Hiram Yale of Wallingford, Connecticut, engaged English workmen to come to America, the spinning method succeeded here also. For a while the new process stemmed the decline in the sale of pewterware, or Britannia metal, as it was now called. But a new era had arrived, a time when almost every designer and artisan aspired to devise new and exaggerated forms and decorative features. Neither pewter nor the new 'hard metal' could be successfully adapted to these shapes, and for the present-day collector pewter made after 1850 is not of interest.

British Pewter

Pewter is an alloy, the principal component of which is tin, with minor additions of brass, lead, and antimony. History records so many varieties, however, that it is impossible to dogmatize.

Pewter has been used in Britain for centuries, beginning with the Roman occupation. But for practical purposes the mid-fourteenth century may be taken as a starting point; for it was during this period that the London Guild promulgated its first ordinances for the control of the Craft. The Pewterers' Company of London had a right to a certain proportion of the Cornish tin, and farmed it out to its members and to provincial Guilds. Pewter succeeded treen (wood), leather, and horn, with, naturally, some overlapping; but at first it was within the reach of only the well-to-do. Inventories of the goods of nobles, knights, and bishops give long lists of vessels, mostly employed in the kitchens of their vast establishments. As time passed its use spread, until by the mid-seventeenth century there was scarcely an article in the plenishing of house or tavern that could not be obtained in pewter. The Church, too, particularly

Right Pewter plateau engraved in the centre with the Royal Arms encircled by the garter with supporters and the initials C.R. Beneath is the Royal motto and the inscription 'Vivat rex Carolus Secundus, Beati pacifici, 1662'. On the rim are the initials C.T.A. within a wreath. Victoria & Albert Museum

Tankard engraved with a portrait of William III, dated 1698. Victoria & Albert Museum

Top Porringer, late 17th century. Victoria & Albert Museum

Above Pair of marriage plates, 1720. Jellinek & Sampson

after the Reformation, enlisted the services of the pewterer to supply its needs in regard to alms dishes, alms plates, and sacramental vessels: especially flagons, which were required in order to implement the Jacobean Canon Law concerning the service of wine to the Communion table. The craft of the pewterer, rigidly controlled by the Guilds, was at its zenith in the seventeenth and early eighteenth centuries, and the workshops turned out a profusion of dishes, plates, flagons, tankards, spoons (in which category, incidentally, are found the earliest surviving specimens of pewter), salt cellars, candlesticks, basins, bowls, beakers, measures, inkstands, and (later) shoe buckles, mantel ornaments, and snuff-boxes; a formidable catalogue. Such was the reputation of British pewter, gained not by decoration but by good proportion and functional fitness, that a very large export trade was established.

MARKS

Among the ordinances of the London Guild was one which made it obligatory for a new master pewterer to invent for himself a mark, or 'Touch', as it was called; to register it by striking it upon a touch plate at Pewterers' Hall; and thereafter to strike it upon his wares. The Great Fire of 1666 destroyed Pewterers' Hall, and with it the touch plates. But the system was revived in 1668, when all pewterers were required to restrike upon a new plate, and it continued into the beginning of the nineteenth century, by which time nearly 1,100 touches had been struck upon five plates. In Scotland the Edinburgh Hammermen's Guild also had touch plates. These cover the period *c.* 1580–1760, and contain 143 touches.

It is with the aid of these touches, together with other material in the Archives of the Pewterers' Company, that the periods, and often the names, of London pewterers from about 1640 can be ascertained. In many cases dates appear in touches; these dates, however, represent the year of registration and not the year of manufacture. As the pewterers did not use the date letter either, the actual year in which any article was made cannot be determined, as it can in the case of silver; but it will lie between the date of registration and the date, where known, of the pewterer's death, or within a reasonable span of working life.

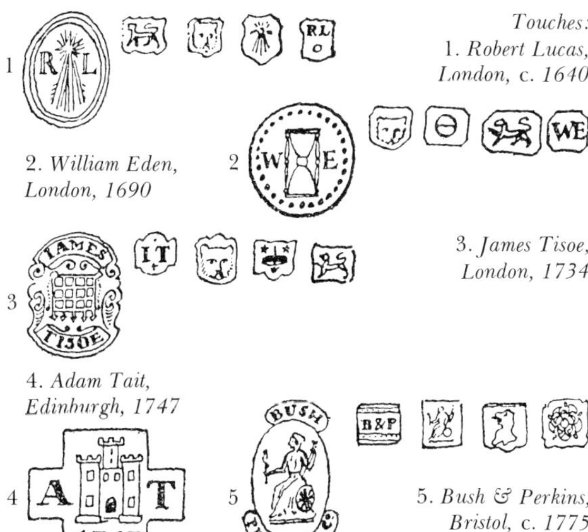

Touches:
1. *Robert Lucas, London,* c. *1640*
2. *William Eden, London, 1690*
3. *James Tisoe, London, 1734*
4. *Adam Tait, Edinburgh, 1747*
5. *Bush & Perkins, Bristol,* c. *1775*

Right Flagon said to have come from Monk Hasleton Priory, Seaton Carew, Durham, early 18th century. Victoria & Albert Museum

Other marks were also applied to pewter, including quality marks, excise marks, deacons' marks (in Scotland), and marks erroneously called 'hallmarks'. The latter were small punches, usually four in number, resembling those used on silver plate; one of them usually contained the maker's initials. These latter marks had no authority whatever, either in law or craft regulation, and indeed at one time, following a complaint by the Goldsmiths' Company their use was prohibited by the Pewterer's Company. Pewterers, nevertheless, continued to apply them, and as they are often helpful in deciphering a partially obliterated touch, we may be grateful for this disobedience. Examples of touches and 'hallmarks' are illustrated here.

Enormous quantities of pewter articles were remelted as scrap, a fact which has naturally stimulated interest in what remains. These 'period' pieces occupy an honoured position in the world of antiques today. In the third quarter of the eighteenth century the competition from cheaper materials began to make inroads on the trade, and soon the demand was too small to make it profitable. The tendency to ignore regulations, and the abolition of the Company's right of search for 'false wares', foreshadowed the end; and although pewterware was still made and a few fresh outlets were devised, the Craft was, by 1800, a shadow of its former self. From that date antiquarian interest disappears.

American Wrought Iron

The fabrication of American wrought iron can be said to have begun in 1607 when James Read, a blacksmith, went ashore at Jamestown, Virginia, with the first group of English settlers. But these first American pieces, as with all wrought iron for years to come, must have been American in name only, for certainly the early smiths who emigrated to the colonies in Virginia and New England must have continued to fashion objects in exactly the same manner as they had learned in their native England.

An American style of work cannot be discerned with any degree of clarity until about the beginning of the eighteenth century. Add the fact that wrought iron is seldom dated and almost never signed and it becomes apparent that the would-be collector of early American hardware is faced with a considerable problem in authentication at the very outset. Yet, in spite of these difficulties, there is a great deal of wrought iron which shows characteristics which have come to be regarded as typically American. Its characteristics are simplicity, lack of ostentatious ornamentation, and an appearance of utility. The whorls, scrolls, and other purely decorative effects so often found on ironwork of the Old World are conspicuous by their absence on most American pieces. Even the objects made by the Pennsylvannia–German smiths, probably the most intricate American ironwork, show a certain restraint that marks them as being of the New World. Nowhere is this tendency towards simplicity better exemplified than at Williamsburg, Virginia, the pre-Revolutionary capital of Britain's wealthiest and most aristocratic colony. The most sophisticated articles in the whole of the enormous collection are a few pairs of shutter hinges from the 'Palace' of the Royal Governors. These have been decorated very modestly by a suggestion of foliation on the ends. The remainder of the iron house hardware of that very imposing building is quite plain and hardly to be distinguished from the hardware used on the houses of some of the humbler residents of the town.

It is hard to explain this characteristic simplicity of American wrought iron. The collector can only note that differences exist and make use of them as an aid in identification.

The foregoing is not meant to imply that American iron is without aesthetic appeal. The well-designed hinges, latches, and shutter fasteners used on early American houses supplement the architecture beautifully. A Suffolk door latch from Connecticut which has had its cusps shaped into the outline of a pine tree by a few cuts with a file and cold chisel exhibits a charm of its own, as does a Pennsylvania latch bearing the simple outline of a heart or tulip. Even the perfectly plain H and HL hinges of Virginia express the dignity and durability of the houses to which they are attached.

Though the colonist often complained about the high cost of ironwork, this complaint was caused by the high cost of blacksmith's labour rather than by a scarcity of material. All of the iron used in the first few years of the struggling new colonies in Virginia and Massachusetts had to be imported from the mother country, but the early settlers were quick to set about finding a means of supplying themselves. Small test furnaces were built at Jamestown in the early years of that settlement, and it is known that a fully-fledged ironworks was being constructed at Falling Creek, Virginia, in 1621. This enterprise was, unfortunately, wiped out during the Indian massacre of 1662. This setback delayed iron production in Virginia for many years, but early in the eighteenth century furnaces were again in operation, and by 1750 Virginia was exporting iron bars in considerable quantities to England, in addition to supplying her own smiths. In the North the industry was successfully established in the seventeenth century. A furnace was built in 1685 at Saugus Center, Massachusetts, and was successfully operated for many years. By 1750 New England furnaces, as well as those of Pennsylvania and Virginia, were exporting great quantities of iron bars which were sometimes made into finished articles in England and shipped back to the country of origin for sale.

Practically all American hand-forged iron was made in the material known as wrought iron until about the middle of the nineteenth century, when various grades of mild steel began to be widely used for blacksmith work. These mild steels, particularly the variety known as hot rolled, are generally used today by the few remaining blacksmiths for their everyday work and, on occasion, reproductions of antique pieces. The use of this material often furnishes the collector with a clue as to the age of a piece of ironwork, particularly if it is rusty. A typical object made of wrought iron rusts to a 'grainy' appearance with the grain generally running in the direction in which the piece was formed or 'drawn' by the smith. Mild steel rusts to an evenly pitted, 'orange peel' surface with no indication of grain. The collector should apply this test with caution, however, since it is not infallible. Some genuine old iron exhibits the surface appearance of steel, and some genuine wrought iron is still available from Sweden and is being worked today. It should be noted that a limited amount of fine steel was available to the colonists and was used primarily in tools and weapons, and that cast iron has existed since the first furnace was built, but both of these topics are beyond the scope of this discussion.

Some of the finest American wrought iron is combined with, or embellished by, other materials, such as wood, copper, and brass. Candlestands frequently have brass finials and drip pans, and lamps of various types are often equipped with brass or copper reservoirs. Fireplace implements, too, are commonly decorated with brass finials which add greatly to their appeal. Among the articles esteemed by many collectors are the countless variety of kitchen ladles, skimmers, spoons, and forks which combine iron, brass, or copper in their make up. Some of these pieces even have the contrasting metal cleverly inlaid in their handles, and it is among this group of highly individual utensils that the signed and dated piece is most often found.

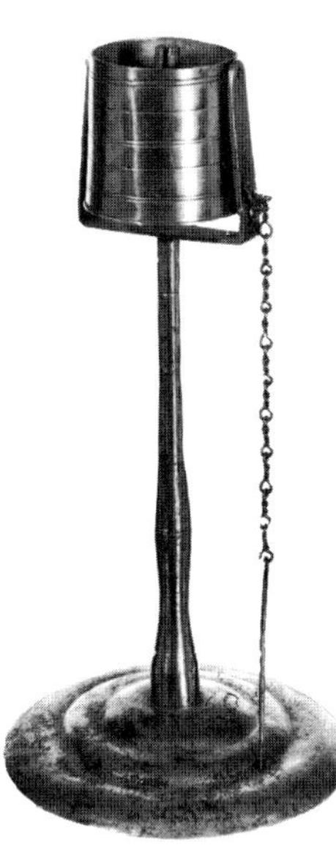

Iron grease lamp with a brass chain for the pick and a cup of brass with a copper bottom, signed by Peter Derr, Berks County, Pennsylvania, dated 1855. Collections of Greenfield Village and the Henry Ford Museum

The would-be collector of American wrought iron should acquaint himself with the various types of material which are likely to be encountered and which are worthy of acquiring. It is often found that a single category offers sufficient variety and interest to occupy the antiquarian for a lifetime, and some fine collections have been assembled in this manner. Others have collected in a wholesale manner and, although expensive, this has resulted in several major museum displays. Still others have known deep satisfaction in collecting pieces of all categories to fit their private homes, disposing of individual pieces as better ones were found. Whatever method is adopted it will be found that iron can be grouped in the following general classifications:

TOOLS AND IMPLEMENTS

This category includes the tools of artisans and farmers as well as some of the implements of the soldier, except swords and firearms. Many tools are made of a combination of wood, wrought iron, and steel, so that the tool collector often confines himself to this one group of objects and is not thought of as a collector of wrought iron.

FIREPLACE AND KITCHEN EQUIPMENT

This group is probably one of the largest and certainly the most diverse type of American iron. It includes such things as andirons, trivets and toasters, spits, hooks, pokers, and trammels, etc. A great deal of individuality is displayed by pieces of this type, since they were often made to order to fit a given fireplace or cooking necessity. It should be noted that most iron pieces which were signed or dated will be found in this group.

BUILDERS' HARDWARE

Hinges, hasps, shutter fasteners, foot scrapers, and the like constitute this group, and it is here that regional characteristics most often come to light, partly because of the fact that many of these pieces are still attached to the houses for which they were made, and peculiarities of different parts of the country can be noted by the astute collector. Nails, too, were an important product of the early smith, and they offer an interesting study by themselves.

CABINET HARDWARE

This group consists mostly of hinges and catches from chests, boxes, and furniture. Though a small group, it often includes some exquisitely fashioned articles.

VEHICULAR HARDWARE

Structural and decorative parts of coaches, carriages and wagons are included in this group, to which little attention has been paid by the collector as yet. Tool boxes from Conestoga wagons have been avidly sought for, however, and are often fitted with ironwork of unusual decorative interest.

ORNAMENTAL IRON

Fences, gates, railings, weathervanes, and other similar pieces. As might be expected, this group of rather expensive, custom-made objects often exhibits the ultimate in the iron worker's skill. There are few collectors who specialize in these things, largely because of the difficulties in housing and displaying such bulky objects, as well as the fact that they are usually an integral part of the structure for which they were designed and are not apt to be available unless a house is demolished. It should be noted that many of the beautiful iron railings and grille works in Charleston and New Orleans are not wrought pieces. They are cast and, as such, are examples of the founder's art rather than that of the blacksmith.

LIGHTING DEVICES

Many types of lighting devices were made, wholly or in part, of wrought iron. These range from simple grease lamps to more elegant candlestands and even, on occasion, to brackets or stands for gas and kerosene lights. Collections of wrought-iron lighting devices are not generally made as such, however, but are included with more comprehensive collections dealing with lighting.

For the student of American wrought iron there are many excellent museum collections on display. All of the larger 'outdoor' museums, such as the ones at Shelbourne, Vermont; Old Deerfield, Massachusetts; Old Sturbridge, Massachusetts; Williamsburg, Virginia, and Greenfield Village at Dearborn, Michigan, have major collections of iron of all types. The period rooms in the larger art museums and most historic house museums as well as local historical societies have a certain amount of blacksmith work represented in their displays. At the Museum of the Bucks County Historical Society at Doylestown, Pennsylvania, and at Landis Valley, near Lancaster, Pennsylvania, there are truly enormous collections of wrought iron of all types. Farther west, there is an extensive collection of implements in the Museum of the Ohio Historical Society at Columbus, Ohio, and a very large and comprehensive collection of wrought iron in the Henry Ford Museum at Dearborn, Michigan.

Chinese and Japanese Bronzes

Bronze is an alloy of copper and tin, the proportions of each metal varying according to the purpose for which it is to be used. Other metals are sometimes added for special purposes. The addition of zinc yields brass, and that of lead makes the metal more fluid and easier to pour into moulds.

Exposure to weather leads to surface changes which are actually a form of corrosion; quite often the surface becomes a bright copper green. Burial induces more extensive corrosion according to the nature of the soil. The corrosion may be green (malachite), blue (azurite), black, brown, or a combination of all these colours. These colourful products of corrosion are termed patination, and a fine patination is especially valued. The soil of China is particularly noted for inducing effects of this kind which can sometimes be described as spectacular. The later bronzes of China and Japan are often given an artificially induced patination which should not be interfered with.

Bronze altar-vessels of a well developed type appear quite sudenly in China in the middle of the second millennium B.C., and they have been excavated in considerable quantities. Even those dating back to the Shang dynasty (*c.* 1600–1027 B.C.) are by no means as rare as their age would suggest.

In the days of Yü the Great of the Hsia dynasty (2205–1760 B.C.), according to legend, nine great tripod cauldrons (*li*) were cast which later disappeared, and from ancient descriptions it seems as though they were decorated with the *t'ao ti'eh* mask in relief. This motif decorates a very large number of bronzes of the Shang and the following Chou dynasty. There are many versions of it, but essentially it is an animal head which has been split in two from the back as far as the nose, and then opened out, so that elements of the design corresponding to the eye, ear, and so forth lie on either side of the central point. Similar motifs are still employed by the Indians of the North West Pacific Coast, and, like the *t'ao ti'eh*, they are totems. All these masks are variable in their elements because they are schematic representations of several different animals. The *t'ao ti'eh* mask, its original meaning long forgotten, occurs in recent times as porcelain decoration.

Left Bronze tripod vessel (*ting*), Chou dynasty (1027–771 B.C.). Victoria & Albert Museum

Right Wine vessel (*tsun*), bronze inlaid with gold and silver, in the form of a phoenix, Sung dynasty (960–1280). Victoria & Albert Museum

The forms of these ancient altar-vessels are fairly numerous, and they fall into well-marked categories, some of which were repeated in porcelain in Ming (1368–1644) and Ch'ing (1644–1912) times, and were even copied by European porcelain makers. The earliest decoration is in low relief, but towards the end of the Shang dynasty an exaggerated high relief became the rule, and this style persisted during the early part of the Chou dynasty which followed.

The purpose of these vessels, however, changed. During the Shang dynasty they were used for religious purposes, but in the Chou period, to which inscriptions testify, they came to be gifts from the emperor to his favoured subjects.

Towards the end of the Chou dynasty styles began to change and animals were represented much more naturalistically, inspired by the animal bronzes of the nomads of the Ordos Desert, and this style persisted into the Han dynasty (206 B.C.–A.D. 220), when bronze began to be replaced by other material.

Throughout the whole period hitherto discussed many objects of bronze, other than vessels, were made for everyday use. These include chariot fittings like linch-pins and bells, weapons ranging from the dagger-axe (*ko*) to the crossbow lock of sophisticated design which dates from the Han dynasty, furniture mounts, belt buckles, mirrors, and many more, and at the end of the Chou dynasty the practice of inlaying bronzes with gold, silver, turquoise, malachite, and even lacquer was started.

From the Han dynasty till the Ming period few bronze vessels appear to have been made, and those were archaic in style. It has been estimated that in the region of ten thousand ancient vessels are in existence, none of which have survived above ground since the time of casting; all have been excavated. In 955 A.D. the Emperor Shih Tsung ordered all bronze vessels in private hands to be seized for melting. When the Sung Court fled south before the Mongols the Imperial collection of ancient bronze vessels was destroyed. At this time the *Hsüan Ho Po Ku Tu Lu*, an

Far left Archaic bronze *chia*, Shang dynasty (*c.* 1600–1027 B.C.). Christie, Manson & Woods

illustrated treatise of the twelfth century on ancient bronzes, inspired many copies, and the practice of applying an artificial patination began at this time.

Little or nothing in bronze was made during the Yüan dynasty (1280–1368), but the metal again became popular during the Ming dynasty, especially during the reign of Hsüan-tê (1426–35). Little is definitely known of Chinese bronzes from the Ming period onwards. Soame Jenyns suggested that zinc (the addition of which converts bronze to brass) was first added at this time, and certainly some bronzes of excellent quality, with the reign-mark, of Hsüan-tê cast into the base, have light yellow glints suggestive of brass.

Bronzes no longer conformed to archaic forms, and ornament like the *t'ao ti'eh* became very degenerate and hardly recognizable. Naturalistic ornament, however, is frequent and well executed. Copies of the ancient bronzes were made once again during the reign of Ch'ien Lung (1736–96) of the Ch'ing dynasty.

There is very little Chinese bronze sculpture earlier than the Han dynasty, although there are a pair of Mongolian ponies in the William Rockhill Nelson Gallery of Art in Kansas City and a lively little pony of early Han date, the type known from contemporary relief sculpture, was shown in the London Chinese Exhibition of 1973. It is probable that at one time a considerable amount of bronze sculpture existed but it has long since been melted down. A Chinese legend has it that in 121 B.C. the general Chang Ch'ien pursued Mongol raiders far into the deserts of Turkestan, and there discovered golden (i.e. gilt-bronze) statues 10 feet (3 m) high which he brought back to the Court of the Emperor Wu. With the introduction of Buddhism in A.D. 67 sculpture in bronze became more frequent, but little is definitely known till 338, which is the date of a statue of Sakyamuni now in Chicago. This was the work of a nomadic Tatar tribe who had established themselves in China as the northern Wei dynasty. Other dated sculpture from the same source exists, influenced by Graeco-Buddhist work from the north-west frontier of India.

In more recent times, and particularly in the eighteenth century, small figures of Kuan-yin, Buddha, and other religious or quasi-religious figures have been made, and are not uncommon. They are variable in quality, but little is known of them otherwise, and they are usually difficult to date.

Very little work has been done on early Japanese bronzes, but as in China, the introduction of Buddhism in 552 was accompanied by an increased interest in metalwork, and by the eighth century, when the Court had removed to Nara, work in gilded copper especially was of very high quality. The craftsmen of the time excelled in the manufacture of objects from sheet-copper rather than by casting, but, in 752, during the reign of the emperor Shomū, a seated Buddha 53 feet (16 m) high, cast in poured sections soldered together, was erected in the grounds of the Todaiji Monastery. Others of the same sort, some even larger, were cast subsequently, the last being erected in 1891.

These, however, are hardly of interest to the collector. Many small and attractive objects of bronze made principally in the eighteenth and nineteenth centuries come from Japan, such as incense-burners (*koro*), vases of all kinds, figures of dragons and other supernatural creatures, living animals like deer, fish, tortoise, and so forth, and figures of Gods and Immortals.

The Japanese are adept at providing their bronzes with patinations like a rare lobster-red to copper. The *shakudo* alloy contains gold which yields a black surface with violet glints, and *shibuichi*, half-copper, half-silver, exhibits a silver-grey. By the *mokumé* technique several sheets of differently coloured copper or bronze were brazed together and then scored with cuts and drilled part-way through. The metal was then hammered out into a thin sheet, giving an excellent imitation of wood-grain. Most Japanese bronzes contain a considerable proportion of lead to facilitate pouring and to lower the melting point of the metal. Like the Chinese, the Japanese used moulds of refractory fire-clay for casting, but in Japan there was, apparently, some difficulty in procuring clay which was sufficiently refractory, and this made it imperative to lower the fusion temperature of the alloy as far as practicable.

The use of enamel for decorating bronze was a western technique introduced into China in the Yüan dynasty, but little used till the Ming dynasty. The most prolific period, however, was the eighteenth century when some large and imposing decorative pieces ornamented with *cloisonné* enamels were made.

The Japanese did not begin to make objects decorated with enamels until well into the 19th century, but they very quickly mastered the technique, and introduced a type of *cloisonné* in which the wires normally bounding the *cloisons*, or cells, were removed altogether. Specimens are usually plates and vases, and of no great interest, apart from technical aspects.

Glossary

Agricultural motifs (horse brasses). Stock patterns appealing to country carters included the wheat-sheaf; cart horse and wagon between the horns of a crescent or set in a star; shepherd and windmill; wagoner carrying a whip; plough; the nine elms; sickle; and, of course, many variants of the horse.
Alloy. A composition of two or more metals intimately mixed by fusion.
Animals (horse brasses). Horses are most frequent. Sporting subjects include greyhounds and other dogs, stags, foxes and fox masks, and hares. Lesser-known motifs are elephants, sometimes inscribed Jumbo and Alice, and elephant and castle; lions and lion masks; bear and staff, camel, boar, squirrel, and cat.
Antimony. A metallic element used for hardening of alloys.
Astronomical (horse brasses). Outlines of horse brasses from the beginning appear to have been mainly in astronomic forms. The sun was usually represented as a sunflash, sometimes as a disc with rays and often enclosed within a serrated edge frame. The crescent moon, emblem of Diana, was extremely popular. Less frequent was the man-in-the-moon, cast full face and with rays. Stars with eight points were considered to have some mystic influence regarding horses, and with five points were believed to make any driven horse safe against the dangers of the road.
Barker of Bath. An artist in sporting scenes, Benjamin Barker was engaged by William Allgood as foreman decorator in the late 1770s. He was the father of the celebrated artists, Thomas and Benjamin Barker of Bath, both of whom were born at Pontypool and decorated trays for Allgood. Thomas specialized in rustic groups and figures of shepherds and woodsmen; Benjamin was celebrated for his landscapes.
Barrel (horse brasses). This was the obvious motif for brasses worn by brewers' dray horses. In the majority of designs the barrel was set vertically in an elongated crescent to which it was attached by struts. The crescent was later extended to form a circular ring into which the cast barrel might be brazed. These rings might be smooth, pierced, with or without serrated rim. Alternatively, the cast barrel with hoops in relief remained unframed and hung as a pendant either vertically or horizontally with the bung to the front, a strap loop being cast on the upper edge. A group of three tuns or barrels, arms of the Brewers' Company, was frequent. Some breweries hung as the lower brass on a martingale a flat shield engraved with the firm's name, address, and date.
Beddington Lock. Typical gilded wrought-iron rim lock of fine quality. Case and striking plate are enriched with panels fret-cut from cold annealed steel and riveted in two layers to the cover plate. Each pair of pierced panels is separated by cast-iron columns, and slender lengths of twisted wrought iron conceal joints between the various units. The central panel, displaying the arms of Henry VII and VIII, moves to reveal the keyhole.
Bell (horse brasses). The lower brass or brasses on a martingale might contain a small swinging bell cast from bell metal. In some of these the brass itself might follow the silhouette of a bell, with a tiny loose bell set in a bell-shaped perforation. In others a lavishly patterned brass contained a loose bell in the centre.

A set of bells might rise vertically above the horse's collar. In the eighteenth century these were of latten, and those of rolled brass in the nineteenth century were further toughened by hammering. The bells were hung in three or four rows, each row ringing its own chord. Each set hung within a shallow rectangular cover of leather-lined brass, the leather preventing the bells striking a discord upon the metal hood. Four-row sets were most unusual: in these the lowest row, containing five bells, was known as the lead; the next, of four bells, the lash; the third and fourth rows, each containing three bells, were termed body and trill. A single bell might hang in the terret.
Bellows. Contrivances for making a draught artificially, dating from very early times. Mention is made of bellows in wills from 1500 onwards, but as they suffered hard usage, survivors are seldom earlier than the seventeenth century; and any of that date are a great rarity. They received their due share of attention and were decorated in many styles. Carved and inlaid wood, wood overlaid with leather or silver, and even finely stitched needlework were used to ornament them. Lacquered examples were made in the first quarter of the eighteenth century. Apart from the small handbellows, which were often decorative rather than useful, more business-like machines were made; doubtless for the use of those servants on whom the warmth of the house depended. These standing bellows were in heavy wooden frames, and rested on the ground firmly, to be worked by means of a lever. Another type, lighter in weight, was operated by turning a wheel which was linked to the mechanism by a cord. This last type dates from the early nineteenth century.

The construction of the bellows has not changed in the course of the centuries. It comprises two shaped boards with a spring to keep them apart, held together by a loose leather hinge. One of the boards is pierced in the centre and fitted with a flap of leather on the inside, which acts as a valve, letting air enter, but not allowing it to escape except by way of the nozzle.
Betty lamp. A simple grease lamp, usually made of wrought iron, and consisting of a shallow cup with a

The Beddington lock showing case covered with hand-pierced and cast iron decorative panels. The centre panel displays the coat-of-arms and supporters as borne by Henry VII and Henry VIII. Enriched with gilding, early 16th century. Victoria & Albert Museum

Indicating lock of cast and engraved brass. Signed 'Johannes Wilkes de Birmingham Fecit', English, *c.* 1680. Victoria & Albert Museum

vertical handle and an indentation in which a wick was placed. Those made of two cups, one below the other, are generally called Phoebe lamps.

Bird, Edward, R. A. Painted japanned trays with historical scenes during and after his apprenticeship with the Ryton firm in Wolverhampton from about 1786 to the mid-1790s. He became Historical Painter to Princess Charlotte of Wales before his death in 1819.

Birds (horse brasses). A bird motif was usually brazed within a narrow plain or perforated ring having a serrated edge. The bird is usually more carefully finished than the frame and often in a different alloy, suggesting that they were acquired from specialists. The birds include the pelican in her piety, that is, feeding her young with blood drawn from her breast, and symbolic of maternal solicitude. This was used in some districts as a face piece on a brood mare. The peacock, considered sacred to Hera, a goddess of fertility, is seen either full face with a fanned tail, walking, or side view with trailing tail. Other birds include the old English gamecock, eagle, and phoenix, the latter dating from 1870. Souvenir pieces are also found.

Bismuth. A metal added to harden pewter. Also called tin glass.

Blowing tube. Forerunner of, and contemporary with, the bellows was a long metal tube widening from a mouthpiece and with a short projection at the base to raise it from the ground. The tube was placed where the draught was needed, and the user simply blew down the mouthpiece.

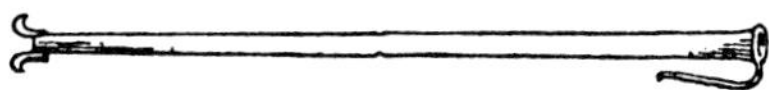

Blue steel. Lockplates in this metal date from late in the seventeenth century and formed contrasting backgrounds for pierced latten enrichment riveted over them and polished. The steel plates were blued by heating on sand.

Bolt. The securing unit of a lock which shoots out of the lock case into a socket or staple in the doorframe. A dead bolt is one capable of being moved both inward and outward by the key.

Borders. Usually in imitation of inlaid gold or silver. The most common ranged from the simple star – used also as an all-over pattern – stripes, and intersecting loop patterns to elaborate combinations of scrolls and flowers, rosettes and tendrils. From about 1820 until 1845 the tray rim and the margin of the panel might be decorated with a single pattern, usually gilded or bronzed, leaving the centre plain.

Bramah lock. The first lock to be operated by a small conveniently carried key, invented by Joseph Bramah in 1784. The key did not act directly upon the sliding bolt, but through the medium of the rotating barrel, thus anticipating Yale's cylindrical lock of 1848. Insertion of the key pushed back a number of sliding plates until notches at different positions came into line, allowing the barrel to be turned and the bolt withdrawn.

Brander. A pierced metal plate, with a half-loop handle by which it was suspended from a pot hook. It was used principally in Scotland for the making of brander bannocks – oatmeal cakes.

Brass. Late in the sixteenth century lock cases began to be made from latten plates. A simple lock case might be raised from the plate, but more frequently it was constructed by brazing suitable plates into a box. This was covered by a removable plate. Keyholes might be strengthened by an applied plate cut from latten and brazed in position. Other brass lock cases were enriched with corner spandrels: at first these were for strengthening purposes only; later they were decorated with punched and engraved work; towards the late seventeenth century spandrels were ornamentally pierced.

Locksmiths found English latten to be of poor quality, pitted with flaws and inclined to split during manipulation. Dutch latten was preferred as softer to work, smoother of surface, capable of taking on a higher polish, and easier to engrave. English latten was of necessity used during periods when the importation of brass and latten was prohibited to protect English brassmen. Fine lock cases in this flawed metal may be dated between 1660 and about 1680.

Brazier. In place of, and in addition to, a fireplace, heating was sometimes provided by a portable iron brazier which burned coke. At a later date the fuel was charcoal. A brazier was at Trinity College, Cambridge, in 1866, and had been in use there 'for upwards of 160 years'.

Braziers, charcoal. Smokers' braziers for table use were in great demand before the days of friction matches. These were low-footed bowls standing upon trays to prevent scorching the table top, and held small ember tongs used to lift the glowing, smokeless court charcoal to the smoker's clay pipe. In some instances the brazier was fitted with an almost horizontal handle. The brazier for heating a japanned kettle was placed in a low cylindrical vessel, from the rim of which rose four brackets to hold the kettle, and mounted on four ball or bracket feet. It was decorated to match the accompanying kettle.

Brander

Britannia metal. A hard form of pewter containing antimony and copper and dating from about 1800 onwards. Japanners shaped hollow ware by spinning this metal in a lathe. In about 1820 this was superseded by a special copper alloy evolved for spinning.

Bullet. A projection or some other formation in a keyhole to suit a corresponding groove cut into the bit of the key.

Butler. Family of tinsmiths from Connecticut who established the business in East Greenville, New York. Aaron Butler was born about 1799 and died

1860. Associated with him were his daughters Ann, Minerva, and Marilla.

Carron. The Carron Ironworks, Falkirk, Scotland, opened in 1759 and was responsible for the making of much fireside equipment. Small andirons (or rests for fire irons) of early nineteenth-century pattern are found with the name of the firm cast on the fronts. Many of these have been re-cast from the original moulds, in the present century, but in these instances the name 'Carron' appears at the back of each piece.

Case. The exterior box of a lock containing the mechanism and action.

Cast iron. A form of iron containing a relatively high percentage of carbon (approximately four per cent) and characterized by hardness and brittleness. Cast iron cannot be worked in a forge but is shaped by being poured into moulds while in a molten state.

Catch plate. A device on a rim night latch which holds the bolt in or out.

Cauldron (kettle). One of the oldest of all cooking utensils and recorded from the earliest times. They were first made of sheets of bronze, hammered to shape and riveted together; later they were of cast bronze. From the sixteenth century they were made of cast iron, and formed an important item in the equipment of the 'down hearth'. Small-sized cauldrons were known in some regions as 'crocks'.

Far right Ormolu candelabra made by Dietrich Anderson, English, *c.* 1760. Glaisher and Nash Ltd, London

Bronze cauldron, English, mid-17th century. Arthur Davidson, London

CHANDELIER MAKERS (ENGLISH)

Addison, Richard. Made chandelier for Canterbury Cathedral, 1685. Freeman of Founders' Company. Died 1690/1.

Dickinson, Richard. 'Mr Dickinson the Brasier' was to make three chandeliers for St Lawrence Jewry, London, 1678. Buried at St Lawrence Jewry, 30 June 1681.

Giles, John. Signed chandelier at Framlingham, Suffolk, 1742. Admitted to Founders' Company, 1716. Master 1740–1. Died September 1743.

Giles, William. Signed chandelier at St Nicholas-at-Wade, Kent, 1757. Admitted to Pewterers' Company, 1737. Master 1769. Admitted as Love-Brother to Founders' Company, 1758. Died January 1771.

Hawes, Patrick. 'Mr Hawes' supplied chandeliers for Barbers' Hall, 1744. Admitted to Founders' Company, 1721. Master 1753–4. Died 1769/70.

Marshall, Robert. Signed chandelier at Leatherhead, Surrey, 1763 (*Marshall Fecit*). Admitted to Founders' Company, 1738. Died insolvent 1771.

Meakins, Richard. 'Mr Meakings ye founder' probably supplied chandelier for St Michael, Crooked Lane, London, 1690/1. Was to have preference for making chandeliers for St Margaret Lothbury, 1690–1. Freeman of Founders' Company. Master 1686–7. Died 1705.

Mist, Mary. Signed chandelier at Wollaston, Northamptonshire, 1777 (*Mist Long Acre Fecit*). Widow of Thomas Mist who died 1766/7. Had son in partnership, 1771; succeeded by Henry Mist, 1778.

Peter, Charles. Signed chandelier at Wymondham, Norfolk, 1712. Admitted to Founders' Company, 1709. Died 1766/7.

Shrimpton, Russel & Co. Probably supplied the chandeliers for Society of Antiquaries, London, 1781.

Sutton, Jacob. Supplied chandelier for St Mary Woolnoth, London, 1727; made lecterns for Salisbury Cathedral and St Paul's Cathedral, 1714 and 1720.

Taylor, Thomas. Supplied chandeliers for St Stephen Walbrook, London, 1679. Died 1679.

Townsend, John. Made chandeliers for Allhallows, Lombard Street, London, 1764/5. Admitted to Pewterers' Company, 1784. Master 1784. Died 1801 (?).

Makers in the Provinces include the following:

Birmingham

Cocks, John. Signed chandelier in nave at Prestbury, Cheshire, 1814. Succeeded Thomas Cocks & Son,

1808. Not in business, 1815.
Cocks, Thomas & Son. Signed chandeliers (*Cocks & Son*) at Yardley Hastings, Northamptonshire, 1808, and Wrenbury, Cheshire, 1839 (?). Called Cocks & Taylor, 1801 and before.
Haywood, James. Signed chandelier at St Harmon, Radnor, 1771. Appears in Birmingham rate books 1751–75.

Bridgwater, Somerset

Bayley, John. Signed chandeliers at Stogursey, Somerset, 1732, and Lympsham, Somerset, 1744.
Bayley, Thomas. Signed chandeliers at Mark, 1758, Ilminster, 1762, Old Cleeve, 1770, Burnham, 1773, Kingston, 1773, and Stogumber, all in Somerset.
Pyke, Thomas. Signed chandelier at Guildhall, Exeter, 1789.
Street & Pyke. Signed chandeliers at St Sidwell, Exeter, 1774, and Over Stowey, Somerset, 1775.

Bristol

Bill, Francis. Signed chandelier at Dunster, Somerset, 1740. Died 1754.
Rennells, Richard. Signed chandelier at Yeovil, Somerset, 1724. Died 1730 (?).
Rice, Roger. Signed chandeliers at Pilton, Somerset, 1749, and Axminster, Devon, 1750. Admitted Burgess of Bristol, 1740. Of Clifton, 1754.
Wansborough, —. 'Mr Wansborough' made chandelier for Evercreech, Somerset, 1761.
Wasbrough, Hale & Co. Signed chandelier at Hatherleigh, Devon (undated).

Chester

Brock, —. 'Mr Brock' supplied chandeliers for Malpas, Cheshire, 1726, and Gresford, Denbigh, 1747. Probably was Thomas Brock, admitted Freeman of Chester, 14 October 1697, buried at St Peter, Chester, 7 May 1755.
Thomas, John. Signed chandelier at St Marcella, Denbigh, 1753. Apprentice of Thomas Brock; admitted Freeman of Chester, 26 May 1752.

Chester or *Manchester* (?)

Davenport, William. Signed chandelier in chancel at Prestbury, Cheshire, 1712.

Wigan, Lancashire

Brown, —. 'Mr Brown' supplied chandeliers for Kirkham, Lancashire, 1725 and 1733.
Tarlington, George. Supplied chandelier for Deane, Lancashire, 1737/8.

Cheap locks. Cases and parts for mass-produced locks were first made in 1796 by Isaac Mason, Willenhall. These were punched and bolstered from sheet iron by the flypress.
Chestnut servers. These urn-shaped containers might be oval or round, their bodies raised from copper in two halves and vertically joined. From about 1800 to 1820 they were spun from Britannia metal; from about 1820 they were spun from a special copper alloy. The vessel was supported on a spreading foot, round or square, and a short, slenderstem. It usually had lion mask and ring handles of cast lead gilded and with a domed cover surmounted by a gilt acorn or other simple finial.

Chestnut servers were handed with coffee and contained Spanish chestnuts, boiled and then roasted. They were served hot, and were lifted from the server with a fork; their husks were removed at table and they were eaten with salt.
Chimney crane. Known in Scotland as a 'Swey', this was a bracket of wrought iron from which a cauldron or tea kettle was suspended. Cranes were of many types: large and small, simple and complicated. In the case of the latter the pot could be raised or lowered and swung to any position over the fire.
Coal containers (coal box, hod, purdonium, scuttle). It can be well understood that owing to the hard usage they received, the life of these was short. There appear to be no examples surviving from before about 1800, and most of them have been reproduced in quantity in this century.

Scuttles made of sheet copper are described as being of 'bucket' or 'helmet' shape; the latter modelled on the fifteenth-century helment, the salade, inverted, and with a moulded base and swing handle.

Covered boxes of mid-nineteenth-century date were of japanned metal with gilt decoration, and the hinged lids were often fitted with a panel of shaped glass with 'back painting,' of flowers or landscapes. The handles of these boxes and their accompanying shovels were often of white china.

Chestnut urn and cover, in Pontypool japanned ware, two gilt handles with acanthus moulding. Black japan with flower spray, flowering shrubs with bowl in red and silver with a golden tinge from the varnish. National Museum of Wales

Coal vases. Replaced coal scuttles in wealthy homes from 1840 when the Nasmyth hammer was introduced into japanning factories. They were intended to remain decorating the fireside and be filled from buckets, unlike scuttles, which were carried into the cellar. The coal for the first time was concealed beneath an ornamental cover. Fearncombe of Wolverhampton displayed at the Great Exhibition a coal vase in the shape of a nautilus shell resting on coral, the cover handle representing a seahorse. Others were in the shape of miniature Gothic fonts and great tureens.
Cobirons. These are similar to andirons, but are usually quite plain in design and have rows of hooks on the standards on which spits could be placed. Some examples of cobirons have basket-like tops, and it has been suggested that they are 'cressets' for holding a light. Alternatively they may have been intended for containing a cup used in basting meat.
Cock's-head hinge. A form of H-hinge in which each termination is formed into the silhouette of a cock's head.
Coffee pots. Made in the shapes and sizes associated with silver, usually in baluster curves or cylindrical with inward-sloping sides, and with wicker-covered handles. Such a vessel was ornamented in the fashionable styles current at the time of manufacture, often with a scene on each side. It stood upon a tripod, also japanned, containing a charcoal brazier.

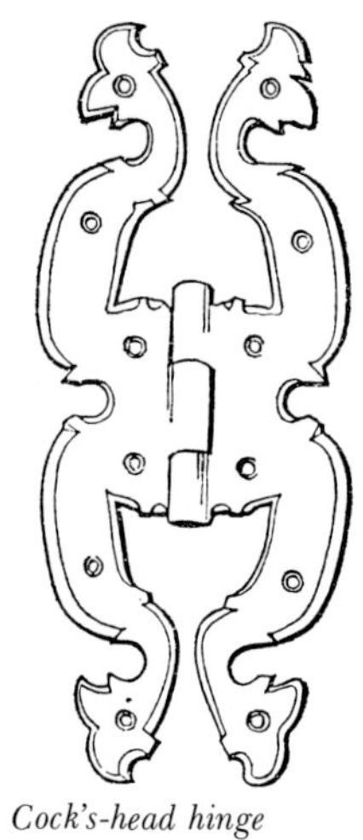
Cock's-head hinge

Curfew

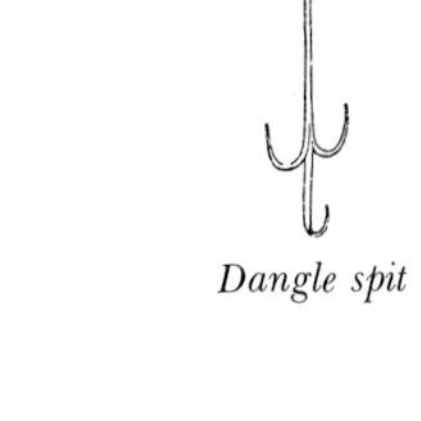
Dangle spit

Coffee-pot with tortoise-shell ground, Pontypool. National Museum of Wales

Cover. A plate screwed over the lock case covering the mechanism and holding the working parts in place.
Cran. An iron trivet fitted over the fire for supporting a kettle, girdle plate, etc.
Creepers. These, in pairs, were small irons of similar shape to andirons, between which they were placed in the hearth. Creepers were of very simple design, and they came into use when andirons grew elaborate and costly.
Cresset. Generally an iron basket affixed to a rod and designed to hold wood or other fuel for lighting purposes.
Cross garnet hinge. A type of strap hinge one leaf of which is a horizontal strap and the other a vertical strap; when in position like a letter T lying on its side.
Crystallized decoration. Patented in 1816 by Edward Thomason, Birmingham, and marketed as *moiré* metal. The patent took advantage of the fact that when tinned iron plate is held obliquely to the light it reveals figured patterns. After processing it was silvery in appearance, and covered with stars and other well-composed geometrical figures: it was varnished at once to preserve its brilliancy. In the 1830s Ryton and Walton discovered that splendid effects could be obtained by staining the tin green, lake, yellow, and other colours. This was coated several times with japanner's varnish. Pictures were painted over this ground with outstanding effect by flower painters from the Potteries. Under the name of crystallized ware many japanners issued a variety of domestic goods such as trays and waiters, tea chests, work boxes, tobacco boxes, and lamps.
Curfew (*couvre-feu*). To enable the fire to be kept alive during the night or when left unattended, a metal cover was placed over it. This cover, known as a 'Curfew', was roughly in the shape of a quarter-sphere and had a handle affixed to it. Old specimens are very rare, and existing ones are of brass or copper with embossed ornament.
Dangle spit. A non-mechanical type of spit which operated in the manner implied by its name. It hung downwards, twisting one way and another on a rope as the latter wound and unwound itself, clockwise and anti-clockwise, sometimes with the aid of two weighted arms.
Decoration. Ornament on early brass lock cases consisted of designs composed of arches, points, and lines applied by means of steel punches cut with a wide range of simple motifs. Stock pattern repeats were drawn on parchment and the outlines picked out in closely spaced pinholes. The parchment was laid upon the surface of the unpolished latten and sprinkled with fine charcoal or chalk. This was rubbed through the pinholes, leaving an outline design to guide the craftsmen.

Cover plates by the end of the seventeenth century might be cast throughout in princes metal with all-over decoration in relief and chased and engraved. Delicate filigree work was associated with exquisite reticulated perforations: these might be laid over plates of blue steel. The brass cover plate and the keyhole escutcheon might have applied steel ornaments cut in delicate, lace-like patterns.
Door furniture. Includes locks, knobs, keyhole escutcheons, finger plates, door closers, hinges, catch plates, and so on, all made to match until early Victorian days.
Dovetail hinge. A butterfly hinge, the leaves of which resemble two dovetails joined at the narrow part.
Down hearth. A slab of stone or metal raised slightly above the level of the floor of the room, forming the earliest and most simple type of fireplace. The first versions were centrally placed in a room, and smoke rose to escape through a louvre in the roof. The down hearth built in one side of the room with a flue communicating with the outside has remained in use in cottages to this day.

Dutch metal. Alloy of copper and zinc used in place of gold leaf in decoration.
Dutch oven. An open-fronted oven, usually raised on legs, placed before the fire and used for cooking. Dutch ovens were made of sheet iron, brass, and even of pottery.
Engraving. Introduced from Italy in the early seventeenth century. By the time of Charles I groups of highly skilled lock-case engravers were established in London and Wolverhampton. All-over designs were incised with gravers, chisels, and flatters forged from Venice steel – probably of Damascus origin. Steel cases were softened before engraving, and after rehardening were fire-gilded to prevent rust.

Some of the most superb brass rim locks were made during the period 1660–1790. The covers were ornamented with elaborate all-over engraving, and sometimes further enriched by the addition of a high relief motif cast in prince's metal or pinchbeck extending across the latch end of the cover to which it was riveted. Fashionably such decoration depicted the coat-of-arms or monogram of the owner, but a great variety of designs is found.
Escutcheon. A plate surrounding the keyhole or swinging over the keyhole.
Escutcheon-lift latch. A trick latch resembling the common Norfolk type which is operated by lifting a sliding escutcheon plate rather than the more usual system of pressing a thumb plate.
Face piece (horse brasses). A brass suspended on the forehead of the horse. A merchant's catalogue of the 1890s captioned such a brass, 'cart-horse face piece'. It is often stated that Queen Victoria's portrait on horse brasses in the early years of her reign was responsible for the name face piece as a generic term.
Fireback. This slab of cast iron, sometimes referred to as a 'Reredos', stood at the back of the fireplace, protected the wall, and reflected the heat of the burning fuel. Firebacks were made by the simple means of pouring the molten metal on to a prepared bed of sand in which a pattern had been impressed. The patterns were carved in wood, and were either of a full-sized design or in the form of single ornaments which were composed into a whole to suit the taste of the maker or his client.

The iron firebacks of Sussex are the best known; others were made in Yorkshire, Derbyshire, and in the Forest of Dean. Many were imported from Holland late in the seventeenth century and onwards. It is often difficult to determine the origin of one from another; the firebacks with scenes from the Bible or mythological subjects are usually said to have been of Dutch make, but these were copied in England, and there is no certainty on the point. In Holland the castings were made thinner than in England, but this feature also was adopted here. The earliest English firebacks were of a wide, low shape, but by the mid-seventeenth century tall ones, of 'Tombstone' style, were introduced.

There are firebacks recorded which bear the coats-of-arms and initials of English sovereigns from Henry VII to James II; others commemorate the defeat of the Spanish Armada (1588), Charles II and the Boscobel Oak (1651), and similar personages and events of widespread contemporary interest.
Fireboard (fire screen). A decorative panel used to conceal the fireplace cavity when no fire was burning. In the Victoria and Albert Museum is one of wood painted with a vase of flowers, and at Osterley is another covered with tapestry to match the hangings of the room in which it stands.

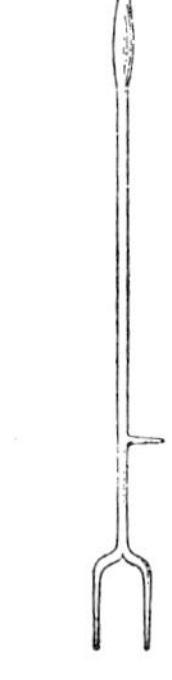
Firefork

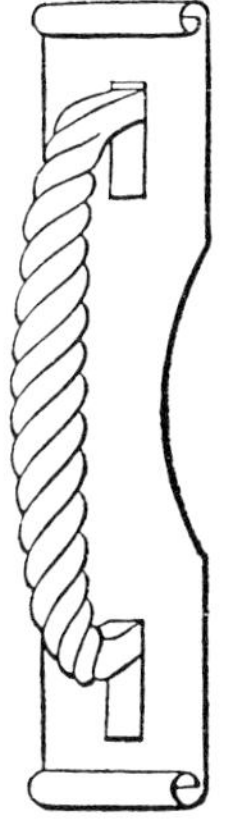
Escutcheon-lift latch

Nineteenth-century examples in the French Louis XV style were of gilt metal, chased and pierced, in the form of a fan which folded up when not in use.
Firedog. Andiron, especially one of the lower and simpler sort.
Firefork. An instrument made of wrought iron, some 4 feet (122 cm) or more in length in order that the user would be away from the heat when moving burning logs in the hearth. Usually it had two stout prongs, but some examples have a spike at one side about three-quarters of the way down from the handle. The firefork was the forerunner of the poker, and it went out of general use when coal replaced wood as a fuel.

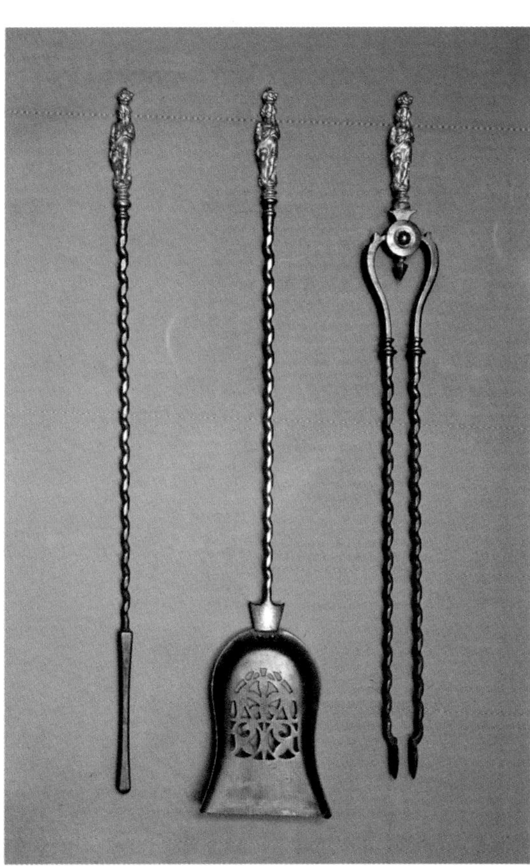
Fire irons of wrought iron with brass finials, late 18th century. William Job, London

Fire irons. In the days of wood fuel these comprised tongs, brush, and firefork. For coal, the principal addition was a shove, and the poker was substituted for the firefork. The shovel was often pierced so that the coal might be sifted, and the smaller pieces chosen for starting the fire. Late in the eighteenth century the pierced designs were still current, but their retention had become no more than a decorative feature.

The implements were variously ornamented, and although the working parts were of steel or wrought iron, this did not preclude the craftsman from making the handles of more costly metals. The sets of fire irons enriched with silver, at Ham House, have been described and illustrated frequently since they were seen and commented upon by John Evelyn when he was there in 1678.

Steel fire irons of eighteenth-century pattern have been much reproduced in the present century.

Flatware. General term for plates, platters, dishes, etc.

Footman. The name given to a four-legged trivet made to stand in front of the fire in the sitting room or parlour. They were made of wrought iron or brass, or partly of each, and commonly had front legs of cabriole design. The top was often pierced with a central hole so that it could be carried. The footman dates from the second half of the eighteenth century onwards.

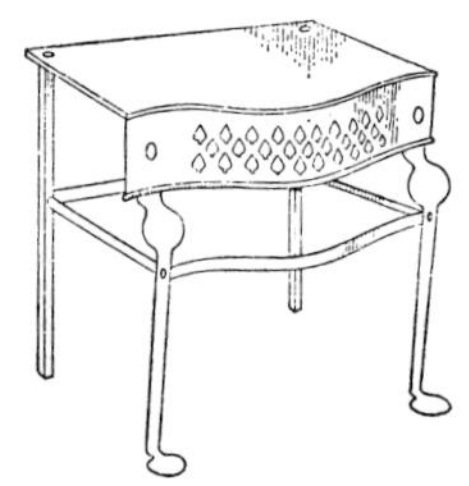

Footman

French tôle peinte (painted sheet iron). Has the same origin as English japan work. The Oriental influence was strongly felt. There is a similarity to the English work in the shape and designs of some pieces thought to be French. This leads to the belief that plain and decorated English products were exported to France. It is known that japanners and painters travelled between the two countries, which confirms the belief and adds to the difficulty of identifying the work. The terms *tôle*, or toleware, have come into rather general use in the United States, however, for all wares of this class regardless of place of production. Japanned tin plate, or japanned tinware can be used more appropriately.

Hasps

Girdle plate. A flat iron sheet on which oatcakes were baked in Scotland. They were of two types: those with a half-loop handle which were attached to the pot hook and the cakes cooked while suspended; and those with a small handle projecting at one end for manipulation. The latter type was placed on a cran.

Gridiron. This was placed over the centre of the fire for cooking, and comprised a number of parallel bars on which meat, etc., rested during the process. Early gridirons were of simple pattern and made of wrought iron. Later ones sometimes had the bars channelled and leading to a trough at the front, which had a spout for pouring out the gravy and fat collected in it.

Gridiron

Grisset. An elongated, cup-like, iron basin, generally with a handle, for holding grease so that rushes can be drawn through it to prepare rush lights. These devices are fairly rare.

Ground colours. In Birmingham and Wolverhampton, according to the specification of John Baskerville's patent of 1742, japanned grounds might be of 'fine glowing Mahogany colour, Black in no way inferior to the most perfect India Goods, or in imitation of *Tortoiseshell*'. Against these might be painted flowers and foliage in colours. At this time Pontypool grounds were black, chocolate, crimson, and tortoiseshell. By the late 1770s Pontypool had introduced new colours, the range including dark green, puce, tomato red, orange, canary, grey, and ultramarine blue. These were coated with varnish displaying an attractive golden tinge.

There is no evidence to show that the basic methods of japanning either in the Midlands or in London differed from those of Pontypool, but tinned rather than tin plates were used, methods of application were less costly and finish less rich although possessing a lustrous surface. Brilliant colours were soon competing with those of Pontypool. The *Dictionary of Arts & Sciences* (1763) described these as yellow, vermilion, red, lake, blue bice, indigo, green, brown, purple, and flesh white.

In the 1820s a fine green japan was developed, an ideal ground for the fashionable Oriental themes in gold. This costly colour was used only on the finest work, and is frequently found in a remarkably successful series decorated with exotic birds, such as peacocks, parrots, cockatoos, flowers, and foliage, sometimes with a playing fountain.

Guard. A fixed unit within a lock preventing fake keys from turning, or to prevent a lock-picking instrument from reaching the bolt or levers.

Hasp. A hinged strap generally used with a pin or lock to secure a door or chest.

Heart. These horse brasses appear to have ornamented the check rein. One series of hearts was stamped in silhouette, sometimes in bold relief, perhaps more frequently with a flat surface. Plain hearts were cast within circular perforated frames, rayed piercing sometimes encircling closely spaced circular perforations: variations are numerous. A series of designs in which the heart is cast in the round has a secondary heart rising in relief from the centre. Rare is the heart within a heart, that is, a heart in relief with its centre pierced by a smaller heart. Three or six small hearts arranged into the shape of a larger heart proved an acceptable design during the 1890s, the surface of each heart highly burnished.

Heraldic (horse brasses). Owners of private stables and country estates considered it a pleasant conceit to use face pieces displaying their coats-of-arms or crests. These appear to have been introduced by Daniel Moriarty of Oxford, who supplied them to order in gilded silver: hallmarks show them to date from the late 1830s. Moriarty also made heraldic face pieces in German silver, and these might be gilded or silver-plated. The majority, however, were cast from a pinchbeck alloy – usually prince's metal – and gilded. Robert Hughes of Finsbury specialized in heraldic face pieces from the 1840s until the mid-1860s, supplying them to the commission of saddlers throughout the country.

Estate brasses in the form of a cipher, with or without a coronet, have been noted, the cipher being in a ring or crescent with or without a serrated rim. In later examples of cheap-quality brass the frame was drilled with closely spaced perforations. Engraved crests and ciphers have been noted on early Victorian sunflash brasses.

H hinge. A common type of early hinge the leaves of which are formed of vertical straps and affixed to each other by short horizontal straps in the centre so as to resemble the letter H. The HL hinge has an extra horizontal strap extending from one extremity of the H.

Hollow ware. A general term for vessels designed to hold liquids.

Horse brasses with horse motifs. Belle Johnson, Antiquarius

Horse motifs (in brasses). The most popular appear to have been the prancing horse of Kent and the horse combatant. Horses carrying sprays of oak leaves in their mouths are associated with the various estates of the Duke of Norfolk. Models include also winged horses, steeplechasers, and racehorses, cart horses, generally facing to the right, horses' heads in profile and full face. These are given various mountings, from plain crescents and wide rings to the complicated geometric perforated patterns of the 1890s and later. A horse's full face usually looks out from a quatrefoil opening, the mount having a circular outline which may be scalloped. Casting and the quality of the metal are generally poor, thus discounting Walsall as a source of origin. A series of cart horses were stamped in relief on plain discs with serrated rims. Horses are to be found framed by horseshoes, pierced or moulded with nail holes, and in almost closed crescents – usually pierced. An interesting though late series are those brasses in which a tiny horse is displayed within a wide pierced inner border enclosing a wide outer border with a serrated edge. The fully harnessed horse cast in the round with a pendant loop rising from the saddle should be classed as a souvenir. It has proved possible to assemble a collection amounting to about eighty brasses bearing horse motifs, without any duplicates.

Horseshoes (horse brasses). In this symbol of good luck the opening, in most instances, hangs downward. Those noted have been cast, and many contain a profile portrait of a horse's head looking to the left. This might be cast separately and brazed into a stamped horseshoe. In others a driven horse is shown facing to the right. A stamped or cast horseshoe with nail holes may contain a trotting horse on a slender bar joining the horns of the shoe. Others display horses apparently copied or adapted from heraldic crests.

Iron and steel. The English iron industry, to which the fireside owes so much of its equipment, was centred on those places where there was assurance of ample supplies of wood – the essential fuel for melting the ore and for causing chemical changes in it. Iron is divisible into two distinct types: with little carbon content it becomes malleable and is steel or wrought iron, and with more than the minimum of carbon remaining in its composition it is cast iron. All three forms of the metal had their place and purpose at the fireside.

From the fourteenth century until about 1800 the wooded areas of Sussex were the seat of great activity, and the foundries established there grew famous for their products. While the ore had been worked from as early as the time of the Roman occupation, it was in the fourteenth century that a great expansion took place and new methods were brought into use. Today there remain traces of slag ('cinder') from the long-dormant workings, sited near streams which once provided power for the needed draught.

In the sixteenth century Buxted was noted for the making of cannon of cast iron, which were first produced in 1543, together with the ammunition. No less well known were the Sussex firebacks, and a number of these have been identified with certainty as having been made in that area. One, inscribed 'Richard Lenard Founder at Bred Fournis' (*Bred*: Brede) is dated 1636, and another depicts the burning at the stake of an earlier iron master, Richard Woodman, and his wife; a couple who suffered that fate in the religious persecutions of Queen Mary in 1557.

Japan. Black asphaltum varnish for coating metal in imitation of lacquer.

Japanner. One who coats the surface with asphaltum varnish. Later it was used in a broader sense in regard to both decoration and manufacture.

Japanning. Was defined by eighteenth-century technical writers as 'the covering of wood or metals by grounds of opaque colours in varnish which when varnished and dried may afterwards be decorated with painted ornament, in gold and colours, or left plain'.

The secret of the surface lustre which characterized the finer work was to cover the opaque coloured grounds with several coats of clear japan varnish. Each application was followed by stoving at 280° F. in a cupboard-shaped iron oven. This firmly fused the surface, made it extremely hard, and prevented the peeling and cracking that spoilt Continental japanning. This surface was excellent for painting and gilding.

Kettle tilter ('Idle back', 'Lazy back', 'Handy maid'). A simple device of wrought iron for tilting the kettle when water was wanted from it. Not only was there no need to soil the hand by touching a smoke-blackened kettle, but the handle of the tilter projected outside the fireplace, was cool, and there would be no risk from scalding steam or water. The kettle was suspended over the fire in the tilter, which in turn hung from a pot hook or crane.

Knocker latch. A combination door knocker and latch. Turning the knocker opened the latch.

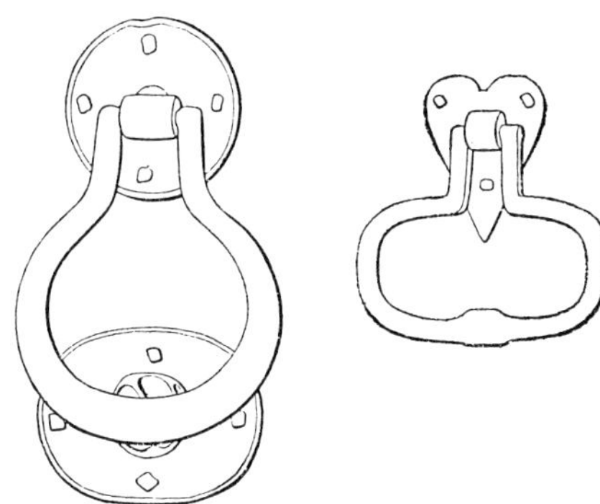

Latch. A lock having a bevelled spring bolt which is self-acting when closing a door. The bolt is then withdrawn with a handle. No key.

Latten. Plate made from brass ingots and composed of copper and calamine and beaten into sheets with heavy horse- or water-powered battery hammers. Horse brasses made from latten are rare. Originally they displayed hammermarks on the back and front: years of polishing may have removed all traces of these from the front of a horse brass, but they remain visible at the back. It must be emphasized that latten was not an alternative name for brass, but was a term distinguishing hammered sheets from brass made by other processes.

Leather. Collectors of horse brasses tend to display them on martingales or other leather straps taken from harness. Until early in the present century such leather was almost invariably horsehide tanned with oak bark and notable for its lightness and strength. Cowhides, appreciably heavier, were sometimes used in the nineteenth century. Years of rubbing against the horse and cleaning with wax polish have made it more pliant than modern leather.

Lever lock. The earliest was patented in 1778 by Robert Barron, its mechanism a system of fixed wards in combination with two pivoting or lifting tumblers which he termed levers, held in position by a steel spring. Attached to the tumblers were stumps or studs which retained the bolt in its locked position. Only its own individually made key, cut in steps of different radii, corresponded with the varying lifts of the two tumblers, so that the latter were raised to the exact height to bring the studs into line with the slot in the bolt, and thus allow the top step of the key to act upon the stump and unlock it. Any attempt to pick the lock was frustrated by a number of upper transverse notches in the bolt. This rendered it impossible to tell when the tumblers had been lifted correctly; from this developed, in the early 1800s, the ordinary lever lock. The lever itself is a piece of flat, shaped metal of which one or more must be lifted simultaneously but differently by the various strips in the key to block the bolt either in the open or a locked position. All levers swing on the same pivot. By about 1850 the stump was attached to the bolt.

Lockplate. The background to which all the pins and stumps are riveted and over which the cover is fixed.

Locomotive (horse brasses). Special horse brasses displaying locomotives were issued by more than twenty railway companies for their dray horses, each picturing its favourite type of engine, some including a driver. They were used in association with a brass bearing the monogram or initials of the company pierced into flat plate: later the full title was engraved. A series of saddlers' stock locomotives, intended for martingales, consisted of a set of six locomotives illustrating development from Stephenson's Rocket until the time when these brasses were made, in 1880. Complete sets have been built up from single acquisitions. A rare brass of the mid-Victorian period is a plain crescent engraved with the Rocket.

Martingales. A broad band of leather or series of straps, extending from the noseband or reins to the girth. By keeping the horse's head down this band prevents the animal from rearing or throwing back its head. From the early 1850s the martingale was hung with brasses as standard equipment. Saddlers usually attached brasses selected at random, but included types most favoured in the district. The topmost brass might be cast in the form of the emblem used by the saddler as his trademark; the lowest brass was often a lunar crescent punched with the saddler's name and address above the engraved inscription 'Saddlery and Harness' and the date recording the year in which the harness was made. Rare indeed are special name and date brasses, such as the plain heart, handcut from rolled plate brass and engraved with the horse's name and the date of its birth.

Measure. A vessel of standard liquid capacity.

Meat fork. Used at the fireside when cooking. It usually had two prongs and was very little (if at all) different from a toasting fork.

Mechanism of locks. Consists of fixed obstructions – wards, guards, and bullets – and movable detainers such as tumblers and levers.

Mortice lock. Concealed from view by inserting it into a hole cut into the door edge. In most early mortice locks only the brass knob remained visible, the keyhole masked by a swinging escutcheon. Decoration might be added in the form of an ornamental endpiece matching the adjoining striking plate: these might be engraved, pierced, or cast and chased, often displaying the owner's coat-of-arms or cipher.

A new style of lock furniture associated with mortice locks was introduced during the mid-1760s. This set consisted of an expansive backplate of chased and gilt cast brass, in scrollwork designs symmetrically arranged with festoons of husks centring on the door knob and flanked with a keyhole escutcheon and a matching dummy escutcheon. The centre rosette and the escutcheon harmonized with the knob. In some instances the dummy was replaced by a small knob operating a night latch.

Mug. A handled drinking vessel without cover.

Night latch. A spring bolt lock operated by a key from outside and a knob from inside.

Norfolk latch. A type consisting of a handle affixed to a large, one-piece escutcheon plate.

Oak leaf and acorn. Motifs favoured during the 1890s and later. A single well-modelled acorn might be enclosed within a wide frame pierced with holes in the form of concentric circles. Others were pierced in complicated patterns. Oak leaves and acorns cast as a single spray are usually within a lunar crescent; in others the crescent is stamped and a spray, cast and chased, is set within held by brazing. The acorn points upward when alone, downward in a spray of foliage.

Paktong. A Cantonese word for a natural alloy of copper and nickel to which zinc was added. The resulting metal was similar to the 'German' or 'nickel' silver discovered in Europe in 1849. The Chinese employed paktong for a variety of purposes, including furniture hinges and decorative mounts. Generally, it is yellowish-white in colour. Paktong came from Yunnan Province and was exported to the West in ingot form in the eighteenth century, where it was used for ornamental purposes, like the casting of candlesticks. The term in Mandarin is *pai-tung* (white copper).

Patterns, casting (horse brasses). Fine brasses such as heraldic crests were cast from master patterns skilfully carved in hard mahogany. These remained the property of the purchaser, and so were used only for limited editions, never commercially. More usually master patterns were carved from pear wood, and from these a number of casting patterns were prepared, usually in a tin-lead alloy. These produced clear-cut relief work. Some of these pewter casting patterns have been mistaken for actual horse brasses, and as such are sometimes included in collections.

Pear shape. A term used in identifying a curved or pyriform shape in hollow ware.

Perforated ornament. Fashionable on silver and ceramics from the 1770s was also introduced to japanned ware. Most perforations were handsawn and finished by filing: a few, such as vertical pales, were die-punched. Perforated borders are notably found on waiters and on the 'hand tea tables' used for setting out the porcelain or Queen's ware tea service. Although such ornament is usually associated with Pontypool, it was also applied to the japanned ware of Birmingham, Wolverhampton, Bilston, and London.

Pewter. An alloy, chiefly of tin, with varying proportions of copper, lead, antimony, or bismuth.

Pin locks. These were usually in oak, the flat bolt passing completely through the locks, one end expanded to engage in the jamb socket, the other shaped to form a handle. Three recesses were sunk into the top edge, into which loose pins fell from above when the key was removed, thus holding the pin immovable. Pin locks were opened by inserting a wooden key into an aperture immediately above the bolt handle, and lifting it slightly. Projections on its upper surface raised the locking pins so that the bolt might be withdrawn from its socket.

Pintle. A pivot pin for a hinge.

Pipe kiln. A tubular wrought-iron frame with a handle at the top and feet at each end. Clay 'churchwarden' pipes were placed in the kiln in order to clean them when they had become foul, and the pipe kiln and its contents were then put into an oven. It is said that in country districts the local baker performed this task.

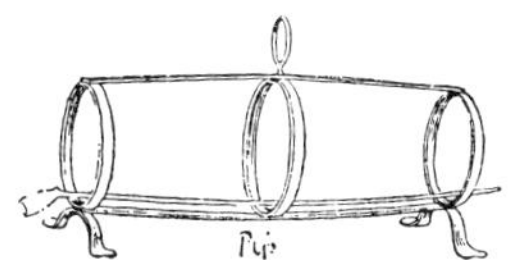

Far right Pewter whale oil lamp with bull's eye reflectors, American, 19th century. American Museum in Britain

Far right Pin lock of oak with bolt, loose pins and key, Scottish. Egyptian in origin, this type of lock was introduced to Britain by the Phoenician traders nearly three thousand years ago. Science Museum, London

Left Quart mug, the barrel inscribed 'Edward Hill at Ye Red Lyon in Ye Pouttery 1676', English, Victoria & Albert Museum

Below pewter candlestick (*left*), first half of the 17th century. The Grainger candlestick (*centre*) cast in relief with the arms of the Pewterers' Company and the name of William Grainger (Steward of the Company in 1620), dated 1616. Candlestick with maker's touch (*right*), the initials S.B. over a star with a lozenge on lip, last quarter of the 17th century. All English. Victoria & Albert Museum

Plate lock. In these the working parts were exposed, being riveted to a heavy hatchet-shaped plate of wrought iron fixed flat against the door. The iron bolt worked in slides and engaged in a striking plate fitted to the door jamb. The visible working parts might display some decoration. By utilizing only the minimum number of parts, at a time when iron and steel were highly expensive, plate locks were made at comparatively low cost. Antique plate locks are of iron made close-textured by hammering: the Victorian type have cast or rolled iron plates.

Plate warmer. This stood before the fire in kitchen, living room, or dining room, to heat the plates preparatory to the serving of a meal. Several types of plate warmer have been recorded; all date from the eighteenth and nineteenth centuries, and the surviving examples are not numerous. One variety is in the form of a wrought-iron revolving stand on a tripod base with upright bars to hold the plates in position. Another kind is similar to a Dutch oven, and has a handle so that the whole apparatus, complete with warmed plates, might be brought from the fireside to the table. A third type is the cat: an ingenious arrangement of three turned wood or metal rods, arranged crosswise to form a double-ended tripod that could stand either way up.

Pontipool. The industrial japanners of Birmingham and South Staffordshire found it convenient to market their japanned metal under the name of 'Fancy Pontipool Ware', the spelling serving to distinguish it from the Allgood japanned ware.

Pontypool. The name given to japanned ware made by the Allgood family at Pontypool, Monmouthshire. Their many agents sold Allgood productions as 'Pontypool Japan', and their London agent Edward Binyon, Fenchurch Street, London, advertised in 1783 that his was 'The Original Warehouse for the Real Ponty-Pool Japann'd Ware'. The terms 'Pontypool' and 'Pontipool' distinguished japanning on metal from japanned wood and Clay's japanned paper ware dating from 1772.

Porringer. A small, handled bowl or basin used for liquid or semi-liquid food, ranging in size from 2½ to 6 inches (6.4–15.3 cm).

Portraits (horse brasses). In addition to royal personages a few late Victorian and early Edwardian celebrities were commemorated on horse brasses. The politicians were Gladstone, Lord Randolph Churchill, Joseph Chamberlain, Disraeli, and Lloyd George from 1908. Disraeli's portrait is usually enclosed in a border of primroses or primroses encircled with a narrow pierced rim. Baden-Powell, Lord Roberts, and Kitchener decorated driven horses at the time of the Boer War, and Nelson during the Trafalgar centenary year of 1905.

Pot hook (Cottrall, Jib crook, Hanger, Tramelle, Hake). A wrought-iron device that was in use from medieval times for suspending a pot over the fire. By means of a ratchet it could be adjusted for height. In Scotland the same means was attained by using a chain and hook, known as a 'Jumping Rope'.

Prince's metal. A brass alloy evolved in the 1670s and tinged to the colour of gold. The metal was heated until slightly red and laid to pickle in a diluted spirit of vitriol. After removing dirt and scale by washing, it was immersed for a moment in aquafortis, dried, and burnished with a bloodstone.

Punch. A die for striking the maker's touch or other identification or decorative marks into metal.

Pontypool argyll (gravy maker), late 18th century. Loot, London

Plate warmer

Plate warmer of wrought iron, 18th century. Victoria & Albert Museum

Pot hook

Rattail. The tapering extension of a spoon handle unto the underside of the bowl.

Rattail hinge. A type usually found on cupboards in which there is a downward extension, serving as a brace, of the pintle. This extension is curved and terminated with a decorative device.

Rim lock. The mechanism is entirely closed within a rectangular metal case and attached to the inner surface of a door. In addition to the locking bolt, such a lock might have an independent smaller knob operating a spring catch to prevent the lock from being opened from the outside. Both of these entered the striking plate screwed upon the jamb.

Royal (horse brasses). Portraits of Queen Victoria are to be found in four types. Bun portraits taken from the coinage were issued early in her reign, and crowned 'young heads' from 1850. 'Widows' with three-quarter veiled bust and small crown date from the jubilee year of 1887, while less rare is the full profile designed by Thomas Brock and first issued on the coinage of 1893. This portrait appears on diamond-jubilee brasses, many of which are inscribed with the date, but the difference in the portrait anyhow distinguishes the 1887 from the 1897 issue. The diamond jubilee was responsible too for horse brasses in the shape of a Victoria Cross surmounted by a royal crown and inscribed '1837 Diamond Jubilee 1897'. Others were in the form of openwork Maltese crosses. *Heart-shaped* brasses with the front in bold relief and burnished might be engraved 'Victoria Jubilee 1887'.

Prince of Wales' feathers were made in several varieties. At first they were mounted in plain circular frames; then came a series with the three feathers stamped and set in a cast ring; and finally, they were in shaped outlines. Edward VII is found full face and in profile, both as Prince of Wales and as king. A dozen variations have been noted, each cast in a single piece. The coronation horse brasses were inscribed 'God Save the King 1902'.

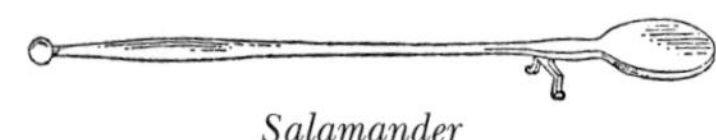

Salamander

Salamander. A bar of wrought iron with a thick round or oblong piece at one end; somewhat like a long-handled shovel in appearance. The larger end was heated until it became red hot, and then held near bread, cake, etc., in order to brown it.

Saw piercing. The design was pounced upon the plate, which, if of iron or steel, was softened by annealing. It was then drilled so that the saw piercer

could pass his delicate bow saw through holes and remove surplus metal. After finishing with a file the surface was engraved. The metal was then hardened.
Scallop shells (horse brasses). Single examples cast and burnished date from the 1880s. Sets in graduated sizes were stamped from about 1890, and these are not uncommon.
Sheet tin or **tin plate.** Thinly rolled iron coated with tin.
Side hinge. A hinge consisting of only one leaf, usually placed in a vertical position, acting on a pintle.
Single reed. A single moulding around the edge of a plate rim as compared to multi-reeded rims, where two or more mouldings form the edge.
Skewer. Small iron pin for holding meat on a spit.
Skillet (Posnet, Pipkin). Medieval skillets were shaped like cauldrons, and it was not until the sixteenth century that this ancestor of the modern saucepan became recognizable. These later skillets had no feet, but were made with the sides sloping outwards so that the circumference of the top was greater than that of the base. The handle was popularly used for advertising the name of the maker or for the spreading of texts such as 'Ye Wages of Sin is Death'. They were made of bronze.
Smooth rim. A flat, unadorned plate rim, where the reinforcing moulding appears on the underside of the rim.
Souvenirs (horse brasses). The motifs used are innumerable and include portraits of George V, Queen Alexandra, George VI, Queen Mary, the rare Edward VIII, Queen Elizabeth II, Sir Winston Churchill, Field Marshal Viscount Montgomery. Souvenir birds include duck, eagle, emu, lyre bird, magpie, ostrich, raven, and swan. The range of souvenir horse brasses designs extends to many hundreds.
Spider. A three-legged skillet, or sometimes a long-handled skillet.
Spinning. A process by which a thin metal sheet is pressed against a wooden core in a spinning lathe to be forced into shape.
Spit. A metal bar with which meat was pierced and placed on cobirons before the fire for roasting; as the bar was rotated all sides of the meat received the heat equally. The spit had prongs in the centre, and a grooved pulley at one end to connect by chain or rope to some sort of motive power: human, animal, or mechanical. This motive power, if human or animal, was termed a 'turnspit', and if mechanical a 'Jack'. Illustrations in early manuscripts show that boys were employed as turnspits, and by the sixteenth century spit jacks were in use. These latter were made of brass and iron, and were driven by large weights of stone or metal, which descended slowly into pits dug for the purpose to increase the length of fall. Like the weights of a clock, once they had completely run down they were wound up again. Another mechanical method of turning the spit was by a fan fitted in the mouth of the chimney, which was operated by the rising draught. A further method was the employment of dogs, specially trained for the purpose, which were confined in a small treadmill fixed to the wall of the kitchen. At the end of the eighteenth century spring-driven jacks were in use, and culminated in the neat bottle jack, brass-cased and driven by clockwork.

When not in use the spits were kept in the spit rack: a row of hooks at either end above the fireplace.

Spit

Spun hollow ware. Bodies of urn vases were sometimes spun in Britannia metal from about 1800 and in copper from about 1820 when a special copper was evolved suitable for spinning in the lathe. Spinning was profitable only if orders were substantial.
Steel. Early locksmiths used Venice steel for their finest work, but otherwise a long-wearing steel capable of taking a good heat at the forge was difficult to obtain. Quality was variable and continued so until after the mid-eighteenth century. English steel made in the Forest of Dean had become the locksmith's first choice. Springs were made from gad steel imported from Germany. Less costly goods were made from Yorkshire or Sussex steel.
Stock lock. A plate lock let into a rectangular block of oak and thereby attached to the door by bolts or rivets, later by screws. The mechanism in some stock locks was covered with an iron plate decorated with pierced designs, usually trefoil or cinquefoil, with a matching plate covering the wooden block. From the mid-eighteenth century the mechanism was almost invariably covered with a solid iron plate.
Strap hinge. A simple hinge consisting of two horizontally placed iron straps.

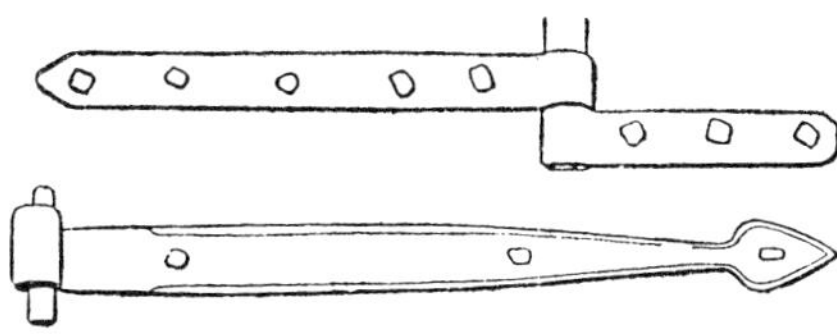

Striking plate. The metal plate fixed to a door frame into which the bolt of a lock is shot by the key. The plate is provided with a lip on which the bolt strikes.
Stump. A circular pin within the case of a lock to guide the different working parts. In lever locks it works in the gating, that is, a slot cut in the lever.
Suffolk latch. A type of latch consisting of a handle terminating in large decorative cusps but lacking an escutcheon plate.
Suites. In large houses rim locks from the 1660s might be made in matching suites, a different key for each lock and a master key capable of opening the entire series. Such a suite of Queen Anne locks was fitted to doors in the apartments of Marlborough House, London, where they still function silently.
Sunflash (horse brass). A face piece, extremely popular in Kent, was originally a disc of latten with its centre hand-raised into a high dome or boss and encircled with a wide, flat rim. This extended almost across the horse's face and weighed about six ounces. In rolled brass the outer rim might be serrated. In some examples of the 1850s–80s the flat rim was pierced with twelve triangular rays extending outward to the rim which, from the early 1870s, might be encircled with drilled perforations. The entire brass, including dome and perforations, might be stamped from 1880. Sometimes the dome might be surrounded by a series of concentric circles in relief, number and width varying. A splash of colour might be given from the mid-1890s by fitting into the raised centre a boss of coloured glass or enamelled china: colours noted include yellow, green, dark blue, red, ringed red, white, blue. A series of uncommon rectangular sunflashes had incurved clipped corners and a central dome against a plain ground: others were shield-shape. Some late cast examples display the sunflash on a wide and elaborately patterned rim.

Terret (horse brasses). These, more correctly termed fly terrets, are also known as swingers and flyers. The terret is a vertical ring set between the horse's ears and in which swings a horse brass with both faces finished and polished. Such brasses are smaller in diameter than the ordinary horse brass, and instead of a strap loop a solid eye was placed at right angles, fitting into a pair of lugs at the top of the ring. This was held in position by a screw pin which permitted free swinging. Frequently the full figure of a horse, cast in the round and chased, hung within the ring, or a horse's head, or an heraldic crest. Tradesmen might display a motif associated with their work, such as a hooped barrel shaped in the round. The terret might be surmounted by a tall cylindrical brush, often with dyed bristles, blue and red being common. In other instances there was a tiny bell.

Tin iron. Midland japanners from 1784 used fine-quality plate rolled from a special iron containing charcoal instead of coke. This was evolved specially for japanners by a Wolverhampton iron master and sold under the name of tin iron. The majority of japanned ware was hand-shaped or spun until the introduction of the drop hammer between 1815 and 1820. A heavy stamp head wound up by a winch was allowed to fall on a sheet of iron laid over a sunk die. Repeated blows forced the metal into the required shape much more speedily than had been possible previously, and larger work could be handled. Patrick Nasmyth's first steam hammer was bought by the Walton firm in 1840 making them first in the field to produce finely shaped, heavy work at prices hitherto impossible.

It was the Midland japanners' use of improved qualities of tin iron, together with the introduction of more efficient japanning stoves, japans, and varnishes during the 1790s that brought about the eventual decline of Pontypool.

Tinned plate. Iron sheet, tin iron from 1784, the surface only being coated with tin.

Tin plate. Rolled iron soaked in molten tin which penetrated its entire texture and gave the whole a silvery white colour. The tin used was pure-grain tin made in the form of shot.

Toaster. These were either in the form of standing toasters or the familiar fork, and were used for the toasting of both bread and meat. The fork needs little mention beyond pointing out that it almost always has three prongs. A variation of it is the toast holder, which has two short upcurved arms at the end of a long handle.

Toaster

Standing toasters are rare and vary much in design. Four in the Victoria and Albert Museum are worthy of description. Two of them have simple tripod bases and central pillars with turned finials. On each pillar is a bell-shaped fitting with three prongs for holding the food to be toasted, and these are adjustable for height. Another is in the form of a circular trivet with a three-pronged fork, also adjustable up and down. The fourth type stands on the ground and is like a table toast rack for only one slice of bread, and it has a long handle projecting at the back. The latter type was for use at a down hearth, and all four were of wrought iron.

Tortoiseshell decoration. Fashionable throughout the second half of the eighteenth century.

Tortoiseshell japan was laid over silver leaf or on a white ground. The rich glowing crimson type required gold or silver leaf to be laid over a white ground. This was clouded and stained with yellow or reddish-yellow varnish to resemble tortoiseshell. Then followed numerous coats of clear varnish, each being stoved.

Trammel. An adjustable device used for hanging a pot from a crane or the lug pole of a fireplace. Many lighting devices are also equipped with a trammel so that they may be raised or lowered.

Trays. The principal articles of japanners' manufacture were trays and waiters made from tinned sheet iron of thickness varying from 24 to 30 gauge. Trays are rectangular, square or oval, and measure 12–21 inches (30.5–53.4 cm) across: waiters are circular. The corners of early trays were folded and riveted: by 1780 they were cut and welded. Narrow handholds might be cut in the rim or D-shaped handles of gilded brass riveted to the sides. Oval trays with plain turn-up rims appeared about 1800 and a few years later came scalloped and gadrooned rims. From about 1820 trays were shaped under the drop hammer, thus greatly reducing the cost. By 1839 there were seventeen factories in Wolverhampton and ten in Birmingham devoted to the production of tray blanks in iron.

Japanned trays might be sold in sets of three, four, or six in graduated sizes with matching decoration, but papier mâché sets of trays had outmoded the metal by the mid-1840s. Each japanner carried some 2,000 different patterns. The weekly output in Wolverhampton in 1840 was estimated to be more than 50,000 trays including about 2,000 sets.

Victorian brass candlesticks, watercan and trivet, English

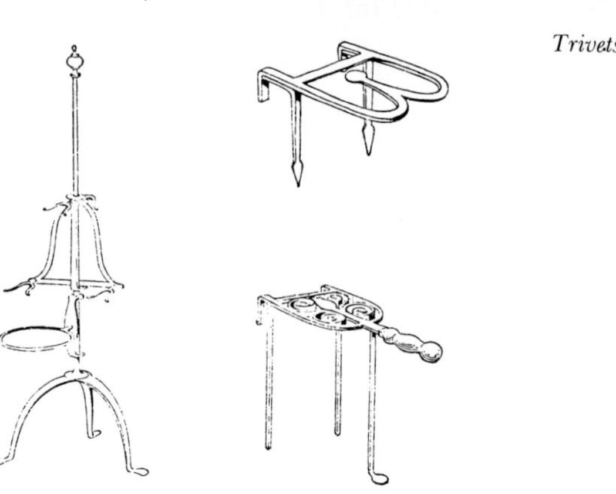

Trivets

Trivet (Brandis(e)). Strictly a three-legged stand on which utensils might rest before the fire, but the word is used to cover many types of stand. The trivets of the seventeenth and eighteenth centuries were usually circular and of wrought iron; sometimes they had a projecting handle. Later versions, also on three legs, were of an oblong shape with one end curved and fitted with a handle, while the far end had curved projections to fit over the firebar of a grate. Others dispensed with legs, and were made to hang on the front of a stove; of this last type many were made in the nineteenth century of cast iron with pierced brass tops.

Tumblers. Units in the mechanism to retain the bolt of a lock. These are immovable to any but the right key, which lifts them to pre-determined heights and shoots the bolt.

Coffee urn with oval body in Pontypool japanned ware, with opening for charcoal brazier at rear and tap in front. Decorated with bands of gilded ornament and a rustic landscape with figures and sheep, by Thomas Barker. National Museum of Wales

Urns, tea and coffee. From the late 1780s until the 1820s japanners made urns heated by charcoal-burning braziers. In its simplest form the body of a japanned urn was cylindrical, the lower third perforated to contain the brazier. The Levno urn, dating from about 1800, had a cylindrical body containing a central tube for conveying heat through the urn from a brazier burning in a perforated cube-shaped box below, often raised on four lion-paw feet of gilded brass.

The vase-shaped urn until the 1820s was hand-shaped in copper and heavily tinned within. It was usually mounted upon three cabriole legs with feet of ivory, ebony, boxwood, or other insulating material so that the urn might stand upon a rectangular tray decorated to match. This held the spirit lamp within a low cylindrical box with perforated sides.

Usk. A breakaway factory established by two of the Allgood brothers in 1761, seven miles from Pontypool and operated by them until early in the nineteenth century. Maintaining that they were the original makers of Pontypool japan, they marketed their ware under that name.

Varnishing. Painted decoration was varnished to preserve it from the ravages of wear and in the case of trays and waiters from disfigurement by scalding liquids. Such varnish needed to possess a glaze both durable and transparent so that the glow of the colours beneath should not be diminished. Fat varnishes were eventually discovered to possess these qualities. The standard formula called for two parts copal, one part linseed oil, two parts essence of turpentine. This was applied with a large flat brush manipulated with a single backward-and-forward motion, the result being an absolutely smooth surface. Considerable skill was essential in this, for undulations and ridges disfigured the uniform reflection of light over the picture.

Waiters. Japanners listed their circular trays as waiters, sizes ranging from 6 to 20 inches (15.2–50.8 cm) with occasional nineteenth-century giants measuring as much as 30 inches (76.3 cm). They were fashionable by the mid-eighteenth century, usually decorated in the tortoiseshell style. They were hammered up from thinly rolled iron plates. Tin plate was used at Pontypool and in London; tinned in Birmingham and Wolverhampton. Early examples have rather deep galleries slightly flaring and perforated. These, by the late 1780s, were superseded by solid rims enriched with gilded lines. A full-sized circular japanned waiter became a fashionable background to the tea equipage with its hissing urn.

Walsall. The centre of the English saddlery and coach-furniture trade in the nineteenth century. Specialist firms were engaged in the manufacture of brass enrichments for leather harness, a trade highly flourishing by 1851, when White's Walsall Directory listed no fewer than twenty-seven harness-furniture manufacturers who were also brass founders. The horse-brass trade as an industry rather than a handcraft dates from the 1840s. The Walsall harness-furniture men evolved a special brass alloy of close texture, golden hue, and capable of burnishing to a high, flawless brilliancy.

Ward. A fixed projection in a lock to prevent a key from entering or turning unless correctly shaped.

Wheatsheaf (horse brasses). Known in heraldry as a garb, the wheatsheaf was highly popular in northern counties. Luxuriant sheaves might be inserted between the upward-pointing horns of a plain crescent which might have a serrated outer edge; or they might be framed within a star or a perforated ring; or cast in bold relief on the surface of a plain shield. The majority are one-piece castings, but a stamped series will be found, the wheatsheaf within a plain crescent.

Wilkes, John. A well-known locksmith of Birmingham responsible for a series of signed locks, most of them in latten, some in blue steel serving as a background to applied brasswork, or in engraved steel. Wilkes became celebrated for his detector lock, of which many examples exist *in situ* in England and on the Continent. This lock is ornamented with the figure of a late Caroline soldier in relief. The left leg is extended by pushing a secret catch, and this reveals the keyhole. The toecap of the boot then points to a number on the dial, by which the number of times the door has been opened is registered, as each turn of the key causes the number to change. The lock bolt is released by pushing back the hat.

Wolverhampton. The finest English locks have been made here from early in the seventeenth century. In 1660 Wolverhampton paid a hearth tax on eighty-four locksmiths' hearths and there were ninety-seven in nearby Willenhall. The Georgian locksmiths of Wolverhampton maintained a high reputation.

Wrought iron. Literally iron which has been worked or formed by a blacksmith. The term has also come to mean a type of iron which contains practically no carbon but a considerable amount of slag, which often gives it a grainy appearance. Wrought iron is readily worked and welded in the forge, and is characterized by great toughness and ductility. Wrought iron cannot be hardened by heating and sudden cooling as steel can be; consequently it is unsuitable for the cutting edges of tools.

Wrought iron gates of Burghley House, probably by Jean Tijou (active 1690–1712). The original design appears in Tijou's *A New Book of Drawings*, 1693. Tijou and his family fled from France and came to work in England

Wrought iron bracket with delicate leaf and scroll decoration, English, mid-18th century. Victoria & Albert Museum

Below Porringer, late 16th century, and broth bowl engraved 'Lincoln's Inn 1704', English. Victoria & Albert Museum

Bottom Two from a set of six Irish pewter plates, late 18th century. Arthur Davidson, London

Terms used in Pewterwork

(A) SADWARE

The pewterer's term for plates, dishes, and chargers.

Plate. Up to 12 inches (30.5 cm) diameter.
Dish. 12–18 inches (30.5–45.8 cm) diameter.
Charger. Over 18 inches (45.8 cm) diameter.

Types of Sadware

Broad rim. Having a rim proportionately wider than the normal.
Cardinal's hat. A deep dish with broad rim.
Marriage plate. One item of a garnish (*q.v.*) decorated with engraved symbols as a souvenir of marriage.
Narrow rim. Having a rim formed solely of multiple mouldings.
Octagonal rim. Self-explanatory.
Paten. A broad rim plate, or a tazza (*q.v.*) used in the administration of Holy Communion.
Plain rim. Self-explanatory.
Sexagonal rim. Self-explanatory.
Single reed. Having one moulding around the edge of the rim.
Tazza. A name commonly (but erroneously) given to a plate supported upon a spreading foot.
Triple reed. Having a rim with multiple mouldings around the edge.
Wavy rim. Having a rim of alternate convex and concave curves.

(B) HOLLOW WARE

The pewterers' term for flagons, tankards, measures, pots, mugs, beakers, etc.

Types of Hollow ware

Beaker. A drinking vessel, resembling the modern tumbler.
Bleeding bowl. A porringer (*q.v.*) marked internally with lines of liquid capacities.
Flagon. A large vessel from which other vessels are filled.
Loving cup. A drinking vessel with two handles, originally used for toasting. General term for twin-handled cups.
Measure. A vessel of a standard liquid capacity, used in taverns for serving into drinking vessels.
Porringer. A shallow vessel with flat, horizontal handle(s), for semi-liquid foods.
Pot (mug). A tavern drinking vessel.
Quaich (Gaelic). A Scottish form of porringer, having two lugs (*q.v.*) and, in its smaller sizes, used for spirits.
Tankard. A drinking vessel, usually domestic.

(*Note.* The terms caudle cup, cupping bowl, and posset cup are sometimes applied, without much authority, to some vessels of the cup or porringer class.)

Pewter tankard, English, 18th century. Marks: leopard's head, lion passant and a buckle inside W.E. with an hour glass. Victoria & Albert Museum

Names used in connection with hollow ware

Baluster. A tavern measure, bulging below, concave above.

Beefeater. A flagon having a lid somewhat resembling the headdress of the Yeomen of the Tower of London.

Bun lid. Self-explanatory. Many flagons of this type have finials rising from the bun.

Dome lid. Self-explanatory.

Flat lid. Self-explanatory, seventeenth century.

Guernsey. A baluster-shaped measure, encircled by two broad bands, and having a heart-shaped lid and twin acorn thumbpiece; peculiar to Guernsey, Channel Islands.

Haystack. More properly Haycock, which it resembles. An Irish tavern measure, made chiefly in Cork.

Jersey. A plain baluster-shaped measure, with lid and thumbpiece as in Guernsey; peculiar to Jersey, Channel Islands.

Moulded base. Self-explanatory. The hollow formed is external.

Ovolo base. Having a base formed by a plain projecting quarter-curve. The hollow formed is external.

Pot belly. A Scottish tavern measure with broad belly and narrowing neck.

Skirt base. Having a wide, spreading base, the hollow formed being internal.

Tappit hen. A Scottish measure, i.e. a 'hen with a top to it' (fanciful). The true tappit hen holds 1 pint Scots (equals 3 pints English), but the term is usually applied to all capacities.

Tulip (pear). A tankard or mug with body shaped as described.

West Country. A tavern measure with bulging body tapering to a narrow spouted neck. Of West Country origin; more numerous in copper.

York acorn. A flagon of acorn shape, peculiar to Yorkshire, having a dome lid with acorn-shaped finial.

York straight side. A flagon with tapering body, the base without projection but defined by multiple concentric mouldings. Of North Country origin.

Thumbpieces by which a lid is raised

Billet, purchase. Alternative names for thumbpiece.

Bar-and-heart. A plain, wide thumbpiece, pierced by a heart and surmounted by a thick bar.

Bud. Two ovoids rising from a common stalk and resembling bursting buds.

Chairback (either solid or pierced). Self-explanatory.

Erect. A tall, solid block found on early seventeenth-century flagons. A lighter, curving form is found on Scottish measures, notably tappit hens.

Hammerhead. Self-explanatory.

Love bird. Twin birds, their beaks jointed, surmounted by a volute.

Ram's horn (full or embryo). Self-explanatory.

Shell (full or embryo). A thumbpiece formed of a ribbed or plain escallop shell.

Sprayed leaf. A thin, wide, fan-shaped thumbpiece with deeply-gouged lines radiating from the foot in a leaf pattern.

Twin acorn. Two acorns rising from a wedge attached to the lid.

Twin cusped. Two semi-spheres rising from a broad base.

Volute. Twin spiral scrolls, chief feature of the Ionic capital, rising from the lid attachment.

Wedge. A thumbpiece formed by the extension of the lid attachment upwards to a point.

(C) SPOONS

Spoons. Spoons are known by their stem terminals (knops or finials). Some, being unique, have no common name; other names are self-explanatory. The following have general acceptance; descriptions are given where necessary.

Acorn.

Apostle.

Ball (Globe).

Baluster. A small bulge topped by a button.

Diamond. Multi-sided, tapering to a point.

Hexagon. Six-sided and of melon shape.

Horned headdress. A female bust surmounted by the lofty, mitre-like headdress worn in the early fifteenth century.

Horse hoof.

Lion (rampant or sejant).

Maidenhead. A female bust understood to represent the Virgin Mary. Similar silver spoons are described in a fifteenth-century inventory as 'Cum ymaginibus Beatae Mariae in fine corundum'.

Pied de biche (hind's hoof). Post-Commonwealth, with flat stem and broad, flat terminal, twice notched at the top. Some are decorated with cast busts of William and Mary or Anne.

Pumpkin. A ball vertically gadrooned.

Puritan. A Commonwealth spoon with flat stem and no terminal.

Rat tail. A tapering extension of the stem down the back of the bowl.
Seal. A baluster, but topped by a flat disc.
Slipped in the stalk. The commonest pre-Commonwealth spoon with plain stem cut off on the slant.
Split end. As *pied de biche*.
Stump. Pre-Commonwealth, with plain stem cut off square.
Wavy. As *pied de biche* but without notches.
Writhen. A ball diagonally gadrooned.

(D) GENERAL

Booge. The curved portion of a plate, etc., joining rim to bottom.
Box inkstand. A rectangular inkstand with one or two wells, drawers beneath.
Bulbous salt. A globular salt cellar with shallow circular depression.
Capstan salt. A salt cellar shaped like a ship's capstan.
Drip shield. A wide, circular or multi-sided collar between the base and stem of a candlestick to prevent grease from falling upon the hand.
Drum. The body of a flagon, tankard, etc.
Entasis. A slight bulge between base and lip of a flagon, tankard, etc.
Finial. An erect terminal sometimes added to the lid of a flagon, or the terminal of a spoon.
Gadroon. A geometrical design of small cast ribs, usually radiating from a centre.
Garnish. A household set of plates and dishes.
'Hallmarks'. Small punches used by pewterers in imitation of those used by silversmiths.
Hammered. Showing the marks of the pewterer's hammer all over. A strengthening device used on dishes, plates, etc. Normally found on the booge (*q.v.*) only.
Knop. *See* Finial.
Loggerhead. A circular inkstand with a wide flat base, still used in banks.
Lug. An ear (Scots); the handle of a quaich (*q.v.*).
Sand dredger. A box with perforated top, for containing sand, which was used before blotting paper was introduced.
Spool salt. A salt cellar resembling a flattened hourglass.
Standish. An inkstand formed by a rectangular flat plate standing upon four feet, and having a curved edge. Upon the plate stand inkwell, dredger, etc., and there is usually a drawer beneath for quills.
Touch. The pewterer's trademark (*see* Introduction).
Touch plate. A flat sheet of soft pewter for recording touches.
Treasury inkstand. A four-footed oblong box, with double lid centrally hinged, containing four compartments for the accessories. So called from an example in the Government Department of that name.
Trencher salt. A low, oblong octagonal salt cellar, with oval bowl.
Wriggle work. A form of decoration made by rocking a gouge from side to side in its progress.

MIRRORS

British Wall Mirrors

Before the fifteenth century, in spite of the fact that the process of silvering glass was understood, it would seem to have been little used, and mirrors were made of highly polished plates of metal. Glass had not then the clarity it later attained, and a carefully burnished piece of gold, silver, steel, or other metal was likely to provide a more accurate reflecting surface. Limited in size, it is doubtful whether such mirrors were hung on a wall or merely stood on a convenient piece of furniture. For a considerable period, along with other comparable luxuries, their ownership was confined to the wealthy.

Glass mirror plates became a monopoly of the republic of Venice, where Murano was the centre of the glass-making industry on the continent of Europe and whence knowledge of the process had come from Germany some time about the year 1500. There is no evidence that they were made in England until early in the seventeenth century, when John Aubrey, the antiquarian, noted in his *Brief Lives* that a man named Robson had commenced their manufacture. In 1618 Robson's enterprise was taken over by Sir Robert Mansell, who by 1623 employed some five hundred men in the 'making, grinding, and foyling of looking glasses'.

Half a century later a glassworks was started at Vauxhall by the Duke of Buckingham, and in due course became famous.

Mirror plate was first made by what was termed the 'broad' process. In this, briefly, the liquid glass was taken up from the furnace on a blowing tube and blown into the form of a large bubble. Two opposite surfaces of the bubble were cut off; the tube remaining was then slit along one side and the whole flattened. The sheet of glass was cooled, ground, and polished until it was as flat and smooth as possible. In spite of the care it received in the two last treatments, the resulting plate was not always satisfactory. Principally it was found that however skilfully the craftsmen blew the glass, it was extremely difficult to ensure that it was of an even thickness over the entire surface; in addition, there was understandably a limit to the size that could be made in this manner.

Late in the seventeenth century, French glass makers introduced the process of glass casting. The molten glass was poured on to a bed of metal, was swiftly spread evenly over it and rolled flat while it was still hot. Much larger and truer plates could be made by this method, which was also quicker in spite of the fact that the plates had still to be slowly cooled, and then ground and polished. The casting process was used for a short while in England about 1690, but it did not find favour and for some reason was given up. In 1773 'The British Cast Plate-Glass Company' was incorporated, and factories were opened at Southwark and at St Helen's, Lancashire. The venture succeeded in producing glass to supplant the imported French plates, and the company remained in being until the outset of the present century.

The actual 'silvering' of the glass is misnamed, as the precious metal is not among the constituents that were used. A sheet of tinfoil and a quantity of mercury were the principal ingredients, and by their use the English and Continental craftsmen of the past produced the mirror plates of which so many have survived the wear and tear of the centuries to bear witness to their skill. The tin-and-mercury amalgam remained in general use until about 1840, when it was replaced by a process that does merit the name of 'silvering', for by a discovery of the German chemist J. von Liebig, a coat of the metal is deposited chemically on the glass.

The framing of mirrors during the seventeenth and eighteenth centuries took many forms, and was the subject of careful study from men of artistic talent ranging from Grinling Gibbons and William Kent to Thomas Chippendale and Robert Adam. At the beginning of the period the pieces of glass were of small size and the frames were usually contrastingly large. Elaborate settings of carved wood, of embroidered stumpwork, coloured beads, ebony, and tortoiseshell, or of chased plaques of silver, were among the many that surrounded comparatively insignificant pieces of mirror glass, and were the workmanship of the most skilled craftsmen of their time. No material, save gold itself, was so costly that it is not found to have been formed into a surrounding for the glass that reflected the features of Caroline beauties.

By 1675 the framing had grown less varied and the well-known 'cushion' type was coming into use. Following the customary rectangular form, it was usually veneered with walnut, often in the form of 'oysters' of selected grain. More decorative versions were heavily inlaid with marquetry, rare examples were of incised Chinese lacquer, and others, rarer still, overlaid with embossed silver may be seen still at Windsor Castle and at Knole.

As it became possible to manufacture glass in sheets of larger size, it was found that not only the frame but also the mirror within it had decorative possibilities, and also that a nearly square shape was not necessarily the most suitable. Perhaps inspired by the Galerie des Glaces at Versailles, completed by Le Brun for Louis XIV in 1682, and by the success of the French in casting large plates, English houses began to be ornamented with mirrors in profusion. These mirrors were for the decoration of the rooms in which they were placed, and not primarily for personal admiration as had been earlier examples.

The increase in the size of the glass was countered

Far right Mirror with frame of straw-work, English, 1670–80. Victoria & Albert Museum

by a shrinkage in the size of the frame. To such a degree did this change sweep into fashion that for a while, about the years 1690–1700, the frame almost vanished altogether, and was replaced by a surround of strips of glass decorated with cutting or with patterns in *verre églomisé*. The French may well have inspired the larger mirror, but undoubtedly the Venetians were responsible for this mode of bordering it.

Following the 'frameless' era came the introduction of the gilt frame; in turn following the new taste for gilt furnishings. Whereas polished cabinet work returned shortly to favour, the mirror frame remained gilt. Few, if any, were in any other finish after 1750, and before that date the exceptions were in a minority. These last comprise the walnut-veneered mirror frames of small size assigned popularly to Queen Anne's reign, much reproduced in recent years, but, if genuine, dating more probably from the time of George I; and the larger mirrors of George II date with gilt enrichments on a ground of polished Virginia ('red') walnut.

The placing of mirrors in a room began to assume a regularity that has remained little changed. Above

Above Three-panel landscape overmantel mirror in narrow gilt frame with borders of *verre églomisé*, English, *c.* 1685. Mallett & Son, London

Left above Mirror in cushion frame, the borders and cresting japanned and decorated with Oriental designs and inset with panels of coloured and gilt rolled paper-work under glass. English, *c.* 1700. Victoria & Albert Museum

Left Oval mirror, one of a pair with ornate gilt frames by Thomas Johnson, 1761

Far left Queen Anne mirror in frame of gilt gesso, English, *c.* 1712–20. Mallett & Son, London the fireplace was the most popular position, and there the framing sometimes formed an integral part of that most important feature. Some of these overmantel mirrors incorporated within their extensive frames an oil painting, and examples of the type, dating from about 1740–60, are found usually with landscape or floral pictures. A simpler variation of the large overmantel mirror, the 'landscape' mirror, came into vogue early in the eighteenth century, gradually grew squarer in shape as the years wore on, and in the succeeding century exchanged width for height. Upright mirrors were placed on the narrow walls (piers) between windows, and pier glasses, as they were called, were widely employed from their first introduction about 1700. Further, in those great mansions that boasted suites of state rooms, mirrors were hung at their far ends to reflect one into another and artificially increase their length.

As with the design of furnishings in general, the design of mirror frames varied almost from year to year and month to month, but they may be grouped conveniently under a number of headings. This is the case with many of the smaller and simpler gilt gesso mirrors, which are assigned to the period of Queen Anne (1702–14), although most are rather later in date. The larger, more heavily designed mirrors with pediments of classical type, are attributed to a foremost architect of the day, William Kent.

Following the vogue of the so-called 'Kent' or 'architectural' frame came the first signs of the combination of French, Gothic, and Chinese styles that culminated in the well-known Chinese Chippendale. From a few years prior to 1754, when Thomas Chippendale's volume of designs was published, mirror frames were modelled elaborately with exotic birds, Chinamen, goats, sheep, seashells, and flowers (among much else), and the carver was able to give full rein to his agile chisel. Many of these frames were from the designs of Linnell, Johnson, Lock and Copland, and others, but all are assigned popularly to Chippendale, whose book conveniently summarized the styles of his time for posterity.

Above Pier glass with *chinoiserie* gilded frame, supplied to Nostell Priory by Thomas Chippendale, 1770

Left Carved and gilded pier glass designed by Robert Adam, 1777. Osterley House

Left Oval giltwood mirror of the Chippendale period, *c.* 1760. Glaisher & Nash Ltd., London

Right Pier glass in the manner of Benjamin Goodison, *c.* 1745. Victoria & Albert Museum

Mirror in frame of carved and gilt wood of classical architectural form, *c.* 1740. The cartouche and carving indicate the beginning of the Rococo style. Victoria & Albert Museum

The various motifs figured by Chippendale, combined or singly, remained in vogue until the introduction of classical themes by Robert and James Adam. In common with the furniture which became fashionable in the 1770s, the mirror frame was ornamented with urns, honeysuckle, husks and paterae. The delicacy of the work proved often to be beyond the resources of the wood carver, and many of the detailed and flimsy ornaments were of composition on a wire core or were cast in lead.

By the second half of the eighteenth century the pier glass had reached very large proportions. Sheets of mirror glass supplied to the Earl of Mansfield in 1769, and still at Kenwood, London, measure 74 inches (188 cm) in height, and a plate measuring 91 inches by 57½ inches (231 × 146 cm) was supplied by Chippendale's firm in 1773.

Oval mirrors were made in the 1730s and remained popular throughout the century, during which their framing followed the prevailing patterns in each decade. Distinctive and rare were the Irish mirrors of the last years of the eighteenth century. These were of oval shape, and framed with one or more rows of clear or coloured glass facets.

Finally, there is the familiar convex mirror. This was introduced from France, and the majority of surviving examples date from 1800 and later. They had been made several centuries earlier, and one is depicted in Van Eyck's picture in the National Gallery, London, painted in 1434. Van Eyck's mirror is in a simple gilt frame; its more modern counterpart usually bears a carved eagle above the deeply turned gilt border in which are placed small gilt balls. Usually a ball is suspended from the beak of the eagle, and in some examples the frame is flanked by arms for candles; the arms of gilt brass fitted with cut-glass drops. Rare convex mirrors are more elaborately and individually carved, and are known with the frames surmounted by an ornament in the form of the crest of the owner, or with dolphin-shaped side supports.

American Mirrors

THE EARLY RECORDS

Instructing farmers about to settle in frontier areas of the United States in 1789, Benjamin Rush pointed out, 'There are several expensive parts of household furniture that he should leave behind him for which he will have no use in the woods, such as a large looking glass. . . .' This advice suggests the reason for the paucity of information about mirrors in America in the early seventeenth century. That they were in use by 1644 is substantiated, however, by the inventory of the estate of Joanna Cummings, of Salem, Massachusetts, which lists a mirror valued at three shillings.

A study of the published probate records of Essex County, Massachusetts, discloses that between 1644 and 1681 at least ninety-four mirrors were owned in that area.

These records reveal that usually the mirrors were placed in the hall or the parlour, the main gathering room in the early homes. Less frequently, they were used in the chamber or bedroom. One of the earliest records of one person's owning more than one mirror occurs in 1661 in the estate of Robert Gray, of Salem: 'In the parlor . . . one large lookinge glass . . . In the litle Chamber . . . a lookinge glass and 3 pictures.'

By the eighteenth century their usage became less limited, and the following advertisement appeared in *The Boston News-Letter* of 25 April/2 May 1715: 'Looking-Glasses of all sorts, Glass Sconces, Cabbinetts, Writing Desks, Bookcases with Desks, old Glasses new Silvered, and all sorts of Japan-work, Done and sold by William Randle at the Sign of the Cabinnett, a Looking-Glass Shop in Queen-Street . . .'

A manuscript book containing inventories taken in New York City between 1742 and 1768 indicates that out of twenty-one colonists of varied circumstances, nineteen possessed at least one mirror. Notable among these are the three owned by Joseph Leddell, pewterer, in 1754: one listed simply as a 'looking glass', one 'with black frame', and one 'with japanned frame'. William Wright, chandler, possessed one old mirror and a 'Small looking glass and sconces, old', in 1757. Rice Williams in 1758 had one small mirror and an overmantel mirror.

At this time overmantel mirrors placed above the fireplace on the chimney breast, were frequently found in American houses where they are known as chimney glasses.

Another type of mirror was the pier glass, intended for use on the wall between two windows. 'All sorts of peer glasses' were advertised as early as 1732 in the *South Carolina Gazette*.

Benjamin Franklin's inventory taken in 1790 reveals a variety of mirrors. In one chamber there was a dressing-table glass valued at £2 and in Mr Franklin's chamber, a pier glass worth £2 and a mirror. There was a mirror in the parlour, two mirrors valued at £12 in the dining room, and one in the Blue Room. This indicates the wider use and the variety of mirrors in America by the end of the eighteenth century.

That these were no longer simply utilitarian objects but also an important part of the decorative scheme is indicated by Abigail Adams's letter to her sister on 9 June 1790, in which she asks that her large mirror be sent from her house in Braintree to Richmond Hill. 'This House', she explains, 'is much better calculated for the Glasses, having all the Rooms Eleven foot high.' A similar reference is found in the diary of the Reverend William Bentley, of Salem, Massachusetts, in October 1801, when he speaks of a Mr West's house: 'The Mirrors were large and gave full view of every one who passed, and were intended for the house in town but were exchanged as those for this Seat were too large.' This is the earliest known use of the term *mirror* in American writings, *looking glass* being the proper term prior to that time.

By 1840 mirrors had become commonplace items in American homes. Two paintings by Henry Sargent, done in the early nineteenth century, provide one of the first visual records of the use of mirrors in American interiors. *The Tea Party* shows the use of horizontal, rectangular mirrors above the fireplace in each of two parlours and a vertical, rectangular pier glass between the two windows of one parlour. *The Dinner Party* shows a similar, though simpler, pier glass between the windows in the dining room.

AMERICAN-MADE MIRRORS

How early mirrors were made in America is uncertain. From the beginning, plate glass had to be brought from the old country. William Wood in his *New Englands Prospect* in 1634 suggested to future colonists, 'Glasse ought not to be forgotten of any that desire to benefit themselves, or the Country: if it be well leaded, and carefully pack't up, I know no commodity better for portage or sayle . . .' Certainly from an early date there was some reframing of old mirrors. This practice of utilizing the glass in a new-fashioned mirror continued well after the Revolutionary War, as indicated by the advertisements of Samuel Kneeland, one of which appeared in the Hartford, Connecticut, *American Mercury* on 12 November 1787, 'N.B. Old Looking Glasses repaired, fram'd and gilt in the neatest manner, so as to look equal to new ones.'

STYLES AND TYPES

The earliest mirrors probably were framed in simple cove-moulded rectangular frames made of oak and pine, perhaps painted or, towards the end of the seventeenth century, veneered with walnut. In the last quarter of the seventeenth century a crest was added at the top, in a separate piece which is often missing today. Because the crest was cut from a thin piece of wood, it frequently warped and curved backward in spite of braces put on the back to correct this tendency. Often the crest was pierced in an elaborate pattern similar to the carved cresting rails on William and Mary chairs. One of the earliest surviving examples of mirrors made in this country has a frame made of white pine, native to New England, and is painted to give a tortoiseshell appearance. This mirror belonged originally to the Pepperell family of Kittery, Maine.

Another variety of mirror with a crested design was that called today in America a courting mirror. These mirrors were set in wide moulded frames with stepped crests. Set in between the mouldings were pieces of simply painted glass decorated with bright-coloured leaves and flowers. Many of these mirrors,

though their origins are uncertain, are found today in New England along with the wooden cases in which they were carried.

In the early eighteenth century the moulding of the frame around the mirror became more elaborate, being rounded at the upper corners. By 1720 this moulding had changed from the cove moulding to a channelled moulding. The most popular type of cresting on mirrors of the first half of the eighteenth century was a solid, scrolled cresting. At this time a scrolled skirt was often added at the base of the mirror as well. Often the bevelled glass was set into the frame in two pieces since many of these mirrors were as much as 5 feet (152.4 cm) high, and glass was precious, especially in large sheets. Because the upper section could not easily be used to reflect a particular image, the glass in that area was sometimes engraved with a floral pattern or a heraldic device.

Above Pepperell family mirror in frame of white pine, painted to give a tortoiseshell appearance. Probably New England, *c.* 1700. Henry Francis du Pont Winterthur Museum

Far right Mirror in painted pine frame, probably New York, 1725–35. Henry Francis du Pont Winterthur Museum

Right Bleeker family mirror, the frame of tulipwood, red pine and spruce with japanned decoration in gilt, 1729–40. Henry Francis du Pont Winterthur Museum

This was particularly true of mirrors made between 1725 and 1750.

Towards the middle of the eighteenth century, japanning became a favourite method of decorating mirror frames. The largest known American example with japanned decoration was probably made in New York between 1729 and 1740 and was owned by Jon Johannes Bleeker. Made of soft pine, it is decorated on a black ground with raised Oriental and European designs in gilt. It was in New York at this time, too, that Gerardus Duyckinck advertised in the *Weekly Journal* in 1736, 'Looking-glasses new Silvered and the Frames plaine, japand or Flowered . . . made and sold, all manner of painting done.'

A simpler version, originally used on the Luyster farm in Middletown, New York, and made between 1725 and 1735, has exotic gilt decoration on a cerulean-blue ground. Many frames were made of walnut in these same designs and were not painted. One of the most popular designs of all, this style continued to be made throughout the eighteenth century and well into the nineteenth century. Such mirrors can be dated only by their diminished crests, the use of later classical motifs, or the type of moulding surrounding the glass itself.

By the middle decades of the eighteenth century the moulding of frames became further elaborated by having an inner border which was carved and gilded. Especially in Philadelphia and also elsewhere, the cresting of these mirrors was often decorated in the centre with a gilded shell, at first a solid, symmetrical shell which, with the advent of the rococo taste, became pierced and asymmetrical. By this time mahogany was the favoured primary wood. A fine example of this particular type of mirror was made between 1762 and 1767 and labelled by John Elliott, Sr, of Philadelphia. This same John Elliott with Isaac Gray owned the Philadelphia Glass Works about 1773–7, a natural association for a cabinet maker who made numerous mirrors. The first label Elliott used, while at his shop on Chestnut Street from 1756 to 1761, was printed in English and German. From 1762 to 1767 he was working on Walnut Street at the Sign of the Bell and Looking Glass, where he advertised in 1763 that he also 'quicksilvers and frames old glasses, and supplies people with new glasses to their own frames; and will undertake to cure any English looking glass that shows the face either too long or too broad or any other way distorted'.

Concurrently popular in the mid-eighteenth century was the architectural type of mirror surmounted by a broken-arch pediment and a phoenix or eagle finial. This type of frame usually had pendent swags of leaves and flowers on each side, and often had the architectural outlines emphasized by gilt and carved egg-and-dart or leaf mouldings. Bearing a close relationship to the architectural patterns of British designers like James Gibbs or Abraham Swan, these frames were quite suitable for filling wall panels similarly derived from the designs of these men. Crosseted corners in the upper section of the frame, more elaborate scrolling below the base of the glass, and rosettes with streamers in the volutes of the pediment are features which enhanced these designs.

Generally the glass in the architectural examples was in one section as, for example, in a mirror by William Wilmerding. This mirror is documented by a bill of sale dated 'New York, Augst. 25th 1794 Mr Jacob Everson Bo^{t}. of William Wilmerding 1 Looking Glass – £8 – .' The beaded oval decoration and delicate gilt branches in the pediment verify the date of 1794, although the rest of the frame reflects a style at its height in the third quarter of the century. William Wilmerding advertised in New York City between 1789 and 1794. After 1798 he was listed in New York directories as a merchant. Wilmerding's label, which appears on a mirror owned by John S. Walton, New York, is most interesting, as it shows a portable dressing box, a cheval mirror with a pedimented crest, a dressing stand with an oval-shaped mirror, a mirror with a widely pitched pediment and eagle finial, and another surmounted by an urn filled with ears of wheat, a new style introduced in the last decade of the eighteenth century.

As the rococo taste became firmly established, frames became more elaborately scalloped, gilt ornament increased, the inner mouldings became undulating and even pierced with rocaille details. Cartouches as well as gadrooned vases filled with three-dimensional flowers and occasionally papier mâché figures filled the pediment.

One of the most beautiful examples of mirrors in the rococo taste is the lightly carved white-and-gold frame which belonged to the Cadwalader family in Philadelphia. The delicate C-scrolls, fanciful columns, and pendent leaves and flowers are the very essence of the rococo style. A strikingly similar mirror, undoubtedly from the same hand, was made for Richard Edwards, proprietor of the Taunton Furnace in Burlington County, New Jersey, by John Elliott, of Philadelphia, and bears the label which he used between 1768 and 1776. A third frame of this type is in the Metropolitan Museum of Art and is distinguished by having glass behind the open areas between the inner moulding and the outer scrolls.

Cadwalader family mirror by James Reynolds of Philadelphia, the frame of white pine and tulipwood, *c.* 1770. Henry Francis du Pont Winterthur Museum

A contemporary of Elliott, James Reynolds, advertised in Philadelphia 'carved and white, carved and gold, carved mahogany pier, sconce, pediment, mock pediment, ornamented, or raffle frames, box, swinging, or dressing glasses . . .' Thomas Jefferson in 1792 recorded in his account book that he 'gave James Reynolds ord[er]. on bank of U.S. for [$] 141.33 in full for looking glasses', and again in 1793 he paid him $99.53 for framing mirrors.

Shortly after the War of Independence the new classical style began to penetrate mirror designs. One of the earliest intrusions of this new taste was in the oval-shaped mirror set into the older-style frame. A happy combination showing this transition is the dressing table made by Jonathan Gostelowe, a Philadelphia cabinet maker noted for his serpentine chest of drawers. This mirror along with a chest of drawers was made in 1789 for Gostelowe's bride, Elizabeth H. Towers.

FEDERAL PERIOD

With a similar oval-shaped face, but showing the subsequent assimilation of the classical style, is a bedroom mirror, in the Museum of Fine Arts, Boston,

Sheraton-style dressing glass, veneered and inlaid, probably carved by Samuel McIntyre, *c.* 1800. Museum of Fine Arts, Boston

the carving of which is attributed to Samuel McIntyre, of Salem, Massachusetts, about 1800. Delicate string inlay, veneers of flame wood, carved laurel swags, beading, and cornucopias all betray the Federal period of design.

Another inlaid mirror of this type, with French feet, was labelled by Stephen Badlam, Jr (1751–1815), a cabinet and mirror maker in Dorchester, Massachusetts. Probably these mirrors in the new style were similar to those advertised in 1784 by Willing, Morris, and Swanwick as having been stolen from their Philadelphia counting house, 'Two oval Swinging Glasses with Mahogany frames and black and white string edges – one marked on the back 52s, 6, the other 35s.'

In the early nineteenth century these bedroom glasses followed furniture styles in the use of plain dark mahogany surfaces. Often they were supported on brass ball feet. At the same time the chest of drawers with an attached mirror supported by a large scrolled frame became a more common furniture form, especially in the Boston and Salem area. This general type of furniture had been made in New York City during the Chippendale period in the form of a chest of drawers, the top drawer of which contained a collapsible mirror and many compartments for organizing the accoutrements of dressing.

Ordinary mirrors, now frequently made in pairs, similarly took up the new decoration, so that the frames for glasses made between 1790 and 1810 were frequently oval, surmounted by fragile classical urns, banded with beading or flat water leaves carved around the base. From these urns sprang wired and gilded gesso ornaments of ears of wheat, rosettes, thin classical scrolls, laurel swags, and acanthus leaves. At the base of the oval frames were more leaves, a patera, and often the favoured feather motif of the Prince of Wales. Usually the innermost moulding immediately surrounding the glass was an edge of beading.

This type of frame was readily developed into the more heavily ornamented frame of the early nineteenth century. One example made for Elias Hasket Derby, of Salem, Massachusetts, has a naturalistic, carved eagle above the three-feathers motif, coarsely carved leaves, and entwined dolphins at the base. The moulding immediately around the glass is reeded with a twisted-rope design in the centre instead of beading. This is an enormous mirror, slightly over 6 feet (2 m) high, which Abigail Adams undoubtedly would have preferred to see in a room where the walls were at least 11 feet (3.4 m) high. Another large, oval-shaped mirror, now in the Museum of Fine Arts, Boston, and owned originally by Elizabeth Derby, is attributed to John Doggett, a well-known picture framer and mirror maker in Roxbury, Massachusetts, whose trade label is itself inscribed within a frame which is surmounted by an eagle on three feathers and which has entwined dolphins at the base.

The final development in this type of mirror was effected when the glass became round and convex, in the style of the French mirrors to which Sheraton referred in his *Dictionary*. Having large eagles at the top, which could be associated with the Great Seal of the United States, and outlined by heavy ball carving, an exaggeration of the classical beaded moulding, these mirrors are often mistakenly cherished above others as American made, although they were largely imported from England and France during this Greek Revival period. When candle arms are added they are popularly called *girandoles*, a somewhat loose application of a term belonging to lighting devices.

At the same time, the architectural type of frame continued in the classical period, with a flat cornice gradually replacing the earlier broken-arch pediment. The term tabernacle has sometimes been applied to the flat cornice type. Classical columns flanked the glass, and the upper section was usually filled with painting. Detail on these frames became less refined after 1810, beading being replaced by heavy ball ornament, twisted-rope mouldings, and surfaces left smooth and undecorated. A chaste example of an architectural-type mirror made in 1810 is particularly interesting in that not only does it bear the label of Peter Grinnell & Son, of Providence, Rhode Island, but also its painted glass or *églomisé* panel at the top is signed by the painter, 'B. Crehore, Aug. 27, 1810'. The painted wall-of-Troy border around the rustic scene gives ample evidence that this frame belongs to the period of the Greek Revival.

An alternative method of decorating the upper section of these frames was to substitute gilded plaster decoration for the *églomisé* panel. A labelled example of this sort made by John Doggett is in the Metropolitan Museum of Art, and has the figure of *Fame* above a floral festoon upheld by two trophies of the Prince of Wales feathers and a bow knot. John McElwee advertised in the *Pennsylvania Packet* on 7 May 1800, that he had 'Also for sale on a liberal credit, a quantity of Composition Ornaments, and Moulds of every pattern necessary for the Looking Glass business'.

During this final period in the first half of the nineteenth century, there were many well-known names among mirror makers. Barnard Cermenati worked at No. 10, State Street in Boston and Newburyport, Massachusetts, and in Portsmouth, New Hampshire. Stillman Lathrop, when he moved to Boston in 1806, continued his old business in Salem through an agent, George Dean. Wayne & Biddle succeeded James Stokes in Philadelphia and produced many architectural mirrors with landscapes and seascapes in the *églomisé* panels.

Glossary

Adam, Robert (1728–92). The eminent architect who, in common with his predecessor, William Kent, paid much attention to the interior decoration of his buildings. Adam designed mirrors, principally pier glasses, and many of them remain in the houses for which they were made. A great number of Robert Adam's original designs are in Sir John Soane's Museum, Lincoln's Inn Fields, London.

Bevelling. The angular shaping of the surface at the edges of a mirror plate was performed by grinding and then polishing the glass. A patent for a method of doing this with the aid of water power was granted in 1678. Much glass for mirrors had the edges bevelled, but the finish was not always employed for large plates after the middle years of the eighteenth century.

Bilbao mirror. Name given to type of mirror in frames veneered with sheets of pink marble imported from Europe to America at the end of the eighteenth century and in the early nineteenth century.

Chimney glass. American term for mirrors designed to fit the chimney breast above the fireplace in a room.

Chippendale, Thomas (1718–79). Cabinet maker and designer. Two large mirrors at Kenwood, London, were designed by Robert Adam and supplied by Thomas Chippendale in 1769.

Constitution mirror. American term for a rectangular mirror in an architectural frame with a broken-arch pediment and shaped apron; reason for use of this term not known.

Courting mirror. American term for mirror of unknown origin, held in moulded, step-crested frames set with panels of glass painted with multicoloured leaves and flowers, usually accompanied by crude wooden boxes in which they were carried.

Dressing glass. American term for mirror attached to dressing table.

Gibbons, Grinling (1648–1720). Carver and designer of Dutch birth and English domicile. He was 'discovered' by the diarist John Evelyn. Gibbons's distinctive and realistic carving exists in the form of mirror frames, but much of the work assigned to him is by his contemporaries, and much is of considerably later date.

Gilding. The process of applying gold, beaten into the thinnest of foils, to a surface. It is divided into two types according to the nature of the mordant by which the gold is made to adhere to the article.

Oil gilding used a preparation of solidified linseed oil, and the resulting finish was the more durable and least expensive of the two, as it could be employed directly on to the surface of the woodwork. Oil gilding would not burnish.

Water gilding required the woodwork to be painted

Mirror in carved gilt frame, English, by Robert Adam, 1772. The acanthus scrolls of the cresting support two female figures and frame an oval looking glass. The commode and *torchères* are by John Cobb, 1772. Corsham Court with several layers of a preparation somewhat like plaster, known as gesso. Gesso was made with a base of glue prepared by boiling scraps of parchment or glover's leather in water. To this was added *bole armoniac*, or *Armenian bole* (a fine clay, now known as gilder's red clay), and some tallow, suet, or beeswax. The coats of gesso were smoothed to as perfect a surface as possible, and then wetted piecemeal to moisten the glue and cause the gold leaf to adhere as it was applied. After allowing time for drying, the gold was burnished where required with the aid of a dog's tooth or a piece of polished agate.

Water gilding was the method principally employed for woodwork, but it was sometimes used in conjunction with the oil process; the latter on flat surfaces that did not need to be burnished.

About 1720 the gesso surface was often ornamented by being stamped with a tool that covered it with tiny circles. Shortly after that date a granulated finish was in use; this was obtained by sprinkling sand on the wet gesso before applying the gold leaf.

Girandole. Wall light, sconce, and girandole are recognized generally as being vague and interchangeable terms. In England a girandole is usually a branched support for candles, generally with a mirror backing; used in America to describe the type of convex, circular mirror surmounted by an eagle, with or without candle branches, which is called, in England, a convex mirror.

Gumley, John. Glass maker and furnisher, living in London in the eighteenth century. A mirror with the name *Gumley* carved on a small gilt plaque is at Hampton Court Palace, and another with 'John Gumley 1703' is at Chatsworth.

Girandole looking glass of poplar and pine, American, 1810–20. Mabel Brady Garvan Collection, Yale University Art Gallery

Japan and Lacquer. Lacquer was not only embellished with painting on the surface, but was also incised with designs; this latter being known as 'Bantam' or 'Coromandel' lacquer. Both types of lacquerwork were used in the framing of mirrors. Mostly the lacquering was done in England, but examples are known that were made from Oriental panels, cut to the required size and fitted on a framework.

Jensen, Gerreit (known also as Garrett or Gerrard Johnson). Cabinet maker and 'glasse-seller', who supplied much furniture to the Royal Household from 1680. A tall mirror at Hampton Court tallies with the description on his bill rendered in 1699, and it is assumed that Jensen had the monopoly of supplying overmantel mirrors and pier glasses to the royal palaces during the reign of William and Mary.

Johnson, Thomas. Designer and wood carver of London. He published a volume entitled *Twelve Girandoles* in 1755, and a more ambitious work, *One Hundred and Fifty New Designs*, between 1756 and 1758. Johnson's designs are very fanciful, and appear to be almost incapable of realization. However he boasted that they 'may all be performed by a master of his art'. A mirror at the Victoria and Albert Museum corresponds with one of his designs, as do a pair of mirrors at Corsham Court, Wiltshire. It is assumed that he worked to his own patterns, but it cannot be taken for granted that anything coinciding with his designs was necessarily from his own hand.

Kent, William (1686–1748). An architect who also planned the landscaping of gardens, painted pictures, and was one of the first of his profession to lavish as much care on the interior of a house as he did on the building of it. He was an exponent of the Palladian style, and his name has been given to the mirrors with frames of 'architectural' type that were fashionable in the years 1730–40.

Linnell, John. Cabinet maker and carver, many of whose designs for mirrors and other furnishings have been preserved and are in the Victoria and Albert Museum. He worked in the period 1760–90, and his designs are mainly in the prevailing 'Chippendale' style. He executed work at several of the country mansions that were then building or being refurnished, including Shardeloes, Bramshill, and Castle Howard.

Makers and designers. It is difficult after the lapse of two centuries or more to differentiate between designers, dealers, and actual makers of mirrors and mirror frames. There would seem to have been much intermingling of these three functions, and it is generally not possible to state who did make any particular specimen. This is particularly the case where a designer and carver published his patterns, which were then available for anyone to copy.

In some instances original bills have been preserved, in others the designs of frames have been traced to their originators, and in a very few instances the name of the maker (or supplier?) is found on the piece. (*See* Chippendale, Gibbons, Gumley, Jensen, Johnson, Kent, Linnell, and Moore.)

Mansell, Sir Robert. A financier who organized the English glass industry in the first half of the seventeenth century, and who eventually controlled glasshouses all over the country. He imported skilled workers from Murano, and successfully made mirror glass.

Moore, James (? 1670–1726). Cabinet maker, in

Carved and giltwood overmantel mirror, the cresting formed as Ganymede and the Eagle. After a design by Thomas Johnson published in 1758. English. Victoria & Albert Museum

partnership with John Gumley from 1714. Moore is known to have made much furniture decorated with gilt gesso, on some of which his name is incised. He was concerned in the furnishing of Blenheim, and it is assumed that some gilt pier glasses and tables there were made and supplied by him.

Stumpwork. A type of fine needlework of which much is in relief; figures, etc., being made to stand out by a stuffing of wool or cottonwool. Caskets were covered with this type of work, and small mirrors were set within panels of it laid down on a wood framework.

Tabernacle mirror. Generally applied to the Sheraton mirror with flat cornice under which is a row of gilt balls above a scene painted on glass; columns at sides.

Vauxhall. A manufactory of plate glass was commenced here about 1665 by George Villiers, second Duke of Buckingham. John Bellingham approached the Duke with a secret process for making mirrors, and as a result the Vauxhall factory was started and Bellingham was given the post of manager. Glasshouses continued to operate in Vauxhall until the end of the eighteenth century, and old mirror plates are often referred to today as 'Vauxhall'.

Verre églomisé. Glass decorated at the back with designs in colour and gold and silver foils. It is a method that has been practised for many hundreds of years, but for some reason is named after an art collector, J. B. Glomy, who died in France in 1786. Borders of *verre églomisé* in arabesque patterns and with coats-of-arms were used to frame mirrors *c.* 1695.

Panel picture embroidered in silk and wool petit-point on canvas, English, *c.* 1705. Lady Lever Art Gallery

Lace

Lace is fabric at its most exquisite: it is ornament with a cultured sophistication requiring neither colour nor gloss. Not until the splendid days of the late fifteenth century did it develop in Europe, and then it was art-conscious, craft-proud Italy that first rejoiced in such an ultimate in embroidery technique as the stitching of patterns 'in the air'.

To the collector today old lace is an endless, absorbing passion, but to the beginner its very complexity may prove daunting, with its many sources and techniques, and its terms complicated by four centuries of peasant craftsmanship in Italy, Flanders, France, England, and elsewhere. This survey can distinguish only among the more renowned laces, and any serious collector is well advised to study museum collections, such as the selection, for example, at the Victoria and Albert Museum.

As a first essential the collector must recognize that two basically different kinds of lace were made, quite apart from the application of the term to various cords and gimps. These are here distinguished by their most usual names of needlepoint and pillow lace. The use of the term 'point' alone is merely confusing.

European needlepoints were first made in Italy; pillow lace may have originated in Italy, or in Flanders, where it certainly preceded Flemish needlepoints. Needlepoints developed from cut- and drawn-thread embroidery; pillow lace from knotted fringes and the network generally known as *lacis*. But by the seventeenth and eighteenth centuries, when man, woman, and child wore lace as the *sine qua non* of elegance and taste, the differing techniques produced results superficially similar. Even the needlepoints tended to lose their early exquisite characteristic of *bride* and *picot* in favour of the less imaginative grounded laces made in short lengths and joined, until these in their turn were debased by the invention of lace making by machinery pioneered by John Heathcoat in 1809.

The basic difference between needlepoint and pillow lace is summed up in the fact that needlepoint lace was made with a single thread and a needle using embroidery stitches dominated by buttonhole stitch, and pillow lace was made with a multitude of threads wound, for convenience, upon bobbins, so that the lace could be created in a range of twists and plaits combining various numbers of threads. The difference is fundamental and soon becomes recognizable at a glance, although the collector may still be puzzled by a minority of mixed laces and the lace effects developed with machine-made net.

England's own contribution to this craft has been unspectacular, but for this the lace factors may be blamed rather than the women and children who created it, for the English thread was poor – a characteristic too of much modern handmade reproduction lace. English spun flax was never of superb quality, and thread imported from Flanders in the eighteenth century might cost £90 a pound.

In the abbreviated glossary below it has not been possible to include all the synonymous terms used by Europe's lace makers, but it has seemed most useful to adopt the most familiar rather than to adhere rigidly to the English, which, indeed, long ago absorbed many of the more charming Continental words and phrases.

Terms used in lace-making

À jours. *See* Fillings.

Alençon. Needlepoint, established 1665. The early Venetian influence soon became less important than lighter, fine-threaded Flemish pillow-lace notions, but like Argentan lace, it was regarded as a heavy winter lace. By 1700 or 1720 the famous grounded *point d'Alençon* was evolved with rich fillings and a stiff *cordonnet* and *picots* sometimes including horsehair. This was mainly a narrow lace for borders and caps and was reintroduced in the nineteenth century, more flimsy and often on a spotted ground. A softly looped hexagonal mesh was made first and the pattern put in, worked in close buttonhole stitch. *See* Point de France.

Antwerp. Pillow lace, strong and heavy looking, the patterns outlined in a *cordonnet* of thick untwisted thread and made at the same time as the *fond chant* ground. The style of pattern has given this the name of pot lace or potten kant, from the substantial two-handled vase usually prominent in it. This motif was fantastically popular in the eighteenth-century embroideries. It appeared also in Normandy laces.

Argentan. Needlepoint, established 1665. Resembled Alençon lace made ten miles away until they developed meshed grounds. The so-called Argentan lace was made also at Alençon, the work tending to be larger and more perfect than so-called Alençon, with bold patterns and a hexagonal ground, sometimes *picotée*, worked over in tiny buttonhole stitches. *See* Point de France.

Argentella. Needlepoint, variant of point d'Alençon, with a large dotted mesh. *See* Œil de perdrix.

Arras. Pillow lace, sometimes spelt orris in old records. Usually associated with a coarser version of Lille, but with scalloped edges. George I had 354 yards of it for his coronation. *See* Point de France.

Ava Maria lace. Pillow lace in long strips with a plaited lozenge ground made at Dieppe until the mid-nineteenth century.

Binche. Pillow lace made with very fine thread and such a close texture that the pattern was almost lost. Gradually it became more open and eventually lost its delicacy. It had much in common with early Valenciennes and some suggestion of Brussels *point d'Angleterre*.

Blonde. Pillow lace, silk, made in the Arras, Lille, and Chantilly regions from the 1740s, first in unbleached Chinese silk but soon in white and black. Had a ground of the Lille type, loosely twisted.

Bobbin lace. Alternative term for pillow lace, but distinguished from bone lace in early inventories as being coarser, of thicker thread requiring large bobbins.

Bobbins. Spools wound with thread for pillow laces, a separate bobbin for each thread. English bobbins are distinctively ornamental, light and dainty for Honiton and Buckinghamshire lace, but often weighted with spangles, or beads, for the coarser laces.

Bone lace. A term sometimes specifically applied to gold and silver lace, but more often also to all good quality pillow lace, as distinct from needlepoints. It has been variously argued that the name referred to the sheep's trotter bones sometimes used as early bobbins and to the bone pins used in place of metal pins to shape the pattern – fish bones on occasion. Metal pins were priced in 1543 at as much as 6*s* 8*d* a thousand. The term has been applied also to the ivory effects of Venetian raised point. It was the accepted term until the early eighteenth century for much pillow lace, and there are many records of its cost: such as 1*s* 4*d* a yard for narrow bone-lace edging in 1594, and 2*s* 4*d* a yard in 1685.

Brides. French term usually preferred to the English bars or ties, used to connect and support the pattern where there was no net ground. Found mainly in needlepoints and mixed laces.

Brussels. Needlepoints and pillow laces. Needlepoint was made from 1720, but took second place to the pillow laces. The ground was a plain looped mesh, and late in the century there was a tendency to restrict the slower needlepoint work to the pattern and introduce a pillow-lace ground. Pillow laces include *bride*-linked tape lace of the seventeenth century succeeded by grounded laces, the ground worked after the pattern, its hexagonal mesh consisting of two sides with four threads plaited four times and four sides of two threads twisted. Patterns in the mid-eighteenth century included many rococo-Oriental extravagances. The Brussels *point plat appliqué* was a pillow lace of the late eighteenth century with a net ground supporting small sprigs worked separately.

Bucks point. Pillow lace, mainly showing the influence of Lille and with much use of Lille's ground (*fond clair*) although often in company with *fond chant* and the soft Mechlin mesh. The patterns were lightened with attractive fillings and outlined with gimp wide and flat. There was some direct copying of Mechlin.

Caen. Pillow lace imitating the silk blondes of Chantilly from the mid-eighteenth century.

Carrickmacross appliqué. Not a real lace, as the pattern was cut from cambric, applied to net, and given needlepoint fillings.

Carrickmacross guipure. As above but with needlepoint *brides* instead of net.

Silk blonde pillow-lace veil, the pattern of a different silk from the ground, probably made at Caen, mid-19th century. Victoria & Albert Museum

Chantilly. Pillow lace, silk with *fond chant* ground and some use of *fond clair*. *See* Blonde.

Cinq trous. Ground found in some Flemish lace in which the threads crossing to form the mesh left five small holes.

Clothwork. *See* Toilé.

Collar lace. Early seventeenth-century term for imported Venetian point laces, simple and largely geometrical in vandyke outlines. A few designs are considered identifiable as English.

Coralline point. Needlepoint, variant of Venetian flat point with confused patterns and very many *brides picotées*.

Cordonnet. French term usually preferred to the English gimp or trolly thread for the more substantial outline often given to the solid pattern motif. It might be composed of several threads whipped or buttonholed together, as in Venetian raised point; or be one thread whipped or buttonholed, as in Alençon; or be a different coarser thread as in Mechlin.

Cutwork. Suggested by drawnwork, but lighter and more conspicuously ornamental, as part of the fabric was cut away and the holes filled with geometrical patterns worked with needle and thread, and at its most advanced consisting of buttonhole stitch, double loop, darning and knotting stitch. It was important in Elizabethan England.

Devonia lace. Honiton product of the 1870s with flower petals raised in relief by tension on the threads.

Dieppe. Pillow lace suggesting simplified Valenciennes. *See* Antwerp; Ave Maria lace.

Drawnwork. Forerunner of real lace. Made from linen with some threads drawn out and the remainder variously grouped and whipped over to form geometrical patterns.

Dresden 'lace'. Drawnwork on muslin.

Dutch. Pillow laces made from the 1660s, tightly woven and solid looking, often with closely grouped scrolls suggesting heavy flowerheads. The grounds included the *cinq trous*. Huguenot refugees brought to Dutch lace something of the old Valenciennes style.

English lace centres. Established in Honiton and other parts of Devonshire; Olney, Newport Pagnell,

Stony Stratford, and Aylesbury, Buckinghamshire; Bedford and Woburn, Bedfordshire; Northamptonshire; Wiltshire; Dorset; Suffolk. *See* Bucks point; Devonia; Honiton; Midlands.

Essex. First region in England to develop tambour 'lace'.

Fillings. Synonymous with the French *à jours* or modes for the fancy open stitches introduced in the pattern spaces in both needlepoints and pillow laces.

Fine drawings. Synonymous with French *point de raccroc*, the delicate work of joining lengths of lace net.

Fond chant. A six-pointed star ground found in so-called *point de Paris*: English Midlands laces and trolly lace; Chantilly lace, etc.

Fond clair. Synonymous with *fond simple* for the mesh ground in Lille lace, with four sides formed of two twisted threads and two sides of crossed threads. This sometimes suggests diamond rather than hexagonal meshes, depending on the tightness of the work.

Footing. Upper edge of a piece of lace.

Genoa. A centre for gold and silver plaited gimps, and hence developed pillow lace. Alternatively, some consider pillow lace began in Flanders.

Gold and silver. Plaited border laces of gold and silver wire, exported from Genoa as early as the sixteenth century.

'Greek' lace. A name given to drawn- and cutwork embroidery, often combined with geometrical needlepoint or pillow lace. When the British occupied the Ionian Isles they brought home great quantities, but probably most of it was imported from Italy while the Isles belonged to Venice.

Ground. Synonymous with the French *fond* or *réseau* and basically meaning any background to a lace pattern, but usually restricted to a mesh or net so that grounded laces are contrasted with those where *brides* support the pattern. Some grounds are best known by their French names. *See* Fond chant; Fond clair.

Grounded laces. Laces with meshed backgrounds to their patterns, allowing more freedom of design than the alternative linking of *brides* found in early needlepoints. The mesh might be made along with the pattern, as in, for example, Valenciennes; it might be worked around the pattern afterwards as in *Brussels point d'Angleterre*; or worked first and the pattern put into it as in Alençon; or worked separately with completed pattern units attached to it as in *Brussels point plat appliqué*. The grounds are considerable aids in identifying old laces, since in pillow laces the tiny hexagons or lozenges are composed of different numbers of threads variously twisted and plaited.

Guipure. Term used confusingly for needlepoint or pillow lace without grounds supported by *brides*.

Hampshire, Isle of Wight. 'Lace' made in running stitch on machine-made net.

Hollie point. Sometimes holy point. Needlepoint in which the pattern was created by leaving spaces or holes in the close *toilé* which was built up with rows of a kind of twisted buttonhole stitch. A dainty lace used in the eighteenth century for babies' caps, shirts, etc.

Honiton. Pillow lace, the best and the first made in England, described as bone lace in about 1620 in Westcote's *View of Devonshire*, and continuing until about 1725. Suggestive of *point d'Angleterre* with the ground worked round the pattern, but with less attractive pattern shapes. Honiton net, made from costly Antwerp thread, and of excellent quality, was an important product in the eighteenth century. Honiton appliqué lace was made with motifs of pillow lace applied to this net ground, but the net was soon machine-made, with the flower motifs reduced to meaningless ugly shapes. Late in the nineteenth century Honiton made a tape pillow lace with *brides*, sometimes in needlepoint, instead of a mesh ground, and also Devonia lace.

Collar and cuff of Devon pillow lace, sometimes known as guipure as it lacks the meshed ground, first half of 19th century. Victoria & Albert Museum

Ireland. Records show that lace was made in quantity, 1650–1780, but the earliest known dates from the nineteenth century. *See* Carrickmacross; Limerick; Youghal.

Kat stitch. Really *fond chant*, but frequently found in Bedfordshire lace (*see* Midlands lace) and given legendary association with Katherine of Aragon.

Knotted lace. Made in sixteenth-century Italy with short lengths of thread or thin cord. When longer threads were introduced bobbins were developed to carry them, first of lead then of wood or bone, and the threads were twisted and plaited instead of knotted.

Lacis. French term for darned patterns on netting

Two borders of pillow lace, attributed to Honiton, second half of 18th century. Victoria & Albert Museum

in vogue in sixteenth-century Italy, a direct preliminary to pillow lace.

Lille. Pillow lace, sometimes black, very popular in late eighteenth-century England, but never as a dress lace. Its somewhat meagre patterns were heavily outlined in flat glossy trolly thread and set in a plain *fond clair* mesh.

Limerick. Tambour 'lace' introduced from England in the nineteenth century.

Machine-made lace. Can be identified by the meticulous evenness of the work, exactly repeated patterns and smoothly woven *toilé*. The edges tend to be weak and the whole lace light. Stitches are mostly woven or twisted, with no buttonholing and little plaiting.

Maltese lace. Pillow lace made from 1833, the designs including 'wheat grains' grouped in fours to make Maltese crosses.

Mechlin. Pillow lace, much imported to England, although it must be remembered that all Flemish laces until the seventeenth century were called Mechlin in England. Queen Anne, who prohibited French lace, allowed imports from the Low Countries. The earliest that can be identified, however, dates only to the 1720s. It developed handsome rococo patterns outlined in a separate, heavier flat thread, the pattern and ground being made together in one operation. The ground was the familiar hexagonal mesh in which four sides were of two threads twisted and two sides were of four threads plaited three times. Structurally this was nearly the same as the Brussels ground, but the effect was altogether less stiff and angular. Other grounds were sometimes used such as the *œil de perdrix*. The spotted patterns of the 1770s onwards consisted of rows of small sprays and the mesh was also variously spotted, the whole effect being subdued in the soft muslin manner of its day, but dull. Some lace in Mechlin style was made in Denmark in the eighteenth and early nineteenth centuries.

Midlands. Pillow lace made in Buckinghamshire, Bedfordshire, Northamptonshire. This appears unlikely to have more than legendary association with Katherine of Aragon. It may have been introduced by Flemish and French refugees from Mechlin and Lille. With local variants the style was mainly similar to Bucks point. Baby lace was made in great quantity, often little more than dotted work on a clear Lille ground. Maltese lace was made in the later nineteenth century, but usually without the tiny Maltese crosses. Black and white blonde laces were made 1860–70 and there was some woollen lace. *See* Bucks point.

Milan. Pillow lace. James I specifically prohibited 'all lace of Millan and of Millan fashion'. In the later work identified today the pattern was worked first and the ground put round it at all angles.

Mixed lace. Associated with Genoa and Naples, the pillow-lace tape patterns supported by needlepoint *brides* or a coarse ground.

Modes. *See* Fillings.

Needlepoint lace. The ultimate development from cutwork with threads tacked on to a parchment pattern as the basis for stitches worked with a needle and a single thread. An outline was drawn on parchment stitched to two thicknesses of linen and this outline covered with threads exactly tack-stitched in position about every quarter of an inch. This outline was buttonholed over closely to form the *cordonnet*, and on this the lace was created, the solid areas of pattern – *toilé* – in close rows of buttonhole stitch and these linked and supported by connecting buttonholed *brides* or a regular mesh ground of buttonholed or looped stitches. It must be emphasized that a single thread on a needle was used throughout so that there could be no plaiting or weaving effects such as characterized pillow lace. The lace was released from the parchment by cutting between the layers of linen.

Œil de perdrix. Synonymous with *réseau rosacé* and *fond de neige* or snowflake ground – the most effective of the grounds used in Argentella needlepoint and the pillow laces of Valenciennes and some Binche and early Mechlin. Each of the irregular spidery meshes had a dot in it.

Orris lace. *See* Arras.

Patterns. Followed the same trends irrespective of

methods. Briefly, the earliest were geometrical, followed in the sixteenth and early seventeenth centuries by flower and scroll forms leading to the full floral grace of Renaissance work. There was some pictorial work around the mid-seventeenth century. The 1720s to 1770s were dominated by rococo inconsequence and rigid, angular flower bouquets, followed by the late eighteenth-century muslin effects spotted and dotted with small bouquets, bees, and so on.

Picot. French for the purl or tiny loop ornamenting *bride* or *cordonnet*.

Pictorial lace. Made in the mid-seventeenth century and resembling the raised embroidery now known as stumpwork and with similar use of raised canopies, loose hangings, beads, seed pearls, and disproportionate details to fill in the background.

Pillow lace. The most usual name for laces made

Above Needlepoint lace fashioned into a pictorial panel depicting The Temptation of Adam and Eve in the Garden of Eden, English, early 17th century. Victoria & Albert Museum

Far right, above Border of needlepoint lace in geometrical and formal flower pattern, early 17th century. Victoria & Albert Museum

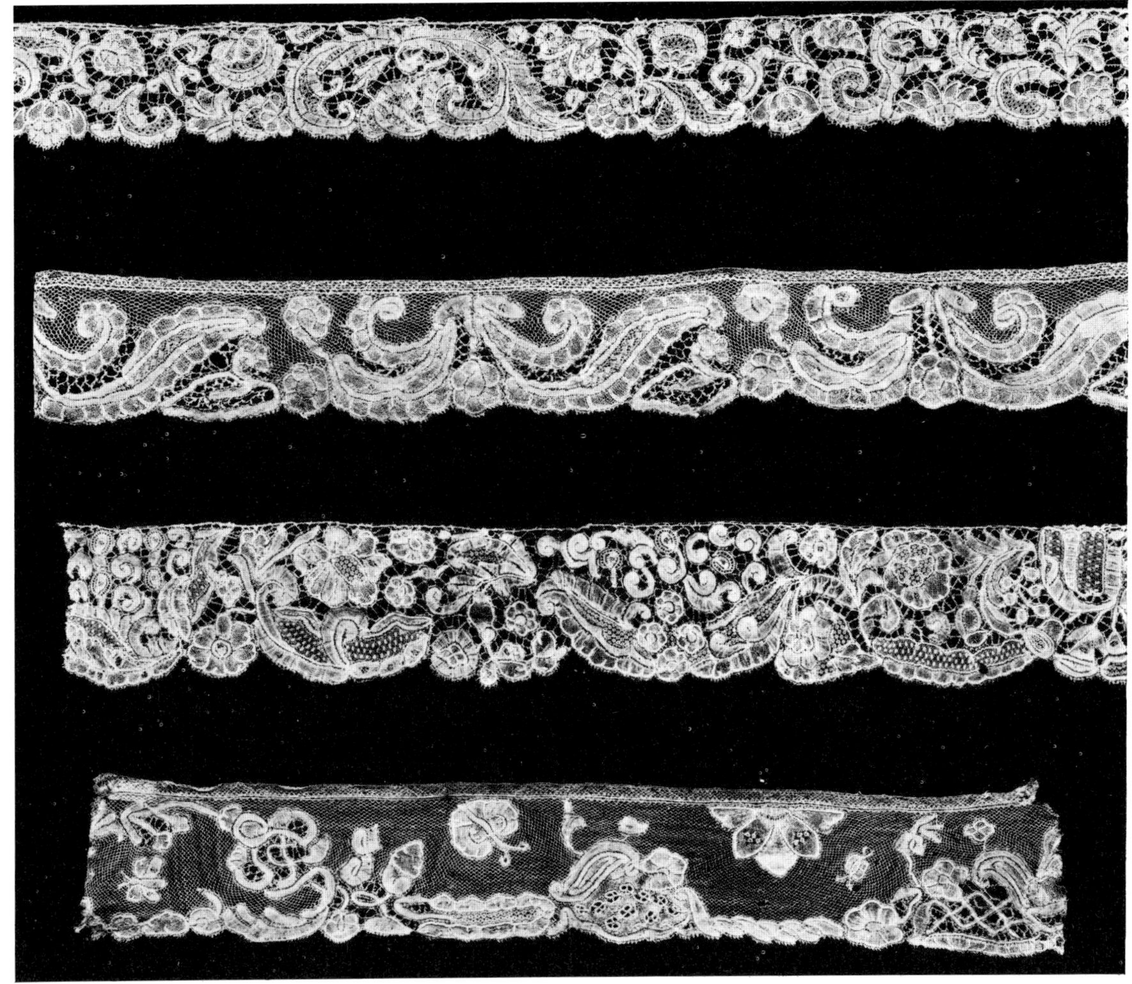

Right Borders of English pillow lace: the example third from top shows the pattern worked in with the meshed ground and associated with Honiton before the introduction of applied sprigs, the design being a crude version of the acorn and butterfly, found, for example, in old Brussels lace. Victoria & Albert Museum with bobbins as distinct from needlepoints, although those too were worked on cushions. Padded boards were used at first.

Point d'Angleterre. Pillow lace of Brussels, not English. English dealers sohnamed it in 1662 when Flemish lace was prohibited in England and France. It is the loveliest of Brussels laces, distinguished by the raised rib of plaited threads outlining leaves, etc., in a pattern which was loosely woven and edged elsewhere with rows of open stitches. The ground was worked after the pattern and was the Brussels hexagonal mesh, sometimes accompanied by the snowflake ground associated with Valenciennes.

Point d'Angleterre à brides. Pillow lace, variant of above, the meshed ground supplemented by *brides picotées*.

Point de France. Needlepoint. Some collectors limit the term to French raised *bride*-lined laces in contrast to grounded needlepoints made in the eighteenth century. Designs were more flowing than in the raised Venetian needlepoints. The term is more usually accepted in its original usage for the lace made at a number of towns where the craft was established in 1665 with State support, under Venetian tutelage, including especially Alençon.

Point de Paris. Pillow lace believed to be the first made in France, but there is no proof that this had any association with a coarse type of lace now sold by that name.

Point lace. All French laces, including pillow laces, so that it is impossible to reserve the term for needlepoints.

Points d'esprit. Small square dots scattered over the mesh ground, as in Lille pillow lace.

Pot lace. *See* Antwerp.

Punto in aria. Italian term, stitch in the air, for the beginnings of lace, the cutwork fabric reduced to a strip supporting the needlepoint work. The transformation was complete when the line of fabric was replaced by threads laid over the pattern drawn on parchment. The earliest work consisted of simple little vandykes worked wholly in buttonhole stitch.

Réseau. *See* Ground.

Spanish. The name Spanish point was variously applied to loosely woven gold and silver lace, much imported from Italy; to a raised needlepoint resembling the Venetian, similarly imported, and to silk laces mainly from Chantilly and Bayeux until Spain made her own.

Suffolk. Pillow lace, simple and less expert than the Midlands lace and with similar indications of Lille inspiration. Coloured worsted lace was also made.

Tambour 'lace'. First made in Essex. Imitation lace worked with a tambour hook on machine-made net.

Toilé. French term usually applied in preference to the English clothwork or mat for the solid part of the pattern. In needlepoint it was composed of rows of stitches, buttonhole or loop. In pillow lace the multiple threads achieved an effect of weaving.

Trolly. Pillow lace, coarse, made especially in the eighteenth century in Devonshire, with heavily outlined patterns in a *fond chant* ground.

Trolly thread. Gimp outlining the pattern in Lille lace.

Valenciennes. Pillow lace. True Valenciennes is reputed to have been made in the town and false Valenciennes in the region around, the countrywomen continuing the older style of ground when the townswomen developed a new one early in the eighteenth century, although both were 'true' in that they were worked pattern and ground in one operation. False Valenciennes included lace with mixed grounds while true Valenciennes had a clear open diamond mesh worked with four – later three – plaited threads. Patterns were mostly the old Flemish scrolls and conventional flowers without a *cordonnet* and worked with such exactitude that it became important, and rare, for one worker to complete a whole piece. Around the mid-eighteenth century the four pieces for a lady's cap and lappets might cost £45 and represent two or three years' work. Since the early nineteenth century this lace has been made largely in Belgium.

Venetian flat point. Needlepoint with a solid *toilé*, the fillings few and simple and the *brides* numerous and decked with *picots*.

Venetian grounded point. Needlepoint meshed lace introduced to follow the eighteenth-century French fashion and much resembling Alençon. The patterns were in the rococo mood of their time and somewhat florid.

Venetian pillow lace. A minor product dating to the early days of pillow lace and much resembling early needlepoint.

Venetian raised point. Needlepoint. This had a distinctively thick multi-thread *cordonnet* and no mesh ground. It was used on the ends of men's cravats in the seventeenth and early eighteenth centuries and had a sumptuous effect of carved ivory.

Venetian rose point. Needlepoint, lighter than raised point. The *cordonnet* might have two or three rows of *picots* and more *picots* were introduced on the many *brides* which were dotted with tiny roses suggesting a powdering of snowflakes – hence its alternative name *point de neige*. Popular in England in the seventeenth and early eighteenth centuries for men's falling collars, ruffles, etc.

Wiltshire. Pillow lace, a coarse simple version of the Midlands laces.

Youghal. Needlepoint, reproducing the Venetian flat point and rose point. This lovely lace was developed in Co. Cork in the late 1840s, but later was largely replaced by crochets.

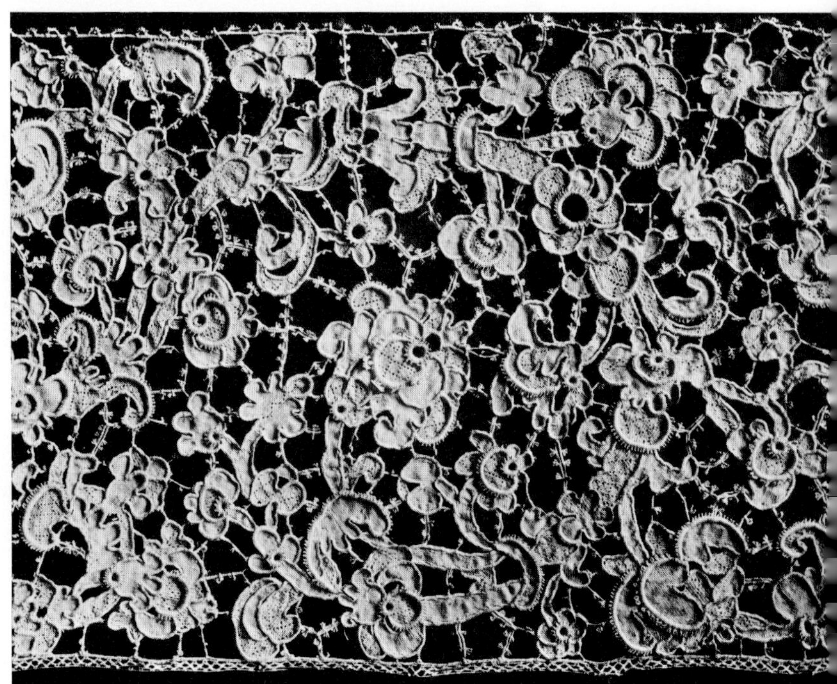

Part of a flounce of rose point, an exquisite needlepoint, the conventional flowers and scrolls linked with *Brides picoteés*, Venetian, 17th century. Victoria & Albert Museum

Sampler by Lucy Symonds, Boxford, Massachusetts, 1796. Victoria & Albert Museum

American Needlework

In America the professional embroiderer has always been the exception. The great bulk of the needlework for which an American origin can be claimed was produced by amateurs – women who employed this age-old craft to beautify their homes and clothing or, in a later period, young ladies demonstrating the genteel accomplishments acquired at school. This accounts for the difficulty of giving exact dates to many of the oldest and most interesting examples that have survived. Embroideresses in remote parts of the country probably continued, as they do today, to work in styles long since abandoned elsewhere, whether for lack of newer models or simply because they liked the old ways best; they evidently copied nature as well as the transmitted pattern and drew on imagination as needleworkers have always done.

Names and dates in the embroidery are not always a certain means of identification. Leaving aside the possibility that such 'signatures' and dates may have been added recently, we can easily imagine how an especially ambitious project, begun by one worker, could have been carried on by her daughters, or even her granddaughters, who would work into it the name of their ancestress and some significant date of her life as a sort of domestic memorial. Not only is it impossible to trace the makers of many 'signed' pieces, but the towns, buildings, and human figures depicted in needlework are only rarely to be identified with real places or people. And, it need hardly be pointed out, family histories not bolstered by other evidence are as unreliable here as in the case of other types of antiques.

It is difficult even to say when the story of American needlework properly begins. An early regulation in the Massachusetts Bay Colony forbade the wearing of 'cuttworke, embroidered or needle worke capps, bands, & rayles', indicating that at least some of the community were exposed to this temptation, but the objectionable finery may have been obtained from abroad. Inventories of the late 1600s, which indicate a rising standard of comfort, frequently list 'wrought', 'needleworked', or 'Turkey' chairs, cushions, carpets, cupboard cloths, and hangings. Though many of these embroideries, like other furnishings of the colonists' homes, undoubtedly came from the mother country, there is just as much reason to think that some were made in America.

The Turkeywork chairs, cushions, and carpets mentioned in early wills and inventories represent a type of needlework that had come into fashion in England in the late sixteenth century. Simulating the colourful rugs imported from the Near East for the homes of wealthy Europeans, Turkeywork was made by pulling heavy wool through canvas or coarse linen, knotting it, and cutting the ends to form a pile. Turkeywork carpets were used for table covers, just as Oriental rugs were at this time. In an inventory of 1676 twelve Turkeywork chairs are valued at 960 pounds of tobacco, twice the amount estimated for the same number of leather-covered chairs. Among the very few pieces of American furniture that have survived with their original Turkeywork upholstery are two chairs, now in the Metropolitan Museum of Art, that date from about this time.

A set of embroidered bed hangings, also in the Metropolitan Museum, is probably typical of many that added warmth and cheerful colour to the American homes of the late seventeenth century. According to tradition, these hangings were made by the three successive wives of Dr Gilson Clapp, an Englishman who went to America about 1666 and settled near Westchester, New York. The story, like others that have come down the years with cherished pieces of embroidery, cannot be corroborated, but the work itself represents a type that came into style in England in the late 1500s and remained popular for nearly a century with women of the middle-class provincial society from which most of the American colonists came. Embroidered with red wool in outline, blanket, and seed stitches, the panels have narrow scalloped borders enclosing a ground on which dots, birds, squirrels, and stags pierced with arrows alternate with floral sprays in a close, all-over pattern. Motifs of this sort were originally copied from manuscripts and early printed books on natural history, herbals, and, in the case of the deer pierced with an arrow, books of emblems and devices; they were later redrawn for the use of embroiderers and published in such works as Shorleyker's *Schole House for the Needle* (1624) and the engravings of Peter Stent and John Overton, among others.

The painted and resist-dyed Indian chintzes imported into Europe from 1630 on opened up a rich source of design to the needleworker. Before the middle of the century, small repeating patterns like that on the Metropolitan Museum hangings had been superseded by typical motifs from the chintzes – the great flowing tree that rises out of a low mound or hillock, with all sorts of exotic birds and butterflies in its scrolling branches and human figures standing on the schematized earth at its base, and the detached, naturalistic flower sprays scattered irregularly over the ground. Embroideries in this style are probably what most people think of first as crewel-work, though the name is just as properly applied to those described above.

The word crewel actually designates the loosely twisted, worsted yarns with which the design was worked. Early newspaper advertisements of crewels, 'cruells', etc., indicate that imported yarns were available in the major cities, but evidently much of the early needlework produced here was worked with materials spun, woven, and dyed at home. Crewels were supplied commercially in several grades, from coarse to fine; homemade yarns were bound to vary widely in weight and texture. The ground is usually linen or twilled cotton; homespun linen is most common in American examples. One invariable characteristic of crewelwork is that the ground material is never entirely obscured by the embroidery, though this may cover more or less of the space. It is generally held that in American work the motifs are smaller and sparser, more of the ground is left showing, and the whole effect is more 'open' than in English crewelwork. The patterns inspired by the Indian chintzes demanded a more naturalistic treatment than those in the preceding style, and were accordingly worked in yarns of various rather than a single hue. At first rather sombre, with many dark blues and greens relieved only by dull tan or mustard yellow, the colour schemes lightened in the course of the following century. Early crewelwork was carried out in a variety of stitches, outline or stem stitch (often spoken of as crewel stitch), Oriental, and long and short stitch being the most usual. Chain stitch gained favour in the 1700s.

Besides bed hangings, coverlets, and curtains, cushions, chair covers, and many smaller objects were decorated with crewelwork. A notice in the *Boston Gazette* of 1749 calls attention to the loss by theft of a 'Woman's Fustian Petticoat, with a large work'd Embroidered Border, being Deer, Sheep, Houses, Forrests, &c.' Several petticoat bands preserved in museums today have patterns that might be described in the same words.

Before the 1700s were well advanced, life in most parts of the American colonies had become relatively safe and easy. In the large cities accumulating wealth brought leisure and the desire for agreeable surroundings in its train. Houses were built and furnished with primary consideration for the comfort and aesthetic enjoyment of their occupants. Among the new forms that served this requirement, easy chairs, sofas, card tables, and fire screens in particular were well designed for the display of fine needlework, and the lady of the house, free of the heavier duties of earlier homemakers and able to call on the professional services of a tailor or mantua maker for the family's clothing, willingly took up the task of embellishing them. Contemporary newspaper advertisements offering instruction in various kinds of embroidery among other handicrafts speak for the popularity of this occupation. As early as 1719, an insertion in the *Boston News-Letter* announced that at the house of Mr George Brownell young gentlewomen and children would be taught 'all sorts of fine Work . . . embroidery in a new way, Turkeywork for Handkerchiefs two ways, fine new Fashion Purses, flourishing and plain work . . . Brocaded work for Handkerchiefs and Short aprons upon Muslin', as well as dancing. Among the 'Curious works' taught in New York in 1731 by Martha Gazley, 'late of Great Britain', were 'Nun's-Work', and 'Philligree and Pencil Work upon Muslin', all probably types of embroidery, though this teacher also offered artificial fruit and flower making, wax work, and 'Raising of Paste'. 'Flowering', 'flourishing', 'Dresden flowering on catgut (canvas)', and 'shading with silk or worsted, on Cambrick, lawn, or Holland' may take in all the colourful floral embroidery found on women's gowns, petticoats, aprons, pockets, and other

Detail from a crewel embroidered petticoat band, 18th century. Museum of Fine Arts, Boston

accessories of the period, as well as the fine work in silk on satin and velvet 'wedding' waistcoats for men.

Tent stitch and cross stitch are frequently mentioned. The first, known today as petit point, is worked on a firm but not too closely woven ground material in rows of short, slanting stitches, each stitch crossing diagonally an intersection of the threads of the ground. Imitating as it did the effect of woven tapestry and offering comparable strength and durability, this kind of work was much appreciated in the eighteenth century, as it is today, for the coverings of chairs and sofas, and it lent itself well to all-over patterns of small, naturalistic flowers and leaves that suited the light, graceful forms of Queen Anne and Chippendale furniture. Cross stitch scarcely requires description; worked in woollen yarns, it was an alternative to tent stitch for upholstery in the 1700s.

A third type of needlework that was frequently used for upholstery and other purposes in this period was called flame stitch or Hungarian stitch. Its rainbow-like effects were created by making horizontal bands of short, parallel stitches from one side of the work to the other. All the stitches in one row are the same length, but the rows themselves may rise and fall in zigzag patterns of great complexity. Wool or silk yarns were used for flame stitch, depending on the purpose of the work.

Most of the newspaper advertisers who offered instruction in needlework also had materials and patterns to sell. A notice inserted in the *Boston News-Letter* in 1738 by a Mrs Condy reads significantly, 'All sorts of beautiful Figures on Canvas, for Tent Stick [*sic*]; the Patterns from London, but drawn by her much cheaper than English drawing.' David Mason, 'Japanner', was also ready to provide 'Coats of Arms, Drawings on Sattin or Canvis for Embroidering'. Mrs Condy supplied 'Silk Shades, Slacks, Floss, Cruells of all Sorts, the best White Chapple Needles, and everything for all Sorts of Work'. 'Shaded crewells' and 'worsted Slacks in Shades' were also advertised.

Outside the cities and in the more modest urban homes, women continued to decorate their curtains, chair covers, bed furniture, and clothing with colourful crewels up to the end of the century and even later. Among fashionable city folk, however, this useful work had gone out of style. For one thing, the new Hepplewhite and Sheraton furniture that came in during the last quarter of the 1700s required more delicate coverings. Pattern-woven silks and satins were used on chairs and sofas in preference to needlework, and the needlewoman, relieved of this last duty, turned to decoration pure and simple, spending her new leisure on needlework pictures and similar 'fancy work'.

Pictorial subjects had, of course, been a frequent choice for furniture covers, fire screens, and other objects worked with woollen yarns in tent stitch and cross stitch earlier in the century. A group of thirty-six embroidered panels from New England, presumably the work of young ladies at a Boston finishing school in the mid-1700s, is widely known as the *Fishing Lady* series because of the name given to the central figure in the pastoral scene depicted. Considerable research has been devoted to tracing the source of this design, evidently one or more English prints.

The embroidered pictures of the late 1700s and early 1800s, however, differ from these last examples

Sampler by Nabby Ford, Portland, New Hampshire, 1799

in their general spirit and intention as well as by the materials and techniques employed in their making. The designs, including landscapes, pastoral scenes, views of architecture and ships, maps, portraits, biblical and mythological subjects, memorials, flower pieces, and allegorical compositions, were worked mainly in floss or twisted silk in a variety of stitches. Large areas like sky or background, as well as faces and other details, were often painted in. The ground material might be fine linen, canvas, silk, or satin. Such pictures were customarily framed like paintings, with a broad margin of black glass setting off the rather delicate colours of the embroidery. Perhaps the most typical of this group are the 'mourning pictures', depicting an urn or monument, often inscribed with a name or epitaph, a willow, symbol of sorrow, and one or more figures that may be meant to represent survivors of the deceased. Numbers of these are dedicated to the memory of George Washington. That the drawing of the figures is ordinarily competent points to the use of prepared designs, kept in stock by the vendors of other materials for needlework and traced or 'pounced' (by rubbing coloured powder through a pricked paper pattern) on the ground material desired. Many of the most elaborate embroidered pictures are the work of schoolgirls, and testify to the young needlewomen's completion of a course of formal instruction. The school conducted by the Sisters of Bethlehem, a Moravian religious order, in Pennsylvania was famous for the fine needlework developed and taught there in the eighteenth century.

In America as elsewhere, girls and young women had long made samplers to demonstrate their mastery of useful and decorative stitches and to record motifs and patterns for future use. Very few American samplers survive from the seventeenth century; the oldest, preserved in Pilgrim Hall in Plymouth, Massachusetts, was worked by Lora Standish, daughter of Captain Myles Standish, 1653. These early samplers, truly exemplars or patterns, as the name indicates, are long, narrow linen panels, on which the needlework is disposed in horizontal bands. Borders and small separate designs in various stitches, cutwork (*reticello*), drawn-thread work, and needle lace (*punto in aria*) are found on them. An alphabet or inscription or both is usual, and the maker's name and the date of the completion of the work were almost invariably added. In the course of the 1770s the inscription, which might be a motto, a verse or verses from scripture, or a selection from some such volume as Isaac Watts's *Divine Songs for Children*, occupied an increasingly prominent place, until the sampler became virtually a vehicle for the lettering and numbers. By this time, the shape had changed as well, tending to be square or oblong with the length little greater than the width. A border, which might be either a slender, running vine or a wide band of flowers, framed the embroidered text, and any remaining space was filled in with such motifs as flowers, fruit and leaves, birds, animals, and human figures, all more or less crudely drawn and worked most often in cross stitch or tent stitch. Bright, gay colours were the rule. After the 1830s, both design and workmanship deteriorated. The wide availability of patterns and materials for the popular Berlin woolwork of the mid-nineteenth century seems to have put an end to all more individual expressions in embroidery.

An effort has been made in this account to introduce the chief varieties of American needlework in some historical sequence, but it should not be forgotten that their periods of popularity overlapped and coincided with those of other techniques. Concurrently with the vogue for embroidered silk pictures there was a great fashion for tambour work, so-called from the shape of the two hoops between which the foundation material was stretched while being embroidered. A tambour needle, with a hooked end, was used, and the thread was drawn up through the material to form a chain stitch on the right side. Sheer muslin and crêpe were worked in tambour for ladies' caps. The same method, used on machine-made cotton or silk net, produced a lace-like effect that was much used for wedding veils, shawls, fichus, and edgings (tambour lace). 'Darned net', embroidered with a needle of the usual sort, was used for the same purposes. Satin stitch was worked in white thread, most often silk or linen, on the gossamer white linen, cotton, and silk dress materials of the 1830s. Large handkerchiefs of the finest white linen were embellished with drawn-thread work and incredibly fine satin-stitch embroidery in white. Mull, a cobwebby silk muslin brought from India, was embroidered in silk with motifs copied from Indian shawls or chintzes.

Needlework portrait of Benjamin Franklin, Berlin work, 1853. New Hampshire Historical Society

The fashion for white on white extended to needlework in coarser materials that give a very different effect. Heavy white cotton bed covers were embroidered with long strands of candlewicking, the typical design of a basket of flowers or a patriotic motif framed by a flowering vine being worked in small running stitches that stand out on the surface of the material and are sometimes looped and cut to make protruding tufts.

Among other types of American needlework that interest collectors are the towel covers made by Pennsylvania–German housewives in the late eighteenth and early nineteenth centuries to hang over and conceal the common towel on its rack in the kitchen. These are long strips of linen, often made up of two or more small towels sewn together, decorated with simple cross-stitch motifs representing birds, hearts, flowers, and human figures. Many are finished off with bands of lace or knotted fringe.

The rare wool-on-wool coverlets, of which a notable example comes from Old Deerfield Village, Massachusetts, apparently represent another regional speciality. Practically all of the small group so far recorded are thought to come from the Connecticut River Valley. Their bold, all-over designs, carried out in woollen yarns on a ground of heavy woollen fabric, seem to acknowledge the same exotic source as the crewel embroideries on linen. Most of the known examples are dated, the earliest 1748, the latest 1826.

An interesting survival of European customs may be seen in the early embroidered hatchments still preserved in some museums today. A hatchment was a coat-of-arms on a lozenge, meant to be carried in the funeral and displayed on the outside of the house of a person who had recently died. It consisted ordinarily of a diamond-shape wooden panel (or canvas stretched on a wooden frame of the same shape), painted black with the arms of the deceased on a shield in colour. In New England, at least, hatchments were copied in embroidery as memorials; the designs were carried out in coloured silks and gold and silver threads, which were couched or worked in long and short stitch and sometimes covered the entire surface of the panel.

American Quilts and Coverlets

Quilts and coverlets are primarily bed coverings created for warmth; while counterpanes and bedspreads are decorative covers for the bed produced with no thought of contributing to the comfort of the user. The quilts and coverlets of the nineteenth century, which were primarily utilitarian in their purpose, are the kinds most available to the collector today. They were produced in great quantity, and a remarkable number have survived in good condition. Many of them are very attractive in colour and pattern. The discriminating collector can make good use of them in the decoration of the home. Some knowledge as to their period, however, is desirable if they are to be fitted into their most appropriate setting. An understanding of the techniques involved in their production will make them more interesting and appreciated.

Most eighteenth-century quilts and counterpanes are very large, often 9–12 feet (274–366 cm) square, as they were used on the high beds of the period and often covered the stacked featherbeds and pillows which were placed on the main bed during the day to be spread on floor and settle for sleeping at night. These early covers were usually made of simple homespun or of imported English, French, or Indian printed or painted cottons and were often not quilted at all but used only as counterpanes.

As a rule the design of the textile will give a clue as to its approximate age. During the seventeenth and eighteenth centuries the designs of bed covers tend to develop from a base and to flow outward and upward as in the typical tree-of-life design. They may be symmetrical horizontally but not vertically, and there are rarely borders. In the nineteenth century this gradually gave way to more formalized patterns. At first the central design remained free and was surrounded by symmetrical borders; but later, that too disappeared and the whole design became balanced. After 1825 the designs tend to become geometrical in repeating units. Naturally there was a great carry-over of these designs and much copying of older pieces so that a typical eighteenth-century design may well appear as late as 1860. In this case the materials used may date the piece. Fortunately many women were very proud of their work and both signed and dated their more elaborate productions.

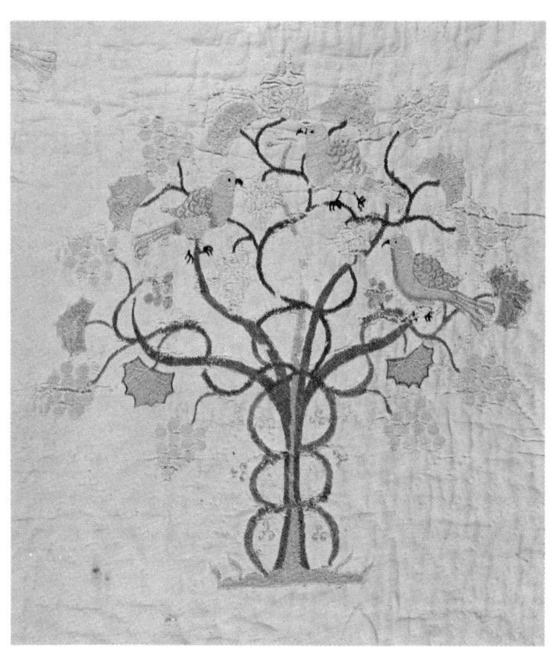

Coverlet, crewel embroidery on a quilted background, mid-18th century

Crewel-embroidered bedspreads, or counterpanes, were produced in the eighteenth century. Often a complete set of bed furniture was embroidered, including canopy or tester, curtains, and sometimes a skirt. The design was produced in the traditional English way with coloured wools worked in various stitches on a homespun linen ground. The well-known tree-of-life design was most popular, but often scattered motifs are found. These usually have the same Eastern feeling, although the subject matter may be the original idea of the maker.

Among the most interesting of the bed covers, though they are rare, are the wool-on-wool covers or bed rugs which have large scrolling or tree-of-life motifs worked in woollen yarn on a background of natural coloured woollen blanketing. While the technique is often mistaken for hooking, it is usually a product of the needle. Several strands of single-ply woollen yarn were stitched through the ground in a running stitch taking short stitches through the fabric and leaving loops of yarn on the surface. The entire surface is usually covered with a deep pile which is uncut. These textiles often resemble in appearance the woven-pile bed rugs of Scandinavia which are called *Rya*. Some have pile in various shades of blue with natural-coloured wool; while others combine these with shades of yellow, brown, and green. The designs appear to stem directly from the early crewelwork. Sometimes the woollen sheeting or blanket used for the background is pieced together from fabric in several different weaves, suggesting that it may have been a secondary use of partly worn material. These bed rugs are usually 7 or 8 feet (213–244 cm) square. Most of them are found in the New England area, particularly in the Connecticut River Valley from Vermont, Massachusetts, and Connecticut. Many are dated, the earliest 1724, and the latest in the early nineteenth century.

When cotton cloth became available from the factory soon after 1815 it was used for counterpanes, just as was the earlier chintz, but it needed to be decorated by hand. It was sometimes printed at home by means of carved wooden blocks or stencils. These block-printed or stencilled counterpanes were occasionally made into quilts, and it is in this condition that they are most often found today. The designs are simple and resemble to great degree the appliquéd quilts of the period. The colours usually used were red, green, and yellow.

After 1800 many bedspreads were made of cotton cloth, the earliest handwoven, embroidered in various stitches with cotton roving or candlewicking. These are all-white counterpanes, with sometimes simple, sometimes elaborate, designs and are often signed and dated. There is usually fringe applied to three sides. The designs become geometric after 1825, and there is often tufting combined with the embroidery stitches.

Closely resembling these embroidered spreads are the all-white woven counterpanes, made on the loom. A cotton roving was raised in loops over a wire to form the pattern on a background of plain cotton. Some of these were produced at home and some by professional weavers. The homewoven ones are usually seamed, while the others were woven full width and often numbered and dated. These woven tufted spreads can be distinguished from the embroidered variety by the heavy roving, which is continuous across the width, forming a heavy rib where it is not looped on the surface for the design. Stars often form a part of the design with swag borders. These were made from about 1800 to 1820.

QUILTS

There were at this period also all-white quilts made to serve as counterpanes. The interlining of cotton wadding is very thin and the quilting stitches very fine. The pattern may be very elaborate, and often extra padding was introduced from the back after the quilting was completed, in order to accent certain parts of the design. This usually consists of a large central medallion, urn, cornucopia, or basket of fruit or flowers with a series of surrounding borders. Companion pieces, such as bureau covers, were often made as well as separate pieces to cover the pillows. These white quilts may usually be assigned to the first quarter of the nineteenth century.

The technique of quilting developed because three layers of cloth are warmer than one, and has been employed for centuries. Clothing has been made for both warmth and protection, as in the quilted cotton garments of China and the quilted padding worn under medieval armour. Counterpanes have probably been quilted in every century from the fourteenth to the twentieth. In the seventeenth and eighteenth centuries bed hangings and table covers were also among the household articles quilted. Clothing also came in for its share of this technique, and articles included petticoats or underskirts, waistcoats, slippers, jackets, and dresses. Petticoats are the most usual surviving articles in this group, and their patterns are inclined to follow rather closely the bed coverings of the period.

In American bed quilts this technique of quilting is often combined with designs, pieced or patched (appliquéd), of coloured fabrics in order to furnish a colourful, as well as warm, article of bed clothing. The important era of American quilt making extended from about 1750 to 1860. Quite naturally, many more examples have survived from the nineteenth than from the eighteenth century.

The quilted woollen bed covers, which are often called Linsey-woolseys, are not often made of that staple household fabric. Rather, they are composed of a top layer of woollen or glazed worsted fabric dyed dark blue, green, or brown, with a bottom layer of a coarser woollen material, either natural or a shade of yellow or buff. The filling is a soft layer of carded wool, and the three layers are held together with quilting done with homespun linen thread. While some of these may date from the eighteenth century, many were made during the first half of the nineteenth. The design of the quilting is often a simple one composed of interlocking circles or crossed diagonal lines giving a diamond pattern. The earlier woollen quilts are thinner and the designs tend to be finer and more elaborate. The size of these quilts may also be a clue to their age, as in the nineteenth century they tend to be blanket size, while in the eighteenth they are likely to be large bed covers, occasionally with cutout corners for the bedposts.

While the eighteenth-century cotton counterpanes were made of whole cloth, usually imported, and therefore confined to the households of the well-to-do, the ordinary housewife soon came to realize that the expensive patterned chintzes would go much farther if they were first cut up into design units and applied to a linen or cotton ground. The central part of the design of the chintz appliqué counterpane was often the tree, cut from the chintz generally in one piece and applied to the plain fabric ground with the birds and insects found in these designs applied separately. Borders were then cut from smaller-figured chintz and sewn on all four, or sometimes only three, sides. There were often two or three of these bands, of varying patterns and colours, separated by bands of plain fabric. At a later period a back was added and a thin layer of carded cotton or wool placed between to be stitched in place by the finest of handsewing. This was almost always a simple running stitch in America; while in England and on the Continent a back stitch was more generally used. The quilting often followed the outlines of the appliqué in the central design, which set it off in a raised manner. The plain ground was often simply quilted in closely spaced diagonal rows.

In the later part of the eighteenth century came the first of the pieced quilts. The central design was often a large rising sun motif or Star of Bethlehem covering almost the entire bed with the familiar chintz floral patterns cut out and appliquéd to the square and triangular blocks of plain white fabric which filled in the star corners. A chintz border was usually added to complete the quilt top. This star pattern, which continued to be popular for a century or more, was composed of diamond-shaped pieces of small-patterned chintz and calico which were carefully arranged so that the colours radiated from the centre to the points. After 1800 the appliqué filling the corners gave way to pieced blocks arranged in a smaller star pattern. The sewing of these pieced patterns had to be most carefully done, as the seams had

Chintz appliqué bedspread, motifs from chintz and printed cottons with embroidered details, dated 1782. Henry Francis du Pont Winterthur Museum

to be perfectly regular if the finished design was to lie flat and even.

The earliest coloured quilts made of remnant patches must have been just that, with the odd-shaped pieces sewn down to a fabric backing; but by 1800 women began to use the more convenient method of making the quilt top in units of blocks and setting these together, either in parallel rows or diagonally, with strips of latticework or with alternate white blocks. These smaller units could be pieced or appliquéd very conveniently and then assembled and quilted in simple or elaborate designs. If plain white blocks were used in setting the pattern blocks together these were often quilted elaborately; while the quilting in the pieced or appliquéd blocks followed rather closely the construction lines of the block.

The patterns for quilting were often marked on the fabric by snapping a chalk line for the diagonal lines or chalking around a cardboard pattern for the more elaborate designs. Household objects, such as cups, saucers, and plates, were often used as patterns for simple quilting. Pencil, chalk, charcoal, and soap were used for the marking. Background designs included: the horizontal, the crossbar, diagonal, diamond, and double and triple crossbars and diamonds. Running designs for borders and lattice strips included: running vine, princess feather, rope, ocean wave, and serpentine. Designs for the plain blocks were: feather wreath, clam shell, wheel of fortune, spider's web, pineapple, bouquet, weeping willow, star crescent, heart, American eagle, fan, star and crown, oak leaf, bellflower, acanthus, swirl, and dove of peace. Many designs were based on the always adaptable feather motif.

Pieced quilts are generally geometric in design, as it is much easier to seam two small pieces of fabric together if the seams are straight and not curved. There are thousands of designs for these quilts, and many have fanciful names. The same pattern was known by different names in various sections of the country, and often the same name would be used for several totally unrelated patterns. There are star patterns named for every state in the Union. A few of the more interesting names are:

Cross and Crown	Puss-in-the-Corner
Goose Tracks	Bourgoyne Surrounded
Hen and Chickens	Pine Tree
Bear's Track	Flying Dutchman
Peony	Feather Star
Flying Geese	Drunkard's Path
Lincoln's Platform	Robbing Peter to Pay Paul
Stepping Stones	Dutchman's Puzzle
Morning Star	Wheel of Fortune
King David's Crown	Cats and Mice
Joseph's Coat	Hearts and Gizzards
Jacob's Ladder	Grandmother's Fan
Sunflower	Dresden Plate
Delectable Mountains	Winding Warp
Log Cabin	Turkey Tracks
Rose of Sharon	Irish Chain

These pieced or appliquéd quilts of the nineteenth century were usually made of plain coloured or printed cotton fabrics combined with white. Many were made of random bits of carefully hoarded fabric, and in this case some of the fabrics may be much earlier than the actual date of the making of the quilt. Often the quilt which is best preserved, because carefully kept for use on special occasions, is the one made of two or three colours of fabric which were especially purchased for its construction. Many quilts of this type were made during the 1830s and 1840s of turkey red and green cottons appliquéd on white grounds. It is probable that many of them were brides' quilts, as even though the customary dozen quilts were made of scraps, it would have been that final masterpiece for which new materials would most likely have been purchased. These quilts were often made of identical blocks in a basket or flower design and set together with white blocks on which were lavished the most elaborate quilting. Often each block is quilted in a different design.

The technique of making the quilt top in separate blocks led to a special type of quilt during the 1840s and 1850s. This was known variously as a signature, autograph, friendship, bride, presentation, or album quilt. These quilts were made for a special person. Friends or wellwishers each supplied a pieced or appliquéd block of her own chosen pattern which she usually signed in Indian ink. These friends gathered for an afternoon and assembled and quilted the quilt, which was then presented to the honoured guest. They were often made for a favourite minister or a minister's wife. These are among the most interesting of the nineteenth-century quilts and, if the colours are compatible and the various blocks well chosen and arranged, they may be very lovely as well.

During the late Victorian era the patched covers of the seventeenth and eighteenth centuries were revived but in a more elaborate form. These were the 'crazy quilts' made of scraps of silk, satin, and velvet. Like their earlier counterparts, they were made of small irregular-shaped pieces appliquéd to a base fabric, but now the seams were often covered with embroidery stitches and sometimes the patch itself had a design painted or embroidered upon it. These were often most attractive in colour and design, but occasionally a good example is found. They were impractical as bed coverings, owing to the material from which they were made, so they were made up into smaller sizes for use as couch throws, piano covers, and other parlour ornamentation of the period.

COVERLETS

Detail from an appliqué comic coverlet, 19th century. American Museum in Britain

Unlike quilts, which were made of already woven fabric, coverlets are woven into patterns on the loom. They may be either the product of the housewife and her family or of the professional weaver. During the early years of the settlement of America not much patterned weaving could have been done. It was all the housewife could do to supply her large family with the everyday clothing and household fabrics which were necessary. The materials for their manufacture were scarce. Sheep were not raised in great numbers and flax was a time-consuming crop. Cotton was obtainable only in limited quantities and at a high price. The housewife spun the flax which she had raised into linen yarn and wove materials for sheets and shirts, underclothing, and towelling. The refuse tow from its processing she converted into sacking and coarse tow cloth. She spun the wool from her sheep into yarn and wove it into heavy material for the clothing of the men and boys and outer garments for the whole family, as well as blankets for the bed. Only when the hardships of the first years had decreased and more time and material were available could she turn her hand to producing the patterned textiles which would adorn her home as well as keep her family warm and protected.

The patterns of these fabrics were not invented by her but were based on a long-continuing tradition. Perhaps she had brought with her some family textiles or perhaps only the written formula for their weaving. These weaving drafts were freely interchanged and travelled through all the colonies. It is likely that the first really intricately patterned fabrics were produced by professional weavers who emigrated to America from the various countries of Europe, bringing with them the old patterns of their homeland. It is certain that the early eighteenth-century pattern books printed in Germany were brought to America and used. The weavers of England and Scotland who came were well trained if they had successfully completed their apprenticeship. They certainly brought with them the patterns which they had been taught to weave. This was true of all the migrant weavers, for German, French, Dutch, Scandinavian, Scottish, and English all contributed their traditional textile designs and techniques to America.

In the category of woven coverlets must be included those woollen blankets also produced on the loom but decorated with embroidery so that they fulfilled both the purpose of warmth and decoration. Rose blankets are among these. They were woven of soft white wool in the simplest weave of the home loom. It is probable that the ones with a raised nap were woven at a slightly later date than the others either at home or in a factory. After weaving and finishing they were decorated with embroidery in coloured woollen yarns. The pattern used was a stylized wheel design of loose stitches. This decoration was often in two corners and sometimes in all four. The colours used were those readily dyed at home with the natural dyestuffs generally available. Rose, green, yellow, tan, brown, black, and sometimes blue are found. Rose blankets were being produced in the period from 1810 to 1840 in both New York and Pennsylvania and probably throughout New England. They were among the items of domestic manufacture which were being encouraged by the prizes awarded by agricultural societies of this period.

Material was also woven especially for making embroidered bedspreads. These often resemble plaid blankets in design. White or natural-coloured cotton was used with blue woollen yarn and woven in a twill weave. Then, after the strips were assembled, a design was embroidered in coloured woollen yarns in the spaces of the plaid. A fringe was often added to finish the edge.

The coverlets produced in their entirety on the loom include several types and techniques. In the order of their complexity, they are: overshot, also known as float weave; summer-and-winter weave; block or double-weave geometric; and the two types of flowered coverlets which are in the so-called Jacquard weave.

Due to the width of the home loom, coverlets were woven in two or more strips, each 2½–3 yards (228.5–274.4 cm) long and seamed together when finished. They were usually about 84 inches (213.4 cm) wide if in two strips. Sometimes a separate woven fringe was sewn on the sides while the ends of the warp threads formed the fringe at the bottom.

Coverlets are found in shades of blue, blue and red, brown, brown and tan, black, madder rose or rust, yellow, green with rose or yellow, and more rarely in scarlet. The dyes used in producing these colours were the ones most readily available and the ones considered to be most permanent. The most satisfactory dyestuff available was indigo. This had to be purchased from a shop or from the pedlar in the country, but it was widely available from the earliest days. Much was grown in the south during the latter half of the eighteenth century, but a large amount was always imported. Indigo produces a fast blue colour on all fibres, and this may be varied considerably in shade. It was also used to produce shades of green by dyeing with it either before or after a yellow dye was applied. The process of dyeing with indigo was an unpleasant one because of the smell of the fermenting indigo vat, which demanded particular care, as the vat had to be maintained at a constant warm heat to keep the fermentation from stopping. Other dyes were easier to apply. The brilliant scarlet was obtained from cochineal, an insect raised under cultivation in Mexico, by boiling the dried and powdered insects with a solution of tin dissolved in acid. As this dyestuff was probably the most expensive of all, it was not often used for homewoven coverlets. The common shades of red were obtained from madder root, which could be purchased as a ground powder or could be raised in the garden. Dyeing with this material followed a standard procedure used for many natural dyestuffs. First the woollen yarn was boiled in a solution of alum or of alum and cream of tartar, and then in a bath with the madder root. Shades from rose to deep lacquer red and rust were obtained. This was the second most popular dye for coverlets, as it was almost as fast to light and washing as indigo blue.

Yellow was obtained from goldenrod and sumac, tan from alder bark and butternut hulls and roots, dark brown from hickory or black walnut hulls and roots, and black by dyeing first with walnut and then with indigo. Other herbs, barks, roots, and berries were used with the alum process for dyeing various shades. Most of these were rather dull in tone due to the natural impurities in the dyestuffs, and most of them faded to some degree in time. Imported dyewoods from South and Central America generally available during the eighteenth and nineteenth centuries included logwood, Brazilwood, and fustic, but the domestic weaver was inclined to trust to the familiar dyestuffs.

The simplest type of coverlet to produce was in the overshot weave, which could be woven on the limited four-harness loom which was to be found in almost every home. It was made of linen warp and woollen weft in the eighteenth century and of cotton warp and woollen weft in the nineteenth. These coverlets are confined, by the limitations of the loom used, to simple geometric patterns, but there are literally thousands of patterns, as the combinations of four blocks in different order and proportions are infinite. Like the names of quilt patterns, the names of coverlet patterns were often very fanciful, reflected the historical events of their day, or were based on the resemblance, either real or fancied, to some familiar object. The fact that these names show late American historical connections does not mean that they were created at that time. The same old pattern with its origin in Europe was renamed by the weaver to modernize it. Geographic and historical names include:

England Beauty	Downfall of Paris
Monmouth	London Beauty
Governor's Garden	King's Flower
Southern Beauty	Queen's Delight
Tennessee Flower	Western Beauty
Indian Trouble	Jackson's Purchase
Federal Knot	Federal City
Indian Wars	Whig Rose

Those bearing resemblance to familiar objects or merely fanciful include:

Double Bow Knot	Snail Trail and Cat Tracks
Church Windows	True Love's Vine
Rose in the Bush	Irish Chain
Snowball	Wheel of Fortune
Blooming Leaf	Snow Drop
Ladies' Delight	Bachelor's Button
Ladies' Fancy	Fox Trail
Free Mason and Felicity	Young Man's Delight
Cards and Wheels	Bachelor Among the Girls
Nine Snowballs	Forsaken Lover
Chariot Wheel	Gentleman's Fancy
Blazing Star	
Pine Bloom	

The overshot weave is a three-thread construction. There is one warp, usually a two-ply linen or cotton; a binder weft, usually the same material as the warp, but often a single ply and slightly smaller in grist; and the pattern weft, which is a coloured woollen yarn. This may be either single or two-ply, and is always larger than either the warp or the binder weft. The pattern of the overshot is three-tone: dark, light, and half-tone. The dark spots or blocks which form the real design are composed of several pattern wefts where they overlie the basic cotton or linen ground. These are called 'floats', 'skips', or 'overshots'. The light spots are the basic ground fabric where the pattern threads lie below it, and the half-tones are formed between the dark and light spots where the pattern weft is bound closely into the ground. Most frequently this type of coverlet is in a four-block pattern. The rectangular blocks may vary in size and proportion, but all the blocks in a horizontal row are the same height, and all the blocks in a vertical row are the same width in any single piece of weaving. This weave was used in all of the Colonies, and travelled westward with the settlers into the new states. Many of these coverlets are still in existence, but most of those surviving were woven in the first half of the nineteenth century.

Coverlets were sometimes woven in the summer-and-winter weave, but this weave did not have as wide a distribution geographically as the overshot weave. These are found most often in New York and Pennsylvania. The opinion of many is that this weave was either brought to America by German immigrants of the early eighteenth century or was developed by them after arrival. A weave closely resembling it and in identical patterns was common in the Schleswig–Holstein area in the seventeenth and eighteenth centuries, where it was used for bed curtains.

Summer-and-winter weave produces a fabric which is two-toned and reversible. On the side where the coloured woollen pattern weft predominates it is dark and on the reverse side, where the light warp and binder weft predominate, it is light. From this it receives its name. It is in fact a small overshot weave in blocks which may be of any size and proportion and may overlap or combine. The pattern is still geometric, but it may be more intricate than the overshot. The fabric is extremely flexible, and the threads being so intimately bound together, it is structurally more sound and wears better than the overshot weave.

The same colours are found in this weave as in the others, since they were the ones commonly available. Indigo blue is the most common, followed by madder rust and rose. More than one colour of pattern weft is never used in summer-and-winter weave. This weave requires a loom slightly more elaborate than the overshot weave, and therefore was used only by the more experienced home weaver. It is doubtful that it was often the product of the professional. These coverlets were probably produced during the first twenty-five or thirty years of the nineteenth century.

Another weave sometimes encountered in Pennsylvania resembles summer-and-winter and can be woven with the same patterns. The blocks, however, show a pattern of bird's-eye weave. It is probable that this technique is an interpretation of the linen patterns found in the German weaving books.

Block or double woven geometric coverlets are among the most beautiful preserved today. These were undoubtedly most frequently the work of the professional craftsman, as few homes would have contained the elaborate loom required for their manufacture. According to the account books of these professionals, they were producing block coverlets during the period from 1820 to 1840. At this same period the same men were weaving the even more elaborately patterned flowered coverlets. These professional weavers were usually Scotsmen who immigrated to America after having already learned their trade. It is reasonable to assume that such weaves were in use in Scotland, but the patterns are identical with the ones used by the Germans for summer-and-winter weave and are to be found in the German weaving books of the eighteenth century as well as the Scottish weaving books of the early nineteenth century. In both of these published sources they seem to have been intended as patterns for linens.

In colour they follow the style of the day, most often in deep indigo-blue woollen yarn which was usually supplied by the housewife, combined with a natural-coloured cotton yarn which was factory spun and supplied by the weaver. Sometimes red and blue were used in the same coverlet, giving a red, white, and blue colouring.

This technique produces a fabric which is really a combination of two fabrics in one. One is a plain-woven coloured woollen, while the other is a plain-woven natural-coloured cotton. Rarely is the second of linen. Two warps are required on the loom, and these are woven together in such a way that the design is produced by the interchanging of the two basic fabrics. It is completely reversible, a block on the one side of coloured woollen fabric being backed on the reverse by a block in natural cotton. Like the summer-and-winter weave, these blocks may overlap and combine, but the pattern is always geometric. Block coverlets, like summer-and-winter and overshot, were woven on the narrow loom; so that two strips were always necessary to produce a full-width coverlet.

The fancy flowered coverlets, now usually called Jacquard coverlets, were always the work of the professional weaver who often referred to them as carpet coverlets. Many of these were woven by Scottish weavers who were already weavers of carpets in the same double weave and with similar patterns. The German weavers of Pennsylvania also produced many of them. They were being woven as early as 1818 in New York State, but the earliest dated one to come to light so far is marked 1821. They were probably first woven in New York and Pennsylvania and later in Kentucky, Ohio, Indiana, and Illinois. In the opinion of some students the coverlets woven during the most active period, the 1830s and 1840s, were woven on the drawloom; while later ones were woven on hand-operated looms with the help of the Jacquard attachment. It was not too difficult to install the Jacquard attachment on the old drawloom, but there was a patent carpet loom used in Scotland which was earlier than the Jacquard and might very well have been in use in America in the 1830s. Many of these flowered coverlets were certainly woven by power in full width on looms with Jacquard attachments in the 1860s and 1870s. These later coverlets have one-piece patterns, usually with a large central medallion surrounded with elaborate borders. The designs are finer and less clear cut than the earlier coverlets. In this late period appear the scarlet-red coverlets which are suitable for rooms decorated in the Victorian manner.

The earliest of these flowered coverlets are always in the double weave, but instead of being confined to geometric patterns, the weaver could use naturalistic designs. While many weavers used the same repeating medallion designs for the central portion of the coverlet, making one wonder if there were not a published pattern book now unknown, the borders were often most individual in treatment. These might contain designs of eagles, scrolls, festoons, flowers, birds, trees, buildings, portraits, or mottoes, and the weaver could include the name of the person for whom the coverlet was woven, the date, the place, and his own signature. The earliest ones are likely to be more restrained in design and more pleasing to the eye.

Many of these coverlets produced in Pennsylvania and westward in Kentucky, Ohio, and Indiana during the 1830s and 1840s are not in double weave but in a single or damask weave. These are often in two or more colours of woollen yarn. Damask table linens in cotton and linen and cotton and wool were produced by some New York weavers in the identical designs of their double-woven coverlets.

Needlework and Embroidery other than American

The intimate and personal quality of embroidery and needlework has a wide appeal to the average collector, and examples of ancestral skill, handed down from generation to generation, often form the basis of a collection. Embroidered pictures, small screens, and samplers, which can adorn the walls of a home, are naturally more popular than less exhibitable objects. Complete quilts and coverlets are usually more expensive, and do not so readily come within the range of the small private collector. Yet even fragmentary examples of old embroidery have their interest, and almost all types of embroidery can be put to decorative uses.

A study of the embroidery and needlework of all countries and periods shows that while each group has its own special characteristics, certain designs, colouring, and stitchery are common to many of them, even in the case of widely separated countries. Tracing the possible sources of pattern and the interpenetration of influences can be a fascinating and rewarding study.

The type of stitch employed is generally regulated by the type of design. For example, geometric patterns are usually worked in cross or tent stitch on canvas or on a loosely woven material in which the

Open wire basket, satin and threaded coloured beads, English, *c.* 1670. Lady Lever Art Gallery

warp and weft threads can be counted to facilitate the accurate working of the pattern. The bewildering number of stitches listed in any encyclopedia of embroidery is somewhat misleading. The variety of stitches is, in fact, not so great as it would at first appear. The vast majority are nothing more than slight variations of a comparatively few basic stitches or the combination of two simple stitches. Some of the most effective embroidery is worked only in one simple stitch and, generally speaking, great variety of both stitches and colour do not give satisfactory results. A study of fine examples of embroidery will generally reveal that where a great variety of stitches is used only one colour is employed, as in English whitework. Alternatively, where many colours are employed only one stitch is used, as in the fine chain-stitch embroidery of the Dutch East Indies.

Embroidery is one of the oldest of the applied arts, but the average collector is little concerned with the embroidery of antiquity, or even of the Middle Ages. In England there is a flourishing tradition of domestic embroidery from the sixteenth century onwards.

Below Stool cover, damask, woven in silk and silver and gilt strips with appliqué embroidery, English, late 19th century. Victoria & Albert Museum

Bottom Prayer-book cushion, silk petit-point (tent stitch). Worked to commemorate the defeat of the Armada in 1588 and the discovery of the Gunpowder Plot in 1605, English, *c.* 1606. Lady Lever Art Gallery

Elizabethan embroidery is essentially English in character, and most of the designs are based on typically English flowers – roses, carnations, pansies, honeysuckle, and many others, interspersed with butterflies and insects. Embroidery was widely used to decorate bodices, coifs, night caps, and other items of costume and for domestic articles such as hangings, pillowcases, and cushion covers. Another class of Elizabethan embroidery consisted of table and floor carpets embroidered in tent stitch on canvas, but, unlike the smaller articles, many of these were the work of professional embroiderers.

The chief feature of Stuart embroidery is the bed curtains and hangings worked in crewel wools on a linen and cotton twill. The 'tree of life', based on Indian models, was the favourite pattern. Stumpwork was widely used during this period to decorate caskets and mirror frames and for embroidered pictures. Quilting reached a high standard during the late seventeenth and early eighteenth centuries, and was widely used for household articles and for dress. A great variety of embroidery is found throughout the eighteenth century, both for costume and furnishing. Silk generally replaced wool as the most popular medium, with a consequent refinement of both design and execution. Elaborately embroidered quilts and pillowcases, often made in sets, are especially characteristic. In the first half of the century embroidered aprons were extremely popular, and throughout the century embroidery was widely used to decorate waistcoats.

In France the general development of embroidery was similar to that in England, but there were certain marked differences in style and technique. For example, in the sixteenth century more use was made of applied work, and in the eighteenth century *chinoiserie* and rococo styles had a greater influence on embroidery than in England. Towards the end of the eighteenth century chenille embroidery and tambour work had a considerable vogue in France.

A great variety of embroidery was produced in Italy. In the sixteenth century embroidered linen bands (*see* Assisi work) and various kinds of cutwork are characteristic. Another type of embroidery was worked in floss silks on a net ground. Applied work reached a high standard in Italy, particularly for pilaster hangings. In the seventeenth century altar frontals, chalice veils, and vestments were produced in large numbers, usually with elaborate floral designs in silk and gold thread. The widespread use of laid work is also characteristic of Italian embroidery.

Spanish embroidery has much in common with Italian work, but the general tendency was to use brighter colours, and Moorish influences are often apparent. The use of painting on the satin to obtain effects of shading and a greater variety of colours is a feature of Spanish applied work. A type of embroidery produced both in Spain and Portugal during the sixteenth and seventeenth centuries was worked in closely twisted cord or string, which was usually brown or white. The cord was often plaited or knotted or woven in basket-like effects to give greater variety of texture. The designs were geometrical or floral.

The most notable German embroideries date from the fourteenth and fifteenth centuries. These are, of course, very rare and cannot readily be collected. They consist mainly of church furnishings and are executed in undyed linen thread on a linen ground. The subjects are mostly religious. Other embroideries in coloured silks imitated the well-known Cologne orphreys, which were woven in silk and gold thread.

Both the Near and Far East have produced a

Mirror frame of silver thread, purl, chenille and silks, framed in tortoiseshell, English, *c.* 1665. Lady Lever Art Gallery

wealth of notable embroidery, and most of the main groups are dealt with under separate countries. There is, in fact, no country in the world where embroidery has not flourished at one time or another either as a simple peasant art or on a more sophisticated level. The field of embroidery and needlework is so vast that it has only been possible briefly to touch upon some of the main points. But even such a brief survey gives a hint of the amazing variety of work that can be collected.

Glossary

Algerian embroidery. The most characteristic feature is the colour scheme, which is in subdued mauves and purple. The motifs of palmettes, flowers, and scrolls recall the Turkish work of Asia Minor. Large hangings for the doorways opening on to the inner courtyard of the house were made in three long panels joined together by coloured silk ribbons. Similar patterns decorated towel scarves, used by Algerian women to dry their hair, and hooded head scarves. The finest embroideries date from the eighteenth or early nineteenth centuries. Satin, brick, and double-running stitches are most frequently found, often with the addition of eyelet holes.

Algerian palmette

American patchwork. American patchwork quilts of the eighteenth and nineteenth centuries show an amazing variety of patterns of much greater elaboration than English examples. There are over three hundred named designs, many of them with a religious origin. One of the most striking and commonest traditional patterns is the 'Star of Bethlehem', an eight-pointed star worked either as a single central motif surrounded by smaller stars or as a number of small stars of equal size regularly arranged on a white ground. Other quilts were made with applied coloured patches on white grounds elaborately quilted with geometrical, feather, or floral designs.

Applied work. The sewing of patches on to the surface of a material so that they form a pattern. The edges of the pattern are usually outlined by embroidery. In the Middle Ages applied work was used as a cheaper substitute for tapestry, and during the Renaissance the figured brocades and velvets were imitated by this method. In the sixteenth and seventeenth centuries applied work was widely used for altar frontals and vestments, for hangings, chair covers, and horse trappings. Outstanding were the pilaster hangings, usually of plain velvet with appliqué of satin outlined by couching, which were made in Italy and Spain. In England during the sixteenth and seventeenth centuries motifs of animals, floral sprigs, and insects were worked in tent stitch on canvas and then cut out and applied to cushion covers and hangings. Needlepoint lace motifs, in silk and metal thread, were similarly applied to workboxes and embroidered pictures.

Aprons. Embroidered aprons were introduced in France as part of fashionable attire during the last quarter of the seventeenth century, and were popular in England during the first half of the eighteenth. The aprons are usually of cream or yellow silk with scalloped edges, embroidered in coloured silks and metal thread, chiefly with floral designs. Muslin and whitework aprons are also found.

Assisi work. A type of embroidery (so-called from the modern embroidery made in Assisi) in which the ground is covered in long-armed cross stitch, leaving the pattern reserved in plain linen. It is usually found in borders or strips, and the earliest examples date from the sixteenth century. The patterns include formal designs in typical Renaissance style, figure subjects, including hunting scenes, and stylized birds and animals. Red silk is most commonly used, but green and brown are also found. A similar type of embroidery comes from Azemmour in Morocco, but the designs are more geometric, often of birds, and somewhat bolder in style.

Beadwork. The earliest surviving English beadwork dates from the seventeenth century. Particularly interesting are the shallow baskets, almost tray-shaped, with a flat bottom and sloping sides, decorated entirely with small coloured glass beads sewn on linen canvas. Pictorial subjects, similar to those of the contemporary embroidered pictures, are most common. Caskets were also decorated in this manner, and some have miniature gardens inside the lid with freestanding flowers made of glass beads mounted on wire. Beadwork purses are also found during the seventeenth, eighteenth, and early nineteenth centuries. Beadwork was commonly used to decorate garters.

Bed valances. Valances or pelmets for four-poster beds are usually found in sets of three, the average

Bead-work picture, 18th century. Mallett & Son, London

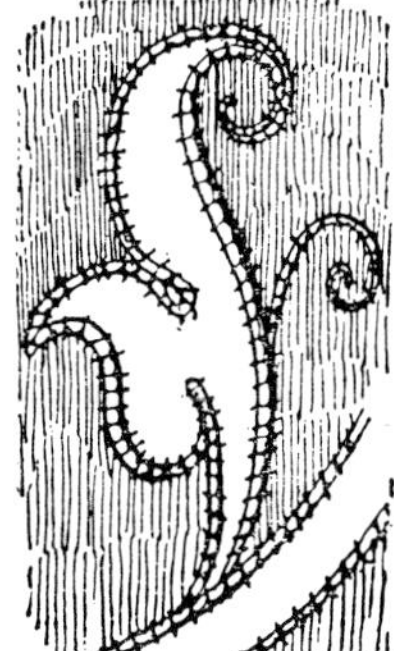

Applied work

length being about 6 ft 6 ins (198.2 cm), the depth 1 ft 8 ins (50.8 cm). Elizabethan bed valances often depict religious or mythological subjects, worked in tent stitch on canvas. In the second half of the seventeenth century valances were embroidered in crewel wools to match the bed curtains.

Berlin woolwork. A type of embroidery in coloured worsteds on canvas in which designs printed on squared paper were copied by counting the squares of the canvas. The designs were published in Berlin and were first imported into England about 1810, but did not reach the country in large numbers until after 1830, the fashion reaching its height about the middle of the century. The first designs were often worked in silk or glass beads, but the garishly coloured worsteds imported from Berlin (which gave the work its name) became the general medium, and tent or cross stitch the usual method of execution. The designs were usually of flowers, depicted with great naturalism, but pictorial subjects, frequently biblical, were also popular. Samplers on long strips of canvas showing various patterns worked in Berlin wools are also found.

Blackwork. The name given to a type of Elizabethan embroidery worked in black silk on linen. It was used widely for both household articles and costume, particularly on long pillow covers, bodices, coifs, and night caps. Gold thread is often found in conjunction with blackwork, and coiling-stem designs were most frequently used. Elaborate diaper filling patterns, worked in back stitch, are a feature of this work, and the effect is often similar to the woodblock-printed lining papers of the period. Blackwork is also found in Spain.

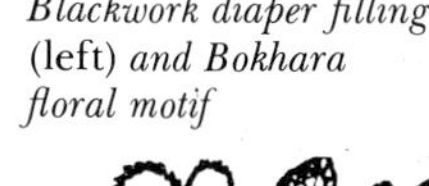

Blackwork diaper filling (left) *and Bokhara floral motif*

Panel embroidered in Berlin wools in cross stitch on white flannel ground, *c.* 1850. Victoria & Albert Museum

Bokhara work. The term generally applied to the bright-coloured embroideries of western Turkestan. Large floral sprays or a diapered ground filled with flowers are the most common patterns, and diagonally laid Oriental stitch and chain stitch are most frequently used. Large coverlets and divan covers are most common, and the finest specimens date from the eighteenth century, although nineteenth-century examples are more numerous.

Bookbindings. Embroidered bookbindings were produced in England and Europe as early as the sixteenth century, but most surviving examples date from the seventeenth. The finest examples are usually of French or English origin, but Dutch and Flemish bindings also reached a high standard, and elaborate examples were produced in Italy. Early seventeenth-century bindings in England were often of petit-point embroidery in coloured silks on a silver-thread ground. Later examples were usually on white satin embroidered in silks and gold thread and enriched with sequins and pearls. A common scheme of decoration was an oval portrait medallion surrounded by floral sprigs, birds, and insects, the spine divided into four or five compartments with a flower, insect, or animal in each. The books are set either with silver clasps, or single or double ties of ribbon of plaited silk. In England the fashion for embroidered bindings died out at the end of the seventeenth century, but in France it continued until about 1810.

Broderie anglaise. A type of whitework (known also as Ayrshire, Eyelet, Madeira, or Swiss work) in which open spaces are cut or punched with a stiletto. The edges of the holes are then overcast. The finest specimens of this type of work, which was used chiefly for sleeve frills, baby clothes, and underwear, were produced in the late eighteenth or early nineteenth centuries.

Caskets. Embroidered caskets were more common in England during the seventeenth century than on the Continent, and were produced to hold toilet articles, jewels, writing materials, and as workboxes. Stumpwork, beadwork, and petit point were most generally employed, and the subjects are similar to those of the embroidered pictures of the period. In France, Germany, Spain, and Italy embroidered caskets decorated with pearls are also found.

Chinese embroidery. Although embroidery has flourished in China for centuries, most of the existing specimens date from the eighteenth or nineteenth centuries. Embroidery plays an important part in Chinese costume. The most magnificent are the Imperial court robes of the Manchu Dynasty (1759–1912). The Emperor's dragon robes were usually yellow with four front-facing dragons on the upper part and five profile dragons on the lower, and in addition the Twelve Symbols, fire-coloured clouds, and the eight Buddhist symbols. Only the Emperor was allowed to wear all twelve symbols – the sun, constellation, moon, mountain, dragon, flowery bird, temple cups, water weed, millet, fire, axe, and the symbol of distinction. The heir apparent had a similar robe but without the twelve symbols, and princes of the first to fourth degrees wore similar robes to the heir apparent. An interesting type of summer robe was embroidered on gauze in the Chinese equivalents of tent and Florentine stitches, which gave the effect of a woven fabric. In addition to the robes worn by the princes, the eighteen high-ranking officials of the Court had special insignia on their robes, usually known as Mandarin squares. The nine civil officials had birds on their squares and were designated, in descending order, by a white crane, golden pheasant, peacock, wild goose, silver pheasant, Eastern egret, Mandarin duck, quail, and Paradise flycatcher. The nine military insignia were animals – a unicorn, leopard, panther, tiger, black bear, mottled bear, tiger cat, seal, and rhinoceros. Many other embroidered robes are found – the informal court robes, theatrical and priest robes. Ladies' robes were often embroidered with butterflies, the emblems of happiness. It is not possible to go into the symbolism of many of the motifs found in Chinese embroidery, but the symbols most frequently found are the Buddhist 'Eight Emblems of Happy Augury' and the Taoist 'Attributes of the Eight Immortals'. The former are the parasol, the fish of gold, the vase, the lotus, the seashell, the mystic diagram, the standard, and the wheel. The latter are the fan, the sword, the gourd, the castanets, the flower basket, the bamboo tube and rods, the flute, and the lotus. The dragon and the phoenix, the mythical bird of China, are among the most popular decorative motifs. Flowers of all kinds are found, the commonest being the magnolia, prunus blossom, orchid, chrysanthemum, peony, narcissus, and lotus. A variety of stitches is found in Chinese embroidery, including French knots (often known as Peking stitch), satin stitch, and a special kind of couching, which consists of twisting two silk threads together, which gives the effect of a fine knobbly cord. Appliqué is also found, particularly on fan cases, cushions, and purses. The separate motifs are sometimes worked on stiffened gauze or tough paper and then applied to the ground. Sleeve bands, long narrow strips of silk or satin about 3½ inches (9 cm) wide, show a remarkable variety of pattern. Landscape scenes, figure subjects, and floral designs are embroidered in coloured silks or sometimes only in couched gold thread. Canton embroidery is remarkable for its naturalism and is worked in brightly coloured floss silks, mainly in satin and split stitches. A type of embroidery in black or dark-blue silk or cotton on linen comes from Yunnan Province.

Casket with rising lid and two doors. Flat couched stitch in coloured floss silks, English, *c.* 1665. Lady Lever Art Gallery

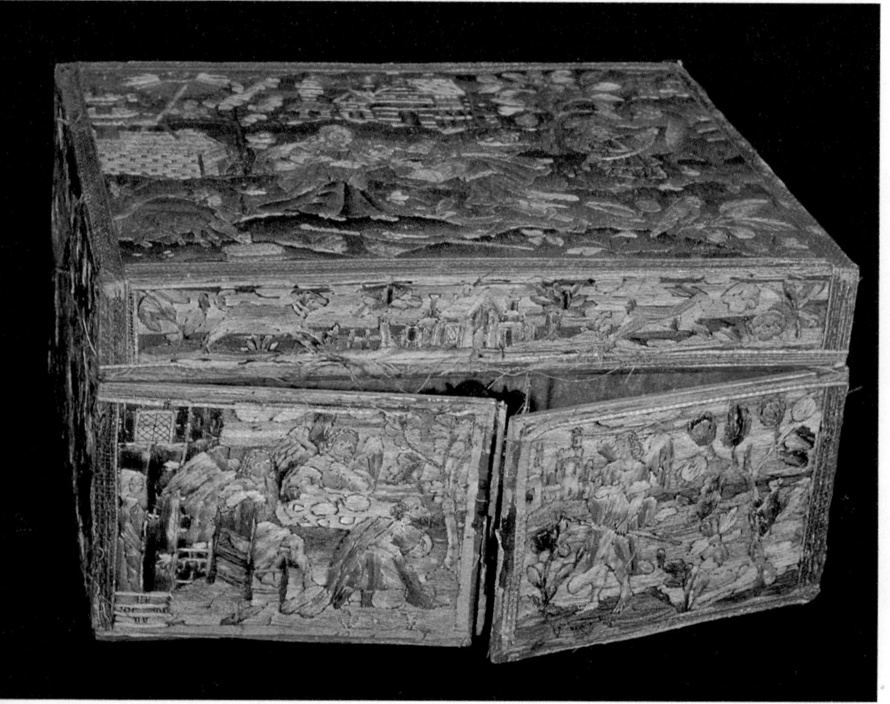

Coif (not made up)

Coif. A close-fitting cap formed of one piece of embroidery seamed along the top of the head. These are often found unpicked or not made up, and are therefore difficult to recognize. The Elizabethan coifs were embroidered in coloured silks and metal thread, or in black silk, in patterns of coiling stems or less frequently with diaper patterns.

Colfichet. The name given to small embroidered pictures, originating in Italy in the late eighteenth century, worked in floss silks on paper so that each side was alike. They were used either as bookmarkers or placed between two sheets of glass.

Cretan embroidery. Most surviving Cretan embroidery is of the eighteenth century. Embroidered skirts are the most characteristic feature, the embroidery consisting of a deep frieze worked round the lower edge in brightly coloured floss silks. The patterns are a mixture of floral motifs, conventional vases of flowers, human figures, and animals. There is a combination of Italian and Turkish influences. The carnation is the most popular flower, and the siren, prevalent in the folklore and art of Italy, appears frequently. Originally, in the earliest Cretan embroideries, the siren had two fish-like tails which curled upwards and were grasped one in each hand, but with frequent copying the tails often became carnations, and the siren a human being with legs and feet. Covers and pillowcases with similar designs are also found, sometimes with a pair of human figures in the centre surrounded by a floral border. A great variety of stitches, including Cretan feather, herring-bone, satin, stem and chain stitch were employed. The designs are mostly worked in many bright colours, but monochrome schemes, usually in red or dark blue, are also found.

Crewelwork. Crewelwork is embroidery in thin worsteds, and is the term usually applied to the curtains and bed hangings of linen and cotton twill embroidered in coloured wools during the second half of the seventeenth century. This type of work is often called Jacobean embroidery. The designs were based on the printed cotton 'palampores' (chintz hangings) which were imported into England at that time. The tree of life, with waving stems of acanthus-like foliage rising from a hillocked ground, was the most popular pattern. The embroidery was either polychrome or worked entirely in shades of green which has often faded to a dull indigo. Coiling stems and an asparagus pattern are also found.

Dutch East Indian embroidery. Embroidered coverlets were produced in the Dutch East Indies in the late seventeenth and early eighteenth centuries. The designs copied the painted chintzes of the period, and the embroidery, worked entirely in chain stitch in coloured silks, is so fine that at a first glance it appears like a printed cotton. Dresses and skirts made of similarly embroidered material are also found.

Embroidered pictures. A great variety of embroidered pictures is found in England from the mid-seventeenth century onwards. Pictorial compositions as part of the decoration of a cushion or valance are not uncommon earlier, but it was not until later that the fashion for working purely decorative pictures as an end in itself was evolved. Subjects from the Old Testament were most popular, also allegorical figures of the Virtues, Vices or the Senses, or a king and a queen. Stumpwork was the most popular medium for pictures during the second half of

Needlework picture depicting a girl with lion, watercolour on silk, late 18th century

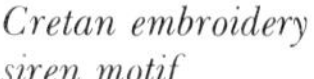

Cretan embroidery siren motif

Crewelwork asparagus pattern

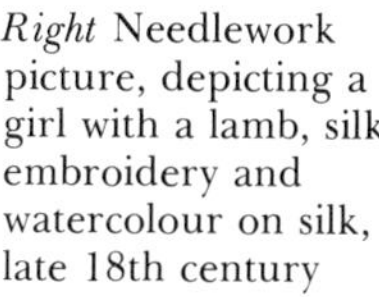

Right Needlework picture, depicting a girl with a lamb, silk embroidery and watercolour on silk, late 18th century

the seventeenth century, but beadwork was also employed.

The pictures of the early eighteenth century are generally worked in tent stitch on canvas, and pastoral or *chinoiserie* subjects are most common. During the second half of the eighteenth century subjects were mostly taken from popular paintings or engravings. The designs were either printed or drawn on the material. Portions of the background and the faces and hands of the figures were painted in water-colours and the rest of the design worked in coloured silks. Other pictures were worked in black silk, or even hair, in fine stitches, to simulate etchings. Simple landscape subjects or portraits of eminent people are most common.

During the third quarter of the eighteenth century copies of oil paintings in coloured wools were made by industrious needlewomen, the most famous being Miss Linwood. The introduction of Berlin woolwork gave rise to embroidered pictures on squared canvas, and by about 1830 these had virtually eclipsed all other types.

Greek Islands embroidery. *See also* Cretan embroidery.

The embroidery of the Greek Islands may be classed as peasant embroidery inasmuch as it was made by the women for their own use and not intended for sale. Although each island, or group of islands, had its own individual characteristic patterns, intermarriage brought a pattern from one island to another, and varieties of the same pattern are found in different places. Most existing specimens date from the eighteenth or early nineteenth centuries. The group can best be subdivided as follows.

Ionian Islands. This group consists mainly of bedspreads, bolsters, and pillowcases worked in fine cross stitch and drawnwork. The designs consist of stylized birds, particularly peacocks, and deer, together with floral and purely decorative motifs. Red, blue, green, and yellow are the dominant colours, and the designs show a marked Italian influence. Another group of bed furnishings are worked in fine split and darning stitches, with rich floral patterns intermingled with human figures, double eagles, parrots, cocks, and sometimes ships. These show a Turkish influence, and are somewhat similar to the work produced at Skyros (*see below*).

Epirus. The embroideries produced in the Epirus, particularly at Yannina, the principal town, are characterized by floral motifs, mostly variations of the Turkish rose spray, worked mainly in herringbone stitch.

The Cyclades. Most characteristic are the bed curtains, valances, and pillowcases. The main patterns are variations of two basic motifs known as the 'Queen Pattern' and 'King Pattern'. These patterns are common throughout the Cyclades, but certain islands have distinctive features. Melos is characterized by the use of the Queen Pattern, worked entirely in red silk, while at Amorgos the King Pattern is dominant. Naxos is characterized by the use of a leaf-and-star diaper, derived from the King Pattern, worked chiefly in red silk.

Dodecanese. The embroidery of Rhodes, the chief island, is worked in thick red and green floss silks in cross stitch. The stitch is not pulled tight on the right side of the work, which gives the embroidery a slightly raised appearance. Embroidered bed tents are the main feature of Kos, where the chief motif is the Glastra, combined with Maltese crosses and stars. The Glastra is also found at Rhodes. Patmos employs a version of the Cycladic King pattern.

Dodecanese Glastra motif

North Greek Islands Skyros figure

Cyclades Queen Pattern (top) *and King Pattern*

North Greek Islands (The Northern Sporades). The best-known embroidery of this group comes from Skyros. Bedspreads and pillowcases are embroidered with lively designs of human figures, animals and birds, particularly cocks and peacocks, and floral motifs. The designs have a distinct Oriental flavour and recall the patterns of later Turkish faïence.

Hollie work. A type of whitework embroidery popular during the Georgian period, particularly for babies' clothes and bonnets. It was worked on fine linen lawn or cambric in white thread. Delicate openwork patterns, worked without any foundation in the manner of needlepoint lace, were inserted into holes cut in the material, which were previously edged with buttonhole stitch. Alternatively, the threads of the ground material were drawn out one way only and the pattern worked on the remaining threads.

Indian embroidery. The finest existing Indian embroideries date from the Mughal period, and show a marked Persian influence, but the drawing and colouring of the floral motifs is usually bolder. The group comprises articles of costume, prayer mats, and wall hangings. In the late seventeenth and early eighteenth centuries embroidered coverlets and hangings were produced for export in large numbers. The flowering-tree motif was the most popular, but many of the designs were adapted to suit European tastes and were worked from patterns sent out by the English, French, and Dutch trading companies. Quilted bedspreads, with designs showing strong Persian influence, were also made. In the early nineteenth century elaborately embroidered shawls were made in Kashmir in imitation of the more costly handwoven variety. Most other types of Indian embroidery fall into the category of peasant art, being indigenous to local regions. A common feature of Sind, Cutch, and Kathiawar embroidery is the use of small circular insets of mirror glass. The Cutch embroideries are worked mainly in chain stitch with a needle like a crochet hook, and an interlaced stitch is also used. Articles of costume, trappings for cattle, and wall hangings are decorated with sprigged patterns and floral diapers, and a peacock motif is often incorporated into the design of skirt borders. The 'toran', a kind of pelmet with a series of tabs at the lower edge, is characteristic of Kathiawar, and a special feature is the almost universal habit of leaving a small corner of the work unfinished. A specialized type of work comes from Chamba. Elaborate pictorial designs, derived from the contemporary schools of hill painting, were embroidered on fine muslin in satin stitch in bright-coloured silks. A kind of whitework, known as Chikan, comes mainly from Uttar Pradesh in the Ganges Valley. Floral motifs, and patterns representing grains such as rice and millet, are worked on muslin in white cotton.

Jacobean embroidery. *See* Crewelwork.

Japanese embroidery. The art of embroidery was practised in Japan from the sixth century onwards, and reached a high standard of excellence, but most surviving examples must be assigned to the nineteenth century. The finest embroidery was used on the 'kimono', the loose, wide-sleeved robe worn by both sexes; the 'obi', the broad sash worn round the waist; and the 'fukasa', the embroidered squares which covered the lacquered boxes in which ceremonial presents were offered. The most characteristic stitches are satin, long and short (used particularly for realistic feather effects), couching, and knotted stitch (French knots). Appliqué is also used, and gold thread, consisting of strips of gilt paper twisted round a cotton or silk core, is used in conjunction with coloured silks or on its own. Painting is also combined with embroidery, and some materials are printed with a resist, or tie-dyed before being embroidered. Cranes, landscape, and floral subjects, particularly the chrysanthemum, are popular designs.

Long pillow covers. Long pillow covers, or 'pillow beres', to give them their contemporary name, unlike the cushion covers, were always worked on linen and were used in the bedroom. The most usual size for Elizabethan examples was about 35 by 20 inches (89 × 50.8 cm), and the back of the cover, which was left plain, has rarely survived. All-over patterns of the coiling-stem type were most popular, and 'blackwork' was frequently employed. In the late seventeenth and early eighteenth centuries pillow covers embroidered entirely in yellow silk are often found; also examples quilted in white linen thread or cotton.

Moroccan embroidery. In the eighteenth and nineteenth centuries practically every city in Morocco had its own characteristic type of embroidery. From Rabat come bolster- and pillowcases embroidered in floss silks, mostly dark blue, purple, and yellow. The designs are of highly conventionalized flowers very solidly worked in herring-bone, satin, and buttonhole stitches. The Tetuan embroideries, usually curtains, are worked in patterns which recall the artichoke or pomegranate motifs of Asia Minor. As in Algiers, mauve is the dominant colour. The embroideries of Fez, Meknez, and Sale have certain common features. The embroideries are reversible and are worked in double and quadruple running stitch, cross stitch, and basket stitch. The designs are geometrical, and are worked by counting the threads of the material. The group comprises mainly pillow- and bolstercases and samplers. Another group, worked in long-armed cross and back stitches, comes from Azemmour, and the designs show a marked similarity to the Italian and Spanish embroidered borders of the sixteenth century. The work of Chechaoen shows a marked Hispano–Moresque influence, and tile-like geometric patterns are worked on divan covers in stem, herring-bone, and cross stitches.

Opus Anglicanum. The name given to English ecclesiastical embroidery of the thirteenth and fourteenth centuries. The art of embroidery had flourished in England from Saxon times, but it reached its highest peak of excellence in the thirteenth century, and was known all over Europe as 'opus anglicanum'. The figures and other details are mostly worked in fine split stitch with backgrounds of couched work. A great deal of 'opus anglicanum' was exported to the Continent, where some of it still remains. Towards the middle of the fourteenth century the standard of both design and execution began to decline.

Patchwork quilts. *See also* American patchwork and Resht work.

In England patchwork quilts did not originate until the eighteenth century, and most surviving examples date from the end of the eighteenth or the early nineteenth centuries. Most patchwork patterns were geometrical or formal, such as the 'honeycomb', which was composed entirely of hexagons, and was the most popular design. Other patterns, such as the 'shell' and various 'feather' patterns, were taken from traditional quilting designs. True patchwork consists of a mosaic of fragments of materials sewn edge to edge, but some so-called 'patchwork' quilts are, in fact, applied work, as, for example, are those quilts where floral motifs are cut out from chintzes and applied to the ground of the quilt.

Persian embroidery. *See also* Resht and Bokhara.

No Persian embroidery of a date earlier than the sixteenth century has survived, and most existing specimens date from the seventeenth to the nineteenth centuries. The embroideries may be divided into three main classes: (1) Covers from northwest Persia embroidered in coloured silks, mainly in double darning stitch on cotton. The embroidery covers the whole ground, and the patterns of hooked and angular arabesques and medallions recall the designs of Caucasian rugs. Other covers, worked in the same technique, have patterns of figures, animals, and flowers of similar design to the contemporary 'hunting' carpets, brocades, and tilework. (2) Nakshe (women's trousering). These rectangular panels are of cotton, embroidered in coloured silks in diagonal parallel bands of floral patterns. Woven Nakshe are also found, and the embroidered type followed the designs of the more expensive brocade. (3) Prayer mats and bathmats worked in coloured silks, with crimson and green predominating, on a white ground, which is usually quilted. The patterns are floral, and a common design is a central medallion surrounded by a network of flowering plants, the whole enclosed in a running floral border.

Pincushions. Rectangular embroidered pincushions, about 10 by 6 inches (25.4 × 15.2 cm), were popular in England from about 1600 to 1700. They were mostly of linen, embroidered in silk and metal thread in tent stitch or in silk in rococo stitch, with designs of floral sprigs. Those which are studded with pins on the reverse side, arranged in a pattern and often with the date, were probably used as christening presents. Smaller pincushions are often found in the workboxes of the period.

Purses. English embroidered purses of the sixteenth and seventeenth centuries are usually flat and about 5 inches (12.7 cm) square, fastened by a double drawstring at the top. The ground is canvas, usually embroidered in tent or cross stitches in coloured silks and metal thread. Coiling tendrils with typical English flowers are the commonest patterns. Embroidered leather purses of this date are much rarer. Beadwork purses are also found in the seventeenth century. Mottoes are common on French purses, but are rare on English examples. In the eighteenth century purses became more commonplace, and with the introduction of the knitted or crocheted stocking purse embroidered purses died out.

Quilts. *See also* Patchwork.

A quilt is a coverlet with a layer of wool, flock, or down between two pieces of material with lines of stitching, usually back stitch, passing through the three layers. In England quilting is a traditional craft, and it reached the height of popularity and excellence in the seventeenth and eighteenth centuries.

During the first half of the seventeenth century quilted doublets and breeches were worn, and during the eighteenth century quilted satin petticoats were fashionable. Quilted bed coverlets were made in great numbers from the late seventeenth century onwards. In addition to the pattern formed by the quilting stitch, which was sometimes purely geometrical, sometimes of elaborate floral arabesques, the quilts were often further ornamented by embroidery in coloured silks. In the late seventeenth and early eighteenth centuries coverlets and pillowcases were often quilted entirely in yellow silk. Others had a small quilted diaper background with floral or *chinoiserie* motifs embroidered in coloured silks.

Another type is 'corded' quilting (often known as Italian quilting, although there is no evidence to support an Italian origin). This type of quilting, employed for decorative rather than utilitarian purposes, was extremely popular in England during the eighteenth century. Two layers of material, usually fine white linen, were sewn together in an elaborate design, often of scrolling arabesques worked by means of two parallel rows of stitching about a quarter of an inch apart. A cord was then inserted between the two rows of stitching through small holes cut in the back of the material. Quilting was also practised in most European countries, notably Sicily and Portugal, and in Oriental countries, particularly India and Persia.

Sampler by Elizabeth Lawson, American, 1833

Corded quilting

Raised work. *See* Stumpwork.

Resht work. A type of mosaic patchwork produced at Resht, Persia, during the eighteenth and nineteenth centuries for covers and prayer rugs. The designs are inlaid in coloured felts with outlines and details worked in coloured silks in chain stitch and couched work. Inferior examples are often not true patchwork, as the small pieces are applied to the ground and not inlaid. A similar type of work was produced in Ispahan.

Resht work

Ribbonwork. Embroidery in fine, narrow silk ribbons often combined with chenille thread and aerophane, a kind of muslin gauze. This type of work originated in the third quarter of the eighteenth century and was popular in both England and France, particularly for dress trimmings, bags, handscreens, and other small articles.

Sampler. An embroidered panel originally intended as a reference sheet of stitches and patterns and later as an exercise for a beginner.

English samplers. The earliest surviving English samplers date from the first half of the seventeenth century. These are worked on loosely woven linen in coloured silks and metal thread, and are generally shorter than those of the second half of the century. Tent, rococo, and plaited-braid stitches are common on these samplers, and the patterns are arranged in a haphazard way. Animals, birds, and floral motifs, similar to those found in contemporary bestiaries and herbals, are mixed with geometrical designs.

Right Sampler panel of needlepoint lace, comparable with contemporaneous raised embroidery, first half of 17th century. Victoria & Albert Museum

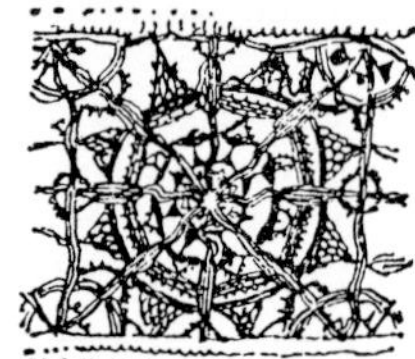

Reticella motif

In the second half of the seventeenth century the samplers are long and narrow on a finer linen, with the patterns formally arranged in horizontal rows. They are worked mainly in pale-coloured silks, chiefly in double-running, cross, and satin stitches with floral and geometrical borders showing a marked Italian influence. Another common type is the whitework sampler of cut- and openwork with designs taken from Italian *reticella* (a kind of needlepoint lace). Many late seventeenth-century samplers are a mixture of these two types.

By the eighteenth century the sampler had become a child's exercise. They are generally squarer in shape and are usually signed and dated. The introduction of the alphabet, religious texts, and mottoes or verses is common, and the colours are generally brighter. A more specialized type is the *Darning Sampler*, which was introduced into England from Holland about the middle of the century. These samplers are worked in darning stitches in ornamental patterns in coloured silks, mostly in squares, but sometimes in floral motifs. Another popular type from about 1770 until 1840 was the *Map Sampler*, that is an embroidered map worked in outline, usually in stem stitch in black silk, sometimes enclosed in a floral border.

German samplers. Samplers worked in horizontal bands, similar to English examples but often coarser in execution, are found in the latter half of the seventeenth century. Many of the designs, even in eighteenth- and nineteenth-century samplers, are taken from the pattern books of Hans Sibmacher, of Nuremberg, which were published in 1591 and 1604. An interesting variety with elaborate motifs worked in fine cross stitch in black cotton was produced in the Vierlande, near Hamburg, during the first half of the nineteenth century. The motifs included conventional flowers in pots and geometrical devices packed closely all over the sampler.

Dutch samplers. Most of the surviving samplers are of the eighteenth century, and are generally broad and square. Cross stitch is most frequently used, and the motifs, which are detached, include human figures, animals, buildings, and elaborate alphabets.

Spanish samplers. Seventeenth- and eighteenth-century Spanish samplers are usually large, either square or rectangular and worked in a series of conventional floral or geometrical borders. In the square samplers the borders are worked round all four sides and the centre is filled with sacred emblems, the Hapsburg eagle or a monogram. In the rectangular samplers the borders are worked in horizontal rows. Drawnwork bands are often included both in whitework and in coloured silks. Vivid colours are characteristic of Spanish samplers, but in many cases the silks have faded to pastel colours. Samplers similar to the English cross-stitch variety of the nineteenth century are also found in Spain.

Mexican samplers. These show similar designs to the Spanish, but they are generally smaller, and dated examples are usually of the nineteenth century. Whitework samplers, with flowers, animals, and initials, are also found in Mexico.

Moroccan samplers. See Moroccan embroidery.

Stomacher. The breastpiece of fifteenth- to eighteenth-century European female dress which was usually embroidered or jewelled. In some cases the stomacher formed part of the corset, when laced at the back, but when the corset was laced at the front the stomacher was made as a separate piece and pinned over the corset lacing. Few stomachers earlier than the eighteenth century have survived. The basic V shape of the stomacher, tapering to a point at the bottom, varied with successive changes in fashion until it died out with the introduction of the Empire style of dress. Continental examples are often elaborately shaped at the lower end, and French examples are usually more ornate than those of English origin.

Stumpwork (or Raised work). Raised embroidery, in which portions of the design were padded to give a three-dimensional effect, was widely used in England from about 1625 to the end of the century to decorate caskets, mirror frames, and bookbindings, and for embroidered pictures. The type of work originated from the raised ecclesiastical embroideries of the fifteenth and sixteenth centuries in Italy and Germany, and was used earlier for church work in England. Scenes from the Old Testament, the Judgment of Paris, and other mythological subjects, or representations of a king and queen were most popular. The interspaces of the designs were filled with quaint beasts, birds, and sprigs of flowers.

Turkeywork floral spray

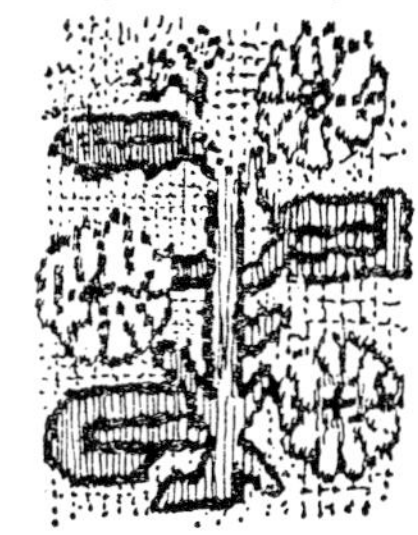

Turkish rose spray

Tambour work. A form of chain stitch, worked with a steel hook, popular in England and France during the late eighteenth and early nineteenth centuries. The name originated from the way the fabric to be embroidered was stretched over a round frame in the manner of a drumskin.

Turkeywork. This type of work, in knotted wool on linen, though strictly speaking carpet knotting, is usually classified as embroidery. It was popular in England during the seventeenth century, chiefly for chair backs and seats and loose cushions. The designs are usually of floral sprigs somewhat geometrically treated.

Turkish embroidery. Turkish embroidery may be divided into two main classes. The older type comprises curtains worked in darning stitch or couched work. The patterns consist of repeating designs of an ogival type with pomegranate or artichoke motifs, or vertical waving stems bearing conventionalized leaves and flowers. Red and blue are the predominant colours, and the darning stitches are usually worked diagonally to imitate the twill weave of the more costly silks. The second group consists of towels, kerchiefs, sashes, and bedspreads worked in coloured silks, gold and silver-gilt thread. The towel borders show an amazing variety of patterns, including the rose spray, vases of flowers, and various designs of mosques and cypresses. The earlier embroideries were worked mainly in double running stitch, but by the early nineteenth century other stitches were also used.

Victorian Embroidery

BERLIN WOOLWORK

In the field of embroidery the first thirty years of the Victorian era were dominated by the fashion for Berlin woolwork, which virtually ousted all other types of decorative needlework. The vogue was indeed so widespread that Mrs Henry Owen opens her preface to the *Illuminated Book of Needlework* (1847) with the words 'Embroidery, or as it is more often called Berlin wool-work . . .'.

The designs used for the work were handcoloured on squared paper and were copied stitch by stitch on to square-meshed canvas, each square of the design representing one stitch of embroidery. Its immense popularity no doubt lies in the fact that it required almost no skill in execution other than that of threading the needle and an ability to count. The first Berlin patterns were published in 1804; and although a few patterns reached England almost immediately, their use did not become widespread until 1831. In that year a Mr Wilks of Regent Street, London, began importing both the designs and the wools for working them direct from Berlin, including many designs which were prepared specially for the English market. According to the Countess of Wilton (*The Art of Needlework*, 1840), no fewer than 14,000 different patterns had been published in Berlin between 1804 and 1840.

Before Mr Wilks began importing the wools, which were manufactured in Gotha and dyed in Berlin, the patterns had been worked mainly in silks, but by 1840 the use of wool had become general.

Floral themes formed a high proportion of the patterns, particularly of those intended for upholstery. In the early 1840s wreaths and bunches of flowers were set against a light background. But by 1850 black backgrounds were more common and served to emphasize the harsh, brilliant colours of the wools. Oversize blooms – cabbage roses, huge bell-like flowers, arum and Victoria lilies – were drawn with great naturalism. The height of achievement was when, by means of elaborate shading, the flowers appeared to stand out in relief from the background. In most surviving examples, the full brilliance is now lost through fading, as the dyes used were fugitive.

Exotic birds, particularly gaily coloured parrots and macaws, were often introduced into the designs. A favourite combination, used for screen panels, was a life-size parrot, together with an ornate vase of mixed flowers drawn with the detail of a Dutch flower painting, and a basket of luscious fruit.

When used for upholstery there was little attempt to relate the design of the Berlin woolwork to the style of the furniture. In a few cases gothic ornamental detail was introduced to harmonize with a 'Gothic' chair, but, generally speaking, furniture in the prevailing styles of 'Louis Quatorze', 'Elizabethan', or François Ier', to mention only three, were adorned with the same type of naturalistic floral pattern. For upholstery the whole of the canvas was usually covered with stitchery, but many chairs, as well as screens, pictures, and piano fronts are found in which the Berlin woolwork appears to have been worked direct on a plain woollen ground. This effect was in fact achieved by tacking the canvas to a piece of plain material and taking the embroidery stitches through both canvas and material. When the design had been worked, by the usual method of counting the squares, the threads of the loosely woven canvas were withdrawn one by one, leaving the design on the plain material.

Although floral themes were most general for upholstery, engravings of popular contemporary paintings were widely used as subjects for the Berlin patterns and were used for embroidered pictures or fire screens. Landseer's paintings, particularly such subjects as *Dignity and Impudence* (1840) or the *Monarch of the Glen* (1851), made impressive wool pictures, but more modest subjects, of a single pet dog or cat reposing on a tasselled cushion, were even more popular. Many versions have survived, either as framed pictures or on the tops of footstools. Biblical subjects, particularly from the Old Testament, or famous historical paintings and romantic landscapes were among the most favoured designs. The Royal Family also received considerable attention from the Berlin pattern makers. The Prince of Wales (later King Edward VII) appeared in various guises. A panel, originally in the possession of Queen Mary, shows him in Highland dress, and the same picture was used for a printed cotton in 1847. Mrs Merryfield, an early critic of Berlin woolwork, writing in the *Art Journal* of 1855, deplores the use of 'the young Prince of Wales as a sailor depicted on a footstool so that on the stool he was lying on his back . . . and subjected to the indignity of being trodden

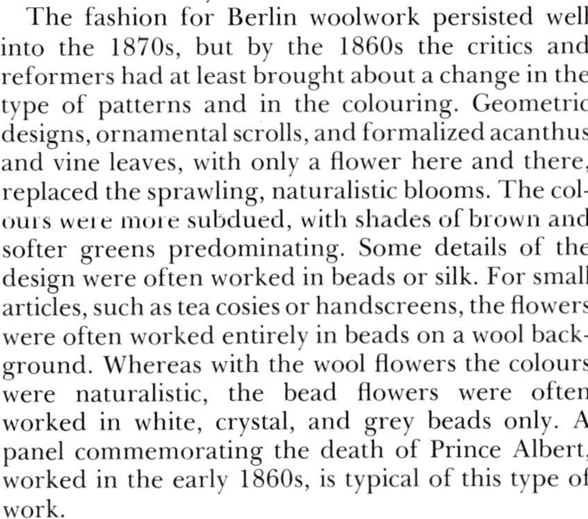

Chair back in Berlin wools, cross stitch on canvas, *c.* 1850. Victoria & Albert Museum

underfoot. In the good old days,' she continues, 'the greatest honour held forth to a conqueror was that he should set his foot upon the necks of princes . . . and his enemies should be his footstool . . . although we may acquit the English ladies of such disloyal thoughts and intentions.'

Berlin woolwork was mostly worked in cross or tent stitch, but other types of canvas stitches were employed, particularly after 1850. One of the most popular, known at the time as 'Leviathan' or 'railway stitch', because it covered the ground so quickly, was in fact no more than a double cross stitch worked on four squares of the canvas instead of one. A stitch known as 'perspective stitch' consisted of straight stitches of graduating lengths worked in different colours to form cubes, which appeared to project from the canvas.

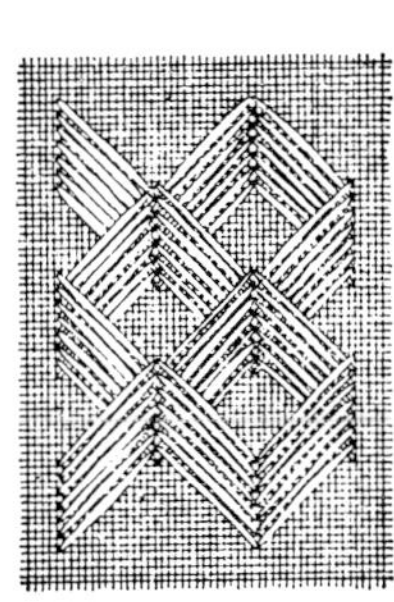

Perspective stitch

A popular variation, which combined the use of beads, silk, and chenille with the Berlin wools, was known as German embroidery. Raised Berlin woolwork, introduced in the 1840s, was another common variant. Parts of the design, either individual flowers, a bird, animal, or other details, were worked in plush stitch in a series of loops which were afterwards cut to give the effect of a thick pile carpet. A large picture of *Joseph presenting his Father to Pharaoh* (in the Victoria and Albert Museum) has the collars of the robes worked in this way to imitate thick fur.

The fashion for Berlin woolwork persisted well into the 1870s, but by the 1860s the critics and reformers had at least brought about a change in the type of patterns and in the colouring. Geometric designs, ornamental scrolls, and formalized acanthus and vine leaves, with only a flower here and there, replaced the sprawling, naturalistic blooms. The colours were more subdued, with shades of brown and softer greens predominating. Some details of the design were often worked in beads or silk. For small articles, such as tea cosies or handscreens, the flowers were often worked entirely in beads on a wool background. Whereas with the wool flowers the colours were naturalistic, the bead flowers were often worked in white, crystal, and grey beads only. A panel commemorating the death of Prince Albert, worked in the early 1860s, is typical of this type of work.

From the 1860s onwards, Berlin woolwork was less generally used for upholstery, except for small footstools or music stools, or for loose cushions for chairs and sofas. The printed patterns were also put to other uses. In the 1860s there was a brief fashion for antimacassars, made of coarse net, darned in colours from the Berlin patterns.

REVIVAL OF EMBROIDERY

Although Berlin woolwork was not finally ousted until after 1875, even in the 1840s critics were protesting at its deadening effect in debasing the art of embroidery. The earliest attacks came from ecclesiastical quarters. In the 1840s both the Anglican and Roman Catholic churches took a particular interest in embroidery. Many new churches were being built which needed altar furnishings and vestments. In the Catholic church the main instigator of the revival of church embroidery, based on medieval models, was A. W. N. Pugin (1812–52), the leading Gothic revivalist of the nineteenth century. In the Church of England the Oxford Movement played an important part in the revival, and the most prominent individual was the architect G. E. Street (1824–81), who, together with his sister and his friends the Blencowes, founded the Ladies Ecclesiastical Embroidery Society with the aim of producing church needlework of a high standard. By the 1850s there was a manifest improvement in the standard of ecclesiastical embroidery, but, although by this time the art periodicals had joined in the campaign against Berlin woolwork, there was little sign of a comparable advance on the domestic front. It was not until the 1870s, largely through the influence of William Morris (1834–96), that secular embroidery showed the same improvement.

'MORRIS' EMBROIDERIES

William Morris's first experiments in embroidery were made in 1855 when he was working in G. E. Street's office. He had an embroidery frame made and worsteds dyed to his specification and set about the task with his own hands. This experimental piece, a repeating pattern of flowering trees and birds with a scroll above bearing the words 'If I can' now hangs at Kelmscott Manor, Oxfordshire. Morris's wife, in a note (British Museum Add. MSS 45341) to Mackail, his first biographer, tells how he initiated her into the art soon after their marriage in 1859: 'He taught me the first principles of laying the stitches together closely so as to cover the ground smoothly and radiating them properly. Afterwards we studied old pieces and by unpicking etc. we learnt much.' Their first joint efforts consisted of a series of embroidered decorations for Red House, built for them by Philip Webb. The bedroom walls were hung with indigo-dyed serge, with flowers designed by Morris simply worked in crewel wools. For the dining room a more elaborate scheme of figure embroideries, designed to imitate tapestry, was attempted. This scheme consisted of twelve female figures, based on Chaucer's *Illustrious Women*, with trees between them and a running band of flowers at their feet, united by a background of coiling floral stems on a blue-serge ground. Only seven of the figures were completed, three of which survive made up into a screen for Lady Carlisle after they were removed from Red House. The figures were worked separately on a coarse linen mainly in crewel wools, but with some silk and gold thread, and cut out and applied to the woollen ground. Two unfinished panels, one of a nude female figure and one of a tree, were in the possession of the late Mr Halcrow Verstage. Two of the original designs are in the Victoria and Albert Museum: and were it not for the fact that the corresponding finished panel for one of them survives, it might well be thought that they were cartoons for stained glass rather than embroidery.

The embroideries exhibited by the newly established Morris firm at the 1862 International Exhibition were of the same medieval inspiration and were described by the *Ecclesiologist* as 'some most antique looking tapestry hangings'. It seems clear that most of the early Morris embroideries were intended primarily as a substitute for tapestry, and they were even described as such by the American novelist Henry James when he visited the Morris workshops in Queen Square in 1869. One of the most ambitious was an embroidered frieze, designed by Morris and Burne-Jones for the huge dining room of Rounton Grange, Northallerton, in 1872. This embroidery now hangs at the William Morris Gallery, Waltham-

Panel depicting St Catherine designed by William Morris for Red House, Bexleyheath, wool and silk embroidery on serge, 1860

stow. Apart from this frieze and the Red House panels, little of Morris's early embroidery work has survived, and his influence and achievements in the field of embroidery have too often been assessed by the embroideries produced by the firm after about 1875, many of which were not designed by Morris himself.

The characteristic 'Morris' embroideries, worked chiefly in darning stitches in floss silks, do not appear until the late 1870s: and most of the surviving examples, in fact, belong to the 1880s or even later. It was the work of Catherine Holiday, wife of Henry Holiday the stained-glass and mosaic designer, which probably first inspired Morris to produce designs for *portières*, coverlets, and cushions to be sold by the firm. She was a skilled embroideress, and Morris was so impressed by her work that he commissioned a vast quantity of work from her. The letters between Morris and Mrs Holiday, published by Philip Henderson in his *Letters of William Morris to his Family and Friends*, provide a fascinating picture of the close co-operation between designer and executant. Morris was so satisfied with Mrs Holiday's work that he entrusted the technique and colouring to her, and had the silks specially dyed to her specifications by Thomas Wardle at Leek. Several examples of her work survive in the possession of her family showing fine stitchery and delicate colouring. The effect of Morris's embroidery designs depended very much on the skill of the executant and on the choice of materials. For example, the Victoria and Albert Museum possesses two versions of a coverlet designed by Morris in 1880. One is worked in crewel wools, with elaborate shading in the manner of seventeenth-century crewelwork: the other is worked in silk almost in outline, and the effect is so different that it is hard to realize that they were both worked from the same design. Since the Morris firm sold not only finished work, executed in their own workshops, but also ready-traced goods and patterns to be worked by the customers themselves, different versions of the same design are often found. The embroideries worked by Morris's daughter May and her assistants, after she took charge of this section about 1880, have, however, a uniform appearance, being worked in floss silks chiefly in darning stitches.

Until about 1880 all the embroidery designs were from Morris's own hand. But thereafter, although Morris's designs continued to be worked, most of the new designs were from the hand of May Morris, or J. H. Dearle. It is not difficult to distinguish May Morris's designs from those of her father. They are stiffer and less flowing, with a broader, simpler treatment. It is more difficult to distinguish the work of J. H. Dearle from that of Morris himself. Dearle joined the Morris firm as an apprentice at the age of eighteen in 1878 and became Morris's chief assistant. He absorbed Morris's personal style so thoroughly that it is often almost impossible, in the absence of documentary evidence, to tell a design of his from one of his master. The Pigeon Portière, designed by Dearle soon after Morris's death, is almost indistinguishable from a design by Morris, and shows the same characteristic treatment of swirling acanthus leaves that typify so many of Morris's own designs.

THE ROYAL SCHOOL OF ART NEEDLEWORK

The interest aroused in embroidery by William Morris led to the foundation of several organizations for the promotion of the art. The first, and the most important, was the Royal School of Art Needlework founded in 1872 under the Presidency of H.R.H. the Princess Christian of Schleswig-Holstein with the twofold aim, according to the prospectus, 'of restoring Ornamental Needlework, for secular purposes, to the high place it once held among decorative arts, and to supply suitable employment for poor

Screen with three panels, embroidered in floss silks, designed by May Morris and executed in the Morris workshops under her direction, *c.* 1890. Victoria & Albert Museum

gentlewomen'. The organizing committee of distinguished ladies, most of whom were themselves skilled embroideresses (including Lady Marian Alford, author of *Needlework as Art*, 1886), had by 1875 assembled a staff of over a hundred workers who executed finished work and also undertook the repair of historic embroidery. Designs were commissioned from leading architects and designers of the day, including William Morris, Sir Edward Burne-Jones, Walter Crane, Selwyn Image, G. F. Bodley, and Alexander Fisher. Designs adapted from historic embroideries were also prepared by the staff.

Permanent exhibitions of the work of the School were held in the premises at Exhibition Road, South Kensington. An impressive exhibit, including a series of wall hangings designed by Walter Crane and a number of works designed by William Morris, was sent by the School to the Philadelphia Centennial Exhibition of 1876. One of the Morris pieces, a large *portière* with peacocks and vines, is now in a collection at Cincinnati. The most important surviving group of embroideries by the school, however, are those made in the 1880s for 93, Park Lane, London. The decorations consisted of an exact copy of the Pomona tapestry (woven at Merton Abbey in 1885), worked entirely in floss silks which cover the whole ground of the fabric. The figure of 'Pomona' was designed by Burne-Jones, and the background and inscription by William Morris. On the staircase are a series of figure panels designed by Burne-Jones to follow the curve of the stairs, and in the entrance hall a large panel entitled Music, also designed by Burne-Jones.

Among upwards of fifteen other organizations of varying size designed to promote the sale and improve the standard of embroidery were the Ladies' Work Society (founded about 1875) and the Decorative Needlework Society (1880). A rather more specialized body for the promotion of embroidery was the Leek Embroidery Society, founded in 1879 by the wife of Thomas Wardle, of Leek, the silk printer and dyer and lifelong friend and associate of William Morris. The designs issued by the Society, which were usually repeating patterns, were printed by woodblock on tussore silk. The coloured silks for working these designs were specially dyed at Wardle's factory in Leek, and the gold thread was imported direct from the manufacturers in China. Many specimens of Leek embroidery, as it was called at the time, were worked on a block-printed silk which was originally produced as a furnishing fabric, the lines of the pattern being completely covered by embroidery. Some of the designs were made by Thomas Wardle himself, who adapted a number of patterns from Indian art, including one called the 'Ajunta', taken from the famous cave frescoes. Other designs were commissioned from leading architects and designers such as R. Norman Shaw and J. D. Sedding. All types of domestic work were produced, but the Leek Embroidery achieved its fame primarily in the ecclesiastical field, and during the 1880s and 1890s many churches commissioned embroidery from the Society.

The basic principle adhered to by all these organizations was that a true revival of embroidery as an art could come about only through a knowledge and study of old embroidery. This attitude of mind is well summed up by Lewis Day (1845–1910) in *Art in Needlework* (1900): 'Design was once upon a time traditional, but the chain of tradition has snapped and now conscious design must be eclectic – that is to say one must study old work to see what has been done, and how it has been done, and then do one's own in one's own way.' It was this point of view which led, during the 1870s for the first time, to a serious study of old embroidery. Loan exhibitions of both old and modern work were held throughout England, the most important being that held at the South Kensington Museum (now the Victoria and Albert Museum) in 1873, another held at the Liverpool Art Club (1875), and one which took place at the Edinburgh Museum of Science and Art (1877).

Leek embroidery

Once it had begun, the revival of embroidery, initiated by societies such as those mentioned above, was swift, and the ideas spready rapidly to the general public.

ART NEEDLEWORK

By the mid-1870s art needlework was firmly established, and by 1880 the craze was as widespread as the Berlin woolwork which it had supplanted. But it exhibited more varieties. The *Dictionary of Needlework* (Caulfield and Saward, 1882) defines art needlework as 'a name recently introduced as a general term for all descriptions of needlework that spring from the application of a knowledge of design and colouring, with skill in fitting and executing. It is either executed by the worker from his or her designs or the patterns are drawn by a skilled artist.' By no means all of the work classified under this rather pretentious term deserved the name. Elizabeth Glaister, author of several books on embroidery, sums up the fashion thus: 'Many people think that no more is needed than to work in crewels on crash instead of as formerly in Berlin wool on canvas. Others think that if the work be in "dowdy" colours it may pass under the sacred name of Art. Others again show a blind and touching faith in South Kensington [i.e. The Royal School of Art Needlework] and maintain that "Art Needlework" is only to be had there; while a more enterprising friend replies that most of the shops have it now, though you cannot get it at the "Stores", and she buys hers at "Whiteleys". All would say that it is a modern invention, much in fashion just now, and therefore they must by no means neglect it' (*Needlework*, Art at Home Series, 1880).

The chief characteristic of art needlework, whatever the technique, was the use of rather sombre colours, no doubt as a reaction against the harsh and gaudy colours of the Berlin wools, and in contemporary periodicals the embroidery shops advertised their silks and crewels as being in 'quaint and artistic colours'.

Crewel stitch

The most popular form of art needlework was crewelwork, usually worked in crewel wools, but also in silks, and mostly worked on crash, linen, Bolton sheeting, or, for heavy curtains and *portières*, on serge, diagonal woollen cloth, or velvet. The chief stitch employed in the work was crewel stitch, which was nothing more than an irregularly worked stem stitch. In the United States, where the craze was as widespread as in England, it was known as South Kensington stitch. The direction of the stitch followed the shape of the leaf or flower or other motif. Other simple stitches, including long and short stitch, satin stitch, chain stitch, and French knots, were frequently employed. The name was derived from the 'crewelwork' curtains of the late seventeenth century, and a number of the designs issued were based on the historic models.

Although no elaborate stitchery was required, the work needed some considerable skill in execution and interpretation. The ideal was considered to be for the needlewoman to make her own design, yet many patterns for crewelwork were issued. These were simply outline drawings, and the direction of stitch, choice of colours, and shading was left to the worker.

Outline drawing for crewelwork

As with almost all types of embroidery, floral themes remained the most popular, but stiff garden flowers, conventionally treated, replaced the naturalistic roses and exotic blooms of Berlin woolwork. Sunflowers, madonna lilies, irises, daffodils, and narcissi were among the most popular. If roses are found, they are wild roses, formally treated. Berries, sprays of bramble or cherry, or strawberry plants were favourite subjects.

Birds were a popular subject. But instead of the gaudy parrots of Berlin woolwork, waterfowl, cranes and herons, peacocks, swallows, or even the humble sparrow were most favoured. Both the types of bird and the treatment were derived from Japanese art. This Japanese influence, which to some extent affected all the decorative arts in the 1870s and 1880s, is apparent in a wall hanging, designed by the architect and designer Thomas Jekyll (1827–81) for an ironwork pavilion at the Philadelphia Exhibition of 1876. It was worked on a heavy cotton sheeting in crewel wools and silk by a group of Norfolk women.

The larger birds, such as the peacock or heron, were considered particularly suitable for screen panels. Japanese arrangements, with waterplants and ducks at the bottom, and flying birds and a suggestion of a cloud or spray of blossom above, are also found on many screens.

Art needlework, unlike Berlin woolwork, was not really suitable for upholstery, but it ran riot elsewhere. The crochet, lace, and silk antimacassars of the early part of the reign were replaced by tidies of linen, embroidered in crewels, and laid on the backs and arms of chairs and sofas. Elizabeth Glaister (*Needlework*, 1880) recalls that 'when art brought crewels into fashion, and crewels made swifter progress than art, many rooms were filled with pieces of linen, hung over the furniture in such quantity as to recall a washing day, each decorated with a spray of brightly coloured flowers'. Embroidered cloths disported themselves on the tops of sideboards and occasional tables, and in the bedroom, behind the washstand, and on the chest of drawers.

Curtains and *portières* provided ample scope for decoration. For winter use curtains and *portières* were made of serge, diagonal woollen cloth, or velvet. The ground was usually dark: brown, deep red, olive green, or indigo. A contrasting dado at the bottom was a common form of decoration, and appliqué embroidery was employed for this type of scheme. Typical of this type of work were the curtains designed by Princess Louise for the state rooms of the new Town Hall at Manchester in 1877. The curtains have a dado of darker velvet on a deep-red cloth ground with a bold pattern of applied sunflower and leaves with several threads of crewel sewn round each leaf and flower. A wide border of dark blue, decorated with applied circles of yellow-brown cloth, surrounds the whole. Somewhat similar were the curtains worked for Queen Victoria by the Royal School of Needlework, and designed by the Hon. Mrs Percy Wyndham. These curtains still hang in the private apartments at Windsor, and also have a bold design of sunflowers enriched by the use of gold thread. 'Powderings' of sprigs of flowers was another favoured type of curtain ornamentation, also simple repeating patterns worked in outline in crewel wools.

Decorative wall hangings, worked in outline in crewel wools, usually almost in monochrome, were

Screen panel, embroidered in silk and gold thread on satin. Worked by Miss E. D. Bradby, dated 1899. The inscription is from Psalm XCIV, verse 14. Victoria & Albert Museum

also popular during the 1870s. The panel designed by Burne-Jones and Morris, in the Victoria and Albert Museum, is a typical surviving example, and a series of similar panels hangs at Ammerdown, Radstock, Somerset. Figure panels of this type, for use either as wall hangings or screens, were also designed by Walter Crane and Selwyn Image.

For counterpanes and coverlets Persian tile patterns were much favoured, or single flowers set in an all-over diamond diaper. Mantel borders and piano fronts were generally considered to need rather formal types of design, and the art of the Italian Renaissance provided the inspiration in many cases. Formal pots of flowers, scrolls, dolphins, or grotesque beasts were combined with floral ornament to make symmetrically arranged, long, horizontal panels.

Italian Renaissance embroidery designs were revived as borders for 'chair tidies'. The Cretan skirt borders (acquired by the South Kensington Museum in 1876) were also recommended by Elizabeth Glaister as suitable models for tidies.

So widespread had the fashion for art needlework become that almost every piece of household linen, from bathmats to dessert doilies, was given some sort of embroidered decoration: and patterns suitable for the embellishment of almost any article could be readily bought.

While the great mass of art needlework was composed from patterns prepared by others, the period produced a number of skilled embroideresses (as well as those connected with the Royal School of Art Needlework) who were artists in their own right. Outstanding among them was Phoebe Traquair (1852–1936), who was a mural painter, enameller, and illuminator as well as an extremely gifted needlewoman. Noted examples of her work are four panels, each of which took several years to complete. The panels depict an allegorical representation of four stages in the spiritual life of man, inspired by Walter Pater's account of Denys d'Auxerrois in his *Imaginary Portraits*. Almost equally skilled was Mary J. Newell (1860–1947), who was originally trained as a

Wall hanging worked in shades of brown in crewel wools. Designed by Sir Edward Burne-Jones and William Morris for the Royal School of Art Needlework, *c.* 1870. Victoria & Albert Museum

painter at the Birmingham School of Art. After two years' study in Paris she returned to the School to teach embroidery from 1882 to 1919. Her figure panels, which were usually of medieval subjects, show a marked influence of the work of Burne-Jones. Both Phoebe Traquair and Mary Newell were members of the Arts and Crafts Exhibition Society, founded in 1888, and embroidery featured prominently in all the Society's exhibitions.

The fashion for art needlework continued until the end of the century. There was little change, however, in the type of designs favoured or in methods of execution. There is in fact little essential difference between either the basic principles or the designs in Lockwood and Glaister's *Art Embroidery* (1878) and Lewis Day's *Art in Needlework* (1900).

It is true, however, that towards the end of the period an entirely new approach to embroidery was evolved at the Glasgow School of Art in 1894 under the direction of Jessie R. Newbery (1864–1948), the wife of the Principal, and Ann Macbeth (1875–1948). The tendency was towards simple, flat designs with broad area of appliqué, and patterns that arose directly out of the stitches themselves. The work of the Glasgow School, the influence of which soon spread throughout England, does not, however, belong to the Victorian era in spirit, but was a pioneering effort which laid the foundation for the embroidery of our own time.

The following types of embroidery, not mentioned in the general survey, are peculiar to the Victorian period:

Arrasene embroidery. A variation of chenille embroidery used mainly for curtain borders, mantel borders, and screens, where the pile of the arrasene (a fine wool or silk chenille thread) was not injured by friction. It was worked on canvas, silk, velvet, or serge, in tent stitch, stem or crewel stitch, and couching.

Braiding. Embroidery executed by means of couched braid chiefly in designs of arabesques or continuous scrolls.

Breton work. A type of embroidery derived from Breton peasant costume worked in coloured silks and gold thread, mainly in chain and satin stitch and used for the borders of garments, necktie ends, and small articles such as bookmarkers.

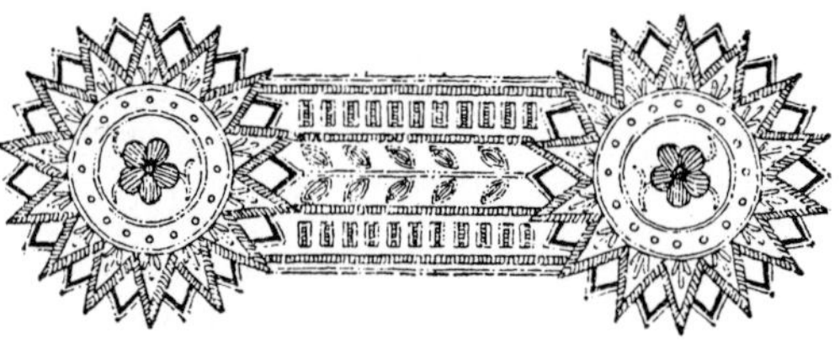

Broderie anglaise. A type of whitework, first introduced during the 1820s, which remained popular for costume embroidery throughout the Victorian era. The designs, which were either purely geometric or of conventionalized flowers and leaves, consisted of a series of cut holes, worked round in buttonhole stitch.

Cretonne appliqué (called also *Broderie perse*). Was composed of groups of flowers, leaves, birds, etc., cut out from printed cotton and applied to a plain ground, usually black. The edges of the motifs were worked round in buttonhole or overcast stitches. Details, such as the veining of the leaves or the centres of flowers, were picked out with embroidery in coloured silks.

Guipure d'art. A type of embroidery worked in white thread on a netted foundation in the manner of sixteenth-century *lacis* and often classified as lace.

Mountmellick embroidery. A type of whitework, first introduced about 1830 at Mountmellick in Queen's County, Ireland, and revived as a local industry in the 1880s by a Mrs Millner. It was worked on a stout white satin jean in white knitting cotton, which gave a raised effect to the work. The designs were naturalistic, passion flowers, blackberry sprays, oak leaves, and acorns being the most favoured patterns. Many designs for this type of work were issued by Weldons and other publishers in the late 1880s and 1890s.

POTTERY AND PORCELAIN

As a craft, the making of earthenware vessels and effigies is as ancient as the recorded history of man. If, however, we exclude those examples which come chiefly within the province of the archaeologist (*See* Antiquities), the general study and collecting of ceramics begins at a period not earlier than the T'ang dynasty (A.D. 618–906). This dynasty saw the full flowering of the art of the Chinese potter, and the invention of the beautiful translucent porcelain, that was to become at once a most prized and elusive material to its would-be imitators.

The following survey provides a concise and reliable guide for those who wish to trace the history and varied techniques employed in the making of pottery and porcelain throughout a period of more than a thousand years.

In the main text the dates, places of manufacture, materials, and characteristics of Chinese and European ceramics are set out in chronological order. There are also sections describing the productions of Russia and America. To this is added a glossary supplying copious additional information, together with the names of individual artists, technical terms, and methods of decoration. Line drawings illustrate examples of various types of ware and the principal marks of each factory.

American

Pottery

'I Like fine things Even when They are not mine, And cannot become mine; I still enjoy them.' This, translated from Pennsylvania dialect, appears on a *sgraffiato* plate signed by Johannes Leman, made before 1830 at the Friedrich Hildebrand pottery near Tyler's Port, Montgomery County, Pennsylvania.

Everything needed for the production of pottery was present in America – everything but the most important, enough encouragement. Potter's clays were abundant. The common red-burning clays (for bricks, roof tiles, coarse redware) occurred in shales at or near the ground's surface, and their use since earliest days had called for only the simplest kilns and equipment. Buff-burning clays of finer texture were employed since the seventeenth century for experimental wares of every grade, and in the 1800s provided a range of factory-made wares from Bennington to Baltimore, and westward along the Ohio River.

White-burning pipe clay had been used by the aborigines. In a court trial of 1685, at Burlington, New Jersey, the potter, 'Wm. Winn Attested sayth that hee can finde noe Clay in the Countrey that will make white wear', but white tobacco pipes were made as early as 1690 in Philadelphia, where in 1720 they were advertised by Richard Warder 'Tobacco Pipe Maker living under the same Roof with Phillip Syng Gold Smith'. And by 1738 'an earth' (the true kaolin, white china clay) was found by Andrew Duché 'on the back of Virginia', a vein of unaker running through the Carolinas into Georgia, exposed on river banks or along old stream beds.

Stoneware clays were absent in New England, but supplies were fetched by boat from northern New Jersey and Staten Island. At the Corselius (afterwards Crolius) pottery on Potbaker's Hill, 'the first stoneware kiln or furnace was built in this year 1730' on lower Manhattan Island. In January of that year in Philadelphia, Anthony Duché and his sons had petitioned the Assembly for support in 'the Art of making Stone-ware', to which they had been applying themselves 'for severall Years past'.

If the wanted clays were not near at hand, coastwise vessels and riverboats brought them. Materials for glaze or decoration were of simple and available sorts. Fuel for the potter's kiln was everywhere in this forested land.

Men with technical knowledge were here among the first. Brick making was reported by 1612 in Virginia, 1629 and 1635 in Salem and Boston. Roof tiles or 'tile Earth for House covering' appeared in Massachusetts court orders of 1646, and 'tylemakers' prospered in Virginia by 1649. The potter Philip Drinker arrived in 1635 in Charlestown, and that same year at nearby Salem the 'potbakers' William Vinson (Vincent) and John Pride were recorded. One 'extraordinary potter' came in 1653 to Rensselaerwyk (Albany) on the ship *Graef*, and a Dirck Claesen 'Pottmaker' was established by 1657 at Potbaker's Corner, in New Amsterdam. The thumping of the potter's wheel was soon heard in every colonial town of consequence, and for New England alone (says Lura W. Watkins) 250 potters were recorded by 1800, twice that number by 1850. How many more were never mentioned at all?

Place names like Potter's Creek, Clay City, or Pottertown give a clue to the spread of activity – four states had a Jugtown, seven more a Kaolin.

All that was lacking was a proper market. In numbers the colonists were so few, a total of 200,000 by 1690 and the five leading towns accounting for only 18,600. The population nearly doubled every twenty years, so that by 1776 its total reached 2,500,000 (about equally divided between the five Southern and eight Northern provinces) and Philadelphia, with 40,000 souls, was the second city in the British dominions. Ninety per cent of the population was on the land, and for the most part comprised a sort of

Salt cellar group, painted in enamel colours and gilt. Mark: a shield with the arms of Austria in underglaze blue, probably from a model by Johann Josef Niedermeyer, Vienna, *c.* 1750. Victoria & Albert Museum

Redware cup, 1780, and dish, the dish with slip decoration and glaze. John Judkyn Memorial, Bath

village society. The complaint was everywhere the same as in Virginia, that 'for want of Towns, Markets, and Money, there is but little Encouragement for tradesmen and Artificers'. It was all very well for a Boston official to say (1718) that 'Every one Incourages the Growth and Manufactures of this Country and not one person but discourages the Trade from home, and says 'tis pitty any goods should be brought from England', but fashion preferred what was imported, and the colonial potter found little demand except for useful wares.

In the South (where tobacco was the cornerstone of the finances of Chesapeake society until 1750, followed by wheat and corn; where rice was the staple in Carolina from 1700, indigo from about 1745) the English character of plantation life was strongly marked. The local commodities were exchanged for English luxuries, and except for rude plantation crafts, nothing much was to be expected here. Andrew Duché and the mysterious Samuel Bowen, two early Savannah potters, were marvels who appeared far ahead of their time.

England's suppression of all colonial manufactures was a sternly established policy. General Thomas Gage expressed the official attitude when writing to Lord Barrington in 1772 that it would be 'for our interest to Keep the Settlers within reach of the Sea-Coast as long as we can; and to cramp their Trade as far as can be done prudentially'. But he was unaware to what an extent people had already moved inland, away from the agents who supplied English goods; nor had he perceived the rapid advance made in American manufactures since the French and Indian Wars of 1754–63.

Yet pot makers lagged in this general improvement. Through the colonial years and far beyond, coarse red-clay pottery – jugs and jars, plates and bowls, mugs and milk pans – formed the principal output of small potteries everywhere. New England's glacial clays made excellent redware, which was partly supplemented by grey stoneware from the time of the Revolution, or more extensively after 1800. Always popular, ordinary redware survived the competition offered by cheap and serviceable factory-made wares from the 1830s, and in country districts lasted through the nineteenth century, lingering within present memory.

REDWARE

In kitchen and dairy, or for table use alongside pewter and common woodenware or 'treen', the simple forms of this sturdy folk pottery were washed or splashed with pleasant colour – glazed with browns and yellows, rich orange to salmon pink, copper greens, a brownish black made from manganese. For this the least equipment was needed: a horse-powered mill for grinding and mixing clay, a homemade potter's wheel, a few wooden tools, with perhaps a few moulds as well. The maker might be no more than a seasonal or 'blue-bird' potter who worked when his other affairs permitted, and carried his output by wagon through the near vicinity; or the larger and full-time potshops might employ untrained lads (William Scofield of Honeybrook got 'one skilled potter from every 16 apprentice boys') or migrant journeyman potters of uncertain grades.

There were no secrets in this simple manufacture. Since 1625–50, at the Jamestown colony, potters everywhere had made useful everyday ware of much the same sorts, in its own time used up, smashed up, never regarded as worth preserving.

Of this class, an early and curious milk pan is credited to Andrew Duché, who advertised (April 1735, the *South Carolina Gazette*) to supply 'Butter pots, milk-pans, and all other sorts of Earthenware of this country make'. The story of its discovery over a decade ago was told by Ruth Monroe Gilmer in *Apollo* for May 1947.

Found at Guyton (in the Salzburger area forty-five miles inland from Savannah) this heavy, thick and flat-footed pan was apparently made from river-bank clays, quoting its owner: 'the body densely textured and mottled reddish brown, as if made from shale and ball clay . . . the glaze a clear straw-coloured lead used all over . . . the glazed bottom flat, without rim or ridge of any kind'.

Not long after Duché's time, another Southern pottery was established by a colony of Moravians, who in 1753 moved from Bethlehem, Pennsylvania, to the wilderness region of Wachovia, North Carolina. Here the United Brethren founded a communal society served by Brother Gottfried Aust as potter. He fired his first kiln at the village of Bethabara in 1756, making redware, clay pipes, stove tiles, and from 1761 conducted public sales which attracted buyers from a surprising distance (Rice, *Shenandoah Pottery*, pp. 271–7). The enterprise was transferred in 1768 to Salem, North Carolina, where by 1774 far superior wares were achieved, and production lasted to around 1830.

Still another venture in this region was the so-called Jugtown Pottery, in a settlement peopled *c.* 1740–50 at Steeds, North Carolina, by a group of colonists from Staffordshire. Apparently the plainest of 'dirt dishes' were made here (1750?) by Peter Craven, first of his family, and latterly the place became known as Jugtown, for the common vessels it supplied to Southern distilleries. Languished and long forgotten, the pottery was revived in 1917 at a hamlet amusingly named Why Not?

Far north, New England must have been brimming with small but able potters. In 1775 (says John Ramsay in *American Potters and Pottery*) the two Essex County, Massachusetts, towns of Danvers and Peabody had seventy-five potters, and there were twenty-two Peabody potters at the Battle of Lexington.

Redware bowl with dark brown glaze and stylized bird decoration, 18th century. American Museum in Britain

Early New England potters

Their wares were given ample and excellent record in Lura Watkins's book (*Early New England Potters and Their Wares*, Cambridge, Massachusetts, 1950) in which the illustrations show what Puritan austerity characterized the general output. Simple and appropriate forms were enough, with richly coloured glazes to satisfy the eye and only with occasional attempts at further decoration.

Pennsylvania-German

For the Pennsylvania-'Dutch' (that is, *deutsch* or German) Frances Lichten has provided a full report in her *Folk Art of Rural Pennsylvania*. In the 'Dutch counties' settled in the eighteenth century by Swiss Mennonites, and by Germans from the Palatinate, pottery was made which was in wide contrast to New England work, marked by a love of colour, a play of ideas, and an engaging humour.

The flat Pennsylvania fruit pie dish or *poischissel* was a distinctive article; or the pots for apple butter called *epfel buther haffa*; the saucered flowerpots or *bluma haffa*. Fluted turk's head cake moulds were produced in all sorts and sizes, and there were standing pottery grease lamps not seen in New England, quaint banks and bird whistles, double-walled tobacco jars displaying skilful pierced work. (See *Pennsylvania-German Folk Art* by Frances Lichten, p. 401.)

Shenandoah Valley

Just south of Pennsylvania, a numerous and flourishing group of potters worked throughout the nineteenth century in a hundred-mile stretch of the Shenandoah Valley. Foremost were the Bell family, founded by Peter Bell, who from 1800 to 1845 produced 'erthingwear' at Hagerstown, Maryland, and Winchester, Virginia. His eldest son, John Bell (1800–80), worked 1833–80 at Waynesboro, Pennsylvania, and was followed by five sons who continued the business until 1899. John's brothers, Samuel and Solomon, were in partnership from 1833 at Strasburg, Virginia, where the factory continued until 1908.

Midwest

Fairly typical of what was made through Ohio and Indiana, where a variety of pottery and stoneware clays were abundant, a washbowl and jug, buff-glazed inside, is stamped on one handle *Zoar*, on the other 1840. The Society of Separatists (called Zoarites) were one of many religious sects gathered in communal settlements that flowered and died in the nineteenth century, themselves coming in 1817 from Württemberg and prospering in 1819–98 at Zoar, in Tuscarawas County, Ohio. In a long list of trades and crafts practised here, we find weavers and carpenters, a printshop and bindery, a fine blacksmith shop, and of course a pottery. Red roof tiles (one is dated 1824) are still seen on a few houses, and in 1834 the Society was selling 'porringers' to farm folk in the vicinity. The services of an outsider were engaged, Solomon Purdy, a potter recorded in 1820 at Putnam; in 1840 at Atwater. Until 1852–3 the Zoar associates still produced common brownware, and black- or buff-glazed redware.

Decoration

Last of the everyday wares, and different from the others, a buff pottery painted (sometimes stencilled) with manganese brown belonged to New Geneva, Pennsylvania. So wholly unlike the Dutch-country pottery seen farther east, this sober stuff with hard, unglazed tan body was made in 1860–90 by James Hamilton of New Geneva, in the southwestern corner of Pennsylvania, and very likely (see *Antiquarian* for September 1931) also across the river at the A. & W. Boughner pottery in Greensboro.

Long employed by redware potters everywhere, a simple and most effective method of decoration was by the use of diluted clay or 'slip', which from a cup fitted with one or several quills was trailed on the surface of a piece in flourishes or perhaps words like *Lemon Pie*, names like *Louisa*. Made by George Wolfkiel at Hackensack, New Jersey, during the panic of 1837, were slipware platters woefully inscribed *Hard Times in Jersey*.

Above Redware jug coated with cream slip and decorated with brown and green glazes, 19th century. American Museum in Britain

Far right Blue-painted grey stoneware crock with decoration of a deer, by Edmands & Co. (working 1850–68 at Charlestown, Mass.), *c.* 1850. Greenfield Village and Henry Ford Museum

Right Slipware plate, *sgraffiato* decoration, glazed earthenware, Pennsylvania, late 18th century. Metropolitan Museum of Art

For such, a slab of clay was flattened with the wooden beater (one of them shows a beautifully worn and polished thumbprint) and smoothed like pie-crust with a wooden rolling pin. When half-dried, the raised lines of slip would be pressed into the soft or 'green' surface of the unfired dish, its edge would be trimmed and then notched with a wooden coggle wheel.

Far more ambitious was *sgraffiato* (scratched) ornament, for which redware was thinly coated with cream-colour slip and this cut through to expose the darker body. Plates often showed a border inscription written with a sharp tool, and parts of the design might be enhanced with added colours. Widely known in European peasant pottery, this technique was a favourite of the Pennsylvania-Germans from perhaps 1733 (a shaving basin, p. 197 in Barber's *Tulip Ware*) and furnishes surely the most decorative examples in American redware.

STONEWARE

The family of stonewares, a varied company, was made of finer and denser clays and fired in a kiln much hotter than for earthenware (above 2,000° F.), resulting in a hard body for which 'no other glazing need be used than what is produced by a little common salt strewed over the ware' (1785). The salt vapour supplied a roughish, glassy coating that was colourless. According to the clays used and the temperature of the kiln, wares ranged from the familiar grey body to buff or cream, even a dark brown.

Fine grades of stoneware approached the quality of porcelain, such as the 'white stone Tea-cups and sawcers' (thin-bodied white Staffordshire, later with scratch-blue decoration) sold 1724 in Boston, or the 'Basket-work't plates' (of salt glaze with embossed and pierced lattice borders) which arrived from England in 1758 and 1764. Next century a middle grade of 'figured stone pitchers' and Toby jugs of 'superior stone' in buff and brown earned praise and awards in 1829–30 for David Henderson of Jersey City.

The popular class of stonewares considered here were chiefly utility articles: common crocks, jugs, or churns, along with other things made for amusement, such as whistles and money banks, bird or animal figures. Most of it was greyware, and after about 1800 the vessels were usually coated inside with brown Albany slip.

The favourite decoration was freehand painting in cobalt blue, or rarely brown. Initials and dates, birds or flowers and scrolls, might be emphasized with scratched lines or die-stamped flowerets, though after about 1850 stencilled designs were widely used.

Many redware potters made stoneware also, and from *c.* 1800 often marked their work with a die-stamped name and perhaps the place. But later than 1850 and especially in the Midwest, crocks might show the name not of their maker but of some wholesaler to whom they were supplied.

Stoneware was developed because of fear of poison from lead-glazed wares. 'Preceding the glorious Revolution', said a long notice in the *Pennsylvania Mercury* on 4 February 1785, 'here and there, were a few scattered Potteries of Earthen-Ware, infamously bad and unwholesome, from their being partially glazed with a thin, cheap washing of Lead.' This lead glaze, attacked by acid foods, 'becomes a slow but sure poison, chiefly affecting the Nerves, that enfeebles the constitution, and produces paleness, tremors, gripes, palsies, &c.' It was hinted that the Legislature should enact 'discountenancing the use of Lead in glazing Earthen-ware', and further that 'a small bounty, or exemption' might encourage stoneware potters.

Whatever justice there was in this alarm, it had long been discussed among potters. The apocryphal date 1722 appears on a large open-mouthed stoneware jar (Robert J. Sim, *Some Vanishing Phases of Rural Life in New Jersey*, p. 43). At least we have seen 'the first stoneware kiln or furnace' erected 1730 near the Collect Pond in New York, by William Crolyas (Crolius). And we have heard Anthony Duché that same year claiming to have made stoneware 'for severall Years past' in Philadelphia. Others soon sought to learn the mystery.

Isaac Parker of Charlestown (Boston) was one of these, a redware maker who eagerly sent for a man 'trained in the stoneware potter's art'. What arrived in Boston on 14 July 1742, aboard the brigantine *Mary* (Watkins, *Early New England Potters*, pp. 35–8) was James, son of Anthony Duché and brother of Andrew the porcelain maker. Two months later, Parker could report to the General Court that he had 'now' learned the secret of stoneware making. Parker died forthwith; but by December 1742 his widow Grace with James Duché as co-partner was granted a fifteen-year monopoly, and in April 1745 their firm (called Thomas Symmes & Co.) advertised 'blue and white stone ware of forty different kinds'. Duché disappeared next year, probably returned to Philadelphia, and death in 1754 released Mrs Parker from a failing enterprise.

Nor was the failure surprising, since New England afforded no stoneware clay and was put to the expense of getting it from New York. Indeed, the major source of supply for all American stoneware was for many years the rich deposit of fine blue clay centred at South Amboy, New Jersey, and extending to Staten Island and Long Island.

From this bed Adam Staats, a potter of Horse Neck (Greenwich), Connecticut, dug clay in 1751, on a five-year lease between 'the Said adam States' and the town trustees of Huntingdon, Long Island. He knew its qualities, having worked at Cheesequake or 'Chesquick' Creek (South Amboy) before appearing in 1743 in New York.

With seemingly one exception, other early stoneware makers, if not in the locality, were at least within easy range of the New Jersey blue-clay beds. This exception occurred far south, where the Moravians at Salem, North Carolina, burnt their first kiln of stoneware (according to Brother Aust's diary) in May 1774, instructed by an English journeyman potter William Ellis, who came the year before from Pine Tree 'where he had been working'. At this inaccessibly inland town local clays must have answered.

Naturally, these opening years of the Revolution saw vigorous increase in stoneware potting. First by a boycott to express political discontent, and then by war itself, the domestic market was largely cut off from its accustomed foreign sources of supply, the Thames-side potteries at Fulham and Lambeth, and the furnaces of the Rhine Valley.

Blue-painted grey stoneware shards carrying the dates 1775 and 1776 (*Antiques*, March 1944, pp. 122–5) have been found along Cheesequake Creek, presumably from a pottery operated by General James Morgan, who in 1779 filed a claim for 'a kiln of Stoneware not burnt' that British soldiers had destroyed. Also dated 1775, *July* 18/*JC* is a stoneware jug (Metropolitan Museum) from the New York factory of William Crolius II. By 1778 a certain Bernard Hamlen advertised for return of a horse strayed from his 'Stoneware Potting Manufactory at Trenton' (Clement, *Our Pioneer Potters*, p. 20).

By a potter who sometimes stamped his ware *C. Crolius Manhattan-Wells* and was working by 1794 is a brownish stoneware batter jug with die-stamped blue flowerets and leaves, scratched: *New York, Feby 17th* 1798/*Flowered by Clarkson Crolius/Blue*. The New York Historical Society, its owner, also possesses the maker's actual stamp and other tools. This was Clarkson, Sr (1773–1843), a grandson of William 'Crolyas', the stoneware potter of 1730. Clement, *Our Pioneer Potters*, reviews (pp. 21–5) the complicated record of the Crolius dynasty (fifteen potters in all) who worked in New York until *c.* 1870 when Clarkson, Jr retired.

The first Crolius and one 'Johannes Remmi' or de Remy (John Remmey I) married the Cornelius sisters, Veronica and Anna. But a supposed business partnership of Remmey & Crolius in 1742–4 finds no supporting records. The Remmeys followed their separate way from 1735 until today. When the New York factory failed in 1819–20 one great-grandson continued at South Amboy until 1833; another had gone to Philadelphia about 1810, where (with a side venture at Baltimore from 1818 to *c.* 1835) the firm is still established.

A reason is easily seen for the flurry of new stoneware factories that appeared around 1805. From 1804 to 1812 the seizure and impressment of 10,000 American seamen into the British Navy led to a series of Congressional Acts (1806–9) that prohibited trade with England. With the Embargo Act of

Below Blue-painted brown stoneware batter jug, inscribed 'New York Feby 17th 1798/Flowered by Clarkson Crolius/Blue'. New York Historical Society

1807 (one of the causes of the War of 1812) imports dropped to one-third, and American potters had to supply a domestic market cut off from foreign sources.

Xerxes Price, who stamped his jars *XP*, was working at Sayreville (South Amboy) as early as 1802 and until 1830. Peter Cross, whose mark was *P. Cross/Hartford*, appeared 1805 to *c.* 1818 in Connecticut. Samuel Wetmore in 1805 began the enterprise at Huntingdon, Long Island, that later would become Brown Brothers. And from an unidentified maker (Watkins, *New England Potters*, p. 83) came sober brown-stained jars with '*BOSTON.* 1804.' impressed.

In Albany the able Paul Cushman from 1809 to 1832 made both redware and stoneware, on the hill 'a half mile west of Albany Gaol'. Not far east was Bennington, Vermont, where Captain John Norton in 1793 had started a potworks continued by the family for a century, until 1894. By tradition, stoneware was made here in 1800; in 1810 wagons were fetching clay across the hills from Troy, and in January 1815 the diary of Hiram Harwood says the Nortons 'were making ware of both kinds, stone and clay' (Spargo, *Potters of Bennington*, pp. 9, 11–13). But the flourishing period was from 1828 to 1832, when the proprietors had begun to use clays from South Amboy and Long Island.

In the Ohio country the earliest recorded stoneware potter was Joseph Rosier, working by 1814 near Zanesville; but by 1840 (says John Ramsay) there were more than fifty such potters through the area. Excellent clays were here in plenty, and potters of all sorts were attracted to the Midwest. East Liverpool with its fine Ohio River clays was to overtake northern New Jersey, which itself has been called 'the Staffordshire of America'.

By this time stonewares were a factory-made product that devoted less attention to form, more to decoration. Typical are a four-gallon crock made in 1850–68 by Edmands & Co. and the grey churn made in 1850–70 in the State of New York, a freely drawn, blue-painted deer on one, a whimsical bird on the other. Still later the decorations might be stencilled, to save labour. After the mid-nineteenth century a cylindrical shape was much used for crocks.

Government reports for 1900 showed an American output of stonewares valued at $1,800,000, but of redwares only $400,000 (Ramsay, p. 18), and the latter mostly from Ohio and Pennsylvania. The old order of work was indeed disappearing.

SOME BETTER WARES

In between the common grades of work, on one hand, and porcelains, on the other, American potters made constant boast of producing wares 'allowed by the nicest judges to exceed any imported from England'. These were always 'on the very lowest Terms' – terms that were often based not on cash but barter, and perhaps 'the potter will take in Pay, pork, tar, wheat, corn or tobacco' (Maryland, 1756). Though claiming so much, theirs were mostly small and experimental ventures, poorly financed and showing a high mortality rate. Edward Rumney in July 1746 bravely undertook 'to sett up a Pottery' at Annapolis, having 'furnished himself with Persons exceedingly well skilled (in the making of) all sorts of Potts, Pans Juggs, muggs &c.' Within four months his business was already offered at public vendue, even 'two Potters and several Horses'. A more ambitious project was that factory in New Boston which advertised in October 1769 'for Apprentices to learn the Art of making Tortoiseshell, Cream and Green-coloured Plates' (or Queensware and so-called green-edge Leeds). After this solitary notice, only silence. From the dismal number of such failures, Lord Sheffield's *Observations on the Commerce of the United States* (1791) seems not too prejudiced in saying: 'Manufactures of glass, of earthenware, and of stone mixed with clay, are all in an infant state.' Yet across this fairly cheerless scene moved many potters of sound experience. Who were these lost men? Some are known only from one passing mention in early records, or for a solitary example of ware 'said to be' by John Doe, a potter. Unlike the silversmiths, who were often men of public consequence, potters enjoyed relatively slight notice.

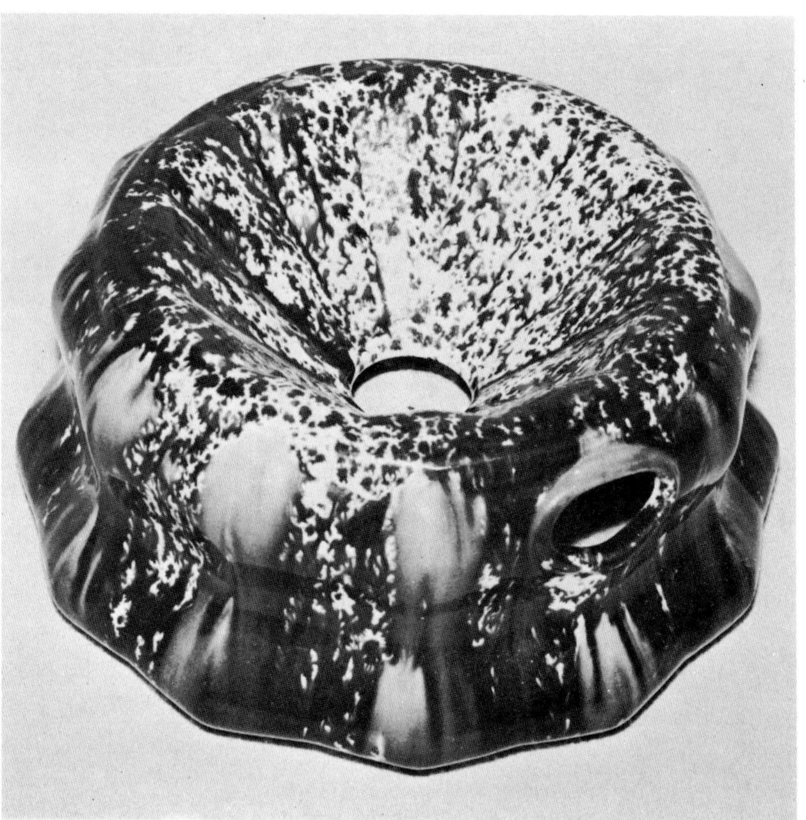

Mottle brown glazed yellow earthenware cuspidor, Lyman, Fenton and Company, Bennington, Vermont, 1849–58. Carborundum Museum of Ceramics Collection, Niagara Falls

And where are their products, of which enormous amounts once existed? How to account for the total disappearance of examples from our first whiteware furnace (1688–92 at Burlington, New Jersey), where Dr Daniel Coxe said his agents made 'a great quantity of White and Chiney ware'? What has become of all the 'Pennsylvania *pencil'd* bowls and sugar dishes' praised for their 'beauty of colours and elegance of figures', the work of Alexander Bartram who 'has got a Pot-house' in Philadelphia and advertised 1767–73? Where is one specimen of 'General Washington's bust, ditto in Medallions, several images part of them not finished', which in 1784 were offered at the sale of Jeremiah Warder's kilns in the North Liberties (Philadelphia)?

An answer might be that because American work of the better grades must compete with the imported, it attempted close imitation, and nowadays the American ware (so seldom marked, until after 1800)

languishes unrecognized, mistaken for English. Thomas Baker who advertised 1756 in St Mary's County, Maryland, was only one who made 'ware of the same kind as imported from Liverpool, or made in Philadelphia'.

In their day the 'compleat Setts of Blue-china, Enamuel'd ditto' shown in the Boston imports lists of 1737 probably had no equal here. But the 'new fashion'd Turtle-shell Tereens' of Whieldon's ware (1754) were soon copied by colonial potters. The same were described as 'Tortorise-ware' in Boston and New York lists of 1771, along with other Whieldon–Wedgwood types such as 'Colly flower, Mellon, Pine-apple, Aggitt'. Also in 1771 came 'Queen's Ware' to Boston, the 'Plain Cream-colour' to New York.

Creamware

Nothing approached the popularity of creamware, or lasted longer. Its inventor Josiah Wedgwood called this (1767) 'the Cream colour, alias Queens-ware, alias Ivory'.

John Bartlem or Bartlam ('one of our insolvent master potters', complained Wedgwood in 1765, who was hiring hands to go to his 'new Pottworks in South Carolina') was producing creamware by 1771 at Charleston. Messrs Bartlam & Co. in October 1770 had opened a manufactory on Meeting-street, 'the proper Hands &c. for carrying it on having lately arrived here from England'. Three months later it 'already makes what is called Queen's Ware, equal to any imported'. But a grant of £500 from the Assembly did not save it from disastrous labour troubles.

William Ellis, one of the Bartlam workmen, appeared in December 1773 at Salem, North Carolina, where Brother Aust's diary said 'he understands how to glaze and burn Queens Ware'. The Moravians built a suitable kiln, and the following May 'Ellis made a burning of Queensware'. He departed the same year and in 1783 Wedgwood referred to this Ellis as now 'of Hanley' (Staffordshire), calling him the sole survivor of Bartlam's enterprise.

Philadelphia became the centre of creamware manufacture. Here in 1792 the Pennsylvania Society for Encouragement of Manufactures and the Useful Arts offered a $50 prize for specimens 'approaching nearest to queen's-ware'. John Curtis, having dissolved the partnership of Curtis & Roat in July 1790, continued with 'the cream-color'd' from 1791 to 1811 at his Pottery-Ware Manufactory in Front Street, Southwark. Three others soon appeared: Alexander Trotter (who in 1809 had 'lately established a Queens-ware pottery on an extensive scale'; the Columbian Pottery); Daniel Freytag (maker in 1810–11 of a 'fine earthenware, the paste resembling queen's-ware'); and David G. Seixas (producing from 1816 a cream-colour 'similar to the Liverpool').

In New York 'a new Cream Ware Manufactory' was established in 1798 at Red Hook Landing, where J. Mouchet made Tivoli Ware 'with colored edges'. Nor had Alexander Trotter retired in 1812–13 (Spargo, p. 180), but reappeared 1815 in Pittsburgh, with Trotter & Co. advertising 'Queensware similar to the Philadelphia'.

The undiminishing popularity of this ware is reflected (*American Collector*, June 1940, p. 11) by one item in a ship's list of 1827: '532 doz. ordinary quality dinner plates, cream colored or blue and green edges', in a shipment of mixed pottery from Liverpool to Portsmouth, New Hampshire.

Yellow earthenware bowl, American Pottery Company, Jersey City, New Jersey, 1828–45

Another decade later, the Staffordshire potter James Clews arrived in 1836 at Louisville, Kentucky, where creamware had been made since 1830 by the Lewis Pottery Co. With the backing of Vodrey & Lewis, Clews built a large factory downriver at Troy, Indiana, and the first kiln of the new Indiana Pottery Co. was fired in June 1837. A blue-printed snuff jar with the mark *Clews's Manufacturer's* is a good sample of the ware made here only in 1837–8, Clews then returning to England because the local clays proved disappointing.

After that time, fine creamware was scarcely heard of, though poor and coarser wares of cream or ivory colour were widely made, e.g. the 'attempts at cream colored' reported 1850–1900 at the Shaker colony in Amana, Iowa. The Bennett Pottery might be listed in 1847 in the Pittsburgh directory as 'makers of domestic Queensware', but through the Ohio country this name was understood to mean a cream-bodied earthenware with rich brown glaze.

Rockingham

This was the common utility ware made by everyone from the 1840s to 1900, a yellowware dappled or streaked with lustrous manganese brown glaze. Its quality ranged from coarse splattered yellow to a rich brown tortoiseshell, and this ware was used for every sort of article, doorknobs or pudding pans, hound-handled jugs or lamp bases, cuspidors or picture frames.

Little was marked, and 'Bennington' as a generic name is wrongly applied to wares the bulk of which were made elsewhere, principally at East Liverpool and down the Ohio River, or by the Bennetts of Pittsburgh and Baltimore, by a hundred factories large and small. At Bennington Julius Norton first made Rockingham or 'flint' glaze (as it was generally called) in 1841. Henderson had produced it in 1829: 'Flint Ware both embossed and plain', in what the New York *Commercial Advertiser* called 'elegant pitchers . . . in a new style [which] if not too cheap will be accounted handsome'.

As an improvement on quiet brown Rockingham, a brilliant glaze flecked and streaked with colours was patented by Lyman, Fenton & Co. in November 1849 and examples carried a special *Fenton's Enamel* mark (Spargo, *The A.B.C.*, p. 21, mark D). Oddly, this *1849*

Figure of a lion, earthenware, with flint enamel glaze, by Daniel Greatbach, Bennington, 1852–8. Metropolitan Museum of Art

mark is found also on common Rockingham, or even on white Parian, and continued in use all through the U.S. Pottery Co. period (1853–8).

This colour-flecked glaze was not new; Fenton's patent referred only to a way of producing it with powdered colours. If a hot-water urn and the famous lion are examples of the best Bennington work, Fenton's enamel was widely pirated, being produced at East Liverpool as early as 1852 (Ramsay, p. 76). Pairs of Bennington lions in plain Rockingham or *1849* enamel, made with or without the platform and showing either a curly or the sanded 'coleslaw' mane, appeared 1851–2 and are attributed to Daniel Greatbach, though he did not arrive at Bennington until December 1851 or January 1852, remaining as chief modeller until the factory closed (Spargo, *Bennington Potters*, pp. 227–8).

PRINTED WARES

Doubtless because the Staffordshire and Liverpool makers supplied such a torrent of cheap and attractive printed pottery, in an endless range of patterns and colours, the development of printed wares made scarcely a beginning here. True, a 'rolling press, for copper-plate printing; and other articles *made use of* in the China Factory' were advertised August 1774 when the Bonnin & Morris properties were offered. Apparently it was their intention to produce Worcester-type porcelains with printed blue decoration, but no examples are known today, if indeed they were made at all.

Not until 1839–43 are American-made subjects encountered (Clement, *Our Pioneer Potters*, Plates 10–13), all four from the Henderson works, which since 1833 had been called the American Pottery Manufacturing Co.

In 1839 the pattern *Canova* was printed in light blue, cribbed from a design by John Ridgway of Hanley. The United States eagle and shield occurs on 6½-inch (16.5 cm) jugs also in light blue. In transfer print with added colours, the *Landing of Gen-Lafayette/at Castle Garden, New-York/16th August 1824* is seen on a larger jug and footed punch bowl at the New York Historical Society, the same jug with a 15½-inch (39.4 cm) oval cistern appearing No. 243 in the Van Sweringen sale of 1938 at Parke-Bernet Galleries. In *Antiques*, May 1931, p. 361, this view is assigned to 1843, when historic Castle Garden (formerly Fort Clinton) was leased to Christopher Heiser.

A black-printed W. H. Harrison memorial jug was made in 1841, when the ninth president died after one month in the White House. Below the repeated portraits of Harrison (from the J. R. Lambdin portrait, engraved by R. W. Dodson and published 1836) is shown the American eagle; above is the 'log cabin' symbol of the Harrison-Tyler presidential campaign, with *The Ohio Farmer*. When the same subject was issued a year before, during that campaign against the New York aristocrat Martin Van Brenu, the log cabin was lettered *To Let in 1841*.

The cabin so lettered, and the portrait entitled *Harrison & Reform*, occur on Staffordshire teaware or copper-lustred mugs, the former marked *Manufactured/for Robt H. Miller/ALEXANDRIA. D.C.*, an importer who advertised 30 October 1840 that he was expecting 'supplies of ware with Harrison and Log Cabin engravings, from designs sent out to the Potteries by himself' (*Antiques*, June 1944, p. 295, and February 1945, p. 120).

The Henderson jug carries a black-printed mark AM. POTTERY/MANUF^{G}C^{O}/JERSEY CITY, and for it (says Lura W. Watkins) 'printing plates were executed by Thomas Pollock, an American engraver'.

Slightly earlier (1837–8) is a blue-printed creamware jar for snuff made to order of Hezekiah Starr, a tobacconist at No. 27 Calvert Street, Baltimore. It has the mark *Clews's Manufacturer's*.

James Clews the English potter had a factory at Cobridge (Burslem) which 'was noted for its cream-colored ware' in the 1820s, but to American collectors is chiefly known as a source of transfer printed pottery showing American historical views. When the J. & R. Clews factory closed in 1836, James (*c.* 1786–1856) came to America and at Louisville, Kentucky, found the firm Vodrey & Lewis, makers

Far right Mottled brown glazed earthenware pitcher, Harker Taylor and Company, East Liverpool, Ohio, *c.* 1850. Newark Museum

of creamware since 1829.

Clews, being 'a man of fine presence and a fluent talker', persuaded Jacob Lewis and others to back him; the Louisville factory was closed, and a new Indiana Pottery Company established in January 1837 across the river at Troy, Indiana. Neither the workmen nor the Ohio River Valley clays suited him, and after disappointing efforts to make creamware in 1837–8 he returned to England. The factory under various proprietors made yellow and Rockingham wares until finally demolished in 1875.

A pot for *Macabau, Scotch & Rappee SNUFF* is probably not unlike those creamware 'pickle, pomatum & druggist pots' made in 1798 by J. Mouchet in New York. Another nearer its own time and area is the 10-inch (25.4 cm) brown-glazed jar, also found in Indiana, made for the tobacconist H. Thayer and carrying the mark of a Cincinnati maker *Franklin Factory/1834/S. Quigley/S. Quigley* (*Antiques*, August 1928, p. 162).

Only one more example of American printed ware deserves mention, a late blue platter, *Pickett's Charge, Gettysburg* (Ramsay, Fig. 86), with oak-leaf border picturing four generals who served that day in July 1863. Its blue eagle mark is for Edwin Bennett of Baltimore, who worked in 1841 at East Liverpool with his brother James (he was formerly with Clews at Troy) and from 1846 operated his own factory in Baltimore. His *Pickett's Charge* appeared in 1870 and was re-issued in 1901.

LATE WARES

It might be felt that Rogers Groups have no place here, being not of fired clay but plaster casts taken from clay models. But in their day these enormously popular figure groups were fondly accepted as ceramic sculpture, an 'art' expression that filled bare space in the Victorian parlour. And indeed they exerted a large influence upon potters who then produced Parian or other figure work.

John Rogers (1829–1904) created his patented story-telling groups in New York, from 1859 to 1893. Cast in reddish plaster and painted a sad putty colour, these low-priced groups were issued in vast editions, in 1886 *The Elder's Daughter* 'weight 100 lbs packed, price $12'. If sentimental, obvious, and sometimes silly, the subjects were well modelled; and their themes were from the Civil War, from domestic life of the time, or popular legends. Collections may now be studied at the New York Historical Society and at the Essex Institute, Salem.

Rookwood ceramic objects, late 19th century: *Left* ewer with dragon motif, marked with initials of Albert R. Valentien; *centre* vase with portrait of Chief Joseph of the Nez Percés, signed W. P. McDonald; *right* bowl with Japanese flower motif. Metropolitan Museum of Art

Majolica

During this same period, a new pottery called majolica won wide favour; a coarse earthen body with coloured lead glazes, it appeared in useful wares, leaf-shaped dishes, and ornamental work of every description. In 1851 Minton had exhibited majolica at the Crystal Palace, and Wedgwood was producing it by 1860. Meanwhile, American potters adopted it; Edwin Bennett by 1853 at Baltimore, and Carr & Morrison of New York in 1853–5. In the 1880s it was a staple of potters everywhere, from the Hampshire Pottery (James Taft's) at Keene, New Hampshire, to the Bennett and Morley firms in East Liverpool. Best known is Etruscan majolica, made in 1879–90 by Griffen, Smith & Hill at Phoenixville, Chester County, Pennsylvania.

An excellent example of Etruscan majolica in the Brooklyn Museum shows surprising likeness to the 'Colly flower tea potts' imported a century earlier (Boston, 1771). Developed in 1754–9 by Wedgwood when a junior partner to Whieldon, cauliflower ware had a vogue in 1760–80. The match for the later tea pot is seen in the Burnap Collection (No. 320, catalogue, 1953, the Nelson-Atkins Gallery of Art, Kansas City, Missouri). According to John Ramsay, 'the first cauliflower teapot' was made by James Carr in New York, Dr Barber adding that Carr & Morrison (1853–88) only made majolica 'for a period of about two years', 1853–5.

Porcelain

Allowance must always be made for the extravagant claims constantly offered by struggling potters who nervously looked for support. Small enterprises might make the loudest noise, asserting that they operated a China Manufactory and calling their ware porcelain, though they did not possess the requisite materials. Even if they did, it was one thing to know how, but another to produce a successful china.

The early 'pottery att Burlington for white and chiney ware' (1688–92) surely achieved no more than white tin-glazed delftware. Indeed, England herself had done no better at that time. Half a century must pass before porcelains of even an experimental grade were actually made here.

The ideal, of course, was true hard-paste porcelain like the Chinese, with which all potters had long been well familiar. This was the ware always preferred by fashionable and wealthy persons, who bought so much of it that by 1754 the General Court of Massachusetts passed an Act placing special excise on 'East-India Ware, called China-ware'.

It should be noted that in August 1738 samples of this Chinese ware were sent by the Earl of Egmont (most active of the Trustees of the colony of Georgia) to a certain master potter in Savannah. These samples were to serve as models for one Andrew Duché, already mentioned, first of the three pre-Revolutionary porcelain makers.

Duché (sometimes Duchee, Deshee, Deusha) was third son of the stoneware potter Antoine (Anthony) Duché. Born in 1710 in Philadelphia, he married twice in 1731, worked first at Charleston (1731–5) and then at New Windsor (1735–7) across the river from Augusta, finally at Savannah (1738–43), where he had been assured that 'all reasonable encouragement' would be given him by General James Oglethorpe, founder (1733) of the colony of Georgia. Indeed, he received a grant of £230 and built a pottery, where (say local records of 1743) he 'found out the secret to make as good porcelain as is made in China'.

The late Mr Hommel and Mrs Gilmer have published extensive notes on Duché, the subject of happy excitement in research circles; and a further hoard of unpublished facts, graciously made available by Mrs Gilmer, might have assisted persons sceptical of Duché's true achievements.

As for his porcelains, Oglethorpe in 1738 already reported to the Trustees that Duché had found 'an earth' (kaolin, china-clay) and baked it into china. By February in the next year he had discovered 'a whole mountain of stone' (petuntse?) in the Salzburger area, near Ebenezer; and in 1740 Duché found 'a quarry of Ironstone' on the five-acre lot of William Gough. For while conducting his experiments to perfect porcelain, Duché supplied the vicinity with useful articles of common earthenware or ironstone, and stove tiles for the settlement forty miles inland.

On 17 March 1738, he had requested of the Trustees 'two ingenious pot painters', and special supplies including 'a Tun weight of Pig lead, 200 wt of blew smalt such as potters use, 300 wt of block Tin, and an Iron Mortar & pestle'. The wanted materials (though skimped in their amounts) were sent him in August, and the 'two servants' came in July 1739 on the ship *Two Brothers*. Duché here had all the requirements for blue-decorated porcelain, and skilled helpers to finish it.

Found in 1946 at Charleston, his unique bowl is heavy for its size, slightly translucent but not resonant. Thanks to the Earl of Egmont's samples, its blue decoration resembles Chinese work but employs a local vernacular, with a band border of white oak leaves, a calyx of slim fern fronds below. If it bears no mark, Mrs Gilmer rightly asserts it is 'marked' all over. This bowl of experimental grade is just such as Duché would produce from the materials he had and working under the particular conditions.

The story of his after-years belongs not here so much as in English accounts of porcelain making. Drawn into political squabbles, Duché came into disagreement with Colonel William Stephens, who was secretary to the Trustees; ostensibly to plead the cause of the dissatisfied settlers, he left Savannah in March 1743 and appeared in London by May the next year.

Our concern with him centres on his contact with the proprietors of the Bow factory, Edward Heylin and Thomas Frye, who obtained the following December a patent for 'invention of manufacturing a certain material, whereby a Ware may be made of the same material as China'. Their secret (apparently communicated by Duché) was 'an earth, the produce of the Chirokee nation in America, called by the natives *unaker*'.

This same year, Duché waited upon William Cookworthy, who in a letter of May 1745 discusses 'the person who has discovered the china earth, calling it *kaulin* and saying that the finder is going for a Cargo of it'. Cookworthy has seen 'several samples of the china-ware of their making', and understands that the requisite earth is to be found 'on the back of Virginia'.

Jug painted with polychrome flowers and gilt. The initials E.S. painted in gilt under the spout are believed to be for the original owner, Elizabeth Slater. Tucker factory, 1828. American Museum in Britain

What profitable arrangements were made by Duché? We hear no more of him as a potter. From 1750 to 1769 he is a 'merchant' and prosperous landowner in Norfolk, Virginia. In 1769 he returned to Philadelphia, and here (described as a 'gentleman') he died in 1778.

Much briefer is the account of a second porcelain maker, the elusive Samuel Bowen. In 1745 one Henry Gossman, aged eighteen, and 'son of a very poor helpless widow of Purisburg, South Carolina' (a Swiss Huguenot settlement on the river above Savannah), was apprenticed or 'bound to a potter'. This would appear to be Samuel Bowen, now occupying the potworks vacated by Duché two years before.

Not until November 1764 did an English newspaper (the *Bristol Journal*) report that 'This week, some pieces of porcelain manufactured in Georgia was imported', but added that 'the workmanship is far from being admired'. Two years later (says Alice Morse Earle) Samuel Bowen was awarded a gold medal from the English Society for the Encouragement of Arts, Manufactures, and Commerce 'for his useful observations in china and industrious *application of them* in Georgia' (italics ours). Two years later, in March 1768, he was thanking the Georgia Commons 'for the Benefits he had received by their Recommendation of him'. Nothing further is known of Bowen.

Bonnin & Morris

Recovering quickly from the French and Indian Wars (the American phase of the Seven Years War, 1756–63), the colonies had enjoyed since mid-century a rising prosperity, an established society, and a higher standard of living. Philadelphia in 1770 was a rich and fashionable centre, likely to support a porcelain factory. 'The China-Works now erecting in Southwark' (1 January 1770) was 'compleated, and in motion' the following July, and for just short of two years gave continual report in newspaper advertisements (Prime, *Arts & Crafts*, pp. 114–24).

The China Proprietors were Gouse Bonnin (from Antigua) and a Philadelphia Quaker named George Anthony Morris. The latter retired in April/May 1771 and removed to North Carolina, where he died two years later while Bonnin in November 1772 was sulkily 'embarking for England without the least prospect of ever returning to this continent'.

They were financed by a £500 advance from the father of Dr James Mease (Barber, pp. 98–100), who got nothing in return but a blue-painted dinner service, from which one broken basket in the Worcester manner is all that survives (Philadelphia Museum). This piece and four others, all with a factory mark *P* in blue, were the 'known' output of Bonnin & Morris.

From the evidence, their ware seems to have been a fine grade of white earthenware, though their 'first Emission of Porcelain' was announced in January 1771, and that same month in an appeal to the Assembly they described the 'Manufacture of Porcelain or China Earthen Ware . . . a sample of it we respectfully submit'. Indeed, they achieved a translucent porcelain.

Their clay came from White Clay Creek, near Wilmington (Barber, p. 99) and they advertised in July 1770 for 'any quantity of horses or beeves shank bones', implying the attempt to make bone china. But in August 1772 Bonnin had 'lately made experiments with some clay presented by a Gentleman of Charles Town, South-Carolina'. Could this have been John Bartlam? Although a few years earlier, Richard Champion of Bristol had received (1765) a 'box of porcelain-earth' from his brother-in-law Caleb Lloyd of Charleston. The firm's first notice (January 1770) had referred to 'the famous factory in Bow, near London', as if this were their ideal.

In October 1770 'nine master workmen' arrived in Captain Osborne's ship. Three months later 'a quantity of Zaffer or zaffera' was wanted, and by July the factory could supply 'any Quantity of Blue and White Ware'. As their agent, Archibald M'Elroy in Second Street was exposing a 'General Assortment of AMERICAN CHINA' in January 1771 and next September 'both useful and ornamental Enamelled China'. The factory in January 1772 needed 'Painters, either in blue or enamel'.

Blue-painted sweetmeat dish in style of Bow or Plymouth. Mark: P in blue. Bonnin and Morris of Philadelphia, 1771–2. Brooklyn Museum

Only their blue-printed wares are recognized today, such as a finely modelled sweetmeat dish found in New Jersey, or a tea pot with charming *chinoiserie* and large initials *WP*. This latter came from a Philadelphia Quaker family in which it had always been known as 'the William Penn teapot', unaccountably, since the Proprietor was in his grave by 1718.

To the next name in American porcelains it is a leap of forty years. Mentioned in 1810 as 'of New Haven', a certain 'Henry Mead, physician' appeared in the New York directory for 1816–17. This was the alleged maker of a solitary all-white vase (Plate 19, Clement's *Own Pioneer Potters*) on the evidence of a paper label: *Finished in New York* 1816. A little late then, 'In 1819 the manufacture of Porcelain . . . was commenced in New York by Dr H. Mead' (J. Leander Bishop, *History of American Manufactures*). No less confusing, the doctor's obituary notice (1843) said that 'he commenced at Jersey City'.

Records are far more satisfactory for the Jersey Porcelain & Earthenware Company, established in December 1825, in Jersey City and sold in September 1828 to David Henderson. In 1826 this firm won a silver medal at the Franklin Institute, for the 'best china from American materials', though what competition might they have had? Fragments of hard-paste porcelain have been unearthed on the factory site, and praise of a visitor to the factory in 1826 (Clement, p. 68) was for articles 'either of white biscuit, or of white and gold in the French style'. Dr Barber in 1902 described one gold-banded white bowl 'made in 1826', then in the Trumbull-Prime collection at Princeton but now lost.

Tucker porcelain

Coming now to the first really successful chinaworks, we need little more than to correct and abbreviate the oft-told accounts of that well-documented Philadelphia enterprise of 1826–38, Tucker porcelains. More than half a century ago, Dr Barber devoted a chapter (pp. 126–53) to these well appreciated wares, *Antiques*, June 1828, pp. 480–4, adding further reports.

Born of a prosperous Quaker family, William Ellis Tucker (1800–32) began in 1826 his earnest experi-

Tucker porcelain

Parian ware pitcher, 'Niagara Falls' design, Bennington, 1852–8. Metropolitan Museum of Art

ments in porcelain making, at the Old Waterworks building in Philadelphia. That year he bought (in brief partnership with one John Bird) a property near Wilmington, Delaware, that yielded feldspar, and another at 'Mutton Hollow in the state of New Jersey' that provided kaolin or blue clay. In 1827 his porcelains won a silver medal at the 4th Franklin Institute exhibition, and in 1828 another, for ware comparing with 'the best specimens of French China'.

Examples of his earlier work are three pieces *c.* 1827 with painted scenes not in the familiar sepia, but darker brown. A cup showing the *Dam and Waterworks at Fairmount* is apparently after the Thomas Birch drawing published 1824 (the same used on blue-printed Staffordshire pottery of 1825–30, Nos. 249–50 and 535–6 in Mrs Larsen's book). The *Old Schuylkill Bridge* occurs on a cordate scent bottle owned by a Tucker descendant (*Antiques*, October 1936, p. 167). Again the subject is used on blue Staffordshire and in very rich taste was employed on a Hemphill jug of about 1835 (*Antiques*, June 1928, p. 481).

In 1828 a younger brother, Thomas Tucker (born 1812), became an apprentice, and William himself formed a partnership (1828–9) with John Hulme, as Tucker & Hulme. From this time came a large tea service factory-marked and dated 1828 (*Antiques*, October 1933, p. 134) with typical 'spider' border in gold, wrongly said to enjoy 'the distinction of being the first *complete sett* of china manufactured in this country'.

In 1831 Tucker established still another partnership, Tucker & Hemphill (with Alexander Hemphill), and that year his porcelains won a silver medal at the American Institute, New York. William Tucker died in 1832, and from 1833 to 1836 the factory was continued by Alexander's father, Judge Joseph Hemphill, with Thomas Tucker as manager. The Hemphill period displayed rich taste, with enamel painting in Sèvres style and a lavish use of gold. Its masterpiece was a large vase made in 1835 by Thomas Tucker, the gilt-bronze handles designed by Friedrich Sachse and cast by C. Cornelius & Sons of Philadelphia.

'The Tucker Masterpiece', porcelain vase in salmon and gold with colours and gilt bronze handles. Made in 1835 by Thomas Tucker. Philadelphia Museum of Art

The first quality of work about 1835 is seen in a mug with gold scrollwork and coloured scene entitled *Baltimore* in black script underfoot. Five cups from a set of *Presidents* must be dated towards the factory's close, since Jackson's portrait is from the *National Portrait Gallery of Distinguished Americans*,

published in 1834–6. Judge Hemphill retired in 1837, and Thomas Tucker rented the factory a year, closing it in 1838.

After a curious lapse of a decade, when porcelains were wholly neglected, five factories deserve notice as producers of such ware on a commercial scale.

Bennington

In 1843 Julius Norton, a Vermont potter, brought from England one John Harrison, a modeller at the Copeland works, where the year before a waxy white porcelain called Parian or Statuary Ware had been perfected (*see* Glossary). Harrison's experiments from October 1843 to mid-1845 were interrupted by a disastrous fire, and he returned to Stoke. During 1845–7 the firm of Norton & Fenton set this work aside; but from 1847 to 1850 the reorganized Lyman & Fenton was producing successful whitewares, including Parian. An example is the Daisy and Tulip jug in white porcelain, showing the Fenton's Works mark of 1847–8, though variants of this design continued for some years.

With new financing and expansion in 1851–2, Christopher Webber Fenton developed blue-and-white porcelains or rarely tan, still rarer the green-and-white. Much work was unsigned, but the familiar *U.S.P.* ribbonmark of the United States Pottery Co. (1853–8) is found 'principally upon porcelain pitchers and vases, both the white and blue-and-white, and upon some Parian pieces' (Spargo, *The A.B.C.*, p. 19).

From the latter years of the factory, which closed in 1858, came whole dinner or tea services of heavy, gold-banded porcelain (Spargo, *Potters of Bennington*, Plate XXVII). Kaolin had been obtained from Monkton, Vermont. Pitchers displayed at the Crystal Palace exhibition in New York (1853–4) were 'made of the flint from Vermont and Massachusetts, the feldspar from New Hampshire, and the china clays from Vermont and South Carolina'.

Greenpoint

First of two factories at Greenpoint (now Brooklyn) was Charles Cartlidge & Co., operating 1848–56. The proprietor was a Staffordshire (Burslem) man, who at once brought over his brother-in-law Josiah Jones to model 'biscuit busts of celebrated Americans'. A 9-inch (22.9 cm) likeness of General Zachary Taylor in 1848 (Barber, pp. 446–7) was followed by Daniel Webster, John Marshall, and others, in what the firm always described as bisque porcelain. From buttons and cameos the firm's output ranged to inkstands and chessmen, cane heads and endless other novelties, which at the Crystal Palace in 1858 won a silver medal 'for the excellence of the porcelain body and the gilding'.

Second of the Greenpoint enterprises was that of William Boch & Brother, founded 1850, which exhibited at the Crystal Palace as makers of door hardware and bone-china table goods. Thomas Carl Smith, who became manager in 1857, acquired the shaky business in 1861, reopened it as the Union Porcelain Works in 1862, and by 1864–5 had changed over to hardpaste porcelain.

Karl Müller came to the factory in 1874, as chief designer and modeller, creating many once-famous subjects eyed nowadays with disfavour, and others of quality and virtue; among the latter was a bisque porcelain pitcher *The Poets*, which in 1876 was a presentation piece to E. J. Brockett. Finely moulded heads of Milton, Ossian, Shakspeare (*sic*), Dante, Homer, and Virgil are seen with trophies and allegorical figures above and below. To the red-painted factory mark is added an impressed (later, printed) bird's head, the symbol adopted in 1876.

Other porcelain

Of minor importance is the Southern Porcelain Manufacturing Co., established in 1856 at Kaolin, South Carolina by William H. Farrar, who had been a Bennington stockholder. Numerous potters followed him here, the modeller Josiah Jones as manager in 1857, when the Cartlidge factory closed, and next year (when Bennington also failed), Fenton was there briefly on his way to Peoria, Illinois, where he built an unsuccessful works. Until fire destroyed the factory in 1863–4 only 'a fair porcelain' was produced at Kaolin, such as the coarsely designed *Corn* pitchers of 1859–61 (Barber, pp. 188–9). But to this site six miles from Augusta, potters were still attracted as they had been in Duché's time more than a century before.

From an inconspicuous beginning in Trenton, New Jersey, in 1863 there grew two years later the firm of Ott & Brewer, whose workshop, called the 'Etruria Pottery', proved the training ground for several potters of stature. For his own part, John Hart Brewer produced in 1875–6 a series of fine Parian portrait busts of Washington, Franklin, and U.S. Grant, modelled by Isaac Broome (Newark Museum, Clement's *Pottery and Porcelain of New Jersey*, Nos. 217–19 and Plate 44). The firm, dissolved in 1893, is especially remembered as a maker of American Belleek in the 1880s.

One of the Ott & Brewer apprentices was Walter Scott Lenox, later their decoration manager, who in 1889 formed the Ceramic Art Company, and in 1896 established the distinguished firm of Lenox, Inc. – since 1918 known as the makers of White House state services, and porcelain for the American embassies.

'Electra' pedestal, Union Porcelain Works, designed by Karl Müller, 1876. Metropolitan Museum of Art

MOULDED WARES

The later porcelains and the wares that follow were of a new order. The factory period had arrived about 1830, product of an industrial revolution that showed a parallel in mechanization of the glass industry, as freeblown glass gave way to pressed. In the ceramics field new types of pottery were no longer thrown on the potter's wheel but shaped in moulds. Forms were now created by designers and mass-produced by professional workmen; the simple potshop was transformed into a factory, where output was large and the price small.

Parian

Being made from liquid clay, Parian ware had to be poured into moulds. Bennington had been first to introduce 'this exquisite material, the happy substitute for marble in statuettes' – indeed, in 1852 had advertised it by the latter name, as 'Figures in Parian Marble'. The snowy ware was everywhere a favourite after the 1850s, made from Vermont to the Carolinas, or in Ohio by William Bloor of East Liverpool in 1860. And so much was its formula varied, one often doubts whether to call an example Parian or bisque porcelain.

But fear and outrage had swept the workers, at seeing 'the old usages of the trade broken up' (Wedgwood and Ormsbee, p. 95). Labour strikes in 1834–43 were followed by a panic of Staffordshire workmen in 1845–6, when they thought their livelihood threatened by the invention of pot-making machines.

The nonpareil of all moulded work was a 10-foot (3 m) monument made 1851–2 at Bennington and displayed 1853 at the Crystal Palace (Barber, Fig. 74). In three tiers of marbled or 'scroddled' ware, of the colour-flecked Fenton's Enamel, and of brown-streaked Rockingham, it was topped with the Parian figure of a 'woman in the act of presenting the Bible to an infant'. Just below, a portrait bust also in Parian represented Mr Fenton himself, peeking through a classic colonnade.

In America David Henderson of Jersey City, who has been called 'the Wedgwood of America', was pioneer in the manufacture of moulded wares. His fine buff stoneware jug marked *Uncle Toby*/1829 was advertised as *Toby Philipot* (*sic*) in 1830. A very similar but larger one was made in 1838–45 at the Salamander Works (1825–96) in Woodbridge, New Jersey. This is a jug of rich chestnut-brown colour with yellow-glazed interior. A Daniel Greatbach model with grapevine handle was made at Bennington, with normal Rockingham glaze but mismarked *Fenton's Enamel/Patented* 1849.

American Belleek

Belonging with the porcelains, last of the late wares is American Belleek, a thin, highly translucent, feldspathic body which is cousin to Parian, finished with a pale pearly glaze. Irish Belleek (*see* Glossary) was seen at the Centennial Exhibition in 1876, and excited the admiration of American potters.

Some time between 1880 and 1882 the Trenton firm of Ott & Brewer brought over the potter William Bromley, who had developed Irish Belleek, and by 1882, produced 'the first piece of belleek porcelain made in America' (a square tray). A fancy shell-shaped pitcher marked *W.S.L.*/1887 was produced at their works by Walter Lenox, who later brought two Belleek workmen to his own Ceramic Art Co. (1889–96) and further developed the ware at Lenox, Inc., from 1896. Edwin Bennett had achieved the production of Belleek by 1886 at Baltimore, and the Columbian Art Pottery (established 1893) made it by 1895 at Trenton.

Perhaps best of the American Belleek was 'Lotus Ware' a product of Knowles, Taylor & Knowles at East Liverpool, 1891–8. In 1887 Isaac W. Knowles had brought over Joshua Poole, manager of the Irish factory, and before 1889 made a finely moulded and fragile ware that in the 1890s earned much favour.

Belleek and majolica, or the art tiles and 'studio wares' that flourished alongside Rookwood from the 1880s, cannot yet be classed as antiques. Yet with Tiffany glass and other late work of quality, they have gained wide acceptance among collectors. In 1879 the 3rd edition of W. C. Prime's *Pottery and Porcelain of All Times and Nations* (which devoted a total of six pages to 'Pottery and Porcelain in the United States') began with these words: 'Ten years ago there were probably not ten collectors of pottery and porcelain in the United States. Today there are perhaps ten thousand. . . .' What would he think of the range and vigour of collecting today?

Cup and saucer and cream-jug, marked with a shield with the arms of Austria in underglaze blue, Vienna, early 19th century. Victoria & Albert Museum

Austrian

Porcelain

At Vienna Claudius Innocentius Du Paquier, assisted by Christoph Conrad Hunger from Meissen and Samuel Stoelzel, an arcanist Meissen, founded his own factory in 1717. He started by producing tableware derived from silver shapes, decorated with Chinese motifs and exotic flowers. About 1725 German flowers and European subjects were introduced in colours and in *Schwarzlot*, a black monochrome heightened with gold. This technique, used earlier by Johann Schaper, of Nuremberg, for the decoration of glass and pottery, was first applied to porcelain by Daniel Preissler (1636–1733) in Silesia, whence it became a characteristic feature of Vienna ware. Du Paquier figures formed at first parts of vessels only, supports, handles, or finials, but gained independence about 1730 and came into their own. The mingling of rustic pottery tradition with the urbanity of Meissen models gives these wide-eyed figures an air of wondering surprise at their own appearance in crinolines rather than in peasant skirts.

Vienna mark

Financial difficulties forced Du Paquier to sell his factory to the State in 1744, when a complete reorganization took place. At that time the Vienna mark, a shield incised or, more often, in underglaze blue, was first introduced. New findings of kaolin in Hungary (1749) and sound management finally brought prosperity to the enterprise. L. Dannhauser and J. J. Niedermeyer modelled figures of great charm, imparting the rhythmic grace of Austrian rococo to courtiers and market vendors alike. During the latter part of the century the transition to classicism took place under the direction of Konrad von Sorgenthal (1784–1805). Tableware in the manner of Sèvres has coloured grounds and gold decoration of restrained design, including medallions with portraits or landscapes. Figures of the period are often formed in biscuit to reproduce the effect of antique marbles. These figures are clad in stylized Greek gowns, and their timid character seems due to a certain slackening of creative power. However, the factory carried on until 1864.

Stork mark of The Hague

Belgian

Porcelain

In Belgium, unaffected by the French Vincennes–Sèvres monopoly, the factory of Tournay was founded in 1751 by François-Joseph Péterinck, under a monopoly granted by the Empress Maria Theresa. Robert Dubois, formerly at Chantilly and Vincennes, was appointed director in 1753, and the soft paste now produced, though not free from Meissen influences, is entirely French in spirit. The shapes of useful and decorative objects are simple and restrained, in spite of the flowering of the rococo style elsewhere. Much of the Tournay porcelain is left in white; and one wonders whether this is due to a genuine preference for the appealing pureness of the glaze, as it is in Nymphenburg, or whether coloured and gilt decoration was at times suppressed, out of reverence for the French crown. There is also a group of Tournay plates and dinner services with contemporary Dutch decoration, which the factory originally sold in white. They are easily recognized by the stork mark of The Hague, applied in overglaze blue.

Faïence

Faïence has been made in Belgium from the sixteenth century onwards, at various places, including Antwerp, Liège, Tournay, and Brussels.

It is not widely known or collected, but the work of Corneille Mombaer's factory, founded in 1705, is of some interest and distinction.

No mark was used – but a rather streaky glaze, and the bold blue, green, and yellow colouring is distinctive. A few examples are signed and dated.

The most attractive pieces are tureens in the form of vegetables, fruits, birds, and fishes. Dishes with fruit modelled in the round and various figures were also made. Work continued here into the nineteenth century.

Chinese, Korean and Japanese

Chinese

Chinese civilization is often credited with a far greater antiquity than the facts will support. The earliest pottery, the funerary wares of Kansu Province, hardly antedate 2000 B.C. Chinese art generally, however, is remarkable for its continuity. The altar vase with the trumpet-shaped mouth known as the *tsun*, first to be found in bronze during the Shang dynasty (1523–1028 B.C.), is a familiar shape in porcelain as late as the eighteenth century, and was even copied in the 1750s by European porcelain factories. Motifs of decoration alter to some extent with the passing of time, some lose their meaning and

Left Neolithic jar painted with abstract patterns in pigments, made in north west China, *c.* 2500 B.C.

Right Vase of unglazed earthenware painted in unfired colours, Han dynasty (206 B.C.–A.D. 220). Victoria & Albert Museum

significance, but even after three thousand years they are often still recognizable. The *tao ti'eh* mask, a very early bronze motif, occurs as painted ornament on the porcelain of the emperor Ch'ien Lung (1736–96), even though by this time its totemic meaning had been lost in the mists of time.

The Shang and Chou dynasties were noted for superb bronzes, but hardly for their ceramics. A fine white stoneware was made during the Shang period, but the only complete specimen is in the Freer Gallery in Washington. Glazes first appear during the second century B.C., probably the result of wood-ash falling on the surface of a pot during firing. A lead silicate glaze had been developed before the Han dynasty (206 B.C.–A.D. 220) had well advanced. This, green or brownish-green, was probably discovered independently of the West, although the Roman world, already skilled glassmakers, had produced a green lead pottery glaze about the same time.

The most familiar Han dynasty pottery objects are the *hu*, a baluster-shaped jar based on a bronze prototype, and found glazed and unglazed; the green-glazed 'Hill' jar, a cylindrical jar with a moulded conical cover representing the Taoist Isles of the Blest; and the 'Hill' censer, like a stem-cup with an integral saucer and a similar mountainous cover to the 'Hill' jar.

The origin of the pottery *hu* is not difficult to see. Some have moulded ring handles integral with the body, instead of the loose ring handles of the bronze version. The *tao ti'eh* mask which occurs on some of them was an ancient bronze motif, even in Han times. Some of the finest specimens have a hunting frieze of figures and horses in relief running round the shoulder, usually called the 'flying gallop', which also has bronze affiliations.

Excavators have brought to light many tomb-figures and other objects of grave-furniture, such as models of servants and retainers, farm animals, domestic appliances like cooking stoves, such farm buildings as pig-sties, and even the house itself. Generally the figures are smaller and less realistically modelled than those of the T'ang dynasty (618–906), but are nevertheless lively and evocative of the life of the period. They testify principally to an agricultural way of life rather than the Court life of the T'ang period.

Neolithic earthenware jar with swirling abstract design

Han dynasty vessel with band of animals and figures in moulded relief

The body of Han dynasty wares is either dark grey, when objects are unglazed and decorated with unfired pigments (rarely lacquer), or dark reddish-brown, when a glaze is present. Glazed pots were fired mouth downwards, with consequent small glaze defects at the rim. The glaze is finely crackled, and usually iridescent due to burial, since all Han pottery has been excavated or recovered from tombs.

The fall of the Han dynasty was followed by a period of strife during which very little of importance was made, but a Tatar Kingdom was established in northern China as the Northern Wei and produced tomb-figures in a blackish-grey body decorated in red and white slip and unfired pigments which stylistically bridge the gap between Han and T'ang figures. Yüeh celadon from Shensi Province first occurs during this period, and is discussed under the heading of Celadon.

The T'ang dynasty is a period of enormous importance in Chinese ceramic history, and a time of unprecedented expansion which coincided with comparative freedom from foreign invasion.

Contacts with Persia and the Middle East generally were many, and the influence of classical Greece, the delayed product of Alexander the Great's conquests, reached China, and is apparent in the form of some T'ang pottery, such as pilgrim-bottles and the decoration of certain urns.

An important aspect of T'ang pottery is the potter's mastery of coloured glazes, either alone as monochromes, or in combination. The glazes are of the lead silicate variety, and colours are green, blue, dark blue, yellow, orange, straw-colour, and brown. These were applied over a lightly-fired buff earthenware body soft enough to be cut with a knife or marked with the fingernail. Both tomb-figures and jars were often decorated with glazes of several colours sponged on, giving a dappled effect. These glazes, like the monochromes, rarely come down to

Offering dish, white earthenware decorated in green yellow with incised lines to prevent the colour from running, T'ang dynasty (618–906)

the base, but usually stop short about one-third or two-thirds of the way from the top.

Although much of the production was soft earthenware, the hard-fired wares were not entirely neglected. The earliest literary reference to Yüeh celadon belongs to the eighth century. The earliest *Ying ch'ing* occurs during the T'ang dynasty; so does the earliest Ting ware. There are several stonewares with a dark brown or a black glaze. Important evidence for the dating of T'ang wares comes from excavations at Samarra on the River Tigris, where the Caliph Mu'tasim built a pleasure palace in 838 which was abandoned in 883. The numerous fragments of T'ang pottery found here could not possibly have been made after the latter year.

Indications of T'ang date: flat base and glaze which stops well short of foot

Ko yao ware

The tomb-figures of this period were first brought to the attention of Western collectors in the 1920s with the import of such models as the fighting horses by George Eumorfopoulos. They had only been discovered a decade or so before, when a railway-cutting was driven through a T'ang graveyard. These models in the lively naturalness of their modelling were quite unlike anything previously known in Chinese pottery. The horses were a breed from Feraghan, instead of the Mongolian ponies which normally occur as an ornamental motif in Chinese art, and camels vigorously modelled are extremely impressive.

Ladies of the Court, musicians, servants, tomb-guardians, and many other subjects are usually decorated with coloured glazes, but are sometimes covered only with a straw-coloured glaze, or the glaze is omitted altogether.

With the coming of the Sung dynasty, which began in 960 and ended with the Mongol invasion of 1279, wares fall into well-marked categories the origin of which is, for the most part known and traceable to definite kiln-sites. During this period the emphasis was on stonewares with a monochrome feldspathic glaze, of which six are esteemed to a point where they are termed 'classic'.

These classic wares are Ju yao, made at Ju Chou in Honan Province; Kuan yao, first made at Kai-fêng fu (Honan Province) and, after 1127, at Hang Chou; Ko yao and Lung Ch'üan yao, made at Lung Ch'üan in Chekiang; Ting yao, made at Ting Chou in Chihli: and Chün yao from Chün Chou in Honan. The word *yao* means *ware.* These wares are considered in more detail under the appropriate headings, but all of them represent distinct and important technical advances, especially in the mastery of the feldspathic glaze fired at the same temperature as the

Typical Sung forms

Left Tomb guardian, earthenware splashed with coloured glazes, T'ang dynasty (618–906). Victoria & Albert Museum

Right Kuan yao octagonal bottle, Southern Sung dynasty (960–1279)

Black Ting bowl bound with copper at the rim, Sung dynasty (960–1279). Percival David Collection, London

body, and in the achievement of colour variations by controlling the atmospheric content of the furnace.

Although not among the classic wares the black glazed tea-bowls and other objects from Chien-an in Fukien Province and the very similar wares from Honan, are also important. They were especially esteemed by the Japanese for use in the Tea Ceremony, and by them called *temmoku.* The body is a dark grey coarse stoneware covered with a thick treacly glaze which ends in a roll just above the base. The Chien potters devised many decorative variations to the simple glaze. With streaks of brown it was called 'hare's fur'. The 'oil-spot' glaze, with silvery iridescent spots, was in great demand among the Japanese Tea Masters.

The most striking departure from the pattern set by Sung wares generally came from the kilns of Tzŭ Chou in Chihli Province, where a coarse greyish stoneware, sometimes covered with a white slip, was employed to make jars, often of dramatic or monumental form, and other wares. Painted decoration was employed in novel ways which had not hitherto been used in the decoration of pottery, and which were to play their part in the development of painted decoration in the Ming and Ch'ing dynasties.

Buff stoneware bottle with white glaze painted in brown-black with a plant and a butterfly, Tzŭ Chou type, probably Sung dynasty (960–1279). Victoria & Albert Museum

Painting was principally executed with a brush in black or brown slip, broadly and with great dexterity and economy of line. Towards the end of the Sung dynasty a few pieces simply painted in red and green enamel occur, and the technique of enamelling as a method of decorating pottery had been learned from Persia. Also from Persia came underglaze blue, where it had been used since the ninth century. There are literary references to the use of underglaze blue during the Sung dynasty, but no certain example till the Yüan dynasty. Many other techniques, apart from painting, were employed at Tzŭ Chou, including *sgraffiato* and carved decorations on large jars, the latter being among the most impressive survivals of the period. Although the Tzŭ Chou kilns were in existence in T'ang times, and are still flourishing today, the wares seem to have been very little esteemed in Sung Court Circles, probably because of their divergence from the admired classic wares.

The greater number of surviving wares from the Yüan dynasty (1280–1368) are celadons of one kind or another which are separately discussed (*see* Celadon). These are usually decorated with elaborately carved floral ornament. It is, however, at this time that porcelain of the kind with which we are most familiar begins to emerge. White translucent, glazed, and painted, the finest wares were made at the Imperial Kilns at Ching-tê Chên in Kiangsi Province, where kilns had existed from very early times. The Percival David Foundation, London, has an altar vase of this kind painted in underglaze blue which is dated 1351. It has now been established that the use of underglaze copper red in painted decoration had its beginnings about the same time, and a few exceedingly rare specimens have survived. The Mongol dynasty's connections with Persia were close. Chinese commentators write of the employment of 'Mohammedan blue' (*hui ch'ing*) in decorating porcelain at this time, and porcelain ewers with a bridge spout of the period are closely based on those of Persian metalwork.

The Mongols were defeated, and the native Ming (Bright) dynasty established in 1368 by Hung-wu. By now the kilns at Ching-tê Chên were well established and during the reign of Yung-lo (1403–24) produced a porcelain referred to as *t'o t'ai* (bodiless) because it was little more than paper-thin porcelain sandwiched between two layers of glaze. This suggests a complete mastery of both material and firing techniques. In the same reign the so-called 'secret' decoration (*an hua*) was first employed. The design was incised into the body of a very translucent porcelain with a needlepoint, or painted on to the unglazed surface in white slip. After glazing the piece had to be held to the light to see the decoration. This was evidently popular, because it was repeated later in the Ming dynasty, and again in the eighteenth century.

The general characteristics of Ming porcelain are a fine grain body, white in colour, tinged buff on the unglazed footring. Glazes are usually fairly thick and sometimes more or less hazy with bubbles. They are often slightly uneven, with a bluish tinge due to traces of iron which also confer the buff colour on the footring. The musliny texture of the glaze surface which the Chinese call 'chicken skin' occurs quite commonly, and 'pinholes' in the glaze surface are also common. Most Ming wares lack the precise finish

Ming wares

of those made in the following Ch'ing dynasty. It is an error, however, to think of them as necessarily heavy and clumsily potted. It is true that wares like celadon dishes, and the large early blue-and-white dishes, have this character, but they were made originally to withstand the hazards of transport by ship or merchant caravan, and are not representative of wares intended for home consumption. Ming potters were not usually very careful about neat and precise finish, unlike eighteenth-century potters who, in this respect, often approached modern Western factory standards, but the scale of values is different, and Ming porcelain painters were capable of superbly free drawings of natural objects, like aquatic birds amid reeds, observed with a sly and subtle humour unmatched at any other period.

The reign of Hsüan-tê (1426–35) is noted for the excellence of its blue-and-white wares, and for those decorated in underglaze copper red. Stem-cups with three red fish or fruit began in this reign, although eighteenth-century versions are far more numerous. Porcelain painted with underglaze blue was made in large quantities, lotus flowers amid scrollwork and aquatic birds being favourite subjects. The colour, a blackish blue, seems as though drawn into thicker spots at intervals, the 'heaped and piled' blue of the Chinese commentator, a feature repeated in the archaizing wares of the eighteenth century.

Not a great deal is known about enamel painting at this time. The author of the *Po Wu Yao Lan*, writing in 1625, referred to them as 'deep, thick, and piled on, and consequently not very beautiful'.

Below Blue-and-white bowl with floral decoration, bearing the reign mark of Hsüan-tê (1426–35), Ming dynasty

Bottom *Tou Ts'ai* jar showing the earliest type of enamel painting and painted with the six-character mark of Ch'êng Hua (1465–87), Ming dynasty

By the reign of Ch'êng Hua (1465–87) the situation had altered. Blue-and-white was being neglected and excellent quality enamelled porcelain produced. The reason for the unpopularity of blue-and-white, according to the *Po Wu Yao Lan*, was the failure of supplies of a good cobalt blue. It is about this time that the method of applying enamels directly to the unglazed body (*émail sur bisque*) was first practised. This gives an entirely different effect from enamels applied on the glaze, and although nothing exists which is certainly as old as this, later examples are much sought.

The most important innovation was the introduction of the *tou ts'ai* or contrasting colours. This was a combination of underglaze blue and enamel colours, the latter laid on the glaze within underglaze blue outlines. The most representative examples of this particular group are the 'chicken cups', so called from the subject of their decoration. These were repeated in the eighteenth century.

The following reign of Hung Chih (1488–1505) is noted for the introduction of a yellow ground, and that of Chêng-tê (1506–21) for the revival of blue-and-white porcelain, no doubt due to the acquisition of fresh supplies of Mohammedan blue, a supposition made the more probable by the existence of specimens from this reign bearing Arabic inscriptions. During this period copies of enamelled wares from earlier reigns were made, and an innovation is a decoration of incised dragons coloured green on a yellow ground. Although Chêng-tê porcelain is scarce, by this reign it becomes possible to date specimens with a far greater degree of certainty. The reign of Chia Ching (1522–66) is also noted for the fine quality of its blue-and-white, and in this reign underglaze copper red more or less disappeared, to be replaced by overglaze iron red, sometimes called tomato red.

The palette termed *Wan Li Wu Ts'ai* (Wan Li five colour decoration), which in the second half of the seventeenth century developed into the *famille verte* palette, was actually first employed in the reign of Chia Ching. *Wu Ts'ai* is a combination of underglaze blue and enamel colours.

The reign of Wan Li (1573–1620) to a great extent continued styles already existing under Chia Ching, but many more wares now began to be made for export to the West. Even Western pewter forms, such as the plate with the condiment ledge, occur towards the end of the reign, just as Chinese forms were copied in European tin-enamelled ware. The export porcelain of this reign was known to the Dutch as *Kraak porselin* (carrack porcelain), because this is what they were capturing from Portuguese carracks intercepted on the high seas. The blue of these wares is greyish, and often pale. They lacked precise finish, but the painting is lively and lacks the stiffness of contemporary wares for home consumption. The export wares of the period are not especially rare today, and they commonly appear in the Dutch still-life painting of the seventeenth century.

Towards the middle of the seventeenth century a new kind of blue-and-white porcelain occurs. The body is cream-white rather than blue-white, and the underglaze blue is a pure sapphire. Many of the vases are almost indistinguishable from those of the reign of K'ang Hsi (1662–1722) of the Ch'ing dynasty, except that the base is flat and unglazed, and a few rare specimens bear a cyclical date a few years

The Ming dynasty came to an end in 1644 and was replaced by invaders, the Manchus, who were Tatars from Manchuria. In Chinese, this dynasty was called Ch'ing (Purity), and it became noted for the wares made during the reign of three emperors – K'ang Hsi, Yung Chêng (1722–36) and Ch'ien Lung (1736–96).

The wares of the Ch'ing dynasty (1644–1912) are truly enormous in their variety, and by this time a great deal of technical knowledge and experience had been acquired. Wares now began to be potted with far greater precision, and a production-line system was introduced at Ching-tê Chên by which manufacture and decoration were broken down into a large number of separate operations, each performed by one man. Even decoration was split into its components, with one man painting figures, one birds, and another trees. This system, described in reports sent to Europe by Jesuit missionaries, was undoubtedly known to Josiah Wedgwood when, towards the end of the eighteenth century, he began to rationalize his own production. The employment of these methods necessarily brought changes in their train which were hardly salutary. The spontaneity and humour of a good deal of Ming porcelain painting disappears, to be replaced by a 'tighter', less adventurous style which gives more attention to detail and less to fluency of line in drawing. Ch'ing porcelain is too often a display of technical virtuosity which lacks the sensitivity of early wares.

The greater number of enamelled wares of this period fall into two categories known as *famille verte*

Chia ching ware

Top Wu Ts'ai square baluster jar bearing a six-character mark within a rough square, Chia Ching (1522–66), Ming dynasty. Christie, Manson & Woods

Far right Porcelain dish painted in *famille rose* enamels, mark and reign of Yung Chêng (1723–35), Ch'ing dynasty. Victoria & Albert Museum

San ts'ai *ware*

before the end of the Ming dynasty. This group, precursors of K'ang Hsi blue-and-white, is termed 'Transitional'. These remarks serve to emphasize that, for the most part, the use of dynasties and emperors in trying to assign dates to wares and their development is a useful, but artificial, convention, since at all periods there was a good deal of overlapping, and wares produced in small quantities in one period might not receive attention till a later one when they were produced in greater quantities.

An important variety of ware about which there is very little definite information is that known as *San ts'ai*, or three-coloured, made principally in the fifteenth and sixteenth centuries. Surviving examples are mainly vases, garden-seats, and large bowls, and decoration is by means of brilliantly coloured lead silicate glazes kept from intermingling by threads of clay which separate the elements of the design. The usual colours are dark blue, turquoise, and aubergine of variable shade and intensity, and the body may either be stoneware burnt to a dark brown where unglazed, or porcelain. Specimens are difficult to date, or to assign to a kiln or kilns.

It is equally difficult to date, and award a provenance to, stoneware objects of various kinds, like the decorative ridge-tiles covered with coloured glazes which continued some of the T'ang tradition.

The important wares of Tê Hua and Yi-Hsing are discussed in the glossary, and celadons continued to be made at Chü Chou, to where the Lung Ch'üan kilns were removed early in the Ming dynasty. Floral decoration is characteristically Ming in style, and it has been suggested that a ring bare of glaze and burnt to a reddish-brown within the footring is indication of a Ming date, which accords well enough with observation.

and *famille rose*. Two other categories – *famille noire* and *famille jaune* – are less well known because specimens are fewer. *Famille noire* refers to a relatively small number of vases – beloved by George Salting and the Empress Dowager – which have a black ground washed over with translucent green enamel in conjunction with flowers in the *famille verte* palette. *Famille jaune* has a yellow ground, instead of black.

Enamelled porcelain was first separated into these categories in the middle of the nineteenth century by Albert Jacquemart on the basis of the colour predominating, and the subject is further discussed in the glossary. Towards the end of the eighteenth

Vase decorated with the copper based *sang de boeuf* glaze, K'ang Hsi period (1662–1722), Ch'ing dynasty

century the *rose* and *verte* palettes were combined to form *rose-verte*, a colour scheme employed for export wares of debased and overcrowded design painted at Canton.

Underglaze copper-red was employed for both archaizing wares and those painted in contemporary styles, and the Ch'ien Lung potters mastered the difficult art of combining copper red and cobalt blue. A very important group of wares developed, during the reign of Ch'ien Lung, from copper used in this way. These are the *flambés* – copper glazes fired in a reducing kiln, some of which are called *sang de boeuf* from a fancied resemblance to ox-blood. This colour was not attainable in Europe till almost the end of the nineteenth century, when its secret was discovered by Bernard Moore in Staffordshire. The *flambé* glazes are usually streaked or suffused with blue, or bear a blue splash, or splashes, much in the same way as Sung dynasty Chün ware. The *sang de boeuf* glaze is generally to be found on large pieces – jars, vases, and bowls – but the delicate peachbloom glaze, which belongs to the same category, is only to be found in small pieces, like those made for the scholar's table. Peachbloom is a pink of variable shade and density which has occasional faint green specks. Good specimens were much prized in eighteenth-century China, and inferior copies were made in Japan which are still good enough to deceive the unwary.

Monochrome glazes are especially numerous throughout the eighteenth century. The *rose* enamel was thus employed, and the coral red monochrome was derived from iron-red. There were several yellows, of which the Imperial yellow is the best known. This is a dark brownish-yellow lead glaze. Brown glazes, sometimes termed *café au lait*, cover vases with *famille rose* floral painting in fan-shaped reserved panels. These are sometimes termed Batavian ware because they were shipped by the Dutch from Batavia, one of their Far Eastern entrepôts. The so-called mirror-black, to be found principally covering *rouleau* vases decorated with delicate patterns in oil-gilding which have often now worn off, is related to the old Honan black glazes, and has nothing to do with *famille noire*. The wash of green enamel is missing. Some of the greens described by Chinese commentators are difficult to identify. Names like cucumber green, camellia leaf green, and apple-green are typical. Turquoise and blue lead glazes, usually covering small pieces and figures, continue a type first introduced during the Ming dynasty.

K'ang Hsi wares

The Ch'ing dynasty developed some not particularly happy novelties, such as *porcelaine lac burgautée* – porcelain painted over with lacquer and inlaid with mother-of-pearl. Imitations in porcelain of jade, lacquer, bronze, rhinoceros horn, and even grained wood, were also made.

Belonging to this period is the so-called Chinese 'soft-paste' porcelain. This is not a soft-paste in the European sense, but an opaque, fine-grained, white porcelain with a crackled glaze painted in underglaze blue. The glaze, according to Chinese sources, contains *hua shih* (slippery stone), once thought to be soapstone but, since analysis reveals a complete absence of magnesium oxide, may in fact be pegmatite. Pieces are small, and of good quality.

During this period vast quantities of porcelain were made for export to the West, largely of European form, with decoration specially commissioned, but also of such Japanese wares as Kakiemon and

Imari decorations in demand in the West. There is little doubt that this trade had a debasing effect on Chinese taste generally which becomes more evident as the nineteenth century progresses.

The reign of the first nineteenth century emperor, Chia Ch'ing (1796–1820), who should not be confused with the Ming emperor, Chia Ching, has little or nothing of importance to show, apart from the snuff bottle, the best examples of which are in hardstones of one kind or another. The *graviata* decoration, in which the body was covered with incised decoration painted over with opaque enamels, began in the reign of Ch'ien Lung and continued into that of Tao Kuang (1820–51). The *rose-verte* palette was commonly employed for wares (especially export wares) with a lumpy, musliny glaze. Enamels became increasingly opaque instead of translucent, and tended to cover most of the available surface. During the reign of Tao Kuang some good copies of the more showy wares of the early decades of the eighteenth century were made, such as the large ewer and stand decorated with a fruiting peach on a bough which runs to the rim of the stand and continues over on to the back.

Ching-tê Chên was burned down in 1853 and rebuilt in 1864; during the reign of Kuang Hsü (1874–1909) the factory produced copies of such eighteenth-century glazes as *sang de boeuf*, apple-green, *famille noire*, and peachbloom which are hardly deceptive. Modern wares are of negligible importance.

This is a very brief outline of the wares which came from the better known kiln sites. There were many other smaller kilns throughout China, about which little is known. There are also many specimens, about which little can be said, that originated in one or other of them. The discovery of 'waster' dumps has led to the identification of some wares, and this process is likely to continue in future.

In the last fifty years or so vast quantities of pottery and porcelain of all periods have been discovered in China by itinerant antique dealers and shipped to the West. Much was bought from grave robbers who concealed the sources of their 'finds', which has not helped the dating and attribution of some things. Some of the wares thus exported were forgeries and reproductions discussed below.

Spurious wares

Copies of early Chinese wares are of two kinds – those made in a spirit of emulation and veneration, and those made for fraudulent purposes. Of the two, the first category is the more numerous. One comes across stories of Palace officials who purloined a fine vase or bowl and replaced it with an exact copy, but

Left *Blanc de chine* Fukien teapot and beaker decorated in raised relief with flowers, K'ang Hsi period (1662–1722), Ch'ing dynasty

Right Yüeh ware celadon jar decorated with a soft smoky-olive glaze, Six Dynasties (220–589)

Yung Chêng wares

these are apocryphal. The potter can make a passable copy of a particular type; it is far more difficult, if not impossible, to make an exact copy of a specific object. Some of the archaizing wares of the eighteenth century, like Yung Chêng imitations of Hsüan-tê blue-and-white or underglaze red stem cups, can be deceptive unless one is well acquainted with the earlier ware.

Generally, it may be accepted as certain that, whenever in the past there has been a fashion for a particular type of ware, forgeries will have been made. This applies to K'ang Hsi blue-and-white, and the *famille noire* vases, much sought after towards the end of the nineteenth century, although few of them would deceive anyone of experience. The closest copies of export wares have not been made in China, but by Samson of Paris and Herend of Hungary, the latter making, also, good copies of *famille verte.*

By far the greater number of forgeries are of T'ang tomb-figures, especially the ambitious models, like camels and fighting horses, and the most deceptive provide a stringent test of connoisseurship. The most difficult are the unglazed models decorated with unfired pigments, but the subject is separately discussed in the glossary.

CHINESE LOWESTOFT AND EXPORT PORCELAIN

The first Chinese porcelain to leave the country where it had been made were pieces that had been manufactured for use in China itself. They had been brought home to the West by those few travellers who had penetrated the then unknown Orient. It was not until the seventeenth century that porcelain began to be made and decorated in China especially to the order of European buyers.

Cup, saucer and cream jug painted with a scene of the Crucifixion in Schwarzlot, first half of 18th century. Museum of Fine Arts, Boston

The Jesuit Fathers

The Europeans who were concerned in the first place with the production of porcelain in China were the French Jesuit Fathers. These men, of whom the most famous in this connection was Père d'Entrecolles, began to establish themselves in the country in about A.D. 1600. It was not until some fifty years after this date that a tangible result of their presence became apparent. This was the making of pieces of porcelain bearing representations of the crucifix accompanied, in many cases, by the letters *I.H.S.* It is uncertain whether they were made for export to Japan for the use of Christian converts in that country or for export to Europe. Whatever their intended destination, a few examples of these early wares, decorated in blue on a white ground, exist today, and their designs have an unquestionably European inspiration. However, in some instances, with a typically Chinese tolerance, Buddhist symbols have been incorporated in the patterns.

About half a century later there was a further output of religious designs. On this occasion there is no doubt that the products were made for export. Large quantities of porcelain were manufactured on which were painted copies of the Crucifixion and other biblical scenes from both the Old and the New Testaments. Some were in full colours, but mostly they were in *Schwarzlot.* While the majority were in the form of plates and dishes, there are in existence also a number of secular articles, such as tea sets, which were doubtless for display rather than for use, painted quite inappropriately with such designs.

Armorial decoration

The most popular form of decoration that was called for from China by patrons in England, Europe, and America generally, was heraldic. Just as it was the fashion that silver plate should bear the arms or crest of the owner, so it became the vogue with porcelain. This may be accounted for by the fact that the shapes of the majority of the articles were copied from pieces of silver, which it was intended that the porcelain should replace, and it was not unnatural that such decoration as the originals bore should be copied in addition.

The making of porcelain in European forms commenced at the beginning of the eighteenth century. Such pieces can be dated by a combination of factors: the shape of the article; the style of decoration and the colours used in painting it; the type of porcelain used in the manufacture; and, in some cases, by the armorial bearings. With the aid of the latter it is possible sometimes to date a piece of china to within a few years. It may so happen that a marriage or a death caused a change to have taken place in the emblazoning of a coat-of-arms, and from this it can be found during which years the particular bearing was current.

In a few cases the original accounts have been preserved in a family, together with the china to which they relate. One such example is the bill, now preserved in the British Museum, referring to the

Above Cup and saucer, pencilled Lowestoft, *c.* 1785. Essex Institute, Salem, Massachusetts

service shipped from Canton in 1731 for a member of the Peers family. Two pieces of the actual china are in the same museum. Such careful and fortunate preservation of the original documents is, of course, very exceptional, and goes far to help in dating many other similar pieces.

Variety of articles

The output of porcelain for export was not confined by any means to articles solely for use at the table. Any attempt to provide a complete list of the many different things that were made would be doomed to failure. In this type of porcelain it is not untrue to suggest that there is nothing new under the sun, and frequently it is surprising to find what the Chinese potters and painters attempted to copy in a medium that was often completely unsuitable. However, although the result was usually a technical success, it must be agreed that it was far from being also an artistic one.

Next in popularity to table services were punch bowls. These were made in many sizes and decorated in an infinite variety of styles. Many bear the scene of an English fox hunt round the outside, and some of these are completed by having the fox painted on the inside of the bowl. Others have accurate copies of European paintings and engravings, such as Hogarth's *Calais Gate*, of which a fine example in full colours is in the Victoria and Albert Museum, London. Others refer to political events, of which the bowl with caricature portraits of John Wilkes and the Lord Chief Justice Lord Mansfield is typical. Others bear externally, say, a group of flowers, but beneath the base is a well-painted amorous scene, best kept concealed from the general gaze.

A list of other utilitarian articles could be a lengthy one, and would include: candlesticks, cache pots (in which a flowerpot stands), water cisterns, shaving bowls, chamber pots, wall brackets, salt cellars, pepper and sugar casters, knife handles, snuffboxes, tea caddies, and beer tankards.

Figures

Apart from such articles intended for daily use in the home, pieces that could serve none other than a decorative purpose were also made. Figures with attempted European features and in Western clothing are typical. There are also figures of animals copied from Dutch Delft pottery, and from other originals. An interesting group in the Victoria and Albert Museum, London, is that of a man and woman dancing. This is known to have been first modelled at the Meissen factory by Eberlein about the year 1745 and, besides the Chinese copies, it was also imitated in England at Chelsea. Few other groups can have been made at so many different factories in so many countries within the space of

Below, left Pair of covered vases of European form, *c.* 1800. Museum of Fine Arts, Boston

Below, right Candlestick, painted in *famille rose* enamels, first half of 18th century. Victoria & Albert Museum

about fifteen years. In the category of figures may be included jugs. Copies of jugs of the Toby type also exist in Chinese eighteenth-century porcelain.

The factories
The articles enumerated above were all made in one or other of the great factories grouped at Ching-tê Chên and decorated, with the exception of blue-and-white pieces, mostly at the port of Canton. Figures, groups, and other pieces were made also at the factories of Tê Hua in the Province of Fukien. The porcelain made there was of a distinctive creamy-white colour, and was not usually decorated in the East. Much of it was imported into Holland and Germany and coloured in those countries. Small groups composed of figures wearing recognizably European costume are found in this ware, also tankards with rounded bodices and reeded necks taken from a model known in Rhineland stoneware. This type of porcelain, which dates from the mid-seventeenth century, is known as *blanc-de-Chine.*

Above The Grand Turk punch bowl, the interior inscribed 'ship Grand Turk at Canton 1786'. Peabody Museum, Salem, Massachusetts

Porcelain plate painted in underglaze blue with figures of European musicians, the border with Chinese landscapes, early 18th century. Victoria & Albert Museum

One further group of eighteenth-century export porcelains was decorated in underglaze blue, together with iron-red and some slight gilding. It was based on that exported from Japan, and is known by the name of the port whence the original was sent to the West, Imari.

Late in the eighteenth century exportations from China included a large proportion of so-called Mandarin wares. These were painted with panels of figures within minutely patterned borders. In the next century came the Canton style, which features butterflies and flowers on a celadon-green ground.

Apart from a knowledge of the role played by the various East India Companies in trading with the Orient, little is known of the details of how this large trade was handled.

The Lowestoft myth
It must be admitted that the word 'Lowestoft' applied to this section is a complete misnomer. In actual fact there is no real connection whatsoever between Lowestoft, a fishing port in Suffolk on the east coat of England, and the porcelain produced in the factories of China. Certainly a type of porcelain was made for some years in a factory established at Lowestoft. The decoration applied to many of the productions of these minor works comprised bouquets of pink roses and groups of figures and was, by a coincidence, very similar to the decoration then current on porcelain from the Far East. This English porcelain itself does not compare at all with the hard Oriental product, and the two are not likely to be confused.

The widespread misapprehension over the origin of the Chinese pieces arose from an error in an early edition of Chaffer's *Marks and Monograms*, and, in spite of repeated corrections over the past twenty-five years, collectors and dealers in both England and the United States continually refer to Chinese porcelain made to European order as 'Lowestoft'. From being applied, in the first place, to pieces with a particular type of floral decoration, the term has been extended to cover the whole group of export porcelains, and today almost any piece of Chinese porcelain which displays in shape and decoration any obvious sign of European influence is still sometimes designated by this inappropriate term.

The American China trade
Once the United States had won independence and was free to trade directly with other countries than England, Americans lost no time in entering the China Trade. They did not found an East India Company: individual merchants sent out their own ships and each was a separate venture. The first to sail to the East was the *Empress of China*, a former privateer, which left New York for Canton on 22 February 1784, and arrived during the summer. Major Samuel Shaw, former aide-de-camp to General Knox, was supercargo on this voyage – an extremely important post, for on the supercargo depended not only financial success of the venture but also diplomatic relations with the Chinese. Shaw acquitted himself well, laying the groundwork for future trade between his country and China, and bringing home a cargo that inspired many American merchants to join in the hazardous but lucrative China Trade.

Ships set sail to the Orient from New York, Philadelphia, Boston, Norfolk, Charleston, and other ports. By 1790 twenty-eight American ships had made the voyage. Before 1800 one merchant trader alone, Elias Hasket Derby of Salem, had sent out forty-five ventures. The China Trade became the

Dish with underglaze decorated in Fitzhugh pattern with the American eagle in the centre. Metropolitan Museum of Art

most profitable branch of American shipping, and presently threatened the monopoly of Britain's powerful East India Company. It reached its peak with the development of the clipper ship in the 1840s, and by the time steam replaced sail its great colourful days were over. But long before then literally tons of Chinese porcelain, along with tea and spices, silks and cottons, lacquer, and other exotic luxuries, had been brought into ports up and down the Eastern seaboard. Some survives still in the families for whom it was made.

Chinese porcelain for the American market

In general, American-market porcelain from China is less elaborate and less varied than what was made for Europe. This is partly because it covers a shorter period, partly because the taste of this period was for the neoclassic, more restrained than the rococo of the preceding era. Moreover, by the time Yankees were trading to the East, the production of export porcelain had become a highly developed commercial operation, and a large proportion of the ware was turned out in stock patterns of simple design instead of being specially made and decorated to individual order.

PRINCIPAL CHINESE DYNASTIES AND REIGNS

Shang	*c.* 1600–1027 B.C.
Chou	1027–771 B.C.
Spring and Autumn annals	770–475 B.C.
Warring states	475–221 B.C.
Han	206 B.C.–A.D. 220
Six dynasties	220–589
T'ang	618–906
Five dynasties	907–60
Sung	960–1280
Yüan	1280–1368
Ming	1368–1644
Hung Wu	1368–98
Yung-lo	1403–24
Hsüan-tê	1426–35
Ch'êng Hua	1465–87
Hung Chih	1488–1505
Chêng-tê	1506–21
Chia Ching	1522–66
Lung Ch'ing	1567–72
Wan Li	1573–1620
T'ien Ch'i	1621–7
Ch'ung Chêng	1628–44
Ch'ing	1644–1912
Shun Chih	1644–61
K'ang Hsi	1662–1722
Yung Chêng	1722–36
Ch'ien Lung	1736–96
Chia Ch'ing	1796–1820
Tao Kuang	1820–51
Hsien Fêng	1851–61
T'ung Chih	1862–74
Kuang Hsü	1874–1909
Hsüan T'ung	1909–12
Chinese Republic	1912–
Hung Hsien (Yüan Shih-k'ai)	1916–

Armorial pieces, bearing the arms of Pennsylvania. New York Historical Society

Korea

Korea occupies a position to the north of China which, in effect, puts it midway between China and Japan, and in the past it has done much to influence art in Japan by transmitting Chinese influences. The pottery and porcelain of Korea is original both in form and decoration, and some Korean products rank with the finest Far Eastern wares.

The earliest pottery of which there is record belongs to the Silla dynasty (57 B.C – A.D. 936). The body is grey and of variable hardness, unglazed, and decorated with incised patterns, or impressed with the mesh of coarse textiles (the so-called 'mat markings'). These wares are, in some respects, similar to those of the Northern Wei in China. Also belonging to the Silla period are some jars and bowls with an olive-green or brown glaze resembling Chinese proto-porcelain, but wares of this kind are not easy to allocate between China and Korea.

The Koryu dynasty (918–1392) produced wares which were analogous to those of china, and especially to the Yüeh and Northern celadons. The base of Korean celadons is glazed all over, with small 'stilt' marks within the footring which indicate the position of kiln supports. Although contemporary with the Sung dynasty, the Koryu potters turned more often to T'ang wares for inspiration. A characteristic Koryu technique, which hardly occurs elsewhere in the Orient, is termed *mishima* in Japan. The *mishima* decoration was inlaid into the raw clay surface in black and white clay in conjunction with a celadon glaze. The name is derived from a small island midway between Korea and Japan at which wares of this kind were transhipped. The same period is also noted for celadons with deeply carved and pierced ornament.

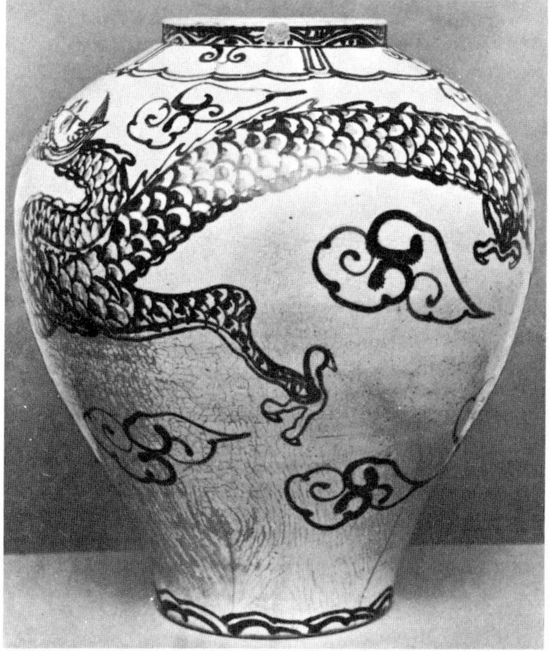

Porcelain jar with painted decoration, Yi dynasty, 17th or 18th century. Victoria & Albert Museum

Ting-type porcelain is among the finer wares of the period. Circular boxes and covers are often of exceedingly fine quality. *Ying Ch'ing* also occurs in fairly typical Korean forms, so it is evident that it was made locally. Painting in brownish black, first practised towards the end of the period, probably owes much to the products of Tzŭ Chou. Decoration of this kind – usually floral scrolls, aquatic birds and flying birds amid cloud scrolls – occurs on jars and vases, and is noted for the exceptional quality of the drawing.

During the Yi dynasty (1392–1910) the *mishima* decoration was continued in the early years, and from the sixteenth century a type of porcelain, often opaque, with a greyish glaze, was clumsily wrought, but superbly decorated with swift, sure brushwork with birds, floral and foliate, and abstract motifs, painted in blackish-blue, or sometimes copper red.

Korean forms generally differ considerably from those of China; spouted vessels based on the gourd, and cups and stands, are examples. The popular *Mei Ping* form was shared with China. Lobed forms, and floral scrolls carved and incised under the glaze, are fairly typical. Much surviving Korean ware is in the form of bowls of one kind or another, and especially sought are the small circular boxes of Ting or *Ying Ch'ing* types with moulded or incised decoration.

Japanese

Although much less is definitely known about Japanese pottery and porcelain than about Chinese wares, the porcelain of Japan has, in the past, often been much more eagerly sought, especially that decorated in the manner of Sakaida Kakiemon. When the Meissen factory began to copy Oriental porcelain in the 1720s they derived inspiration from the Japanese porcelain collection of the Elector, Augustus the Strong, which he had obtained from Dutch suppliers, and when Augustus bought a palace to house his collection he called it the Japanische Palais. In France, about the same time, a factory at Chantilly belonging to the Prince de Condé devoted itself to copying the decorations of Kakiemon. The copies of Chelsea in the early 1750s were so close that they have occasionally been mistaken for Japanese.

Following the reopening of trade with Japan by Commodore Perry of the U.S. Navy in 1853 Japanese pottery and porcelain once more became extremely fashionable, attracting the attention of collectors like the brothers Goncourt in Paris, and during the last quarter of the nineteenth century Japanese influence played an important part in the development of Art Nouveau.

The ceramic art in Japan is very ancient, but the early wares are hardly known in the West. The earliest is a black coiled pottery known as Jomon ware, once thought to belong, at the latest, to the first millennium B.C. but now considered to have its origin at a much earlier date. Yayoi pottery is more or less contemporary with the Chinese Han dynasty, and the latter variety includes tomb-figures known as *haniwa*, so called because they encircled burial mounds. *Haniwa* means, literally, 'clay circle'. These wares are hardly to be seen outside specialist museum collections.

Until the Nara period (710–794), when the Court established itself at Nara, no very great technical advances were made. The principal manufacture was a grey bodied stoneware, unglazed, and Korean in style. At this time potters began to master coloured glazes, and such centres as Bizen, Omi, Iga, and Owari first made domestic wares.

At the beginning of the thirteenth century Kato Shirozayemon journeyed to China to study the art of potting, especially the making of black-glazed teabowls, then much valued by the Japanese for use in the Tea Ceremony (*cha-no-yu*) and by them called *temmoku*. On his return he founded kilns at Seto (Owari) where he started to make similar bowls.

Towards the end of the sixteenth century the victorious Hideyoshi returned from Korea, bringing potters with him. They settled at a number of new centres like Kyoto, Karatsu, Takatori, and Satsuma, and started to produce wares in current Korean styles. Under the influence of the Tea Masters fashion in Tea Ceremony wares began to change from the Chinese Sung dynasty black glazed wares to more summarily made and decorated Korean peasant wares.

A Korean potter named Ameya (d. 1574) devised a new and popular type of teabowl which was first made about 1525, and continued by his son, Chojiro. These teabowls were brought to the notice of Hideyoshi in 1588, and he awarded Chojiro a gold seal engraved with the word *raku*, which means 'enjoyment' or 'felicity'. The manufacture of *raku* ware spread widely. It was a kind of earthenware fired at a very low temperature on a hearth, and covered with a treacly glaze which fused at a similar temperature. At first black or dark brown, then light red, the *raku* glaze became straw-coloured in the seventeenth century, and then green, cream, and other colours, either alone or in combination. The ware itself was thick and roughly potted, usually with an irregular shape and surface. Often the form was deliberately distorted still further by squeezing it before firing.

In origin the Tea Ceremony was Zen Buddhist, and the utensils were required to be of refined and simple shapes covered with a good glaze of restrained colour or colours, but the introduction of *raku* ware led to a cult of the primitive which caused the arbiters of taste, the Tea Masters, to search for objects of unique form with striking accidental glaze effects. This cult has not, in the past, appealed to English collectors, but it has found a good deal of favour in France, even in the nineteenth century. The collection of the Goncourt brothers was sold in the 1890s, the sale catalogued by Samuel Bing, whose gallery, L'Art Nouveau, gave its name to the style.

Another development took place at Awata early in the seventeenth century, where a cream coloured stoneware with a finely crackled glaze was first made. This became the medium for some distinguished painting by Kenzan (1660–1743). Even more celebrated was Ninsei, more or less contemporary with Kenzan, who painted in enamel colours and silver and gold. The Dohachi family worked in styles similar to those of Ninsei, and a school of enamelling grew up in and around the region. The earliest Satsuma pottery belongs to the end of the eighteenth century when it was enamelled sparsely and in good taste. The type of grossly overdecorated 'Satsuma', developed towards the end of the nineteenth century to appeal to the uniformed taste of the West for the quaintly Oriental, is hardly to be taken seriously.

Bizen ware, made at Imbé in Bizen Province, is traditionally said to date from the fourteeenth century. The later wares are in a red or bluish-brown stoneware (the latter colour often with a metallic sheen) in which were made Tea Ceremony wares, vases, and figures of animals. The body is not unlike

that of Yi-Hsing stoneware, the wares of which were copied.

Banko wares take their name from that adopted by an amateur potter, Gonzayemon (1736–95), whose output was both varied and prolific. He copied *raku* wares, Satsuma, the Ming 'red and green family', Dutch delft (then being imported into Japan) and the work of Kenzan and Ninsei. Some of these wares were continued during the nineteenth century by the man who bought the original formulae.

Japanese pottery is a very difficult field. It is badly documented, and attributions are frequently uncertain. A pot in the style of a particular artist was often signed with his name as a tribute, much in the same way as the Ch'ing potters in China put Ming reign-marks on their porcelain. Japanese pottery is difficult to classify because wares made in different places may be given the same name. They may be called by the name of a province, a town, the principal market, the name of a Tea Master, or that of a ruling prince. Potters rejoice in several names. For instance, Kenzan was called Ogata, Shinsho, Sansho, Shinzaburo, and so on. For the most part, therefore, there is little point in trying to arrive at exact attributions or dates. Specimens of the work of masters like Kenzan and Ninsei are rare in Japan, and there must be few, if any, in the West, even in France where more attention has been devoted to Japanese pottery than anywhere else. The collector is therefore forced to rely on taste rather than knowledge to an extent which prevails in few other fields.

A different scale of values applies to Japanese porcelain, partly because it was never greatly influenced by the Tea Masters. Traditionally the art of

Left Baluster jar, early Kakiemon, decorated with enamel colours, *c.* 1670

porcelain-making was brought to Japan from China by Gorodoyu-go Shonsui in the first half of the sixteenth century. Little use was made of the knowledge for nearly a hundred years, and the first kilns were established in the early decades of the seventeenth century at Arita in Hizen Province close to a source of raw materials. The first wares were painted in underglaze blue, but the first Sakaida Kakiemon (born 1590) is reputed to have learned the art of enamelling in colour around 1644. Enamelling remained the secret of the Sakaida family for many years thereafter.

In 1641 the Dutch were given a trading concession and were awarded a trading station on the minute island of Deshima at Nagasaki, which was small enough to be circumnavigated during the course of a leisurely after-dinner promenade. Very soon large quantities of Arita porcelain, made to order, were being shipped to Holland. Arita was sometimes willing to make special export shapes, but they were less inclined to decorate to order. They did, however, supply porcelain 'in white' for export which the Dutch painted in their own studios in Antwerp and Delft.

By the last decades of the seventeenth century the third Sakaida Kakiemon was painting Arita porcelain in an attractive asymmetrical style, with a distinctive palette consisting of a soft iron-red, a bluish-green, light blue, yellow, and (occasionally) slight gilding. Specimens in which the blue is underglaze are the earliest. This style became so popular in Europe that vast quantities were imported and extensively copied. The Chinese also copied the Japanese wares for the European market and their own. Their copies lack the bluish-green, while the Japanese red is thicker and darker. Chinese wares also lack the 'stilt' marks (three or four defects in the glaze inside the footring), which are invariable in the case of Arita wares and Chelsea copies. These 'stilt' marks were the points of support in the kiln during firing.

The most attractive features of Kakiemon decoration is simplicity, and a careful balancing of areas of white porcelain against the painted decoration, with a carefully judged asymmetry which is a characteristic of most Japanese art.

The shapes employed by the Arita kilns differ considerably from those of China. Octagonal deep dishes, bowls, and vases are frequent, and those of square section not uncommon. Some difficulty may have been experienced in firing objects of circular section without distortion in the natural mixture of clay and fusible rock employed. Japanese porcelain is usually thicker than comparable Chinese wares, and the glaze has a musliny texture, not unlike the Chinese 'chicken skin', due to the body being fired to biscuit before glazing. When this effect is absent an attribution to a Japanese kiln becomes very doubtful.

Typical Kakiemon patterns are the 'quail' the 'tyger and wheatsheaf' (Korean tiger pattern), the 'banded hedge', the 'Hob in the Well', and many more. The 'quail' pattern is still being used today in European factories.

Also from Arita, beginning at the end of the seventeenth century, are wares, principally dishes and vases, decorated with a blackish underglaze blue, and a thick, dark red as the predominating colours. They were usually painted with chrysanthemums and otther flowers, and often with patterns derived from textiles, or with the *mon* (a Japanese heraldic device).

Far right Arita plate decorated in enamel colours in a style inspired by Chinese *famille verte*, first half of 18th century

Dish decorated in underglaze blue and overglaze enamels with a Kabuki theatre scene, Imari, mid-17th century

These wares, made almost entirely for export, were called 'Imari', from the name of the port of shipment near Arita. They were imitated by the Chinese, and they continued to be made until well into the nineteenth century, when both the blue and the red became darker and coarser. The addition of reddish-brown, purple, black, and lilac-blue to the Arita palette are definite evidence of a nineteenth century date.

While Arita was the largest and best known of the seventeenth- and eighteenth-century porcelain factories of Japan there were others producing wares of notable quality. The kilns at Kutani in Kaga Province were established in 1664 and closed about 1692. Ao Kutani was decorated with a fine and distinctive green within black outlines, while Ko Kutani is noted for brilliant enamel colouring on a brownish-red patterned background. Saiko Kutani (revived Kutani) belongs to the nineteenth century and was made by kilns in Kaga Province. Early Kutani porcelain is extremely rare.

A factory was founded in the middle of the seventeenth century at Okawachi in Hizen Province by the Prince of Nabeshima helped by Korean potters. Some of the best work has points in common with the Chinese *tou ts'ai* (contrasting colours). The designs are outlined in underglaze blue and the colours applied in thin washes. This Ming technique was revived in China itself during the reign of Yung Chêng (1722–36).

About 1710 the Prince of Hirado was responsible for the founding of kilns at Mikawachi (Hizen Province), where Korean potters had been working since the seventeenth century. The wares were small, but of good quality, well painted in a pale underglaze blue, with a certain amount of relief decoration. Celadons were made both at Arita and Mikawachi in imitation of Sung dynasty types, but the body is porcelain rather than stoneware.

These comprise what might well be called the 'classic' wares of Japan. They are becoming much rarer in Europe than they were because Japanese collectors have been buying them back for some years past. Still fairly common are nineteenth-century wares from places like Seto (Owari), Kyoto, Mikawachi, and Shiba. Both Mikawachi and Shiba produced a kind of 'eggshell' porcelain often in the form of tea-services for export. Quality is variable. Kyoto imitated Sung dynasty celadons and the Ming 'red and green' family. Seto made enormous vases painted all over which were exported to Europe towards the end of the nineteenth century. Porcelain imitations of *cloisonné* enamels on copper were made in the same place.

The commercial porcelain of the nineteenth century for export to the West was often made and decorated to the specification of Western merchants, who had astutely gauged (or should it be 'plumbed'?) Western popular taste. This was a source of considerable apprehension to Japanese official circles, and to Western critics, like Walter Crane. A Japanese Government contribution to the Philadelphia Centennial Exhibition of 1876 was an exhibition of pottery and porcelain in native taste. This exhibition later came to England and was purchased by the South Kensington Museum (now the Victoria and Albert Museum). A small handbook by Sir A. W. Franks, compiled with the aid of Japanese experts, was published, and provided a foundation for a more scholarly appraisal of Japan's contribution to the ceramic art. Today, the Victoria and Albert Museum has the most representative public collection of Japanese wares in England, and there are several important English private collections, principally of porcelain.

Danish

Copenhagen Porcelain

Attempts to make porcelain in Denmark did not meet with any real success until F. H. Müller, an extremely able chemist employed at the Danish Mint, began production in 1771.

Tureen and cover, Copenhagen, 1780–90. Victoria & Albert Museum

The hard-paste porcelain made by Müller resulted from lengthy experiments with kaolin deposits discovered on the island of Bornholm in 1755 by Niels Birch.

An earlier undertaking by Louis Fournier, who had been at Sèvres in Chantilly, made only soft paste, and lasted no more than six or seven years (1759–66). Fournier's rare productions are usually marked with an 'F' accompanied by the number '5' (for Frederick V of Denmark).

Various German workmen and arcanists, including the unreliable C. C. Hunger, had also offered their services, but these had been declined.

Müller was, however, assisted by J. G. von Langen, a mining engineer from Fürstenberg, who became advisor to the factory.

In 1744 a company was formed with Queen Juliane Marie as chief shareholder, and a year later it obtained a privilege.

On Langen's advice A. C. Laplau, a Fürstenberg modeller and arcanist, was employed in 1776, and with his help both the paste and techniques of production were much improved. In spite of this, financial difficulties caused the company to be taken over by the King in 1779. It then became the Royal Copenhagen Porcelain Manufactory (Den Kongelige Porcelainfabrik Copenhagen), a title retained until the present day; though Royal ownership ended in 1867.

The mark adopted from 1775 was three wavy lines, symbolizing Denmark's main waterways to the Baltic (the Sound, the Great and Little Belts). This, surmounted by a crown, and with varying inscriptions, has also been retained.

Twenty years of prosperity under the Crown was followed by a marked decline in the first half of the nineteenth century. Damage was caused to the factory during the bombardment by the British fleet under Admiral Gambier in 1807, and by 1822 the number of painters employed had dwindled to two. Modern revival dates from the appointment of Arnold Krog (1856–1931), an architect and designer of great ability, who became Art Director in 1885, following the removal of the factory from Købmagerade to Smallegrade, Frederiksberg.

Porcelain made during the first period (1772–9) was of a bluish-grey tone, but by 1780 it had become whiter and more translucent. The shapes and decoration in underglaze blue were at first much under the influence of Meissen and Fürstenberg. From the beginning of the Royal period a classical style pre-

Covered chocolate cup and saucer, 1780–90. Victoria & Albert Museum

vailed and the palette was greatly increased. Rams' heads, architectural motifs, and pierced basketwork borders were favoured; also silhouettes in black or grey monochrome, historical portraits and landscapes with ruins. Some nineteenth-century biscuit figures and reliefs are after Bertel Thorvaldsen.

Copenhagen's greatest achievement was the famous 'Flora Danica Service', probably intended for the Russian Empress Catherine II. It was started in 1789–90, but Catherine died in 1796, and the service, which was still incomplete in 1802, is now in the Rosenborg Castle, Copenhagen.

The decoration of the 1,602 pieces was determined by the administrative director Theodor Holm, statesman and botanist, and the painting executed by J. C. Bayer, who had already illustrated Holm's book on Danish fungi. The shapes are neoclassical, painted with naturalistic botanical subjects taken from the earlier parts of a great work on Danish flora, started by Oeder and published between 1761 and 1883. Fruit and flower baskets are ornamented with flowers modelled in the round by Søren Preuss.

Dutch

Pottery

When the name of a substance, such as nylon, or a product, such as Leica, is adopted immediately into the vocabulary of every civilized nation it is convincing proof of both its novelty and its worldwide appeal. The use of the name of a small Dutch town, Delft, spelt in a variety of ways, to describe more or less any blue-and-white earthenware in a score of different languages, leaves us in no doubt of the absolute pre-eminence enjoyed by the wares produced in that town over a period of some 150 years. It is the purpose of this chapter to give, briefly, the history of the evolution of those wares, to distinguish the various types, discuss their merits, and give some guidance to collectors.

EARLY FLEMISH AND DUTCH MAJOLICA

The technique of painting in high-temperature colours on a tin-enamel surface came north over the Alps from Italy early in the sixteenth century. We know that a potter from Castel Durante, Guido di Savino, who took the name of Guido Andriesz, settled in Antwerp in 1508, and we may take that date as the beginning of the school of South Netherlands majolica, which flourished for a hundred years and more. Other Italians, from Brescia and Venice, soon followed, and important commissions, especially for coloured tile pavements, have survived. Soon the drug pots and dishes began to acquire local characteristics which made them, in spite of their colouring, unmistakably non-Italian. The strong blue, green, deep orange, and yellow, with manganese outlines, were reminiscent of Urbino and Faenza, but were soon applied in characteristic groups of fruit, surrounded by circular bands of colouring. Two Italian motifs, which were to become Netherlandish specialities, were the strapwork, evolved from the cartouche, and the grotesques, derived via Urbino from Raphael's decorations in the Vatican – decorations themselves copied from ancient Rome. Unlike its Italian prototype, this Netherlands majolica seems to have been made only in 'useful' wares.

By the third quarter of the century, Antwerp potters are known to have moved farther north, just as Jaspar Andries (believed to be a son or grandson of Guido di Savino) moved to England in 1567 and began the long history of 'English Delft' some years before such wares were ever made at Delft itself. We

Polychrome dish, enamelled earthenware painted in colours, on blue ground, probably Rotterdam, *c.* 1620. Victoria & Albert Museum

have records of such Antwerp potters in Amsterdam (1584), Dordrecht, Middleburg, Rotterdam, Haarlem (1573), where they flourished, and eventually in Delft (1584).

It is extremely hard to classify these impressive early pieces, or to say with certainty that a particular piece was made in the North rather than in the South. The bold dishes, not unlike our 'blue-dash chargers', were tin-enamelled on the front only, the back being covered with a transparent lead glaze, showing the greyish yellow of the clay. There is no evidence, from excavation, that the wares decorated with *groteschi* of Urbino type were ever made in the North. Certain plain blue-and-white drug pots, with a gadroon border, are held to be Dutch. A type of plate with birds and animals painted on a dark-blue

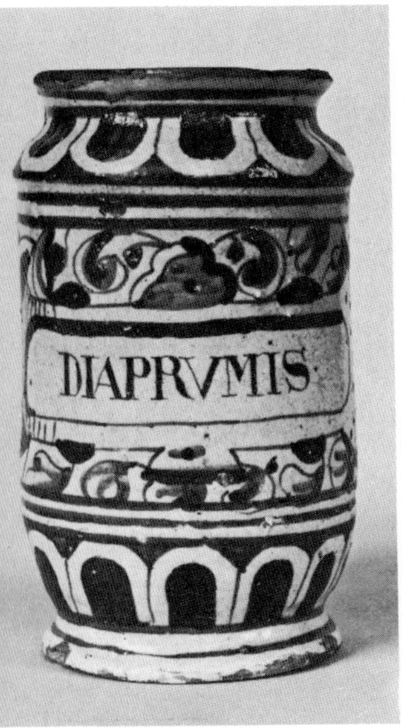

ground seems, on the evidence of the large quantity of fragments excavated, to be exclusively North Netherlandish, and was probably made at Rotterdam, as were the majority of the plates with stylized rosettes or chequered patterns. Pots and dishes in which the colours are exceptionally strong, and have been less well assimilated with the glaze, so that they seem almost to be in relief, are held, partly on the evidence of tiles, to be of North Netherlandish make, as are those which add dark-blue grapes to the conventional clusters of apples and pomegranates.

Northern also are the plates with raised knobs on the border and bearing pious inscriptions such as *Eert Godt altijt* (Honour God always), a type which, starting as early as 1580, even crops up in blue-and-white in the late eighteenth century. The palette used in these is unpleasing: a very strong blue, a pure bright ochrous orange, and a vivid opaque light green. It occurs in a number of plates with similar borders showing milkmaids (sometimes with a date) and coats-of-arms (generally imaginary), nearly all of which date from the first quarter of the seventeenth century. These, with the gadrooned *albarelli* and the blue-ground plates mentioned above, give us a fairly accurate picture of the North Netherlands majolica, which we can amplify by the study of the tiles. The few more elaborately decorated pieces which have survived seem to be almost certainly of South Netherlands and Antwerp origin, to which city may also be ascribed any pieces showing a pure, clear lemon yellow. It is worth commenting that an inscription in Dutch, or Flemish, cannot be considered as evidence one way or another.

Above Blue monochrome drug jar, north Netherlands, *c.* 1620. Rijksmuseum, Amsterdam

Right Polychrome plate, enamelled earthenware painted in blue, green and yellow, *c.* 1600. Victoria & Albert Museum

Suffice it to say that by the close of the sixteenth century majolica was being made in a great number of Dutch towns, with Haarlem perhaps achieving the greatest technical perfection and Rotterdam producing the greatest quantity, especially of tiles. Dishes were still covered with lead glaze on the back: a practice which was not wholly abandoned until near the middle of the next century. Very little of it was marked, and none of the marks may be ascribed with any certainty to a particular maker, any more than pieces can be attributed, except by conjecture, to a particular place of origin.

All these early wares, the incunabula of Dutch pottery, are of Italian inspiration, however much design and colouring may have undergone a local modification. They are vigorous and confident, unsophisticated and unpretentious, attractive in their own artistic right as well as in the problem of origin which each separate piece poses to collector, dealer, and museum expert alike. Yet they remain essentially derivative, a late offshoot of a great tradition. Dutch majolica, in the making of which the Northern potters were building up an invaluable tradition of knowledge and skill, still awaited the external impulse which was to give it a new direction, a life of its own, and was to help it develop, with all the vigour of a young and prosperous nation, into something specifically and uniquely Dutch, one of the great monuments of ceramic art which, in its turn, fertilized and influenced the whole field of ceramic activity in Europe.

This external impulse came, in 1602, from the landing of the first large cargo of Chinese porcelain in Amsterdam. Chinese blue-and-white pieces had long been known and the material treated with awe as something wellnigh magical. This arrival in quantity, however, caused a revolution in taste. At first it was only the decoration which was imitated, and from about 1610 onwards we have a series of chargers with deep-blue borders on which appear, in reserves, the conventional Wan Li designs of Buddhist emblems, etc. For a while these were combined with centre decorations done in the old Netherlands palette of blue, bright green, ochre, and reddish brown, and the Chinese frame might surround a Dutch landscape, fruit bowls, or a Madonna and Child. But soon the blue-and-white monochrome swept all before it, and a dish of that type appears in the arms of the Haarlem potters (1635). An important further consequence of greater familiarity with Chinese originals was that it became customary to apply tin-enamel to the back of the dish as well as the front, in order more closely to imitate porcelain. The earliest surviving fragment thus glazed back and front is dated 1622.

Far right Dish painted in colours, probably Haarlem, first half of 17th century. Fitzwilliam Museum

From now on, for over a hundred years, the decoration of by far the greater part of Dutch earthenware was to be Chinese in character. That it was not slavishly imitative but developed a character of its own is largely for technical reasons. The softness of the glaze, into which the decoration seemed to melt, was one such factor. More important, and more of an obstacle to any too minute copying, was the fact that the decorators were painting on to a highly absorbent ground, on which their colour dried instantly, allowing no retouching and demanding a swift and confident brush stroke. Some pieces were indeed made which, at first glance or behind the glass of a museum cabinet, are impossible to distinguish from K'ang Hsi originals. But soon the introduction of manganese outlines, the combination of Chinese with baroque motifs, the illustrating of scenes from Dutch life, all helped to create that intensely individual character which distinguishes Dutch Delft from the Chinese decoration which inspired it and from the innumerable imitations which were made, all over the rest of Europe, from the second half of the seventeenth century onwards.

'Dutch Delft': it may seem doubly tautological to use the phrase, but one can avoid it no longer. The first of these Wan Li dishes were probably made at Haarlem, whence the earliest recorded potters in Delft had come. Yet by 1650 Delft had established a predominance it was never to lose. Potteries continued to produce good work in Haarlem, Friesland, and elsewhere, while Rotterdam became the great manufacturer of tiles. Yet qualitatively and quantitatively, Delft stood alone in its high repute for the production of luxurious wares of every shape and every degree of elaboration. This was in part due to its convenient geographical position, between the estuaries of the Rhine and the Meuse and the rest of Holland, and near to the North Sea. But no town in Holland lacks access to the country's waterways. The rise of Delft must be ascribed to the chance of a combination of propitious circumstances. The geographical position, the arrival of large quantities of blue-and-white ware from China, the rapidly increasing prosperity of the country, seeking a new outlet for capital, and the sudden decline of the important Delft brewing industry, suffering from the competition with English beer (by 1667 only 15 of over 180 breweries were still working). This last was possibly decisive, as the buildings were thus made available for those who wished to set up a pottery. In fact, many potteries took over the names of the breweries they replaced: the Three Bells, the Rose, the Peacock, the Greek A, and many others which have become familiar to lovers of Delft. The new industry doubtless also profited by the rebuilding of much of the town after the explosion of the powder magazine in 1654. As the second half of the seventeenth century began, the industry at Delft was launched on the greatest period of its existence, in which it was to continue with unabated prosperity until well into the second quarter of the eighteenth century.

Plate in blue monochrome with lead glaze, dated 1718. Rijksmuseum, Amsterdam

For convenience it will be best to discuss the wares produced at Delft according to types of colouring: blue-and-white, polychrome high-temperature, and polychrome produced in the muffle kiln. This is, however, a division of convenience only. It should be remembered not only that blue-and-white remained the staple and most characteristic product right until the decline of the industry at the end of the eighteenth century but also that it was in blue-and-white, after the abandoning of the North Netherlandish majolica palette, that the first great triumphs of Delft earthenware were made.

BLUE-AND-WHITE

In the second half of the seventeenth century the wares made fall into two main classes. Earliest perhaps were the large dishes known, from the Chinese porcelain brought round the Cape, as *Kaapsche Schotels*. These show the traditional late Ming border round a central octagon or hexagon in which are drawn waterfowl or deer of conventional Chinese pattern, or a bowl of peonies and other flowers standing on a low table on a terrace. One is immediately impressed by the great size of these dishes, most of which are at least 18 inches (45.3 cm) across, by the remarkable thinness of the potting, which is in fact as thin as the porcelain it strives to imitate, and by the extreme delicacy with which the elaborate fretted backgrounds are drawn. It was on these dishes that the outlining in black or dark manganese was first applied, the *trek* which became so distinctive a feature of Delft. Here also we notice the introduction of the *kwaart*, the final coating of lead glaze, applied to the front only, giving a special brilliance to the finished article. Few of these pieces, which were mostly made between 1660 and 1700, are dated or marked, though a fine specimen in the Rijksmuseum, Amsterdam, unusual also in its brilliant white, as opposed to bluish, glaze, bears the exceptionally late date 1718.

Alongside these Oriental designs developed the wares whose decoration sought its inspiration nearer home, drawing especially on the vast wealth of

Landscape panel in blue monochrome after Berchem, Delft, dated 1658. Fitzwilliam Museum, Cambridge

engraving and etching produced as an offshoot of the great contemporary School of Dutch painting. Here we see the last vestiges, and the only undoubtedly Northern examples, of the Urbino grotesques so popular at Antwerp. In blue monochrome, they surround such pictures as the famous one of the young Prince of Orange, and gradually fine down to a strip of decoration round some purely Dutch biblical scene. Work of this quality was primarily meant for display, as is shown by the large number of plaques which have survived from the early period. The etchings of Berchem were specially popular sources, and there is no doubt as to the superlative quality of the workmanship.

In spite of all that enthusiastic perusers of marks have conjectured, it seems most likely that these finer works were executed as special commissions by special artists, working as *Hausmaler*. We know from inventories that there was a fashion for 'porcelain landscapes' sometimes described as 'in ebony frames'. To these must be added the small, but often illustrated, group of portraits of Protestant divines. These portraits are clearly the work of gifted artists, not of copyists, and the small hole at the top of each rectangular plaque makes it clear that it was meant to hang.

Supreme among these independents is Frederick Frijtom, whom we can trace as an immigrant to Delft in 1658, where he remained until his death in 1702. A number of highly elaborate landscape plaques have survived, such as we find mentioned as by him, in contemporary wills and inventories. They are of such quality as to expose the wishful thinking underlying the ascription to him of clumsier work. Even more remarkable are the plates, of which some two dozen have survived, showing simple landscape scenes of woodland and riverside within a broad border left severely unornamented. Such unpretentious little views have a close affinity with the innumerable landscape etchings being produced at the time by Waterloo and others. Yet these are original works of art. On the exceptionally brilliant white ground the scenes are drawn in a series of lines and dots, distance being conveyed by a more delicate, finer touch and an ever paler blue. They are unlike anything else ever made and belong to the supreme ceramic masterpieces of all times and countries.

It was in the last twenty years of the century that the industry began to be organized into larger groups, and it is from then onwards that we find greater numbers of marked pieces. At one time it was believed that these marks were those of individual artists, but a closer examination has shown that the same mark occurs on pieces clearly by a number of different hands, or on pieces which, for stylistic reasons, must have been made long after a particular supposed author was dead. The marks are now taken to refer to the owners or lessees of the various potteries, the capitalists who were venturing into the rising industry. Some of these can be shown to have managed several different factories at different times.

In this first great period various marks are pre-eminent. Perhaps the earliest pieces are those marked *SVE*, in monogram. These date from the period 1675–86, when Samuel van Eenhoorn ran the 'Greek A' factory – the only one with which his name is connected and one which had a long, distinguished history under a number of famous potters. The figures on *SVE* pieces are almost always outlined in black or purplish *trek*, and are mostly decorated with Chinese scenes. The glaze is bluish, and the monochrome blue varied, in the same piece, from deep to pale, often with a strong mauve tinge. Samuel van Eenhoorn was followed, in the same factory, by Adrianus Kocx, whose monogram *AK* is found on many of the most ambitious pieces made between

Two Delft plates painted in blue monochrome by Frederick Frijtom, *c.* 1670. Victoria & Albert Museum

1690 and 1700, and who also produced, in a particularly brilliant blue, some of the closest replicas of K'ang Hsi blue-and-white. A closer study of *AK* pieces shows very clearly how these factories worked. Normally such pieces were made in standard baroque shapes and decorated with a mixture of baroque and Chinese designs. Special commissions were clearly farmed out to special decorators, men whose skill was something very different from that of the average workman. Pieces commissioned by William and Mary for Hampton Court (for which the bills, dated 1695, have survived) were based on the designs of Daniel Marot, who also designed the parterres in the garden. The very delicate draughtsmanship on these famous vases, considered in conjunction with the finest landscape and portrait plaques and the work of Frijtom, suggests that quite apart from the standard pottery production, gifted artists, working rather in the manner of *Hausmaler*, frequently tried their hand in the new medium, just as, in 1711, Sir James Thornhill, Hogarth's father-in-law, decorated and inscribed a splendid series of plates with the signs and emblems of the Zodiac.

On Kocx's death in 1701, the factory was continued by his son Pieter Adriaensz Kocx, who died soon after. His widow continued the work, using his *PAK* monogram, far into the eighteenth century. We shall come across it again in discussing polychrome wares. It seems certain that the *AK* mark was widely copied by contemporaries (it is even found on Chinese porcelain) and probably that the factory continued to use it for some time after 1700.

The factory of Rochus Hoppesteyn, at the Moor's Head, produced some of the most distinctive, and most highly prized, work of the late seventeenth century. It is akin to that marked *SVE*, but the glaze is bluer and more brilliant, the *trek* darker, the drawing firmer, and many pieces are made notable by a skilful use of gold and an unusually clear and brilliant cornelian red. His mark was *RHS* in monogram, to which a Moor's Head is sometimes added. Closely associated with these pieces, and possibly produced in the same factory, is a series of large vases and fine dishes, ornamented in blue with scenes from Italian engravings, surrounded by arabesque borders in a paler version of the Hoppesteyn colours – including a foxy red and an olive green. The palette is distinctive, and once seen cannot be mistaken. Most of this group are marked with the monogram *IW*. For many years this was believed to refer to the father of Rochus Hoppesteyn, but that attribution is no longer considered tenable. It is more likely to be the mark of an independent decorator.

Perhaps most prolific of these early decorators and factories, was that which marked its productions with *LVE* in monogram. This mark, very often accompanied by numbers and by individual potters'

Below, left Wig stand, enamelled earthenware painted in manganese purple outline and blue mark SVE in monogram, Delft, late 17th century. Victoria & Albert Museum

Below Teapot, yellow on black, LVE factory, Delft, *c.* 1720 (unmarked). Fitzwilliam Museum

monograms, occurs on innumerable pieces of blue-and-white made between 1700 and 1720. Most are of a bold and brilliant blue, with a highly shiny *kwaart*. The use of *trek* is rare, and the decoration tends to be crowded. It is also found on an important group of black-ground pieces. The mark is that of Lambertus van Eenhoorn. It has long been fashionable to divide this monogram between him and Louwijs Victoorsz. This theory, which still has its doughty champions, seems untenable. There is no clear stylistic break to suggest a dividing line; the monogram is clearly *LVE* or *LVF*, and Victoorsz never wrote, or could have written, his name with an F. The desperate suggestion that the F stands for *fecit* is irreconcilable either with what we know of factory practice or the non-existence of any other instance of the word being used by a Delft potter.

Last, but among the very best of all, must be considered the wares made at the 'Rose' factory, almost all of which are of quite exceptional quality. Most famous, perhaps, is a series of blue-and-white plates of New Testament scenes, within a border of cloud-borne *putti*. But there are also dazzling imitations of *famille verte*, a unique bottle with Near Eastern decoration, and a magnificent polychrome set of five massive vases of K'ang Hsi design, now in the Victoria and Albert Museum. The factory mark was either the word 'Roos' or a capital R, often surrounded by groups of dots, and sometimes, though more rarely, a stylized drawing of a rose.

Blue-and-white continued as the main product of the Delft factories throughout the eighteenth century. Designs became more stereotyped, Oriental being modified first with baroque motifs of lambrequins and the like, then with the more asymmetrical curls and graces of the rococo. Artistically there was a decline in freshness and originality from about 1730, though much attractive earthenware continued to be made. In 1764, chiefly to protect themselves against 'pirate' competition, the leading makers deposited their marks at the Town Hall. For that period, therefore, we have a reliable hand list. The best makers in the second half of the century were:

Jar and cover decorated in blue monochrome, mark LVE, by Lambertus van Eenhoorn, Delft, *c.* 1700. Fitzwilliam Museum, Cambridge

Tulip vase in blue monochrome, Delft, *c.* 1700, tin-glazed enamelled earthenware. Fitzwilliam Museum

	Mark
The White Star	a star
The Claw	a leg with claws
The Greek A	capital *A* with initials
The Porcelain Axe	a hatchet
The Ewer	LPK
The Three Bells	three bells

Plates, jugs, and the like were produced decorated with scenes from various trades, or of the months, biblical scenes, shepherds and shepherdesses, coats-of-arms, beautiful interlaced ciphers, and loyal references to the House of Orange. In the 1760s and 1770s the repertoire became restricted and repetitive, and a few familiar designs, such as those of a large tree laden with fruit, of a 'fan' of peacocks' feathers and of a goddess with a cornucopia were made indiscriminately by all the surviving factories. Special mention must be made of the large drug pots and tobacco jars, simple pieces with standardized decoration, but handsome and satisfying in both shape and design.

The Delft industry survived the twofold competition of the enormously increased import from China and the rise of the German hard-paste porcelain. Yet by 1770 it was hard hit by a new rival: English creamwares, which captured the European market by their lightness, cheapness, and Louis XVI elegance. By 1790 only ten factories were still in production, and early in the nineteenth century only two were still making tin-enamelled wares, and the prosperity not only of the industry but also of the town whose name it had spread all over the civilized world had come to an end.

POLYCHROME WARES

The coloured wares made in Delft fall into two main groups. Those fired in high-temperature colours and those fired in the muffle kiln.

(a) *High-temperature colours.* From the late seventeenth century onwards the Delft potters added to their original blue and manganese a dull, coppery green, an iron red, and, rarely, a clear yellow. The red was a novelty in European ceramics, and was introduced at Rouen at about the same time. The whole Delft high-temperature colour scheme was, however, distinctive and unlike anything else. Many coloured replicas of Ming Ch'ing transitional pieces were made, the most popular being the sets of vases intended for the chimneypiece or the top of a Dutch cupboard. Of these the most famous were the reeded, octagonal vases, of great height, covered with a strewn decoration more reminiscent of Oriental embroidery than of any Chinese ceramic prototype. This design, in which the rusty iron red predominates, was known as 'cachemire', a name which suggests an Indian rather than a Chinese origin. With the exception of *SVE*, the same factories produced these coloured pieces as made the blue-and-white, *LVE* being once again the most prolific. The peculiar palette of Hoppesteyn and the monogrammist *IW* has already been discussed. The Rose factory, as ever, produced an exceptional variety, pieces having little in common except their high quality.

The high-temperature colours continued to be used far into the eighteenth century, among other things on the rococo scrollwork, in relief, surrounding plates, barber's bowls, plaques, etc., on which the main decoration was in blue or manganese.

Pagoda of enamelled earthenware, blue monochrome decoration, Delft, early 18th century. Mark AK in blue. Arms and motto *fiel perodesdicado* of John Churchill, first Duke of Marlborough. Victoria & Albert Museum

Delft punch bowl commemorating the Peace of Ryswyck, dated 1697. Victoria & Albert Museum

(b) *Muffle-kiln colours.* Quite apart from the wares more closely in line with the main trends of European faïence, which attempted more and more to compete with the minutiae and brilliant colouring of hard-paste porcelain, Delft produced very early in the eighteenth century a special imitation of the Japanese porcelain made at Arita, and known throughout Europe as 'Imari' ware. In these most distinctive Delft wares the iron red and blue predominate, supplemented by touches of pure lemon yellow, transparent manganese, and a translucent copper green. At first these were all fired in the high-temperature kiln, but as soon as gold was added to produce the 'brocaded Imari', the muffle kiln was used increasingly, and the opaque colours of the *famille rose* were imitated more and more. Plates, cruets, jugs, and the usual sets of five or seven vases were the main objects produced. Many bear in red the *PAK* mark of Pieter Adriaensz Kocx's widow. Others, including some of the most original and most brilliantly executed, the letters *AR* in monogram. Once again, a confident traditional attribution is found untenable, and the significance of the initials remains in doubt. In both these groups the paste is of a very brilliant and warm white, without a hint of blue in it, and the body itself is slightly pinkish.

It was after 1760 that attempts were made to rival the jewel-like brilliance of German porcelain. Small boxes, pipe stands formed as sleighs, pickle trays, butter dishes, and the like were made, decorated with 'Watteau' scenes, or reminiscences of Herold or even – and it is almost the only time it is found on Delft – with a version of the 'Kakiemon' designs so ubiquitous in European porcelain of every kind.

(c) *Coloured grounds.* In addition to the two main types of polychrome wares described above, must be described the important and highly prized group of coloured grounds.

The most famous, and most prized, of these are the black grounds. These are of two kinds. The earlier type consists of a black enamel painted all over a dark-red clay body, and subsequently decorated in olive green and yellow, sometimes with touches of brilliant opaque light blue, red, and green. It seems that these were intended to imitate lacquer, a novel material enjoying an enormous vogue at the time, and that the olive green and yellow were meant to simulate gold. Such of these rarities as are marked mostly bear the *LVE* monogram.

The later type, closely associated with *Delft Doré* bearing the *PAK* and *AR* marks, has the black ground painted over the white body, leaving reserves to be painted in colours, the whole being fired in the muffle kiln. There are also pieces treated in this way but decorated in the usual high-temperature palette.

Delft tea caddy with black enamel decoration painted to imitate Chinese lacquer. Mark IF or LVE, *c.* 1700. Victoria & Albert Museum

Apart from the black grounds, there are pieces with deep-olive, chocolate, emerald-green, yellow and turquoise grounds. Each colour seems to have been the speciality of one particular maker, though not all pieces are marked. Thus the turquoise and emerald-green ground, with their ornamentation of brilliant opaque yellow, dark manganese lines, and occasional touches of underglaze blue, often bear the mark *IHL* in monogram. Chocolate grounds bear a *CK* in monogram, yellow grounds bear the *3 Astonne*, whereas the large and distinguished group of deep olive-green pieces nearly all bear the mark *LVD*, the last two initials in monogram, as the evidence of the decoration. The olive and chocolate grounds would seem to date from the first quarter of the eighteenth century, the brighter grounds from the third quarter. Mention must also be made of the deep-blue ground pieces with white ornament, generally in conscious though heavy-handed imitation of a well-known Nevers type. Most of these were made early in the eighteenth century at the *Paeuw* pottery. The blue was painted over the white ground, the white decoration added next, no reserves being left uncovered by the deep cobalt blue.

Delft arbour group, mid-18th century. Fitzwilliam Museum

FIGURES

Many figures were made at Delft, most of them in the middle fifty years of the eighteenth century. A distant echo of Meissen, these personages sit awkwardly round candlesticks or small pots. They are much prized rarities, but to anyone not inflamed by a collector's cupidity they seem curiously bad for two reasons. The lesser plastic wares, such as lidded butter boxes, in the shape of boys on goats or eagles, or having the lid shaped as a plover, or grebe, or other marshland bird, are excellent in their simple way and far more pleasing than the analogous boxes made at Marieberg and elsewhere. A favourite type is where the box is in the shape of a curled pike (or even two) with a smaller fish in its mouth. All these pieces are simply coloured with effective lines of colour over the main patches, to suggest feathers, features, and so on. Many bear the marks of the *Axe*, *LPK*, or the *3 Astonne*. The other reason for surprise at the feebleness of the more ambitious figures is that the Delft potteries showed no lack of plastic skill elsewhere.

We do not refer to the very rare and rather absurd Delft violins. These were triumphs of misdirected cunning, only redeemed by the very high quality of the figure painting with which they are decorated, or to the bird cages, which, again, are merely very rare. But plastic skill of a very high order is shown in the numerous types of complicated tulip vases, in which from pyramid and obelisk, or from less easily defined shapes, innumerable orifices sprout upwards and sideways. The masterpieces of the type may be seen in the Long Gallery at Hampton Court and are illustrated in the article by Mr Arthur Lane already referred to. But slightly less ambitious pieces are by no means uncommon and may be seen in many museums and private houses. It is perhaps significant that all these date from the earlier years, round 1700, whereas the pseudo-Meissen figures and the butter pots are later.

DUTCH FAÏENCE MADE IN OTHER TOWNS

Haarlem, as already stated, was early among the places where North Netherlands majolica was made, and a group of tiles with either simple patterns of small motifs arranged in a diagonal cross or attractive animal figures in blue surrounded by a wreath of blue and ochre 'peacocks' feathers', is, on slender evidence, associated with the town. There is no doubt that blue-and-white ware was made at Haarlem until late in the seventeenth century. A few signed pieces by M. van Eems have survived, and there is a record, dated 1642, of a dispute and an agreement between the Verstraetens, father and son, as to which should make majolica and which 'Dutch porcelain' (i.e. blue-and-white faïence). The Haarlem plates tend to have Dutch scenes rather than Oriental designs, to be deep in the bowl, and to be painted in a very bright light blue, closely resembling that of Frankfurt. The town seems to have produced no wares in the eighteenth century, probably owing to the overwhelming competition of the Delft potteries.

Friesland, situated farther away from metropolitan Holland, and nearer the export market of Germany, produced a very great quantity of rather second-class goods throughout the eighteenth century.

The wares of Harlingen and Bolsward are difficult to identify. Harlingen is credited, among other things, with some very late tea-pot stands, in greyish-white faïence with simple Louis XVI and Empire decoration. Bolsward is even harder to identify, in spite of a magnificent document in the shape of a huge, widely reproduced, tile picture of the inside of a pottery on which one can study most of the processes involved. It is roughly painted in a pale and slaty blue. Much so-called 'Peasant Delft' was undoubtedly made there, and production continued through the nineteenth century until the present day.

With Makkum it is possible to be more definite. Many plates are dated, and quite a few are inscribed. The painting is less fluent than that at Delft, but it is firm and convincing for all that. The blue is dark and slaty, and there is a preference for floral borders and firmly drawn biblical scenes. Marriage plates and alphabet plates were a popular line.

Between 1755 and 1773 a faïence factory at Arnhem produced goods of the finest quality, in a fully understood rococo idiom, and entirely divorced from anything else made in Holland. The beautiful white enamel, decorated with flowers or scenes after French engravings, the amusing tureen shapes, and the firm, crisp lines of tripod coffee pots, close to the admirable Dutch silver of the period, all combine to give Arnhem a high place among the faïence of rococo Europe. It can best be studied in the Musée du Cinquantenaire, Brussels, and the town museum at Arnhem.

TILES

Throughout the period under review an enormous number of tiles were produced in Holland and exported all over Europe in vast quantities. Indeed, for many people, these are the most characteristic examples of 'Delft'. Ironically, though produced to some extent in that town, by far the greater part were made in Rotterdam or in the various Friesland potteries.

The majolica tiles, dating from early in the seventeenth century (earlier types were almost certainly made at Antwerp), are of reddish clay and are well over half an inch (1.3 cm) thick. They show four-tile patterns of grapes, tulips, and pomegranates, in the usual Netherlands majolica palette, with blue and

Left Polychrome dish, enamelled earthenware painted in blue, brownish red and yellow, probably Rotterdam, *c.* 1600. Victoria & Albert Museum

Right Polychrome tile with painted decoration of pomegranates, first half of 17th century. Victoria & Albert Museum

Blue and white milk pan, probably from a set made for the dairy at Hampton Court. Mark AK in blue, Greek A., 1690–4. Victoria & Albert Museum

orange predominating. They were intended as wall tiles – a Spanish rather than an Italian use – and the designs may have been prompted by those used on Spanish leather. To these were soon added figures of animals in circles, with a simple dark-blue corner motif, the creatures rising on mounds of bright green and ochre, with occasional touches of manganese. The corner motifs soon became large fleurs-de-lis. By 1630 the Chinese fashion had radiated out from Delft, and blue-and-white tiles became universally popular, at first enclosed in a bold and effective late Ming fret. It is odd that actual Chinese scenes, so popular elsewhere, were always uncommon on tiles. At first large figures of animals, soldiers and officers, horsemen and ladies were the main subjects of decoration. As the seventeenth century moved on, these figures grew smaller and at the same time the corner motifs shrank and became insignificant. To the repertoire were added children, *putti*, marine monsters, innumerable and very attractive ships, from men-of-war to fishing smacks, and an immense variety of small landscapes. Round the turn of the century manganese replaced blue to some extent, especially in the Bible scenes, which from then on enjoyed enormous popularity. In the eighteenth century manganese, or more rarely blue, grounds were introduced, round a central scene painted in blue. All these types were imitated abroad, especially in England. A very few polychrome tiles in the colours of the muffle kiln have survived, but there is nothing to equal the extent or the quality of the polychrome tiles made in Liverpool in the second half of the eighteenth century, by which time the Dutch industry was declining both in quantity and in quality of output.

Tile pictures have always been popular. Apart from such masterpieces as the huge allegorical scene in the Victoria and Albert Museum – a special commission carried out, brilliantly, after a design by a stained-glass painter – there are innumerable harbour scenes and townscapes on quite a large scale. Most satisfactory are perhaps the huge flower pieces, in their baroque vases, which adorned the kitchens of several palaces in Germany and France. These are painted in the high-temperature colours and are akin in feeling to the 'cachemire' vases.

Innumerable small scenes of six or eight tiles, showing cats, dogs, windmills, horses, bird cages, in fact almost anything, were let into walls of plain tiles in kitchens and dairies, very much as pictures hanging on the wall.

In all their huge production it is difficult to be certain of date or provenance. Thin tiles are eighteenth-century – the thinner, the later. Manganese is not much found before 1700. A slate blue and coarse white suggests Friesland. The subject is as inexhaustible as philately, with which it has points of affinity. Once one has felt the fascination of tiles one is an addict for ever, and one may promise oneself, with reasonable confidence, the discovery of an endless series of minor variants on the central themes. The collections at the Victoria and Albert Museum, at the Huis Lambert van Meerten, Delft, in the Boymans Museum, Rotterdam, and in the store rooms of the Rijksmuseum, Amsterdam, are the essential places of pilgrimage.

FORGERIES

Few ceramic groups have been so extensively forged as Delft, and, for various reasons, faïence is easier to imitate convincingly than hard-paste porcelain. Hannover describes a visit to Samson's workshop in Paris, where he could compare original pieces side by side with the replicas, and all collectors would do well to heed his warning against buying important Delft pieces without a long pedigree.

The *AK* and *CK* monograms are the most frequently forged of the earlier marks, and the forgers show a strong preference for 'important' reeded vases and for plates in sets, showing the months or some industry such as whale fishing or tobacco curing (a famous faked set of this last, in the cellars of a great English national collection, is illustrated by Knowles). The *PAK* mark is also much forged, especially on *Delft Doré*. The standard of skill in the best forgeries is very high, but the following points may prove helpful.

Suspect any piece in which the blue has an ultramarine tinge, or in which the paste feels hard or faintly granular. In genuine pieces the exposed body of the clay feels soft to the fingernail. Suspect any *AK* mark followed by a group of numbers, and any *PAK* piece of 'Imari' on which the painting is not convincingly neat and controlled.

There is the further problem of distinguishing Delft from German wares, such as those made at Frankfurt and Hanau. It should be remembered that on the German wares the blue used is much starchier and brighter, the use of *trek* is rare, there is a preference for lobed dishes, which are uncommon in Holland, and that narrow-necked jugs are very common in Germany and very rare in Delft. It should also be remembered that Delft plates are remarkably thin and remarkably light.

Northern French wares, such as white-lobed plates with a central motif of a cherub, a fleur-de-lis or a portrait head, and a frequently found series of puzzle jugs with blue and orange tulips, can soon be recognized by a family likeness and by the fact that the glaze is harder and more parchment-like to the touch.

Good-quality Delft is always very highly glazed yet soft to the touch, and it should be noted that crazing is very rarely found on any genuine piece.

Porcelain

In Holland Meissen workmen, unemployed during the Seven Years' War, helped to produce hard-paste porcelain at Weesp from 1759 on. The factory, with all moulds and plants, was transferred to Oude Loosdrecht in 1771, and thence to Amstel.

English
Pottery

The making of pottery in England is continuous back to, and beyond, the Roman occupation. Before the later Middle Ages, however, the pots made were technically of the simplest. The dominant invention in the post-Roman period was the discovery of lead glazing, by which clay, sprinkled with powdered galena of lead and fired at a reasonably low temperature, could be covered with a watertight glass-like coating. The decorative techniques used by the medieval potter were few and simple, and it is by their primary shapes that medieval pots make their greatest appeal. Since, however, they are seldom recovered intact, this quality can rarely make its due aesthetic impression, and medieval pottery is rather the preserve of the archaeologist than of the connoisseur and collector. Its technical character, however, is very important for the subsequent history of English pottery. By the sixteenth century a considerable degree of refinement had been achieved. Small, neat pots were now produced with a whitish buff body and a solid, satisfactory green lead glaze; and a second class of pottery was made of a very hard red body with a dark-brown, almost black, lead glaze.

This century, however, also saw a notable innovation. Ever since the medieval period Italian potters had been making an earthenware (*maiolica*) with a dense and smooth white glaze produced by the suspension in a lead glaze of opaque white particles of oxide (ashes) of tin. This was not only more hygienic and cleaner-looking than ordinary lead glaze, but served as an admirable base for painting in various metallic colours. The resultant popularity of *maiolica* induced Italian potters to follow their markets and settle in other European countries. One great centre of this transplanted industry was Antwerp, and from there in 1567 two potters came and settled in Norwich, moving to London in 1570.

Slipware harvest jug with *sgraffiato* decoration. Inscribed 'The Potter fashioned me complete as plainly doth appear for to supply the harvest men with good strong English beer. Drink roundrey jolly reapers and when the corn is cut we'll have the other jug boys and cry A Neck A neck.' Abel Symons, 1813

SEVENTEENTH-CENTURY DELFTWARE

The earliest dated piece of certainly English delftware (anachronistically so-called from the commanding position of Delft in the Netherlands tin-glazed pottery industry later in the century) is a dish of 1600 in the London Museum. Outside an Italianate arabesque border derived from *maiolica*, it has an edging of blue dashes, the earliest appearance of a motif which links together a large class of later polychrome dishes. These 'blue-dash chargers' were used for decorative purposes, being placed on court cupboards or hung on walls. The earliest are painted with fruit and floral designs based on foreign models, but figure designs appear at least as early as 1614. No specifically English type was evolved, however, until the 1630s, when, among other biblical subjects, the story of the Fall was represented, to be repeated in innumerable examples well into the eighteenth century. A characteristically English series of chargers bearing effigies of ruling monarchs or national heroes begins with a representation of Charles I dated 1653. Among the most striking 'blue-dash chargers' are those decorated with boldly stylized tulips painted in green, blue, orange, yellow, and sometimes red. They are rarely dated, although there are examples of 1668 and 1676. The most characteristic specimens were made about 1650–80,

Blue dash charger bearing the arms of the Wavers' Company, dated 1670

but a piece dated 1628 is known. Equally effective are the rare specimens of similar date with abstract patterns, usually of spirals and feather-like groups of curves, painted in blue, yellow and purple.

The majority of the 'blue-dash chargers' employed the polychrome palette taken over from Netherlands majolica. From the 1620s onwards, however, English delftware also began to imitate the blue-and-white colour scheme, and the designs, of contemporary imported Chinese porcelain. This development appears to be connected with the opening of a pottery in Southwark, by one Christian Wilhelm about 1625. The earliest dated piece is a wine bottle of 1628 painted with a design of birds, insects, and rocks in blue. Similar designs are found on spouted posset pots (from 1631) and on mugs, whether barrel-shaped (from 1629) or tapering and straight-sided (from 1635). The blue of these Southwark wares was sometimes supplemented by purple. This and another Southwark pottery, together with the original Aldgate pottery founded in 1571, made all the English delftware of the second quarter of the seventeenth century, including many 'Lambeth' types. The Lambeth potteries did not commence operations until about 1660.

One notable type of 'Lambeth' delftware continued the blue colouring of the Chinese-imitated wares, but confined it to inscriptions or simple heraldic devices, leaving plain a large surface area of the incomparable dense smooth white glaze of the period. The forms most favoured were mugs (dated examples from 1650 onwards), stemmed goblets (from 1659), posset pots (from 1650), and articles for the apothecary's shop – drug jars for liquid and dry medicaments, and pill slabs. The virtues of this type are best seen, however, in the wine bottles, used for bringing the wine to table; numerous examples are known dating from the second and third quarters of the century. They normally bore no more decorations than the name of the wine, the date, and a simple calligraphic scroll.

Sometimes the beautiful glaze was left totally undecorated, as is sometimes the case with the horned biconical salt cellars, the candlesticks, and other forms closely modelled on contemporary silverware or pewter.

It is difficult, and often impossible, to distinguish the London delftware of the later seventeenth century from that manufactured at the potteries founded at Brislington (near Bristol) about 1650 and in Bristol itself in 1683.

SEVENTEETH-CENTURY STONEWARE

Just as the importation of Netherlands majolica had brought the majolica potters in its wake, so efforts were made in Elizabeth I's reign to start a manufacture of salt-glazed stoneware pots, to compete with those imported in great quantities from the Rhineland in the wine trade. This is known from documentary sources only. It is only when we come to the patent taken out in 1671 by John Dwight, of Fulham, that actual pots can be associated with the documentary evidence.

A number of known types may be identified as Dwight's work. Two yellowish-brown mottled 'bellarmines' were found on the site of his pottery and are preserved. Dwight must have made many more such under a contract to the Glass Sellers' Company in 1676. Akin to them, but more elaborate, are some brown and marbled pear-shaped bottles, with applied reliefs which roughly correspond with a set of brass stamps said to have come from the Fulham pottery site. Of a similar material, but usually white in colour, is a splendid series of figures of mythological personages, and portraits of royalty and of Dwight's own daughter, all now in public collections. Less rare are some small globular handled mugs with vertical reeded necks, made of mouse-coloured or marbled stoneware. These are occasionally so thinly potted as to be translucent.

In 1693 Dwight brought a lawsuit in defence of his patent rights against a number of defendants. It is clear from this that salt-glazed stoneware was being made in several parts of the country – Burslem in Staffordshire (by the brothers Thomas, Aaron, and Richard Wedgwood); Nottingham (by John Morley); Southampton and Southwark. The Staffordshire wares have been identified in a series of simple mugs with brown, grey, or speckled appearance. The Nottingham stonewares are marked by a peculiar lustrous brown surface, and were frequently decorated with incised or impressed designs. Small globular mugs, with decoration pierced through an outer wall, were characteristic of the seventeenth-century

Below Delft documentary Jacobite bowl painted in the centre with a portrait of King James, inscribed 'T. Lilly 1732', Bristol or Brislington

Below, right Loving cup, brown salt-glazed stoneware with incised decoration, Nottingham, 1719. Museum & Art Gallery, Nottingham

Nottingham products. The manufacture continued more or less unchanged throughout the eighteenth century.

Dwight's most serious rivals, however, were the brothers John and David Elers, of Fulham, also cited in 1693. They appear to have had some connection with Dwight, and their work at Fulham cannot be distinguished from his. Shortly after 1693, however, they migrated to Bradwell Wood, near Newcastle-under-Lyme in Staffordshire, and there started to manufacture unglazed tea-table ware from the local red clay. These imitated the red stonewares of Yi-Hsing, imported in large quantities with the China tea itself during the seventeenth century. A number of globular mugs, cups, and tea pots decorated with applied moulded relief have been identified as their work. Their clay had run out by 1699, but in that short time the clean quality of their workmanship seems to have made an impression in Staffordshire which contributed to the rise of the pottery industry there.

Slipware bowl decorated with a figure of a king by Ralph Simpson, *c.* 1680. Victoria & Albert Museum

SEVENTEETH-CENTURY LEAD-GLAZED EARTHENWARE

Contemporaneously with the relatively refined wares described in the two foregoing sections, simple lead-glazed earthenware continued to be made in country districts in the sixteenth-century tradition. Thus at Wrotham in Kent, there was a school of pottery which probably had its beginning in the sixteenth century, although the earliest dated piece is a tyg of 1612. The Wrotham wares were usually of red clay decorated with white pipe clay, the former appearing red-brown and the latter straw-coloured under the lead glaze. The pipe clay was either applied in pads and then stamped with small decorative motifs, or used as a 'slip' for writing inscriptions, much as a cake is iced. The shapes of Wrotham pottery are primitive and without great distinction. Its greatest merits lie in the freedom and well-judged spacing of the trailed inscriptions, and in the warm colours of the clay. Similar virtues endow the pottery found in the London area, but probably made in the Harlow district of Essex, about the middle of the seventeenth century ('Metropolitan' slipware).

The green-glaze tradition of medieval times was continued at York (Walmgate) throughout the seventeenth century, the forms made being large jars or milk pots decorated with rosettes. A similar survival of green and yellow glazing is to be noted in the West Country, in Devonshire, Somerset, and Glamorgan, and continued into the eighteenth, and in some cases the nineteenth, century. Such pottery was often decorated with incised (*sgraffiato*) designs.

In other parts of the country, however, the potters used no more than the natural colours of their clays. The Wrotham repertory of simple clay techniques was greatly extended, mainly in Staffordshire. The chief innovation was the use of a wash of white clay on which clays of various tones of red and brown (and, exceptionally, greenish grey) could be trailed as desired. Areas of the darker colour could then be enlivened with dots of white. The resultant wares – notably the great dishes bearing the names of Thomas and Ralph Toft – have a freedom of design and a mellow vivacity of tone unsurpassed in peasant pottery. Their unsophisticated themes – mermaids, Adam and Eve, or King Charles in the oak tree – give them an added charm. Such dishes were also made by members of well-known potters' families in Burslem, such as Simpson, Glass, Meir, etc., and date from the 1670s until the first decades of the eighteenth century. Small cups, posset pots, and various forms of jug were also made. These relatively elaborate wares were no doubt special commissions outside the potter's normal work on simple pots for kitchen and dairy.

Yet more technical innovations followed, notably the use of various simple stamped devices, and (most effective of all) a technique of combing the trailed slip into feather and arcade patterns in dark and light tones.

EIGHTEENTH-CENTURY EARTHENWARE AND STONEWARE

The refinements described in the preceding paragraph properly belong to the opening years of the eighteenth century, and the second and third decades of that century saw further innovations, which were clearly inspired by the whiteness and fineness of porcelain. The first step was the use of washes of imported white Devonshire clay laid over the local clay. The second was more fundamental, and consisted in adding calcined flint to a clay body, giving it lightness both of weight and colour, and a refractory character which enabled it to be fired at a high temperature, giving a stoneware which could be salt-glazed: at a lower temperature it became a cream-coloured earthenware, and from this point onwards (in the 1730s) there ceases to be a clear distinction between stoneware and earthenware potters.

The manufacturing methods of the period seem to derive from the tradition left behind by the Elers. Not only did the shapes employed stem from theirs (indeed, the whole idea of making teawares was an innovation in Staffordshire), but they were decorated by the applied relief technique. This was not only used on the red stoneware tea pots but was applied to lead-glazed earthenware. In one class of wares, popularly attributed to John Astbury, but certainly also made by Thomas Whieldon and others, pads of pipe clay stamped with a variety of simple designs were applied on a red ground. The same colour contrasts were observed in tea wares decorated with stamped flowers, vine leaves, etc., in white

Tea pot, salt-glazed stoneware painted in enamel colours, Staffordshire, *c.* 1755–60. Victoria & Albert Museum

placed on a darker ground, and joined together by freely-scrolled stems made of clay rolled between the palms. The spouts and handles, usually modelled to simulate a gnarled branch ('crabstock'), were also of white clay. The range of these colour contrasts was extended by using glaze colours applied in patches over the relief.

This art of colour glazing was probably in some degree due to the generally improved control of glazes made possible by the substitution of a liquid glaze mixture (in which the piece, lightly fired to an absorbent 'biscuit' condition, could be dipped) for the powdered glaze which had previously been applied by sprinkling. The new colours included a mottled brown ('tortoiseshell') and an all-over black, and added a range of soft tones of blue and grey, green and yellow. These colours were combined in delicate harmonies on the refined light-toned mid-eighteenth-century wares associated particularly with the name of Thomas Whieldon. Colours were also used to enliven the simple but animated figures made in this period – mainly clay tones and occasional patches of green on the earlier pieces associated with Astbury, and the full range of glaze colours in the figures of the 'Whieldon' class.

Colour contrast was further exploited in a ware made by kneading together clays of contrasting colours, to produce marbled effects ('agate ware'). Since excessive manipulation spoiled the markings of these pieces, moulding was used, both for the lead-glazed teawares and the little figures (often cats) made in salt-glazed stoneware.

Moulding, indeed, was becoming increasingly important. The earliest form of this process was the pressing of clay into metal moulds but far more significant was the introduction, shortly before 1740, of the plaster-of-Paris mould. From a positive master mould in alabaster or the like was taken an impression, from which in turn a number of mould blocks were made in salt-glazed stoneware. From these were taken the final multiple plaster-of-Paris moulds, into which a liquid slip was poured. The water was absorbed by the plaster, leaving a fine film of clay adhering to the mould. This process enabled any number of pieces to be made from a single original, and was the crucial first step towards mass production in the Potteries. It was particularly suited to the making of fine white stoneware for the tea table, and it is mainly among the tea pots of the period 1740–50 that the most original English moulded wares are to be found. These display a fantasy and humour which link them with the earlier slipwares, and which disappear in the more sophisticated second half of the century. These models are frequently by, or are attributed to, the block cutter Aaron Wood.

Thrown and turned stonewares, however, continued to be made and were decorated either with relief – in white on a drab body (often miscalled 'Crouch' ware) or in white gilt on a white body – or by incised designs into which cobalt was rubbed to produce blue lines on the white ground ('scratch blue').

The appearance of this stoneware readily prompted comparison with porcelain, and it was natural that the decoration of porcelain should be copied. This enamelling technique (*see* Enamel) seems to have been introduced by immigrant artists from Holland, where English stoneware was much imported. In its developed form, however, it has an entirely English character, and employed a striking palette, which included blue, green, turquoise, and pink, often used in startling combinations. Transfer printing in a beautiful russet red was also done on stoneware by John Sadler of Liverpool and probably others.

The whole of this phase is summed up in the career of Thomas Whieldon, of Fenton Low, near Burslem. On the site of his factory there have been found wasters of almost all the types described, and it is very likely that he was the great innovator of this intensely active period. It is perhaps significant that in 1754 he

Coffee pot, earthenware with mottled glaze, Staffordshire, *c.* 1782. Victoria & Albert Museum

Figure of a mounted Hussar, Astbury-Whieldon type, *c.* 1745. City Museum and Art Gallery, Hanley, Stoke-on-Trent

Vase of black stoneware with white reliefs (jasper ware), Wedgwood, late 18th century. Museum and Art Gallery, Nottingham

took as his partner the man who was to become England's most famous potter – Josiah Wedgwood (1735–95).

It is important to understand Wedgwood's contribution to English pottery. His greatest qualities were those of organizer, businessman, and technician. As an artistic influence he is less easy to assess. He was quick to associate himself with the incipient neoclassical movement in art of the 1760s, and he found a kindred spirit in Thomas Bentley, his partner from 1769 in the manufacture of ornamental wares. On these he now concentrated, in an effort to find ceramic bodies suitable for the incorporation of his classical ideals, and produced a whole series of fine-grained stonewares left unglazed. These included 'black basaltes' (which when painted with matt-red enamel could be used to imitate Greek red-figure vases), and *rosso antico*, resembling terracotta. In 1775 he finally perfected a body which would enable him to imitate the cameos of antiquity – a fine-grained stoneware capable of being coloured by a number of different metallic stains ('jasperware'). Countless vases, cameos, medallions, mounts, etc., were made in it, and these are the productions most readily associated with his name. Although he employed the best artists he could find to model the reliefs with which these wares are decorated, and although he applied to them the most rigorous technical standards, they are to the modern taste rather cold in their devotion to classical purity, and sentimental in their rendering of more homely themes.

Alongside the decorative wares, however, Wedgwood continued the more practical wares of his partnership with Whieldon. One is of particular importance. This was cream-coloured lead-glazed earthenware, which he had perfected by 1760 and which was called 'Queen's ware'. This possessed the practical advantage of being tough but not excessively hard (salt-glazed stoneware tended to wear out silver spoons and forks), and added to this a slight fashionable ornamentation in the neoclassical style, painted in enamel. It was immensely popular, becoming the standard English body and being copied extensively on the Continent. Much was disposed of undecorated, to be transfer-printed by Sadler and Green, of Liverpool, or enamelled in independent workshops, where some of the most charming painting was carried out in red and black or polychrome.

Although Wedgwood was the outstanding figure in the history of English pottery, there were numerous other potters, in Staffordshire, Yorkshire, and elsewhere, who ran him close. The late eighteenth century was, in fact, characterized by mutual copying of materials and designs within the two main divisions of decorative stonewares and cream-coloured useful wares. There were some, however, who continued the older styles, notably the Ralph Woods,

Bird nesting groups by Ralph Wood Jr, Staffordshire, *c.* 1810

father and son. Their fame rests chiefly on the figures and groups, which, simply modelled with due regard to the limitations of lead-glazed earthenware in rendering sharp profiles or fine detail, are glazed in the harmonious quiet tones of the 'Whieldon' palette. They are among the best things in English eighteenth-century pottery.

EIGHTEENTH-CENTURY DELFTWARE

The Chinese influence on English delftware becomes more pronounced in the late seventeenth and the eighteenth centuries. It shows itself not only in the blue-and-white palette but also in a polychrome scheme probably derived from the Chinese porcelain of the *famille verte.* This colour scheme, although used to render 'Chinese' designs, was also employed for purely European themes (a windmill, a swan, etc.). The painting of this early eighteenth-century phase was broad and vigorous, the colours bold and strong. Towards the middle of the eighteenth century, however, when the baroque in art was giving way to the rococo, the painting becomes more delicate and the palette softer. The shapes often have the lobed and fretted outlines favoured in the mid-eighteenth century and were probably inspired by silverware. The subject matter of the painting is equally of the period, with fantastic Chinamen fishing or boating in imaginary landscapes, or tall elegant European ladies moving amidst slim trees in a landscape. The influence of Chinese porcelain is everywhere noticeable, in the designs of peonies and bamboo, or the border patterns of diaper or 'cracked ice'; in ground colours of 'powder blue' (also much copied in manganese purple) and *bianco-sopra-bianco* (white-on-white) borders in imitation of the incised patterns on some Chinese porcelain. All these designs were executed in the 'high-temperature' colours (those that are painted on the glaze-dipped 'biscuit' and fired with it). Only in the second half of the eighteenth century were enamel colours used and then only rarely, this development, like that of transfer printing on delftware, being peculiar to Liverpool.

Tea pot with blue-printed decoration, New Hall, *c.* 1795. City Museum and Art Gallery, Hanley, Stoke-on-Trent

The rococo gave way to the neoclassical style in the course of the 1760s, but by 1770 the manufacture of delftware was on the wane and neoclassical decoration is therefore relatively rare, being restricted in the main to floral festoons.

Throughout the eighteenth century delftware was used for propaganda purposes, with inscriptions and themes reflecting the political passions of the moment ('God Save King George', 'Calvert and Martin for Ever', etc.). It was also frequently topical, recording the taking of Chagre in 1740 or Lunardi's balloon ascent in 1783.

The repertory of forms of eighteenth-century delftware greatly extended that of the seventeenth century. Despite the unsuitability of the material, tea pots, cups, etc., were made for the tea table. Bowls, 'bricks' (small perforated box-like vases), wall pockets, and vases for flowers reflect the increased refinement of eighteenth-century living. 'Puzzle jugs' were made at all the main factories, and bottles and basins of exiguous dimensions answered the toilet needs of the period. The most numerous forms by far, however, were plates,

Blue mug painted with the arms of the Blacksmiths' Company, inscribed 'Brother Vilkin let us drink whilst we have breath for there is no drinking after death.' Joseph Piper, 1752, Delft dishes, and bowls. Tiles were made at all the factories.

By about 1790 the manufacture of delftware ceased. The Bristol potteries were all closed or turned over to other purposes before 1780, and those of Liverpool (begun about 1710) shortly afterwards. Only the Lambeth wares continued to be made into the 1790s, but they, too, were doomed by the competition of creamware.

THE NINETEENTH CENTURY TO 1830

By 1800 the pottery industry was well on the way to industrialization as we know it today. The different centres lost much of their individual character, and it is often impossible, in the absence of a mark, to say whether a piece was made in Staffordshire, Yorkshire, Liverpool, Scotland, or on Tyneside. Individual firms often copied shamelessly the materials and designs of their competitors.

The basic commodity on which this flourishing industry was built was cream-coloured earthenware in a wide range of varieties. Enamelling and printing were the chief methods of decoration, but in an atmosphere of breathless industrialization the quality of hand painting was declining rapidly, being in some cases reduced to mere daubs of colour, as in the opaque dirty-coloured enamels which ousted the clear glaze colours on figures of the type produced by the Woods (their final declension is seen in the wares of Walton, and others about the end of our period); or in the dabs of high-temperature colours (brown, green, and blue predominating) which emphasize the relief on wares of the 'Pratt' type.

A method of decoration more in harmony with the spirit of the time was printing, and by the second quarter of the century underglaze-blue printing became the most widespread decorative technique in use, the wares so made having a worldwide market. Overglaze printing, mainly in brown and black, was also widely practised.

A fresh decorative resource of the nineteenth century was the use of 'lustre' painting, the favourite colours being 'silver' and pink. Lustre was frequently applied in solid areas, the pink sometimes in conjunction with black printing, but the most effective use of the medium was by painting designs in a 'resist' which left them standing in reserve on the (usually silver) ground.

Earthenware plate, blue and white, from the Carmanian series showing 'The head of the harbour at Cacano', Spode, *c.* 1815

An innovation of this period was an earthenware body dubbed 'stone china', more solid than cream-coloured earthenware and usually greyish in appearance. Similar in character, but patented at a later date, was the 'ironstone china' of C. J. and G. Miles Mason (from 1813).

Stoneware went on being made up to the end of our period. The unglazed black basaltes and coloured jasperwares continued into the nineteenth century unaltered in technique but with decoration to suit the changing taste of the time. To Wedgwood's repertory of colours were added others, notably a green invented by Samuel Hollins of Shelton, a white associated with Castleford, and a drab much used at Herculaneum (Liverpool) and elsewhere. In the early nineteenth century it was a common practice to decorate these stonewares in opaque enamel colours.

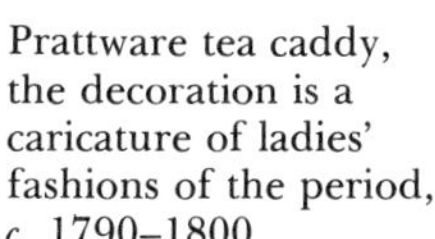

Prattware tea caddy, the decoration is a caricature of ladies' fashions of the period, *c.* 1790–1800

Rogers earthenware plate, blue and white, showing a scene of India or Asia Minor, *c.* 1815

The stoneware of the London area (Lambeth and Mortlake) continued in the crude style of the eighteenth century, with relief and incised decoration on unpretentious brown and grey wares, such as mugs for public houses, spirit flasks, and the like.

English Porcelain

THE EIGHTEENTH CENTURY

The first porcelain known in this country was imported from China and, being rare, was very expensive. The high price was an inducement to imitate it. This was done in Italy in the sixteenth century, and again in France from 1673 onwards. The material made, however, was a 'soft-paste' porcelain only in outward appearance like the Oriental. It was not until 1709 that true 'hard-paste' porcelain was made in Europe, at Meissen (near Dresden). Meissen porcelain thenceforward became all the rage, and was imitated in its turn. The making of porcelain in England was part of this general imitative movement.

Above Three painted 'Sparrow-beak' cream jugs: *Left to right* Lowestoft, *c.* 1780; Worcester, *c.* 1770; Bow, *c.* 1755. The Worcester is decorated with Chinese figures and the other two with floral motifs

Goat and bee jug, based on a contemporary silver design with the boat forming the base of the jug, Chelsea, *c.* 1745, marked with an incised triangle. Cecil Higgins Art Gallery, Bedford

Although numerous experiments were made earlier, it was not until the 1740s that English porcelain is known to have been made. The earliest dated piece is a Chelsea jug of 1745, and although the Bow factory's patent dates from 1744, it is unlikely that much porcelain was made before the second patent of 1749. Both these factories worked in the French soft-paste tradition, but at Bow was developed what proved to be England's greatest contribution to porcelain chemistry – the use of bone ash. This greatly reduced the risk of collapsing in the kiln, a fault to which soft-paste porcelain is particularly prone. A further novel ingredient was introduced at a factory founded at Bristol in 1749. This was soapstone (steatite), which made the porcelain body more resistant to sudden changes of temperature – a very desirable characteristic in tea-table wares.

Soft-paste porcelain alone was made in England for the first twenty years. In 1768, however, William Cookworthy, of Plymouth, took out a patent for the making of true porcelain, and in 1770 transferred his factory to Bristol.

English porcelain was put to most of the uses for which china is employed today. In particular, it was devoted to the dinner table and the tea table.

At first English porcelain tended to follow closely the forms of Meissen, and (often by way of Meissen) of Oriental china. Another potent influence on porcelain shapes, however, was that of silver. At Chelsea, perhaps because Nicholas Sprimont, the proprietor-manager, was a silversmith by training, this influence was particularly strong; and specific instances of exact copying can be cited. Tablewares (particularly tureens) made in the forms of animals, birds, and vegetables exemplify the contemporary rococo taste.

Although a fair proportion of the earlier porcelain was left undecorated (save, perhaps, for sprays of leaves and flowers applied in relief in imitation of those on the *blanc-de-Chine* porcelain of Fukien), the greater part was 'enamelled' in various colours and styles. These, too, were imitated from Meissen, where, after a phase of close copying from the Oriental, a completely European manner of decoration was being evolved. As a complement to the 'Indian' flowers of the Kakiemon porcelain was evolved a style of naturalistic European flower painting (*deutsche Blumen*), at first stiff, formal, and large in scale, but later painted with greater fluency and less pretension. All these styles were taken up at Chelsea and Bow. From Meissen, too, was derived a manner of painting in which tiny figures were depicted against a background of landscape within panels. From the same source were derived the vignettes of gallants and ladies, or of grotesque Chinese, which were borrowed ultimately from Watteau.

Soon after the middle of the eighteenth century the role of Meissen as the fashion-leading European porcelain factory was assumed by the French royal factory at Sèvres, and the change is reflected in English porcelain. Notable among the styles borrowed were the rendering (both in painting and in gilding) of 'exotic' birds in the manner of Hondecoeter, and the use of rich-coloured grounds, particularly a royal blue, a green, and a rich wine red, the colours being further enriched by lavish gilding. These styles were particularly favoured at Worcester and at Chelsea in the 'gold anchor' period. When French taste reacted from the lush exuberance of the

Above Figure of a Bagpiper with dog, Derby, *c.* 1760

Above, right Vase and cover with gilt *chinoiserie* design, Chelsea, gold-anchor period, 1758–70

Sugar basin and cover, mark D intersected by an anchor, Chelsea–Derby, *c.* 1770–84. Victoria & Albert Museum

rococo and entered upon the sober phase of the Louis XVI style, English porcelain followed suit. To the extravagances of the Chelsea 'gold anchor' wares succeeded the restrained garlands, wreaths, and neoclassical urns of the combined Chelsea-Derby concern, and this style was also followed at the recently founded Bristol factory.

One form of porcelain decoration may confidently be claimed as an original English contribution. This was transfer printing, a process first introduced in the enamel industry before 1756, but used at Bow probably in that year. By 1757 its chief exponent, Robert Hancock, had moved to Worcester, where it was to be most extensively used. A similar process was used at Liverpool to decorate tiles at about the same time, but its application to porcelain there probably dates somewhat later. Transfer printing is also occasionally to be seen on Chelsea, Derby, Longton Hall, and even Bristol porcelain. The prints were sometimes washed over with colours to give the effect of polychrome painting. The overglaze method of transfer printing was before long adapted for printing in underglaze cobalt blue.

Most characteristic of all in an art which catered for the extravagant and carefree taste of the rich in the eighteenth century were the figures in porcelain. These, too, were the invention of Meissen. In Germany porcelain figures and groups were used to replace the sugar and wax figures which were combined into scenes and panoramas on the tables at great banquets. This idea, as well as the actual Meissen models, was transplanted to England, and porcelain figures were used for table decoration until almost the end of the century. Such figures had to be modelled so that they could be viewed from any point, but from about 1760 figures and groups became popular also as ornaments for chimney-pieces and cabinets, and these, being intended for a front view only, were modelled accordingly, and were often provided with a leafy bower or background (*bocage*).

Figures were (and are) made by cutting the original model into parts suitable for making moulds. The corresponding clay parts taken from the moulds were reassembled by the 'repairer', who, although not necessarily a modeller of any originality, needed special aptitude for the work. The 'repairers'' marks sometimes found on figures do not, therefore, indicate the identity of the original modeller. When not derived directly from Continental originals, English porcelain figures were frequently inspired by engravings, and sometimes by sculpture in other materials. They were seldom entirely original work.

Far right Table centrepiece for sweetmeats, *c.* 1760–5. This piece has the patch marks seen so often on Derby wares caused by the clay pads on which it stood during firing

Figures were usually decorated in enamels, and, in the appropriate period, gilt. Sometimes, however, they left the factory in the white, in which state they are usually found today. The original intention was almost certainly to paint them in unfired ('cold') colours, traces of which may sometimes be noted on otherwise plain pieces. Such work was probably done outside the factories by independent decorators.

The neoclassical movement of the later eighteenth century inspired the use of an unglazed 'biscuit' porcelain to resemble marble. Figures and groups in this material were a speciality of the Derby factory, but were also made elsewhere.

THE NINETEENTH CENTURY TO 1830

Of the great eighteenth-century factories, only Worcester and Derby survived into the nineteenth century. The neoclassicism of the previous century lingered on and developed into the heavier Regency style. In this field there seems to have been some borrowing from the greater Continental factories. There was a general tendency to use heavy all-over decoration, and this is seen most clearly in the gaudy 'Japan' patterns common to Derby and the Staffordshire factories, of which many began to manufacture porcelain about or soon after 1800. In Staffordshire much of the decoration common on pottery was extended to porcelain – lustre painting, overglaze printing, etc. Nearly everywhere the English bone-china body as finally evolved by Josiah Spode II was becoming standard, and this fact and the general mutual copying of designs make for a certain monotony in the porcelain of this period.

A notable exception was provided by the beautiful glassy soft-paste porcelain made at Nantgarw and Swansea by William Billingsley, and later at Coalport. These porcelains were much sought after by the independent London dealers and decorators. To Billingsley was also due a naturalistic manner of flower painting in which the highlights were wiped out with the brush. This style, although evolved at Derby before 1800, only became general after that date. In the hands of subsequent painters it hardened into a somewhat arid formalism, and the flowers were often rendered against a heavy-coloured ground.

Towards the end of our period the rococo style was revived, and porcelain was decorated with asymmetrical scrollwork, often emphasized by brassy gilding. Beige, grey, maroon, and other coloured grounds, were favoured and are commonly associated with the Rockingham factory, although used elsewhere. Much use was also made of elaborate incrustations of flowers, particularly at the Coalport factory.

Cup and saucer, painted and gilt, Coalport, *c.* 1810

Tureen and cover, mark impressed C.W., Nantgarw, Swansea, 1817–20. Victoria & Albert Museum

French

Faïence

The art of tin-enamelling earthenware was probably introduced into France during the sixteenth century by migrant potters from Spain and Italy. Early French wares, such as those made at Lyons, show the dominating influence of Italian majolica techniques, and both Florentine and Genoese artists are recorded as having worked there in the first half of the sixteenth century. The term faïence, derived from the Italian town of, Faenza, was, however, not in general use until about 1610.

The development of an independent style began at Nevers, which was the last city to receive the wandering Italians. From 1632 onwards new establishments sprang up there, and from then until the end of the eighteenth century the industry continued to thrive, notably at Rouen, Moustiers, Marseilles, and Strasbourg.

Nevers had carried forward the finest Italian traditions, as a result of privileges granted to three brothers of the Conrade family, who came from Albrissola near Genoa. A departure is first seen in a well-defined type decorated in imitation of Chinese blue-and-white porcelain, imported into Europe in the seventeenth century. Another innovation for which the potters of Nevers became famous was a

Right Faïence plate, *istoriato* style, showing Paris presenting the golden apple to Venus, Lyons, second half of 16th century. Victoria & Albert Museum

Below, far right Dish of tin-glazed earthenware painted in polychrome, Moustiers, *c.* 1750. Victoria & Albert Museum

Below Faïence vase painted with Old Testament scenes in the colours of the Nevers Palette, Nevers, early 18th century. Victoria & Albert Museum

deep-blue glaze, on to which was painted in opaque white, yellow, and orange, the so-called 'Persian' motifs of flowers and birds. Their pseudo-Oriental character led Brongniart (Director of the Sèvres Museum) to classify them as Persian, and the ground colour is generally known as *bleu persan.* The shapes were either Oriental or baroque, and coinciding with the Chinese imitations, were beautiful pictorial subjects, painted from engravings after Raphael, Frans Floris, and the baroque masters Poussin, Van Dyck, and Simon Vouet.

In 1647 the factory at Rouen, owned by Edme Poterat, obtained a fifty-year monopoly for the whole of Normandy. A very distinctive kind of ornament originating there was the somewhat monotonous repetition of symmetrical patterns painted in blue on a white ground. Known as *style rayonnant*, it consists of elaborately scrolled and foliate decoration converging inwards in pendants (*lambrequins*) towards the centre of a dish or plate: alternatively, the pattern was 'reserved' in white on a blue ground. Variations, introducing *ferronnerie*, figures, and slight architectural motives, were taken from engravings by Jean Berain (*style Berain*).

Faïence was at first regarded as only suitable for use by the bourgeoisie, and below stairs in the houses of noblemen. At the beginning of the eighteenth century, however, a national emergency caused Louis XIV and his courtiers to send their silver plate to be melted down at the Mint, and this provided the faïenciers with an unexpected opportunity to sell their wares in a very different market. Those nearest Paris naturally benefited most, and numerous Rouen services painted with the arms of famous families testify to the patronage of the nobility.

In the south, Moustiers and Marseilles at first adopted the prevailing styles. Pierre Clerissy, assisted by a painter François Viry and his sons Gaspard and Jean Baptiste, founded the industry at Moustiers in 1679. Through successive generations the business was handed down to his grandson Pierre II, who, until 1757, continued it with such success that he

Far right Coffee pot painted in blue, Strasbourg, *c.* 1750. Victoria & Albert Museum

became a landed nobleman. His enterprise also attracted others to the district.

The fashionable blue-and-white palette used on early Moustiers shows great distinction. Some fine dishes painted by Viry depict hunting scenes taken from engravings by Antonio Tempesta, also biblical subjects after Leclerc's engraved illustrations in the Bible de Sacy, published in Paris, 1670. The early eighteenth century saw the adoption of the *style Berain.*

Foremost among the other factories was that of Jean Baptiste Laugier and his brother-in-law Joseph Olerys. It lasted from 1738 to 1790. The use of polychrome was introduced to Moustiers by Olerys, who had already worked at the Alcora factory in Spain (1727–37). From the *style Berain* it passed to a phase characterized by elaborately framed pictures and festooned borders *décor à guirlandes.* Biblical and allegorical scenes with figures painted in small detail are believed to have been executed by Olerys. Emerging from this came a period of grotesque figures, dwarfs, clowns, birds, etc., scattered irregularly among fantastic vegetation. The painting is sometimes in orange, purple, or yellow monochrome.

From the latter part of the seventeenth century until the time of the French Revolution, faïenciers were thriving in or near Marseilles, its maritime trade providing great opportunities for expansion. An establishment in the suburb of Saint-Jean-du-Désert was directed by Joseph Clerissy, brother of Pierre, who came from Moustiers to take over in 1679 a factory started by potters from Nevers. Joseph died in 1685, but the family retained control of the business until it closed in 1748. Its connections with Nevers and Moustiers are obvious, and were reflected in its productions. In the town of Marseilles an important factory was run by Joseph Fauchier, whose management dates from 1710. Here too the influence of the earlier factories was evident, though the interpretation was more robust. In addition to other wares Fauchier made some excellent large figures, wall fountains, and crucifixes. He died in 1751, and his nephew Joseph II, who carried on the business, was elected an Associate of the Academy of Painting and Sculpture at Marseilles. He is also credited with the invention of a very fine yellow ground colour, though this feature is common to all the Southern factories.

Other important establishments were those of Leroy, Bonnefoy, Savy, and Perrin (the last-named was known as Veuve Perrin, because it was carried on by the widow of the founder). Savy, who was in partnership with her from about 1761 to 1764, invented a green enamel, used as a wash over drawings in black outline. *Chinoiseries* after Pillement were particularly well done at Veuve Perrin.

Somewhat straggling flowers in green monochrome are common on Marseilles wares. Excellent marine subjects arranged as still life typify its marine environment.

Eighteenth-century faïence colours were of two kinds. Those known as *grand feu* were painted on to the glaze and fired with it. Blue, copper green, manganese purple, orange, and antimony yellow withstood this high-temperature firing. Others proved intractable, and in order to include them, pieces were first glazed and fired. Enamel colours fluxed with glass and lead could then be applied and fixed at a low-temperature *petit feu.* These provided varying

shades of red, crimson, pink, etc. The most famous, 'purple of Cassius', was obtained from gold.

Perhaps the best known of all French faïence was that made at Strasbourg, where, in 1732, C. F. Hannong conveyed to his sons Paul and Balthasar the factories at Strasbourg and Haguenau, which he himself had founded. Paul at first managed the main branch, but in 1738 both establishments passed into his hands.

The interchange of French and Germanic rococo styles was particularly noticeable at Strasbourg, owing to its close proximity to the German border. This influence was further heightened by the arrival of A. F. von Löwenfinck and his wife Seraphia from Höchst in 1749, followed by that of J. J. Ringler in 1753. Another German, W. Lanz, was chief modeller between 1745 and 1754.

Hannong showed great capabilities. Besides increasing the *grand feu* palette, he was the first French faïencier to adopt the full range of *petit feu* colours; among which the 'purple of Cassius' has already been mentioned. Gilding was first used in 1744 on pieces presented to Louis XV. Modes of decoration between 1749 and 1760, the year of Hannong's death, begin with borrowed Chinese and Japanese motives. Stylized *fleurs des Indes,* introduced by Löwenfinck, were followed by naturalistic *fleurs fine,* the *deutsche Blumen* of Meissen.

The forms are mostly rococo, employing elaborate scrolls, shells, etc. A great variety of articles was made, including clock cases, vases, figures, wall fountains, and tureens modelled in the form of vegetables.

Offshoots of Strasbourg were at Niderviller, Les Islettes, Lunéville, and Saint Clément.

Of the others, Sceaux, near Paris, was by far the most important. Its first owner, de Bey, an architect, made nothing significant, but in 1749 he enlisted the services of an itinerant craftsman Jacques Chapelle, who became sole proprietor ten years later. An application to make porcelain had been suppressed owing to Vincennes' monopoly, but Chapelle succeeded in making a quantity of admirable faïence, which was, by intention, closely akin to Sèvres porcelain. The shapes were at first mostly rococo. Tureens of animal and vegetable forms were also made. Later the neoclassical style of Louis XVI prevailed. Sceaux colours were strong and of excellent quality.

At the close of the eighteenth century the coming of the French Revolution, combined with competition from Wedgwood's creamware, spelt ruin for the faïence industry.

For lead-glazed wares see glossary under *Palissy.*

Porcelain

In France soft-paste porcelain, decorated with underglaze-blue arabesques in the style of Berain, had been made at Rouen since 1673. During the early eighteenth century new factories were established at St Cloud, Chantilly, and Mennecy, which all centred in and around Paris. St Cloud porcelain, rarely pure white but of soft ivory tonality, continues at first with traditional underglaze-blue lacework borders. Thereafter a distinctive raised and tooled gold decoration, heightened with coloured enamel, was introduced, which the young Hunger copied at Meissen, Vienna, and Venice, as mentioned earlier. Contemporary silver determines the shape of useful articles, bowls, covered jars, and cache pots with reeded or gadrooned borders and mask handles. Applied plum-blossom relief in white after the Chinese, and painted Kakiemon motives after the Japanese, are additional features. At Chantilly, which the Prince de Condé chose as a place for a factory in 1725, white tin glaze on soft-paste porcelain forms the background for simplified Japanese decorations in asymmetrical order, expressive of the playful mood of French rococo. Snuffboxes and fashionable pieces for the tea table are covered with these slight but clearly defined and self-confident designs in bright colours, which establish perfect balance of form and decoration. Mennecy, the last of these earlier factories, was founded in 1734, at the rue de Charonne in Paris, whence it moved to Mennecy in 1748, and later to Bourg-La-Reine. Imitating St Cloud and Chantilly at first, they soon attained great technical skill, but the primeval freshness of earlier patterns was not always maintained. The mature style of Mennecy was chiefly inspired by that of Vincennes. Few figures were produced in these three factories up to the middle of the century, since soft paste did not lend itself easily to moulding in the round, and there was danger of collapse in the kiln during the firing.

Vincennes mark, 1756 (left) *and* Porcelaine Royale *mark*

Pair of blue-and-white cylindrical jars and covers with silver mounts, St Cloud, first half of 18th century. Christie, Manson & Woods

The factory of Vincennes, installed in 1738 in an abandoned royal palace, was transferred to Sèvres in 1756, where it flourishes to this day. A monopoly protecting the factory from competition, allowed Vincennes exclusive rights in the making of porcelain and in decorating it with figure subjects and gilding. This monopoly forbade the engagement of Vincennes workmen elsewhere and provided for the punishment of deserters. As further protection, a factory mark, consisting of the royal cipher, two crossed *L*s, was introduced in 1753, and a date letter added at the same time. Thereafter the name *Manufacture royale de porcelaine* was assumed well before the time (1759) when the King finally bought the concern. In spite of the original intention to rival Meissen, a desire intensified after the exchange of presents between Augustus III and Louis XV on the occasion of the marriage of the former's daughter, Maria Josepha, to the Dauphin in 1748, hard paste was not produced until more than twenty years later. But in 1753, when P. A. Hannong's factory at Strasbourg was affected by the monopoly granted to Vincennes, the opportunity of learning the secret presented itself. However, only some of it seems to have been extracted from Hannong, and no French sources supplying kaolin and petuntse had as yet been discovered. These difficulties prevailed until 1769, when the right clay was found near Limoges. Meanwhile Hannong had to destroy his porcelain kilns at Strasbourg and founded the factory at Frankenthal. The new hard-paste porcelain, made concurrently with soft paste, was marked with a crowned version of the crossed *L*s and named *Porcelaine Royale* to distinguish it from the *Porcelaine de France*.

The earliest Vincennes, which is unmarked, includes *jardinières*, jugs, ice pails, and trays of simple shape. Among the factory's first achievements are decorations in blue monochrome with flesh tones added, and the earliest of the many famous ground colours, a dark and sometimes mottled *gros bleu*. Occasionally gold decoration is used alone, but more frequently in combination with *gros bleu* grounds and reserved panels, which are painted with figures and birds in landscapes, or with silhouetted birds among blossoms. And while, as yet, there are but few figures, the modelling of naturalistic flowers in imitation of 'Saxe' proved to be the factory's greatest success,

Statuette of Diana asleep, Vincennes, *c.* 1755. Victoria & Albert Museum

forming five-sixths of the total sales value. Such flowers were used for *bocages*, they formed parts of candelabra, clocks, and other decorative objects, which often included porcelain figures. Occasionally we hear also of a whole bouquet of these flowers; there is one at Dresden which the Dauphiness Maria Josepha sent to her royal father in 1748–9, to show that Vincennes could equal Meissen.

Biscuit porcelain, as a medium for figure modelling, was first mentioned in 1753, and soon began to displace glazed and coloured kinds. The influence of Boucher upon early biscuit groups of children and pastorals is felt strongly until such time as the sculptor E. M. Falconet entered the factory. During his nine years at Sèvres Falconet created models which were entirely original and belong to the best in the factory's history. After his departure for Russia in 1766 it became an established practice to employ sculptors as modellers, who made reduced versions of well-known monuments, and adapted classical models for reliefs. By 1780 pastorals had completely gone out of fashion, superseded by mythological and contemporary literary subjects, presented in a somewhat lifeless manner, following neoclassical taste.

Above Bleu celeste coffee cup and saucer, turquoise background with border of dark red and white and gilded garland decoration. The medallion shows a rural scene. Sèvres, *c.* 1780

Biscuit porcelain figure *The Kiss* by Étienne-Maurice Falconet, after Boucher, Sèvres

The most characteristic of all Sèvres decorations are paintings enclosed in panels, reserved upon various coloured grounds, each shade in succession a triumph: turquoise (*bleu celeste*) in 1752; yellow (*jaune jonquille*) the following year; pea green in 1756; and the pink known as *rose Pompadour* again a year later. Finally, the strong, even *bleu du roi*, of such unequalled brilliance that an all-over pattern called *œil-de-perdrix*, consisting of tiny gilt dots within rings and white circlets, was often applied to soften the effect. Festoons of flowers were also popular. Landscape and figure decorations, which are frequently signed at Sèvres, tend to become more sumptuous than they had been on early Vincennes porcelain. They adopted the manner and style of oil painting, surrounded by a framework of richly chased and burnished gold. A rare form of decoration, from about 1781–4 onwards, is the so-called jewelled Sèvres, with drops of translucent coloured enamel fused over gold or foil, simulating precious stones.

The breakdown of the Sèvres monopoly about 1770 gave other French factories their long-expected chance. Henceforth hard-paste porcelain was made in various small centres at Paris, some under the protection of the Royal family. In the east Strasbourg and Niderviller opened factories, and at Lunéville biscuit-porcelain figures were made of the famous *terre de Lorraine*. The discovery of kaolin in the vicinity of Limoges prompted the brothers Grellet to establish a hard-paste porcelain manufacture in 1771, and with it a flourishing industry in the Haute-Vienne district of France.

German

Faïence in the Seventeenth and Eighteenth Centuries

The extraordinary variety and complexity of German faïence derives from the central position of the country, open to influences from Western, Eastern, and Southern Europe, and from the fact that, until well into the nineteenth century, it was divided into innumerable independent states, free cities, and principalities, many of them no bigger than an English parish, few larger than an English county.

It will simplify matters if the productions of North and South Germany are considered separately. This is, however, a division of convenience. All over Germany potteries were exposed, in different degrees of intensity, to the same influences and caprices of fashion, and especially in the eighteenth century, influenced and imitated each other. There is no

Three German faïence vases, *c.* 1755. Victoria & Albert Museum

region of European ceramic study where questions of provenance and attribution can prove more difficult. It is this quality of uncertainty, this wide scope for further research, that makes German faïence such a peculiarly attractive field for the collector.

NORTH GERMANY

Hamburg

No documentary evidence survives to give details of the seventeenth-century Hamburg potteries, which were among the very earliest faïence factories in all Germany. Yet we know from dated specimens, which are numerous (the earliest known being dated 1624), that there was a flourishing production in the middle fifty years of the seventeenth century. The wares are very characteristic, strongly painted in a good, sometimes rather blackish, deep blue. Many pieces bear coats-of-arms, with bold mantling, sometimes the arms of the city itself, more often the pseudo-heraldic achievement of some non-armigerous merchant. Dates and initials are very common, as are merchants' marks. Plates and chargers are sometimes scalloped and almost always decorated with the typical Wan Li export ware border of alternate segments of flowers and scrolls, precious objects and the like. These contemporary Oriental porcelains enjoyed an immense vogue and were copied in many places, most notably, besides Hamburg, in Holland and Portugal. The Dutch versions, known as *Kaapsche Schotels*, are larger and more finely drawn.

Far right Hamburg dish, mid-17th century. Victoria & Albert Museum

Hamburg dish, dated 1643

The Portuguese are more difficult to distinguish from the Hamburg dishes, except by the mercantile decoration mentioned above, which strongly suggests Hamburg. An unusually wide foot rim and a hint of blackish purple in the blue generally denotes a Portuguese origin, as does a more granular glaze. There is no doubt that there was a close trading and artistic connection between these two maritime states.

Most characteristic of all are the Hamburg jugs. These stand a foot (30.5 cm) high and are shaped like a pear with the point downwards, leading into a broadly splayed circular foot. The neck of the jug is high, narrow, and slightly tapering. The front, where not decorated with the arms and merchants' marks referred to as occurring on the plates, bears vaguely allegorical figures. The painting is predominantly blue, enlivened occasionally with touches of a very pure, strong yellow, and more rarely with green and red. These jugs, clumsy yet vigorous, are much sought after.

No factory mark, as opposed to potter's mark, is recorded, and the Hamburg factory seems, for some reason unknown, to have ceased production about the year 1670.

In the eighteenth century a Hamburg faïence factory specialized in the production of blue-and-white tiled stoves. Very few 'useful wares' can be ascribed to it with certainty, but the tiles made were of the highest quality – perhaps the most successful rococo tiles made anywhere – and one would expect an equally high standard of decoration of any other productions of the factory.

Berlin and Potsdam

There were four factories in Berlin and its immediate neighbourhood during the period under review. The wares are difficult to differentiate, since the craftsmen copied one another. There are no definitive factory marks and, in all cases, the body is reddish in tone. The two earliest factories were founded by Dutchmen: one, by Pieter van der Lee, in Potsdam (1678), which soon moved into the town and continued well into the eighteenth century; the other, founded in 1699 by Cornelius Funcke, came to an end by 1760. A third factory was started in the middle of the eighteenth century by Lüdicke, who later moved to Rheinsberg and in the end specialized in creamware to rival English products. In Potsdam itself Rewend's factory prospered for some thirty years from 1739.

Berlin

The products of these factories form a curious group. There is a distinct preference for bold baroque shapes and reeded bodies, for double gourds with unusually narrow necks, and for combinations of cylinder and octagon not seen elsewhere. Yet throughout this ambitious variety runs a marked vein of provincialism. The shapes themselves are seldom convincing, the waisted foot misses the elegance to which it aspires: lids, especially, often look absurdly small for the vase they crown.

Most of the decoration is in a strong rather matt blue, with ever-recurring motifs of swans and peacocks, sometimes in a reserve of scroll cloud which must derive from Isnik ('Rhodian') wares of the previous century. A similar Near Eastern source must account for a remarkable group of vases, in a variety of typical Berlin shapes. Here, on a turquoise ground, are portrayed Levantine ships with their lateen sails left white, or, more rarely, reserves with *chinoiseries* in manganese. These are attributed to Funcke's factory and are quite unlike anything else in European faïence.

Hannoverisch-Münden

The most notable wares from this Northern pottery, with its easily recognized mark of three crescent moons (drawn from the arms of its founder, von Hanstein), are vases and, more rarely, tureens, with double walls and panels of open basketwork. These are painted in rather pallid high-temperature colours, as are the vaguely pastoral scenes, a very long way removed from the 'Watteau' originals which inspired them. There was also much blue-and-white, only distinguishable from the main bulk of North German eighteenth-century faïence when it bears the factory mark.

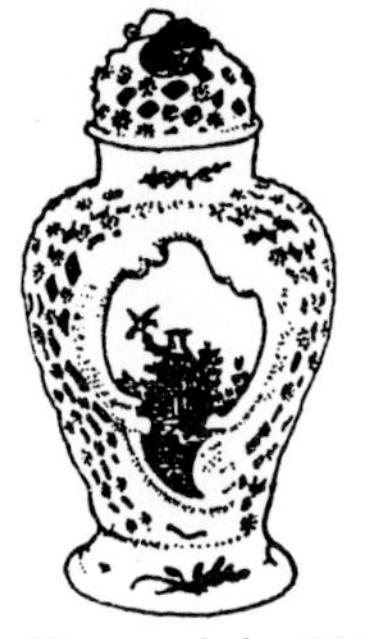

Hannoverisch – Münden

Brunswick

The elder of the two Brunswick factories – the Herzogliche Fabrik, whose wares are generally marked V H in monogram – began by producing pottery which was clearly Dutch-inspired. Some immensely tall tulip vases exist, remarkably well potted and painted with schematized trees with sponged foliage. The factory produced a number of figures, no coarser than those made at Delft, most occurring in blue monochrome as well as in simple high-temperature colours. This same predilection for plastic effects is shown in various baskets and plates with open basketwork edges and, more notably, in the relief ornament on various covered vases of heavy rococo shape, generally painted in blue and manganese. The Brunswick factory, with its early date and attractive, simple colouring, in which a curiously flat cobalt blue is characteristic, exerted a wide influence, and mention must also be made of jugs and mugs on which the crowned monogram AR, sometimes in cobalt blue, is shown on a powdered-manganese ground. These are often, wrongly, associated with Queen Anne: the cipher is that of Augustus Rex.

A rival to the Ducal factory was Chely's pottery, which after a short career (1745–57) amalgamated with it. Here again the local enthusiasm for plastic shapes was in evidence, and work of a high standard was produced, including figures of blackamoors and street vendors, rather thickly coloured, and some excellent butter dishes in the form of a duck brooding a clutch of fruits and nuts. Chely's mark was a monogram of crossed *C*s, like that later used at Ludwigsburg and Niderviller. In vases and useful wares ornamented in cobalt blue a similarly high standard of painting was maintained, distinguishing the work from the superficially similar productions of other factories.

Brunswick, marked B C

Brunswick, marked

Schleswig-Holstein

Until 1848 Schleswig-Holstein belonged to Denmark, and the important group of factories in this area is sharply differentiated from the mainstream of German eighteenth-century faïence. As ever, once the borders of Scandinavia are approached, a lively and sophisticated understanding of and feeling for rococo is immediately noticeable. The faïence produced in this Northern outpost is among the most charming ever produced anywhere. The shapes are original without being provincial, the painting is fully worthy of the Strasbourg and Marseilles work which inspired it, yet distinctive and excellent in its own right.

A Scandinavian characteristic of these factories is that their marks tend to consist of groups of two or, more often, three or four letters, placed underneath one another and separated by horizontal lines.

Thus:	Schleswig	S	S
		–	–
		R	L
			O
			–
			E
	Criseby and Eckernförde		–
			B
			–
			Z
			K
			–
	Kiel		B
			–
			L

It will be seen that the factory initial comes first – below are mainly potters' marks.

Schleswig, perhaps the least impressive of the major factories in the group, produced mainly useful wares, including the 'Bishop' bowls, painted in manganese and colours, as blue-and-white was a jealously guarded monopoly at Copenhagen.

Johann Nikolai Otte, who had been involved in the founding of the Schleswig factory, was also responsible for the founding of a factory on his own estate at Criseby, near Eckernförde. His initial is the O above the E in the mark given. Otte's master stroke was the engagement of two important artists: Johann Buchwald and his son-in-law, Abraham Leihamer. Buchwald had had experience at Höchst and Fulda, at Hölitsch in Hungary, and Rörstrand in Sweden. He was later to leave Eckernförde for Kiel and Stockelsdorff, and in all three places was responsible for the peculiar distinction of the work produced. At Eckernförde were made admirable tureens and plates of French silver shape, *surtouts de table* and tureens with heavy relief ornament. All were of excellent quality. The white glaze has a mauve tinge: the decoration is mostly of 'natural' flowers, freely and brilliantly painted in muffle colours in the Meissen manner.

Kiel, signed Leihamer fecit

Buchwald moved on to Kiel in 1769, remaining there, with his son-in-law, until 1772, and this brief reign marks the golden age of the factory founded by Tännich in 1763. Yet the whole ten years of the Tännich–Buchwald dynasties rank very high in the history of European faïence.

The tin enamel at Kiel was of exceptional whiteness, and the colours, applied in the muffle kiln, were of astonishing brilliance. A bold crimson, close to that of Strasbourg, was used for flowers and for picking out detail left in relief. A violet, a clear yellow, and a very pure copper green, shaded with black, added further to the palette.

In addition to useful wares, all sorts of elaborate shapes were made: watch holders, inkstands, barber's bowls, baskets, and tureens. Among the most characteristic were the punch bowls in the form of a mitre (for the popular drink 'Bishop', a sweet punch made with spice and oranges): these are plump and roundly confident in shape, with true ceramic feeling. The Kiel pot-pourri jars, or *Lavendelkrüge*, are of a shape which does not occur elsewhere: a pear-shaped, flat-shouldered body rises above a spreading foot, with a high-domed, fluted, and pierced lid covered with applied twigs and flowers. Finally, one must mention the wall cisterns and bowls, in wavy variations of a basic shell pattern. A famous polychrome set, in the Copenhagen Museum, illustrated in colour by Hannover, must rank as one of the supreme masterpieces of European faïence – or indeed of all ceramic art.

The factory at Stockelsdorff produced many wares akin to those of Kiel, coming under the same management and similar influences. Special lines were plates with basketwork edges, helmet-shaped jugs, and a form of pear-shaped covered vase more controlled and more deeply satisfying than that of the Kiel pot-pourriers. These are often decorated with

Vase and cover, tin-glazed earthenware painted in colours, Stockelsdorff, Schleswig-Holstein, *c.* 1775. Victoria & Albert Museum

Left Dish decorated with flowers, Schleswig-Holstein, 1775. Victoria & Albert Museum religious and other scenes after engravings by Nilson, and the knob on the lid is frequently in the form of a figure. This was sometimes humorous, sometimes a cloaked Madonna or a nun. But the great glory of Stockelsdorff both was and is in its faïence stoves, of which there are a number at Hamburg and in other North German museums. The factory was found in 1771, when already the springs of rococo inspiration were running dry, and many of the Stockelsdorff stoves were of an opulent neoclassicism. Yet the finest were the late rococo ones, either decorated in the delicate *chinoiseries* by Leihamer or left plain, rising tall and elegant above their cast-iron foundation in an exquisite balance of contrasting curves.

In all these factories a main source of design lay in the work of the Augsburg engraver, J. E. Nilson, and it was in part through him that they reached, in their Northern fastness, so high a pitch of sophistication. One more Holstein factory must be mentioned, Kellinghusen. Here the pottery is far from sophisticated; it is in fact peasant ware, but so individual and decorated with so sure a sense of ceramic values, that it merits a place in any collection. The best-known type consists of useful wares – most frequently plates, decorated in high-temperature colours with stylized flowers and leaves, within a densely designed border of foliage. The dominant colours are an ochrous yellow and a yellowish green, with blues and brownish reds to add the stronger touches. Both design and colour scheme are unlike anything else, and once seen can never be mistaken. These delightful things continued to be made until halfway through the nineteenth century.

Plate painted with floral decoration, Kellinghusen, Schleswig-Holstein, *c.* 1800

With the remaining Northern factories it is only possible to deal selectively. On the Eastern frontier, projecting right into Poland, the Upper Silesian factory at Proskau enjoyed a brief heyday in the third quarter of the eighteenth century, as did the closely associated Glienitz. Both produced wares in a derivative Strasbourg style, Glienitz boasting a particularly fine crimson and a deep copper green, shown to best effect by the black outlining and shading. Proskau colours were more delicate. Here, as at Glienitz, a speciality was vases with highly modelled naturalistic flowers and in a number of figures, including one of a monk in a white habit. During the earlier years the factory mark was a rather florid P: from 1770 to 1783 a D:P:.

A forest region with unlimited fuel and plentiful clay, it was inevitable that Thuringia should have as many faïence as it had porcelain factories. Apart from some fine baroque tureens, most of the work is undistinguished and, unless clearly marked, indistinguishable. The Erfurt factory may be taken as typical. In addition to much robust blue-and-white of manifestly Dutch inspiration, some of it is decorated with amusingly naïve *chinoiserie*, and the main productions were the familiar *Krüge*, or beer mugs. No problem in German faïence is more difficult than that of assigning these to their various factories, for they were made everywhere, and are seldom marked otherwise than with a potter's initial. Yet certain characteristics suggest Erfurt, or more certainly Thuringia: bold drawing, thick manganese outlines, trees of olive green with highly stylized leaves outlined in dark manganese, and a general *art paysan* character. The typical Thuringian high-temperature palette, in which cobalt and manganese predominate over a muddy yellow, a green made from mixing blue and yellow rather than from copper, and a dry 'sealing-wax' red which lies on top of the glaze. A word of caution must be given against dating such pieces by the pewter lids with which they are nearly always fitted. Old lids were often used again for new pots, and new inscriptions as often added to mark the presentation of a piece already ten or fifteen years old. Erfurt also produced the oblong boxes in the shape of pug dogs, coloured olive green and black, ugly but entertaining and endearing, which were also made at Bayreuth.

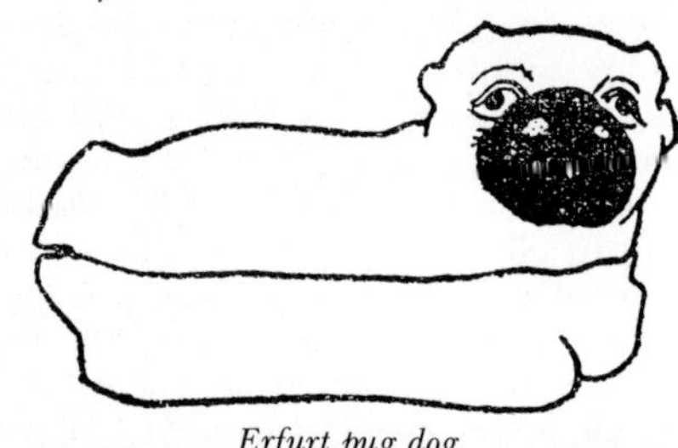

Erfurt pug dog

Far right Plate, tin enamelled earthenware painted in enamel colours, Fulda, Hesse, *c.* 1740. Victoria & Albert Museum

Near the southern limits of Northern Germany, in Hesse, the short-lived factory of Fulda (1741–58) produced wares of the most consummate brilliance, worthy of the exquisite porcelain to be made later. The famous Meissen painter Löwenfinck came to Fulda from Bayreuth and must be held responsible for much of the sophisticated accomplishment of the work produced.

Over a rather dark red material Fulda spread a very pure white enamel. Much of the decoration was in muffle colours, heightened with gold, and both the painting and the firing were of superlative quality. Vases were decorated in a transposed *famille verte* style of great individuality, notable for a brilliant emerald green, while in reserves are harbour scenes, based on and in no way inferior to those made popular by Herold at Meissen. Blue-and-white wares were produced in a vivid violet blue, often described as 'copying ink-coloured', outlined with manganese. Two splendid altar candlesticks, over 2 ft 6 ins (76.2 cm) high, in the Cassel Museum are masterpieces of baroque in shape and ornamentation. Simpler objects, such as plates, showed a sensitive appreciation of K'ang Hsi blue-and-white, far closer to the original in spirit than most of its innumerable imitators could achieve. Some of the finest pieces were signed by Löwenfinck or his wife. But the usual factory mark consists of the letters F. D. over some other initials. The F. D. mark is also found on a few of the famous *famille verte* plates of a Chinese fairy riding on a roebuck, traditionally ascribed to Bayreuth.

SOUTH GERMANY

The great seventeenth-century factories founded at Frankfurt-am-Main and the nearby Hanau were for long considered to have been the earliest in Germany. Though they have now yielded pride of place to Hamburg, their importance, both in output and influence, remains unchallenged. Yet before we consider them we should glance briefly at two other factories which produced, as it were, the incunabula of German faïence. Nuremberg, with its strong trading link with Venice, is considered as the source of a group of mid-sixteenth-century South German majolica, painted mainly in blue and characterized by carefully drawn arabesque foliage borders. Most of the known pieces are dated from the middle years of the century and are safely tucked away in German museums, though a famous small plate in the Victoria and Albert Museum shows their quality and the strongly German character of the drawing, clearly derived from Northern woodcut or engraving. Nuremberg majolica seems to have been made well into the first twenty years of the seventeenth century, but to have left no direct progeny, though much interesting and attractive South German peasant ware, including the splendid Habaner dishes from Moravia, shows a kindred Italianate inspiration.

The other group of German faïence 'primitives' is that frequently signed L.S. and ascribed to Lorenz Speckner. Most unmistakable of this group are the flat-sided square bottles, the earliest of which is dated 1618. Such pieces are often inscribed with bold square lettering and coats-of-arms and decorated with strongly stylized flowers of possibly Near Eastern origin, drawn as if with a pen and heavily cross-hatched. It is, among other things, this highly characteristic drawing which links the bottles to a group of *albarelli* and spouted drug jars, on which it is combined with the spiral whorls which have given the type its name. They appear to have been made until after 1668, though in the later wares the glaze is coarser and the drawing, created for penmanship, has lost its tense vigour when applied with a brush. It seems certain that this group was a faïence sideline of the Kreussen stoneware factory, possibly made to meet specific orders for the furnishing of apothecaries' shops.

Jug with stylized floral decoration, spiral fluting and rope-twist handle, Hanau, *c.* 1700. Fitzwilliam Museum

Hanau

The factory was founded in 1661 by two Dutchmen, Behagel and van der Walle, who had first tried to obtain permission to set up shop in Frankfurt. With Frankfurt, it was perhaps the most productive of all the German factories. Its rather coarse blue-and-white wares were made in most of the usual shapes, specializing in the various ribbed and pleated dishes, in the narrow-necked jugs known as *Enghalskrüge* and rather squat pear-shaped pitchers and tankards. The standard cylindrical beer mugs do not seem to have been made there.

The Hanau wares, naturally enough, showed strong traces of their Dutch foundation and have indeed often been mistaken for Delft. Yet the pottery produced is thicker, less deftly painted, and lacks the lead ŏverglaze, or *kwaart*, which gave the finest Delft such brilliant finish. The subjects, too, are easily distinguishable. The direct imitation of Chinese designs was soon abandoned and never wholly assimilated. Vaguely turbaned figures with their hands in their sleeves and a generally low standard of painting are indices of Hanau origin. *Chinoiserie* was soon discarded for isolated flowers and birds interspersed with groups of four or five dots to suggest smaller flowers. Some of the flower painting, in cobalt blue and outlined with manganese, has the pedantic charm of early illustrations to herbals and must have been inspired by engravings.

The factory soon evolved its own special bunch of flowers, arranged symmetrically round a central large-petalled flower left white, above which rises a second flower, while others radiate to left and right. The whole is highly stylized, and a characteristic feature is the drawing of the leaves, carefully hatched with the final third, towards the point, filled in in monochrome. The total effect is of a robust peasant art, instinctively skilful but in no way sophisticated. To the modern eye by far the most satisfying Hanau wares are the armorial jugs and pitchers. The heraldic decoration, with rich mantling or supporters, is neat and small, showing a firm sense of spacing and allowing the blue painting to be set off to best advantage by the excellent white of the tin enamel. The charm of these pieces is much akin to that of the similarly decorated Lambeth sack bottles, but the drawing is firmer and the result more confident and thus more convincing.

Hanau continued right through the eighteenth century, attempting a variety of baroque shapes with some agreeable but unsensational decoration in muffle-kiln colours. There was at first no factory mark, though a roughly shaped incised crescent occurs so frequently that it may be accepted as a sure sign of Hanau origin. Later a monogram of A and V, for van Alphen, and the word Hanau itself, are often found.

It has been claimed that the spiral fluting of the *Enghalskrüge*, their rope-twist handles and the manner in which the handle is impressed into the main body are signs of Hanau origin, but Riesebieter and others have shown that identical evidence might be brought forward in support of a number of other South German factories.

In distinguishing the wares of Hanau from those of Frankfurt it is safer to judge by the less brilliant glaze, by the preference for certain designs outlined above, by the fact that Frankfurt hardly ever used the four-and-five-dot flowerets, by a strong suspicion that dark manganese outlining indicates Hanau, and finally by assuming that coarser quality and inferior painting are a pointer to Hanau rather than Frankfurt, to which splendid factory we can now turn.

Frankfurt-am-Main

In 1666, five years after Behagel and van der Walle, the founders of the Hanau factory, had been refused leave to found a pottery in Frankfurt, a French workman from Hanau succeeded in obtaining permission. He was financed by Johann Christoph Fehr, who by the next year was the sole proprietor of the factory. It was during the ownership of Fehr and his sons, 1666–1723, that the finest wares were made, though production continued until about 1770.

Blue-and-white dish with *chinoiserie* decoration, Frankfurt. Victoria & Albert Museum

The faïence of Frankfurt is, at its best, characterized by great brilliance of colouring and materials, combined with superb drawing. A final lead glaze, or *kwaart*, was sometimes added to the enamel, as was done at Delft. This gave an almost glassy finish and imparted a rich depth to the colour. The blue most often used was an exceptionally bright cobalt, so striking that once seen it is always recognizable, and this blue is set off by the pure milky whiteness of the tin enamel. The drawing is hardly ever outlined by the black or deep manganese *trek* so often used in Delft.

Most of the shapes favoured resemble those of Hanau. The decoration of the *Enghalskrüge* tends to be spread over the whole jug, whereas at Hanau it is usually divided into three zones: neck, body, and foot. Moreover, the body of the Frankfurt jugs is pear-shaped, narrowing down bit by bit towards the foot, while the Hanau body is more often spherical, separated from the splayed foot by a narrow waist. Double and treble gourd vases were popular at both factories, but the Frankfurt type has a straight cylindrical neck, the Hanau showing a preference for a spreading trumpet. Beer mugs were made with necks only just narrower than the swelling bodies,

Enamelled earthenware teapot decorated with Chinese motifs, Frankfurt-am-Main, *c.* 1700. Fitzwilliam Museum

and these were not often made elsewhere. Frankfurt showed two other marked preferences: many very large vases were made, some standing a full 3 feet (91.4 cm) high and more, impressive objects, though the swelling shape is often inflated and clumsy, lacking the controlled baroque excellence of the larger, architectural pieces made in Holland. There was also a fondness for eight- or nine-lobed dishes, the lobes being decorated with alternating motifs, which never quite worked out when nine lobes were involved. One final shape must be described as being very much a Frankfurt speciality and one which one often sees attributed to Lambeth, Bristol, or Delft. We refer to the circular, lidded, two-handled posset bowls, some 3 inches (7.6 cm) deep. The majority are decorated with pseudo-Chinese scenes, and most are in blue-and-white. Yet there is a large class where the painting is in very pale manganese with either an equally pale sage green or lemon yellow, or a combination of both. The motif is generally that of the 'philosopher squatting in a rocky landscape', always a great favourite at Frankfurt, and the glaze is more often a greenish blue, common to many potteries in the last decade of the seventeenth century, rather than the dazzling white for which the factory is famous.

Like innumerable seventeenth-century factories, Frankfurt began by more or less faithful copies of Wan Li export wares. These Chinese motifs were agreeably rendered and show us either the familiar solitary sage or parties of vaguely dallying Orientals, grouped among boldly painted trees and plants. Among these the most typical are well-drawn and well-understood clumps of giant plantain, very close to their late Ming originals, and fir trees whose foliage, shown by curious sixfold palmettes of radiating strokes, repeated over and over again, is almost a guarantee of Frankfurt draughtsmanship. Yet the great splendours of the factory arose only when it broke away from direct copying and evolved a style of its own. This had as its central theme the widespread lotus leaf on its tall stem, like an elegant parasol being blown inside out.

A series of great dishes, intended for display rather than use and measuring 18–20 inches (45.7–50.8 cm) across, bears witness to the standard reached. At first glance they are difficult to distinguish from the equally imposing *Kaapsche Schotels* being produced in Delft at much the same time. Yet the thicker body, the colouring and, it must be admitted, a certain controlled elegance in the drawing, betray the Frankfurt dishes, as does the broad flat brim round the strongly recessed centre. The masterpieces of the series, still very close to their Chinese originals, are two splendid specimens in the Hamburg Museum. Of these one can only say that the drawing reaches a pitch of combined strength and delicacy which was never equalled in any other blue-and-white earthenware.

For many years the lotus leaf remained, on dishes, gourd vases, and jugs, the dominant Frankfurt motif. Gradually the designs of which it was a component became simpler, the drawing less refined, and the lotus leaf itself more highly stylized, until in the end it resembled two symmetrical bunches of holly leaves round a central flower, boldly drawn by artists who no longer had any clear idea of what it was they were drawing. Other effective borders of flowers and leaves, painted freely and without hard outlines, were evolved from Dutch and Italian sources, and a notable series of plates with biblical subjects was based on baroque engravings. The factory closed in the 1770s, having never produced inferior work and, in its prime, earned its place among the greatest of European potteries.

Höchst

In 1746 two Frankfurt businessmen, Göltz and Clarus, founded a faïence factory at Höchst, near the electoral city of Mainz. As their chief associate they had the Meissen porcelain painter Adam von Löwenfinck, of whom we have already heard at Fulda. Löwenfinck's peregrinations through the faïence and porcelain factories of the eighteenth century make a fascinating chapter in the art history of the period. He was a highly skilled painter and produced admirable work wherever he went. Short though his stay was, for he deserted to Strasbourg in 1749, he may be considered as largely responsible for the exceptional quality of the faïence made at Höchst. He brought with him from Fulda Georg Friedrich Hess, and soon summoned further painters, including his younger brother, from Meissen.

From the first, very little blue-and-white was made at Höchst, the painting being chiefly in enamel colours and with a conscious imitation of porcelain. Many decorative shapes were made, besides plates and dishes. Specially common were rococo tureens and sauceboats of a shape familiar in Strasbourg and northeastern France, and wide-mouthed, pear-shaped vases of a shape not found elsewhere. In all these the glaze is of a brilliant, milky white. The rocaille work on the tureens is picked out in crimson and blue, the vases are often decorated with delicate landscapes, either in polychrome or in black, the whole surrounded with an elaborately asymmetrical rococo frame, later to become familiar on the useful wares made in Höchst porcelain.

The factory was also renowned for those essentially rococo *trompe-l'œil* pieces, dishes formed as turkeys, capercailzies, pheasants, jays, pug dogs, boars' heads, or cabbages, artichokes, and bundles of asparagus. The drawing is delicate and refined, the stylization controlled: nowhere else, except in Strasbourg, were these amusing objects so beautifully made.

Many Höchst pieces are marked with the wheel, generally six-spoked and rather roughly drawn. To this are often added the initials of the painter, Friedrich Hess and his son Ignaz, Johannes Zeschinger, and others who have not been identified. Production seems to have ended early in the 1760s, but in its short life the factory produced wares of exquisite quality, very close to porcelain in inspiration and effect, which deservedly hold a proud place in any private or public collection and are fully worthy of the famous Höchst porcelain to which they formed in some sort the prelude.

As was stated in the introduction, the traditional ceramic division into North and South Germany is a division of convenience only. Fulda in the north, Hanau and Frankfurt in the south, all belong to Hessen-Nassau and to Prussia, and Höchst lies but some twenty miles from Frankfurt. But with Ansbach, a hundred miles to the southeast, we are well into Bavaria. Here the southern-ness is no longer a convenience of cataloguing, but a solid geographical and ethnological fact, and we can state without fear

Far right Richly decorated jug, Ansbach, second half of 18th century. Christie, Manson & Woods

of contradiction that, of all the South German faïence factories, four reign supreme: Ansbach, Nuremberg, Bayreuth, and, farthest south of all, Künersberg.

Ansbach

The factory was founded early in the eighteenth century, shortly after 1708, under the special protection of the Margrave of Brandenburg, who soon forbade the sale of Frankfurt and Hanau wares within his territories. The dominating figures in its history were the various members of the Popp family, associated with it from about 1727 and in sole charge from 1747 until the turn of the century. In the earlier period no factory mark was used, but from the 1760s the signature A.P. (= Ansbach. Popp) was adopted.

The factory began by making blue-and-white wares of Dutch type, often on a bluish ground similar to that favoured at Bayreuth. In the 1720s a restrained variant of the Rouen *lambrequins* was invented, and subsequently introduced, by an Ansbach potter, Wackenfeld, to Strasbourg, where it enjoyed great popularity. During this early period were made the *Enghalskrüge*, decorated with the small birds and groups of dots typical of the Hanau prototype, and only distinguishable by the hue of the bluish glaze, and a less spherical body.

Octagonal dish painted in blue with mark S, Ansbach. British Museum

The two chief glories of the Ansbach factory date from the second third of the century. The first of these was a version of 'brocaded Imari', not unlike the famous *Delft Doré*, though less successful. Ornamental pieces, including some vases 2 ft 9 ins (83.9 cm) high, were painted in strong underglaze blue and then lacquered with red and gold. These colours were insecure, indeed the muffle kiln seems never to have been used at Ansbach, and the gold is often badly worn. The second, and more famous, speciality was the so-called Ansbach *famille verte.* This seems to have been a closely guarded secret and to have been made during a short number of years only, possibly only during the 1730s, though a reference in a contemporary book of travel suggests that the secret had been known at least ten years before. The characteristic colours of this type are a transparent viridian green and a strong violetish blue, both lying thick upon the paste and translucent as enamel. To these are added a yellowish green, red brown, sulphur yellow, and a liberal use of manganese, successfully re-creating the aubergine of the Chinese originals. The designs are mostly Oriental, but the colouring is also applied with baroque formal strapwork. The effect is extremely rich and much admired, though often the decoration is overcrowded and provincial in character. The shapes were mainly Oriental, lidded or beaker-shaped vases, often with part of the design in relief.

In later years the factory continued to make wares painted in underglaze blue, notably some very tall twelve-sided vases (just under 3 feet (91.4 cm) high) painted in a local and strongly characteristic version of Delft–Oriental.

One cannot leave Ansbach without mentioning the polychrome tiles, painted in the green, yellow, blue, and manganese of the high-temperature palette. Though ultimately derived from the Dutch, these tiles show an extreme originality, with their gay portrayal of local characters, huntsmen, landed gentry, *chinoiseries* based on the engravings of J. Chr. Weigel, stags, pheasants, parrots, and, in one case, a pottery vendor in his booth, inscribed 'A.P. 1763'. They are 7½ inches (19 cm) wide, half as wide again as the standard Dutch tiles, and are indeed unique in every way. An entire room in the Residenz at Ansbach is lined with them, a bewildering and enchanting spectacle for anyone who has once succumbed to the lure and fascination of the study of tiles.

Nuremberg

With its strong trading connection with Italy Nuremberg had already produced, in the middle of the sixteenth century, the earliest truly German

Tankard with pewter lid, Nuremberg. Victoria & Albert Museum

majolica. Yet production had died away by the middle of the next century and when in 1712 two merchants decided to follow the fashion of the day and embark upon a faïence venture, they had no thread of tradition to guide them. Their first technical expert was J. C. Ripp, who had been apprenticed in Delft, and came to Nuremberg via Frankfurt, Hanau, and Ansbach. We trace him later at many factories, but he seems to have been a quarrelsome man and he only stayed at Nuremberg for a year. This was enough to launch the pottery on safe Delft–Frankfurt lines. Yet it soon deserted these and developed a baroque style of decoration more peculiarly its own than any other factory. One characteristic was a tendency to cover as much of the surface as possible with painting. It is not indeed until the full tide of rococo that European ceramic art rediscovers the knack of leaving areas unadorned. At Nuremberg, as at Bayreuth, every available square inch was covered with the so-called *Fiederblätter* or feathery leaves of fern or hemlock, curling this way and that in balanced symmetry. The best years of the factory were still dominated by the *Laub und Bandelwerkstil*, the formal foliage and strapwork of the baroque age. Much of the work was still in underglaze blue, most often on a bluish ground, and a favourite motif is that of a basket of fruits and flowers, crowned with birds. When high-temperature colours were attempted they were confined to a bold blue, a dull green, brilliant lemon yellow, and a manganese varying from pale lilac to near black. Red was seldom used. The glaze is often so brilliant as to suggest the use of *kwaart*, though that technique is not known to have been employed.

The usual wine jugs of Hanau–Ansbach type were made either with the birds and dots decoration and thus almost indistinguishable or with a bold and lavish all-over design of flowers. The painting on the cylindrical mugs is superior to that done in most places. Well-drawn scenes from the Bible or classical mythology, splendid coats-of-arms, or landscapes set in a formal framework of debased *lambrequins* are the best-known types. In addition to large reeded dishes, Nuremberg created two highly original shapes. The first was that known as the *Sternschüssel*, or star dish. In these a central depression in the shape of a large or small six-pointed star is surrounded by heart-shaped hollows, in between the points of the star, the whole being covered with lavish decoration of curling foliage. Nothing quite the same seems to have been made elsewhere, though Bayreuth, too, made imitative star dishes of its own. Although they resemble sweetmeat or pickle dishes, they were probably meant for show only. Remembering the brass dishes for which Nuremberg was long famous all over Europe, we may conjecture a metal origin for this curious design. The other peculiar pattern was that of small, squat tea pots, shaped as eight-sided pyramids on ball feet, and equipped with a fanciful spout and even more flamboyant handle. The shape does not occur elsewhere except in Böttger's red stoneware, and must originally have been designed by some Dresden court silversmith, such as Irminger.

No factory mark was used at first, but from about 1750 a monogram of NB is often found, as are the signs for the planets Jupiter, Venus, and Mars. On the other hand, painters' signatures or initials are extremely common, the most familiar being that of Kordenbusch, who was also the factory's most important artist. The mark, a capital K, is nearly always accompanied by three dots, arranged as a triangle standing on its apex, and these are also found unaccompanied. So many pieces, of such different degrees of accomplishment, are found with these marks that they most probably indicate Kordenbusch's workshop rather than that the pieces came from his hand. The earlier years of the factory were the best and, though it continued production until as late as the middle of the nineteenth century, the quality of the wares declined steadily from about 1770.

Hausmaler tankard painted with a landscape scene, Nuremberg, first half of 18th century. Christie, Manson & Woods

Nuremberg Sternschüssel

Tea pot with stylized decoration, enamelled earthenware, Bayreuth, *c.* 1735. Fitzwilliam Museum

It was in Nuremberg that the majority of the *Hausmaler* worked, independent painters and enamellers who decorated jugs, tankards, and dishes bought undecorated from the potteries. They showed a preference for the wares of Hanau, with their very white glaze, and of Frankfurt and Ansbach. These outside decorators were in the main recruited from those who had enamelled glass or silver, and they do not all show an equal appreciation of ceramic values. Yet at their best, in black or purple monochrome at the end of the seventeenth century, in the rich autumn-tinted fruits and flowers which followed, or the delicate muffle-kiln colours of the mid-eighteenth century, their works count as among the most desirable of all ceramic objects, and are as highly valued as they are rare. The collector should bear in mind, when confronted with a German faïence object of unusually rich decoration, the names of such *Hausmaler* as Schaper, Heel, and Helmack, and the Augsburg engraver Bartholomäus Seuter. He should also bear in mind the possibility of forgery.

Bayreuth

The factory was founded in 1713 and for some sixty years was one of the best known and most productive of all German potteries. The brown-glazed and rarer yellow-glazed wares, delicately decorated with silver or gold arabesques and *chinoiseries*, were made in the earliest years of the factory and are justly famous. The type is often confused with Böttger's stoneware, but a brief examination will show that it is not a stoneware at all, but a porous, reddish earthenware, covered with a coloured lead glaze. The manufacture of faïence began slightly later. Throughout, the major part of the production was in blue-and-white, the blue being distinguishable for the minute bubbles within the pigment, which give a milky brilliance to the whole.

All the usual South German shapes were made, and some which are not so usual, such as candlesticks, butter dishes disguised as fruit, birds, logs and the like, and hideous jugs in the form of top boots. The standard of painting was very high. On more ordinary wares, sometimes in high-temperature colours, often in a combination of blue and manganese, the favourite decorations were groups of tall, vaguely Italianate castles and a boldly effective design of flowers, highly stylized and almost chintzy in appearance. In such wares broad bands of blue gave strength to the ensemble. The 'birds on basket' motif was also very popular at Bayreuth. The more ambitious wares included tall, covered cups and dishes with strapwork borders surrounding monograms, notably that of Georg Friedrich Carl, Margrave of Brandenburg–Bayreuth, and coats-of-arms brilliantly executed and showing the innumerable quarterings of which the German nobility was so notoriously enamoured.

Two groups of Bayreuth wares must count as its masterpieces, each produced by a peripatetic painter whom we have met elsewhere. Adam von Löwenfinck was at Bayreuth from 1736 to 1741 and must be held responsible for a group of *famille verte* dishes, trays, and tankards, dispersed among various German museums. These pieces are unsigned, but in their drawing and colouring, in the spacing of that drawing upon the object decorated, they show a sophisticated control and elegance that makes the *famille verte* of Ansbach, for instance, seem clumsy and countrified and has won for these rarities a place among the masterpieces of all European *chinoiserie*. During the same period, but more briefly, the Vienna painter Dannhöfer worked at Bayreuth. He too created an intensely personal group of objects, decorated with the black-and-red baroque arabesques familiar on Vienna porcelain of the Du Paquier period. Some German experts attribute Löwenfinck's *famille verte* to Dannhöfer, working at Fulda. Of pieces manifestly by the same hand (and not, as it seems to us, Dannhöfer's) some bear the Fulda mark, FD, and at least one that of Bayreuth, BK.

Towards the end of its time the Bayreuth factory broke with its past and produced some charming wares with moulded decoration, notably dinner plates and tureens with a border pattern in pinks and greens, of sprays of wild flowers springing from a rococo shell, centred round a charmingly drawn moss rose, and even more notably a looking-glass frame in the Neues Schloss at Bayreuth.

The factory's period of greatest prosperity was during the direction of Knöller (1728–44). Its wares are recognizable by the quality of the blue, by the type of design, and by the odd fact that the spur marks on the underside of plates and dishes have been filed flat, the resulting scratches still showing on either side, though sometimes covered with a final coat of glaze. At Bayreuth, however, the marks are uniquely helpful and for once give a sure aid in dating pieces. For the earliest period no marks are known, but from Knöller onwards all is simple. The marks, often over a line below which are painters' initials, are as follows:

Knöller period.	1728–44. B. K.
Fränkel and Schreck.	1745–47. B. F. S.
Pfeiffer and Fränkel.	1747–60. B. P. F.
Pfeiffer.	1760 onwards. B. P.

Künersberg

This factory is the southernmost and also the latest founded of the factories we describe in detail. Küner, a successful financier of the small town of Memmingen, had founded a new town outside its gates and named it Künersberg and here, in about 1745, he set up a faïence factory. Not much is known of its short history, but it had almost certainly closed down by 1770. The earlier pieces are often, but not always, marked either KB or Künersberg, in full. The first dated piece (1745) is a tankard in the Hamburg Museum. Against a rambling landscape and a white-clouded sky of almost urbinesque brilliance, a sheep, a goat, and a kid are shown cropping the grass or munching the shoots of a vine. The combination of delicate drawing and broad brush strokes, of warm colours with colder greys and blues gives this famous specimen an altogether exceptional quality and leads one to think that it was probably a trial piece, a demonstration of what the new factory and its first manager, Conradi, could do. Though seldom resembling it, the subsequent wares were of great excellence. The *Enghalskrüge* are elongated, slender variants on a familiar theme. Two-handled vases and wall sconces, both decorated in relief, formed part of the wares painted in underglaze blue, as did plates and dishes decorated in dark blue with a very clearly drawn version of the Rouen *lambrequins*, transmuted by Ansbach and Strasbourg. Yet with its brilliant white enamel Künersberg was bound to yield to the mid-eighteenth-century feeling for the elegant colours of the muffle kiln, and it is here that its most charming productions were made. Vases and plates were painted with porcelain-style landscapes, in vignettes surrounded by delicate gilding. Plates of French or North Italian 'silver' shape were decorated with flowers or coats-of-arms similar to those made later at Lenzburg in Switzerland, as were dishes

Künersberg

with still-life scenes of fruit, tumbling out of upset hampers. Most delightful of all, and peculiar to Künersberg, are the coffee jugs and tea pots decorated with sporting scenes in two shades of green, black, or characteristic nut brown, and pale blues and yellows. Nor must one forget the small patchboxes, their lids decorated on each side, sometimes with 'souvenir' views of Memmingen, sometimes with little 'Watteau' figures which recapture, in their discreet colours, not only the gaiety of the rococo but also something of its tenderness.

In this first survey of German faïence in the seventeenth and eighteenth centuries we have had to omit much. Strasbourg, intensely Germanic both in its antecedents and its personnel, is universally accepted, outside Germany, as one of the glories of French ceramic culture. We have considered the principal productions of some twenty-five leading factories out of a total of something like eighty. Of those omitted Abstbessingen, Crailsheim, Jever, and Durlach appeal strongly to the writer's affection, but the majority are minor factories, some of them excessively short-lived and most of them producing derivative work under the shadow of the greater centres. Those discussed will suffice to show how wide is the variety, and how great the riches, of the German faïence achievement. Less confident, but also less standardized and less mass-produced than Delft, less urbane than French faïence, less intimate than English Delft, it must be considered in its own right, standing in the centre of European culture, sincerely individual, as a major branch of European ceramic art. When we consider how few of the pieces in this enormous production are marked, how much uncertainty still exists and to what extent experts still disagree, we may realize that here is a vast field calling for exploration, for all those delights of recognizing similarity in difference, of attribution and counter-attribution, of hope deferred and unexpected good fortune, which are the lifeblood of collecting and compared with which progress through some more accurately charted ceramic region is as a stroll, pleasurable but unexacting, through the known niceties of a municipal garden.

German Porcelain

The foundation of the Saxon factory at Meissen in 1710 marks the actual beginning of porcelain making in Europe, where its commercial value to a court

Coffee pot and cover painted in enamel colours and gilt, marked crossed swords in underglazed blue, Meissen, *c.* 1740–50

in need of money was at once recognized. Johann Friedrich Böttger, an alchemist in the service of Augustus the Strong, Elector of Saxony and King of Poland, discovered in 1710 a red stoneware 'which surpasses the hardness of porphyry'. During the following year this red stoneware was offered for sale at the Leipzig Easter Fair. Almost immediately rival factories appeared, one at Plaue on the Havel, where a Prussian minister found red clay on his estate, another at Potsdam, encouraged by the King of Prussia himself. But neither of these factories was progressive, whereas Böttger succeeded in replacing the red clay with white kaolin. Thus he produced the first real porcelain in Europe, called Böttger ware, after the inventor, and sold at the Leipzig Fair from 1713 on. Above the entrance of Böttger's laboratory, where the King had virtually kept him a prisoner, there is a significant inscription: 'God, our creator, has made of a goldmaker a potter' (*Gott unser Schoepfer hat gemacht aus einem Goldmacher einen Toepfer*).

The earliest porcelain tableware followed the shape of contemporary silver, and the first modeller, Johann Jacob Irminger, was a Saxon court silversmith. Some of this porcelain is decorated with applied floral motifs, some with enamel, gilding, or lustre colour, which is a pale mother-of-pearl coating obtained from gold, the outcome of another of Böttger's experiments. The earliest figures show dependence upon ivory statuettes, and ivory carvers are known to have found employment at the Meissen factory. A figure of the King himself, in heroic attitude, made first in red Böttger ware and later in white with enamel colouring, belongs to this period, and is attributed to the Saxon ivory carver Johann Christoph von Lücke.

With the rediscovery of underglaze blue at Meissen, the first factory marks were introduced. A pseudo-Chinese sign of square shape is the earliest mark recorded, followed by the so-called Caduceus, in turn replaced by the letters K P M (*Königliche Porzellan Manufaktur*), until, in 1724, the Crossed Swords, taken from the King's arms, were permanently adopted. Special commissions executed for the King himself bear his initials AR (*Augustus Rex*) in underglaze blue. Incised signs are usually factory assembly marks, and are intended for the convenience of workmen or 'repairers' rather than for individual distinction.

Meanwhile Johann Gregor Herold experimented with colours and, among others, produced a clear yellow ground which found the King's special favour, since it recalled the Imperial colour of China. Herold's *chinoiserie* subjects, based upon engravings, became an established fashion, followed in the later 1730s by harbour views with figures which reveal the influence from Delft. In spite of the complete anonymity which Herold enforced upon his workers, it is sometimes possible to trace the style of individual artists, such as Hunger and Löwenfinck, since they were able to sign work done elsewhere, when visiting other factories. Such moving about by porcelain workers was often caused by financial gains resulting from the disclosure of the technical secrets of one factory to another.

Painted porcelain was more costly than white ware, and outside painters, (*Hausmaler*), often executed private orders upon request. The Meissen factory suffered from such competition, and introduced measures to prevent the further sale of undecorated porcelain, unless imperfect or of a discontinued pattern. But we may be glad that the competition existed, for some of the *Hausmaler*, mainly those centred at Augsburg and Dresden, display an originality of design which would have been difficult to attain under the levelling influence of Herold's strong personality.

With the employment at Meissen of Johann Gottlob Kirchner in 1727 the great period of porcelain sculpture begins. Misled at first by his ambitious royal patron, who commissioned large-scale statues for the Japanese Palace, Kirchner modelled figures which did not obey the innate laws of the new material. His powerful, fantastic animals, in white, are again more distinctive as remarkable *tours de force* rather than as cabinet pieces for the porcelain collector.

J. J. Kändler, who became chief modeller at Meissen in 1733, was the first to recognize the possibilities

K.P.M.

Meissen marks

Cup and cover and saucer, marked with crossed swords and a star in underglaze blue, Meissen, early 19th century. The cup is decorated with a hand-painted portrait of the painter Angelica Kauffmann, probably from the engraving by F. Bertolozzi after Reynolds. On the saucer Ariadne is deserted by Theseus on the Island of Naxos with Cupid weeping at her feet, probably from the engraving by E. G. Kruger after the painting by Angelica Kauffmann in the Dresden Gallery. Victoria & Albert Museum of the new material, and to exploit its inherent qualities. His Italian Comedy figures seem to dance on the shelves of china cabinets, and his fashionable ladies to swing their crinolines in rhythmic movements, anticipating Mozart's minuets. Even conventional tableware takes a share in plastic decoration, and the 'Swan Service', which Kändler modelled for Count Brühl (1737–41), reveals his creative genius in the many variations on the theme of swans. Kändler's birds were all studied from nature, since Augustus the Strong kept a large collection of domestic and rare specimens at the Moritzburg.

Meissen figures and groups served often as table decorations, replacing earlier ones of wax or sugar. The themes are suggested by court amusements, from theatrical characters performing with baroque exuberance to disguised princesses and shepherds of sophisticated elegance. Mythological and allegorical subjects are never absent: river gods, seasons, continents, or the arts, all richly endowed with the graces of eighteenth-century society. Watteau scenes begin to appear on Meissen porcelain about 1738–40. At that time the King's daughter, Maria Amalia Christina, married Charles IV, King of Naples, and the famous service with green monochrome Watteau decoration, made as a wedding gift, established the new fashion. The increased demand for French engravings as sources of designs was satisfied by J. C. Huet, brother of the painter, who became the factory agent in Paris. Kändler himself did not undertake the journey to Paris until 1749, when Maria Josepha, another of the King's daughters, married the Dauphin. After Kändler's return, French influence gained in intensity at Meissen. Elongated figures, painted in soft colours, turn into pleasing conversation pieces and an air of sentimentality pervades, replacing the whimsical mood and vigour of earlier days.

Figure of a cook boiling eggs, Meissen, *c.* 1753–63. Victoria & Albert Museum

Kändler was assisted by a few gifted modellers, and Peter Reinicke, as well as Johann Friedrich Eberlein, deserve special credit. Friedrich Elias Meyer, appointed after Eberlein's serious illness in 1748, belonged to a younger generation, and the aging Kändler had some difficulty in ruling this self-willed pupil. Meyer's figures are easily recognized by their small heads and slender proportions, to which richly moulded and gilt scroll bases lend additional height. The young artist did not stay at Meissen for long, but in 1761 followed a call to the newly established Prussian factory at Berlin.

With the outbreak of the Seven Years' War in 1756, the Meissen factory suffered a heavy blow. The Prussians occupied the town, and the King and his ministers fled to Warsaw. Frederick the Great had thirty boxes of porcelain dispatched to Potsdam, and placed further orders for table services and snuff-boxes at the factory, some of which were copied later on at the Berlin factory. After the war Meissen never regained its former unchallenged lead. A number of other factories, patronized by German rulers and princes, had meanwhile been established, producing porcelain of local character and refreshing charm. They add much variety and colour to the gay company of German eighteenth-century porcelain figures, and enhanced the attractions of the tea trays and dinner tables of contemporary society. At Meissen an academic (neoclassical) period followed under the French modeller Acier and the director, Count Camillo Marcolini, with an ever-increasing production of dinnerware. The disaster of the Napoleonic Wars brought these activities to an end.

Pair of figures *das Fliehendes Mädchen* and *der Erschreckte Knabe*, Höchst. Christie, Manson & Woods

In spite of all efforts to keep the secret of porcelain making as a source of wealth for Saxony alone, itinerant technicians (arcanists) would offer information for sale. Thus the Saxon enameller and gold worker Christoph Conrad Hunger, having been at St Cloud first, made his way from Meissen to Vienna and Venice, each time taking an active part in the establishment of a new factory.

The factory at Höchst started in 1750, at the place where Adam von Löwenfinck, the migrant Meissen painter, had founded a faïence factory four years earlier, but he had left for Strasbourg shortly before. The factory was granted a monopoly by the Elector of Mainz, who later on subsidized it. Meissen influence is obvious in pieces produced in the initial years, and some early figures are copies. But the modellers J. Chr. L. Lücke and Simon Feylner show independence. The set of Italian Comedy figures attributed to Feylner is remarkable for freedom of movement; each actor is placed upon a high pedestal, in the manner of contemporary garden sculpture, taking a bow in the limelight. As the rococo period advanced J. Fr. Lück created idyllic groups on richly scrolled openwork bases, similar to those he designed at Frankenthal a few years later. L. Russinger (1758–65), afterwards at Fulda, modelled the famous table decoration known as 'The Chinese Emperor', while J. P. Melchior, a friend of the young Goethe, finished some of the figures which formed part of the group after 1765. Melchior's own works include portrait medallions, busts, and reliefs, some produced in biscuit. After Melchior's departure for Frankenthal and Nymphenburg, the factory closed down. The mark applied to Höchst porcelain and faïence is the wheel of Mainz, either incised or in colour, above or below the glaze.

Höchst wheel of Mainz mark

In 1751 the Berlin merchant W. K. Wegely, helped by workers from Meissen and Höchst, started a factory which produced tableware, often in white, as well as figures after Meissen and Höchst models. Frederick the Great encouraged Wegely at first, but later on showed dissatisfaction with his results, whereupon the factory closed down in 1757. One of the modellers, E. H. Reinhard, sold the secret of porcelain to Gotzkowsky, who started production in 1761, assisted by artists who had fled from Meissen during the Seven Years' War. In 1763 the Berlin factory was sold to Frederick the Great, and it became State property, which it has remained ever since. F. E. Meyer, from Meissen, and his brother, W. Chr. Meyer, modelled at Berlin some of the best figures made during the third quarter of the eighteenth century; otherwise the factory is better known for tableware. Wegely's mark is a W and numerals in underglaze blue. Gotzkowsky's a G. Subsequent marks include a sceptre and the letters KPM (*Königliche Porzellan Manufaktur*), again in underglaze blue.

Wegely and Gotzkowsky marks

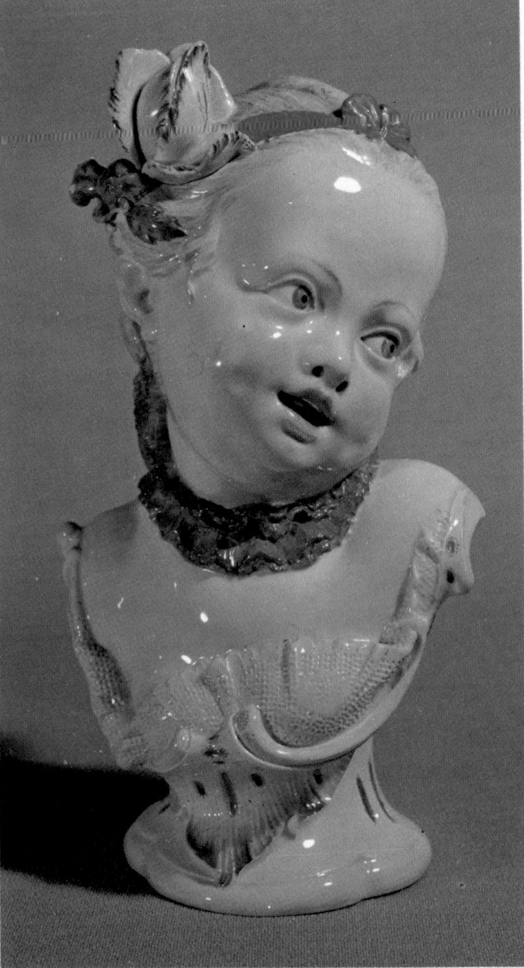

Porcelain bust of a girl from a model by F. A. Bustelli, marked with impressed shield from the arms of Bavaria, Nymphenburg, *c.* 1761

At Neudeck, near Munich, porcelain was made from 1753 on, due to the initiative of Count Sigmund von Haimhausen and the arcanist Ringler. In 1761 the factory moved to a building in the palace grounds at Nymphenburg, where it continues to this day. The first two modellers, Ponhauser and Haertl, were succeeded in 1754 by Anton Bustelli of Locarno (1723–63), the greatest creative genius in porcelain. He recaptured the playful mood of the rococo period and gave it permanence in figures, often rendered in pure white, or in restrained colours, so that light and shade bring out the innate charms of the new material. Bustelli's figures show great affinity to style with those of Ignaz Günther and other contemporary Bavarian sculptors; whereas C. Lindeman and C. Purtscher painted on tableware figure subjects which were inspired by J. E. Nilson and Augsburg engravers of the period. Bustelli's successor, D. Auliczek, continued along established lines, but showed his originality by modelling animal groups of a type not hitherto attempted. In 1797 J. P. Melchior, formerly at Höchst and Frankenthal, came to Nymphenburg, where, following the taste of the time, he modelled his sensitive portrait busts and medallions in biscuit. The Nymphenburg mark, the *Rautenschild* from the arms of Bavaria, is usually shown upon the base, impressed as part of the decoration.

The factory at Frankenthal, founded in 1755 by P. A. Hannong from Strasbourg, owes its existence partly to the French monopoly protecting Vincennes, which prevented the foundation of similar privately owned ventures. Hannong crossed the Rhine and was granted a monopoly by the Elector Palatin. He started his factory near Mannheim; it was sold to the Elector Carl Theodor in 1755, and was closed in 1799, in consequence of the war with France. Among the gifted modellers attracted to Frankenthal, I. W. Lanz (1755–61) and Konrad Link (1762–6) are noted for large allegorical groups and hunting scenes of great originality. Link was succeeded by K. G. Lück in 1766. With Melchior as modeller (1779–93) the influence of Höchst is felt, and the fashion for biscuit portrait medallions was introduced. The tableware of Frankenthal owes much to France, repeating popular bird patterns of Vincennes and Sèvres. The marks on Frankenthal porcelain vary, showing Hannong's initials until 1756, and thereafter a quartering from the arms of the Palatinate, occasionally also the lion from the same arms. The initials of the Elector Carl Theodor, with or without crown, appear after 1762, all in underglaze blue.

The factory at Ludwigsburg near Stuttgart was founded in 1758, with the help of the arcanist Ringler, who had previously made porcelain at Höchst, Strasbourg, and Munich. The best work belongs to the period of 1760–7, while the change from rococo to classicism took place under G. F. Riedel and the court sculptor W. Beyer, who left in 1767 for Vienna. Of real originality are miniature groups by J. Jean Louis, ranging from allegorical and satirical subjects to representations of the 'Venetian Fair', depicting tradesmen in their booths. The latter became popular after the return of the Duke from Venice, and were modelled on actual fairs held at Stuttgart from 1767 on. Ludwigsburg tableware, made under G. F. Riedel, is often decorated with birds and flowers: the jugs and tea pots are usually supported upon three

Above Comport hand-painted and gilt by G. F. Kersting, from the table service presented to the Duke of Wellington by King Frederick Augustus II of Saxony. Meissen, *c.* 1818

Far right Albarello (drug jar) decorated in blue, green, yellow and orange with inscription close to rim, Faenza, *c.* 1500. City Museum and Art Gallery, Hanley, Stoke-on-Trent

Nymphenburg Rautenschild *mark*

Frankenthal marks

Ludwigsburg marks

legs. The manufacture came to an end in 1824. The early mark of Ludwigsburg porcelain consists of interlaced *C*s with or without crown, substituted by the stag's horns, from the arms of Württemberg.

Other factories under princely patronage founded in Germany during the third quarter of the eighteenth century include Ansbach (1758–1860), Kelsterbach (1761–8), (1789–1802), Ottweiler (1763–*c.* 1770), Fulda (1765–90), Cassel (1766–88), Kloster Veilsdorf (1760), Limbach (1762), and Wallendorf (1763). The misfortunes of Meissen during the Seven Years' War made their sudden growth possible, but few outlasted the founder's personal interest. The demand for porcelain decreased with the change from an extravagantly decorative style, for which porcelain was eminently suited, towards the pale tranquillity of neoclassical marble and biscuit sculpture. During the last quarter of the century, and after the conclusion of the Prussian war, Meissen, rivalled by Vienna only, continued under Count Camillo Marcolini to supply the German market with tableware and decorative porcelain. But change of taste and lack of inspiration forced the factory to follow other styles created at the royal manufactory at Sèvres and elsewhere.

Italian

Majolica

The name *maiolica*, first applied to the lustred Spanish pottery of Valencia, imported into Italy via the Balearic Island of Majorca, later became a generic term, embracing not only the whole range of tin-glazed Italian earthenwares but also those of other countries working in the same tradition.

The growth of the industry in Italy dates from about the second half of the fifteenth century, when there were already establishments at Orvieto (Umbria), Florence and Siena (Tuscany); Pisa was the port to which the Spanish wares were shipped, and Faenza (Emilia). The great influence of the latter place has caused the term faïence to be adopted for another large class of tin-enamelled pottery, particularly on the Continent. Rome, Padua, Cortono, and Todi have also been identified as places of manufacture.

Very early Italian majolica shows a marked Spanish influence, employing the same palette of green and purple applied to a white ground. Some 'Florentine green' dishes, and the famous 'impasto-blue-painted' Tuscan 'oak-leaf jars' are notable but very rare examples. There are, however, numerous blue-and-white and blue-and-lustred pieces, together with exceptionally fine tile pavements, in the Spanish manner. This influence is seen principally in the painting, as the shapes adhered more or less to native traditions.

Towards the end of the fifteenth century Italian majolica developed a new and indigenous style, and for the next fifty years or so there were produced some of the most beautiful examples of European painted pottery.

Faenza has already been mentioned as one of the most important centres. From the last quarter of the fifteenth century to the end of the sixteenth, its out-

put was copious and of an extremely high quality. Moreover, emigrant workmen, establishing themselves elsewhere, helped to spread its influence. A documentary piece, now in the Musée de Cluny, is a magnificent plaque inscribed with the name 'Nicolaus de Ragnolis' and dated 1475. There are also many tiles bearing similar inscriptions. Some pieces are decorated with gothic scrolls and foliage, others have peacock-feather motifs and varied diapering. Inverted-pear-shaped vases with flat handles; tiles and drug jars (*albarelli*) painted with grotesques, busts, or coats-of-arms in rich polychrome, are typical. A method known as 'contour framing' outlined a design by surrounding it with a white halo. In some instances the whole ground was stained with a single colour. The palette is manganese purple, dark blue, orange, yellow, and copper green. Seven or eight highly accomplished artists, identified on stylistic grounds and by monograms, painted many wonderful panels and dishes with mythological and biblical subjects; some of the latter are after Raphael. A quantity of commoner wares was also made.

At Deruta (Umbria), where potteries exist to the present day, fine polychrome and lustred pottery is known to have been made between about 1490 and 1545, though the earliest is hard to distinguish from that of Faenza. The style was much under the influence of the Umbrian school of painters. Characteristic colouring, besides a warm yellow and manganese purple, was a strong blue in combination with lustre. The colours were inclined to run, and, as has been pointed out by Bernard Rackham, the tin glaze is sometimes cut through to the clay body (*sgraffiato*) to obviate this difficulty. Many dishes and plates have profile busts painted in circular reserves surrounded by intricate designs, and in a class known as 'petal back' the lead-glazed reverses are decorated with imbricated floral patterns. Deep shading in blue to accentuate an outline was another device. Subjects were also rendered in relief. After the middle of the sixteenth century the quality declined and was never revived.

By the beginning of the sixteenth century the industry had become well established. Pharmacies were adorned with beautiful sets of drug vases and jars, and the great dishes, *piatti da pompa*, were displayed on sideboards and tables.

Castel Durante (near Urbino), renamed Urbania in 1635, was probably under the patronage of the Dukes of Urbino. The earliest dated specimen, 1508, bears the arms of Pope Julius II. It is also signed by Giovanni Maria, recognized as one of the great painters of majolica. Perhaps the most notable contribution of Castel Durante was the *istoriato* painting of Nicola Pellipario, working there between about 1515 and 1527. This kind of narrative painting is usually spread across the whole surface of a dish or plate. It was brought to its highest state of perfection by this master, and extensively copied elsewhere.

Gubbio, also in the Duchy of Urbino, was famed for its magnificent gold and ruby lustres. The best period comes within the first thirty years of the sixteenth century. Some of the finest pieces were gadrooned or embossed to give full play to the refulgent brilliance of the lustre colours. The master of this art was Giorgio Andreoli, 'Maestro Giorgio', a native of Intra in Lombardy, who became a citizen of Gubbio in 1498. Much already decorated majolica was sent to Gubbio to be enriched with lustre.

Caffaggiolo (near Florence), a renowned centre of Tuscan potting, was, for a time, under the patronage of the Medici family, whose arms and mottoes appear on some of its wares. The earlier work shows the influence of the Florentine masters, particularly Botticelli; Donatello's work was also copied. A family named Fattorini made pottery in the neighbourhood

Left Albarello (drug jar) painted in blue, green, yellow and orange, Deruta, *c.* 1560. City Museum and Art Gallery, Hanley, Stoke-on-Trent

Right Plate painted by Jacopo showing a majolica painter at work, Caffaggiolo, *c.* 1510. Victoria & Albert Museum

Saucer painted with Cupid and his bow, Hewelcke factory, Venice, *c.* 1761–3. Victoria & Albert Museum

in 1469, and were at Caffaggiolo from about 1506 onwards. The subjects are boldly painted in strong colours. They reflect Florence's individual status and depict, besides religious and classical subjects, scenes of pageantry, triumphs, shields of arms, and trophies. 'Peacock-feather' ornament was also used here. Typical themes are: a rich blue, used as a background; lemon yellow, orange, and green; also lustre, and a dark cherry red peculiar to the factory. The best work was done between 1506 and 1526.

The painter Titian is recorded as having supervised the making of majolica at Venice in 1520. Much that was made there from about 1530 is characterized by the admixture of cobalt blue with the white enamel glaze. This produced a greyish-blue surface called *smaltino*, on to which were painted designs in dark blue and opaque white. Their Chinese origin shows the influence of Oriental importations. *Istoriato* painting in the manner of Urbino was developed later.

Italian Porcelain

The first successful attempt to produce porcelain in Europe was made at Florence about 1575 under the patronage of Francesco de' Medici. Inspired by contemporary blue-and-white Ming ware, an artificial porcelain was produced for a short time only, which contained some kaolin, the pure infusable clay used in China, mixed with powdered glass and frit. Medici porcelain, proudly marked with the cupola of the cathedral and the 'F' of Florence, is decorated in underglaze blue of varying intensity, which gently melts into the glaze. The flowering of the faïence industry during the seventeenth century is due in no small measure to the untiring quest for the secret of porcelain manufacture. This faïence, or earthenware, which fuses at a low temperature in the kiln, is usually dipped into opaque tin glaze, which, while hiding impurities of texture, is admirably suited to be the recipient of coloured decoration.

Venice, with its great glass industry, is also an early centre for true porcelain. Chr. C. Hunger, the Meissen gold worker and arcanist, reached Venice from Vienna in 1720, bringing with him the secret of porcelain making. This he disclosed to the brothers Francesco and Giuseppe Vezzi, former goldsmiths, who launched an enterprise which flourished until 1727. Cups without handles and saucers with coloured decoration, and tea pots with acanthus-leaf reliefs are characteristic of this factory, which took as models not only Meissen and Vienna porcelain but also Italian silver. Monochrome or coloured decoration reveals that lightness of touch which one has come to associate with Venetian art in general. Vezzi porcelain is marked va, VENA, or VENEZIA, in underglaze blue or overglaze red.

Va VEN: Venezia

N. F. Hewelcke and his wife, Dresden dealers who had left Saxony during the Seven Years' War, secured rights to manufacture porcelain 'in the style of Meissen' at Venice in 1758. Thus the market continued until 1764, when Geminiano Cozzi started to manufacture aided by the Venetian senate. From then on, figures, snuffboxes, cane handles, and tablewares were made; the latter all marked with an anchor in red. This enterprise lasted until 1812. Porcelain was also made at Lenove (1762–1825) and Este, from 1781.

The most beautiful and important Italian porcelain was made at the Royal Palace of Capodimonte, where Charles, King of Naples, established a factory in 1743.

His interest in the project was aroused through his marriage to Maria Amalia of Saxony, daughter of Augustus III of Poland, who brought him as part of her wedding dowry a great quantity of Meissen porcelain.

Attempts to rival the German production were at first frustrated by an inability to discover the secret of making a suitable paste. Following unsuccessful attempts to lure arcanists from the Doccia and Vienna factories, a chemist of Belgian extraction, Livio Ottavio Schepers, was employed. He too proved unsatisfactory and was dismissed in 1744, when his place was taken by his son, Gaetano, who supplied a successful recipe for the making of soft paste.

Giuseppe Gricci was the chief modeller and Giovanni Caselli remained in charge of the painting until his death in 1754. Both Gricci and Schepers continued at Buen Retiro when the manufactory was removed there in 1759.

In addition to the tablewares, snuffboxes, cane handles, and vases were made from an early period, when the influence of Meissen was still a factor. Tea services are recorded as having been painted with figure subjects, seascapes, landscapes, battle scenes, etc., by Giuseppe della Torre. Oriental designs included the raised prunus motif of *blanc-de-Chine*, common to most early European factories.

The porcelain is frequently unmarked, but the Bourbon fleur-de-lis in blue or gold was used both here and at Buen Retiro. It is generally impressed on figures.

Capodimonte's greatest achievement was the decoration of a porcelain room at the Palace of Portici (1757–9). Removed to the Capodimonte Palace in 1805, it has remained there to the present day.

Many beautiful figures were modelled by Gricci; they include subjects from the Italian Comedy and peasant types. A very noticeable characteristic is the extreme smallness of the heads. The colouring and soft creamy quality of these pieces is something which has never been surpassed.

Set of comedy figures, Capodimonte, *c.* 1765. Victoria & Albert Museum

Contrary to popular belief, the white or coloured figure subjects in relief on vases and other wares have nothing to do with Capodimonte. They originated at Doccia, and have since been widely reproduced in debased forms. Nineteenth-century Doccia examples are marked with the crown N of Naples, but crude copies are still made elsewhere.

The Doccia factory was founded by the Marchese Carlo Ginori in 1735, and carried on by his son Lorenzo from 1757 to 1791.

Karl Anreiter, an independent decorator from Vienna, was engaged in 1737. His son, Anton, later became a painter at the factory. Both left in 1746. The chief modeller was Gaspare Bruschi.

By 1740 good progress earned Ginori a privilege for making porcelain in Tuscany. The best period was 1757–91.

Small figures of the Italian Comedy among other subjects are particularly attractive, though on the whole Doccia colouring is inclined to be hard and the glaze rather dry in appearance. A hybrid hard-paste body was very liable to firecracks.

About 1770 white tin glaze was used. Large white groups of biblical and mythological subjects, mounted on rococo bases, were well modelled in the Italian baroque manner. In these pieces the fire-cracking is usually extensive.

The factory mark of a star, taken from the Ginori arms, was introduced towards the end of the eighteenth century.

Bowl and cover with floral decoration, Capodimonte, 1750s. Victoria & Albert Museum

The concern remained in the hands of the Ginori family until 1896, and still bears their name.

Porcelain marked with an N surmounted by a crown, together with the monogram F.R.F., was made at the Royal Naples factory, started in 1771 by Ferdinand I, as an attempted revival of his father's enterprise at Capodimonte.

The porcelain is of a soft, glassy paste and highly translucent. Early products recall those of Capodimonte, where some of the painters had worked. An Academy of the Nude was started in 1781, when a classical style was adopted. Many of the later figures are in biscuit. Large services were decorated with scenes and neoclassical subjects.

The original factory lasted until 1807, when it was sold to the French firm, Jean Poularde Prad & Company.

Russian

Porcelain

Russian porcelain, being little known or collected in the West, has often been mistakenly judged as an inferior imitation of that from the more famous German, French, and Austrian factories which preceded it, and therefore hardly worthy of being studied as a ceramic art with a character, artistic quality, and history of its own. Closer acquaintance, however, reveals many distinct and individual qualities, which at their best can rival the standard set by the finest West European products, although the first Russian factory started later, and only began to flourish after a series of calamities.

Peter the Great had sent scientific experts on Russian trade caravans to Peking, with strict instructions to find out from the secretive Chinese the exact manner in which they made their porcelain. But his emissaries returned home none the wiser. It was not until 1744 that his exuberant daughter, the Empress Elizabeth, entrusted a vagrant German, C. K. Hunger, then employed in Stockholm, with a written contract to 'found in St Petersburg a factory for making Dutch plates and pure porcelain, as it is made in Saxony'. Hunger had started life as a goldsmith's apprentice, later sought out Böttger, the famous director of the first hard-paste Meissen factory, and was employed as a gilder there in 1727. He wrote to the Empress Elizabeth that he had been responsible for organizing the Rörstrand ceramic factory in Sweden (whence he had in fact been summarily dismissed).

He belonged to that familiar class of restless international adventurers, in which even the eighteenth century abounded. Lavish in promises, he knew how to advertise his very scanty talents, and thereby win the confidence of highly placed people. From the start, his behaviour in Russia aroused suspicion. His first firing in the kiln was a total failure, but he always found plausible excuses. Eventually he exhausted the patience of the director, Baron Cherkasov, who complained that during three years Hunger had turned out barely a dozen cups, and even they were crooked and discoloured.

A Russian priest's son, Dmitri Vinogradov, who had studied chemistry in Marburg, was then ordered

A group of three figures, a peasant woman and man, and a priest, 18th century

to extract from Hunger all the secrets of porcelain manufacture, to supervise him, and never to leave him alone for a single moment. In 1747 he replaced Hunger, who was dismissed. Undoubtedly Vinogradov gave himself heart and soul to experimental work, especially with the ingredients of the paste and glaze, and scientific methods of firing in the kiln. He produced some good though limited results, but he suffered from bouts of drunkenness, which made him violent and unreliable. In 1752 Baron Cherkasov, who took porcelain seriously, had Vinogradov fastened to an iron chain, perpetually watched and in his turn forced to write down every technical recipe that he knew. He died in 1758 at the early age of thirty-nine.

After this painful initiation the Imperial Factory came into its own during the reign of Catherine II (1762–96). She made a thorough personal inspection of the factory in 1763, and at once ordered highly skilled painters, modellers, and craftsmen to be engaged, regardless of expense, from Germany, Austria, and France. Catherine had a passion for building, and for filling whatever she built with beautiful and magnificent objects, without any prejudice about their national origin. For her new Imperial Hermitage and Tsarskoe Selo she collected pictures, sculpture, and porcelain from all over Europe.

Reacting against the lush and gaudy baroque encouraged by her predecessor, she promoted a sterner classical temper in architecture, and admired an architectural dignity in decorative art. Her best and favourite architects were Italians. 'I want Italians,' she told her agent, Grimm, 'because we already have enough Frenchmen who know too much and design ugly buildings.' She bought up all the portfolios of Clérisseau's drawings and aquatints, made during a tour of Italy, minutely depicting Italian ornamental plasterwork, arabesques, vase construction, and Pompeian detail. This decorative Italian strain, often nostalgically reflected by northern temperaments, also found expression in Russian porcelain, where it recurred throughout the following century. At the same time Catherine herself, being a pure German and a usurper, tried hard to personify some more ideal aspects of her adopted country, and was keen on giving scope for native Russian themes in art.

Many West European porcelain factories had begun by working in the manner initiated either by the Chinese or by their immediate predecessors. The first Russian factory was no exception, for it frankly emulated Meissen as the best and leading European exponent of ceramic art. Catherine ordered a well-known dinner service from Meissen ('The Hunter's Service', because it was decorated with diverse hunting scenes). But characteristically, as soon as some plates and dishes became broken, she insisted that the Imperial Factory should make all replacements. And these turned out hardly inferior to the originals, although the paste was less uniformly white, showed the bluish tint of Russian kaolin, and the painting was recognizably freer and more naïve.

The Chinese Empire, being uncomfortably close, appeared less romantic to Russia than it did to Western Europe at that time. And the Western fashion for fantastic whimsical *chinoiseries* found less favour there. Moreover, in Russia, any craving for the exotic could be fully gratified at home. A book by the German traveller, J. Georgi (translated into Russian in 1776), called *Description of the Races inhabiting the Russian Empire*, attracted attention chiefly by its lively coloured illustrations. These formed the starting point for a whole new series of porcelain figures, showing many characteristic types, wearing picturesque national or regional costumes.

Perhaps they were partly inspired by earlier racial figures from the Meissen modeller, Kändler, but

Tartar archer after J. Kändler and P. Reinicke of the Meissen factory in Germany, Popov Factory, Moscow, 1810

they drew upon original and local raw material. Their striking success led to the creation of a further series, illustrating Russian peasants, tradesmen, craftsmen, etc., wearing their professional clothes and carrying the emblems of their work. These provide delightfully idealized genre studies of Russian life in the late eighteenth and early nineteenth centuries.

Jean Rachette, son of a French sculptor but born in Copenhagen, came to the Imperial Factory as a modeller in 1779. He took responsibility for launching both these series of porcelain figures, which were often as remarkable for their balanced rhythmical composition as for their pure and sensitive modelling and colourful brilliance. This foreigner's talented interpretation of native Russian themes launched a new tradition, which was drawn and enlarged upon by later Russian porcelain factories throughout the nineteenth century. Rachette remained active until 1804, when he was granted the rank of State Counsellor in recognition of his great services to art. Paradoxical though it sounds, foreign artists who came to work in Russia were often more inspired by original Russian subjects and environment than native artists, who went out of their way to imitate the latest Western fashions, whether they were bad or good.

Figure of a Samoyed woman, St Petersburg, late 18th century. Victoria & Albert Museum

Another line, developed in the Imperial Factory at this time, glorified Catherine and the achievements of her reign. On many vases her head appears in medallion form with the helmet of Minerva. On another a Cupid crowns with a laurel wreath her interlaced initials, while a double-headed eagle holds out an olive branch of peace. A vase at Gatchina depicts her greeted by a whole group of allegorical female figures, *Abundance*, *Humanity*, *Science*, *Justice*, and *Industry*, while *Chastity*, with modest downcast eyes, holds up a mirror to the Empress. The so-called 'Arabesque Service', though decoratively inspired by frescoes excavated at Herculaneum, also served to illustrate Russian naval victories.

But the majestic dinner services and vases, ordered by Catherine, already differed both in colouring and form from the Meissen porcelain of the period. They were severer, more compact in line, less elaborate and mannered in execution. In the 'Cabinet Service' (first ordered as a present for her favourite, Count Bezborodko) the artistic splendour of luxuriant Italian ornament prevailed over national self-glorification. Together with exquisite detail, similar to that in the Arabesque service, it is distinguished by a broad gold band, encircled by garlands of delicate flowers, with oval medallions in the centre, depicting Italian architectural scenes, sometimes with human figures.

Having mastered ceramic technique and form in the eighteenth century, the art of modelling, painting, and gilding porcelain reached its high point and boldest native originality in the first half of the next century under Alexander I and Nicolas I. At the same time preoccupation with new experiments in colour contrast was accompanied by a diminishing concern with purity of form. This led to a looser relationship between sculptural design and painted decoration. The latter tended to predominate. Intense malachite and emerald greens, rich lapislazuli blue, delicate mauves and buffs and deep maroon, more and more took the place of pure and dazzling white as favourite colours for the background. But exquisite miniature painting, often framed in white panels, was made to blend effectively with these coloured grounds.

Catherine's son, the Emperor Paul (1796–1801), although he was a certifiable megalomaniac and hated his domineering mother, inherited her passion for good porcelain. He particularly liked medallions with paintings of landscapes and fine buildings, and he started a branch of the Imperial Factory near his own palace at Gatchina. It is recorded that, the day before he was murdered, he received a new dinner service he had ordered, painted with Russian architectural scenes, and, admiring it together with members of his family, pronounced that day to be the happiest in his whole life.

Alexander I (1801–25), despite the Napoleonic Wars which dislocated his reign, did not neglect the factory, which continued to recruit first-class artist-craftsmen, regardless of nationality. As a rule each new foreign craftsman was (very sensibly) put under contract to teach two Russian apprentices. The most important foreign painter, Schwebach, who had worked for twelve years at Sèvres, was prominent in launching a new genre of decoration, depicting soldiers in battle scenes, and Asiatic figures seen against Russian landscapes.

In 1806 Alexander was persuaded to issue a decree imposing a prohibitive tariff on the import of foreign porcelain into Russia. By stimulating internal competition, this measure made private porcelain factories start to multiply. Some were straightforward business ventures, run by enterprising merchants. Others, like that run by Prince Yusupov at his palace of Arkhangelskoe, were designed to gratify the taste of wealthy connoisseurs, and to provide unique presents for their personal friends. The Miklashevsky factory, started by a landowner who had found china clay on his estate, and employing his own serfs, won a gold medal at an exhibition in Petersburg in 1849. Its most striking work was a huge porcelain iconostasis with blue and gold columns, made for the owner's village church at Volokhitin. One generous landowner, who detected a natural talent for modelling and carving in a young serf called Kudinov, arranged for him all facilities to start his own porcelain factory in 1818, and later gave him his freedom. This factory was managed by the Kudinov family, whose name it bore, until 1881, lasting longer than many others founded in the same period, which did not survive the Emancipation of 1861.

The main difference between Russian and European porcelain at this time depended less on style (which was everywhere neoclassical) than on choice of themes and mode of artistic interpretation. While the Sèvres factory concentrated on glorifying Napoleon and his deeds, the Imperial factory started to specialize in majestic and graceful vases, with an astonishing variety of shapes and decoration. Events of the patriotic war in 1812 also provoked a vogue for battle scenes with soldiers and officers wearing splendidly gay uniforms.

In 1814 the Russians learned from a French prisoner of war the process of making transfer prints of colour blocks on porcelain. This practice was later adopted by private commercial concerns; but the directors of the Imperial factory rejected it as a semi-mechanical device, good enough for the quick salesmanship required by Western bourgeois mass production, but unworthy of the Russian court and

Dinner service made for Nicholas I and used at the coronation of the Tsars, Imperial Porcelain Factory, St Petersburg, 19th century. Christie, Manson & Woods

Imperial Porcelain Factory marks

aristocracy, which demanded and appreciated first-class hand painting.

Nicolas I (1825–55) was more exacting than his predecessor. He required splendid and dignified porcelain to decorate the royal palace, examined every piece personally, and gave little encouragement to his director's scheme to make the Imperial factory pay its way by selling surplus products to the public. During his reign the vases were superbly painted, although they began to show too many scenes directly copied from Old Master paintings in the Hermitage. But some of the most lively and exquisite paintings depicted flowers, fruit, or exotic birds, and were made on the flat centres or borders of plates and dishes. One of the Russian painters, Paul Ivanov, excelled in modelling porcelain flowers and foliage in high relief. At the 1851 Crystal Palace exhibition in London the Imperial Factory was awarded a medal for its exhibit.

During the reign of Alexander II (1855–81) orders for the palaces and members of the Imperial family rapidly declined. Emancipation of the serfs in 1861 also led to the closing down of numerous private factories, which had depended on serf craftsmen, formerly trained by their masters and foreign artists. Taste grew more stereotyped and stale, and art began to be overshadowed in importance for its patrons by the fashionable concentration on social reforms.

In 1871 the Empress told the director of the factory that he must fight against academic stagnation, and aim at more vitality, diversity of shapes, painting, and style. She suggested he might start to take some helpful examples from English porcelain. The chief sculptor, Spiess, was thereupon dispatched to England, whence he brought back many specimens from English factories. Despite the decline of interest among its patrons, the Imperial Factory still had superb artists, and the flower painting on some of its vases remained as perfect as in the earlier period, reminiscent of the most luxuriant Dutch seventeenth-century 'still life' style.

Alexander III (1881–94) on his accession gave orders for the Imperial Factory to be given the best possible technical and artistic opportunities. A survey taken at this time admitted that a quite disproportionate number of administrative officials demoralized the best craftsmen, and that many incompetent workmen were engaged or retained, merely because they happened to be children or relatives of members of the staff. Regularly once a year Alexander gave instructions about projects submitted to him. Far from being a stuffy philistine, his own taste was definite. He encouraged a dignified and massive simplicity. Towards the end of his reign, however, he showed a preference for the pale, cold blues and greys of the late Copenhagen style. He ordered one important and elaborately painted dinner service for the court. This was described as the 'Raphael Service' because the motifs in it were taken from Raphael's Vatican decorations, which had been copied in the eighteenth century for the Hermitage in Petersburg.

Under Nicolas II (1894–1917), who had inferior personal taste and no love for art, the standard rapidly declined. During his reign little original work was done, except perhaps in Easter eggs, and the best porcelain consisted of replacements or additions to services previously commissioned by his more cultured predecessors.

The first mark of the Imperial Factory in the reigns of Elizabeth and Peter III consisted of a black or impressed double-headed eagle, and, more rarely, an impressed anchor. From the time of Catherine II, and under all subsequent emperors, the mark consisted of the reigning sovereign's initials painted under the glaze, usually in blue, but sometimes in black or green. Except in the reign of Catherine, these initials are surmounted by the Imperial crown. Some pieces, made in the reign of Alexander II, have the Emperor's initial surrounded by a circular wreath. Many pieces are unmarked, since marking was first made compulsory by Nicolas I.

Though the Imperial factory usually launched the style and themes for other Russian porcelain manufacture, it was followed and frequently surpassed in quality by several private factories. The most notable of these was started about 1756 by an Englishman,

Vase painted with a portrait plaque, exhibited in 1862, Imperial Porcelain Factory, St Petersburg. Bethnal Green Museum

Francis Gardner, who appears to have first settled in Russia in 1746. It was successfully carried on by his descendants until 1891, when it was sold to the giant Kuznetsov porcelain and faïence combine. The factory was situated in the Gjelsk region, near Moscow, where local clay, which proved suitable for porcelain, could be used. Gardner started with a German manager called Gattenberg, who later joined the Imperial Factory, and he employed a well-known German painter, Kestner. But these and other foreigners taught many Russian craftsmen, principally serfs, who gradually replaced them, as soon as they had mastered the various techniques; so that the number of foreigners employed in key positions steadily diminished in course of time.

Eighteenth-century Gardner groups and figures of a sentimental pastoral character are still close to Meissen prototypes, and so are its rare figures representing characters from the Italian *Commedia dell'Arte*. The academician, G. Miller, who visited the Gardner factory in 1779, noted that 'its quality is equal to that of any foreign factory'. He found only one defect: 'that its glaze is less white than the Saxon. But they are trying to remedy this, and have gone quite far towards success.' (A. Selivanov: *Farfor i Fayans Rossiyskoy Imperii* (Vladimir, 1903, p. 22). Not only did Gardner already compete with the Imperial factory, but he even obtained orders from the court of Catherine II for specially designed services.

Miller remarked with admiration on the beauty of one of these, decorated with architectural scenes and classical ornament. Gardner also produced for the Court four separate dinner services decorated with emblems of the Russian orders of knighthood.

By the beginning of the nineteenth century the work of the Gardner factory had grown emancipated from imitation of foreign models. In particular, its figures of Russian peasant types and craftsmen reveal a dignified simplicity, remote from the increasing sophistication of Sèvres and Meissen figures that were being made at that time. The best of these also show a mastery of sensitive modelling and sculptural poise, accompanied by a bold and brilliant range of colour combinations, and frequently by skilful contrasts between matt and glazed painting used on the same figure. All these innovations and refinements illustrated how Russian modellers and painters were freshly and independently inspired by this new art, and were reaching beyond what they had learned from foreign masters, while introducing native themes and decorative colouring drawn from their traditional Russian background.

The Gardner factory could not escape the general decline in visual art which oppressed the second half of the nineteenth century throughout Europe. But in a number of its individual products it still maintained the exacting standard of an earlier age. Some of its figures of national types, especially Asiatic ones, are modelled with extraordinary finesse, even in the 1880s, though the colouring tended to be cruder than it was in the previous decades. But many of the peasant figures of this late period are mannered and 'literary'. Some are painfully coarse and clumsy, and seem like drunken caricatures of their serene and charming predecessors. In this period Gardner also embarked on mass-produced tea services, gaily painted with roses in white medallions against deep blue, red, or green grounds. Many of them were for export to the Turkish Empire or Central Asia, and carry Arabic lettering under the Gardner factory mark. They are widespread enough to be familiar to many people who have never seen the rarer and finer kinds of Russian porcelain.

Gardner porcelain had a wide variety of marks in the 140 years of its existence. Different shapes of the Latin letter G, painted underglaze in blue or black, were most frequent in the late eighteenth and early nineteenth centuries. Occasionally the mark is similar to the Meissen crossed swords with a star. In the first quarter of the nineteenth century the full name of the factory, impressed either in Cyrillic or Latin characters, becomes more frequent. In the second half of the nineteenth century the mark is usually the Moscow St George and Dragon crest, surrounded by a circle, bearing the full name of the factory, at first impressed, and later painted in green or red. In the last decades of the factory's existence the double-headed eagle was added to the design, and this elaborate mark continued after the Gardner firm had been absorbed by Kuznetsov.

One of the most important factories, stimulated by the protective tariff of 1806, was started in that year in the village of Gorbunov near Moscow, by a certain

Right *Popov Factory marks, 1811–72*

Left *Gardner Factory marks*

Karl Milli. It was taken over in 1811 by a Moscow merchant, A. Popov, who gave his name to the factory, which, together with his son, Dmitri, he personally built up and directed until he died in the 1850s. A decade later it was sold by the Popov family, and passed rapidly from one new owner to another. In the 1870s it belonged to an Armenian, and finally to a Russian merchant who liquidated the whole enterprise.

This factory made most money out of porcelain services designed for country inns. But it also specialized in a small output of extremely fine artistic pieces. The Popov porcelain highly valued by collectors consists of figures of Russian types, dancing peasants, and elaborate dishes featuring flowers or fruit in high relief, which in the quality of their modelling and painted designs are equal to the best of the Gardner and Imperial factories. There is a remarkable figure of a negro in the Sèvres museum, illustrating Bernardin de St Pierre's novel, *Paul et Virginie*. Large-scale ceremonial bread and salt dishes with brilliant floral borders, were another speciality of Popov. The mark of this factory during the whole period of its existence consisted of an impressed or underglaze blue monogram, showing the initials of the founder.

The Kornilov factory, started in 1835 by two brothers of a merchant family in Petersburg, engaged skilled artists and craftsmen from the Imperial, Gardner, and Popov factories. It quickly acquired a reputation for artistic excellence, and as early as 1839 won a gold medal at the Moscow ceramic exhibition. The owners spared no expense and trouble to bring their products to perfection, and for this purpose commissioned original drawings from leading artists of the day. The gorgeous colouring, rich gilding, and decorative finesse of Kornilov products soon became well known, and they were sought after by collectors. But they remained much more expensive than the corresponding Gardner porcelain.

In the last decades of the nineteenth century this factory started mass production of cheap porcelain wares for export. Connoisseurs can detect the difference at a glance. The distinction is made still easier by the fact that all the Kornilov porcelain after 1861 is marked with the full name of the firm in underglaze blue, whereas prior to that date similar marks had always been in red.

Right *Kornilov Factory marks*, c. *1830*

In 1817 there were about forty-five porcelain factories in Russia, many of them very small. In the 1870s the number had risen to seventy, and it fell to fifty towards the end of the century. As time went on the larger factories swallowed up the small ones, or forced them out of business. By the beginning of the twentieth century, the giant M. Kuznetsov combine had eliminated so many competitors that it was responsible for about two-thirds of the total quantity of pottery and porcelain produced throughout the Russian Empire.

Only the Imperial Factory, which remained outside commercial competition, escaped from the degeneration of a period in which cheapness and transient popular novelty were rapidly conquering pure artistic quality. Working solely for the court, it maintained a surprisingly high level of craftsmanship and decorative brilliance up to the very end of the nineteenth century, and even during the uninspiring reign of Nicolas II.

Group painted in colours and gilding, Buen Retiro, mid-18th century. Victoria & Albert Museum

Spanish

Buen Retiro Porcelain

There is so little Buen Retiro porcelain outside Spain that the proper place to study it is in that country. This fact is remarked by Arthur Lane in his fine monograph on Italian porcelain, which includes a section on Buen Retiro, as an extension of the Capodimonte factory.

When Charles III, Bourbon King of Naples, inherited the crown of Spain in 1759 he transported to Madrid artists, workmen, and materials from Capodimonte, where he had started a factory in 1743.

The new establishment was erected in the grounds of the royal palace of Buen Retiro, and by May 1760 work began there under the administrative direction of Giovanni Bonicelli who in 1781 was succeeded by his son Domingo.

The actual making of porcelain was at first in the hands of the chief arcanist Gaetano Schepers and the artistic director Giuseppe Gricci. Schepers died some time after 1764 and Gricci in 1770, after which the management passed successively into the hands of their sons.

Production was much hampered by difficulties arising from the composition of the paste, a situation further complicated by a feud between the Gricci and Schepers families. These factors, together with enormous costs, brought about a steady decline. Disastrous experiments between 1798 and 1802 caused the abandonment of soft-paste manufacture, and after 1805 the wares were hard paste and of utilitarian character. Occupation by French troops in 1808 finally brought about the closing of the factory, and an attempted revival at La Moncloa between 1817 and 1849 was of no artistic importance.

The finest period was during the lifetime of the founder, who died in 1788. Rococo and *chinoiserie* styles were quickly superseded by the early neoclassical (Louis XVI) influence of Sèvres, though the interpretation is unmistakably Spanish.

The earlier paste, which has a beautifully soft brilliance, is often slightly yellow in tone; latterly it became of a hybrid variety owing to difficulties experienced with the composition and materials.

Gricci's first great undertaking was the Porcelain Room in the Palace of Aranjuez (1763–5). Here, the magnificent mirror frames, brackets, vases, groups of *putti*, and Chinese figures among elaborate scrollwork, remain to the present day. A great chandelier in the form of a Chinaman and a monkey holding a palm tree is now in the Royal Palace on the outskirts of Madrid.

Many of the figures, which formed a great part of the factory's output, were modelled by Gricci himself. Naked infants, often representing the continents and seasons, were grouped on scrolled rococo bases; others are of rustic subjects. Tableware, snuff-boxes, holy-water stoups, and a variety of trinkets were also made.

The colouring is soft and the painting particularly characterized by stippling. Where gilding is used it has a warm and distinctly mellow tone. The eighteenth-century mark was the Bourbon fleur-de-lis, either painted or incised, as at Capodimonte. From 1804 to 1808, it was an MD surmounted by a crown.

Spanish Pottery

The history of Spanish pottery goes back to medieval times, when it was dominated by Islamic traditions, imposed by Arab and Moorish invaders, who brought with them the art of making tin-glazed and lustred earthenware. The best-known and most important type dates, however, from the

Hispano–Moresque tin-glazed earthenware lustre plate bearing the arms of Isabel of Castile and Ferdinand, King of Sicily, Manisses, *c.* 1468–79. Victoria & Albert Museum

period of reconquest, when a synthesis of Near Eastern and European styles is seen in the so-called Hispano-Moresque wares.

From the beginning of the fifteenth century onwards Valencia, and particularly the suburbs of Paterna and Manisses, were the chief centres of the industry. Here, under Christian rule, Moorish potters produced wares decorated in a hybrid style, in blue and white, and blue enriched with gold lustre.

Arabesques and inscriptions in Arabic gradually merged with Christian emblems and epigraphs in gothic lettering; together with bold heraldic devices and foliate patterns of great power and distinction. Human figures were more rarely depicted.

Albarelli and great dishes, superbly painted with the armorial bearings of famous French and Italian families, such as those of René of Anjou and Lorenzo de' Medici, indicate the high esteem in which these wares were held; indeed, it was asserted in a contemporary writing that 'Manisses work was gilded and painted in masterly fashion, with which the whole world is in love—pope, cardinals and princes ordering it by special favour, and marvelling that things of such excellence and nobility could be made from clay'. Gadrooned and relief-decorated pieces appeared towards the end of the fifteenth century, while arabesques and diapered patterns of Persian origin were still in use.

The diminishing number of coats-of-arms appearing in the sixteenth century prove the decline in aristocratic patronage, and, though the manufacture has continued, there has been no revival of its previous excellence.

ALCORA

An important factory making faïence at Alcora (Valencia) was founded in 1726–7 by the Count of Aranda, who secured the services of Édouard Roux and Joseph Olerys, formerly of Moustiers.

On the death of the founder the factory was carried on by his son, and continued to make fine-quality faïence, together with some porcelain, until the latter half of the eighteenth century; after which, nothing of any merit was produced.

During the period of Olerys's employment (1727–37), the style was very similar to that of Moustiers (*see under* French Faïence).

Some fine pictorial painting on large panels and oval plaques with moulded frames was done by Miguel Soliva. After Olerys's departure, elaborate rococo forms were adopted, and a recipe for lustre was obtained from nearby Manisses in 1749.

A number of excellent busts were made at Alcora, and a magnificent portrait of the Count of Aranda is in the collection of the Hispanic Society of America, New York.

Swiss

Porcelain

Switzerland has not produced much porcelain, and since it is bordered by Germany and France it is not surprising that Zürich porcelain is of the German type and Nyon porcelain of the French type.

ZÜRICH

At Schooren near Zürich, a company, including the poet Salomon Gessner, started to produce soft paste in 1763, and two years later hard paste, with kaolin brought from Lorraine. Gessner occasionally supplied his own designs for the decoration of plates, which bring to mind the vignettes in his *Idyllen*, published in Switzerland about this time. Whether he actually painted some himself is uncertain. The factory's best period lasted up to 1790; its output included original figures of great charm, some influenced by artists from Lorraine, others closer to Ludwigsburg, from whence the modeller J. V. Sonnenschein had come.

From 1766 to 1790 the factory was under the technical direction of Adam Spengler, whose son John was a modeller at the Derby factory (1790–5).

NYON

Hard-paste porcelain was also made at Nyon, near Geneva, from about 1780, by Ferdinand Müller of Frankenthal and Jacques Dortu, who had been at Berlin and Marieberg. Dortu, whose technical knowledge provided a good-quality white paste, eventually became sole director, 1809–13. In the latter period English-style earthenware was made.

A variety of pieces were competently painted in the current Paris mode, with scattered sprigs of flowers, butterflies, beribboned trophies, garlands, and diapers. The coloured grounds of Sèvres and commoner Meissen patterns were also imitated. Figures are very rare.

The mark of a fish in underglaze blue has been used by Hamann of Dresden (1866), and also as a rebus in the perch (fish) of the Paris decorator Perche (about 1825).

Far right Agateware cream jug, in imitation of a silver form, *c.* 1750. (*See* Glossary overleaf.)

Glossary

Absolon. *See* Independent decorators.
Adam. A number of potters of this name worked in Staffordshire in the late eighteenth and early nineteenth centuries.
Adam and Eve. A favoured subject on delftware 'chargers' (first dated example 1635, but continued well into the eighteenth century) and slipware, also for stoneware 'Pew' groups.
'AF' mark. *See* Bow.
Agateware. Wares made in imitation of agate. They were made either of differently coloured clays, mixed, and with the colours going right through the body of the piece, or the effect was achieved by means of coloured clays on the surface of plain pottery. (*See* illustration previous page.)
Albany slip. The diluted, creamy state of a fine clay found near Albany, New York, on the bank of the Hudson River. Of rich dark-brown colour, sometimes used as a glaze, or after *c.* 1800 for coating the interior of salt-glazed stoneware vessels. In 1843, the New York Geological Survey said it was 'known and shipped all over the country'.
Albarello. A cylindrical jar made to contain ointments or dry medicaments. The neck is grooved for tying on a parchment cover. Those with a spout were for liquids.
Allen, Robert (1744–1835). An artist at the Lowestoft, Suffolk, porcelain factory from 1757, and manager there from about 1780. On the closing of the works in 1802 Allen set up as an enameller of white porcelain on his own account. A Chinese tea pot and cover in the Schreiber Collection at the Victoria and Albert Museum, London, has the body painted with a Crucifixion scene, the cover bears some flowers, and the base is signed: *Allen, Lowestoft.* The religious scene was painted in China, and the flowers probably in Lowestoft by Allen, who added his name to the whole.
'A' mark. *See* Bow.
Anchor mark. *See* Chelsea, Bow, Derby, Davenport.
An hua ('secret') decoration. Faint engraving or painting in white slip, visible only against the light; found especially on early Ming and eighteenth-century white porcelain.
Arcanist. Workman knowing the secret of pottery making in general, and of porcelain making in particular.
Arcanum. Chemical composition and technique of porcelain making.
Arrowmark. *See* Worcester and Pinxton.
Art pottery. Also called studio ware. Much ornamental work in what Dr Barber (writing in 1893) considered 'elegant decorative forms' appeared after the Centennial, 1876. Rookwood faïence (*q.v.*) was especially admired, also the wares of Chelsea Keramic Art Works (1872–89 at Chelsea, Massachusetts) developed by Hugh C. Robertson from 1891 as the Chelsea Pottery, from 1895 as Dedham Pottery. Art tiles (*see* Barber, pp. 343–84) flourished in the 1880s, notably John G. Low's from 1789 at Chelsea, Massachusetts.
Astbury. A family of Staffordshire potters. To John Astbury (1686–1743) were attributed (questionably) the first use of white clay washes and of calcined flint in earthenware manufacture. The name 'Astbury' is applied to red earthenware with applied white reliefs, and to small figures in white clay enlivened with touches of red clay and dabs of colour in the glaze. Both were probably also made by other potters.

Wares marked 'Astbury' impressed were made by a later Astbury (after *c.* 1760).
'Astbury' type. Classification of Staffordshire pottery in which red and white clays are combined under a transparent lead glaze. Similar wares covered by a glaze splashed with metallic oxides are generally styled 'Astbury-Whieldon'.

Far right Astbury-Whieldon type group, earthenware with mottled lead-glaze, Staffordshire, *c.* 1740. Art Gallery and Museum, Brighton

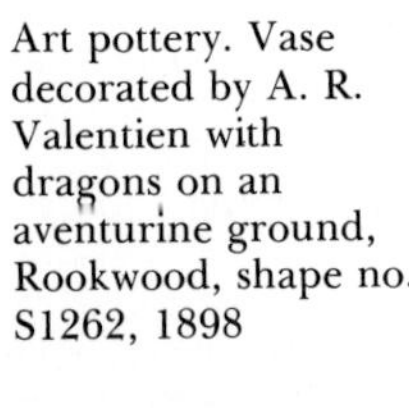

Art pottery. Vase decorated by A. R. Valentien with dragons on an aventurine ground, Rookwood, shape no. S1262, 1898

Ballot box. A common name for a salt kit (*q.v.*).
Bamboo. The bamboo is found in China in wild and cultivated varieties, and from the Sung dynasty onwards it has probably been represented more frequently than any other plant-form. Many small vessels, like spouted wine-pots, were modelled as sections of the bamboo cane, especially in the stoneware of Yi-Hsing. It symbolizes longevity, and represents Buddha, with the prunus and pine representing Kung-fu Tzŭ (Confucius) and Lao-Tzŭ respectively.
Bamboo ware. A variety of stoneware, of a darker tint of brown than the caneware, introduced by Josiah Wedgwood in 1770.
Barm pot. Pot for storing barm or yeast (*see also* salt kit).
Basaltes. The name given by Josiah Wedgwood to his fine-quality stoneware introduced in 1766.
Bat. Chinese, *fu*, Japanese, *Komori.* The number of vocables in the Chinese language is far too small to give one to each idea, noun, or subject. This is overcome by the use of tones, which determine the meaning of a word. For example, said in one tone *fu* means bat, in another tone it means happiness. To give a porcelain bowl decorated with bats is to wish happiness to the recipient. Five bats represent the Five Blessings – longevity, wealth, serenity, virtue, and an easy death. This peculiarity of the Chinese language is the key to the symbolic meaning of a great deal of the decoration of porcelain. The bat in Japanese decoration has no such meaning, and has been copied from China.
Batavia. A trading station of the Dutch East India Company in Java (*see* Batavian ware).
Batavian ware. Porcelains with lustrous brown-glazed grounds and panels of *famille rose* decoration;

named after the Dutch trading station in Java through which they reached Europe in the first half of the eighteenth century.

'Battle for the Breeches.' Theme of popular imagery concerning marriage occurring on seventeenth-century slipware and as a subject for nineteenth-century spill vases. Possibly made by Obadiah Sherratt.

Baxter, Thomas (1782–1821). Painter, worked independently (*see* Independent decorators), and at Worcester (1814–16 and 1819–21) and Swansea (1816–19): painted figure subjects, landscapes, shells, flowers, etc.

Bear jug. Model in the form of a bear hugging a dog, illustrating the sport of bear baiting. The detachable head serves as a cup. Made in Staffordshire and Nottingham, eighteenth century.

Bellarmine. Big-bellied stoneware bottle with a bearded mask in relief, named after Cardinal Bellarmine (1542–1621). Frequently cited in contemporary literature and used in magic and witchcraft. Also called 'Greybeards'.

Belleek. A light, fragile feldspathic porcelain cast in moulds, with lustrous pearly glaze. Invented *c.* 1860 by William Goss of Stoke, improved by William Bromley at the Irish factory of David McBirney & Co. (founded 1857 at Belleek, Co. Fermanagh), which by 1865 won a medal at the Dublin Exhibition. Produced at many American factories 1882–1900 and called lotusware by Knowles of East Liverpool.

Bellringers' jugs. Jugs for serving ale to bellringers, kept in the church tower, as at Macclesfield, or in the home of a ringer.

Belper (Derbyshire). *See* Bourne & Co.

Bennington. A name widely, and wrongly, applied to brown Rockingham wares in general. The Vermont town had two establishments, a lesser stoneware works of the Norton family (1793–1894) and the enterprising factory of Christopher W. Fenton, 1845–58 (called the U.S. Pottery Co., from 1853). Fenton produced a diversity of wares, from common yellow and flint enamel (*q.v.*) to porcelains and Parian.

Berain, Jean (1637–1711). French engraver and draughtsman. *Dessinateur* to Louis XIV. Creator of a style of ornament used on French faïence and porcelain. Also his son, Jean II (1674–1728).

'BFB' mark, impressed. *See* Worcester.

Bianco-sopra-bianco. An opaque white pigment used for decorating a tin glaze of slightly contrasted colour.

Bennington ware

Right Biscuit porcelain group 'Three Virgins distressing Cupid', after Angelica Kauffmann, marks D, Ds35 and a triangle incised, Derby, *c.* 1785

Mug painted with a view of Chatsworth by William Billingsley, marked on the base with a P. Pinxton, *c.* 1800

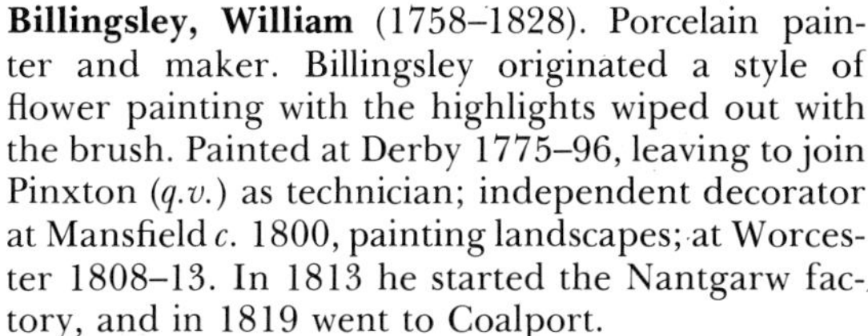

Billingsley, William (1758–1828). Porcelain painter and maker. Billingsley originated a style of flower painting with the highlights wiped out with the brush. Painted at Derby 1775–96, leaving to join Pinxton (*q.v.*) as technician; independent decorator at Mansfield *c.* 1800, painting landscapes; at Worcester 1808–13. In 1813 he started the Nantgarw factory, and in 1819 went to Coalport.

Bird call. Pottery whistle in the form of a bird. Sometimes built into old chimneys as a charm against evil spirits.

Bird fountain. Wall bracket with a projecting socket for water, made in blue-printed, lustred, or enamelled earthenware, eighteenth and nineteenth centuries.

Biscuit. Unglazed porcelain or, more rarely, pottery, as a medium for statuettes and reliefs, used since the middle of the eighteenth century under the influence of the classical revival. The material more nearly resembles marble than porcelain. Falconet created some of the earliest Sèvres models, Melchior some of the later portraits, at Höchst, Frankenthal, and Nymphenburg. (*See* Derby, Bristol.)

Bisque. Unglazed or 'biscuit' porcelain.

Black. *See* Brown and Black glazes.

'Black basaltes' or **'Black Egyptian'.** An unglazed line-grained black stoneware perfected by Wedgwood *c.* 1769 and much imitated elsewhere. Decorated with relief, gilding, or enamelling.

Black printing. 'A term for applying impressions to glazed vessels, whether the colours be black, red, or gold' (William Evans, 1846).

Blake, William. The artist, poet, and visionary, was

employed to draw and engrave a catalogue of Wedgwood cream-coloured wares in the years 1815 and 1816. The engravings run to eighteen in number and illustrate 185 pieces of domestic china. Eight of the actual copper plates are still in existence, but have been altered since they left Blake's hand. Some correspondence between the artist and Josiah Wedgwood is printed by Geoffrey Keynes in *Blake Studies* (1949). Sixteen of the engravings are reproduced in W. Mankowitz's *Wedgwood*, Keynes gives two, one of which is not in Mankowitz's book.

Blanc-de-Chine. *See* Tê Hua porcelain.

Blue-and-white porcelain. Decoration with painting in cobalt blue under the glaze has continued ever since its introduction. It is both attractive and economical, requiring one firing only. Some fourteenth-century wares depict plants and animals within floral scroll borders. The classic fifteenth-century Ming reigns of Hsüan-tê and Ch'êng Hua produced perhaps the finest of all blue-and-white, with perfect forms, superb glaze, rich colour, and lively yet restrained painting of dragons and floral scrolls. A deep violet blue was used in the Chia Ching period, and sixteenth-century painting is freely executed in 'outline and wash' technique. As well as the traditional subjects, ladies on garden terraces, playing boys, and animals in landscapes are now depicted. Much Ming porcelain now in European collections came from the Near East or south-east Asia, to which it had been exported in many styles and qualities. From about 1600 the East India Companies imported into Europe thin porcelain plates and bowls with indented edges, painted with emblems and figures in wide panelled borders. The 'Transitional' period wares of the mid-seventeenth century, e.g. cylindrical vases and bottles with tulip designs, bold landscapes and figure subjects, are often finely painted. The paste of K'ang Hsi period wares is fine and white, and for the best pieces a brilliant sapphire blue was used, applied in overlapping flat strokes, as on the famous 'prunus jars', with sprays of plum blossom reserved in white. Decorative vases and 'useful' wares are extremely varied in shape and decoration. Landscapes and scenes from literature, with elegant ladies or huntsmen, are common, and a great variety of panelled, brocaded, and bordered designs with flowers (aster and tiger-lily patterns, lotus, chrysanthemum, etc.), as well as the traditional animals and emblems. Ming reign marks were often used; that of K'ang Hsi rarely. The Yung Chêng and Ch'ien Lung periods produced little besides revivals of early Ming styles, and export wares of declining quality. Later eighteenth-century services made to European order ('Nankin china') are rather coarse, with thick glazes, and crowded designs of the 'willow-pattern' type.

'Blue-dash chargers'. *See* English pottery.

Blue or **lavender glazes.** Especially fine porcelains with the high-temperature cobalt-blue glaze were made during the Ming reigns of Hsüan-tê and Chia Ching; it was also used in coarser wares decorated with raised white slip designs, and in the 'three-colour' class. During the Ch'ing dynasty the colour was varied by dilution or addition of manganese purple to produce a variety of tones. K'ang Hsi deep-blue glazes are generally overpainted with gilt designs, or appear in conjunction with underglaze blue or red painting; they include the 'powder' blue (*q.v.*). Several shades of lavender and pale blue, such as the *clair-de-lune*, were at their best under Yung Chêng and Ch'ien Lung; when fine imitations of the crackled Sung Kuan and Ko wares were also made.

'B' mark. *See* Bow, Bristol (hard-paste porcelain), Worcester (Dr Wall and Flight & Barr) and Pinxton.

Bocage. A background of flowers and leaves, usually on figures and groups intended for a frontal view only.

'Boccaro' ware. A misnomer for Yi-Hsing stoneware.

Body. The composite materials of which potter's clay is made – the ware itself, usually pottery or stoneware; for porcelains the word *paste* is preferred (as hard paste, soft paste).

Bone-ash or **bone china.** The white ashes of bones were used in Bow porcelain from 1748, and subsequently in the modified hard-paste porcelain which from *c.* 1800 became the standard English body.

Boulton, Matthew (1728–1809). In partnership with John Fothergill (to 1781), and with John Watt, was a manufacturer of metalwork at Soho, Birmingham. He mounted Wedgwood cameos, etc., in cut steel and in gilt bronze. Writing to Bentley in 1768 Wedgwood said: 'We have an order from Mr Boulton for some bodys of vases for mounting, which I must either comply with or affront him, and set him a-trying to get them elsewhere . . .'

Bourne & Co. Stoneware potters at Belper (from *c.* 1800), Codnor Park (from 1833), and Denby (from 1812) in Derbyshire. Mark: 'Bourne'.

Bow (soft-paste porcelain). The Bow factory, possibly active in 1744 (when E. Heylyn and Thomas Frye took out a patent), was certainly working before

Figure of a Turkish dancer, porcelain painted in colours, mark two dots in blue, Bow, *c.* 1765. Victoria & Albert Museum

1750. In 1748 Frye took out a second patent, the ingredients including bone ash; the resultant phosphoric acid in the paste is diagnostic. Frye remained manager until 1759. After 1763 the history of the factory is uncertain, but it is stated to have closed in 1775 or 1776, the moulds being removed to Derby.

Bow specialized in useful wares, but many figures were also made. The porcelain is characterized by a creamy colour, a tendency to stain brown, and an occasional black specking. The early (*c.* 1750) white wares were often decorated by applied moulded sprigs.

The colours on the earlier Bow porcelain (to *c.* 1765) include a characteristic rose purple and opaque light blue. Imitation Kakiemon and *famille rose* painting was much practised; since much Bow porcelain, however, was outside-decorated (*see* Independent decorators), the painting is a fallible guide. Much porcelain painted in underglaze blue of a vivid, intense tone was made. Transfer printing, mainly in russet and purplish black, was employed *c.* 1756 (*see* Hancock).

Bow figures may often be distinguished by the modelling of the head, rather small and doll-like, with only slightly modelled chin and cheeks, and a *retroussé* nose. They are rather heavy, and often have a square hole cut behind for an ormolu embellishment. The characteristic rococo vase, from *c.* 1755, has four feet and in front a pendant scroll, all picked out in rose purple.

Towards the end a palette including a pink and a watery green was adopted; the opaque blue enamel was replaced by a darker translucent colour.

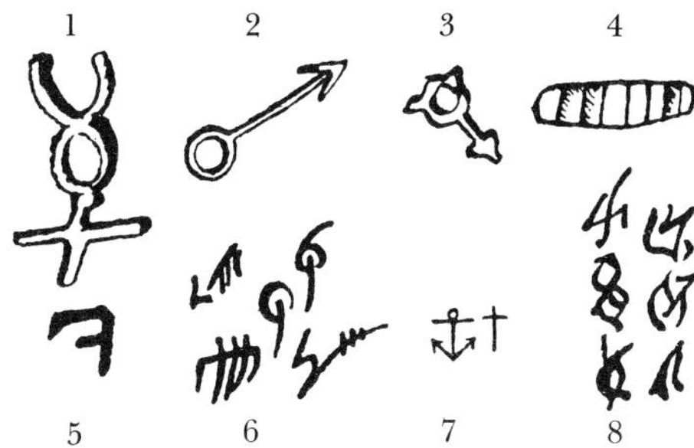

MARKS: 1–3 above *c.* 1750; CT, R, W, AF & D (incised), B, T°, T, and 4 above (impressed) are probably repairers' marks of *c.* 1750–60; B, G, '13', various simulated Chinese characters (e.g. 6 above), and 5 above, in blue, occurs on blue-and-white porcelain *c.* 1755–65; various numerals and initials in enamel were used on useful wares; I, A, a crescent, two dots, and 7 above, in blue, and various forms of 8 above in brownish-red occur on late figures, etc., *c.* 1760–75.

Brampton (Derbyshire). Brown stoneware pottery, second half of eighteenth and nineteenth century.

MARKS: 'Oldfield & Co.', 'S. & H. Briddon'.

'Brinjal' bowls. K'ang Hsi porcelain bowls with incised flower sprays coloured yellow and green on an aubergine- (Anglo–Indian: *brinjal*) purple ground, in glazes applied 'on the biscuit'.

Brislington. Delftware pottery from *c.* 1650 to 1750 (*see* Bristol, delftware).

Bristol (delftware). A pottery at Brislington, near Bristol, was founded by Southwark potters *c.* 1650; it in turn colonized a factory in Bristol (Temple Pottery, 1683–1770, when delftware was abandoned). Others were St Mary Redcliffe's (*c.* 1700–77) and Limekiln Lane (*c.* 1700–54).

Early Bristol delftware is difficult to distinguish from Lambeth, and the later from that of Liverpool. The glaze, however, often had a distinctive lavender-blue tone, and the early red (*c.* 1700) stands out in appreciable relief. The *bianco-sopra-bianco* borders usually include a cone motif and curved sprays of leaves. Characteristic Bristol shapes include a plate with straight sides forming an obtuse angle with the bottom; puzzle jugs with openwork necks formed by intersecting circles; flower 'bricks' pierced with a square hole at the top and mounted on small bracket feet, and (seventeenth-century) porringers having a circular handle with corrugations radiating from a central hole.

Bristol (hard-paste porcelain). About 1770 the Plymouth factory moved to Bristol. In 1773 the factory and rights were bought by Richard Champion, and in 1781 sold to a combine of Staffordshire potters (*see* New Hall). The Plymouth models were continued, and it is sometimes impossible to distinguish the work of the two factories. Both suffered from technical defects (*see* Plymouth), and Bristol thrown wares show in addition spiral marks known as 'wreathing'. Useful wares were, exceptionally, painted or printed in underglaze blue, or printed in overglaze enamel. The more normal enamelling was in perceptible relief; the colours included a characteristic 'juicy' red, clear yellow, and bright translucent green. The decoration reflected Sèvres styles. Figures were much made often with a rockwork base. 'Biscuit' presentation plaques, with applied flowers framing portraits, coats-of-arms, etc., were a speciality.

MARKS: a cross or B (sometimes both), in greyish-

Figure of Summer, hard-paste porcelain, Bristol, *c.* 1775. Fitzwilliam Museum blue enamel; crossed swords imitating Meissen, in underglaze blue or greyish-blue enamel, T° impressed.

Bristol (soft-paste porcelain). In 1749 a factory using soapstone as an ingredient was founded in Bristol. Until recently called 'Lowdin's', it is now known to have been started by William Miller and Benjamin Lund. In 1752 it was advertised as transferred to Worcester, and it is usually impossible to distinguish Bristol from the earliest Worcester porcelain. Certain sauceboats, however, and figures of a Chinaman, bear the mark BRISTOL(L) in relief, impressed. Underglaze blue (and occasionally manganese brown) and enamel painting were practised, usually in styles copying Chinese export porcelain. (*See also* 'Scratch cross' porcelain.)

MARKS: *see* Worcester.

Brown and black glazes. These colours derived from iron are among the high-temperature glazes of Sung stonewares (e.g. Chien ware); and coffee-brown glazes occur on Ming porcelain. The lustrous glazes of the Ch'ing dynasty – the Chinese *tz'ŭ chin* ('brown gold') – range from pale *café-au-lait* to deep golden brown. 'Nankin yellow' is the pale golden brown added to some blue-and-white; the darker 'dead leaf brown' framing *famille rose* painted panels is Batavian ware; and *café-au-lait* was sometimes overpainted in *famille verte* enamels. All appear also as monochromes. The superb glossy K'ang Hsi mirror black was generally enamelled with gilt designs. Produced by an admixture of manganese with iron, it should not be confused with the *famille noire* black (*q.v.*). During the Yung Chêng and Ch'ien Lung periods mottled or speckled brown glazes such as the 'iron rust' and 'tea dust' were favoured, and another class faithfully imitate the character and patina of archaic bronze and silver vessels. Crackled wares with transparent brownish glaze, often with stamped designs in unglazed relief, are principally nineteenth-century.

Bull baiting. Pottery groups showing a bull goring or tossing a dog, often upon table bases supported by six legs, popular *c.* 1830–5. Said to have been made by Obadiah Sherratt.

Bussa. Large earthenware pot commonly kept in old Cornish cottages for salting down pilchards.

Butter pot. Cylindrical earthenware vessel made to hold fourteen pounds of butter, made at Burslem in the seventeenth century for use at Uttoxeter market. An Act of 1661 regulated abuses in the manner of making and packing the pots.

'Cadogan' tea or **hot-water pot.** A copy of the Chinese peach-shaped wine jug, filled through an orifice in the base and constructed on the principle of a non-spillable inkwell. (*See* Rockingham).

Café-au-lait. *See* Brown and black glazes.

Calligraphy. Chinese copying of European handwriting was purely mechanical and, as may be expected, many mistakes occurred in the transcription of verses, mottoes, and inscriptions sent from the West. Letters were omitted, or formed into unpronounceable diagraphs, and the letter *N* was rendered frequently as n. A typical mistake of another type was the careful copying of a coat-of-arms on each piece of a service, with the addition of the words *These are the Arms of myself and my wife*, which had been written on the pattern sent from England.

Cane-coloured ware. Unglazed fine-grained buff stoneware, sometimes decorated with blue, etc., enamels, made by Wedgwood, Turner, Elijah Mayer, etc., late eighteenth century.

Canton. The principal port on the coast of China for trade with Europe in the eighteenth and nineteenth centuries (*see* East India Company). Porcelain was brought to Canton by river from Ching-tê Chên. From the middle years of the eighteenth century increasing quantities of the porcelain were sent unpainted, and decoration was applied to order by artists in enamelling shops at the port. 'Canton' is the familiar name for a nineteenth-century Chinese porcelain exported to Europe. It bears a decoration of butterflies, flowers, etc., on a celadon-green ground.

Canton potteries. Chün-type wares reputedly made here from Sung times remain unidentified, but may include the soft-glazed, sandy-bodied Ma Chün. Certain wares with opaque, crackled grey, purple, and blue glazes are possibly as old as Ming. Stonewares with grey or brown bodies and various glazes, ranging from opaque grey or blue to the streaked *flambés* of purple, red, and green, continue till the present day. Very large jars, vases, etc., were made for outdoor use, sometimes with elaborate applied work, and numerous small animal figures serve as incense burners, water pots, etc. Enamelling workshops at Canton decorated porcelain in the *famille rose* style for export, as well as the 'Canton enamels' painted on copper.

Capacity mug. Cylindrical measure made in stoneware, earthenware, mocha ware, etc., from the seventeenth century. The presence of a royal cipher or an excise stamp provides a clue as to date.

Carpet balls. Used in the Victorian game of carpet bowls, made in brown stoneware or white earthenware coloured with starry, ringed, or flowery patterns. A set comprised six patterned and one white or self-coloured balls. Made in Scotland and Staffordshire. The Parr family of Burslem specialized in them.

Castleford (Yorkshire). Pottery founded by David Dunderdale *c.* 1790, making creamware, black basaltes, and other characteristic Leeds and Staffordshire wares. Best known for unglazed relief-decorated white stoneware, usually called 'Castleford' but certainly also made elsewhere. Wares marked 'D.D. & Co., Castleford' are authentic productions: these do not include pieces with enamelled landscapes with blue-outlined panels.

Castle Hedingham. Pseudo-medieval and Tudor pottery was made here by Edward Bingham (b. 1829). Sometimes mistaken for authentic fifteenth-, sixteenth-, and seventeenth-century wares.

Cats. Figures made in striped salt-glazed stoneware ('agateware') and earthenware in the mid-eighteenth century (Staffordshire); also in delftware.

Solid agate cat, Staffordshire, *c.* 1750

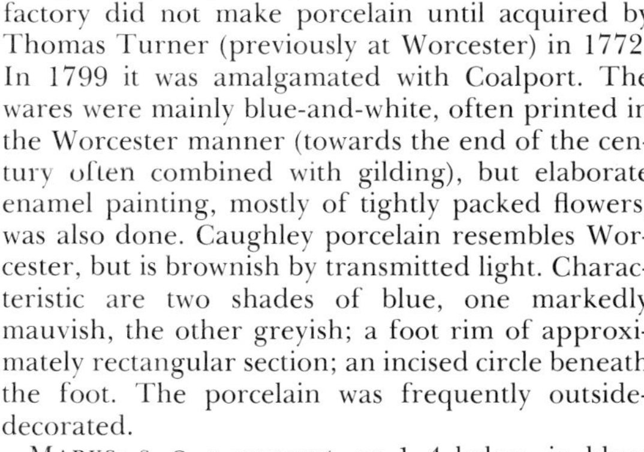

Caughley (soft-paste porcelain). This Shropshire factory did not make porcelain until acquired by Thomas Turner (previously at Worcester) in 1772. In 1799 it was amalgamated with Coalport. The wares were mainly blue-and-white, often printed in the Worcester manner (towards the end of the century often combined with gilding), but elaborate enamel painting, mostly of tightly packed flowers, was also done. Caughley porcelain resembles Worcester, but is brownish by transmitted light. Characteristic are two shades of blue, one markedly mauvish, the other greyish; a foot rim of approximately rectangular section; an incised circle beneath the foot. The porcelain was frequently outside-decorated.

MARKS: S, C, a crescent, or 1–4 below, in blue; SALOPIAN, impressed.

Left Tea pot, pineapple ware, Whieldon-Wedgwood type, *c.* 1750. City Museum and Art Gallery, Hanley, Stoke-on-Trent

'Cauliflower' ware. Green- and yellow-glazed earthenware, often in the form of cauliflowers, pineapples, etc., made by the Whieldon–Wedgwood partnership about 1750–70.

'CD' mark. *See* Coalport.

Celadon. A glaze ranging in colour from olive-green to sea-green. Celadons from Lung Ch'üan form one of the classic wares of the Sung dynasty. The term, celadon, is a corruption of Salah-ed-din (Saladin), Sultan of Egypt who, in 1171 sent forty pieces of this Chinese ware as a gift to Nur-ed-din, Sultan of Damascus. A less credible explanation is that a shepherd in Honoré d'Urfé's seventeenth-century romance, *L'Astrée*, whose name was Céladon, wore a costume of greyish-green colour somewhat resembling that of the glaze of this name. Celadons were especially sought in the Near East in the days of Saladin because they were reputed to break, or change colour, if poisoned food was placed in them, and relatively few specimens found their way to the West until much later. Until the eighteenth century celadon glazes covered stoneware bodies; during the eighteenth century the glaze was also employed on porcelain. The colour was derived from iron, usually by washing the body over with a ferruginous slip before glazing, followed by firing in a reducing atmosphere.

There are literary references to the earliest type of celadon made at Yüeh Chou as far back as the third century, but specimens surviving are hardly older than the Sung dynasty. The glaze is greyish-green in colour over a grey stoneware body, and incised or carved decoration is the invariable rule. Fragments resembling Yüeh ware have been found at Samarra.

The origin of the Northern celadons is still uncertain, but specimens have been found in Honan and Korea, and the incised, combed and moulded decorations suggest affinities with both Ting and *Ying Ch'ing* wares. The body is a grey hard-fired stoneware, with a glaze olive-brown in colour which is usually crazed.

The finest of the Sung dynasty celadons were made at Lung Ch'üan. The body is a hard-fired greyish white stoneware, and the glaze colour is variable, from sea-green to a greyish-green. Where the

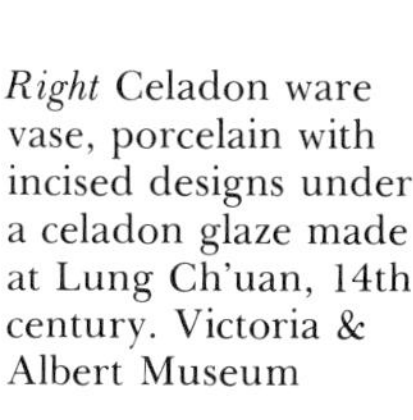

Right Celadon ware vase, porcelain with incised designs under a celadon glaze made at Lung Ch'uan, 14th century. Victoria & Albert Museum

body is unglazed it has burned to a reddish brown, especially on the foot, and this effect was sometimes used as a form of decoration, when dragons in relief on the upper surface were left unglazed to form a contrast with the green glaze. The glaze itself is thick, and hazy with minute bubbles. By far the greater number of surviving wares are dishes, large and heavily potted, which were made in enormous quantities for export. A type of celadon, usually small bottles and vases, has brownish spots on a green glaze. These the Japanese call *tobi seiji* ('buck-wheat' celadon). Also popular in Japan was a type of bluish-green celadon known as *Kinuta*; *Kinuta* means 'mallet', and this is the shape of a famous vase preserved in Japan. Large vases carved with floral and foliate ornament belong to the Yüan dynasty; a dated example is in the Sir Percival David Collection, London.

The kilns of Lung Ch'üan were removed to Chu Chou early in the Ming dynasty, where dishes were produced with floral decoration stylistically similar to the early Ming painted dishes. Probably made at a kiln in the region of Lung Ch'üan is a ware known as Ko, which has a dark body, a greyish glaze, and a well marked crackle. (*See* Kuan.)

Chaffers, William. Editor of the famous works *Marks and Monograms on Pottery and Porcelain*, first published in 1863. He was responsible for the error by which a great quantity of Chinese porcelain was ascribed to the English Lowestoft factory. At this distance of time it seems strange that such a mistake ever should have occurred, and even stranger that some of the greatest ceramic experts of the period should have joined the argument, and produced complicated theories that were no less remote from the truth.

Farmyard clock case with a dog chasing a fox out of a chicken house, Chelsea, marked with a red anchor, *c.* 1755

Chai ware. A ware made at Ching Chou (Honan Province) and known from Chinese literary sources. It was made during the short period of the Five Dynasties. Its colour, wrote an eighteenth-century commentator, was 'blue as heaven after rain seen through a rift in the clouds'. A stoneware pillow in the Sir Percival David Collection bears an incised poem by the emperor Ch'ien Lung calling it Chai ware, but it is virtually indistinguishable from Chün.

Champion, Richard. *See* Bristol.

Chelsea (soft-paste porcelain) (1745–84). The finest and most significant English eighteenth-century porcelain. The earliest wares ('triangle' period: *see* Marks) were of a milk-white glassy porcelain showing 'moons'. They were often left white, and decorated only with moulding, frequently closely imitating silverware. Small flower sprays to conceal blemishes in the paste, and occasionally rather stiff 'botanical' flowers drawn in Meissen style were sometimes added in enamel.

Plate decorated in the Japanese Kakiemon style, with scalloped rim, Chelsea, *c.* 1750–2

In the succeeding 'raised anchor' phase (*see* Marks) the use of painted decoration was greatly extended, the Japanese Kakiemon manner being much copied. Meissen porcelain inspired other decorative styles; these include a more developed flower painting and harbour scenes (to which are related Æsop's *Fables* subjects). A warm brown is characteristic. The extremely rare transfer prints were perhaps done at the Battersea enamel factory. Figures are rare – mainly dwarf-like ('Callot') or Italian Comedy types, characterized by bright-red cheeks. Bird figures were suggested by Meissen. From 1749 at latest Chelsea was managed by Nicholas Sprimont (1716–71), a silversmith from Liège, and the continuity of the Chelsea style is unbroken in the succeeding 'red anchor' period.

In this period the repertory and skill of the Chelsea painters were increased to include figures and landscapes in purple monochrome; 'botanical' flowers copied from illustrated herbals or even from nature; polychrome figural compositions derived through Meissen from the French Masters. Underglaze blue was used, but rarely. Characteristic of the useful wares were three small projecting 'spur marks' within a ground-down foot rim. Tureens and dishes simulating birds, animals, vegetables, etc., were much favoured. Most notable, however, were the very numerous figures. Their subjects may be roughly divided into mythological and 'abstract' (e.g. sciences, seasons); trades, hunting and pastoral life; Italian Comedy characters and 'exotics' (e.g. Turks, Chinese). They are superbly modelled and sparingly coloured, so as to reveal the beautiful porcelain material. A plain mound base is normal. Mainly of this period also were the 'Chelsea toys' – tiny étuis, scent bottles, patchboxes, etc., exquisitely modelled and painted, and showing a rich fancy in the invention of (mostly amorous) conceits.

In 1758 bone ash was introduced in the Chelsea body. The frequently 'crazed' glaze tends to run into greenish glassy pools; the grinding of foot rims persisted. This 'gold anchor' period is marked by ever-increasing sumptuousness. Coloured grounds (royal or 'Mazarin' blue, pea green, turquoise, and claret) were copied from Sèvres, and gilding was lavishly used. Elaborate rococo scrollwork was used on figures and vases, etc. The painters' repertory was enlarged to include elaborate mythological scenes after Boucher or Rubens, or Pillement *chinoiseries*; 'exotic' birds in polychrome enamels on white or in gilding on a ground were inspired by Sèvres; groups of fruit became favourite subjects. The Kakiemon subjects were discarded, but Japanese patterns resembling elaborate textile designs ('brocaded Imari') continued in favour. In figure modelling a broader style and a larger scale were introduced. Elaborate *bocages* were made and the figures were richly and elaborately painted and gilt.

In 1769 the factory and its contents were sold, in 1770 passing into the possession of Wm Duesbury and John Heath, of Derby.

Chelsea marks

1 2 3

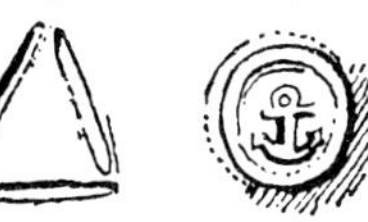

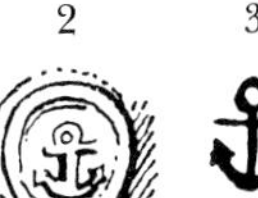

MARKS: 1 left, incised (*c.* 1745–50); 2, in relief (*c.* 1749–53); 3, in red (*c.* 1753–60), in gold (*c.* 1758–69); 'R', impressed, a repairer's mark (*c.* 1760–5).

Ch'êng Hua period (1465–87). The rarest porcelains of this classic reign employ coloured enamels over sparing underglaze blue outlines (*tou ts'ai* enamels); and this style was much imitated from the seventeenth century. The blue-and-white 'palace bowls' were more slightly potted and decorated than previously. The reign mark is much used on later wares.

Chesterfield (Derbyshire). Brown stoneware pottery, second half of eighteenth and nineteenth centuries.

Chia Ching period (1522–66). Ming reign noted for painted blue-and-white of rich violet tone, and the development of brilliantly coloured enamel painting, chiefly in red, green, yellow, and turquoise. Coloured glazes, too, were used, sometimes in combination (e.g. yellow and green), covering incised designs 'on the biscuit'. Heavily potted blue-and-white jars and dishes were much exported to the Near East. The reign mark was used in K'ang Hsi times.

Chia Ch'ing period (1796–1820). In this period the later Ch'ien Lung styles continued, but with poorer glaze and less lively drawing in enamelled wares. Iron-red enamelling was popular, and heavily-potted wares with thick blue or celadon-green glazes may be mentioned.

Ch'ien Lung. During the reign of this emperor, who was on the throne from 1736 to 1796 and who abdicated at the advanced age of eighty-six, was produced much of the porcelain decorated to the order of Europeans. The Emperor Ch'ien Lung was a noted patron of the arts, and encouraged the making of porcelain in his country. He was interested in Western culture, and there is no doubt that he encouraged the making of many pieces of china based on the design of French articles sent as presents to Peking from the King of France, or ordered from Paris by the Jesuits at the command of the Emperor.

Chien ware. This production of Fukien Province during the Sung dynasty consisted principally of small conical tea bowls. A very granular grey-black stoneware, with thick treacly brown or black glazes, often streaked with fine golden lines ('hare's fur'), or spotted and dappled, was arrested above the foot. These effects result from the varied response of iron to kiln conditions. Known to the Japanese as *temmoku* ware. Other brown and black wares from Kiangsi, Honan, or Tzŭ Chou, have a lighter body.

Chill. Earthenware oil lamp shaped like a large candlestick with lipped cup large enough to hold two cups of 'train' (pilchard oil), used in Cornwall before candles. Sometimes rendered Stonen Chill.

China clay. A white-burning natural clay (kaolin) used with china stone (petuntse) to produce true porcelain. It was the *unaker* of the Cherokees, found 'on the back of Virginia' and through the Carolinas, into Georgia. Wedgwood imported 'the Cherokee earth', and in 1777 wrote to his partner saying that 'it is really used in all the Jaspers'.

'China' dogs. Mantelpiece ornaments in the form of spaniels, Welsh sheepdogs, French poodles, greyhounds, etc., made in earthenware, and sold extensively in Wales and the West Country. Made by Sampson Smith, James Dudson, William Kent, and many others in Staffordshire and Scotland; rarely marked.

China 'Imari'. Imitations of the Japanese export porcelain, with strong decoration in greyish underglaze blue and enamel colours, especially iron red, and prominent gilding; made in the first half of the eighteenth century.

China stone. Feldspar, decomposed granite (petuntse). Fuses at great heat, combining with china clay to produce porcelain.

Chinese export porcelain.

Decoration.

1650 The earliest designs on Chinese export porcelain were of a religious character. The blue-and-white pieces, dating from this time, painted with religious scenes and emblems, are the subject of some argument as to whether they were made for use by Christian converts in China and Japan rather than for export to the West.

1700 Still with decoration in blue are cups, saucers, etc., painted with European figures, and inscriptions in French. Coloured figures were made.

1725 At about this time the first pieces painted with English and other coats-of-arms in colours began to be made in quantities. In these early importations the coat-of-arms is usually of a large size with elaborate mantling. (Mantling: the scrollwork, etc., surrounding the actual coat-of-arms.)

Schwarzlot decoration, especially of religious subjects, was also exported.

1750 The coat-of-arms grew smaller and the mantling was simplified.

Right Chinese export porcelain dish, painted in colours with the Royal arms of England and inscription in Dutch, early 18th century. Victoria & Albert Museum

Far right Two blue and white jugs decorated in a *chinoiserie* pattern, Worcester, *c.* 1765 and 1758

1770 The coat-of arms was usually in a simple shield.

1790 The coat-of-arms was in a spade-shaped shield, and the rest of the piece is plainly decorated with the gold star, or some similar bordering. The surface of the china is often of the texture of an orange skin. In contrast, the complicated Mandarin patterns were also being made.

1825 Butterflies and flowers painted on a celadon-green ground were becoming popular, the so-called Canton style.

MARKS: Marks are not generally to be found on Chinese porcelain made for export. Two pieces of blue-and-white in the Victoria and Albert Museum are marked; a bottle bears a capital G and beneath a plate is the word 'BEVERE'. A pattern plate bears the name *Syngchong* on the back. There is a plate, also in the same museum, inscribed *Canton in China 24th Jany. 1791* (*see* Syngchong).

'Chinese Lowestoft'. A misnomer for Chinese export porcelain.

Ch'ing dynasty (1644–1912) reign marks. (*See* opp.)

Ching-tê Chên. The town situated on the south bank of the River Ch'ang, where pottery and porcelain has been made, almost without cessation, for many centuries. In the early years of the eighteenth century the population ran to a million persons, all of whom were employed, it was stated, in the production of porcelain that was fired in some three thousand kilns. Rare Ching-tê Chên porcelain figures are those with *famille verte* or early *famille rose* enamelling. Fine models of birds and animals decorated with coloured glazes were made during the eighteenth century, and especially those in turquoise have been imitated.

Chinoiserie. Fantastic decoration in gold, silver, or colours, depicting an exotic world with Chinese figures, surrounded by flowers, birds, and animals, attending court ceremonies or pursuing such diversions as are centred around the tea table. These decorations were in no way indebted to Oriental sources, but to European engravings and travelogues published in Holland and Germany in the second half of the seventeenth century and later. The Augsburg *Hausmaler* of the early eighteenth century developed a distinct style of *Goldchinesen*, occasionally in silver, whereas Johann Gregor Herold, at Meissen, preferred to work in bright colours from his own etched designs. A later type of *chinoiserie* adopted in the 1730s shows larger figures of Europeans in Chinese guise, taken from French sources, including Pillement, Watteau, and Boucher.

Christening goblet

Christening goblets. Footed four-handled loving cups with whistles attached for calling for replenishment, especially associated with Wiltshire, and used for christening, harvest homes, etc. A favourite inscription is HERE IS THE GEST OF THE BARLY KORNE GLAD HAM I THE CILD IS BORN. Dates from 1603 until 1799 recorded.

Chü-lu Hsien ware. A white ware made during the Sung dynasty at Chü-lu Hsien in Chihli Province, not far from Tzŭ Chou. The principal survivals are jars and vases in a cream-coloured stoneware which sometimes have a stained and crazed glaze as a result of burial.

Chün ware. Ware made at Chün Chou in Honan Province during the Sung and Ming dynasties. The glaze varies in colour from lavender to opalescent blue and it is often suffused or splashed with reddish-purple. The body is a stoneware, brown where unglazed, and the glaze finishes in a roll just above the base. The glaze is thick and full of minute bubbles, and here and there are small marks shaped like a V or a Y which the Chinese call 'earthworm tracks' and regard as a sign of genuineness. They result from the opening of a fissure in the glaze in the early stages of firing which closed in the later stages. Bowls of characteristic form, flower-pots, bulb-bowls, and stands are the most often seen, and Chinese numerals (from 1 to 10) incised into the base of flower-pots refer to the size.

'Soft' Chün has a similar glaze, but the body has received a 'softer' firing. The glaze itself is often

Ch'ing dynasty reign marks

大清順治年製

Shun Chih (1644–61)

大清康熙年製

K'ang Hsi (1662–1722)

大清雍正年製

Yung Chêng (1723–36)

大清乾隆年製

Ch'ien Lung (1736–96)

嘉慶年製

Chia Ch'ing (1796–1820)

大清道光年製

Tao Kuang (1820–51)

大清咸豐年製

Hsien Fêng (1851–61)

大清同治年製

T'ung Chih (1862–74)

大清光緒年製

Kuang Hsü (1874–1909)

denser, more inclined to be opaque, and crackled. The body is buff in colour. Most specimens are of Ming date, and the earliest are doubtfully Sung.

'Fatshan' Chün comes from Kuangtung Province in the south, in the region of Canton. The glaze is thick and dappled with a number of colours which give it a resemblance to Chün. Specimens are hardly likely to be earlier than Ming, and some seem no earlier than the nineteenth century. (*See* Reducing atmosphere.)

'Church Gresley'. A factory was apparently working at Church Gresley, Leicestershire, 1794–1808, but its porcelain remains virtually unidentified.

Clair-de-lune. *See* Blue glazes.

'Claret' ground. *See* Chelsea, Worcester.

Clay. Special plastic earths of varying grades and colours, from coarse red-burning clay fit for bricks or tile making to the blue clays required for stoneware, the fine white kaolin used for porcelains.

Cloisonné ware. Enamelled metal on which the colours of the design are separated by thin metal *cloisons*. A similar technique employing clay *cloisons* was used in the Ming 'three-colour' pottery.

'C' mark. *See* Caughley.

Coalport (soft-paste porcelain). John Rose started a pottery at Jackfield about 1780, and shortly afterwards moved it to Coalport (Shropshire) almost opposite the Caughley factory, acquired in 1799. The Swansea and Nantgarw moulds and stocks were bought up (1819–24), and W. Billingsley's services obtained (1819). The Coalport porcelain, previously indistinguishable from that of Caughley, became white and translucent like the Welsh porcelain. Billingsley's style of flower painting was introduced, but much Coalport porcelain was painted by independent decorators. The 'revived rococo' style at Coalport (*c.* 1830) was characterized by lavishly applied flowers, bright green enamel, light-coloured gilding, and flower decoration with pink-printed outlines washed over in colours. Coalport copied Chelsea porcelain.

MARKS: the name, or script 'CD', in blue.

Cockpit Hill, Derby. Probably made slipwares, early eighteenth century; from *c.* 1751 to 1779 Staffordshire-type pottery, latterly printed creamware.

Codnor Park. *See* Bourne & Co.

Combed slip. A technique in which a marbled or feathered effect is achieved by brushing together, while wet, two or more different-coloured slips.

Compagnie dessin (French: Company pattern). The French name for porcelain made to European order in the Far East, and imported by the *Compagnie des Indes*, the French East India Company.

Contour framing. A method of emphasizing a design by means of a line following the edge, but leaving a white margin.

Cookworthy, William. *See* Plymouth.

Copeland. *See* Spode.

Costrel. Flat, circular bottle with loop handles for suspension from the shoulder, used by field workers.

Cottages. Used as night-light shields, pastille burners, and mantelpiece ornaments. The latter frequently represent the scenes of sensational crimes, such as the Red Barn at Polstead (Maria Marten) or Stanfield Hall (the Rush murders). Porcelain models were made at Rockingham, but probably far more frequently in Staffordshire, mainly second quarter of the nineteenth century.

Cow milk jug. Model of cow with mouth and tail forming spout and handle. Filled from an aperture in the back. Based upon a Dutch model introduced into England about 1755. Made in Staffordshire, South Wales, Yorkshire, and Scotland.

Crackle. French, *craquelure.* The formation of a fine network of cracks over the surface of a glaze is, in European wares, a defect which is caused by a disagreement in the rate of shrinkage between body and glaze during cooling. From the Sung dynasty onwards the Chinese induced an effect of this kind deliberately as a form of decoration, and to a considerable extent they were able to control it. Usually the appearance was enhanced by red or black pigment rubbed into the cracks.

Crackle decoration is to be found on such Sung dynasty wares as Ju, Kuan, and Ko, or on archaizing wares made later, notably during the reign of the emperor, Yung Chêng. The Chinese distinguish between a large, bold, crackle, termed 'crab's claw', and a much closer and smaller network termed 'fish roe' crackle. The former developed first, and was accentuated with black pigment; the latter, developing at a later stage, was coloured red. Crazing of the glaze of some excavated wares, such as those of Chû-lu Hsien, are not, of course, intentional, but the result of burial.

Cradle. Presentation piece for a newly married couple, having the same significance as the *La Fécondité* dish. Slipware specimens recorded from 1673 until 1839. Used as a hold-all or pipe tray.

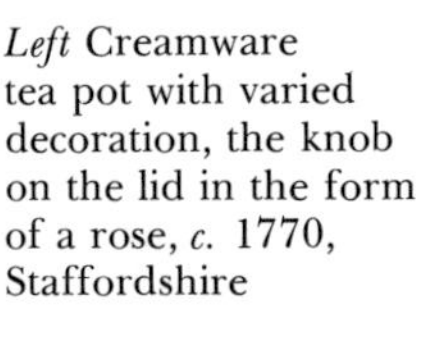

Left Creamware tea pot with varied decoration, the knob on the lid in the form of a rose, *c.* 1770, Staffordshire

Cream-coloured earthenware or **Creamware.** A lead-glazed earthenware with light body made of pale clay and usually containing calcined flint, perfected in Staffordshire about 1740–50. It began to oust other tablewares about 1760. It was made extensively in Staffordshire, Yorkshire, and elsewhere, and enjoyed a world market in the late eighteenth and early nineteenth centuries. It could be decorated with pierced, moulded, enamelled, or printed designs. It was the most mentioned of American imports, their potters constantly claiming to equal the English.

Crescent mark. *See* Bow, Caughley, Worcester.

Crich (Derbyshire). Brown stoneware pottery, second half of eighteenth century and perhaps earlier.

Cross mark. *See* Bristol (hard-paste porcelain), Plymouth, Worcester.

'Crouch' ware. Staffordshire ware said to have been made before the mid-eighteenth century, sometimes wrongly identified with stoneware having white reliefs on a drab ground. Perhaps a variegated stoneware or an earthenware imitating it. 'Crouch' ware is sometimes identified with 'Crich'.

'CT' mark. *See* Bow.

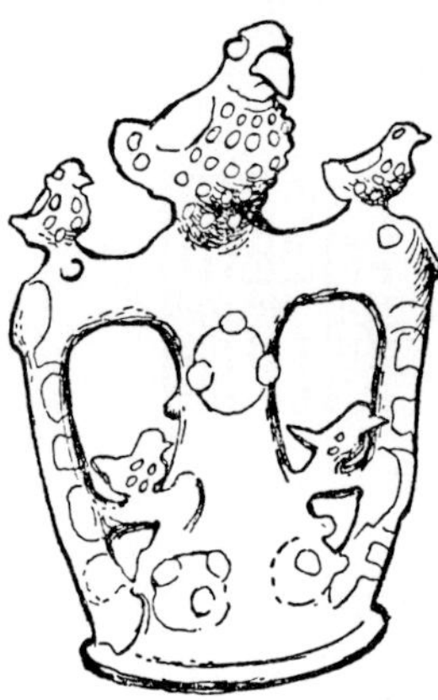

Cuckoo

Cuckoo. Bird call in the form of a large spotted bird perched upon a fence, with four smaller birds. Commonly made in slipware, nineteenth century.

Daggermark. *See* Bow.

Daniel, Ralph. A Staffordshire potter credited with the introduction, before 1750, of plaster-of-Paris moulds, and with being the first English enameller of salt-glazed stoneware.

Davenport. Family of potters at Longport (Staffordshire). From 1793 made cream-coloured and other earthenware, and, from the early nineteenth century, porcelain.

MARKS: an anchor or 'Davenport', sometimes both.

Delftware. Earthenware coated with a glaze made opaque by the addition of tin ashes, named after Delft in Holland, which became an important centre of manufacture in the seventeenth century.

Jar and cover with Chinese decorations in blue monochrome, Delft, late 17th century. Mark LV monogram. Fitzwilliam Museum

Denby (Derbyshire). Brown stoneware pottery, late eighteenth and nineteenth centuries (*see* Bourne & Co.).
Dendritic. Having tree-like markings.
D'Entrecolles, Père François Xavier. A Jesuit missionary who went out to China in the year 1698. At a time when all the nations of Europe were trying actively to discover the secrets of porcelain manufacture he informed his compatriots of the methods of the Chinese potters. Two long letters, detailing with accuracy all that he had seen and heard, were written by him in 1712 and 1722, and published later in Paris. These documents are still the basis of much of our knowledge of porcelain making in China. Père d'Entrecolles died in Peking in 1741.

The letters have been translated into English, and are accessible in *Porcelain: its Nature, Art and Manufacture* by William Burton, London, 1906.
Derby (soft-paste porcelain). Porcelain was made in Derby by 1750, and by 1756 there was a prolific factory, established by W. Duesbury and John Heath.

Sauceboat decorated in underglaze blue with an oriental brocade pattern on the outside and a river scene inside, Derby, *c.* 1765

Many figures were produced, often avowedly copying Meissen. The early figures are characterized by bases having a 'dry edge' (bare of glaze) and a hole underneath formed as if countersunk for a wood screw; light weight, pale colours, and often a blue-toned glaze. About 1760–70 a richer palette (including a characteristic dirty brownish turquoise) was used, with gilding; the figures almost always have three or four dark patches below the base. The early tablewares were characterized by painting of flowers with stems rendered as trembling hairlines, and of birds and moths by a distinctive hand (the 'Moth painter').

In the early period blue-and-white and printed decoration are rare. There was no regular factory mark.

In 1770 the Chelsea factory was acquired. Although some work continued there, the Chelsea style was largely abandoned. The figures of this 'Chelsea–Derby' period are characterized by rather weak modelling, and a lighter palette of pink, pale green, and a *clear* turquoise. Many were made in 'biscuit'. The tablewares were finely potted and fastidiously painted, mainly with neoclassical designs, but fine flower painting was also done. On more elaborate pieces coloured (opaque bright blue and brownish claret are characteristic) and striped grounds were combined with miniature-like painting of landscapes and classical subjects. The porcelain of this period is commonly marked (*see* below).

Duesbury died in 1786 and was succeeded in turn by his son (d. 1796 or 1797) and Michael Kean (until 1811). This (1786–1811) is the 'Crown Derby' period proper. The figures continued the old models, and 'biscuit' was extensively used. The useful wares are characterized by the use of figure and landscape subjects on diapered or pale-coloured grounds. Naturalistic flower painting was introduced (*see* Billingsley).

In 1811 the factory was bought by Robert Bloor (went insane, 1826), and the period 1811–48 is known by his name. The figures (mainly old models) have opaque paint-like enamels and profuse brassy gilding. On useful wares the elaborate 'revived rococo' and Japanese 'brocaded Imari' styles largely supersede the neoclassical.

MARKS: script 'Derby', incised (*c.* 1750); (at left) 1, in gold or red ('Chelsea–Derby' period); 2, in gold (*c.* 1770–80); 3, in enamel or gold (*c.* 1784); 4, incised on figures, and 5, in enamel or gold (*c.* 1784–1810); 6, in purple (1795–6); 7, usually in red, and 8, printed in red (Bloor period).

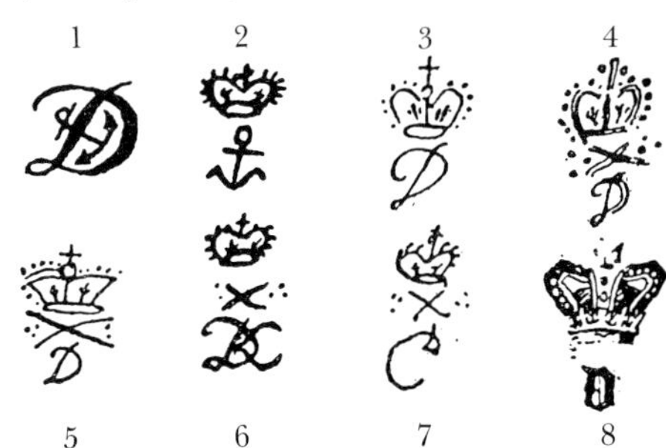

Derbyshire. Slipware was made at Bolsover until about 1750; brown stoneware at Brampton and Chesterfield from the second half of the eighteenth century; at Crich somewhat earlier, and by Bourne & Co. at Belper (from *c.* 1800), Denby (from 1812), and Codnor Park (from 1833). (*See* Tickenhall, Cockpit Hill.)
Devonshire. Rustic lead-glazed earthenware was made (mainly at Barnstaple, Bideford and Fremington) from the seventeenth century onwards. The characteristic ware was of red clay with designs incised through a white slip, under a yellow-green glaze.
'DK' mark. *See* Derby.
'D' mark. *See* Bow, Derby.
'Doctor Syntax.' Fine underglaze blue transfer prints representing the adventures of Doctor Syntax, used as tableware decorations by James and Ralph Clews, Cobridge, *c.* 1821. Pottery figures were also popular. *The Tours of Dr Syntax in Search of the Picturesque* by Dr Clombe, with illustrations by Thomas Rowlandson, published 1815–21, were a satire upon the writings of the Rev. William Gilpin.
Don Pottery (Swinton, Yorkshire). Made creamware and other Leeds-type pottery, early nineteenth century.
Dots mark. *See* Bow.
Doulton (Lambeth). Stoneware pottery, founded 1818, making mainly industrial brown ware.
Dragon. By far the commonest motif of decoration on Chinese porcelain, the dragon with five claws is a symbol of the Emperor, with four claws it represents princes of the blood, and with three claws it was intended for high officials. The dragon represents Spring, and it is the Spirit of the Waters which brings rain to the young crops. It is a mild and beneficent creature (apart from some Buddhist dragons called Nagas), and the Blue Dragon is a Taoist temple guardian. Dragons are often found in pairs in pursuit of something called a 'flaming pearl' which is

Blue-and-white temple vase with dragon motif and dated inscription, 1351, Yüan dynasty. Percival David Collection

probably intended to represent the sun. The Dragon is one of the Four Supernatural Creatures, the others being the Phoenix, the Kylin, and the Tortoise. It also represents the East from the Four Quadrants. The Dragon does not have the same connotation in Japan, where it was adopted as a motif of decoration from China. The Japanese dragon has three claws, unless it is part of a decoration copied from Chinese sources.

Duesbury, William (1725–86). Independent decorator in London 1751–3; controlled porcelain factories at, successively, Derby (1756–86), Chelsea (1770–84), and perhaps Longton Hall (1760) and Bow (1763 onward). His son, also William (1763–96 or 97) owned the Derby factory 1786 until his death.

Dwight, John (*c.* 1637–1703). Potter, of Fulham, from about 1671.

Easter eggs. 'Nest' eggs decorated, inscribed with the name of the recipient, and given as Easter and birthday gifts.

East India Company. The Honourable East India Company was incorporated in 1600, and had a monopoly of trade between England and the East. Factories (warehouses) were established for trading with China during the second half of the seventeenth century at Tongking, Amoy, Tainan (on Formosa), and at Gombron in the Persian Gulf. None lasted for more than a few years. In 1715 Canton became the principal port, and the Chinese side of all business came under the regulation of the *Co-hong*, a closed corporation of the local merchants. The Company formed a Council of Supercargoes to deal with them.

In addition to the ships belonging to the East India Company, licences were granted to the vessels of other traders, and there were in addition numerous unlicensed and unprincipled interlopers. Before long the vessels of the licensees and the unlicensed outnumbered those of the Company and, in turn, the total number of British vessels outnumbered those of all the other trading companies of the European nations. The factories of the various trading nations fronted the Pearl river, and contemporary views of them are found on porcelain and in paintings on canvas and glass. The East India Company was dissolved in 1858.

East India Company china and 'Compagnie des Indes' china. The wares imported by these trading companies. The former continued till 1854.

'Eggshell' porcelain. *See* Famille rose. Thin-bodied white bowls of Yung Lo (1403–24), with faint incised or slip-painted designs, were copied in the K'ang Hsi period. Some modern Japanese porcelains are eggshell thin.

Egyptian black. Hard stoneware body heavily stained with manganese.

Ehret, G. D. Born at Heidelberg in 1708, became one of the most celebrated botanical artists of the eighteenth century. His work inspired some of the botanical designs on Chelsea porcelain. He died in 1770.

Eight Buddhist Emblems, The. The *Pa chi-hsiang* which are frequently used as painted decoration on porcelain. They are LUN, a flaming wheel (the wheel of the Law); LO, a conchshell, a wind instrument used in religious ceremonies; SAN, a state umbrella; KAI, a canopy; HUA, a lotus, emblem of purity; a vase; YU, a pair of fishes, a symbol of connubial felicity; CHANG, an endless knot.

Eight Horses of Mu Wang, The. Mu Wang was an Emperor of the Chou dynasty who travelled around his kingdom in a chariot drawn by eight horses. He visited the Goddess, Hsi Wang Mu, in her western garden, where grew the tree which bore the Peach of Immortality. The eight horses occur in painted decoration, especially relaxing from their day's labours.

Eight Immortals, The. In Chinese, the *Pa-hsien*. The Eight Immortals are Taoist legendary figures who accompany Lao Tzŭ (Shou Lao). Lao Tzŭ himself is easily recognizable from a large and protuberant forehead. The Immortals include CHUNG-LI CHUAN, a fat man with a feather fan and the peach of longevity; LÜ TUNG-PIN, carrying a sword and a fly-whisk; LI T'IEH KUAI, a lame beggar with a stick or crutch who carries a gourd; TS'AO KUO-CH'IU, carrying his tablets of admission to the Sung Court; LAN TS'AI-HO, with the flower basket and spade of the gardener; CHANG KAO, sometimes seated on a mule facing the tail, carrying a peach, a feather fan, or a bamboo tube drum; HAN HSIANG TZŬ, carrying a flute, and HO HSIEN KU who is an immortal maiden with a peach or a lotus.

These personages appear quite commonly in painted form, or as ceramic figures, with Lao Tzŭ in addition. They also occur on some eighteenth-century European porcelain in painted form and as figures; for instance, the early white Bristol figure of Li T'ieh Kuai.

Eight Precious Things, The. The *Pa pao*, frequently the subject of painted decoration. They comprise a pair of rhinoceros horn cups, a musical stone of jade, the artemisia leaf, a jewel, a coin, a painting, a pair of tablets, and a symbol of victory. The *Pa pao* are closely related to the Hundred Antiques (*q.v.*).

Eight Trigrams, The. The *Pa Kua*, or Eight Trigrams, are a series of eight sets of three lines, broken and unbroken, which represent natural forces – heaven, wind, earth, water, fire, thunder, vapour, and mountains. They occur fairly frequently as decoration, moulded or painted, on Ch'ing porcelain especially. Commonly they occur on a vase-form which is a cylinder squared on the exterior, derived from an ancient jade astronomical instrument and known as a *tsung*. The Eight Trigrams are also employed in the *Book of Changes* of the Warring States period for purposes of divination and for forecasting the future.

Elers, John Philip and **David.** Stoneware potters, originally silversmiths, of German extraction, settled in England before 1686. Worked in Fulham about 1690–3, at Bradwell Wood about 1693–8.

Enamel. Enamel painting on porcelain, a decoration in vitreous colours which fuse upon the glazed surface in the muffle kiln at a low temperature. On soft-paste porcelain the enamel sinks deeply into the fusible lead glaze. On hard-paste porcelain it is not absorbed.

Encaustic painting. Josiah Wedgwood was granted a patent in 1769 for: 'The purpose of ornamenting earthen and porcelaine ware with an encaustic gold bronze, together with a peculiar species of encaustic painting in various colours in imitation of the antient Etruscan and Roman earthenware.' He prepared a number of substances by which were produced the following colours: red, orange, white, green, blue, yellow, and both a matt and a 'shineing' black. The principal use for these colours was in the decoration of the basaltes body, which was modelled and painted in imitation of ancient Greek ware.

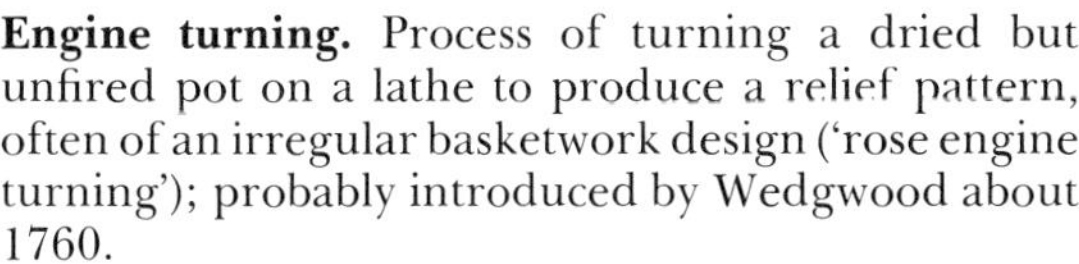

Tripod incense-burner of red earthenware with lustre glaze, Etruria Wedgwood factory, dated 1805. Victoria & Albert Museum

Right Tureen and cover decorated in enamel colours and gilt in *famille rose*, 18th century. Metropolitan Museum of Art

Engine turning. Process of turning a dried but unfired pot on a lathe to produce a relief pattern, often of an irregular basketwork design ('rose engine turning'); probably introduced by Wedgwood about 1760.

Etruria and 'Etruscan' vases. *See* Wedgwood.

Faïence (also **fayence**). The term, derived from the Italian town of Faenza, was adopted in France at the beginning of the seventeenth century to describe tin-glazed earthenware. It has since been loosely applied to all kinds of white pottery.

Famille noire. K'ang Hsi wares enamelled in *famille verte* style, generally 'on the biscuit', with dry black ground colour, made lustrous by a covering of green glaze. The large vases with superb floral designs have fetched great sums, encouraging forgeries and skilful redecoration of old pieces. Cups and bowls are less rare. A few marked examples are of the Yung Chêng period.

Famille rose. Porcelain painted in a palette which includes an opaque *rose* enamel derived from colloidal gold. The colour is the same as the European purple of Cassius, invented by Andreas Cassius of Leyden about 1675 and taken to China by Jesuit missionaries before 1700. It was first used at Peking for painting on enamel on copper, and appears to have reached Ching-tê Chên about 1700. Most painting using this colour, however, was executed in the Canton studios. The finest examples of *famille rose* porcelain painting belong to the reign of Yung Chêng, and to this reign belong plates painted in meticulous detail on the front with, on the back, an unbroken ground of *rose* enamel, except for the space within the footring – the so called 'ruby-back' plates. As the century progressed the colour was increasingly employed for export wares, and quality deteriorated. Towards the end of the century it formed part of a palette known as *rose-verte* used, for the most part, to decorate run-of-the-mill export wares such as the 'Mandarin' types.

Famille verte. This, and the other *familles*, are the result of an arbitrary classification based on the predominant colour in the palette employed which was made by Albert Jacquemart in the middle of the nineteenth century.

All of them belong to the Ch'ing dynasty and the best work in all categories was done between 1662 and about 1760. The *famille verte* is a development of the *Wan Li wu ts'ai*, or Wan Li five-colour decoration, dating from the end of the sixteenth century. The *verte* is a brilliant transparent green enamel. The earliest examples also have passages of underglaze blue later to be replaced by an enamel blue. Surrounding the enamel blue on many pieces is a slight 'halo', to be seen when light falls on the glaze at an angle. This does not occur on *every* genuine specimen, but it has not yet been seen on a spurious piece. A forger who was also a first-class ceramic chemist might conceivably be able to reproduce the effect, since the probable cause is known, but it is very unlikely.

'Fazackerley' colours and patterns. *See* Liverpool (delftware).

'FBB' mark. *See* Worcester.

Feeding bottle. Flattish oviform article with a small circular aperture at the top and a small nozzle.

'Feldspathic glazes'. Those containing feldspar rock, an essential ingredient of porcelain glazes; but used also on stonewares (*see* main article).

'Female archer'. Subject of 'Pratt'-type jugs and earthenware figures intended as satire upon the smart archery parties popular in 'high' society, 1800–50. Sometimes known as the 'fair toscopholite' or 'toxophilite'.

Ferronnerie. A style of ornament resembling wrought-iron work.

Ferruginous. Containing iron oxide and, therefore, reddish brown in appearance.

Ferrybridge (near Pontefract, Yorkshire). Pottery making Wedgwood-style stoneware and creamware, late eighteenth and early nineteenth centuries. From 1796 to 1806 the firm had Ralph Wedgwood as partner, and used the mark 'Wedgwood & Co', impressed.

Fitzhugh. A Chinese pattern very popular in America was the profuse floral arrangement known as Fitzhugh (said to be a Yankee version of Foochow). The wide, distinctive border is composed of pomegranates, butterflies, and latticework, and the centre is filled with four large medallions of flowers and emblems. The border alone sometimes frames enamelled motifs, as on George Washington's Cincinnati service. Enamelled decoration is also combined with the complete design, usually in the form of a monogram, occasionally of an eagle, placed in the centre. Though most often in underglaze blue, Fitzhugh occurs also with overglaze colour – green, brown, or orange.

Flambé glazes. Glazes in which kiln conditions produce variegated colour effects, e.g. on some Chün wares of the Sung dynasty, the eighteenth-century copper-red wares, and Canton stonewares.

Flasks. In form of fish, mermaid, constable's baton, horse pistol, boot, potato, cucumber, barrel, or a figure of some royal or political celebrity, commonly made in brown stoneware or 'Rockingham'-glazed earthenware, early nineteenth century. Chief centres: Denby, Chesterfield, Brampton, Lambeth. (*See* Reform Flasks.)

Flaxman, John, R.A. A well-known sculptor who was employed by Josiah Wedgwood from 1775 to 1787. Much of his work has been identified; it includes a number of plaques in relief, some portraits, and a set of chessmen. His father, also named John, supplied plaster casts of antique busts to Wedgwood, and some confusion has resulted in the classification of the work of father and son.

Flight & Barr; Flight, Barr & Barr. *See* Worcester.

Flint enamel. *Fenton's Enamel*, an improvement on the brown Rockingham glaze, patented 1849 by Lyman, Fenton & Co. of Bennington, Vermont, but soon copied by East Liverpool and other factories. Metallic powders dusted on the glaze produced streaks and flecks of colour. *See* Rockingham.

'Florentine-green' dishes. Mid-fifteenth-century majolica dishes painted in green, orange, and purple, at Florence.

Flowers. Porcelain, usually mounted on ormolu branches, were made at Chelsea and Derby as embellishments for porcelain figures, etc.

Flower symbolism. Flowers (and plants and trees generally) are used very widely in the decoration of porcelain in the Far East, and an elaborate symbolism is attached to most of them. The seasons are represented by the prunus (Winter), the tree peony (Spring), the lotus (Summer), and the chrysanthemum (Autumn). A favourite subject since the days of K'ang Hsi has been prunus blossom in white against a pulsating blue ground irregularly divided up by lines to suggest the cracked ice of the thaw.

A flower is associated with each of the months – January, the prunus or plum; February, the peach; March, the tree peony; April, the cherry; May, the magnolia; June, the pomegranate; July, the lotus; August, the quince; September, the mallow; October, the Chrysanthemum; November, the gardenia; December, the poppy. The bamboo (*q.v.*) is a longevity symbol, and is very commonly represented. The lotus is associated with Buddha and Kuan-yin. The peony represents sexual love; the peach, immortality; the 'Buddha's hand' citron (*citrus medica*), wealth; and the omegranate, cut to reveal the seeds, a numerous ogeny.

The *ling chih* fungus (the *fomes japonicus*) grows on trunks and is an emblem of immortality. It grew e Taoist Isles of the Blest, and the deer (a longevmbol) often carries one in its mouth. Kung-fu Confucius), Lao Tzŭ, and Buddha, the Three Friends, are represented by the prunus, pine, and bamboo respectively.

'F' (and F reversed) **mark.** *See* Bow, Worcester.

'Fretted-square' mark. *See* Worcester.

Fuddling cups. Cups of three, five, or more conjoined compartments communicating internally, made at Donyatt and Crock Street, Somerset, seventeenth and eighteenth centuries.

Fuddling cups

Fukien. *See* Tê Hua porcelain.

Fulham. *See* Dwight, Elers. In the eighteenth century massive mugs of brown-and-grey salt-glazed stoneware were made, with applied reliefs of hunting scenes, topers, etc.

Garniture de Cheminé. Set of five vases, two trumpet-shaped beakers, and three covered vases, usually of baluster shape, a combination originating in China, whence adopted by most European faïence and porcelain factories.

Gaudy Dutch. The popular name for a gaily decorated Staffordshire pottery produced *c.* 1810–30 for the American trade.

Gaudy Welsh. Also gaudy ironstone. Later wares (*c.* 1830–45 and 1850–65) made in England for the American trade.

'German flowers' (deutsche Blumen). Contemporary name for naturalistically painted flowers, introduced as porcelain decoration at Meissen about 1740. *Ombrierte Teutsche Blumen*, flowers with shadows, are a variation. Later the treatment became freer, and smaller flowers, arranged in sprays or bouquets, were scattered over the whole surface until, under classical influence, they were confined between conventional rims and borders.

Giles, James. Owned a decorating establishment in London about 1760–80, where much Bow and Worcester porcelain was painted.

'Girl in a swing' family of early porcelain figures (mostly white) having Chelsea affinities; by some conjecturally ascribed to dissident workmen from Chelsea, *c.* 1750.

Coffee pot and cover with decoration of finches, Meissen, *c.* 1760

Glaze. A shiny coating, rendering porcelain impervious to liquids while lending brilliance to its surface. In China body and glaze were fired together. At Meissen the body was fired first at a low temperature (*Verglühbrand*), then dipped in a liquid glaze mixture and subjected to firing at a higher temperature. Glazes can be translucent, opaque, or coloured. The chemical composition is dependent upon that of the body beneath, lead and salt glazes being applied to pottery and soft-paste porcelain, feldspathic glazes to hard-paste porcelain.
'G' mark. *See* Bow.
Gold star. A pattern commonly used as a border for tea and dinner services, etc., towards the end of the eighteenth century, and in the early years of the century following. It is in the form of a band of dark-blue overglaze enamel, with small gold stars set on it at intervals. It was, and is, very popular in America.
Gombron. In the early part of the seventeenth century the English East India Company established a factory at the port of Gombron, in the Persian Gulf. As a result of this, native Persian ware and Chinese porcelain imported into England from this source were referred to indiscriminately as 'Gombron ware'. As late as the 1770s Horace Walpole wrote of 'two basins of most ancient Gombron china', which may have been either Persian or Chinese. The modern name of the port is Bandar Abbas.
Gotch. East Anglian word for a large stoneware jug.
'Granite' ware. A creamware with minutely speckled glaze resembling granite, late eighteenth and nineteenth centuries.
Greatbach, William. Potter, of Lane Delph, Staffordshire. Some creamwares with black transfer prints washed over in colours bear his name, probably as maker (some dated 1778).
Green glazes. Apart from the celadon wares, *see* Medium- and low-temperature glazes.
Gretna Green. Popular black print showing a runaway couple being married by the Gretna blacksmith, accompanied by the verse, 'Oh! Mr Blacksmith, ease our pains: hand tie us fast in Wedlock's Chains'. Known alternatively as 'The Red Hot Marriage'.
'Greybeards'. *See* Bellarmines.
Grey hen. Stoneware liquor bottle.
'Greyhound' jugs. Jugs with greyhound handles and relief decorations of sporting subjects.
Griffin mark. *See* Rockingham.
Ground colours. Areas of coloured glaze as a background to painted or gilt decoration, often in reserved panels; chiefly yellow, deep blue, claret, green, and turquoise.
Hackwood, William (d. 1839). Wedgwood's principal modeller from 1769 to 1832. Hackwood spent much of his time in adapting the antique, but is known also to have done some original work. Occasionally he signed his work with his name in full, or with initials.
Hancock, Robert (1730–1817). Engraver. Hancock probably learned transfer printing at the Battersea enamel factory (1753–6), subsequently practising it at Bow (1756), Worcester (1757 at latest, until 1774), and Caughley (1775).
Han dynasty (206 B.C.–A.D. 200). *See* Chinese pottery.
Hard paste. Hard paste (or true) porcelain is compounded of 'china clay' (kaolin) and powdered feldspathic rock ('china stone' or petuntse). It is glazed with petuntse. Under intense heat (about 1450° C) the petuntse fuses into a kind of natural glass. The clay, which will only fuse at 1600° C, holds the object in shape during firing. True porcelain cannot be cut by an ordinary steel file.
Hausmaler. Independent faïence and porcelain painters of Germany, working on white porcelain from Meissen, Vienna or on Chinese export ware, in competition with legitimate factory decorators. Hence the reluctance of the Meissen factory to sell white porcelain, and the introduction of the KPM mark as protection against outside painters. At Augsburg Johann Aufenwerth, his daughter Sabina, members of the Seuter family and others painted *chinoiseries* in gold and silver, framed by conventional lacework borders, which occasionally include contemporary scenes. In Silesia and Bohemia *Schwarzlot* and coloured monochrome decoration are more characteristic, originally derived from Dutch glass workers. Jacobus Helchis and Ignaz Bottengruber excelled in these techniques on Vienna porcelain. At Dresden Christoph Conrad Hunger combined the gold relief technique of St Cloud with that of Saxon glass decorators. There also seems to be proof that Meissen factory workers occasionally undertook outside work. During the second quarter of the century Johann Friedrich Metzsch and R. Chr. von Drechsel, of Bayreuth, painted figures in landscapes with palace architecture or harbour views, enclosed in ornamental borders with shell motives, sometimes painted in purple monochrome.
Hearty good fellow. Toby jug in form of a swaggering standing figure clasping a jug.
Hens and chickens. Emblems of Providence, hence frequent use as adornments of money boxes.
Hen dish. Oval, basket-shaped egg dish with cover in the form of a sitting hen.

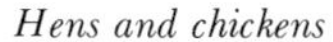
Hens and chickens

Herculaneum. *See* Liverpool (creamware).
Historical blue. Also 'Old blue'. Staffordshire pottery transfer printed with scenes of actual places, notable persons, historic events. These deep-blue prints of the 1820s were followed by light colours about 1830 and into the 1840s.
Ho-ho bird, or *fêng-huang*. The phoenix.
Hollins, Samuel. Potter of Shelton, Staffordshire, late eighteenth century. Made chiefly Wedgwood-type stonewares.
MARK: S. HOLLINS (impressed).
He was succeeded by his sons.
MARK: T. & J. HOLLINS (impressed).
Honan wares. Black- and brown-glazed wares of the Sung dynasty, probably made in Honan Province.
Horn mark. Imitated from Chantilly, at Worcester and Caughley.

Hsüan-tê period (1426–35). Classic reign for blue-and-white porcelains of very fine, richly glazed materials. A certain rhythmic vitality is found alike in the contours of vessels and in their painted lotus scrolls, flying dragons, etc. Blackish spots sometimes mottle the cobalt pigment. Underglaze copper-red painting, white wares with faint incised or slip designs (*an hua*), blue or red monochromes, and the use of yellow enamel grounds, are found. Later times (especially the eighteenth century) 'borrowed' the reign mark, and also made admirable copies of the wares.

Hull (Yorkshire). Pottery founded 1802, making Staffordshire-type earthenware.

MARK (from 1825): 'Bellevue Pottery Hull' and bells.

Hundred Antiques, The. The *Po ku*, frequently employed as painted decoration, are a collection of instruments and implements used in the arts and sciences, such as water pots, brushes, tablets, musical instruments, etc. 'Hundred' in this context means 'many'.

'Image toys'. Contemporary designation of mid-eighteenth-century Staffordshire figures.

Imari. A port in Japan which gave its name to a porcelain made at Arita and decorated in a distinctive style in underglaze blue, iron red, and gold. Similar patterns in these colours on Chinese porcelain are known also as Chinese Imari.

'I' mark. *See* Bow. Wrongly attributed to Isleworth.

Impasto. A method by which the colour is applied thickly so that it stands out in relief.

Imperial Russian service. Known also as the 'Frog' service. Josiah Wedgwood received the order to make this enormous service of cream-coloured earthenware in March 1773. It was for the Empress Catherine of Russia, and was to be placed in her palace near St Petersburg (Leningrad), known as *La Grenouillière*. The device of a green frog was painted in a shield in the border of each piece. The service numbered more than nine hundred pieces, each of which bore at least one painting of an English view, the obtaining of which caused a great deal of difficulty. The cost of the actual ware came to £51 8*s* 4*d*, but the decoration and other charges raised the final total to nearly £2,500. The Empress is believed to have paid £3,000 for it, and Wedgwood wrote: '. . . there will not be near the proffit upon this service that we have upon our commonest painted goods'.

The painting of the service was done at Chelsea, where Wedgwood had an enamelling establishment under the supervision of Thomas Bentley. It was commenced in April 1773, and when the newly acquired showrooms at Portland House, Greek Street, were ready for opening in June of the year following it was found that a sufficient number of pieces of the service had been completed for an exhibition to be made of it. The service was shown there with success, and was seen by many famous people, including Queen Charlotte. It is at present in the Winter Palace at Leningrad.

Independent decorators. Porcelain in the eighteenth and early nineteenth centuries was often obtained in the white and decorated by enamellers working outside the factory. Notable were W. Duesbury; J. Giles; Baxter (father of Thomas Baxter), who decorated Caughley and Coalport porcelain in a workshop near Fleet Street (early nineteenth century); T. M. Randall and R. Robins, of Spa Fields, decorated Coalport, Swansea, and Nantgarw for the London dealers (*c.* 1815–25).

Salt-glazed stoneware was also enamelled outside the factory (e.g. by W. Duesbury), as was creamware (e.g. by Robinson and Rhodes at Leeds about 1760–70 and by Absolon at Yarmouth). (*See also* Pardoe.)

Dish decorated in the *istoriato* style, Siena, *c.* 1730. City Museum and Art Gallery, Hanley, Stoke-on-Trent

India ware. The term in general use in England during the eighteenth century for imported Chinese porcelain. It gained currency owing to the fact that the East India Company held a monopoly of trade with the East. It sold the goods it imported by auction at India House, London. This building in the City was demolished in 1861.

Inlaid decoration. Process used by medieval potters for decorating paving tiles (Cleeve Abbey, Westminster Abbey) and by Sussex potters, *c.* 1790–1850, for useful and ornamental wares. The decoration was formed by impressing the body with punches or with printers' types, and filling in with clay of a contrasting colour, usually white on red.

Iron-red. Chinese – *fan hung*. One of the principal Chinese enamel colours which first appears towards the end of the Sung dynasty. During the reign of Chia Ching (1522–66) it replaced underglaze copper red, and it was also employed as a ground colour. An iron red ground decorated with lotuses in gold was much prized by the Japanese and referred to by them as *Kinrandé*. Iron-red when used as part of painted decoration during the Ming period causes a 'halo' to develop on the surface of the glaze immediately surrounding it. Whilst it is not invariably present on genuine examples, it never occurs on later copies.

'Ironstone china'. Variety of 'stone china' (*q.v.*) (*see* Mason). Produced experimentally 1740–3 by Andrew Duché at Savannah. Wares of heavy grade similar to the Mason ironstone were a staple of American makers from 1860 to 1900 under such names as white granite, opaque porcelain, flint china, with so-called hotel china and semi-porcelain appearing about 1885.

Isleworth (Middlesex). Pottery run by Joseph Shore and R. and W. Goulding, making Staffordshire-type pottery, late eighteenth century. Relief-decorated tea pots, etc., marked 'S. & G.' and some Worcester blue-and-white porcelain have been wrongly attributed to Isleworth.

'Istoriato' painting (Italian 'storied'). It is especially associated with Urbino, though not invented there. Essentially pictorial, it frequently covers a whole plate or dish, leaving no border.

Italian Comedy figures. Characters from the Italian Comedy were popular as porcelain models, mid-eighteenth century, chiefly Pantaloon, Isabella, Cynthio, Pierrot, Harlequin, Columbine, Captain, Doctor, Advocate.

Jackfield (Shropshire). Old-established pottery, making (*c.* 1750–75) black-glazed earthenware, usually decorated with unfired painting and gilding.

'Japan' patterns. Term indiscriminately used of both Chinese and Japanese designs in the eighteenth century. Chinese *famille verte* and *famille rose* patterns were copied, as well as the Arita wares known as Imari (often with sumptuous floral and 'brocaded' designs in underglaze blue, enamels, and gilding) and Kakiemon (enamelled in red, green, blue, turquoise, and yellow).

Jasper dip and Jasperware. A fine-grained unglazed stoneware perfected by Wedgwood in 1775.

Normally white, it could be stained with different metallic colours (chiefly blue, lilac, sage green, and black). From about 1780 this colouring could be superficial only ('jasper dip'). Wedgwood's jasperware was much copied elsewhere.

'Jesuit' china. Porcelains of the first half of the eighteenth century painted with Christian subjects supplied by Jesuit missionaries, principally in black monochrome or *famille rose* enamels. The Jesuits brought to bear the first Western influence on the Chinese potters and painters. They first came to reside in the country towards the end of the sixteenth century.

Johanneum. The Dresden building containing the porcelain collection started by Augustus the Strong. Inventory marks, begun 1721, engraved on the wheel and coloured black, show numbers and letters to classify the type of porcelain, including Chinese and Japanese export ware.

Joney or **joney grig.** A dialect term for a chimney ornament in the form of a dog. A well-known Burslem pottery in the nineteenth century was known as a 'doll and jona' (figure and dog) works.

Ju-i. A sceptre with cloud-scroll head, emblem of fulfilled wishes.

Ju ware. One of the six classic wares of the Sung dynasty which was made in the Imperial kilns at Ju Chou (Honan Province). For many years Ju ware was known only from often conflicting literary references, some of which were obviously inaccurate. A ritual disc acquired by Sir Percival David refers to the opening of the kiln in 1107, and it is known that it closed in 1127. Specimens are exceedingly rare.

Kakiemon III. Japanese potter of Arita, credited with the first application of enamelling to Japanese porcelain (*c.* 1660). A class of Japanese ware with subtle asymmetrical decoration, named after him, and much copied in Europe during the eighteenth century, particularly at Meissen, Chantilly, and Chelsea.

Kaolin. *See* China clay.

'Keep within compass'. A popular 'morality' used as decoration for earthenware by John Aynsley (1752–1829), showing the rewards of virtue and the punishments of sin.

Kiln. Used to fire body and glaze of hard-paste porcelain at about 1,200–1,400° C. (*grand feu*).

'Kinuta' celadon. *See* Celadon.

Ko ware. *See* Kuan ware.

Kuan ware. One of the classic glazes of the Sung dynasty. The name means 'Imperial' ware, and it was made for Court use, at first at K'ai-fêng in Honan Province and, after 1127, at Hang Chou. It has a greenish-grey glaze with a well-marked crackle which is virtually opaque, and it resembles, to some extent, a type of ware known as Ko, which has a greyish-white glaze, also with a well-marked crackle accentuated by red and black pigment. By tradition Ko ware was made by the elder of two brothers named Chang, *Ko* meaning 'elder brother', but the brothers Chang may well be legendary. Despite the resemblance there is no relationship otherwise between Kuan and Ko, the latter being made at Lung Ch'uan. (*See* Crackle.)

Kuan-yin. A Buddhist Goddess, originally the Indian Avalokiteshvara who changed sex when translated to China. The change seems to date from the Sung dynasty. As the Goddess or Mercy, Kuan-yin was widely popular throughout China and the subject of innumerable figures in the white porcelain of Tê Hua. She is sometimes depicted carrying a child, and in this form has been confused with a Chinese version of the Virgin Mary.

Ku Yüeh Hsüan. The name means 'Ancient Moon Pavilion' and is derived from an inscription which occurs on some examples. It is applied to small pieces made towards the middle of the eighteenth century and decorated with enamel colours in a similar technique to that employed by contemporary European factories. The technique was first employed for glass painting.

Kylin. More correctly, *ch'i-lin.* A term often erroneously applied to the Dog (or lion) of Fo (Buddha). The *ch'i-lin* has the head of a dragon, a scaly body, deer's hooves, a bushy tail, and a single horn. Its appearance always portended some auspicious event. Despite its appearance it was too gentle even to tread on living grass. The *ch'i-lin* occurs comparatively rarely in either painted or modelled form.

Lambeth (delftware). 'Lambeth' is often used to denote the London delftware potteries generally, namely: Aldgate (1571–*c.* 1780), Southwark (Pickleherring Quay, *c.* 1620–1770, and St Saviour's, *c.* 1630–*c.* 1760), Vauxhall (perhaps late seventeenth century–*c.* 1800), and Lambeth (Howard House, Church Street, *c.* 1665–1770, and Fore Street, first half of eighteenth century–late eighteenth century).

Characteristic of Lambeth are (seventeenth-century) porringers with oval handles having a central oval hole or heart-shaped perforations; posset pots with curved profile; plates (*c.* 1690 onwards) having a sloping rim, and almost vertical sides curving into a flat base; (eighteenth-century) flat-based flower 'bricks' perforated with round holes; puzzle jugs with narrow in-curved necks, often with V-shaped perforations; wall pockets somewhat resembling a rain-water drainhead; trinket trays of one central star-shaped and five outer lobed compartments. The Lambeth *bianco-sopra-bianco* design usually includes flattened spirals.

Lambrequins. Originally applied to drapery, but later extended to all forms of pendant, lace-like (vandyked) decoration.

Lead. Was employed for lead glazing either as a dry powder (galena, native lead sulphide) or a liquid (litharge, lead oxide). 'Baron' Stiegel the glass maker was buying 'Litterage' for lead glass in 1772. In scarce times one Ohio potter obtained lead by collecting and burning the lead foil with which Chinese tea was packaged.

Le Compte, Père Louis. A Jesuit missionary who published in Amsterdam in 1697 *Memoirs and Observations made in a late Journey through China.* The book was issued in translation in London in the same year. Le Compte devotes several pages to porcelain and mentions that blue-and-white was the principal product. He adds that the European merchants foolishly bought anything that the Chinese were willing to sell.

Leeds (Yorkshire). A pottery was founded about 1760 by two brothers Green. Fine creamware, frequently enamelled outside the factory, was a speciality. Pierced decoration was common. Most of the late eighteenth-century Staffordshire-type wares, including a few simple figures, were made.

MARKS: HARTLEY GREENS & CO. and LEEDS POTTERY, either alone or repeated in a cross. The old moulds were re-used at Slee's pottery (Leeds) from 1888, and were marked like the original wares.

Above, left Early deep creamware jug enamelled in black and red, Leeds, *c.* 1770. Victoria & Albert Museum

Above, right Water-bottle, enamelled earthenware painted in enamels of a similar type to certain Staffordshire salt-glazed wares, Liverpool, *c.* 1750. Fitzwilliam Museum

Mug, decorated by the so-called Trembly Rose painter, Longton Hall, *c.* 1755. Victoria & Albert Museum

Leeds horse. Large model of horse on a rectangular plinth made specially at Leeds, and probably used as the sign of a horse leech.

Limehouse. A short-lived porcelain factory before 1750. Its productions are unidentified.

Ling lung. Pierced openwork, as found on some seventeenth- to eighteenth-century blue-and-white porcelain bowls, and on elaborate vases of Ch'ien Lung and later date.

Lions (Dogs) of Fo (Buddha). These lions were originally temple guardians. They are often miscalled 'dogs', and they are also sometimes confused with the much rarer Kylin (*q.v.*). They were made in pairs, the male playing with a ball and the female with her cub. They occur as painted decoration and also as figures from the Ming dynasty onwards, in a variety of bodies and glazes. The best are enamelled on biscuit. Most specimens belong to the eighteenth and nineteenth centuries, and many are completely modern.

Littler, W. *See* Longton Hall.

Liverpool (creamware). A pottery, founded 1793–4, and in 1796 renamed 'Herculaneum', made cream-ware, often transfer-printed in blue or black, and other Staffordshire-type wares. MARK: HERCULANEUM (impressed). In U.S. Liverpool was a generic name given to creamware made 1780–1825 by Liverpool but also certain Staffordshire potters, especially in jugs black transfer-printed with American-historical subjects.

Liverpool (delftware). Delftware began in Liverpool in 1710 and was thereafter manufactured at numerous potteries (eight in 1750 and twelve by 1760), including some making porcelain. After about 1770 the industry declined, until by 1780 there were only three potteries. Liverpool delftware is often indistinguishable from Lambeth and Bristol. Typical of Liverpool is a foxy red, often used, together with blue, yellow, and green, in designs of flowers and Chinese lattice fences ('Fazackerley' colours). Red was also frequently used to edge rims. The Liverpool blue sometimes tends to cause a depression in the glaze. Liverpool *bianco-sopra-bianco* borders consist of rosettes separated by curved sprays of leaves. Characteristic Liverpool shapes are: plates with sides forming an obtuse angle with the bottom; mugs, both bell-shaped and cylindrical, with a spreading foot; bottles with a distinct foot-rim; large vases painted in blue; puzzle jugs with neck perforations of rosettes with heart-shaped petals; cornucopia wall-pockets for flowers; trinket trays, some with dishes fitting into an outer lobed tray; flower bricks with large, round (sometimes square) holes on top and a waved edge below or four solid ball feet; round dishes with low vertical rims painted with fishes ('charpots'); bowls decorated with ships. Liverpool delftware was occasionally decorated in overglaze enamels and gilt. Transfer-printing was also employed, particularly on tiles.

Liverpool (soft-paste porcelain). (1) Richard Chaffers (1731–65) from at latest 1756 made porcelain of Worcester type, a common form being a bulbous mug with an incised cordon above the foot, enamelled with a Chinese scene in polychrome. Chaffers was succeeded by Philip Christian. (2) Seth, James, and John Pennington made porcelain, especially bowls, painted in a bright 'sticky' blue. (3) To Zachariah Barnes are traditionally ascribed pieces roughly printed in a smudgy dark blue. (4) Samuel Gilbody was making porcelain by 1761 at latest, and (5) W. Reid, by 1756. In general, Liverpool porcelain is characterized by foot-rims vertical or undercut on the inner surface; flat bases to mugs; areas of blue ground marbled in gold; a blued glaze giving a 'thundercloud' effect where thick under the base.

'L' mark. *See* Worcester, Longton Hall.

'Long elizas'. A corruption of the Dutch *'lange lijzen'*, the gawky ladies often depicted on K'ang Hsi blue-and-white.

Longton Hall (soft-paste porcelain). Excavations on the site of this factory, together with documents traced by Dr Bernard Watney, prove that it was founded 1749–50 by William Jenkinson, who, in 1751, took into partnership William Nicklin and William Littler. Nicklin took no part in the work of the factory, which was managed throughout by Littler. In 1755 Jenkinson sold the majority of his shares to Nathaniel Fermin, who died soon afterwards. Robert Charlesworth also became a partner in this year, obtaining a major financial interest in the establishment. He dissolved the partnership in 1760, causing the factory to close down. Dr Watney's discoveries show that the wares thought typical of Longton Hall, including the 'snowman' family, were in fact made there, while many of its useful wares have been wrongly attributed to other factories. Characteristic of Longton Hall porcelain are a rich blue used as a coloured ground, sometimes over-painted in opaque-white enamel; vessels simulating melons or formed of overlapping leaves; a distinctive yellowish green; painting with roses delineated by a trembling outline; and a relief border-design of strawberries and leaves. The porcelain is commonly heavy and glassy, with a palish-green translucency betraying large bright flecks and frequent imperfections. The Longton Hall figures have been identified in a class characterized by poses half-turned to right or left; scrolled bases, often picked out in red; costume diapered with stars and small formal motifs, rather than flowers; and outlining of eye-lashes, often in red. The rare gilding is usually poor.

MARK: As diagram in blue.

(*See also* 'Snowman' family.)

Lotusware. *See* Belleek.

'Lowdin's' factory. *See* Bristol.

Lowestoft (soft-paste porcelain). This factory (1757–*c.* 1802) specialized in table- and teawares, usually decorated with Chinese derived patterns in underglaze blue or enamels. There is a strong affinity with Bow, their blue-and-white porcelain being sometimes almost indistinguishable. Both used bone ash. The Chinese and rococo styles persisted longer at Lowestoft than normally elsewhere, but towards 1800 slight 'sprig' patterns became popular. Primitive underglaze-blue printing was done. Lowestoft characteristics are wedge-shaped foot rims, and workmen's marks in blue inside them. There was no recognized factory mark, but (e.g.) Meissen and Worcester marks were copied. The very rare Lowestoft figures include swans, sheep, cats, and *putti.* Paris fakes of Lowestoft and genuine pieces redecorated are occasionally found.

'Lowestoft' china. Chinese porcelain of the eighteenth century with European-style decoration, once mistakenly attributed to this English factory.

'Lund's' factory. *See* Bristol.

Lung Ch'üan celadon. *See* Celadon.

Lustre. A sheeny surface film deposited on pottery or porcelain by firing metallic pigments in a 'reducing' (smoky) atmosphere (early nineteenth century). 'Silver' lustre was made with platinum and pink and mauve lustre with gold, which on a red body also produced copper. Lustre could be either applied in 'solid' areas or used for painting, often combined with printing. Alternatively, designs were painted in a glycerine or shellac medium and the piece dipped in lustre mixture. On removal of the medium, the pattern remained in negative on a lustre ground ('resist' process).

Lustre jug made to commemorate Queen Victoria's marriage on 10 February 1840, bearing portraits of Queen Victoria and Prince Albert

Longton Hall mark

Lustre colour. A pale mother-of-pearl shade containing some red, found on early Meissen porcelain, used either as background colour, for painted designs, or for overglaze marks. Probably the outcome of one of Böttger's experiments in search of the Chinese underglaze red.

Plate from the Venice workshop of Maestro Lodovico (d. 1550), decorated with a rondel showing a river and castles in blue within a coloured border. Victoria & Albert Museum

Majolica (from *maiolica*), the name first used in Italy to describe the lustred wares of Valencia. It was later extended to all varieties of Italian tin-glazed earthenware. By a further extension, it was applied to the pottery of other countries, painted in the traditional colours. Majolica is a nineteenth-century English name for lead-glazed pottery of sixteenth-century French style. Enormous quantities were distributed as premiums in the 1880s in America.

Manchu dynasty. The Ch'ing dynasty (1644–1912).

Mandarin. Late eighteenth-century decoration of groups wearing official dress, painted in panels within borders of elaborate diaper and other patterns.

Mandarin porcelain. Chinese porcelain made for export towards the end of the eighteenth century and thereafter. Panels of figures and floral subjects in a *rose-verte* palette are framed with borders in underglaze blue; gilding is the rule. Most of the designs are debased and overcrowded, and the glaze on later examples is often lumpy and uneven. Today most Mandarin porcelain is bought for interior decoration. It is of small interest to the serious collector.

'Marbled ware'. *See* Agateware.

Marks. Signs of origin on porcelain, applied either in underglaze blue, impressed, incised, or painted above the glaze. Marks are usually applied beneath the base, though occasionally, as for instance on Nymphenburg figures, they may form part of the decoration. Generally they indicate the factory, but marks can also refer to a painter or 'repairer', some are factory *assemblée* or warehouse signs for the convenience of workers, as are the early Herold period lustre marks; or else they may help to control gold supplies handed to individual decorators, as do gold numerals on tea services with *chinoiserie* decoration.

Martabani ware. Chinese celadon transhipped at the port of Moulmein on the Gulf of Martaban. Copies of celadons made in Persia in earthenware were later sometimes thus called.

Martha Gunn. Female Toby jug modelled in the likeness of Martha Gunn (1727–1815), the Brighton bathing woman.

Mason. Potters of Lane Delph (Staffordshire and Liverpool). Miles Mason (d. 1822) made porcelain. His son, C. J. Mason, patented 'Ironstone China' in 1813, commonly blue-printed or painted with 'Japan' patterns.

MARKS: usually the name in full.

'Mazarin' blue. *See* Chelsea.

Medium- and low-temperature glazes. Certain coloured glazes are applied to the already baked biscuit porcelain, which is then refired at 'medium' temperature. Such were the glazes of the Ming 'three-colour' class; monochromes, among which the yellow and turquoise blue were especially popular; and bowls and dishes with coloured glazes covering incised designs of dragons, flower sprays, etc., which were still made throughout the following dynasty. The K'ang Hsi, Yung Chêng, and Ch'ien Lung monochromes are remarkable for their wide range of rich, luminous colours and fine shapes. Turquoises are particularly distinguished from the Ming and more modern pieces by their clear brilliance. Greens include a leaf colour, dark green, olive green, and speckled cucumber green, as well as the much-prized apple green, which is applied over a crackled white glaze. Various light yellows are distinguishable,

and one with a deeper, brownish tint. A deep purple and paler, brownish aubergine were produced with the aid of manganese. Occasionally glazes are splashed with two colours – e.g. turquoise with purple, and green with yellow (tiger skin or 'egg-and-spinach').

Low-temperature glazes are the familiar enamels of overglaze painting, and were fired in the muffle kiln. Very various in shade, they include most of the colours of the *famille verte* and *famille rose*, and are

Martha Gunn toby jug decorated with coloured glazes, by Ralph Wood, *c.* 1770, Burslem, Staffordshire. City Museum and Art Gallery, Hanley, Stoke-on-Trent

Minton mark

often opaque. A mustard yellow and opaque light green, for example, resemble colours found on Ch'ien Lung painted wares. The opaque, mottled 'robin's egg' blue, spotted with lavender and crimson, is one much revived during the nineteenth century.

In dating these wares shape and finish, especially of the foot, should be carefully considered: for the same quality is not achieved in nineteenth-century and later pieces.

Mei Ping. A vase having a very short, narrow neck with an outcurving rim and a bulbous body at the top which curves inwards to a base of smaller diameter. The *Mei-Ping* vase was intended to hold a single spray of prunus blossom. The shape first appears during the Sung dynasty and was subsequently made in China, Korea and Japan.

'Merry man' plates. Delftware plates, usually simply decorated, forming a series of six, normally inscribed: (1) 'What is a merry man'; (2) 'Let him do what he can'; (3) 'To entertain his guests'; (4) 'With wine and merry jests'; (5) 'But if his wife do frown'; (6) 'All merriment goes down'. Late seventeenth and first half of eighteenth century.

'Metropolitan' slipware. Lead-glaze red-bodied earthenware with white slip decoration (inscriptions, simple rosettes, stars, coils, etc.), made in the London area about 1630–70.

Mille fleurs. Decoration with panels of growing plants reserved on a flower-covered ground: employed from the Ch'ien Lung period.

Ming dynasty (1368–1644) reign marks. (*See* right.)

Minton, Thomas (1765–1836). After apprenticeship at Caughley, Minton worked for Josiah Spode. In 1796 he set up for himself at Stoke, first making pottery only (much blue-printed), but from 1798 to 1811, and again 1821–5, porcelain too. Excellent transfer printing in black and brown was done.

MARKS: 'M' or as diagram, in blue.

Right Minton vase exhibited at the Exhibition of 1862, bearing the rare puce mark used only on ceramics made for that exhibition

Left Porcelain jar with high shoulders and short neck, decorated with a brilliant yellow enamel, 16th century, Ming dynasty. Bluett & Son, London

Mishima. Celadon wares, principally bottles and vases, inlaid with black and white clays in a variety of motifs usually floral. The technique was first employed in Korea during the Koryu dynasty and manufacture was extended into the following Yi dynasty. The wares were later copied in Japan. The name is derived from the Island of Mishima midway between Korea and Japan, where wares of this kind were transhipped, and perhaps even made.

'M' mark. *See* Minton, Pinxton.

Mocha. Ware decorated with coloured bands into which tree, moss, or fern-like effects have been introduced by means of a diffusing medium, described by William Evans (1846) as 'a saturated infusion of tobacco in stale urine and turpentine', made from about 1780 until 1914. Named from mocha quartz.

Moco, moko. Buff- or redware mottled by spattering coloured slips over the surface before glazing. A cheap nineteenth-century substitute for mocha.

Money boxes. Made at most country potworks from medieval times. Usual forms comprise houses, chests of drawers, globes, fir-cones, pigs, and hens and chickens. Associated with the custom of the 'Christmas box'. (*See* overleaf.)

Money boxes

Chinese tripod vessel (*li*) with hollow legs, incised grey earthenware, *c.* 2000 B.C.

Monochrome-glazed porcelain. These are divisible into two classes: (i) with high-temperature glazes, fired in one process at the full heat of the kiln – such as white, blue, copper red, celadon green, and brown or black; (ii) the remainder, with medium- or low-temperature colours (*q.v.*).

'Moons'. Patches of higher translucency observable in some porcelains.

'Mr and Mrs Caudle'. Relief decoration on brown stoneware spirit flasks, made about 1846 by Doulton of Lambeth, and based upon Douglas Jerrold's *Punch* papers ('Mrs Caudle's Curtain Lectures'). One side shows 'Mr and Mrs Caudle in Bed', the other 'Miss Prettyman'.

Muffle. Kiln used for low-temperature firing (*petit feu*) of about 700–900° C. The porcelain piece is enclosed in an inner chamber 'muffle', out of contact with flames or smoke, hence the name. It is used to fuse enamel painting into the glaze of faïence and porcelain.

Nanking porcelain. Only blue-and-white Chinese porcelain made at Ching-tê Chên for export, and shipped through the port of Nanking, should be so-called. This type of porcelain, however, was routed through Nanking as a matter of course, while porcelain was sent 'in white' southwards to Canton to be enamelled for export, whence it was shipped to the West.

Nantgarw (Glamorgan, soft-paste porcelain). A porcelain factory at Nantgarw was started in 1813 by W. Billingsley and, after transfer to Swansea (1814–16/17), continued until Billingsley left for Coalport (1819), and afterwards (probably for decoration only) until 1822 under W. W. Young.

At Swansea (*q.v.*) the beautiful but uneconomic Nantgarw material (white, glassy, and translucent) was adapted to produce: (1) a body with a greenish translucency ('duck's egg'), and then (2) one with a minutely pitted surface and yellow translucency (*c.* 1817).

The porcelain of both factories, although often simply decorated on the spot with 'Billingsley-style' flowers, birds, etc. (*see* Pardoe, Baxter), was keenly sought after by London dealers and decorators, who were responsible for much elaborate decoration. A raised border pattern of floral panels was favoured at both factories.

MARKS: NANT-GARW / C-W impressed, used at both Nantgarw and Swansea; 'Swansea' impressed or written in red or gold, on (1) above; SWANSEA with a trident, impressed, on (2) above.

Neale, J. *See* Palmer.

Neolithic pottery. The principal Chinese Neolithic wares come from cemeteries at Pan-Shan and Ma-Chang in Kansu Province. They are difficult to date accurately, but a date in the region of 2000 B.C. is generally accepted. These pots were made by coiling or on a 'slow' (i.e. hand-turned) wheel. The body is reddish-brown, and most are painted with bold, abstract, swirling patterns in black, white, red, and purple-brown pigments. Kansu is the gateway to China from the West, and urns related in style have been found as far west as the Ukraine. More or less contemporary with these wares are some pots in a grey body with impressed or incised ornament which suggests the use of a 'beater' bound with string. Most known specimens are either globular in shape, or in the form of a hemispherical vessel with three hollow legs for standing over a fire. Known as a *li*, this later became the prototype of a bronze vessel of the same name.

Newcastle-on-Tyne. Potteries here (St Anthony's 1780 onwards, and St Peter's about 1817 onwards) made inferior creamware.

New Hall (Shelton, Staffordshire). In 1781 the Bristol patent for hard-paste porcelain was bought by a Staffordshire combine, which in 1782 established a factory at New Hall. Hard-paste porcelain decorated with simple, mainly floral, patterns was produced until about 1810, when a glassy bone china was adopted.

MARKS: pattern numbers prefaced by 'N' or 'N°'; on bone china, 'New Hall' within a double circle, printed.

'N' and 'N°' mark. *See* New Hall.

Northern celadon. Sung wares probably from Honan Province, with grey porcellaneous body burnt brown where exposed, and usually glazed base. The glaze is often glassy and olive green to brown in tone. They include beautifully shaped bowls, pear-shaped vases, and small shallow dishes superbly carved with plant forms or free designs incised with a comb.

Nottingham. Stoneware pottery from late seventeenth century to about 1800, making wares thinly potted and overlaid with a lustrous ferruginous wash. Pierced, impressed, or incised decoration was common. Latterly almost indistinguishable from Derbyshire stoneware.

'Oak-leaf' jars. Mid-fifteenth-century Tuscan drug jars decorated with foliage in impasto blue.

'Oil-spot' glaze. Some of the so-called Honan brown and black glazes of the Sung dynasty bear attractive silvery spots which are caused by precipitated iron crystals.

On-glaze. Decoration applied after the ware has been glazed and fired.

'Opaque china'. *See* Swansea.

'Orange jumper'. Local subject on Yorkshire cream-coloured earthenware made at the Don pot-

Owl jug

tery, *c.* 1808, depicting a coarse-featured local horse breaker who acted as messenger for Lord Milton in the 1807 election. He is clothed in orange, the 'colour' of Lord Milton. Orange tawny was considered the colour appropriate to the lower classes.

Owl jug. Jug with a separated head forming a cup, made in slipware, *c.* 1700, and white salt-glazed stoneware, *c.* 1720–75. The proverb 'Like an owl in an ivy bush', used of a vague person with a sapient look, may explain its convivial associations. Jugs in the shape of owls (or *Eulenkrüge*) were also made in Germany in the sixteenth century, providing one of the earliest examples of the use of tin glaze in Germany. There are about fifteen known examples dating between 1540 and 1561. They have moulded relief feathers and sometimes shields of arms in oil paint and cold gilding on their breasts.

Palissy, Bernard (*c.* 1510–*c.* 1590). A celebrated French potter. Palissy's great reputation rests on the fine coloured glazes used on his wares. He was originally a painter of glass, and after a period of travel in France, settled at Saintes. His ambition to become a potter was aroused, according to his own account, by the sight of a beautifully decorated cup. After many costly experiments he succeeded in making pottery and decorating it with mingled colour glazes. His *figulines rustiques* (pottery with rural subjects modelled in relief) brought him the patronage of the Constable de Montmorency, who, on one occasion, had him released from prison by declaring him *inventeur des rustiques figulines du roi.* The subjects of these *figulines* include snakes, lizards, shells, fishes, etc., modelled on a ground of rockwork and moss. The glazes provide a harmonious blending of blue, purple, brown, yellow, and green. He decorated a grotto at the Tuileries in this manner to the order of Catherine de' Medici; but, as a Huguenot, was obliged to flee from Paris in order to escape the massacre of St Bartholomew's day. Eventually imprisoned in the Bastille de Bucy, he died there about 1590. Genuine specimens of his work are extremely rare, but it has been extensively copied.

Palmer, Humphrey. Potter of Hanley (Staffordshire), 1760–78, rivalled Wedgwood in making black basaltes (1769) and jasperware. Bankrupt in 1778, he was helped by J. Neale ('Neale & Co.', subsequently (1784) 'Neale & Wilson'). Their lead-glazed earthenware figures are notable for neat modelling and clear, bright enamel colours.

Pancheon. Large shallow earthenware bowl with sloping sides used for settling milk.

Pap dish. A shallow boat with a tubular spout for feeding infants.

Pardoe, Thomas (1770–1823). Painted porcelain at Derby and Worcester, pottery at Swansea (1797–1809); became independent enameller in Bristol (1809–21); decorated Nantgarw porcelain (1821–?1823). Painted mainly 'botanical' flowers.

Far right Cabinet cup painted by Thomas Pardoe, Nantgawr, Swansea. National Museum of Wales

Far right Parian ware vase, drab ground decorated with passion flowers and foliage in relief. Minton, 1854

Sauce boat with decoration of a lady in the bath by Bernard Palissy, French, early 16th century. Victoria & Albert Museum

Parian or statuary ware. Fine-grained, waxy feldspathic porcelain resembling white Parian marble, developed in the 1840s by Copeland and Minton; much admired at the Crystal Palace exhibitions in London and New York (1851 and 1853). Soon a favourite of American makers, chiefly for portrait busts and parlour ornaments. (*See* previous page.)
'Parson and clerk'. Figure group showing a drunken parson being led home by the faithful Moses, first made by Enoch Wood (1759–1840) as a sequel to the 'Vicar and Moses'. A satire on the drinking, hunting squarson type of incumbent.

Pastille burners. Box-like containers, often in the form of cottages, churches, or summer houses, with detachable perforated lids for burning cassolette perfumes. These consisted of finely powdered willow-wood charcoal, benzoin, fragrant oils, and gum arabic. Extremely popular, 1820–50.
'Patch family'. *See* Derby.
'Paul Pry'. Model for pottery figures and Toby jugs based upon the meddlesome hero of John Poole's comedy of that name, 1825.
Peach-bloom glaze. A pink glaze mottled with a deeper red with small spots of brown and green. This much prized reduced copper glaze was principally employed to cover small pieces, such as the water-pots used on the scholar's table of which there is a fine example in the Victoria and Albert Museum. The best examples belong to the reign of K'ang Hsi: Japanese copies are sometimes deceptive.
Pearlware. A white variety of the cream-coloured pottery ('Queen's Ware') introduced by Josiah Wedgwood about 1779. It had a nacreous glaze, hence the name given to it.
Peasant style. Ornament derived from peasant art: specifically earthenware painted in the 'resist' lustre style with a restricted palette of colours.
'Pebbled' vases. Vases with marbled surface (*see* Agateware, Wedgwood).
Peever. A piece of slate or stone used in the game of hopscotch, also a disc of pottery, so used, coloured and lettered in the name of the owner. Made at Alloa and elsewhere in Scotland, nineteenth century.
'Peggy Plumper'. Crude decoration showing Peggy Plumper sparring with Sammy Spar for mastership of bed and board, accompanied by a long rhyme 'about wearing the breeches'.
Peking bowls. Bowls of Ch'ien Lung or later date, with painted *famille rose* medallions reserved on a single-coloured ground covered with engraved scrollwork; said to have been sent as yearly tribute to the Emperor at Peking.

Pastille burner

'Pelican in her piety'. A Christian emblem representing the old popular fallacy that the pelican feeds her young with her own blood. Used on Staffordshire slipware.
Penny bank. Earthenware money box in the form of a house or chest of drawers.
Petuntse. *See* China stone.
'Pew groups'. In salt-glazed stoneware depicted seated figures, sometimes playing instruments (*see also* Adam and Eve). Conjecturally attributed to Aaron Wood.
Phoenix. Correctly, the *fêng huang* in Chinese, and the *ho-ho* in Japan. This bird, a kind of long-tailed pheasant, is a symbol of the Empress of China. Sometimes called the Vermilion Bird, it represents Spring from the Four Seasons, and the South from the Four Quadrants.
'Piatto da pompa'. An elaborately decorated dish made entirely for ornamental display.
Piggin. A small milk pail. A pig wife is a woman who sells crockery.
Pilchard pots. Made in North Devon, South Wales, and Cornwall for the West Country fishermen, and known by size as 'gallons', 'bussas', and 'great crocks'.
Pilgrim bottle. *See* Costrel.
'Pineapple' ware. *See* 'Cauliflower' ware.
Pinxton (soft-paste porcelain). The Pinxton (Derbyshire) factory (1793–1813) was started with the technical assistance of W. Billingsley, a fine translucent white porcelain being made. In 1799 Billingsley left, and a coarser Staffordshire-type porcelain was made. The decoration followed Derby styles. A yellow ground is notable.

MARKS: 'T' and 'M', impressed, 'P', in various enamels; 1 below in blue, 2 in purple, 3 and 4 in red enamels.

190

1 2 3 4

Pipkin. Earthenware cooking vessel.
Pirlie-pig. Earthenware money box. 'Pig' is a North Country word for an earthen jar: 'pirlie' is a diminutive indicating something of slight value.
Pitcher mould. Mould made of clay and fired.
Plymouth (hard-paste porcelain). In 1768 William Cookworthy, a Plymouth apothecary, took out a patent for hard-paste porcelain. The factory was moved to Bristol about 1770. Plymouth porcelain suffers from technical defects – smoky glaze discoloration, firecracks, warping, etc. The enamels (often of a dirty tone) frequently stand out in relief. A characteristic brownish red was much used on the rococo bases of figures. These formed an important part of the factory's production. Painting in blackish-toned underglaze blue was practised.

MARKS: (1) as diagram, in underglaze blue, blue or red enamel, or gold; (2) occasionally a cross, alone or with (1), either incised through the glaze or in enamel or gilt; (3) 'T' and 'T°' impressed.
'P' mark. *See* Worcester, Pinxton.
Pope and Devil. Reversible bell-shaped cup showing the Pope in his triple tiara when held one way up,

and the Devil when reversed. Sometimes inscribed 'When Pope absolves, the Devil smiles'. Late eighteenth century.

Porcelain. Translucent, vitrified ware made of china clay and china stone fused at great heat – the 'true' or hard-paste porcelain. Soft-paste or artificial porcelain is made of white clay and a glassy grit, in some cases with bone ash added as a flux. A type of porcelain made from clay and soaprock (steatite) is also classified as soft porcelain. From continual experiments, the formulas varied endlessly, and many marginal 'porcelains' are accepted if they show translucence.

Porringer. Child's basin for broth or porridge.

Portland vase. This vase, which is in the British Museum, London, is in the form of an amphora about 10 inches (25.4 cm) in height. It is made of glass of a deep-blue colour, over which is a layer of white glass. The body of the vase is cut in relief with scenes from the story of Peleus and Thetis. It dates from the first century A.D. The base, which does not belong to the vase, is of the same materials, and is carved with the bust of a youth wearing a Phrygian cap. When in the possession of the Duke of Portland it was loaned to Wedgwood, who made many successful copies.

'Portobello' ware. Made at Tunstall, Staffordshire, *c.* 1830, in imitation of banded and 'Pratt'-type wares made at Portobello in Scotland.

Posset. Beverage comprising hot ale, milk, sugar, spices, and small pieces of bread, toast, or oatcake, said to have been a common supper beverage in Staffordshire and Derbyshire on Christmas Eve. Enjoyed widespread popularity.

Posset pot. Straight- or curved-sided vessel with loop handles and spouts, generally covered with a slanting or dome-shaped lid, and occasionally crowned with an elaborate knob, used for posset, and made in delftware and slipware, seventeenth and eighteenth centuries.

Potiche. Large, broad-mouthed jar, often of 'baluster' shape, with cover; favoured from Ming times.

Pottery. In the broadest sense is 'any receptacle or vessel made of clay' by the potter. But the name is saved for earthenwares fired at low temperatures (600° C. or more) as distinguished from stoneware or porcelain, fired at much greater heat.

Pottle pot. Quart pot.

Powder blue. Chinese, *chui-ch'ing*, French, *bleu soufflé*. An underglaze-blue ground termed *bleu soufflé*, or 'blown blue', because it was blown on in powder form through a bamboo tube with a silk screen at one end. It was especially employed to decorate *rouleau* vases which usually had panels reserved in white for painted decoration. Most powder-blue porcelain was made at the end of the seventeenth century and in the early decades of the eighteenth. It was extensively copied in Europe, for instance by the Worcester factory in the 1760s.

'Pratt' type. Wares made at the end of the eighteenth and the beginning of the nineteenth centuries, decorated in a distinctive palette of colours, consisting of drab blue, dirty brown, ochre, orange, yellow, and dull green. Made in Staffordshire by Pratt and others; also in South Wales, Liverpool, Sunderland, and Prestonpans.

Prattware jug decorated with a dragoon approaching a military encampment, *c.* 1790–5

Printing. The process of printing, or transfer printing, on pottery and porcelain is carried out by means of 'inking' an engraved metal plate. An impression is then taken on thin paper and applied to the article to be decorated. The engraving, being printed with a special ink and used while it is still wet, is thus transferred. This is done on a piece that has been glazed already, and when it is fired the printing sinks into the glaze and a smooth surface results.

The invention is an English one, and its use was practised in the first place at the Battersea enamel works, near London, in 1753. Shortly afterwards it was in use at Worcester and at Liverpool. John Sadler and Guy Green, of the latter town, claimed credit for the original invention, stating that they had made it in 1749. No evidence in favour of this claim has come to light.

The invention proved a workable and economical one, Sadler and Green stating that they had within the space of six hours 'printed upwards of twelve hundred tiles of different colours and patterns, which, upon a moderate computation, was more than one hundred good workmen could have done of the same patterns in the same space of time by the usual way of painting with the pencil'.

By the year 1764 Wedgwood is known to have been sending plain cream-coloured pottery to Liverpool to be decorated by Sadler and Green by the transfer process. A typical example, a tankard dating from about 1775, is in the Victoria and Albert Museum.

Printing in blue, which was done by a similar process but prior to the application of glaze to the article, was developed at Worcester soon after the invention of the first process, and outstripped the latter in popularity. It was employed extensively at Caughley and by Spode, but a meat dish bearing the Wedgwood mark, dating from about 1840, is exhibited in the Victoria and Albert Museum.

Proto-porcelain. Hard-fired stoneware dating from the Han dynasty. It has a grey body covered with a feldspathic glaze which is olive-brown in colour. The glaze has a tendency to coagulate into drops. Technically these wares, usually globular jars, are the precursor of later porcelains.

Punch. Beverage consisting of spirits blended with hot milk or water, sugar, and flavoured with lemon and spice.

Punch bowl. Large basin for serving hot punch, sometimes called a 'jorum'.

Purple of Cassius. Discovered by Andreas Cassius of Leyden, in the middle of the seventeenth century. It involved dissolving gold in nitric acid and sal ammoniac.

Puzzle jug. Vessel made in earthenware, delftware, or stoneware with a hollow tube round the lip opening into three or more spouts, and connected with the inside by the hollow handle. Sometimes there is a hole under the top of the handle. The neck is pierced with ornamental motifs, and usually inscribed with a challenge to the drinker. To empty the vessel without spilling the contents it is necessary to stop all the apertures except one, and to drain it by suction.

Queen's ware. Cream-coloured earthenware improved and marketed by Josiah Wedgwood. He named it 'Queen's ware' in honour of Queen Charlotte, the wife of George III.

Red and green family. Although a combination of iron-red and green enamels antedates the reign of Wan Li, large jars, vases, and *potiches* thus decorated, and belonging to this reign, are usually referred to as the 'red and green family'. In China these wares are among the forerunners of the *famille verte*, and they were also popular in Japan.

Red glazes and enamels. The copper-red glazes and underglaze pigment should be distinguished from the vermilion-toned iron-red enamel colour. This was much used in Ming times, is prominent in the K'ang Hsi *famille verte*, and appears also on some *famille rose* wares, and as a monochrome glaze from Yung Chêng.

Reducing atmosphere. A kiln atmosphere heavily charged with carbon monoxide is termed 'reducing'. Its effect is profoundly to modify the colours yielded by certain metallic oxides, particularly iron and copper. Celadons, and the purple suffusion of Chün glazes, underglaze copper red, and the later *flambé* glazes, are all the product of firing in a reducing atmosphere.

The Chinese often achieved the desired concentration of carbon monoxide by feeding the furnace with wet wood.

Redware. Or red-clay pottery. Simple lead-glazed wares of soft, porous body ranging in colour from pinkish buff to reds and brown. (*See also* Slipware, Sgraffiato.)

Redware

Reform flasks. Brown salt-glazed stoneware spirit flasks made by Doulton (Lambeth), Stephen Green (Lambeth), Oldfield (Chesterfield), and Joseph Thomson (Wooden Box Pottery, Hartshorne), in the form of prominent politicians and royalty, at the time of the Reform Bill, 1832. Personalities portrayed included William IV, Queen Adelaide, Lord Grey, O'Connell, Brougham, Richard Cobden, and Lord John Russell.

Reform flask

Registry mark. Appearing on English wares in two cycles, 1842–67 and 1868–83. A lozenge with code letters and numerals assigned by the 'Registration of Designs' Office.

Relief decoration. There are various ways of producing relief decoration: by freehand modelling, free incising or piercing, or, more frequently, by pressing soft clay in plaster moulds; also by impressing the surface of soft-clay objects with cut-metal stamps. Occasionally separately moulded low reliefs are applied to the surface.

Repairer. Repairer, or *bossierer*, workman responsible for assembling the porcelain clay impressions from moulds, attaching heads, limbs, etc., and finishing the figure, which was usually modelled by another artist. Incised and impressed marks on figures and groups often refer to these repairers.

Reserved. A surface left plain to receive decoration.

'Resist' lustre. On-glaze decorative process used generally with silver lustre, giving an effect of a light or coloured decoration against a metallic background. The ornament is painted on the ware with a 'resist', covered with the metallic solution, and fired; the infusible 'resist' being removed by polishing with whiting afterwards.

'Rice-grain' decoration. Small perforations filled with transparent glaze; a technique adopted from Persian pottery, popular during the eighteenth century.

Ridgway. Staffordshire potters at Hanley (1794 onwards) and Cauldon Place, Shelton (from 1812), making mainly stone china, but also porcelain.

'R' mark. *See* Chelsea, Bow.

Rockingham (England). Little is known about 'The Rockingham Works' (near Swinton, Yorkshire) founded about 1750, but from 1787 to 1806 it was allied to the Leeds Pottery, after which it passed to the Brameld family. The wares are almost indistinguishable from those of Staffordshire or Leeds. Distinctive, however, were a streaky dark-brown glaze, and a special ('Cadogan') type of tea pot. Porcelain (soft paste) was made from 1820 in the contemporary florid taste (*see* Introduction, English porcelain). Some figures were

made, including dogs, models and cottages, etc.

MARKS: BRAMELD and ROCKINGHAM, impressed, and as diagram below, opposite.

Rockingham (U.S.). A common yellow ware with lustrous brown manganese glaze, mottled or streaked. The popular misnomer is 'Bennington ware', but it was made at countless American factories from the 1840s onward. East Liverpool produced 'probably fifty per cent of the total' (*see Antiques*, Jan. 1946, pp. 42–4).

Rookwood faïence. *See* Art Pottery. The Rookwood Pottery at Cincinnati, Ohio, was founded in 1880 by Mrs Maria L. Nichols (later Mrs Bellamy Storer), first making tablewares, but by 1889 receiving a gold medal at the Paris Exposition for its now widely recognized art wares.

'Rose engine turning'. *See* Engine turning.

Rosso antico. The name given by Wedgwood to his red stoneware, which was a successor to imitations of the 'Boccaro' ware imported from China in the seventeenth century. It was decorated by being polished on a grindstone and by means of 'engine turning' applied on a lathe.

'Ruby-back' plates. *See* Famille rose.

Sadler, John (1720–89), of Liverpool. Decorated with transfer prints pottery, porcelain, and enamels obtained from various sources – notably delftware tiles (from 1756) and Wedgwood's cream-coloured earthenware (from 1761).

Below Cream coloured salt-glazed cow cream jug, Staffordshire, *c.* 1745. City Museum and Art Gallery, Hanley Stoke-on-Trent

Salt-glazed stoneware. Stoneware in which the glaze is formed by throwing common salt into the kiln when it reaches the maximum temperature. The salt decomposes, forming sodium oxide and hydrochloric acid, the former combining with the alumina and silica of the surface of the wares to form a thin coating of glass.

Salt kit. Dome-topped ovoid jar surmounted by a knob and loop handle with a wide circular aperture at one side; used for storing salt, etc.

Samson. This Paris porcelain factory is well known for clever copies of old armorial Chinese porcelain, which have been made there for more than half a century. The coats-of-arms are often those of Great Britain or of France, or of some famous person, such as Lord Nelson. Examined closely, these copies should not deceive the collector, but in an ill-lighted room a costly mistake might easily be made. Samson's productions sometimes bear a simulated Chinese 'seal' mark or a disguised 'S' beneath the base in red.

Samson figure of a bird, 19th century

'S. & G.' mark. *See* Isleworth.

San ts'ai (three-colour) ware. Generally implies the Ming three-colour ware, but also describes porcelains enamelled 'on the biscuit' in *famille verte* yellow, green, and purple during the K'ang Hsi period, and hence also Ming porcelains with this technique.

'Scratch blue'. Decoration characteristic of white

salt-glazed stoneware comprising incised floral arabesques and inscriptions into which clay stained with cobalt was rubbed. Examples dated from 1724 to 1776 recorded.

'Scratch-cross' porcelain. Mainly mugs and jugs, marked underneath with an incised cross and/or strokes inside the foot rim. Analogies with Worcester and Bristol (soft-paste) porcelain suggest that they were made at one or both factories, *c.* 1751–5.

Schwarzlot. Black monochrome decoration, sometimes heightened with iron red or gold. This technique, originating with Dutch glass workers and Nuremberg faïence painters, was probably first applied to porcelain by Daniel Preissler (1636–1733) of Bohemia, whence it became characteristic for the decoration of du Paquier porcelain, executed by Jacobus Helchis and others.

Sgraffiato. Cutting away, incising, or scratching through a coating of slip to expose the colour of the underlying body. Popular technique in South Wales, Devonshire, Somerset, and Staffordshire. In the U.S.A. used on redware, especially the Pennsylvania–German showplates.

An important class of lead-glazed earthenware of this type was made in Italy from the fifteenth century onwards. The great centre was at Bologna. Incised patterns were sometimes reinforced by adding touches of coloured pigment, and by staining the glaze with metallic oxides.

Shou. A Chinese ideogram which is actually a wish for longevity. It occurs in a large number of stylized, ornamental forms. The word *Shou* also means peach, and for this reason the peach is a common symbol of longevity. The words *fu shou* mean a bat and a peach respectively, but the same words also mean happiness and long life. Hence the two things are often associated in porcelain decoration.

Shrinkage. The contracting of porcelain after firing by about one-seventh of the size of the mould. Hence the supports, in the shape of tree trunks or rockery, to prevent contortion after the cooling process. The supports take the weight of the body off the legs, which at maximum temperature would not be strong enough to hold it.

Shu fu ('Privy Council') ware. Yüan dynasty porcelain of Ching-tê Chên with slightly opaque, bluish-tinged glaze covering moulded relief designs of flying cranes, lotus sprays, and the characters *shu fu*.

Siamese twins. The 'monstrous' birth in Somerset, 19 May 1680, recorded on a *sgraffiato* dish and Bristol Delft platter. The Kentish Siamese twins, Eliza and Mary Chulkhurst (d. 1734, aged 34), occur on redware copies of the 'Biddenden' cake.

Skillet. Earthen saucepan with three legs.

Slip. A clay watered down to a creamy consistency and normally used either to coat a pot of another colour or to decorate it with lines or dots produced by means of a spouted can.

Slipware. Earthenware decorated with white or coloured slip. (*See also* Combed slip, Sgraffiato, Trailed slip, and Inlaid decoration.)

Smaltino. The contemporary Italian name for a pale-blue tin glaze on sixteenth-century Italian *maiolica*; especially at Venice.

'S' mark. *See* Caughley.

'Snowman'. Family of porcelain figures, with glaze partially obscuring the modelling. Mainly of animals, often with a clumsy rosette on the base, made at Longton Hall about 1750.

Snufftaker. Standing Toby jug in the form of an ugly man taking a pinch of snuff, usually with a deep purple-brown lustrous 'Rockingham' glaze.

Soapstone. An ingredient in Bristol (soft-paste), Worcester, Caughley, and Liverpool porcelain. (*See* English porcelain.)

Soft-paste ('frit' or 'artificial') porcelain. Is compounded essentially of white clay mixed with a glassy substance. In England bone ash was used in some grit porcelains as a flux. (*See also* Soapstone.)

Somerset. Lead-glazed pottery, with incised designs and glaze stained green in patches, was made at Donyatt from mid-seventeenth century onwards, and at Crock Street in the eighteenth and nineteenth centuries.

Southwark. *See* Lambeth.

Spatter. A cheerful range of wares with sponged colour and painted designs, made *c.* 1820–50 in Staffordshire for the American market.

Spinario. Figure of boy extracting a thorn from his foot, copied from statue in the Capitoline Museum, Rome.

Spode. Josiah Spode I (1733–96), once a workman of Whieldon, started a pottery at Stoke-on-Trent about 1770. His son, Josiah Spode II (1754–1827) added porcelain (*c.* 1810) to the productions, and is considered the inventor of 'bone china'; in 1805 'stone china' was manufactured. W. J. Copeland became a partner in 1813, and manager in 1829.

MARKS: 'Spode', impressed, in blue and red, blue-printed, etc., and as diagram, blue-printed.

'Sponged' ware. A crude, easily recognized peasant style originally made by Adams of Tunstall, and, because of its 'bright fancy character' (Jewitt), extensively exported.

Sprigging. The term used to describe the method of ornamenting wares by means of applied reliefs. The 'sprigs' are moulded separately and attached to the plaque, vase, or other object by means of water or thinned clay. Wedgwood used sprigging for the decoration of his jasperware.

Steen. Originally an earthen vessel with two ears to hold liquids, later used for bread, meat, or fish.

'Stone China'. A hard white earthenware containing china stone, made as a cheap substitute for porcelain in Staffordshire from 1805.

Stoneware. A variable family of hard, high-fired wares mostly salt-glazed, from the thin white Staffordshire stonewares of 1720–50 to heavy crocks and jugs of blue-painted grey stoneware so common in the nineteenth century.

Stubbs, George, R.A. The painter who excelled in the delineation of the horse was an acquaintance of Josiah Wedgwood. In 1777–8 the latter was attempt-

Slipware

Vase of stoneware, gilt and painted with pictures of Queen Victoria and the Crystal Palace, Charles Meigh and Sons, Hanley, exhibited in 1851. Victoria & Albert Museum

ing to assist the painter, who wished to attempt enamel painting by using large plaques of china for the purpose. Three of these made of creamware, one of which is a panel 36 inches (91.4 cm) in height, painted with a portrait of the potter by Stubbs, are in the Lady Lever Art Gallery, Port Sunlight. Stubbs also designed some cameos with equestrian subjects, and painted on canvas a characteristic 'conversation' portrait of Mr and Mrs Josiah Wedgwood and their family. This was exhibited at the Royal Academy in 1780.

Spode mark

Sunderland (Co. Durham). Several potteries here made creamware, often decorated with transfers and/or pink lustre (late eighteenth and early nineteenth centuries).

Sung dynasty (960–1280). *See* Chinese pottery.

Stoneware

Supper set. For this style of article there is a contemporary notice from which its introduction can be dated with reasonable accuracy. Mrs Philip Lybbe Powys, who carefully recorded the events in her daily life in a series of diaries covering the years from 1755 to 1809, entered under the year 1797:

> 'August 31st. – In the morning we went to London a-shopping, and at Wedgwood's, as usual, were highly entertain'd, as I think no shop affords so great a variety. I there, among other things, purchas'd one of the newly-invented *petit soupee* trays, which I think equally clever, elegant, and convenient when alone or a small party, as so much less trouble to ourselves and servants.'

Sussex. Rustic lead-glazed earthenware was made in Sussex (at Cadborough, Chailey, Brede, Rye, Wiston, Dicker, Burgess Hill, etc.) from the second half of the eighteenth century onwards. The characteristic ware was a red pottery decorated by incisions or stamped depressions (often printer's type) filled with white clay.

Sussex pig. Pottery jug with a loose head used as a cup, enabling the user to drink a hogshead of liquor without disquieting aftereffects. Peculiar to the Sussex factory of Cadborough, Rye, nineteenth century.

Swansea (Glamorgan). (1) 'The Cambrian Pottery' (1765 onwards), mainly run by L. W. Dillwyn from 1812 until 1831, made most of the typical contemporary Staffordshire wares, including a white earthenware ('opaque china') and a creamware with a rippling surface, blue-printed or painted in lustre or colours (botanical painting done by Thomas Pardoe; birds, butterflies, and flowers by W. W. Young). At this factory was made the Swansea porcelain (*see* Nantgarw). (2) 'The Glamorgan Pottery' (*c.* 1813 onwards) made earthenwares of the same types as (1) above.

'Swatow' ware. Porcelains with thick, 'fat' glaze and roughly finished, glazed, gritty base, made in South China and probably exported from Swatow, especially to Japan. Dishes, with wild, powerful painting in red, green, and turquoise enamels and similar underglaze-blue wares date from the late sixteenth to seventeenth centuries; also celadon, light-brown and pale-blue monochromes with white slip flowers.

Syngchong. A dealer in Canton *c.* 1800. A large bowl belonging to the Corporation of the City of New York, bearing a view of the city and the arms of the corporation, and dated 1802, is inscribed on the outside of the rim of the base: *This bowl was made by Syngchong in Canton, Fungmanhe Pinxt.*

T'ang dynasty (A.D. 618–906). *See* Chinese Pottery.

T'ang figures, forgeries of. There have been forgeries of T'ang tomb-figures from the time when these first became popular in Europe. The unglazed figures are the most deceptive, but experience teaches that, however convincing the quality of the modelling may be, the body will have been fired at a higher temperature than genuine examples, and will therefore be harder and less absorbent. A useful (but not completely certain test) is to wet the finger-tip with saliva and dab it on an unglazed part. If the moisture is absorbed like ink on blotting-paper the figure is probably genuine. If it remains on the surface and is not absorbed the specimen is likely to be spurious. Glazed figures present less of a problem. The T'ang lead silicate glazes exhibit a finely-meshed crackle under a magnifying glass, and it is doubtful whether a single genuine specimen exists without this feature. Modern forgeries either have no crackle, or one with a larger mesh. On excavated specimens the green glaze is likely to have degenerated to a greater extent than the yellow. A forger can induce glaze iridescence, but not selective deterioration.

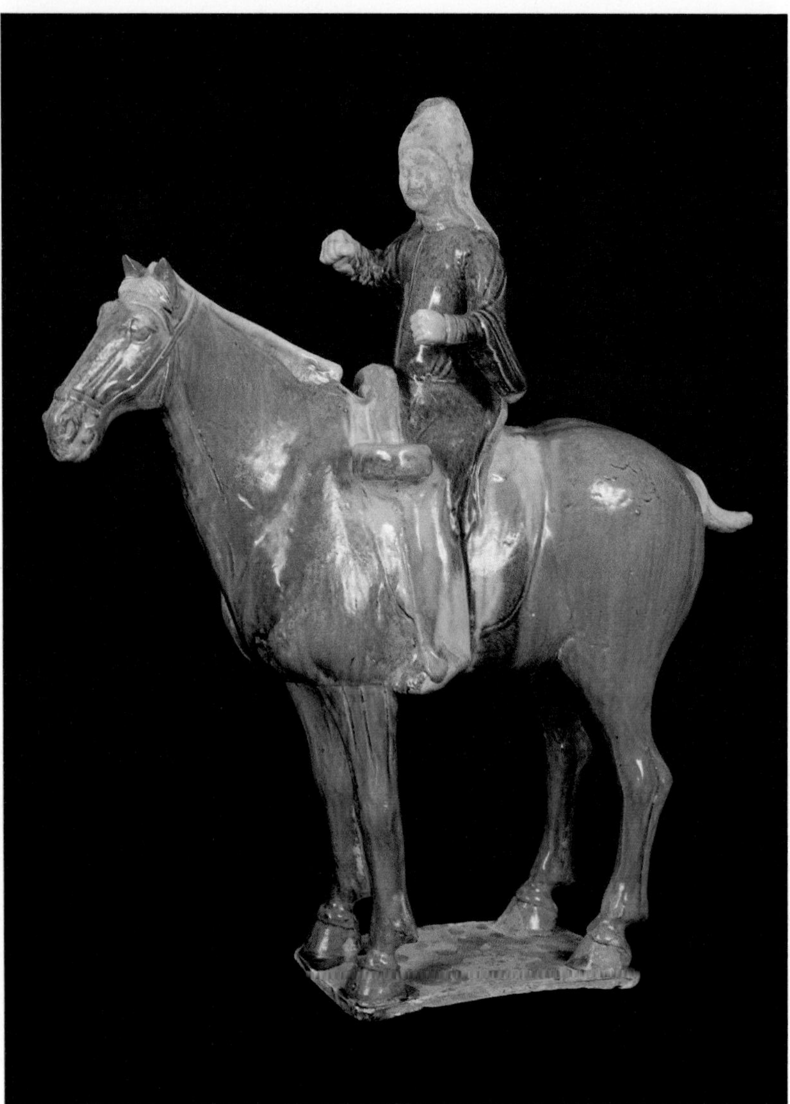

Glazed tomb figure of a mounted drummer, T'ang dynasty (618–906). Christie, Manson & Woods

All T'ang figures, being of soft earthenware, are likely to have some degree of restoration, but it is necessary to beware of specimens which have been assembled from largely unrelated fragments. Chinese restorers are very skilful, and they know that if a minor piece of restoration is just about visible to a buyer he will conclude that this is the sum total, and not look for more or less invisible repairs elsewhere. The ultra-violet lamp is very useful in the detection of repairs, revealing the site and extent by a colour different from that exhibited by unrestored parts.

Tao Kuang period (1820–51). Characteristic wares are those minutely painted in *famille rose* style, employing low-toned enamels, and *graviata* coloured grounds. *Tou ts'ai* decoration was also popular. The body is coarser than in eighteenth-century wares, and the glaze has an oily sheen.

Taws. Marbles or small balls made in earthenware.

Teapoy. An incorrect name for a tea caddy.

Tê Hua porcelain. A fine white porcelain with a glaze aptly described by Hobson as looking 'like milk jelly' made at Tê Hua (Fukien Province) from the sixteenth century onwards. In colour it ranges from cream-white to chalk-white, and the former colour is likely to be the earlier. Early examples, also, are often firecracked, like the more primitive European porcelains. Little is known of wares manufactured in the district before the introduction of the porcelain which became known in Europe as *blanc-de-Chine*, but by the seventeenth century the kilns at Tê Hua were the largest in China after Ching-tê Chên, and its wares were extensively copied by almost every eighteenth-century European porcelain factory, especially the familiar type decorated with prunus blossom or tea-blossom in relief. The kilns specialized in the production of figures, the most frequent being the Buddhist goddess, Kuan Yin, in many poses. Especially sought today are figures of European merchants. Early figures particularly were often made with detachable head and hands, and with holes pierced in the face for the provision of a moustache and beard of natural hair. A few examples of Tê Hua porcelain painted in enamel or lacquer colours are known. Those painted in lacquer colours are obviously European work. Those painted in enamels may have been decorated in one of the Canton studios, or in Europe. It seems unlikely that the factory would have been responsible. The kilns are still working and modern figures of Kuan Yin are not unusual.

Temmoku. Japanese name for wares with lustrous brown glazes, especially Sung Chien wares.

Texts. Wall plaques with lustre 'frames' and cottage mantelpiece ornaments in the shape of pedimented façades enclosing a clock, sun, and moon, and boldly lettered scripture verses ('PREPARE TO MEET THY GOD'), nineteenth century.

'TF' mark. *See* Bow, Worcester.

Tickenhall (Derbyshire). Pottery has been made at Tickenhall since the Middle Ages, but 'Tickenhall' ware usually connotes a hard, dark-brown lead-glazed earthenware decorated with shaped applied pads of white clay (seventeenth century), although the name is sometimes loosely applied to other slipwares.

Tiles. All the main English delftware factories made tiles (Lambeth and Bristol, late seventeenth and eighteenth centuries, Liverpool and Wincanton, eighteenth century). Some very rare relief-moulded salt-glazed stoneware tiles are known. Creamware tiles were made at Liverpool and in Staffordshire (late eighteenth century).

Ting. The small three-footed cauldron used as an incense burner.

Tin glaze. Lead glaze made opaque by the addition of tin ashes.

Ting ware. One of the classic wares of the Sung dynasty. Ting ware is a porcelain of variable translucency, orange by transmitted light, which was made at kilns near Ting Chou (Chihli Province) from the T'ang dynasty onwards. The finest variety is *pai* (white) Ting, and most surviving specimens are bowls, either with moulded or carved and incised ornament, the latter being the most valued. The bowls were fired mouth downwards in the kiln, and the unglazed rim is usually bound by a copper or silver band. The glaze on the exterior is inclined to run into drops, which the Chinese call 'teardrops' and regard as a sign of genuineness.

Most of the finest Ting ware is ivory-white in colour, but there are literary references to black, red, and purple Ting. Of these, one or two specimens of black Ting exist, notably in the Percival David Foundation, London, and the Schiller Collection, Bristol, but the other two have not been identified. The

Chinese recognize two other varieties of Ting ware – *tu Ting* (earthen Ting) and *fên Ting* (flour Ting). Tu Ting has a yellowish glaze and a coarse body, and probably belongs to the Yüan dynasty. Fên Ting has only been conjecturally identified. Ting ware is often divided into northern and southern types, since manufacture was moved south about 1127 under pressure from invading Mongols. Of the other white wares of the period made in various places, perhaps the best known are those of Chü-lu Hsien. Although *Ying Ch'ing* ware has a faintly blue glaze instead of white it has some points of resemblance otherwise with Ting ware.

'Tithe pig'. Figure subject in porcelain and earthenware, also used as decoration of mugs and jugs accompanied by such rhymes as 'In Country Village lives a Vicar/Fond as all are of Tithes and Liquor'. A well-known Toby jug is inscribed 'I will have no child tho the X pig'. The collection of tithe in kind was abolished by the Tithe Commutation Act, 1836.

'T' and 'T°' marks. Probably for the modeller Thibaud (Bow, Bristol, Plymouth).

Toad mug. Surprise mug with a large toad inside, seen only as the vessel is emptied, and causing consternation because of popular superstitions connected with toad poison. Often inscribed 'Tho' malt and venom seem united, etc.'. Made at Sunderland, late eighteenth to the end of nineteenth centuries.

Tobi seiji ('buckwheat celadon'). Japanese name for brown-spotted Sung celadon wares of Lung Ch'üan.

Toby Fillpot. Nickname of a noted toper, Harry Elwes, who, through contemporary engravings, served as model for the original Toby jug.

Toby jugs. Are shaped like a man seated holding a mug of beer and a pipe, his tricorn hat often forming a detachable lid. Made by Ralph Wood and numerous Staffordshire and Yorkshire imitators, late eighteenth and nineteenth centuries. Many variants are recorded. Also produced at various U.S. factories.

Toft. An often-recurring Staffordshire name on slipware (late seventeenth and early eighteenth centuries), probably that of the potters (*see* Introduction, English pottery).

Ewer, Henri II ware, the design based on 16th-century patterns, probably by Charles Toft, exhibited in 1862. Victoria & Albert Museum

Torksey (Lincolnshire). W. Billingsley is supposed to have made porcelain here (1802–3). Some rare pieces of coarse material and primitive decoration (cup and saucer in the Victoria and Albert Museum) have been identified.

Tortoise. Representing the North from the Four Quadrants and Winter from the Four Seasons, the Tortoise is one of the Four Supernatural Creatures. Its shell was used for oracular purposes during the Shang dynasty and the markings thereon were probably the origin of the Eight Trigrams. In Japan the water-tortoise occurs on Arita porcelain in the style of Kakiemon. It trails a quantity of water-weed and this was misunderstood in Europe which led to it being called the 'flaming tortoise'. The Japanese call it *minogame* or 'raincoat tortoise' because the trailing weed was thought to resemble the Japanese straw raincoat.

Tortoiseshell glaze. Mottled glaze stained with manganese and cobalt used by Thomas Whieldon, of Fenton.

'Tortoiseshell ware'. A Staffordshire earthenware with mottled, usually brown, lead glaze (mid-eighteenth century).

Tou ts'ai (**'contrasting colour'**) **enamels.** Delicate, sparing designs in underglaze blue set off by transparent enamel colours, chiefly red, yellow, and green; their jewel-like quality was perfect under Ch'êng Hua (1465–87). Deceptive imitations and new-style wares were made under Yung Chêng and Ch'ien Lung; and again revived under Tao Kuang (1820–51).

Trailed slip. Slip applied by trailing it from a spouted or tubular vessel.

'Transitional' period. The years of the seventeenth century between the Ming period of Wan Li and the K'ang Hsi revival, when blue-and-white and Ming 'five-colour' style wares of some quality were made.

Turner, John (d. 1788). Potter of Stoke and Lane End (Staffordshire), made fine creamware and Wedgwood-type stonewares. His sons continued until 1803.

MARKS: TURNER and TURNER & CO., impressed.

Turquoise blue glazes. *See* Medium-temperature glazes.

Tyg. Beaker-shaped drinking vessel with from two to twelve handles.

Tzŭ Chou ware. The Tzŭ Chou neighbourhood (Chihli Province) has made stonewares from before the Sung dynasty until the present day. The characteristic body is hard and greyish white, covered with slips and glazes of creamy-white, brown, or black, and occasionally green colour, often ingeniously combined. The Sung wares are remarkable for bold, sensitive shapes – especially tall, swelling vases and jars with loop handles at the shoulder. Plates and dishes are rare. One type of decoration has leafy floral designs strongly incised or carved through the glaze to reveal another colour beneath. Another is bold painting in brown or black. Black painting under a turquoise glaze was popular about the fourteenth century. Red, green, and yellow enamel painting is sometimes of Sung date. Ming wares employed similar techniques, and elaborate landscape and figure subjects became more common; but there is a marked decline in their vitality.

Unaker. *See* China clay.

Underglaze blue. Well known from Chinese porcelain, particularly of the Ming period. David Köhler, assisted by Johann Georg Mehlhorn, both working under Böttger at Meissen, rediscovered the secret of applying cobalt blue beneath the glaze. Apart from its decorative qualities, their discovery made it possible at Meissen to introduce the well-known factory mark of two crossed swords in underglaze blue in 1724.

Underglaze colours. Until the nineteenth century only a few metallic oxides, notably cobalt, stand the high temperature of the glaze firing. Manganese purple was occasionally used.

Underglaze copper red. Legend has it that this colour was unattainable until a potter sacrificed his life by throwing himself into the furnace, whereupon the ware emerged shining and perfect. Unlike most legends, this one could well have some foundation in fact, since the combustion of a body would induce the reducing atmosphere essential for the development of this colour. To the Chinese underglaze copper red is 'sacrificial red' (*chih hung*), but this has nothing to do with the legend, and it probably refers to the use of the colour for religious vessels. It was first used during the Yüan dynasty, but specimens from this date are exceedingly rare. By the beginning of the fifteenth century it was being used to decorate stem-cups, often with three red fish or three peaches, of a type repeated in the eighteenth century. For reasons unknown copper red was replaced by iron-red during the reign of the Emperor Chia Ching, but it was being produced once more by the reign of K'ang Hsi, when some vases with a pale celadon ground and landscapes (*shan shui*) in underglaze blue and copper red in reserved panels are a remarkable technical achievement. This combination is rare at any period, since blue develops in an oxydizing atmosphere and red in a reducing atmosphere, so extremely close control over this aspect had to be exercised. It is usual to find that one colour or the other is more or less deficient.

Underglaze decoration. Decoration applied to biscuit pottery before the addition of glaze.

Venisons. Bowls 'made to fit into one another . . . in capacity ranging from a pint to a peck' (George Bourne), made at Frimley, Cove, and Farnborough, *c.* 1800–50.

'Vicar and Moses'. Popular satire on the drinking parson, showing a clergyman asleep in the pulpit with the parish clerk conducting the service. First made by Ralph Wood of Burslem, *c.* 1775.

Wall, Dr. *See* Worcester.

Wall pocket. Flower or spill vase shaped as a mask, fish, or cornucopia, made in Staffordshire salt glaze, and in Liverpool and Lambeth Delft, eighteenth century.

Walton, John, Burslem. Made small earthenware figures, often with *bocages* and painted in opaque enamels (*c.* 1820–30).

MARK: WALTON, impressed.

Wan Li period (1573–1620). Most of the Chia Ching styles were continued. Porcelain with enamels and underglaze-blue painting (the *wu ts'ai*) are especially characteristic. The numerous blue-and-white export wares are very variable in quality, often with poor blue and careless drawing. Pieces expressly intended for Europe become common.

Warburton. Family of potters of Hot Lane, Cobridge (Staffordshire), late eighteenth century. Made creamware.

MARK: WARBURTON, impressed (rare).

Wassail bowl. Two-handled loving cup passed clockwise around the company on convivial occasions.

'Wassailing'. Originally a rite to ensure fertility in cereals, fruit crops, and cattle, but later a term of abuse to describe Christmas revels.

Webber, Henry. A modeller employed by Josiah Wedgwood between the years 1782 and 1794, both at Etruria and at Rome with John Flaxman. He was engaged in the copying of the Portland Vase.

Webber received a gold medal from the Royal Academy in 1779. On that occasion he gave his address as 'Etruria', and his association with Wedgwood may be ante-dated perhaps from the accepted period given above.

'Wedgewood' mark. Used by W. Smith, Stockton-on-Tees, mid-nineteenth century.

'Wedgwood & Co' mark. *See* Ferrybridge.

Wedgwood, Josiah W. (1730–95). After apprenticeship with his brother and participation in a works at Stoke, entered into partnership with Thomas Whieldon in 1754. These associations made him master of the contemporary Staffordshire pottery techniques in most branches, and in 1759 he set up for himself, first at the Ivy House, Burslem, subsequently at the Brick House Works (1764). In 1768, in partnership with Thomas Bentley (1730–80), he built a new factory, called 'Etruria', for making ornamental wares. At these two works he produced: (1) green and yellow-glazed 'cauliflower', etc., wares; (2) creamware from about 1765, called 'Queen's ware',

Right Black basalt tea pot with enamelled decoration of flowers, Wedgwood, *c.* 1840–50

Black basalt urn, Wedgwood and Bentley, *c.* 1770. City Museum and Art Gallery, Hanley, Stoke-on-Trent

enamelled either in the factory or at an establishment in Chelsea, or sent in the white to various outside enamellers or to Liverpool for transfer printing (*see* Sadler); (3) 'marbled' wares; (4) 'pearlware', from about 1779; (5) unglazed stonewares: (*a*) black basaltes from about 1767, (*b*) red (*rosso antico*) often rose-engine-turned, from about 1763, (*c*) cane-coloured, (*d*) 'jasper' in various colours, from about 1774 and 'jasper dip' from about 1780.

Additions to the repertory after Wedgwood's death were 'silver'-lustred pottery (up to about 1810), pink lustreware, and bone porcelain (1812–16).

Wedgwood wares after *c.* 1770 were nearly always marked 'WEDGWOOD' impressed; 'WEDGWOOD & BENTLEY' or 'W. & B' occur on decorative pieces 1768–80.

(*See also* English porcelain.)

'Welsh' ware. Shallow meat dishes with feathered slip decoration, in form like a gardener's trug, commonly made in Staffordshire, Sunderland (Scott's 'Superior Fireproof') and Isleworth, under this name.

Whieldon, Thomas (1719–95). Potter of Fenton Low, Staffordshire, from 1740–80, and one of the foremost makers of his day, manufacturing all the known contemporary types of ware – 'agate' and 'marbled', 'tortoiseshell', 'Astbury', and 'Jackfield' wares; earthenware with dappled coloured glazes, unglazed red stoneware and salt-glazed stoneware, sometimes with 'scratch-blue' patterns.

(*See also* English pottery: eighteenth-century earthenware and stoneware; Wedgwood.)

'Whieldon' ware. Ware made in cream-coloured earthenware under a glaze splashed with metallic oxides to give tortoiseshell or mottled effects, made by Thomas Whieldon (1719–95) at Fenton, and others.

White porcelain. White porcelain was first made during the T'ang dynasty. To the Sung period belong the creamy-white Ting and bluish-tinged *Ying Ch'ing* wares, with their lively incised or impressed decoration. The Yüan *shu fu* ware marks the growing importance of the porcelain manufacture at Ching-tê Chên.

Despite the Ming predilection for colour, excellent white wares were still made, notably during the fifteenth century, with *an hua* (secret) decoration. During the Ch'ing dynasty white was the colour of court mourning and not greatly employed. Decorated with incised designs and carved or applied relief work, wares are often reminiscent of the Sung and Ming.

Much use was made of 'soft-paste' opaque glazes and painting in opaque white slip (*pâte-sur-pâte*), and small pieces were made with 'soft-paste' body.

The technique of pierced openwork (*ling lung*), as in the 'rice-grain' decoration, was employed with considerable ingenuity. Unglazed (biscuit) porcelain vases with landscapes or figures carved in relief are of Ch'ien Lung or later date. Wares with intentionally crackled glazes and the numerous *blanc-de-Chine* wares are discussed elsewhere.

Blue-printed oval dish with 'Willow pattern'. Printed mark of Bovey Tracey Pottery, Devon, mid-19th century

'Willow pattern'. A blue-printed pseudo-Chinese design, traditionally ascribed to T. Minton at Caughley, *c.* 1775–80. Many variants were made elsewhere.

Wincanton (delftware). A pottery was run by the Ireson family between at least 1737 and 1748. Blue and manganese painting only are known. A powdered-manganese ground is characteristic.

Wirksworth. Wirksworth porcelain, probably made about 1800, remains unidentified. New Hall wares are often mistakenly attributed to Wirksworth.

'W' mark. *See* Worcester.

'W(***)' mark. *See* Wood, Enoch.

Wood, Aaron (1717–85). The most renowned mould cutter for Staffordshire salt-glazed stoneware. (*See* Pew groups.)

Wood, Enoch (1759–1840). Son of Aaron Wood. Modeller and potter of Burslem, in partnership with Ralph Wood, 1783–90, and with J. Caldwell, 1790–1818 ('Wood & Caldwell'); thereafter the firm was 'Enoch Wood & Sons'. Most of the current types of stoneware, earthenware, and probably also porcelain, were made; notably earthenware figures with enamelled decoration.

MARKS: the various styles of the firm, and probably W(***) on porcelain, all impressed.

Wood, Ralph (1715–72) and his son Ralph Wood (1748–95). Potters of Burslem. The elder Wood made salt-glazed stoneware from at least 1749 until 1770. Later productions were figures, reliefs, and Toby jugs in lead-glazed earthenware with soft colours.

MARKS: R. Wood, RA. WOOD, BURSLEM impressed.

Worcester (soft-paste porcelain).

'Dr Wall' period (1751–83)

A factory was founded in 1751, and in 1752 incorporated the Bristol factory. The period 1751–83 is called after Dr John Wall (d. 1776), a leading partner, although, in fact, William Davis (d. 1783) managed the factory.

Soapstone was used in the porcelain, and is revealed on analysis by a high percentage of magnesia. The porcelain is greyish (greenish by transmitted light) with a thin, hard-looking, and 'close-fitting' glaze, which often shrinks away from the foot rim underneath. The potting is fine and 'crisp'. In the early period moulding, after silver models, was much used. The earliest painting, indistinguishable from the Bristol, is characterized by *chinoiseries* in polychrome enamels or underglaze blue. By about 1760 a distinctive Worcester style evolved, including European figure and landscape subjects, often in a soft purple monochrome; polychrome flower sprays and birds; fantastic Chinese landscapes in panels on a yellow ground; and pseudo-Chinese subjects painted in a thin linear style in black ('pencilled'). Transfer printing in overglaze black, lilac, and brownish red was much used from 1756/7 (*see* Hancock); underglaze-blue printing was occasionally practised from 1759.

The period about 1765–75 is characterized by the adaptation of Kakiemon and 'brocaded Imari' designs.

In 1769 Chelsea painters migrated to Worcester and elaborate decoration in Sèvres style dates from this time, with figure subjects and particularly exotic birds, in panels on coloured (blue, claret, apple-green, turquoise, and lavender) grounds, which were frequently diapered, the commonest pattern being an imbricated dark-blue ground ('scale blue').

Tea pot painted blue with *chinoiserie* scenes, Worcester, *c.* 1755

Fine, slightly dull gilding is characteristic, painted in lacy scrollwork designs. Much porcelain was decorated in the workshop of J. Giles.

Towards 1780 neoclassical designs (urns, festoons, etc.) and modified Sèvres Louis XVI styles were introduced. Landscapes and classical figure subjects within medallions were favoured. A bright-blue enamel like that of Chelsea–Derby was used, and gilding was frequently employed alone in floral, etc., designs.

Blue-and-white porcelain characterized by a deep indigo tone formed a large part of the output, whether painted or (from 1759) printed.

Figures are exceptionally rare (a Turk, a Gardener, and a Sportsman, with their companions, and a Nurse and a Child).

Imitations are known both in soft and hard paste, and in Staffordshire earthenware.

MARKS: 1 and 10 below (in red), 2–12 (in blue), probably workmen's marks, on Bristol or early Worcester (*c.* 1750–2); 13, in red, 14–16 and 18, in blue, painters' marks, *c.* 1752–70; 17, in blue, 19 in various colours (chiefly blue), much used to about 1795; 20, in blue, much used (1755–83). (*See also* 'Scratch cross'.)

'Flight', 'Flight & Barr', etc. (1783–)

In 1783 the Worcester factory was bought by

Far left Worcester 'Dr Wall' period yellow-ground cabbage-leaf mask jug (1751–83). Christie, Manson & Woods

Wrotham slipware jug by George Richardson, dated 1651. Christie, Manson & Woods

Thomas Flight. In 1792 Martin Barr was taken into partnership, and with the admission of other members of the family, the firm became successively 'Barr, Flight & Barr' (1807) and 'Flight, Barr and Barr' (1813–40).

The style of this period reflected the prevailing neoclassical taste, with areas of marbling and figures in panels, the best by James Pennington and Thomas Baxter. The gilding became brassy and unsympathetic.

MARKS (apart from names written in full): 'B' or 'DB', incised (to 1809); the initials of the partners, 'BFB' and 'FBB' under a crown, impressed.

Chamberlain's

In 1783 Robert Chamberlain left the Worcester factory and set up as a decorator. From about 1800, however, a greyish porcelain resembling Flight and Barr's was manufactured.

Chamberlain's work reflects the contemporary styles, but is notable for profuse gilding, and the production of vases, etc., in the most florid 'Japanese' taste.

MARKS: the name.

Grainger's

Thomas Grainger at first (1801) decorated porcelain obtained elsewhere, but latterly manufactured a fine white and translucent porcelain.

MARKS: the name.

'Wreathing'. *See* Bristol.

Wrotham (Kent). Slipware pottery (seventeenth and early eighteenth centuries). (*See* Introduction, English pottery.)

Wu ts'ai (five-colour) wares. This generally implies the characteristic Wan Li period wares, painted in underglaze blue and enamel colours (red, green, yellow, and purple). Some, however, date from Chia Ching; and they continue into K'ang Hsi's reign, when the *famille verte* was introduced.

Yang-yin. Symbol frequently used as part of porcelain decoration which represents the male-female principle in nature. It is circular in form, and resembles two tadpoles (one light, one dark) placed head to tail. It is often used in conjunction with the Eight Trigrams (*q.v.*).

Yellow. *See* Medium- and low-temperature glazes.

Yellow ware. Utility ware moulds (baking dishes, etc.) of cream or buff clays with transparent glaze ranging from pale straw colour to deep yellow; it became Rockingham (*q.v.*) when given a mottled brown-manganese colouring. Widely made *c.* 1830–1900.

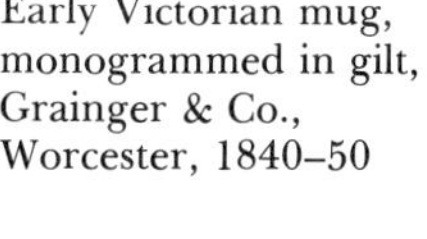

Early Victorian mug, monogrammed in gilt, Grainger & Co., Worcester, 1840–50

Yi-Hsing ware. Red or brown unglazed stoneware made at Yi-Hsing (Kiangsi Province) from the latter years of the Ming dynasty onwards. Among its products in the seventeenth century were small spouted wine-pots which became popular with the Tea Masters of Japan, and they were also included with shipments of tea to the West as a convenient way of making the new drink, instead of making and storing large quantities to be reheated as required, as was at first the custom. These red ware teapots were equally popular in Europe, and they were copied by Arij de Milde in Holland, Dwight and the Elers brothers in England, and Böttger at Meissen. There is little definite information about the history of the Yi-Hsing kilns.

The colour of the stoneware ranges from red, through buff, to brown, and there is sometimes more than one colour present in a single piece. Plain, almost undecorated, objects of simple form are among the best, but highly modelled objects based on natural forms, like the 'Buddha's hand' citron, are also to be found, and forms based on the bamboo are common. Incised inscriptions are fairly common, and calligraphy is sometimes the only decoration.

The kilns are still working, and even imprecise dating is usually difficult. The best criterion of judgment is quality.

Ying Ch'ing wares. *Ying Ch'ing* is a Chinese dealers' term which means 'shadowy blue'. It is a thin, translucent porcelain which burns to a reddish colour where unglazed. The glaze is a faint blue in colour, the blue being deepest where the glaze is thickest. Like Ting-ware bowls, those of the *Ying Ch'ing* variety were fired mouth downwards, and the unglazed rim is usually bound by a copper band. Decoration is incised, moulded, and combed, as in the case of Ting wares, and, to some extent, Northern celadon, to both of which *Ying Ch'ing* bears a resemblance in certain particulars, especially decoration. The greater number of surviving specimens are bowls, ewers, and vases. Covered boxes are much rarer. The type appears to have been made at several places from the T'ang dynasty onwards, including Korea, and it has survived in relatively large quantities, although forgeries undoubtedly exist.

Yorkshire. Trailed and marbled slipwares were made at Howcans, Swill Hill, Burton-in-Lonsdale, Midhope (eighteenth century onwards). (*See also* Leeds, Don Pottery, Castleford, Ferrybridge.)

Yüeh ware. Celadon ware with grey porcellaneous body and thin, pale, greyish-green, or buff glaze, made in Chekiang Province from about the third to eleventh centuries. Early examples often borrowed forms and moulded decoration from bronze work. Later pieces may be delicately potted, with lobed sides and delicately incised designs.

Zaffer. Cobalt oxide in powder form, from which was made smalt (a powdered blue glass), the blue colouring used by potters. Bonnin & Morris in January 1771 wanted 'a quantity of Zaffre' for their blue-painted porcelains. The potter John Bell wrote to his brother Samuel in 1848 that 'graffree is calcined cobalt or fly stone which is the same thing', warning him that this 'coulering matter is rank poison'.

L'Amant Surpris

PRINTS

Far right Florida, ritual with trophies from defeated enemies, engraving by Theodore de Bry after John White. Bodleian Library

The collecting of prints is one of the oldest pastimes of amateur and connoisseur alike. The reasons are not far to seek. It is one of the most rewarding: there can be few fields of collecting where an ever-widening knowledge can yield treasures acquired for an ever-diminishing outlay; prints can be easily stored, and the choicest can adorn the walls. And then there is the variety, both in media and kind; lovers of prints can never tire of the incisiveness of a fine proof etching or engraving, where the ink has a deeply satisfying richness and clarity. A collector of prints usually knows exactly what he is looking for; and when he has acquired an impression of a long-sought print the pride of possession gives way to a desire to obtain a yet finer and rarer impression. It must never be forgotten that many of the greatest masters of European painting regarded the print as a worthy medium for their genius.

There is yet another variety, ranging from Japanese colour prints to American silhouettes, the etchings of Rembrandt to English mezzotints. The field is so inexhaustible that the collector of prints can decide for himself whether to specialize or to sample all the delights in every sphere.

American

Engravings and Woodcuts

For the collector, American prints in the wider sense of the word begin with the views of the second half of the sixteenth century, engraved and published in Europe from 1590 onwards; while in the narrower sense they are restricted to prints produced in America, beginning in the middle of the seventeenth century. John Foster of Boston illustrated the books he printed with woodcuts which are the first American prints to which a maker's name can be attached; they hardly merit the word artistic. However, his name stands out in the anonymity of seventeenth-century American engravings, surrounded, as it were, by a number of crude productions by unknown craftsmen who were most likely printers or silversmiths working with simple tools and having little or no training.

Theodore de Bry, a Flemish engraver and copperplate publisher who resided in Frankfurt from 1588 until his death in 1598, engraved for his collection of *Great Voyages* the first views and pictorial accounts of the North American mainland with its native inhabitants, their tribal customs, their villages and the flora and fauna of the newly discovered country. Some of the engravings were made after the paintings by Jacques Le Moyne de Morgue, the French explorer who had journeyed to Florida with

Left L'Amant Surpris, mezzotint by Charles-Melchior Descourtis after F. J. Schall, late 18th century. British Museum

the Huguenots under René de Laudonnière in 1564. Twenty years later Le Moyne wrote a narrative of his explorations and illustrated his account, entitled *Brevis Narratio*, with forty-three sketches which de Bry engraved and published in 1591. A year earlier de Bry had engraved the drawings by John White, the artist who had accompanied Sir Walter Raleigh on his unsuccessful expedition to Virginia in 1585, and a second time as 'Governor of the Colonie' in 1587. Of the seventy-five watercolours by John White – the 'first' English watercolours – de Bry engraved twenty-three to illustrate Thomas Hariot's account, *A Briefe and True Report of the New Found Land of Virginia*, for his Virginia volume of the *Great Voyages*, and later two others for the work on Florida. The twenty-three watercolours by John White are now preserved in the British Museum, while of Jacques Le Moyne's small paintings only one is known to exist, in the possession of an American collector; the others are presumed lost. De Bry's collection of *Great Voyages* was issued in a number of editions and translations. Some of the later publications based their illustrations on those which appeared in de Bry's work, but, in addition to these, other travel books written by European explorers and travellers were illustrated with new pictorial material. In Sir Francis Drake's *Expeditio* of 1588 appears the first view of a town within today's limits of the United States, the town of St Augustine in Florida; while the earliest known engraved view of New York, the so-called Hartger's view, was issued with the small book entitled *Beschrijvinghe van Virginia, Nieuw Nederlandt, Nieuw Engelandt* ... published in Amsterdam in 1651. John Ogilby's *America* (London, 1671) contains views of a number of ports in this hemisphere, and in Father Louis Hennepin's *New Discovery of a Vast Country* (London, 1698) there is possibly the earliest view of Niagara Falls. Not only do the early views appear in books, but also as insets on handsome maps like the important maps of the Visscher series published in the middle of the seventeenth century.

Parallel, although on a very different level artistically, was the production of illustrated books in colonial America. The crudity of the early cuts, either wood or type-metal, is more than made up for by their historical importance in the development of the American graphic arts. Their naïve charm somewhat compensates for their lack of artistic quality. It is to John Foster of Boston, who established his printing shop in 1675, that the credit goes for being the first American-born 'artist' to have made engravings in this country. His woodcut portrait of Richard Mather, the Massachusetts clergyman (1670), is known in only five impressions. Almost as rare are his other woodcuts, a seal for the Massachusetts Bay Colony in 1675 and a map of New England which appeared in William Hubbard's *Narrative of the Troubles with the Indians* (1677).

It was not until the beginning of the eighteenth century that single prints were published, apart from book illustration. Again the earliest were published in Europe, although drawn in America and advertised for sale in the colonial newspapers. William Burgis was the first to supply large single views of American cities. Very few copies of these views, however, are known to exist, either in first states or in later, second, states, but they can be studied in public collections which are fortunate enough to own them. William Burgis's panoramic views of New York (1719) and Boston (1722) were engraved by John Harris of London and published there, copied and plagiarized by later engravers, no doubt to satisfy the great demand of a curious public eager to know what the new country looked like. In studying these early views we find that some are fairly accurate renderings, others slightly fictitious, while still others, like the colourful *vues d'optique*, show a remarkable fantasy and lack of knowledge of conditions in a pioneering country. These handcoloured – amusing rather than puzzling – peepshow prints, with reversed lettering in the top margin, and the text often in both German and French, were published in the second half of the eighteenth century in Augsburg and Paris to be used in mirrored boxes and carried around by itinerant showmen.

Not more than about a dozen engravers were working in colonial America in the eighteenth century, and these were primarily engaged in illustrating books, including several Bibles and periodicals. It was from Europe that the colonists received their large prints to be hung on the walls of their homes or, in some few cases, kept in portfolios.

The post-Revolutionary period brought a radical change in the conditions in the field of print making in this country. Professionally trained painters and engravers arrived in increasing numbers from England and Scotland and settled in Boston, New York, or Philadelphia, where publishers were ready to employ them. Among these was John Hill. The English artists brought with them the knowledge and techniques of the highly developed art of watercolouring, which had such a vogue in eighteenth-century England, while the engravers were equipped to handle the aquatint process, so well suited to reproduce the watercolours. The beginning of the nineteenth century saw an increased production in the numbers of town and local views and, because of their artistic and picturesque quality, these views are among the most attractive to today's collector. The aquatints were coloured, either by hand or printed from several plates, limiting the use of the process usually to topographical work – to the picturesque rather than mere landscape. Very few attempts were made to use this technique for portraits, which are more suitably engraved in either stipple or mezzotint.

The growing periodical literature gave increasing opportunity for employment to engravers. This had

Newburgh, coloured aquatint from the *Hudson River Portfolio* by John Hill after W. G. Wall. The Old Print Shop, New York

Norfolk from Gosport, Virginia, aquatint by John Hill after Joshua Shaw, 1821. New York Public Library

already been done by American editions of British encyclopedias published in Philadelphia, although there was little chance given for artistic development and imagination. Banknote engraving was another field for many excellent engravers, who had to meet the high standards of workmanship required for such meticulous work. The first half of the nineteenth century has been called the 'Golden Age of Engraving', brought to a close by the activities of a number of art societies which sponsored annual distribution of large engravings to their membership, the most prominent being the Apollo Association, later called the American Art Union, 1839–51. Unfortunately the invention of a number of mechanical ruling devices for use in engraving began to spoil the artistic quality of many of the prints produced towards the middle of the century, which deteriorated to mere hack work. Finally, the photomechanical processes liberated the engravers from mere reproductive work and gave the field of print making a new lease of life.

VIEWS

The earliest views of American towns appeared in books published in Europe, but they can often be found as separates, either with or without the accompanying text. Single prints of American scenery were not published till the early eighteenth century, and among the earliest are the very rare Burgis views of New York (1719) and Boston (1722), the Boston Lighthouse and the view of the New Dutch Church in New York, dedicated to Governor Rip van Dam. Of equal importance are the panoramic views of Charleston, South Carolina, by B. Roberts (1739) and the Scull-Heap view of Philadelphia (1754). The Carwitham views of Boston, New York, and Philadelphia, published for Carington Bowles of London some time after 1764, are based chiefly on earlier views, although with a character of their own. These coloured line engravings, signed by John Carwitham, are among the most attractive, although very scarce; later states with alterations exist: however, they are not as valuable.

In 1734 the earliest view of Savannah was engraved by Pierre Fourdrinier after a drawing by Peter Gordon, a bird's-eye view, showing the newly settled town with its straight streets and large squares for markets amidst a wilderness. The view of Philadelphia depicting the House of Employment, Alms House, and Pennsylvania Hospital, about 1767, was engraved by John Hulett after a drawing by Nicholas Garrison, and is another of the important early views of an American city.

One of the handsomest of large collections of topographical prints of North America and the West Indies in the middle of the eighteenth century is the *Scenographia Americana*. This collection, which was published in London in 1768, contains twenty-eight engraved plates. In some cases it has been augmented to include as many as seventy-four, reproducing the drawings made by British army and navy officers. Matching in importance the *Scenographia Americana* is another set of views, the *Atlantic Neptune*, a collection of as many as 275 maps, charts, and views brought together for the British Admiralty by J. F. W. Des Barres during the years 1763–84. This publication includes aquatinted views of American ports.

Following the Revolution a number of very beautiful views were executed by newcomers to America, some using the relatively new aquatint process for reproducing watercolours. Saint-Mémin, in addition to his prolific output of profile portraits, made two charming etchings of New York in 1796. The well-known London aquatinter Francis Jukes reproduced four watercolours by Alexander Robertson, the Scottish artist who had come to New York around 1794 and opened the Columbian Drawing Academy together with his brother Archibald. Included in this set of four views are *New York from Hobuck Ferry* and *Mount Vernon* in 1799.

At the turn of the century William and Thomas Birch, father and son, drew, engraved, and published a set of twenty-eight line engravings entitled:

Second Street North from Market Street to Christ Church, Philadelphia, line engraving by William and Thomas Birch, from the series *The City of Philadelphia as it appeared in 1800*

Line engravings by William and Thomas Birch, from the series *The City of Philadelphia as it appeared in 1800*: *Top The House intended for the President of the United States, in Ninth Street, Philadelphia. Above Arch Street Ferry, Philadelphia*

The City of Philadelphia as it appeared in 1800. The dates on individual plates range from 1798 to 1800. A later edition was published by Birch in 1806 and re-issued by Desilver in 1841. The aquatints by J. Cartwright in the Atkins and Nightingale series of American views are all very rare. They were made after the paintings by George Beck of Philadelphia and published in London between 1800 and 1810. A decade later W. G. Wall executed his watercolours for the justly famous *Hudson River Portfolio*, a series of twenty aquatinted views engraved by John Hill and published by Henry J. Megarey in New York about 1825. Together with William J. Bennett's nineteen views of American cities published in the 1830s, they make up the finest and most desirable group of coloured aquatints in America. In a different style altogether are two other publications containing views of the city of New York. These are the small, well-executed engravings of the Bourne *Views of New York City* (1831) and the Peabody *Views of New York and Environs* (1831–4). Both series contain double plates with accompanying text and were issued in parts.

Among the last aquatinters in this country who engraved views of American scenery were Robert Havell, Jr, who had come to New York after completing the engravings of Audubon's *Birds of America* in London. Havell made two panoramic views of New York, one from the North River (1840), the other from the East River (1844); a view of Hartford, Connecticut, and a view of Niagara Falls. Another was Henry Papprill, who engraved the Catherwood view of *New York from Governor's Island* in 1846, and in 1849 his bird's-eye view of New York from the steeple of St Paul's Church, after a drawing by John W. Hill, published by Henry J. Megarey. Modern impressions, or re-strikes, exist of many of the listed views, and in some cases the original copperplates have been preserved and are owned by public institutions. It is, therefore, advisable for collectors to study the literature on these prints before buying any of them. Sidney L. Smith re-engraved a number of rare American views, but these are all clearly signed and identified; in themselves they are very attractive and in some instances also rare.

WOODCUTS AND WOOD ENGRAVINGS

Mention may be made of the extremely rare, crude, anonymous German woodcut of about 1505 which depicts the Indians of the northern shores of South America and is 'the first pictorial representation of any part of the mainland of the western hemisphere'. This cut is known in two states and shows the Indians with fearful evidence of cannibalistic habits.

It was not until the middle of the seventeenth century that woodcuts were first printed in colonial America by John Foster of Boston. Not till the eighteenth century, and well into the middle of it, did the artistic quality of the woodcuts improve, decorating pages of farmers' almanacs and broadsides describing cruel deeds and crimes or advertising travelling entertainers. Crude as they are, these cuts have a quaint charm and may attract the collectors of folk art as well as the social historian. James Franklin of Boston and his younger brother Benjamin in Philadelphia are both credited with having made some woodcuts and metalcuts in their printing shops. The Revolution inspired broadsides in the nature of political caricatures, while the post-Revolutionary period created pictorial evidence of the growing national strength and geographical expansion. At the turn of the century Alexander Anderson, a New Yorker, introduced to this country Thomas Bewick's white-line technique of cutting the design on the end grain of the woodblock instead of on the plank. In this manner Anderson executed nearly 10,000 cuts during his lifetime, for books, periodicals, and commercial ephemera; even if not of great artistic quality, they reflect a certain high standard of craftsman-

Top Buffalo from Lake Erie, aquatint by William J. Bennett after a sketch by J. W. Hill, 1836. One of the series *Views of American Cities.* The Old Print Shop, New York

Above City of Washington from Beyond the Navy Yard, aquatint by William J. Bennett after George Cooke, 1833. New York Public Library

Top right The Country Store, wood engraving by Alexander Anderson. New York Public Library

ship. Among the few other known wood engravers of the first half of the nineteenth century is Abel Bowen, who is known for his large historical woodcut in three sections, *View of Colonel Johnson's Engagement near the Moravian Town*, 5 October 1812, as well as for some cuts for book illustration. Other wood engravers active in the second quarter of the century, supplying illustrations for books and magazines, were Alfred A. Lansing, John H. Hall, Abraham J. Mason, Joseph Alexander Adams, and Benson J. Lossing.

HISTORICAL SUBJECTS

The first historical print produced in America was Samuel Blodget's *Battle of Lake George*, 8 September 1755, which was published in Boston, 22 December of that year. An English copy was published a year later in London, and like the American edition was accompanied by a pamphlet describing this battle of the French and Indian war. Henry Dawkins's *Paxton Exhibition* in Philadelphia in 1764 records a historical event in which Benjamin Franklin played an important part. It is also the earliest known street view of this city. Paul Revere's engravings of the British ships landing their troops in Boston Harbour, 1768, and his print of the 'Bloody Massacre' in Boston on 5 March 1770, are foundation stones of American historical engraving. The original copperplate of Revere's *Boston Massacre* is still preserved in the office of the State Treasurer of Massachusetts.

During the Revolution a set of four crude, but highly important historical prints were engraved by Amos Doolittle, showing the *Battles of Lexington and Concord* in 1775 after paintings by Ralph Earl. Doolittle also engraved a view of the façade of Federal Hall in New York City after a drawing by Peter Lacour, depicting George Washington's first inauguration in 1789 on its balcony. Another print of the Revolutionary period was made by Bernard Romans, whose *Exact View of the Late Battle of Charlestown* (Bunker Hill), 1775, was re-engraved by Robert Aitkin on a reduced scale and published in the latter's *Pennsylvania Magazine* for September 1775 (issued probably in October of that year) and called a *Correct View* ... Robert Edge Pine's painting of *Congress Voting Independence* exists in an unfinished line and stipple engraving by Edward Savage, *c.* 1794.

The war of 1812 produced the following prints: *The Capture of the City of Washington by the British Forces*, 24 August 1814, a line engraving by an unknown engraver published by John Ryland; John Bower's rather crude prints of the *Battle of Patapsco Neck*, 12 September 1814 and the *Bombardment of Fort McHenry near Baltimore*, on 13 September 1814; a pair of aquatints by Robert Havell, Sr, of the *Attack on Fort Oswego, Lake Ontario*, 6 May 1814 and *Storming of Fort Oswego*, published in 1815; *The Battle of New Orleans*, 1815, *and Death of Major General Packenham*, a line engraving by Joseph Yeager of Philadelphia. Historical prints of the Mexican War were executed almost entirely in lithography.

COLLEGE VIEWS

Among the earliest college views is the Burgis view of Harvard, *Prospect of the Colledges in Cambridge in New England*, in 1726; another early Harvard view was engraved by Paul Revere in 1768. *William and Mary, c.* 1740, the second oldest college view in America, was engraved after a drawing possibly made by the colonial botanist John Bartram. The earliest view of Princeton appears in the New American Magazine

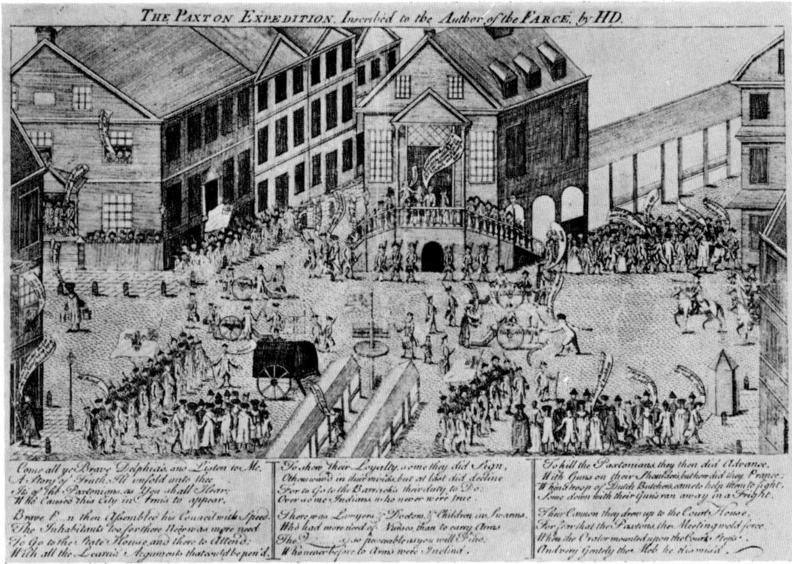

Above The Paxton Expedition, engraving by Henry Dawkins, 1764. I. N. Phelps Stokes Collection, New York Public Library

for 1760 entitled *Auld Nassovica*, while the second oldest view of this college was engraved by Henry Dawkins (*North-West Prospect of Nassau-Hall*), and was published as a frontispiece to *An Account of the College of New Jersey* (Woolbridge, New Jersey, 1764). Yale College is first shown in an engraving by Thomas Johnston from a drawing by John Greenwood and published by James Buck, *c.* 1749. King's College (Columbia) is shown prominently in a view of New York from the collection of the *Scenographia Americana* (1768). One of the last college views in the eighteenth century appeared in the *Massachusetts Magazine* for February 1793; this is a view of Dartmouth College in New Hampshire. Beginning with the nineteenth century, the number of college views increases rapidly. Alvan Fisher drew a 'North East View' of Harvard as well as a 'South View', which were engraved and published in 1823. The University of Virginia appears as an inset on a map of the state published in 1825 and engraved by B. Tanner. J. H. Hinton, in his *History and Topography of the United States* (1830–1), included views of Amherst College, Massachusetts, and Kenyon College, Ohio. William Henry Bartlett drew a view of Yale College in 1839 which was engraved and issued in N. P. Willis's *American Scenery* (1840). J. W. Barber's view of *New Haven Green with Buildings of Yale College* is much sought after by collectors, as is the view of Dartmouth College by Christian Meadows, 1851.

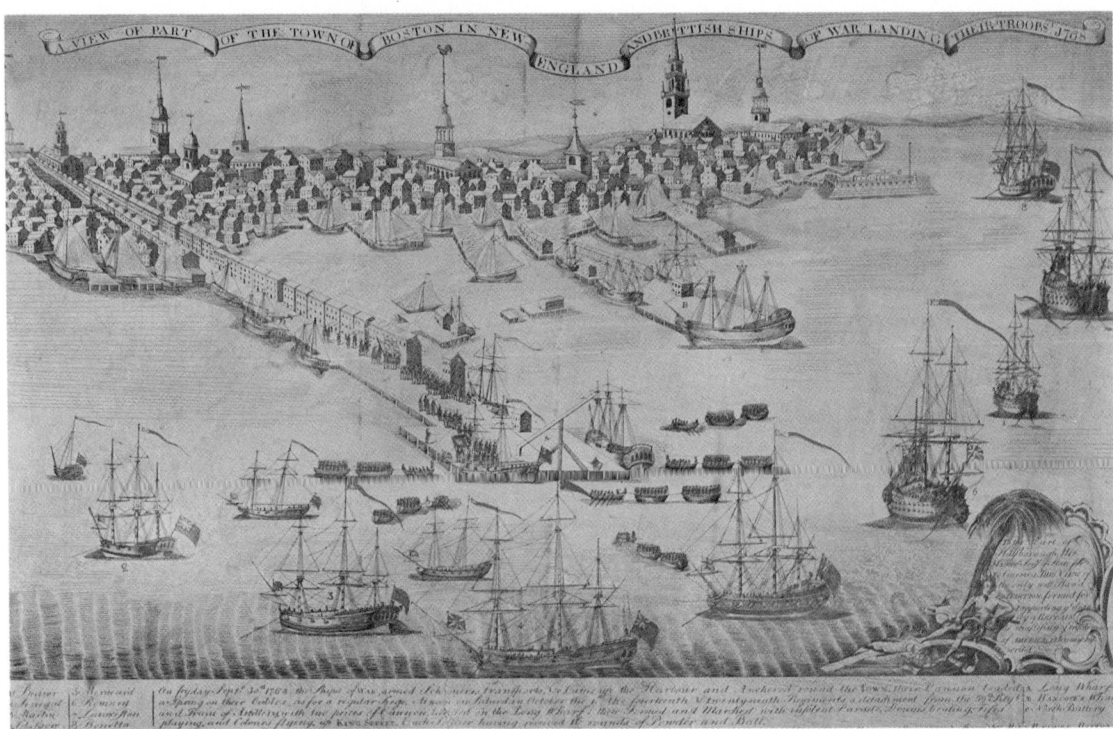

Right British ships landing their troops in Boston Harbour, etching by Paul Revere, 1768

Below View of the Battle of Concord, Massachusetts, 1775, by Amos Doolittle, line engraving after Ralph Earl. New York Public Library

PORTRAITS

From among the great number of portraits executed in America in the period under discussion a few may be mentioned here either for their historical importance or for their artistic merit. The first woodcut portrait produced in America was made by John Foster, the Boston printer, in 1670. This is the portrait of Richard Mather, the New England clergyman and grandfather of Cotton Mather, whose por-

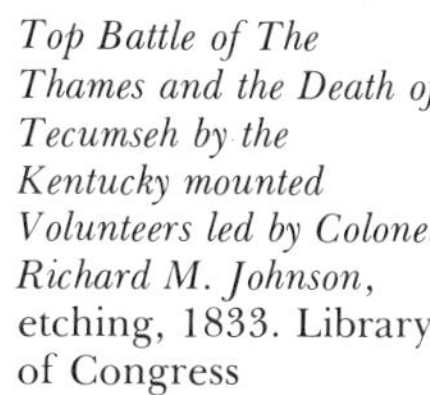

Top Battle of The Thames and the Death of Tecumseh by the Kentucky mounted Volunteers led by Colonel Richard M. Johnson, etching, 1833. Library of Congress

Above A view of the President's House in the City of Washington after the Conflagration of 24th August 1814, aquatint by W. Strickland. Library of Congress

trait was engraved in mezzotint by Peter Pelham, a London-trained engraver who had come to America and executed a series of mezzotint portraits of clergymen about 1727. Paul Revere engraved the portraits of Samuel Adams, Benjamin Church, John Hancock, Jonathan Mayhew, and others. Amos Doolittle, the engraver of four important battle scenes of the Revolution, also engraved a number of small portraits. Late in the eighteenth century Charles Willson Peale made a few and very rare mezzotint portraits of Benjamin Franklin, Lafayette, William Pitt, and George and Martha Washington. John Norman is credited with having made the first engraved portrait of George Washington in 1779 as well as a series of other historical portraits. H. Houston of Philadelphia did some meritorious portrait engravings in stipple, as did Edward Savage, a native American engraver who had studied in London. His important portraits are those of John Adams, Benjamin Franklin, and George Washington. Cornelius

Top Portrait of the Rev. Jonathan Mayhew, line engraving by Paul Revere. New York Public Library

Above Portrait of John Jay, engraving by Cornelius Tiebout after Gilbert Stuart, 1795. New York Public Library

Tiebout is called the first American-born engraver of any artistic talent. He engraved portraits of George Washington, John Jay after Gilbert Stuart, and the generals of the American Revolution. Charles B. J. Févret de Saint-Mémin, a French nobleman who, while earning his living in New York and Philadelphia by making profile crayon drawings with the aid of the *physionotrace* and reducing them with a pantograph on to the copperplate which he then etched and aquatinted, executed about 800 portraits of distinguished American ladies and gentlemen. Another engraver who used the aquatint process for portrait work was William Strickland. David Edwin was an excellent and prolific engraver of stipple portraits and has been called 'the American Bartolozzi' by Stauffer. James Barton Longacre executed some very fine stipple portraits, among them one of Andrew Jackson after a painting by Thomas Sully (1820). Longacre is also responsible for many of the plates in the *National Portrait Gallery* (1834–9), in four volumes, which he published together with the painter James Herring. Asher Brown Durand, before becoming known as the father of American landscape painting, was a very fine engraver of portraits in line. J. F. E. Prud'homme did fine portrait work in stipple, while John Rubens used both stipple and mezzotint for his many portrait engravings.

No other person in America has been so much portrayed as George Washington. Hart, in his catalogue of the engraved portraits of George Washington, lists 880 entries with several states adding up to a number close to 1,500. The largest number of these are engravings after the paintings by Gilbert Stuart.

City of Cleveland from Reservoir Walk in 1856. Western Reserve Historical Society

American Lithographs

Lithography began to be used in the United States soon after the painter Bass Otis did two drawings on stone in 1819–20. Otis apparently had no idea of the possibilities of lithography, but they were soon realized and utilized. Only about seven years later Rembrandt Peale, in his copy of his own painted portrait of Washington, showed real understanding of what could be done by this new process.

That the new process had importance through possible service to business appeared from the start. What concerns us here is that this exploitation for profit has provided a very large storehouse of documentary material. And historical documentation is an important function of antiques.

It is an impressive, many-sided picture of American life and its rural and urban setting that is presented in this mass of publications serving popular interest and demand.

Portraits there are in large number, including many good ones. Among those who signed them were Henry Inman, Albert Newsam, Charles Fenderich, F. D'Avignon (who did a series of drawings in delicate, silvery grey, after daguerreotypes by Brady), L. Grozelier, C. G. Crehen (portrait of the painter W. S. Mount) and Fabronius. There are also the numerous portraits of North American Indians by J. O. Lewis, King, and Catlin.

Views of natural scenery were done by Charles Gildemeister, E. Whitefield, Mrs Frances F. Palmer (who drew a number of country scenes for Currier & Ives), Charles Parsons, and others. Pictures of rural life were offered by various artists, among them Louis Maurer (his *Preparing for Market*, 1856, is full of detail in picturing farmyard appearance, wagon construction, harness). In these the life of the gentleman farmer is often accentuated, and they present also an interesting record of suburban architecture.

City views were numerous, naturally, giving expression to local pride in urban development. Avoiding a catalogue, here are a few names: Peter Maverick, A. J. Davis the architect, C. W. Burton, and Max Rosenthal. Interest in the city and its life brought also pictures of city types, including such valuable items as the series on New York's volunteer firemen, by Louis Maurer. Other human figures thus preserved are the 'Bowery B'hoy', and people skating on ponds in parks and elsewhere, with a show of changing fashions in dress. Dress brings to mind the uniforms of military companies, of which there is a notable array in drawings such as those by A. Hoffy and F. J. Fritsch. (The latter's large prints of the 38th Regiment, Jefferson Guards, 1843, and the First Division, 1844, have been collected as highly interesting New York views). To this record of military dress are to be added the many illustrated sheet-music covers of marches dedicated to various military companies, many of them grenadier guards wearing the French high bearskin shako. These covers usually show uniformed members of the company in question, and they give a valuable record of militia uniforms that is scattered and apparently cannot be found in any collected form.

Transportation is another speciality dealt with in lithographs. Railway prints are numerous; Gen. Wm. Barclay Parsons brought together a considerable number of them. Sailing vessels were portrayed by Charles Parsons and others in good number.

Sports were also much pictured. Hunting and fishing scenes, ably done by A. F. Tait and Louis Maurer, bear the stamp of actual experience and interest and add their part to the colourful panorama of our social life. Horse races were naturally a popular subject. Pictures of trotting races and trotters show changes in the form of vehicle used. The numerous portraits of individual horses, running and trotting, included one of Hambletonian, the famous sire of trotting horses, shown with his

Top Buffalo Hunt, Chase, drawing and lithograph by George Catlin

Above Wall Street East from and including Broadway, Winter 1833–4, lithograph by Peter Maverick after Hugh Reinagle. New York Historical Society

owner at Chester, New York.

There was also the separately published political caricatures of obvious importance to the historian. Large collections of these may be seen in the New York Historical Society, the American Antiquarian Society, Worcester, the New York Public Library, the Library of Congress, and other institutions.

Theatre posters illustrate still another phase of American social life. Designed by Matt Morgan, H. A. Ogden and H. F. Farny, among others, and printed by various firms such as the Strobridge Lithographic Co., many of these productions are so large as to make preservation a problem. However, they have been collected, and towards the end of the nineteenth century there came a vogue, almost a craze, which resulted in numerous articles and books, exhibitions, and much collecting activity. Advertising art also made use of lithography, and examples of this are finding their way into collections of industrial subjects. Still other specialities come to mind, for instance Christmas cards, for the designing

Top Passed Midshipman, U.S. Navy, drawn on stone by A. Hoffy, lithograph by P. S. Duval. The Old Print Shop, New York

Above Death of General Andrew Jackson, lithograph by N. Currier, 1845. American Museum in Britain

New York Crystal Palace, For the Exhibition of Industry of all Nations, lithograph by N. Currier after Frances Palmer, 1853. New York Public Library

of which Louis Prang enlisted the services of well-known artists.

All this pictorial material evidently had its appeal, to which the public made a response that is reflected in the productiveness of the many lithographic printing firms. The name of Currier & Ives is apt to come first and most easily to mind, but there were plenty of others competing with them.

In the enormous mass of material here hinted at there is very much of great interest and value to collectors and historians, and in fact to anyone interested in the development of American social and political life. It is to be noted also that from the 1840s and 1850s drawings of similar subjects and interest, engraved on wood, were appearing in illustrated weeklies and comic papers.

Quite naturally he who collects as well as he who writes history should carefully examine this output of the nineteenth century before choosing. For instance, the sentimental bits relating to domestic life have no great interest save in showing what the public bought. The Civil War battle scenes put out by Currier & Ives are quite negligible. But when the same firm issued pictures based on actual contact of the artist with the scene depicted, as in the pictures of New York City's volunteer firemen, or hunting subjects, or country life, we were given valuable pictorial illustration of social history.

Here, then, is a rich field to delve into. Critical discrimination in choice will still leave a full storehouse, a crowded one, of pleasure and profit.

American Marine Prints

Naval pictorial art emerged in America as soon as national pride demanded it. It was not until the country became a nation on its own, with a navy of its own, that pictures of naval and maritime accomplishments were created. American primitive art had started in colonial days, but its subjects were those close to the hearts of the people and their everyday life.

The task of recording pictorially the history of the country from its colonial days until after its independence from England fell upon artists and engravers of foreign lands. There was a dearth of material produced even in the mother country.

THE REVOLUTIONARY WAR

It was not until the outbreak of the Revolutionary War that an American warship sailed the seas, and it was later before there appeared an American picture

The 'Phoenix' and the 'Rose' Engaged by the Enemy's Fire Ships and Galleys on the 16 August 1776, engraving by J. F. W. Des Barres after Dominic Serres, 1778. National Maritime Museum

of an American ship. The people were too busy fighting the war to have time to paint or engrave its events. It fell upon well-established British and French artists and engravers to be the 'combat artists' of the American Revolution.

Joseph F. W. Des Barres of London published *The Atlantic Neptune* in 1777, a book of charts 'for the use of the Royal Navy of Great Britain'. Among the charts appeared sketches of landfalls and port views. One of the most handsome of these aquatints shows *The 'Phoenix' and the 'Rose' Engaged by the Enemy's Fire Ships and Galleys on the 16 August, 1776*. This naval action was the first important one of the American Revolution, and the print the first view of the war to be published.

Naval historians consider the Battle of Lake Champlain in October 1776, early in the war, to rank in importance with Admiral De Grasse's fleet action off Chesapeake Bay at the war's end. Although lost by the Americans, the Lake Champlain action was important because it delayed the advance of British troops until winter set in. Contemporary engravings published in London by Robert Sayre and John Bennett record this battle.

Naturally enough these prints published in England generally record British victories. Other examples are two prints which appeared in *The Naval Chronicle* in 1814 showing the disembarkation of British troops on Long Island on 22 August 1776, and Sir George Collier's victory over a small Continental fleet in Penobscot Bay, 13 August 1779. A map, engraved by William Faden, London, 1778, is illuminated with drawings of warships which took part in the action off Mud Fort in the Delaware River on 22 October 1777. Lieutenant W. Elliott, Royal Navy, also produced an aquatint of this attack, an action not entirely favourable to the British.

Pictures of naval engagements of the Revolutionary War were few, indicative perhaps of the lack of importance which the British placed upon the war. There was one engagement, however, which is generously depicted, the battle between the *Bon Homme Richard* and the *Serapis*, off the coast of England on 23 September 1779. Although it was a victory for Captain John Paul Jones, it is also remembered with pride in England because the *Serapis*, although sunk, achieved its purpose of protecting a convoy of merchant ships, and because of the gallantry of the British commander, Captain Richard Pearson. British artists produced pictures of the battle, the most notable of which is the line engraving published by John Boydell after a painting by Richard Paton.

THE QUASI-WAR WITH FRANCE

It was not until the quasi-war with France, 1799–1801, that the first completely American prints appeared. Edward Savage, an American-born engraver of Philadelphia, brought out a pair of aquatints in 1799 depicting the action between the *Constellation* and the *Insurgent*, the principal engagement in this naval war.

THE WAR WITH TRIPOLI

Several naval subjects appeared at the time of the romantic war with Tripoli (1801–5). This war was the result of attacks by the Barbary pirates on American shipping in the Mediterranean, and in it the United States managed to convince the Barbary States that she was an established nation. There were incidents in the Tripolitan War which captured the imaginations of Americans interested in the fortunes of their young navy. Print makers were ready with depictions of Stephen Decatur's bold destruction of the captured frigate *Philadelphia*, and of the unfortunate explosion of the fireship *Intrepid* before she was able to destroy enemy ships in the harbour of Tripoli. The former is recorded in an aquatint by Francis Kearny, published in New York in 1808. An illustration of the *Intrepid* incident appears in *The Port Folio* in 1810. Charles Denoon drew interesting views of the loss to the Tripolitans of the *Philadelphia*, and Preble's bombardment of Tripoli.

THE WAR OF 1812

The war of 1812 was principally a naval war, and from the pages of its history emerge names of naval engagements which have been pointed to with pride by Americans ever since. Artists and print makers have not been the least among the naval historians to make these battles famous.

The city of Philadelphia was the centre of artists and engravers of naval pictures at the time of the war of 1812. Thomas Birch (1779–1851), who had taken up marine painting in 1807, was the artist of many well-known engagements of the war: the *Constitution* and the *Guerrière*, August 1812; the *Wasp* and the *Frolic*, October 1812; the *United States* and the *Macedonian*, October 1812; the Battle of Lake Erie, September 1813; the *Peacock* and the *Epervier*, April 1814; and the *Constitution* versus the *Cyane* and the *Levant*, February 1815; all American victories.

Engravers of these Birch views were Cornelius Ticbout, Francis Kearny, Denison Kimberly, Samuel Seymour, Benjamin Tanner, Alexander Lawson, William Strickland, P. S. Duval, and Abel Bowen, most of them of Philadelphia, and all of them well known in the world of print makers.

The battles named above were also painted by J. J. Barralet, Michèle Corné, Thomas Sully, Thomas Chambers, W. A. K. Martin, and George Thresher. Prints were published by Freeman and Pierce, William Kneass, J. R. Smith, Samuel Walker, William Smith, Joseph Delaplaine, H. Quig, J. Baillie, D. W. Kellogg and Cammeyer & Acock.

Other well-remembered American victories have

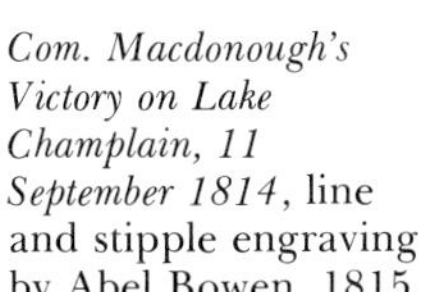

Com. Macdonough's Victory on Lake Champlain, 11 September 1814, line and stipple engraving by Abel Bowen, 1815

been recorded in prints and paintings, such as the engagement between the *Constitution* and the *Java*, December 1812; the *Hornet* and the *Peacock*, February 1813; the *General Pike* and the *Wolf*, September 1813; the *Enterprise* and the *Boxer*, September 1813; Macdonough's victory on Lake Champlain, September 1813; the bombardment of Fort McHenry, September 1814; and the battle of Lake Borgne, Louisiana, December 1814. Outstanding among the pictures of these battles is an engraving by Benjamin Tanner after a painting by Hugh Reinagle of Macdonough's victory; a lithograph by H. R. Robinson of the victory of the *Enterprise*, and an aquatint of the bombardment of Fort McHenry by J. Bower showing 'the bombs bursting in air', as seen on that occasion by the writer of the *Star Spangled Banner*, Francis Scott Key.

A number of naval prints originated in periodicals contemporary with the war of 1812. *The Naval Monument* was one of these. Most of the engravings are by Abel Bowen, W. Hoogland, W. B. Annin, and Wightman after originals by Michèle Corné. Works of Corné are also reproduced in *The Naval Temple*. Thomas Birch drew for another periodical, *The Port Folio*, and Samuel Seymour did the engraving. Printed later (1840) was the *United States Military Magazine*, which carried lithographs by J. Queen after J. Evans and Thomas Birch. This magazine specialized in pictures of uniforms. Portraits of naval officers are reproduced in the *Analectic Magazine* appearing in 1813.

THE WAR WITH ALGIERS

The fifth war fought by the U.S. Navy was brief and almost bloodless. Algiers attempted extraction of tribute money from American ships, as had her neighbour, Tripoli. She had a free hand in such practice until the war with England ended. In June 1815, however, squadrons under Decatur and Bainbridge appeared off Algiers, as the result of which threat the Dey released American prisoners and signed a treaty. This short chapter in our naval history is illustrated with several small prints, principally appearing in magazines of the day. One of the best shows *The U.S. Squadron, under the Command of Com. Decatur at anchor off the City of Algiers, June 30th, 1815*, published in New Haven by N. Jocelin and G. Munger.

PORTRAITS OF NAVAL SHIPS

A classification of naval picture, different from the 'naval action picture', is the ship 'portrait' which shows the likeness of a ship when not engaged in battle.

The best-known and most frequently painted ship of the U.S. Navy is the *Constitution*. She was one of a group of frigates to be built by the Congress when the infant republic first realized the need for a regular navy, and she remains afloat today, 160 years after her launching.

One of the earliest portraits of the *Constitution* is an engraving by Abel Bowen (1790–1850) of Boston, the publisher of *The Naval Monument*. The artist was William Lynn. The Senefelder Lithographic Company produced another portrait of 'Old Ironsides' about 1830 after a drawing by William Marsh, Jr, copied on stone by James Kidder. The same print appeared later under the name of William S. Pendleton, who took over the Senefelder presses after 1831. Other portraits of this famous ship are: lithographs by J. Baillie, three by P. S. Duval after J. Evans, 1840; engravings by J. Thackara; a drawing by O. E. Linton.

Just as there was a surge of shipbuilding activity a few years after the Revolutionary War which added famous frigates to the American Navy, so was the war of 1812 followed by the creation of great ships-of-the-line. Four of these, the *Washington*, *Independence*, *Franklin*, and *Columbus*, were built in the last years of the war. The names of later ones indicate the start of the practice of naming battleships after states. They were the *North Carolina*, launched in 1820; *Delaware*, 1820; *Ohio*, 1821; *Pennsylvania*, laid down in 1822 but not launched until 1837, and *Vermont*, launched in 1845 after twenty-seven years' building.

These impressive ships were popular subjects with artists, engravers, and lithographers. The *Delaware* seems to have been the most popular of all. J. Hill shows her on the stocks at Gosport (now Norfolk), Virginia. A pair of lithographs published by Childs & Inman after J. G. Bruff show her entering America's first dry dock (still in use) at Gosport Navy Yard in 1836. There are three oil paintings by James C. Evans and an Endicott lithograph after an Evans painting. A tempera in the Roosevelt Collection shows the *Delaware* off Naples. N. Currier produced a small folio print. A lithograph by F. W. Moore seems to be after an Antoine Roux painting.

The *Ohio* was lithographed by J. C. Sharp, Endicott & Co., and N. Currier. A view of the launching of the *Pennsylvania* appears as a lithograph published by Lehman & Duval, and there are portraits by Gibbs & Co. and N. Currier. Currier, in fact, published prints of all these ships-of-the-line. A spirited view of the *Pennsylvania* in a storm is in an aquatint by W. J. Bennett after J. Pringle. The *North Carolina* was painted by Henry Walke and Cammillieri. She was lithographed by Ensign & Thayer and appears on a sheet-music cover.

THE PEACETIME NAVY

During some eleven years scattered throughout the country's first forty years, the American people had been at war. The period of quiet which followed gave the nation three decades in which to build up its economy. The navy was active during these years, playing its part in the protection of merchant marine and the expansion of American trade.

One phase of this period had to do with the opening of the Far East to American trade. In 1842 Commodore Lawrence Kearny sailed to China to protect interests of the United States in incidents connected with the British–Chinese Opium War. Kearny's work extended further and before he was through he had done much to increase China's trade with America. A formal trade treaty was made the following year by Caleb Cushing, who sailed for China in the steam frigate *Missouri*. A pair of lithographs published by Day & Haghe, London, and one by N. Currier, show the untimely end of the *Missouri* by fire at Gibraltar while on the way to China. Cushing continued his voyage in the frigate *Brandywine*.

The treaty which Cushing brought back was ratified by Congress and was returned to the Chinese Government by Commodore Biddle in the ship-of-the-line *Columbus* in company with the sloop-of-war *Vincennes*. Before returning to the United States, Biddle made the first attempt to open the fast-closed

Troy, taken from the West bank of the Hudson in front of the United States Arsenal, aquatint by William J. Bennett, 1837. New York Public Library

trade door to Japan. A lithograph by Wagner & McGuigan after drawings by John Eastley shows the *Columbus* and *Vincennes* in the Bay of Jeddo (Tokyo), surrounded by hundreds of Japanese craft. These boats finally helped to tow the American ships out of the Bay, 'rejoicing', as the title puts it, 'that they had rid themselves so easily of such a number of Barbarians'.

Although Biddle's visit to Japan failed, he learned customs and protocol which were valuable to Commodore Matthew C. Perry in his successful venture on the same mission in 1853. Lithographs by Sarony & Company and others by Hatch and Severin show Perry's imposing squadron at Jeddo and details of the theatrical pomp which the astute Perry knew would appeal to the Japanese. Perry's official report, a two-volume publication, is generously illustrated with lithographs by Sarony & Company.

Two prints, one by J. L. Keffer and one by J. H. Bufford, Boston, bring to mind one other incident which occurred in this period when the door to the Orient was being opened. Commander A. H. Foote with the sloops-of-war *Portsmouth* and *Levant* was attempting to withdraw American neutrals from Whampoa lest they become involved in British–Chinese hostilities in 1856. Despite an understanding with Chinese authorities, the American ships were fired upon and denied passage beyond the 'barrier forts'. The prints show the exchange of fire and the landing of a force of Americans to attack the forts from land.

Captain Ingraham Vindicating American Honor is the title of a lithograph by Endicott & Company recalling an incident which took place in the harbour of Smyrna in July 1853. Martin Koszta, a naturalized American citizen, was arrested by Austrian officials and held aboard a warship in the harbour. Commander Ingraham, of the sloop-of-war *St Louis*, took the initiative in the situation, anchored abreast of the Austrian warship and, with loaded guns, demanded Koszta's release. As a result, the man was placed in neutral hands ashore.

The Boston lithographers, Lane & Scott, brought out a print of the departure from Boston of the sloop-of-war *Jamestown* for Ireland, laden with food for the relief of victims of the Irish famine. The Irish people replied with a lithograph (published by W. Scraggs) of the *Jamestown* entering the Cove of Cork, 13 April 1847. The caption states the print to be 'commemorative of the splendid generosity of the American government in dismantling a ship of war for a Mission of Peace and Charity'.

A handsome lithograph was published in England at the time of the joint British–United States venture of laying the Atlantic telegraph cable in 1856. This print, published by W. Foster, London, shows the U.S. Steam Frigate *Niagara* together with H.M.S. *Agamemnon* laying the cable.

THE MEXICAN WAR

In 1846 the controversial Mexican War broke out over the disputed Texan frontier and ended in the annexation of the territories of Texas, New Mexico, and California, and the establishment of the Rio Grande River as the United States–Mexican border. The U.S. Navy's principal part in this war was to transport General Winfield Scott's army to Vera Cruz, whence it could move on Mexico City, carrying the war to the heart of Mexico.

Lieutenant H. Walke, U.S.N., served aboard the bomb brig *Vesuvius* in the naval operations against Mexico. Possessed of artistic talents, he made paintings of the movements of the ships in this expedition. Eight of his views were produced as lithographs by Sarony & Major under the title *Naval Scenes of the Mexican War*.

Another U.S. Navy lieutenant, Charles C. Barton, drew Mexican War scenes of the landing of General Scott's army which P. S. Duval, Philadelphia lithographer, reproduced on stone. In Frost's *Pictorial History of the Mexican War* appeared a spirited picture of the Vera Cruz landing, lithographed by Wagner & McGuigan. Nathaniel Currier, alert as ever for news pictures, secured from a midshipman a sketch for his lithograph, *Attack of the Gun Boats upon the City and Castle of San Juan de Ulloa* (Vera Cruz).

CIVIL WAR

The story of the navies of the Civil War is one of blockade and blockade running, a few engagements between individual ships, river warfare, some 'amphibious' operations, and attacks from the sea on near-impregnable forts.

When President Lincoln ordered the blockade of Southern ports the Union Navy consisted of scarcely twenty-five vessels.

The New York lithographers Endicott & Company have left a telling record of the Union Navy's answer to Lincoln's order for the blockade. With what soon amounted to monotony, the Endicott lithographic stones rolled out print after print of newly constructed gunboats. The portraits themselves vary little, and the names even were similar, being of Indian origin: *Winooski*, *Ascutney*, *Lenape*, *Mackinaw*, to mention but a few, with *Grand Gulf and Fulton* added for variety.

The answer of the Confederates to the blockade was the 'blockade runner', which dashed through the blockade with greater speed than the Federal guard ships could muster, to bring the South imports necessary to carry on the war. Unfortunately there were few artists to record these craft and their existing exploits.

Some Confederate vessels acted as privateers. The U.S. revenue cutter *Aiken*, seized in Charleston at the outbreak of the war, was converted to the privateer schooner *Petrel*. On her first cruise she was chased by the U.S. Frigate *St Lawrence*. After a brief action the schooner sank. The Philadelphia lithographer, L. Haugg, published a handsome print to commemorate this incident.

One of the most notable exploits of the war was the cruise of the Confederate raider *Alabama* under Raphael Semmes. During this eleven-month cruise the *Alabama* captured sixty-nine prizes. The successful voyage was brought to an abrupt end in June 1864, when the raider was cornered in Cherbourg harbour by the U.S. sloop-of-war *Kearsarge*. The Confederate ship unhesitatingly went forth to meet her opponent, but after a battle of less than two hours, she struck her colours and sank. This, one of the few duels of the war, was popular in story, song, and picture. An artist named Xanthus Smith, an enlisted man in the U.S. Navy, has left several paintings of the engagement, and W. F. Mitchell and C. Oliver did watercolour drawings of it. Prints include French lithographs, a pair of small folios by Currier & Ives, a chromolithograph by L. Prang & Co., and a sheet-music cover by L. R. Rosenthal.

The renowned battle between the first ironclads, the *Virginia* (ex-*Merrimac*) and the *Monitor*, was a popular subject for prints and paintings. The *Merimac*, as a steam frigate before conversion by the Confederates, appears in a portrait lithographed by L. H. Bradford & Company. Currier & Ives have pictured her on her first appearance as the ironclad ram *Virginia*, sinking the frigate *Cumberland*.

The fight of the *Virginia* and *Monitor*, which revolutionized naval history, took place on 9 March 1862. Among the many contemporary pictures it inspired are lithographs by Casimir Bohn, Henry Bill, Endicott, Hatch, and Currier & Ives. The battle though not in itself a decisive one, was ostensibly a victory for the *Monitor*. A lurid print published by Currier & Ives shows *The Destruction of the Rebel Monster MERRIMAC off Craney Island, May 11, 1862*.

There followed the construction or conversion of ships of the types of both of these vessels. The rams, similar in appearance to the *Virginia*, were later seen particularly on the Mississippi River and are recorded especially in lithographs by Currier & Ives. Vessels of the design of the *Monitor* were built in numbers by the Federal Navy. Endicott published a series of lithographs, over a dozen, of monitors also having Indian names, as *Manhattan*, *Weehawken*, *Monadnock*, and *Wassuc*.

The firm of Currier & Ives, lithographers, was in its prime at the time of the Civil War. The 6,000-odd titles published by these prolific print makers cover a wide range of subjects. Many had to do with current events and were, in effect, forerunners of the presentday newspaper pictures. In consequence we find the firm furnishing its 'readers' with views of the latest developments at the 'front', including the naval 'front'. Thus a list of Currier & Ives naval prints, in order of publication, becomes a chronology of the naval war.

The Mississippi River was the Confederate front in the west. Important naval operations took place on the river and its tributaries. One of the key points first to be won with the aid of Commodore Foote's fleet of Union gunboats was Fort Henry, Tennessee, on 6 February 1862. This action is recalled in a Currier & Ives print, as is the Battle of Shiloh, 6 April 1862. Middleton, Strobridge & Company, lithographers of Cincinnati, who produced a series of Civil War battle scenes, also depicted this battle. Proceeding southward, the fleet engaged in *The Bombardment and Capture of Island Number Ten, April 7, 1862, by the Gunboat and Mortar Fleet*, another Currier & Ives title.

Meanwhile a fleet under Admiral Farragut entered the mouth of the Mississippi. A woodcut published by Howard Brown after a drawing by William Waud records the *Bombardment of Forts Jackson and St Philip*. A drawing by William McMurtrie shows the fleet lying before New Orleans, before proceeding northwards to 'engage the Rebel Batteries at Port Hudson (Louisiana) March 14th, 1863', as the Currier & Ives title reads. A dramatic chromolithograph by L. Prang shows the Union fleet as from a Confederate battery near Port Hudson. The last major engagement on the Mississippi was the Battle of Vicksburg, in which the Naval forces took part, as is evidenced by the title, *Admiral Porter's Fleet Running the Rebel Blockade of the Mississippi at Vicksburg, April 15th, 1863*. Other naval operations followed but with the river opened and the Confederacy divided, the navy had done most of its work in the west.

A 'combat artist' of the Civil War, worthy of special mention, was Alfred Waud. He was employed by *Harper's Weekly* as a 'war correspondent'. Most of Waud's pencil sketches had to do with the operations of the army, but there were many drawings of naval activity done in his admirable style. The Library of Congress owns most of his work.

It was difficult to blockade the coast off Hatteras, North Carolina, owing to generally unfavourable weather, so the Federals decided early in the war to get a foothold on shore in order to prevent blockade runners from bringing supplies in at this point. Currier & Ives recorded this operation in a print entitled *The Bombardment and Capture of the Forts Hatteras and Clark at Hatteras Inlet, N.C., by the U.S. Fleet under Commodore Stringham and the Forces under Genl. Butler, August 27th, 1861*.

The Victorious Bombardment of Port Royal, S.C., November 7, 1861, by the United States Fleet under the Command of Commodore Dupont, a Currier & Ives print, depicts the action which gave the South Atlantic Blockading Squadron a much-needed base of operations at a point between Charleston and Savannah.

The Savannah River was closed to Confederate use after *The Bombardment of Fort Pulaski, Cockspur Island, Georgia, 10th and 11th of April 1862*, as the title of the Currier & Ives lithograph puts it.

We turn to prints by Endicott and W. H. Rease to give a prelude to the siege of Charleston. These lithographs show the monitor *Weehawken* fighting rough weather on the way south to attack, with other monitors, the invulnerable Fort Sumter. The action was disastrous to the Union naval forces and proved an unfounded reliance on this new type of vessel.

Fort Sumter proved a stronghold hard to silence. Other Currier & Ives prints show that it was 'bombarded' frequently. The print, *The Siege of Charleston, Bombardment of Fort Sumter and Batteries Wagner and Trigg . . . August 1863* depicts the climax of the naval war at Charleston and the silencing of Sumter, though the town was not abandoned until General Sherman's arrival by land.

Wilmington, North Carolina, was one of the last important strongholds on the coast to be captured. A fleet, comprising over 150 warships and transports, was assembled for the amphibious assault which the Currier & Ives print, *The Bombardment and Capture of Fort Fisher, N.C., January 15, 1865*, depicts. Endicott & Company also produced a print of this battle, which took place three months before the Confederate surrender at Appomattox.

American Railroad Prints

THE BEGINNINGS

The first incorporated railroad to perform transportation service in the United States was the Granite Railway, organized in Quincy, Massachusetts, in 1826: it was horsedrawn. The first full-sized steam locomotive to operate on rails here was the *Stourbridge Lion*, brought from England in 1829. As early as 1825 Colonel John Stevens demonstrated a steam railway in Hoboken, New Jersey. The *American Railway Journal*, which began publication in 1832, carried a wood engraving of the *Stourbridge Lion* on its mast for several years. Otherwise there are no contemporary prints of these interesting 'firsts'.

The *De Witt Clinton* was the first practical American steam locomotive to operate. It ran from Albany to Schenectady, beginning 31 July 1832. On that day a dextrous observer, William H. Brown, cut a silhouette of the train. In 1869, Leggo & Company of Montreal made a lithograph from the silhouette. Although not contemporary, the lithograph gives a clear picture of the first locomotive of the New York Central.

Equally important is the lithograph by Ed. Weber of a view of Ellicott's Mills, the first stopping place of the Baltimore & Ohio Railroad. Begun in 1828, the road was used as horsedrawn means for carting granite blocks from which, incidentally, the Carrollton Viaduct was built. A print of this viaduct shows one of Ross Winians's locomotives with steam up and two cars attached, ready to leave for Baltimore. The print dates from about 1837.

With the full development of lithography in the United States, railway prints came into their own. It is interesting that this process, easier and cheaper than the etching and engraving processes favoured in Europe, formed the bulk of American railroad prints. A list of known early American railway prints was published by the Railway and Locomotive Historical Society in 1934. Of the 326 items listed, by far the greater number are lithographs, only fifteen having been executed in other techniques.

Ellicott's Mills, end of first section of Baltimore & Ohio Railroad, drawing and lithograph by Ed. Weber, Baltimore, *c.* 1837

De Witt Clinton (Mohawk & Hudson Railway), lithograph by Leggo & Co., Montreal, Canada, 1869, from Brown's silhouette of 1832 in Connecticut Historical Society. The Old Print Shop, New York

LOCOMOTIVE PRINTS

Among the most prized items on the lists of collectors of railroad subjects are prints of early locomotives. They are actual portraits of the engines themselves. They were engineer scale drawings transferred to the lithographic stone and include a mass of detail often showing even the decorative panels which had been painted on the engine and tender. The prints were large and bright and bold in colouring, but the engine is not shown in motion. They were used as advertisements by the builders and were circulated among their agents and railroad companies.

One hundred and fifty of these locomotive prints are included in the Railway and Locomotive Historical Society list. Forty-four builders are listed. Often the same lithographer was employed over a period of years by a firm, and we find the same print maker's name appearing again and again. J. H. Bufford is one of these. He lithographed the *Auburn*, *Amoskeag*, *Ontario*, *Gazelle*, *Jervis* and *Saturn* for the Amoskeag Manufacturing Company. For the Boston Locomotive Works he did the *Buffalo*, *Norwalk*, *Lisle*, *Rapid*, *Sacramento*, *Boston*, *Fashion*, *Ysabel*, and *Marquette*. For other manufacturers he did the *Express*, *Janus*, *State of Maine*, *Forest State*, *Shelburne*, *Minnehaha*, *Rough and Ready*, *Calumet and Tender*, *President and Tender*, *New Englander and Tender*, and *Northerner* (*sic*.).

Julius Bien did the following lithographs for M. W. Baldwin: *Locomotives* 4-4-0, 4-6-0, *and* 0-8-0, *Baldwin & Co. Locomotives*, *Baldwin's Coal Burning Boiler*, *Baldwin Engines Types C*, *D*, *and E*, *Thomas Rogers*. Bien's partner, Sterner, did *Baltic*, *Young America*, and *Superior* for Breese & Knowland. Richard Norris & Son, locomotive builders in Philadelphia, hired L. N. Rosenthal and A. Brett to portray the *Auburn*, *Meredith*, *Sagua la Grande*, *Wyoming*, *Union*, and at least four others.

Thomas S. Sinclair lithographed the *Massachusetts* for Hinkley & Drury of Boston; the *John C. Breckenridge and Tender*, for the Lancaster Locomotive Works; the *Assanpink* for the Trenton Locomotive Works; and a miscellaneous lithograph called *Track Across the Susquehannah River*. The lithography firm of Tappan & Bradford published some of the finest examples of the locomotive print: *General Stark* for the Amoskeag Manufacturing Company; *Columbia*, *Mercury*, and *Ariel* for other manufacturers. Charles H. Crosby and also Tappan & Bradford worked on the stone for William Mason, the builder in Taunton, Massachusetts, and brought out the *Armstrong*, *Phantom*, *Highland Light*, and *Janus*. John Sartain, probably the leading mezzotint engraver in the United States in his time, scraped *Three Locomotives with Baldwin Plant in Background*; *The Baldwin Works*; and *Certificate of the Franklin Institute*, which is, technically, a railroad print.

Donald McKay built the *Arkansas*, and C. H. Crosby's lithograph of this engine is a gem. The *Arkansas* is shown in the Far West. Two U.S. troopers appear lower right. Indians, of which there are seven, are in a state of agitation occasioned by this, their first view of a locomotive. The most remarkable figure in the piece is the fireman, who is wearing a pigtail and Chinese dress. He is one of the thousands of Chinese who were encouraged to emigrate to the United States, where they played an important part in the construction of the railroads in the West.

No doubt the very popularity of these gay and decorative prints accounts for their scarcity today. Cheaply framed, if at all, they were hung in railroad stations, offices, barns, bedrooms, and bagnios, where they were thrown away when damaged. Those kept in the files of the manufacturing firms were discarded as their prototypes were replaced by newer and better models.

VIADUCTS AND BRIDGES

When the road beds were laid out bridges and viaducts were required. They were viewed as wonders at the time of their building, and shared some of the enthusiasm accorded the locomotives. The type of construction varied according to the materials available locally. There is a peculiar satisfaction in contemplating the old prints and reflecting that our ancestors' ingenuity served them well in overcoming obstacles to their progress.

In the vignette of *The Carrolton Viaduct*, published by Endicott & Swett in 1831, we see the solidly constructed viaduct straddling the glen, its beautiful arch and well-built buttressed walls made of granite from the quarry at nearby Ellicott's Mills. The horse-drawn railway coach is practically bursting with passengers as it proceeds majestically.

Portage Bridge, lithograph by Compton & Co., Buffalo, New York after J. Stilson, *c.* 1865. Kennedy Galleries, New York

Thirty years later we find a larger print lithographed by Compton & Company after a drawing by J. Stilson. It is called *Portage Bridge* and represents a bridge of the Erie Railroad in Western New York. Of timber construction, it had a cross walk from which pedestrians could contemplate the waterfalls below. The legend on the print states that 1,602,000 feet of timber and 108,862 pounds of iron were used in its construction. In the picture a steam locomotive chugs across this wonder of engineering, pulling two freight and five passenger cars.

Currier & Ives's *Railroad Suspension Bridge near Niagara Falls* appeared at the same time as the *Portage Bridge*. Lithographed from a painting by Charles Parsons, it designates as engineer John A. Roebling, whose name was to become a household word in America after the building of Brooklyn Bridge.

American Autumn, Starucca Valley viaduct, Erie Railroad, chromolithograph by T. Sinclair, after Jasper Cropsey, Philadelphia, 1865. Kennedy Galleries, New York

Across the Niagara Bridge, suspended by cables from huge stone towers, goes the train, while below, on the underpath, horsedrawn carriages proceed.

A beautiful chromolithograph done in 1865 by Thomas Sinclair is entitled *American Autumn*. It shows the Starucca Valley viaduct on the Erie Railroad, which was said to be the longest viaduct in the country at that time.

RAILROAD ACCIDENT PRINTS

Lithography lent itself well to tabloid reporting, and John Collins published *Accident on the Camden and Amboy Railroad near Burlington, New Jersey*, 29 August 1855, shortly after the disaster. *The Abolition Catastrophe*, a political cartoon published by Bromley & Company is another story. Hullmandel & Walton published *Accident on the Baltimore and Ohio Railroad* in 1853. John L. Magee published *The Dreadful Accident of the North Pennsylvania Railroad, 14 Minutes from Philadelphia*, 17 July 1856.

PRINTS WITH HISTORICAL SIGNIFICANCE

Charles Parsons's *Panama Railroad – View of the Culebra or the Summit* shows the first railroad which operated between the Atlantic and Pacific Oceans. It is dated 1854. Currier & Ives's *Across the Continent* commemorates the completion of the railway across the North American Continent. Schile & Company also issued no less than three coloured lithographs under this title. These prints are more noted for dash than accuracy.

Railroad scenes of the Civil War include: *The Invasion of Pennsylvania*, a coloured woodcut by Berghaus; *Volunteer Refreshment Saloon, Supported Gratuitously by the Citizens of Philadelphia, Pa.*, published by B. S. Brown and printed in colour by W. Boell; *Lookout Mountain near Chattanooga, Tennessee*, by Donaldson & Elmes; *Military Post, Cowan, Tennessee*, by Henry Eno; *Tracy City, Tennessee*, also by Eno; *Away to the Front*, by MacClure, MacDonald & MacGregor; and *Camp at Melville, Md.*, by Sachse & Company.

WESTERN PRINT MAKERS OF RAILROAD ITEMS

Information concerning Western print makers is small, and examples of their work are much appreciated by collectors. A few titles are: *The Way Not to Build the S.P. Railroad* – anonymous and with no date; *What we want in California. From New York Direct, Family and Fireside*, by Britton & Rey; *San Diego, Cal.*, by George H. Baker. This is an interesting field for collectors with pioneer instincts.

Strangely enough, early railroad prints before 1860 were comparatively few among the Currier & Ives productions. The first railroad print issued by Nathaniel Currier is a small folio entitled *The Express Train*, and was taken from a banknote of the Fort Jervis Institution. Undated, it shows the engine before the addition of a headlight. *The American Express Train*, after Charles Parsons, published in 1855, is a large folio. It was re-issued with an overprint in the sky, *Adams Express Co.*, with that company's advertising legend in the margin. The large *Express Train*, published in 1859 after a painting by Parsons, is almost a duplicate of the former, but in reverse. All of these prints show entire trains in motion with smoke issuing from the stack and with landscape backgrounds.

The most important railroad prints done by Currier & Ives, however, were those issued towards the end of or shortly after the Civil War. These are imaginative to the point of being theatrical, are not accurate as to detail, are well drawn and highly coloured, and seek to dramatize some important railroad incident. We find such titles as *The Lightning Express Trains Leaving the Junction*; *Night Scene at an American Railway Junction*; *The Great West*; *American Railroad Scene, Snow Bound*; *Through to the Pacific*; *Prairie Fires of the Great West*; and *Across the Continent, Westward the Course of Empire Takes its Way*. The Currier & Ives productions are among the most charming of the railroad prints.

Mention should be made of the long series of 'comics' issued by Currier & Ives, those caricaturing new railroad conveniences such as the 'accommodation train', stops for refreshments at the station, entanglements with cattle, and so on, plus the amusing group of *Darktown* prints.

MUSIC SHEETS, BANKNOTES, AND STOCK CERTIFICATES

Any event which kindles public interest and enthusiasm is usually a theme of popular poetry and song. Railroading was no exception. One finds numerous titles referring to this industry, and most have lithographed representations of railroads on their covers. Perhaps the earliest in this field are the marches dedicated, at the time of the inception of the Baltimore and Ohio Railroad, to Charles Carroll of Carrollton, the last surviving Signer of the Declaration of Independence. The marches were dedicated to him and the other directors of the company. The event took place on the Fourth of July 1828 and *The Carrollton March* and *The Baltimore and Ohio March* were sold on the streets on that momentous day. *The Lion Quickstep* was played for the first time at the opening of the railroad to Westborough (Boston), 15 November 1834. *The New Orleans and Great Northern Railroad Polka* was published in 1854. The galops, polkas, quicksteps and even 'steam galops' generally bore names at least as exuberant as the pictures on their covers. Amusing collectors' items, they yet offer important sources for certain elusive railroad data.

Banknotes and stock certificates of the early period utilized railroad material for decoration. On its notes of 1833 the Bank of Tecumseh, Michigan, used a picture of a railroad train with a sharp-pronged cowcatcher on little wheels. This device was actually used by Isaac Dripps of the Camden and Amboy Railroad in 1832. The engraving also shows the iron bonnet on the smokestack devised to arrest the burning embers belched forth from the engine. The first trip of the *De Witt Clinton* and near incineration of the passengers had made the necessity for such an invention obvious. There is no doubt that the engravers of the notes, Rawdon, Wright & Hatch of New York, had actually seen this train in operation and have left us an accurate picture of it.

Catalogues of railroad subjects offered for sale often list old stock certificates which have a current value only because of the railroad items engraved on them. These vignettes have a charm of their own, which comes from the fact that the spectator generally holds them and looks at them close up. The New York Public Library has a fine collection of vignettes, many of which portray railroads.

American Silhouettes

In 1767 Benjamin Franklin wrote home from London: 'I send you the little shade that was copied from the great one.' This 'great' shade – presumably lifesize – was a silhouette of Franklin, now lost, made by Patience Wright, the New Jersey Quakeress then established in England. However, the earliest mention of silhouette work done in America is found in a letter written in 1799 by Harriet Pinckney, a South Carolina belle, in which she mentions her 'shade' by Thomas Wollaston. The whereabouts of the profile are unknown; it is probable that the artist was an amateur.

Foremost among the notables of the period, George and Martha Washington were innumerably portrayed by amateur silhouettists, among whom were their granddaughter Nelly Custis, Samuel Powell, Mayor of Philadelphia, and Miss Sarah de Hart, of Elizabethtown, New Jersey. The work of Major André – his own self-portrait, his studies of General Burgoyne, Major Stanley, 'Becky' Stedman – is naturally of high historical interest. Such 'shades' when encountered speak for themselves eloquently enough.

However, with the advent of the nineteenth century, the growing popularity of silhouette soon created a real demand, and the sporadic manifestations of amateurs were supplemented by the steady production of a group of professionals. One of the earliest among these was Moses Chapman of Salem, Massachusetts (*c.* 1780–1821), no relation to Chapman of Virginia so far as is known. The Salem silhouettist was not a particularly gifted artist; his work is correct but undistinguished. But he was an innovator in the sense that he made use not of the silhouette proper but the outer contour usually discarded by the cutter. This, placed on a black ground, paper, silk, or any other material, furnished a striking effect. Chapman employed the tracing and cutting machine invented by Chrétien in France, the *physionotrace*, but occasionally still cut freehand.

The possibilities of silhouette work by this 'hollow-cut' process were to be fully realized by Charles Willson Peale (1741–1827), the extreme example of Yankee ingenuity and business sense, who resolved to bring about the mass production of silhouettes. He actually achieved this by means of the *physionotrace*, complemented by an ingenious stencil machine (invented by his assistant Isaac Hawkins) which is described as enabling 'any steady hand in a few moments' to 'produce a correct indented outline'. Peale was eminently successful financially, but it is obvious that the works executed entirely by this means are almost devoid of artistic value. The work of Peale himself must, at least in some cases, be excepted. He was a serious, really excellent artist and craftsman, having been in succession, though more often simultaneously, a saddler, clockmaker, silversmith, taxidermist, soldier, legislator, educator, and scientist (naturalist and archaeologist). He established his own museum in Philadelphia, largely devoted to natural history. Of the three stamps he used on silhouettes, *Museum* is the most usual; *Peale's Museum* comes next, and rarest is the plain mark, *Peale*; all three are embossed in roman capitals.

Peale's nephew, Charles Peale Polk (1767–1822), made profiles on gold background, the rarest type of American silhouettes.

Not on a level with Peale the elder, but something more than an amateur was Samuel Folwell (1765–1813), whose first avocation had been the engraving of bookplates in New Hampshire. Having moved to Philadelphia, then the metropolis of the arts in America, Folwell, in order to meet active competition, turned to various occupations, among them miniaturist, profilist, worker in hair (as were most profilists), and in his spare time, school teacher. His most famous work, the profile of George Washington, is firm and delicately chiselled. A Folwell silhouette is *rarissima avis*.

William Doyle was born in Boston in 1769, the son of a British soldier. He divided his admiration equally between Peale and Miers. To Miers he paid artistic homage, and he strove to emulate him, but never attained to the subtle effects of the English artist. He did rival Peale, if not as an artist, at least as a museum founder. His business enterprises, in co-operation with another silhouettist, David Bowen (whose only date, 1791, is found on a portrait, *George Washington and his lady*), were quite successful, in spite of disaster by fire. Doyle generally copied the Miers bust curve, but interrupted it halfway with an odd little nick that is extremely characteristic. He was known to have done some works on plaster, but none was thought to exist until a unique discovery of such a profile on 'composition'. He signed in careful script, but never stamped.

Henry Williams (Boston, 1787–1830) was fully as versatile as any of his colleagues, and in addition was a professor of electricity and a modeller in wax. His method was the usual hollow-cut technique, and his advertisements offered '16 different sizes down to a quarter of an inch', this last no doubt intended for setting in jewelry. His work is very rare.

'Todd' must remain just that; his first name is not known. He was approximately a contemporary of Doyle and Williams, and an album with about 2,000 examples of his work is in the collection of the Boston Athenaeum. It provides a delightful and lively record of costumes and types, in an unpretentious and effective clean-cut style without any pen flourishes. The stamp *Todd's Patent* is the only signature. Most valuable perhaps, Todd kept a meticulous record of his sitters' names, with dates of posing.

William King (active 1785–1805) wielded his magic 'Patent Delineating Pencil' in Salem and vicinity. Possibly it may have been his own invention; he is spoken of as 'an ingenious mechanic but full of projects & what he gains in one he loses in the other'. In an advertisement published in 1806 King claimed to have executed upwards of 20,000 silhouettes. Yet today it is rare to find even one.

Daniel Wadsworth by William Bache. Wadsworth Atheneum

In perfect contrast to King was the serious and honest William Bache, who was to raise hollow cutting to the level of art. Born on 22 December 1771 (at Bromsgrove in Worcestershire, England), Bache emigrated to Philadelphia when he was twenty-two years old. His career as a profilist took him far and wide through the south, particularly Louisiana, where he did some excellent work, and later to the West Indies. In his short career as a profilist he produced much and created a new style, being the first hollow cutter to paint on his paper backings details of dress such as a transparent collar ruffle. At his hands, hollow cutting lost rigidity and coldness. A true artist, he was equally skilful in cut-and-pastel work and in painted silhouettes.

The last days of silhouette, before the advent of daguerreotype sounded its doom, saw its richest flowering. Among a host of lesser lights, which limitations of space preclude mentioning, there emerges William Henry Brown, who was born in Charleston, South Carolina, in 1808, died there in 1883. Brown was something of a prodigy; his first silhouette, of Lafayette, was executed at the age of sixteen. In contrast to the usual American practice, Brown was a freehand cutter. His style is pure and severe, without extraneous embellishments of gold or colour. This is silhouette in the finest sense of the word, which implies denudation to the point of artistic asceticism. The characterization of subjects is superb, but is always rightly held subservient to the artistic conception. Brown was an artist and social observer, and, as a result of this, has given us a more enduring record of his age than the most slavish hollow cutter.

Brown's greatest accomplishment was the compilation of the *Portrait Gallery of Distinguished American Citizens*, published at Hartford, Connecticut, in 1846. To this album of lithographs he furnished both text (biographical notes) and illustrations, the subjects being shown against backgrounds which he did not execute himself, but must have supervised and in many cases suggested. These are of great historical interest. Almost the entire edition of the *Portrait Gallery* was destroyed by fire shortly after publication, so that copies are of the utmost rarity.

The prestige of freehand cutting quite did away with the hollow cutting by machine that had satisfied earlier: silhouettists now were 'scissorgraphists'. William James Hubard ('Master Hubard', born in England in 1807, died 1862) was advertised as a child prodigy, starting on his career at the age of twelve. There is scepticism on this point now, and it is thought, on good grounds, that he may actually have been fifteen at his debut. He later became a pupil of Sully and a competent portrait painter in his own right. His highest success was won in Charleston, and he finally settled in the south. The Valentine Museum in Richmond, Virginia, has a collection of his work.

A successor, Master Hankes, was also born in England. Hankes's career started in Salem, Massachusetts, in 1828. He may have been an early anonymous associate of Master Hubard, helping to satisfy the press of business. When he appeared under his own name he was only moderately successful, doing best of all in Baltimore. Returning to New England after this tour, Master Hankes disappears from view. His talent, however, was not mean, as seen in his portrait of Dr E. Holyoke of Salem.

Phenomenal also, but far inferior artistically, were

Portrait of Dr Edward Augustus Holyoke of Salem, by Master Hankes. Essex Institute, Salem, Massachusetts

Miss Honeywell and Master Nellis. The first, born without arms, contrived to cut with scissors held in her mouth. Her work may have fully satisfied many, but it is probable that most of her patronage was due mainly to compassionate interest. Little of it has survived.

Of Sanders K. G. Nellis we know nothing but his name from an advertisement. Also armless, he made use of his toes in place of fingers. Mention is made merely on the chance that some vestige of his pathetic industry might turn up at some future date.

A history of silhouette in America must necessarily include mention of the work of visiting artists from abroad, whose works represent a documentary study of national interest.

Charles Balthazar Julien Févret de Saint-Mémin (born in Dijon in 1770, died 1852) was a French *émigré* originally destined to a military career. A gifted amateur artist in happier days, he developed under pressure of financial necessity into a masterly professional. Although he undertook to furnish the American market with silhouettes, his most important work was in the related form of coloured profiles in life size, and engravings, of which he executed a large number during his stay. In style, he combined eighteenth-century grace and the cold intensity of Davidesque neoclassicism. Much of this is reflected in his silhouettes, which have purity of line and a very special flavour of French elegance.

Augustin Amant Constant Fidèle Édouart (1789–1861) was the universal silhouettist – his subjects ranging all the way from dignified historical portraits to humorous genre scenes. In addition to his huge European output (see the article on British and Continental silhouettes), his ten years' stay in America resulted in a unique and priceless record totalling upwards of 10,000 silhouettes. Much of this was lost in a shipwreck, that is, the careful record of duplicates kept by the artist; many of the originals have survived. But Mrs Nevill Jackson was still able to refer to her photographic files of the remaining 3,800 American Édouart silhouettes as 'in such number as no other nation possesses'.

Édouart's style was that of a purist of genius: no adornments, no shading of any sort, gold or otherwise. He allowed himself at most a slit of white for the gentlemen's neckcloths, but within the bounds of this self-imposed economy achieved extraordinary linear expressiveness.

British

Prints

Reduced to its simplest analysis, a print is merely a drawing or a painting transferred to a plate of copper or zinc, a block of wood, or a stone. The word 'print' is a generic term applying to several methods – line engraving on wood and copper, etching, soft-ground etching, drypoint, aquatint, mezzotint, and lithography, and some knowledge of each technique is an aid to appreciation.

Engraving had reached a state of perfection on the continent of Europe at least a hundred years before its advent in England; but it was not long before an indigenous school was established.

During the last years of the sixteenth century William Rogers, the first important native-born engraver, was busy with plates expressive of a glorious reign and event. Appropriately, one of his most famous works was in honour of Elizabeth I. It commemorated the victory over the Spanish Armada, and was called *Eliza Triumphans*. It is a full-length effigy of the Queen, elaborating details of her fantastic costume, and is dated 1589. More historic than aesthetic, it is none the less a landmark in English engraving.

Working contemporaneously with Rogers was Thomas Cockson, who illustrated Sir John Harrington's metrical translation of Ariosto's *Orlando Furioso*. His best plates, however, are the equestrian portraits of the Earls of Devonshire, Essex, Cumberland, and Nottingham. Carefully cut after good drawings, these engravings, if somewhat formalized have considerable distinction.

Rogers and Cockson set a course for portrait engraving in England. Unlike portrait painting, it was an art that could be shared by many, and print sellers and publishers were not slow to take advantage of a profitable accessory to their trade. William Hole, another engraver of that time, is also remembered for his portraits, including that of George Chapman used in the 1616 edition of his translation of Homer.

With William Faithorne (1616–91) the engraved portrait reached a splendour that loses nothing by comparison with the work of any other master of the burin or graver. He cut many plates after Van Dyck, Dobson, and Walker. Faithorne understood the painter's mood and interpreted it as one might translate a poem from one language into another, without losing its original inspiration. Faithorne's print represented a warm and intimate personality. His line is bold and vital, and his feeling for character, colour, and texture is absolutely convincing. The artist's life was not without adventure, for he took up arms in defence of the Royalist cause, was captured at Basing House garrison and confined in Aldersgate. On being released, Faithorne went to France, where he was fortunate in making friends with the Abbé de Marolles, who allowed him to study his enormous collection of about 120,000 prints by all the great masters of engraving and etching. While in France Faithorne also worked with the famous engraver Robert Nanteuil, thus consummating his own style. He returned to England with the Protector's permission, and enjoyed many years of success in his profession. Notable plates by him are portraits of Prince Rupert, Oliver Cromwell, William Sanderson, Charles II, Barbara Villiers, William Prince of Orange, and Margaret Smith.

The artists so far mentioned cut direct on the copper, a method known as line engraving, which, after being inked, was put under the press.

A line engraver and etcher of much originality in animal, bird, and fish subjects was Francis Barlow (1626–1702). His 110 etchings for Æsop's *Fables* are of exceptional interest to students and collectors.

It was Wenceslaus Hollar (1607–77) who introduced the art of etching into England. He came here with the Earl of Arundel, whom he met at Cologne. A Czech from Prague, Hollar adapted himself to English ways, married an English woman, attached himself to the Royalist cause, and was taken prisoner, strangely enough, at the same time as Faithorne at

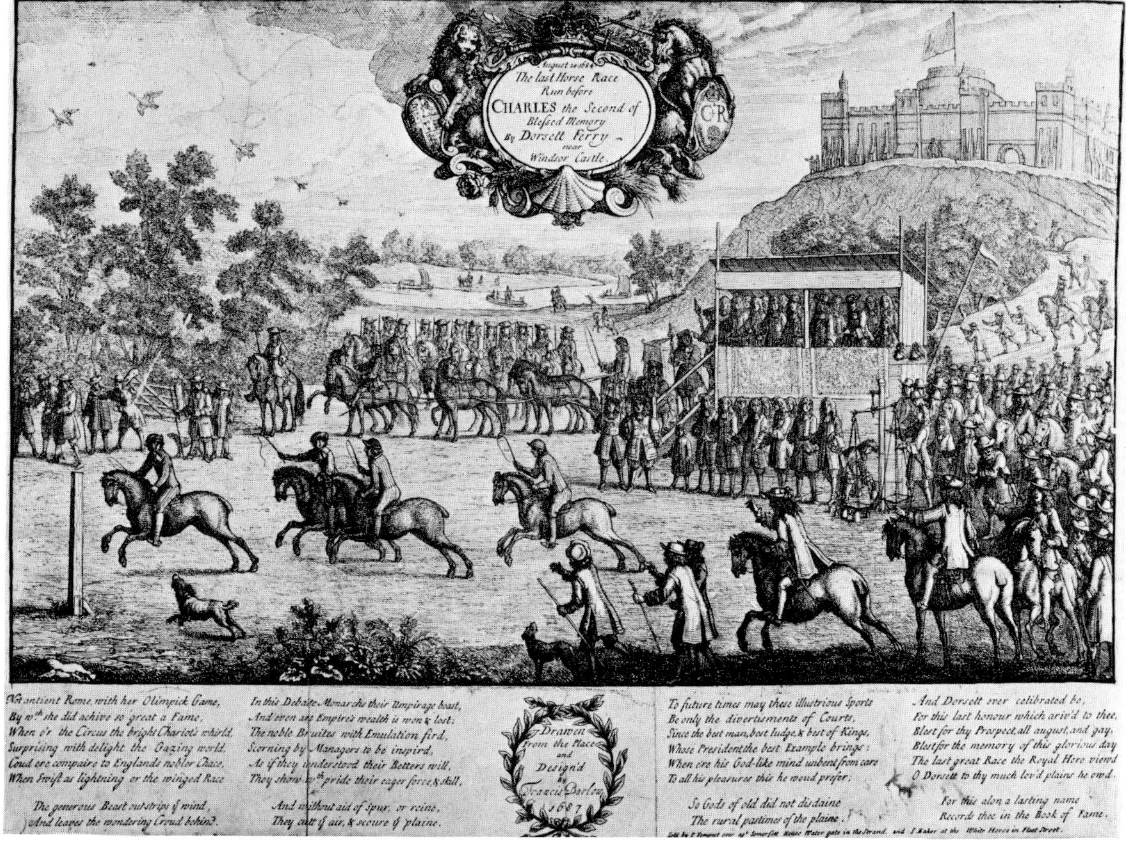

The Last Horse Race Run Before Charles II, near Windsor Castle, etching by Francis Barlow, 1684. British Museum

Basing House. Retiring to Antwerp, whither his patron, the Earl of Arundel, had withdrawn, Hollar lived there from 1644 to 1652, after which year he returned to England, where he spent the rest of his life. A versatile and spirited artist, Hollar etched over 2,500 plates – interpretations of religious and classical paintings, portraits, and townscapes. His great panorama of London, views of other cities, and studies of feminine costume form a microcosm of England and Europe as they were during the seventeenth century. Essentially a realist, Hollar's accurate yet vibrant line is instinct with acute, if unimaginative, observation.

An amateur of some importance who was a friend of Hollar's, and influenced by him, was Francis Place (1647–1728). Among the first of the English topographical artists, Place toured the country recording views in monochrome, which he afterwards etched in a style akin to Hollar's. He also engraved mezzotint portraits.

Etching differs from line engraving in that the drawing is not incised in the copperplate but produced by the biting effect of hydrochloric or nitric acid. The plate is first covered with a thin ground of wax. The drawing is done on the wax, the etching needle sufficing only to open lines or channels into which the acid will bite when the plate is immersed therein. The strength of the bitten line depends

The South Prospect of Bridgnorth in the County of Salop, line engraving by S. and N. Buck, 1732. Samuel and Nathaniel Buck were largely responsible for the creation of a home market in topographical prints in England

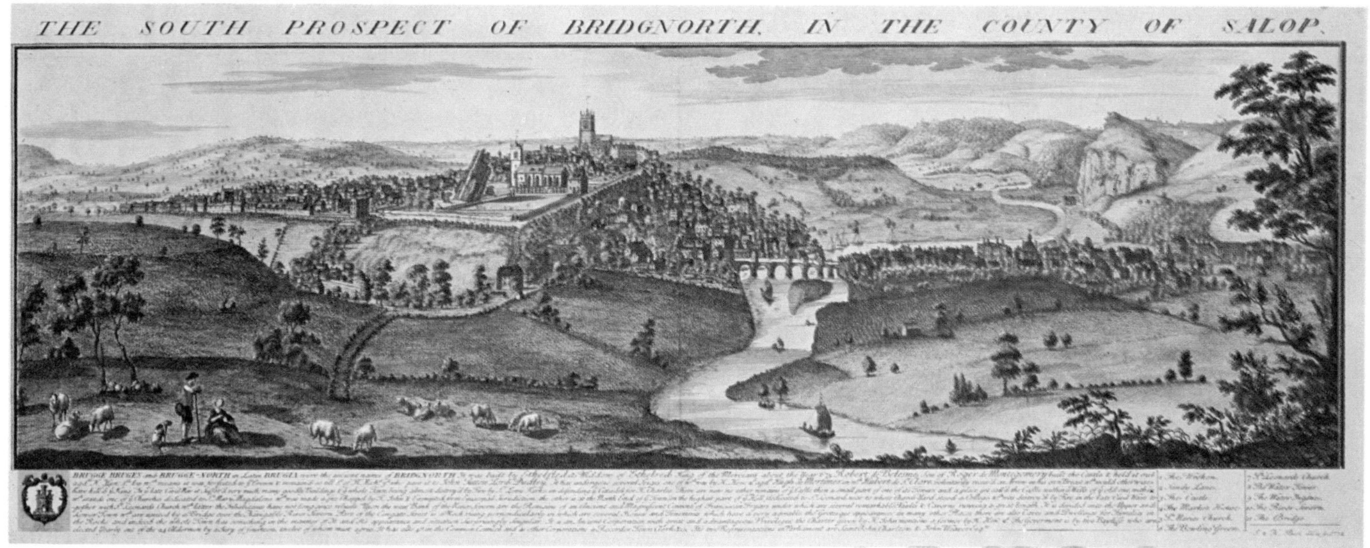

upon the length of time the plate is left in the mordant. Lines that have been bitten deeply enough are 'stopped out', i.e. protected by a special varnish while other lines, in their relative degrees of strength or delicacy, are brought to completion.

A variant of the etching method is known as soft-ground etching, which, in printing, suggests the grain and texture of the paper on which the drawing is made. In this method the drawing is transferred to the etching ground by a tracing.

The evolution of the English print in the seventeenth century, whether line-engraved or etched, is concentrated in the work of Faithorne, Hollar, Barlow, and Place, all of whom were associated with one another.

Though George Vertue (1684–1756), himself a competent artist and esteemed historian of art, deplored the decline of engraving in the first half of the eighteenth century, the century as a whole produced a veritable flood of prints of every conceivable subject in every kind of technique. For separate prints, and as illustrations for books, the copperplate had become indispensable. It was William Hogarth (1697–1764), however, who proved that the engraving which reproduced the subject picture could be of immense monetary gain to artist and print seller alike. Twelve hundred persons are said to have subscribed a guinea each for a set of *The Harlot's Progress*.

Beer Street, etching by William Hogarth, 1751. Victoria & Albert Museum

Thus the commercial value of the print became paramount and resulted in an ever-increasing number of clever craftsmen. Hogarth's own line engravings had no other purpose than to translate the painting as obviously as possible in all its details. His prints were designed to gratify popular taste in its widest sense. As an engraver, therefore, he is not in the first class.

If Hogarth was a rapid worker with the burin, William Woollett (1735–85) was slow and deliberate, and would take many months on a plate, which no doubt accounted for his feeling such intense relief when the work was finished that he signalized it by firing a cannon from the roof of his house. His engraving after Richard Wilson's picture *The Destruction of the Children of Niobe* set the seal on the fame of one of the most prominent reproductive landscape engravers. Woollett's chiaroscuro effect, wrought with an infinity of intricate lines, especially in his plates from Wilson's pictures, catches some of the poetic solemnity of Wilson's mood. Woollett was also a portait and animal engraver. A well-known print by him is *The Spanish Pointer*, and he did many others after George Stubbs. Woollett, like other eighteenth-century line engravers, started his plates with a preliminary etching as a guide to the general design.

Equally celebrated in his time, but principally for historical and religious subjects, was Sir Robert Strange (1721–92), who gained an international reputation as well as a knighthood for his plates after Van Dyck and other Dutch and Italian masters.

Of the same period were William Sharp, who began as a craftsman engraving guns and pewter, and later achieved a position in the art comparable with Woollett's; Richard Earlom, celebrated for his plates after Claude; and William Pether, interpreter of Rembrandt. These three used the mezzotint method.

While so many eighteenth-century engravers were engaged in reproducing paintings, either by old or contemporary masters, William Blake (1757–1827) relied on his own mystical mind for invention and ideal imagery. At his best an inspired poet, Blake was eminently gifted for the task of illuminating Holy Writ and the poetry of his time. For original composition, devout feeling, and refinement of line his designs for *The Book of Job* are outstanding in the history of the art. They should be studied in conjunction with the earlier plates for Young's *Night Thoughts* and the seven for Dante's *Divine Comedy*, on which Blake was working during the last year of his life. An unusual and little-known line engraving is that entitled *Christ with a Bow Trampling on Satan*, believed to be one of the poet-painter's last works.

Another supreme artist in the creative style was Thomas Bewick (1753–1828). Regarded as the restorer of the art of engraving on wood, he designed a vast number of prints of birds and animals.

Prints from copperplates reached a crescendo in the late eighteenth and early nineteenth centuries. Portrait, classical, historical, topographical, genre, architectural, marine, sporting, and satirical subjects found a ready market. Novel variants known as the crayon or chalk and pastel manners further stimulated public interest. A charming example of the crayon or pastel style is the print entitled *Alinda* by William Ward (1762–1826). The object was to suggest the graceful texture of the chalk drawing,

Top left Chairing the Members, Plate 4 from *The Election*, 1758, etching by Hogarth

Above Cottage Industry in the Kitchen, mezzotint by William Hincks, 1791. British Museum

Top right Hare Shooting, by G. Moreland, stipple engraving by C. Catton, 1790

Above right Portrait of Joseph Wright of Derby, mezzotint by James Ward after a self-portrait, 1807

and the etching ground was perforated with various needles and other tools. Ward was a pupil and assistant of John Raphael Smith, and he engraved works after Sir Joshua Reynolds, and George Morland, who was Ward's brother-in-law. He was equally skilled in what is known as the stipple engraving, the main technique of which is the use of innumerable dots and flicks to suggest modelling and gradation.

The stipple method was also practised by L. Schiavonetti and A. Cardon, who collaborated in one of the most successful series of prints ever created, *The Cries of London*, after Francis Wheatley, R.A. Schiavonetti was greatly influenced by, and worked for some time with, Francesco Bartolozzi, who enjoyed phenomenal success with his stipple engravings, notably a set of portraits of the time of Henry VIII, after drawings by Holbein, published by John Chamberlaine in 1792–1800.

Yet another novelty was the aquatint, introduced into England by the Hon. Charles Greville, who communicated the principle to Paul Sandby, R.A. Greville is said to have bought the secret from Jean Baptiste le Prince, a French engraver. As soon as Sandby had shown the way by publishing *Twelve Views in Aquatinta from Drawings taken on the Spot in South Wales* (1775), he had many followers. The name of James Malton is familiar to collectors, for his aquatinted Dublin views, published 1792–9, while his brother, Thomas Malton, is known for his London and Westminster views, dated 1792–1801, and Oxford views dated 1802. Other accomplished aquatinters were William Daniell and his uncle, Thomas Daniell, for Oriental scenes and views of Great Britain. D. and R. Havell and J. C. Stadler were also masters of this method of engraving.

Boxing, racing, hunting, and other sports

The Vale of Aylesbury Steeplechase, aquatint by C. & G. Hunt after F. C. Turner, 1836. British Museum

attracted scores of aquatinters. *The Interior of the Fives Court with Randall and Turner Sparring*, for example, is crowded with interest. The painting is by T. Blake and the print by Charles Turner (who, among other important works, engraved twenty-four plates after J. M. W. Turner's *Liber Studiorum*).

Many of the foreground figures are portraits of personalities connected with the 'fancy'. We learn from a key that Jem Belcher is among them, but the famous pugilist died long before the print was made. Lifeguardsman Shaw, also a champion boxer, and one of the soldiers in uniform, was killed at Waterloo; but it was not infrequently the convention to commemorate in prints the figures of celebrities who had been popularly connected with sport.

Settling Day at Tattersalls, aquatint by Charles Hunt after James Pollard, 1836

What better impression could be gained of Tattersall's as it was in the last years of William IV than from the print entitled *Epsom* by Charles Hunt, after J. Pollard? It is an aquatint full of figure, sartorial, and architectural ingenuities. Charles Hunt (*fl*. 1820–50) has about 120 plates to his credit, including many of racehorses.

Sporting art and the Alken family are synonymous, and they exhausted every aspect of the subject. Henry T. Alken (1785–1851) was the best artist in several generations, and certainly no other sporting painter expressed with keener fun and more accurate knowledge the 'ritual' and predicaments of hunting, racing, fishing, and shooting. To detail all the prints, either by Alken himself or other engravers after his pictures and drawings, would necessitate volumes. Dates appear on prints from 1813 to 1859 inclusive. Some interesting examples are *Shooting Discoveries* (1816); *How to Qualify for a Meltonian*, aquatinted by 'Ben Tally Ho', Alken's pseudonym; *On the Road to the Derby* (1819); *The High Mettled Racer*, in which set he collaborated with T. Sutherland (1821); *First Steeplechase on Record, or the Night Riders of Nacton*, engraved by J. Harris (1839).

First Introduction to Hounds is also by J. Harris, dated 1850, and is probably from a picture by Samuel Henry Alken, Henry T. Alken's son, who signed himself H. Alken, thereby causing no little confusion to students of this family of sporting artists.

James Pollard was another versatile painter who provided engravers with plenty of sporting 'copy'. F. Rosenberg's plate of *The Yard of the Swan with Two Necks*, showing the Royal Mails preparing to start for the West of England, is a very rare print.

Coaching, which reached its zenith during the time of George IV, provided many lively subjects for the engraver, and a splendid coaching print is

The Start for the Memorable Derby of 1844, aquatint after J. F. Herring Senior. Fores Ltd, London

T. Sutherland's *The Peacock, Islington*, after Pollard (1823). Sutherland is a very subtle master of aquatint. Another coaching subject of exquisite quality is T. H. A. Fielding's *Elephant and Castle* (1836), also after Pollard.

The heroic and hazardous years from 1793 to the eclipse of Napoleon at Waterloo brought a patriotic sentiment into the print world, and many plates were made with a naval interest, such as *Representation of the Battle of Trafalgar* by J. Yeakes, after T. Whitcombe. The antics of Napoleon repeatedly touched off 'salvoes' of satirical squibs, and two contemporary geniuses who delighted the public by 'despoiling' the Corsican ogre, when they were not ridiculing home affairs, political and social, were Joseph Gillray (1757–1815), and Thomas Rowlandson (1750–1827), some of whose plates can be very coarse and violent. An amusing Rowlandson drawing, etched also by him for the purpose of the aquatint by Thomas Malton, is *A Sudden Squall in Hyde Park*. It shows the panic among 'fashionables' caught in a shower. Joseph Grego, in his book on Rowlandson, identifies the figure on horseback as the Prince of Wales, and that standing in the lofty phaeton is Lord Barrymore. Prints after Rowlandson should be studied in *The Microcosm of London* series (1808–10), *Dance of Death* (1815–16), and other publications by the enterprising Rudolph Ackermann.

Aquatinting is a method of etching in tone. In pure aquatint no lines are necessary, but most of the specimens mentioned above and those generally in vogue during its heyday included the use of line. The copperplate must first be prepared with a ground either of powdered asphaltum or resin dust or a spirit solution, which produces a tiny porous, reticulated surface into which the acid bites, leaving a tone

Far right Exhibition Staircase, engraving by Thomas Rowlandson, 1794. Victoria & Albert Museum

Right Juvenile Monstrosities by George Cruikshank, 1825. Victoria & Albert Museum

Part of the French display at the Great Exhibition, 1851, lithograph published by the Dickinson Brothers

so minutely even all over as to print like a wash drawing. Variety of tone in aquatint, like degrees of strength in line etching, is obtained by 'stopping out'. The Malton print after Rowlandson is a typical example of the method. The general effect is as of a watercolour. Pure aquatint tones make up the sky. Figures and buildings are delineated.

By the turn of the nineteenth century the craft had become crystallized in the works of many gifted performers who supplied the print sellers and public. They served a utilitarian purpose. Here and there a few great original artists – John Crome, Thomas Girtin, and J. M. W. Turner – made use of the copperplate with individual distinction. Crome's *Mousehold Heath*, Girtin's softground *Views of Paris and Its Environs*, acquatinted by F. C. Lewis and other engravers (1802–3), Turner's pregnant outlines as the basis for full-tone plates, may be cited as masterpieces of creative engraving.

The medium of the copperplate, however, was temporarily superseded by lithography, the new invention for multiplying prints. Lithography, as its name implies, means writing, or drawing, on stone. Brought to England in the first decade of the nineteenth century, it particularly attracted the watercolour painters, notably Richard Parkes Bonington. His best lithographs are to be found in that sumptuous publication *Voyages pittoresques et romantiques dans l'ancienne France*, sponsored by the French Government, the first volume of which was published in 1822. Among other English artists who contributed to this work were Samuel Prout, J. D. Harding and Thomas Shotter Boys. No lithographer excelled Boys in his handling of this method of art expression. Two classics on the subject are his *Picturesque Architecture in Paris, Ghent, Antwerp, Rouen, etc.* (1839) and *London as it is* (1842). *Entrance to the Strand from Charing Cross* is one of many superb architectural lithographs by Boys.

The virtue of lithography is that the print from the stone has the appearance of an original drawing, and many lithographers drew direct on the stone. The line is neither incised nor raised. The chalk or crayon used must contain a certain amount of grease. The drawing complete, the stone is sponged with acid, which fixes the drawing, but the acid is removed before it has time to bite into the stone. The stone is then moistened with water, and as grease and water will not mix, the greasy drawing rejects the water, while those parts of the stone untouched by the chalk absorb it. Greasy ink on a roller is then passed over the stone and adheres to the drawing only for the purpose of the print.

An important figure in lithography was Charles Joseph Hullmandel (1789–1850), who is credited with having invented the method whereby lithographs could be printed with oil colours direct from the stone instead of being tinted afterwards by hand. He thus developed a method that made the chromolithographic print the most popular style of reproduction during, at least, the second quarter of the nineteenth century.

South Devon Railway, View of Landslip near the Parson and Clerk Rock between Dawlish and Teignmouth, engraving on stone by F. Jones, lithograph by W. Spratt, 1852.

Mezzotints

The mezzotint was brought to its highest point of perfection in England during the second half of the eighteenth century, and although its depth and subtlety of tone, delicacy and velvet-like texture had always been admired, it was only during the last three decades or so of the nineteenth century that the first large collections began to be formed – notably those of Lord Cheylesmore (the whole of which was left to the British Museum), H. S. Theobald, Fritz Reiss, and Martin Erdmann, not to mention countless smaller collections. During the first thirty years of this century mezzotints enjoyed a reputation in the art auction rooms of London bordering on absurdity: in 1923 £3,045 was paid for Valentine Green's *The Ladies Waldegrave*.

The best mezzotinters have highly individual styles; yet it must be emphasized that the mezzotint is essentially an interpretive print: the original is generally an oil painting, usually a portrait. There is little doubt that many mezzotints, in so far as two media are comparable, are superior to their originals: compare, for example, John Raphael Smith's *Mrs Carnac* with Reynolds's original in the Wallace Collection. Although many mezzotints have been printed in colours, the effect being often very impressive, the mezzotint depends on its rich tonal qualities for its effect of colour, thus rendering real colours superfluous, even distracting: so one must expect a mezzotint to be printed in black or deep shades of brown. Anyone who has seen a row of well-framed mezzotints ranged along a wall cannot fail to have been impressed by their decorative effect; their purely tonal colouring seems to enhance nearly all normal colour patterns of the average interior.

A mezzotint is produced by roughening, or grounding, a highly polished sheet of copper all over with a rocker, an instrument resembling a chisel but having a curved serrated edge with cutting teeth. The blade of the rocker is rocked to and fro in hundreds of crisscross lines until the plate is so roughened that there is no discernible pattern. The grooves caused by laying the ground hold the ink. If the plate were inked over at this stage and an impression taken on a sheet of paper a uniformly deep black image would result. In order to produce a mezzotint the ground has to be scraped. With a scraper, a tool with a flat, curved blade finely sharpened, the engraver scrapes away at the ground on to which the design has been sketched, smoothing down those portions which are to be lighter than the rest, and continuing until the right contrast of light and dark tones has been produced to complete the design. If the engraver wants a highlight he polishes that particular part of the surface with a burnisher. It will have become apparent from the process described that the mezzotint is ideally suited to effects of moonlight, the representation of dress and velvet hangings, and softness of facial expression: in fact, all the trappings of a portrait.

The mezzotint was invented by Ludwig von Siegen (1609–76), a soldier in the service of William VI, Landegrave of Hesse-Cassel. Von Siegen was a lover of the arts and particularly of engraving. The first finished mezzotint was a portrait of the Landgrave's mother, *The Landegravine Amelia Elizabeth* done in the year 1642. Von Siegen kept the process secret until twelve years later when he met a fellow soldier artist and engraver, none other than Prince Rupert. The Prince at once saw the possibilities. Before long he produced a mezzotint, *The Executioner of John The Baptist* after Ribera, the intensity and power of which has seldom been equalled in this medium. The quality of this print may in part be due to the strange appearance of early mezzotints, which have all the primitive force of an entirely new medium, but more particularly because of obvious indications that the process was different from that commonly used during the next 200 years. Thus it was that Prince Rupert introduced the art to England, where it rapidly took roots. Abroad, where the line engraving held first place, the mezzotint flourished little and indeed became known as 'the English Manner'.

One of the first to work in 'The English Manner' was a Dutchman named Abraham Blooteling (1634–98), already distinguished abroad for his line engravings. During his four years in England from 1672 he engraved a number of mezzotint portraits after Lely with considerable success; perhaps the finest was his *James, Duke of Monmouth*. The honour of producing the first dated mezzotint by an Englishman falls to William Sherwin (*fl.* 1669–1711). This was a portrait of Charles II dated 1669. The weakness of this print is its coarse texture, a fault with most early mezzotints. Sherwin was a talented amateur. Another was Francis Place (1647–1728), who was quickly drawn to the new medium, producing a few smooth-toned mezzotints. With Isaac Beckett (1653–1719) we come to the first English mezzotint engraver who practised extensively and may be said to have founded a school. As with most mezzotinters of this period, a large proportion of his prints are after the fashionable portraitists of the day, first Lely, then Kneller. He engraved about 100 known plates in which he shows a skilful use of the scraper, although tending at times to a deadly monotony. Occasionally he achieved sufficient grace to rival John Smith. A typical example of Beckett at his best may be seen in his *Lady Williams* after Wissing. One of the most interesting of this early group was George White (1684–1732). He tended to use the etched line in combination with the scraper, a practice common to both the earliest and the latest mezzotint engravers. He was, perhaps, the first to show the affinity between artist and engraver which characterizes the best mezzotints, in his broad, fluent strokes, which catch the spirit of brushwork in oil painting. This is particularly evident in his *William Dobson* after Dobson.

John Smith (*c.* 1652–1742), the first of the great masters of the mezzotint, produced nearly 300 portraits, ranging in quality from dull to excellent. Unfortunately a great number of Smith's plates were extensively printed from after his death. Thus impressions from these plates, faded and ghostly, are commonly met with, and others, when he destroyed the plates, are extremely rare. An early impression of one of his prints, such as *Mrs Arabella Hunt* after Kneller or *Charles XII of Sweden* after Von Krafft, shows Smith to have been master of his medium. In

Charles XII of Sweden, mezzotint by John Smith after David von Krafft, 1701

the latter print the sensitive face of the great soldier set in the flowing curls of his periwig and the steely glint of the armour are engraved with refinement and vigour, characteristic of the subject of the portrait. Indeed, the qualities of John Smith's style at its best are sensitivity, strength, and a kind of watery lucidity, which can be most readily admired in some of the very small subject plates after Titian, Correggio, and other Italians. These tiny crystallizations from great originals are among the most lovely of all mezzotints.

If Smith dissipated his energy in overproduction, John Faber the younger (1684–1756) spread his rather meagre talent over more than 400 plates. Occasionally, in prints like his *Lady Christiana Moray Abercairny* after Davison and his very rare *Lute-player* after Franz Hals, he was equal to the best of John Smith. He is chiefly remembered for his forty-eight portraits of the Kit-Kat Club after Kneller and the twelve *Beauties of Hampton Court*. He lived to engrave portraits after Sir Joshua Reynolds.

During the first forty years of the eighteenth century the mezzotint went into a decline; for the stiff and awkward style of the fashionable portraitists of that period gave little encouragement, and it was due to the work of two engravers in Dublin, Andrew Miller and John Brooks, that the art was kept alive. The rise of Reynolds, Romney, and Gainsborough gave the mezzotint exactly the kind of stimulus it needed, and one by one the Dublin engravers came to London, so that in a short time the mezzotint flourished again until it quickly attained a glory never surpassed.

Of the Irish group, James McArdell (1729–65) was the greatest. In his short life of thirty-six years he engraved over 200 plates, and he is the first to have engraved to any great extent after Reynolds. Scarcely any of his plates are without distinction, and the finest have few equals. He was matchless in his ability to stimulate the actual texture of costumes. His best plates glow with the most radiant kind of virtuosity, so that one is compelled to turn to them again and again. His *Duchess of Ancaster* after Thomas Hudson is one of the most beautiful female portraits and one of the greatest mezzotints ever engraved. This must always be one of the first to be sought by the collector. The sweetness of expression, elegance of pose, and the luxuriant dexterity with which the dress is engraved combine to produce a print of consummate brilliance. The same power may be seen in his *Lady Mary Coke* after Ramsay, and again in his *Lords John and Bernard Stuart* after Van Dyck. Others of special quality are *Lady Charlotte Fitzwilliam* after Reynolds and *Mrs Middleton* after Lely. McArdell's contemporary and fellow Irishman Richard Houston (1721–75) is chiefly remembered for his powerful interpretations of Rembrandt. Of his prints after Reynolds, *Harriet Powell* has always been popular.

With Edward Fisher (1722–85), another of the Irish school, we come to a powerful engraver who earned Reynolds's unfair rebuke that he paid too much attention to unnecessary details. On the contrary, Fisher showed great skill in his handling of tone surfaces. Of his sixty-odd plates one must single out *Lady Elizabeth Keppel* after Reynolds. This plate went through five states. In the third state the inscription was carefully erased so as to stimulate a first state. An early state will reveal the true richness and variety of this dignified print, in which Fisher

Mary, Duchess of Ancaster, mezzotint by James McArdell after Thomas Hudson, 1757

makes skilful use of the etching needle. His *Hope Nursing Love* after Reynolds combined strength with sweetness, and has a sumptuous tonal quality. Yet another Irishman, John Dixon (1730–1800), had great merit. His *Duchess of Ancaster* after Reynolds is a powerful print. The same must be said of his *Rembrandt's Frame-maker* after Rembrandt. The last of the Irish group, James Watson (1739–90), was an engraver of considerable delicacy and technical skill, though sometimes lacking in strength. His many plates have a consistently high quality, and he is said to have always destroyed an unsatisfactory plate rather than re-engrave on it. Of his male portraits *Dr Johnson* and *Thomas Burke* after Reynolds and *Augustus Hervey* after Gainsborough are noteworthy. Among the women, prints like his *Countess of Suffolk* after Read and *Mrs Hale* after Reynolds are typical.

William Pether (1731–1821) is placed slightly apart from the main stream. He engraved some very powerful mezzotints, few of them portraits. His best are after Rembrandt and Joseph Wright of Derby. *A Philosopher giving a Lecture on the Orrery* shows him to be a master of brilliant artificial-light effects. Richard Earlom (1743–1822), an engraver justly famous for his versatility and skill, produced some fine mezzotints after Van Huysum, Snyders, and Mario de' Fiori. These flower pieces, market scenes, and *The Concert of Birds*, in particular, after the last of these make a welcome break from the tradition of portraiture.

The great period of the mezzotint may be said to fall between approximately 1770 and 1810, and we come now to the school of mezzotinters who brought the medium nearest to perfection during the time of Reynolds's mature period.

Few names shine as brightly in the history of the mezzotint as that of Valentine Green (1739–1813). A native of Worcestershire, he learnt to engrave in mezzotint after a short spell of line engraving, and during his life produced some hundreds of plates. His style, at its best, is distinguished by the utmost delicacy and smoothness, and by the most meticulous handling of tone surfaces: at its worst his prints are flat to the point of monotony. The brilliance of his best plates and the skill with which Reynolds's portraits are translated to the engraver's medium have placed his plates among the most highly prized of all, a fact once reflected in the auction rooms, where hundreds of pounds were paid for single impressions. Out of a score of outstanding plates may be mentioned his *Maria Cosway* after herself, a portrait of haunting beauty, *Valentine Green* after Abbott, a fine male portrait, and of the many portraits after Reynolds: *The Duchess of Rutland* (for which £1,555 has been paid in the auction room), *The Duchess of Devonshire* (£1,333 was paid in 1924), *The Ladies Waldegrave*, a lovely but rare print, *Lady Elizabeth Compton*, and the sensitive and sophisticated print of *Louise, Countess of Aylesford*. From a host of prints after other artists one might add the suavely executed *General Washington* after Peale.

The name of Thomas Watson (1748(43?)–81) also stands high among mezzotinters. His powerful style is characterized by great depth and warmth of tone. His famous *Lady Bampfylde* after Reynolds for long held the record auction price of 1,200 guineas in the Huth sale of 1905. The large triple portrait known as *The Three Graces* after Reynolds is a print of most impressive richness and dignity. *Warren Hastings* after Reynolds is a notable mezzotint. In a set of six prints entitled *The Windsor Beauties* after Lely, Watson engraved with the assurance of a master. In 1778 Watson took William Dickinson (1746–1823) into partnership. Dickinson was a fine engraver with a stylistic affinity to Watson. The treatment of backgrounds, in the suggestion of thundery skies, rich foliage, and streaks of light became a convention with later engravers. Dickinson had the lighter touch, and in two full-length portraits after Reynolds, *Diana Viscountess Crosbie* and *Mrs Mathew*, he placed himself in the first rank. Characteristic of his grace and vigour are *Miss Benedetta Ramus* and *Mrs Pelham feeding Chickens.*

With one or two notable exceptions, John Jones (1745–97) is chiefly remembered as an engraver of male portraits. He had a bold painterly style which may be seen in his many portraits after Romney, of which his *Edmund Burke* is a fine example. The fascination of *Madame Giovanni Baccelli* is vividly conveyed in his full-length portrait after Gainsborough.

By far the most generally talented of them all is John Raphael Smith (1752–1812). An artist in his own right, J. R. Smith handled the mezzotint with the freedom and assurance of an original artist. His powerful style, changing with ease from boldness to restraint according to the nature of the subject, leaves mere interpretation far behind. Of the many superb prints after Reynolds, Romney, and Gainsborough, one can only list a few. The serenely beautiful print of *Mrs Carnac* (with an erstwhile sale record of £1,218) deserves pride of place; not far behind is his *Mrs Musters*; *Lady Catherine Pelham Clinton* and *The Children of Walter Synnot* are very appealing child subjects; and *Colonel Tarleton* is a vigorous portrait. Romney is no less well served in his large *The Gower Family*; the stylish costume in *Miss Cumberland* is accomplished with wonderful *panache*. Out of dozens of equally desirable prints may be mentioned *Lady Elizabeth Compton* after Peters, *The Fruit Barrow* after Walton, typical of his many genre pieces, and lastly his immensely powerful *John Philpot Curran* after Lawrence. George Morland's bucolic scenes were ably translated by J. R. Smith.

Left Miss Benedetta Ramus, mezzotint by William Dickinson after George Romney, 1779

Right Mr Samuel Chiffney, winner of the Derbys of 1818 and 1820, mixed method print by F. C. Turner, 1807. British Museum

John Dean (1750–1805) was a mezzotinter of unusual refinement, whose few plates have more charm than vigour. James Walker (1748–1808) engraved one or two fine plates, notably *Mrs Musters* and the rare *Admiral Sir Hyde Parker*. John Young (1755–1825) is chiefly remembered for his attractive plates after Hoppner, including the famous *The Godsall Children*. Gainsborough Dupont (1767–97) engraved twelve of his uncle Thomas Gainsborough's works, of which *Colonel St Leger*, pendant to J. R. Smith's *George, Prince of Wales*, is a fine example. Charles Phillips (1737–73) is remembered solely for his rare and lovely print *Nelly O'Brien* after Reynolds.

Even during J. R. Smith's lifetime, the mezzotint was on the decline. This was partly due to a similar decline in portraiture: the latent harshness and facility of Lawrence's portraits were less suited than the softer and richer tones of Reynolds's canvases to translation into the medium of mezzotint. William Ward (1766 and 1826) was scarcely less good than his master J. R. Smith. While he excelled at portraiture he is chiefly remembered for his fine prints of farmyard and ale-house scenes after his brother-in-law George Morland. His many portraits include the rare circular print, *Elizabeth, Countess of Mexborough*, the very popular *Daughters of Sir Thomas Frankland*, and *The Salad Girl* (*Mrs Phoebe Hoppner*), all after Hoppner. The full-length portrait of *Henry Beaufoy* is an attractive print after Gainsborough. James Ward (1769–1859), in his life of ninety years, engraved only in his early period. He at least equalled his brother in quality, if not in output, producing mezzotints in a vigorous and powerful style. The affectations first noticeable in Thomas Watson's prints are more pronounced in James Ward's. His extremely rare and beautiful print *Mrs Michael Angelo Taylor as 'Miranda'* after Hoppner is one of the most desirable of all mezzotints. A fine portrait of *Joseph Wright of Derby* after himself is also worthy of note.

S. W. Reynolds (1773–1835) produced a great number of plates, the best of which are his earliest. His *Duchess of Bedford* (1803) is perhaps the last of the great full-length portraits of women in mezzotint. Charles Turner (1774–1857) engraved a variety of subjects on a very large number of plates. Only his earliest work is of real interest, and shows him to be a good interpreter of Raeburn. His *Lord Newton* after this artist reveals Turner at his best. Samuel Cousins (1801–87) engraved a great quantity of plates after Lawrence, many of them on steel, the pernicious invention of a certain William Say (1768–1834) dating from 1820. This invention may be said to have dealt the deathblow to the mezzotint as a medium. A print engraved on steel, a harder-wearing metal than copper, will produce well over a thousand good impressions, but the result lacks the marvellous quality of a mezzotint engraved on copper, which can produce only about two dozen perfect impressions before the plate begins to wear. A brief and final mention must be made of David Lucas (1802–81), whose talented plates after Constable's landscapes, seem to underline the suitability of the medium to portraiture.

Mezzotints are fragile and should be well cared for, and protected against dirt, exposure, or too much handling. It is then that they will give most pleasure.

European

Prints

'Almost every man of taste is in some degree a collector of prints', wrote Joseph Strutt in 1785, when the vogue for print collecting was at its height and no gentleman's library was considered complete without a bulging portfolio of etchings and engravings. The same could hardly be said today, but there are signs that the tide of taste is changing once again. Now that paintings and drawings of high quality are becoming annually scarcer and more expensive, an increasing number of collectors are turning their attention to works by the outstanding etchers and engravers of the past, and discovering that these prints are no mere 'second-best' alternatives, but individual works of art of considerable interest and great beauty.

Prints may be divided into two main categories, the original and the reproductive, the former being those etched, engraved, or lithographed by the artists who provided the designs, and the latter those executed by one artist after the paintings or drawings of another. The appeal of original prints need hardly be laboured, for they often form as important a part of an artist's output and give as clear an impression of his personality as his work in other mediums. Indeed, many great artists found in print making, usually in etching, an alternative means of self-expression. Reproductive prints should not, however, be slighted. Dürer usually and Holbein invariably employed skilled craftsmen to transfer their designs to the printer's block, and throughout the subsequent centuries artists who were uncertain of their abilities as cutters and engravers called on specialists to perform these technical parts of their work. The process of reproductive engraving is a difficult one, requiring not only a virtuoso's command of the burin but also an intuitive understanding of the master's painting or drawing. Great reproductive engravers (like Marcantonio Raimondi) have possessed both technical ability and also a high degree of interpretative artistry. Both reproductive and original prints were widely collected in the past, and both types were extensively faked. The collector must therefore be on his guard against forgeries, especially of the most valuable prints.

FAKES

'Woe to you! you thieves and imitators of other people's labour and talents. Beware of laying your audacious hands on our works,' wrote Dürer at the end of a series of woodcuts, but his words were little heeded, and few artists have suffered more than he from the wiles of thieves and imitators. Even in his own time his woodcuts were plagiarized with varying degrees of fidelity and his monogram was freely applied to indifferent works by other artists. The simple lines of the woodcut provided fakers with some of their easiest work, and early prints have been imitated in freehand by the use of new blocks which reproduce the old designs, by lithograph, and by zincograph. Most of these fraudulent prints were copies of well-known works, but one nineteenth-century forger was sufficiently enterprising and, we may now say, sufficiently rash, as to fabricate a whole series of cunning pastiches called the *Saints of Basle*, which he dated 1414 and which enjoyed such a success among unsuspecting collectors of incunabula that it went into three editions, marked by miniscule differences of state. Rembrandt's etchings were copied freehand and in the mid-eighteenth century Benjamin Wilson etched an 'original' Rembrandt landscape which hoaxed Thomas Hudson. But his reputation has suffered more harm from his own plates, some fifty of which survived him and were unscrupulously used to multiply impressions long after his death. To repair the damage of frequent use these plates had to be heavily re-worked, and the prints made from them have none of the sparkling freshness of those Rembrandt pulled himself. In the detection of forged prints the study of watermarks is, alas, of little avail, since most competent fakers took the precaution of printing or drawing their impostures on paper of the correct period. The only sure method of showing up a dubious print is to compare it with a similar work of undoubted authenticity in one of the great collections of Europe or America.

The prints mentioned in this section are those valued primarily for their aesthetic or technical merits, but there are, of course, many others, the main interest of which lies in their subject matter. These include portraits, topographical views, caricatures, and representations of historical events, many of which have great charm. Their importance to the historian is obvious, but the collector of fine prints concerns himself with them only if they have independent artistic qualities.

INCUNABULA

The earliest surviving European prints date from the first half of the fifteenth century. They represent religious scenes and were mostly printed in monasteries, usually from wooden blocks but sometimes from metal plates. Designed principally for an unlettered public, they have none of the sophistication of contemporary manuscript illuminations, but are characterized by an engaging peasant naïveté of conception and rustic virility of line. By 1457, however, the art of the woodblock carver had developed to such a degree that he was able to produce the superb two-colour initials to Fust and Schoeffer's Latin Psalter. In the 1450s and 1460s fine line engravings were being printed in Germany not only of religious themes such as *The Death of Mary* but also of such decidedly secular subjects as *The Gardens of Love*.

Martin Schongauer (*c.* 1430–91), the first great German line engraver, emerged at Colmar in about 1453. A master of his medium, able to give his prints a greater subtlety of tone than any of his predecessors, he was also a religious artist of great power, as is shown by his brilliant engraving of *Christ Falling Beneath the Cross*. His near contemporary, Israhel van Meckenem (d. 1503) executed a number of religious engravings as well as a series of a dozen very attractive genre scenes. Meanwhile, the art of line engraving had been introduced into Italy by Maso Finiguerra (1426–64), a Florentine niellist whose work shows the strong influence of Antonio Pollaiuolo (1432–98). Unfortunately Pollaiuolo's own graphic work is known by only one plate, the superb and mysterious *Battle of Ten Nudes*, which shows his complete mastery of the medium and is drawn with the same sinewy strength as his paintings. In northern Italy, Andrea Mantegna (1431–1506) was producing engravings in a similarly fine but somewhat harder style. Before the century had ended the *Hypnerotomachia Poliphili* illustrated with numerous highly sophisticated and elegantly simple woodcuts was published in Venice. Within 100 years the art of the woodcutter and engraver had developed from infancy to maturity.

Battle of Ten Nudes, engraving by Antonio Pollaiuolo (1429–98). Metropolitan Museum of Art

SIXTEENTH-CENTURY PRINTS

First among early sixteenth-century print makers was Albrecht Dürer (1471–1528), who executed etchings, line engravings, and drypoint engravings as well as designing the woodcuts for which he is principally remembered. His prints are technically flawless, having an elegant sensitivity of line and subtlety of tone which demonstrate his perfect understanding of the potentialities of each medium he employed. Moreover, the extraordinarily wide range of their subject matter – religious, mythological, and allegorical – reveals him as one of the great personalities of the age of Humanism and the Reformation. As to the aesthetic value of his prints, suffice it to say that he is the only major European artist whose stature would be undiminished if he were known only by his graphic work. Hans Holbein (1497–1543) showed a similarly nice regard for the woodblock medium in his *Dance of Death* series, and in the Netherlands Lucas van Leyden (1494–1533) adapted his style to the needs of the copper plate. Among Italian line engravers of this period Marcantonio Raimondi (1480–*c.* 1530) is probably the greatest, though his work was largely reproductive. Notable French engravers do not appear until later in the century, the earliest of interest being Jean Duvet (1485–*c.* 1561), whose works, especially the *Apocalypse* series, seem to recreate the fervid mysticism of the Middle Ages.

The art of etching, which was developed in Germany at the beginning of the century and practised by Dürer, was introduced into Italy in about 1520. Here it was taken up by Parmigianino (1504–40) and later by Federigo Barocci (1528–1612), who executed a few exquisite plates in this medium. The most notable etchers of the later sixteenth century were, however, the group of Netherlandish landscape painters which included Pieter Breughel (1525–69), Jan Breughel (1568–1625), and Paul Bril (1554–

Left Wood block and print from *The Passion* by Albrecht Dürer, 1510

Below Saint Eustace, woodcut by Albrecht Dürer. Christie, Manson & Woods, London

1626). The chiaroscuro process also originated in Germany and was introduced by Ugo da Carpi (*fl. c.* 1455–1527) into Italy, where it was found a perfect means for the reproduction of mannerist designs. Towards the end of the century it was much used in the Netherlands by Hendrik Goltzius (1558–1616) and Abraham Bloemaert (1564–1661).

SEVENTEENTH-CENTURY PRINTS

The seventeenth century may well be regarded as the golden age of etching which was practised by a considerable number, one might almost say the majority, of leading painters. Moreover, the period is marked by the emergence of a number of highly interesting artists who are known principally, if not solely, for their works in this medium. At the beginning of the century in France, Jacques Bellange (*fl.* 1600–16) evolved a highly sophisticated and fantastic personal style, based on a strange medley of mannerist influences, which he expressed in a few etchings of scenes (mostly religious) populated with small-headed, long-necked women in sweeping robes. Another latter-day mannerist etcher was Jacques Callot (1592–1635), who worked from 1611 to 1621 at the Medici court, where he executed vast plates of Florentine festivities and tiny grotesques of prancing, gesticulating, and grimacing pantaloons, hunchbacks, and dwarfs. A note of seriousness crept into his work after his return to France and in 1633 he etched the terrifying yet very beautiful *Grandes Misères de la Guerre*, which eloquently expressed his horror at the atrocities of the Thirty Years' War. Callot's Florentine pupil, Stefano della Bella (1610–64), brilliantly developed the fantastic strain in his master's work and also executed some delicate topographical plates. Abraham Bosse (1602–76), who collaborated with Callot in Paris, applied himself to the semi-satirical rendering of genre scenes. A French artist of a very different stamp. Claude

Lorrain (1600–82), etched some of his idyllic visions of the Roman Campagna and that more volatile landscape painter, the Neapolitan Salvator Rosa (1615–73), etched a few plates of bloodthirsty *banditti* and *Landsknechte*.

In the Netherlands Sir Anthony van Dyck (1599–1641) showed himself a masterly etcher in twenty-two prints (mostly portraits) which he produced in the late 1620s. Another notable Flemish etcher of this period was Hercules Seghers (*c.* 1590–*c.* 1635), who executed prints of landscapes and other subjects in a wholly individual manner and experimented by printing them on tinted paper or linen. But the outstanding figure of the century is, of course, Rembrandt (1606–69), who began his work as an etcher in about 1628.

Right La Toilette de Venus, mezzotint by Jean-François Janinet after François Boucher, British Museum

Below Landscape with Sportsman and Dogs, etching by Rembrandt van Rijn, *c.* 1652. Art Gallery and Temple Newsam House, Leeds

More than any other great artist, Rembrandt found an ideal means of self-expression in the art of etching, and for a full understanding of his personality his works in this medium must be given as much prominence as his paintings and drawings. Tireless in his search for expression, he experimented not only with problems of composition and form but also with technical matters, combining the drypoint with the etching needle to obtain some of his finest effects. His 300-odd prints, varying in size from the tiny *Beggars* to such grandiose plates as *The Death of the Virgin*, testify to his remarkable virtuosity as a craftsman no less than to his fecundity as an imaginative artist. With equal success he was able to represent the icy calm of a Dutch winter landscape and the stormy drama of *The Descent from the Cross*, the beautiful and resigned face of his mother and the angry countenance of a starving beggar. Furthermore, his etchings supplement the incomparable autobiography presented by his self-portraits in oil, showing him truculent in youth, pompously prosperous in maturity and utterly disillusioned in his last years. Few artists have rivalled the technical perfection of Rembrandt's etchings, and none has approached his ability to express the profoundest thoughts and emotions in this medium.

Below Nymph jumping over the clasped hands of two Satyrs, etching by Jean Honoré Fragonard, 1763. Fitzwilliam Museum

EIGHTEENTH-CENTURY PRINTS

At the beginning of the century, in France, Antoine Watteau (1684–1721) made a few etchings of gossamer delicacy; many of his drawings were etched by his pupil François Boucher (1703–70), who also did original work in this medium. Later, Jean Honoré Fragonard (1732–1806) etched a few plates of nymphs and satyrs which have the same gay lightness of touch as his drawings. But the greatest French contribution during this period was in book illustrations printed from line engravings designed by such master hands as H. F. Gravelot (1699–1773), Charles Eisen (1720–78), Charles N. Cochin (1715–90), and a host of others, some of whom engraved the architectural fantasies of Lajoue, the rococo furniture designs of Meissonnier, and the gay *chinoiseries* of Pillement. To obtain their effects of cobweb brittleness most of these artists employed a mixture of etching and engraving.

In Italy the most productive centre of print

making was Venice, where Giovanni Battista Tiepolo (1696–1770) and his son Giovanni Domenico Tiepolo (1727–1804) produced many lovely etchings of *capricci* and religious scenes. Canaletto (1697–1768) also etched *capricci* and some shimmering views of the lagoon. Moreover, a group of line engravers, of whom Marco Pitteri (1707–86) was probably the ablest, produced admirable prints after the drawings of G. B. Piazzetta and other contemporary masters. The most remarkable of Venetian graphic artists was, however, Giovanni Battista Piranesi (1720–78), who spent most of his working life in Rome, where he etched phantasmagoric scenes of imaginary prisons and scarcely less imaginative and dramatic views of classical ruins.

NINETEENTH-CENTURY PRINTS

The cult of the picturesque greatly increased the demand for topographical prints in the early nineteenth century. Perhaps the most notable artist to produce such works was Bartolomeo Pinelli (1781–1835), whose etching, engravings, and aquatints of Rome and the Campagna populated with picturesque bandits fighting, peasants gaming, and spruce young couples dancing the *saltarello* have greatly contributed to the northerner's romantic vision of Italy.

Soon after the beginning of the nineteenth century, lithography ousted nearly all other means of colour reproduction and provided artists with an alternative to etching. Many great artists, including Géricault, Delacroix, and Blake, essayed the new medium, but none as successfully as Francisco Goya (1746–1828). Goya found both lithography and aquatint excellent mediums in which to express his devastatingly satirical message, and his prints are among the finest ever made. Later in the century, lithography was employed by the two great French masters of caricature, Gavarni (1804–66) and Honoré Daumier (1808–79).

Top L'Aveu Difficile, mezzotint by Jean-François Janinet after Nicolas Lavreince, 1787. British Museum

Above A Perspective View from St Mark's Pillar to the Dalmatian Wharf, line and stipple engraving by G. Lereau after Canaletto

Silhouettes

Although its origins go back to classical antiquity, the silhouette as we recognize it today most likely originated at the end of the seventeenth century. Doubtless various influences contributed to its subsequent popularity, but probably the greatest stimulus it received came from the publication of Johann Kaspar Lavater's *Essays on Physiognomy* in the 1770s, in which, as well as claiming the silhouette to be the most faithful of all types of portrait, the author used many such portraits for illustrating his work.

At about this time silhouettes became fashionable and their popularity spread everywhere, finding admirers so diverse in character as Goethe, George III of England, and Catherine the Great of Russia.

The earliest silhouettes were probably scissor cuts. One was that of William and Mary, said to have been cut by Elizabeth Pyburg (*fl.* 1699). Indeed, these early cut silhouettes have great charm, and are much sought after by collectors. Some of them – especially those of Francis Torond (1743–1812) – are of great rarity.

Above Bacchus, etching by Francisco Goya after Diego Velázquez

Right Église et Ferme d'Eragny, four-colour etching by Camille Pissarro, 1890. William Weston Gallery, London

Left Le Chapeau Épingle, nine-colour lithograph by Pierre Auguste Renoir, 1898. William Weston Gallery, London

The mid-nineteenth-century interest in the past brought about the revival of nearly all the old methods of reproduction for 'artistic' purposes. After about 1850 the lithographic and line-engraving processes were principally used for commercial purposes, while the crafts of woodblock cutting, etching, and drypoint engraving were reserved for artists; though relatively few of them attained an understanding of the mediums in which they worked. However, some revivalist engravers like William Hooper (1834–1912), who cut the Renaissance style woodblocks for books printed at the Kelmscott Press, achieved very fine effects. Several Impressionist painters, including Edgar Degas and Édouard Manet, created prints of exquisite quality.

But charming though these old cut silhouettes are, the art's highest peaks have undoubtedly been reached by artists producing painted work. It is generally agreed that one of the greatest silhouettists of all was John Miers (1758–1821), whose work is painted as finely as the most delicate miniature. Although not so prolific a worker as Miers, Isabella Beetham (*fl.* 1750), whose work was painted mostly on the reverse side of convex glass, is, so far as quality is concerned, at least his equal.

At the end of the eighteenth century the silhouette went into a period of decline, from which it was rescued mostly through the efforts of Augustin Amant Constant Fidèle Édouart, a French refugee who came to England in 1814. Édouart, a freehand cutter, initiated the second and last great period of English silhouettes. His output was enormous (he cut something approaching 250,000 likenesses), and this fact, coupled with the publication of his (now excessively rare) *Treatise* on the subject, published in 1835, gave a great impetus to the numerous and often very able school of amateur silhouettists that arose at the time.

The Continent, too, produced a large number of good silhouettists during the eighteenth and nineteenth centuries. The art flourished particularly in Germany. Goethe himself was a cutter, and mention must also be made of the delicate and lacy cutwork of Christina Luise Duttenhofer (1776–1829) and that of Philipp Otto Runge (1776/7–1810). France produced A. Forberger (1762–1865) and E. P. Sideau (*fl.* 1782); and Austria H. Loeschenkohl (*fl.* 1780) and Leopold Gross (*fl.* 1790). In fact, most European countries can boast at least one or two silhouettists of some standing.

Although silhouette work continues to be used even today, its heyday as a form of portraiture ended with the invention of photography. It is one of the few fields still open in which the collector can occasionally obtain genuine rarities at reasonable prices.

Japanese Prints

Seventeenth and Eighteenth Centuries

The Japanese print was 'discovered' soon after the opening up of the country to foreign visitors in 1854, and considerable impetus was given to the formation of collections later in the century by the enthusiasm of the French Impressionists and their protagonists, who found much that appealed to their aesthetic scenes, ever tuned to receive the new, the adventurous, the unacademic, in the calculated design and arbitrary use of form and colour, of the Japanese print designers. The most immediately attractive of these exotic engravings were the colour prints of the late eighteenth century, but in the methodical way of the European art historian it was not long before the origin of these gay pictures was traced back to black outline prints of the seventeenth century.

Indeed, the earliest wood engravings made in Japan belong to a very remote period. Some can reliably be given to the eighth century and, as wood engravings are still being published in Japan, the term 'Japanese print' might conceivably embrace everything from the crude Buddhistic cuts of an almost legendary antiquity to the pseudo-Picasso abstractions of postwar Tokyo artists. Specifically, however, the term is usually held to apply to the productions of a certain school of mainly Yedo artists, the Ukiyo-ye, which arose in the mid-seventeenth century, and whose work was virtually ended by the time of the Restoration in 1868.

The collector may not wish to limit himself strictly to this school: book illustrations of great beauty and originality were designed during the Tokugawa or Yedo period (1615–1868) by painters of various other schools whose styles differ vastly from the Ukiyo-ye. Nor need strict regard be given to the limits of the period: one needs to study the illustrated books of the early seventeenth century for the light they throw on the development of the designer's art; and though it is convenient to consider 1868 as a date closing a particular chapter of Japanese art, specimens of the work of artists who flourished thereafter may well be included in a collection, if for no other purpose than to exhibit the changes the 'Western invasion' brought about.

At the outset it should be remarked that Japanese prints are all woodblock prints and were issued as much in bound or book form as in the form of separate broadsheets. Folding albums (*gwajo*) and picture books (*yehon*) must come within a collector's purview, for no study of the art of the Japanese print as a whole can be complete unless the prints in books are considered side by side with those published as separate sheets. Moreover, whereas practically all the broadsheets were produced by the Ukiyo-ye school, artists of the classical, naturalistic, and impressionistic schools were responsible for some of the loveliest and most remarkable picture books ever printed, East or West.

TECHNIQUE

Wood engraving is the traditional, and almost exclusive, means of reproduction in Japan, as in the East generally. By the inheritance of the centuries-old lore of the craft, and by a rigorous apprenticeship, engravers were capable of almost incredible feats in making a facsimile of an artist's brush drawing. The painter-engraver was unknown: the engraver was a skilled craftsman whose sole task was to make a faithful reproduction of the artists' designs, just as the German engravers made facsimiles of Dürer's designs.

The wood used was normally cherrywood 'on the plank', in contrast to 'on the end grain' as in Europe since Bewick's day. The drawing, made on thin paper, was usually pasted face down on to the block, and the paper then scraped to render the drawing perfectly visible. The engraver or, more properly, cutter, for he used a cutting knife not an engraving tool, made incisions along both sides of the lines, afterwards removing the wood between, leaving the lines in relief.

The printer was, in his way, as much artist-craftsman as the engraver. The ink was brushed on to the block pigments being mixed with a little rice paste to give them consistency, and the impression taken by placing paper over the face of the block and burnishing the back with a rubbing implement called a *baren*. When colour printing from blocks was introduced a great deal devolved upon the printer. Black-ink proofs were taken from the 'key blocks' prepared from the artist's drawing, and the proofs then pasted down on to additional blocks, a separate one for each colour to be printed, the artist indicating on each proof, for the engraver's guidance, the area to be printed in the chosen colour.

In making a colour print, the same sheet of proofing paper had to pass first over the 'key block' and then over each colour block in turn. Accurate 'register' was achieved by a simple arrangement of a rightangle cut in the blocks at one side with a corresponding guideline cut at the opposite side.

In addition to the increase in the number of colour

blocks used, various refinements were introduced to embellish the prints, mentioned in the account that follows:

THE 'UKIYO-YE' OR 'PASSING WORLD' SCHOOL

The greatest single impetus to the development of Japanese print came from Hishikawa Moronobu (1626–94). Though not the titular founder of the Ukiyo-ye school (which came to be the Popular school identified with the common people, notwithstanding the fact that its founder was an aristocrat named Matabei), Moronobu came at a time when there was a rapidly expanding demand for illustrated literature of every kind – classical poetry, legend, novel, everyday happenings, descriptions of the well-known landmarks of the country, and especially of the capital, Yedo. Owing to his tutelage in several different schools of Japanese painting, he was capable of drawing in a number of styles, but his most justifiably admired prints and book illustrations show the early Ukiyo-ye style at its best. The bold line and undulating swing in the drawing, coupled with a compact and rhythmic pattern in the design, are characteristics that mark the work of all succeeding Ukiyo-ye artists, and in his treatment of his subject matter we discern already the sophistication, the raciness, and the vulgarity that, in greater or lesser degree, are in the make up of all subsequent prints of the school. Apart from his development of book illustration as an art, Moronobu is also credited with the production of the first separately printed sheets, called *ichimai-ye*.

Contemporaries of Moronobu, responsible for much fine work in book illustration, were Hinaya Ryūho, Yoshida Hanbei, Ishi-Kawa Ryusen, and Sugimura Jihei, all more or less independent of Moronobu. A little later there were Moronobu's direct pupils, Moroshige and Morofusa.

Towards the end of the seventeenth century prints began to be issued to record the *Kabuki* drama, the popular plays that were filling the Yedo theatres with devotees whose fanaticism was not only equal to the strain of day-long performances but also gave rise to a demand for pictures of favourite actors in their roles in the latest 'thriller'. Women were debarred from the stage, and female parts were played by men, some actor families specializing in women's roles. It was natural that the People's Theatre should have been recorded by the Ukiyo-ye artists, and actor prints are as numerous in their output as portraits of the reigning courtesans, the other principal subject.

Among the earliest to make these prints was Torii Kiyonobu (1664–1729), a great artist who had much influence on the development of the actor print, and whose own gift of expressive draughtsmanship and swirling design was never equalled. His pupils and followers include many of the best designers of the early eighteenth century – Kiyomasu I (1696?–1716?); Kiyomasu II (1706–65); Kiyonobu II (1702–52?), Kiyoshige, Kiyotada, Kiyotomo, and Terushige.

Most of these early prints were handcoloured, at first with *tan*, a strong red-lead pigment, later with more elaboration. Printing of colours by woodblocks did not occur until many years later.

Other powerful 'Primitives', as artists up to the introduction of colour printing in 1764 are called, are a group of four or five artists bearing the name Kwaigetsudō, whose superb *kakemono-ye* are among the rarest and the most coveted of all Japanese prints; and Nishikawa Sukenobu (1674–1754), whose work is almost confined to book illustrations, in which the rough boldness of his contemporaries is tempered with a grace and gentleness that was to have an immense effect upon aftercomers. Another great artist, a publisher, too, with a flair for technical devices, was Okumura Masanobu (1686–1764). Owing something to Moronobu, Kwaigetsudō, and Sukenobu, and passing through phases when the influence of each of these masters predominated in turn, Masanobu's fusion of strength and grace produced some of the loveliest prints of the first half of the seventeenth century. To him is probably attributable the introduction of *urushi-ye*, the lacquer prints' with applied metal dusts, whose glint still catches the eye, as it was meant to catch the eye of the Yedo purchaser over 200 years ago. His pupil Toshinobu (active 1725–50) also made some very attractive prints of this type.

About 1740, or soon after, occurred the momentous substitution of block printing of the colours for the hand application that had prevailed hitherto.

Okumura Masanobu has been credited with the introduction of the two-colour process, but by 1740 a number of gifted artists were working in the medium, any one of whom was capable of making the innovation. The most prominent were the Torii masters, Kiyonobu II, Kiyohiro (active 1737–68), and Kiyomitsu (1735–85), all carrying on in the family tradition of actor-print designing, and Nishimura Shigenaga (1697–1756), whose later work shows the trend towards a new ideal of womanhood that was to lead to the exquisite fragility of Harunobu's child-woman. The prints of the Ukiyo-ye school were not only a mirror of the life of the time, the daily events, the customs and festivals but also the glass of fashion. In them one follows the changing predilection of the Yedo male for women of Junoesque amplitude of form in the early years of the eighteenth century, garbed in clothes decorated with patterns that have large pictorial motifs, to the diminutive *musume* of the 1760s, disporting herself in silks that have the most intricate of pretty designs worked upon them. With this change, quite a gradual one, but speeded up after the introduction of the *beni-ye* prints, came another, no less significant, in the subjects portrayed, an introduction of a more domestic setting, of scenes from play or legend or even daily life, that are in some way made to seem idyllic, to belong to a never-never land of the Japanese artists' imagination.

This magical world is perhaps most the creation of Shigenaga's pupils – Ishikawa Toyonobu (1711–85), Suzuki Harunobu (1739?–70), Isoda Koryūsai (active 1764–80), and Kitao Shigemasa (1739–1819). Toyonobu was the earliest, and, under the name of Shigenobu, designed handcoloured prints before 1737. His later work, contemporary with that of Kiyomitsu and Kiyohiro, has an indivdual charm that has caused one Japanese enthusiast to call him the 'lyric poet of Ukiyo-ye'. Harunobu has been accredited – rightly or wrongly, it hardly matters – with the introduction of the full colour print which made its appearance about 1764. The innovation coincided with the issue of a flood of calendar prints for the year 1765, a number of which are known to have been designed by Harunobu. Between 1765 and his premature death in 1770 Harunobu designed

Left Two Geishas and a maid by Kitao Shigemasa, unsigned, *c.* 1778. British Museum

Right The actor Bando Mitsugoro as a Daimyo, by Katsukawa Shunshō, *c.* 1775–80

hundreds of prints that design, colouring, and an exquisite fancy combine to render among the most charming of all the prints of this school.

The introduction of polychrome printing was more the culmination of a gradual development than a sudden innovation, for three and four blocks had been used with entrancing effect by Toyonobu, Kiyomitsu, and Kiyotsune between 1760 and 1765, but the year 1765 is used as an arbitrary line between the 'primitives' and their successors. Thereafter, while there is little new technically in the production of the print once Harunobu and others had introduced a whole range of lovely colours hitherto untried, and the printers had perfected relief printing, blind printing or *gauffrage* and the use of gold and silver dusts and mica backgrounds, many great artists arose to make the fullest use of the perfected medium.

Koryūsai was not only a master of that most typically Japanese, and most exacting, format the *hashirakake*, the long panel print designed to hang on pillars, but he also popularized the large *ōban* sheet with pictures that are really 'fashion plates' showing the reigning beauties in the latest creations of the *hautcouturiers*. Katsukawa Sunshō (1726–92) brought to the narrow *hoso-ye* actor print wonderful powers of dramatic design, and tutored a whole school of artists, most of whom, like Shunkō, Shunjō, Shundō, Shunyen, and Shunsen, repeated almost exactly the style of their master, while Shunyei, though associated with the theatre, developed on more individual lines. Ippit-Susai Bunchō (active 1760–79) is sharply distinguishable from all his contemporaries, however similar his subject matter, for qualities that spring more, we feel, from an unusual personality than from any especial adroitness of hand. He was equally at home in the theatrical print as in the idyllic composition in Harunobu's vein.

Birds and Flowers by Isoda Koryūsai, *c.* 1775

After Harunobu's death in 1770 and Koryūsai's retirement about 1780, Torii Kiyonaga (1752–1815), came to the fore, and in the 1780s was responsible for a vogue for tall women of regal mien, who now ousted the dimimutive *musume* from favour. The diptych and triptych forms, in which the design is carried over two or three sheets, had an especial appeal to Kiyonaga, and through his magnificent example became popular formats with all succeeding Ukiyo-ye artists. As the creator of the currently fashionable feminine 'type', Kiyonaga influenced practically all his contemporary print designers, except perhaps the conservative, Shunshō, Shunchō, and Shunzan, originally pupils of Shunchō, and Shunman, who had studied under Shigemasa, were perhaps the most successful followers of the Kiyonaga model, the work of each having certain distinguishing traits, the recognition and identification of which is one of the subtler pleasures of connoisseurship. Kitao Masanobu (1761–1816), another pupil of Shigemasa's, designed some splendid prints in the early 1780s and seemed to vie for a time with Kiyonaga as the arbiter of fashion in Ukiyo-ye, but deserted painting for literature when quite a young man.

Women cutting and measuring stuff for dresses by Kitagawa Utamaro. British Museum

Beauty at her toilet by Kitagawa Utamaro, *c.* 1795. British Museum

Throughout its history, the Ukiyo-ye school received the stimulus from a new genius in its midst just when the influence of the last was beginning to wane. So now, as Kiyonaga went into retirement about 1790, Kitagawa Utamaro (1753–1806) became this new and revitalizing force. Beginning as a devotee to the Kiyonaga manner, and producing many lovely prints before 1790 rather in his style, Utamaro was afterwards responsible for a number of innovations – three-quarter-length 'portraits' with mica backgrounds; large portrait heads in which the design relies on the outlined features of the face and the decoratively coiffured hair; and, for a time, affectedly elongated girls whose extravagant height he used both to show to best advantage the glorious clothes they wear and to create sweeping and decorative compositions.

Chōbunsai Yeishi (active 1780–1800) was another artist who came to his maturity under the benign influence of Kiyonaga. He brought to his designs a refinement that makes his courtesan of the hour and his princess of olden times indistinguishable. His pupils, Yeishō, Yeiri, and Yeisui, were also responsible for prints of unusual refinement.

Two artists stand somewhat apart from their fellow print designers of the last decade of the eighteenth century: Toshūsai Sharaku (active 1794–5) and Yeishōsai Chōki (active 1782–95). The actor prints of Sharaku are phenomenal, even in company with the most powerful productions of such gifted contemporaries as Shunshō, outstanding in this field, or Shunyei, whose large 'portrait heads' preceded those of Sharaku by several years. His sudden emergence as a print designer, his short career, and his *faire brutale*, consitute the great mystery of the Ukiyo-ye. Chōki, much influenced by Kiyonaga, Utamaro, and Sharaku, designed a small number of prints of beauties, mostly printed on mica backgrounds, that are as distinctive among the *bijin-ye*, from subtleties of design and vague distortion of forms, as Sharaku's are among the theatrical prints.

The last years of the eighteenth century saw the beginning of a deterioration in the standard of print- and picture-book production, which seems to have been a reflection of changing social conditions in Yedo, the growth of the demand for prints, a consequent increase in the output of the artists, and a coarsening of the fibre both of those that purchased and those that made the prints. Certain it is that stronger causes than a simple failure of powers in the artists have to be found for the degeneration which set in at the end of the century. It infected the later

work of Utamaro and of his pupils Hidemaro, Tsukimaro, and Kikumaro, and of his followers like Yeizan, Bunrō, and Ryōkoku, but it is most glaring in the prints of Utagawa Toyokuni (1769–1825) and his pupils.

Toyokuni (a pupil of Toyoharu (1733–1814)), founder of the Utagawa subschool and himself principally remembered for *Uki-ye* (or 'perspective pictures'), was an accomplished artist who, in the 1790s, designed many fine prints, though one thinks of him more as a plagiarist of Utamaro, Sharaku, and Shunshō than as an artist of originality. Some of his early actor prints, however, are superb, and it is in comparison with these that his later work, almost entirely theatrical, seems so slipshod and vulgar.

Of the vast number of pupils of Toyokuni, it is possible to mention only a few. Apart from Kunimasa, whose 'large heads' are as rare and as much sought after as Sharaku's, most of the pupils were prolific and their prints are common. Kunisada (1786–1864), who later took over the name of Toyokuni (being the third of the name, since Toyoshige, another pupil, had already used it from the death of Toyokuni I in 1825 until his own death in 1835), produced enough fine prints to prove he was capable of great things, but his enormous output of actor prints succeeds only in overpowering us with a welter of riotous pattern and colour.

Kuniyoshi (1797–1861) is more interesting, and is justifiably renowned for his great battle pieces founded on the events of the clash between warring clans in medieval Japan. His landscapes are also noteworthy.

But the first half of the nineteenth century produced its own great master – Katsushika Hokusai (1760–1849) and Andō Hiroshige (1797–1858). Hokusai's life spans a vast number of changes in the art of the Ukiyo-ye school, and his own early work, contemporary with that of Kiyonaga and Shunshō, has something of the style and much of the charm that was in the air they breathed in that halcyon period. But his finest work was in landscape, a new development in Ukiyo-ye art, and in prints of birds and flowers that take something from the *kwachō* of

Above Two actors as a man and a woman in a scene from a play by Utagawa Toyokuni, polychrome, *c.* 1795–6. British Museum

The Momokawa tea-house at Edo by Kunisada. Victoria & Albert Museum

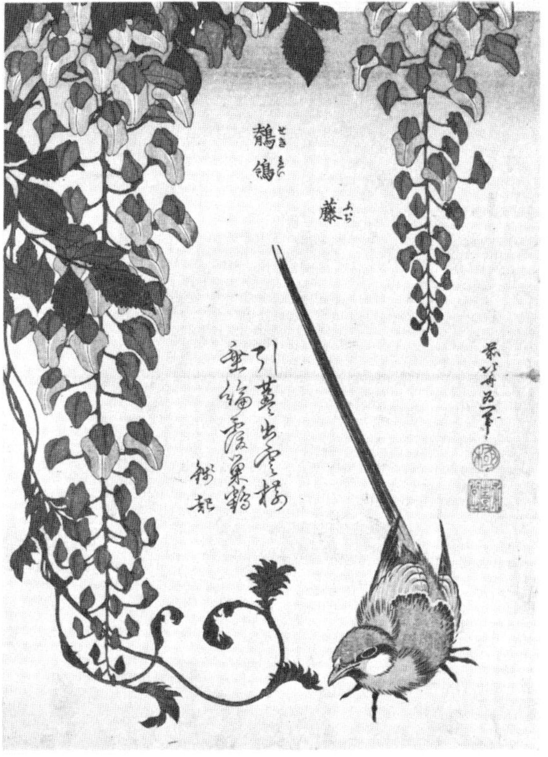

Left Wagtail and Wisteria, one of the set *Flowers and Birds* by Katsushika Hokusai, *c.* 1828. British Museum

Top left The actor Matsumoto Koshiro IV in role by Toshūsai Sharaku, polychrome with mica background, 1794. British Museum

Top right Mount Fuji by Kuniyoshi, *c.* 1842

Above Fuji in clear weather from the series *Fugaku Sanjurokkei*, thirty-six views of Mount Fuji by Katsushika Hokusai, *c.* 1823–9. Victoria & Albert Museum

the aristocratic masters of China and Japan. These prints are probably the best known of all Japanese prints and maintain their hold upon us whatever fashions in collecting may decree: 'others abide our question . . .'

Hiroshige is another artist whose work of most account is in landscape and whose lovely renderings of the Japanese scenery, his capture of transient atmospheric effects by the skilful use of the utmost art at the colour printer's command, has endeared him to most Western collectors. Keisai Yeisen (1790–1848) was also capable of fine things in landscape, but his *bijin-ye* suffer from the faults of vulgarization that vitiate so many of these late artists' gifts.

Most of Hokusai's pupils developed a talent, which Hokusai had had in large measure, for designing *surimono*, and collections can be formed of these enchantingly conceived and exquisitely printed little sheets of greeting, invitation, or commemoration. Shinsai, Taitō, Hokkei, Gakutei, and Shigenobu excelled in this miniature art.

Disparagement of the prints of the 'decadence' has become what has been called the 'correct' view of Japanese prints. On the other hand, the wholesale condemnation of everything produced after 1800 is manifestly wrong, and many things of real merit can be collected from the vast mass of prints surviving from the period. Picture books, for reasons hard to find, were often much better printed during this

Above Tonosawa, from the series *Hakone Shichito Zu-e*, pictures of the seven hot springs of Kakone, by Hiroshige, *c.* 1847–50. Victoria & Albert Museum

period than the prints, and offer a rich mine of material to the collector.

COLLECTING

'Orthodox lines' would probably be a matter for dispute, for collecting today is conditioned largely by what remains to collect. Even a great fortune, and a long period of patient collecting, would not be able to bring together collections on the scale and of the scope of those of, say, Hayashi or Happer. One tendency nowadays is for small but select collections to be formed of a hundred or two outstandingly lovely prints, with no particular deference to chronology or completeness, or even to artists' traditional reputations – the supreme example of this type is the famous Ledoux Collection. Another method is for specialization, with a focus either on one period or one artist, or even on a particular type of print, for instance, *surimono*, or illustrated novels, or landscape prints.

Right An unidentified actor as Kosanro Ichijosei, a heroine of the play *Suikoden* by Hokkei, *c.* 1830. Victoria & Albert Museum

Far right Aquatint on etching, *Nanny's Boy*, from *Los Caprichos* by Francisco Goya, published 1799

Left Anger, by Kiyomine after a triptych of *Joy, Sorrow and Anger* by Nishimura-Ya Yoachi, *c.* 1815. Victoria & Albert Museum

Far right Aquatint, *The Grand Leicestershire Steeplechase*, after H. T Alken, 1829. British Museum

Condition and 'state' are naturally of the utmost importance. Much reprinting from the original blocks was done contemporaneously, and many of the best prints have been copied, with intent to deceive or otherwise. Expertise in distinguishing the genuine first impression from reprints and facsimiles comes only through seeing and handling multitudes of specimens of all kinds, so that one learns the telltale variations in colour and in the texture of the paper, the surest guides where it is not possible to compare the actual woodcut lines with those of a known authentic impression.

The collector's ideal should, of course, always be a first impression in immaculate, unfaded condition, but very few prints, and even fewer *yehon*, have survived in that state. Originally they were sold to the commoners of Yedo, the prints to be exposed to the light and to the discolouring fumes of charcoal fires, the picture books to be thumbed through, often without the care we pay to them as 'works of art'.

Value of prints and books, therefore, turns on three things: the stature of the artist; the comparative rarity of his work; and condition. A few artists' prints could only be secured – if ever the chance occurred – at very high prices; any print by Kwaigetsudō and certain rare masterpieces of Toyonobu, Kiyonaga, and Utamaro are of this order. Fine prints by most important artists of early period are also expensive, but hosts of good prints can be obtained relatively cheaply. The finest *yehon* will be expensive, but those who collect with an eye to acquiring representative examples of an artist's work (and are not too concerned about the charge of 'heresy' that some will make against them) can pick up odd volumes and detached sheets for a modest outlay. Every collector will find his own level of outlay and his own particular sphere for specialization.

Glossary

TERMS

Aquatint. A colour print which emulates the pale washes of watercolour and was sometimes finished by hand in watercolour. Jean Baptiste le Prince (1734–84) is usually credited with having invented the process in about 1768, but an aquatint background appears to have been used in a portrait of Oliver Cromwell, signed *Velde sculp.* in the seventeenth century. Ploos van Amstel (1726–98), who imitated Old-Master drawings, L. M. Bonnet (1735–93), and P. G. Floding (1731–91) were producing prints which closely resemble aquatints in the 1760s. Le Prince contented himself with monochrome, usually sepia, washes, but his follower, François Janinet (1752–1813), initiated the practice of printing in several colours which was successfully developed by P. L. Debucourt (1755–1832) for his scenes of high life. The one great artist to make use of

aquatint was Goya, who employed it for his *Caprichos* and *Proverbios*. The process won great popularity in England.

Black line. In the black-line process of engraving, used mainly for woodcuts, the white or negative parts of the design are cut away from the block.

Block book. A type of book produced before the invention of movable type in which each page was printed from a single block on which both text and illustration had been cut. The recto and verso of each page were printed on separate sheets, which were stuck together. Among the earliest of such volumes are the *Exercitium super Pater Noster* and an *Apocalypse* printed between 1430 and 1450. The *Ars Moriendi* appeared a little later. A few block books, including the *Biblia Pauperum*, the *Canticum Canticorum*, and *Speculum Humanæ* Salvationis, were produced after movable type had come into use.

Broad manner. The name given to a style of line engraving practised by certain Florentine craftsmen in the later fifteenth century. Broad-manner engravings imitated the style of open-pen drawings with lines drawn in parallel strokes having light return strokes between them.

Bronzing. The name of the metallic shading on some silhouettes. In some cases this was used with beautiful effect, particularly by John Miers, who used real gold. It was usually, though not exclusively, used on painted work.

Burin or **graver.** A sharp metal instrument used to incise lines on metal; made in many sizes and forms.

Chiaroscuro. Chiaroscuro prints are made from a number of woodblocks to show several tones of a single colour. Black outlines are provided by the first or key block and degrees of colour by two or three successive blocks. The process demands care to ensure that the blocks are correctly superimposed. In Germany this method of making prints was practised

Chiaroscuro woodcut, *Triumph of Julius Caesar*, printed from three blocks in black and two shades of olive green by Andrea Andreani after Mantegna. Christie, Manson & Woods

after 1508 by Lucas Cranach (1472–1553), Hans Baldung Grün (*c.* 1476–1545), Johann Wechtlin (*fl.* 1506–26), and others. It was introduced into Italy by Ugo Da Carpi (*fl.* 1455–1527) and extensively practised throughout the sixteenth century by such artists as Antonio da Trento (*fl.* 1510–50) and Andrea Andreani (1584–1610). Netherlandish artists who produced chiaroscuro prints included Hendrik Goltzius (1558–1616), Abraham Bloemaert (1564–1651), and Frederick Bloemaert (1610–69). The process was revived in the eighteenth century in England, notably by J. B. Jackson (*fl.* 1701–54) and John Skippe (1742–96). Chiaroscuro blocks were sometimes used in combination with etched or engraved plates in both England and France at this period. In Venice the process was used by Antonio Maria Zanetti (1680–1757) to execute a series of reproductions of drawings by Parmigianino. Towards the end of the nineteenth century chiaroscuro was again revived by Charles Shannon (1863–1937) and others.

Colour print. The earliest colour prints were made from a series of woodblocks like those used for chiaroscuro prints but each impregnated with ink of a different colour. This process was first used for the bichromatic initials in Fust and Schoeffer's Latin Psalter (1457), and later for illustrations to books published by Ratdolt at Venice (*c.* 1482–6) and for liturgical books published at Augsburg (1487–1516). During the eighteenth century various attempts were made to print in the full range of colours from metal plates, and J. C. Le Blon developed an unsatisfactory process depending on Newton's theory of the three cardinal colours. At the end of the century more successful colour prints were produced by aquatint and later by lithography. The art of colour printing from wooden blocks was revived at the end of the nineteenth century, notably by Camille Pissarro (1831–1903). Colour prints made from a single plate repainted after every printing were produced by a few seventeenth-century line engravers (notably Johannes Teyler) and later by stipple engravers and mezzotint scrapers.

Conversation. A silhouette representation of a group of people – usually a family – engaged together in some domestic pursuit. Some of its finest exponents were Francis Torond, a French refugee who worked in Bath and London, Johann Friedrich Anthing (1753–1823), a native of Gotha, who produced some outstanding conversations of the Russian Imperial Court, which he cut or painted at St Petersburg, Augustin Édouart, William Wellings (late eighteenth century), Charles Rosenberg (1745–1844), and J. Dempsey (early nineteenth century).

Counterproof. A print made from a damp impression and not a plate. It is much weaker than an ordinary impression and presents the subject in reverse. Artists usually made counterproofs in order to have a print in the same direction as the plate to assist them in making alterations to the plate.

Crayon engraving. A process in which etching and engraving were combined to render the lines of a chalk drawing. Roulettes with heads designed to reproduce the grain of a chalk line were used to prepare the plate for biting with acid. After the plate had been etched, burin, drypoint, and roulette were used direct on its surface. This process was much employed for the reproduction of Old Master drawings, mainly by artists who otherwise worked in stipple or mezzotint.

Decorative border. These were sometimes used as settings for silhouettes. They were of two kinds: (*a*) *Printed*. These were used in much the same way as the nineteenth-century photographers' cards, as cheap settings for the cut portraits which were pasted on them. They were particularly favoured by Continental silhouettists. (*b*) *Painted*. These were usually painted as an intrinsic part of the silhouette portrait, but sometimes were painted under frame glass in *verre églomisé*.

Del. Short for *delineavit* or *delineaverunt* – Latin for he or she or they drew. To be seen after the artist's name, usually on the lefthand side of the print.

Drypoint. A process of engraving on a metal plate with a solid rod of steel shaped like a pencil which is drawn (not pushed like the burin) across the plate and throws up a rich burr. This burr is allowed to remain on the plate, holds the ink, and imparts a velvety tone to the print, but is soon worn down. Only the first fifty impressions, or even fewer, show the full effect. The first prints scratched in a manner similar to that of drypoint were made by the anonymous German *Master of the Amsterdam Cabinet* in about 1480. Dürer engraved three outstanding drypoint plates, and in Italy Andrea Meldolla (Schiavone) (d. 1582) used drypoint in conjunction with etching. The process was brought to a high pitch of perfection by Rembrandt, who occasionally produced pure dry points but more often used the drypoint pencil to finish his etchings. In the late eighteenth century drypoint was revived in England by Thomas Worlidge (1700–66) and Benjamin Wilson (1721–88): and in the early nineteenth century by David Wilkie (1785–1841), Edward Thomas Daniell (1804–42), and many others. It has been much used by modern etchers.

Engraved background. These were used by some cutters as settings on which to mount their portraits. A. Édouart used them widely and even used printed accessories such as newspapers, scrolls, etc., to place in the hands of his subjects.

Engraved silhouette. Books of printed silhouettes were popular in the eighteenth and nineteenth centuries, and the collector should be cautious of any such portraits framed up to look like genuine cut or painted examples. The books themselves are well

Far left Drypoint, *Le Bain*, by Pablo Picasso. Christie, Manson & Woods

Left Etching, *Idee pittoresche sopra la fugga in Egitto*, by Giovanni Domenico Tiepolo, *c.* 1775. Christie, Manson & Woods

worth collecting. On the other hand, it must be remembered that some silhouettes of celebrities were printed especially for framing.

Etching. A process of print making in which the plate is not engraved or cut with a tool but bitten (etched) with acid. The artist draws with an etching needle on a copper plate which has been covered with a ground composed of various waxes, gums, and resins. The needle cuts through the ground to expose, without incising, the plate, which is then immersed in acid (usually nitric) until the lightest lines have been sufficiently deeply etched. These lines are then covered with protecting varnish and the plate is replaced in the acid bath until the darker lines have been etched. This process is repeated as often as the artist desires. Sometimes the plate is finished in drypoint. The process of etching allows the artist a greater freedom of hand than that of engraving, but also demands a high degree of proficiency. Etchings by the greatest masters have a lightness of touch and depth of tone which can otherwise be obtained only in a drawing.

As a method of decorating iron, etching was extensively used by armourers, especially in Germany, in the second half of the fifteenth century, and the first etched prints were probably made by Daniel Hopfer

Left above Etching, *Abraham entertaining the Angels*, by Rembrandt van Rijn. Christie, Manson & Woods

Left Etching, *Les Grandes Misères de la Guerre*, by Jacques Callot, 1633. Christie, Manson & Woods (*fl.* 1493–1536), an armourer of Augsburg, in about 1500. The earliest dated etching was made in 1513 by Urs Graf (*c.* 1485–1529). Dürer etched a few plates between 1515 and 1518, and many minor German engravers occasionally worked in this medium during the first half of the sixteenth century. Etchings were first produced in Italy in about 1520 by Parmigianino and Schiavone, but the most notable sixteenth-century Italian etcher was Federigo Barocci (1528–1612). In the Netherlands etchings were executed in the first half of the sixteenth century by Lucas van Leyden (1494–1533) and Dirick Vellert (*fl.* 1511–44) who were followed by an important group of painters, including Pieter Breughel (1525–69), Jan Breughel (1568–1625), Hans Bol (1534–93), and Paul Bril (1554–1626), all of whom etched landscapes. From the beginning of the seventeenth century until our own times many of the greatest European painters have occasionally practised etching, while many artists of noteworthy ability have confined themselves almost exclusively to this medium.

Fine manner. The name given to a style of engraving practised at Florence in the later fifteenth century, notably in the workshop of Maso Finiguerra (1426–64). Fine-manner prints have something of the appearance of washed drawings with close lines of shading and crosshatching. The style is distinct from broad manner practised at the same time.

Glass-coloured print. Painted copies of prints which enjoyed much popularity in England in the eighteenth century. A glass-coloured print was made by pasting a print – usually a mezzotint – on to a sheet of glass and then rubbing the paper away. The sheet of glass was then painted on the inner side.

Glass print. Certain nineteenth-century artists, including Corot, Daubigny, Théodore Rousseau, and J. F. Millet, produced 'glass prints' by exposing sensitized photographic paper beneath sheets of glass covered with an opaque ground from which the required design had been removed with an instrument like an etching needle. Such prints closely resemble etchings in effect.

Glass silhouette. Silhouettes painted on to glass by one of the following methods: (*a*) *Verre églomisé* and *gold-glass engraving*. Silhouettes of this kind were produced by the Parisian artist A. Forberger (1762–1865), who backed his portraits with gold leaf or blue wax and often gave them floral borders, and W. A. Spornberg, a Swede, who worked at the end of the eighteenth century in Bath, and whose profiles are backed with red pigment and usually surrounded by a geometrical border. (*b*) *Painting on to the reverse side of flat or convex glass*. This was a common form of silhouette painting, and one capable of giving very effective results, particularly on those painted on convex glass, mounted over white backgrounds on to which their shadows could be thrown. Work of this kind was painted by Walter Jorden (late eighteenth century), Isabella Beetham, Charles Rosenberg (1745–1844), W. Rought (early nineteenth century), and many others.

Several silhouettists, among them John Miers, mounted their ordinary painted work beneath convex glass with *églomisé* borders, and Mrs Beetham often combined *églomisé* mounts with portraits in plain black painted on the underside of the same glass. At least one silhouette in a glass millefiori paperweight is on record.

Impression. Any print made from a block, plate, or stone is termed an impression. The number of impressions that can be pulled depends upon the fineness of the artist's technique and the softness of the medium he employs. Whereas one of Rembrandt's more delicately etched plates or a drypoint plate yielded barely fifty impressions, a steel engraving might produce several thousands. Some recent artists have destroyed their plates or stones after taking a limited number of impressions.

Incunabula. Prints or printed books produced before 1500; also called incunables.

Ivory was sometimes used as a ground for silhouettes. It was particularly favoured for silhouettes intended for insertion in jewelry.

Jewelry and trinkets. Some of the art's most pleasing examples are set in jewelry and trinkets. Rings, brooches, and snuffboxes were particularly favourite repositories for shades. Some of John Miers's tiny shades, some less than half an inch high, are in such settings under coverings of rock crystal. Silhouette jewelry is of the greatest rarity.

Line engraving. Line engravings are printed from finely polished metal plates, usually of copper but sometimes of iron, pewter, silver, or steel, on which the engraver has incised the design with a burin. At the side of the line the burin leaves a burr of displaced metal which would hold ink and is therefore cut away with a scraper. In drypoint engravings the burr is left on the plate.

Decorations were incised on gold, silver, and base-metal surfaces from the earliest times and throughout the Middle Ages, but not until the first half of the fifteenth century were plates engraved for the purpose of printing on paper. The earliest dated line engraving is one of a series of prints of the *Passion* executed by an anonymous craftsman in 1446. Many similar prints dating from the same period or a little later have also been preserved, but the names of their engravers and the exact dates of their production are unknown. The first major artist in this medium was Martin Schongauer (*c.* 1430–91), whose works stand between the somewhat primitive engravings of such anonyms as the *Master of the Banderoles* or the *Master E.S.* and the highly polished works of Albrecht Dürer and Lucas Van Leyden. The earliest known Italian line engraver was Maso Finiguerra of Florence, who began his career as a goldsmith working in *niello*. Two notable *quattrocento* artists, Antonio Pollaiuolo and Andrea Mantegna, executed works of superb quality in this medium, and Leonardo da Vinci has occasionally been credited with line engravings, though only one has even a slight claim to be by him. The art of line engraving was practised by several north Italian artists in the early sixteenth century, notably Jacopo de' Barbari (1450–*c.* 1516), Benedetto Montagna (1480–1540), Giulio (*fl.* 1482–1514), and Domenico Campagnola (*fl.* 1511–63).

Whereas etchings were frequently executed by painters, line engravings made after the early years of the sixteenth century were usually the work of specialists who copied the designs of greater artists. Some, like Marcantonio Raimondi (1480–*c.* 1530), were interpretive artists of genius, but the majority were humble craftsmen able to achieve little more than the rough outlines of the works they copied. Perhaps the most notable and original were those who engraved perspective views of architecture. Fine

original engravings were produced in France in the 1550s by Jean Duvet (1485–1561) and Étienne Delaune (1518–95), while certain artists, such as Domenico de' Barbieri (1506–70) and Jean Viset (*fl.* 1536), executed fine prints after Fontainebleau school paintings. In the early seventeenth century Abraham Bosse (1602–76), who wrote an important treatise on the art of etching and engraving, showed himself a master of the burin, as well as the etching needle, especially in his original genre scenes. Most other seventeenth-century engravers confined themselves to reproductive work, and Rubens employed several in his studio to make plates after his paintings. In England line engravings were produced in ever-increasing quantities after 1540. Most are, however, book illustrations, and very few are of conspicuously high quality.

The widespread vogue for the collection of prints, especially those after the most famous paintings by Old Masters and portraits of contemporary celebrities, gave a great impetus to the production of line engravings in the eighteenth century. Several artists, as for example, Sir Robert Strange (1721–92), subsisted solely by making engravings after portraits and Old Masters, while some advanced neoclassical painters, such as Gavin Hamilton, found that they could make more money and secure a far wider reputation from the sale of engravings than from the pictures that provided the designs. Most of these painters, however, employed engravers rather than applying themselves to the burin, and some suffered from the diffusion of piratical prints after their works. Among the most notable eighteenth-century engravings were those produced as illustrations to books by such artists as H. F. Gravelot (1699–1773), Charles Eisen (1720–78), and Jean Michel Moreau (1741–1814). The art of the line engraver deteriorated sharply after the beginning of the nineteenth century with the increased use of steel plates.

Lithograph. Lithographs are printed from absorbent stone blocks impregnated with chalk and have the effect of chalk drawings. The artist may either draw his design in specially prepared greasy lithographic chalk directly on to the stone or on paper with a gummed surface from which it can be transferred to the stone. In the latter instance the impressions are usually pulled by a craftsman.

The lithographic process was at first used only for making black-and-white prints, but its possibilities for colour printing were developed early in the nineteenth century. In Germany lithography was much used for reproducing the more famous pictures in the Munich and Dresden galleries between 1820 and 1850. Perhaps the greatest artist to employ lithography was Francisco Goya, but Théodore Géricault (1791–1824) and Eugène Delacroix (1798–1863) were among many others who designed for the medium. Later in the century Édouard Manet

Above Line engraving, first state, *Skaters before the gate of St George at Antwerp*, by Frans Huys after Pieter Breughel the Elder. Christie, Manson & Woods

Right Lithograph, *He is not here: for He is risen*, by Benjamin West, 1801. Victoria & Albert Museum

Lithograph, *The Transept, Interior of the Crystal Palace in Hyde Park*, by J. Nach, printed and published by Dickinson Brothers, 1851

Lithograph in four colours, *Le Boulevard*, by Pierre Bonnard, 1899. William Weston Gallery, London

Lithograph, *Les Oies Bords de Rivière*, by Alfred Sisley, 1897. William Weston Gallery, London

(1832–83) and Fantin-Latour (1835–1904) both produced notable lithographs. The greatest modern master of the medium was probably Pierre Bonnard (1867–1947).

Lithotint. When the design was washed on with a brush and greasy ink the effect of a watercolour was produced, and this was by some firms named a 'lithotint'.

Machine cutting. Silhouettes produced by a mechanical profile machine, of which there were many forms. Such work may usually be distinguished by a certain hardness and lack of freedom in its outlines. There were, however, a few machine cutters who produced commendable work. One such was Mrs Sarah Harrington (*fl.* 1775), whose shades are full of vivacity. On the whole, however, machine cutting is the art's most debased form.

Maculature. A weak impression. The copper plate or block from which prints are taken must be inked after each impression has been pulled; a maculature is a second impression taken without re-inking, usually to extract the rest of the ink from the lines.

Manière criblée. Prints in the *manière criblée*, sometimes called 'dotted prints', are taken from a metal plate engraved in the same manner as a white-line woodblock. The name is derived from the groups of dots made on the plate with a punch to break up otherwise black areas of background. Prints of this type were made in the late fifteenth and early sixteenth centuries, especially in Florence, and there are isolated examples of *manière criblée* prints by Giuseppe Scolari of Vicenza and Urs Graf. The method was revived in England towards the end of the eighteenth century.

Mezzotint. Literally 'half tint'; a method of engraving which renders tone rather than line. The process is as follows: a copper plate is roughened with a mezzotint rocker which makes a series of uniform indentations, each with a burr to hold ink, and provides the black background; the artist then removes the burr with a scraper where he wishes to obtain the lighter portions of the plate with a burnisher to obtain highlights. As the quality of the print depends on the delicacy of the burr, few impressions can be taken before the plate is flattened in the press. Finished prints are somewhat delicate and liable to deteriorate.

The mezzotint process was extensively practised in the Netherlands, but became so popular in England before the end of the seventeenth century that it acquired the name, *la manière anglaise*. In the late seventeenth century and throughout the eighteenth century mezzotints after paintings (usually portraits and later of genre scenes often executed primarily for reproduction by this means) were produced in considerable quantities by English artists, including Isaac Beckett (1653–1719), John Smith (1652–1742), John Faber the elder (*c.* 1660–1721), John Faber the younger (1684–1756), James McArdell (*c.* 1729–65), John Dixon (*c.* 1730–1800), Richard Earlom (1743–1822), Valentine Green (1739–1813), and John Raphael Smith (1752–1812). In the nineteenth century Turner's *Liber Studiorum* was executed by a combination of mezzotint and etching, and David Lucas (1802–81) scraped a series of landscapes after Constable.

Monotype. Plates painted with oil colour instead of ink yield a single impression which is called a monotype. This process was occasionally used by G. B. Castiglione (1616–70), William Blake (1757–1827), and Edgar Degas (1834–1917).

Niello. A method of ornamenting metalwork used by goldsmiths in the second half of the fifteenth century. A small metal plate, usually of silver or gold, was engraved and the lines filled in with a black

Mezzotint, *Mrs Musters* by James Walker after George Romney, 1780

substance composed of lead, silver, copper, and sulphur. The plates were an end in themselves, but occasionally their makers seem to have taken prints from them, or from sulphur casts of them, probably as records of their work. The art of niello was closely bound up with the development of line engraving in Florence, and its most notable exponent was the engraver Maso Finiguerra.

Painted silhouette. These were produced in a number of techniques on various materials, ranging from paper to glass.

Paste print. Paste prints were made in the fifteenth century from metal plates, similar to those used in the *manière criblée* process, on which a glutinous ink or paste was used, so that gold leaf or tints of colour could be added.

Plaster shade. Shades painted on slabs of plaster, often with beer as the medium. This was at one time a common background, and it undoubtedly was effective, its snowy depth giving the greatest possible contrast and sharpness to the black of the shade. Probably the greatest master of this type of silhouette was John Miers. Another was W. Phelps (*fl.* 1788), although shades by the latter are excessively rare. Great care should be exercised in handling shades painted on plaster, as they are exceedingly fragile and will often crack at the smallest impact. Neither should any attempt be made to brush off dust that may have accumulated on them through the years, as they scratch very easily. If a plaster shade requires attention, it should be given to a specialist to do what is necessary.

Plate mark. The name given to the indentation made by the edges of the plate on the print. This mark forms the frame of an etching or line engraving, but is rarely visible on woodcuts or lithographs. Impressions of etchings or engravings cut within the plate mark are said to be clipped and are of considerably less value than those on which the mark is to be seen.

Porcelain. Porcelain was sometimes, particularly at the end of the eighteenth century, decorated with silhouette portraits, usually of royalty, though sometimes of other celebrities. The factories of Royal Worcester, Royal Copenhagen, Dresden, Meissen, Berlin, and Sèvres all produced porcelain of this type. And objects so decorated include mugs, chocolate pots, *jardinières*, cups, saucers, plates, vases, and simple plaques. No silhouette porcelain is common, and most of it is rare.

Profile. A silhouette portrait in which features other than the outline are drawn, sometimes in great detail. Silhouettes in which features and hair are drawn in gold paint on a black ground come into this category. Some profiles are merely miniatures painted in sharp outline. Edward Foster of Derby (1761–1865) painted many portraits of this type.

Remarque proof. A print on which the engraver or etcher has added a little sketch or token in the margin as a sign of state. This practice of marking prints was fashionable in the late nineteenth century.

Samtteigdrucke. Known in French as *empreintes veloutées* and occasionally referred to in English as 'flock prints'. They were printed from ordinary black-line woodblocks on which a glutinous ink or paste had been used. Before the ink dried the impression was sprinkled with powdered colour, which gave it a velvety surface. Such prints were executed only in the fifteenth century and are very rare.

Sand grain. A sand-grain aquatint is obtained from a plate which has been pulled through the press with a piece of sandpaper to roughen its surface.

Scissor work. Silhouettes cut freehand from paper. Although this technique is not capable of giving great refinement of finish as any of the painting methods employed, it is nevertheless capable of giving very striking effects of a different kind. Its most notable quality is the uncompromising sharpness it gives to the outlines of its subjects. It is possible for a cutter, by holding several thicknesses of paper together, to cut as many duplicates at the same time, thus giving several 'originals'. The most prolific cutter of all was A. Édouart. Other noteworthy cutters were Francis Torond, 'Master' William James Hubard (1807–62), who achieved notoriety as a protégé, and the ill-fated Major John André (1751–80), who was hanged by the Americans as a spy in the Civil War. One method used was to cut out the portrait as a hollow from a piece of black paper or material.

Scraped lithograph. A lithograph executed by a reverse process which gives the impression the appearance of a mezzotint. The whole surface of the stone is covered with lithographic chalk, which the artist scrapes away to bring out highlights and on which he draws with a point to obtain white lines.

Shade. A silhouette portrait in which the face is painted in black. Ideally, the whole portrait should be in black, but sometimes clothes, nosegays, or other details are inserted in colour, but the face itself must have no detail at all apart from that of its outline. J. Buncombe, who practised from *c.* 1745 to *c.* 1825 at Newport, Isle of Wight, painted fine shades of soldiers in which the uniforms are shown in colour and in great detail. Edward Foster of Derby often painted faces in brown, blue, or some other colour, and unless details are shown in the faces, such may also be termed shades. But this treatment is really a departure from the best practice. The most effective shades are those with faces painted in pure black on an unadulterated white ground.

Silhouette. The name usually given collectively to shades and profiles. It is derived from that of Étienne de Silhouette (1709–67), the parsimonious finance minister of Louis XV. He was an amateur cutter of shades. As such portraits were cheap, they were dubbed *à la Silhouette*, as indeed at the time were all cheap objects. He was not the originator of the art.

Silhouette of unknown woman by William Bache, American, early 19th century. Essex Institute, Salem, Massachusetts

Soft-ground etching. A soft-ground etching imitates the effect of a pencil or chalk drawing. The soft ground, a mixture of ordinary etching ground with tallow, is laid on the plate and a sheet of paper stretched over it. The design is then drawn on the paper in pencil in such a way that the ground adheres to the paper beneath each stroke. The plate is then immersed in acid. Soft-ground etchings are often difficult to distinguish from crayon engravings, which obtain a similar effect by different means.

State. At various stages in the making of a print a single impression or group of impressions may be pulled. Each group of impressions is termed a state. Rembrandt, for instance, made numerous alterations to his etchings, some of which exist in as many as five states. The term state 1 is given to the earliest group of impressions pulled from the plate; state 2 to those pulled after the first alterations have been made; and so on. It is often difficult to ascertain which state was considered final by the artist, as some later alterations were made to repair damage to a worn plate. State 1 usually provides the rarest but not necessarily the most satisfactory group of impressions; the later states were often pulled after the plate had been heavily worn and had been re-worked, sometimes by another hand. Connoisseurs of states should, however, be warned that, even in the eighteenth century, unscrupulous dealers were not above creating unique first-state impressions of Rembrandt etchings by deleting details from an ordinary first-state print.

Steel engraving. Steel plates which suffer less wear in the press and thus yield a greater number of impressions than copper plates were first used by line and mezzotint engravers in the early nineteenth century. Such plates are, however, difficult to work, and the resulting impressions – known as steel engravings – are somewhat harsh. Later in the century it was discovered that a steel facing applied by electrolysis to a copper plate added equal durability without cramping the engraver's style.

Stipple engraving. On stipple engravings depths of tone are shown by conglomerations of dots and flicks of varying density. The plates from which these prints are obtained are covered with an ordinary etching ground through which the darkest portions of the design are picked out with an etching needle or roulette. The plate is then steeped in acid until the dots are sufficiently deeply bitten, and is finished with a stipple graver used directly on the metal.

Coloured stipple engraving, *Duck Shooting*, by C. Catton after G. Moreland, 1790

Stippled shading (applied without the aid of acid) was occasionally used by sixteenth-century Italian engravers, including Giulio Campagnola, Marcello Fogolino, and Ottavio Leoni, but the stipple process was not fully developed until the mid-eighteenth century. It was then taken up by Francesco Bartolozzi (1728–1813), a Florentine who executed most of his work in this medium in England, where it enjoyed great popularity. Indeed, most late eighteenth-century stipple engravings were executed by English artists or foreign artists working in England, and the process remained popular throughout the nineteenth century.

Sulphur tint. Sulphur-tint aquatints are produced by dusting powdered sulphur above a layer of oil on the surface of the aquatint plate. Particles of the sulphur corrode the plate in a delicate grain, which gives the appearance of a colour wash to the prints.

Trade label. Silhouettists, particularly in the eighteenth and early nineteenth centuries, often used trade labels which they fixed on the back of the frames containing their works. These labels in themselves form a fascinating subject for study. If still in place, covering the aperture at the back of a frame, a label can often be taken as at least a partial guarantee that the original contents of the frame have not been tampered with.

White-line engraving. The reverse process to black-line engraving. The block provides a black background on which the white lines of the design are incised.

Woodcut. Woodcuts or xylographic prints are obtained from blocks of wood, usually a soft wood like beech, apple, pear, or sycamore, sawn with the grain and about ⅞ inch (2.2 cm) thick (thicker blocks were used for the earliest prints). The woodblock process developed out of the medieval practice of printing patterns on textiles from wooden forms, but it does not seem to have been used for printing on paper or parchment until the late fourteenth century. As early as 1377 playing cards were in use in Germany, but none has been preserved, and it is not certain whether they were printed from woodblocks or painted individually. The earliest surviving woodcuts, dating from the first half of the fifteenth century, are of scenes from the Passion of Christ and the lives of the Saints which were distributed to pilgrims at various shrines and seem to have been printed in monasteries. Early in the fifteenth century volumes of woodcuts, known as block books, were produced in Germany. After the invention of movable type (at a date which has never been ascertained, but probably in the 1450s) woodcuts were extensively used for book illustrations; the earliest-known date from between 1460 and 1464. Among the first major artists whose works were reproduced in woodcuts were Albrecht Dürer (1471–1528), Hans Burgkmair (1473–1531), Albrecht Altdorfer (*c.* 1480–1538), Lucas Cranach (1472–1553), Lucas van Leyden (1494–1533), and Hans Holbein (1497–1543). These artists seldom cut their own blocks, however, and names of most of the carvers are lost. One of the most notable was Hans Lutzelburger (d. 1526), who made some of the blocks for Holbein's *Dance of Death* and illustrations to the Old Testament. Mid-sixteenth-century woodblock cutters included Giuseppe Scolari (*fl. c.* 1580), Jost Amman (1539–91), Virgil Solis (1514–62), Tobias Stimmer (1539–84), and Bernard von Salomon (*c.* 1508–61). The popularity of woodcuts waned towards the end of the sixteenth century, and the medium was little employed until the late eighteenth century, when it was taken up by William Blake and others. In the late nineteenth century black-line woodcuts based on fifteenth-century prototypes were extensively used to illustrate finely printed books; some of the most notable were cut for the Kelmscott Press by William Hooper (1834–1912) after designs by William Morris and Edward Burne-Jones.

Wood engraving. The wood engraving differs from the woodcut in being taken from a block of hard boxwood cut across the grain. This process permits finer effects than those obtainable from woodcut blocks. Thomas Bewick (1753–1828) developed the art of wood engraving (by the white-line process) towards the end of the eighteenth century. He was followed by three pupils: Charlton Nesbit (1775–1838), Luke Clennell (1781–1840), and William Harvey (1796–1866).

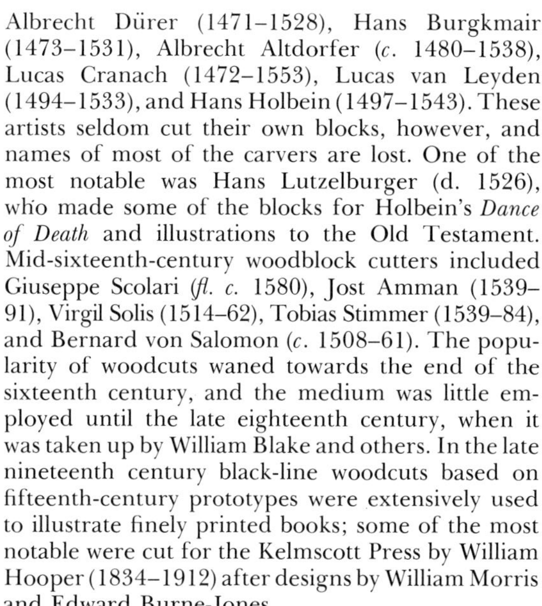

Wood engraving, first state, *The Ploughman*, or *The Christian ploughing the Last Furrow of Life*, inscribed by Edw. D. Calvert Inven. et. Sculp., 1827

Left Woodcut, *St George on horseback slaying the dragon*, by Lucas Cranach. Christie, Manson & Woods

AMERICAN ENGRAVERS

Aitken, Robert (1734–1802). Printer and publisher, originally from Scotland, who issued the *Pennsylvania Magazine* 1775–6. He supposedly re-engraved on a reduced scale the view by Bernard Romans of the Battle of Bunker Hill: *A Correct View of the Late Battle at Charlestown*, 17 June 1775, which appeared in the *Pennsylvania Magazine* for September 1775.

Allen, Luther (1780–1821). Engraved *A South West View of Newport, R.I.*, after a drawing by S. King, 1795.

Anderson, Alexander (1775–1870). Wood engraver, born in New York of Scottish parents, studied medicine, but turned to wood engraving, introducing to America the 'white-line' technique of Thomas Bewick. He made about 10,000 cuts for books, periodicals, bill heads, advertisements, etc.

Atlantic Neptune. A large collection of about 275 views, maps, charts, etc., of ports in North America, published for the British Admiralty under the direction of Joseph F. W. Des Barres during the period 1763–84.

Bakewell, Thomas. London publisher of the second state of the famous Burgis view of New York, called the Bakewell re-issue of 1746.

Barber, John Warner (1798–1885). Engraver and publisher of New Haven, Connecticut, whose interest in history led him to illustrate and publish the following books: *History and Antiquities of New Haven* (1831); *Connecticut Historical Collections* (1836); *Views in New Haven and Vicinity* (1825). Very much sought after by collectors is his view of New Haven Green with the buildings of Yale College.

Barralet, John James (1747?–1815). Philadelphia painter and engraver; chiefly a designer of views engraved by others. Came to America in 1795 from Ireland.

Bartlett, William Henry (1809–54). Artist, whose numerous sepia drawings were engraved by others for books such as N. R. Willis's *American Scenery* (1840), which was issued in parts.

Beck, George. Landscape painter, located in Philadelphia from 1798 to 1807, drew the views of American scenes published by Atkins & Nightingale in London, *c.* 1801–9.

Bennett, William James (1787–1844). Painter and engraver of aquatints, born in England. A pupil of the Royal Academy and of Westall, he came to America in 1816. Known for his series of *Views of American Cities*, the finest colour aquatints in this field; also for the three *Street Views in the City of New York* published by H. J. Megarey in New York in 1834; two views of the Great Fire of New York in December 1835 (after N. V. Calyo), and *The Seasons* after George Harvey (1841).

Bingham, George Caleb (1811–79). Portrait and genre painter whose paintings were engraved by John Sartain, Gautier, and Thomas Doney, and widely distributed, especially to the members of the American Art Union.

Birch, Thomas (1779–1851). Landscape and marine painter, son of William, with whom he worked. Later became known for naval subjects of the war of 1812, which were engraved by Tiebout, Tanner, and Lawson.

Birch, William (1755–1834). Born in England, active as an enamel painter, engraver, and print publisher. He came to Philadelphia in 1794. His earlier engraved work was done in stipple. Drew and engraved, together with his son, a series of twenty-eight views of the City of Philadelphia issued in 1800, either plain or coloured; also a series of small views of the *Country Seats of the United States* (1808).

Blodget, Samuel. First American-born artist to draw an eye-witness account of a historic event, the view of the *Battle of Lake George*, engraved by Thomas Johnston, Boston, 1755, also published by Thomas Jefferys in London, 1756. This is the first historical print engraved in America. Both the English and American issues were accompanied by a pamphlet describing the battle.

Bourne, George M. Publisher of the so-called Bourne *Views of New York City*, 1831. There are nineteen double plates, all but the first six copyrighted in 1831. Charles Burton drew most of these views, while James Smillie engraved the greater number of the plates. The New York Historical Society owns original drawings of eighteen of the views, while fifteen of the remaining twenty are in the Smillie Collection of the New York Public Library. The New York Historical Society owns all but three of the copperplates.

Bowen, Abel (1790–1850). Copper and wood engraver, known for his line and stipple engravings of public buildings in Boston for Snow's *History of Boston* (1825) and for a woodcut in three sections of the *View of Colonel Johnson's Engagement with the Savages near the Moravian Town*, 5 October 1812. Publisher of the *Naval Monument*, partly illustrated by him.

Bower, John (*fl.* 1809–19). Philadelphia engraver who executed two important battle scenes of the war of 1812; *The Battle of Patapsco Neck*, 12 September 1814, and *The Bombardment of Fort McHenry near Baltimore*, 13 September 1814.

Bry, Theodore de (1528–98). Flemish engraver and publisher of the earliest prints depicting North American Indians, their villages and customs, appearing as part of his collection of *Great Voyages* published in 1590 and 1591.

Left The Bay of Annapolis, lithograph by Currier & Ives, *c.* 1880

Far left Library and Surgeons' Hall in Fifth Street, Philadelphia, line engraving from the series *The City of Philadelphia as it appeared in 1800* by William and Thomas Birch, 1799

Buck, James. Boston publisher of the first view of Yale College in 1749, engraved by Thomas Johnston after a drawing by John Greenwood.

Burgis, William. Early eighteenth-century publisher of maps; an artist whose panoramic views of New York and Boston were engraved by John Harris of London and published in 1719 and 1722 respectively. He also drew a view of Harvard College, issued in 1726, a view of the Boston Lighthouse and the New Dutch Church in New York. These views are among the most sought after by collectors; only a few recorded impressions are known.
Burt, Charles (1823–92). Engraver, born in Edinburgh, came to New York in 1836. Engraved portraits and illustrations for books, some large 'framing' prints for the American Art Union; after 1850 worked almost exclusively on banknote engraving.
Calyo, Nicolino V. (1790–1884). Painter who came to New York from Italy and is known for two aquatint views of the Great Fire in New York in 1835 engraved by William J. Bennett; also for a series of Street Cries of New York (now at the Museum of the City of New York).
Cartwright, John. English engraver of the aquatint series of American scenes by George Beck of Philadelphia, published by Atkins & Nightingale of London from 1801 to 1809. (Not to be confused with T. Cartwright.)
Carwitham, John. Active 1723–64. London engraver for Carington Bowles: his name appears on three important and attractive views of New York, Boston, and Philadelphia. His name appears on the second states only of these prints, which were issued after 1764, although the three cities are depicted between 1731 and 1755. The Boston view is probably based on the Burgis view of 1722; the Philadelphia seems to copy the Scull-Heap view of *c.* 1754.
Casilear, John W. (1811–83). A good line engraver who turned to painting of landscapes.
Catherwood, Frederick (1799–1854). English artist, architect, and engineer, known for his views of Central America and his view of *New York from Governor's Island*, 1846, which was engraved in aquatint by H. Pappril.
Charles, William. Engraver and etcher who came to America from Scotland in 1801 and died in Philadelphia about 1820. Known for his caricatures of the war of 1812.
Clover, Lewis P. New York publisher of William J. Bennett's aquatints, 1834–8.
Cooke, George (1793–1849). Maryland artist, known for the four views in the Bennett series of American Cities: Charleston, South Carolina, Richmond, Washington, and West Point.
Copley, John Singleton (1737–1815). Painter (stepson of Peter Pelham), who is known to have made only one mezzotint, the portrait of the Rev. William Welsteed of Boston, 1753.
Davis, Alexander Jackson (1803–92). New York architect whose drawings of private homes, towns, and colleges from 1820 to 1850 were engraved by a number of different engravers.
Dawkins, Henry. Active in New York by 1754, also in Philadelphia, as an engraver of bill heads, maps, caricatures, but known chiefly for his *View of Nassau-Hall* (Princeton College) which appeared as a frontispiece in Blair's *An Account of the College in New Jersey* (Woodbridge, New Jersey, 1764). Dawkins died probably in 1786.
Des Barres, J. F. W. English cartographer and artist who prepared the *Atlantic Neptune* for the British Admiralty, 1763–84.
Dewing, Francis. English engraver and printer in Boston who engraved and printed the earliest and most important plan of Boston, the *Bonner Map* of 1722, known in five states and republished three times: in 1733, 1743, 1769.
Doney, Thomas. New York mezzotint engraver whose print after Bingham's *Jolly Flatboatmen* was distributed by the American Art Union to its members in 1845. Contributed mezzotints to periodicals.
Doolittle, Amos (1754–1832). Engraver of New Haven, Connecticut, known for his crude but important set of four views of the Battles of Lexington and Concord in 1775 after Ralph Earl, as well as a view of Federal Hall in New York, after a drawing by Peter Lacour, showing George Washington's first inaugural ceremony on its balcony, April 1789.

Federal Hall the Seat of Congress, line engraving by Amos Doolittle after a drawing by Peter Lacour, 1790

Durand, Asher Brown (1796–1886). Engraver of portraits, subjects (John Trumbull's *Declaration of Independence*, 1820), and banknotes. In 1836 he turned to painting and came to be known as the 'Father of American Landscape Painting'.
Earl, Ralph (1751–1801). American portrait painter whose original drawings of the Battles of Lexington and Concord, 1775, were engraved by Amos Doolittle.
Edwin, David (1776–1841). Engraver, born in England, came to Philadelphia in 1797. Excellent engraver of portraits in stipple, including portraits of generals.
Fay, Theodore Sedgwick (1807–98). Editor of *Views in New York and its Environs* published by Peabody & Co., New York, 1831–4, a collection of thirty-eight engraved views on sixteen plates, including a map and descriptive text, issued in parts (only eight of the proposed ten were published) after drawings by J. H. Dakin, A. J. Davis, and others, and engraved by A. Dick, among others.
Foster, John (1648–81). Boston printer and engraver, credited with the first signed portrait in colonial America, the portrait of Rev. Richard

Mather; also a seal of the Massachusetts Bay Colony and a map of New England which served as a frontispiece for William Hubbard's *A Narrative of the Troubles with the Indians in New England* . . . Boston, printed by John Foster, 1677. These are woodcuts.

Greenwood, John (1727–92). American-born artist who did etchings and mezzotints in eighteenth-century Europe. There is no record of his having made prints in America. Born in Boston, he worked in Holland and England.

Harris, John. London engraver of the William Burgis views of New York and Boston.

Harvey, George (*c.* 1800–*c.* 1877). English painter who resided in America between 1820 and *c.* 1842. Known for his *Atmospheric Views of North America* in watercolours, of which only four were engraved in aquatint by William J. Bennett and published under the title: *Primitive Forest in America, at the four seasons of the year*, London, 1841.

Havell, Robert, Jr (1793–1878). English engraver who came to America after completing Audubon's *Birds of America* published in London. He engraved in aquatint a number of views of American cities, among them two panoramic views of New York, one of Hartford, Connecticut, Boston, and Niagara Falls in 1845.

Heap, George. Map maker, map seller, and surveyor who drew one of the most important early views of Philadelphia, the so-called Scull-Heap view of 1754.

Hill, John (1770–1850). London-born artist who came to New York in 1816. Known for the aquatint plates in the *Hudson River Portfolio* after the paintings by W. G. Wall, published by Megarey, New York, *c.* 1825; also engraved Joshua Shaw's *Picturesque Views of American Scenery* (Philadelphia, 1819) and seventeen aquatints for *Lucas' Progressive Drawing Book* (Baltimore, *c.* 1827).

Broadway, New York, aquatint on etching by John Hill after Thomas Hornor. New York Public Library

Hill, John William (1812–79). Son of John Hill; made some aquatints, but known chiefly for the views which were engraved by others.

Hill, Samuel. Boston engraver of portraits and views for the *Massachusetts Magazine* between 1789 and 1796.

New York from Brooklyn, etching by Thomas Hornor, 1836–9. New York Public Library

Hornor, Thomas. English watercolour artist and engraver who came to New York in 1828. *Broadway, New York* (*c.* 1834) was drawn and etched by this artist, but aquatinted by John Hill. An unfinished etching of a panoramic view of New York from Brooklyn, *c.* 1837, and an unfinished wash drawing of a bird's-eye view of City Hall Park, are in the collection of the New York Public Library.

Hudson River portfolio. A series of twenty views drawn by W. G. Wall and engraved by John Hill. Four of the first issued views were engraved by J. R. Smith. Published by Henry J. Megarey, New York, *c.* 1825. 'The finest collection of New York State views'; originally planned to include twenty-four plates, issued in six numbers of four views each. Only five numbers with a total of twenty views were actually published.

Johnston, Thomas (1708–67). Boston engraver of the *Prospect of Yale College*, 1749, after a drawing by John Greenwood, published by J. Buck; also of *The Battle Fought near Lake George*, 1775; *Plan of Boston* after W. Burgis, and a *View of Quebec*, 1759.

Jones, Alfred (1819–1900). English-born engraver who worked in New York, known for some large engravings distributed by the Apollo Association, among them Mount's *Farmers Nooning*, engraved in 1836, distributed in 1843.

Jukes, Francis (1747–1812). London aquatint engraver, specializing in views and marine scenes. Engraved Henry Pelham's *Plan of Boston*, 1777; four aquatints after watercolours by Alexander Robertson, including the views of *New York from Hobuck Ferry* and *Mount Vernon*, 1799.

Krimmel, John Lewis (1787–1821). Philadelphia artist, whose *Election Day at the State House, Philadelphia*, 1815, was engraved, but left unfinished, by A. Lawson. Joseph Yeager made an aquatint after his *Procession of Victuallers of Philadelphia*, 1821.

Lawson, Alexander (1773–1846). Born in Scotland, came to Philadelphia in 1793. Engraved plates for A. Wilson's *Ornithology* and a number of periodicals; *Perry's Victory on Lake Erie*, 1813, after a painting by T. Birch; *Election Scene at the State House, Philadelphia*, 1815, after J. L. Krimmel (unfinished plate).

Longacre, James Barton (1794–1869). Engraver specializing in stipple portraits. Noteworthy among these is the portrait of Andrew Jackson after the painting by T. Sully, 1820. Together with James Herring, a portrait painter, published the *National Portrait Gallery of Distinguished Americans*, 4 vols, 1834–9.

Maverick, Peter (1780–1831). Son and pupil of Peter Rushton Maverick, 1755–1811. Conducted a large engraving and publishing business in New

York, turning to lithography about 1824. Best known for his view of Wall Street (lithograph) after Hugh Reinagle.

Meadows, Christian. New England engraver and apparently a counterfeiter, active about 1840–59; known for one of the most desirable college views, the Meadows' View of Dartmouth College, Hanover, New Hampshire, 1851.

Megarey, Henry J. New York publisher of *The Hudson River Portfolio*, a set of twenty aquatint views engraved by J. R. Smith and John Hill after the watercolours by W. G. Wall, 1821–5; Street Views in the City of New York (Fulton Street and Market, South Street from Maiden Lane, Broadway from Bowling Green), a series of three views engraved by W. J. Bennett, *c.* 1834.

Mount, William Sidney (1807–68). America's first genre painter, whose paintings were reproduced by a number of engravers as well as lithographers and widely distributed in America and in Europe.

Norman, John (1748–1817). Architect and landscape engraver from London who worked in Philadelphia and Boston. Engraved portraits of heroes of the Revolution and a portrait of George Washington in 1779. Worked also for New York publishers.

Okey, Samuel. Mezzotint engraver from London who worked in Newport, Rhode Island, 1773–5; is known for having been America's first engraver to reproduce Old Master paintings.

Papprill, Henry. Aquatint engraver who worked in New York in the 1840s. He engraved two large views of New York, one after F. Catherwood called *New York from Governor's Island*, 1846 (the Papprill–Catherwood view) and *New York from the Steeple of St Paul's Church*, after a drawing by J. W. Hill, 1849, re-issued in 1855.

Parkyns, George Isham (*c.* 1749/50–after 1820). English artist and aquatint engraver who came to Philadelphia in 1795, planning a series of twenty aquatint views, of which, however, only four were executed. These are: *View of Mount Vernon*, *Annapolis, Md*, and two views of *Washington*. Parkyns is also the author of *Monastic and Baronial Remains*, 1816.

Peale, Charles Willson (1741–1827). Painter and founder of a museum in Philadelphia; he engraved a few, rare, mezzotint portraits.

Pelham, Peter (*c.* 1684–1751). Earliest engraver in America; came from England to Boston in 1726 as an experienced mezzotint engraver; did a series of portraits of American clergymen, among them the portrait of Cotton Mather, 1727. Stepfather of John Singleton Copley.

Prud'homme, John Francis Eugène (1800–92). Engraver of stipple portraits, and plates for periodicals and banknotes for the U.S. Treasury Dept. in Washington.

Revere, Paul (1735–1818). Boston's most famous silversmith and a patriot who was also an engraver of three important historical prints. These are: *The Landing of the British troops in Boston* (1768) issued in 1770; the so-called *Boston Massacre* in 1770; a *View of Harvard College* in 1768. He also engraved a number of plates for the *Royal American Magazine*, 1774–5; the Massachusetts paper currency, 1775–6, and some portraits and political caricatures.

Roberts, Bishop. English artist who drew the most important early view of Charleston, South Carolina, in 1739, which was engraved by W. H. Toms and published in London. Roberts died in October 1739.

Robertson, Alexander (1772–1841). Scottish artist who established, together with his brother Archibald, the Columbian Drawing Academy in New York, *c.* 1795. Four of his watercolour views were engraved in aquatint by Francis Jukes of London.

Robertson, Archibald (1765–1835). Painter and etcher, born near Aberdeen, Scotland. Studied in Edinburgh and London from 1782 to 1791, when he came to New York. Painted a portrait of George Washington at the request of the Earl of Buchan. From 1792 to 1821 he worked in New York as a painter, chiefly in watercolour, and as a teacher of drawing. Established the Columbian Drawing Academy in New York, *c.* 1795.

Robertson, Archibald (*c.* 1745–1813). British naval officer during the Revolutionary period, who, like several fellow officers, made sketches of American ports and naval engagements. The Spencer Collection of the New York Public Library owns a large part of these original drawings. He is not to be confused with the aforementioned artist.

Rollinson, William (1762–1842). English-born engraver of stipple portraits for magazines, who became interested in banknote engraving, inventing a mechanical ruling device. Best known for his portrait of Alexander Hamilton, published in 1804, after a painting by Archibald Robertson; and for his aquatint view of New York, 1801, which was printed in colours.

Romans, Bernard (1720–84). Engraver, engineer, and cartographer from Holland whose eyewitness view of the Battle of Bunker Hill, Boston (*Exact View of the Late Battle at Charlestown, June 17th, 1775*) was published in America in 1775; an almost identical engraved plate was published in London in 1776; a reduced re-engraving was made by Robert Aitkin for the *Pennsylvania Magazine* for September 1775.

Far right Exact View of the Late Battle at Charlestown, June 17th, 1775, engraving by Bernard Romans

Saint-Mémin, Charles Balthazar Julien Févret de (1770–1852). French *émigré* who came to the United States in 1793, staying in New York and Philadelphia, earning a living by making crayon profile drawings with the aid of the *physionotrace* and reducing them with the pantograph to fit a circle of about 2 inches (5.1 cm) in diameter on to a copper plate which he then etched and finished in aquatint and some roulette work. In this manner he made about 800 portraits of distinguished Americans; he is also known for two views of New York. Returned to France, where he became the director of the Museum of Dijon in 1817.

Sartain, John (1808–97). Prolific engraver in mezzotint who came to America from England in 1830 and settled in Philadelphia where he died in 1897. He was also a publisher of several illustrated magazines. His larger plates are in line, among them the engraving after Bingham's *County Election* and *Martial Law* (Order No. 11).

Savage, Edward (1761–1817). Painter and engraver, generally credited with the first aquatint made in America: *Action between the Constellation and L'Insurgent*, 1798, published 1799. Originally a goldsmith, he learned to engrave portraits in stipple and in mezzotint in London. Known for his portraits of George Washington and an unfinished engraving of the *Congress Voting Independence* after a painting begun by Robert E. Pine.

Scenographia Americana. A collection of views in North America and the West Indies, engraved by Sandby, Grignion, Rooker, Canot, Elliot, and others from drawings taken on the spot by several officers of the British navy and army. Printed in London for John Bowles, Robert Sayer, Carington Bowles, Henry Parker, 1768. This collection contained originally twenty-eight plates, but was in some cases augmented to as many as seventy-four plates.

Scull, Nicholas (d. 1762). A native of Pennsylvania who became a cartographer and Survey-General of the Province of Pennsylvania in 1748, under whose direction the so-called Scull-Heap *East Prospect of the City of Philadelphia*, 1754, was made.

Seymour, Samuel. Philadelphia engraver, active 1797–1820, who engraved portraits and views after the paintings by Thomas and William Birch, among them views of Philadelphia, New York, and Mount Vernon.

Shaw, Joshua (1776–1860). Landscape painter who came to America in 1817 and drew the originals for *Picturesque Views of America* which were engraved in aquatint by John Hill (Philadelphia, 1819–20) and published by Moses Thomas and M. Carey & Son.

Smillie, James (1807–85). Born in Scotland, came to New York in 1828. Engraved a great number of fine landscapes, largely after his own drawings; a series of four allegorical prints of the *Voyage of Life* after Thomas Cole. From 1861 he worked almost exclusively on banknote engraving. Some of his large plates were issued as membership prints by the American Art Union.

Smith, John Rubens (1775–1849). Born in England, son of the engraver John Raphael Smith, 1752–1812. Worked first in Boston and then in New York where he painted, engraved, and directed a drawing school. For a while he worked also in Philadelphia. He engraved portraits in stipple and mezzotint and did some views in aquatint for the Hudson River Portfolio, as well as naval subjects.

Strickland, William (1788–1854). Philadelphia engraver and architect who was one of the first to engrave in aquatint in America; executed some small views and a few portraits. Although unsigned, except for the vignette on the title page, Strickland did the ten plates for *The Art of Colouring and Painting Landscapes in Water Colours*, published by F. Lucas, in Baltimore, 1815.

Tanner, Benjamin (1775–1848). Engraver in both line and stipple; publisher in Baltimore. He engraved some large plates of portraits and naval subjects relating to the Revolution and the war of 1812. Among these are *Macdonough's Victory on Lake Champlain*, *Perry's Victory on Lake Erie*, published 1 January 1815.

Tennant, William. Princeton graduate, class of 1758, who drew the view of *Nassau Hall* (Princeton), 1764, which was engraved by Henry Dawkins.

Tiebout, Cornelius (*c.* 1773–1832). The first American-born engraver who produced good stipple portraits; also some small landscape prints for the *New York Magazine*.

Toms, William Henry (*c.* 1700–*c.* 1750). London engraver of the important Roberts's view of Charleston, South Carolina, published in 1739.

Trenchard, James. Engraver, active in Philadelphia in the 1770s, who did some portraits and views, among them a view of the State House in Philadelphia after a drawing by Charles Willson Peale, 1778, as well as illustrations for the *Columbian Magazine*.

Trumbull, John (1756–1843). Painter of historical subjects, among them the *Declaration of Independence*, which he commissioned A. B. Durand to engrave in 1820. Credited with engraving a caricature depicting the Loyalists, published in New York in 1795. Elkanah Tisdale engraved nine satirical copperplates for Trumbull's *M'Fingal, a modern epic poem in four cantos* (New York, printed by John Buel, 1795).

Turner, James. Engraver who moved from Boston to Philadelphia, where he died in 1759. Engraved portraits and views for books and magazines and is known for his maps of Boston, the Middle Colonies (1755), and Philadelphia.

Wall, William Guy (1792–after 1862). Dublin-born landscape artist who resided in New York from 1818 till 1836, returning once more in 1856. In the 1820s he painted the watercolours which were engraved for Megarey's *Hudson River Portfolio*; also known for views of New York: *New York from Weehawk*, and *New York from Brooklyn Heights*, 1823, *City Hall*, 1826.

City Hall, New York, aquatint by John Hill after W. G. Wall, 1826. The Old Print Shop, New York

Yeager, Joseph (*c.* 1792–1859). Engraver in Philadelphia from 1816 to 1845, who worked for Philadelphia publishers. Known for his aquatint of the *Procession of Victuallers of Philadelphia*, 1821, and his line engraving of the *Battle of New Orleans and Death of Major General Packenham*, 1815. Together with William H. Morgan published many children's books.

AMERICAN LITHOGRAPHERS

Autenrieth, C. Name appears on a set of lithographs of New York views in decorative borders published by Henry Hoff, New York, 1850.

Barnet & Doolittle, New York. First American lithographic firm, 1821–2.

Beyer, Edward (1820–65). Drew originals for Beyer's *Album of Virginia*, a desirable set of views containing representations of the fashionable spas of the ante-bellum South, drawn in America but lithographed Berlin, Dresden, 1858.

Bien, J. New York lithographer, active 1850–68. In 1860 issued Audubon's *Birds of America*, elephant folio, in chromolithography.

Bowen, J. T. Lithographer, New York, 1835–8. Moved to Philadelphia, 1838–44; issued a good series of twenty views of Philadelphia after J. C. Wild.

Britten & Rey. San Francisco lithographic firm, *c.* 1849–*c.* 1880; of great importance for scenes of the Gold Rush.

Brown's Portrait Gallery of Distinguished American Citizens. Lithographs from twenty-six silhouettes cut by W. H. Brown, published with decorative backgrounds by Kellogg, Hartford, 1845. Most of original edition destroyed by fire; has been published in facsimile about 1930.

Burton, C. Artist, active 1830–50, New York. Did work for Sarony & Major, Pendleton, Michelin.

Buttersworth, James. Marine painter whose subjects were lithographed by Currier & Ives.

Cameron, John. Lithographer and artist, active 1852–62, New York; best known for horse subjects done for Currier & Ives, but did work indepen dently, or with other lithographers.

Castelnau, Francis. French traveller in America, 1838–40; published *Vues de l'Amérique du Nord*, Paris, 1842; illustrated in lithography.

Catlin, George (1796–1872). Artist and lithographer, traveller in Far West in the 1830s. Best known for *North American Indian Portfolio*, folio, with lithographs (London, England, published by the author, 1844); later published in America.

Childs, Cephas G. Philadelphia lithographer, active 1823–58; associated at various times with Pendleton, Kearny, Inman, and Lehman.

Currier & Ives. The leading American lithographic firm, founded by Nathaniel Currier in New York in 1833. James M. Ives became a partner in 1857. The firm was in existence until 1906. Publishers of popular subjects, including sporting subjects, genre, comics, etc., and employing such artists as Louis Maurer, A. F. Tait, Fanny Palmer, Charles Parsons, Thomas Worth, and James Buttersworth.

Durrie, George H. (1820–63). Painter, born and worked in Connecticut. Did the originals of the best-known farm and winter scenes published by Currier & Ives.

Duval, Peter S. Philadelphia lithographer, active 1831–79; associated at times with Lehman, Huddy, Prang and others.

Endicott. An important name in American lithography. Firm began as Endicott & Swett in Baltimore, 1828, and moved to New York 1830; active under various names until 1896.

Hoff, Henry. New York lithographer, active 1850.

Hoffy, Alfred. Philadelphia artist and lithographer, active 1840–60. Did drawings of military costumes in Huddy & Duval's *U.S. Military Magazine*.

Top The Life and Age of Man, Stages of Man's Life from the Cradle to the Grave, lithograph by James Baillie, 1848

Above The Life and Age of Woman, Stages of Woman's Life from the Cradle to the Grave, lithograph by N. Currier, 1852

Huddy & Duval. Philadelphia lithographers, 1839–41; published *U.S. Military Magazine*, 3 vols, prized for costume plates.

Imbert, Anthony. Active 1825–35 as pioneer lithographer, New York. His work for Colden's *Erie Canal Memoir*, 1826, the first outstanding American work.

Inman, Henry (1801–46). Painter; member of Philadelphia lithographic firm, Childs & Inman, 1831–33.

Jevne & Almini. Leading Chicago lithographic firm, established about 1866. Publishers of *Chicago Illustrated* 1830.

Kearny, Francis. Philadelphia engraver and lithographer; member of the firm of Pendleton, Kearny & Childs, *c.* 1829–30.

Kellogg, D. W., later **E. B. & E. C. Kellogg.** Lithographic firm of Hartford, also in New York and Buffalo; the most prolific firm after Currier & Ives; established 1833; subjects included sentimentals, portraits, book illustrations.

Klauprech & Menzel. One of the best Cincinnati lithographic firms; active 1840–59; views of Ohio a speciality.

Lithograph, *Castle Garden*, by Imbert & Co., New York, 1825–8. New York Historical Society

Below Lithograph, *The National Lancers with the Reviewing Officers on Boston Common* by Moore, from drawing on stone by F. H. Lane after C. Hubbard, Boston, 1837. Library of Congress.

Koellner, August (1813–*c.* 1878). Artist and lithographer, best known for fifty-four well-drawn views of American cities lithographed by Deroy, Paris, published by Goupil, Vibert, 1848–51.
Lane, Fitz Hugh (1804–65). Marine artist, born in Gloucester, Massachusetts. Did originals of town views; having worked at the lithographic firm of Pendleton in Boston, he put some of his own work on stone.
Lehman, George (*c.* 1800–70). Painter, engraver in aquatint, lithographer; worked in Philadelphia with Duval and also with Childs.
Leighton, Scott. Painter of horses for Currier & Ives.
Matthews, A. E. Artist, known for *Pencil Sketches of Colorado*, 1865, lithographs by J. Bien, New York, and *Pencil Sketches of Montana*.
Maurer, Louis. One of the Currier & Ives artists, whose speciality was sporting subjects, including field sports, represented by *Deer Shooting*, *On the Shattagee*, and horse subjects, such as *Trotting Cracks on the Snow*.
Michelin, Francis. Lithographer, Boston 1840; moved to New York 1844; worked to 1859.
Milbert, J. French artist, in America 1815–23. Author of the *Itinéraire Pittoresque du Fleuve Hudson* . . . issued in Paris in thirteen parts beginning 1826 and containing fifty-three numbered views in lithograph.

Nagel, Louis. Lithographer, in New York 1844; Nagel & Weingaertner, 1849–57. Went to San Francisco in 1862, where he was associated with Fishbourne & Kuchel.
North American Indian Portfolio, 1844. Lithographed in England by Daye & Haghe, after George Catlin.
Otis, Bass. Made the first American lithograph, Philadelphia, 1818–19.
Pendleton. Important lithographic firm, Boston, New York, Philadelphia, 1825–*c.* 1866.

Above right Lithograph from Rembrandt Peale's portrait, *George Washington*, by Pendleton. Library of Congress.

Below Lithograph in two tints, *The Hippodrome*, by Sarony and Major, 1853. New York Public Library

Robinson, H. R. New York lithographer, active 1832–51. Showed the news value of the lithograph with his view of the New York Fire, 1835, issued a few weeks later; also the arrival of the steamship *Great Western* in New York harbour, 1838; his *Peytona and Fashion* was the first print of an American horse race, 1842 (also issued by N. Currier).
Sarony, Napoleon (1821–96). Expert lithographer and artist working in New York alone and with others, as Sarony & Major, also Sarony, Major & Knapp; withdrew from lithography about 1867.

Tait, A. F. (1819–1905). Leading sporting painter of the nineteenth century; not a staff artist of Currier & Ives, but many of his scenes of field sports were issued in lithograph by them.
Walton, Henry. English artist known for attractive town views in New York State, such as Ithaca, Elmira, Binghampton, and Watkins Glen; was in Ithaca 1836–46. Work issued in lithograph by Bufford and others.
Whitefield, Edwin. Active *c.* 1854, artist and publisher of largest series of American city views in lithograph, printed by F. Michelin, Endicott & Co., Lewis & Brown.
Wild, J. C. Artist, came to Philadelphia in 1838. The firm of Wild & Chevalier issued lithographs of Philadelphia. Later Wild went to Ohio, St Louis, and Davenport, Iowa, where he died in 1845. Wild drew originals for *The Valley of the Mississippi*, published 1840 by Chambers & Knapp, St Louis.
Worth, Thomas. Artist, worked for Currier & Ives; best known for horse subjects, such as *Trotting Cracks at the Forge*; also comics.

AMERICAN RAILROAD-PRINT MAKERS

Bien, Julius. Active New York 1850–68.
Brett, Alphonse. Active Philadelphia and New York 1852–64.
Bufford, John H. Active Boston and New York 1835–1870s.
Crosby, Charles H. Active Boston 1852–72.
Currier & Ives. Active New York 1834–1907.
Duval, Peter S. Active Philadelphia 1831–93.
The Endicotts. Active New York 1830–96.
Rosenthal, Louis N., and family. Active Philadelphia 1852–70.
Sartain, J. Born 1808 and died 1897.
Sinclair, Thomas. Active Philadelphia 1839–89.
Swett, Moses. Active New York, Boston, and Washington 1830–7.

Lithograph, *Carrolton Viaduct*, by Endicott & Swett from drawing on stone by Moses Swett, *c.* 1831. Kennedy Galleries, New York

Tappan & Bradford. Active Boston 1848–53.

AMERICAN SILHOUETTISTS

Andrews, Mrs M. (d. 1831). Illustrated reminiscences of Washington, D.C.
Banton, T. S. Early nineteenth century, New England.
Bascom, Ruth (1772–1848). Gill, Massachusetts. Her silhouettes are frequently adorned with details of metal foil.
Brooks, Samuel. Boston, 1790.
Brown, J. (*c.* 1812–20). Salem, Massachusetts.
Chamberlain, William (*c.* 1824). New England.
Colles, J. (*c.* 1778). New York.
Cottu, M. (*c.* 1811). A French *émigré*.
Cummings, Rufus (*c.* 1840s). Boston.
Doolittle, A. B. (*c.* 1807). Son of Amos Doolittle, the engraver.
Doolittle, S. C. (*c.* 1810–20). Worked in South Carolina.
Edwards, Thomas (1822–56). Boston.
Ellsworth, James (*c.* 1833). Worked in Connecticut.
Griffing, Martin (1784–1859). Cripple, itinerant. New England.
Harrison, A. H. (1916). St Louis, Missouri.
Howard, Everet (*c.* 1820).
Jones, F. P. (early nineteenth century). New England.
Joye, John? (b. Salem, 14 March 1790). Active, Salem 1812.
Letton, R. (*c.* 1808). Showman and silhouettist.
Lord, Philip (1814–40). Born in Newburyport, Massachusetts. Active 1830–40. Made use of silver and gold in shading.
Metcalf, Elias (1785–1834). New York. Travelled in Guadeloupe, Canada, New Orleans, and West Indies.
Mitchell, Judith (b. 1793, married 1837). Quakeress, Nantucket, Massachusetts.
Perkins, George (*c.* 1850–55). Salem. Did some original work and numerous replicas of the silhouettes of William Henry Brown. Often confused with the originals.
Rogers, Sally. Armless cutter. Active New York, 1807.
Rossiter (active 1810–11). Hanover, New Hampshire.
Seager (*c.* 1834). Cutter, New Bedford, Massachusetts. Halifax, Nova Scotia, 1840, Boston, 1845–50.
Stewart, Rev. Joseph (active 1806). Hartford, Connecticut.
Valdenuit, M. de. Assistant to Saint-Mémin. Silhouette work is often signed *Vnt & S. M.* or *Drawn by Valdenuit and Engraved by St. Mémin.*
Vallée, Jean-François de la (1785–1815). Portrayed Washington. Active Virginia, Philadelphia, New Orleans.
Waugh (active 1835). North Carolina.
Way, Mary (active 1811). New London, Connecticut.
Williams, Henry (1787–1830). Boston.

BIRD PRINTS

History. All, or almost all, bird prints were to start with part of a book. Whether it is ethically agreeable to pull books to pieces and to sell their engravings separately need not affect the collector so much as the print dealer. Some books such as Dr Thornton's *Temple of Flora* or Audubon's *Birds of America*, were in effect collections of prints which have finally found their way into book form.

Bird books with coloured plates make an interesting subject for collectors, but they demand a very considerable capital outlay and a libary of some size. The individual coloured prints take up little space and can be collected reasonably cheaply. Furthermore, it is possible to specialize and to collect, for example, prints of, say, a robin or a bird of paradise, or to limit oneself to English, French, or German prints.

Coloured bird prints started to appear in books around 1730, with handcoloured copper engravings which continued until about 1830, though at the beginning of the nineteenth century the French produced wonderful stipple engravings of birds and flowers, partially printed in colours by a method unequalled before or since and touched up by hand. Handcoloured lithographs began to appear around 1830, and chromolithographs, printed in colour, after 1850. All these types have their own special interest, while Audubon's *Birds of America*, giant aquatint engravings which appeared between 1827 and 1838, are unique.

Almost all bird prints come from Germany, France, or Great Britain; a few from Italy and Holland, some of very good quality. And a very few, not very interesting, from Scandinavia. The Germans excelled in copperplate engravings, the French in stipple engravings partly printed in colour, and the British in lithographs. Audubon's aquatints stand above all competition, but as loose plates are on sale almost exclusively in the United States, they are not easy to collect, as well as being very expensive.

Most, but not all, prints have the name of the artist on them, usually but not always in the bottom lefthand corner; and again most, though slightly less often, have the name of the engraver, this usually in the bottom righthand corner. In addition, the name of the printer sometimes appears, under the title or elsewhere. A list of the abbreviations used to indicate artist, engraver, or printer will be found below. Meanwhile it must be pointed out that some confusion can be caused to the collector by the naming of complete sets of prints after the author of the book rather than the artist. Thus bird prints painted by Barraband are usually referred to as Levaillant's birds, since Levaillant's name is on the title page of the books in which these prints appeared. Quite often, however, the author was the artist.

Albin, Eleazar. Author and artist. His *Natural History of Birds*, 3 vol, quarto, 1731–8, is the earliest of all collections of coloured bird prints, with 306 in handcoloured engravings. Also produced in 1737, twenty-three engravings, very small, of British songbirds.

Audebert, Jean Baptiste. Author and artist. Produced *Les Oiseaux Dorés ou à Reflets Métalliques*, 1802; 190 very fine engravings printed in colours by a method invented by Audebert himself. There were two sets of these plates, the ordinary one with lettering in black, the superior in gold. Printing in colours had been performed in various ways since 1730. It consists basically only of putting the colours on to the engraved plates and pressing them on to the paper, rather than printing the paper in monochrome and colouring it later. The French, however, performed feats of colour printing which gave us these prints, almost all Redouté's flower books and the illustrations to Levaillant's bird books, which have never been surpassed. Most of these engravings, however, were printed in colours and finished by hand.

Audubon, John James Laforest. The author and artist of the most famous of all collections of bird prints, *The Birds of America from Original Drawings made during a Residence of Twenty-five years in the United States*, published between 1827 and 1838 in four volumes, size double elephant folio, easily the largest bird prints ever done. There were 435 handcoloured aquatints, of which Lucy Audubon drew Plate 404, but Audubon himself the rest. The first ten were engraved by W. H. Lizars, and the remainder by Robert Havell and Robert Havell Junior, who also revised later editions of the first ten plates, adding their name. It is likely that not more than 300 copies of each print were produced. This is by far the most valuable of any collection of bird prints, and for a collection of this size the capital value is therefore staggering. No other bird prints are in the same class. The most expensive flower prints, the engravings from Dr Thornton's *Temple of Flora*, number only thirty-five, of which the first and only good printing comprised not more than 400 copies of each. Audubon prints are very rarely on sale individually in Britain, and are, moreover, outside the scope of the ordinary collector.

Barraband, Jacques. Artist. Drew most of the pictures reproduced by François Levaillant in his very important series of exotic birds published between 1796 and 1816.

Bessa. Artist, mainly famous for his drawings of flowers, which were almost comparable to Redouté, but drew some of the pictures for R. P. Lesson's *Histoire des Oizeaux Mouches*, 1828–33, and *Illustrations de Zoologie*, 1832–5.

Bock, Johann Carl. Artist. Helped to illustrate Bernhard Meyer's *Naturgeschichte der Vögel Deutschlands.*

Bolton, James. Author and artist for *Harmonia Ruralis*, 2 vols, quarto, 1794–6, with eighty handcoloured engravings. Other editions of this well-known collection appeared until 1845.

Bonaparte, Prince Lucien Charles Laurent. Author of *American Ornithology or the Natural History of Birds inhabiting the United States not given by Wilson*, 4 vols, folio, 1825–33, with twenty-seven handcoloured engravings by T. R. Peale, A. Rider, and J. J. L. Audubon; and of *Iconographie des Pigeons*, large folio, 1857–9, with fifty-five handcoloured lithographs by P. L. Oudart, F. Willy, and E. Blanchard.

Borkhausen, Moritz Balthasar. Author of *Deutsche Ornithologie*, 2 vols, folio, 1800–17. Illustrated by H. Curtmann and the Susemihl family. A very rare collection, reprinted 1837–41.

Boucquet, Louis. Artist. Illustrated L. J. P. Vieillot's *Histoire Naturelle des Plus Beaux Oiseaux Chanteurs de la Zone Torride*, 1805–9.

Brookshaw, George. Author and artist of *Six Birds accurately Drawn and Coloured after Nature*, folio, 1817; six handcoloured lithographs. Brookshaw also drew the famous 'Pomona Britannica' series of fruits.

Brown, Peter. Part author with Thomas Pennant and artist of *New Illustrations of Zoology*, quarto, 1776; fifty handcoloured engravings.

Buffon, Comte Georges-Louis Leclerc de. Author of the famous *Histoire Naturelle Générale*, 1749–1804. Many editions of this book, a number with coloured plates, were published, but the important illustrations to it are those drawn by François Nicholas Martinet, which numbered 1,008 in all, appearing between 1770 and 1786. Size: small folio, and de luxe edition, larger folio. Attractive plates with a gold-panel line drawn round each, they represent one of the largest of all single collections.

Catesby, Mark. Author and artist of *The Natural History of Carolina, Baltimore and the Bahama Islands*, large folio, 1731–43; 220 handcoloured engravings (109 of which are of birds). These are the earliest of all American bird prints. Reprinted in 1748–56 and in 1771; and in Germany in 1750 and 1757.

Chromolithograph. The lithograph only requires one stone for printing, but the chromolithograph needs as many stones as colours are to be used on the finished print. A different colour is applied to each stone, and the various stones are applied in succession to the same paper until the complete picture is achieved. It is obvious therefore that to produce a really fine chromolithograph was both a cumbersome and an expensive process, so that while some magnificent examples appeared, there were far more prints which tended to be cheap and nasty. The very important series of illustrations by Keulemans and others for the works of Richard Bowdler Sharpe were all reproduced in chromolithography, but in most cases the printing and colouring leave much to be desired. A comparison of one of these prints with one of the handcoloured lithographs from Gould's *Birds* will make this inferiority immediately plain.

Copper engravings. Until the arrival of the lithograph all bird prints, save the few reproduced by aquatint, were taken from copper plates on which the necessary lines had been scratched with an engraving tool. The results naturally varied according to the skill of the artist or the engraver; in many cases the artist was his own engraver. Almost all bird prints, then, from 1730 to 1830 are copper engravings, and some later still, though the handcoloured lithograph was responsible for the important work in the later period.

Descourtilz, Jean Theodore. Author and artist of two works on Brazilian birds. The earlier published in Paris in 1834 with sixty-six handcoloured lithographs: the later published both in Rio de Janeiro and London in 1856 with forty-eight handcoloured lithographs. Both large folio. These prints are much sought after, as they stand almost alone in portraying only South American birds.

Donovan, Edward. Author and artist of several collections between 1794 and 1826; all octavo size and depicting both British and exotic birds.

Edwards, George. Author and artist of *A Natural History of Uncommon Birds and Gleanings from Natural History*, in all seven volumes, quarto. With 362 very fine handcoloured engravings, mostly of birds. Edwards's bird prints are some of the most important, and were reprinted in London, Amsterdam, and Nuremberg, the last edition being in 1805. The colouring of these printings varies, but even the later ones are still good, while the printing of 1802–5, which produced only twenty-five of each print, is perhaps the best coloured of all.

Elliot, Daniel Giraud. Author and part artist of a number of important collections of bird plates published in New York and London. All handcoloured lithographs, large folio size, and showing grouse, pheasants, birds of paradise, hornbills, and other birds. The other artists were P. L. Oudart, J. Wolf, J. Smit, E. Shephard, W. S. Morgan, and J. G. Keulemans.

Frisch, Johann Leonard. Author of one of the most enjoyable of all bird books, *Vorstellung der Vögel in*

The Long-tailed Humming-bird, engraving by George Edwards, 1742

Deutschland, containing 255 handcoloured engravings, folio size, drawn by F. H. Frisch, P. J. Frisch, and J. C. Frisch. Published Berlin 1733–63, and re-issued 1764 and 1817. These lovely prints are unfortunately very rare.

Gabler, Ambrosius. Part artist of Bernhard Meyer's *Naturgeschichte der Vögel Deutschlands*, 1799–1807.

Gould, John. Author and also largely artist of the most complete and most famous collection of bird books, depicting over 3,000 different birds. All Gould's plates are folio and all are handcoloured lithographs: the principal subjects are British Birds, European Birds, Humming-birds, Birds of New Guinea, Birds of Australia, Birds of Asia, Toucans, Trogons, Partridges of America, and Himalayan Birds. His fellow artists were: his wife, E. Gould; Edward Lear, H. C. Richter, William Hart, and Joseph Wolf. The artists did their own lithography, and the printing was done by C. Hullmandel and, to a lesser extent, by Walter and Coln. The dates of the prints, which are all of very fine quality, range from 1831 to 1888. Gould himself died in 1881.

Graves, George. Author and artist of *British Ornithology*; 144 octavo handcoloured engravings, 1811–21.

Gray, John Edward. Author of *Gleanings from the Menagerie and Aviary at Knowsley Hall*, containing seventy-nine handcoloured lithographs. Nine of these are of birds and are drawn by Edward Lear, who was at that time (1846–50) curator to Lord Derby at Knowsley.

Hart, William. Artist of a number of the plates in Gould's *Birds*.

Hayes, William. Author and, with the other members of his family, artist of *A Natural History of British Birds*; forty handcoloured folio-size engravings, 1771–5; and of *The Birds of Osterley Park*; 101 handcoloured engravings, quarto size, 1794–9. Both very attractive series. Many of the plates are signed in ink by the artists.

Hergenroder, J. M. Part artist of Bernhard Meyer's *Naturgeschichte der Vögel Deutschlands*.

Huet, Nicholas. Part artist of Temminck's *Nouveau Recueil de Plantes Coloriées d'Oiseaux*.

Hullmandel, C. Printer of almost all the lithographs for Gould's *Birds*.

The Lyre Bird, lithograph, drawn by John Gould and Elizabeth Gould for Part III of *The Birds of Australia*, 1841. Victoria & Albert Museum

Jardine, Sir William. Author of Jardine's *Naturalist's Library*, published in forty volumes between 1833 and 1843. Size small octavo. The first fourteen volumes were devoted to various sorts of birds, and the plates were drawn by Edward Lear, William Swainson, James Stuart, and others; each volume contained about thirty plates. Not very exciting to look at, they have been used a great deal in recent years to cover tablemats.

Keulemans, John Gerard. Artist and lithographer. Produced about 800 plates of birds altogether during the latter part of the nineteenth century, notably for D. G. Elliott and R. Bowdler Sharp.

Knip, Antoinette Pauline Jacqueline Rifer. Artist. Illustrated *Histoire Naturelle des Tongoras, des Manakins et des Todiers*, by Desmarest with seventy-two plates, 1805, printed in colour and produced herself *Les Pigeons*, large folio, 1809–11, with 147 coloured plates. Madame Knip, who was the accredited Natural History Painter to Queen Marie-Louise, produced in *Les Pigeons* one of the finest of all sets of bird prints. The first eighty-seven are printed in colours and finished by hand, engraved by J. C. Macret. The remainder are lithographs, hand coloured except for a few engravings by Dequevaubiller or Guyard.

Langlois. French printer, who printed partly or wholly in colours, very finely, many books, notably among bird books those by Levaillant and Vieillot.

Latham, John. Author and artist of *A General Synopsis of Birds*, quarto, 1781–5, with many supplements and reprints. The final total of handcoloured engravings was 193.

Lear, Edward. Lear wrote and illustrated the famous *Nonsense Rhymes*, limericks, etc., and produced many books with topographical plates. He was also famous as a painter of birds. His own illustrations of the family of Psittacidae, or Parrots, folio, 1830–2, with forty-two handcoloured lithographs, are very fine plates. He also did many of the drawings for Gould's *Birds*, for Jardine's *Naturalist's Library*, and J. E. Gray's *Knowsley Menagerie*.

Lesson, René Primevère. Author of many bird books published between 1828 and 1839. All fairly small octavo or royal octavo, illustrated with plates printed in colour and finished by hand, drawn by J. G. Prêtre, P. L. Oudart, A. G. Bevalet, Bessa, and others. In all responsible for more than 700 bird plates, of which the best known are of birds of paradise, flycatchers, and colibris.

Levaillant, François. Producer until surpassed by Gould of the largest series of works on exotic birds, including the parrots, birds of Africa, birds of paradise, birds of America, etc. In all nearly 700 engravings, printed in colour and finished by hand. Most of his collections were published in two editions, a folio and a larger folio, the latter 'grand papier' edition being the better coloured. The artists were J. F. L. Reinold and J. Barraband, with various engravers, but almost all were printed magnificently by Langlois.

Lewin, William. Producer and artist of several bird books. His *Birds of Britain*, 1795–1801, quarto, with 336 handcoloured engravings, is of moderate interest, but the first edition of this work, 1789–94, limited to sixty sets, is unique, in that all the illustrations are watercolours drawn and painted by Lewin himself.

Lizars, W. H. Engraver of the first ten aquatints in Audubon's *Birds of America*.

Lord, Thomas. Artist and author of Lord's *Entire New System of Ornithology*, folio, 1791; 111 handcoloured engravings.

Lorenzi, Lorenzo. One of the artists for Manetti's *Storia Naturale Degli Uccelli*.

Manetti, Xaviero. Author and part artist of *Storia Naturale Degli Uccelli*. Large folio, Florence, 1767–76; 600 magnificent handcoloured engravings. A superb collection of bird prints: the other artists were L. Lorenzi and V. Vanni.

Martinet, François Nicholas. Artist. Drew the 1,008 pictures for the great edition of Buffon's *Histoire Naturelle*. Martinet also drew and engraved thirty-one plates for François Salerne's *Histoire Naturelle*, a French edition of John Ray's *Synopsis Methodica Avium*.

Meyer, Bernhard. Author of *Naturgeschichte der Vögel Deutschlands*, folio, Nuremberg, 1799–1807. A very fine collection of engravings drawn by A. Gabler, J. M. Hergenroder, and J. C. Bock.

Meyer, Henry Leonard. Author and artist of *Illustrations of British Birds*, folio, 1835–41; 313 handcoloured lithographs; and *Coloured Illustrations of British Birds and Their Eggs*, octavo, 1841–50; 432 handcoloured lithographs.

Miller, John Frederick. Author and artist of the *Cimelia Physica*, large folio, 1796, with sixty handcoloured engravings (forty-one of birds).

Morris, Francis Orpen. Author of *A History of British Birds*. Originally published 1851–7, 6 vols, royal octavo, with 358 handcoloured lithographs, and reprinted often. The illustrations are disagreeable in all editions.

Murray, G. Engraved some of the pictures for Wilson's *American Ornithology*.

Nozeman, Cornelis. Author of *Nederlandsche Vogelen*, 5 vols, large folio, Amsterdam, 1770–1829; with five handcoloured title pages and 250 handcoloured engravings by J. C. Sepp. A splendid collection of prints.

Oudart, Paul Louis. Artist. He did illustrations for Prince Bonaparte, D. G. Elliot, and R. P. Lesson.

Pennant, Thomas. Author of the *British Zoology*, folio, 1761–6; with 132 handcoloured engravings, 121 of birds, all engraved by P. Mazell; drawn by various artists, including P.Paillon and George Edwards.

Reinold, Johann Friedrich Leberecht. Artist. Drew the pictures for Levaillant's *Birds of Africa*.

Richter, H. C. Artist. Drew some of the pictures for Gould's *Birds*.

Rider, A. Artist. Helped to illustrate Bonaparte's *American Ornithology*.

Selby, Prideaux John. Drew illustrations of *British Ornithology* – 222 huge double-elephant folio handcoloured engravings (nearly as large as Audubon's *Birds of America*). Issued between 1821 and 1834.

Sepp, Jan Christian. Illustrated Nozeman's *Nederlandsche Vogelen*.

Sharpe, Richard Bowdler. Author of a number of works issued between 1868 and 1898 and illustrated in chromolithography by J. G. Keulemans, William Hart, J. & P. Smit, and others. Quarto or folio, they show birds of paradise, kingfishers, swallows, etc. The plates are interesting ornithologically but not aesthetically.

Smit, Josef. Artist. Drew some of the illustrations for Elliott's *Pheasants and Birds of Paradise*, for Gould's *Birds*, and for R. Bowdler Sharpe.

Susemihl, Johann Conrad, Johann Theodor and Erwin Eduard. Drew between them most of the illustrations to Borkhausen's *Deutsche Ornithologie*.
Swainson, William. Drew many of the illustrations for Jardine's *Naturalist's Library*; also produced *Zoological Illustrations* with 334 handcoloured lithographs, 1820–33, and *A Selection of the Birds of Brazil and Mexico*, seventy-eight handcoloured lithographs all drawn by himself.
Temminck, Coenrad Jacob. Author of *Nouveau Recueil de Planches Coloriées des Oiseaux*, a tremendous, but not so attractive sequel to the edition of Buffon's *Natural History*, with plates by Martinet. The plates, 600 handcoloured engravings by N. Huet and J. G. Prêtre, were issued in both quarto and folio size between 1820 and 1839.
Vanni, Violante. Artist. Drew many of the plates for Manetti's *Storia Naturale Degli Uccelli*.
Vieillot, Louis Jean Pierre. Author of several works published in Paris between 1805 and 1830, with folio coloured plates by P. L. Oudart and J. G. Prêtre. The most important are *Les Oiseaux Chanteurs de la Zone Torride* (seventy-two engravings printed by Langlois), *Les Oiseaux d'Amérique* (131 plates printed by Langlois) and *La Galerie des Oiseaux* (324 handcoloured lithographs). All very fine plates.
Walter. Printed a number of the plates for Gould's *Birds*.
Warnicke, J. G. Engraved some of the illustrations to Wilson's *American Ornithology*.
Watermarks. It is sometimes possible to date a print which is not otherwise dated by inspecting the watermark. Most handmade paper had a watermark in it, and this watermark often included the date. It is a fair inference, though not quite always true, that the date of the watermark will be little if any before the time of the making of the print. To inspect the watermark hold the print up to a strong light, when it will at once stand out.
Wilson, Alexander. Author and artist of the fine folio work in nine volumes, published in Philadelphia in 1808–14, called *American Ornithology*, with seventy-six handcoloured plates engraved by A. Lawson, J. G. Warnicke, G. Murray, and B. Tanner. Though not comparable artistically to Audubon's *Birds of America*, these plates were considerably earlier and were the first done of American birds in America. Bonaparte's book was a supplement to this.
Wolf, Joseph. Artist. Drew many of the illustrations for Gould's *Birds*.

JAPANESE PRINTS

Ban. Size (*see* Chūban, Kōban and Ōban).
Baren. The burnisher used in hand printing from blocks.
Beni. A pink or red pigment obtained from saffron flowers.
Beni-ye. Pink picture: generally applied to two-colour prints, in which the *beni* was used with one other colour, usually green.
Beni-zuri-ye. Pink-printed pictures, a more correct term for the two-colour prints.
Bijin-ye. Pictures of beautiful girls.
Chūban. A vertical print about 11 × 8 inches (28 × 20.3 cm); medium-sized.
Fude (or **Hitsu**). A brush; also painted with a brush.
Gauffrage. Blind printing, producing an embossed effect without colour.
Gwa. Picture or drawing; drew (at the end of an artist's signature).
Gwafu. Book of sketches.
Gwajō. Album of folding pictures.
Harimaze. Sheets printed with two or more irregularly shaped subjects, to be divided up by the purchaser.
Hon. A book.
Hoso-ye. Small, vertical, narrow picture, about 12 × 6 inches (30.5 × 15.3 cm).
Ichimai-ye. Single-sheet pictures.
Ishi-zuri. Stone print.
Kabuki. Dramatic performances.
Kakemono. Hanging picture, rolled up when stored.
Kakemono-ye. Prints in the form of hanging pictures, usually about 26–28 × 10–12 inches (66–71 × 25.4–30.5 cm).
Key block. The engraved block from which the outline of the picture was printed.
Koban. A size smaller than the chūban, about 8 × 7 inches (20.3 × 17.8 cm).
Kwachō. Bird and flower pictures.
Meisho-ki. Guide books to famous places.
Mon. Badge or device serving as a sort of heraldic emblem for actors, courtesans, and others.
Naga-ye. Kakemono-ye.
Nishiki-ye. Brocade pictures, colour prints.
Ōban. Full-size, 15 × 10 inches (38.1 × 25.4 cm).
Sumi-ye. Ink pictures, i.e. printed in black only.
Surimono. Literally 'printed things', especially prints used for greetings or to mark special occasions.
Tan-ye. Pictures coloured by hand with *tan*, a red-lead pigment.
Tanzaku. Narrow, vertical prints, inscribed with verses, about 14 × 6 inches (35.6 × 15.3 cm).
Tate-ye. Upright pictures.
Uchiwa-ye. Fan-shaped pictures.
Uki-ye. 'Perspective' prints.
Urushi-ye. Lacquer prints.
Ye-goyomi. Pictorial calendars.
Yehon. Picture book.
Yoko-ye. Horizontal pictures.

The actor Bando Mitsugoro III as the wrestler Shirafuji Genta in the play *Kachi-sumo* produced at the Ichimura theatre in the third month of Bunkwa 7 (1810) by Toyokuni. Victoria & Albert Museum

A woman at her mirror from the series *Azuma sugata Genji awase, Genji comparisons*, by Eizan, *c.* 1830. Victoria & Albert Museum

WORLD

SCIENTIFIC INSTRUMENTS

left Navigation instruments in use before 18th century. Included are a sand glass, a globe, dividers and a map of the known world. Also, *bottom left* a mariner's astrolabe; *centre* a cross staff; *top* a Gunter's scale; *bottom* a sector. National Maritime Museum

THE SCOPE OF THIS CHAPTER

Contemporary interest in the history of science has led to a wider appreciation of early scientific instruments. These, until fairly recently, were collected and studied by only a few pioneers. This field, almost as extensive as science itself, includes medical and dental instruments, pharmaceutical equipment, chemical and physical apparatus, all of which, however, must be excluded, because of their rarity or specialized appeal, from a brief article addressed primarily to collectors. Large astronomical instruments from observatories, whose size alone would deter most collectors, are also omitted. This chapter is confined to those instruments comprised in the old phrase, 'mathematical instruments' – the smaller astronomical and surveying instruments, drawing and calculating instruments, microscopes, and some of the apparatus used by the natural philosophers of the eighteenth century. Most of these instruments were made by professional instrument makers to accepted designs for use by the practitioners of some profession (such as surveying) or for the interested layman.

HISTORY

(i) *The Islamic East.* Very few scientific instruments have survived from Babylonian, Egyptian, Greek, or Roman antiquity. The Muslim conquest of Syria in the seventh century A.D. brought the Islamic peoples into contact with Hellenistic scientific knowledge, which was soon made available in translation and supplemented by further mathematical knowledge from India. The flowering of Islamic scientific activity in the succeeding centuries involved a development of the craft of instrument making and resulted in improvements of the classical instruments.

The earliest surviving Islamic instruments are astrolabes. The astrolabe,[1] a complicated observational and computing instrument, was for many centuries the most important precision instrument available to astronomers. Until about the sixteenth century in Europe, centres of instrument making are associated with schools of astronomers: for example, the Toledo astronomers in Muslim Spain in the eleventh century. The history of the astrolabe will serve here as an illustration of the spread of astronomical and mathematical knowledge and of the making of associated instruments, such as celestial globes, sundials, and quadrants.

The earliest extant astrolabes[2] were made in Syria in the late ninth century. Based on Hellenistic models, the early astrolabes were soon improved by the addition of scales using trigonometrical knowledge derived from India. At the beginning of the tenth century the manufacture of astrolabes had already

Right Persian astrolabe, brass, made by Khalîl Muhammad b. Hasan 'Alî and decorated by Muhammad Bâqir Isfâhanî, probably in Isfahan, 1119 A.H. (i.e. A.D. 1707/8). The front (*near right*) shows the typical Persian foliate pattern ('ankabût), and decorated throne (kursî) and the suspension cord ('ilâqa); the reverse shows the diagram of sines, the graphs of arcs of the signs of the zodiac and azimuths of the Qibla, shadow-square, astrological tables, and the signatures (in the two cartouches below the alidade, pivot). National Maritime Museum begun in Persia, at Isfahan, and certain stylistic features of the earliest Persian astrolabe remained typical of eastern Islamic astrolabes throughout their history. During the succeeding nine centuries, Persia remained an important centre of instrument making. Scientifically the astrolabe remained unchanged. Such improvements as there were were mainly in the decoration of the instruments, which, by the seventeenth and eighteenth centuries, were lavishly ornamented with engraving. In the middle of the sixteenth century there appears to be a break in the tradition of astrolabe making in Persia. A revival in the latter part of the century may have derived its inspiration from Mogul India, where astrolabes were first made about 1570. Certain European influences are to be seen on Persian astrolabes about this time.[3] This is a complex and unstudied aspect of the instrument's history.

In Muslim India the history of the manufacture of astrolabes and other scientific instruments runs parallel to its history in Persia from the late sixteenth century until the early nineteenth century, by which time in both regions the craft had degenerated. In non-Muslim India there was what was probably an independent tradition of instrument making. The astrolabes are engraved in Sanskrit and appear to derive from an early Islamic source, perhaps from the instruction which the eleventh-century Islamic scientist, al-Birûnî, gave to the Brahmins, and of which he speaks in his history of India.[4] However, the surviving Sanskrit instruments are all later than Jai Singh's revival of Hindu astronomy in the late seventeenth and early eighteenth centuries.

(ii) *The Islamic West (the maghrib).* Islamic science spread westwards to Spain about two centuries after the Muslim conquest. The ninth Umayyad Caliph at Córdova, akl-Haam II, (961–76), imported books from Syria and Egypt and encouraged the public teaching of science. Maslama b. Ahmad al-Majritî (d. *c.* 1007), the first great Spanish scientist, wrote a treatise on the astrolabe, from which the whole tradition of western Islamic (and therefore European) astrolabe making probably stems. The earliest known western Islamic astrolabes date from the eleventh century.[5] After the Christian reconquest of Toledo in 1085 the way was open for an unchecked transmission of Islamic knowledge to medieval Christian Europe.

(iii) *Europe.* The work of the early translators from Arabic, who had begun to acquaint Europe with the achievements of Islam (if only in order to be able to combat the heresy more effectively), was reinforced by the translations sponsored by Alfonso el Sabio of Castile (1221–84) in the *Libros del Saber*, and the scientific activity in Catalonia and southern France. The Sicilian court of Frederick II may also have played an important part.

Some of the earliest instruments engraved in Latin script may indeed have been made in Spain by Muslim, or recently Christianized, craftsmen. Soon, however, France, Germany, Italy, and England had their own centres of instrument making. The work of the Judaeo-Provençal mathematician, astronomer, and zoologist, Prophatius (*c.* 1236–*c.* 1304), Johannes Regiomontanus (1436–76), Georg Hartmann of Nuremberg (1489–1564), Gemma Frisius (1508–55) of the University of Louvain, and others led to the introduction of new instruments and the improvement of older instruments. The Arsenius family at Louvain, relations of Gemma Frisius, made instruments to his design which were sold throughout Europe, partly through the agency of the Plantin printing house. The exquisite craftsmanship of the Arsenius workshop perhaps reached its peak in the work of Erasmus Habermel, at the Court of Rudolph II in Prague, and was reflected in the work of the Fleming, Thomas Gemini, and of Humfrey Cole, the two greatest instrument makers in England in the sixteenth century. Already, at the beginning of the sixteenth cen-

Right Ivory diptych dial (*left*) signed Fait par Charles Bloud à Dieppe, the leaves engraved with scrolls, the cover with conventional sundial calibrated with twice 12 hours with additional 8-12-4 polar dial, 17th century; *left back* English brass quadrant engraved with initials TM with pin-hole sights and Zodiac signs, 18th century; *right back* small Islamic wood quadrant of orthodox design, reverse with sinecal quadrants, signed Unjani; *right* ivory diptych dial probably by Jacob Karner and twice stamped 3, cardinal points indicated in German, short pin gnomon, early 17th century; *centre* ivory sundial in the form of a barrel, threaded at one end to reveal a portable sundial with painted compass card and folding gnomon, probably German, 17th century; *front* small silver Butterfield type dial signed Chapoto à Paris, with folding bird gnomon, *c.* 1700. Christie, Manson & Woods

Left Ivory tablet dial (*far left*) signed Leonhart Miller, dated 1636; *centre* ivory magnetic analemmatic dial signed C. Bloud à Dieppe, *c.* 1670; *right* tortoiseshell and silver tablet dial signed Charles Bloud à Dieppe. Christie, Manson & Woods

Right French Butterfield-type dial made by Nicolas Bion in Paris for the Eastern (probably Turkish) market, silver, *c.* 1700. The maker signed in Arabic script within the hour scales. Adjustable bird gnomon. National Maritime Museum

tury, workshops of craftsmen who specialized in the manufacture of the popular types of instrument, such as the ivory diptych dials, had been established at Nuremberg and Augsburg. The latter town, to which the beautiful work of the two Schisslers had brought fame in the sixteenth century, is especially associated with the manufacture, during the seventeenth and eighteenth centuries, of the small octagonal universal equinoctial sundials which bear its name. The manufacture at Dieppe, *c.* 1660, of a particular type of magnetic azimuth sundial by Charles Bloud and others, and the small universal horizontal sundials of the type associated with the name of Michael Butterfield of Paris about the same time, are further examples of the production in quantity of small popular instruments by the craftsmen instrument makers, who had replaced the scholar or astronomer who either made his own instruments or closely supervised their construction by an artisan who might specialize in some other field. The finest instrument makers of the seventeenth and early eighteenth centuries – such as Elias

Allen (*fl.* 1606–54), Henry Sutton (d. 1665), and John Rowley (d. 1728), of London, and Pierre Sevin (*c.* 1665–83) of Paris – not only produced excellent examples of the popular instruments but also collaborated with scholars (e.g. Allen's association with the mathematician William Oughtred, 1575–1660) to produce new types of instrument.

By the end of the seventeenth century a number of factors had produced a fundamental change in the work demanded of the professional instrument makers. The development of the telescope, the enhanced accuracy of clocks and watches, the influence of the work of Tycho Brahe, who had realized the need for more accurate astronomical observations, and above all the increasing momentum of scientific discovery, made many of the traditional instruments outmoded and required an increasing specialization if the desired precision of ever more complex new instruments was to be achieved. The fate of the astrolabe in Europe is illustrative of the change. As a time-telling instrument it was no longer required. Telescopes had replaced it for astronomical observations, and, for surveying, specialized instruments, such as the circumferentor and theodolite, were favoured. The dawning 'Age of Reason' had no use for an instrument conceived by astrologers.

After the work of Isaac Newton and the publication of several popular works explaining his scientific ideas, the eighteenth century finally accepted the Copernican (heliocentric) system. The simple armillary sphere, designed to illustrate the Ptolemaic (geocentric) system, for centuries had been the universal instrument for the demonstration of cosmological theory. It was superseded by the complicated orrery with its trains of gears for showing the movements of the planets around the sun. The orrery, together with the airpump, the loadstone, and the frictional electrical machine, served to demonstrate the 'New Philosophy' and to satisfy the popular interest in the natural sciences. The development of the dividing engine and other aids to precision helped to produce a class of professional instrument makers who were technologists and scientists rather than merely embellishers of traditional designs, applying themselves, like Tycho, to the solution of problems in the very design of the instruments. Such were men like John Bird (1709–76) and Jesse Ramsden (1730–1800); others like Benjamin Martin (1704–82) and George Adams (*c.* 1704–73) made a wide range of instruments and wrote on associated scientific subjects.

(iv) *Islamic countries in the eighteenth and nineteenth centuries.* In Islamic countries, where the impetus had gone out of scientific discovery since medieval times, the traditions lingered on, encouraged by occasional influences from Europe.[6] Many of the latter Islamic instruments are of considerable interest. An early nineteenth-century quadrant from the *maghrib* should be despised by no collector. It may well prove as good an example of a Prophatius astrolabe-quadrant as he is likely to find.

(v) *The Far East.* Few important Chinese or Japanese instruments are found in the European market. Chinese geomancers' compasses of lacquered wood are not rare, and other types of compass are found. Chinese and Japanese sundials of lacquered wood, ivory, or metal are somewhat rarer. They are mostly based on European models, though one particular type seems to be of Chinese origin. A hitherto unrecognized scientific instrument is the *hsüan-chi*, a circumpolar constellation template (*cf.* the European nocturnal), formerly sought only by the jade collector.

MATERIALS

The interdependence of the concentration of instrument making at certain places and the convenient supply of materials is an interesting line of inquiry which has been suggested by Monsieur Henri Michel of Brussels. For instance, he has pointed out that southern Germany and the Netherlands developed as such centres in the late sixteenth century in connection with the trade in rolled (as opposed to beaten) brass plates, a monopoly of the Fugger family; similarly, the availability of a very large quantity of ivory at Dieppe, brought there by ship in the fourteenth century, led to the development of an ivory-carving industry, and later, in the latter half of the seventeenth century, to the manufacture of ivory sundials.

Most instruments are of brass or bronze, which in the late eighteenth and the nineteenth centuries was usually lacquered. In view of the great variety of alloys used for the older instruments, it is sometimes difficult to distinguish between brass and bronze. Copper has occasionally been used. It is also notably the material of which a number of faked instruments were made. All three metals were often silvered or gilded.

The scales, especially of many European instruments of the seventeenth, eighteenth, and nineteenth centuries, are silvered in the same way as the chapter rings of old clocks. Fire gilding is not infrequently found on instruments of the sixteenth and seventeenth centuries, and was used with beautiful effect by Erasmus Habermel.

Iron and steel were rarely used except for small parts. Silver was popular in the seventeenth centuries for finely made small sundials. It was the most commonly used material for Butterfield-type sundials and for the hour scales and calendar scales of the ivory magnetic azimuth dials of Bloud type. Other small instruments frequently made of silver were universal equinoctial sundials and equinoctial ring dials. From Islam, only one instrument, an astrolabe, is known which is made entirely of silver,[7] but silver and gold were sometimes used for damascening.[8]

Stone has mostly been used for large outdoor sundials, but several small seventeenth- and eighteenth-century German horizontal table sundials were made of Solenhofen stone, the inscriptions and decoration being very finely carved.

Wood, after brass and silver, is probably the most common material and has been used in many ways. Many instruments exist of plain incised wood. Pearwood and boxwood, for instance, are characteristic materials of one type of English nocturnal of the seventeenth and eighteenth centuries. Sets of Napier's bones and mathematical rules and scales are also commonly of wood, covered with a thin layer of plaster. Wood was an obvious choice for the gores of globes. The gores, printed from engraved plates, were posted on the plaster, coloured with watercolour and finally varnished. A similar technique was used to produce instruments which could be sold more cheaply than those made of brass, or which could be made by a layman. Astrolabes and quadrants, for instance, were made by engraving the instrument (or its component parts) on copper plates from which many copies could be printed. The printed sheets were pasted on to wooden boards or pasteboards which were cut to the desired shape. Georg Hartmann of Nuremberg (*c.* 1530), Johann Krabbe of Münden (*c.* 1580), Philippe Danfrie of Paris (*c.* 1590), Henry Sutton of London (*c.* 1650), and the unfortunate John Prujean of Oxford (*c.* 1690) were makers who occasionally used this technique. It was also used in Italy in the eighteenth century for small quadrants and vertical sundials. Some of the early books on scientific instruments, such as those of Peter Apian (1495–1552) of the University of Ingolstadt, and Johann Krabbe, include full-size plates which may be cut out by the reader in order to make instruments in this way. Certain woods were especially suitable for particular uses. Boxwood was ideal when scales had to be engraved on the wood itself, as in the manufacture of mathematical rules. *Lignum vitae* was found to be excellent for the lens mounts of microscopes and

Compass set in a turned ivory case with lid, Italian, late 16th century. National Maritime Museum

telescopes and was commonly used for this purpose in the seventeenth century. In the following century mahogany was favoured for the tubes of telescopes.

In Persia and Turkey, during the eighteenth century and the early part of the nineteenth, quadrants, *Qibla*-indicators, sundials, and dialling instruments were made of wood and lacquered in yellow, red, black, and gold. (Dealers and collectors have unjustly neglected the attractive and interesting instruments made in this way.) Chinese geomancers' compasses were similarly made.

Pasteboard (which has been mentioned as a support for printed scales), together with papier mâché, covered with tooled leather or vellum, was used in the seventeenth century for the tubes of microscopes and telescopes.[9] These materials, with coverings of fish skin and shagreen, served also in the eighteenth century for the small cases containing drawing instruments or pocket sundials.

Ivory and bone have been used for instruments since medieval times, and are the usual materials for the diptych, or book, dials of the sixteenth century. In combination with wood, they were used with most satisfying effect for the inlay of German miners' compasses of the late sixteenth and seventeenth centuries.

THE INSTRUMENT MAKERS

Numerous techniques and disciplines are involved in the design and construction of scientific instruments. Much work still remains to be done on the more detailed aspects of their history, especially on the instrument makers themselves. A large proportion of instruments were not signed or dated by their makers. In particular, the earliest non-Islamic instruments of Europe are anonymous; the first of such instruments to bear their maker's name are those by Hans Dorn (*c.* 1480), Georg Hartmann, Pier Vincenzo Danti (*c.* 1490), and Euphrosynus Vulpariae (*c.* 1520). The late Professor L. A. Mayer showed that most Islamic instruments were made by men who were, in a sense, professional astronomers. In Europe, in recent periods, instruments were mostly the work of professional instrument makers who often specialized in narrow fields. In other periods the situation is more complex. In medieval times, in the sixteenth and seventeenth centuries, and even later, the craftsmen were often masters of several disciplines, enabling them not only to produce works that combined scientific precision with ornamental beauty but also sometimes to improve the design unaided by professional mathematicians. Yet most early instruments of the western world were made by metal workers carefully instructed by an astronomer or a mathematician. Such were the Arsenius, who followed the designs of their uncle, Gemma Frisius. Perhaps it was the lack of such supervision that caused Erasmus Habermel, a maker of the greatest ability and aesthetic sense, to perpetrate the same gross error on every one of his astrolabes. The link between those craftsmen who engraved copper plates for printing and those who engraved brass plates as instruments has already been mentioned. Thomas Gemini, for instance, is remembered not only as the maker of two fine astrolabes for Elizabeth I and of other fine instruments but also as the engraver of the plates for the first English edition of Vesalius. A seventeenth-century Spanish engraver, Juan Batista Morales, made in his later years one of the finest known universal equinoctial dials. Conversely, in the eighteenth century, Edmund Culpeper (1660–1738), famed for his microscopes and sundials, appears also as the engraver of an ecclesiastical monumental brass. Another versatile maker of this type was Philippe Danfrie, who wrote and printed, in Robert Granjon's *caractères de civilité*, a book on a surveying instrument (*graphomètre*) he had designed. Collaboration between different trades is also suggested by the use of bookbinders' tools on the leather and vellum coverings of microscope and telescope tubes.

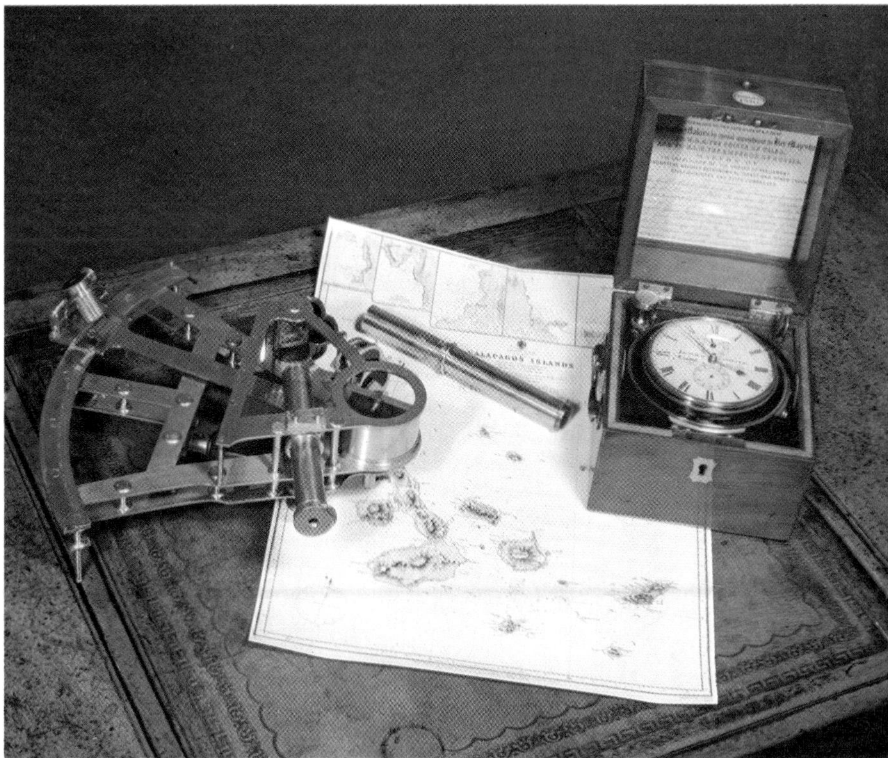

A map, chronometer and sextant as would have been used in the early 19th century. National Maritime Museum

RESTORATION AND CLEANING

Any historical object should be restored as little as possible. Under-restoration is decidedly the lesser one of two evils.

There is no point in leaving instruments in a dirty condition, though most collectors will prefer a little dullness on an instrument to the glare of shiny brass. A rub with a clean soft cloth, perhaps after careful application of some soap and water, is often sufficient and is the only appropriate treatment for gilt or silvered brass and copper. A form of liquid cleaner made for use with fine silverware can, however, be safely used on silvered brass and copper to remove the tarnish. Seriously tarnished brass or silver work should be cleaned with a non-abrasive cleaner, e.g. of the impregnated wadding type. Decayed lacquer on nineteenth-century brasswork may be removed with a suitable organic solvent, followed by further cleaning as described above.

For the leather tube coverings of microscopes and telescopes, and for leather instrument cases, the use of the British Museum leather dressing[10] is recommended, preceded, if the leather has suffered from acid decay, by a previous application of a 7½ per cent aqueous solution of potassium lactate.

FAKES

Faked scientific instruments, made with sufficient skill to deceive the specialist, are uncommon. The majority of fakes are crude. A large group of reasonably skilful fakes, including many instruments attributed to Habermel, have been described by Price, and examples of this group of fakes still occasionally appear on the market. Several faked Persian astrolabes have been sold and are of sufficient quality to pass unnoticed, except by those familiar with details of the mathematical designs and the traditional Arabic epigraphy.

COLLECTIONS AND SOURCES OF INFORMATION

Nothing can replace a detailed study of the important collections of instruments. In the British Isles there are comprehensive or otherwise notable collections in the Museum of the History of Science, Oxford;*[11] the National Maritime Museum, Greenwich;* the British Museum and the Science Museum, London;* the Whipple Museum of the History of Science, Cambridge; and the Royal Scottish Museum, Edinburgh. Abroad, the Conservatoire des Arts et Métiers, Paris,* the Museo di Storia della Scienza, Florence,* the Deutsches Museum, Munich, the Mathematisch-Physikalischer Salon, Dresden, the Rijksmuseum voor de Geschiedenis der Natuurwetenschappen, Leiden,* the Musée de la Vie Wallone, Liège,* the Adler Planetarium, Chicago,* the New York Historical Society,* the Museum of Islamic Art, Cairo, the Przypkowski Collection, Jedrzjow, and the firm of Nachet, Paris,* have valuable collections. Important instruments, however, are found in many other museums, such as the Benaki Museum, Athens; the Arab Museum, Baghdad;* Harvard University, Cambridge (Mass.);* the Museum of the Jagiellonian University, Cracow; the Musées Royales d'Art et d'Histoire, Brussels; the Landesmuseum, Innsbruck; the Hessisches Landesmuseum, Kassel; the Hermitage Museum, Leningrad; the Wellcome Historical Medical Museum, London (whose collection includes a few astronomical instruments); the Lüneburg Museum; the Victoria and Albert Museum; the Museo Naval, and the Museo Arqueológico Nacional, Madrid; the Germanisches Museum, Nuremberg; the Bibliothèque Nationale, Paris; the Národní Techniké Museum, and the Umělecko-průmyslové Museum, Prague; the Kunsthistorisches Museum, Vienna; and many others.

There are a few good books of a general nature on various classes of instrument, and these are listed in the bibliography at the end of this book. These are often the main source of information for the serious student. Many of the old books on instruments are of much more than historical interest and remain of great practical use to the collector. An extensive bibliography of the ancient and modern literature of the subject may be compiled by consulting the bibliographies in the works of R. T. Gunther, L. A. Mayer, D. W. Waters, E. Zinner, the Supplement to the Catalogue of the Billmeir Collection,[12] also the catalogues of such booksellers as Messrs William Dawson & Sons, Malcolm Gardner, Maggs Bros., Henry Sotheran, and E. Weil (all of London), and Herbert Reichner (Stockbridge, Massachusetts), F. & G. Staack (Camden, New Jersey), and Zeitlin & Ver Brugge (Los Angeles). The Science Museum, London, and the Museum of the History of Science, Oxford, both have excellent libraries, which include most of the important books. The latter also possesses the Lewis Evans Library, probably the finest collection of the older literature on astrolabes, dialling, and mathematical instruments generally.

The available lists of instrument makers do not entirely cover the field, and there are some serious gaps. Islamic makers have been exhaustively treated by L. A. Mayer. German and Dutch makers of the eleventh to the eighteenth centuries and their instruments have been listed by E. Zinner. There is also a useful list of makers from the northern Netherlands in M. Rooseboom. English mathematical practitioners of the sixteenth and seventeenth centuries are well covered by E. G. R. Taylor. French instrument makers may be found in M. Daumas. Many European astrolabe makers are listed in H. Michel.

English makers of the eighteenth and early nineteenth centuries, French makers of the sixteenth century, and American, Italian, and Spanish makers have not been adequately studied. Some information on English makers of the eighteenth and nineteenth centuries, Italian makers in general, and American makers in Philadelphia may be found in Clay & Court, M. L. Bonelli, and H. E. Gillingham respectively. There is a useful general list of makers in the Nachet catalogue. Otherwise recourse must be had to the instruments themselves, to the indexes of makers at the Museum of the History of Science, Oxford, and the Science Museum, London,[13] and to such original sources as trade cards.[14]

As might be expected, the dating of unsigned instruments involves a combination of the comparative study of instruments, an assessment of their place in the history of artistic design, and, occasionally, scientific aids.[15]

COLLECTING TODAY

Scientific instruments are much more sought after than even a few years ago. Consequently their rarity and prices have increased. Most of the finest instruments pass through the hands of a few specialist dealers or are sold by auction, mainly in London and Paris. It is, however, still possible to find at modest prices many of the more common instruments. The low price of sectors and Islamic quadrants, for example, is not in proportion to their historical interest.

N.B. No attempt is made in the following Glossary to list all early scientific instruments or the many technical terms associated with them. The glossary is merely a selection of some of the most interesting and least familiar instruments and of some of the terms likely to be encountered in descriptions of them.

NOTES

1) For notes on the various instruments mentioned in this introduction, see *Glossary*.
2) There are examples in the Museum of the History of Science, Oxford, the Bibliothèque Nationale, Paris, the Museo Nazionale, Palermo, and the Museum of Islamic Art, Cairo.
3) See above, p. 581 and footnote, *ibid.*
4) Edward C. Sachau (trans. and ed.), *Alberuni's India. An Account of the Religion, Philosophy, Literature, Geography,*

Chronology, Astronomy, Customs, Laws, and Astrology of India about A.D. *1030*, 2 vols, London, 1910,vol. I, p. 137.
5) There are examples in the West-Deutsche Bibliothek, Marburg, the Museum of the History of Science, Oxford, the British Museum, London, and in the Royal Scottish Museum, Edinburgh (dated A.D. 1026–7 and therefore the earliest dated maghribî astrolabe; see *Illustrated London News*, 19 October 1957).
6) European influences on later Islamic instrument-making have been unjustly neglected. Two examples may be mentioned. A Persian astrolabe, in the National Maritime Museum, Greenwich (No. A. 35–36.678), has obviously been influenced by the work of the Arsenius family at Louvain in the sixteenth century (see above). The *rete* has the characteristic Arsenius pattern, and a small compass has been inserted in the bracket; the latter feature is also found on a few other late Islamic astrolabes. Another Persian astrolabe, in the Hermitage Museum, Leningrad (No. VC512), is engraved with the projection associated with Juan de Rojas, a pupil of Gemma Frisius. At a later date further European influences penetrated to Islamic science through the attempt in Turkey, in the early eighteenth century, to study European science aided by the work of a renegade Hungarian printer and publisher, Ibrahim Mütaferrika.

Of similar interest is the revival of Hindu science by Jai Singh (1686–1743), who used European as well as Islamic and Hindu works, and sent a mission to Europe in quest of astronomical knowledge. This resulted in a curious blend of old and new learning.
7) Museum of the History of Science, Oxford, No. 55–6, dated A.D. 1350–1 or 1311–12.
8) E.g. on the astrolabe of 1227/28 by 'Abd al-Karîm al-Misrî, in the Museum of the History of Science, Oxford, No. G(1C), 103.
9) E.g. the fine instruments by John Marshall of London (1663–1725).
10) Available from Messrs Baird & Tatlock, London.
11) Asterisks by the names of museums indicate that partial catalogues or useful descriptive guides are available of the collections in these museums.
12) Now in the Museum of the History of Science, Oxford.
13) The Science Museum has in preparation a comprehensive list of English instrument makers.
14) The Gabb Collection included many trade cards of instrument makers (now in the Science Museum).
15) E.g. the use of the precession (52) protractor for astrolabes, and the magnetic variation marked on the compasses of sundials.

Glossary

Alidade. A rule with sights for use with a plane table; on astrolabes, etc., a rotable diametrical or radial arm, sometimes equipped with sights, for measuring altitudes, etc.

Armillary sphere. An instrument for demonstrating cosmological theory, consisting of a skeleton celestial sphere composed of rings representing the meridian, the equator, the tropics, the ecliptic, etc., on which various fixed stars are usually marked by pointers. Within the sphere are representations of the planets. Most armillary spheres are constructed according to the Ptolemaic (geocentric) system and have a small terrestrial globe in the centre. Examples survive from medieval times to *c.* 1700, when a few Copernican (heliocentric) armillary spheres were made.

Astrolabe. The most important astronomical and astrological computing and observational instrument from Hellenistic times to *c.* 1700; also used for surveying. It consists essentially of (i) a thick plate with a cavity (Latin: *mater*; Arabic: *umm*) on one side, into which fit (ii) one or more plates (Latin: *Tympanum*; Arabic: *safîha*); the latter are engraved with stereographic projections of the celestial sphere for various latitudes. Over the uppermost plate is (iii) a rotatable star map (Latin: *rete*; Arabic: *'ankabût*). (i), (ii), and (iii) are assembled by a pin and wedge ('horse') which also hold the alidade on to the back of (i), where are engraved scales of degrees and other scales and tables of use to the astronomer or astrologer. A bracket or 'throne' (Arabic: *kurst*) and ring attached to (i) enable the whole instrument to be suspended vertically when in use.

Stylistically and historically, astrolabes fall into several distinct groups. It is usual to distinguish among Islamic astrolabes, the Syro-Egyptian, the Persian, the Indo–Persian, and the Hispano–Moorish (*maghribî*) instruments, all of which have their own characteristics. Medieval European instruments are classified as Hispano–Moorish, 'semi-quatrefoil' or 'trefoil', Y-type, and late Gothic.

Some astrolabes (known as 'universal astrolabes') use a projection which may be used in any latitude. Such are the projections associated with az-Zarquellu (the *sapha ar zachelis*), Gemma Frisius, and Juan de Rojas.

The mariner's astrolabe was a deliberate simplification of the astrolabe made for nautical use in Portugal towards the end of the fifteenth century. The *rete* and plates of the usual astrolabe are omitted; the instrument consists essentially of a heavy pierced disc with a suspension ring. Around the edge of the disc are engraved scales of degrees, and the instrument is equipped with an alidade. It was used solely for measuring altitudes.

Astrolabe-quadrant. *See* Quadrant.

Astronomical compendium. A small rectangular, circular, hexagonal, or octagonal box, usually of gilt brass, sometimes in the shape of a book with clasps, containing several astronomical devices, such as sundials, a nocturnal, a lunar volvelle, a wind rose, a compass, and tables of latitudes. In addition, it may include an astrolabe, a quadrant, tide tables, a map, or a set of drawing instruments. Mostly of the sixteenth and seventeenth centuries.

Astronomical ring. A rare observational instrument, derived from the armillary sphere, which may be used to perform some of the functions of an astrolabe for time telling and surveying. Revived by Gemma Frisius.

Circumferentor. A surveying instrument consisting of a graduated circle of degrees over which moves an alidade. The Holland circle type has four sights (separated by 90°) on the main circular plate. A semicircular version of a circumferentor is known as a graphometer. Both usually have a ball-and-socket joint for tripod mounting: sixteenth to eighteenth century.

Compass, magnetic. Among special types of compass are the meridian (or trough) compass, which is in a narrow rectangular box and the needle of which can move only a few degrees on either side of the meridian, the surveyor's compass, which is made for use with or attachment to a plane table and has often a reversed compass card, and the miner's compass used in the surveying of mines and the charting of mineral rights, which has a characteristic numeration of the points of the compass.

A particular type of Islamic compass, often combined with a sundial, is the *Qibla*-indicator (*Qibla-numa*) giving the azimuth of the Qibla (i.e. the direction of Mecca) when the instrument is aligned on the meridian at various places inscribed on the instrument.

The Chinese geomancer's compass consists of a small magnetic compass set in the centre of a round lacquered wooden board. Surrounding the compass are circular scales of cyclical characters and *kua* symbols used in the art of geomancy (*feng shui*).

Cross, surveyor's. A simple sighting instrument, often combined with a compass, consisting of a cylinder or box with slit sights at 90°, sometimes 45°, intervals.

Dial or **sundial.** The terms used in classifying the numerous types of sundial often overlap, as some of the terms refer to the scientific principle of the dial's design, others to the form of the instrument. Universal dials are those which may be adjusted for use in more than one latitude. Altitude dials and directional dials constitute the two main classes of dial. The former depend for their operation on the variation of the sun's altitude during the day; the latter on the variation of its azimuth or its hour angle measured along the equinoctial circle. Dials which are not self-orientating include compasses and must be aligned on the meridian; dials which are neither fixed nor suspended when in use must also be levelled, and sometimes include plummets or spirit levels for this purpose. A few of the terms used in describing the dials in each class are listed in alphabetical order below (those marked * are altitude dials; those marked †, directional dials).

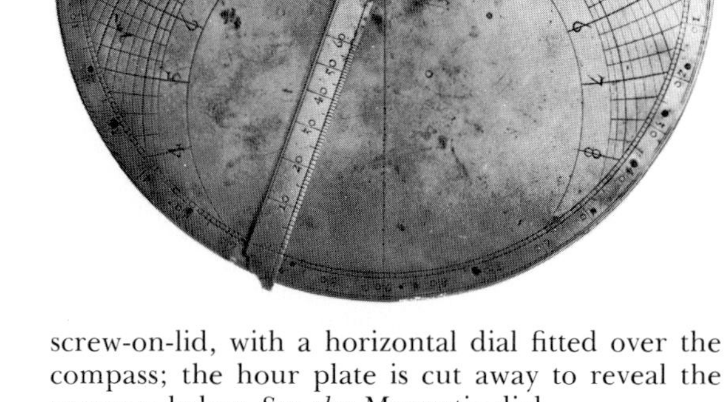

Combined azimuth and astronomical dial, English, signed Rob. Davenport fecit, circular, brass, first half of 17th century. Christie, Manson & Woods

Analemmatic dial, made by E. Baradelle (Baradelle the younger) in Paris, brass, late 18th century. National Maritime Museum

Analemmatic.† A self-orientating dial (therefore requiring no compass) which includes an hour arc and an azimuth dial on the same hour plate.

Augsburg.† Pocket octagonal universal equinoctial dials, particularly associated with the town of Augsburg in the seventeenth and early eighteenth centuries. Also popular in France in a slightly different form.

Azimuth.† A pin-gnomon dial with concentric hour scales graduated in the solar azimuth angles for each month of the year; *see* Magnetic azimuth.

Bloud.† A form of diptych dial, usually of ivory, associated with Charles Bloud and other Dieppe makers, *c.* 1660; the main feature is a magnetic azimuth dial, but usually polar, equinoctial, and string-gnomon dials are also included.

Butterfield.† A small octagonal, oval, or rectangular universal horizontal dial, often of silver, associated with Michael Butterfield and other Paris makers of the seventeenth and early eighteenth centuries. Similar horizontal dials, but without the adjustable gnomon with the latitude index in the form of a bird's head and beak, are also found.

Compass.† A compass, usually in a round box with a screw-on-lid, with a horizontal dial fitted over the compass; the hour plate is cut away to reveal the compass below. *See also* Magnetic dial.

Crescent.† A self-orientating small pocket dial of silver and gilt brass associated with Johann Martin and Johann Willebrand of Augsburg (early eighteenth century); it derives from the universal equinoctial ring dial. The hour ring is cut into two semi-circles set back to back. There is a crescent-shaped gnomon which slides on a declination scale.

Cruciform (or *crucifix*).† A multiple universal dial of cruciform shape in which the arms of the cross form the gnomons.

*Cylinder.** Also known as shepherd's dial, particularly the unsophisticated wooden versions which were made until recently in the Pyrenees. The hour scale is marked on the outer surface of a vertical cylinder. The gnomon projects horizontally from the top of the cylinder.

Diptych.† A dial made of two hinged leaves, usually of ivory, sometimes with coloured engraving, sometimes in the form of a book with clasps. Contains usually universal equinoctial, vertical, and horizontal string-gnomon and pin-gnomon dials. Mostly made at Nuremberg in the late sixteenth and early seventeenth centuries.

Equatorial. See Equinoctial.

Equinoctial.† A dial the hour scale of which is set parallel to the plane of the equator. As the hour scale is circular, it may be simply and accurately divided; one of the most common forms of dial, usually made universal.

Universal equinoctial dial, Chinese, made by Fung Shu Sui in Tsinan, lacquered wood, 19th century. Needham's type B (4,310 ff.), possibly indigenous to China and dating back to the Sung period (960–1279). National Maritime Museum

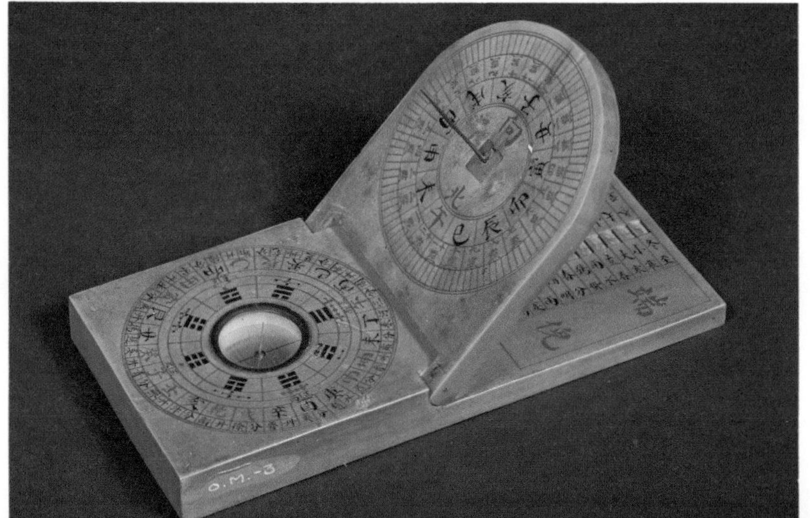

Geminus. See Rojas.
Globe (or *spherical*).† An equinoctial dial consisting of a sphere on which the hour circles are engraved: often made of stone.
Horizontal.† A dial in which the hour scale is horizontal, and which has a gnomon of which the shadow-casting edge is parallel to the Earth's axis – the usual garden sundial is of this type.
Inclining.† A horizontal dial made universal by including a means of tilting the hour plate from the horizontal for adjustment to different latitudes. Most inclining dials of the eighteenth century resemble large compass dials, but small versions for use in a few latitudes are often included in the small gilt-brass *victoria* (small pocket dials usually of gilt brass) and astronomical compendia of the sixteenth and seventeenth centuries.
Magnetic (*compass*).† A small dial, mostly of the eighteenth and nineteenth centuries, wherein a magnetic compass card is marked with hour lines (as for an ordinary horizontal dial) and also carries the gnomon. As the compass card aligns itself on the meridian, so the dial is orientated.
Magnetic-azimuth.† A dial in which a magnetic compass needle indicates the time, when the dial is directed towards the sun; instead of having separate hour scales for the varying azimuth of the sun throughout the year, some dials of this type have an elliptical hour scale, or the pivot of the compass needle is adjustable by means of an index moving over a calendar scale. Bloud dials have an adjustable hour scale.

Right Equinoctial ring dial, English, signed on the reverse of the chapter ring Made by Tho. Wright, brass, early 18th century. Christie, Manson & Woods

Below Mechanical universal ring dial, English, signed Rich. Glynne Londini Fecit. Christie, Manson & Woods

Mechanical. Used of an equinoctial dial, having a radial index which is turned towards the sun; the tip of the index then shows the hour, and a small hand, geared to the equinoctial hour plate (which is toothed), shows the minutes on a smaller dial face.
Navicula. See Regiomontanus.
Pin gnomon. Any dial whose gnomon consists of a short vertical or horizontal pin; the shadow of its tip indicates the time.
Poke. See Ring.
Polar.† A dial of which the plane of the hour scale is parallel to the Earth's axis; rare, usually found only on polyhedral and Bloud dials.
Polyhedral.† A multiple dial, usually cube-shaped, but other polyhedra and the surfaces of caskets were used; a dial was drawn on each face. In eighteenth-century Germany D. Beringer and others made cube dials of wood on which were pasted coloured printed scales: large polyhedral dials of stone were used as garden dials.
Rectilinear. See Regiomontanus.

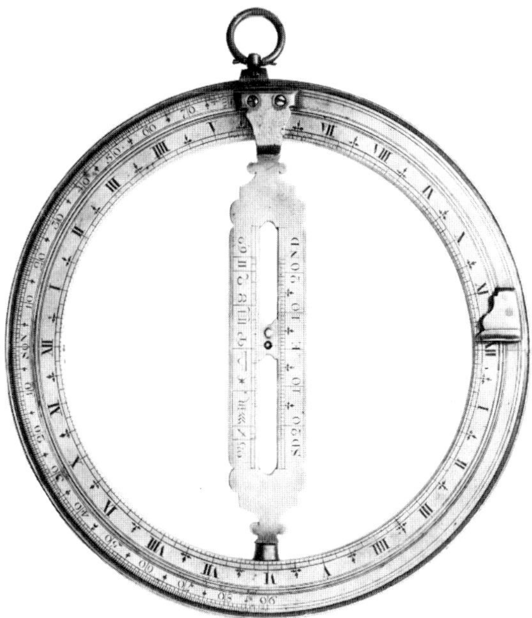

Regiomontanus.* Also known as universal rectilinear dial; a complex vertical dial sometimes found on the back of a nocturnal in the sixteenth and seventeenth centuries; also separately, especially in Italy in the seventeenth and eighteenth centuries with a particular (i.e. for one latitude only) rectilinear dial on the reverse. A very rare form of Regiomontanus dial in the shape of a ship is known as navicula.
Ring. The simplest form of ring dial (also called poke dial)* consists of a single ring with a sliding collar in which is a small hole; the collar was adjusted to the solar declination and the ring suspended and turned towards the sun so that sunlight passing through the hole indicated the time on an hour scale engraved within the ring. An equinoctial ring† dial is a self-orientating universal dial, consisting of a meridian circle and an equinoctial hour ring within which is a gnomon consisting of a pierced slider on a declination scale ('bridge'); after adjustment for latitude and solar declination, the dial is suspended and turned until sunlight passing through the hole in the slider falls on the equinoctial ring where it indicates the time.

Universal equinoctial ring dial, English, made by Hilkiah Bedford, Holborn Conduit, London, brass, *c.* 1670. There are two rings, a meridian ring and an equatorial ring, also a bridge bearing a slider, adjustable for solar declination, in which is a pin-hole serving as a gnomon. National Maritime Museum

Rojas.* Also called Geminus; a vertical universal dial based on a simplification of the universal astrolabe projection associated with Juan de Rojas, a pupil of Gemma Frisius; often found on the back of nocturnals.
Scaphe (*cup-dial*).* A dial with the hour lines engraved on the inner surface of a hemisphere, shallow bowl, or a goblet.
Shepherd's. See Cylinder.

Horizontal string-gnomon dial, French, unsigned, ebony and ivory, *c.* 1620. National Maritime Museum

String gnomon (*string style*). Any dial in which the gnomon is a taut thread.
Universal ring. See Ring.
Vertical. Any dial in which the hour scale is vertical (e.g. vertical disc* dial, vertical plate* dial, and the vertical form of an ordinary horizontal dial†).
Window. A vertical dial painted on a pane of glass for insertion in a window.

Gunnery instruments. Many instruments were made for the use of gunners, e.g. levels, combined with sights, for use with cannon; sectors and rules with scales correlating the weight and sizes of shot of different materials and showing the necessary charges; and calipers for measuring bore and shot.

Hours. Not all horary systems divide day and night into twenty-four equal hours, numbered in two series of twelve. Among other systems used on Islamic and European astrolabes, quadrants, and sundials, the following may be mentioned: planetary (unequal or Jewish) hours resulting from a division of the periods from sunrise to sunset and from sunset to sunrise each into twelve equal hours (noon and midnight are therefore the sixth hours), the hours vary in length from day to day, and except at the equinoxes, day hours differ in length from the night hours; Babylonian hours (*horae ab ortu solis*), which are equal hours counted up to twenty-four from the first hour after sunrise; and Italian hours (*horae ab occasu solis*), which are similarly counted from the first hour after sunset. In the pre-1873 Japanese system of time keeping the periods from sunrise to sunset and from sunset to sunrise were each divided into six equal *toki*. The *toki* were numbered, starting at midnight and again at midday, 9, 8, 7, 6, 5, and 4. The 'hour' lines on Japanese sundials are, therefore, marked with numerals indicating the 5th, 4th, 9th (midday), 8th, and 7th *toki* of the day.

Loadstone. A piece of magnetic iron ore, magnetite, usually ground symmetrically, equipped with steel or iron pole pieces and a keeper, and mounted in a metal frame with a suspension ring. Popular in the seventeenth and eighteenth centuries for 'philosophical' experiments and for magnetizing the compass needles of pocket compasses and sundials. A spherical loadstone reproduces in miniature the magnetic system of the Earth and is known as terella.

Microscopes are either simple (with one lens) or compound (with several lenses). The earliest simple microscopes, such as those of Leeuwenhoek or Musschenbroek type, and the earliest compound microscopes, such as those made by John Marshall, *c.* 1700, are very rare. In the eighteenth and nineteenth centuries there were many types of compound microscope, known by names derived from their function (e.g. botanic, universal), their form (e.g. drum, chest-type, screw-barrel), their place of origin or a maker associated with them (Cuff, Culpeper, Gould, Joblot, Lyonnet, Nuremberg), or some variation of the normal form (aquatic, lucernal, reflecting, solar).

Napier's bones. A pocket calculator, for multiplication and division, invented by John Napier of Merchiston. The commonest type consists of loose square-sectioned 'bones' or rods, with a series of numbers divided by diagonal lines on each of the four sides of each 'bone'; the 'bones' lie on a small tray which slides into a case. Another type has rotatable cylindrical 'bones' fixed in a box.

Orrery, English, published for and sold by J. Addison, Regent Street, London, Globe-maker to George IV, brass, ivory, printed and coloured paper scale and star map mounted on wood base, *c.* 1800. The planets and their satellites up to and including Uranus are shown, the earth and moon are modelled in greater detail than the other heavenly bodies and are linked to each other and the sun by gear work. National Maritime Museum

Nocturnal. An instrument used to find the time by night. It consists usually of a disc with a handle, with a smaller disc and an index arm attached to the centre of the main disc by a pierced rivet. The small disc is set to the date; the pole star is sighted through the hole and the index arm moved until it cuts a particular star of the Great or Little Bear, when it will indicate the time. Regiomontanus or Rojas dials are often found on the backs of nocturnals.

Orrery. The eighteenth-century successor to the armillary sphere; a hand- or clockwork-driven machine for demonstrating the motion of the planets about the sun, and in the larger and more elaborate types showing also the movements of the satellites of the planets. Usually the earth and moon are made to a larger scale than the other planets so as to show their motions relative to each other and to the sun in greater detail. Orreries were especially popular in England. The first true orrery appears to have been made by George Graham and Thomas Tompion, *c.* 1709. Inspired by this machine, John Rowley made, *c.* 1712, a similar instrument for Lord Orrery, which, according to Richard Steel, the essayist, was named 'orrery' by Rowley in honour of his patron.

Quadrant. Consists essentially of a flat plate (of wood or metal) in the shape of a quarter of a circular disc; the simplest form has a scale of 90° along the curved edge and a plumbline and bob suspended from the apex of the right angle. Equipped with a pair of sights on one radial edge, it could be used for finding angular elevations of heavenly bodies or in surveying. Islamic quadrants usually have on one side a nomograph of the sines and cosines of the angles marked on the arc. This is known as a sinecal quadrant (*quadrans canonis* or *vetustissimus* in medieval Europe). Another type of quadrant had a diagram of planetary hours above the scale of degrees. This required a sliding bead on the plumbline and was improved by the addition of a zodiacal scale for ascertaining solar declination. An adjustable zodiacal scale rendered the quadrant universal (*see* Dial). This was the medieval *quadrans vetus*. European quadrants of the sixteenth, seventeenth, and eighteenth centuries were made with hour lines for ordinary Italian and Babylonian hours, and include many ingenious new designs. Seventeenth-century English quadrant designs include those associated with Allen, Collins, and Gunter.

An astrolabe-quadrant is a reduction to a quarter of a circle of the essential lines of the stereographic projection on the *rete* and plates of an astrolabe. The commonest type is that described by Prophatius in the thirteenth century (the medieval *quadrans novus*). The typical Islamic quadrant is engraved on one side as a Prophatius astrolabe-quadrant, and on the other as a sinecal quadrant.

Qibla-indicator. *See* Compass.

Sector. A mathematical instrument consisting of two flat equal arms hinged together as in a joint rule. The arms bear various scales which were used for the solution of numerous problems in practical geometry, surveying, dialling, and gunnery. For instance, to divide a given line into the same proportions as a scale on the sector, it is only necessary to open the sector until the ends of the two arms are as far apart as the length of the line and to drop verticals from the scale to the line: hence the French name, *compas de proportion* (which must not be confused with the English proportional compass). Three main types of sector are distinguishable by the types and lay-out of the scales engraved on them, viz. the English, French, and Dutch types. Surveyor's sectors are equipped with sights and sometimes a ball-and-socket mounting. Some of the fine sixteenth- and seventeenth-century triangulation instruments are also based on the principle of similar triangles.

Sundial. *See* Dial.

Telescopes are either refracting or reflecting. In the latter type the light is focused by means of a speculum mirror. In the Newtonian reflecting telescope the mirror reflects the light through a prism to an eyepiece mounted at the side of the upper end of the telescope tube. In the Gregorian reflecting telescope the light is reflected on to a second smaller mirror at the upper (open) end of the tube and thence back to an eyepiece mounted behind a hole in the centre of the mirror. Unlike terrestrial telescopes, astronomical telescopes give an inverted image.

Telescope made by Sir Isaac Newton in 1671

592

SILVER

Egyptians, Assyrians, Phoenicians, Greeks, Romans, all the ancient civilizations delighted in the splendour of wrought silver. The Old Testament abounds in references; Homer wrote of silver wine bowls; Horace of the silver brilliance in the Roman home. Long before the Romans came to Britain the Celts were embossing, chasing, punching, and engraving their magnificent silver ornaments and drawing wire for exquisite silver filigree. Gold may suggest greater magnificence, but silver has always offered peculiar opportunities to the creative artist-craftsman, and specimens remain representing every period and style from the Gothic to the present day.

Entirely pure silver is too soft to work and other white metals render it brittle, but copper proved a satisfactory alloy, in the proportion of 11 oz 2 dwts silver to 18 dwts copper – the quality recognized in Britain and known and revered throughout the world as sterling. Unfortunately, however, it is difficult to detect far larger proportions of alloy in the silver, and in London, Paris, and other Continental centres the master silversmiths early formed themselves into guilds for protection from such unfair competition. The London Goldsmiths' Company, especially, has proved remarkably successful in upholding the sterling quality ever since its establishment in the thirteenth century. In the early sixteenth century a Continental visitor exclaimed that all the shops of Rome, Milan, Venice, and Florence together could not rival the gold- and silverwork on sale in London, and English hallmarked silver retains a unique position to this day.

American

The art of the silversmith (or goldsmith, as the craftsmen called themselves) flourished early in colonial America, with a skill and sophistication not found in the other crafts. The styles were basically English, as the earliest goldsmith whose work has come down to us was, like many subsequent ones, trained in London. Robert Sanderson emigrated after a nine years' apprenticeship to arrive in Massachusetts in 1638. Richard Storer had served only five years in a London goldsmith's shop before he came to Boston in 1635, yet he was able to instruct his young half-brother, John Hull, in 'the trade of a goldsmith', until he 'through God's help obtained that ability in it, as I was able to get my living by it'. Storer's work, and that of John Mansfield, the first trained goldsmith in New England, are unknown today. Hull was one of the most active early Boston citizens, and upon being appointed mintmaster recorded again in his diary that the Court permitted him to take his friend, Robert Sanderson, to be his partner. Most of the silver fashioned by these men bears the mark of each partner, and most of it survives from having been given to churches. Marks were not a requisite on plate fashioned in the colonies, and wrought plate was a commodity as valuable as its weight in coin, and more useful. Hence, a good proportion of the silver owned by the first churches had served a period of domestic use; and the tankard, caudle cup, beaker, and standing cup are ecclesiastic as well as secular forms. Porringers are unknown today in church services; it is probable that this shallow bowl with a flat, pierced, horizontal handle was always a domestic piece. Inventories disclose that it was always a popular one, whereas the seemingly equally domestic dram cup lost favour in the early eighteenth century.

Spoons, too, a household's first possession in the precious metal, followed English styles; although those with slipped in the stalk or puritan handles are rare today, suggesting re-fashioning into the ensuing forms. Another seventeenth-century Boston worker in precious metal, William Rouse, has left a few pieces in distinctly English style; yet the journal of Jasper Danckaerts, visiting in Boston, reveals that he was 'Willem Ros, from Wesel. He had married an Englishwoman and carried on his business here. . . . We were better off at his house, for although his wife was an Englishwoman, she was quite a good housekeeper.'

The first native craftsman was Jeremiah Dummer, born of English parents in 1645 and recorded as his apprentice in Hull's diary of 1659. Indentures for apprentices followed those of England, and in Boston the legally required term was seven years. Dummer's contract called for eight years. His work, too, was largely in English styles; exceptions are his seventeenth-century columnar candlesticks like ear-

Far right Caudle cup by Robert Sanderson, Boston *c.* 1680

Left The Vivyan Salt, silver-gilt, set with glass panels painted with scenes from Jeffrey Whitney's 'Choice of Emblems', published in 1556. Surmounted by a goddess bearing a sword and scales, and the canopy inset with glass plaques of the heads of four Roman emperors. London hallmark 1592–3. Victoria & Albert Museum

The Huguenot, Bartholomew LeRoux, who is known to have been working in New York in 1689, wrought similar handles for his generous 'brandy bowl' now owned by Yale University, but left the sides similarly unadorned save for the grooves to indicate panels. LeRoux trained his own sons, John and Charles, and the Dutch-named Peter Van Dyck, who, in the manner of apprentices, married his master's daughter. Onckelbag and Kierstede in New York's first generation vie for the richest productions, although Jacobus van der Spiegel's tankard at Yale University has no rival in its intricacy of engraving. Tankards were fashioned with great skill by all the Dutch New Yorkers, although the form was not one found in their homeland. To the English vessel, elaboration of handle and base moulding, and frequently of the cover too, gave a distinctly local style well exemplified in the one by Peter Van Dyck.

When, in the last years of the seventeenth century, the craft developed in Pennsylvania, the first tankards had simplified New York base mouldings, although porringer handles were derived from New England styles. New York porringers almost always show a regional character; the early handles had intricate cuttings that left no room for the owners'

lier French ones copied in England, and his punch bowl of 1692, which is Portuguese in derivation. He is credited with having introduced cutcard work and gadrooning into colonial silversmithing. Some of his contemporaries, documented apprentices of Hull as were the Samuels, Paddy, and Clark, have left no known work; Timothy Dwight, similarly trained, is known by only two pieces, yet each of a skill to make the scarcity of his work the more surprising. John Coney, whose work survives in greater quantity and variety than any of the others, reasonably seems to have learned his craft from the same source. His earliest sugar boxes are in rich Charles II style, as are his cherub-laden caudle cups or punch bowls, yet the majority of his pieces are simple.

Sanderson had three sons whom he trained, yet only one is known by his work today. Hull's sons all died in infancy; his daughter Hannah, however, married Samuel Sewall, who has been called the colonial Samuel Pepys; his diary records activities of 'Cousin Dummer', 'Mr Coney', 'Tim', and their successors. Thomas Savage, whose small porringer's handle is very much like the simple early ones by Dummer, was by witness of Sewalls diary the master of Samuel Haugh.

Dummer's generation saw the beginning of the craft in New York, which, although then under English rule, still held to Dutch traditions. The very names of the earliest craftsmen, Van der Burgh, Onckelbag, Kip, and Kierstede, proclaim their origin. Cornelis van der Burgh was the first native New York goldsmith; he died in 1699. His best-known beaker – the basically Dutch form which had, however, been incorporated into English plate in Jacobean days – was engraved with illustrations by Adriaen van der Venne from a Dutch book of poems; his broad two-handled panelled bowl shows the form most characteristic of New York plate. A simpler one, yet characteristically New York by its six embossed panels and similar caryatid handles, was made by Jesse Kip, who is thought to have taught the craft to Cornelius Kierstede.

Above Caudle cup and cover, showing English and Dutch influence, made by Gerrit Onckelbag for the christening of Judith Bayard, 13 December 1696, New York. Yale University Art Gallery

Right Porringer by John Coney and Peter van Inburgh, Boston, late 17th or early 18th century. Yale University Art Gallery

Punch bowl of pumpkin shape and panelled sides with *repoussé* and chased floral decoration and engraved with the initials of Theunis and Vroutje Quick (married in 1689), by Cornelius Kierstede, New York, first quarter of 17th century. Metropolitan Museum of Art

initials proudly proclaimed on others, and in the eighteenth century cuttings were starkly simple in a handle of distinct solidity. New York spoons, too, had been different in their first styles of case-shaped handles with hoof or caryatid terminal, whereas Philadelphia's earliest are the trifid ends, of which the greatest surviving number in the colonies are from New England.

Rhode Island, at the turn of the eighteenth century, was training goldsmiths, probably in Boston. Samuel Vernon, the first from that colony whose work has survived, occasionally employed the meander wire and stamped base moulding of New York

Tea set by Paul Revere, presented in 1799 to Edmund Hartt, builder of the frigate *Constitution*, Boston. Museum of Fine Arts, Boston

derivation. Connecticut became the home of Boston-trained John Potwine and the New Yorker, Cornelius Kierstede, who was without doubt that colony's unsurpassed craftsman. In the south, although English goldsmiths, apparently seeking metal, had arrived in Virginia earlier even than in New England, no goldsmiths are known to have plied their craft until the eighteenth century. In Virginia, which still preferred to order its fine plate in London, small wares and repairs continued to be the goldsmith's chief role until Revolutionary days. Cesar Ghiselin, who was Philadelphia's first goldsmith, moved to Annapolis to become Maryland's first – as Johannis Nys, in Philadelphia in the late 1690s, went on to start the craft in Delaware. In South Carolina the Legares from New England and Stoutenburghs from New York started a craft of which little now remains.

Meantime, in the city of Boston, John Coney had taken a Huguenot lad to be his apprentice. Apollos Rivoire anglicized his name and as Paul Revere became famous through his son and namesake. Coney had had no sons to carry on; but John Burt, believed to have been his apprentice, had three sons to continue the proud craft, one of whom worked throughout the second half of the century. Although there were numerous goldsmiths in Boston at that period, the patriot Revere and Benjamin Burt seem to have shared the earlier importance of John Coney and Jacob Hurd. Edward Winslow had been an apprentice of Jeremiah Dummer, as had, undoubtedly, John Noyes and, probably, John Edwards. No parallel is found for Winslow's four sugar boxes, all dated in the early 1700s. Dummer, Winslow, and Edwards, in partnership with Allen, fashioned the three surviving standing salts of colonial make. A third maker of sugar boxes in the early 1700s is thought to have been Daniel Greenough of New Hampshire where, for the most part, less ambitious pieces were fashioned. Early in the eighteenth century, Salem, Newburyport and other towns supported goldsmiths, but important works seem to have been largely restricted to the main centres of the craft.

John Edwards was the scion of a three-generation craft tradition; his sons, Thomas and Samuel, were almost exact contemporaries of Jacob Hurd. The last, by the quality and variety of his work and importance of his clients, seems to have taken Coney's place in Boston for approximately a quarter of a century. His sons, Nathaniel and Benjamin Hurd, and his apprentice, Daniel Henchman, all worked in the third quarter of the century and left an occasional rococo piece, though New England obviously still preferred simple lines and fine proportions. Jacob Hurd was commissioned by the maritime court to make its admiralty oar; the Court of Vice-Admiralty in New York ordered one from Charles LeRoux. The latter fashioned a gold box for Andrew Hamilton, an official presentation piece now owned by the Historical Society of Pennsylvania. An earlier gold

Far right Loving cup presented to Edward Tyng for a naval victory in King George's War, by Jacob Hurd, Boston, 1744. Yale University Art Gallery

gift had been made in 1693 by Cornelis van der Burgh for Governor Fletcher, but it is known only by documentation.

In Albany the Ten Eyck family of goldsmiths was flourishing; the early Koenraet had sent his son Jacob to be an apprentice of Charles LeRoux. A generation earlier Kiliaen Van Rensselaer, apprenticed to Jeremiah Dummer in Boston, had found living in that staid town to be rather simple. Kiliaen's work is unknown, but Koenraet and his sons, Jacob and Barent Ten Eyck, have left examples of their fine workmanship. Barent fashioned for Daniel Cruyn in 1755 a gorget engraved with the British Royal arms, also engraved on the Admiralty Oars. Throughout the eighteenth century, and in all colonial centres, British designs set the styles for colonial craftsmen. Samuel Sympson's *Book of Cyphers*, published in London in 1736, is known to have been used in New York and Rhode Island. John Singleton Copley painted Nathaniel Hurd with the 1724 edition of Guillim's *Display of Heraldry* at his elbow, and many craftsmen followed the heraldic designs in this oft-published work.

There are more portraits of silversmiths than of other craftsmen. Copley painted Revere in his shirt sleeves, though at a highly polished workbench, with a pear-form tea pot in his capable hand; and depicted Rufus Greene, an apprentice of William Cowell, who, in turn, had learned his craft with Dummer. Nathaniel Hurd sat for his miniature portrait on copper to Copley, and to an unidentified limner in watercolour on ivory. William Gilbert of New York sat to James Sharples, as did Joseph Anthony of Philadelphia to Gilbert Stuart; but none of these portraits proclaim the sitter's profession as Copley twice had done.

trade in all its branches. Many were also spreading into other fields which were then, but not now, allied to it. Dentistry was an achievement of several goldsmiths, best known among them, no doubt, the patriot Revere. Nathaniel Hurd had turned to engraving so that, at his early demise in 1777, it was as an 'ingenious engraver' that he was extolled. Revere's engravings were sometimes executed carefully, but the best known of his were political cartoons, carelessly and hastily executed. He gave up his craft entirely for the five years of the Revolution, but resumed to work in the newest English fashion practised also by Benjamin Burt, both of whom continued into the early years of the 1800s. Revere printed continental currency; Ephraim Brasher of New York minted the famous and now very rare Brasher doubloon. Like the earliest mint in Massachusetts, it was not entirely legal, but extremely convenient. Myer Myers of New York, whose work also spanned the rococo through classic styles, showed usually a preference for simplicity. His dish ring is unique in known American silver, and his bread basket made for the same patrons, Samuel and Susanna Cornell, came to public attention with the publication of Mrs Rosenbaum's book on Myers.

Philadelphia had three families of three-generation craftsmen who almost spanned the eighteenth century. Philip Syng, Jr, fashioned the standish used at the signing of the Declaration of Independence; his father and son, both of the same name, owe their present-day reputation to him. Francis Richardson had a namesake and a Joseph among his sons. The latter – who imported much English plate and worked in richest styles – had sons Joseph and Nathaniel as successors. Peter David, and his son and grandson John were capable crafts-

Right below Coffee pot by Joseph Anthony Jr, Philadelphia, 1785. Greenfield Village and Henry Ford Museum

Below Covered sugar bowl and coffee pot by Simeon Soumain (*c.* 1685–*c.* 1750), New York. The straight sides indicate the first half of the century. Museum of Fine Arts, Boston

The shift to English styles in New York was undoubtedly broader in scope than the influence of such London-trained craftsmen in that town as Simeon Soumain and Daniel Christian Fueter, two well-known names in its goldsmithing annals. The latter advertised employing a chaser from Geneva, yet the average goldsmith was still carrying on his

Porringer and spoon inscribed *S.S. Junior* by Paul Revere, Boston. Worcester Art Museum, Massachusetts

men, but probably owe their reputation today to their family adherence to the craft rather than to their individual practice of it. Richard Humphreys was selected by the Continental Congress to fashion its rich presentation urn to Charles Thomson, Secretary of the Congress, and by George Washington to make camp cups.

The silversmithing family of Faris in Annapolis was founded by William, who has been characterized as 'the most picturesque figure among eighteenth-century Maryland silversmiths'. His accomplishments included clock and watch making, portrait painting, and work as a cabinet maker, dentist, innkeeper, and tulip grower. He has left the only known manuscript book of silver designs in the colonies, and had three sons whom he trained in silversmithing.

Unique in America was Baltimore's endeavour in the early 1800s to establish a guild system similar to that so long in existence in England and on the Continent. For a brief time, starting in 1814, silver made in Baltimore was marked at a hall and identified by a date letter; this compulsory marking was abolished in 1830. By coincidence, perhaps, this is the period when American silver was becoming, through the taste of the time and introduction of machinery, a commodity of far less appeal than that of the previous two centuries.

British

The collector who turns his activities to the silver wrought in the British Isles in past centuries enters a field of exploration in the antique which yields to no other sphere of collecting in extent and interest, and is indeed of greater range and possessed of more possible varieties of specialization than many other forms of applied art. This breadth of subject may well be a discouragement to the beginner as he comes to realize that English plate survives from the sixteenth century downwards in great quantity on account of its intrinsic value, which has encouraged its safe keeping, and of its comparative indestructibility. But this same high rate of survival affords a reasonable prospect, whatever particular form a collection may take, that sufficient examples will appear in the market to make pursuit and selection of desirable pieces a practical and enjoyable pastime.

Many ardent collectors must have had their first interest in the subject aroused by stumbling attempts to decipher the hallmarks on some inherited piece of plate, and by the subsequent realization that every normal piece of English silver bears its own documented evidence of age and origin. To this, no doubt, may have succeeded a rush of marks to the head and an attempt to acquire every piece that falls in one's path for the pleasure of identifying and labelling it. Slowly a deeper appreciation of the subject grows as more pieces are handled, standard works consulted, and museums and exhibitions visited. The pieces of the puzzle fall into shape and the collector sees his subject as a whole and realizes the often quite small part of it he can expect to make his own particular sphere. There are, of course, lovers of old silver who never become real collectors on a set plan. They merely acquire pieces which please the eye and for which they have some specific domestic need. They are not greatly exercised over questions of period, style, or craftsmen, so long as the piece 'goes' with their general taste and décor; though it is true that appreciation of the quality of workmanship, line, and proportion will be sharpened with practice, despite any indifference to the historical relationship of the piece. From this general interest, however, a more particular study may easily spring, once the first general 'furnishing' phase is over.

Right The Lambard Cup, silver-gilt, probably by John Bird 1578. It bears the arms of England, those of the Drapers' Company and those of Sir William Cordell, Master of the Rolls. The inscriptions reads 'A Proctour for the Poore am I and remember theim before thow Dye 1578'

James I beaker, maker's mark a crescent in a shaped shield with three pellets below, London, 1607. Thomas Lumley, London

What lines is specialization likely to take in silver? There is first the national division of England, Scotland, and Ireland. The silver of each country shows distinct characteristics and certain specific forms which do not occur, unless as exceptions, in either of the other types, and many collectors like to concentrate on the native work of their own country. The study of Scottish silver is perhaps the most rewarding, since there was a smaller output of silver in Scotland at all periods. Up to the mid-eighteenth century at least any piece, however simple, possessed a sharp individuality which often seems to vanish into the smoothness of repetition in its English counterpart produced in far greater numbers.

Inside national divisions it will always be possible to focus attention on the other methods of specialization to be considered. The most obvious is undoubtedly that of period: and so inherently of style. A study of the trend of prices in relation to the comparative number of pieces of any particular period available will show that it is not necessarily scarcity alone that determines a price or the demand for the period which the price reflects. There are distinct fashions in collecting as there are in every other form of activity. These trends in popularity move slowly, and there are crosscurrents which at times may confuse the direction of the main stream. But if we stand far enough off we can see the movement. The serious collector of a chosen period will rise above popular fancies of the moment and find his own reward.

Far right Dessert basket centrepiece supported by three caryatids on a double tripod plinth, silver-gilt with glass liner, by Paul Storr, 1810–11

The next form of specialization is that of a particular type of piece as it was made at different periods, allowing a study of its development, decoration, and social use. The enormous varieties of form which wrought plate has taken makes this a very worthwhile pursuit. Here, again, one may detect fashion. At times tankards may be out of, and teapots in favour. This form of collecting is undertaken perhaps less seriously than others, but it has its devotees. I have seen a collection of taper sticks of all dates and styles; a whole herd of cow cream jugs; a large array of casters, and so on. The assembly of a particular class of object in sufficient numbers to form comparisons contributes a great deal of knowledge of the subject and reveals aspects of workmanship and design not immediately recognized from isolated examples seen at intermittent intervals.

The most highly specialized form of collecting is that of early spoons. These, from their personal associations and their usefulness, have survived in greater numbers than any other single form of wrought plate, and provide a very wide field for collectors. Since the spoon is naturally the first piece of plate required, it early became the established christening gift and was made in many small provincial centres where little other silver was ever made. It thus provides by far the greatest number of examples of rare provincial silversmiths' marks. Much work has been done and much remains to establish the definite ascription of many of these marks. Spoon collecting therefore brings an extra reward to its devotees in the study the subject entails. The main types of spoons are indicated in the glossary to follow, but the present scope cannot permit of any detailed account of rare provincial types or the larger subject of the marks on such pieces. The established collector will know where to turn for his information. The beginner is advised to take the advice of an established collector or specialist dealer.

Above Pair of sauce boats by Paul Lamerie, London, 1740. Thomas Lumley, London

Standing salt, enclosing a standing figure within the column, and mounted with scrolled carayatids, maker's mark a swan's head erased, silver-gilt and crystal, London, 1549. Trinity College, Oxford

Perhaps the most rewarding form of specialized collecting, and one practically ignored, is that of studying the work of one maker. This has been done as regards the whole Huguenot school of the early eighteenth century, in the incomparable Farrer Collection now in the Ashmolean Museum, Oxford. Few attempts have been made to assemble the work of one craftsman, other than that of Paul Lamerie or Paul Storr. There has been an enthusiasm in America for Hester Bateman's work. But there seems a certain frenzy in the scramble for pieces by her which suggests that keenness has swamped discrimination. One other individual family of silversmiths, that of Augustine Courtauld, his son Samuel,

and the latter's wife Louisa, has received worthy attention promoted by the interest of his present-day descendants. But there are very many other excellent craftsmen of whose work never more than a few pieces have been seen together at a time, and who would be worthy of greater attention. This interest can scarcely be extended to pieces made before 1697, from which date the surviving records of Goldsmiths' Hall provide the identification of makers' marks. The maker's name provides the personal touch which seems necessary to an appreciation of his work; though there are outstanding silversmiths, particularly of the seventeenth century, known only by their marks, such as the maker who used a hound sejant and whose work possesses great individuality and outstanding merit worthy of special attention.

Those who prefer to collect silver, not as specialists but simply to enjoy the use of beautiful plate, will find their opportunities widened by the exercise of ingenuity in transforming the original purpose of a piece to a modern use. The late eighteenth-century Argyle or gravy warmer serves excellently for a small coffee pot; the sharp-pointed skewer opens letters as if made for the purpose; the pierced mazarine or dish strainer, mounted on a dark wood tray can be enjoyed afresh for the intricacy of its arabesque piercing; large oval tea caddies or early tankards make excellent biscuit boxes, wine coolers can be used as flower vases, and so on. Few pieces, except the rarities of the sixteenth century, need be considered purely as cabinet or decorative items.

The would-be collector may well be attracted by the study of hallmarks, and it is often apparent how a facility for interpreting these indications of age and provenance excites the envy of the beginner. The scope of this guide to silver precludes any serious attempt to explain the system or to show examples to illustrate its working. But there is room for brief advice. Most important factor is that no one mark, whether it is date letter, town-, or maker's mark, should ever be relied upon alone for evidence of date or provenance, or forced to support some point of view which has no other evidence of style, workmanship, or period to back it. Even when a complete set of marks is present it is easy to misread them by overlooking relative evidence. For example, although the cycles of London date letters are varied in succession, certain superficial resemblances occur at various periods. The capital Roman O, for instance, for 1809, is not very dissimilar from the small o for 1829. Whereas with the former letter the leopard's head used is crowned, that of the latter cycle is uncrowned. Once this is appreciated, confusion becomes impossible. Again, two Court letter cycles were used, commencing respectively in 1638 and 1697. In the former the Sterling Standard marks of leopard's head and lion passant were in force, whereas the latter cycle began with the introduction of the Britannia Standard with the figuremark, from which it takes its popular name, accompanied by the lion's head erased. The only time the second Court cycle of letters can occur with leopard's head and lion passant is on gold plate of the time. Other examples of this nature could be adduced, but enough has been said to point to the need for a careful weighing of all the evidence provided by the marks. In this respect collectors would be well advised to avoid the use of pocket lists of marks which provide the cycles of date letters alone without the accompanying standard marks. A countercheck should always be made with the maker's mark, which can be identified in the standard works of Sir Charles Jackson, Chaffers, or Cripps. The date at which the mark was entered at Goldsmiths' Hall or of incorporation in a provincial guild provides a *terminus a quo* for the piece. Latest possible date for a maker is less easily determined. But without definite evidence to the contrary, a working life of thirty years should be considered long enough, and many makers seem to have a shorter working time than this. A further check is provided by re-entry of a mark in a new form at a known date.

Even such a brief discussion as this cannot overlook the matter of false and transposed marks. These

Richard Chester Steeple cup, silver-gilt chased and *repoussé*, maker's mark FT monogrammed, London, 1625–6. Victoria & Albert Museum

Two mugs: *left* by Timbrell and Bentley, London 1713; *right* by Nathaniel Locke, London, 1716

Left Saucepan, probably used for heating brandy, by William Fleming, 1726

two categories must be distinguished. By the former is meant reasonably close imitations of old marks made by fakers in the late nineteenth century for the express purpose of deceiving. It is almost impossible to recommend any firm method of detecting such imitations. Their recognition must spring from the experience of much handling of plate. This promotes an 'eye' for a genuine mark, either in its fresh, clearly struck state in some position not subject to wear or in an exposed position which has suffered the wear and polish of centuries. On the other hand, we may note certain points which may lead to the detection of a false mark. Many deliberate forgeries appear to have been perpetrated by fakers whose lack of knowledge led them to use marks of some date at variance with the style of the piece they were attempting to reproduce, or even to invent some new form of vessel which has no authentic prototype of the date to which the marks would assign it. Here a knowledge of the characteristics of the particular period suggested by the marks is essential. Again, a certain type of false mark, struck with soft-metal punches, gives the appearance of wear, often in positions normally protected from rubbing, such as the bases of jugs or tankards. Common sense will raise immediate doubts of such pieces. Marks obtained from castings of genuine examples are harder to recognize at first sight. Comparison of presumed date and style may still provide the first clue. Sets of table silver, spoons, and forks sometimes bear cast marks. A close examination of a number of the suspects side by side will often reveal that the marks are spaced and related to each other in exactly the same degree in each piece, revealing a master die for all, in place of the infinite variations obtained in genuine individually struck marks.

Transposed marks fall into two categories. There are, first, the genuine old pieces of plate, known colloquially as 'duty dodgers', made by a silversmith working in the contemporary style of his day, who, to avoid the expense of submitting his work to the Assay, inserted into the new piece a set of marks taken from some old and possibly worn-out piece on his hands. Often he completed the deception by adding his own mark, striking it over the earlier maker's mark, if this was visible. Such pieces were felonious evasions of the hallmarking laws at the time, and, although clearly genuine examples of antique plate of their period, remain illegal in the eyes of the unaltered law of today. But the new Hallmarking Act, 1973, to come into force in 1975 envisages recognition of such pieces by a special exemption mark.

The other form of transposed mark is the nineteenth-century faker's device, usually handled with more cunning than the imitative forging of marks, and needs constant watchfulness to detect. It is possible, particularly when the piece is oxidized by lack of cleaning, to detect the solder line surrounding marks let into a plain surface. But when the joint of the applied plate of marks is masked, for instance,

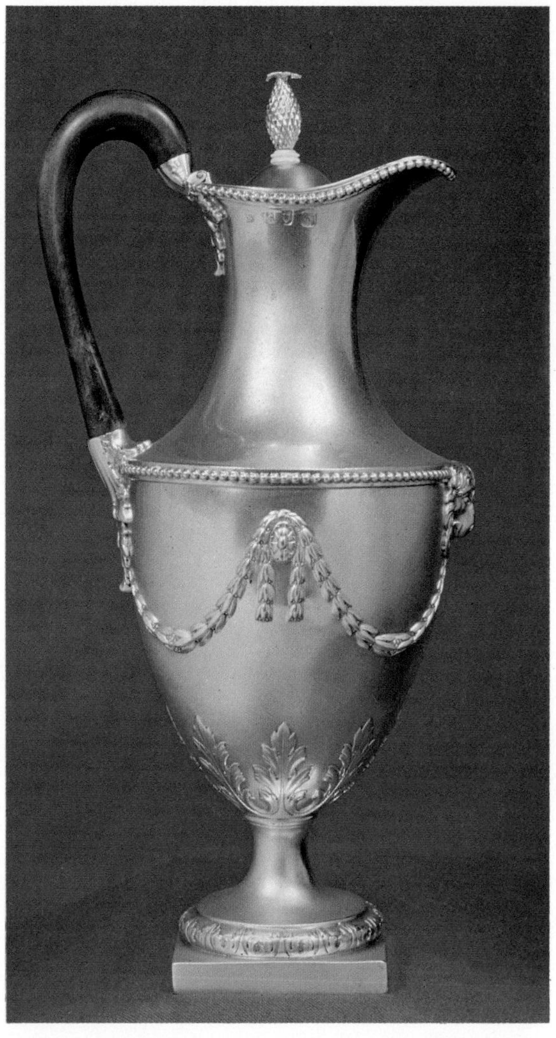

Chocolate pot, chased and *repoussé*, 1773–4. Victoria & Albert Museum

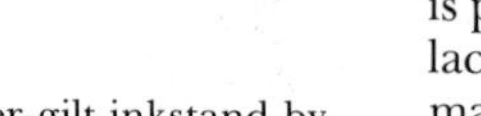

Silver-gilt inkstand by Robert Hennell, 1789

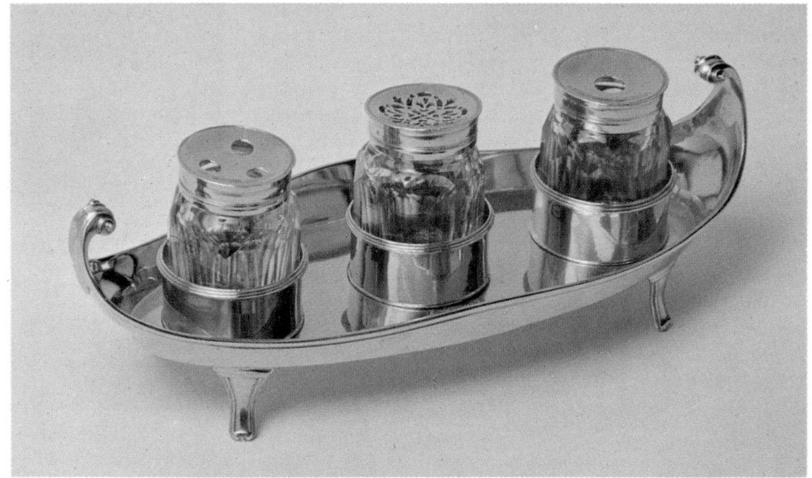

Pair of silver-gilt sugar-vases by Benjamin and James Smith, London, 1810–11. Part of the ambassadorial service used by the first Duke of Wellington in Paris. Wellington Museum, Apsley House, London

by a separate cast base applied to a coffee pot or sauceboat, detection may be harder. There may possibly be a small pinhead blowhole to allow the imprisoned air expanded by the heat of the solder to escape. This is an invaluable clue. This may, however, be dispensed with by a clever craftsman and detection will be increasingly harder. Mistakes of style, form, and decoration will probably also occur in such pieces.

A further type of illegal plate must also be mentioned. This is represented by pieces which have either been altered in form, though retaining their original metal and marks, or have had additional sections added to change their decoration or purpose. They are also illegal, since additions made to hallmarked plate should also be marked at the time they are added. Often such alterations were carried out to private order so as to provide a new purpose for an outmoded or disused piece. The commonest example is that of a seventeenth- or eighteenth-century covered tankard with a spout added at the front to convert it to a jug. If the spout, in the hands of an honest silversmith who knew the law, was made of standard silver and the piece sent to the Assay office for the additions mark to be impressed, this would be in order. But the great majority of such pieces, having been privately ordered, possibly from the local country silversmith, were not so marked, and remain illegal. The discerning collector will not be interested in such pieces, but the beginner should be warned.

Another form of alteration which is not illegal is that of the addition of later decoration. Plain pieces of the seventeenth and eighteenth centuries in every form were the prey of the prevailing Victorian taste for lavish embossing of fruit, flowers, animals, and other motifs with which the craftsmen of the time fondly hoped to enrich their predecessors' handiwork. The recognition of such later work can be achieved only by the experience of handling; by seeing as much genuine period decoration as possible; by a study of the essential forms of plain pieces which the student must learn to perceive below the overgrowth of later years. This is sometimes complicated by pieces with some original decoration to which later work has been added. Again, there exists the necessity for continual handling of every type of piece and the slow cultivation of an eye for what is and what is not original.

Much has been heard in recent years of the value of antiques as an investment. In precious metals there is an underlying feeling of security in the intrinsic value of the pieces apart from any rarity value in the collector's market. On the other hand, it is apparent from a study of prices over a wide range of years that changes in fashion can affect values very considerably. The genuine enthusiast will scarcely consider the question of a potential return or profit on his outlay. No monetary value can be put to the intangible assets his collecting activities will produce for him in the thrill of the chase and in pride of possession. Even allowing for the decline in the purchasing power of money, it is growing more and more apparent that there is an ever-widening circle of appreciation for the beautiful products of past

Far right Pair of beakers with coat of arms and unusual engraving of shooting scenes by J. E. Edwards, 1812

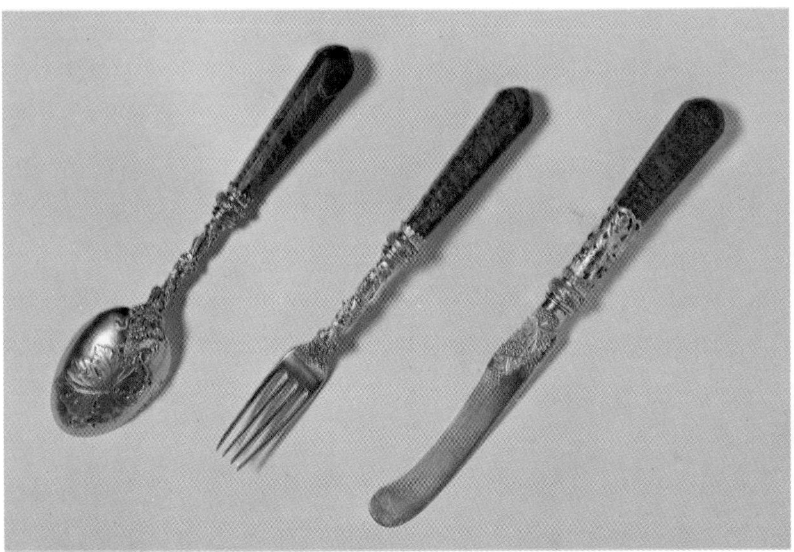

Silver-gilt knife, fork and spoon with lapis lazuli handles and grape vine decoration, London, 1825

centuries. So long as a civilized existence continues, such appreciation must promote the desire to share in inherited treasures. The collector links the past with the future and is happy in the part he plays.

Scottish

For the purposes of the collector, Scottish silver spans a period from the late seventeenth to the early nineteenth centuries. Pieces dating from the sixteenth century or before are rare indeed; although the craftsmanship reflected by some of them is of a standard that suggests long experience and a considerable output, while the appearance of anything hitherto unknown from the first half of the seventeenth is an event. Most of the choicer things which now come on the market belong to the eighteenth century.

The general characteristics of Scottish silver are not obvious ones. If anyone new to the subject thinks he will be able to recognize what is Scottish by its manifestly Celtic shape or by the crop of thistles engraved on it, he is mistaken. There are only two or three types of vessel which are exclusively national. On the other hand, the Scottish goldsmith had an outlook and an approach quite different from those of his colleagues south of the Border. In the first place there lay behind him no sumptuous tradition such as produced the extravaganzas of Cellini or the Nuremberg craftsmen. He had not even the elegant patrons to foster in him any of the assured, sophisticated design sense of a Lamerie. The virtues which his circumstances developed in him were directness, a canny respect for the metal, and a real love for its beauty unadorned. Simplicity and functionalism are therefore the marks of Scottish silver at least until a taste for the rococo spread northwards in the mid-eighteenth century, and they laid a restraining hand on ornament for another generation or two after that. The ornament, when it is present, is often heavy handed by English or foreign standards. Yet if it has not the crispness or the precision, at least there is nothing stereotyped about it, and this often lends a life and sparkle which make the piece good to live with.

Foreign influences were numerous. Silver mirrors the country's social history. French imports probably dominated the late medieval scene, if the Gothic tabernacle heads of the St Andrews University maces or verges are significant. Low Countries influence is marked among the Communion plate of the east coast in the seventeenth century, and the Scandinavian link in some of the tankards of the Restoration period. In 1707 the Union opened the door wide to an English impact which inevitably, although only after a century, imposed itself completely on the Scottish goldsmiths.

Above Quaich, engraved with roses and initials by Charles Blair, Edinburgh, 1736. Royal Scottish Museum

Highland plaid brooch dated 1701. National Museum of Antiquities, Scotland

Scottish silver was perhaps at its most distinctive in the second half of the seventeenth century. This is the period when the quaich was being translated from wood into silver, when the so-called 'thistle' cups were being made, when sugar casters and tankards and, above all, spoons still had an unmistakably Scots accent. For the collector, however, it is a period which demands a fairly long purse, as well as a good deal of patience. Quaichs of various sizes do turn up at intervals. It is rather less difficult to find a silver-mounted wooden quaich, transitionary pieces which have a peculiar charm, especially those in which the staves are of alternating woods. Unfortunately shrinkage has often rendered the staves loose, and even the silver mounts, and to tighten them permanently and satisfactorily is very difficult indeed. Nothing in all the range of treen is more graceful, however: and this grace is inherited by the earliest of the all-silver quaichs, becoming lost as the more sophisticated goldsmiths of the eighteenth century turned the quaich into a mere twin-handled bowl.

The thistle cup is perhaps even more rare and expensive. What it was used for has never been clear. It was certainly not made in sets like tea cups, though pairs are found occasionally. It seems to have come into fashion about the end of Charles II's reign. The exuberant ornament which was such a feature of this reign in England is not nearly so marked in Scotland, incidentally. The Scots possessed less high hopes of the restored monarchy than did their neighbours.

The massive simplicity so characteristic of the best Scottish silver achieved its peak in the early years of the eighteenth century. Men like Colin McKenzie and James Sympsone in Edinburgh were making sober pieces of considerable importance, such as tankards, two-handled cups, fruit dishes, and coffee pots. As a rule they are devoid of any ornament except for such details as thumbpieces and finials and the coats-of-arms which are not excelled by Scots engravers of any other period. The coffee pots, whether octagonal or round in section, are among the loveliest things of their kind. They are, however, excessively rare. Spoons, commonly of the rat-tail form, offer more hope for the collector, but even these are not numerous of such early date. It should be remembered that a fair proportion of the energies of the goldsmiths was being diverted to the manufacture of Communion plate, since many churches were still not properly equipped in the reign of Queen Anne.

Tankard by Colin McKenzie, Edinburgh 1711, and a pair of candlesticks by Thomas Ker, Edinburgh, 1707. Thomas Lumley, London

Below right Covered cup, one of a pair, with gadrooned decoration, by Robert Keay, Perth, *c.* 1790. Royal Scottish Museum

Below Tea service by William Aytoun, Edinburgh, 1733. Thomas Lumley, London

The 1730s and 1740s are in many ways the Golden Age of Scottish silverware. At the same time modest, domestic pieces were being produced in large numbers in Edinburgh, Glasgow, Aberdeen, and to some extent in smaller places. Collectors can still secure prizes belonging to this period. Tea pots are eagerly sought after, notably those by such makers as James Ker and William Aytoun. They are variations of the 'bullet' type, sometimes flattened a little, sometimes nearly spherical, and in earlier examples the spouts are usually quite straight. A few still have their stands, which greatly enhance their appearance – and their value. The corresponding cream jugs and sugar basins are as difficult to find as the tea pots. Local lairds and ministers often had their domestic silver made in the nearest city, even in burghs of the size of Banff or Elgin, and a small amount of this probably remains in the districts where it has always been. The best hunting ground used to be, and possibly still is, the northeastern counties, which were fairly prosperous towards the close of the eighteenth century and yet isolated enough from Edinburgh to make it possible for the burgh craftsmen to develop their trade. The simple pieces which resulted have great charm, and are well suited to the collector who wants good old craftsmanship with which he can live.

In Edinburgh and Glasgow the second half of the eighteenth century brought closer imitation of southern styles, and elaborate ornament makes it much less easy to distinguish what is Scottish. The swing of fashion can be traced even in the output of a single maker, such as Patrick Robertson. His rococo of the 1760s becomes classicism in the 1770s, when Craig's New Town was beginning to take shape and Robert Adam was building his Register House. The more recognizably Scottish work from now right on into the nineteenth century came from centres such as Aberdeen, Perth, and Inverness, where styles were conservative and treatment more individualistic than in the sophisticated south. Much table silver was made in small places as far north as Tain. These attractive provincial pieces ceased to be made after 1836, when a Statute required all Scottish silverware to be assayed in Edinburgh or in Glasgow.

With Scottish as with English silver, almost the first

Left Tea urn by John Main, Edinburgh, 1732. Royal Scottish Museum

Right Tankard with applied decoration to the handle by Thomas Ker, Edinburgh, 1699. Thomas Lumley, London

thing the collector looks for is the hallmark. The standard reference work is still the Scottish section of Sir Charles Jackson's *English Goldsmiths and Their Marks*; although a great deal has been learned since it was written, especially about the provincial goldsmiths. Briefly, the Edinburgh hallmarking system has been in operation since the middle of the sixteenth century. When the date letter was added in 1681 this brought the normal complement of marks on Edinburgh silver to four, at which it remained until the sovereign's head was added in 1784. Glasgow instituted the date letter in the same year as Edinburgh, so far as we know, but its appearance was most irregular until as late as 1819. Aberdeen and the other burghs do not seem to have had a regular date stamp. Indeed, the hallmarking of all places other than Edinburgh is full of pitfalls for the collector. The form of the townmark is only of very general help in dating a piece, a matter which really has to be decided by the maker's punch. Sometimes the townmark has such a range of variations that it opens wide the door of speculation, as when the dromedary mark of Inverness beguiled Jackson into including the Calcutta elephant among the symbols of the Highland capital. Many small provincial pieces, however, have no 'hallmark' other than the maker's punch carrying his initials. This is true of a high proportion of the table silver, and then only familiarity with the actual punch, considered in relation to the style of the piece, enables one to hazard an identification at all. This is perhaps not quite such wild guesswork as it may seem, since the makers in towns such as Banff or Elgin were few, and it is possible to acquire a 'feel' for their products. A few of those in the north and east of the country were itinerant, and stamped pieces now in one town, now in another, which adds to the problems of the collector.

Far right above Embossed and chased tazza with the mark of Ernst van Vianen, Utrecht, 1602. Victoria & Albert Museum

Near right Clock with a silver and silver-gilt case by Hans Conraedt Breghtel, The Hague, *c.* 1600. Victoria & Albert Museum

Far right Nautilus shell standing cup, mounted in silver-gilt, Utrecht, 1613. Victoria & Albert Museum

Dutch

If all the Dutch silver of the sixteenth and seventeenth centuries had been melted into bullion, as indeed the greater part of it was, hardly a single fashionable style would have been lost. The Dutch masters of painting so faithfully recorded the tradition of contemporaneous silverware in such minutely detailed domestic scenes that reproductions of old silver have been made directly from pictures in museums. This was a great creative era during which Dutch silversmiths wrought their fashionable plate into designs of almost riotous magnificence.

Some of this silver is still in existence. The Earl of Yarborough, for instance, possesses a celebrated historic tazza-shaped cup and cover of the sixteenth century. This cup, commemorating the naval victory of the Dutch over the Spanish in the Zuyder Zee on 11 October, 1573, was made in 1574, probably as a thanks-offering from the citizens of Enkhuisen to William the Silent for their deliverance from Spanish domination. It is elaborately embossed and chased with marine scenes, including a view of the Zuyder Zee with ships and towns. The ornament includes sea monsters and tritons and the arms of William the Silent.

Dutch silver of the early seventeenth century was richly chased with scenes of farm life, domestic themes, rural landscapes, and other homely subjects. Then, from the 1640s until the end of the century, fashion demanded symbolical, allegorical, legendary, mythological, and classical subjects. Ornamental motifs were acquired from every possible source, resulting in a motley assemblage of escutcheons in Renaissance styles, such as winged heads, cherubs, satyrs, acanthus leaves, heraldic shields, all surprisingly well harmonized.

Distinguished among the many Dutch silversmiths of the late sixteenth and early seventeenth centuries were Adam van Vianen, the elder, and Johannes Lutma. The former sponsored grotesque designs, and his fantastic enrichments influenced silversmiths in London of Charles II's reign working from his book of designs engraved by Th. van Kessel and published in 1641.

Although van Vianen was born in about 1555, none of his work made before 1610 is known to have survived. His masterpiece is the noble rose-water ewer and basin belonging to the City of Amsterdam. The basin is exquisitely chased with scenes from the Dutch and Spanish War, enclosed in panels on the wide rim; in the depression is a representation of the battle of Nieuwpoort, 1600, and the raised centre displays the arms of Amsterdam and the date 1614. The ewer is enriched with three panels depicting similar scenes. A second member of this celebrated family, Christian van Vianen, entered the service of Charles I, for whom he made, in 1637, vessels for St George's Chapel, Windsor. These, unfortunately, were melted for bullion during the civil war. A large dish, decorated with dolphins and dated 1635, is in the Victoria and Albert Museum.

Dutch connoisseurs consider Johannes Lutma to have been a greater silversmith than Adam van Vianen, but surviving works are too few for accurate judgment. Lutma delighted in depicting marine life, adapting it most gracefully to his patterns. Remaining pieces include two funeral shields dated 1633, intended to be deposited on the coffins of Guild Masters in accordance with Dutch custom; a famous ewer and basin commemorating the opening of Amsterdam Town Hall in 1655; and a dish signed by him in 1641 similar to one shown in his etched portrait of his close friend Rembrandt.

Circular punch-bowl by Reynier de Haan, The Hague, 1778, with engraved guilloche decoration. Christie, Manson & Woods

Handsome drinking horns have been recorded in paintings by Dutch artists. Horns were costly gifts presented to Guilds by prominent members and used at Guild banquets. The most celebrated drinking horn belonged to the Guild of St Sebastian in 1565. This horn, richly mounted with figures in the round representing the saint's martyrdom, is seen in Bartolomew van der Helst's portrait group of the Guild officers painted in 1653. Three years later the artist included it again on a canvas portraying four high officers of the Archers' Guild. The magnificent horn presented to the Guild of St George in 1566 also takes its theme from the story of its saint. This was recorded by van der Helst in his painting of the banquet held in the hall of St George's Guild to celebrate the Peace of Munster in 1648.

Silver beakers were important articles of plate. First they were used as drinking vessels commemorating peaceful achievements or events. After the Reformation they were used also as sacramental cups engraved with conventional arabesques and flower sprays, sacred subjects, Biblical scenes, sym-

bolical personifications, and views of churches. Sacramental beakers, usually gilded, are recorded in the still-life paintings of Pieter Claesz and Willem Heda.

In the seventeenth century the beaker, with a moulded circular foot and slightly spreading sides, was usually decorated with all-over engraving. Typical is a beaker struck with the Delft hallmark for 1633: it is divided horizontally by a central corded rib, the upper part engraved during the second half of the century. By 1700 and during the eighteenth century decoration was commonly chased.

Silver galleons or nefs on wheels were made by Dutch silversmiths in enormous numbers from the 1660s for use in the service of wine. Such a vessel was fully rigged: and the wine was contained in the hull and was poured into glasses through the wide-open mouth of the figurehead. Richly ornate examples were made throughout the eighteenth century.

Dutch silver tankards are now comparatively rare, yet they are conspicuous in still-life paintings, notably those by Willem Heda. It was fashionable for them to be engraved with historic scenes, many taken from prints by the engraver Bastiaen Stoopendaal. The engravings depict Queen Mary, consort of James II of England, with her infant son, later known as the Old Pretender; the escape of James II, represented by three figures in a barge; the departure of the Prince of Orange for England in 1688; and William III opening the English parliament in 1689.

Characteristic of Holland and not made by silversmiths elsewhere were the tall, elegant holders for single glasses of wine. These were made in sets of a dozen. They are seen in many paintings, notably those by Jan Steen and Willem van Aelst. The City of Amsterdam possessed a set of five stamped with the Amsterdam date letter for 1609 and the maker's monogram L.C. Others have been noted made two centuries later.

The three cups most representative of Dutch conviviality are the windmill cup, the bridal cup, and 'Hans in the cellar', made from the sixteenth to the nineteenth century and exported profitably to other European countries. The windmill cup was filled

Right Windmill wager cup, maker's mark a pear, Dordrecht, 1599 or 1620. Christie, Manson & Woods

Left Pair of silver-mounted wine bottles, The Hague, 1689. Victoria & Albert Museum

Below Pair of salts by Adrien de Grebber, Delft, 1601. S. J. Phillips, London

Below right Teapot, with beaded decoration by Svalte Striebeck, Amsterdam, 1792

with wine and handed to the guests of the party who, by blowing through a slender tube, set in motion the sails of a tiny windmill which operated a pointer around a numbered dial. The wine had then to be consumed in a single draught before the windmill sails ceased revolving. Failure to accomplish this feat involved drinking as many cupfuls as were indicated on the dial. A variant contained a globular openwork cage containing a silver die placed between the windmill and the bell-shaped cup. One of Johanne van Haensbergen's paintings illustrates a wager cup in use. Windmill cups might be engraved with the figures of Faith, Hope, and Charity.

The bridal cup, more often used as a wager cup, was in the shape of a young woman with both arms raised, holding aloft a swinging bowl. Her wide skirts formed a drinking cup which the bridegroom was expected to empty without spilling any wine from the smaller vessel now swinging perilously below. He would then hand his bride her share of the wine.

Hansje in den kelder or 'Hans in the cellar' was brought out when a birth was expected in the family, so that host and friends could drink the health of the mother and her baby. As the wine was poured into the cup, its increasing weight lifted a domed lid in the centre, and to the delight of all a tiny silver model of a child would automatically emerge.

The brandy bowl is another characteristic piece of seventeenth- and eighteenth-century plate expressive of the Dutchman's native sociability. This vessel was reserved for intimate family gatherings and was filled brimful with brandy and raisins, eaten direct from the bowl with silver spoons. Its early shape was octagonal or heptagonal, and it was engraved with symbolical figures, sometimes associated with the family, and often fitted with mask handles. An oval form evolved in the 1670s and continued throughout the following century, the handles flat and chased, as seen in Metsu's *The Collection*.

Few early Dutch salts and casters remain, and reliance regarding their shapes must be placed on paintings by Heda, Pieter Claesz, Jan Steen, de Heem, and Dou. Silver candlesticks are rare, too, but they can be seen, for example, in Terborch's *Guitar Lesson*. Those with clustered columns appear over and over again on Gerard Terborch's pictures. Boxes, often gilt, were made specially for costly peppers and spices.

Ordinary domestic silver made in large quantities during the eighteenth century was influenced by French design, and much gilded. There was a great demand for table bells, tobacco boxes, charcoal

braziers, tea canisters, tea pots, kettles, tea urns (from 1760), trays and waiters, cake baskets, and candlesticks. When it is realized that finer silver was made in at least thirty-four different towns in Holland before 1800, it became obvious that many silversmiths concentrated on plain domestic ware for everyday use by the gentry.

Dutch silver was of sterling quality for finely wrought ware: ordinary domestic plate contained nine per cent more copper alloy.

French

French silver plate until the mid-sixteenth century was dominated by the formal restraint of Gothic design, decoration being chiefly confined to wide bands of lettering. The centre of the silversmiths' craft was in Paris, where workshops were originally established near the Pont-au-Change, a covered bridge which ended at the steps of Notre-Dame Cathedral. Early in the fifteenth century silversmiths gradually moved to the section of the River Seine bank now known as the Quai des Orfèvres. Little French silver of the Gothic period now remains. The British Museum houses a gold and enamelled cup attributed to about 1380, decorated with scenes from the life of St Agnes. Although altered from time to time, enough of the original remains to show that these French silversmiths were superb craftsmen.

The Italian Renaissance influence was introduced by Benvenuto Cellini late in the reign of Francis I (1515–47). He visited Paris in 1540 and was persuaded to establish a school for silversmiths, where for five years under his vigorous guidance pupils wrought magnificent ecclesiastical and domestic plate so that the Gothic formality was soon superseded by silver embossed with intricate and fanciful designs often containing human figures. The demand by the French nobles for silver plate enriched in the Italian manner became so immense that Paris attracted many master silversmiths from Italy.

Little now exists, however, of the gorgeous silver designed and made during this period: to gain an idea of its exact appearance students refer to the many contemporaneous prints of domestic scenes. The engravings by J. A. Ducerceau (1510–84) and René Boyvin (1530–98) illustrate an extensive array of fashionable silver, its surfaces virtually covered with strapwork and elaborate *repoussé* figures.

When Henri III founded the Order of the Saint Esprit in 1578 he presented a silver-gilt bottle in the Italian style, believed to have been made by the master silversmith Noel Delacroix and now in the Musée du Louvre. In the same year Henri levied a high tax on silver plate, his purpose being to discourage the manufacture of luxurious services, and so direct more silver to the Royal Mint to remedy the drastic shortage of bullion.

Elegance of form characterized French plate of the seventeenth century, plain surfaces contrasting with lavishly florid covers and handles. Immense numbers of *écuelles* were made, tableware peculiar to France but closely resembling contemporaneous English porringers and used for serving spoon meat. The *écuelle* was a two-handled shallow bowl raised from thick-gauge plate, with cover and standing plate. The majority were enriched with engraved cutcard work and ornamental finials. Handles usually projected horizontally, either decoratively pierced or engraved on the upper surface: others were wrought in the shape of leaves or other motifs, such as the coiled snakes associated with wine tasters.

Most of France's finest domestic silver was sacrificed in 1681, when Louis XIV commanded a nationwide melting at the behest of the powerful group of bullionists. Few outstanding pieces of plate escaped the general confiscation, apart from those that had been sent abroad. These included the magnificent silver-gilt toilet set, covered almost entirely in *repoussé* work, made by Pierre Prevost in 1670 and now in the possession of the Duke of

Right Pair of silver-gilt tazze, Paris, 1583. S. J. Phillips, London

Far right *Écuelle*, the cover with snake handle, Paris, 1670

Devonshire. This set once belonged to William of Orange and Princess Mary, who were married in 1677: their arms are engraved on each of the twenty-two pieces. Louis XIV's melting did not prevent silversmiths from producing plate as handsomely wrought as formerly. A pair of octagonal stands, pierced and chased with foliage, strapwork, and medallion heads, formerly in the collection of Lord Brownlow, were made at Bayonne in 1690.

At the opening of the eighteenth century French silversmiths were continuing fashions in plate evolved over a long period, but when Louis XIV moved his Court to the splendour of Versailles, French taste under the influence of Daniel Marot, developed for massive, heavily decorated plate, including toilet tables with matching stools and mirror frames, as well as extensive toilet services. Applied ornament included arabesques, lambrequins, and masks. Superb craftsmanship was carried out under the masters Sebastien Leblond and Jean Baptiste. The death of Louis XIV in 1715 began a short era of simplicity, with piercing a fashionable style of ornament.

This trend was succeeded by forty years of showy rococo design. This greatly appealed to hostesses eager to load their tables with glittering arrays of plate. The outstanding master in this work was Justin Aurèle Meissonier, who interpreted the rococo at its most florid. Under his influence the decoration of French domestic plate reached a high standard of radiance. Louis XV appointed him royal silversmith.

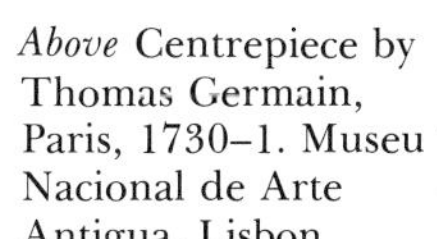

Above Centrepiece by Thomas Germain, Paris, 1730–1. Museu Nacional de Arte Antigua, Lisbon

Left Louis XV ewer and basin by Sebastien Igonet, Paris, 1733, with the *poinçons* of Hubert Louvet. Christie, Manson & Woods

Below Design for a candlestick and an inkstand dated 1728 from *Oeuvre de Juste-Aurèle Meissonier.* Victoria & Albert Museum

Other celebrated silversmiths of this period were Claude Ballin, the younger; Paul Charvel; Robert Joseph Auguste, a prolific worker; Antoine Boullier; Edmé Balzac; and Claude Augustus Aubry. Thomas Germain and his son François were accounted high among the silversmiths of Paris. The elder possessed a flair for bold design and skilful handling of the sumptuous and ornate. An immense tureen made for Louis Duc d'Orléans, son of the Regent, is a notable feat of craftsmanship. The cover is piled high with all kinds of game, meat, fish, and vegetables, with boars' heads for handles, and the stand supported by boars' feet. François rivalled him in creative skill and in the quantity of his productions, which were in continual demand at the Continental Courts. Little remains of the plate produced by Thomas, but several sumptuous pieces by his son have survived, notably at Lisbon and Leningrad. Louis Lenhendrick, a contemporary, supplied fantastic plate in the rococo style to the Russian Court.

Rococo was succeeded by neoclassicism, a style thoroughly suited to the French temperament. These new patterns acquired fashion appeal when the celebrated Delafosse published designs which overcame early prejudice and influenced silversmiths throughout France. The neoclassic continued until the Revolution, when once again fashionable domestic plate was confiscated by the government for conversion into bullion. The result is that French silver wrought earlier than 1790 is extremely scarce, much scarcer than that of other Continental countries. Many people, however, possessed no more than a single lightweight article of undecorated silver such as a spoon, beaker, wine taster, or *écuelle.* Little of this fell into the hands of the bullionists, and examples are plentiful.

Prior to the Revolution enormous quantities of

Wine taster by C. J. Fontaine, Paris, 1768–75. S. J. Phillips, London

silver plate had been made, much of it with consummate skill. Paris alone supported more than 500 master silversmiths, and in every town throughout the country at least one member of the craft was fully occupied. A law was enacted in 1784 requiring each of the 176 silver communities or guilds in France to register in Paris an invariable mark by which their work could be identified, with the date indicated by the last two ciphers of the years. Such a community mark was usually identified with the region in which the silversmith operated: such as a rose for Provence, a grape cluster for Theims, an artichoke for Laon, a cannon for Mézières, scissors for Thouars, lace bobbins for Valenciennes, a lion's head for Lyons, a rock for Rochefort, a bear for Vesoul, a squirrel for St Germain-en-Laye, a ship for Brest, a fish for Dieppe, and a cat for Meaux.

The provincial silversmiths were not slavish imitators of the Parisian designers and craftsmen; many of them established less lavish localized styles. These were too widespread to be much affected by competing models, and each jealously guarded autonomy discouraged any tendency towards uniformity. Each community restricted membership, and no trained craftsman was permitted more than one assistant.

Silver-gilt cream jug decorated with formal leaves and honeysuckle, Paris, *c.* 1800

The period of Napoleon's Empire emphasized the elgance of classicism in silver plate by such masters as Marc Jacquart, Martin Biennais, Henri Auguste, and J. B. Odiot. The Château de Malmaison houses four pieces from a silver-gilt dinner service made by Auguste to the command of Napoleon I, who presented it to the City of Paris. The soup tureen and stand are typical of Empire classicism: the bowl is encircled with a border of classical figures in relief, repeated on the stand, which is supported by four figures of winged lions. The cover finial consists of a seated classical figure. The Emperor's favourite was Biennais: many historic services by this master have survived.

During the next thirty years or so there was a close resemblance between French and English silver plate. An English silversmith's catalogue published in about 1850 illustrates numerous designs found also struck with French hallmarks. For instance, a silver-gilt vase-shaped coffee pot made in 1825 by Marc Augustin Lebrun, Paris, was constructed of units of plate – none of it hand-raised – to which cast and chased ornament was soldered (palm leaves and bulrushes, swans, fountains, and dolphins).

Above Louis XVI oval soup tureen and stand from the Orloff service by Jacques Nicolas Roettiers, Paris, 1770. Christie, Manson & Woods

The *Jury's Report of the Great Exhibition*, 1851, records in connection with French silver plate: 'The beauty of elegance of the individual forms and ornamental details is a thorough study of ornamentation; figures are perfect parts of many compositions and might be oxidized to emphasize their beautiful workmanship. Ornament is in low relief over the surface generally and parcel gilding gives expression when design is confused by excess. The plateaus on which tea cups, cream and sugar vessels are arranged are ornamented in niello.' The electrotype process of reproducing elaborately worked silver was now in use: the copies were, of course, in unalloyed silver. A pioneer of this branch of silver working was F. A. Thouret, Paris, who produced replicas of many cups, including one representing the 'Rape of the Sabines' and the 'Cup of Fulda'.

One of the most prolific of Parisian silversmiths during this period was J. F. Rudolphi. One fashionable piece, of which he made many, was a round tripod worktable constructed entirely from units of cast silver. The top consisted of a hollowed flat plate with a mask of a Naiad in the centre surrounded by Titans and Naiads, the rim ornamented with applied masks, birds, and foliage. The pillar resembled a stem of reed foliage, ornamented with kingfishers: upon the three claws were a bird's nest being attacked by a rat, and an intoxicated infant Bacchus.

In France it is compulsory for a standard mark, either 950 or 800, to be struck by the State Assay Office, and it is illegal to sell below these standards in France, although silver of lower quality may be exported. The maker is also required to strike his mark.

German

Vienna, home of the German emperors from the time of Rudolf IV in the fourteenth century, was the centre of early silversmithing. Here assembled the craftsmen whose brilliant wares eventually brought fame to the German states. It was the custom in Vienna to provide Court appointments to master goldsmiths resident within the city. These men were exempt from guild regulations, and none was compelled to strike his plate with any mark.

The German Gothic period in silver, about 1150–1550, was one of exceptional magnificence. Crocketed and pinnacled, enriched with exquisite figurines of saints, gilded and enamelled, set with precious stones and gems, much of this silver was designed for ecclesiastical purposes, such as monstrances and reliquaries, huge candlesticks and chalices. A favourite cup form late in the period was the small castle on slender stem and lobed foot.

Mazers and drinking horns were mounted in silver and usually engraved with Gothic lettering or leaf ornament. Mazers were often elaborate, the wooden bowl being fitted with a silver foot bearing the arms of its owner in enamel and the cover being surmounted by a silver figure, such as a falcon holding a heraldic shield upon which the arms were repeated.

By 1500 the free city of Nuremberg and the German town of Augsburg were supporting many prosperous master silversmiths with an enormous output of Gothic plate, much of it exported. Wenzel Jamnitzer, who went from Vienna to Nuremberg as late as 1534, became one of the most celebrated silversmiths in the Gothic style. Many German silversmiths had been apprenticed in or near Vienna, and consequently produced plate now counted as German, although very few pieces exist. These prove beyond doubt that no other European country made silver plate of comparable workmanship.

The Italian renaissance affected the design of domestic plate during the sixteenth century, making it renowned for its gorgeous ornamental detail, including new motifs, such as *putti*, urns, satyrs, nymphs, and acanthus leaves: the Church authorities preferred the formality of Gothic design until about 1600. Pineapple cups and columbine cups of superb craftsmanship were made by every aspirant to mastership. These were constructed according to guild rules and were masterpieces to prove dexterity of hammerwork and a sensitive touch in the chasing.

Altar monstrance elaborately mounted in silver-gilt made by M. Wollbaum, Augsburg, *c.* 1600

Below Ebony cabinet with silver mounts by Boas Ulrick (1550–1624). Augsburg, *c.* 1600. Victoria & Albert Museum

Silver-gilt and enamelled overlay tankard, *c.* 1600

Silver-gilt model of a rearing bull, the body with tooled hide and detachable head, by Hans Keller, Nuremberg, *c.* 1590. Christie, Manson & Woods

Germany's well-organized guild life favoured the production of plate such as wine cups, tankards, beakers, wager cups, and the like. There was little ecclesiastical patronage after the Reformation, and silversmiths found their profits among the solidly prosperous burghers. Every collection of German plate inevitably contains a preponderance of drinking vessels. Doctors from the fifteenth century advised every man who could afford it to drink from vessels of precious metals as a protection against infection.

Certain drinking vessels were used exclusively by Germans, mostly at their guild meetings. These include the giant *Riesenpokal* and the *Jungfrauenbecher*, a double cup – that is, one-stemmed cup supporting a precisely similar cup brim to brim. Some fantastic cups were fashionable in the shape of figures, birds, and animals, such as the parcel gilt lion passant, its tongue formed as a spout and the tail reflexed over the back; and the lion sejant with a detachable head and a finely chased mane.

Specialist designers working on a freelance basis became established in the sixteenth century and included Albrecht Altdorfer (1480–1538); Peter Flütner, whose *Kunstbuch* was published in 1549; Virgil Solis (1514–62); Hans Rosamer (*fl.* 1520–34); Bernard Zan (*fl.* 1580s); Hans Sibmacher (*fl.* 1555–95); Georg Wechter; Paul Flindt. Ornament on English Elizabethan and Jacobean silver was influenced by these German artists.

Cups were often masterpieces of lavish design, but their stems might be wrought of copper and heavily gilded. In others the cover, stem, and foot were in gilded copper, only the bowl being in silver, and that of quality lower than sterling.

Cups in which the liquor was held in nautilus shells were in great demand. The shell was cleaned by grinding until its mother-of-pearl surface showed unflawed and iridescent: it might then be all-over engraved. The upper curve was decorated with silver such as with the reptiles associated with Jacob Frick of Constanz. The shell bowl was held firmly by four hinged straps of silver rising from an expansive oval base of embossed silver. Many handsomely engraved examples were made at Augsburg for a century from the 1550s.

Silver-mounted coconut cups were largely exported during the same period. In these the bowl was meticulously carved with religious or personal subjects and held by three silver straps. Daniel Michael, Augsburg, from 1580 made silver-gilt mounted figures of cocks, the body consisting of a coconut, the head detachable to form a drinking vessel, and the hinged wings and tail in openwork silver.

Globe cups, German productions of the seventeenth century, were never very fashionable. They resembled terrestrial and celestial globes and were sold in pairs. The globes were supported by carefully modelled figures of Atlas kneeling on plinths of baroque design, often chased with dolphins and shells. These cups appear to have been used mainly for ornament.

Wager cups of the type associated with Dutch silversmiths were produced prolifically in Germany, particularly in Augsburg. Both those in the form of a windmill and those shaped as a woman holding aloft a swinging cup were made from the late fifteenth century until the 1850s.

Parcel-gilt nef by Esaias Zur Linden, Nuremberg, *c.* 1610. S. J. Phillips, London

Nefs of richly wrought silver were produced in hundreds of patterns from the fourteenth century, and one maker exhibited at the Great Exhibition, 1851. They were originally in almost universal use among the nobility and higher clergy. Until the mid-eighteenth century these sometimes massive pieces of plate, resembling perfectly rigged galleons, were often the work of specialist nef workers in Nuremberg and Augsburg. In the British Museum is an example made in 1581 by Hans Schlott, Augsburg, with a clock incorporated in its design.

Tankards were fashionable from the sixteenth to the eighteenth centuries, many of them parcel gilt. The beaker-shaped body was decorated with masses of chased embossments and engraving, virtually no plain space being left on body or lid; the handle was an elaborate casting such as caryatid or claw. A 7-inch (17.8 cm) tankard made by Kaspar Bauch, Nuremberg, 1580, is covered with strapwork, masks, birds, and bunches of fruit, with a female bust handle and with a thumbpiece in the shape of an infant bacchanal. There was also a vogue in Danzig for setting the body with numerous coins, all from a single state such as Brandenberg, or Prussia, and chasing the intervening spaces with foliage and scrollwork on a matted ground. Several struck with the mark of P. Overdieck, Hamburg, late in the seventeenth century, are encircled with frieze designs of bacchanalian figures and have grotesque scroll handles. Others by Cornelius Poppe, of the same period, are encircled with Roman emperors' heads.

Beakers were made throughout the collector's period of German silver plate, invariably in thick-gauge metal, Hamburg, Breslau, and Strasbourg being the specialist centres. Many are fitted with finialled lift-off covers, and their capacities are usually pint or half-pint, although other sizes are found. Early beakers might have ball feet, but a moulded or gadrooned foot rim was more usual. A typical beaker by Matthias Gelb, Augsberg, 1670, is worked in *repoussé* and chased with *amorini* astride dolphins in a seascape. Many in the eighteenth century were engraved with inscriptions in praise of wine.

The baroque and rococo styles extending from 1600 to 1760 were recognized by the Church, and their architects realized the decorative value of silver and designed handsome altar frontals, delicate monstrances, and enormous candlesticks. Silversmiths during this period made full use of the baroque flame-like curve on which they based many of their designs and ornaments.

German silversmiths excelled the Dutch until early in the seventeenth century, when the latter began embossing plate in a style acknowledged to be the finest in European silver of the period. This fashion was superseded by the Louis XIV style during the third quarter of the century. The Germans then turned their attention to much plainer domestic plate, producing small wares in enormous quantities in a metal less than sterling, but also making huge wine fountains and cisterns, magnificent centrepieces, and entire dinner services and tea equipages.

There was a late seventeenth-century and early eighteenth-century vogue for associating agate with silver mounts, such as candlesticks and drinking cups, later copied by Wedgwood in agateware with silver rims. Silver gilt and agate tea services made from agateware consisted of a tea pot with hexagonal sides, each set with a pink and brown agate medall-

Parcel-gilt beaker, maker's mark II in oval, Augsburg, *c.* 1680. The view is taken from an engraving by M. Merian of Frankfurt, *c.* 1646. Christie, Manson & Woods

Coffee pot by Johann Christoph Engelbrecht, Augsburg, 1749–51. S. J. Phillips, London

ion, two oval boxes for tea and sugar, and four brown agate tea cups and saucers, the cups with moulded silver feet and the saucers in fluted silver.

Ordinary domestic ware continued as the mainstay of the German silversmiths during the eighteenth and nineteenth centuries and included tea pots, jugs, tea canisters, coffee pots, tazzas, ewers, and basins in styles little different from the English rococo, neo-classic, and regency, but always in metal of a quality lower than sterling.

The cathedral city of Osnabrück in Hanover, of which George IV was created archbishop a few days after his birth, wrought much domestic silver for the English royal family. Examples have been noted engraved with the crest of George II as Prince of Wales, and with the arms of George III; but none of this is of sterling quality.

The German standard for silver is 800 parts per thousand, compared with 925 parts per thousand for sterling, the alloy being copper. The German silversmith may strike his personal mark and the standard mark, but neither of these is compulsory. It is not illegal in Germany to sell silver plate below recognized standards. German silver plate could be imported freely into Britain, but was difficult to sell owing to the absence of the sterling hallmark. The Foreign Plate Act of 1842 required German plate, if it were to be sold, to be assayed and struck with a mark if it is of sterling quality: any found to be below sterling was to be rejected and battered. By rigid adherence to their demand for sterling quality the Goldsmiths' Company successfully prevented the entry of German silver for sale. This Act, and the low standard of German silver, accounts for its absence from the Great Exhibition, 1851.

Papal rose, gold and sapphires, presented in 1562 by Pius VI to Duchess Ann, wife of Albrecht V of Bavaria. Residenzmuseum, Munich

Italian

Italian silver and gold of the Renaissance and earlier periods has for long been admired by all connoisseurs. Such works as the Pistoia altar, numerous reliquaries, processional crosses and croziers, the exquisite gold roses given by the popes to various sovereigns, and Benvenuto Cellini's magnificent gold salt cellar at Vienna, are among the outstanding examples of the European goldsmiths' and silversmiths' craft. But only in recent years has the silver of late periods won the attention of collectors. One of the chief reasons for this neglect was probably the difficulty which collectors experienced in their attempts to identify the marks on Italian silver. Two books published in 1959 – Signor C. G. Bulgari's dictionary of Roman silversmiths and the catalogue of an exhibition held at the Poldi Pezzoli Museum, Milan – have, however, made it possible to identify most of the townmarks and the Roman makers' marks. It may safely be predicted that the new interest in Italian silver of the seventeenth, eighteenth, and early nineteenth centuries will soon spread from collectors in Italy to the rest of Europe and America.

To eyes trained on the relative severity and solidity of the best English plate, much Italian baroque and rococo silver may, at first, seem a little too showy, not to say meretricious. Although Italian silversmiths produced numerous vessels marked by a restrained elegance of design, they excelled in the production of richly ornamented and often fantastic works. It must also be admitted that very few pieces of Italian silver reveal that exquisitely controlled sense of form and decoration which marks the finest works of French silversmiths. However, the same might be said in a comparison of any of the arts of eighteenth-century Italy and France. Exuberance is the outstanding quality of the best seventeenth- and early eighteenth century Italian silver. And even in their later, severer, neoclassical works, the *argentieri* seem to have had difficulty in restraining their sense of fantasy, making coffee pots in the form of urns with leaping greyhounds or goats as handles, crowning tureens with statuettes of river gods, fashioning lamps as Egyptian slaves.

There is a bold virility in the curves which decorate many large and small examples of Italian plate of the late seventeenth and eighteenth centuries. These pieces are also marked by a sculpturesque quality which is the other distinguishing feature of the best Italian silver. Such a relief as that by Luigi Valadier and many crucifixes and giant candlesticks like those at Lisbon, may indeed be regarded as minor masterpieces of Italian sculpture. But this sculpturesque quality is also evident in much domestic plate: the magnificent tureens made at Turin and Genoa, for instance, or such a boldly modelled object as the oil lamp in a private collection at Milan.

Marks and regional characteristics. Silver objects produced in different parts of Italy naturally show variations of style similar to those which mark the regional schools of sculptors and painters. The five most important centres for the production of silver were Rome, Turin, Venice, Genoa, and Naples, where the practice of hallmarking silver of approved quality seems to have been almost invariable in the eighteenth century. The study of marks has, however,

Altar cross and two candlesticks of rock crystal mounted in silver-gilt, enamelled. Attributed to Valerio Belli of Vicenza, *c.* 1520. Victoria & Albert Museum

revealed that fine work was produced in many other places. The list of notable Italian silversmiths printed below reveals how many, born and trained in various parts of Italy, worked principally in Rome. It is therefore rash to attribute silver to different regions purely on stylistic grounds. Silversmiths of the five main centres of production did, however, have their specialities.

Roman silversmiths naturally specialized in ecclesiastical plate, for which there was a particularly brisk market not only among the prelates resident there but also the numerous visitors. The Roman hallmark – the crossed keys of St Peter with either the Papal tiara or the ceremonial umbrella – may thus be found on much ecclesiastical silver in all parts of Europe. Silver reliefs and statuettes, of mythological as well as religious subjects, seem to have been made in Rome more frequently than elsewhere. It is interesting to note that Roman silversmiths adopted the neoclassical style in the early 1770s, a decade or more before their colleagues in other towns.

At Genoa the art of making silver filigree flourished as nowhere else in Italy, though unfortunately few pieces bear the city's mark (a tower). Another speciality of Genoese silversmiths were *trembleuses*, which appear to have been made nowhere else. Much mid-eighteenth century Genoese plate reveals the influence of France. The French influence on the silversmiths of Turin was stronger and eighteenth-century Turinese *écuelles* might easily be mistaken for French work. The Turin hallmark – the arms of the House of Savoy – may also be found on many tureens, coffee pots, and sugar bowls which have a French elegance of design. Venetian silversmiths seem to have specialized in rather highly embossed decorations, and they produced some of the finest bookbindings and *cartagloria* frames made in Italy. The Venetian hallmark – the winged lion of St Mark – also appears on many simple domestic objects, some of which seem to show the influence of English plate. Many objects bearing the Naples hallmark – the first three letters or the full name of Napoli, with a crown above – are also very simple. But Neapolitan silversmiths are more famous for such exuberant and sometimes rather gimcrack productions as vases of silver flowers. Other towns

Below Candlestick with Venice mark, 18th century. Victoria & Albert Museum

where fine silver was produced included Bologna, Florence, Mantua, Messina, and Palermo.

SOME NOTABLE ITALIAN SILVERSMITHS

Agricola, Giuseppe (1717–1804). A German originally named Bauer who began to work in Rome in 1739 and obtained his patent in 1745. His mark (initials) is to be found on several pieces of domestic plate dating from the second half of the century. Two of his sons Luigi (1759–1821) and Vincenzo (b. 1769) became gem engravers.

Left Silver- and parcel-gilt bowl, Venice, *c.* 1500. Victoria & Albert Museum

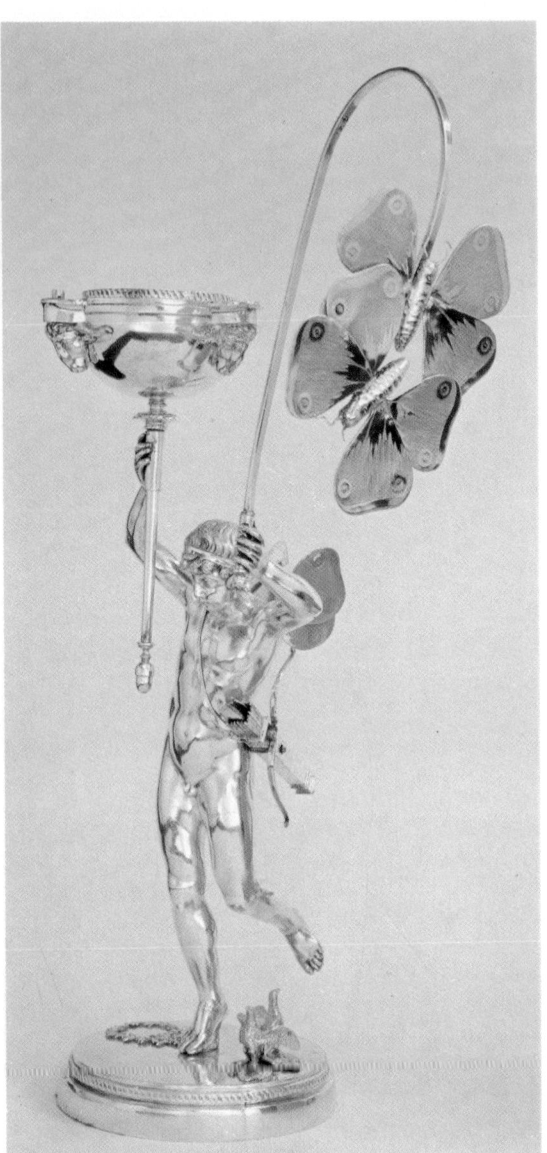

Lamp in the form of a figure by Giovacchino Belli, Rome, 1805. Victoria & Albert Museum

Arrighi, Giovanni Francesco (1646–1730). Roman, obtained his patent in 1683. He worked much for Cardinal Cybo and provided plate for several Roman churches. His mark (a lion's paw) appears on a pair of candelabra in the church of S. Maria Assunta in Capranica (Viterbo). His sons Agostino (1682–1762) and Antonio (1687–1776) were also silversmiths, employing marks similar to his. Antonio obtained his patent in 1733. His most notable work is the magnificent silver and lapis lazuli altar frontal, made to the design of Agostino Corsini and Bernardo Ludovisi for the royal chapel in Lisbon, between 1747 and 1749. He also produced grandiose works for Roman churches.

Bartalesi, Urbano (1641–1726). Sienese, was in Rome by 1660. His mark (a wolf, the Sienese arms) is found on domestic and ecclesiastical plate. His son, Stefano (1692–1737), took over his workshop in 1726 and employed the same mark.

Bartolotti, Giuseppe (1709–75). Roman, obtained his patent in 1731. His mark (a fish) is found on several pieces of mid-eighteenth-century domestic plate. The same mark (changed in 1790 to an upright fish between the initials CB) was used by his son, Carlo (1749–1834), who obtained a patent in 1777. A very handsome tureen with ram's head handles and a river god seated on the cover, made *c.* 1785–95, is in the collection of Dr Massimo Spada.

Belli, Vincenzo (1710–87). Founder of a very important family of silversmiths working in Rome, was born in Turin. He is first recorded at Rome in 1740 and obtained his patent next year. His marks (initials) is to be found on much ecclesiastical and domestic plate, a fine example being the ewer and basin (1772–83) in the Palazzo Venezia in Rome. His son Giovacchino (1756–1822) followed his calling, obtaining his patent in 1788, and produced some very fine silver in a strongly neoclassical style. Giovacchino's son, Pietro (1780–1828), also became a silversmith, obtaining his patent in 1825. Many of his designs for silver are in the Cooper Union Museum, New York. In the fourth generation Vincenzo II (*fl.* 1828–59), Pietro's son, took over the workshop, obtaining the patent in 1828. Among his numerous works (marked either with his initials or full name) one of the most outstanding is a coffee pot, based on one of his father's designs, with a handle in the form of a greyhound and a triton as spout (collection of G. Colonelli, Rome). He also produced a silver statuette of Menelaus with the body of Patroclus (modelled on the antique group at Florence) which was bought by the Earl of Jersey in Rome between 1828 and 1848, and is now in the collection of Dr Massimo Spada.

Benzi, Tommaso (1644–1723). Born in Genoa but went to work in Rome, where he obtained his patent in 1697. His mark (the head of a bearded man) appears on a monstrance in the church of S. Giovanni dei Genovesi, Rome.

Birelli, Bernardino (1707–67). A Roman, he obtained his patent in 1733. His mark (a lion with a book) has been found on several pieces of plate, including a pair of candlesticks in the collection of Professor Carlo Pietrangeli.

Boroni, Bartolomeo (1703–87). Born in Vicenza but was working in Rome by 1725. He obtained his patent in 1730. Among other works he provided the gilt-copper crown and sceptre for the coffin of the Young Pretender, made two reliquaries of solid gold to the design of Piranesi, and in 1774 produced several *decorazioni* for the Vatican after designs by Mengs. Three of his sons became silversmiths: Giuseppe, who used his father's mark (a monogram of Maria), was responsible for much work that has survived, including a Crucifix and six candlesticks of silver and lapis lazuli in the church of S. Biagio at Fabriano.

Carlier, Michele (1665–1741). Born in Ath in France, but had settled in Rome by 1688. Two years later he received his patent. He was much employed by Cardinal Camillo Cybo, for whom he made, among other objects, a gold reliquary adorned with diamonds and amethysts which was given to the Duke of Gordon in 1726. His mark (a cross on a pedestal) appears on three *cartagloria* frames in the cathedral at Poggio Mirteto.

Italo-French soup tureen and cover by J. Beya with crowned M mark, 1762. Christie, Manson & Woods

Cellini, Benvenuto (1500–69). Born in Florence, was probably the greatest of all Italian goldsmiths and one of the most notable sixteenth-century sculptors. His famous autobiography presents a fascinating account of an artist's life in the late Renaissance. His literary fame has naturally attracted numerous attributions to his name, but the magnificent salt in the Kunsthistorisches Museum, Vienna, is the only surviving work in precious metals that can with certainty be ascribed to him.

Cervosi, Angelo (1661–1720). A Roman who obtained his patent in 1690. A fine engraved salver in the collection of Mr Edward Burnett Lawson bears his maker's mark (a stag).

Chiocca, Matteo (1702–58). A Roman who obtained his patent in 1737. In 1739 he became silversmith to the city of Rome and the producer of chalices for the Camera Capitolina. In this capacity he made the chalices (varying from thirty-four to forty-three per year) which were given by the *Magistrato* to the various churches of Rome on their patronal festivals. His mark is therefore found on much ecclesiastical plate in the city (a sun with initials). He was succeeded by his son Giuseppe (1743–1812), who obtained his patent in 1739 and also produced numerous chalices for the *Magistrato.*

Colleoni, Corinzio (1579–1656). Born in Gallese, working in Rome by 1596, obtained his patent in 1612. Between 1616 and 1654 he made numerous chalices given by the *Magistrato* to the churches of Rome. In this work he was followed by his nephew Bartolomeo (1633–1708), who provided chalices between 1658 and 1701. The third Colleoni to hold this post of silversmith to the *Magistrato* was Bartolomeo's nephew, Agostino (1663–1746), who made many chalices between 1714 and 1738. The three Colleoni used as a mark a leopard's head rendered in different ways.

De Alessandris, Flavio (1668–1744). Born at Narni and obtained his patent at Rome in 1692. He worked also in Naples. His mark (a spread eagle) appears on six large candlesticks in the church at Polaggia. His son, Paolo (1696–1773), obtained his patent in 1739 and made for the church of São Roque, Lisbon, six large candelabra between 1748 and 1750. A *cartagloria* frame in the convent of S. Caterina at Fabriano also bears his mark (the diadem of the Holy Trinity).

De Caporali, Lorenzo (*c.* 1712–77). Born at Civitavecchia and worked in Rome, where he obtained his patent in 1745. His son, Antonio (1755–1832), obtained his patent in 1783. Several pieces of neoclassical silver bear his mark (a halberdier which was used by his father, the initials R. L. C., another which reads D.N.D./Vedov L.C., and finally, A 42 C.).

De Castro, Antonio (*fl.* 1565). A Portuguese silversmith who made for Franco Lercaro in 1565 the magnificent ewer and basin now in a private collection in Venice, and another in the Wallace Collection.

Fedeli, Stefano (1794–1870). A Roman who obtained his patent in 1815. Among his works the most notable is a statuette representing *The Return of Ulysses*, formerly in the collection of the Earls of Jersey, later in that of Dr Massimo Spada, Rome.

Fornari, Antonio (1734–1810). A Roman who obtained his patent in 1760. His mark (initials with a star beneath or full name) has been found on ecclesiastical and domestic plate.

Gagliardi, Giuseppe (1687–1749). A Roman who obtained his patent in 1742. For the King of Portugal in 1745 he made a magnificent pair of silver gilt *torchères* more than 9 feet (274 cm) high, now in the Museum of Religious Art, Lisbon. He also made for his patron a silver-gilt statue of the Madonna, some 6 feet (183 cm) high, on a model provided by G. B. Maini. His son, Leandro (1729–1804), also worked for the King of Portugal, making four reliquaries, holy-water bucket, censer, and incense boat which

Set of knife, fork and spoon by Antonio Gentili da Faenza, late 16th century. Metropolitan Museum of Art

were sent to Lisbon. The reliquaries have vanished, but the other objects survive.

Gentili, Antonio (1519–1609). Born in Faenza and went to Rome in about 1550. In 1582 he made for Cardinal Alessandro Farnese a silver-gilt crucifix and a pair of candlesticks now in the Treasury of St Peter's, Rome.

Ghini, Simone (1410–*c.* 1475). Born in Florence, in about 1435 he went to Rome, where he was employed in making ceremonial swords and also papal roses, one of which survives in the Palazzo Communale, Siena.

Giardini, Giovanni (1646–1721). Born at Forlì, he was in Rome by 1665, and ten years later obtained permission to open a workshop. Together with his younger brother Alessandro (1655–1718), he made the bronze relief for the monument of Queen Christina of Sweden in 1700. His mark (a basket of flowers) is to be found on a reliquary at Gubbio and several vessels in the treasury of St Peter's. In 1714 he published a book of somewhat fantastic designs for silver.

Giardoni, Francesco (1692–1757). A Roman who obtained his patent in 1729. His mark (a bee) appears on a statue of San Felice in the cathedral at Foligno. He also made two statuettes of silver on models by Bernardino Ludovisi. His brother Carlo (1693–1764) appears to have specialized in making silver statues, but none is known to have survived.

Grazioli, Giuseppe (1717–92). Born at Fermo, obtained his patent at Rome in 1749. His mark (initials) has been found on a reliquary in the cathedral at Piperno and on domestic plate.

Guizzardi, Martino (1561–*c.* 1652). A Roman, who obtained his patent in 1583. In 1614 he made the silver case for the body of St Agnes in the church of S. Agnese, Rome.

Jacomini, Samuele (1625–1707). Born at Manzan in Lorraine, he was working in Rome in 1653 and obtained his patent there in 1661. A jeweller rather than a silversmith, he specialized in the production of rings, jewelled crosses, and reliquaries. A richly worked baroque chalice by him, dated 1690, is in the Cathedral at Gnesen.

Ladatte, Francesco (1706–87). Born in Turin and trained in Paris and Rome. Most of his life was passed in his native city, where he worked much for the House of Savoy as sculptor and *ciseleur.* He is also known to have produced works in silver, notably a monstrance for the basilica at Superga, but none of these survives.

Landi, Marc' Antonio (1688–1732). A Roman who obtained his patent in 1716. His marks (a heart and later a bunch of grapes) have been recognized on several pieces of ecclesiastical plate.

Lorenzini, Nicola (1710–67). A Roman who obtained his patent in 1756. In 1759 he made a magnificent silver lamp for the church of the Consolazione at Todi, now in the Museo Civico, Todi.

Lotti, Santi (1599–1659). Born at Viterbo, he was in Rome by 1621 and obtained his patent in 1629. He made chalices for the *Magistrato* of Rome to give to

Pair of sauce boats, Venice, second half of 17th century. Victoria & Albert Museum

churches in the city. In the cathedral of S. Severino (Macerata) there is a large silver statue of St Severino made by Lotti in 1659.

Mariani, Domenico Gabriele (1697–1756). Born at Ronciglione and worked in the shop of Giuseppe Nipote at Rome from 1725 until 1753 when he obtained his own patent. His mark (three stars) has been found on some fine domestic plate.

Mascelli, Luigi (*c.* 1770–1825). A Roman who obtained his patent in 1804. He seems to have specialized in the production of small gold boxes which are marked with his initials.

Menniti, Giacomo (1643–1714). A Roman who obtained his patent in 1668. His mark (the shield of the city of Rome) is found on ecclesiastical and domestic plate, notably a fine simple ewer in the collection of S. E. Silvio Innocenti.

Merlini, Lorenzo (1666–*c.* 1745). Born in Florence, he went to Rome in 1694, returned to his native city in 1702, and went back to Rome in 1715. A sculptor and architect, he occasionally worked in silver and obtained his patent as a silversmith in Rome in 1719.

Miglié, Natale (1649–1720). Born at Dôle in Burgundy, he was in Rome by 1665 and obtained his patent in 1673. A holy-water bucket dated 1710 in the church of S. Maria Assunta, Rome, bears his mark (an anchor). His son, Simon (1679–1752), who used the same mark, made three lamps for the church of São Roque, Lisbon, between 1745 and 1749.

Mola, Gaspare (1567–1640). Born at Coldré (Como), he went to Rome and was working for the mint there by 1625. His masterpiece is a large, elaborately worked plate of silver, partly gilt, made for the Boncompagni family to record the reform of the calendar and now in a private collection in Venice.

Monti, Francesco (1662–1708). A Roman who obtained his patent in 1696. His mark (a rampant unicorn) has been found on six reliquaries in the church of S. Giovanni dei Portoghesi, Rome, and several other pieces of ecclesiastical silver.

Moretti de Amicis, Antonio (1611–87). A Venetian, was in Rome by 1640 and obtained his patent in 1652. He worked much for the Chigi family, and many pieces of the silver for their chapel in the cathedral at Siena bear his mark (the heads of two Moors facing each other).

Ossani, Francesco (*fl.* 1800–29). Obtained his patent in Rome in 1801. His mark (initials) appears on several pieces of domestic plate of great elegance and simplicity.

Petroncelli, Lorenzo (1724–1801). A Roman who obtained his patent in 1758. His mark (a bee) has been found on several very fine pieces of domestic plate.

Pieri, Pietro Paolo (1658–1718). Born in Villach, Germany, and went to Rome before 1671, obtaining his patent there in 1685. His mark (a dove) is found on silver in the cathedral of Sutri and Pergola.

Reali, Raimondo (*c.* 1714–78). A Roman who obtained his patent in 1742. His mark (initials) is found on a reliquary in the cathedral at Pisoniano and the bust of a Saint at Capranica Prenestina.

Sangeni, Carlo (*c.* 1770–1836). A Roman who obtained his patent in 1815. He worked much for the Vatican and made an elaborately engraved walking stick for Pius VI. This is now in the Vatican Museum.

Sanini, Giovanni Felice (1727–87). Born at Lucca and went to work in Rome in 1741, obtaining his patent in 1747. He provided silver for the King of Portugal, and several of his works are now in the Museum of Religious Art, Lisbon, notably a crucifix on which the figure of Christ was made by G. B. Maini.

Scarabello, Angelo (1711–95). Born at Este. His most famous work is the gilt-bronze doorway to the chapel of the relics in the Santo at Padua.

Spagna, Paolo (1736–88). A Roman who obtained his patent in 1772. His mark (a pair of dividers with an S between them) appears on much domestic and ecclesiastical plate, including the silver bust of St Rufino in the cathedral at Assisi.

Spezzani, Giuseppe (1627–1710). A Florentine who went to Rome in 1640 and obtained his patent there in 1654. Two of his sons, Cosimo (1663–1717) and Giovanni Girolamo (1665–1748), became goldsmiths using similar marks (a centaur). Cosimo made four reliquaries now in the Cathedral at Sezze.

Spinazzi, Angelo (*fl.* 1720–85). Born at Piacenza, obtained his patent at Rome in 1721. He made two

Below Bowl and cover on three scroll feet, 18th century. Victoria & Albert Museum

Below right Pair of silver candlesticks, mark TB monogram with fleur-de-lis, and PM, *c.* 1720. Victoria & Albert Museum

large candelabra for the King of Portugal (Museum of Religious Art, Lisbon), worked much for the Vatican and made the large silver altar frontal now in the Cathedral at Siracusa.

Taglietti, Fantino (1574–*c.* 1650). A Roman. Between 1627 and 1647 he was employed in making chalices to be given by the *Magistrato* to the churches of Rome. His masterpiece is the silver statue of St Ambrose on horseback, of 1641, in the Cathedral at Ferentino, which bears his mark (a rose).

Valadier, Andrea (1695–1759). Founder of a very important family of Roman silversmiths, was born at Aramont in the south of France and began to work in Rome in 1720, obtaining his patent in 1725. Two sons, Giovanni (1732–1805) and Luigi (1726–85), both became silversmiths. Giovanni's mark (initials beneath a fleur-de-lis) is found on much fine silver of the Pius VI period. Luigi (his mark was either initials between three fleur-de-lis, or his full name) made numerous domestic and ecclesiastical vessels, also the model of Trajan's Column (together with B. Hecher) now in the Residenz at Munich. Both his marks were used after his death by his son, Giuseppe (1762–1839), who was also an architect. Both father and son produced silver in the neoclassical style. Many of Giuseppe Valadier's designs are in the Cooper Union Museum at New York.

Vendetti, Antonio (1699–1796). Born at Cotanello in Sabina and obtained his patent in Rome in 1737. He is represented in the Museum of Religious Art, Lisbon, by three *cartagloria* frames made for the church of São Roque between 1744 and 1749. They bear his mark (a spread eagle).

Venturesi, Mattia (*c.* 1719–76). Born at Forlì, was in Rome by 1738 and obtained his patent there in 1762. His mark (a lion's paw with a star below) has been found on a great many pieces of domestic and ecclesiastical plate.

Vincente, Giovanni Antonio (1636–95). Born at Perugia, was in Rome from 1655 to 1659 and returned in 1672, when he obtained his patent. His mark (a unicorn) has been noticed on several pieces of ecclesiastical plate, including the reliquary of the Holy Shroud in the Cathedral at Amelia.

Two coffee pots by Daniel Schebs, Brevik, *c.* 1760. Kunstindustrimuseet, Oslo

Norwegian

A limited amount of Norwegian silver from the Middle Ages – spoons, jewelry, church plate, and drinking vessels – still exists. But as most of it is now kept in churches and museums in Norway, it is of little interest to the collector. Post-Reformation silver made in Norway is, on the other hand, eminently collectable. There is a lot of it about, and important pieces frequently come on the market in Norway and Denmark and in Britain.

The fact that so much old Norwegian silver can be found in Britain can to some extent be explained from the very close contacts which have always existed between the two countries, especially in the fields of commerce and shipping. Most pieces of Norwegian silver in Britain seem, however, to have found their way there during the nineteenth century as tourist souvenirs for British visitors to Norway. Especially important are the activities of English-born Thomas Bennett (b. 1814), who settled in Oslo in 1848 and founded Norway's first travel agency. Bennett transformed travelling in Norway from being a dangerous job for intrepid and hardy explorers to a comfortable pastime for people of leisure. Early in his career the sale of Norwegian antiques (some genuine, others copies) to his customers, the vast majority of whom were British, had become an important part of his business. A description of Bennett's premises in Store Strandgade 17, Oslo, in 1873, tells of an extensive stock of Norwegian silver tankards, jugs, belts, woodcarvings, paintings and etchings, maps, books: anything, in fact, that demonstrated Norwegian life in ancient and modern times to the foreign visitor.

The more quaint and picturesquely 'Norwegian' the souvenirs were, the more they were sought after by the Victorian travellers, and it is easily noticeable that most Norwegian antiques found in Britain today are of types with no close English parallels. During the 1920s Norwegian silver began to trickle back to its country of origin, and when finally the Norwegian museums began an organized campaign to bring back the more important pieces from Britain, no less than three of the tall welcome cups (*q.v.*), which are the most picturesque of all silver types made in Norway, were brought to light, apart from any number of peg tankards and spoons of medieval type (though mostly of later make: *see* Spoons). In spite of the many antique dealers and private collectors from Norway who have been looking for Norwegian silver in Britain since, pieces still continue to appear, both in the art auction rooms and in private collections.

GUILDS

The earliest silver made in Post-Reformation Norway was produced during the early and middle part of the sixteenth century by German goldsmiths, working for the Hanseatic merchants in Bergen. Their products were naturally very closely related in style to contemporary north German silver. Not until the late sixteenth century did an indigenous goldsmith's art develop. The goldsmiths in Bergen organized themselves into a guild as early as 1568, and at the beginning of the seventeenth century the activities of goldsmiths working everywhere in the Danish–Norwegian kingdom were regulated through a series of royal decrees. The craft was to be

Jewel box by Jens Kahrs, Bergen, 1753. Kunstindustrimuseet, Oslo

carried on in the towns only, and the goldsmiths in all the major cities were organized in guilds. The system of masters, journeymen, and apprentices was properly regulated and the standard of the metal fixed. Hallmarking was made compulsory (*see* Marks). Powerful guilds now developed both in Christiania (as Oslo was then called) and Trondheim. By far the strongest guild, with the greatest number of members, was that in Bergen. Until about 1840 Bergen was the biggest city in the country, and old Bergen silver is preserved in greater quantities and in more varied styles than that from any other town. During the eighteenth century loosely organized guilds appeared in some of the medium-sized towns like Stavanger and Bragernes (Drammen today), and even in some of the smaller townships on both sides of the Oslo fjord. These smaller guilds seem to have worked under the supervision of the guild in the nearest big city.

The guilds in Bergen, Trondheim, and Christiania seem to have worked in comparative isolation from each other, and the silver from each of the three towns has its own stylistic peculiarities and its own chronological development. During the Renaissance, and for a time between 1740 and 1790, Bergen silver was of quite exceptional quality, while the guild in Trondhjem seems to have had a particularly fine period during the latter part of the seventeenth century. The finest Christiania silver was made during the early part of the eighteenth century and during the decades preceding 1800.

All the goldsmiths' guilds in Norway worked in close connection with the large and powerful organizations on the Continent. The guilds in Norway, Denmark, and Germany worked according to similar rules and had the same ceremonial at their meetings. German was the common language spoken by all members, and journeymen from all three countries travelled over the whole area. That there should be important stylistic similarities in the products of German, Danish, and Norwegian goldsmiths is only natural. The guild system was abolished in Norway in 1839.

SOCIAL BACKGROUNDS

Norwegian silver from the sixteenth to the nineteenth centuries has essentially a bourgeois character. During the 400 years of political union with Denmark (1397–1814) the monarch of the 'Twin Kingdoms' resided in Copenhagen, and the spectacular orders for silver from the King and his Court were given to the goldsmiths of the capital. The most important patrons of the Norwegian goldsmiths were officers, clergy, civil servants, and the merchants in the coastal towns. Some of the latter had great wealth. They lived elegantly in their spacious town houses and comfortable country homes, and their collaboration with the goldsmiths was sometimes unusually inspiring. Some encouraging orders were also occasionally given for church plate.

Dish by Jens Christensen Seested, Trondheim, *c.* 1690. Kunstindustrimuseum, Trondheim

Christiania mark, c. 1630–c. 1820: a crowned C, sometimes with the last two figures of the year fitted into the bend of the letter

Beaker with lid by Albert Groth, Christiania, *c.* 1710. Kunstindustrimuseet, Oslo

MARKS

The earliest marked silver made in Norway is that produced by the German goldsmiths for the Hanseatic merchants in Bergen during the early and middle part of the sixteenth century. The chief trading commodity of the Hansa merchants was dried cod from Arctic Norway. Their coat-of-arms was a crowned fish with an eagle, their goldsmiths' mark a crowned fish. Sometimes their works also carried a maker's mark, but none of these can now be identified.

The rules about marking laid down during the seventeenth century do not seem to have been very

From c. 1820: the city arms, i.e. a sitting St Halvard contained in a shield

Trondhjem mark, from c. 1700: a rose or six-pointed star

From the mid-18th century to the beginning of the 19th century: the city gate with seven balls underneath

strictly enforced, but quite a lot of silver from the period is marked with town and maker's mark. During the early and middle part of the eighteenth century wardens were appointed in the various guilds to ensure that the marking was properly carried out. From then on we find occasionally, though not always, complete sets of marks with townmark, maker's mark, warden's mark, and the mark for the year and the month of production. Gold products of the proper metal standard are marked with an impressed *c.*

The chief townmarks are: *Bergen.* From *c.* 1580 until the middle of the eighteenth century: a crowned B. Occasionally the figures of the year are applied to the top or sides of the letter.

From the middle of the eighteenth century to the beginning of the nineteenth: the city gate with seven balls in two rows underneath, four in the top row and three in the bottom. On late eighteenth-century pieces are sometimes found the figures of the year applied to the sides of the gate.

Russian

The knowledge and aesthetic reputation of Russian metalwork have suffered, like those of other Russian arts, from the scanty interest shown by many *Westernized* Russians, over-corrected later by an unnecessary attempt to demonstrate unique gifts of dazzling national originality, peculiar to Russian craftsmen. In fact, the best Russian plate assimilated a bewildering variety of influences, both from East and West, and foreign artists of diverse nationalities appear to have played a prominent part in its creation from earliest times.

Tankard, Moscow mark, 1750. Victoria & Albert Museum

That artificial controversy, involving national vanity, as to whether foreign or native craftsmen, imported fashions or tradition, predominated, is less important than clear visual evidence that many talented foreigners worked in a different manner when they were employed in Russia, that they taught Russian apprentices (who might surpass their masters), and did more to stimulate than impede the growth of some characteristic styles and techniques while on Russian soil. The French architectural historian, Viollet le Duc, likened Russia to a vast laboratory, in which the art of contrasting races mingled in the creation of something intermediate between Asia and the West. Exuberant bejewelled magnificence from India and Sassanian Persia, curly calligraphic motifs from Islam, the naïve wooden crafts of a changeless Slav peasantry, combined with a sternly ascetic Byzantine strain and with many refined secular fashions from Italy, Germany, and France.

Far right Large parcel gilt nielloed beaker and stand, unmarked, *c.* 1680. Christie, Manson & Woods

Three of the most typical and striking genres brought to perfection by silversmiths in Russia were of course practised previously in the Byzantine Empire, namely niello, filigree work, and patterns in coloured enamel, especially *cloisonné.* Niello, in the characteristic manner used in Russia, demanded an expert draughtsman as well as a master engraver; for the design was first drawn upon the silver, then chased, so as to lower the pattern, after which the hollowed sections were filled with a black enamel alloy. The article was then heated in a kiln until the enamel fused with the silver. Finally, it was polished, until the black design or lettering became flush with the surface of the silver.

Filigree, the art of making intricate patterns out of malleable gold or silver wire, was known from ancient times in Russia as *skan.* It was favoured for decorating the covers of sacred books and the surrounds of icons, and the silver wire was usually soldered against a solid silver background. Nineteenth- and twentieth-century excavations from burial mounds and the sites of ruined towns have also revealed many early filigree ornaments dating from the ninth to the thirteenth centuries. The Russian style of filigree developed a strikingly compact geometrical composition of spiral scrolls merging in a rhythmic flow against smooth or embossed surfaces.

Many Greek enamellers worked in Kiev prior to the Mongol invasion, but the Russian iconographic expert, P. Kondokov, maintained that in the eleventh and twelfth centuries Russian enamellers on precious metals under the Kiev Grand Princes did work as fine as that of the best Byzantine Greeks, because of obvious mistakes in rendering classical draperies on the enamelled figures, and because it introduced a turquoise blue unknown in Byzantium.

The destructive lust of Mongol hordes, who overran and occupied the greater part of Russia in the mid-thirteenth century, obliterated much of early Russian art, and most of all gold and silver vessels, which were easily looted, broken, or melted down. In Kiev alone six hundred churches were left as smoking ruins by the Mongols. But after the sack of Kiev, the chief centre of fine silver craftsmanship shifted to Novgorod, which escaped the Mongols, and where many specialized artists continued to work for the monasteries and churches until the end of the fifteenth century, when it was annexed by resurgent Moscow. The silverwork of Novgorod, and that of Kostroma, another local centre, is generally regarded as cruder and more provincial than that of earlier Kiev or later Moscow, but first-class specimens, both of sacred and lay silver, have survived.

Novgorod's close trade relations with the Hanseatic towns attracted North German artists to work in Russia, where scope seems to have been given to their talents. This may be the origin of a crystal barrel in an elaborate silver-gilt setting, presented by the Metropolitan of Novgorod to the Tsar Ivan III when he annexed that city in 1478. This exuberantly pagan work illustrates the extent and power of Renaissance influence in northern Europe during the fifteenth century. The sides of the mount are chased with bacchanalian scenes, and a nude young Bacchus sits on the lid, pouring wine into a beaker.

Moral servitude to copying Byzantine models and paralysing fear of cunning Tartar conquerors were overcome in integrated Moscow, though it had taken two centuries to shake off the Tartar yoke. The healthier, more self-confident Russian state of mind was reflected in a vigorous upsurge of decorative art in the sixteenth century. Foreign envoys who visited Russia at this time bore witness to the dazzling splendour and abundance of gold and silver vessels, encrusted with precious stones as large as nuts, used at royal receptions and feasts in the Moscow palaces. The Church was equally lavish in using the precious metals to make its ceremonies more majestic and impressive. Unfortunately much of this gorgeous work was in its turn destroyed during the anarchic *Time of Troubles* in the early seventeenth century.

After the Poles had been driven out, the more stable Moscow period of the early Romanov Tsars enabled Russian work in precious metals to reach a high peak of artistic style and a distinct kind of international originality. Within the recently consolidated Empire, artists of all races and skilled in all techniques, flocked to the new capital. But the Moscow Tsars (long before Peter the Great) also invited silversmiths from Holland, and Persia.

One striking feature of early seventeenth-century Russian silver is the chasing of finely stylized foliage and flowers in all-over patterns, which became thicker and more complicated as the century proceeded. Filigree was now rarely plainly soldered on sheets of metal, but was filled with polychrome enamels, in which white, blue, and yellow tones predominated. Towards the end of the century geometrical *cloisonné* began to give place to miniature portrait paintings in enamel colours, a genre which became wide spread in the eighteenth century.

Tankard, silver-gilt on niello ground ornamented with flowers and foliage enclosing medallions of Samson and Delilah, The Temptation of Joseph, Judith and Holofernes, and on the lid The Judgement of Solomon. Late 17th century. Victoria & Albert Museum

Some provincial towns also began to flourish artistically at this time. Solvychegodsk, largely belonging to the great merchant family, the Stroganovs, who opened up trade in Siberia, produced superb examples of free painting with enamel colours direct on silver surfaces. The Stroganovs educated their town by bringing to it exemplary specimens of silver from abroad, and they appear to have encouraged Ukrainian artists, who painted silver bowls and boxes with the most luscious foliage, huge tulips, garlands of daisies and sunflowers, and also with designs of swans, turkeys, lions, and stags.

Ceremonial dishes played an important part in the marriage ceremonies of old Russia. A grandiose specimen dating from 1561, has survived in the Orujeinaya Palata of the Moscow Kremlin. Its interior is chased with a simple but dynamic design of curved concave spirals, radiating from a central double-headed eagle, engraved in niello. The flat rim is adorned with a fine network of stylized foliage, varied by an old Slavonic inscription. Just as in ancient China certain forms in jade or porcelain became revered as classical standards of perfection, repeated with slight variations from one century to another, so did silversmiths in Russia repeat the refined simplicity of this circular dish, its interior curves and flat nielloed rim, right up to the early eighteenth century, when more sophisticated Western fashions prevailed.

Such unique gold and silver vessels were highly cherished by their owners, and hardly ever sold. They changed ownership chiefly by inheritance, or by passing as gifts from Tsar to Patriarch, or to deserving Boyars and other citizens. Sometimes from a disgraced Boyar they would find their way back into the Imperial Treasury. Or, after the death of a conscience-stricken owner, they would be bequeathed to some monastery to promote the repose of his soul.

Two traditional vessels, the *kovsch* and the *bratina*, derived from earlier models made in wood by Slav peasants, had characteristic shapes. These were different to any metalwork made outside Russia. The *kovsch* was a low almost boat-shaped drinking vessel, with a raised handle, like a ladle, principally used at feasts for drinking mead, *kvass*, or beer. Gradually it

Above Silver-gilt and enamel *kovsch* with inscription dated 26 September 1914, by Carl Fabergé, Moscow. Christie, Manson & Woods

lost its practical importance, and became a decorative symbol of honour awarded for some outstanding service to the State. It could also be a reward for some military feat, or for a successful diplomatic or commercial mission. For a long time its shape maintained the same severe simplicity, but during the eighteenth century Western fashions made it more ornate and complicated. Later, in the nineteenth century, came another reaction in taste, which led Fabergé and other eminent silversmiths to produce numerous ceremonial *kovschy*, evidently inspired by older seventeenth-century styles.

The *bratina*, a loving cup without handles, was always globular in shape, with a flat band-like lip, usually inscribed with stylized old Slavonic lettering. On the death of a royal prince, a favourite *bratina* of his was often placed on his tomb in a church, and could afterwards be consecrated for use there as an incense burner. A *bratina* which originally belonged to Tsar Michael, the first Romanov, bears an inscription that it was placed on the coffin of the Tsarevich Ivan Ivanovich to commemorate the murder of that prince by his father (Ivan the Terrible). Though the inscription around the rim sometimes records the name of the owner, or the purpose for which it is dedicated, more often it is a simple toast, or poetic axiom, such as: 'True love is a golden cup, which can never be broken; the soul alone can change it.'

Many persons of high rank had their own *bratina* made for them, and a few notable early specimens have survived. An exceptionally elaborate one, made for Peter Tretyakov, a state official in the first quarter of the seventeenth century, is illustrated in *Antiquities of the Russian Empire* (1852). Its foot is supported by miniature human caryatids, who appear to uphold the bowl on their heads and outstretched hands. The surface of the bowl is richly embossed with an arabesque of flowers and foliage and four heraldic plaques. It is also remarkable in having a coved cover finishing in a long-stemmed silver flower, identical to the one used on Persian and Chinese perfume sprinklers of the same period. The edifying inscription around the rim reads: 'As arms are needed by the warrior in battle, as rain in time of drought, as drink to the thirsty, and as a sincere friend to console in time of misfortune and sorrow, so concord and friendship are demanded from all those who would drink from this cup.' It should be remembered that old Russian drinking customs were embellished by a lot of ritual. The man who proposed a toast had to stand with his head uncovered, empty the cup to the dregs, then turn it upside down over his head, so that all could see that he had emptied it and thereby sincerely wished the health of the person he had toasted.

Though the Orthodox Church resembled Islam in frowning on sculpture of the human figure in the round, as an instrument of idol worship, it permitted carving and chasing in high relief. In this way silver ornament of many kinds, especially the surrounds of icons, allowed remarkable sculptural gifts to be expressed, so long as they were consecrated by a genuine religious purpose. One of the finest surviving early specimens of this kind is the lid from the silver sarcophagus of the Tsarevich Dmitri, made in 1630 by the chief Kremlin silversmith to be placed in the Archangel Cathedral in Moscow. In 1812, when Napoleon occupied Moscow, the body of the sarcophagus disappeared, but the superb gilded lid with its lifesize figure of the young prince, embossed in high relief, is now in the Orujeinaya Palata. The head is worked out with a severe but sensitive fullness, and the whole silver background, partly granulated and partly smooth, is filled in with rich patterns of interlacing foliage.

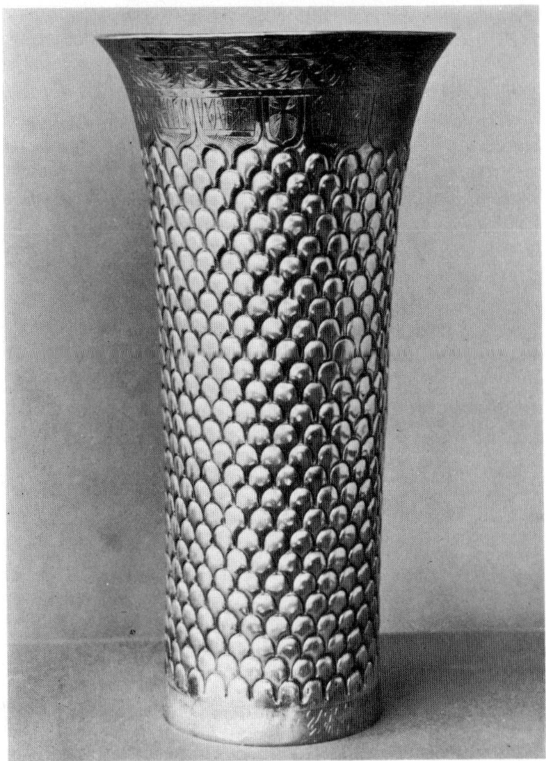

Silver-gilt beaker, 17th century. Victoria & Albert Museum

Until the middle of the seventeenth century the masters of the Kremlin Gold and Silver Chambers served not only the Imperial Court but also the wealthy Patriarchate, which kept a huge staff of artists, craftsmen, and jewellers employed in making church adornments, mitres, crucifixes, censers, and covers

Wine bowl, silver parcel-gilt, chased and embossed, dated 1751. Victoria & Albert Museum

for church books. But in the 1650s the Patriarch Nikon organized his own workshop for this purpose near the Patriarchal palace. About the same time, an exceptionally able and cultured nobleman, the Boyar Khitrovo, was appointed by the Tsar Alexei Mikhailovich to take charge of the Kremlin gold and silver work, a post which he retained for over twenty years. Talent and creative enterprise meant far more to him than national origin. Records show that he employed Poles, Germans, Tartars, Greeks, and Swedes. This happy combination of factors helps to account for the high quality of Russian silverwork during that period. Much of its ornament was derived from Italian Renaissance motifs, especially in its treatment of foliage, figuring graceful main stems, from which sprang numerous symmetrical sideshoots. But the increasing representation of animals and birds more probably derived from Persia, and the love of niello from Greek artists on Mount Athos.

At the turn of the seventeenth century drinking cups of Western European design and huge covered tankards, like those from Augsburg, appeared more frequently in Russia. The early eighteenth century saw the start of St Petersburg silver, which flourished in the hands of many foreign craftsmen brought by Peter the Great to work in his new capital. But one must remember, as had happened often before, that artists from abroad worked differently in their new environment. The Russian Government was strict about maintaining the purity of precious metals, as they were about measures to safeguard against debasement of the currency. Though marking of silver vessels started in the seventeenth century, Peter first made it systematic and universal by a decree in 1700. In 1714 he also allowed foreign craftsmen in precious metals to form their own separate guild. The majority were then from Germany, and their records were kept in German. Swedes took second place, and a number came from Finland.

Catherine II gave the same guilds more definite rules in a decree issued in 1785. The guild consisted of masters, journeymen, and apprentices, as in the West; a 'master' had to have a 'masterpiece' of his work approved, after serving not less than three years as a journeyman. In 1793 the guild of Russian craftsmen in St Petersburg had forty-four masters, and that of foreign craftsmen fifty-nine. The number of masters rose to about 150 at the beginning of the nineteenth century. They often had foreign pupils, but also many Russian ones. The native Russian craftsmen had for long tended to specialize in work for churches, crosses, lamps, and surrounds for icons. A few outstanding artists, like the Frenchman, Ador, who made exquisite jewelled boxes for Catherine II, did not belong to any guild. The Swiss, J. Pauzié, who worked for Peter's daughter, the Empress Elizabeth, completely remodelled the Imperial crown, to 'modernize' it for Catherine's coronation. But, tired of being exploited, as he said, by many of his Russian patrons, he left in 1764, and spent the remainder of his life in his calmer native land. A number of beautifully embossed tall cups and covers in silver gilt were made for the Court during this period.

Towards the end of the eighteenth century, and

Left Moscow tankard, first half of 18th century. Victoria & Albert Museum

Right Cup for brandy, decorated with gadrooning, with an octagonal lip decorated with scroll work on a matted ground, Moscow mark, mid-18th century. Victoria & Albert Museum

Far right Silver and silver-gilt snuff box by Ivan Kaltikov, made in the form of a pack of cards, Moscow, 1825

more markedly in the early nineteenth century, there started a reaction against conventionally classical and stereotyped Western styles, and a reversion of taste to earlier models, to the use of filigree, niello, and coloured enamel, sometimes combined with traditional shapes, and painted directly on medallions. It was by order of the Emperor Nicholas I that the Imperial Academy of Sciences undertook the first large-scale attempt to catalogue and illustrate widely scattered and hitherto little known masterpieces of ancient decorative art and icons preserved in the Russian Empire. The result emerged in the massive illustrated volumes *Antiquities of the Russian Empire* already referred to. These are still the best records available. It is also to the credit of Nicholas I that he had the building of the Orujeinaya Palata in the Kremlin completely renovated and enlarged so that the whole Imperial collection of Moscow gold and silver vessels should be transferred and properly displayed there.

While the range of articles which they made was widening, the best Russian silversmiths in the second half of the nineteenth century returned increasingly for inspiration to Byzantine Muscovite motifs, in particular to more grandiose and massive shapes and to a revival of the old techniques of filigree, niello, and coloured enamel. The latter became a speciality of the Moscow jewellers and silversmiths, Ovchinikov, Klebhikov, and Sazykov, but it was also pursued by Morozov and Fabergé in St Petersburg. Silver-gilt coffee pots and jugs by Sazykov made between 1856 and 1864 illustrate the revival of the older Oriental strain in decorative silver. The massive coffee pots and wine jugs made in the same period show how the old Slavonic type of ornament could be skilfully adapted to contemporary civilized objects of utility. Brilliantly enamelled but dignified tea pots and wine goblets are fine examples of slightly later work from Moscow silversmiths, and a cigarette-case of the period reveals the exquisite painting of miniature peasant scenes on silver. This work reached a high level during this period.

Chocolate pot, Leningrad, 1804. Victoria & Albert Museum

Delicately incised or nielloed architectural scenes, landscapes with figures, on cigarette cases and snuffboxes, were also produced by many good silversmiths at this time. With individual variations, they continued a tradition established in the late eighteenth and early nineteenth centuries. Certain domestic utensils, like tea pots and trays, achieved a harmonious fusion of contemporary European and Russian styles, whereas objects like silver or silver-enamelled glass holders for tea, primarily used in Russia, retained a distinctive Russian character right up to the early twentieth century. The old *bratina* shape was still produced, with certain changes, as can be seen from a nielloed specimen decorated with peasant scenes. The same plate shows a typically European tall cup and cover decorated with a characteristic Russian prancing *troika.*

There is no space to do justice in this context to the master silversmith and jeweller, Carl Fabergé, whose superb work, while justly famous, has rather overshadowed that of other fine Russian silversmiths. His fantastic Imperial Easter eggs, his elaboration in *bijouterie* of classical French styles, have already been well described and documented. But it is sometimes forgotten that he also instilled into old Muscovite Byzantine traditions that fresh touch of Russian idiom, that stimulating *genius loci*, which exercised such a powerful spell over the best foreign artists who worked in Russia. And the 'neo-Russian' products of Fabergé show a classical restraint which is absent from the flamboyant extravagances of some Russian seventeenth-century silver. He skilfully adapted old Russian motifs on various *kovsch* and tea caddies using old Slav folk-lore motifs, filigree spirals, and massive bosses.

This internal renaissance of decorative art in nineteenth-century Russia becomes more understandable when one bears in mind that West European taste, from which Russia had drawn so much, was at the same time going through a series of eclectic revivals. By contrast the best nineteenth-century Russian silverwork preserved an integrity of style, grandeur of design, and finesse of craftsmanship which approximated to eighteenth-century European standards, more rapidly disappearing in the fluid industrial society of the modern West. Of course there is a striking unevenness about the quality of 'neo-Russian' work produced at this time, whether by Moscow or Petersburg silversmiths. While at its best, it is bold, brilliant, and refined, at its worst it can be course, gaudy, heavy, and monotonous. But its best is far better than has yet been widely recognized.

Systematic marking and control of objects made in precious metals came into force in 1700 under Peter the Great. The silver standard is represented by the numerals 84, 88, or 91, which means the number of *zolotniks* of pure silver in ninety-six parts (equivalent in weight one continental pound). The standards for gold are represented by the numerals 56, 72, and 92, indicating the proportions of pure gold in ninety-six *zolotniks.* The four regulation marks were: the maker's initials (sometimes his full name), second, the crest of the city where the silver was tested, third the initials of the assayer (the latter was often followed by the date), fourth, the figures showing the proportion of pure silver. The St Petersburg town mark shows two crossed anchors with a sceptre in the centre, and the Moscow mark a St George and Dragon. After 1896 the townmarks were dropped, and a woman's head with a headdress was adopted as a general hallmark both for gold and silver objects.

Miniature Silver

Miniature silver toys, replicas of furniture, table accessories, and other household equipment, have delighted the children of noble families for at least 500 years. The daughter of Henry II in 1576 commissioned a set of silver toys including 'buffet pots, bowls, plates and other articles such as they make in Paris', to be sent to the children of the Duchess of Bavaria. In the wealthy homes of Holland and Germany miniature silver toys were already commonplace. The plate inventory of the mother of Henry IV of France (1553–1610) records 'a doll's set of silver plenishments set with diamonds'.

In England miniature toys of gold and silver delighted rich Stuart and early Georgian sophisticates, but such trinkets were for adult enjoyment, with an adult subtlety about their very childishness. Today they are particularly fascinating as meticulous records of passing vogues in innumerable household details from rockinghorse to footwarmer. Few early Stuart examples remain, but Christie's on 7 May 1952, sold a miniature goblet, its bowl formed from a nut held in scalloped straps engraved with foliage, supported on a wire scroll tripod stem and a circular pierced foot. This was attributed to about 1630.

Miniature silver in the late seventeenth century closely followed the Court fashions for silver furniture and magnificent toilet sets. Many of these were imported from Holland, but hallmarks prove their manufacture in London for at least a century from 1665, and again in the nineteenth century. Few examples have been noted struck with provincial hallmarks.

Towards the end of the seventeenth century there began a half-century vogue for superb dolls' houses, then known as 'baby houses'. These were individually designed for the rich by architects who might also supervise their construction by cabinet makers. But in those days, when a homely occupation was essential to fill the long hours of the evening, it was not uncommon for them to be made at home. In 1750 the Prince of Wales was 'building baby houses at Kew'.

Group of miniature silver including a settee, Dutch, with English import mark for 1903, table, 1902, and a replica of the coronation chair, 1901. Claire, Barrett Street Antique Market

Miniature furniture and all the accessories found in contemporaneous homes of the rich were bought from specialists in this work, in wood, silver, and other metals. An extensive range might be accumulated over the years, and those in precious metal were treasured and handed down from one generation to another. Modern children would find little to admire in a pair of snuffers and a tray, just large enough to snuff the tiny candles in their miniature candlesticks; but in those days such toys were highly appreciated.

An essential part of the charm of silver toys is their close adherence to the fashions and customs of the time when they were made. The range of objects includes furniture, everything for the tea equipage, tankards and mugs, monteiths and punch bowls, cruet stands, table baskets, salvers, candlesticks, warming pans, and a numerous array of other perfectly constructed miniatures reflecting the tastes of wealthy silver-flaunting families. Toilet sets are superb treasures complete with silver-framed mirror and receptacles for trinkets, soap, unguents, and the rest. Even the men and women, their horses and carriages, soldiers, beggars, parrots, and dogs were fashioned as silver toys. But scarcely less beguiling is, say, a frying pan complete with fish.

George Middleton, a descendant of Sir Hugh Middleton, the celebrated goldsmith and jeweller to James I and Charles I, appears to have been the first London silversmith to become a specialist in the manufacture of miniature silver. He was followed by innumerable other specialists, but few achieved comparable quality.

Miniature silver was sold at the spas, but this was probably the work of London silversmiths. Lady Mary Wortley Montagu wrote in her *Farewell to Bath*, 1736:

> *'Farewell to Deards' and*
> *all her toys which*
> *glitter in her shop.*
> *Deluding traps to girls and boys. . . .'*

The Deards' trade card published by their shop in St James's, London, during the mid-1760s, refers to a 'Variety of Fine Toys', showing that fashionable demand continued.

Much of the existing early miniature silver was made as carefully as jewelry, every piece worked by hand. These silversmiths were notably accurate in copying detail and proportions, and the consistent careful construction and meticulous finish, including engraved ornament and dainty *repoussé* work, suggests the nimble fingers of women assistants. The majority was shaped and wrought from flat plate with the addition of small castings. Wall sconces, for instance, were perfect replicas, the smooth reflecting surface being surrounded by intricate embossed work: a tankard would be rolled from flat plate, seamed vertically and a base inserted. Some of the most attractive hollow ware was hand-raised from the plate: later in the eighteenth century hollow ware was shaped by spinning in a lathe in the style current with factory-made silver. Candlestick stems might be turned from slender cast rods, and applied details, such as handles, feet, and so on, might be midget castings.

Early in the nineteenth century miniature silver consisted of castings, and gilding was frequent. The early Victorians reverted to fine toys, however, entirely handmade. So far as tableware was

A group of miniature silver including a pair of candlesticks, English, 1892, Dutch tankard, *c.* 1890, bird pin-cushion and mirror, English. Claire, Barrett Street Antique Market

concerned these copied the so-called Queen Anne styles.

Some important makers of miniature silver were John Clifton, Augustine Courtauld, Edward Dobson, Anthony Ellines, Joseph Lowe, Isaac Malyn, George Middleton, John Sotro, Viet and Mitchell, and Wetherell and Janaway.

Filigree

In the ancient world it must be supposed that the art of working filigree was mastered at an early stage, at least where the technique or working in silver and gold had attained a reasonably high level. We know that excellent filigree jewelry was produced by the Egyptians, and even in the Far East a very early mastery of the craft must be taken for granted. To Mexico and South America, however, a knowledge of it was first implanted by Spanish and Portuguese craftsmen. There have, moreover, been times when filigree was highly prized. Today, little is seen of it other than as souvenir pieces or products of peasant art.

Filigree is a Latin word, a combination of *filum* (wire) and *granum* (grain). It seems difficult, however, to arrive at a general agreement to the exact etymological implications of the term. In the modern usage followed in this chapter it should be understood to comprise all works in silver or gold (or, rarely, even other metals), in which either the form or merely the ornamentation has been effected by means of thin wire, frequently with the addition of minute grains or balls. Granulation or granulated work remain the correct terms where these grains or balls are used alone, either placed in rows or grouped together, on a solid surface, for decorative purposes.

TECHNIQUE[1]

It is known with certainty that at any rate for the last thousand years filigree wire has been produced by means of the drawplate, a method which was described for the first time by the versatile monk and craftsman Theophilus Presbyter in his *Schedula diversarum Artium*, written probably about 1100.[2] According to him, a thin bar of silver or gold would be drawn by hand with a pair of strong pliers through successively smaller holes in a solid piece of flat iron, the drawplate. This resulted in a thin wire several yards long. During the fifteenth century the process was made less complicated by the introduction of the drawbench, where a small pulley was used.[3] In both cases the process calls for repeated annealing of the wire.

It is calculated that the process of drawing wire was known much earlier than the ninth or tenth centuries, when, according to my knowledge, the earliest existing drawplate was made.[4] It was found in a Norwegian grave, and indicates an earlier mastery of drawplate technique in the more advanced countries of classical antiquity either around the Mediterranean or in the Near East. Here the earliest drawplates may even have been made of hard stone.[5]

However this may be, it is also certain that wire was not produced by means of the drawplate alone. On jewelry found in Norwegian graves dating from the late Roman Empire, wire of extreme fineness is found to have been produced from thin, narrow sheets or strips of silver or gold. These strips have been coiled spiral-wise into long tubes, similar to the insulating sheath coiled around an electric cable, to form thin pieces of wire on which very fine spiral lines may be observed even without a magnifying glass.[6] A similar kind of wire is found in Etruscan jewelry,[7] and the French *savant* Édouard Salin has observed the same on Merovingian pieces.[8] A close examination of antique jewelry would probably show this to be a method generally adopted, at least for very thin wire, by the earliest filigree workers.[9]

Yet a third form of wire was employed by filigree workers of the Migration period, and of the Carolingian and Romanesque centuries. This is the so-called pearl-string wire. During the long span of time already referred to filigree ornamentation was among the forms of embellishment most commonly used: not only in jewelry, bookbindings, crucifixes, and reliquaries, but, for example, in the making of Emperor Otto's crown in A.D. 962. The above-mentioned Theophilus Presbyter also taught how this pearl-string wire was made:[10] with the aid of small, grooved irons the drawn wire was transversely impressed with grooves, one beside the other, to form a series of balls or pearls. The efficiency of the method has been proved through recent experiments carried out by Mr Oscar Sørensen, head of the goldsmiths' class at the Governmental School of Arts and Crafts in Oslo. His experiments have also shown the frequently discussed equatorial grooves (which may be observed encircling the broadest part of each 'pearl', or thickened ball, on a piece of pearl-string wire) to be a natural outcome of the process itself – not, as has been repeatedly argued, a result of aesthetic consideration, a means to 'catch the light' or in any other way enhance the effect. Numerous pieces of Migration and Viking Age jewelry examined by myself prove this beyond doubt.[11]

The use of pearl-string wire was universal until the end of the Romanesque era, but during the eleventh century we meet the first pieces of jewelry in which a twisted, two-cord round wire takes its place. Interesting examples are illustrated by Dr Joan Evans.[12] Now linear surface ornamentation may also be built up by means of single, smooth wires of a rectangular section, placed on end and soldered to the underlying metal – in the manner of metal ribs of *émail cloisonné* left without their enamel fillings. The last and so far final step in this technical development was taken

Antique Eastern gold filigree bracelet.
S. J. Phillips, London

some time before the sixteenth century. After this date, wire of two different kinds are generally seen combined in the same work: for the main lines of the design, a fairly heavy drawn wire of a square or rectangular section was used. For the more detailed parts, or fillings, two thin, round wires were twisted together, then rolled or possibly hammered flat, thus producing a flat wire with a diagonally serrated edge. A similar effect may be obtained by passing a round wire through a screw die, afterwards rolling it flat. The last method produced a slightly mechanical, dry effect. It has been used sporadically in eighteenth-century pieces. But its employment became general, at least in Scandinavia, only after 1800. Several other forms of twisted or plaited wire are also used, mostly for decorative rims and borders.

The *grani* or grains used in filigree work, or in granulated work, are best produced as described by Benvenuto Cellini.[13] He mixed tiny pieces of silver or gold with charcoal in a crucible, and heated it until the metal melted. At that point each little particle contracted into a ball, the balls being sorted according to size by means of a series of riddles.

The complicated and numerous parts which made up a piece of filigree work were kept together by means of solder. It also seems evident that at least the Etruscans employed a simple technique of welding for the granulated work. As the details are not of great importance for the present understanding of the subject, it is sufficient to refer to more detailed treatises.[14] A further study of the technical niceties of filigree may reap rich rewards. It has been suggested that the various forms of wire are typical each of its separate period. Yet an examination of further material over a wider field may well reveal unknown lines of influence and new important centres of technical as well as aesthetic innovation.

HISTORY

Filigree jewelry of the Ancient World may be studied in several large collections on both sides of the Atlantic. Already in Egyptian pieces the intricacies of granulated work and wire ornamentation have been mastered. Greek, and still more Etruscan work must be placed in a class by itself, because of its singular forms and the unparalleled perfection of its granulation. In this last respect, the quality of pieces like the lion clasp in the Pigorini Museum, Rome, has never been equalled.

During the early centuries of the Middle Ages new forms were fostered by the Germanic tribes of the north and west, and important finds from Gotland indicate that during the Viking age this island may have been an important centre of production.[15] A solid gold tenth-century spur and harness trappings covered with granulated work (from Rød, Østfold, Norway) are exceptional pieces.[16] In the Celtic areas of Britain filigree was known, but apparently more sparingly used. In the Byzantine Empire, on the other hand, classical traditions must have been kept alive for a considerable time.

However, precise knowledge of the development is incomplete, mainly because proper attention has never been given to the subject. It must suffice to demonstrate the preference shown in Migration jewelry for pearl-string wire ornamentation, and to suggest a direct link between this and the best period of pearl-string filigree during the subsequent Carolingian and Romanesque eras. From the ninth century on, filigree achieved a place of eminence even in monumental pieces of goldsmithing. Reliquaries, bookbindings, and regalia have been handed down to us, in which jewel-studded wirework enriched with granulation is the chief feature of ornamental design. Outstanding and unique pieces are the gold Imperial Crown and the Imperial Cross and Orb of the Holy Roman Empire, in the Schatzkammer, Vienna. In construction they span from the middle of the tenth until the twelfth centuries.[17]

It seems that in the northern and western countries of Europe this great period of filigree ended as the Gothic style advanced. Now, finely cast architectural detail and twisted and bent scrollwork in stylized imitation of foliage satisfied the demand for intricate and profuse ornamentation. It would seem a reasonable assumption that the strong position of filigree in popular jewelry all over Europe marks a continuation, on a lower social level, of the great age which had lasted from the early Middle Ages until the advent of the Gothic style.

Only in a few centres did the production of high-class filigree continue to prosper. One of the most prominent among them was Venice. While superb pieces remain to us from the Romanesque period in Italy, and sporadically even from the subsequent centuries of the Middle Ages, the Venetian art of filigree held a prominent position even as late as the sixteenth century, when the goblet with silver wirework on a ground of silver gilt now in the Museo di Palazzo Venezia, Rome, was made. The reliquary of St Louis of Toulouse in the Museo degli Argenti, Florence, also gives a fine example of the combination, according to Filippo Rossi so typical of Venice, of filigree and crystal.[18] Signor Rossi dates this piece to the sixteenth century. It seems as likely that the gold filigree, at least, might be placed around 1600 or a little into the seventeenth century. Possibly, also, the 'chrystalline glasse and cover garnished with wyer work of gold, appraised at £30' in the treasury of Charles I, was closely related.[19] It should now be realized that, in Venetian pieces like the ones just mentioned, a new and important stage of technical development had been reached. Between smooth, rectangular-sectioned wire that marks the main lines of the composition, the intricate lines of the fillings are made up of a doubly twisted wire rolled flat. This development marks a crucial change, and much would be gained if we knew how, when, and where it first took place.

Siebenbürgen was another important centre for the production of filigree throughout the late Middle Ages. Here filigree was still popular among the farming population and the nobility of the surrounding principalities, and granulated wire ornamentation was employed on a distinguished series of altar cups. Their bases, stems, and the lower part of the cup were covered with an ornamental display of filigree. This style continued into the sixteenth century.[20]

Besides filigree from Siebenbürgen and Venice, a group of German tankards should be mentioned among the comparatively rare sixteenth-century examples of the craft. Many of them are of the 'poison tankard' type. That is, they have crystal drums set in silver, covered with a mesh of granulated wirework. If the drink were poisoned, the crystal was supposed to burst. Some of the tankards date from the seventeenth century. The earlier ones, however, prove that the art of working in filigree was far from unknown during the Renaissance, even if, possibly, it was less universally practised. The famous poison tankard owned by Clare College, Cambridge, belongs to this group.[21]

With a few, if any, exceptions it seems that before the seventeenth century filigree was conceived as a decorative adjunct, as something added or applied to objects of art. The poison tankards are excellent examples of this. However, this conception was soon to be changed. When, during the seventeenth century, a positive vogue for filigree became manifest in all European countries this not only marked the revival of a technique which apparently, in most places, had been out of fashion for several hundred years, but it was clear that with the old craft everywhere returning to favour, a completely new and intriguing style was also rapidly taking shape.

It is now that we meet, for the first time in Europe, the delicate open lacework which most of us associate with the word filigree. It is no longer used merely as a means to decorate something else, but assumes the character of a constructive material in its own right. Furthermore, it expresses in a rare manner the stylistic ideals of its time. Few branches of the decorative arts are more baroque in their wealth and complexity than filigree, when its web-like flowers and leaves are moulded into plastic shape, enamelled, and then set with coloured stones.

The new way of exploiting an old craft achieved immediate success. It created a demand, as far as can be judged, in all countries of Europe. So popular did the new fashion become that in some countries a new class of worker in filigree was admitted to the trade guilds. In her book *Hispanic Silverwork*, Ada Marshall Johnson has given some details about the production of filigree in Spain. She explains how, in the archives of Sevilla and Toledo, several goldsmith's names occur followed by the word *Filigranero*. At the same period the guilds instituted special test pieces in the form of earrings and rosaries.[22] Statues of a similar kind were known in Sweden[23] and Norway,[24] and it will probably in due course be found that similar arrangements existed in other countries on the Continent at about the same period.

Equally significant is the fact that the very word filigree was only at that time introduced into the Spanish, French, and English languages. In the two latter the word is first encountered in the 1660s, in Spanish it is known somewhat earlier. Introduced from Italy, it was at first given a varied spelling, as in *filagramme* and *philigrin*. Throughout the latter half of the seventeenth century we meet it in contexts which indicate its growing familiarity. This also proves that objects of filigree were of quite common usage.[25]

Pendant brooch of gold filigree and diamonds set in silver on gold, Breton work, early 18th century. S. J. Phillips, London

A new fashion, a new style, a new name to describe it, special craftsmen to cater for the new whim of a sophisticated public. Why and how did it all arise?

It must be stressed that existing knowledge on this point is very incomplete. It may seem far from unlikely that seventeenth-century filigree was born in Italy. The importance of Venice has already been referred to, and it is well known that, at least during the eighteenth century, Genoa was famous for its products.[26] There is another possible solution, however, which may not even exclude the first. What if the original impulse for the new fashion in filigree came from the Far East?

Very little is so far known about the early filigree

of the Orient. The Chinese Emperor Wan-Li (1573–1619) was buried with his two wives, each skull carrying 'a high curved crown, black with gold filigree set with jewels'.[27] These were not European, and it seems unlikely that they represent an influence from one of the few centres where the art may have been practised at that early date. During the latter half of the seventeenth century the Siamese Ambassador to Louis XIV brought splendid pieces of filigree among his gifts.[28] Also, among seventeenth-century references to filigree is one where Lady Ann, wife of Charles II's Ambassador to Spain, Sir Richard Fanshawe, records that among several gifts of filigree which she and her daughters received from Spanish dignitaries or from English countrymen settled in Spain, was a silver box and a small trunk of *filigrana*, made 'in the Indies'. This was in 1665, when she accompanied her husband to his embassy at the Spanish Court. Objects in silver and gold made 'in the Indies' are mentioned by her on several occasions, along with pieces of furniture, such as 'three pair of Indian cabincts of Japan'.[29]

It has to be admitted that no investigation has as yet been undertaken to confirm the validity of what might be called the Oriental theory. Indeed, since filigree has never been seriously studied, such an investigation would have to start with the most elementary examination of museum pieces, few of which are known to exist except by museum curators. They are very rarely published, probably because marked pieces are scarce, and also because somehow the general lack of knowledge about them seems to prevent their inclusion in books on gold- and silverwork.

It will therefore be understood that further research is needed before the main events in the history of filigree can be established with certainty. Until then, the theory of a strong Oriental impulse at the base of its surprising development in the seventeenth century must stand as a fascinating possibility.

Whatever the original impulse for its expanding popularity, the art of filigree *did* flourish: first and foremost, it seems, in Spain. According to Ada Marshall Johnson, Spanish filigree, especially of the northwest, is well known and is of a very fine quality. Fine pieces are found in several churches, the cathedral treasure of Santiago da Compostela in particular being well supplied. They are caskets, reliquaries, chrismatories, and saints' crowns.

Swedish filigree has lately been treated by Dr Carl Hernmarck,[30] who points to its formal reliance on German prototypes. Many leading masters were, in fact, German immigrants. Swedish filigree is conservative and continues the older tradition of wirework used as a decorative foil on a solid base. Famous masters worked in Stockholm and Gotenburg, and filigree cups and mirrors were presented as royal gifts to Tsar Peter of Russia.[31] The craft lasted until the early part of the eighteenth century.

Filigree has been popular in Germany, where Augsburg seems to have specialized in sets of knives, spoons, and forks with filigree handles. As far as is known, however, no special literature exists on the subject, which doubtless deserves wider treatment. The same is true of other European countries, with the exception of Sweden and Norway.

In Norway, research undertaken in connection with an exhibition of filigree sponsored by the Museums of Applied Art in Bergen and Oslo, brought to light a school of masters who produced excellent pieces, starting during the latter half of the seventeenth century, and carrying on through the next.[32] The most prominent among them worked in Bergen, and their production was quite varied; bookcovers, caskets, or miniature chests for keepsakes or jewelry, and many small boxes, oval, round, rectangular or square. A number of curiosities were also made. These included such things as miniature chests of drawers, small filigree ships, a complete, miniature set of furniture – chairs, stools, gueridons, table, all fully equipped with tea cups, tea pots, sugar basins, trays, and candlesticks. These are stamped pieces, made by Johannes Johannessen Müller of Bergen, working from 1723 to 1739. The *pièce de résistance* of this school, however, is a truly monumental piece of work. It is the great filigree casket, formerly owned by the aristocratic Knagenhielm family and now in the Historic Museum, Bergen University. Measuring 17 inches by 11½ inches (43 by 29.5 cm) and 8 inches (20 cm) high it is, as far as is known, unequalled for size, while the workmanship displayed is of a very high order. It is unmarked, but its Bergen origin can now be considered certain. A similar, if smaller, piece in the David Collection, Copenhagen, confirms the impression that the type was by no means confined to Norway. In short, as more and more objects come to light, many of them sumptuously decorated with floral ornamentation rendered in the subtlest of silver filigree, our conception of silversmithing, especially from the seventeenth and eighteenth centuries, is that much advanced. A factor of equal importance is that a similar and probably even richer variety may be found to have existed in other countries from which Norwegian craftsmen drew their inspiration.

Although in leading countries like Spain the *grand époque* of filigree ended as the eighteenth century progressed, its popularity continued. In 1718 Mme de Montespan was amusing herself by harnessing six white mice to a carosse of *filagramme*,[33] and throughout the century the material continued to be put to a great variety of uses. From the neoclassical period until the end of the Empire, a more particular style *à l'antique* became iniversally favoured for gold jewelry. Light earrings were common, crescent-shaped or constructed like flower baskets or cornucopia, or with side-split filigree drops. Delicate

Silver filigree miniature chest, Portuguese, *c.* 1880. Claire, Barrett Street Antique Market

gold wire frames were designed for the miniature medallions then universally in use, whereas boxes, caskets, and so forth no longer seem to have been equally in favour.

Like the products of other crafts, much nineteenth-century filigree made after 1830 was of a revivalistic kind. In Italy, Castellani recovered the Etruscan method of granulation, and delicate gold bracelets and brooches with filigree ornamentation soldered on in the shape of fine wire or grains became fashionable all over Europe. With an increasing interest in folk lore and prehistoric styles, various other branches were studied and refined, prominent among them the ancient Celtic and Scandinavian styles. Various forms of peasant filigree jewelry were re-introduced, and exploited commercially by various firms. Jacob Citroen of Amsterdam carried on a large production, and from the 1850s Jacob Tostrup of Christiania (now Oslo) produced large quantities of provincially inspired filigree jewelry. He was soon followed by others, whose products soon became well known abroad. At the same time, however, a naturalistic style imitating flowers and vegetable forms was also highly popular. The experiments which from the 1880s were carried out to master the technique of *èmail au jour* were based on a thorough mastery of filigree.

Filigree is being produced in many parts of the world today, but mostly, it seems, along less ambitious lines. Souvenirs from the Far East or from the Mediterranean countries may be of very fine workmanship, but apart from this there is little to qualify them as works of art. Even from a technical point of view, modern pieces rarely equal the delicacy of fine antique work. With the advance of mechanization, it is probable that filigree will never again resume its old position among the crafts.

NOTES

1) For a detailed, illustrated treatise see Riisøen and Böe, *Om Filigran. Teknikk, historikk, filigran i norsk eie* (Filigree, its Technique and History. Filigree in Norwegian Ownership), Oslo, 1959.
2) Vol. I. *Revidirter Text, Übersetzung und Appendix* von Albert Ilg, Vienna, 1874. See pp. 160, 162, 260.
3) Numerous illustrations from Delaunay and others reproduced by Marc Rosenberg, *Geschichte der Goldschmiedekunst auf technischer Grundlage*, Frankfurt a.M. 1907–22, 'Einführung'. The earliest-known reference to a draw bench is stated by him to date from 1498 (pp. 94–6).
4) Found in a Viking Age burial mound at Bö, Löten, Hedmark, in the southeastern part of Norway. Exhibited at the Oslo University Collection of Antiquities, No. U.O. – C.9553.
5) As suggested by H. Wilson, *Silverwork and Jewellery*, 2nd ed. in collaboration with Professor Unno Bisei, London, 1951, p. 390.
6) Oscar Sørensen, 'Gullsmedteknisk vurdering av enkelte funn', *Viking*, XV, Oslo, 1951, pp. 204–9.
7) Øyvind Modahl, 'Hvorledes fikk de det til?', *Gullsmedkunst*, No. 6, Oslo, June, 1956, pp. 73–6.
8) Édouard Salin, *La Civilisation Mérovingienne*, Paris, 1957, IIIe Partie, Les Techniques, pp. 44 ff.
9) A possible connection between this process and the methods used by medieval makers of gold and silver thread for the textile industry might well be sought. See Sofus Larsen, 'Kvindeligt Haandarbejde i Middelalderen med særligt Hensyn til Folkeviserne', *Aarböger for nordisk Oldkyndighed og Historie*, III Række, 5. Bind, Copenhagen, 1915, pp. 56 f. My attention was directed to this reference by Dr Odd Nordland.
10) *Op. cit.*, p. 164.
11) See Thale Riisöen and Alf Böe, *op. cit.*, footnote 23. Oscar Sørensen, *op. cit.*
12) Joan Evans, *A History of Jewellery 1100–1870*, London, 1953, pls 1–3.
13) *Opere di Benvenuto Cellini*, Milano, Dalla Società Tipografica de' Classici Italiani, 1806–11, Vol. III, capitolo iii: 'Dell' arte del lavorare di filo, del modo di fare la granaglia, e del saldare', p. 38. Interesting supplementary explanation of Cellini's text is offered by Marc Rosenberg, *op. cit.*, Abteilung: Granulation, p. 10.
14) The problem has been thoroughly discussed by Marc Rosenberg, *loc. cit.* A modern English patent No. 415181, March 1933, may have a bearing on the problem. Our attention was drawn to this reference by the goldsmith Øyvind Modahl, Oslo.
15) M. Stenberger, *Die Schatzfunde Gotlands der Wikingerzeit*, Lund 1947.
16) Illustrated in *The Connoisseur*, October 1958, Vol. CXLII, No. 572, p. 104. On Scandinavian filigree from Carolingian times until the end of the Middle Ages, see Aron Anderson and Alf Böe's articles under Filigran, in *Nordisk Kulturleksikon.*
17) See Hermann Fillitz, *Die Insignien und Kleinodien des Heiligen Römischen Reiches*, Vienna and Munich, 1954.
18) On the position of Venice, see Filippo Rossi, *Capolavori di Oreficeria Italiana* (Swedish edition, Malmö, 1958).
19) J. Starkie Gardner, *Old Silver-Work chiefly English from the XVth to the XVIIIth Centuries*, London, 1903. p. 18.
20) See Charles Pulsky, Eugène Radisics and Émile Molinier, *Chefs-d'œuvre d'orfèvrerie ayant figuré à l'exposition de Budapest*, Paris, Budapest, London, New York, no date; Julius Bielz, *Die sächsische Goldschmiedekunst Siebenbürgens*, Bukarest, 1957.
21) Marc Rosenberg, 'Studien über Goldschmiedekunst in der Sammlung Figdor, Wien', *Kunst und Kunsthandwerk*, Wien, 1911, pp. 354 ff. The Clare College tankard has been studied and described by J. E. Foster and T. D. Atkinson in *An illustrated Catalogue of the Loan Collection of Plate exhibited in the Fitzwilliam Museum, May 1895*, Cambridge, 1896, Cat. No. 28.
22) Ada Marshall Johnson, *Hispanic Silverwork*, New York, 1944, pp. 110 ff.
23) Carl Hernmarck, 'Trådarbeten', *Svenskt Silversmide*, Vol. I, pp. 232–4, Stockholm, no date. Ed by Olle Källström and Carl Hernmarck.
24) Riisöen and Böe, *op. cit.*, p. 56.
25) *Ibid.*, p. 26 f.
26) Examples illustrated in *The Connoisseur*, November 1959, Vol. CXLIV, No. 581, p. 156.
27) Miss Ella Winter in *Illustrated London News*, 11 April 1959, p. 617.
28) We are grateful to Dr Carl Hernmarck for this information. Dr Hernmarck refers to Guiffrey, *Inventaire Général du Mobilier de la Couronne sous Louis XIV*, which it has not been possible to consult.
29) *The Memoirs of Ann Lady Fanshawe*, London and New York, 1907, pp. 139 f., 147, 189.
30) *Op. cit.*
31) E. Alfred Jones, *Old Silver of Europe and America*, London, 1928, pp. 325 f. Jones refers to Filimonows catalogue of the Kreml Collections, and to F. R. Martin, *Schwedische königliche Geschenke an Russische Zaren, 1647–1699*, pl. 50 and p. 21. We have not found occasion to consult these works.
32) Riisöen and Böe, *op. cit.*
33) Letter from Mme de Maintenon to Mme de Caylus, 24 January 1718, referred to in E. Littre, *Dictionnaire de la langue française*, 1863, Filigrane.

Sheffield Plate

Georgian Sheffield plate is beautiful and distinguished, its range of design rivalling that of eighteenth-century handwrought silver. Shortcomings in the processes involved, however, made it difficult to follow the florid cast silver patterns introduced by the silversmiths from 1797 after the Goldsmiths' Company had complained to Parliament that 'plated manufacturers have produced articles of the highest elegance and fashion, many of which are now made with solid silver – borders, shields, ornaments, finished in exact resemblance of real plate – and which do material injury to the sale of wrought plate'.

Beautiful table accessories were no longer the prerogative of the rich. Families of moderate means were now dining from Wedgwood's creamware or Spode's bone china, graced with elegant accessories in radiant Sheffield plate. The effect of this was so devastating upon the silversmith's craft that for the next half-century little wrought plate was made in England.

Soup tureen in the form of a turtle, with a capacity of ten pints. The shell hinges upwards from the neck. City Museum, Sheffield

The fact that Sheffield plate reacted like a single piece of metal when shaped by silversmiths' tools, raised it to an important position during the reign of George III (1760–1820). Skill and time expended upon it by the craftsmen were no less than for solid silver, however. The tax of sixpence an ounce levied upon manufactured silver plate from 1782 had the effect of enabling Sheffield plate to be sold at one-third the price of silver: in 1815 the silver tax was increased to eighteen pence an ounce.

Many enthusiastic collectors prefer the peculiar lustre radiating from plate made by fusing silver over copper to the brilliance of silver plate. Similar patterns were made over such long periods that only a detailed knowledge of the processes involved in Sheffield plating will enable a collector to place examples within closely defined periods.

Sheffield plating is one of the many industries entirely English in origin. The discovery that silver and copper could be united by fusion was made in 1743 by Thomas Bolsover (1704–88), a Sheffield cutler. It is uncertain how Bolsover's achievement came about: the story of the broken silver knife handle and the copper penny bears no investigation, for such a coin was not included in the English coinage until 1797.

Aware that silver and copper would fuse together, he experimented with rolled copper plates and sheets of silver foil. These he fused together as a single entity. With borrowed capital of £170 and Joseph Wilson as partner, Bolsover began to manufacture silver-plated buttons. The venture prospered, and within a year the loan had been repaid with interest. During the following twelve months he experimented further, fusing a plate of silver to an ingot of copper and reducing them to plate thickness by passing between heavy spring rollers. The relative proportions of silver and copper remained unaltered and the copper was silvered on one side only. Bolsover named his production Copper Rolled Plate, and although he did not patent the process, it appears to have remained under his sole control until 1758. During this period he manufactured small circular and oval boxes with pull-off lids hand-embossed in low relief.

Joseph Hancock, a former apprentice of Bolsover's, discovered the single-lapped edge, and, aware of its potential value, had established himself as a competitor by 1758. His vision carried him further, and by installing horse- and water-power he rolled heavier ingots into plates large enough for him to enter the field formerly the prerogative of silversmiths. He issued a wide range of domestic ware, including tea and coffee pots, hot-water jugs, sauce-

Far right Coffee pot made from single-sided plate, the lid and foot worked from two pieces of fused plate placed copper to copper, the upper layer of silver turned over to conceal the copper edges, *c.* 1760. City Museum, Sheffield

pans, all tin-lined, as well as candlesticks. Bolsover, already a rich man, made an unsuccessful effort to follow suit, and eventually sold his business to Hancock.

It was probably to Hancock's workshops that Matthew Boulton (1728–1809) was sent in 1760 by his father, a Birmingham toy maker, who appreciated the potentialities of the silver-plated ware. After mastering the technique, Matthew Boulton returned to Birmingham, and by 1762 was producing plated ware at Soho, two miles to the north. Three years later he founded the Matthew Boulton & Plate Company in Birmingham to organize the sale of silver and

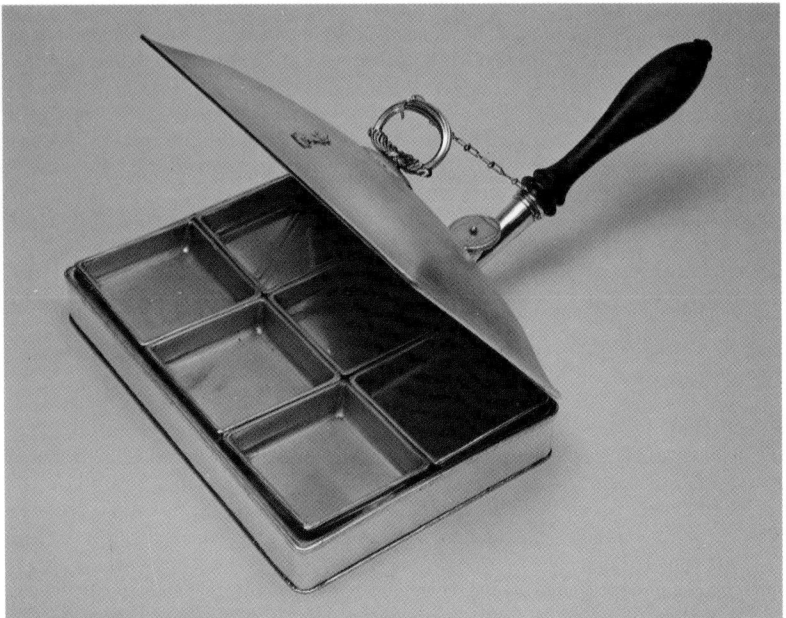

Cheese toaster with hot water compartment, *c.* 1805. City Museum, Sheffield

plated ware, issuing an ever-increasing stream from his factory.

The wide variety of ware issued by the Sheffield platers is shown by illustrated pattern books dating from about 1790. In the Victoria and Albert Museum are several such books, the earliest a folio of eighty-four plates issued by John Green, Sheffield. On the first page is written his name and the year 1792, with a note to the effect that a discount of thirty per cent was allowed. Unfortunately, however, the articles are not priced. The objects illustrated are tea and coffee sets, cake baskets, hot-water jugs, tea caddies, tankards and beakers, tea pots, wine-bottle corks, bottle labels, waiters and trays, cruet frames with glass accessories, toasters, breakfast dishes and covers, soup tureens, chamber candlesticks, wax-taper holders, snuffers and snuffer trays, toast racks, standishes, wine funnels, sand boxes, salt cellars, candelabra, spoons and forks, fish servers, sauceboats and sauce tureens, tumbler stands, egg cups, mustards, sugar basins, table heaters and stands, ladles, oil-bottle stands.

Another catalogue, issued in 1797 by John Cadman, Sheffield, is a folio of seventy plates illustrating similar objects in different patterns, but showing, in addition, tea urns, candlesticks on perspective and half section, and this firm's well-known telescopic candlestick marked 'patent'. Prices have been written in with pen and ink.

A further catalogue, undated but with pages watermarked 1811, illustrates a widening range of ware with the addition of cigar cases, oil lamps to fit candle sockets, combined egg-cup holders and muffineers, tea bells, spirit frames and bottles, knife rests, wine coolers, beefsteak dishes, saucepans, cream buckets, cream ewers, argyles, strainers, and plate covers.

These pieces continued in production throughout the traditional period to the establishment of Elkington's electroplate, during which German silver gradually superseded copper as the foundation for Sheffield plate. The decline was slow, for in 1865 there were nine platers operating in Birmingham, using between them about ten tons of plate annually.

Glossary

Acanthus. Conventional foliage adapted from the capitals of Corinthian columns, used extensively throughout the Renaissance period, sixteenth to seventeenth centuries, chiefly in embossed technique.
Alms dish. Circular dish with broad, flat rim, plain or decorated in prevailing style of period. Single examples of seventeenth-century domestic plates sometimes mistaken for alms dishes.
Altars. Since the early Middle Ages, altar frontals, and sometimes whole altars, have occasionally been made in silver, At Città di Castello, in Umbria, there is a fine twelfth-century frontal which is an important specimen of late Romanesque sculpture. One of the best examples of a complete silver altar is that of St James made, between the thirteenth and fifteenth centuries, for Pistoia Cathedral (cf. *The Connoisseur*, November 1956). Among numerous seventeenth- and eighteenth-century altars that by G. B. Foggini for the Corsini Chapel in the Carmine at Florence, and that of 1730 at Frieburg (near Augsburg), should be mentioned.
Andirons. On the Continent were frequently made in silver for palaces, but few of these heavy pieces of furniture have survived. In the Victoria and Albert Museum there is a very fine rococo one made by Philip Jacob Drentwitt of Augsburg (1747–79). In England rare in silver, but examples occur from Restoration period. Usually of richly chased baluster or vase form and occasionally as caryatid figures. Either cast from solid metal or built up in sections on iron cores.
Annealing. Process of softening the silver by heating over red-hot charcoals, as it became brittle under hammering during the process of raising from a flat sheet.
Anthemion. Conventional foliage resembling honeysuckle blossom found as ornament on pieces in the classical idiom (Greek).
Applied. A term used in connection with ornament; certain parts, such as spouts, handles, covers, were made separately and applied with solder.
Arabesque. Interlaced patterns of flowers and foliage often combined with strapwork (*q.v.*) in sixteenth century and in pierced work of eighteenth century.
Argyll. Gravy container, cylindrical or vase-shaped, resembling small coffee pots with either outer lining or central container (sometimes detachable) for hot water. Introduced about 1770; in favour until about 1830. Not made in Sheffield plate until the late 1780s.
Armour. In the sixteenth century it was not uncommon for the pageant armour of great princes to be made either wholly or partly of silver. The Louvre has a magnificent enamelled gold shield and morion made for Charles IX between 1560 and 1574. A great shield of iron, in the British Museum, damascened with gold and plated with silver, was made by Giorgio Ghisi of Mantua in 1554, and is a notable example of mannerist art.
Asparagus tongs. Introduced in late eighteenth century. Derived from fish slice with spring-hinged upper jaw. Later form of spring-bow form with pierced flat grips. Handle patterns conform to table services. Rare in U.S. silver.

Aspergill. The orb-ended rod or brush used for sprinkling holy water; the handle is often of silver and made to match a holy-water bucket (*q.v.*).
Assay. In silver, the test made to prove that the metal was of required quality.
Assay groove. The wriggled groove by which metal was taken for purposes of assay. Occurs usually in proximity to hallmarks up to the late seventeenth century. This method was practised on the Continent, and is an interesting minor reflection of close historical link between Scotland, where it was also used, and certain European countries.
Bannock rack. Resembles an outsize in toast racks, the silver tray secured to a wooden base. Few examples known date from the second half of the eighteenth century. Bannock is a flat homebaked Scottish cake made from oatmeal, barley, or peasemeal, generally the first, broken into pieces when removed from the girdle and served hot.
Baptismal basin. While many baptismal basins were made specifically for the purpose, there are instances of the bequest of rose-water basins to churches to serve in this capacity, such as the one now belonging to the First Parish Church, Cambridge, Massachusetts, which was made by Jeremiah Dummer of Boston. Earliest baptismal basins are of the seventeenth century.
Baroque. The generic title for the late Renaissance flamboyant style of scrollwork and naturalistic ornament.
Basins. Were frequently made in gold, silver, or mounted crystal, and the decoration of some is so elaborate that one suspects that they were intended primarily for display on the sideboard. A fairly simple Flemish example, of about 1560, with a raised centre, belongs to the Corporation of Guildford. In the Louvre there is a magnificent basin (with its ewer), made at Antwerp 1558–9, chased with scenes of Charles V's expedition to Tunis in 1535. A large Portuguese basin in the Wallace Collection (*c.* 1565) is richly embossed with symbols of the seasons, the elements, and the planets. Basins were used for the essential hand washing before and during meals, but their popularity as decorative pieces lasted until after the introduction of forks and declined in the early eighteenth century.
Basket. Variously used for bread, cake, or fruit. Early examples rare and usually circular. Oval form introduced about 1730 with pierced bodies and swing handles. Wirework bodies with applied foliage, wheat, and flowers popular about 1770. Later examples have solid bodies, engraved decoration, and gadrooned or reeded rims. Circular gilt baskets return after 1800 for dessert use (*see* Cream, Dessert, and Sugar baskets).
Bat's-wing fluting. Graduated gadrooning curved to resemble the outline of a bat's wing and encircling hollow ware.

Simple uncovered beaker, Holland, 16th–17th century

Baptismal basin, 1716

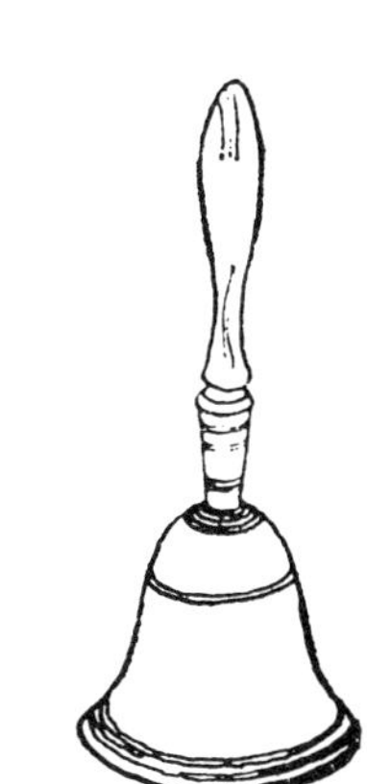

Ivory-handled bell, 1806

Beading. A border ornament composed of small contiguous half-spheres resembling pearls or beads. Commonest in late eighteenth century.
Beakers. Stemless drinking cups were popular in various parts of Europe from the fifteenth until the eighteenth century. In the fifteenth century they were especially popular in Germany, where they usually had covers decorated with overhanging Gothic leaf decoration around the rim. A superb nielloed example of about 1480 is in the British Museum. Some were made in fantastic shapes, like the copper-gilt one in the Victoria and Albert Museum, which is very intricately fashioned to resemble a castle. Norwegian beakers of the sixteenth century usually rest on feet in the form of lions or female busts. Simple, uncovered beakers, much like those made in England at the same time, reached the height of their popularity in the sixteenth and seventeenth centuries in Holland, where they also served as communion cups in Protestant churches. In Hungary very tall beakers, decorated in national fashion, were favoured, and in Italy they were occasionally covered with filigree work. In the United States the early ones were straight-sided with flaring rim, followed by a Queen Anne bell shape on low moulded foot; the body became ovoid in Federal period, *c.* 1800.
Bedwarmers. Were made in silver, but few have survived. One by the French craftsman Charles Petit in 1661 was in the Puiforcat Collection.
Beefsteak dish. Similar to an entrée dish, and described in the 1797 catalogue as fitted with 'the handle to screw off to make a pair of dishes occasionally'.
Beer bowles and **beer cupps.** Encountered in inventories but not distinctly recognizable today.
Beer jug. *See* Jug.
Bekerschroef. A stand for a wine glass, shaped like the stem of a large cup. These objects are peculiar to Holland, where they were made in the early seventeenth century.
Bells. Table bells of silver have been made since the sixteenth century, varying in style with the taste of the times. A famous bell, decorated with snakes, lizards, and insects, made by Hans Jamnitzer at Nuremberg in about 1558, is in the British Museum, and a similar one attributed to the same craftsman, is in the Schatzkammer der Reichen Kapelle at Munich. In England they were rare before the eighteenth century. Usually found with baluster handles, frequently as centrepieces of inkstands until mid-eighteenth century. Later examples have wood or ivory handles. In Scotland it is doubtful if any handbells survive earlier than 1800, with the notable exception of the Holyrood Mass Bell. Two examples of racing bells are preserved from seventeenth century.
Bezel. The added inside rim to make a cover fit more firmly.
Biggin. A form of cylindrical coffee pot with short spout, often with stand and spirit lamp.
Blackjack. Leather tankard occasionally mounted with silver rim, of seventeenth- and eighteenth-century date. Certain examples bearing pretentious historical inscriptions should be viewed with scepticism.
Bleeding bowl. Flat, shallow, circular bowl with one flat, pierced, and shaped handle. Believed to have been used for bleeding, but more probably a form of

individual porringer, by which name American examples are always known. The covers of early skillets (*q.v.*) or saucepans are of the same basic form and were probably the prototype.

Blowhole. A small hole pierced in hollow castings or seamed hollow members as handles, finials, etc., to allow escape of the air expanded by heat when soldered to the main body. Tankards with this feature have long been mistakenly known as 'whistle' tankards, to be used for calling for another drink. This fantasy dies hard.

Bookbindings (*rilegature*). In Italy, from a very early period, books, especially liturgical books, have occasionally been bound in precious metals. In the seventeenth and eighteenth centuries the entire bindings were sometimes made of embossed silver plates. A more usual practice was to decorate the leather- or velvet-covered boards with silver edges and a pattern of scrollwork with central medallion of a religious subject or the arms of the owner. Bindings of this type rarely bear hallmarks.

Bottle tickets. Small plaques, plain or ornamented, engraved or cut with the name of a beverage, with a chain to be hung on the necks of a decanter. Date from the 1730s.

Bowl. An unknown item is the 'silver Bowl with two wooden handles' in a U.S. inventory of 1728; 'a wrought bowl which will hold five pints, with handles' is mentioned in 1758. Slop bowls and slop basins appear in inventories early in the eighteenth century, but are identifiable chiefly in the second half.

Box. Small circular and oval boxes occur from seventeenth century onward, made for patches, comfits, pomades, and other feminine needs (*see also* Snuff and Tobacco box, Pomander, Vinaigrette, and Étui).

Brandewijkom. An oval, two-handled bowl peculiar to Holland, where it was made in the seventeenth and eighteenth centuries. It was used on festive occasions to hold raisins steeped in brandy.

Brandy bowls. Flat, two-handled bowls called *orekovsken* in Denmark, *oreskaal* in Norway, and *dopskal* in Sweden, used for serving hot brandy, were popular throughout the Scandinavian countries in the seventeenth century.

Bratina. A globular, covered cup with a contracted lip (usually decorated with a sententious inscription), peculiar to Russia. It was a form of loving cup, intimately associated with its owner and used at his funeral feast. Sometimes they were richly enamelled and begemmed; a rare example in gold is in the museum at Vienna.

Brazier. Circular bowl with pierced plate in base for burning charcoal as heaters for kettles or dishes. Found late seventeenth century and occasionally in eighteenth, but supplanted by spirit lamp stands (*see also* Chafing stand).

Bread baskets. The opulent form, usually of pierced work and on feet, although a U.S. example by Myer Myers is on a baseband, with bail handle; today called a cake basket, as in the will of Dorothy Quincy Hancock Scott (1830): 'My large silver cake basket requesting her to have it used at the weddings . . . as it had been heretofore.'

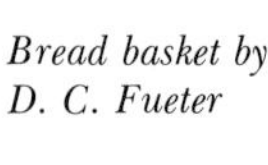

Bread basket by D. C. Fueter

Bridal crowns. The custom for Norwegian brides to wear a crown at their wedding probably goes back to the Middle Ages, but all the examples which now exist in Norway must have been made in post-Reformation times. One particular example, which has names of saints engraved on it, may date from *c.* 1550. Some specimens go back to the seventeenth century, while the majority of existing crowns must have been made in the eighteenth and nineteenth centuries. The crown is made of a ring, from which rise the ornamental parts. From them again ornaments are suspended which glitter and tinkle when the wearer moves about. On some of the best examples the ring (which rested on a padded cushion) is divided into sections, and the ornaments above are cut into heraldic figures of decorative patterns. These are repeated in identical form with each section. Another type consists of a plain cylinder, the top of which has been cut out into the patterns desired, and to them the hanging ornaments are attached. The cheaper specimens are made of silver-gilt copper. Crowns seem to have been most widely used in Western Norway. In fact, the bridal crown is still in use in part of the country, but, like the national costume with which it is usually worn, its traditionalism seems a little self-conscious.

Bright-cut engraving. A particular form of engraving popular about 1790 in which the metal is removed by bevelled cutting, giving a jewel-like, faceted sparkle to the surface.

Far right Bright-cut decoration, detail from a George III sugar-basket by Henry Crawner, 1792

Britannia metal, plating on. Introduced in the early 1820s by Kirkby, Smith & Company, Sheffield. A sheet of pure silver was laid on a flat surface and well heated. Molten Britannia metal was poured over this. When cold it was found to have picked up the silver. The two were then rolled into sheets as for plated copper. Owing to difficulties in assembling, the method was soon abandoned, but examples are to be found from time to time.

Britannia Standard. The Higher Standard for wrought plate introduced in 1697 to prevent the melting down of coinage by silversmiths. It consists of 11 oz 10 dwts fine silver in the Pound Troy (12 oz). Named from the mark of Britannia replacing Sterling mark of lion passant. In force till 1720, when Sterling or Old Standard was restored, the Higher being left as optional, which it still is.

Brooches. The heavy silver Norwegian specimens, made by country goldsmiths or by guild masters for provincial customers, are of special interest. They were used either to hold together the standing collar on the blouse of the national costume (and some of these were worn by both men and women) or rested on the bosom of the wearer as a magnificent ornament. It is among the latter group that the most

Above left Nielloed plaid brooch, Scottish, 1762. National Museum of Antiquities, Scotland

Above Pair of candelabra bearing the crest of Pitt, Baron Rivers, by Frederick Kandler, London 1751 and 1752. Thomas Lumley, London

interesting types are found. Some of these *sölje* brooches are made to patterns that go back to medieval times, like the very fine example with heraldic animals in a circle which is in the Victoria and Albert Museum. Others rely for their effect on hanging ringlets, which are suspended from the edges of the brooch and give a glittering, shimmering effect of a certain primitive beauty. Other examples are made in a mould. Finally there are the filigree specimens, which are lighter and more elegant than any of the other types. Some of the latter are made of very white metal.

Peasant brooches were particularly sought after by English tourists in quest of souvenirs from Norway, and quite a number of them have been found in Britain. It should always be remembered that they have been much copied for tourists during the last eighty to a hundred years. Some of them have very close parallels in Scotland, like the little heart-shaped 'Luckenbooth' brooch or the circular moulded type with the pin to catch (not to stick) into the material of the blouse.

Buckles. For knees, shoes, girdles, and stocks were recorded in great quantity in the U.S. in gold, silver, paste, etc., but comparatively few have survived, and even fewer with maker's marks.

Burnishing. Polishing with a hand tool containing a hard, smooth stone or, in modern times, steel; used to remove planishing marks from the 'planishing teast' or hammer.

Butter dish. Oval pierced bowl and cover with glass liner, usually Irish, dating from the second half of the eighteenth century. English examples rare till nineteenth century, when circular tub-shaped examples occur.

Butter tester. A device found in silver from the mid-eighteenth century akin in shape to a modern apple corer, and sometimes thus called erroneously.

Butt joint. A joint made by soldering two ends of silver on the flat without fold or overlap.

Cake basket. *See* Basket.

Candelabrum. A branched candlestick. In England virtually no survivals before eighteenth century. Stems and base conform to candlestick design. Detachable or fixed scroll branches for two or more lights with finials of various forms. Late examples highly elaborate and many-branched, sometimes with interchangeable *épergne* dishes. In the Portuguese royal collection there is a magnificent rococo one by the French craftsman François Thomas Germain whose pupil, Robert Joseph Auguste, made three great candelabra for the Winter Palace at Petrograd. Silver wall sconces of the seventeenth and eighteenth centuries are commoner, especially in Holland and Germany. A pair of fine candle brackets with tulip-shaped holders, made by Nicholas Verhaar at Utrecht, is in the Brum Collection in that city.

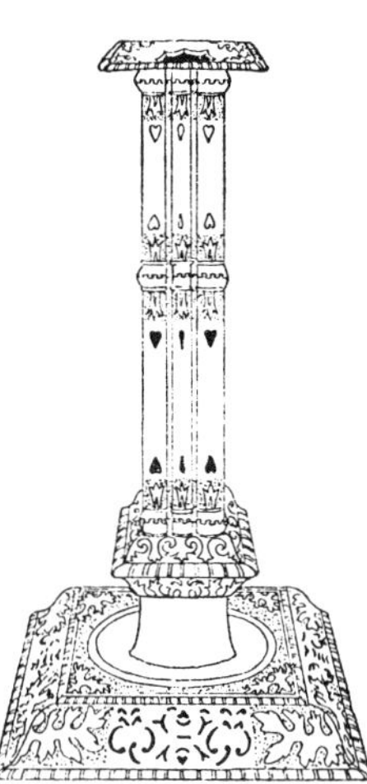

Domestic candlestick, Dutch, 17th century. Victoria & Albert Museum

Candlestick, altar. Either larger version of domestic examples of the period or of Italian Renaissance design with tripod bases. Prickets (spikes) occur in place of sockets.

Candlestick, chamber. Also known as flat candlestick. Usually circular, flat base. Early examples have cast pear-shaped handles, later of scroll or ring form. Extinguishers fit in slots on sockets or handle. Late examples often with snuffers carried in opening in stem. Found from late seventeenth century onwards.

Candlestick, table. In England found in pairs and sets of four or more from Charles II onwards. Stems either of cast baluster or figure form or classical columns in sheet metal, the latter in Adam period die-struck at Sheffield and loaded with resin or lead. Telescopic stems rare in silver but frequent in Sheffield plate. Single candlesticks of silver have been made on the Continent since the sixteenth century in all sizes, for use in churches and houses, varying with the stylistic trends of the times. In the seventeenth century domestic candlesticks were normally square and solid, like the Dutch examples in the Victoria and Albert Museum. They provided great scope for the rococo silversmiths and designers like Meissonier, who made roses sprout and blossom from the hollows of the contorted pillars. In the United States the earliest, 1686, by Jeremiah Dummer, Boston, shows architectural influence, continued in a different form in baluster stems of the early eighteenth century, used by Coney in Boston and George Rideout in New York; fluted columns on square or octagonal bases are seen in work of Boelen and Kierstede. After about 1715 candlesticks were cast in moulds, being raised from a flat piece of silver in the earlier period. Baluster forms continued to be most popular throughout the eighteenth century.

Canes. Inventories from 1697 refer to 'silver-headed canes'; in 1719 the Boston goldsmith, Samuel Haugh, had 'a silver ferril upon an Agget Canes head', and Revere's daybook in 1786 mentions a gold cane head. Many English examples exist.

Canister. A receptacle for tea; Edward Franklin's inventory of 1725 listed 'a Canister Boat for spoons'. This was a wicker basket.
Cann. Drinking vessel, usually of one-pint capacity, like a mug, but always having rounded sides, and standing on a moulded base. The term 'cann' appears in old inventories of the late eighteenth century.

Canoe-shaped cruet stand

Censer, 1767–79. Bayerisches National Museum

Canoe shape. A piece oval on plan with the two ends, seen in elevation, higher than the centre, such as in some standishes and cruet frames.
Canongate silver. Calls for separate mention, since Canongate is now merged in Edinburgh, but until the nineteenth century formed independent burgh with its own trade guilds. Finest period sixteenth century, when some elaborate mazers crowned its output, but good work still done in seventeenth. By end of eighteenth main output was table silver. Feature of list of Canongate goldsmiths is number of apparent foreigners. Close proximity to gates of Holyrood Palace may account for place's prosperity. Canongate silver (mark: stag's head lodged) is comparatively rare and much sought after.
Canteen. Small individual set of knife, fork, and spoon with beaker and condiment box, contained in shagreen case, used for travelling, dating from late seventeenth to late eighteenth centuries.
Caryatid. The cast thumb grips on the handles of caudle cups generally take this form, derived from the classic draped female figure used as a support for an entablature.
Caskets. Large caskets of silver were made in Germany in the sixteenth century, but elsewhere they were usually of other materials, mounted in silver, like the famous Renaissance *Cassetta Farnese* in the Naples Museum. Small wedding caskets for jewelry, no more than 3 inches (7.6 cm) high and fashioned like miniature chests, were made in Holland in the seventeenth century.
Cast. To shape in a mould, which was generally of brass. Certain small parts, thumbpieces, finials for covers, hingeplates, handles for cups, etc., were given their form in the molten state. These were finished by filing and chasing after removal from the mould.
Caster. Found singly or in set of three for sugar, pepper, and with unpierced cover for mustard. Seventeenth-century form cylindrical. In eighteenth century pear-shaped and later of vase form, polygonal or circular in outline. Largely replaced in late eighteenth century by cut-glass examples with silver covers (*see also* Cruet frame, Dredger, Muffineer).

Caster, 1715

Pierced caster cover, 1716

Castwork. Decoration or parts of a vessel cast in a mould and soldered to the main body. Principally used for handles, feet, spouts, and finials. Complete castings occur in candlesticks built up in various sections and in some other pieces.
Celtic decoration. After, perhaps, ninth century anything which can really be called Celtic decoration is most rare on silver, except for some jewelry (*q.v.*). Touches of Celtic feeling occur on croziers and on Dunvegan Cup (fourteenth century), but latter is Irish. Also on Macleod Cup, of late sixteenth century, but this fundamentally Renaissance.
Censer. Occasionally called a thurible. The vessel in which incense is burnt; it is more frequently of base metal than silver. Gothic examples are usually architectural in form, and resemble fantastic spires or octagonal chapter houses. In Renaissance times a simpler, vase-shaped type came into use, and in subsequent periods its decoration varied with current trends in architectural taste. A very fine silver censer of 1767–79 in the Bayerisches Nationalmuseum echoes in its broken curves the decoration of the rococo pilgrimage churches of Bavaria. A few English examples late seventeenth to eighteenth centuries have survived, and the Ramsey Abbey example (fourteenth century).
Centrepiece. A large and often fantastic object, sometimes called a *surtout de table*, used to decorate the centre of a table; in some ways it took the place of the ceremonial salt. One of the most famous is that made by Wenzel Jamnitzer (1546) in the form of a woman, standing on a mound covered with leafy plants, holding on her head a covered dish crowned by a vase of flowers (Rijksmuseum, Amsterdam). A Swedish example of the late seventeenth century has four candle branches, a dish supported by a five-headed dragon, casters for sugar, and shell-shaped dishes for sweetmeats. Rococo silversmiths allowed their ingenuity to run riot when designing such objects, and one of the finest of all was that made in 1730 by Thomas Germain, now in the Museu de Arte Antigua, Lisbon, which stands some 3 feet (91.4 cm) in height, bears two three-branch candleholders, and is enriched with *putti*, dogs, tortoises, and hunting horns. *See also The Connoisseur*, December 1954, p. 259). *See* Épergne.
Chafing dish. Brazier or spirit-lamp stand for hot food.

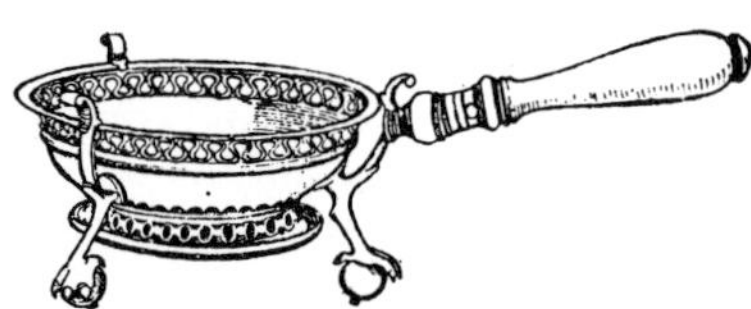

Chalice. The cup in which wine is consecrated at the Eucharist. When intended for the use of the Roman Catholic Church it was invariably made of gold, silver, or silver gilt, frequently enriched with enamel and relief decoration and occasionally encrusted with precious stones. The earliest chalices have a hemispherical bowl on a spreading, knopped stem, and some romanesque examples, like that at Kremsmünster, are decorated with Christian symbols amid interlaced decoration. In the Gothic period the stems were occasionally enriched with buttresses and pinnacles, like the fifteenth-century Venetian one in the Victoria and Albert Museum, but such becrocketed vessels must have been difficult to

Romanesque chalice, decorated with Christian symbols. Kremsmünster

Chalice with stem enriched with buttresses and pinnacles, Venetian, 15th century. Victoria & Albert Museum

handle, and a simpler, more practical type, in which the decoration was limited to engraving on the bowl with enamelling on the knop and foot, was generally preferred. In the fourteenth century a deeper form of bowl came into use, and a pattern was established that did not alter radically until the nineteenth century, when the hemispherical bowl was revived; but the decoration of both bowl and stem varied considerably with the times. In the seventeenth and eighteenth centuries the lip of the bowl was normally left free from the baroque or rococo decoration, which swirled around the lower part to riot on the stem and foot. Many chalices of these periods were enamelled and some decorated with stones; one in the Vatican, made in Rome for the Cardinal of York, being studded with diamonds. Rococo craftsmen occasionally made the stem in the form of a standing figure, as in the example of 1707 in the Church of St Paul, Antwerp. Large numbers of chalices were made by English silversmiths in the mid-nineteenth century.

Chandelier. Hanging candle branches to be distinguished from the standing candelabrum. The two words are the French and Latin forms of the same word. The above distinction is usually observed in English for clarity.

Charger. *See* Sideboard dish.

Charka. A small cup with a single handle, peculiar to Russia; it was used for drinking strong liquors. A characteristic, richly enamelled example is in the British Museum.

Chasing. Relief decoration raised by surface hammering of the metal. Also applied to the finishing given to cast- or *repoussé* work, in which former case roughness or projections may also be filed or cut away (*see also* Flat chasing).

Cheese scoop. Introduced in late eighteenth century for serving cheese. Consists of a short, curved blade with silver shaft and ivory or wood handle. Later examples have silver handles conforming to table service patterns.

Cheese warmers. Shallow, rectangular trays with rounded corners and projecting handles of turned wood. From second quarter of eighteenth century. Attractively simple, but rare.

Cherub's head. A cast cherub mask appears on the curve and at the tip of the handle of New York tankards, at tip in Boston work. The European source of design was identified by Marshall Davidson (*Antiques*, April 1940) in cast ornament of spandrels of Dutch and English clocks of the late seventeenth century. The cherub mask with pendant leafage on handles duplicates a French seventeenth-century *applique de cabinet* (*see* 'Le Bronze', second part of a catalogue of metalwork, Musée des Arts Décoratif). Masks and pendants as used by different silversmiths are so similar as to suggest the moulds were imported.

Chinoiserie. Decoration of pseudo-Chinese inspiration. Occurs at three periods: (i) from about 1680 to 1690 in engraved form; (ii) about 1750 chiefly in *repoussé* and chased form; (iii) about 1820 in the same technique with cast details.

Chocolate pot. Of the same basic form as the coffee pot, from which it can be distinguished by the detachable or sliding cover finial concealing the hole for insertion of the swizzle stick for stirring the chocolate. Many pieces must have been used indiscriminately for both liquids.

Chocolate-pot by Pierre Platel, 1705. The chain attached to the handle has a pin which is removable from the lid hinge to enable the lid to be taken off. Manchester City Art Gallery

Gothic ciborium

Chop dish. Small, flat, two-handled, oblong dish occurring from about 1750 to the 1850s.

Ciborium. The receptacle used for the reservation of the Eucharist. It is normally provided with a hinged cover and a lock. Gothic examples usually have a spire-shaped cover above a cylindrical (occasionally polygonal), font-shaped bowl. Flatter covers, usually crowned by a cross, were introduced at the Renaissance.

Cipher. Double monogram, especially popular on New York tankards. Sympson's *Book of Cyphers*, published in London about 1726. was widely used in America.

Clasps. For books, pocketbooks, and cloaks were shaped plaques on which, to judge by the few remaining ones, a goldsmith could show his imagination and skill in engraving. Clasps for necklaces and bracelets were usually oblong or elliptical and engraved. These are sometimes called lockets.

Coaster. *See* Wine coaster.

Coat-of-arms. Arms on earlier pieces were engraved in a flat-topped shield (on a lozenge for widows or spinsters), surrounded with a plumed mantling. A baroque form with broad, curling acanthus leaves was favoured in New York in early eighteenth century. About 1740 a new style was adopted with imbrication in the framework surrounding the arms; then followed the Chippendale rococo, well exemplified by Revere and Nathaniel Hurd; Guillim's *Display of Heraldry* was largely used by American silversmiths. In the classic period, 1785–1810, the shield showing the arms has floral garlands suspended on either side.

Cobbet pot. In Boston in 1667 John Wilson left 'one chased cobbet pott & Cover' of silver. The *Oxford Dictionary on Historic Principles* lists *Cobbit* as an obsolete form of *Cobbard*, or firedog.

Coffee pot. Introduced about 1680. In England early examples basically of straight tapering form, later polygonal. Pear-shaped bodies appear about 1730 and classical vase forms in the Adam period. Later cylindrical forms often provided with spirit-lamp stands (*see also* Biggin). On the Continent they vary but slightly from one region and date to another. They were normally vase-shaped with a spout, but exotic patterns also occur, like that entwined with snakes and crowned with a toad, which was made at Dresden in about 1700 by J. M. Dinglinger. In the United States the earliest coffee pots, *c.* 1700, were of severe tapering form like the earliest English type, followed by about twenty years later by a modification of the tapering form, being rounded at the base, and standing on a narrow moulded foot. The rococo coffee pot was, like the English, pear-shaped and tall, stood on a spreading foot, and had a domed cover. In the Federal period (late eighteenth and early nineteenth centuries) the coffee pot was an inverted pear with a simple scroll handle of wood; some were made in classical urn shape.

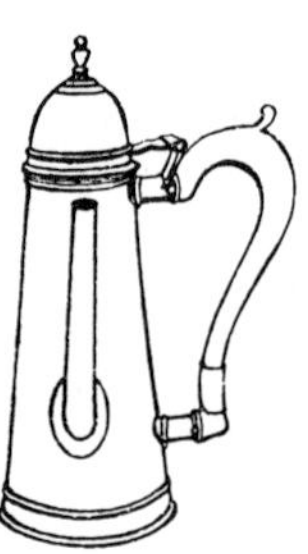

Coffee pot, 1720

Coffee pot, 1770

Coffee pot by John Watson, Sheffield, 1818

Coin. Inlaid in lid of tankards; German and Scandinavian practice, followed in New York and England.

Coin silver. In the United States the stamp, coin, after 1850, signified pieces made from silver coin, 900 parts pure silver, 100 alloy, or less than sterling.

Communion silver. A very important branch of Scottish silverware, although unlikely to have much immediate concern for collectors, as most pieces are still in the hands of the kirks for which they were made. Reformed church demanded entirely new types of vessels, owing nothing to traditional forms, and earliest cups – late sixteenth and early seventeenth centuries – seem to have been modelled either on standing mazers or on secular wine cups. Presbyterianism required participation of all communicants in Sacrament, and cups in populous parishes are frequently large-bowled, and occur in pairs or even fours. Graceful shapes, but little or no ornament. Cups become more stereotyped with advance of eighteenth century. Names or initials and coats-of-arms of donors commonly engraved on bowls, with date of gift. On northeast coast and inland typical cup is of beaker type, modelled on Dutch and German secular beakers, which themselves are sometimes adapted for sacred use and then copied by local goldsmith. A number of handsome basins and lavers from the seventeenth century are still in use in the churches. Earliest is baptismal basin of St John's Kirk, Perth (1591).

Compostiera. A container for stewed fruit, usually in the form of a salver carrying a pair of silver jars normally having glass linings. The containers are often richly worked and have elaborate knobs on their covers. An example made at Turin (now in a private collection at Milan) has a barking dog to serve as the knob of one lid and a cat arching her back on the other.

Corkscrew. A thumbpiece of twisted shape derived from the Dutch form, used especially on New York and English tankards.

Cow cream jug. Small model of cow with open mouth and lid in back. Introduced from Holland about 1755 by John Schuppe, probably a Dutchman. Later examples occur by other makers.

Cream basket. Small vase or boat-shaped basket, pierced or plain, introduced about 1760, often matching larger examples for sugar.

Creamer. In the United States earliest cream pitchers are of second quarter of the eighteenth century and are pear-shaped with collared foot and domed cover. Next came a higher form with larger lip, three cabriole legs, double-scroll handle. This was followed by the inverted pear shape; then the classic helmet.

Cream jug. Early examples of plain pitcher form from Queen Anne to George II. Mid-eighteenth century, pear-shaped bodies on three feet, plain or chased. Classical vase or helmet shape introduced about 1780. Flat-bottomed examples about 1800. After this usually part of tea service *en suite* with tea pot and sugar basin.

Cream jug, 1753

Cream jug by William Ayrton, Edinburgh, 1730

In Scotland a most unusual type is the very rare, spherical covered jug of about 1730–40, matching bullet tea pots. Helmet-shaped jug with upstanding handle, of same period, is equally attractive, but almost as rare. Otherwise development of styles follows southern fashions.

Crozier. The head of the crozier, or bishop's pastoral staff, has often been made of silver. Gothic examples usually have a circle of crocketed niches beneath the volute which contains the figure of a saint. The sinuous curve of the crook naturally appealed to eighteenth-century silversmiths; there is a fine rococo example at Eichstätt.

Crucifixes. Altar crucifixes and processional crosses (which are decorated on both sides) generally follow, somewhat tardily, the stylistic development of sculpture. The Gothic type of cross, which had arms terminating in trefoils or quatrefoils enclosing symbols of the evangelists or half-figures of saints, persisted into the sixteenth century. Italy is particularly rich in silver crosses, some of which were designed by great artists like Antonio Pollaiuolo, who was responsible for the magnificent altar cross in the Museo dell'Opera del Duomo at Florence. A simpler type, introduced at the Renaissance, has generally persisted ever since.

Cruet frame. First examples date from Queen Anne. Made with open rings and central or side handle to hold sets of casters with or without glass oil and vinegar bottles. Later form oblong or boat-shaped, containing silver-mounted glass bottles, casters, and mustard pot (*see also* Oil and Vinegar frame, and Soy frame).

Cruets. The vessels containing the wine and water for use at the Eucharist. Sometimes wholly silver, they are frequently of glass with silver mounts, and follow the patterns prevalent in domestic plate. A fourteenth-century Burgundian cruet in the British Museum is quite plain except for the animal head at its spout. There is a curious pair of fifteenth-century workmanship in the Victoria and Albert Museum – one labelled A for *acqua*, the other V for *vinum*.

C-scroll. A term applied usually to the shape of a handle in form like the letter C; also called 'single scroll'.

Cupping bowl. A misnomer for bleeding-bowl (*q.v.*). Cupping is a suction action not achievable by the shallow bleeding-bowl.

Cups. Silver and gold cups have been made from very early times until the present day, but after the mid-eighteenth century their popularity as drinking vessels declined, and they have since been used mainly for presentation. So great was the diversity of cups in the sixteenth and seventeenth centuries, that no account of all the patterns made can be attempted here, but a list of the principal types would include the following.

Animal cups. Covered cups fashioned like animals – foxes, hounds, deer, unicorns, dragons, elephants, etc. – were made in Germany between the sixteenth and eighteenth centuries, being at the zenith of their popularity from about 1575 to about 1650. Some, made principally at Augsburg, were in the form of groups, St George and the Dragon or Diana riding a Centaur, and a few were fitted with clockwork mechanism so that they could be made to run across a table.

Bird cups. In the form of owls, larks, griffins, pelicans, etc., enjoyed the same popularity as animal cups, but seem to have been more widely made. A Portuguese owl cup of the seventeenth century is in the collection of Comandante Ernesto de Vilhena, and at Clare College, Cambridge, there is a falcon cup made at Antwerp in about 1555.

Silver-gilt stag cup, chased, the head removable, Augsburg, late 16th century. British Museum

Pierced cupping-bowl handle, 1698

Coconut cup, German, 16th century

Caudle cups. Two-handled cups with or without cover, generally of gourd shape; used for caudle, a thin gruel mixed with spiced wine or ale; also used for other drinks; frequently left to churches, they became communion cups. An alternative name for porringer.

Chocolate cups. Boston's famed Peter Faneuil left '6 Lignum Vitae chocolate cups lin'd with silver' in 1743, but they are unknown today.

Church cups. A designation in bequests for standing cups and beakers diverted from domestic to ecclesiastical use.

Coconut cups appear to have been made as early as the thirteenth century, but the oldest survivors are those made in Germany in the sixteenth century. Coconuts, polished and occasionally carved, were enclosed in delicate silver mounts and set upon stems. They appear to have been popular in Holland in the sixteenth century, and to have been introduced into Russia in the seventeenth, shortly before they went out of fashion in western Europe. In Scotland they occur from sixteenth to eighteenth centuries. The nuts were never carved as on the Continent, and mounts were of the simplest kind, with vandyked edges and usually only small amount of engraved pattern, if any. Seem to have attracted provincial makers especially; some of the finest are Dundee products (Bute Collection) of early seventeenth century. Mounts are in most cases crude.

Columbine cups were often, but not invariably, trial pieces made by candidates for admission to the goldsmiths' guilds of Germany. Their complicated form tested the skill of the young craftsmen without trying his ingenuity. Nuremberg was probably the first town to define the form in the sixteenth century.

Communion cups. The Protestant equivalent of the chalice (*q.v.*). Introduced under Edward VI and

Coconut cup and cover, silver mounted. German, Mainz, 1656. S. J. Phillips, London

continued as basic form till the end of the eighteenth century. Deep, beaker-shaped stem, with compressed central knop and circular foot. The accompanying paten usually fits the lip to form a cover (*see also* Paten).

Crystal and hard-stone cups were mounted in silver and gold from the end of the fifteenth century. In the sixteenth century Prague and Vienna were notable centres for this work, which was also practised in Germany and Italy. Rock crystal was much favoured as it was believed to act as a poison detector, but all manner of precious and semi-precious stones – emerald, agate, onyx, chalcedony, jasper, etc. – were also used. The precious nature of the material which could not be wasted in making regularly shaped vessels determined some of the most bizarre patterns and tested the invention of the craftsmen.

Two-handled cups, 1701 (top), *and 1720*

Hard-stone cup

Double cups are intimately identified with Germany, and became increasingly popular there from the end of the fifteenth century. Formed out of a cup of normal pattern with a cover that could be used as a second one, usually a smaller cup intended for the mistress of the house, they were occasionally shaped like double mazers. Hans Petzolt, a conspicuous Nuremberg silversmith of the sixteenth century, made several double cups. Such vessels are rarely found to date from after the middle of the seventeenth century.

Feeding cup. A small, plain, saucepan-like cup with one or two handles and curved or straight spout designed for child or invalid feeding. Found from mid-seventeenth century onwards.

Font-shaped cups. A form of low, circular wine cup on spreading foot, with or without cover, occurring in the first half of the sixteenth century, Extremely rare.

Globe cups, in the form of terrestrial globes, usually supported by a human figure, were made in France, Germany, and Switzerland in the sixteenth and seventeenth centuries. Abraham Gessner of Zürich appears to have specialized in making these vessels, some of which were as much as 20 inches (51 cm) high.

Globe cup

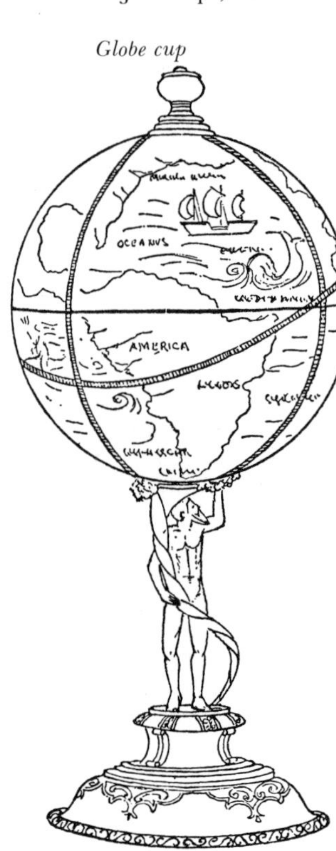

Gourd-shaped cups were made in Germany in the late sixteenth century, inspired by the design of Brossamer and Solis. They frequently stand on twisted-tree stems.

Grace cup. See Wine cup.

Nautilus shells, elaborately mounted as cups in gold or silver, were very popular in Germany some hundred years after 1550. An unusual example of 1580, in the British Museum, is mounted on a foot fashioned like the claw of a bird, and has a shell which was engraved in China. They were introduced into Holland in the sixteenth century. The greatest ingenuity was used in mounting the shells, which were sometimes made to resemble birds and beasts. It must be assumed that these vessels were intended for display rather than use. On occasions, nautilus shells were also made into flasks or cups.

Ostrich eggs, sometimes supposed to be the eggs of griffins or phoenixes, were often mounted as cups (and occasionally made into flasks) in the later Middle Ages. Most surviving specimens are German and date from the sixteenth or early seventeenth

centuries. A notable example is mounted as an ostrich, the eggs serving as the body.

Pineapple cups, with covered bowls, in the shape of stylized pineapples, were distinctive products of Germany (called *Ananaspokal*), where they were made in the seventeenth century. Some stand as much as 30 inches (76 cm) in height.

Spout cup. See Feeding cup.

Standing cups. Large ceremonial or decorative cups on high stems and feet found in every variety of style and decoration down to the end of the seventeenth century, after which they were replaced by the two-handled cup on low foot without stem. Examples without covers have probably lost them in the past.

Steeple cups. Popular term for standing cup surmounted by an obelisk or pyramid finial found in the reign of James I and early years of Charles I.

Stirrup cup. Handleless and footless drinking cup in the form of a fox's or greyhound's mask, based on the classical rhyton and introduced about 1770 for sporting prizes and commemorative trophies.
Thistle cups. An exclusively Scottish type, rather like tea cup, with single S-shaped handle and everted lip. Principal decoration is calyx-like arrangement of *appliqué* lobes rising from foot towards waist, and waist is also encircled by fillet. Handle sometimes enhanced with beaded ornament. Precise use obscure, but cups seem to have been made in some numbers in Edinburgh (also Canongate), Glasgow, Aberdeen, and Inverness. A miniature version also occurs. Range in time short: from about 1690 to beginning of eighteenth century.
Two-handled cups. Introduced in the late seventeenth century, developing from porringer form and gradually replacing the earlier standing cup on high stem (*q.v.*). Normally found with cover. Of great variety of size and decoration. Used for 'loving cup' ceremonies in corporate bodies, race prizes, and display generally.
Tumbler cup. Small, plain drinking bowl with rounded base and straight sides. Extent from mid-seventeenth century onwards.
Wager cup. See Jungfrauenbecher.
Windmill wager cups were shaped like model windmills so that when they were inverted the body of the mill acted as the bowl. They were used for wagers on festive occasions, the drinker having to consume the contents before the sails had stopped revolving. (*See also* Jungfrauenbecher.)
Wine cup. Small, individual goblet on high stem, surviving from the late sixteenth to seventeenth centuries. Also known as Grace cup. Very small examples of mid-seventeenth century have no stem but a small, trumpet-shaped foot (*see also* Goblet). A wine cup of tumbler form was popular in New York.
Miscellaneous. Among many other types of cup the following may be mentioned. They were occasionally made in the form of human heads, one, made by Albrecht Biller of Augsburg between 1696 and 1700, being that of a hideous witch. Cups fashioned like peasants carrying barrels, which act as the bowls, are not uncommon. Presentation cups given to distinguished Dutch sailors in the seventeenth century were often enamelled with sea fights. (For other drinking vessels see: Beakers, Brandy bowls, Bratina, Chalices, Charka, Goblets, *Haufenbecher*, Horns, *Jungfrauenbecher*, Mazer, *Prunkgefass*, *Riesenpokal*, Tankards, *Tazza*, and Wine tasters.)

Far right Cutcard work: elaborate example on a cup of 1715, silver-gilt

Left Ostrich egg, mounted in silver by Garrards, 1838

Right Tumbler cup with a band of matted decoration running round it

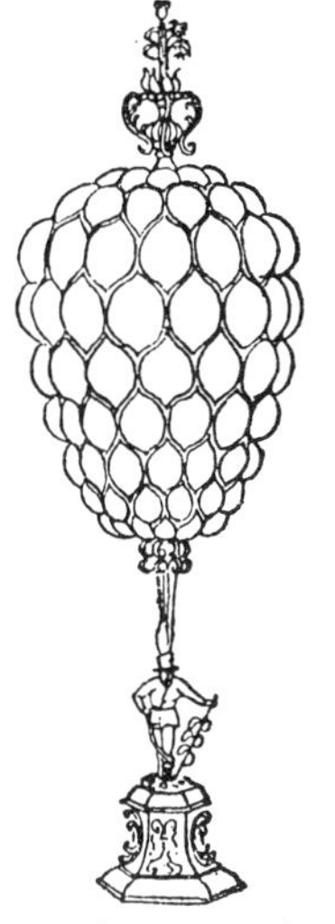

Pineapple cup

Standing cup and cover, 1590

Cutcard work. Flat sheet metal cut into foliage and strap outline and soldered to the main surface to produce relief decoration. Of French origin, introduced in late seventeenth century and later built up in various planes to greater relief.
Date letter. The specific mark of a letter of the alphabet used at the various Assay Offices to distinguish the year of hallmarking. There are no date letters on American silver.
Deacon. In Scotland the chief office bearer of the craft or guild. In Edinburgh the deacon's mark appeared as proof of test among the hallmarks, normally in third place, from the sixteenth century down to the institution of the date stamp in 1681–2, when the assay master's punch replaced the deacon's.
Decanter stand. *See* Wine coaster.
Dessert basket. Oval or circular in form, usually pierced. Met with in sets of various sizes and numbers, the larger often with separate plinth. Introduced in the late eighteenth century. Usually gilt.
Dessert service. Gilt set of plates, dishes and baskets, following the pattern of the contemporary white dinner service. Not common before the late eighteenth century.
Dessert table service. Set of gilt dessert spoons, knives, and forks, either of similar styles to the white table service (*q.v.*), or also found in a number of ornamental vine, foliage, and bacchanalian patterns.
Dinner service. The total assemblage of everything required for the banquet table. Plates, dishes (oval and circular), soup and sauce tureens, entrée dishes, vegetable dishes, and many other items are all found made *en suite* and of the same date.
Dish. Vast dishes, intended for display rather than use, were a speciality of Augsburg in the seventeenth century (of the nineteen gigantic dishes in the Kremlin, fourteen are of Augsburg manufacture). A fine early seventeenth-century Italian example, embossed with the departure of Christopher Columbus, is in the collection of the Marchese Spinola at Genoa. Circular dishes embossed in the centre with flowers or birds, frequently peacocks, were popular in Portugal in the second half of the seventeenth century. A large dish decorated with dolphins by Christopher van Vianen, a member of the famous family of Dutch seventeenth-century silversmiths, is in the Victoria and Albert Museum. In the United States Revere made '4 silver dishes' in 1796 for presentation to the First Church in Boston in the form of the six given in 1764 by Thomas Hancock to the Brattle Street

Church. These in turn are similar to the wholly domestic ones of Winslow's and Coney's make, which have been erroneously called 'alms dishes'. The royal gifts to established churches included a 'receiver' in plate form. 'Issue plates' and 'trencher plates' of silver were recorded in private possession in the 1690s. *See* Entrée, Meat, Second course, Soufflé, Toasted cheese, Vegetable, and Venison Dish.

Dish cross. Spirit-lamp stand with two adjustable arms revolving around the lamp with sliding feet. The lamp sometimes omitted and replaced by a pierced plate for use with separate lamp below. Found from about 1750 to 1850s.

Dish ring. Also called 'Potato ring'. Of Irish origin. Circular dish or bowl stand with straight or incurved sides usually pierced and chased with pastoral or classical motifs. Found from about 1740 onwards, many dating from about 1770. Modern copies should be carefully distinguished.

Dish stand. Importation of 'ex-s with slides and lamps for dish stands' and 'table crosses' with and without lamps were advertised in the second half of the eighteenth century, and a few, also known as dish crosses, with local maker's marks are known.

Dish strainer. *See* Mazarine.

Dolphin. A thumbpiece design, generally on Boston tankards, showing addorsed dolphins with a mask.

Domed. Spheroid form of cover, used on tankards, tea pots, coffee pots beginning in the 1690s.

Double scroll. A sinuous line of S-shape, or composed of reverse curves, employed especially in design of handles.

Doune. Small town on Highland border where making of steel flourished in seventeenth and eighteenth centuries. Pistols were skilfully inlaid with silver, occasionally with gold.

Douter. Scissor-like implement with flat, elliptical 'blades' for extinguishing candles. Not to be confused with snuffers, which have a cutting edge. Douters are comparatively rare and not always recognized as such (*see* Snuffers).

Dram cup. A small, two-handled, shallow bowl, similar to a wine taster, seldom made after the second decade of the eighteenth century.

Draw benches. Used in forming applied mouldings and strap handles.

Dredger. Small, cylindrical pepper pot with side scroll handle of early eighteenth century date. Also called 'Kitchen pepper'.

Dutch silver marks. Dutch miniature silver was struck with the townmark, maker's mark, date and a letter, such as on the three following beakers: Amsterdam, ewer in a shaped shield, 1622; The Hague, wing, 1666; Dordrecht, bunch of grapes, 1653. Of more than two hundred eighteenth-century specimens examined more than ninety per cent bore the townmark of Amsterdam, The Hague, or Leeuwarden: others displayed marks of Utrecht, Haarlem, and Rotterdam.

Silversmiths whose miniature ware has been noted included: *Amsterdam:* sugar bowl by Samuel Strik, 1793; bowls, Lucas Claterbos, 1756 and 1758; set of four table candlesticks, Jan Pondt, 1733; table bell, Hendrik Swiering, 1738; candlestick, Jan Buysen, 1804; tea pot of inverted pear shape, Hendrik Griste, 1776; brazier on three feet, J. P. Dell, 1792; two-handled tray, Roelof Helwig, 1780; pear-shaped coffee pot, H. Nieuwenhuyse, 1762; cruet frame with casters, Reynier Brandt, 1753; oval tray with handles, D. W. Rethmeijer, 1806; caster and mustard pot, W. Warneke, 1771. *The Hague:* cruet frame and casters, Nicholas Radijas, 1764; pear-shaped caster, Cornelis de Haan, 1766; bowl, Reynier de Haan, 1738; vase-shaped casters, G. van der Toorn, 1750; oval tea caddy, J. van de Toorn, 1803; salver, Godert van Ysseldijk, 1753; kettle and stand, F. M. Simons, 1791; pair candlesticks, Jacques Tuiller, 1710. *Leeuwarden:* pair of sauceboats, W. Dominicus, 1767.

Dutch miniature silver imported during the eighteenth century bore the marks of origin, but was also on occasion struck with an English silversmith's mark, showing that Dutch silver was retailed by English makers. Since 1867 all imported plate of sterling or Britannia standard has been struck with a capital F, and from 1904 with an assay-office mark, fineness mark and date letter. The plate laws are strictly enforced in Holland, where there is no legal obligation for the maker's mark to be present.

Dutch toys. These were sold side by side with English productions and for comparable work were slightly less expensive. A collection of Dutch miniature silver might include plain, engraved, or embossed work: pear-shaped coffee pots, money boxes, cups and saucers, sweetmeat baskets, milk cans, braziers, flatirons, frying pans, mortars, mustard pots, chairs, settees, bookcases, toilet mirrors, vases and covers, and many other pieces.

Écuelle, *cover domed and surmounted by finial, 18th century*

Écuelle. A shallow, two-handled, covered dish peculiar to France, where it was a favourite piece of plate in the *Régence* and rococo periods. Late seventeenth-century *écuelles* usually had flat covers with a handle on top, but in the eighteenth century the covers were usually domed and surmounted by finials. A fine silver-gilt example of 1672 is in the Victoria and Albert Museum. Some were provided with a dish, knife, spoon, and fork enclosed in a leather case for travelling. In spite of the strong influence exerted by French silversmiths, *écuelles* were rarely made in other countries, though a few German and Italian (Piedmont) examples are known.

Edgings. *See* Mounts.

Egg and dart. A sixteenth-century border ornament composed of alternating ovolos (*q.v.*) and arrowheads.

Egg and tongue. A similar border ornament of alternating ovolos and pointed mouldings. Usually stamped from a die, but in important pieces may be chased by hand.

Egg frame. Openwork frame holding two and more egg cups with spoons and, occasionally, a salt cellar above. Introduced *c.* 1785.

Embossing. A general term to describe relief work on metal. Strictly applicable only to hammered work (*repoussé*), but extended to cover any technical method resulting in relief.

English plate. A term used by Sheffield platers to

distinguish ware in which the silver was plated on copper from that plated on white alloy such as German silver.

Engraving. Flat line decoration incised on the surface with a cutting tool. The normal method of rendering inscriptions and armorials. Also used at all periods for every variety of ornament. Sometimes combined with 'Flat chasing' (*q.v.*) (*see* Bright-cut engraving).

It was customary for Sheffield plate to be engraved with the coat-of-arms or crest of its owner the more nearly to complete its semblance to silver plate. From about 1815 tea and coffee services, kettles, trays and waiters, and other articles of the tea equipage might be engraved all over with complicated patterns surrounding the heraldic device. To prevent the copper from showing when the silver was cut with a graving tool the whole surface was coated more thickly than usual.

When only coats-of-arms and the like were to be engraved it was at first customary to cut a suitable area of metal clean out of the article and insert a thickly silvered section of metal. The scarcely perceptible joint was masked by wavy borders, but examination of the reverse of a coat-of-arms will show if insertion has been effected.

This method was discarded between 1810 and 1815 in favour of 'sweating on' or 'rubbing in' a circle or shield of four-gauge pure silver of suitable size. The plate to receive the extra silver was heated over a clear charcoal fire, then placed in position and rubbed vigorously with a steel tool until it adhered to the plated copper. After burnishing it was impossible to detect the join except by warming the piece, when a difference in the colour of the silver is noted, the sweated-on piece then showing lighter in hue than the surrounding metal. A small dot was always made in the centre of such shields so that the engraver was sure of his mark.

Entrée dish. A covered dish, early examples usually circular or polygonal. Later chiefly of oblong form or occasionally oval. The covers may have detachable handles, enabling their use as separate dishes. Later examples have silver, or more commonly, plated heater stands *en suite.*

Épergne. Table centrepiece of elaborate design incorporating numerous dishes for fruit, pickles, or sweetmeats. Early examples also fitted with candle branches, casters, and other accessories. Rococo models festooned with flowers, swags, pierced and boat-shaped forms, Chinese pagodas, and Classical temples are all recognized examples (*see also* Centrepiece and Dessert basket).

Etching. Surface decoration bitten-in with acid as in the print process of the same name. Rare in English silver, but occasionally found in the sixteenth century.

Étui. Small case usually of tapering oval form fitted with scissors, bodkin, snuff spoon, etc., for ladies' use. Silver examples chiefly found first half of eighteenth century and in the mid-nineteenth century.

Ewers. Large jugs to carry water for the ablutions at meal times were essential items of plate in the later Middle Ages and the sixteenth century; they were often made of silver and intricately wrought. The most popular type was vase shaped with a grotesque handle, and German examples frequently had disproportionately narrow necks. A fine German ewer of 1559 in the British Museum has a low relief of the Rape of Helen on its body and a handle fashioned like a satyr leaning backwards. They were usually matched with basins, many of which have since disappeared. Spanish ewers of the late sixteenth and early seventeenth centuries tended to be rather small and to stand on short feet. Like cups and basins, they were frequently made in rock crystal or hard stone. Later French and Spanish examples were helmet shaped, but their popularity declined with the introduction of the fork and the change in eating habits.

Ewer with disproportionately narrow neck, German, 16th century

Extinguisher. Conical 'fool's cap' implement with scroll handle usually accompanying chamber-candlestick. To be distinguished from snuffer (*q.v.*).

Feather edge. Decoration of edge of spoon handle with chased, slanting lines.

Filigree work *(filigrana).* Genoa was the most renowned centre for the production of filigree work in eighteenth century Italy. A large variety of such objects were produced here, from tall Chinese-shaped vases to tiny toys and ornaments.

Finial. The small cast ornament at the top of a cover; sometimes acorn-shaped in early eighteenth century; flame-shaped in rococo period, urn-shaped in classic period. Pineapple used also in rococo period, and pinecone beginning *c.* 1782.

Firedog. *See* Andiron.

Fireplace furniture. In English miniature silver dates from the late seventeenth century, when fireplace sets composed of fire basket and fireback, firedogs, fender, tongs, shovel, and poker were made. A number of these by Middleton still remain, in the Westbrooke Baby House and various museums. A collection of eighteenth-century specimens displays chronologically these changes of form and dimensions.

Fish slice. Introduced in mid-eighteenth century. Early examples finely pierced and engraved in fish and floral patterns. Later and soberer models conform to standard table service patterns and have little decoration. Also found with ivory or wood handles. Accompanying fish fork made from *c.*1800.

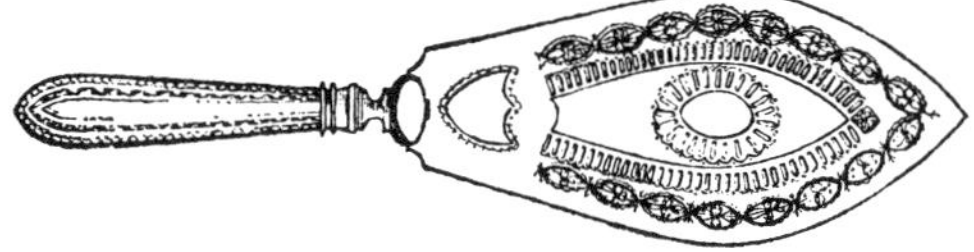

Flagon, 1710

Flagon. Large vessel for serving wine or other liquors. Pear-shaped and cylindrical bodies occur contemporaneously at most periods and are always closely related in form and decoration to tankards. Except for ecclesiastical use, the flagon is rare after the mid-eighteenth century. Fantastic shapes were sometimes used; in about 1610 Melchior Gelb of Augsburg made one in the form of a vine-covered head of Silenus.

Flat chasing. Surface decoration in low relief produced by hammering with small blunt tools. Popular in the early eighteenth century combined with engraving for borders to salvers and other pieces. Widely used in the United States, 1750–85.

Flute. A concave channel originating in classical columns, used either as detached decorative element or in close repeated formation as a border or body ornament. Found extensively on bodies of cups, tankards, and other vessels in late seventeenth century alternating with gadroons (*q.v.*) to form corrugated surface.

Flat chasing in a design of bullrushes, *c.* 1845

Forks. In the later Middle Ages small forks were made in most countries, but they do not appear to have been used for eating meat; it is significant that they were frequently made to match spoons, never knives. Some late fifteenth-century examples are of great delicacy, like that of Flemish workmanship with a rock-crystal handle in the Victoria and Albert Museum. Folding forks were frequently made in conjunction with spoons (*q.v.*). The use of forks for eating meat seems to have originated in Italy in the sixteenth century, and to have spread through the rest of Europe in the course of the next hundred years. A fine sixteenth-century set, consisting of a fork, knife and spoon, each with a handle in the form of a human figure attributed to Antonio Gentili, is in the Metropolitan Museum, New York. The earliest forks were two-pronged, the three-pronged type being introduced in the early eighteenth century. In the eighteenth century the handle of forks, as of spoons and knives, varied slightly with the changes in taste. No English silver forks have survived before the early seventeenth century. Early examples two-pronged, followed by three-pronged form till about 1750 and, occasionally, later. After this four prongs are standard. Stems follow spoon models throughout. Sets of twelve or more survive from Charles II onwards, but are very rare before the eighteenth century.

Forks are extremely rare in American silver, but mentioned in old inventories.

Fountains. Made to stand in the centre of a table and dispense scented water or wine in the course of a meal, enjoyed some popularity in the richest households of the sixteenth century; but few have survived. In the British Museum there is a German example, dating from about 1580, which is formed out of a Seychelle nut with silver-gilt mounts.

Frames (*cornici*). The frames of small pictures were occasionally made wholly or partly of silver in the seventeenth and eighteenth centuries. More familiar are the large *cartagloria* frames designed to stand on altars and hold cards inscribed with prayers. They are often richly embossed with rococo scroll work. Many examples in private collections have been transformed into looking glasses.

Freedom box. Small circular or oblong box, usually gilt, when not gold, presented with script conferring the freedom of a town. Particularly popular in Ireland late eighteenth to early nineteenth centuries. In Scotland, on rare occasions at least, a much larger, silver box seems to have been made to contain the parchment.

Frosting. A rough or mat white surface produced by acid fuming or scratch brushing. Not found before the early nineteenth century, principally used on ornamental and figure work on centrepieces.

Furniture. Silver furniture in the form of sheet metal overlaid on wood survives from the Restoration period, and may have been made earlier. Examples are rare and confined to the Royal Collection and one or two famous houses: Ham or Knole. George Middleton made miniature chairs and day beds of the Charles II type during the 1680s, the 'woodwork' in flat plate silhouettes and chased to resemble turned uprights and stretchers, the seat and back panel pierced to look like woven cane. Gate-leg tables were made by Isaac Malyn and other early eighteenth-century toy makers. Tripod tables by Augustine Courtauld are known with stem and feet cast, the rim of the round top chased to resemble a piecrust edge. Later chairs in the style of Hepplewhite have cast legs and backs.

Gadroon (French: *godron*). A border ornament either hammered or cast composed of radiating lobes of curved or straight form. Principally used on rims and feet of cups and other vessels or to borders of plates and dishes from late seventeenth century onwards.

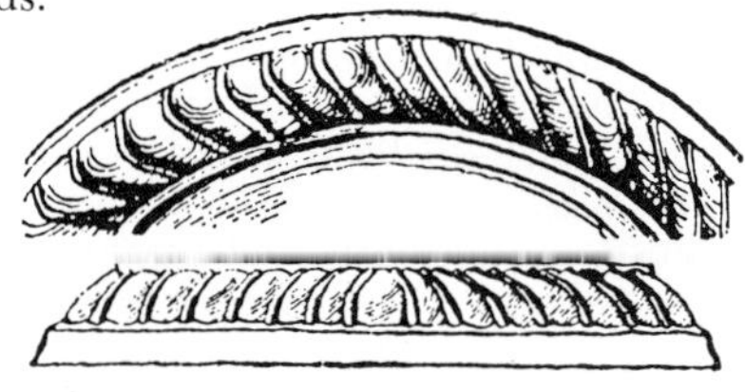

Geometric. Pierced handle of early eighteenth-century porringer; in Boston and Philadelphia, crescent, heart, and tulip; in New York, cross, heart, and diamond.

German silver. Introduced to the plating trade by Samuel Roberts, who was granted a patent in 1830 by which 'a layer of German silver or other white or light-coloured metal was introduced between the silver and copper'. A coating of silver could thus be applied with the knowledge that if it were thin the defect would be far less perceptible than if applied direct to the copper. This method was superseded in 1836 by Anthony Merry's patent by which the copper was omitted, plating the silver direct to a foundation metal of German silver. Stronger and more durable than copper, German silver consisted of nickel, copper; and zinc in varying proportions. Workers in this medium described themselves as 'platers on white metal'.

Gilding. *See* Silver gilt.

Goblets. Silver goblets, closely imitating German glasses with heavy bases and bulbous tops, were popular in Scandinavia in the late sixteenth and early seventeenth centuries. Two Swedish examples in the British Museum have bosses typical of glass decoration. Imitations of glass in silver do not appear to

Left *Gadrooning: salver border, 1694* (top), *and candlestick base, 1762*

Bail handle

Goblet with boss typical of glass decoration, Swedish, late 16th- early 17th century. British Museum

have been usual after the middle of the seventeenth century.

Goldwork. Rare, but appears in New York. Garvan Collection at Yale has eight gold teaspoons and strainer by Soumain, child's spoon with bells by van der Spiegel, rattle by Fueter, necklace by Van Dyck, freedom box by Samuel Johnson; all of New York.

Golf clubs. Practice of reproducing full-sized golf clubs in silver, as trophies, appears to date from about the middle of the eighteenth century. Several of such clubs are still preserved, notably those of the Edinburgh Burgess Golfing Society and of the Royal and Ancient Club at St Andrews. Captains or tournament winners attached silver balls to the shafts, engraved with name. Clubs and balls were quite well modelled, even to reproduction of spiral grip; but unfortunately hallmarks and makers' punches have not been added, so that nothing is known of where they were made.

Granulated band. A form of decoration, generally on beakers, derived from Scandinavian and German work.

Graver. Tool used to engrave silver with initials, coats-of-arms, etc., or to sharpen the chased ornament.

Guilloche. A border moulding composed of interlaced ribbon enclosing foliage rosettes, chiefly used early eighteenth century. Simpler forms occur in sixteenth century.

Hallmark. Strictly speaking, the distinguishing mark of the Hall or Assay Office at which the piece so marked is assayed, e.g. leopard's head for London, crown for Sheffield, etc. Used generally in the plural to denote the whole group of marks employed, viz. Hall, maker's, standard, date letter, and, between 1784 and 1890, the monarch's head duty mark.

There are no hallmarks on American silver. In 1918 Maryland established an Assay Office at Baltimore, but other Assay Offices were non-existent, although in Pennsylvania, beginning in 1753, many attempts were made to have the Assembly enact legislation (*see* Pseudo hallmarks).

Hammermen, Incorporations of. These were the first craft guilds to which the goldsmiths in Scotland belonged. They were influential bodies, which looked after the interests of all metalworkers, among them blacksmiths, cutlers, pewterers, and armourers. Like the great guilds elsewhere, they were highly organized, with strict control over the conduct of their members and apprentices. Religion played an important part in their activities, and they had their own altars or chapels in the Middle Ages, under the patronage of St Eloi. Strict religious control continued after the Reformation.

Hammers. Coney's inventory in 1722 contained '112 Hammers for Raising, Pibling, Swolling, Hollowing, Creasing, Planishing &c.' as well as several 'Two-hand hammers' to give an idea of the painstaking care in handwrought silver.

Hanap. The medieval name for 'standing cup' (*q.v.*).

Handles, Bail. A half-hoop or semicircle hinged on a pair of pivots or looped ears on hollow ware, such as a basket or cream pail.

Hash dish. Circular dish with straight sides, close-fitting cover, and loop or drop-ring handles. Similar to and probably used also as vegetable dish. Often found with open-frame stand and spirit lamp.

Haufenbecher. Literally a piling cup. Alternatively called a *Setzbecher.* Beakers that could be fitted into one another, in pairs and in sets of six or twelve, popularized by the designs of Virgil Solis, were made in Germany in the late sixteenth century, but appear to have gone out of fashion before 1650. Each beaker has a band of moulded decoration around its rim, like a modern picnic cup. They were much used for hunting parties.

Hinges, Book. Found on lids of coffee pots, jugs, and so on. They have a round back resembling a book spine, and the pinjoints, where the base metal is left bare, are concealed beneath slightly ornamental silver caps.

Holy-water bucket. The receptacle for the holy water sprinkled in the *asperges* at the beginning of the Mass. Early examples are normally straight-sided, polygonal or cylindrical, and occasionally waisted; the *bombé*-vase shape came into fashion in the seventeenth century. Handles were occasionally terminated with dragon heads. A good Spanish example of about 1500 is in the Victoria and Albert Museum.

Holy-water stoups (*acquasantiere*). These were made for the house as well as the church. Some are in the form of a large framed relief of the Madonna and Child or other sacred subject, with a small shell-shaped container.

Honey pot. Jar formed as skep beehive with detachable cover and circular dish stand. Made by Paul Storr and others from about 1795 into the nineteenth century.

Hooped cans. The shape is copied from a wooden type, made on the principle of a barrel and with a broad, bulbous body, a narrow cylindrical neck, a thin, straight spout, and a lid. The wooden can was probably in its turn a copy of a metal form. In wood it can be traced back to the seventeenth century. An early eighteenth-century example, with silver mounts, is in the Kunstindustrimuseum in Oslo, but the plain wooden types must at that time have been used mainly in the country. Silver copies are known from Copenhagen as well as from Norway. Both the Danish and the Norwegian examples have a moulded lion on a halberd as handle to the lid. The

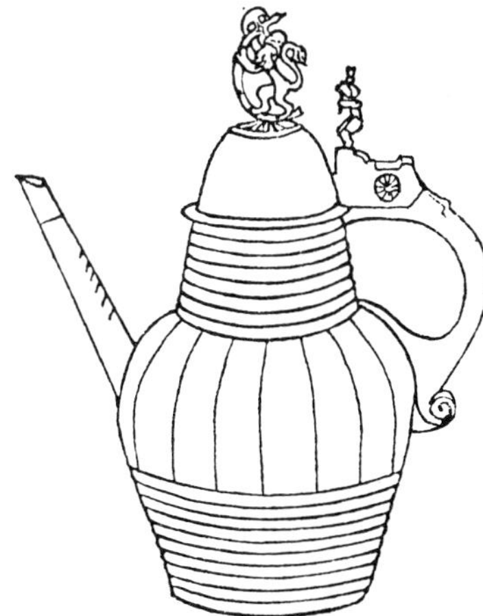

presence of this symbol from the Norwegian coat-of-arms seems to indicate that the type was meant to be romantically 'Norwegian'. The shape was also copied in Danish pewter and faïence and in Norwegian pewter, faïence, and glass. The silver examples are gilt or partly gilt, and sometimes they were made in pairs and accompanied by beakers, shaped like small barrels. They are comparatively rare.

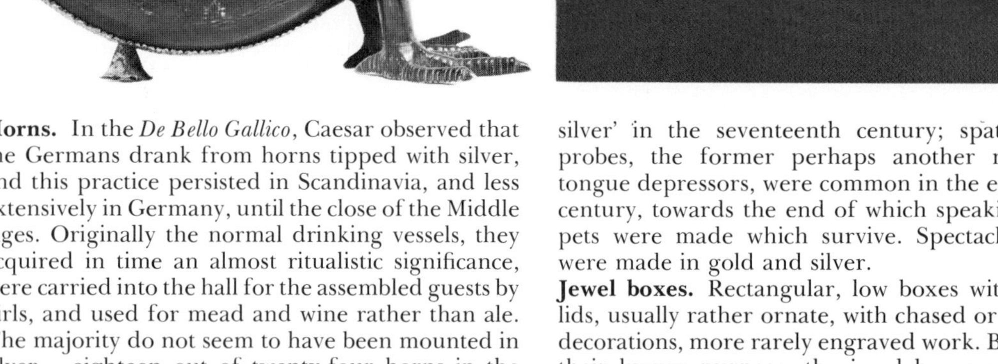

Horns. In the *De Bello Gallico*, Caesar observed that the Germans drank from horns tipped with silver, and this practice persisted in Scandinavia, and less extensively in Germany, until the close of the Middle Ages. Originally the normal drinking vessels, they acquired in time an almost ritualistic significance, were carried into the hall for the assembled guests by girls, and used for mead and wine rather than ale. The majority do not seem to have been mounted in silver – eighteen out of twenty-four horns in the Copenhagen Museum have mounts in copper-gilt. Normally the mounts are simple, but a Norwegian example of 1300 (in the Copenhagen Museum) is decorated with Gothic architectural features, and a Danish one in the British Museum has been made to resemble a bird, mounted on claw feet, the point of the horn fashioned into a tail.

Hot-milk jug. Small pear-shaped or polygonal jug and cover similar in form and decoration to the larger contemporary coffee or chocolate pot but with beak spout. Also found with egg-shaped body on three feet.

Ice pail. *See* Wine cooler.

Incense boat. The vessel in which the incense is carried before it is placed in the censer to burn. Normally it is a fairly simple boat-shaped vessel, and it was occasionally made to match a censer. Many were of base metals or of other materials mounted in silver; a crystal incense boat mounted in silver gilt is in the Victoria and Albert Museum.

In Italy the Gothic tradition of making these vessels in the form of model ships standing on baluster stems survived until the late seventeenth century. The form of the boat was then swallowed up in baroque scrollwork. In the late eighteenth century a simpler outline became popular.

Inkstand. Early name standish. A few examples have survived from pre-1650, but not many recorded before 1680. 'Treasury' type an oblong casket with two centrally hinged lids. Tray form in prevailing style of period persists throughout eighteenth century. Fittings include inkpot, sand and/or pounce box, bell, and taperstick in varying combinations. Glass bottles appear about 1765, together with pierced gallery sides. About 1790 small globe-shaped form introduced. Mahogany desk models with silver tops appear from 1800 onwards.

Instruments for surgery. Made by silversmiths for the wealthy practitioners who could afford this most hygienic material. 'Rasors and Scissors tipt with silver' in the seventeenth century; spatulas and probes, the former perhaps another name for tongue depressors, were common in the eighteenth century, towards the end of which speaking trumpets were made which survive. Spectacle frames were made in gold and silver.

Jewel boxes. Rectangular, low boxes with hinged lids, usually rather ornate, with chased or moulded decorations, more rarely engraved work. Because of their luxury purpose, the jewel boxes are always important pieces, richly ornamented and prettily finished. They came into use in Norway during the early eighteenth century, and the majority of the existing examples are in an elegant rococo style. It has been suggested that the moulded parts may have been imported.

Jewelry. Beads, bracelets, buttons for shirts and cuffs, necklaces, and rings are the most frequently found. In Scotland simple and somewhat crude silver brooches were made in large quantities in the Middle Ages. Usually round or octagonal, with swinging pin. Commonly they have talismanic inscriptions, hailing Christ or the Virgin Mary. Niello decoration sometimes introduced. There is a small group of elaborate brooches mounted with charm stones, which belongs to the sixteenth century: family heirlooms, and it is unlikely any more will turn up to tempt collectors. Field in which collectors may still hope to find a few good things is that of seventeenth- and eighteenth-century Highland brooches. Larger, usually of brass. Smaller silver brooches, which may have been worn by women, are much more rare. Decoration rather crude, chevrons or zigzags, occasionally plant or zoomorphic forms, deteriorating in interest with advance of eighteenth century. The silver brooches all seem to be betrothal tokens, as they carry two sets of initials scratched on. Fairly valuable. Type of brooch most easily acquired is Luckenbooth, heart- or double-heart-shaped little ornament, sometimes set with garnets, related to Scandinavian type. These are also betrothal pieces. Made down to nineteenth century as far north as Inverness. (*See also* 'Mary' brooches.)

Jug. Large jugs, probably used for numerous purposes and variously called beer, wine, claret jugs, or ewers, occur from the early eighteenth century onwards. Usually with pear-shaped bodies plain or chased, circular feet, and finely moulded scroll handles (*see also* Cream, Hot-milk, and Tigerware jugs).

Jungfrauenbecher

Above left Drinking-horn, mounted in copper-gilt on claw feet, Danish, 15th century. British Museum

Above Inkstand, maker's mark indistinguishable, 1759–60. The fretwork is similar to that used on Chinese wallpaper. Victoria & Albert Museum

Two small milk or cream jugs: *left* by Mackay, Cunningham & Co., Edinburgh, 1879, silver-gilt; *right* by J. B. Hennell, London, 1877, cast and chased silver, made in the Egyptian manner

Jungfrauenbecher. A wager cup in the form of a girl with a wide-spreading skirt holding a bowl above her head. The bowl is pivoted so that when the figure is inverted the skirt forms an upper cup and the bowl a lower one. Such vessels were used specially at wedding feasts, when the groom was expected to drink the contents of the larger cup without spilling any of the contents of the smaller, which he passed to his bride. They first appeared in Germany in about 1575, and their fashion continued throughout the seventeenth century, when many were made at Nuremburg. A simpler form, apparently popular in Holland, replaced the head and shoulders of the girl with a mesh ball, which occasionally contained a die.

Kettles and urns. The earliest vessels made for heating water at the tea table are the kettles with a handle and a spout, fitted over a small spirit lamp. A remarkably early example dates from *c.* 1700 and appears strongly influenced by the English Queen Anne style. Some very fine kettles of the same basic shape have twisted ribs in mature rococo. Another type from the same period (about the middle of the eighteenth century) stands on three tall feet and has a pear-shaped body with twisted ribs and a tap. With neoclassicism real urns are introduced. They stand firmly on a base and have internal heating and a tap. Some examples are in the rich and exuberant Louis XVI style.

Keyhole. The name given to the pierced handle of a porringer which has a central pierced design similar to a keyhole, surrounded by interlacing scrolls; introduced first half of eighteenth century and continued in more delicate form to about 1810.

Knife. Silver-handled knives occur at all periods from late seventeenth century onwards, and single rare specimens from earlier dates. Earliest form found in sets has tapering round or polygonal handle about 1690, followed by the pistol handle, its form becoming more decorated in mid-eighteenth century. Later handles of thin stamped sheet metal filled with resin, in many designs, finally about 1800, being made *en suite* with main table service. In Italy knives of the Renaissance period often had silver handles cast in the shape of human figures.

Knife rests. Were of two types and sold by the dozen: (*a*) cross ends joined from their centres by a short rod: in 1797, of Sheffield plate, priced 20*s* a dozen and with ball centres 24*s* a dozen; (*b*) solid or pierced triangular ends joined from each angle by short rods.

Knope. Word used in medieval period to denote finials to cups or spoons. Modern use refers to flattened spherical or polygonal bulbs at centres of stems in Communion cups and candlesticks.

Knurling. Show ridges or bead tooled on borders and handles from early in the eighteenth century.

Kovsch. A boat-shaped vessel with a single handle used for ladling out drinks, such as *kvass* and beer. It is peculiar to Russia, where its popularity lasted until the middle of the eighteenth century. There is a silver example in the Victoria and Albert Museum, and a rare gold one was in the Green Vaults at Dresden.

Ladle, cream. Small ladle with circular bowl and curved handle, similar to sugar sifter and found associated with the latter in sets of sugar and cream vases and baskets.

Ladle, punch. Long-handled ladle for serving punch into glasses. Early examples have oval bowls and tapering silver handles. Eighteenth-century handles usually of horn or whalebone, the bowls sometimes inset with or beaten out of a silver coin. Also known as 'Toddy ladle'. The first had hollow handles of silver, followed by horn handle. Bowls might be double-lipped from 1725.

Ladle, sauce. Basic form has deep, circular bowl and curved stem. In mid-eighteenth century decorative forms with shell bowls and foliage or bird's-head handles occur. Later examples match table service patterns.

Ladle, soup. Similar in form to sauce ladles, but with long stem. Early examples have hooked ends, sometimes formed as eagle's head, etc.; later models match table services.

Lamps. Were occasionally made in silver, conforming in design with those made in glass or other materials. A fantastic Genoese example of the eighteenth century, shaped like a pagoda, is in the collection of Dott. F. Fassio at Genoa.

Lanterns (*lanterne*). Large lanterns, for use on ceremonial occasions, were sometimes made partly or (very rarely) wholly of silver. An outstandingly fine example, apparently made for use at the celebration of the Farnese–Spanish marriage of 1714, is in the Costantino Nigro Collection, Genoa.

Larding pine. A pointed instrument, angular in section, seemingly dating from the late eighteenth century.

Lemon squeezer. A hinged instrument with cup-like depressions to contain the fruit, leverage being

supplied by wood handles. Early nineteenth century.
Limmel. The early form of *lemail*, or scrapings or filings of metal.
Lion passant. The lion walking with dexter paw raised appears in relief on seventeenth-century tankard handles by New York makers. This is not an English style and it is likely that it comes from a Continental source.
Luckenbooths. Wooden booths once situated in the High Street of Edinburgh, near St Giles's Church. Many of city's goldsmiths had shops here, though booths were of small size. Heart brooches associated with name, since no doubt sold here.
Mace. Civic, university, or state emblem of authority derived from medieval war weapon. Usually surmounted by royal arms and crown. Examples date from fifteenth century onwards.
Maker's mark. The distinguishing mark of the individual goldsmith, device or initials struck on every piece of plate from his workshop. First enforced in London in 1363. In the United States marks were not required, but they were usually used. The early marks are composed of the first letters of the maker's given name and surname, generally in a shaped shield, and frequently with some device, such as a fleur-de-lis. In the eighteenth century the full name or the surname and initial were used.

At least fifty London silversmiths' marks have been noted on miniature silver made between 1665 and 1739. These include: *RD* crowned, 1665; *FC* 1669; *G* crowned, 1670; *EM* in monogram, 1677; *CK* under a mitre, 1686; *WP* with a mullet below, 1689; and *IC* over a star, 1691. Later were Edward Jones, 1696; Jonathan Bradley, 1696; Matthew Maden, 1697; John Cole, 1697; William Matthew, 1698; Nathaniel Green, 1698; Matthew Pickering, 1703; Joseph Smith, 1707; Jacob Margas, 1708; James Godwin, 1710; George Smart, 1715; James Morson, 1720; Edward Coven, 1724; John le Sage, 1725.
'Mary' brooches. A double-M brooch usually surmounted by a crown. Scottish betrothal type, early nineteenth century, or later. Thought vainly by many possessors to have been gifts from Mary Queen of Scots to her Four Maries.
Masking spoon. A slender Scottish spoon intended for stirring the tea when 'masking' (Scots for 'infusing').
Matting. A dull, roughened surface produced by repeated punching with a burred tool. Much used in mid-seventeenth century on tankard and cup bodies.
Mazarine. Pierced, flat straining plate for use with fish dishes, supposedly named after Cardinal Mazarin.
Mazer bowls. Made of spotted maple wood and mounted in silver, silver-gilt, or base metals, appear to have originated in Germany, and were popular throughout northern Europe in the later Middle Ages. Double mazers in the form of a large one with a single handle surmounted by a smaller were occasionally made, and this pattern was sometimes copied for double cups. Handles were often richly fashioned; a double mazer in the Wallace Collection has a handle shaped like a Gothic chapel. Large standing examples on high feet found in Scotland and a few in England. Rare after the sixteenth century.
Meat dish. Oval in form. Survivals rare before eighteenth century. Early examples have moulded rims. After 1730 the rims are shaped and gadrooned. From about 1775 beaded rims occur and later shaped mouldings or reed-and-tie patterns. Found in all sizes from about 10 to 30 inches (25.4–76.2 cm) long.
Meat plate. Also called dinner plate. Made in large sets throughout the eighteenth and early nineteenth centuries. Examples of the seventeenth century occur, but practically only as single specimens. Borders conform to those of meat dishes.
Midband. A moulded band slightly below centre of a tankard to strengthen as well as ornament; introduced in late sixteenth century. Also used on large two-handled covered cups.
Milk potts of silver seem to have been the same as cream jugs.
Mirror. *See* Toilet service.
Monstrance (occasionally called an **Ostensory**). The vessel in which the Host is displayed or, less fre-

Double mazer

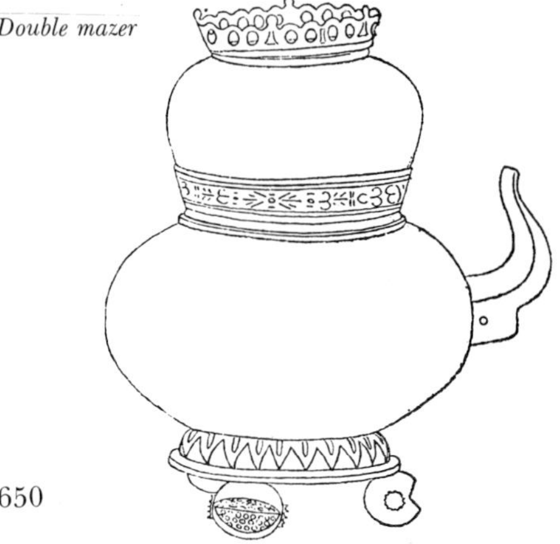

The Belem Monstrance, gold and enamel, with figures of the Apostles kneeling in adoration of the Sacrament, Portuguese, *c.* 1506. Museu Nacional de Arte Antigua, Lisbon quently, in which a relic is shown. They vary in size according to whether they were intended primarily to be placed on an altar or carried in procession. Frequently enriched with enamelling and precious stones, they are among the most magnificent pieces of church plate. Gothic monstrances tended to be of architectural design with a cylindrical container for the Host in the centre. The famous Portuguese Belem monstrance, of the early sixteenth century, shows little figures of the Apostles kneeling in adoration of the Sacrament. In many countries the Gothic pattern persisted until the end of the sixteenth century, when it was superseded by a baroque pattern in which the Host is placed in a cylinder flanked by angels or framed by a flaming sun, the rays of which were often decorated with jewels. A Spanish chalice of about 1600 (in the Victoria and Albert Museum) has a detachable monstrance as a cover; both parts being lavishly decorated with Renaissance motifs. A fine Flemish example of 1670, by Joannes Moermans, is in the Church of Notre Dame at Rupelmonde. One of the most beautiful was designed in about 1740 by the great Bavarian architect, Aegid Asam, for the little Church of St Johannes Nepomuk, which he and his brother built in Munich. A diamond-set monstrance made by Johann Baptist Känischbauer von Hohenreid and Mathias Stegner, in 1699, was in the Church of St Loretto at Prague.

Monteith. Wine-glass cooler with indented rim. Introduced in early 1680s. The rim, at first part of the body, made detachable about 1690. The name said to be derived from that of a Scottish adventurer with notched cloak, although it is very rare indeed in Scotland. Edinburgh example of 1719 belongs to Royal Company of Archers, and is hung with gold archery medals.

Monteith by Philip Brush, English, 1707

Morse. A clasp for fastening a cope, occasionally made of gold or silver and decorated with jewels. The most famous was that made by Benvenuto Cellini for Pope Clement VII.

Moulding. Cast or hammered border or body girdle composed of various arrangements of convex and concave members based on architectural models. Also applied to castings from the mould.

Mounts and edging. A basic problem facing the early Sheffield platers was that of concealing the dark reddish streak of copper visible when the silvered plate was sheared. This problem was never satisfactorily solved by Bolsover, and his ranges of productions were drastically limited.

(a) *Single-lapped edge* (1758–1780s). Joseph Hancock introduced the single-lapped edge in 1758. This required a thicker coating of silver to be applied to the copper than had been customary. The edges of the plated copper were cut with a blunt tool so manipulated that the layer of silver was extended sufficiently beyond the edge of the silvered copper to lap over and effectively conceal the raw edge.

(b) *Double-lapped copper mount* (1768–early nineteenth century). This followed as a direct result of George Whateley's patent of 1678, by which he 'plated silver upon mettal wire and drew the same into small gauge wires'. A thick cylindrical ingot of copper-brass alloy was plated with rolled silver and passed through a series of holes in a drawplate until reduced to the required gauge: the thicknesses of the copper and silver remained in their original proportions. This wire was then passed between polished steel pressure rollers, thus forming a thin, flat ribbon of plated metal silvered on both surfaces and the edges. This was the immediate forerunner of plating on both sides of the sheet.

This paper-thin ribbon was soldered to the silvered edge of the plate, so that it protruded sufficiently over the edge to permit it to lap over the raw edge and be flat against the underside. So skilfully was lapping carried out that upon the plated surface it was difficult to detect the joins.

(c) *Silver-lapped mount* (1775–1815). This followed the introduction of double-plated copper in the early 1770s. A narrow ribbon of paper-thin silver, which might measure as little as one-sixteenth of an inch (1.5 mm) wide, was passed through a small round hole in a drawplate, thus making a fine-bore tube. The seam was then opened throughout its length to the same width as the gauge of the plate upon which it was to be mounted. This was accomplished by fixing into a vice a steel plate of the same gauge as the plated copper. The seam of the tube was inserted into this and opened by drawing the silver along. The resulting U-shaped silver wire was then fitted to the plated edge and soldered into position on both surfaces. These were vigorously burnished until the joins were invisible.

(d) *Solid-silver mounts* (*c.* 1780–*c.* 1830). These ornaments for fine Sheffield plate were cast and hand-chased by silversmiths. They were hard-soldered into position. These hand-chased mounts are sometimes difficult to distinguish from blurred stamped work finished by chasing.

(e) *Drawn-silver wire mounts* (1785–*c.* 1820). Valentine Rawle in 1785 patented a method by which the joints of articles made from Sheffield plate could be strengthened 'by covering the mitres, angles and joints with drawn silver wire, the invention being likewise applicable to wares made round and oval'. Silver wires were drawn in a range of decorative cross-sections – flat, half-round hollow U, sharp L, angles, and curves. These were filled with a mixture of lead and tin, and could easily be shaped by the hand to fit the piece they decorated. Before such mounts were applied to edges silver wire measuring one thirty-second of an inch (0.75 mm) in thickness was soldered beneath the rim. Rawle licensed his patent to other platers.

(f) *Silver stamped mounts* (from early 1790s). These

first appeared on Sheffield plate during the early 1790s, following the introduction of a hard steel capable of making profitable runs on the press when cut in deep, sharp relief. As in drawn-silver wire mounts, the silver was either pure metal or alloyed with brass, but better than sterling. Sterling silver produced finer work both as to colour and durability, but unfortunately wear on the tools was much harder, considerably reducing their useful life. Pure silver mounts were used on common ware as it could be rolled much thinner for stamping without danger of splitting in the tools.

The first mounts to be stamped in silver included bead, thread, and a variety of gadroon patterns. Early in the nineteenth century technical improvements permitted the stamping of mounts composed of festoon and bead, leaf and scroll, laurel leaf, egg and dart, scallop shell and scroll, and others. The under seam was made invisible by vigorous burnishing.

Wide, deeply struck mounts in elaborate rococo designs seldom date earlier than about 1815. Earlier mounts had been struck from silver so thick that the sections could be hard- or silver-soldered into position after filling back hollows with soft solder. From about 1815 thinner silver and soft solder were used.

These mounts were applied to edges in which the copper was already concealed by a silver-lapped mount. The division between the two mounts is unmistakable.

(g) *Improved silver stamped mounts* (from 1824). This method of applying elaborate rococo mounts to Sheffield plate in such a way that the junction between body and mount was rendered invisible, was patented in 1824 by Samuel Roberts of Sheffield, who licensed the process to other platers of repute. After shaping the edge of the ware to be ornamented to follow the indentations of the mounting, drawn silver wire was hard-soldered over the bare copper edge. This was flattened with a hammer until it extended a little beyond the ornamental silver edge. The projecting part of the soldered silver edge was then filed off. Burnishing made the join invisible, even to the inquiring fingernail.

Muffineer. Name for caster (*q.v.*) with low, slightly domed cover. The derivation indicates their use for sprinkling cinnamon on muffins. In the United States a tall caster with high pierced dome, for sugar and cinnamon, a quite different use of the term from the English. Caster is the more common term for all types and sizes in American silver.

Mustard pot, 1796

Mug. Small-handled drinking vessel conforming mainly to tankard shape. A late seventeenth-century neck similar to pottery of the period. Cylindrical forms follow, to be superseded in mid-eighteenth century by bellied bodies and later by hooped barrel forms. Shaped forms return in nineteenth century.

Mustard pot. Mustard taken dry and mixed on the plate was contained in casters with unpierced covers until well into the eighteenth century. A few vase-shaped pots have survived from time of Queen Anne. After about 1760 pierced or plain cylindrical forms appear, to be followed by oval and later spherical bodies. Glass liners, usually blue, are commonly used.

Nef. A vessel shaped like a ship and used in the later Middle Ages for the lord's napkin, knife, and spoon. In 1392 a nef on wheels was recorded in the papal collection. In the sixteenth century ornaments, jugs, and cups were made in the same form, notably in Germany and Switzerland. Many were very elaborate and accurate models, richly enamelled and peopled with little figures of sailors. A Swiss example is in the British Museum, and a wheeled nef, made at Nuremberg in about 1620 and probably intended as a jug, is in the Rothschild Collection on show at the Victoria and Albert Museum. In the eighteenth and nineteenth centuries they were adapted for use in England as wine servers and bottle coasters.

Wheeled nef, silver-gilt salt, German, 16th century

Niello. A black composition composed of silver, copper, lead, and sulphur frequently employed to fill in engraved lines on surface of silver brooches from the Middle Ages to the nineteenth century.

Night light. A square, oval, or circular tray having a central cylindrical candle socket enclosed within a gallery pierced with a double circuit of crosses towards the lower edge. This was fitted with a glass chimney. By burning a fine wax night light, no snuffing was required. An extinguisher was hooked to the handle, a rod extending from its apex enabled it to be inserted down the chimney without lifting it off.

Night light

Nutmeg grater. Found from the late seventeenth century onwards. Formed as circular, oval, spherical, or cylindrical boxes fitted with a steel grater under the cover or down the side, or in hanging form with curved grater at front.

Mug, silver, with banding and incised *chinoiserie* decoration, London 1685

Oar. Civic emblem of mayoral authority in ports over local waters. Admiralty examples also survive.
Oil and vinegar bottle stands. These are usually in the form of small salvers with containers for the bottles and a tall handle to which the stoppers are attached by chains. In Italy mid-eighteenth-century examples are often a riot of rococo curves, but in the neoclassical period a severer type with a central column crowned by an urn came into favour.
Onslow pattern. Design for flatware copied from English design in which the handle is shaped as an Ionic volute.
Ostensory. *See* Monstrance.
Ovolo. A small oval convex moulding chiefly used in repetition as sixteenth-century border ornament. Some use also made of the device in late eighteenth to early nineteenth centuries.
Pannikin. A small silver drinking vessel.
Pap boat. Small, shallow, oval bowl with tapering lip at one end for feeding infants. Surviving examples date from early eighteenth century onwards.
Parcel gilt. Descriptive of plate decorated by the partial application of gilding (*see also* Silver gilt).
Paten. Small circular plate for Communion bread. Medieval examples have shaped central depression and flat rim. Elizabethan paten covers fit the cup and have flat seal foot. Later examples follow this pattern until the entry of the Gothic revival. Small circular footed waiters of *tazze* should not be confused with ecclesiastical pieces.
Pax. A tablet with a projecting handle behind, used in the Eucharist, when it is kissed by the celebrant, the other priests, and, very occasionally, the communicants. It is usually decorated on the front with a sacred symbol, a scene from the Gospel (usually the Crucifixion), or the lives of the saints, engraved, nielloed, or enamelled. A large silver-gilt Spanish pax of about 1530 in the Victoria and Albert Museum has a low relief of St Idelfonso receiving the chasuble from the Virgin.
Peace medal. Late eighteenth-century medals were engraved for presentation to Indian chiefs on occasion of ceremonial visits to the national capital, then in Philadelphia. They are dated between 1792 and 1795, and were the work of Joseph Richardson, Junior, of Philadelphia, who was assayer of the United States Mint.
Peg tankards. The tankard was a communal drinking vessel, and most of them have a row of pegs set in a vertical row inside the drum on the side where the handle is fixed. This was supposed to mark exactly how much each drinker was supposed to consume of the contents. Collectors therefore call them peg tankards.

Although rare in the rest of Europe and the United States, during the greater part of the period under discussion the tankard was the most usual silver vessel of importance to be made and used in Norway. A tankard was a favourite present at weddings, and engraved with the names or initials of the married couple it remained a family memory and a treasured possession for generations.

The Norwegian Renaissance tankard is tall and thin and rests on a base of concave form, which on the more elaborate examples is decorated with chased ornaments. Round the lower part of the drum is a decorative belt, usually moulded into the shape of a rope, while the smooth part of the drum above might be decorated with engraved ornaments. The lid rises in steps to the centre, where a coin is sometimes inserted. Some of the steps may have chased decoration that harmonizes with that on the base. The thumbpiece is moulded into a flat ornamental shape or has the form of a plain turned knob. The late sixteenth-century examples have an almost Gothic slimness, but during the early seventeenth century the shape becomes slightly broader and more sturdy.

Renaissance tankard

A completely new type of tankard was introduced during the latter part of the seventeenth century. The baroque tankard is broad and squat, has a rounded bottom and rests on three feet, moulded into the shape of a lion, a pomegranate, or a ball and claw. The thumbpiece is of a similar shape (2). The earliest specimens date from the 1650s and 1660s and are quite plain, except for an engraved border around the centre of the lid, which is decorated with an engraved inscription or an inserted coin. Some tankards have a small leaf ornament soldered on to the drum where the feet join it, or the same area may be engraved. During the last quarter of the seventeenth century chased ornamentation was increasingly used. This gave a richer and more truly baroque general effect. Chased decoration first became obligatory for the drum round the three points where the feet join it, and soon the border round the central part of the lid became decorated with wreaths of flowers or leaves, chased out into high relief. A number of tankards from Christiania and a few from Bergen have the whole of the drum covered in chased decoration (3). A few examples have human figures introduced into the composition.

Baroque tankard

The basic form of the baroque tankard remained popular until the middle of the eighteenth century, with some modifications in the ornamentation according to the change of taste, from baroque to *Régence*. For provincial customers tankards of the basic baroque shape were made well into the latter

Tankard with chased decoration

part of the eighteenth century with rococo or neo-classical decorations.

Apart from the standard Renaissance and baroque types described, Norwegian tankards can be seen in more unorthodox shapes, with a polygonal body, set with coins or decorated with engravings with a topical significance. A few examples from the mid-seventeenth century have a plain drum, slightly tapering, which rests on a broad plinth. The type is closely related to the contemporary counterparts in England.

Perfume-burner with winged caryatids and claw and ball feet in a tripod arrangement, by Matthew Boulton, late 18th century

Perfume burner. Pierced baluster form vase on scroll feet of late seventeenth-century date. Rare. Less lavish examples made in England until mid-nineteenth century.
Pibling. An obsolete form of pebbling. Coney's inventory included hammers for pibling, undoubtedly to produce the matted surface found on some of his early work.
Pierced work. Fretwork decoration cut with chisel or saw, used alone or combined with embossed work. Found at most periods in naturalistic or formal lattice and diaper designs. The application of ornamental piercing to Sheffield plate was governed by the development of hard-steel tools. The fretsaw was useless, because such cutting exposed the central core of copper in such a way that it could not be concealed. Shortly after the introduction of double plating in the early 1770s, flypresses were used with hardened punches so designed that a layer of silver protruded very slightly beyond the copper, enabling it to be lapped over and thus conceal the telltale line. With adequate burnishing the laps were virtually invisible. At first each pierced motif was pressed singly: by the mid-1790s they were produced in small groups, and the collector will easily detect this work. After about 1820 piercing machines with hard-steel tools did this work more quickly.

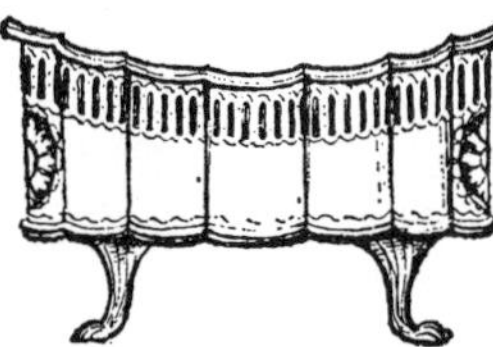

Pierced salt

Pitcher by Paul Revere, c. *1800*

Pincushion. Silver-framed examples survive from late seventeenth century in toilet services or separately and continued to be made by England until 1850s.
Pine-tree shillings. Made by John Hull and Robert Sanderson of Boston, 1652; first silver currency in Massachusetts. Hull was appointed mint master of Colony in that year.
Pipkin. Small vessel, like saucepan with spout and turned wooden handle, for warming brandy.
Pitchers. Early in the nineteenth century Paul Revere adapted in silver the Liverpool pottery pitchers favoured by sea captains; copied copiously today for water pitchers, and in small sizes for cream, one can only speculate on their original use. Revere left three sizes of them in his own inventory, to judge by the listing; and large ones survive from his household.
Planishing. Making flat by hammering with an oval-faced punch, called in the old days a planishing teast.
Plate. The generic term for wrought silver or gold. Later applied by transference to the imitative wares of Sheffield and electroplate (*see also* Meat and Soup plate).
Plateau. A shallow dish on a short stem. A type characteristic of Spain and Portugal in the sixteenth century is derived from Valencia pottery.
Plating. Until the 1790s copper was silver-plated in the actual factories in which the ware was fabricated. Afterwards plating became a specialist trade, being made and stocked in three standard qualities, according to the thickness of the silver. This was sold to the plate workers.

An eight-pound copper ingot alloyed with about one-fifth its weight in brass, and measuring 8–10 inches (20.3–25.4 cm) long by about 3 inches (7.6 cm) wide and 2 inches (5.1 cm) thick, was smoothed and cleaned on the upper and lower surfaces. At first this was done by hand-filing; from about 1820 by steam-driven planing machines.

An ingot of silver was rolled to the required thickness, as needed for varying qualities of metal, the lowest weighing 16 dwt, to cover one face of the copper. This was increased to as much as 8 oz for the very rich plating used before the introduction of silver mountings and for the lavishly engraved work from 1820. The coating of silver required to be more than a mere film, otherwise it discoloured when heated by the soldering iron. A rectangle of silver plate, flawless in texture and unpitted, measuring about one-eighth of an inch (3 mm) less each way than the surface of the copper ingot, was cleaned on one side. The two bright surfaces were then placed together and bedded by placing a heavy iron upon the silver and striking it with a sledge hammer until every part of the two surfaces was in close contact.

A heavily whitewashed piece of thick sheet copper was placed over the silver and firmly bound to the ingot with iron wires, burnt borax and water being applied to the edges of the silver to act as a flux. The ingot was now placed in an oven containing a charcoal fire and its door pierced with a small hole through which the plater could observe its progress. A bright line encircling the edges of the silver told him when fusion had taken place. He immediately removed the ingot and plunged it into diluted spirits of salt. After cutting the wires the ingot was compressed in a rolling machine, repeated annealing being required as it was gradually converted into sheets of specified width and gauge. These sheets, in which silver and copper were perfectly united, were not silvered on both sides until the early 1770s.

Pomander. From the French 'Pomme d'ambre'. Small box for sweet-smelling spices carried to ward off infections. Formed as segmented spheres, skulls, fruits, or other fancies. Used up till the seventeenth century. Partially superseded by vinaigrettes (*q.v.*).

Porringer. Two-handled bowl with or without cover for porridge and spoon meat. Survivals date from

Porringer, 1699

the first half of seventeenth century and last into the nineteenth. Shallow bowls with flat handles commonly called bleeding bowls (*q.v.*), probably also used as small porringers. The two-handled seventeenth-century form in its largest size is one of the most important forms of decorative vessels of its day. In the United States the term applies only to cupping or bleeding bowls. Porringers were popular in miniature during the period of Britannia standard silver.

Potato ring. *See* Dish ring.

Pounce box or **-pot.** Baluster or vase-shaped bottle for sprinkling powdered gum sandarac (pounce) on writing paper. Indistinguishable from sand box (*q.v.*).

Pricking. Delicate needlepoint engraving used principally for armorials and inscriptions in sixteenth to seventeenth centuries and also to a limited extent for naturalistic decoration on small scale.

Prunkgefass. A cup intended for display rather than use. A typical example is the gold cup supported somewhat insecurely on a coral figure, made by Peter Boy in about 1700, in the Schönborn Collection at Pommersfelden.

Przeworsk. A Polish method of decorating belts with chased-silver plaques sewn on to the leather.

Pseudo hallmarks. Devices were occasionally adopted by individual makers of British plate (not silver) from 1835, to suggest English hallmarks.

Punch-bowl racing trophy by William Williamson, Dublin, 1751, engraved by Daniel Pomarde. Christie, Manson & Woods

Punch bowl. Large circular bowl with or without drop-ring handles for preparing punch. Used contemporaneously with Monteiths (*q.v.*) from the seventeenth century onwards.

Punched work. Elementary form of embossing struck with blunt punches grouped in primitive floral designs, principally used in mid-seventeenth century.

Punch ladle. *See* Ladle, punch.

Purchase. *See* Thumbpiece.

Pyx. A small vessel, usually a round silver box, in which the sacrament is carried to the sick. They were frequently richly decorated, like the French one of 1562 in the Victoria and Albert Museum, embossed with the Last Supper and other biblical scenes, and crowned by a standing figure of Christ at the column. Only one authenticated English medieval example has survived; now in Victoria and Albert Museum.

Quaich. A Scottish drinking cup with two or more handles (Gaelic: *cuach*). Originally probably hollowed from solid, by the seventeenth century quaichs were built up from neatly carved staves, beautifully feathered together, the vessels being bound around with withies. Woods often of different kinds, alternating. Handles in this phase formed part of staves and had characteristic 'dip', which should be studied by those wishing to be good judges of a quaich of any period. By latter part of century wood quaichs were being mounted in silver (handle, foot, rim, sometimes plate inside). By third quarter of century quaichs were being made in silver. Stave construction nearly always recalled by incised lines on body, commonly with floral engraving in alternate panels (Tudor rose and tulip; thistles exceptional). Initials of original owners usually appear on handles. In late eighteenth and nineteenth centuries quaich degenerated into mere bowl with handles, often fancifully decorated, sometimes with Gaelic motto. Though sold as quaichs, they should be avoided by connoisseurs. Delightful miniature quaichs were made in the earlier part of the eighteenth century, some in Aberdeen and Inverness. Their prices are more moderate than those of full-sized examples. Quaichs had a very special place in Highland social ritual. Primary use for drinking rather than for food, but some adopted by churches for Communion, and even for offertory purposes.

Raising. The normal technique of forming a hollow vessel from sheet metal by successive rows of hammering on a woodblock, stretching and curving the metal. The silver, hardened by the hammering, is annealed or softened by repeatedly being raised to red-hot heat as required.

Ram's horn. Thumbpiece of twisted form seen on early Boston tankards. It differs from the New York corkscrew.

Rapiers. With silver hilts were fashionable for dress occasions in England, America, France, Russia, and elsewhere in the eighteenth and nineteenth centuries. American examples show little variety whether made by early or late men of New England or New York.

Reed-and-tie. A similar moulding to Reedings (*q.v.*) with the addition of crossed straps simulating ribbons binding the reeding together.

Reedings. A border moulding composed of contiguous parallel convex members. Derived from the convex filling to the lower part of fluting in classical columns.

Regency. Miniature silver made in the early nineteenth century was of smaller dimensions than formerly and confined largely to tea-table ware. Whereas seventeenth- and eighteenth-century productions averaged between 1¾ inches (4.5 cm) and 2½ inches (5.7 cm) in height, the Regency series was normally no more than a third of these measurements. For the most part they were cast with turned interiors and conformed with fashionable plate of the period with all-over decoration in relief. They were never heavy enough to demand hallmarking, and because of the chasing might lack even the maker's mark. They are found fully gilded: gilded within and in white silver.

Reliefs (*rilievi*). Silver reliefs, usually of religious subjects, enjoyed great popularity in Italy from the Renaissance to the late eighteenth century. Many are of such high quality that they may be regarded as minor works of sculpture. Small reliefs were made to decorate paxes in the Renaissance period.

Reliquary. The vessel in which a relic or relics of the saints are kept. Reliquaries have been made in a great variety of patterns, offering the maximum scope for the invention of the goldsmith. Early examples were generally of architectural design, like the reliquary of Pepin d'Acquitain in the treasury of Ste Foy at Conques, which dates from the ninth century and, with its high roof and round-headed niches, resembles a shrine. Some made in the Rhineland in the twelfth century (one is in the Victoria and Albert Museum and another at the Schlossmuseum, Berlin) were made as model romanesque churches. Church-shaped reliquaries followed, a little tardily, the changes in architectural taste, and the shrine of St Elizabeth at Marburg (1236–9) is decorated with a mixture of Romanesque and early Gothic ornaments. Reliquaries in the form of limbs and busts were also made as early as the eleventh century, and held their popularity for some 500 years. They were frequently enriched with precious stones, which have in some instances (the bust of St Agatha at Catania) been so richly augmented by the offerings of the pious that the original work is now practically obscured. The early busts were normally stylized and expressionless, but during the Renaissance period they were treated with greater naturalism. One of the most famous medieval reliquaries is that of the Holy Thorn in the British Museum, which was made of gold richly decorated with enamel and precious stones by a Burgundian craftsman of the fourteenth century. (This object may also be called an Ostensory, as it is intended for the display of the relic.)

During the Renaissance the architectural type of reliquary developed into the coffer-shaped, of which the best example is that of St John the Baptist in the Cathedral at Siena. This type, richly ornamented with reliefs and statuettes, was normal throughout the baroque period. Among the curiosities is the early eighteenth-century reliquary of St Anthony in the Victoria and Albert Museum, which is shaped like a spire.

Replating. The problem of detecting Sheffield plate replated during mid-Victorian days is difficult to solve. Advertisements were consistently inserted in newspapers and elsewhere from 1849 offering to replate at one-third of the original cost. Such pieces have toned down with a century of cleaning and now closely resemble genuine plating. Fused plate is much harder than electroplate, the effect of introducing alloy into the silver, this being plus rolling and hammering. Electroplating tends to soften the foundation metal. Electroplated silver is always white; Sheffield plate has a faintly bluish hue owing to the presence of alloy.

Repoussé work. Relief ornament hammered from the under or inner side of the metal. Usually given added sharpness of form by surface chasing of detail and outline. Common at all periods.

Reproductions. Precautions need to be taken when acquiring miniature toys lacking a full series of marks. Modern copies struck with a bogus date letter or lion passant gardant are far more numerous than originals. Shapes are important: it is, for instance, inconsistent to find a ball-shaped tea urn with a pre-1739 hallmark, as they were not designed for a full quarter century later.

Riesenpokal. Literally a 'giant cup'. The name is usually given to the vast cups, standing up to 40 inches (101.6 cm) in height and usually gilt, intended for ostentation rather than use, and made in Germany in the sixteenth century.

Rings. To commemorate special occasions, and particularly as funeral mementoes, were a common task of the goldsmith.

Rococo. The generic title for the eighteenth-century style of ornament based on shellwork and scrolls (French *rocaille*).

Roses. Golden roses were sent by the popes to princes who had rendered signal service to the Roman Church and, later, to important ecclesiastical bodies. Of the many made in the fourteenth and fifteenth centuries few survive; one of the most notable, the gift of Pius II, is at Siena. All were made by goldsmiths working in Rome.

Rose-water ewer and dish (or **basin**). Used for finger washing at table. Extant examples from early sixteenth century onwards. Dishes usually circular or occasionally oval. Ewers of various form, chiefly vase- or helmet-shaped. Important pieces of decorative plate displaying the highest standards of ornament and design of their periods.

Salad servers. Introduced about 1800 to conform with main table services. Spoons with flattened bowl ends, forks with deep prongs cut into bowl of spoon form.

Salt cellar. Early form known as Trencher Salt (*q.v.*). Basic form in eighteenth century a shallow circular bowl, first on moulded base, later on three or four feet. Oval pierced examples with glass liners introduced from about 1765. Plain boat-shaped model about 1780. Early nineteenth-century examples revert to earlier models, and sometimes match tureens of dinner services.

Salt cellar, 1735

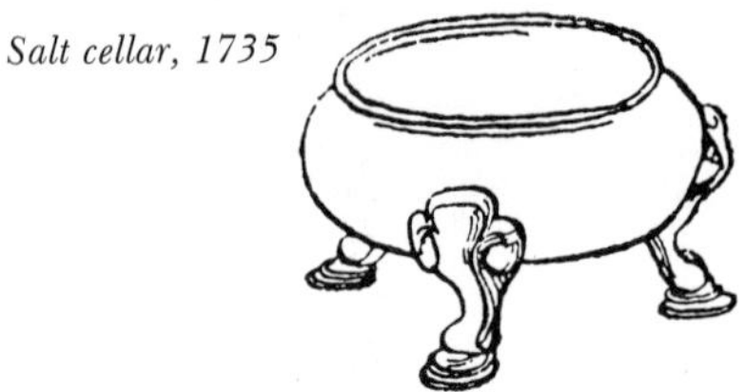

Salts. The ceremonial salt occupied a prominent position on the medieval dining table, and its importance did not decline until the seventeenth century; but the surviving French and German salts of the sixteenth century look plain and insignificant beside English examples of the same date. Some French

Salt, silver-gilt with plaques of Limoges enamel, attributed to Jean II Penicaud, 16th century. Wallace Collection

salts were of great delicacy enriched with Limoges-enamel plaques, like the one in the Wallace Collection; and German salts were occasionally fantastic, as may be seen from the one in the British Museum, which is in the form of a whale supporting a shell on its tail. An exotic pair made at Breslau in about 1600 are fashioned like turkeys with spotted shells for their bodies. The most famous of all salts is, of course, that made in gold by Benvenuto Cellini for Francis I. Dutch silversmiths of the seventeenth century occasionally used human figures or fish for decoration; a beautiful example of about 1625 by Thomas Bogaert of Utrecht, supported by a kneeling girl, is in the collection of the Duke of Buccleuch. In spite of their diminished importance, French rococo craftsmen saw the decorative value of salts as table ornaments, and one of the finest sets ever made, consisting of four double and three single cellars supported by *putti* with feathered Red Indian head-dresses, by François Thomas Germain, was in the Portuguese Royal Collection. (*See The Connoisseur*, December 1954, p. 264.) Salts of Sheffield plate were sold in pairs and catalogued in three qualities, the first two fitted with blue-glass liners: (*a*) tinned inside: (*b*) plated inside with silver edges; (*c*) gilt inside with silver edges. Until 1820 they were made with three or four feet.

Salver. Flat circular plates for presenting other vessels. Early examples have central spreading foot and are often erroneously called *tazze* (*q.v.*). From about 1725 small feet applied at circumference. Circular, oval, and polygonal forms all found, with chased or plain centres. Early borders plain mouldings, followed by shell and scroll, pierced, beaded, or gadrooned patterns (*see also* Waiter).

Samovars or **tea urns.** Though principally connected with Russia, were also made in other countries. A fine rococo specimen by François Thomas Germain was in the Portuguese Royal Collection.

Sand box. Baluster- or vase-shaped pot used for sprinkling sandarac on wet ink. Found as part of inkstands or separately (*see also* Pounce box).

Sauceboat. Introduced in early eighteenth century. First examples have oval moulded bases, later replaced by individual scroll or hoof feet. Handles formed as scrolls, dolphins, eagles' heads, etc. Largely supplanted by tureens in late eighteenth century, with some revival of the boat form in the early nineteenth.

Double-lipped sauceboat, 1722

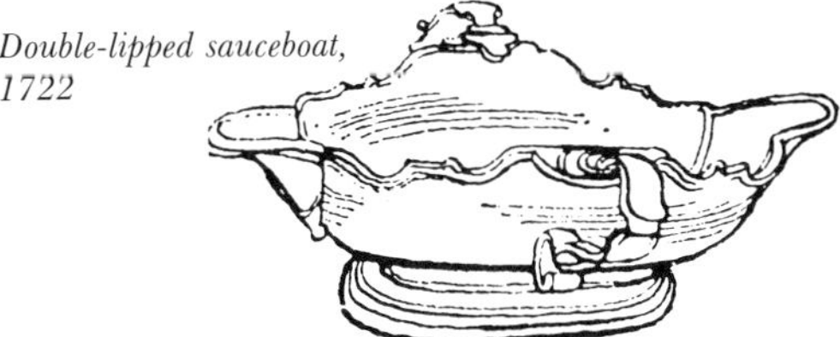

Saucepan. Found throughout eighteenth and early nineteenth centuries. Cylindrical or bellied bodies with projecting wood handles, with or without cover (*see also* Skillet).

Saucepan, 1730

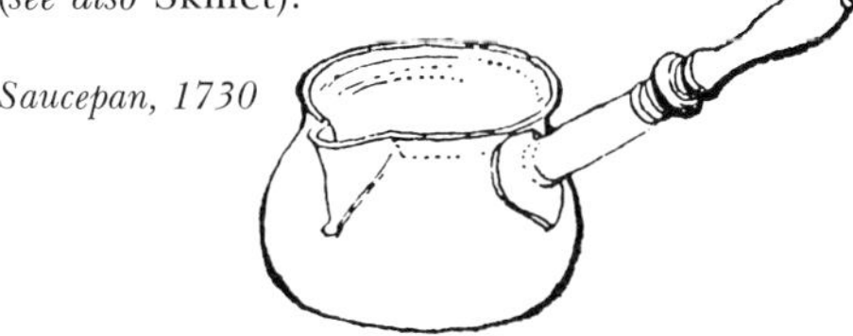

Save-alls. Are recorded with snuffers and extinguishers suggesting use with lighting equipment; Revere recorded in 1797 two with a total weight of 1 oz 16 dwt, so it is not surprising that none are known to have survived.

Scaldini (portable braziers). These were often made of silver and enjoyed more popularity in Italy than elsewhere in Europe. In shape they generally resemble tureens with flat perforated tops. They have hinged handles with wooden centrepieces.

Scent bottle. Of small size for personal use, usually of pear-shaped form with chased or engraved decoration of the period. Very common in mid-nineteenth century. Larger examples in seventeenth-century toilet services.

Sconce. Wall light for candles extant from the Restoration into the eighteenth century. The wall plate usually of cartouche form with embossed decoration and branches for one or more candles. A plain form with rounded top to wall plate and flat pan with single low socket also occurs. The name also used in the past for the normal candlestick.

Seal box. A flat circular or oval box for containing the seal attached to important documents as royal warrants, university degrees, etc. The covers embossed or engraved with appropriate armorials.

Secchielli. Vessels shaped like holy-water buckets, but not necessarily intended for ecclesiastical use. The body of the vessels was usually embossed or engraved. They were used for carrying liquids or ice,

and the same Italian word is used for wine coolers.
Second-course dish. Circular dish for serving entremets and puddings. Conforms in style and pattern to meat dishes and plates of the period, throughout eighteenth and early nineteenth centuries. Sizes range from 10 to about 16 inches (25.4–40.7 cm) diameter.
Serrated. Knotched, used especially of the shaped edge of the rim of tankard lid.
Sewing equipment. Thimbles, scissors, bands on pin balls, hooks, needle cases, bodkins, in gold and silver are known by record more than by surviving specimens.
Shaving dish. Kidney-shaped bowls, usually accompanied by helmet-shaped ewers, enjoyed great popularity in Spain and Portugal in the eighteenth century.

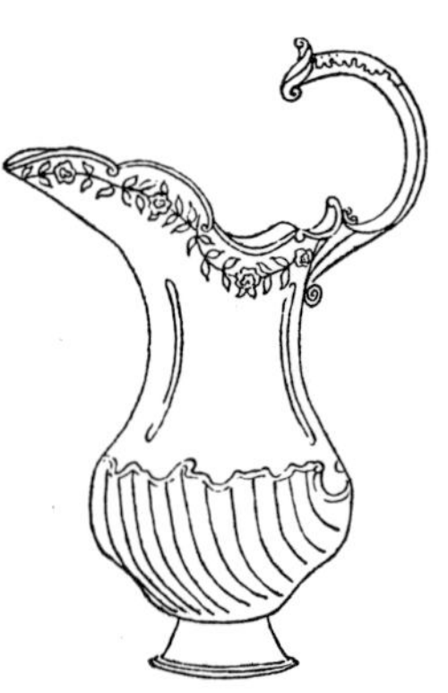

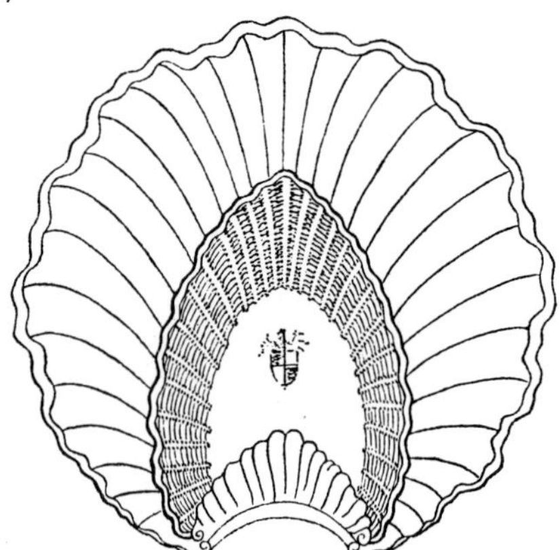

Shaving dish: Kidney-shaped bowl (right) *and ewer*

Shaving pot. Small cylindrical or tapering vessel, usually with detachable ivory or wood handle, stand, and spirit lamp. Introduced in late eighteenth century. Found in fittings of men's dressing sets.
Sheffield plate. The earliest and most effective substitute for wrought silver. Invented by Thomas Bolsover about 1713. Composed of copper ingot fused to a thinner one of silver and rolled to requisite thickness, the metals remaining in the same relative proportions when rolled. First used for buttons and other small articles, but from about 1765 onwards a serious rival to silver in every type of vessel.

The silvered copper could be shaped by any of the hand-raising processes customary in silversmithing, by stamping, or by spinning.

The exterior of Sheffield plate was rarely, if ever, gilded. Sugar basins, cream jugs, mustard pots, and salt cellars were gilded inside as protection against the foods concerned, which tended to corrode silver and produce black spots difficult to remove. In tea services the tea pots were also gilded to match.

It was illegal until 1784 to strike a name or mark upon Sheffield plate. In that year the law was amended so that reputable platers 'working within one hundred miles of the town of Sheffield' might be enabled to distinguish their work by name and emblem.

In England it is an offence to describe as Sheffield plate any ware which has not been manufactured by actually laying silver upon copper. Among the subterfuges adapted to keep within the law is to add the letter 'd' and thus label pieces electrically plated in Sheffield as 'Sheffield Plated'. Some of the original tools are still in use for making Sheffield plate by the original methods.

Collectors of Sheffield plate should be aware that during the 1820s and 1830s large quantities of cheap, thin-gauge, poorly plated ware was imported from France. The copper, which was quick to spin and required no annealing, contained less alloy than its English counterpart, and consequently was of a redder tinge, which imparted a faintly pinkish hue to the thin film of silver.
Shell. Small dish of lifesize scallop shell form introduced about 1700 for butter and other uses. Usually raised, but fine examples occasionally cast from nature.
Shield. The handle frequently terminated in a shield on tankards.
Sideboard dish. A large circular dish primarily designed for display, usually enriched by finely engraved or embossed armorials. Probably derived from the rose-water dish (*q.v.*). Later versions take the form of convex shields richly ornamented for special presentation, e.g. the Waterloo Shield of the Duke of Wellington. Also known as Chargers.
Silver gilt. Silver with an applied surface of gold. Traditional technique known as fire, water, mercury, or wash gilding consists of painting on an amalgam of mercury and gold. The former is driven off with heat and the gold combines with the silver. Modern method of electrogilding employs the use of electric current in a bath of gold solution, producing a deposition of the latter as in electro-silver-plating.
Silver guns. Only two of these silver guns are known, at Dumfries and Kirkcudbright. James VI and I presented them to the incorporated trades of the two burghs for annual shooting competitions. Dumfries gun still being shot for in 1813. No hallmarks on either.
Skewer. Extant meat skewers date from the early eighteenth century. Normally provided with ring or shell top to afford a grip. Later examples conform to table-service patterns.
Skillet. Seventeenth century form of saucepan on three feet for heating gruel or other liquids. Covers of flat cap form with flat pierced handle resembling cupping bowls.
Snuff box. Found in great variety of forms from late seventeenth century onwards, both in solid silver and wood, tortoiseshell, and other materials mounted with silver.
Snuffer. Scissor-like implement for trimming candlewicks. The cutting blade fits into shallow box when closed for holding the snuffed wick, the box having a pricket end for lifting bent-over wire. Survivals common from late seventeenth century. Not to be confused with the conical extinguisher (*q.v.*).
Snuffer stand. Upright container on stem and moulded base into which snuffers fit. Introduced in late seventeenth century, but superseded by trays in the early eighteenth. Some have accompanying candle-socket and/or extinguisher.
Snuffer tray. Oblong or oval tray with or without small feet and scroll or ring handle at side for holding snuffers. Not to be confused with spoon trays (*q.v.*).
Soap box. Spherical box for soap ball, standing on moulded base with screw-on or hinged pierced or plain cover. Can be mistaken for pounce or sand box (*q.v.*), but the spherical form appears to have been peculiar to the soap box.
Soufflé dish. Cylindrical bowl with liner, usually two-handled, to hold soufflés, introduced in early nineteenth century.

Soup plate. Similar to meat plate (*q.v.*) but with deeper centre.
Soup tureen. *See* Tureen.
Soy frame. Oblong or oval stand with ring frame for holding soy or sauce bottles. Introduced in late eighteenth century. Found *en suite* with larger cruet frames (*q.v.*).
Spectacle frames and cases. Appear in inventories in the seventeenth and throughout the eighteenth centuries, and in nineteenth-century silversmiths' catalogues.
Spice box. A general name for caskets of indeterminate purpose of the early seventeenth century, usually of shell outline with scallop lid and shell or snail feet. Later applied to oval caskets of the Charles II period which may also have served as tobacco or sugar boxes. An eighteenth-century version has centrally hinged twin lids with or without a detachable nutmeg grater in the centre.
Spice dredger. A small cylindrical or octagonal piece with a pierced cover and single handle. More survive from the early than the late eighteenth century.
Spinning. Much miniature hollow ware dating from the 1750s onwards was shaped by spinning in the lathe. This was much less expensive than hand-raising with the hammer. It is particularly noticeable among Dutch miniature silver. From the 1770s light domestic hollow ware might be spun by factory methods. Almost invisible circular marks were made on the interior by the tools.
Splayed. A candlestick or other foot is termed splayed when the top and bottom diameters are different.
Spoons. In medieval times spoons, used for consuming thick, sweet liquids, were usually carried as personal possessions and not provided on the table. Some very elaborate early examples have survived, with bowls of shell, agate, or other hard stones, exquisitely mounted in gold or silver. Occasionally they were combined with forks; in the British Museum there is a folding spoon and fork in a Gothic handle which also contains two dice and a pen. With the general introduction of forks, the variations in pattern became fewer. Generally speaking, the fig-shaped bowl remained normal until the middle of the seventeenth century, when it was superseded by the egg-shaped. Incense spoons, used for placing incense in the censer, usually had spade-shaped bowls.
Apostle spoon. Early type of spoon with full-length figure of an apostle or Christ (The Master) as finial. Extant examples date from late fifteenth century till Charles II period. Complete sets of thirteen of very rare occurrence.
Basting spoon. Long-handled, with nearly oval bowl, early examples rat-tailed, presumed to have been used for basting. Similar in form to early punch ladles and probably of general domestic use.
Caddy spoon. Small spoon with short handle for measuring tea from the caddy. Made in numerous fancy forms, leaf, jockey, cap, hand, etc., from about 1780 onwards.
Cherub spoon. A genuine creation of the Renaissance in Norway is the cherub spoon with a drop-shaped bowl and a thin stem which tapers towards the cherub's mask which forms the knob.
Dessert spoon. Introduced in early eighteenth century. Has a parallel development to the table spoon.

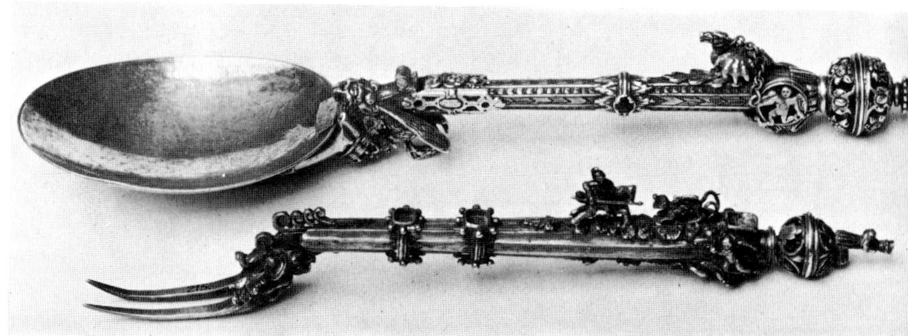

Top Folding spoon and fork, Flemish, 16th century. The prongs of the fork fit into loops at the back of the spoon bowl. The pierced sphere top of the spoon contains two silver dice released by unscrewing a lancet-like pin. The top unscrewed reveals a silver pen, toothbrush and earpick.

Above Basting spoon with tubular handle, by William Fawdery, 1712

Disc-end spoon. In fashion in Scotland 1575–1650, or thereabouts. The main feature varies considerably, but there is always a disc, cushioned from the stem by anything from a short bar to an elliptical member, all cut with the stem in one piece. A set of six of these, inscribed 1575, is in the Bute Collection. The disc end grows into a Puritan type of spoon in the second half of the seventeenth century by merging its members into a simple broadening of the stem, ornament being confined at most to some shallow notches in the top of the stem and some simple line engraving on the face of it. Stem joins bowl without rat tail or other type of reinforcement.
Egg spoon. Not recognized before late eighteenth century. At first found in egg frames and later as part of complete table services.
Grape spoon. Norwegian type, simple and elegant with a drop-shaped bowl and a long thin stem terminating in a bunch of grapes. A similar type is sometimes found, with the knob of the stem shaped like a shell instead of a bunch of grapes.
Gravy spoon. Long-handled spoon similar to basting spoon and indistinguishable in early eighteenth century. Later forms follow main table-service patterns.
Lion sejant spoon. Early form surmounted by a small figure of a seated lion, sometimes supporting a shield at the front. Extant examples date from fifteenth to early seventeenth century.
Maidenhead spoon. Early form with finial formed as a female head with long hair rising from Gothic foliage. Extant from fifteenth to seventeenth centuries.
Marrow spoon. Long, narrow-bowled spoon, usually double-ended with two widths of bowl for eating bone marrow. Alternative version has normal table spoon bowl and marrow bowl in place of handle.

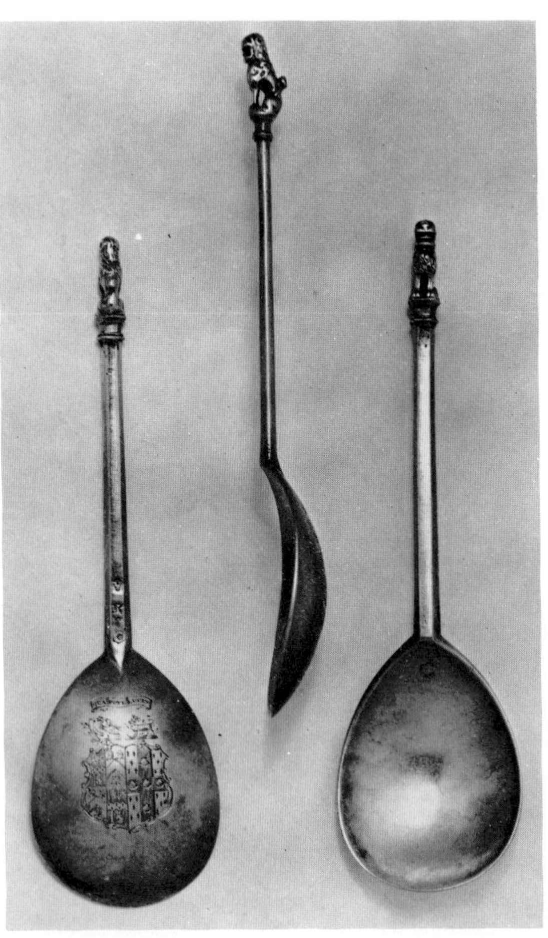

Three from a set of six silver-gilt Elizabeth I Lion-sejant spoons, one 1558, five 1578. Christie, Manson & Woods

Found from early eighteenth century onwards.
Mulberry spoon. See Straining Spoon.
Mustard spoon. Not recognized before mid-eighteenth century. Early examples have long curved stems and deep circular bowls. Later versions conform to main table service patterns with egg-shaped bowl.
Olive spoon. See Straining Spoon.
Puritan spoon. Mid-seventeenth-century form with flat stem with straight top edge, and nearly oval bowl. The earliest form of English flat-stemmed spoon.
Rat-tail spoon. The principal form of the late seventeenth to early eighteenth centuries, distinguished by tapering rib runing down back of bowl. Found with trifid (*q.v.*), dog-nose, and rounded top stems.
Salt spoon. Early examples either small versions of contemporary rat-tailed type or formed as shovels. Many fancy varieties occur in mid-eighteenth century. Later examples conform to main table-service patterns.

Right Silver spoon with a gold seal top, London, 1668. This is a late example, made when the trefid spoon was fashionable

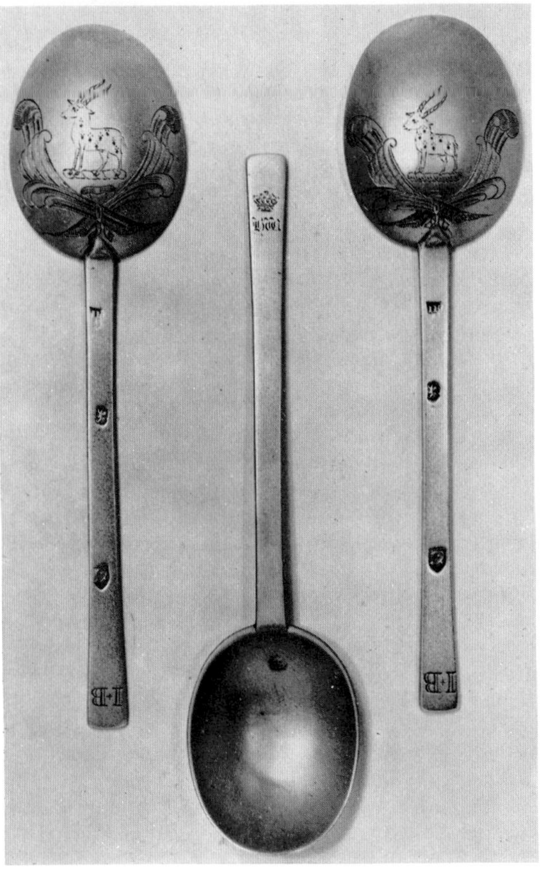

Left Three from a set of six silver-gilt Puritan spoons, maker's mark IK, English, 1670. Christie, Manson & Woods

Seal-top spoon. The commonest surviving form of early spoon with flat, seal-like finial placed on short turned baluster of oval, circular, or polygonal section, and with hexagonal stem. Examples range from fifteenth century till Charles II period. In Scotland the rarest type, of sixteenth and early seventeenth centuries, has been called the seal-top, but has little or no resemblance to English spoon of this name. 'Seal' is little wedge-shaped member with projecting collar where it joins the stem, which is flat instead of hexagonal in section. Bowls also distinctive, and have undeveloped rat tail. Only four examples known at present.
Slip-top spoon. Early form with hexagonal stem with sloping or bevelled end. Examples occur from medieval period until mid-seventeenth century.
Snuff spoon. Miniature version of larger contemporary spoons found in snuff boxes and étuis for taking snuff.
Straining spoon. Spoon with pierced bowl, found either in large sizes for gravy or similar use or in tea spoon size with thin, tapering stem with pricket top, used for skimming motes from tea cups. These latter have been called mulberry or olive spoons, but have no possibly explicable function for such fruits. Their purpose as tea strainers is exemplified by their conjunction with tea spoons in fitted tea-caddy caskets.
Stump-top spoon. Seventeenth-century form with octagonal stem swelling at the end and diminishing to a flattened point. Rare.
Table spoon. Developed as a specific size contrasting with dessert spoon in early eighteenth century. The main constituent of table services and the prototype

for the various patterns evolved (*see* Table service).
Tea spoon. Rarely found in sets before 1700. Conform in general to prevailing styles of larger spoons, but individual patterns in mid-eighteenth century occur, e.g. foliage stems and bowls, shell bowls, and many small devices stamped on bowl backs.
Trefid or *Trifid spoon.* Also known by the French term *pied de biche*. Late seventeenth-century form with flat stem widening to a lobed outline at the top, split by two cuts forming three sections suggestive of a cleft hoof. The ends sometimes curve upwards. Normally found with rat-tailed bowls.
Volute spoon. The stem ends in a palmette with a protuberance below, shaped like a volute.
Writhen-top spoon. Rare medieval form surmounted by spirally fluted ovoid finial.
Spoon tray. Small oval or oblong dish of early eighteenth-century date used for holding tea spoons in the absence of tea-cup saucers. Usually with scalloped and fluted or moulded rims.
Stake. An iron tongue or anvil, on which the silver object is formed. Many kinds of stakes are used, shaped for certain purposes, such as to give an inward curve, a flat surface, etc.
Stamped work. Relief ornament produced by hammering from reverse of the metal into an intaglio-cut die. Commonly used in sixteenth century for strapwork and ovolo borders, and occasionally for larger surface patterns. In late eighteenth century developed on a commercial scale with large dies at Sheffield and Birmingham for candlesticks, dish borders, etc.
Standing dishes. Occasionally, and incorrectly, called *tazze*, have shallow bowls on baluster stems, and were used for sweetmeats or fruit. The interior of the

bowl is often richly adorned with relief decoration, and some have standing figures in the centre (notably those made by Paul Hubner of Augsburg between 1583 and 1614). They were popular, especially in Germany and Holland, from the late sixteenth to the early eighteenth centuries. The British Museum possesses an exceptionally fine set of a dozen made at Augsburg, and there is a notable example, made by Adam van Vianen at Utrecht in 1612, in the Victoria and Albert Museum.
Standish. Early name for inkstand (*q.v.*).
Statuettes (*figurine*). Italian silver statuettes of saints and mythological beings correspond closely with contemporary bronzes on which some appear to have been modelled. Early in the nineteenth century statuettes were occasionally based on Graeco-Roman figures or the works of such neoclassical sculptors as Canova and Thorvaldsen.
Stepped. A term indicating the elevations on a lid, as 'single-stepped' or 'double-stepped'.
Sterling Standard. The normal standard for wrought plate in the British Isles. Established in London in 1300 and in force till 1696. Then replaced by Britannia Standard (*q.v.*) till 1720, when Sterling was restored as legal. Consists of 11 oz 2 dwt of fine silver in every pound Troy (12 oz) of wrought metal, or 925 parts in 1,000. In the United States the word Sterling appears on Baltimore silver, 1800–14, and, after 1860, elsewhere. However, eighteenth-century silversmiths used the same standard as English Sterling, and so advertised their wares.
Stoning. Polishing with an emery stone.
Strainer. Rare survivals of the seventeenth century have circular bowls and tapering hollow handle. Of common occurrence in eighteenth century with two open scroll handles for use as orange strainers in punch-making and for other purposes.
Strapwork. Arrangements of interlaced ribbon and scrollwork mixed with naturalistic foliage and floral patterns, either engraved or *repoussé*, common in sixteenth century. The name is also used for the cast and applied vertical ribs and scrollwork derived from the earlier cutcard work (*q.v.*) much used by the Huguenot school in England in the eighteenth century.
Strawberry dish. A name given to small saucer-like dishes of seventeenth- and early eighteenth-century date, the early examples with punched decoration, the latter with fluted scalloped borders. Probably used for a variety of purposes.
Sucket fork. Two-pronged fork with flat stem, a spoon at other end, used for eating sweetmeat. A rare example by William Rouse, Boston was made before 1689.
Sugar basin. The later form of sugar bowl or basket, with two handles and of oblong, circular, or oval form, usually part of a matching tea service from about 1790 onwards.
Sugar basket. Pierced or plain vase or boat-shaped basket dating from about 1760 onwards with swing handle and glass liner in the pierced examples. Often made with matching cream basket.
Sugar bowl. Found as separate piece in the early eighteenth century of plain circular or polygonal form, usually with low cover. Later combined with two tea caddies matching to form set contained in casket. Small covered bowls for sugar, usually in the form of miniature tureens, were as popular in eighteenth-century Italy as tea caddies were in England. The knobs are fashioned in the form of animals, squatting Chinamen, flowers, nuts, and pineapples, while their bodies are enriched with every type of embossed or engraved, floral, foliated, and abstract rococo ornament.
Sugar box. Like British Charles II sweetmeat box; term adopted in America because of its use in old inventories, with 'sugar chest' or 'sugar trunke'. Seven Boston examples known.
Sugar nippers. An early form of scissor-like sugar tongs with scrolling stems and shell grips of George I and II date.
Sugar shifter. Small ladle with pierced bowl for sprinkling sugar over fruit, etc. Introduced about 1750.
Sugar tongs. Early eighteenth-century examples

modelled as miniature fire tongs. Later examples of spring-bow form with pierced or solid stems, subsequently conforming to table-service patterns. In the United States tongs appear about mid-eighteenth century in a scissor-form ending in cast shell grips; after 1760, bow-shaped 'spring tongs', in which a spring joins the arms.

Swage. A form into which silver might be stamped as the '2 Tests with plaine and flower'd Spoon Swages' of Edward Webb's inventory in 1718 (U.S.).

Sweetmeat basket. Small oval or circular basket introduced about 1740, found separately or on *épergne* branches. Early examples mostly pierced with cast floral borders. Later ones solid and decorated with engraving.

Sword hilts. In Scotland a small number of solid silver basket hilts have survived from the eighteenth century. One by Robert Cruickshank of Aberdeen is in the collection of Her Majesty the Queen. The account book of John Rollo lists sword hilts, including one of basket type for the Duke of Perth.

Table decorations. Small silver objects, figures, animals, miniature coaches, etc., were occasionally made as table decorations in the eighteenth century; in style they are similar to contemporary porcelain figures. Genoese craftsmen appear to have specialized in these objects, which they decorated with filigree work.

Table services. Complete table services in silver did not come into any general use until the eighteenth century, when those made for princely houses were often of the greatest magnificence. Small travelling table services were occasionally made, the most notable being the Italian one which belonged to Cardinal York and is now at Windsor. For main patterns see below.

Feather-edged. Found in the second half of eighteenth century. Stems filled with a narrow border fluting resembling the edge of a feather.

Fiddle pattern. Stems shaped with broad upper section and notched shoulders at bowl end, resembling slightly the basic form of violin body. Introduced early nineteenth century. Found plain, with threaded edges or with stamped shells at top.

Hanoverian. Stems with central longitudinal ridge on the front and upcurved ends. The common form from about 1720 to 1740.

King's pattern. Early nineteenth-century form with shaped stems with waisted hourglass tops decorated with scrolls, shells, and anthemion-like foliage.

Old English Pattern. Perfectly plain form with flat stems spreading slightly to the rounded ends. Common form from mid-eighteenth century onwards. Scottish and Irish varieties show a tendency to more pointed ends to stems.

Onslow pattern. Rare mid-eighteenth century form of stem with upper third decorated with radiating fluting and cast and applied corkscrew-like scroll tops.

Queen's pattern. A less elaborate form of King's pattern, the decoration struck only on the upper surface of the stem and without a shell on the bowl.

Tankard. Drinking vessel for beer with single handle, with or without hinged or, rarely, detachable lid. Appears to have been among the most popular silver vessels made in northern Europe, especially Scandinavia, in the seventeenth and eighteenth centuries. The type that first appeared in Germany in the sixteenth century had a small tapering body, but in the next hundred years patterns became larger and more ornate. In the late seventeenth and early eighteenth centuries tankards set with coins were in demand. In Scandinavia and the Baltic states tankards with tall cylindrical bodies were favoured in the late sixteenth and early seventeenth centuries. Later Swedish examples tended to have shorter bodies which tapered downwards, lower and broader covers projecting over the lip and larger thumbpieces. Heavy, squat ones standing on ball feet were usual in the Baltic states in the later seventeenth century; five massive examples of this type being in the collection of the Kompagnie der Schwarsen Haupter at Riga. In Hungary, tall, hexagonal, octagonal, or cylindrical tankards narrowed in the middle of the body and sometimes decorated with medallions of Roman heads were popular during the seventeenth century.

In England embossed examples occur in sixteenth century. From seventeenth century of strictly plain functional form with cylindrical tapering barrel. Mid-eighteenth century form with bellied barrel and domed lid.

In the United States, in Noncomformist New England, tankards were used rather than flagons in communion service. In New York the tankard was larger and heavier than in New England. Early forms were tapering and cylindrical; the flat-top cover (like English Stuart form) persisted in New York, but Boston adopted a domed cover about 1715 and used a midband on the body. The New York tankard is distinguished by an applied foliated band at the bottom. New York silversmiths frequently used a corkscrew thumbpiece, Boston a dolphin, and many American makers used for ornament on handle a cast cherub's head (*q.v.*). Pear-shaped bodies and domed covers were made in the rococo period, 1750–85, but the flat-top, Stuart tankard was continued in New York past mid-eighteenth century. The tankard went out of fashion in late eighteenth century.

Tankard, ivory mounted in silver-gilt by Didrik Hysing, Stockholm, 1676–1702. S. J. Phillips, London

Taperstick, 1734

Right Tea kettle and stand, maker's mark of Charles Kandler, London, *c.* 1730

Taper box. Small cylindrical box with handle and hole in lid to contain coiled sealing-wax taper. Found from about 1700 onwards (*see also* Waxjack).

Taperstick. Small version of contemporary candlestick to hold sealing taper. Found both in vertical form and with flat base similar to chamber candlestick. Extant from late seventeenth century onwards. In eighteenth century found as central fitting to inkstands.

Tassie. Scots for a drinking cup (French *tasse*).

Tazza (Italian; cf. French *tasse*; Scottish *tassie*). Wine cup with shallow circular bowl. The name, correctly applied to such pieces of sixteenth to seventeenth century, has become erroneously extended to cover flat dishes and salvers on central foot. Its derivation is clear, however, and can have no connotation with the latter pieces.

Tea canister. A small oblong or octagonal canister with cap cover, with or without sliding base, and kept in a tea chest. Vase forms introduced in mid-eighteenth century and accompanied by similar sugar bowls in sets in fitted wood, ivory, or shagreen caskets, to which the name was transferred. Later examples of oval, circular, or oblong form with lock, and interior division to hold two qualities of tea. Were known as caddies.

Tea cup. Rare examples of silver handleless tea cups and saucers survive from *c.* 1700.

Tea cup stand. Circular saucer dish with detachable open frame for holding porcelain cup, found in first two decades of eighteenth century. Very rare.

Tea kettle. Introduced about 1690, the bodies conforming nearly to tea pot form. The early examples have brazier-like stands for charcoal or spirit lamp, later replaced by open frame stand. A very rare feature is the accompanying silver tripod table to hold kettle and stand. Late eighteenth-century examples occasionally have tap in lieu of spout. Tea urns (*q.v.*) largely replaced kettles from about 1765.

Tea pot, octagonal, by Jonathan Lambe and Thomas Tearle, English, 1718–19. Victoria & Albert Museum

Tea canister, 1739

Tea pots. Modelled on those made in ceramics and imported from China, appear to have been made in all countries in the eighteenth century. A very early tea set of Augsburg craftsmanship shows the application of rococo motifs to a pot and jugs. Towards the end of the century, English patterns were occasionally used on the Continent. In England bodies were of pear shape under Queen Anne, spherical from George I to II, followed by inverted pear form early George III and oval flat-bottomed model with stand about 1780. Squat circular forms were introduced in early nineteenth century, with matching sugar basin and cream jug. Tea pots of Sheffield plate were made in shapes following those of the silversmiths, with handles of ivory, ebony, horn, or hardwood.

Tea service. Few examples of matching tea sets before 1785 in England. Some evidence of earlier fashion in Scotland. Services of tea pot, sugar basin, and cream jug common from 1790 onwards with or without coffee pot or hot-water jug with stand and lamp. Kettles very rarely form matching part of service until nineteenth century.

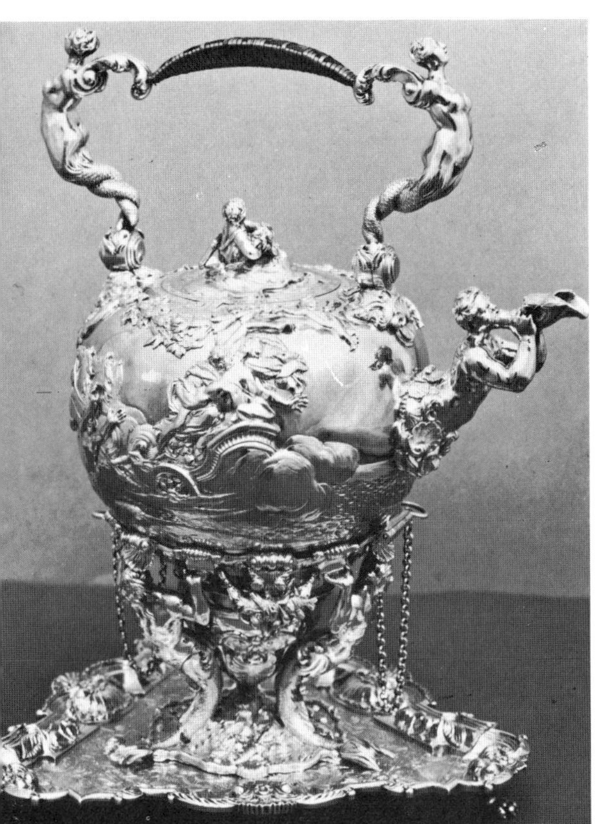

Tea set, three-piece, silver-gilt, with *chinoiserie* decoration, English, 1818

Teasts. Coney's inventory (U.S.) in 1722 had 'spoon teasts'; *see also* Swage.
Tea tray. Large, two-handled oval or oblong trays introduced *c.* 1780. Earlier the purpose was served by handleless salvers used in conjunction with tripod mahogany tables. Trays are among the rarities in American silver, but nine were made by Jacob Hurd, Boston, while Paul Revere's large oval tray made for Elias Hasket Derby in the Garvan Collection is one of the masterpieces of American silver.
Tea urn. Large vase-shaped hot-water urn introduced about 1760 in lieu of tea kettle (*q.v.*). A few earlier examples found in Scottish silver. Body fitted with a compartment at base or suspended in mouth for red-hot heating iron.

Left Tea urn with ivory tap handle, maker's mark of Paul Storr at the Dean Street Workshops of Rundell, Bridge & Rundell, English, 1809–10. Victoria & Albert Museum

Right Tigerware jug, silver-gilt, Elizabethan, London, 1573. S. J. Phillips, London

Threading. One or two narrow lines engraved or stamped as a border to spoon and fork stems and other small pieces.
Thumbpiece. The projecting part above the hinge of a covered vessel whereby the cover might easily be opened with the thumb. On tankards these showed greater variety than on flagons; on a few early chocolate pots a thumbpiece is found. Corkscrew, cusped, dolphin and mask, scrolled, and open thumbpieces denote periods and places.
Tigerware jug. German stoneware bellied jug of the sixteenth century mounted with Elizabethan silver or gilt embossed and engraved neckband, cover, foot, and handle mounts. Rarer examples of this technique are the coloured Turkish faïence jugs and a few English pottery jugs similarly mounted.
Tinkers. Known in Gaelic as *ceardan*, these had a long tradition of metalworking in the Highlands, and some were considerable craftsmen. Responsible for many of the early brooches, and probably for most of the brass and silver brooches of the seventeenth and eighteenth centuries. Sometimes made domestic articles of silver, but in nineteenth century degenerated into menders of pots and pans.
Tinned. Sheffield plate coated with pure tin, deposited on the copper surface by first sprinkling it with sal ammoniac, and then washing with molten tin. Early hollow ware was tinned inside: after the introduction of double-faced plate the backs of large trays and waiters were usually tinned, and the interiors of tea urns, dish covers, coffee pots, and hot-water jugs. Even in the 1820s catalogues describe trays, snuffer dishes, and so on as having either 'tinned' or 'plated' backs.
Toasted-cheese dish. Oval or oblong dish with hinged cover and hot-water compartment below. Sometimes fitted with separate pans to hold the cheese. Introduced in late eighteenth century.
Toast rack. Introduced about 1770. Early examples have detachable wires on oval base. Boat-shaped form *c.* 1790 followed by oblong examples, usually on four feet with ring handle above.
Tobacco box. Flat, oval or circular box with hinged or detachable lid, dating from late seventeenth century onwards. Often finely engraved with armorials or ciphers.

Toddy ladle. *See* Ladle, Punch.
Toilet sets. Of gold or silver were made for the *grandes dames* of the seventeenth and eighteenth centuries. They might contain as many as fifty-three pieces, as did the gold one made for the Empress Maria Theresa by Anton Mathias Domanek in about 1750, and sometimes included, besides pots, brushes, and combs, such objects as bodkins, tongue scrapers, and combined tooth- and earpicks.
Toothpicks and **toothpick cases.** Of silver and gold are not known to have survived in the United States, although mentioned in the seventeenth and eighteenth centuries.
Touch. Maker's mark, impressed with a punch.
Touchstone. A piece of polished 'stone' on which a piece of silver of known quality could be rubbed to compare its mark with that of a piece being assayed.
Toy silver. Miniature models of every form of wrought plate made for children and doll's house use. Sometimes considered to be travellers' sample pieces, but the evidence of specialist makers' marks in this genre establishes their true nature. Rare in America, but a set made for Bethea Shrimpton by an unidentified silversmith is in the Garvan Collection at Yale.
Trembleuses. Little silver trays with stands, usually in the form of leaves, to hold porcelain cups. These objects, which were probably derived from a French pattern, appear to have been a speciality of Genoese silversmiths and to have been made only in the 1750s and 1760s and in mid-nineteenth century.
Trencher salt. Small individual salt cellar with solid sides reaching to the base. Earliest examples date from about 1630. The standard form of table salt till about 1725. Of circular, oval, square, or polygonal form with oval or circular well.
Tulip design. Floral decoration in form of a tulip is found in Boston and New York silver, known through both Dutch and English precedent.
Tumblers. Are the rounded based cups familiar in various sizes.
Tureen. Circular or oval bowl and cover for soup introduced in early eighteenth century. Richly decorated in rococo period. Later of plain classical vase form, becoming elaborate again in the nineteenth century. Small versions of matching design to the soup tureen introduced about 1760 in sets of two or four as alternative to sauceboat.

Eighteenth-century tureens are among the most magnificent examples of Italian plate. Some of them are as much as 18 inches (45.7 cm) high. The knobs on their covers were often modelled in the form of human figures or delicately wrought still-life groups of dead game or vegetables. Usually they were provided with large shallow dishes in which to stand.
Tureen ladles. Appear in Revere's ledgers, but silver tureens of colonial make are rare if existent. A few from the Federal period follow classic forms. John Singleton Copley wrote from Paris of 'Soupp . . . in Silver Turenes' in 1774, which probably would not have been noteworthy had he known them at home.
Urn. *See* Tea urn.
Vase. Sets of large, richly decorated vases and bottles for chimney display date from the Restoration. In the late eighteenth century large models of classical form appear for presentation purposes. In the early nineteenth century the Warwick Vase was reproduced in this way. (*See* illustration overleaf.)

Soup tureen and cover on stand with matching ladle, by Edward Wakelin and William Taylor, London, 1783. Thomas Lumley, London

In the south of Italy altar vases were often provided with bouquets of paper-thin silver or, more usually, silver-gilt, flowers and foliage.
Vegetable dish. Of circular or oval form with straight, deep sides and cover, introduced late eighteenth century (*see also* Hash dish).
Venison dish. Similar to meat dish with channels and well for collecting gravy.
Vinaigrette. Small box with hinged lid and inner pierced grille holding sponge for aromatic vinegar. For ladies' use against faintness and megrims. Introduced late seventeenth century in many varieties of forms, e.g. books, purses, eggs, etc.

Below Selection of vinaigrettes of various shapes. They include a fish, 1817, and a crown, 1820, by Joseph Willmore, Birmingham; a basket of flowers by T. Shaw, Birmingham, 1820; a cow by Wilkinson & Co., Sheffield, 1834; and a musical instrument, French, *c.* 1850. The porcelain vinaigrette (*centre bottom*) is Viennese, *c.* 1850, and was probably worn as a necklace. The earliest examples are the egg, S. Pemberton, Birmingham 1789, and the scallop

Voyding dish or **voyder.** Large dish for collecting broken meats and table remnants. A medieval term. The only known surviving example, a seventeenth-century replacement of an earlier dish, belongs to the Drapers' Company.

Waiter. Small tray for handing wine glass, letter, etc. Conforms generally to salver form (*q.v.*). In eighteenth century often found in pairs *en suite* with the larger salver. The small, early, footed form often misnamed *tazza* (*q.v.*).

Footed waiter, 1724

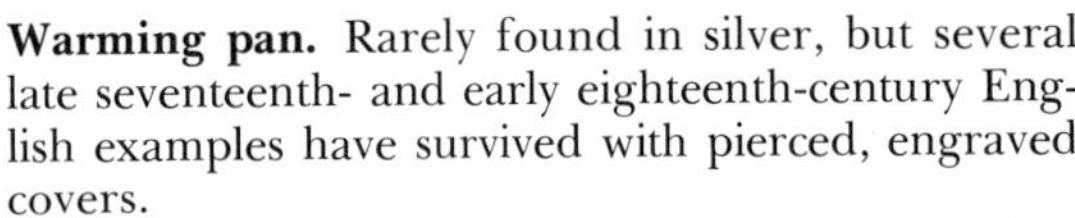

Warming pan. Rarely found in silver, but several late seventeenth- and early eighteenth-century English examples have survived with pierced, engraved covers.

Waxjack, 1795

Water pots. Seemingly appear first in an advertisement in Philadelphia in 1782 as 'milk pots, water ditto . . .' but the beverage was not catered for by colonial goldsmiths.

Waxjack. Openframe stand for coil of sealing taper threaded on central pin and led through nozzle above. Found late seventeenth century onwards. Several enclosed types made after *c.* 1750.

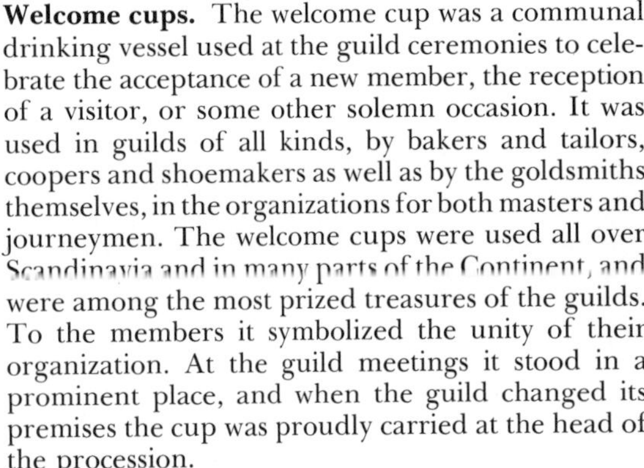

Welcome cups. The welcome cup was a communal drinking vessel used at the guild ceremonies to celebrate the acceptance of a new member, the reception of a visitor, or some other solemn occasion. It was used in guilds of all kinds, by bakers and tailors, coopers and shoemakers as well as by the goldsmiths themselves, in the organizations for both masters and journeymen. The welcome cups were used all over Scandinavia and in many parts of the Continent, and were among the most prized treasures of the guilds. To the members it symbolized the unity of their organization. At the guild meetings it stood in a prominent place, and when the guild changed its premises the cup was proudly carried at the head of the procession.

Occasionally ordinary beakers or tankards did service as welcome cups, but mostly they were tall goblets with ornate stems and lids with elaborate handles in pewter, copper, or, usually, silver. The details of the shape changed with the varying fashions, but generally speaking they were conservative in style. An early eighteenth-century type, with a marked horizontal division of the bowl, rich chased decoration, and a gay figure in moulded work as handle to the lid, was made over a period of forty years in Bergen. Apart from being the traditional welcome cup of the period, it seems to have been the set masterpiece for Bergen goldsmiths. A fine example of this type, unfortunately unmarked, is in the Victoria and Albert Museum.

Sometimes, but not always, the welcome cup carries inscriptions that describe its purpose. Members and friends of the guild had badges made with their names and appropriate inscriptions to be hung on the cup on special occasions. When all the badges were in place the cup was more or less covered. Welcome cups were made in Norway well into the nineteenth century.

Vase, Trafalgar, designed by John Flaxman and made by Digby Scott and Benjamin Smith, London, 1805–6. Bears figures of Britannia Triumphant and a warrior slaying a serpent and the inscription 'Britons Strike Home'

Left Welcome cup, Bergen, 1745–50. Victoria & Albert Museum

Westbrooke baby house. A superlative collection near Baldock, Hertfordshire, of more than fifty miniature silver toys has accompanied this doll's house, which, for nearly 250 years, has been handed down from mother to daughter as an heirloom. The majority of these are struck with London hallmarks of the Britannia standard. A grate with a fireback in *repoussé* work included in this collection is struck with the maker's mark *ID*., also found on a mug, six plates, and four chargers. This is the mark of John Deard, toyman and goldsmith of Fleet Street, who died in 1731. A wall-down hearth with firedogs, tongs, shovel, and poker bear the London hallmark for 1718 and the maker's mark *CL*, showing them to have been made by John Clifton, Foster Lane, a well-known silver toy maker. There are two chairs in the late seventeenth-century style bearing the mark of Matthew Madden of Lombard Street, registered in 1696, and a three-legged pot made by Thomas Evesdon in 1713. A rare detail is a foot stove, such as were used in wealthy homes, in plate silver decorated with ornamental piercing, 'to laye under their feete when they write, or studie, in cold weather, or in their coaches to keep their feet warm'.

'Whistles'. The hole at end of a tankard handle, mistakenly called a whistle, was actually a vent for hot air to be expelled during soldering.

Whistles. With corals and bells for children are depicted in gold and silver in portraits and survive of eighteenth-century craftsmanship from the three centres: Boston, New York, and Philadelphia.

Whistle tankard or **cup.** *See* Blowhole.

Wine-bottle stand. Oval bowl on moulded base for holding the early form of glass wine bottle with rounded base of early eighteenth century. The very rare examples that survive are sometimes mistaken for sugar bowls.

Wine bowls, wine-cups, and **wine tumblers.** Are recorded in American silver annals of colonial time, but not identified in form.

Wine cistern. Large oval vessel on base or separate feet for cooling bottles in cold water or ice. Survivals date from Charles II to the mid-eighteenth century. Important decorative pieces of a high standard of design and ornament.

Wine coaster. Circular decanter or bottle stand for table use. Pierced or solid silver sides, usually with turned wood base. Introduced about mid-eighteenth century. Occur in pairs, set of four, or greater numbers.

Wine cooler. Also known as ice pail. Vessel for holding single bottle. A few survivals from early eighteenth century, but not common till about 1780. Vase or tub shape, and occasionally of double oval form. Occur in pairs or sets of four or more. Usually fitted with liner and flat rim.

Wine fountain. Large vessel-shaped urn with tap in body.

Wine funnel. Tapering funnel with detachable strainer for decanting. Circular stands of saucer form with domed centres were used with the funnels.

Wine label. Pierced or chased label with the name of the wine hung by chain around decanter neck. A rarer form have neck ring in place of chain. Many varieties of form and name, including plain intials, occur from mid-eighteenth century onwards.

Wine tasters. Small vessels, usually two-handled, found in all wine-growing countries, though the Portuguese type with a domed centre, to reflect the colour of the wine, is said to be of English origin.

Wirework. Among the rarest pieces of Sheffield plate are those constructed from plated wires, dating chiefly between 1785 and 1815. They were a direct result of George Whateley's patented invention of 1768, by which copper rods, round, flat, square, and triangular, could be silver-plated. Not until after the expiry of the patent in 1782 was this work carried out on a considerable scale, the demand being chiefly for a wide range of inexpensive table baskets, toast racks, and *épergnes*. The wires at first were cut into short lengths, fitted into holes drilled into rim and base, and soldered into position. Early in the nineteenth century less-expensive wire ware was made by bending lengths of wire into continuous curves forming patterns. These were soldered to rim and base, thus saving the cost of drilling. Ball handles might consist of flat wire curved and spaced with balls or other ornament, or of twisted wire of various sections.

Collectors should realize that dessert, cake and sweetmeat baskets in many period styles have been made by the twentieth-century copyists. Wires in sections other than round are not found in this series, in which the soldering lacks the experience of the old workers.

Wrigglework. A form of engraving employing a zigzag line cut by a rocking motion. Used in conjunction with line engraving at certain periods, principally late seventeenth century, for filling in spaces between engraved lines. Its use may have been copied from the more extensive practice in pewter.

For Further Reading

Note. The place given with each title is not necessarily the only place of publication. Many titles have been issued, for example, both in Britain and the United States.

The Aesthetic Movement; The Arts and Crafts Movement; Art Nouveau; Art Deco, etc.

MORRIS & CO. AND 'JAPONESQUE'

Aslin, Elizabeth, *The Aesthetic Movement*, London, 1969
Briggs, Asa, (ed.), *William Morris: Selected Writings and Designs*, Harmondsworth, 1962
Cook, E. T., and Wedderburn, Alexander, *The Complete Works of John Ruskin*, London, 1912
Ferriday, Peter, (ed.), *Victorian Architecture*, London, 1963
Holman Hunt, W., *Pre-Raphaelitism and the Pre-Raphaelite Brotherhood*, London, 1905
Harrison, Martin, and Waters, Bill, *Burne-Jones*, London, 1973
Watkinson, Ray, *William Morris as Designer*, London, 1967

ARTS AND CRAFTS

Ashbee, C. R., *The Ideals of the Craftsman*, London, 1889
Mackmurdo, A. H., (ed.), *Plain Handicrafts . . . being essays by artists setting forth the principles of designs*, London, 1971
Naylor, Gillian, *The Arts and Crafts Movement*, London, 1971

FIN DE SIÈCLE

Huysmans, J.-K., *À Rebours*, Paris, 1884
Jackson, Holbrook, *The Eighteen Nineties*, London, 1922
Julian, Philippe, *Oscar Wilde*, trans. Violet Wyndham, London, 1969
Pater, Walter, *Studies in the History of the Renaissance*, London, 1873
Reade, Brian, *Aubrey Beardsley*, London, 1967

ART NOUVEAU

Battersby, Martin, *Art Nouveau*, Feltham, 1969
Hillier, Bevis, *One Hundred Years of Posters*, London, 1972
Howarth, Thomas, *Charles Rennie Mackintosh and the Modern Movement*, London, 1952
Lövgren, S., *The Genesis of Modernism: Seurat, Gauguin, van Gogh and French Symbolism in the 1880s*, Stockholm, 1959
Schmutzler, Robert, *Art Nouveau*, New York, 1962
Snowman, Kenneth A., *The Art of Carl Fabergé*, London, 1964
Sweeney, James Johnson, and Sert, Josep Lluís, *Antoni Gaudí*, London, 1960

ART AND INDUSTRY

John, Augustus, *Chiaroscuro* , London, 1952
Lethaby, W. R., (ed.), *The Study and Practice of Artistic Crafts*, London, 1902
Roh, Franz, *German Art in the Twentieth Century*, London, 1958
Rothenstein, Sir William, *Men and Memories*, 2 vols, London, 1931–3
Voysey, C. F. A., *Reason as a Basis of Art*, London, 1906
Yeats, W. B., *The Trembling of the Veil*, London, 1924

BALLETOMANIA

Beaumont, Cyril, *The Diaghilev Ballet in London*, London, 1940
Buckle, Richard, *In Search of Diaghilev*, London, 1955
Spencer, Charles, *Léon Bakst*, London, 1973

ART DECO

Acton, Harold, *Memoirs of an Aesthete*, London, 1948
Battersby, Martin, *The Decorative Twenties*, London, 1969
Battersby, Martin, *The Decorative Thirties*, London, 1971
Fry, Roger, *Vision and Design*, London, 1920
Gloag, John, (ed.), *Design in Modern Life*, London, 1934
Hillier, Bevis, *The World of Art Deco*, London, 1971
Le Corbusier, *Vers une Architecture*, Paris, 1923
Naylor, Gillian, *The Bauhaus*, London, 1968
Russell, Sir Gordon, *Designer's Trade*, London, 1968
Sexton, R. W., and Betts, B. F., *American Theatres of Today*, New York, 1927
Spencer, Charles, *Erté*, London, 1970

Antiquities

GENERAL

Ancient People and Places, (series), Thames and Hudson, London, 1956–
Art of the World, (series), Holle Verlag, Baden Baden
Breasted, James H., *Ancient Times*
Burland, C. A., *Man and Art*, London, 1959
The Cambridge Ancient History, 12 vols, Cambridge University Press, Cambridge
The Cambridge Medieval History, 8 vols, Cambridge University Press, Cambridge
Childe, Gordon, *What Happened in History*, London, 1960
Clarke, G. and Piggot, S., *Prehistoric Societies*, London, 1965
Discovering Art, 12 vols, Fratelli Fabri, Milan, 1961
History of the World, 12 vols, Hamlyn, Feltham, 1969

MIDDLE EASTERN

Akurgal, E., *The art of the Hittites*, London, 1962
Lloyd, Seton, *The Art of the Ancient Near East*, London, 1961
Lloyd, Seton, *Early Highland People of Anatolia*, London, 1967
Mellaert, J., *Earliest Civilisations of the Near East*, London, 1965
Olmstead, A. T., *A History of the Persian Empire*, Chicago, 1948
Oppenheim, A. L., *Ancient Mesopotamia*, London, 1964
Strommenger, E., *The Art of Mesopotamia*, London, 1964

EGYPTIAN AND NORTH AFRICAN

Breasted, James H., *History of Egypt*, London, 1956
Gardiner, Alan, *Egypt of the Pharaohs*, Oxford, 1961
Guillaume, A., *Islam*, repr., Harmondsworth, 1969
Hitti, P. K., *History of the Arabs*, repr., London, 1970
Lewis, B., *The Arabs in History*, repr., London, 1966
Shinnie, P. L., *Meroë, A Civilisation of the Sudan*, London, 1967
Smith, W. Stevenson, *The Art and Architecture of Ancient Egypt*, Harmondsworth, 1958
Spuler, Bertold, *The Muslim World*, 2 vols, Leiden, 1960

CLASSICAL

Bell, H. Idris, *Cults and Creeds in Graeco-Roman Egypt*, Liverpool, 1957

Boardman, J., *Greek Art*, London, 1964
Boardman, J., *The Greeks Overseas*, Harmondsworth, 1964
Cook, J. M., *The Greeks in Ionia and the East*, London, 1963
Cottrell, Leonard, *The Bull of Minos*, repr., London, 1971
Cowell, F. R., *Everyday Life in Ancient Rome*, London, 1968
Finley, M. I., *The World of Odysseus*, Harmondsworth, 1964
Huxley, G. L., *Early Sparta*, London, 1962
James, E. O., *The Ancient Gods*, London, 1960
Jones, A. H. M., *The Decline of the Ancient World*, London, 1966
Jones, A. H. M., *The Later Roman Empire*, 3 vols, Oxford, 1964
Kenna, V. E. G., *Cretan Seals*, Oxford, 1960
Kirk, G. S., *The Songs of Homer*, Cambridge, 1962
Scullard, H. H., *The Etruscan Cities and Rome*, London, 1967
Wellard, James, *The Search for the Etruscans*, London, 1973
Wheeler, Mortimer, *Roman Art and Architecture*, London, 1964
Woodhead, A. G., *The Greeks in the West*, London, 1962

WESTERN AND NORTHERN EUROPEAN

Brøndsted, Johannes, *The Vikings*, Harmondsworth, 1965
Frere-Cook, Gervis, *Decorative Arts of the Christian Church*, London, 1972
Moss, H. St L. B., *The Birth of the Middle Ages*, London, 1935
Rorig, F., *The Medieval Town*, London, 1967
Sturleson, Snorri, *Heimskringla*, Cambridge University Press ed., 1932
Trevor-Roper, H., *The Rise of Christian Europe*, London, 1966
Vasiliev, A. A., *History of the Byzantine Empire*, Oxford, 1953

SOUTH EAST ASIAN

Burland, C. A. and Forman, W., *Marco Polo*, Vienna, 1970
The Cambridge History of India, London, 1922
Hall, D. G. E., *History of Southeast Asia*, repr., London, 1968
Thapar, Romila, *A History of India*, Harmondsworth, 1965
Wheeler, Mortimer, *Early India and Pakistan to Asoka*, London, 1959

NORTH, CENTRAL AND SOUTH AMERICAN

Burland, C. A., *Montezuma*, London, 1973
Burland, C. A., *People of the Ancient Americas*, Feltham, 1970
Dockstader, Frederick, *Indian Art of Central America*, London, 1964
Kendall, Ann, *Everyday Life of the Incas*, London, 1973
Lothrop, S. K., *Treasures of Ancient America*, Geneva, 1964
Mason, J. Alden, *The Ancient Civilisations of Peru*, Harmondsworth, 1956
Miles, Charles, *Indian and Eskimo Art of North America*, Chicago, 1963
Morley, S. G., *The Ancient Maya*, repr., Stanford, 1969
Thompson, J. Eric S., *The Rise and Fall of Maya Civilization*, London, 1956

Arms and Armour

Blackmore, Howard L., *British Military Firearms 1650–1850*, London, 1961
Blair, Claude, *European Armour, c. 1066–1700*, repr., London, 1972
Blair, Claude, *European and American Arms, c. 1100–1850*, London, 1962
Blair, Claude, *Pistols of the World*, London, 1968
Boudet, Jacques, *The Ancient Art of Warfare*, 2 vols, London, 1966
Hayward, J. F., *The Art of the Gunmaker*, vol I, 2nd ed., London, 1965, vol II, London, 1963
Held, Robert, *The Age of Firearms*, repr., New York, 1959
Joly, H. D., *Japanese Swordguards*, London, 1910
Laking, Sir Guy, *A Record of European Armour and Arms through Seven Centuries*, 5 vols, London, 1920–2
Norman, A. V. B., *Small Swords and Military Swords*, London, 1967
Peterson, Harold L., *Arms and Armor in Colonial America 1526–1783*, Pa., 1956
Peterson, Harold L., *Encyclopedia of Firearms*, London, 1964
Robinson, B. W., *Arms and Armour of Old Japan*, London, 1951
Wilkinson, Frederick, *Antique Firearms*, London, 1969
Wilkinson, Frederick, *Small Arms*, London, 1968

Barometers, Clocks and Watches

BAROMETERS

Bell, G. H. and E. F., *Old English Barometers*, Winchester, 1952
Goodison, N., *English Barometers, 1680–1860*, London, 1969
Middleton, W. E. K., *The History of the Barometer*, London, 1964

CLOCKS AND WATCHES

Baillie, G. H., *Watchmakers and Clockmakers of the World*, repr., London, 1966
Britten's Old Clocks and Watches and their Makers, 8th ed., London, 1973
Bruton, E., *Clocks and Watches, 1400–1900*, London, 1967
Bruton, E., *The Longcase Clock*, London, 1967
Cescinsky and Webster, *English Domestic Clocks*, London, 1913
Clutton, Cecil and Daniels, George, *Watches*, London, 1965
Cuss, T. P. Camerer, *The Country Life Book of Clocks*, London, 1967
Cuss, T. P. Camerer, *The Story of Watches*, repr., London, 1967
Drepperd, Carl, *American Clocks and Clockmakers*, New York, 1955
Edey, Winthrop, *French Clocks*, New York, 1967
Lloyd, Alan, *The English Domestic Clock* privately printed, 1938
Lloyd, Alan, *Old Clocks*, London, 3rd ed., 1964
Milham, Willis I., *Time and Timekeepers*, New York, 1941
Nutting, Wallace, *The Clock Book*, New York, 1935
Palmer, Brooks, *A Treasury of American Clocks*, New York, 1967
Rees, Abraham, *Clocks, Watches and Chronometers*, reprint of sections from Rees' *Encyclopaedia* (1819–20), Devon, 1970
Robertson, J. Drummond, *The Evolution of Clockwork*, repr., London, 1972
Symonds, R. W., *A Book of English Clocks*, London, 1947
Symonds, R. W., *Thomas Tompion, His Life and Work*, London, 1951
Tardy, *Dictionnaire des Horloges Français*, Paris, 1971
Thompson, Richard, *Antique American Clocks and Watches*, Princeton, 1968
Wenham, Edward, *Old Clocks for Modern Use*, London, 1951

Carpets and Rugs

Bode, Wilhelm von and Kühnel, Ernst, *Antique Rugs from the Near East*, trans. C. G. Ellis, rev. ed., London 1970
Collingwood, Peter, *The Techniques of Rug Weaving*, London, 1968

Delabere, C. J., *How to Identify Persian and other Oriental Rugs*, New York, 1953
Dilley, Arthur Urbane, *Oriental Rugs and Carpets*, 2nd ed., New York, 1960
Erdmann, Kurt, *Seven Hundred Years of Oriental Carpets*, trans. M. Beattie and H. Herzog, London, 1970
Formenton, Fabio, *Oriental Rugs and Carpets*, trans. P. L. Phillips, London, 1972
Haack, Hermann, *Oriental Rugs: an Illustrated Guide*, trans. George and Cornelia Wingfield Digby, London, 1960
Hubel, Reinhard G., *The Book of Carpets*, trans. K. Watson, London, 1971
Kendrick, A. F. and Tattersall, C. E. G., *Handwoven Carpets, Oriental and European*, 2 vols, London, 1922
Kühnel, Ernst and Bellinger, Louise, *Cairene Rugs and Others Technically Related*, Washington
Ries, Estelle H., *American Rugs*, Ohio, 1950
Schürmann, Ulrich, *Central Asian Carpets*, trans. A. Grainge, London, 1970
Tattersall, C. E. C., *The Carpets of Persia*, London, 1931
Tattersall, C. E. C., *A History of British Carpets*, Leigh-on-Sea, 1934
Tattersall, C. E. C., *Notes on Carpet Knotting and Weaving*, 4th ed., London, 1949
Walker, Lydia LeBaron, *Homecraft Rugs*, New York, 1929
Winthrop, William, *Rare Hook Rugs*, Mass., 1941

Coins and Medals

COINS

Brooke, G. C., *English Coins*, London, 1950
Carson, R. A. G., *Coins, Ancient, Medieval and Modern*, London, 1971
Corothers, Neil, *Fractional Currency*, New York, 1930
Craig, W. D., *Coins of the World, 1750–1850*, Racine, 1966
Crosby, S. S., *Early Coins of America*, repr., 1970
Engel, A. and Serrure, R., *Traité de Numismatique du Moyen Âge*, vols I–III, Paris, 1891–1905
Engel, A. and Serrure, R., *Traité de Numismatique Moderne et Contemporaine*, vols I–II, Paris, 1897–9
Grueber, H. A., *Coins of the Roman Republic in the British Museum*, 3 vols, repr., 1970
Hazlitt, W. C., *The Coinage of the European Continent*, London, 1893
Head, Barclay V., *Historia Numorum: A Handbook of Greek Numismatics*, Oxford, 1911
Head, Barclay, V., *A Guide to the Principal Coins of the Greeks*, London, 1959
Jenkins, G. K., *Ancient Greek Coins*, London, 1973
Linecas, H. W. A., *Collecting*, London, 1970
Mack, R. P., *The Coinage of Ancient Britain*, London, 1964
Mattingly, H. and Carson, R. A. G., *Coins of the Roman Empire in the British Museum*, vols. I–VI, 1923–62
Mattingly, H., *Roman Coins*, London, 1960
Mattingly, H., Sydenham, E. A. et al., *Roman Imperial Coinage*, vols. I–IX, London, 1923–69
Miller, H. C. et al., *State Coinages of New England*, New York, 1920
Seltman, C. T., *Greek Coins*, London, 1960
Stewart, I. H., *The Scottish Coinage*, London, 1955
Vlack, Robert A., *Early American Coins*, New York, 1965
Whitting, P. D., *Byzantine Coins*, London, 1973
Yeoman, R. S., *A Catalog of Modern World Coins, 1850–1964*, Racine, 1965

MEDALS

Belden, B. L., *Indian Peace Medals Issued in the United States*, repr., New York, 1966
Forrer, L. S., *Biographical Dictionary of Medallists*, London, 1902–30
The Medallic History of the United States of America, 1776–1876, repr., New York, 1967

Ethnographica

AFRICAN

Elisofon, Eliot and Fagg, William, *The Sculpture of Africa*, London, 1958
Fagg, William, *Nigerian Images*, London, 1963
Himmelheber, Hans, *Negerkunst und Negerkünstler*, Brunswick, 1960
Leiris, Michel and Delange, Jacqueline, *African Art*, London, 1968
Leuzinger, Elsy, *Africa: The Art of the Negro Peoples*, London, 1960
Paulme, Denise, *African Sculpture*, London, 1962
Sieber, Roy, *African Textiles and Decorative Arts*, The Museum of Modern Art, New York, 1972
Willet, Frank, *African Art*, London, 1971

OCEANIAN

Barrow, T., *Art and Life in Polynesia*, Wellington, 1972
Barrow, T., *Maori Wood Sculpture*, Wellington, 1969
Berndt, Ronald M., (ed.), *Australian Aboriginal Art*, New York, 1964
Bühler, Alfred, Barrow, T. and Mountford, Charles P., *Oceania and Australia: The Art of the South Seas*, London, 1962
Force, Roland W. and Maryanne, *The Fuller Collection of Pacific Artifacts*, London, 1971
Guiart, Jean, *The Arts of the South Pacific*, London, 1963
Kupka, Karel, *Dawn of Art*, Sydney, 1965
Schmitz, Carl A., *Oceanic Art*, New York

AMERICAN INDIAN AND ESKIMO

American Indian Art: Form and Tradition, and exhibition catalogue, New York, 1972
Bunzel, Ruth, L., *The Pueblo Potter*, 2nd ed., New York, 1972
Collins, Henry B., de Laguna, Federica, Carpenter, Edmund and Stone, Peter, *The Far North: 2000 Years of American Eskimo and Indian Art*, Washington, 1973
Colton, Harold S., *Hopi Kachina Dolls*, rev. ed., Albuquerque, 1959
Dark, Philip J. C., *Bush Negro Art*, Tiranti, repr., 1954
Dockstader, Frederick J., *Indian Art in America*, London
Dockstader, Frederick J., *South American Indian Art*, London, 1967
Feder, Norman, *American Indian Art*, New York
Hartman, Günther, *Masken Südamerikanischer Naturvölker*, Museum für Völkerkunde, Berlin, 1967
Kahlenberg, Mary Hunt and Berlant, Anthony, *The Navajo Blanket*, New York, 1972
Ray, Dorothy Jean, *Eskimo Masks: Art and Ceremony*, Seattle, 1967
Siebert, Erna and Forman, Werner, *North American Indian Art*, London, 1967

Furniture

AMERICAN

Andrews, Edward Deming, *The People Called Shakers: A Search for the Perfect Society*, New York, 1953
Bjerkoe, Ethel Hall, *Cabinetmakers of America*, New York, 1957
Burton, E. Milby, *Charleston Furniture 1700–1825*, Narberth, Pa., 1955
Carpenter, Ralph E. Jr, *The Arts and Crafts of Newport*, 1954
Cornelius, Charles O., *Early American Furniture, New York, 1926*
Davidson, M. B., The American Heritage History of Antiques, New York, 1969
Downs, Joseph, *American Furniture: Queen Anne and Chippendale Periods*, rev. ed., New York, 1967
Drepperd, Carl, *Handbook of Antique Chairs*, New York, 1948
Hayward, Helena, (ed.), *World Furniture*, repr., London, 1969

Hornor, William M., *Blue Book of Philadelphia Furniture*, 1931

Kettell, Russell H., *Pine Furniture of Early New England*, New York, 1949

Lockwood, L. V., *Colonial Furniture in America*, 3 vols, New York, 1926

McClellan, Nancy, *Duncan Phyfe and the English Regency*, 1939

Nutting, Wallace, *Furniture Treasury*, 3 vols, New York, 1948–9

Ormsbee, Thomas H., *Field Guide to American Victorian Furniture*, Boston, 1951

Pratt, Richard, *Second Treasury of Early American Homes*, New York, 1954

Stoneman, Vernon C., *John and Thomas Seymour: Cabinetmakers in Boston*, 1959

Williams, H. L., *Country Furniture of Early America*, New York, 1963

CHINESE AND JAPANESE

Ecke, G., *Chinese Domestic Furniture*, repr., Rutland, 1963

Herberts, Dr Kurt, *Oriental Lacquer*, London, 1962

Jahss, M. and B., *Inro, and other forms of Japanese lacquer art*, London, 1970

Kates, George N., *Chinese Household Furniture*, London, 1946

Newman, A. and Ryerson, E., *Japanese Art: A Collector's Guide*, London, 1964

Swann, Peter C., *Introduction to the Arts of Japan*, Oxford, 1958

Swann, Peter C., *Arts of China, Korea, and Japan*, London, 1963

Willetts, William, *Chinese Art*, repr., London, 1965

Yee, Chiang, *Chinese Calligraphy*, London, 1954

ENGLISH

Agius, Pauline, *Late Sixteenth- and Seventeenth-century Furniture in Oxford*, *Furniture History*, VII, (Journal of the Furniture History Society), London, 1971

Ancient Church Chests and Chairs in the Home Counties round Greater London, London, 1929

Ash, D., *Dictionary of English Antique Furniture*, London, 1970

Aslin, Elizabeth, *Nineteenth-Century English Furniture*, London, 1962

Boger, Louise Ade, *The Complete Guide to Furniture Styles*, London, 1961

Bond, Francis, *Wood Carvings in English Churches*, Oxford, 1910

Brackett, Oliver, *Late Stuart to Queen Anne Furniture*, Victoria and Albert Museum, London, 1927

Coleridge, Anthony, *Chippendale Furniture*, London, 1968

Edwards, Ralph and Ramsay, L., *The Connoisseur Period Guides*, London, 1956

Edwards, Ralph, *English Chairs*, 2nd ed., Victoria and Albert Museum, London, 1957

Edwards, Ralph, *Georgian Furniture*, 2nd ed., Victoria and Albert Museum, London, 1957

Edwards, Ralph and Jourdain, Margaret, *Georgian Cabinet-Makers c. 1700–1800*, rev. ed., London, 1955

Edwards, Ralph, *Late Tudor and Early Stuart Furniture*, Victoria and Albert Museum, London, 1930

Edwards, Ralph, *The Shorter Dictionary of English Furniture*, London, 1964

Howard, F. E. and Crossley, F. H., *English Church Woodwork*, 2nd ed., London, 1927

Fastnedge, Ralph, *English Furniture Styles from 1500 to 1830*, repr., London, 1969

Fastnedge, Ralph, *Sheraton Furniture*, London, 1962

Gloag, John, *English Furniture*, rev. ed., London, 1973

Gloag, John, *The Englishman's Chair*, London, 1964

Gloag, John, *Georgian Grace*, London, 1967

Gloag, John, (ed.), *A Short Dictionary of Furniture*, rev. ed., London, 1969

Gloag, John, *A Social History of Furniture Design from BC 1300 to AD 1960*, London, 1966

Gloag, John, *Victorian Taste*, repr., Newton Abbot, 1972

Grandjean, Serge, *Empire Furniture*, London, 1966

Hayden, Arthur, *Chats on Cottage and Farmhouse Furniture*, rev. Cyril G. E. Bunt, London, 1950

Hayward, Charles H., *English Period Furniture*, repr., London, 1971

Hayward, Helena, (ed.), *World Furniture*, repr., London, 1969

Hayward, John F., *Tables in the Victoria and Albert Museum*, London, 1961

Heal, Sir Ambrose, *The London Furniture Makers (1660–1840)*, London, 1953

A History of English Furniture, Victoria and Albert Museum, London, 1955

Honour, Hugh, *Cabinet Makers and Furniture Designers*, London, 1969

Howard, F. E. and Crossley, F. H., *English Church Woodwork*, 2nd ed., London, 1927

Johnston, Philip Mainwaring, *Church Chests of the Twelfth and Thirteenth Centuries in England*, repr. from *Archaeological Journal* LXIV, London, 1908

Joy, Edward T., *Chippendale*, Middlesex, 1971

Jourdain, Margaret, *Regency Furniture*, London, 1946

Lewer, H. W. and Wall, J. C., *Church Chests of Essex*, London, 1913

MacQuoid, P. and Edwards, Ralph, *Dictionary of English Furniture*, repr., London, 1954

Mercer, Eric, *Furniture, 700–1700*, London, 1969

Musgrave, Clifford W., *Adam, Hepplewhite and Other Neo-Classical Furniture*, London, 1966

Musgrave, Clifford W., *Regency Furniture 1800–30*, rev. ed., London, 1970

Nickerson, D., *English Eighteenth-Century Furniture*, London, 1963

Nutting, Wallace, *A Windsor Handbook*, 1917

Nutting, Wallace II, *Furniture Treasury*, 1948

Pinto, Edward H., *Treen*, rev. ed., London, 1969

Ramsay, L. and Comstock, Helen, (eds.), *The Connoisseur's Guide to Antique Furniture*, London, 1969

Roe, Fred, *A History of Oak Furniture*, London, 1920

Roe, F. Gordon, *English Cottage Furniture*, rev. ed., London, 1961

Roe, F. Gordon, *Windsor Chairs*, London, 1953

Sheraton Furniture Designs, preface by Ralph Edwards, London, 1948

Smith, Donald, *Old Furniture and Woodwork*, 2nd ed., London, 1947

Smith, H. Clifford, *Gothic and Early Tudor Furniture*, Victoria and Albert Museum, London, 1930

Steer, Francis W., *Farm and Cottage Inventories of Mid-Essex, 1635–1749*, repr., Chelmsford, 1970

Symonds, R. W., *English Furniture from Charles II to George II*, London, 1929

Symonds, R. W., *Furniture Making in the Seventeenth and Eighteenth Century in England*, London, 1955

Thornton, Peter, *Two Problems ('When was a cupboard not a cupboard')*, *Furniture History*, VII, (Journal of the Furniture History Society), London, 1971

Twiston-Davies, Sir L. and Lloyd-Johnes, H. J., *Welsh Furniture: An Introduction*, Cardiff, 1950

Ward-Jackson, Peter, *English Furniture Designs of the Eighteenth Century*, Victoria and Albert Museum, London, 1959

Wills, G., *English Furniture, 1550–1760*, Enfield, 1971

FRENCH

Dacier, Emile, 'Arts, Style, and Techniques', *Le Style Louis XVI*, Paris, 1939

Dilke, Lady, *French Furniture and Decoration in the Eighteenth Century*, London, 1901

Janneau, Guillaume and Devinoy, Pierre, *Le Meuble Léger en France*, Paris, 1948

Kimball, Fiske and Picard A. and J., *Le Style Louis XV: Origine et Évolution de Rococo*, Paris, 1949

Verlet, Pierre, *French Furniture and Interior Decoration of the 18th Century*, trans. G. Savage, London, 1967

Verlet, Pierre, *French Royal Furniture*, London, 1963

ITALIAN

Lorenzetti, G., *Lacche Veneziane del Settecento*, Venice, 1938

Morazzoni, Guiseppe, *Il Mobile Genovese*, Milan, 1949

Morazzoni, Guiseppe, *Il Mobile Italiano*, Florence, 1940

Morazzoni, Guiseppe, *Il Mobile Veneziane*, Milan, 1958

Odon, William, M., *A History of Italian Furniture from the Fourteenth to the Early Nineteenth Century*, New York, 1966–7

Pignatti, Terisio, *Lo Stile dei Mobile*, Verona, 1951

Glass

AMERICAN

Daniel, Dorothy, *Cut and Engraved Glass, 1771–1905*, repr., New York, 1965

Hunter, Frederick W., *Stiegel Glass*, repr., New York, 1966

Lee, Ruth Webb, *Early American Pressed Glass*, rev. ed., Northboro, Mass., 1946

Lee, Ruth Webb, *Sandwich Glass*, Pittsburg, Penn., 1931

Lindsey, Bessie M., *American Historical Glass*, rev. ed., London, 1967

McKearin, G. S. and H., *American Glass*, New York, 1948

McKearin, G. S. and H., *Two Hundred Years of American Blown Glass*, New York, 1950

Revi, A. C., *American Pressed Glass and Figure Bottles*, New York, 1964

Rose, James H., *The Story of American Pressed Glass of the Lacy Period*, New York, 1954

BRITISH

Ash, D., *How to Identify English Drinking Glasses and Decanters*, London, 1962

Beard, G. W., *Nineteenth-Century Cameo Glass*, Monmouthshire, 1956

Bickerton, L. M., *An Illustrated Guide to Eighteenth-Century English Drinking Glasses*, London, 1971

Bles, Joseph, *Rare English Glasses of the Seventeenth and Eighteenth Centuries*, London, 1926

Buckley, Francis, *History of Old English Glass*, London, 1925

Crompton, Sidney, *English Glass*, London, 1967

Davis, Derek C., *English Bottles and Decanters 1650–1900*, London, 1972

Davis, Derek C., *English and Irish Antique Glass*, London, 1965

Elville, E. M., *English and Irish Cut Glass 1750–1950*, London, 1953

Elville, E. M., *English Tableglass*, London, 1951

Foster, Kate, *Scent Bottles*, London, 1966

Francis, Grant R., *Old English Drinking Glasses*, London, 1926

Hartshorne, Albert, *Old English Glasses*, London, 1897

Haynes, E. B., *Glass Through the Ages*, rev. ed., London, 1970

Honey, W. B., *English Glass*, London, 1946

Hughes, G. Bernard, *Old English, Irish and Scottish Table Glass*, London, 1956

Thorpe, W. A., *English Glass*, rev. ed., London, 1961

Thorpe, W. A., *A History of English and Irish Glass*, rev. ed., London, 1969

Wakefield, Hugh, *19th-Century British Glass*, London, 1961

Westropp, M. S. Dudley, *Irish Glass*, London, 1920

FRENCH

Amic, Yolande, *L'Opaline Française au 19ième Siècle*, Paris, 1952

Barrelet, James, *La verrerie en France de l'Époque Gallo-Romaine à Nos Jours*, Paris, 1953

Chavance, René, *L'Art Française Depuis Vingt Ans: La Céramique et la Verrerie*, Paris, 1928

Galle, Émile, *Écrits Pour l'Art*, Paris, 1908

Rosenthal, L., *La Verrerie Française Depuis Cinquante Ans*, Paris, 1927

SCANDINAVIAN

Polak, A. B., *Gammelt Norsk Glass*, Oslo, 1953

Seitz, H., *Äldre Svenska Glas med Graverad Dekor*, Stockholm, 1936

VENETIAN

Gasparetto, A., *Il Vetro di Murano*, Venice, 1959

Hettes, Karel, *Old Venetian Glass*, trans. Ota Vojtisek, London, 1960

Mariacher, G., *L'Arte del Vetro*, Verona, 1954

Mariacher, G., *Italian Blown Glass*, trans. M. Bullock and J. Capra, London, 1961

PAPERWEIGHTS

Bergstrom, Evangeline G., *Old Glass Paperweights*, New York, 1947

Elville, E. M., *Paperweights and other Glass Curiosities*, London, 1954

Cloak, Evelyn Campbell, *Glass Paperweights*, London, 1969

Hollister, Paul, Jr., *The Encyclopedia of Glass Paperweights*, New York, 1969

McCawley, Patricia K., *Antique Glass Paperweights from France*, London, 1968

Jewelry

Aschengreen, C. Piacenti, *Il Museo degli Argenti a Firenze*, Milan, 1967

Bapst, G., *Histoire des Joyaux de la Couronne*, Paris, 1889

Barsali, Isa Belli, *European Enamels*, trans. Raymond Rudorff, London, 1969

Blakemore, Kenneth, *The Retail Jeweller's Guide*, London, 1969

Bossert, H. Th., *Geschichte des Kunstgewerbes aller Zeiten und Völker*, vol V, Berlin, 1928–35

Bulgari, C. G., *Argentiere Gemmari e Orafi D'Italia. Parte Prima: Roma*, Rome, 1959

Clifford, Anne, *Cut-Steel and Berlin Iron Jewellery*, Bath, 1971

Cooper, Diana and Battershill, Norman, *Victorian Sentimental Jewellery*, Devon, 1972

Evans, Joan, *English Jewellery from the Fifth Century A.D. to 1800*, London

Evans, Joan, *A History of Jewellery 1100–1870*, 2nd ed., London, 1970

Evans, Joan, *Magical Jewels of the Middle Ages and the Renaissance, Particularly in England*, Oxford, 1922

Fillitz, H., *Catalogue of the Crown Jewels and the Ecclesiastical Treasure Chamber*, trans. G. Holmes, Vienna, 1956

Flower, Margaret, *Jewellery 1837–1901*, London, 1968

Gere, Charlotte, *Victorian Jewellery Design*, London, 1972

Gregorietti, Guido, *Jewelry through the Ages*, trans. Helen Lawrence, London, 1970

Guérinet, A., *Oeuvres de Bijouterie et Joaillerie des XVIIe et XVIIIe Siècles*, Paris

Hinks, Peter, *Jewellery*, London, 1969

Hughes, Graham, *Jewelry*, London, 1966

Hughes, Therle and Bernard, *English Painted Enamels*, London, 1951

Lewis, M. D. S., *Antique Paste Jewelry*, London, 1970

Menzhausen, J., *Das Grüne Gewölbe*, Leipzig, 1968

Moses, E., *Der Schmuck der Sammlung W. Clemen*, Cologne

Muller, P. E., *Jewels in Spain 1500–1800*, New York, 1972

Peter, Mary, *Collecting Victorian Jewelry*, London, 1970

Smith, J. Clifford, *Jewellery*, London, 1908

Steingraeber, E., *Antique Jewelry*, New York, 1957

The Treatises of Benvenuto Cellini on Goldsmithing and Sculpture, trans. C. R. Ashbee, 1888, repr., New York, 1967

Twining, Lord, *A History of the Crown Jewels of Europe*, London, 1960

Webster, Robert, *Practical Gemmology*, 4th ed., London, 1966

Metalwork

AMERICAN

Bridenbaugh, Carl, *The Colonial Craftsman*, New York, 1950

Clark, Mary Jane, *Illustrated Glossary of Decorated Antiques*, Vt., 1972

Drepperd, Carl, *Pioneer America: Its First Three Centuries*, New York, 1949

Fuller, John, *The Art of Coppersmithing*, New York, 1911

Hayward, A. H., *Colonial Lighting*, Boston, 1923

Kauffman, Henry J., *American Axes*, Battleboro, Vt., 1972

Kauffman, Henry J., *American Copper and Brass*, Camden, N.J., 1968

Kauffman, Henry J., *Early American Copper, Tin and Brass*, New York, 1950

Kauffman, Henry J., *Early American Ironware*, Rutland, Vt., 1966

Lindsay, J. Seymour, *Iron and Brass Implements of the English and American House*, Boston, 1927

Roberts, Kenneth D. and Jane W., *Planemakers and Other Edge Tool Enterprises in New York State in the Nineteenth Century*, New York, 1971

BRITISH AND EUROPEAN

Allemagne, H. R., de l', *Histoire de Luminaire*, Paris, 1891

Allemagne, H. R. de l', *Les Accessoires du Costume et du Mobilier*, 3 vols, Paris, 1928

Antique Locks, from the Collection of Josiah Parks & Sons Ltd., Willenhall, Staffs., 1955

Bailey, C. T., *Knives and Forks*, London, 1927

Bury, Shirley, *Victorian Electroplate*, London, 1971

Byrne, A. and Stapley, M., *Spanish Ironwork*, The Hispanic Society of America, 1915

Dent, Herbert C., *Piqué: A beautiful Minor Art*, London, 1923

Frank, E. B., *Old French Ironwork*, Cambridge, Mass., 1950

Gardner, J. Starkie, *Handbook on Ironwork*, 3 vols, Victoria and Albert Museum, London

Hamilton, Henry, *The English Brass and Copper Industries to 1880*, repr. London, 1967

Hefner-Alteneck, I. H., *Serrurerie du Moyen Age et de la Renaissance*, Paris, 1870

Himsworth, J. B., *The Story of Cutlery*, London, 1953

Hughes, G. Bernard, *Horse Brasses and Other Small Items for the Collector*, London, 1956

Kippengerger, A., *Die deutschen Meister des Eisengusses im 16 Jahrhundert*, Marburg, 1931

Lindsay, J. Seymour, *Iron and Brass Implements of the English and American House*, London and Boston, 1927

Lister, Raymond, *The Craftsman in Metal*, London, 1966

Lister, Raymond, *Decorative Cast Ironwork in Great Britain*, London, 1960

Singleton, H. Raymond, *A Chronology of Cutlery*, Sheffield, 1966

Smith, R. Goodwin, *English Domestic Metalwork*, Leigh-on-Sea, 1937

Twopeny, W., *English Metalwork*, London, 1904

Wills, Geoffrey, *The Book of Copper and Brass*, Middlesex, 1969

Wills, Geoffrey, *Collecting Copper and Brass*, London, 1962

JAPANNED TIN PLATE

Caffin, Margaret, *American Country Tinware*, Tenn.

DeVoe, Shirley Spaulding, *English Papier Maché of the Georgian and Victorian Periods*, Middletown, Conn., 1971

DeVoe, Shirley Spaulding, *The Tinsmiths of Connecticut*, Middletown, Conn., 1968

John, W. D., *Pontypool and Usk Jappaned Wares*, Newport, Mon., 1953

Jones, W. H., *Story of Japan and Tin-plating*, London, 1900

PEWTER

Cotterell, H. H., *Old Pewter, Its Makers and Marks*, London, 1968

Ebert, Katherine, *Collecting American Pewter*, New York, 1973

Laughlin, Leslie, I., *Pewter in America: Its Makers and their Marks*, 2 vols, Barre, Mass., 1969

Michaelis, R. F., *Antique Pewter of the British Isles*, London, 1972

Montgomery, Charles F., *A History of American Pewter*, New York, 1973

Peal, Christopher A., *British Pewter and Britannia Metal*, London, 1971

Price, F. G. Hilton, *Old Base Metal Spoons*, London, 1908

Rogers, Malcolm A. Jr., *American Pewterers and their Marks*, Southampton, N.Y.

Sunderland-Graeme, A. V., *Old British Pewter, 1500–1800*, London, 1951

AMERICAN WROUGHT IRON

Geerlings, Gerald K., *Wrought Iron in Architecture*, New York, 1949

Short-Hollister, G., *Wrought Iron*, New York, 1970

Sonn, Albert H., *Early American Wrought Iron*, New York, 1928

CHINESE AND JAPANESE BRONZES

Newman, A. and Ryerson, E., *Japanese Art: A collector's guide*, London, 1964

Swann, Peter C., *Introduction to the Arts of Japan*, Oxford, 1958

Swann, Peter C., *Arts of China, Korea and Japan*, London, 1963

Turk, Dr F. A., *Japanese Objets d'Art*, London, 1962

Watson, W., *Ancient Chinese Bronzes*, London, 1962

Willets, William, *Chinese Art*, London, 1958

Needlework and Embroidery

Atwater, Mary Meigs, *The Shuttle-craft Book of American Hand-Weaving*, repr., New York, 1951

Bolton, Ethel Standwood and Coe, Eva Johnston, *American Samplers*, Massachusetts Society of the Colonial Dames of America, repr., 1973

Gray, J., *Machine Embroidery*, London, 1963

Hake, E., *English Quilting, Old and New*, London, 1937

Hall, Eliza Calvert, *A Book of Handwoven Coverlets*, Boston, 1912

Harbeson, Georgiana Brown, *American Needlework*, New York, 1938

Howard, C., *Inspiration for Embroidery*, London, 1966

Ickis, Marguerite, *The Standard Book of Quilt Making and Collecting*, New York, 1949

Jourdain, R., *English Secular Embroidery*, London, 1910

Junton, M. D., Jr., and Rush, William, *Old Quilts*, Maryland, 1946

Kendrick, A. F., *English Needlework*, London, 1967

Little, Frances, *Early American Textiles*, New York, 1931

Peto, Florence, *American Quilts and Coverlets*, New York, 1949

Peto, Florence, *Historic Quilts*, New York, 1939

Robertson, Elizabeth Wells, *American Quilts*, New York, 1948

Wardle, Patricia, *Victorian Lace*, London, 1968

Wingfield Digby, E. F., *Elizabethan Embroidery*, London, 1963

Pottery and Porcelain

GENERAL

Aldridge, Eileen, *Porcelain*, London, 1969

Boger, Louise, *The Dictionary of World Pottery and Porcelain*, London, 1971

Charleston, R. T., *World Ceramics*, Feltham, 1968
Cooper, Emmanuel, *History of Pottery*, London, 1972
Cushion, J. P., *Continental China Collecting for Amateurs*, London, 1970
Hodges, Henry, *Pottery*, Middlesex, 1972
Penkala, Maria, *European Pottery*, Feltham, 1968
Savage, George, *Porcelain through the Ages*, London, 1961
Savage, George, *Pottery through the Ages*, London, 1963
Tait, Hugh, *Porcelain*, London, 1962

AMERICAN

Barber, E. A., *The Pottery and Porcelain of the United States*, New York, 1909
Barber, E. A., *Tulip Ware of the Pennsylvania-German Potters*, Pennsylvania Museum, repr., 1970
Bridenbaugh, Carl, *The Colonial Craftsman*, repr., New York, 1961
Camehl, A. W., *The Blue-China Book*, New York, 1946
Clement, A. W. and Bishop, Edith, *The Pottery and Porcelain of New Jersey, 1688–1900*, Exhibition Catalogue, Newark Museum, Newark, N.J., 1947
Cox, Warren, *Book of Pottery and Porcelain*, repr., New York, 1970
Guillard, Harold F., *Early American Folk Pottery*, Philadelphia, 1971
Laidacker, Sam, *Anglo-American China, Parts I and II*, Bristol, Pa., 1951
Larsen, E. B., *American Historical Views on Staffordshire China*, rev. ed., New York, 1950
The Potters and Potteries of Chester County, Pennsylvania, Chester County Historical Society, West Chester, Pa., 1945
Ramsey, John et al., *American Potters and Pottery*, Boston, 1939
Spargo, John, *The A.B.C. of Bennington Pottery Wares*, Bennington Historical Museum, Bennington, Vt., 1948
Spargo, John, *Early American Pottery and China*, New York, 1926
Spargo, John, *The Potters and Potteries of Bennington*, Boston, 1926
Watkins, Lura Woodside, *Early New England Potters and Their Wares*, repr., Cambridge, Mass., 1968

AUSTRIAN

Hayward, J. F., *Vienna Porcelain of the Du Paquier Period*, London, 1972

BELGIAN

Helbig, J., *La Céramique Bruxelloise du Bon Vieux Temps*, Brussels, 1946

CHINESE, KOREAN AND JAPANESE

Franks, Sir A. W., *Japanese Pottery*, London, 1880
Garner, Sir Harry, *Oriental Blue and White Porcelain*, repr., London, 1964
Garner, Sir Harry, *Chinese and Japanese Cloisonné Enamels*, London, 1962
Gompertz, M. St G., *Chinese Celadon Ware*, repr., London, 1958
Gray, Basil, *Early Chinese Pottery and Porcelain*, London, 1953
Hetherington, A. L., *Early Ceramic Wares of China*, London, 1922
Hetherington, A. L., *Chinese Ceramic Glazes*, repr., South Pasadena, 1947
Hobson, R. L., *Handbook of the Pottery and Porcelain of the Far East*, 3rd ed., London, 1948
Hobson, R. L., *Chinese Pottery and Porcelain*, 2 vols, London, 1950
Hobson, R. L., *The Wares of the Ming Dynasty*, London, 1922
Hobson, R. L., *Later Ceramic Wares of China*, London, 1925.
Honey, W. B., *Ceramic Art of China*, London, 1945
Honey, W. B., *Corean Pottery*, London, 1947
Honey, W. B., *Later Chinese Porcelain*, London, 1927
Jenyns, Soame, *Ming Pottery and Porcelain*, London, 1953
Jenyns, Soame, *Later Chinese Porcelain*, repr., London, 1972
Jenyns, Soame, *Japanese Porcelain*, London, 1965
Jenyns, Soame, *Japanese Pottery*, London, 1970

CHINESE EXPORT

Beurdeley, M., *Porcelain of the East India Companies*, London, 1962
Godden, G. A., *The Illustrated Guide to Lowestoft Porcelains*, London, 1969
Hyde, J. A. Lloyd, *Oriental Lowestoft*, 2nd ed., Newport, Mon., 1954
Jourdain, Margaret and Jenyns, Soame, *Chinese Export Art in the Eighteenth Century*, London, 1950
Le Corbeiller, C., *China Trade Porcelain*, Exhibition catalogue of the China Institute of America, New York, 1973–4
Mudge, Jean McClure, *Chinese Export porcelain for the American Trade, 1785–1835*, Newark, Delaware, 1962
Philips, J. G., *China Trade Porcelain*, London, 1957
Volker, T., *Porcelain and the Dutch East India Company*, Leiden, 1954

DANISH

Christensen, Den Kyl, *Dansk Porcelænsfabrik*, Copenhagen, 1938
Hannover, E., *Pottery and Porcelain*, trans. B. Rackham, London, 1925
Hayden, a., *Royal Copenhagen Porcelain*, London, 1911

DUTCH

Harvard, H., *La Céramique Hollandaise*, Amsterdam, 1909
Sypesteyn, C. H. C. A. van, *Het Oud-Hollandsch Porselein*, Hilversum, 1933

ENGLISH

Barnard, Julian, *Victorian Ceramic Tiles*, London, 1972
Barrett, F. A., *Caughley and Coalport Porcelain*, Leigh-on-Sea, 1951
Barrett, F. A., *Worcester Porcelain and Lund's Bristol*, London, 1966
Barrett, F. A. and Thorpe, A. L., *Derby Porcelain 1750–1848*, London, 1971
Bedford, John, *Old English Lustre Ware*, London, 1965
Bemrose, G., *Nineteenth-Century English Pottery and Porcelain*, London, 1952
Berendson, Anne et al, *Tiles, A General History*, London, 1967
Brears, P. C. D., *The English Country Pottery*, Newton Abbot, 1971
Charleston, R. J., (ed.), *English Porcelain 1745–1850*, London, 1965
Cooper, Ronald G., *English Slipware Dishes 1650–1850*, London, 1968
Dixon, J. L., *English Porcelain of the Eighteenth Century*, London, 1952
English Ceramic Circle, English Pottery and Porcelain Exhibition Catalogue, London, 1948
Eyles, Desmond, *Royal Doulton 1815–1965*, London, 1965
Garner, F. H., *English Delftware*, rev. Michael Archer, London, 1972
Godden, G. A., *British Pottery and Porcelain, 1785–1850*, London, 1963
Godden, G., *English Porcelain – An illustrated guide*, London, 1974
Godden, G. A., *Coalport and Coalbrookdale Porcelains*, London, 1969
Godden, G. A., *Illustrated Guide: Mason's Patent Ironstone China and the Related Ware*, London, 1971
Godden, G. A., *Illustrated Guide to Ridgway Porcelains*, London, 1972
Godden, G. A., *Minton Pottery and Porcelain of the First Period, 1793–1850*, London, 1968
Godden, G. A., *Victorian Porcelain*, London, 1961
Gompertz, G. St-G. M., *Celadon Wares*, London, 1969
Hackenbroch, Y., *Chelsea and other English Porcelain . . . in the Irwin Untermyer Collection*, London, 1957

Holgate, David, *New Hall and Its Imitators*, London, 1971
Honey, W. B., *English Pottery and Porcelain*, rev. ed., London, 1969
Honey, W. B., *Old English Porcelain*, London, 1948
Honey, W. B., *Wedgwood Ware*, London, 1948
Jewitt, L., *Ceramic Art of Great Britain*, rev. ed., London, 1972
John, W. D., *Nantgarw Porcelain*, Monmouthshire, repr., 1969
John, W. D. and Baker, W., *Old English Lustre Pottery*, repr., Monmouthshire, 1966
John, W. D., *Swansea Porcelain*, Monmouthshire, 1958
King, W., *English Porcelain Figures of the Eighteenth Century*, London, 1925
Klamkin, Marian, *The Collector's Book of Wedgwood*, Devon, 1972
Lane, Arthur, *English Porcelain Figures of the 18th Century*, London, 1961
MacKenna, F. S., *Champion's Bristol Porcelain*, Leigh-on-Sea, 1947
Mankowitz, Wolf and Haggar, Reginald, *Concise Encyclopedia of English Pottery and Porcelain*, London, 1957
Mountford, Arnold, *Staffordshire Salt-Glazed Stoneware*, London, 1971
Nance, E. Morton, *The Pottery and Porcelain of Swansea and Nantgarw*, London, 1942
Oliver, A., *The Victorian Staffordshire Figures, A Guide for Collectors*, London, 1971
Pugh, P. D. Gordon, *Staffordshire Portrait Figures and Allied Subjects of the Victorian Era*, London, 1971
Rackham, B., *Catalogue of the Glaisher Collection*, 2 vols, Cambridge, 1934
Rackham, B., *Catalogue of the Schreiber Collection*, vol II, London, 1929
Rackham, B., *Early Staffordshire Pottery*, London, 1951
Rackham, B. and Read, H., *English Pottery*, London, 1924
Sandon, Henry, *Illustrated Guide to Worcester Porcelain 1751–1793*, London, 1969
Sandon, H., *Royal Worcester Porcelain*, London, 1973
Savage, G., *Eighteenth-Century English Porcelain*, London, 1952
Savage, G., *Old English Porcelain*, London, 1952
Shinn, Charles and Dorrie, *Victorian Parian China*, London, 1971
Smith, Alan, *Illustrated Guide to Liverpool Herculaneum Pottery 1796–1840*, London, 1970
Towner, Donald C., *English Cream-Coloured Earthenware*, London, 1957
Towner, Donald C., *The Leeds Pottery*, London, 1963
Watney, Bernard, *English Blue and White Porcelain of the Eighteenth Century*, London, 1963
Watney, Bernard, *Longton Hall Porcelain*, London, 1957
Whiter, Leonard, *Spode, A History of the Family, Factory and Wares from 1733 to 1833*, London, 1970
Williams-Wood, Cyril, *Staffordshire Pot Lids and their Potters*, London, 1972

FRENCH

Damiron, C., *La Faience Antique de Moustiers*, Lyons, 1919
Dauterman, Carl Christian, *Sèvres*, London, 1970
Eriksen, S., *Sèvres Porcelain*, Fribourg, 1968
Honey, W. B., *French Porcelain of the Eighteenth Century*, London, 1972
Landais, Hubert, *French Porcelain*, London, 1961
Lane, Arthur, *French Faïence*, rev. ed., London, 1970
Lane, Arthur, *Nevers Faïence: the High Renaissance and Baroque Styles*, Faenza, 1946
Les Porcelainiers du XVIIIe Siècle Français, preface by Gauthier, S., Paris, 1964
Savage, G., *Seventeenth- and Eighteenth-Century French Porcelain*, London, 1960

GERMAN

Bayer, A., *Ansbacher Porzellan*, Ansbach, 1933
Ducret, S., *German Porcelain and Faïence*, New York, 1962
Ducret, S., *Keramik und Graphik*, Brunswick, 1973
Ducret, S., *Meissner Porzellan bemalt in Augsburg, 1718–1750*, 2 vols, Brunswick, 1971–2
Fürstenberger Porzellan bis 1800, Brunswick, 1965
Hackenbroch, Y., *Meissen and other Continental Porcelain . . . in the Irwin Untermyer Collection*, London, 1956
Hofmann, F. H., *Frankenthaler Porzellan*, Munich, 1911
Honey, W. B., *Dresden China*, London, 1946
Honey, W. B., *German Porcelain*, London, 1947
Lenz, G., *Berliner Porzellan: Die Manufaktur Friedrich des Grossen*, 3 vols, Berlin, 1913
Meister, P. W., *Porzellan des 18 Jahrhunderts: Sammlung Pauls, Riehen*, 2 vols, Frankfurt am Main, 1967; Eng. ed., 1969
Morley-Fletcher, H., *German Porcelain of the Eighteenth Century, The Pauls Collection*, vol I: *Meissen from the beginning until 1760*, London, 1971
Pauls-Eisenbeiss, Erika, *German Porcelain of the Eighteenth Century, The Pauls Collection*, vol II: *Höchst, Frankenthal and Ludwigsburg*, London, 1973
Rückert, R., *Meissner Porzellan 1710–1810*, Exhibition catalogue of the Bayerisches Nationalmuseum, Munich, 1966
Savage, G., *Eighteenth-Century German Porcelain*, London, 1968

ITALIAN

Ballardini, G., *La Maiolica Italiana dello Origini alla Fino del Cinquecento*, Florence, 1938
Eisenhof, Barone Angelo de Eisner, *Le Porcellane di Capodimonte*, Milan, 1925
Erdberg, Joan Prentice von and Ross, Marvin, *Catalogue of the Italian Maiolica in the Walters Art Gallery*, Baltimore, 1952
Fortnum, C. D. E., *Catalogue of Maiolica in the Ashmolean Museum*, Oxford, 1897
Gregorietti, G., (ed.), *Maioliche di Lodi, Milano e Pavia*, exhibition catalogue of the Museo Poldi Pezzoli, Milan, 1964
Lane, Arthur, *Italian Porcelain*, London, 1954
Liverani, G., *Five Centuries of Italian Maiolica*, London, 1960
Rackham, B., *Catalogue of Italian Maiolica in the Victoria and Albert Museum*, London, 1940
Rackham, B., *Italian Maiolica*, London, 1964
Scavizzi, Giuseppe, *Maiolica, Delft and Faïence*, trans. Peter Locke, London, 1970
Stazzi, Francisco, *Italian Porcelain*, London, 1967

RUSSIAN

Emme, B., *Russian Art Porcelain*, in Russian, Moscow-Leningrad, 1950
Lukomsky, G., *Russisches Porzellan*, Berlin 1924
Rodin, I. (ed.), *The State Porcelain Factory*, Leningrad, 1938
Ross, Marvin, *Russian Porcelains*, Oklahoma, 1968

SPANISH

Frothingham, Alice W., *Capodimonte and Buen Retiro Porcelain: Period of Charles III*, New York, 1955
Frothingham, Alice W., *Lustreware of Spain*, New York, 1951
Frothingham, Alice W., *Talavera Pottery*, New York, 1944
Perez, M., *Artes e Industrias del Buen Retiro*, Madrid, 1904
Van de Put, A., *Hispano-Moresque Ware of the 15th century*, London, 1951
Van de Put, A., *The Valencia Styles of Hispano-Moresque Pottery 1404–1454*, New York, 1938

SWISS

De Molin, A., *Histoire Documentaire de la Manufacture de la Porcelaine de Nyon, 1781–1813*, Lausanne, 1904
Ducret, S., *Zürchner Porzellan des XVIII Jahrhunderts*, Zurich, 1944
Ducret, S., *Die Zürchner Porzellanmanufaktur und ihre Erzugnisse, im 18 und 19 Jahrhundert*, Zurich, 1958–9
Wyss, R. L., *Berner Bauernkeramik*, Bern, 1966

MARKS

Cushion, J. P., *Pocket Book of English Ceramic Marks*, London, 1965

Godden, G. A., *Encyclopedia of British Pottery and Porcelain Marks*, London, 1964

Godden, G. A., *The Handbook of British Pottery and Porcelain Marks*, London, 1968

Macdonald-Taylor, Margaret, (ed.), *A Dictionary of Marks*, rev. ed., London, 1966

Rozembergh, A., *Les Marques sur la Porcelaine Russe*, Paris, 1926

Prints

AMERICAN

American Historical Prints, repr., New York, 1972

American Prints in the Library of Congress: A Catalog of the Collection, Baltimore, 1970

Bolton, E. S., *Wax Portraits and Silhouettes*, repr., Boston, 1972

Brewington, M. V. and Dorothy, *Kendall Whaling Museum Prints*, Sharon, Mass., 1969

Brigham, C. S., *Paul Revere's Engravings*, American Antiquarian Society, repr., Worcester, Mass., 1969

Burgess, Fred W., *Old Prints and Engravings*, New York, 1937

Carrick, Alice van Leer, *Shades of our Ancestors*, Boston, 1928

Comstock, Helen, *American Lithographs*, New York, 1950

Comstock, Helen, *American Lithographs of the 19th Century*, New York, 1950

Conningham, F. A., *Currier and Ives Prints: An Illustrated Check List*, New York, 1970

Drepperd, Carl, *Early American Prints*, New York, 1950

Elman, Robert, *The Great American Shooting Prints*, New York, 1972

Jackson, E. N., *Ancestors in Silhouette*, repr., New York, 1973

Jackson, E. N., *A History of Silhouette*, London, 1911

Jackson, E. N., *Silhouette Notes and Dictionary*, New York, 1938

Johnson, U. S., *American Woodcuts 1670–1950: A Survey of Woodcuts and Wood-Engravings in the United States*, New York, 1950

Middendorf, J. W. and Shadwell, Wendy J., *American Printmaking: The First 150 Years*, Washington, 1969

Morse, John D., (ed.), *Prints in and of America to 1850*, Charlottesville, Va., 1970

The William Barclay Parsons Railway Prints, Columbia University Library, 1935

Peters, H. T., *America on Stone*, New York, 1931

Peters, H. T., *Currier and Ives: Printmakers to the American People*, 2 vols, New York, 1931

Piper, David, *Shades*, New York, 1970

Prints Pertaining to America: A list of publications in English, relating to prints about that portion of America now included in the United States with emphasis on the period 1650–1850, The Walpole Society (United States), 1963

Shadwell, Wendy J., *American printmaking, the first 150 years*, New York, 1969

Slater, J. Herbert, *Engravings and Their Value*, New York, 1929

Stauffer, D. M., *American Engravers upon Copper and Steel*, 2 vols, repr., New York, 1964

Stokes, I. N. Phelps, *The Iconography of Manhattan Island 1498–1909*, 6 vols, repr., New York, 1967

Weitenkampf, Frank, *American Graphic Art*, repr., New York, 1970

BRITISH AND EUROPEAN

Allen, Bryan, *Print Collecting*, London, 1970

Bartsch, A., *Le Peintre Graveur*, Vienna, 1803–21

Coke, Desmond, *The Art of Silhouette*, London, 1913

Davenport, Cyril, *Mezzotints*, London, 1904

Frankau, Julia, *John Raphael Smith*, London, 1902

Goodwin, Gordon, *James McArdell*, London, 1903

Hind, A. M., *Early Italian Engraving*, London, 1938–48

Hind, A. M., *Engraving in England in the 16th and 17th Centuries*, 2 vols, London, 1926–31

Hind, A. M., *The Processes and Schools of Engravings*, 4th ed., London, 1952

Hind, A. M., *A Short History of Engraving and Etching*, London, 1921

Lister, Raymond, *Silhouettes*, London, 1953

McLean, Ruari, *Victorian Book Design and Colour Printing*, London, 1963

Naval Prints: The Collection of Sir C. L. Cust, Bart., London, 1911

Robinson, M. S., *The MacPherson Collection of Maritime Prints and Drawings in the National Maritime Museum, Greenwich*, London, 1950

Salaman, M. C., *Old English Mezzotints*, London, 1910

Sitwell, S., Buchanan, H. and Fisher, J., *Fine Bird Books*, London and New York, 1953

Smith, J. C., *British Mezzotinto Portraits*, 4 vols, London, 1884

Vesme, Baudi de, *Le Peintre Graveur Italien*, Milan, 1906

Weber, W., *A History of Lithography*, London, 1966

Weschler, Herman J., *Great Prints and Printmakers*, London, 1967

Whitman, Alfred, *The Masters of Mezzotint*, London, 1898

Wilder, F. L., *How to Identify Old Prints*, London, 1969

Zigrosser, C. and Gaehde, D. M., *A Guide to the Collecting and Care of Original Prints*, London, 1966

JAPANESE

Binyon, L. and Sexton, J. J. O'Brien, *Japanese Colour Prints*, London, 1923

Brown, L. N., *Block Printing and Book Illustration in Japan*, London, 1924

Hillier, J., *Japanese Masters of the Colour Print*, London, 1954

Holloway, O. E., *The Graphic Art of Japan – The Classical School*, London, 1967

Michener, James A., *Japanese Prints: From the Early Masters to the Modern*, Tokyo, 1963

Scientific Instruments

Bradbury, S., *The Evolution of the Microscope*, Oxford, 1967

Clay, R. S. and Court, T. H., *The History of the Microscope*, London, 1932

Cousins, F. W., *Sundials*, London, 1969

Daumas, M., *Scientific Instruments of the 17th and 18th Centuries and their Makers*, trans. M. Jolbrook, London, 1972

Franco, Salvador Garcia, *Catálogo Critico de Astrolabios Existentes en España*, Madrid, 1945

Gould, R., *The Marine Chronometer*, repr., London, 1960

Jones, E. Lancaster, *Catalogue of the Collection of the Science Museum of South Kensington, Geodesy and Surveying*, London, 1925

Herbert, A. P., *Sundials Old and New*, London, 1967

Kiely, E., *Surveying Instruments, their History and Classroom Use*, New York, 1947

King, H. C., *The History of the Telescope*, London, 1956

Mayer, L. A., *Islamic Astrolabists and their Works*, Geneva, 1956

Schroeder, W., *Practical Astronomy*, London, 1956

Taylor, E., *The Mathematical Practitioners of Hanoverian England, 1714–1840*, Cambridge, 1966

Taylor, E., *The Mathematical Practitioners of Tudor and Stuart England*, Cambridge, 1954

Waters, D. W., *The Art of Navigation in England in Elizabethan and Early Stuart Times*, London, 1958

Wolf, A., *A History of Science, Technology and Philosophy in the 16th and 17th Centuries*, rev. ed., Douglas McKie, London, 1950

Silver

AMERICAN

Avery, C. L., *Early American Silver*, repr., New York, 1968
Bigelow, F. L., *Historic Silver of the Colonies*, London, 1914
Buhler, K., *American Silver*, Ohio, 1950
Buhler, K. and Hood, Graham, *American Silver in the Yale University Art Gallery: Garvan and other Collections*, 2 vols, New Haven, Conn., 1970
Buhler, K., *American Silver 1655–1825 in the Museum of Fine Arts, Boston*, 2 vols, Boston, 1973
Clarke, H. F., *John Coney, Silversmith*, repr., Boston, 1971
Clayton, Michael, *The Collector's Dictionary of the Silver and Gold of Great Britain and North America*, London, 1971
Currier, Ernst M., *Marks of Early American Silversmiths*, repr., 1970
Enstro, Stephen G., *American Silversmiths and their Marks*, Southampton, N.Y.
French, Hollis, *Jacob Hurd and his Sons*, 1939
French, Hollis, *Silver Collector's Glossary and a List of Early American Silversmiths and Their Marks*, New York, 1967
Hood, Graham, *American Silver: A History of Style, 1650–1900*, New York, 1971
Kauffman, Henry J., *The Colonial Silversmith*, Camden, N.J., 1969
Jones, E. A., *The Old Silver of American Churches*, privately printed
Jones, E. A., *Old Silver of Europe and America*, London, 1922
Kovel, R. and T., *A Directory of American Silver, Pewter and Silver Plate*, New York, 1961
Phillips, J. M., *American Silver*, New York, 1949
Pick, Franz, *Silver: How and Where to Buy and Hold It*, rev. ed., New York, 1973
Pleasants, J. Hall and Sill, Howard, *Maryland Silversmiths 1715–1830*, repr., 1972
Wills, Geoffrey, *Silver*, New York, 1969

BRITISH

Banister, Judith, *An Introduction to Old English Silver*, London, 1965
Bradbury, Frederick, *British and Irish Silver Assay Office Marks 1544–1968*, 2nd ed., Yorkshire, 1969
Bradbury, Frederick, *Guide to Marks of Origin on British and Irish Silver Plate 1544–1972*, 1972
Chaffers, W., *Gilda Aurifabrorum*, 1899
Clayton, Michael, *The Collector's Dictionary of The Silver and Gold of Great Britain and North America*, London, 1971
Cripps, W. J., *Old English Plate*, 11th ed., 1926
Delieb, E., *Investing in Silver*, London, 1967
Dennis, Jessie McNab, *English Silver*, New York, 1970
Fallon, John, *The Marks of the London Goldsmiths and Silversmiths, Georgian Period c. 1697–1837: A Guide*, Devon, 1972
Gilchrist, J., *Anglican Church Plate*, London, 1967
Goodden, Robert and Popham, Philip, *Silversmithing*, London, 1971
Grimwade, Arthur, *Rococo Silver 1727–1765*, 1974
Guide to Marks of Origin on British and Irish Silver Plate, 1544–1946, 7th ed., 1947
Hayward, J. F., *Huguenot Silver in England, 1688–1727*, London, 1959
Honour, Hugh, *Goldsmiths and Silversmiths*, London, 1971
Jackson, C. J., *English Goldsmiths and their Marks*, repr., London, 1965
Jackson, C. J., *An Illustrated History of English Plate*, 2 vols, 1911
Oman, C. C., *Caroline Silver 1625–1688*, London, 1970
Oman, C. C., *English Domestic Silver*, rev. ed., London, 1968
Oman, C. C., *English Silversmith's Work, Civil and Domestic: An Introduction*, London, 1965
Phillips, Philip, *Paul de Lamerie: Citizen and Goldsmith of London*, London, 1968
Rowe, Robert, *Adam Silver*, London, 1965
Taylor, Gerald, *Silver*, rev. ed., London, 1963
Wardle, Patricia, *Victoria Silver and Silver Plate*, London, 1963
Wenham, Edward, *Old Sheffield Plate*, London, 1955

IRISH

Bennett, Douglas, *Irish Georgian Silver*, London, 1972
Bradbury, Frederick, *British and Irish Silver Assay Office Marks 1544–1968*, 12th ed., Yorkshire, 1969
Ticher, Kurt, *Irish Silver in the Rococo Period*, London, 1972

FRENCH

Carré, Louis, *A Guide to Old French Plate*, repr., London, 1971
Cripps, W., *Old French Silver*, repr., Christchurch, Hants., 1972
Dennis, Faith, *Three Centuries of French Domestic Silver: Its Makers and Its Marks*, New York, 1969
Taralon, Jean, *Treasures of the Churches of France*, trans. Mira Intrator, London, 1966

GERMAN

Brunner, Herbert, *Old Table Silver*, trans. Janet Siligman, London, 1967
Steingraber, Erich, (ed.), *Royal Treasures*, trans. Stefan de Haan, London, 1968

ITALIAN

Bulgari, G. C., *Argentiere Gemmarie Orafi D'Italia. Parte Prima: Roma*, Rome, 1959
Gregorietti, G., *Argenti Italiani*, Milan, 1959

NORWEGIAN

Gammel Bergensk Gullsmedkunst, Catalogue, Vestlandske Kunstindustrimuseum, Bergen, 1937
Gammel Guldsmedkunst, Catalogue, Oslo Kunstindustrimuseum, 1909
Kloster, R. and Krohn-Hansen, T., *Bergen Silver from the Guild Period*, 2 vols, Bergen, 1957
Kristiania-sölv 1604–1854, Catalogue, Oslo Kunstindustrimuseum, 1954
Penzer, N. M., 'Bergen Silver of the Guild Period', *The Connoisseur*, April, 1958

RUSSIAN

Argenterie Russe Ancienne de la Collection Eugène Lubovich, Paris, 1932
Bainbridge, H. C., *Peter Carl Fabergé, His Life and Work*, London, 1949
Benois, A., (ed.), *Art Treasures of Russia*, St Petersburg, 1901
Bunt, C., *Russian Art*, London, 1949
Foelkersam, A., *Inventaire des Palais Impériaux*, St Petersburg, 1907
Guide to Artistic Silver in the Hermitage, Moscow, 1956
Oman, C. C., *The English Silver in the Kremlin 1557–1663*, London, 1961
Porfiridov, N., *Russian Silver and Enamel, Russian Museum, Leningrad*, Leningrad, 1956

List of Museums and Galleries

The following list is arranged under the main subject headings in the book – Furniture, Glass, etc. It does not seek to be exhaustive and covers only major museums and galleries and a few provincial ones which contain a certain number of good examples of the objects indicated; however, many provincial galleries can show one or two good specimens and are usually worth a visit.

The Aesthetic Movement: The Arts and Crafts Movement; Art Nouveau; Art Deco, etc.

BRITISH ISLES

Bethnal Green Museum, London
Bowes Museum, Barnard Castle
Castle Museum, York
City Museum and Art Gallery, Birmingham
City Museum and Art Gallery, Bristol
City Museum and Art Gallery, Manchester
Courtauld Institute Galleries, London
Fitzwilliam Museum, Cambridge
Geffrye Museum, London
Lady Lever Art Gallery, Port Sunlight
Laing Art Gallery and Museum, Newcastle-upon-Tyne
Museum and Art Gallery, Leicester
Tate Gallery, London
University Collection, Glasgow
Victoria and Albert Museum, London
William Morris Gallery, London

EUROPE

Austria
Museum des 20. Jahrhunderts, Vienna
Österreichisches Museum für Angewandte Kunst, Vienna

Belgium
Musée d'Art Moderne, Brussels

France
Musée de l'Art Moderne, Paris
Musée des Arts Décoratifs, Paris
Musée National de Céramique, Paris

Germany
Kunstgewerbemuseum, West Berlin

Norway
Nordenfjeldske Kunstindustrimuseum, Trondheim

U.S.A.

Art Galleries, University of Santa Barbara, Cal.
Brooklyn Museum, New York
Cooper-Hewitt Museum of Design, New York
Freer Gallery of Art, Washington D.C.
Metropolitan Museum of Art, New York
Museum of Modern Art, New York
Philadelphia Museum of Art, Philadelphia, Pa.

Antiquities

BRITISH ISLES

Ashmolean Museum, Oxford
British Museum, London
City Museum and Art Gallery, Birmingham
City Museum, Liverpool
Fitzwilliam Museum, Cambridge
Horniman Museum, London (Pre-Columbian American)
Museum of Mankind, London
National Museum of Ireland, Dublin
National Museum of Wales, Cardiff
Oriental Institute, Oxford (S.E. Asian)
Oriental Institute, University of London (S.E. Asian)
Petworth House, Petworth (Classical)
Royal Scottish Museum, Edinburgh
Scottish Museum of Antiquities, Edinburgh (W. and N. European)
University College, London (Egyptian and North African)
Victoria and Albert Museum, London (W. and N. European)

EUROPE

Czechoslovakia
Národní Muzeum – Historické Muzeum, Prague

Denmark
Carlsberg Museum, Copenhagen (Classical)
Nationalmuseet, Copenhagen

France
Musée des Antiquités Nationales, Paris (W. and N. European)
Musée Guimet, Paris (S.E. Asian)
Louvre, Paris

Germany
Cathedral Treasury, Aachen (W. and N. European)
Ehemals Staatliche Museen, Berlin
Germanisches Nationalmuseum, Nuremberg (W. and N. European)
Glyptothek, Munich (Classical)
Hamburgisches Museum für Völkerkunde und Vorgeschichte, Hamburg (Pre-Columbian American)
Linden-Museum, Stuttgart
Staatliches Museum für Völkerkunde, Munich
Staatliches Museum für Völkerkunde, Munich (Pre-Columbian American and S.E. Asian)

Greece
National Museum, Athens (Classical)

Italy
Museo Archeologico, Florence (Classical)
Museo Civico Archeologico, Bologna (Classical)
Museo Egizio, Turin (Egyptian and North African)
Museo Nazionale Romano, Rome (Classical)
Museo Preistorico Etnografico Luigi Pigorini, Rome (Pre-Columbian American)
Villa Giulia (Etruscan Museum), Rome (Classical)

Netherlands
Tropenmuseum, Amsterdam (S.E. Asian)

Norway
Vikingskipshuset, Oslo (W. and N. European)

Spain
Museo de América, Madrid (Pre-Columbian American)

Sweden
Göteborgs Etnografiska Museum, Gothenburg
Nationalmuseum, Stockholm

U.S.A.

American Museum of Natural History, New York
Boston Museum of Fine Arts, Boston, Massachusetts (Classical)
Chicago Natural History Museum, Chicago, Ill.
Los Angeles County Museum of Art, Los Angeles, Cal.

Metropolitan Museum of Art, New York
University Museum, Philadelphia, Pa.

Arms and Armour

BRITISH ISLES

Abbey House Museum, Leeds
Admiral Blake Museum, Bridgwater
Blair Castle and Atholl Museum, Perth
British Museum, London
Castle Museum, York
Chiddington Castle, Edenbridge
City and County Museum, Lincoln
City Museum and Art Gallery, Birmingham
City Museum and Art Galley, Bristol
Dick Institute, Kilmarnock
Farleigh Castle Museum, Hungerford
Ilfracombe Museum, Ilfracombe
Imperial War Museum, London
Inverness Museum and Art Gallery, Inverness
Laing Art Gallery and Museum, Newcastle-upon-Tyne
Lichfield Art Gallery and Museum, Lichfield
Ludlow Museum, Ludlow
Padiham Memorial Park Museum, Padiham
Preston Hall Museum, Stockton-on-Tees
Rapallo House Museum and Art Gallery, Llandudno
Royal Artillery Museum, Woolwich
Royal Scottish Museum, Edinburgh
St Edward's Hall Museum, Stow-on-the-Wold
The Scott Collection, Glasgow Art Galleries and Museum, Glasgow
Thorpe Prebend House and Museum, Ripon
Tower of London
Victoria and Albert Museum, London
The Wallace Collection, London
The West Gate, Canterbury
The Whitelaw Collection of Scottish Arms, Glasgow Art Galleries and Museum, Glasgow
Yeovil Borough Museum (Wyndham Museum), Yeovil

EUROPE

Austria
Heeresgeschichtliches Museum, Vienna
Landeszeughaus, Graz
Waffensammlung (Kunsthistorisches Museum), Vienna

Belgium
Musée Royal d'Armes et d'Armures, Brussels

Denmark
Tøjhusmuseet, Copenhagen

France
Louvre, Paris
Musée de l'Armée, Paris
Musée des Arts Décoratifs, Paris

Germany
Bayerisches Nationalmuseum, Munich
Deutsches Klingenmuseum, Solingen
Germanisches Nationalmuseum, Nuremberg
Kunstsammlungen Veste Coburg, Coburg

Italy
Armeria Reale, Turin
Bargello, Florence
Museo Civico, Marzoli, Brescia
Museo Nazionale di Castel S. Angelo, Rome
Museo Poldi Pezzoli, Milan
Museo Stibbert, Florence
Odescalchi Collection, Rome
Palazzo di Capodimonte, Naples
Palazzo Ducale, Venice
Palazzo Venezia, Rome
Sanctuaria della Madonna della Grazie, Mantua

Netherlands
Nederlands Leger- en Wapenmuseum, Leyden

Spain
Museo de la Real Armería, Madrid

Sweden
Kungliga Livrustkammaren, Stockholm

Switzerland
Historisches Museum, Basle
Schweizerisches Landesmuseum, Zurich

U.S.A.

Armory Museum, Springfield, Mass.
Cincinnati Art Museum, Cincinnati, Ohio
Cleveland Museum of Art, Cleveland, Ohio
Colonial National History Park, Yorktown, Va.
Colonial Williamsburg Magazine and Guard House, Va.
John Woodman Higgins Armory, Mass.
Metropolitan Museum of Art, New York
Pilgrim Hall, Plymouth, Mass.
United States National Museum, Washington D.C.
Walkers Art Gallery, Baltimore, Md.
West Point Museum, West Point, N.Y.

Barometers, Clocks and Watches

Barometers

BRITISH ISLES

Museum of the History of Science, Oxford
National Maritime Museum, London
Royal Scottish Museum, Edinburgh
Science Museum, London
Victoria and Albert Museum, London
Wallace Collection, London
Whipple Museum of the History of Science, Cambridge

EUROPE

France
Musée de Conservatoire National des Arts et Métiers, Paris

Germany
Deutsches Museum, Munich

Netherlands
Rijksmuseum voor de Geschiedenis der Natuurwetenschappen, Leyden
Teylers Museum, Haarlem

Clocks and Watches

BRITISH ISLES

British Museum, London
Clockmakers' Company Museum, Guildhall, London
Science Museum, London
Victoria and Albert Museum, London
Wallace Collection, London

EUROPE

Austria
Kunsthistorisches Museum, Vienna

France
Musée de Conservatoire National des Arts et Métiers, Paris
Louvre, Paris
Musée des Arts Décoratifs, Paris
Musée du Petit Palais, Paris

Germany
Bayerisches Nationalmuseum, Munich
Deutsches Museum, Munich
Germanisches Nationalmuseum, Nuremberg
Herzog-Anton-Ulrich Museum, Brunswick
Staatliche Kunstsammlungen, Kassel

Netherlands
Rijksmuseum voor de Geschiedenis der Natuurwetenschappen, Leyden

U.S.A.
Boston Museum of Fine Arts, Boston, Mass.
Bristol Clock Museum, Bristol, Conn.
California Palace of the Legion of Honor, San Francisco
Essex Institute, Salem, Mass.
Henry Ford Museum, Dearborn, Mich.
Henry Francis du Pont Winterthur Museum, Winterthur, Del.
Metropolitan Museum of Art, New York
New York University (the James Arthur Collection)
Newark Public Library, Newark, N.J.
Old Sturbridge Village, Sturbridge, Mass.
Pennsylvania Historical Society, Philadelphia, Pa.
Smithsonian Institution, Washington D.C.
Yale University Art Gallery

Carpets and Rugs

BRITISH ISLES
Bowes Museum, Barnard Castle
The Burrell Collection, Glasgow Art Galleries and Museum, Glasgow
City Museum and Art Gallery, Birmingham
Ham House, Petersham (English)
Hampton Court Palace, Hampton Court (late medieval)
Hatfield House, Hatfield
Knole, near Sevenoaks
Osterley Park House, Isleworth (Gobelins and Beauvais)
Victoria and Albert Museum, London
Wernher Collection, Luton Hoo

EUROPE
Austria
Hofburg, Vienna
Kunsthistorisches Museum, Vienna
Österreichisches Museum für Angewandte Kunst, Vienna

France
Louvre, Paris
Musée des Arts Décoratifs, Paris (medieval and later)
Musée de Cluny, Paris (medieval)
Musée des Tapisseries, au Château, Angers
Trésor de la Cathédrale, Rheims (late medieval)

Germany
Bayerisches Nationalmuseum, Munich
Ehemals Staatliche Museen, Berlin
Germanisches Nationalmuseum, Nuremberg
Schloss Nymphenburg, Munich (18th century)

Netherlands
Rijksmuseum, Amsterdam

Italy
Museo Vaticano, Rome (Sistine Chapel)
Palaces and galleries, Florence (especially 16th century)
Palaces and galleries, Rome (16th–18th century)

Spain
Museo de la Catedral, Saragoza (medieval)
Museo de la Catedral, Zamora (medieval)
Palacio Real, Madrid

Switzerland
Historisches Museum, Basle (15th century)
Historisches Museum, Berne (15th century, Tournai)
Landesmuseum, Zurich (15th–16th century)

U.S.A.
Henry Francis du Pont Winterthur Museum, Winterthur, Del.
Metropolitan Museum of Art, New York
New York State Historical Association, New York
Shelburne Museum, Shelburne, Vt.

Coins and Medals

BRITISH ISLES
Ancient House Museum, Thetford
Arbuthnot Museum, Peterhead
Ashmolean Museum, Oxford
British Museum, London
Castle Museum, Norwich
Castle Museum, York
Charterhouse School Museum, Godalming
Chelmsford and Essex Museum, Chelmsford
Church Porch Folk Museum, Winchcombe
City and County Museum, Lincoln
City Museum and Art Gallery, Bristol
City Museum and Art Gallery, Gloucester
City Museum and Art Gallery, Manchester
City Museum, Sheffield
Colchester and Essex Museum, Colchester
Cyfarthfa Art Gallery and Museum, Merthyr Tydfil
Eastgate House Museum, Rochester
Fitzwilliam Museum, Cambridge
Gorey Castle Museum, Jersey
Grosvenor Museum, Chester
Holburne of Menstrie Museum, Bath
Hunterian Museum, Glasgow
Library of the Thoresby Society, Leeds
Lichfield Art Gallery and Museum, Lichfield
Marlipins Museum, Shoreham, Sussex
Municipal Museum and Art Gallery, Tunbridge Wells
Museum and Art Gallery, King's Lynn
National Museum of Antiquities of Scotland, Edinburgh
National Museum of Wales, Cardiff
Philpot Museum, Lyme Regis
Poole Guildhall Museum, Poole
Public Library and Museum, Whitehaven
Public Library, Museum and Art Gallery, Blackburn
Somerset County Museum, Taunton
Spalding Gentlemen's Society Museum, Spalding
Swindon Museum and Art Gallery, Swindon
Ulster Museum, Belfast
Victoria Art Gallery, Bath
Victoria Jubilee Museum, Cawthorne
Wells Museum, Wells

EUROPE
Austria
Kunsthistorisches Museum, Vienna

Belgium
Cabinet des Monnaies et des Médailles, Bibliothèque Royale, Brussels

Czechoslovakia
Národní Muzeum–Historické Muzeum, Prague

Denmark
Nationalmuseet, Copenhagen

France
Cabinet des Médailles, Bibliothèque Nationale, Paris

Germany
Museum für Hamburgische Geschichte, Hamburg
Staatliche Münzsammlung, Munich

Greece
National Museum, Athens

Hungary
Magyar Nemzeti Múzeum, Budapest

Italy
Castello Sforzesco, Milan
Museo Nazionale, Naples
Museo Nazionale, Rome

Netherlands
Koninklijk Penningkabinet, The Hague

Norway
Universitetets Museum, Oslo

Sweden
Statens Historiska Museum, Stockholm

Switzerland
Historisches Museum, Basle
Musée d'Archéologie, Geneva

U.S.A.
American Numismatic Society Museum, New York
Boston Museum of Fine Arts, Boston, Mass.
Carnegie Institute, Pittsburg, Pa.
Smithsonian Institution, Washington D.C.

Ethnographica

BRITISH ISLES

City Museum and Art Gallery, Birmingham
City Museum and Art Gallery, Bristol
City Museum, Leeds
City Museum, Liverpool
City Museum and Art Gallery, Manchester
Glasgow Art Galleries and Museum, Glasgow
Hancock Museum, Newcastle-upon-Tyne
Horniman Museum, London
Hunterian Museum, Glasgow
Ipswich Museum, Ipswich
Museum and Art Gallery, Maidstone
Museum of Mankind, London
National Museum of Ireland, Dublin
Powell-Cotton Museum, Birchington
Rothesay Museum, Bournemouth
Royal Albert Memorial Museum, Exeter
Royal Scottish Museum, Edinburgh
University of Anthropology Museum, Aberdeen
University Museum of Archaeology and Ethnology, Cambridge

EUROPE

Austria
Museum für Völkerkunde, Vienna

Belgium
Musée Royal de l'Afrique Centrale, Tervuren

Denmark
Nationalmuseet, Copenhagen

France
Musée de l'Homme, Paris
Musée des Arts Africains et Océaniens, Paris
Musée Municipal, Angoulême
Musée Lafaille, La Rochelle

Germany
Hamburgisches Museum für Völkerkunde und Vorgeschichte, Hamburg
Linden-Museum, Stuttgart
Museum für Völkerkunde, Berlin
Museum für Völkerkunde, Leipzig
Rautenstrauch-Joest-Museum für Völkerkunde, Cologne
Staatliches Museum für Vökerkunde, Dresden
Staatliches Museum für Völkerkunde, Munich
Völkerkundliche Sammlungen der Stadt Mannheim, Mannheim

Hungary
Magyar Nemzeti Múzeum, Budapest

Italy
Museo Missionario Etnologico, Vatican
Museo Preistorico Etnografico Luigi Pigorini, Rome

Netherlands
Etnografisch Museum, Delft
Haags Gemeentemuseum, The Hague
Museum voor Land- en Volkenkunde, Rotterdam
Rijksmuseum voor Volkenkunde, Leyden
Tropenmuseum, Amsterdam

Sweden
Göteborgs Etnografiska Museum, Gothenburg
Statens Etnografiska Museum, Stockholm

Switzerland
Bernisches Historisches Museum, Berne
Musée d'Ethnographie, Geneva
Musée d'Ethnographie, Neuchâtel
Museum für Völkerkunde, Basle
Museum Rietberg, Zurich
Sammlung für Völkerkunde der Universität, Zurich

U.S.A.
American Museum of Natural History, New York
Art Institute, Chicago, Ill.
Boston Museum of Fine Arts, Boston, Mass.
Brooklyn Museum, New York
Denver Art Museum, Denver, Colo.
Field Museum of Natural History, Chicago, Ill.
Milwaukee Public Museum, Milwaukee, Wis.
Museum of African Art, Washington D.C.
Museum of the American Indian, Heye Foundation, New York
Museum of Ethnic Arts, University of California, Los Angeles, Cal.
Museum of Primitive Art, New York
Peabody Museum of Archaeology and Ethnology, Cambridge, Mass.
Peabody Museum, Salem, Mass.
Robert H. Lowie Museum of Anthropology, Berkeley
Smithsonian Institution, Washington D.C.

Furniture

American Furniture

U.S.A.
Art Institute of Chicago, Chicago, Ill.
Boston Museum of Fine Arts, Boston, Mass.
Brooklyn Museum, Brooklyn, New York
Cleveland Institute of Art, Cleveland, Ohio
Colonial Williamsburg Foundation, Williamsburg, Va.
Detroit Institute of Arts, Detroit, Mich.
Freer Gallery of Art, Washington D.C.
Henry Francis du Pont Winterthur Museum, Winterthur, Del
Metropolitan Museum of Art, New York
M. H. de Young Memorial Museum, San Francisco, Cal.
Museum of the City of New York
Philadelphia Museum of Art, Philadelphia, Pa.
Seattle Art Museum, Seattle, Wash.
Shelburne Museum, Shelburne, Vt.
Wadsworth Atheneum, Hartford, Conn.

BRITISH ISLES
American Museum in Britain, Bath

English Furniture

BRITISH ISLES
Anne of Cleves' House, Lewes
Astley Hall, Art Gallery and Museum, Chorley
Aston Hall, Birmingham
Binning Collection, Fenton House, London
Bowes Museum, Barnard Castle
Broughton House, Kirkcudbright
Burrell Collection, Glasgow Art Galleries and Museum, Glasgow
Castle Museum, York
Cecil Higgins Museum, Bedford
Christchurch Mansion, Ipswich
City Museum and Art Gallery, Manchester
Collection of Wooden Bygones, Oxley Wood House, Northwood
Courtauld Institute of Art, London

Folk Museum of West Yorkshire, Halifax
Ford Green Hall, Stoke on Trent
Geffrye Museum, London
Georgian House, Bristol
Hall's Croft, Stratford
Heaton Hall, Manchester
Holburne of Menstrie Museum, Bath
Lady Lever Art Gallery, Port Sunlight
London Museum, London (Victorian)
Museum of English Rural Life, University of Reading, Reading
Museum of Welsh Antiquities, Bangor (Welsh furniture)
Oak House Museum, West Bromwich
Preston Manor, Brighton
Red Lodge, Bristol
Royal Pavilion Art Gallery and Museum, Brighton
Shipley Art Gallery, Gateshead (Victorian)
State Apartments, Hampton Court Palace, Hampton Court
State Apartments, Kensington Palace, London
St John's Gate, Clerkenwell, London
Temple Newsam House, Leeds
Torre Abbey Art Gallery and Conference Centre, Torquay
Towneley Hall Art Gallery and Museum, Burnley
Valence House Museum, Dagenham, Essex
Victoria and Albert Museum, London
Wallace Collection, London
Wilberforce House, Hull
William Morris Gallery, London (Victorian)
Wythenshawe Hall, Manchester

French Furniture

BRITISH ISLES

Bowes Museum, Barnard Castle
Victoria and Albert Museum, London
Wallace Collection, London

EUROPE

France
Louvre, Paris
Musée des Arts Décoratifs, Paris
Musée Marmottan, Paris
Musée Nissim de Camondo, Paris

Germany
Residenzmuseum, Munich

Netherlands
Rijksmuseum, Amsterdam

Sweden
Nationalmuseum, Stockholm

U.S.A.

Cleveland Museum of Art, Cleveland, Ohio
Frick Collection, New York
Metropolitan Museum of Art, New York
Philadelphia Museum of Art, Philadelphia, Pa.

Italian Furniture

EUROPE

Austria
Bundessammlung alter Stilmöbel, Vienna
Historisches Museum der Stadt Wien, Vienna
Hofburg, Vienna
Österreichisches Museum für Angewandte Kunst, Vienna
Schönbrunn Palast und Park, Vienna

Italy
Ca'Rezzonico, Venice
Museo Civico, Treviso
Museo Comunale Stibbert, Florence
Museo Horne, Fondazione Horne, Florence
Museo Poldi Pezzoli, Milan
Palazzo Pitti, Florence
Palazzo Quirinale, Rome
Palazzo Reale, Genoa
Palazzo Reale, Turin

U.S.A.

Frick Collection, New York
Ringling Museum of Art, Sarasota, Fla.

Glass

BRITISH ISLES

Astley Hall Art Gallery and Museum, Chorley
Bethnal Green Museum, London
Bowes Museum, Barnard Castle
British Museum, London
Castle Museum, York
Cecil Higgins Museum, Bedford
City Museum and Art Gallery, Birmingham
Glasgow Art Galleries and Museum, Glasgow
Harris Museum and Art Gallery, Preston
Haworth Art Gallery, Accrington
Heaton Hall, Manchester
Holburne of Menstrie Museum, Bath
Laing Art Gallery and Museum, Newcastle upon Tyne
Library and Museum, Buxton
London Museum, London
Municipal Art Gallery and Museum, Oldham
Museum and Art Gallery, King's Lynn
Museum, Saffron Walden
Pilkington Glass Museum, St Helens
Public Library and Museum, Castleford
Public Library, Museum and Art Gallery, Blackburn
Public Library Museum, Brierley Hill, Staffordshire
Rossendale Museum, Rawtenstall
Royal Pavilion Art Gallery and Museum, Brighton
Spalding Gentlemen's Society Museum, Spalding
Townley Hall Art Gallery and Museum, Burnley
Ulster Museum, Belfast
Victoria and Albert Museum, London
Wernher Collection, Luton Hoo

EUROPE

France
Musée des Techniques, Paris

Netherlands
Rijksmuseum, Amsterdam

Norway
Kunstindustrimuseet, Oslo

Sweden
Nationalmuseum, Stockholm
Nordiska Museet, Stockholm

U.S.A.

Boston Museum of Fine Arts, Boston, Mass.
Brooklyn Museum, New York
Cincinnati Art Museum, Cincinnati, Ohio
Cooper-Hewitt Museum of Design, New York
Corning Museum of Glass, New York
Henry Francis du Pont Winterthur Museum, Winterthur, Del.
Metropolitan Museum of Art, New York
New York Historical Society

Jewelry

BRITISH ISLES

Bowes Museum, Barnard Castle
British Museum, London
Cheapside Hoard, London Museum, London
City Museum and Art Gallery, Birmingham
Municipal Museum and Art Gallery, Worthing

Museum and Art Gallery, Rotherham
Peter Jones Collection, Walker Art Gallery, Liverpool
Tower of London
Victoria and Albert Museum, London
Waddeston Bequest, British Museum, London
Wallace Collection, London
Wernher Collection, Luton Hoo

EUROPE

France
Musée des Arts Décoratifs, Paris

Italy
Galleria Nazionale dell'Umbria, Perugia
Museo degli Argenti, Palazzo Pitti, Florence
Museo dell'Opificio delle Pietre Dure, Florence

U.S.A.

Currier Gallery of Art, Manchester, N.H.
Maryland Historical Society, Baltimore, Md.
National Gallery of Art, Washington D.C.
Philadelphia Museum of Art, Philadelphia, Pa.
Virginia Museum of Fine Arts, Richmond, Va.

Metalwork

BRITISH ISLES

Bilston Art Gallery and Museum, Wolverhampton
Bowes Museum, Barnard Castle
British Museum, London
City Art Gallery and Museum, Nottingham
John Every Collection, Anne of Cleves' House, Lewes
Laing Art Gallery and Museum, Newcastle upon Tyne
National Museum of Wales, Cardiff
Old Merchant's House, Great Yarmouth
Public Museum and Art Gallery, Hastings
Victoria and Albert Museum, London

U.S.A.

Brooklyn Museum, New York
Colonial Williamsburg Foundation, Williamsburg, Va.
Henry Ford Museum, Dearborn, Mich.
Metropolitan Museum of Art, New York
Old Sturbridge Village, Sturbridge, Mass.

Pewter

BRITISH ISLES

British Museum, London
Castle Museum, Norwich
Castle Museum, York
City Museum and Art Gallery, Birmingham
City Museum and Art Gallery, Bristol
Fitzwilliam Museum, Cambridge
Guildhall, London
London Museum, London
Victoria and Albert Museum, London

U.S.A.

Henry Ford Museum, Dearborn, Mich.
Old Deerfield, Deerfield, Mass.
Shelburne Museum, Shelburne, Vt.

Chinese and Japanese Bronzes

BRITISH ISLES

Ashmolean Museum, Oxford
British Museum, London
Victoria and Albert Museum, London

France
Musée Cernuschi, Paris
Musée des Arts Décoratifs, Paris
Musée Guimet, Paris

Germany
Museum für Kunst und Gewerbe, Hamburg
Museum für Ostasiatische Kunst, Cologne
Ostasiatische Kunstabteilung, Ehemals, Staatliche Museen, Berlin

U.S.A.

Cleveland Institute of Art, Cleveland, Ohio
Freer Gallery of Art, Washington D.C.
Metropolitan Museum of Art, New York
Philadelphia Museum of Art, Philadelphia, Pa.
Seattle Art Museum, Seattle, Wash.
William Rockhill Nelson Gallery, Kansas City, Kans.

Mirrors

BRITISH ISLES

Temple Newsam House, Leeds
Victoria and Albert Museum, London

U.S.A.

Boston Museum of Fine Arts, Boston, Mass.
Colonial Williamsburg Foundation, Williamsburg, Va.
Henry Ford Museum, Dearborn, Mich.
Henry Francis du Pont Winterthur Museum, Winterthur, Del.

Needlework and Embroidery

BRITISH ISLES

Bankfield Museum, Halifax
Burrell Collection, Glasgow Art Galleries and Museum, Glasgow
City Museum and Art Gallery, Hereford
City Museum and Art Gallery, Manchester
Ferens Art Gallery, Hull
Fitzwilliam Museum, Cambridge
Galleries of the Regional College of Art, Manchester
Gallery of English Costume, Platt Hall, Manchester
Hardwick Hall, near Chesterfield
Lady Lever Art Gallery, Port Sunlight
Museum and Muniment Room, Guildford
National Museum of Wales, Cardiff
Thorpe Prebend House and Museum, Ripon
Whitworth Art Gallery, Manchester
Victoria and Albert Museum, London

EUROPE

Germany
Herzog-Anton-Ulrich-Museum, Brunswick
Kestner-Museum, Hanover

U.S.A.

Boston Museum of Fine Arts, Boston, Mass.
Cincinnati Art Museum, Cincinnati, Ohio
Colonial Williamsburg Foundation, Williamsburg, Va.
Cooper-Hewitt Museum of Design, New York
Fine Arts Society of San Diego, San Diego, Cal.
Henry Francis du Pont Winterthur Museum, Winterthur, Del.

Pottery and Porcelain

BRITISH ISLES

Porcelain

Art Gallery and Museum, Cheltenham
Bantock House, Wolverhampton
Bethnal Green Museum, London
Bowes Museum, Barnard Castle
British Museum, London
Cecil Higgins Museum, Bedford

City Museum and Art Gallery, Stoke on Trent
Fenton House, London
Fitzwilliam Museum, Cambridge
Fletcher Moss Museum, Manchester
Glasgow Art Galleries and Museum, Glasgow
Municipal Museum and Art Gallery, Rotherham (Rockingham)
Museums and Art Gallery, Blackburn
Public Library, Museum and Art Gallery, Blackburn
Rapallo House Museum and Art Gallery, Llandudno
Royal Museum and Slater Art Gallery, Canterbury
Usher Art Gallery, Lincoln
Victoria and Albert Museum, London

Pottery

Art Gallery and Museum, Cheltenham
Art Gallery, Oldham
Astley Hall Art Gallery and Museum, Chorley
City Art Gallery, Leeds
City Museum and Art Gallery, Stoke-on-Trent
Colchester and Essex Museum, Colchester
Glaisher Collection, Fitzwilliam Museum, Cambridge
Heaton Hall and Wythenshawe Hall, Manchester
Library and Museum, Buxton
Museum and Art Gallery, Hanley, Stoke-on-Trent
Museum and Art Gallery, Nottingham
Public Libraries, Museum and Art Gallery, Bootle
Public Library, Museum and Art Gallery, Blackburn
Public Museum and Art Gallery, Hastings
Roman Town and Museum, Aldbrough (Roman)
Royal Albert Memorial Museum and Art Gallery, Exeter
Royal Museum and Slater Art Gallery, Canterbury
Schreiber Collection, Victoria and Albert Museum, London
Segontium Museum, Caernarvon
Williamson Art Gallery and Museum, Birkenhead
Willett Collection, Art Gallery and Museum, Brighton
Ypres Tower Museum, Rye

Chinese, Korean and Japanese
Ashmolean Museum, Oxford
British Museum, London
Burrell Collection, Glasgow Art Galleries and Museum, Glasgow
City Museum and Art Gallery, Birmingham
City Museum and Art Gallery, Bristol
City Museum and Art Gallery, Manchester
Fitzwilliam Museum, Cambridge
Lady Lever Art Gallery, Port Sunlight
Royal Scottish Museum, Edinburgh
Sir Percival David Foundation, London University
Temple Newsam House, Leeds
Victoria and Albert Museum, London

EUROPE

Belgium
Musées Royaux d'Art et d'Histoire, Brussels

Denmark
Kunstindustrimuseet, Copenhagen
Nationalmuseet, Copenhagen

France
Musée Cernuschi, Paris
Musée des Arts Décoratifs, Paris
Musée Guimet, Paris
Musée National de Céramique, Sèvres, Paris

Germany
Ostasiatische Kunstabteilung, Ehemals Staatliche Museen, Berlin
Museum für Kunst und Gewerbe, Hamburg
Museum für Ostasiatische Kunst, Cologne

Netherlands
Rijksmuseum, Amsterdam

Sweden
Nationalmuseum, Stockholm

U.S.A.
Boston Museum of Fine Arts, Boston, Mass.
Carnegie Institute, Pittsburg, Pa.
Cleveland Institute of Art, Cleveland, Ohio
Cincinnati Art Museum, Cincinnati, Ohio
Colonial Williamsburg, Williamsburg, Va.
Cooper-Hewitt Museum of Design, New York
Freer Gallery of Art, Washington D.C.
Frick Collection, New York
Henry E. Huntington Library and Art Galley, San Marino, Cal.
Metropolitan Museum of Art, New York
Philadelphia Museum of Art, Philadelphia, Pa.
Seattle Art Museum, Seattle, Wash.
University of Kansas Museum of Art, Lawrence, Kans.
Walker Art Center, Minneapolis, Minn.

Prints

Old English Prints

BRITISH ISLES
British Museum, London
City Museum and Art Gallery, Birmingham
Courtauld Institute of Art, London
Harris Museum and Art Gallery, Preston
Holburne of Menstrie Museum, Bath
Philpot Museum, Lyme Regis
Tate Gallery, London
Thorpe Prebend House and Museum, Ripon
Victoria and Albert Museum, London

Bird Prints

BRITISH ISLES
Natural History Museum, London

EUROPE

Denmark
Universitetsbiblioteket, Copenhagen

Netherlands
Teylers Museum, Haarlem
Zoölogisch Museum, Amsterdam

American Prints

U.S.A.
American Antiquarian Society, Worcester, Mass.
Boston Museum of Fine Arts, Boston, Mass.
Library of Congress, Washington D.C.
Mariners' Museum, Newport News, Va.
Metropolitan Museum of Art, New York
Museum of the City of New York, New York
New York Historical Society, New York
New York Public Library, New York
Philadelphia Museum of Art, Philadelphia, Pa.

Japanese Prints

BRITISH ISLES
Ashmolean Museum, Oxford
British Museum, London
Chester Beatty Library, Dublin
Fitzwilliam Museum, Cambridge
Maidstone Museum and Art Gallery, Maidstone
Whitworth Art Gallery, Manchester
Victoria and Albert Museum, London

EUROPE

Belgium
Musées Royaux d'Art et d'Histoire, Brussels

France
Bibliothèque Nationale, Paris
Musée Guimet, Paris

Netherlands
Prentenkabinet, Amsterdam
Prentenkabinet der Rijksuniversiteit, Leyden

Scientific Instruments

BRITISH ISLES

Museum of the History of Science, Oxford
National Maritime Museum, London
Reading Museum and Art Gallery, Reading
Science Museum, London
Wellcome Museum of Medical Science, London

EUROPE

France
Musée Astronomique de L'Observatoire de Paris, Paris
Musée du Conservatoire National des Arts et Métiers, Paris

Italy
Museo Nazionale della Scienza e della Tecnica 'Leonardo da Vinci', Milan

U.S.A.

Adler Planetarium and Astronomical Museum, Chicago, Ill.
Buffalo Museum of Science, Buffalo, N.Y.
Smithsonian Institution, Washington D.C.

Silver

BRITISH ISLES

Ashmolean Museum, Oxford
Bethnal Green Museum, London
British Museum, London
Burrell Collection, Glasgow Art Galleries and Museum, Glasgow
Cecil Higgins Museum, Oxford
City Museum and Art Gallery, Birmingham (also Sheffield Plate)
City Museum, Sheffield (Sheffield Plate)
Fitzwilliam Museum, Cambridge
Glasgow Art Galleries and Museum, Glasgow
Heaton Hall, Wythenshawe Hall and Fletcher Moss Museum, Manchester
Holburne of Menstrie Museum, Bath
Laing Art Gallery and Museum, Newcastle upon Tyne (also Sheffield Plate)
Ormonde Collection, Bankfield Museum, Halifax
Preston Manor, Brighton
Public Museum and Art Gallery, Sunderland
Royal Scottish Museum, Edinburgh
Ulster Museum, Belfast
Victoria and Albert Museum, London
Wallace Collection, London

EUROPE

Austria
Kunsthistorisches Museum, Vienna

France
Louvre, Paris
Musée Carnavalet, Paris

Germany
Bayerisches Nationalmuseum, Munich
Städtische Kunstsammlungen, Augsburg

Italy
Museo d'Arte Antica, Palazzo Madama, Turin
Museo d'Arte Antica, Palazzo Pitti, Florence
Museo dell'Opera del Duomo, Florence
Museo Nazionale, Messina

Norway
Kunstindustrimuseet, Oslo
Kunstindustrimuseum, Trondheim

Portugal
Museu Nacional de Arte Antigua, Lisbon

U.S.A.

Art Institute of Chicago, Chicago, Ill.
Art Museum, Princeton, N.J.
Baltimore Museum of Art, Baltimore, Md.
Boston Museum of Fine Arts, Boston, Mass.
Cincinnati Art Museum, Cincinati, Ohio
Detroit Institute of Arts, Detroit, Mich.
Henry Ford Museum, Dearborn, Mich.
Los Angeles County Museum of Art, Los Angeles, Cal.
Metropolitan Museum of Art, New York
Philadelphia Museum of Art, Philadelphia, Pa.
Toledo Museum of Art, Toledo, Ohio
Wadsworth Atheneum, Hartford, Conn.
William Hayes Fogg Art Museum, Harvard University, Cambridge, Mass.
Yale University Art Gallery, New Haven, Conn.

Illustration Acknowledgments

Except where otherwise indicated the photographs belong to the museums, galleries, dealers etc. credited in the captions.

Rainbird Reference Books Ltd: 15 bottom, 16 bottom right, 18 top and bottom right, 31 right, 36 centre, 38 right, 39 top, 41 centre, 42 centre and left below, 45 top right and bottom, 46, 47, 50 top, 51, 52, 55, 59 top and centre right, 61 bottom, 64 top and left, 65 bottom left, 66 bottom, 80 bottom, 88 right, 91 all, 98, 100 top left and bottom, 101 top, 105 bottom left and right, 107, 108, 109 bottom, 110, 111, 113, 115 both, 117, 118 both, 119 both, 120, 121, 122 left and top right, 123, 124, 125 both, 126 both, 127 both, 128, 132 bottom, 133 bottom, 134 bottom left, top right and bottom right, 135 all, 136 bottom left, 137 both, 141, 142 top, 144, 145 bottom, 147 all, 175 bottom left, 176 bottom right, 179 both, 185, 189 bottom, 191 left, 192, 193, 194 top, 199 top, 200 top, 201 bottom and right, 205, 211 bottom, 218, 221 bottom, 226, 234, 239 top right and bottom, 240 both, 242 top, 245 top, 247 bottom, 248 bottom right, 249, 250 both, 251 bottom left, 252 both, 253 both, 254, 255, 256 both, 261 top, 264 centre, 265, 266, 270, 274 bottom (top Delomosne & Son, London), 275 top, 278 bottom, 279, 280 top, 290, 298, 299 both, 300 all, 301 all, 302 bottom, 305 bottom, 308, 310 both, 313, 314 all, 315, 316, 320 top, 322, 323, 324 bottom, 327, 328 all, 329, 330, 331, 332 all, 333 top and bottom, 335, 336 top, 337, 338, 339, 340 left, 341, 342, 343, 344, 346, 347 all, 348 top, 351, 353 centre and bottom, 354, 358 top centre, 362 all, 363, 364, 366, 367, 370, 371, 372, 373 all, 374, 376, 380, 387 bottom, 392 bottom, 394, 397, 399, 400, 405, 406 top left and right, 407, 408, 409, 410 bottom, 412, 413, 414 bottom, 417 right, 419 top, 423 bottom, 424 all, 425 both, 426 both, 427, 430, 431 both, 432 all, 433, 434 both, 435 all, 436 both, 437, 438 centre, 439 left, 442 right, 444 both, 445 both, 446 right, 449 bottom left, 451 bottom right, 452, 453 bottom, 455 both, 457 both, 458 both, 459, 460 both, 462 bottom, 463 top, 464, 467 left, 469 bottom, 470 left, 472 top, 474, 478 top, 480 right, 481 right, 482, 483, 485 bottom left, 488 left, 490 right, 492, 493 both, 496, 501 top, 503 top right, 507 left, 512, 518, 521 top left and right, 522 top, 523 top right and bottom right, 525 bottom left and top right, 531 both, 532, 533, 535, 536, 537 top, 538, 539 top left, 540 both, 541 bottom right, 543, 544, 545 right, 547, 549 centre and bottom, 554 all, 555 both, 556 top, 557 top left and bottom left, 559 bottom, 566 left, 567 right, 570 top, 572, 574 top and centre left and right, 575, 577 bottom, 579 top, 581 both, 583 bottom, 588 centre and bottom, 590 both, 591 top, 594 top and bottom, 595 both, 596 both, 597 top, 602 centre and bottom, 603 bottom right, 605 top right, 607 bottom left, 608 left, 609 top, 610 top left, 611 bottom, 613 top, 614 both, 615 both, 616 both, 618 both, 619 both, 620, 621 all, 622 bottom, 623, 624 right, 625 all, 626 bottom, 627, 628, 629, 630, 631, 637 left, 641, 642 left, 648 left, 650, 657, 659 top, 662, 664 right, 666

The Cooper-Bridgeman Library: 12 right, 13, 14 both, 15 top, 16 left, 17 both, 18 bottom left, 20 all, 21 all, 22, 23 both, 24, 26 bottom, 29 top, 30 top and centre, 31 left, 34, 36 top and bottom left, 37 top and bottom, 39 bottom left, 41 bottom, 42 top, 42 bottom right, 43, 44 both, 45 top left, 50 both, 54 right, 58 top right and bottom left, 59 centre left and bottom left, 60, 61 top left, 65 bottom, 67 all, 68 both, 69, 70 all, 71 left, 72 both, 73, 74 left and right, 77 both, 78, 79, 80 top right, 82, 83, 84, 85, 86, 89 both, 90 centre and bottom, 96 both, 97, 100 top right, 101 bottom, 104 both, 105 top, 109 top, 132 bottom right, 134 top centre, 135 bottom left, 136 top and bottom right, 138 both, 140, 145 top, 149 both, 150, 151, 152 bottom right, 153 both, 154 top left and right, 155 both, 156 top centre, top right and bottom, 158 both, 159, 160 both, 161, 163 bottom, 164 bottom, 165 all, 166, 167 right, 168 right, 169 all, 171 bottom, 173 both, 174, 175 top and bottom right, 176 top left, top centre, top right and bottom left, 178 both, 180, 182 top, 188, 190, 197 top, 198 both, 199 bottom, 201 top, 203 top and bottom, 204 bottom, 208 both, 212 top right, centre and bottom, 213, 215, 216 both, 223, 224, 228 both, 229, 230, 232 top, 236, 243, 244 top left and right, 245 bottom, 246 top, 247 top, 248 bottom left, 251 top left and right, 257, 258 top left and top right, 259, 260, 261 bottom, 264 top and bottom left, 271, 272, 275 bottom, 276, 283 bottom right, 285, 286 top, 287 left, 288, 289, 293, 294 bottom, 295 bottom left and right, 296 all, 302 top, 311, 318, 320 bottom, 321, 324 top, 325, 348 centre, 350, 352, 353 top, 357, 358 bottom right, 359 both, 360 top right and bottom, 365, 368, 377, 384, 385 both, 386, 388, 389 both, 392 top, 396, 402, 404, 417 left, 418 all, 419 bottom, 420 both, 421 right, 422 both, 423 top, 428, 429 both, 439 right, 441 both, 442 left, 443, 446 top and bottom, 447 all, 448 both, 449 top and centre left and bottom right, 450 top, 451 top and bottom left, 454 both, 465, 466, 468, 469 top, 470 right, 471, 472 bottom, 473 both, 476, 478 bottom, 479, 480 left, 481 left, 485 top and bottom right, 486 both, 488 right, 490 left, 491, 494, 498 all, 499, 500 both, 502, 503 bottom left and bottom right, 505, 507 right, 509, 511, 513 both, 514 top, 515 bottom, 516, 537 bottom, 539 top right and bottom left and right, 541 top and bottom left, 542 both, 545 left, 548 top, 551 top, 556 bottom, 557 top right and bottom right, 558 both, 559 top left and right, 563 top right, 565, 566 right, 568, 577 top, 579 bottom, 580, 584, 585, 591 bottom, 592, 593, 594 centre, 597 right, 598 left, 599 all, 600 all, 601 both, 602 top, 605 left and bottom right, 606 right, 607 bottom right, 608 right, 609 bottom, 610 bottom, 611 top, 612 top, 626 top, 633 both, 634, 636, 639, 640, 642 right, 643 both, 646, 648 right, 649, 651, 652 both, 654, 659 bottom, 660 right, 663 all, 664 left, 665 bottom, 667

Alinari: 306 both

Cottie Burland: 35

Mark Gerson: 12 left

Angelo Hornak: 26 centre, 28 bottom, 29 bottom left and right, 30 bottom, 62, 71 right, 74 bottom, 80 top left, 139 top right and bottom, 152 bottom left, 182 bottom, 183, 194 bottom left, 195, 200 bottom, 203 left, 206, 209, 214, 244 bottom left, 258 bottom left and bottom right, 280 bottom, 282, 283 bottom left, 305 top, 317 both, 333 centre, 416, 450 bottom, 501 bottom

Orbis Publishing Ltd: 90 top, 102 all, 132 top, 133 top, 134 top left, 326, 378, 517, 519 both, 520 both, 521 bottom left, 522 centre, 523 top left and bottom left, 524, 525 top left and bottom right, 526 both, 527, 529, 568 left, 569, 570 bottom, 571, 573 both, 574 bottom

Picturepoint: 99, 106 both, 246 bottom, 247 centre, 248 top, 277 both, 278 top, 375, 379, 438 top and bottom, 440, 549 top, 550 top

The following illustrations from the Metropolitan Museum of Art are from specific collections: 88 right The James F. Ballard Collection, 133 bottom Gift of Mrs Russell Sage 1910, 134 bottom left Gift of Mrs Russell Sage 1910, 134 top right Rogers Fund 1941, 134 bottom right Gift of Mrs J. Insley Blair 1950, 135 top left Rogers Fund 1936, 137 top Gift of Mrs George Coe Graves 1930, Sylmaris Collection, 137 bottom Kennedy Fund 1918, 140 Edgar J. Kaufmann Charitable Foundation Fund 1968, 142 top Fletcher Fund 1926, 144 Gift of Mrs Charles Reginald Leonard 1957, 145 top Edgar J. Kaufmann Charitable Foundation Fund, 211 bottom Gift of Mrs Russell Sage 1910, 329 Gift of Mrs J. Insley Blair 1946, 406 bottom left Gift of Mrs Robert W. de Forest 1933, 410 top Rogers Fund 1941, 411 left and right Edgar J. Kaufmann Charitable Foundation Fund 1969, 411 centre Gift of Wells M. Sawyer 1945, 414 top Gift of Dr Charles W. Green 1947, 415 Anonymous gift fund 1968, 426 top Gift of the Winfield Foundation, 493 right Gift of the Winfield Foundation, 547 Purchase 1917 Joseph Pulitzer Bequest, 594 bottom Samuel D. Lee Fund 1938, 618 top Rogers Fund 1947

The following illustrations from the New York Public Library are from specific collections: 521 top right Astor, Lenox and Tilden Foundations, 522 top left and bottom I. N. Phelps Stokes Collection

The following illustrations from Yale University Art Gallery are from the Mabel Brady Garvan Collection: 594 top left and centre right, 595 bottom

Index

Figures that refer to illustration captions are in italics and parentheses: those in italics refer to the main subject of the illustration; those in parentheses to additional information contained within the caption.